TEACHER'S EDITION

AMERICAN HISTORY

James West Davidson Michael B. Stoff

PEARSON

Boston, Massachusetts Chandler, Arizona Glenview, Illinois New York, New York

Cover Image: South Dakota, Mount Rushmore with viewscope in foreground. Chris Cheadle/Alamy.

PEARSON

ISBN-13: 978-0-13-330713-9
ISBN-10: 0-13-330713-1

9 16

Authors, Consultants, Partners

[Authors]

James West Davidson

Dr. James Davidson is coauthor of *After the Fact: The Art of Historical Detection* and *Nation of Nations: A Narrative History of the American Republic.* Dr. Davidson has taught at both the college and high school levels. He has also consulted on curriculum design for American history courses. Dr. Davidson is an avid canoeist and hiker. His published works on these subjects include *Great Heart,* the true story of a 1903 canoe trip in the Canadian wilderness.

Michael B. Stoff

Dr. Michael Stoff received his Ph.D. from Yale University and teaches history at the University of Texas at Austin. He is the author of *Oil, War, and American Security: The Search for a National Policy on Foreign Oil, 1941–1947,* coauthor of *Nation of Nations: A Narrative History of the American Republic,* and coeditor of *The Manhattan Project: A Documentary Introduction to the Atomic Age.* Dr. Stoff has won numerous grants, fellowships, and teaching awards.

[Contributing Author]

Jennifer L. Bertolet

Jennifer L. Bertolet is a Professorial Lecturer at George Washington University, where she teaches American history courses, among them Introduction to American History. She received her Ph.D. from George Washington University. In addition to teaching, she has served as an education consultant, a subject matter expert for online teaching and learning, and as an historian and policy consultant specializing in Indian policy and environmental issues.

[Program Consultant]

Dr. Kathy Swan is an Associate Professor of Curriculum and Instruction at the University of Kentucky. Her research focuses on standards-based technology integration, authentic intellectual work, and documentary-making in the social studies classroom. Swan has been a four-time recipient of the National Technology Leadership Award in Social Studies Education. She is also the advisor for the Social Studies Assessment, Curriculum, and Instruction Collaborative (SSACI) at CCSSO.

[Program Partners]

NBC LEARN

NBC Learn, the educational arm of NBC News, develops original stories for use in the classroom and makes archival NBC News stories, images, and primary source documents available on demand to teachers, students, and parents. NBC Learn partnered with Pearson to produce the myStory videos that support this program.

Constitutional Rights Foundation is a nonprofit, nonpartisan organization focused on educating students about the importance of civic participation in a democratic society. Constitutional Rights Foundation is the lead contributor to the development of the Civic Discussion Topic Inquiries for this program. Constitutional Rights Foundation is also the provider of the Civic Action Project (CAP) for the *Economics* and *Magruder's American Government* programs. CAP is a project-based learning model for civics, government, and economics courses.

Reviewers & Academic Consultants

Pearson American History was developed especially for you and your students. The story of its creation began with a three-day Innovation Lab in which teachers, historians, students, and authors came together to imagine our ideal Social Studies teaching and learning experiences. We refined the plan with a series of teacher roundtables that shaped this new approach to ensure your students' mastery of content and skills. A dedicated team, made up of Pearson authors, content experts, and social studies teachers, worked to bring our collective vision into reality. Kathy Swan, Professor of Education and architect of the new College, Career, and Civic Life (C3) Framework, served as our expert advisor on curriculum and instruction.

Pearson would like to extend a special thank you to all of the teachers who helped guide the development of this program. We gratefully acknowledge your efforts to realize Next Generation Social Studies teaching and learning that will prepare American students for college, careers, and active citizenship.

[Program Advisors]

Campaign for the Civic Mission of Schools is a coalition of over 70 national civic learning, education, civic engagement, and business groups committed to improving the quality and quantity of civic learning in American schools. The Campaign served as an advisor on this program.

Buck Institute for Education is a nonprofit organization dedicated to helping teachers implement the effective use of Project-Based Learning in their classrooms. Buck Institute staff consulted on the Project-Based Learning Topic Inquiries for this program.

[Program Academic Consultants]

Barbara Brown
Director of Outreach
College of Arts and Sciences
African Studies Center
Boston University
Boston, Massachusetts

William Childs
Professor of History Emeritus
The Ohio State University
Columbus, Ohio

Jennifer Giglielmo
Associate Professor of History
Smith College
Northhampton, Massachusetts

Joanne Connor Green
Professor, Department Chair
Political Science
Texas Christian University
Fort Worth, Texas

Ramdas Lamb, Ph.D.
Associate Professor of Religion
University of Hawaii at Manoa
Honolulu, Hawaii

Huping Ling
Changjiang Scholar Chair Professor
Professor of History
Truman State University
Kirksville, Missouri

Jeffery Long, Ph.D.
Professor of Religion and Asian Studies
Elizabethtown College
Elizabethtown, Pennsylvania

Gordon Newby
Professor of Islamic, Jewish and Comparative Studies
Department of Middle Eastern and South Asian Studies
Emory University
Atlanta, Georgia

Mark Peterson
Associate Professor
Department of Asian and Near Eastern Languages
Brigham Young University
Provo, Utah

William Pitts
Professor, Department of Religion
Baylor University
Waco, Texas

Benjamin Ravid
Professor Emeritus of Jewish History
Department of Near Eastern and Judaic Studies
Brandeis University
Waltham, Massachusetts

Harpreet Singh
College Fellow
Department of South Asian Studies
Harvard University
Cambridge, Massachusetts

Christopher E. Smith, J.D., Ph.D.
Professor
Michigan State University
MSU School of Criminal Justice
East Lansing, Michigan

John Voll
Professor of Islamic History
Georgetown University
Washington, D.C.

Michael R. Wolf
Associate Professor
Department of Political Science
Indiana University-Purdue University Fort Wayne
Fort Wayne, Indiana

Reimagine Learning

Realize Results. Social studies is more than dots on a map or dates on a timeline. It's where we've been and where we're going. It's stories from the past and our stories today. And in today's fast-paced, interconnected world, it's essential.

Instruction Your Way!

Comprehensive teaching support is available in two different formats:

- **Teacher's Edition:** Designed like a "T.V. Guide," teaching suggestions are paired with preview images of digital resources.
- **Teaching Support Online:** Teaching suggestions, answer keys, blackline masters, and other resources are provided at point-of-use online in Realize.

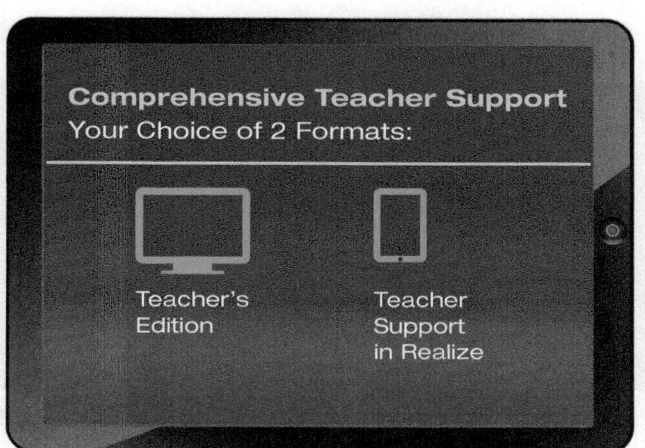

Pearson Mastery System

This complete system for teaching and learning uses best practices, technology, and a four-part framework—Connect, Investigate, Synthesize, and Demonstrate—to prepare students to be college-and-career ready.

- Higher-level content that gives students support to access complex text, acquire skills and tackle rigorous questions.
- Inquiry-focused Projects, Civic Discussions, and Document-Based Questions that prepare students for real-world challenges;
- Digital content on Pearson Realize that is dynamic, flexible, and uses the power of technology to bring social studies to life.

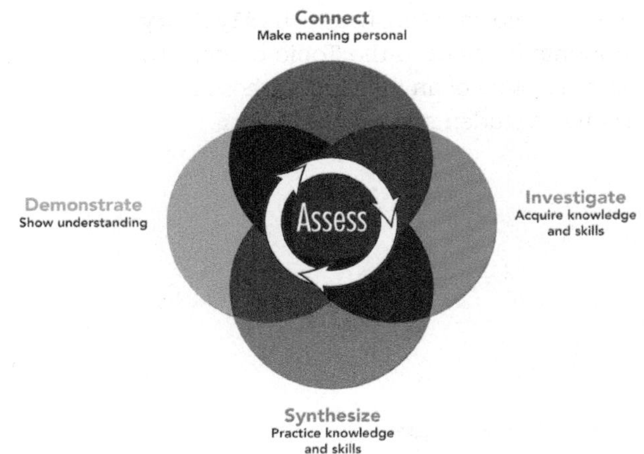

Table of Contents for Today's Learners

Today's learners research new information by using a search engine and browsing by topic. Breaking out of a book metaphor of "chapters," this table of contents is organized by:

- **Topic:** As you decide what you want to teach, you search first for the topic.
- **Lesson:** Within each topic are several lessons where you will find a variety of diverse resources to support teaching and learning.
- **Text:** Each lesson contains chunked information called Texts. This is the same informational text that appears in the print Student Edition.

This organization saves time, improves pacing, and makes it easy to rearrange content.

» Go online to learn more and see the program overview video.

CONNECT! Begin the Pearson Mastery System by engaging in the topic story and connecting it to your own lives.

Preview—Each Topic opens with the Enduring Understandings section, allowing you to preview expected learning outcomes.

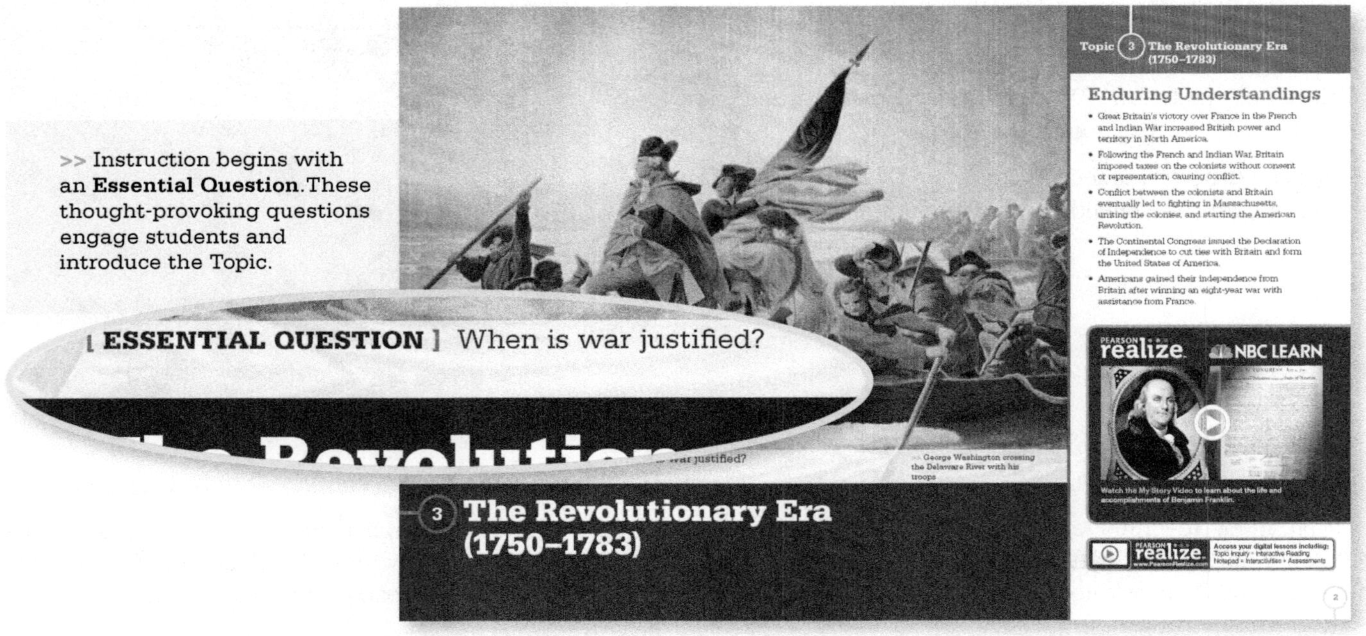

Developed in partnership with NBCLearn, the **My Story** videos help students connect to the Topic content by hearing the personal story of an individual whose life is related to the content students are about to learn.

INVESTIGATE! Step two of the Mastery System allows you to investigate the topic story through a number of engaging features as you learn the content.

>> **Active Classroom Strategies** integrated in the daily lesson plans help to increase in-class participation, raise energy levels and attentiveness, all while engaging in the story. These 5-15 minute activities have you use what you have learned to draw, write, speak, and decide.

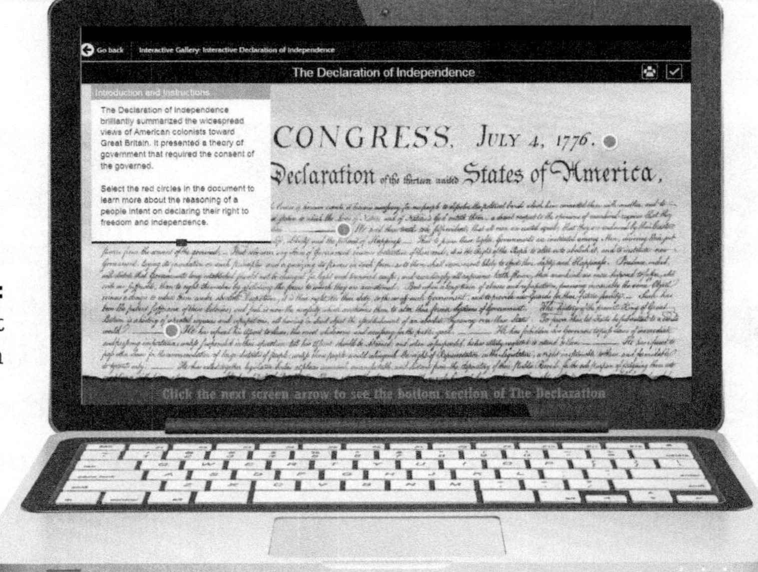

>> **Interactive Primary Source Galleries:** Use primary source image galleries throughout the lesson to see, analyze, and interact with images that tie to the topic story content.

Investigate

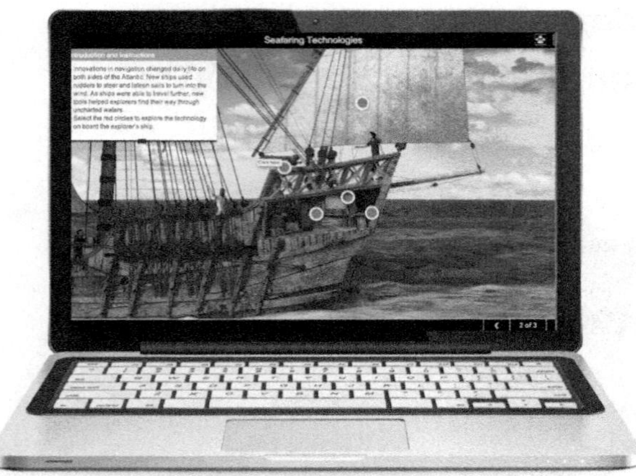

>> Feel like you are a part of the story with **interactive 3-D models**.

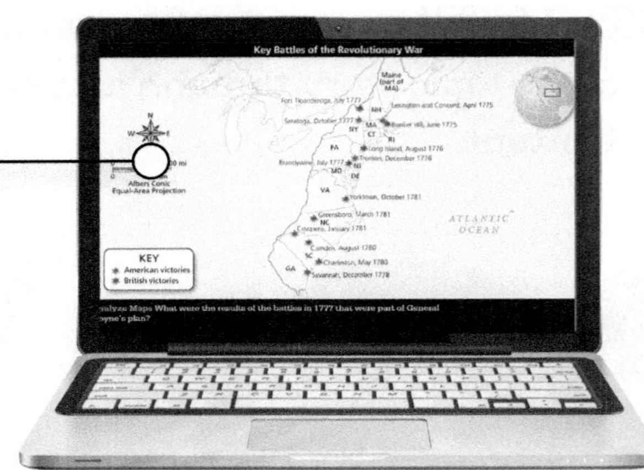

>> Continue to investigate the topic story through **dynamic interactive maps**. Build map skills while covering the essential standards.

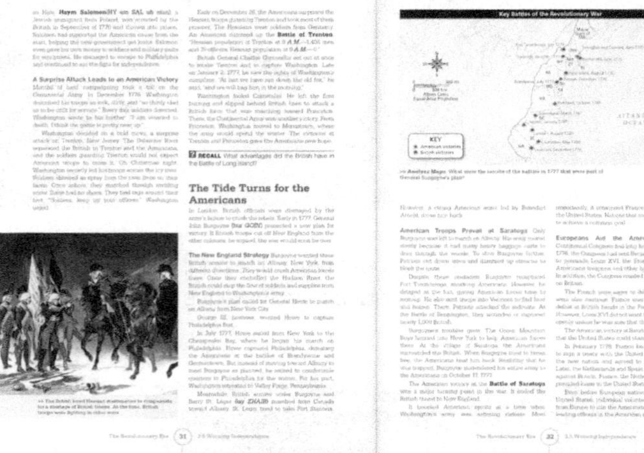

The Tide Turns for the Americans

>> Learn content by reading narrative text online or in a printed Student Edition.

Synthesize: Practice Knowledge and Skills

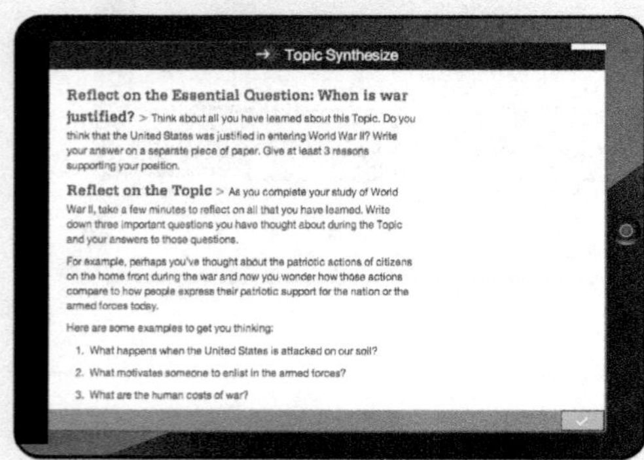

SYNTHESIZE!

In step three of the Mastery System, pause to reflect on what you learn and revisit an essential question.

Demonstrate: Show Understanding

DEMONSTRATE! The final step of the Mastery System is to demonstrate understanding of the text.

PEARSON realize™

>> **The digital course on Realize!** The program's digital course on Realize puts engaging content, embedded assessments, instant data, and flexible tools at your fingertips.

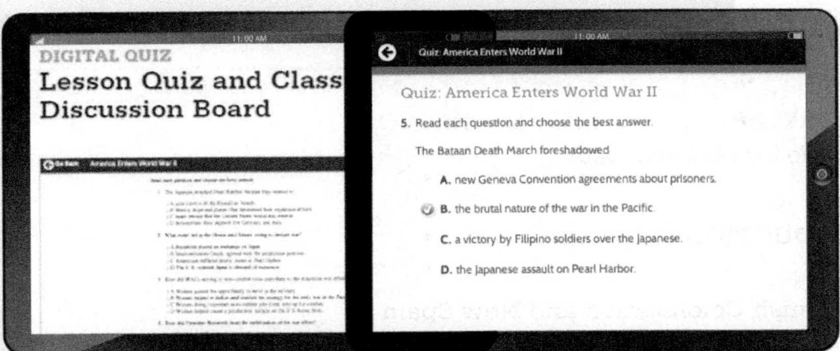

>> **Assessment**. At the end of each lesson and topic, demonstrate understanding through Lesson Quizzes, Topic Tests, and Topic Inquiry performance assessments. The System provides remediation and enrichment recommendations based on your individual performance towards mastery.

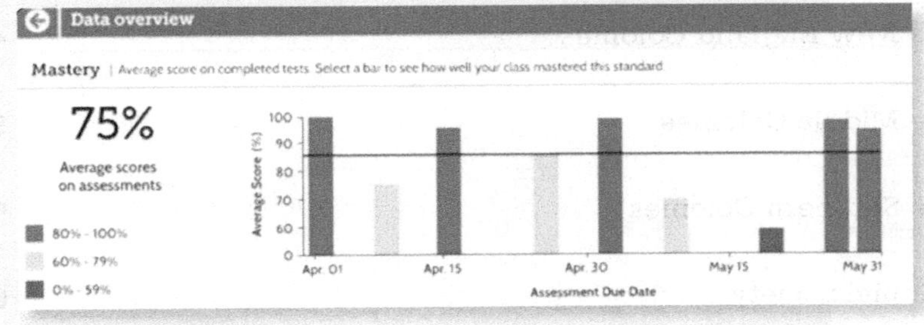

>> **Class and Data** features on Realize make it easy to see your mastery data.

Digital Course Content

Digital Course Content

Topic 8 Sectionalism and Civil War (1820–1865) 291

Topic 9 The Reconstruction Era (1865–1877) 337

Topic 10 Industrial and Economic Growth (1865–1914) 365

Topic 11 The Progressive Era (1865–1920) 406

Topic 17 Meeting New Challenges (2001–Present) 626

Digital Resources

Many types of digital resources help you investigate the topics in this course. You'll find biographies, primary sources, maps, and more. These resources will help bring the topics to life.

Core Concepts

Culture

- What Is Culture?
- Families and Societies
- Language
- Religion
- The Arts
- Cultural Diffusion and Change
- Science and Technology

Economics

- Economics Basics
- Economic Process
- Economic Systems
- Economic Development
- Trade
- Money Management

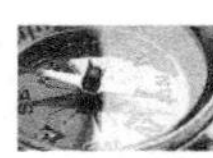

Geography

- The Study of Earth
- Geography's Five Themes
- Ways to Show Earth's Surface
- Understanding Maps
- Earth in Space
- Time and Earth's Rotation
- Forces on Earth's Surface
- Forces Inside Earth
- Climate and Weather
- Temperature
- Water and Climate
- Air Circulation and Precipitation
- Types of Climate
- Ecosystems
- Environment and Resources
- Land Use
- People's Impact on the Environment
- Population
- Migration
- Urbanization

Government and Civics

- Foundations of Government
- Political Systems
- Political Structures
- Conflict and Cooperation
- Citizenship

History

- How Do Historians Study History?
- Measuring Time
- Historical Sources
- Archaeology and Other Sources
- Historical Maps

Personal Finance

- Your Fiscal Fitness: An Introduction
- Budgeting
- Checking
- Investments
- Savings and Retirement
- Credit and Debt
- Risk Management
- Consumer Smarts
- After High School
- Taxes and Income

Landmark Supreme Court Cases

- *Korematsu* v. *United States*
- *Marbury* v. *Madison*
- *McCulloch* v. *Maryland*
- *Gibbons* v. *Ogden*
- *Worcester* v. *Georgia*
- *Dred Scott* v. *Sandford*
- *Plessy* v. *Ferguson*
- *Schenck* v. *United States*
- *Brown* v. *Board of Education*
- *Engel* v. *Vitale*
- *Sweatt* v. *Painter*
- *Mapp* v. *Ohio*
- *Hernandez* v. *Texas*
- *Gideon* v. *Wainwright*
- *Wisconsin* v. *Yoder*
- *Miranda* v. *Arizona*
- *White* v. *Regester*
- *Tinker* v. *Des Moines School District*
- *Roe* v. *Wade*
- *Baker* v. *Carr*
- *Grutter* v. *Bollinger*
- *Edgewood* v. *Kirby*
- *Texas* v. *Johnson*
- *National Federation of Independent Businesses et al.* v. *Sebelius et al.*
- *Mendez* v. *Westminster* and *Delgado* v. *Bastrop*

Interactive Primary Sources

- Code of Hammurabi
- Psalm 23
- The Republic, Plato
- Politics, Aristotle
- Edicts, Asoka
- Analects, Confucius
- First Letter to the Corinthians, Paul
- The Quran
- The Magna Carta
- Travels, Ibn Battuta
- The Destruction of the Indies, Bartolomé de Las Casas
- Mayflower Compact
- English Petition of Right
- English Bill of Rights
- Two Treatises of Government, John Locke
- The Spirit of Laws, Baron de Montesquieu
- The Social Contract, Jean-Jacques Rousseau
- The Interesting Narrative of the Life of Olaudah Equiano
- "Give Me Liberty or Give Me Death," Patrick Henry
- "Remember the Ladies," Abigail Adams
- Common Sense, Thomas Paine
- Declaration of Independence
- Virginia Declaration of Rights
- Virginia Statute for Religious Freedom, Thomas Jefferson
- "To His Excellency, General Washington," Phillis Wheatley
- Articles of Confederation
- Anti-Federalist Papers
- The Federalist No. 10, James Madison
- The Federalist No. 39, James Madison
- The Federalist No. 51
- The Federalist No. 78, Alexander Hamilton
- Northwest Ordinance
- Iroquois Constitution
- Declaration of the Rights of Man and the Citizen
- Farewell Address, George Washington
- Mexican Federal Constitution of 1824
- State Colonization Law of 1825
- Law of April 6, 1830
- Debate Over Nullification, Webster and Calhoun
- Turtle Bayou Resolutions
- Democracy in America, Alexis de Tocqueville
- 1836 Victory or Death Letter from the Alamo, Travis
- Texas Declaration of Independence
- Declaration of Sentiments and Resolutions
- "Ain't I a Woman?," Sojourner Truth
- Uncle Tom's Cabin, Harriet Beecher Stowe
- "A House Divided," Abraham Lincoln
- First Inaugural Address, Abraham Lincoln
- Declaration of Causes: February 2, 1861
- Emancipation Proclamation, Abraham Lincoln
- Gettysburg Address, Abraham Lincoln
- Second Inaugural Address, Abraham Lincoln
- "I Will Fight No More Forever," Chief Joseph
- How the Other Half Lives, Jacob Riis
- The Pledge of Allegiance
- Preamble to the Platform of the Populist Party
- Atlanta Exposition Address, Booker T. Washington
- The Jungle, Upton Sinclair
- Hind Swaraj, Mohandas Gandhi
- The Fourteen Points, Woodrow Wilson
- Two Poems, Langston Hughes
- Four Freedoms, Franklin D. Roosevelt
- Anne Frank: The Diary of a Young Girl, Anne Frank
- Charter of the United Nations
- Universal Declaration of Human Rights
- Autobiography, Kwame Nkrumah
- Inaugural Address, John F. Kennedy
- Silent Spring, Rachel Carson
- "I Have a Dream," Martin Luther King, Jr.
- "Letter From Birmingham Jail," Martin Luther King, Jr.
- "Tear Down This Wall," Ronald Reagan
- "Freedom From Fear," Aung San Suu Kyi
- "Glory and Hope," Nelson Mandela

Biographies

- Abigail Adams
- John Adams
- John Quincy Adams
- Samuel Adams
- James Armistead
- Crispus Attucks
- Moses Austin
- Stephen F. Austin
- James A. Baker III
- William Blackstone
- Simón Bolívar
- Napoleon Bonaparte
- Chief Bowles
- Omar Bradley
- John C. Calhoun
- César Chávez
- Wentworth Cheswell
- George Childress
- Winston Churchill
- Henry Clay
- Bill Clinton
- Jefferson Davis
- Martin De León
- Green DeWitt
- Dwight Eisenhower
- James Fannin
- James L. Farmer, Jr.
- Benjamin Franklin
- Milton Friedman
- Betty Friedan
- Bernardo de Gálvez
- Hector P. Garcia
- John Nance Garner
- King George III
- Henry B. González
- Raul A. Gonzalez, Jr.
- Mikhail Gorbachev
- William Goyens
- Ulysses S. Grant
- José Gutiérrez de Lara
- Alexander Hamilton
- Hammurabi
- Warren Harding
- Friedrich Hayek
- Jack Coffee Hays
- Patrick Henry
- Adolf Hitler
- Oveta Culp Hobby
- James Hogg
- Sam Houston
- Kay Bailey Hutchison
- Andrew Jackson
- John Jay
- Thomas Jefferson
- Lyndon B. Johnson
- Anson Jones
- Barbara Jordan
- Justinian
- John F. Kennedy
- John Maynard Keynes
- Martin Luther King, Jr.
- Marquis de Lafayette
- Mirabeau B. Lamar
- Robert E. Lee
- Abraham Lincoln
- John Locke
- James Madison
- John Marshall
- George Marshall
- Karl Marx
- George Mason
- Mary Maverick
- Jane McCallum
- Joseph McCarthy
- James Monroe
- Charles de Montesquieu
- Edwin W. Moore
- Moses
- Benito Mussolini
- José Antonio Navarro
- Chester A. Nimitz
- Richard M. Nixon
- Barack Obama
- Sandra Day O'Connor
- Thomas Paine
- Quanah Parker
- Rosa Parks
- George Patton
- John J. Pershing
- John Paul II
- Sam Rayburn
- Ronald Reagan
- Hiram Rhodes Revels
- Franklin D. Roosevelt
- Theodore Roosevelt
- Lawrence Sullivan Ross
- Haym Soloman
- Antonio Lopez de Santa Anna
- Phyllis Schlafly
- Erasmo Seguín
- Juan N. Seguín
- Roger Sherman
- Adam Smith
- Joseph Stalin
- Raymond L. Telles
- Alexis de Tocqueville
- Hideki Tojo
- William B. Travis
- Harry Truman
- Lech Walesa
- Mercy Otis Warren
- George Washington
- Daniel Webster
- Lulu Belle Madison White
- William Wilberforce
- James Wilson
- Woodrow Wilson
- Lorenzo de Zavala
- Mao Zedong

21st Century Skills

- Identify Main Ideas and Details
- Set a Purpose for Reading
- Use Context Clues
- Analyze Cause and Effect
- Categorize
- Compare and Contrast
- Draw Conclusions
- Draw Inferences
- Generalize
- Make Decisions
- Make Predictions
- Sequence
- Solve Problems
- Summarize
- Analyze Media Content
- Analyze Primary and Secondary Sources
- Compare Viewpoints
- Distinguish Between Fact and Opinion
- Identify Bias
- Analyze Data and Models
- Analyze Images
- Analyze Political Cartoons
- Create Charts and Maps
- Create Databases
- Read Charts, Graphs, and Tables
- Read Physical Maps
- Read Political Maps
- Read Special-Purpose Maps
- Use Parts of a Map
- Ask Questions
- Avoid Plagiarism
- Create a Research Hypothesis
- Evaluate Web Sites
- Identify Evidence
- Identify Trends
- Interpret Sources
- Search for Information on the Internet
- Synthesize
- Take Effective Notes
- Develop a Clear Thesis
- Organize Your Ideas
- Support Ideas With Evidence
- Evaluate Existing Arguments
- Consider & Counter Opposing Arguments
- Give an Effective Presentation
- Participate in a Discussion or Debate
- Publish Your Work
- Write a Journal Entry
- Write an Essay
- Share Responsibility
- Compromise
- Develop Cultural Awareness
- Generate New Ideas
- Innovate
- Make a Difference
- Work in Teams
- Being an Informed Citizen
- Paying Taxes
- Political Participation
- Serving on a Jury
- Voting

Atlas

- United States: Political
- United States: Physical
- World Political
- World Physical
- World Climate
- World Ecosystems
- World Population Density
- World Land Use
- North Africa and Southwest Asia: Political
- North Africa and Southwest Asia: Physical
- Sub-Saharan Africa: Political
- Sub-Saharan Africa: Physical
- South Asia: Political
- South Asia: Physical
- East Asia: Political
- East Asia: Physical
- Southeast Asia: Political
- Southeast Asia: Physical
- Europe: Political
- Europe: Physical
- Russia, Central Asia, and the Caucasus: Political
- Russia, Central Asia, and the Caucasus: Physical
- North America: Political
- North America: Physical
- Central America and the Caribbean: Political
- Central America and the Caribbean: Physical
- South America: Political
- South America: Physical
- Australia and the Pacific: Political
- Australia and the Pacific: Physical

Creating an Active Classroom

This Social Studies program places a strong emphasis on **Inquiry** in the form of

- Document-Based Questions
- Project-Based Learning
- Civic Discussions

Each inquiry strand requires students to formulate their own arguments based on evidence. To support this learning approach, the program integrates **Active Classroom strategies** throughout each lesson. These strategies encourage students to begin building their own arguments and collecting evidence about the past and present at even the earliest stages of a lesson.

You can use these strategies to help students participate in their own learning as you call upon them to

- draw
- write
- speak
- decide

You'll find a rich variety of these strategy suggestions throughout both the Teacher's Edition and online **Teacher Support** for each lesson.

ACTIVE CLASSROOM STRATEGIES

ACTIVITY NAME	HOW TO ACTIVATE
Quickdraw	· Pair students and give them 30 seconds to share what they know about a concept or Key Term by creating a symbol or drawing.
Graffiti Concepts	· Ask students to reflect on the meaning of a concept or idea and create a visual image and/or written phrase that represents that concept. Allow approximately 3–5 minutes. · Next ask students to post their "graffiti" on the board or on chart paper and ask students to look at all the various responses. · Next discuss similarities and differences in the responses as a group.
Word Wall	· Ask students to chose one of the Key Terms for the lesson and create a visual image with a text definition. Allow approximately 3–5 minutes. · Ask students to post their words on the board or on chart paper and ask students to look at all the various responses. · Discuss similarities and differences in the responses as a group. · Pick a few favorites and post them on the class "Word Wall" for the year.
Cartoon It	· Ask students to make a quick drawing of one compelling image from this lesson on a piece of paper. · Next ask students to turn their drawing into a political cartoon that illustrates a key concept or main idea from the lesson by adding a text caption or text "bubbles." · Ask students to share their cartoons with a partner or within small groups.
Wallpaper	· Ask students to review information they have learned in a topic and design a piece of "wallpaper" that encapsulates key learnings. · Then have students post their wallpaper and take a "gallery" walk noting what others have written and illustrated in their samples.
Quick Write	· Ask students to write what they know about a key idea or term in 30 seconds.
Make Headlines	· Have students write a headline that captures the key idea in a map, photo, timeline, or reading. · Ask students to share their headline with a partner.
Circle Write	· Break into groups and provide a writing prompt or key question. · Have students write as much as they can in response to the question or prompt for 1 minute. · Next have students give their response to the person on their right. That person should improve or elaborate on the response where the other person left off. · Continue to pass each response to the right until the original response comes back to the first person. · Each group then reviews all the responses and decides which is the best composition and shares that with the larger group.

ACTIVE CLASSROOM STRATEGIES

ACTIVITY NAME	HOW TO ACTIVATE
Write 1-Get 3 (or Write 5-Get 4)	· Ask a question with multiple answers, such as: What are 4 key characteristics of ______ (a dictator)? What are the 5 key causes of _____? · Have students write down 1 response and then go around the room asking for 3 other responses. If they think a response is correct, ask them to write it down. · Have students keep asking and writing until they have 3 more responses on their page. · Have students share and discuss responses with the class.
Sticky Notes	· Ask students to spend three minutes jotting down their response to a critical thinking question on a sticky note. · Ask students to work in pairs and share their responses. · Next ssk students to post their sticky notes on the board or on chart paper and read all the notes. · Discuss similarities and differences in the responses as a group.
Connect Two	· Select 10 to 12 words or phrases you think are important for students to know prior to reading a selection. · List the words on the board. · Ask students to “Connect Two” or choose two words they think might belong together, and state the reason. “I would connect ______ and ______ because ______.” Consider posting their Connect Two statements on the board. · As students read the text they should look for evidence to support or refute their Connect Two statements.
Conversation With History	· Ask students to choose one of the people mentioned or pictured in the text and write down a question they would like to ask that person if they could. · Next ask students to write what they think that person would say in response and then what they would say in response to that.
Walking Tour	· Post passages from a reading around the room. · Ask small groups to tour the room and discuss each passage. · Summarize each passage as a class. · Alternatively, assign each small group to a passage and have them summarize that passage for the rest of the class.
Audio Tour	· Ask students to work in pairs. Have the first student give the second a verbal “tour” of a map or graph or infographic. · Have the second student give the first an explanation of what the graphic shows.

ACTIVE CLASSROOM STRATEGIES

ACTIVITY NAME	HOW TO ACTIVATE
My Metaphor	· Post the following metaphor on the board: This (map, timeline, image, primary source) shows that _____ is like _________ because __________________. · Ask students to fill in the metaphor prompt based on their understanding of the source.
Act It Out	· Choose an image in the lesson and ask students to think about one of the following questions as appropriate to the image: · What may have happened next in this image? · What may have happened just before this image? · What do you think the people in this image are thinking? · What do you think the people in this image are saying to each other?
If Photos/Images/Art Could Talk	· Ask the following questions about an image in the course: What do you think the person in this photo would say if they could talk? What's your evidence?
See-Think-Wonder	· Ask students to work in pairs. · Ask them to look at an image, map, or graph and answer these questions: · What do you see? · What does that make you think? · What are you wondering about now that you've seen this? · Have students share their answers with the class.
A Closer Look	· Project a map or image on the board and divide it into four numbered quadrants. · Have students count off from 1 to 4 into four small groups. Have each group look closely at the part of the image in their quadrant. · Have each small group report on what they observed and learned as a result of their focus on this part of the image.
Take a Stand	· Ask students to take a stand on a yes-or-no or agree/disagree critical thinking question. · Ask students to divide into two groups based on their answer and move to separate areas of the classroom. · Ask students to talk with each other to compare their reasons for answering yes or no. · Ask a representative from each side to present and defend the group's point of view. · Note: you can adapt this activity to have students take their place on a continuum line from 1 to 10 depending on how strongly they agree or disagree.

ACTIVE CLASSROOM STRATEGIES

ACTIVITY NAME	HOW TO ACTIVATE
Rank It	· List a group of items/concepts/steps/causes/events on the board. · Ask students to rank the items/steps . . . according to X criteria (which is most important, which had the greatest impact . . . most influential, essential, changed, affected). · Ask students to provide a justification for the ranking decisions they made. · Then ask students to work in pairs to share their rankings and justifications. · Poll the class to see if there is agreement on the ranking. OR · Place stickies on the board with key events from the lesson or topic. · Break students into small groups and ask each group to go up and choose the sticky with what they think is the most significant event. · Ask the group to discuss among themselves why they think it is most significant. · Ask one person from each group to explain why the group chose that event.
Sequence It	· Place key events from a lesson or topic on sticky notes on the board. · Ask students to place the events in chronological order. · You could do this activity with multiple groups in different parts of the classroom.
PMI Plus/Minus/Interesting	· Place students in groups and give each group a 3-column organizer with headings Plus/Minus/Interesting for recording responses. · Ask students to analyze a text or examine an issue and then answer these three questions in their organizer: 1. What was positive about this text/issue? 2. What was negative about this text/issue? 3. What was interesting about this text/issue?

PRINT STUDENT EDITION

Celebrate Freedom

"We hold these truths to be self-evident, that all men are created equal, that they are endowed by their Creator with certain unalienable Rights, that among these are Life, Liberty and the pursuit of Happiness. That to secure these rights, Governments are instituted among Men, deriving their just powers from the consent of the governed. . . ."

Declaration of Independence

Every year, you and your classmates may participate in Celebrate Freedom Week activities. These activities are designed to remind you about some of the important ideas that make our country so special. In your school, you may have school-wide displays or an assembly. Maybe speakers come to share their thoughts or students write essays or make posters or develop presentations. Whatever happens in your school, you will likely take some time to think about America's founding documents, such as the Declaration of Independence.

The Declaration of Independence states some of America's most important ideas about society and government. It has played a key role in shaping America's constitutional republic. As you recite the words, think about why many students join in Celebrate Freedom Week.

Summarize According to the Declaration of Independence, who has rights? Who can take them away?

Paraphrase In your own words, restate the idea in the Declaration about the purpose of government.

Analyze Why do you think many students recite part of the Declaration of Independence when they celebrate Freedom Week?

self-evident, adj., obvious
endowed, v. given; provided
unalienable, adj., not to be taken away
deriving, v., getting from a source
consent, n., agreement

The Bill of Rights

One of the chief ways early American leaders tried to protect individual rights was by adding the first ten Amendments to the Constitution. This section is known as the Bill of Rights. The Bill of Rights guarantees certain legal rights, and it limits the power of the government to interfere with others.

Constructing an Argument Write an essay discussing one of the rights guaranteed in the Bill of Rights.

1. Review the Bill of Rights in the U.S. Constitution in the online Reference Center or at the back of your book. Notice that the Constitution has Commentary on the side of the actual document. This Commentary helps explain the language in the Constitution and can give you some background about each provision. Use the Commentary to help you review the first ten Amendments, or Bill of Rights.
2. Choose one basic right as the focus of your essay. Note that several of the Amendments—including the First, Fifth, and Sixth—are divided into different parts, each dealing with a specific right. You may choose to focus on one part of one of these Amendments rather than the entire Amendment.
3. Research a recent event or situation where the right you have chosen was protected or threatened. This might be an event or situation in your local community or a nearby community, in your state, or somewhere else in the nation. Be sure to use more than one source and to use reliable sources.
4. Begin your essay by naming the Amendment you have chosen, and restating in your own words what the right protects or guarantees.
5. Explain why you believe that right is important to guarantee liberty today.
6. Describe what you think might happen if that right were not protected by the Constitution.
7. Support your opinion with facts you have learned from your research.
8. Don't forget to check and revise your essay, as needed. Be sure to use proper grammar, spelling, and sentence structure.
9. After you write your essay, your teacher may ask you and your classmates to share your views with the class. If so, remember to speak clearly and to present your views using the evidence you gathered for your essay. When listening to others, listen closely and be respectful of their views.

>> The First Amendment protects the right to petition.

Objective 1: **Understand the intent, meaning, and importance of the Declaration of Independence; 2: Recite the opening text from the Declaration of Independence.**

Quick Instruction

Using these materials, students can prepare for Celebrate Freedom Week, by thinking about the importance of the Declaration of Independence and the Bill of Rights. The materials will help you make links between the Declaration and your course of study.

Aa Vocabulary Development: Before students recite the words from the Declaration, review key terms the key terms "self-evident," "endowed," "unalienable," "deriving," and "consent." Ask students to compose a sentence using each word. Then have students paraphrase the excerpt from the Declaration, putting the ideas into their own words.

Further Instruction

Have students recite the key section from the Declaration of Independence, "We hold these truths…" to each other or as a whole class.

Summarize *all men have rights; no one can take them away, because they are unalienable.*

Paraphrase *Sample: Governments are set up in order to protect people's rights.*

Analyze *Sample: They recite the words to remember that our country started because of a beliefs in our rights and we still believe that people have rights today.*

Bill of Rights Teach

Plan Help student review the Bill of Rights found in the U.S. Constitution in the Reference Center or in the back of their books. They might be particularly interested in the First (freedom of religion, speech, press, assembly, and petition), Second (bearing arms), Fourth (searches and seizures). Fifth (criminal proceedings; due process; eminent domain), Sixth (criminal proceedings), and Eighth (punishment for crimes). You might suggest students work in pairs as they consider the provisions of the amendments. This closer study will help each student choose the Amendment on which they want to focus their research.

Explore Students might begin their research with the local newspaper, or they could conduct an online search using key words related to the Amendment they have chosen. As they do their research, remind students to use several sources and to be sure the sources are reliable. Remind them to keep track of information about their sources, such as source name, date, location, and so on.

Communicate Remind students of the basics of a good essay. Have them sketch a rough outline. The thesis statement should directly respond to the assignment. Tell students to start their essay with a clear statement of the thesis, to use specific examples and details to support it, and to finish with a strong conclusion.

ADDITIONAL LESSON RESOURCES

- Print student text
- Declaration of Independence
- United States Constitution
- Pledge of Allegiance to the U.S. Flag
- Celebrate Freedom Resources

Topic 1

The Early Americas and European Exploration (Prehistory–1550)

TOPIC 1 ORGANIZER	PACING: APPROX. 6 PERIODS, 3 BLOCKS
	PACING
Connect	1 period
MY STORY VIDEO **Austin Celebrates His Heritage**	10 min.
DIGITAL ESSENTIAL QUESTION ACTIVITY **How Much Does Geography Affect People's Lives?**	10 min.
DIGITAL MAP ACTIVITY **Physical Features of the United States**	10 min.
TOPIC INQUIRY: DOCUMENT-BASED QUESTION **How Reliable is This Account of the Easter Mutiny?**	20 min.
Investigate	1–3 periods
TOPIC INQUIRY: DOCUMENT-BASED QUESTION **How Reliable is This Account of the Easter Mutiny?**	Ongoing
LESSON 1 The Early Americas	30–40 min.
LESSON 2 Early Europe, Africa, and Asia	30–40 min.
LESSON 3 European Exploration in the Americas	30–40 min.
Synthesize	1 period
DIGITAL ACTIVITY **Reflect on the Essential Question and Topic**	10 min.
TOPIC INQUIRY: DOCUMENT-BASED QUESTION **How Reliable is This Account of the Easter Mutiny?**	20 min.
Demonstrate	1–2 periods
DIGITAL TOPIC TEST **The Early Americas and European Exploration**	10 min.
TOPIC INQUIRY: DOCUMENT-BASED QUESTION **How Reliable is This Account of the Easter Mutiny?**	20 min.

NOTES

TOPIC INQUIRY: DOCUMENT-BASED QUESTION

How Reliable is This Account of the Easter Mutiny?

While Ferdinand Magellan led the first successful expedition to circumnavigate the world, it was not without significant difficulty and sacrifice on the part of his crew. Magellan had difficulty maintaining his leadership, and a mutiny broke out in 1520. Written accounts of the mutiny exist, but in this Inquiry, students will examine the account of the voyage's record keeper, Antonio Pigafetta, to evaluate its veracity.

STEP 1: CONNECT

Develop Questions and Plan the Investigation

Watch the Entry Event and Discuss

Explain to students that they will evaluate the validity of a primary source about the mutiny that took place during Ferdinand Magellan's voyage in 1520 based on language, corroboration with other sources, and information about the author. They will decide whether or not this account of the mutiny is a reliable description of what took place. Review the primary source, including the language it uses, and the corroborating sources on Magellan's expedition. Then have students view the information about the author.

Suggestion: You can have students watch the biography together in class, or assign them to view it on their own.

Discuss: Have students discuss the video as a class or in small groups. Ask students to explain the reasons for Magellan's expedition and why his route matters today. Students should also imagine what challenges the expedition held for Magellan and his crew. Remind students to use examples from the biography in their discussion.

Suggestion: If you'd prefer students to work outside of class time, you can assign them to write down their thoughts or share them on a class blog or discussion board.

PROFESSIONAL DEVELOPMENT

Document-Based Question

Be sure to view the Document-Based Question Professional Development resources in the online course.

STEP 2: INVESTIGATE

Apply Disciplinary Concepts and Tools

Analyze the Documents

Students will work independently to analyze six sources relating to the expedition. Guide students to write down key facts and observations about each source.

Suggestion: Tell students to make a separate list of notes for each source to help them organize their thinking.

Check Your Understanding

Students will answer the multiple choice and short answer questions attached to each document. Students can discuss the answers in pairs or as a class to ensure understanding.

Suggestion: To save time, students can complete the questions on their own and then check their answers in class.

STEP 3: SYNTHESIZE

Evaluate Sources and Use Evidence to Formulate Conclusions

Write Your Essay

Have students prepare the first draft of their essay. Tell students to gather the relevant information from each source and review the notes they took as they examined the documents. Remind students to include evidence from at least one document with information about the author of the primary source and at least two documents that corroborate or conflict with the primary source.

STEP 4: DEMONSTRATE

Communicate Conclusions and Take Informed Action

Complete Your Essay

Have students revise and submit their essays. Remind students to read over their essays for any errors before turning it in.

Suggestion: When students finish drafting their essays, have them exchange essays with a partner to review. Students should look for topic sentences, organization, evidence, facts, and integration of opposing arguments, as well as correct spelling, grammar, and punctuation.

Suggestion: Have students share with the class whether or not they think Pigafetta's account of the mutiny is valid, or reliable, giving evidence from their essays to support their argument.

INTRODUCTION

The Early Americas and European Exploration (Prehistory–1550)

The United States is a vast country encompassing different geographic regions, from icy mountains to some of the driest, hottest deserts on Earth. The first people to settle in the Americas had their way of life shaped by the environment and resources where they lived. The arrival of the first Europeans brought many changes, with both positive and negative results.

CONNECT

MY STORY VIDEO

Austin Celebrates His Heritage

Watch a video about a brother and sister as they learn more about their ancestry.

Check Understanding What musical instrument is essential to Native American culture? *(Drum)*

Determine Point of View What words best describe Austin's perspective about his heritage? *(pride, eagerness to find out more, desire to set a good example)*

DIGITAL ESSENTIAL QUESTION ACTIVITY

How Much Does Geography Affect People's Lives?

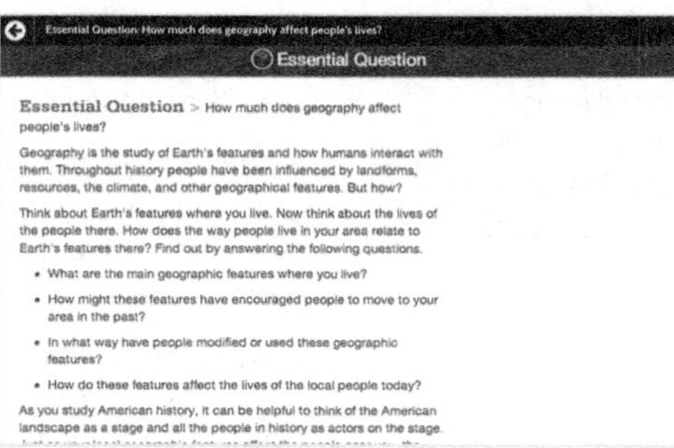
Essential Question: How much does geography affect people's lives?

Essential Question

Essential Question > How much does geography affect people's lives?

Geography is the study of Earth's features and how humans interact with them. Throughout history people have been influenced by landforms, resources, the climate, and other geographical features. But how?

Think about Earth's features where you live. Now think about the lives of the people there. How does the way people live in your area relate to Earth's features there? Find out by answering the following questions.

- What are the main geographic features where you live?
- How might these features have encouraged people to move to your area in the past?
- In what way have people modified or used these geographic features?
- How do these features affect the lives of the local people today?

As you study American history, it can be helpful to think of the American landscape as a stage and all the people in history as actors on the stage.

Ask students to think about the Essential Question for this Topic: How much does geography affect people's lives? Geography is the study of Earth's features and how humans interact with them. What role does it play in shaping societies?

If students have not already done so, ask them to think about the questions in the activity. Then go over the answers as a class.

Compare and Contrast Ask students to pick two areas in the United States with dissimilar geographies and explain how life would differ in each area as a result. *(Midwestern plains and northeastern woodlands; in the Midwest the flat land makes farming easier.)*

Support Ideas with Examples Do you think the amount that geography affects people's lives has changed over time? Why or why not? Provide examples to support your view. *(Geography may affect people's lives less now than in the past. For example, heating and air conditioning mean people can live more comfortably year-round in hot and cold climates)*

DIGITAL MAP ACTIVITY

Physical Features of the United States

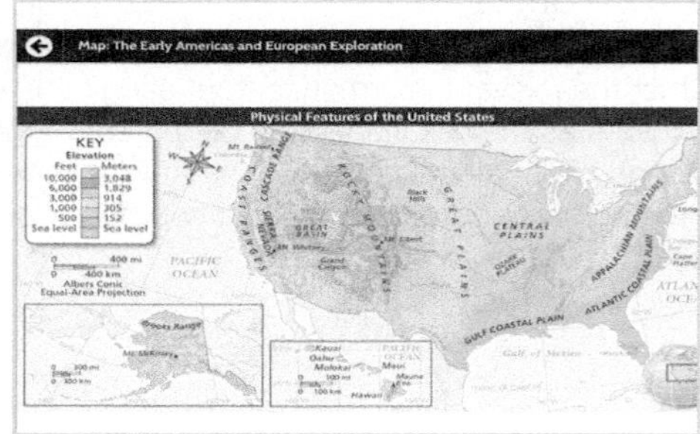

Display the map showing the physical features of the United States. During this Topic students will learn about the early peoples of North America. This map will help them understand the regions in which Native Americans lived.

Analyze Information What region of the United States has the highest elevation? What does this tell you about that area? *(The west; this area is mountainous)*

Analyze Maps Describe three things you notice about the physical features of the United States, based on this map. *(Elevation changes; extensive plains; several large rivers)*

Topic Inquiry

Launch the Topic Inquiry DBQ with students after introducing the topic.

PEARSON realize™ www.PearsonRealize.com Access your Digital Lesson

The Early Americas

Supporting English Language Learners

Use with Digital Text 6, **Early North American Societies.**

Learning, Speaking

Ask one or more volunteers to read aloud the first paragraph of the reading. Then point out certain key words in the text, and invite students to share how prior knowledge helps them to understand the meanings of these words. Ask students to use vocabulary from the reading to ask for more information about the reading content. Prompt students to use a range of vocabulary, from key words and expressions needed for basic communication to more abstract, content-based vocabulary during speaking assignments.

Beginning Identify basic words in the text, such as "complex," "culture," and "migrating." Ask students to work in pairs, using those words in questions and responding to them using prior knowledge related to the content.

Intermediate Have students focus on the second sentence in the reading. Ask students to work in pairs, asking what the words in the sentence mean, and responding with examples from previous lessons of each of the items mentioned in the sentence.

Advanced Have students work in pairs and take turns speaking for a couple of minutes each. Have them use vocabulary to state questions they had about the reading and to explain how prior knowledge, from previous lessons or outside the course, enriches their understanding of the content.

Advanced High Invite students to give extended spoken presentations to one another or to the class. Have them share their questions about the content that use abstract, content-based vocabulary, and have them respond to those questions drawing on prior knowledge in ways that enrich students' understanding of the content.

Use with Digital Text 7, **Culture and Physical Geography of North America.**

Writing

Read aloud the section *Cultures of the Northwest Coastal Region*, or invite volunteers to do so. Prompt students to write explanations with increasing specificity and detail to fulfill content area writing needs.

Beginning Have students reread the first paragraph of this reading aloud. Invite students to ask questions about parts of the paragraph that they do not understand. Then have students explain briefly in writing why people in the Northwest stayed in permanent villages.

Intermediate Ask students to write a brief paragraph explaining how the physical environment affected the ways of life of people in the Northwest.

Advanced Have students write a paragraph explain in detail how the environment of the Northwest was related to the customs of its people.

Advanced High Invite to write an essay explaining in detail how the physical environment of the Northwest was connect to the people's culture, including the custom of potlatches.

D Differentiate Instruction

Use the Differentiated Instruction notes throughout the lesson plan to support the varied skill sets, levels of readiness, and interests in the mixed-ability classroom.

Challenge These notes include suggestions for expanding the activity for advanced students.

On-Level These notes include suggestions for modifying the activity to address different interests or learning styles.

Extra Support These notes include ideas for providing more scaffolding or reading spupport.

Special Needs These notes provide ideas for adapting instruction to support the needs of various special needs students.

NOTES

Topic 1 Lesson 1

The Early Americas

Objectives

Objective 1: Explain how people first reached the Americas.

Objective 2: Describe early civilizations and cultures of the Americas.

Objective 3: Identify the human and physical characteristics of regions.

Objective 4: Analyze how physical characteristics influenced population distribution and settlement patterns.

LESSON 1 ORGANIZER			PACING: APPROX. 1 PERIOD, .5 BLOCKS	
			RESOURCES	
	OBJECTIVES	PACING	Online	Print
Connect				
DIGITAL START UP ACTIVITY **Physical Geography Affects Ways of Life**		5 min.	●	
Investigate				
DIGITAL TEXT 1 **The First Americans**	Objective 1	10 min.	●	●
DIGITAL TEXT 2; DIGITAL TEXT 3 **Olmecs Develop a Civilization; Mayan Civilization**	Objective 2	20 min.	●	●
DIGITAL TEXT 4; DIGITAL TEXT 5 **Aztec Civilization; Incan Civilization**	Objective 2	20 min.	●	●
DIGITAL TEXT 6; DIGITAL TEXT 7 **Early North American Societies; Culture and Physical Geography of North America**	Objective 3	20 min.	●	●
INTERACTIVE MAP **Native American Culture Regions of North America**	Objective 3	10 min.	●	
DIGITAL TEXT 8; DIGITAL TEXT 9 **Religion; The Iroquois League**	Objective 4	20 min.	●	●
INTERACTIVE GALLERY **Housing Adaptations Based on Environment**	Objective 4	10 min.	●	
Synthesize				
DIGITAL ACTIVITY **Adapting to the Environment**		5 min.	●	
Demonstrate				
DIGITAL QUIZ **Lesson Quiz and Class Discussion Board**		10 min.	●	

Go online to access additional resources including: Primary Sources • Biographies • Supreme Court cases • 21st Century Skill Tutorials • Maps • Graphic Organizers.

CONNECT

DIGITAL START UP ACTIVITY

Physical Geography Affects Ways of Life

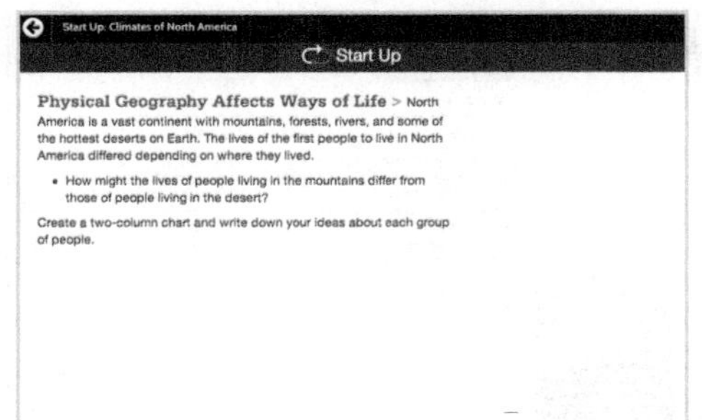

Project the Start Up Activity Ask students to look at the map as they enter and get settled. Then have them discuss their answers with another student, either in class or through a chat or blog space.

Discuss What would people do if they lived somewhere very cold? What about somewhere very hot? *(Use furs for warm clothing; build settlements in shade)* How might people find food if they lived near water? What about in the hills? *(Fishing, hunting, trapping game, gathering plants)*

Tell students that in this lesson they will be learning about how the physical characteristics of the environment shaped where Native Americans settled and how they lived.

Aa Vocabulary Development: Use the Interactive Reading Notepad to preview the Key Terms and Academic Vocabulary in the lesson with students.

FLIP IT!

Assign the Flipped Video for this lesson.

STUDENT EDITION PRINT PAGES: 4–20

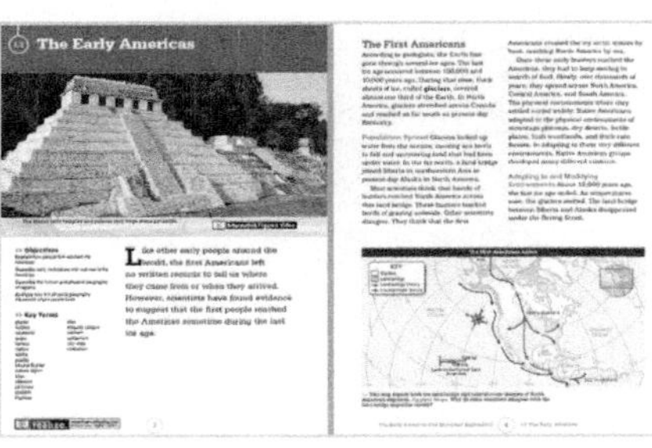

INVESTIGATE

DIGITAL TEXT 1

The First Americans

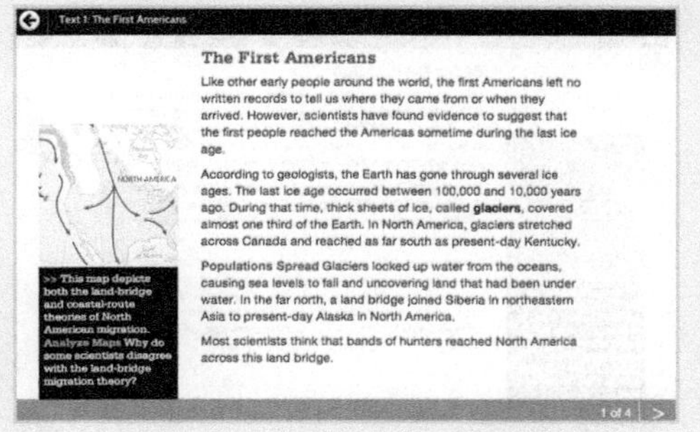

Objective 1: Explain how people first reached the Americas.

Quick Instruction

Project the image on the whiteboard. Explain to students that the physical characteristics of the environment influenced population distribution and early settlements in North America.

Categorize Ask students to describe the physical characteristics of different environments in the United States, such as deserts, mountains, and forests.

D Differentiate: Challenge Ask students to describe the physical characteristics of their environment and explain how these characteristics influence their community.

Further Instruction

Go through the Interactive Reading Notepad questions and discuss the answers with the class. To extend the lesson, have students go through the additional resource Geography: People and Their Environments.

Sequence Events Have students explain the process by which Native Americans spread across and came to settle in North America. *(They arrived on foot over land exposed by lower sea levels, or by sea, and spread across the continent in search of food, eventually building settlements around farming.)*

Make Predictions Ask students to predict how the different geographical regions of North America will impact Native American groups. *(Native Americans will adapt differently to their regions, developing different settlements and ways of life.)*

DIGITAL TEXT 2

Olmecs Develop a Civilization

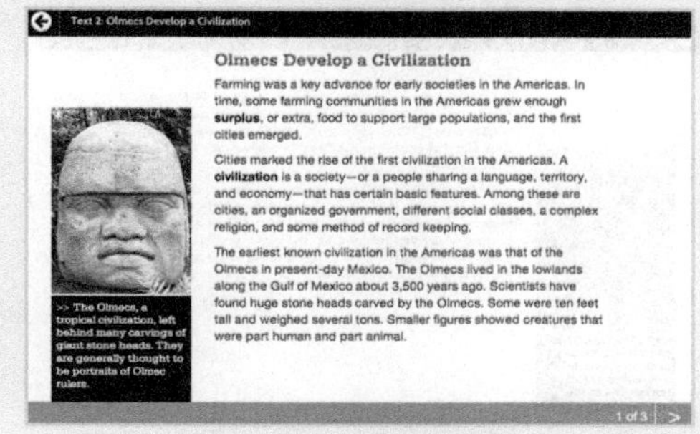

Objective 2: Describe early civilizations and cultures of the Americas.

Quick Instruction

Project the image on the whiteboard. Explain that the Olmecs and the Mayas were two different tropical civilizations that were shaped by the physical characteristics of their environment in Central America. In both civilizations, farmers supported nearby cities and leaders built temples of stone. The Olmecs also built giant stone heads.

Compare and Contrast How might the Olmec and Maya civilizations differ from a civilization built in a colder region? Why? *(There would be more opportunities for farming. The clothing, food, and houses would differ.)*

Further Instruction

Go through the Interactive Reading Notepad questions for *Olmec Civilization and Maya Civilization* with the class, including the graphic organizer asking students to describe the features of the Olmec civilization. Review the features of the civilization on the whiteboard as you go.

Be sure that students understand that the physical characteristics of the environment in Central America influenced features of Olmec civilization. Discuss how both Olmec and Maya settlements were shaped by the geographic region in which the civilizations lived.

The Early Americas

DIGITAL TEXT 3

Mayan Civilization

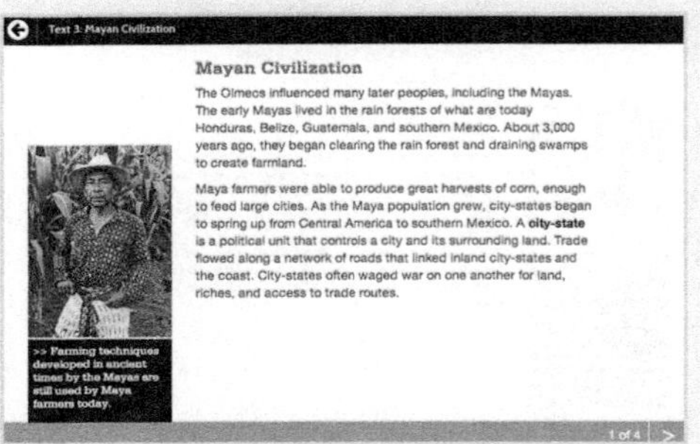

Text 3: Mayan Civilization
Mayan Civilization
The Olmecs influenced many later peoples, including the Mayas. The early Mayas lived in the rain forests of what are today Honduras, Belize, Guatemala, and southern Mexico. About 3,000 years ago, they began clearing the rain forest and draining swamps to create farmland.
Maya farmers were able to produce great harvests of corn, enough to feed large cities. As the Maya population grew, city-states began to spring up from Central America to southern Mexico. A city-state is a political unit that controls a city and its surrounding land. Trade flowed along a network of roads that linked inland city-states and the coast. City-states often waged war on one another for land, riches, and access to trade routes.
>> Farming techniques developed in ancient times by the Mayas are still used by Maya farmers today.
1 of 4

Identify Cause and Effect How did farming cause Olmec cities to grow? *(Farming allowed people to build permanent settlements. Having sufficient food enabled larger populations to grow.)*

Generate Explanations Have students explain why the Mayas' successful farming enabled the civilization to make developments in mathematics and astronomy. *(Successful harvests meant not everyone had to farm. Priests therefore had the time to study.)*

DIGITAL TEXT 4

Aztec Civilization

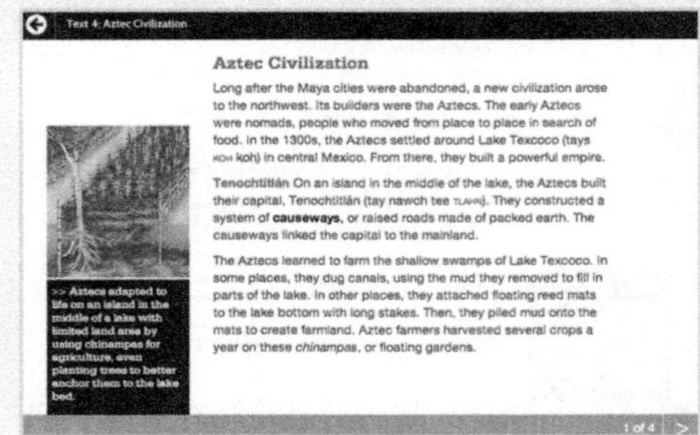

Text 4: Aztec Civilization
Aztec Civilization
Long after the Maya cities were abandoned, a new civilization arose to the northwest. Its builders were the Aztecs. The early Aztecs were nomads, people who moved from place to place in search of food. In the 1300s, the Aztecs settled around Lake Texcoco (tays KOH koh) in central Mexico. From there, they built a powerful empire.
Tenochtitlán On an island in the middle of the lake, the Aztecs built their capital, Tenochtitlán (tay nawch tee TLAHN). They constructed a system of causeways, or raised roads made of packed earth. The causeways linked the capital to the mainland.
The Aztecs learned to farm the shallow swamps of Lake Texcoco. In some places, they dug canals, using the mud they removed to fill in parts of the lake. In other places, they attached floating reed mats to the lake bottom with long stakes. Then, they piled mud onto the mats to create farmland. Aztec farmers harvested several crops a year on these chinampas, or floating gardens.
>> Aztecs adapted to life on an island in the middle of a lake with limited land area by using chinampas for agriculture, even planting trees to better anchor them to the lake bed.
1 of 4

Objective 2: Describe early civilizations and cultures of the Americas.

Quick Instruction

Project the image of Machu Picchu. Explain that the Aztecs were a civilization in present-day Mexico, while further south, the Incas built a civilization along the west coast of South America. The Aztecs settled near shallow swamps, and the Incas in the mountains. Both civilizations altered the land in order to farm.

Analyze Information Ask students to examine the image of Machu Picchu and describe the physical environment where the Incas lived. Then ask how and why the Incas modified their physical environment. *(The terrain was mountainous and rugged. The Incas cut flat areas into the mountains where they could build houses and farms.)*

Further Instruction

Go through the Interactive Reading Notepad questions for *Aztec Civilization and Inca Civilization* with the class.

Be sure that students understand how the physical characteristics of the environment influenced both the Aztecs and the Incas. Discuss the different environments where the two groups lived and the ways these differences were reflected in the civilizations.

DIGITAL TEXT 5

Incan Civilization

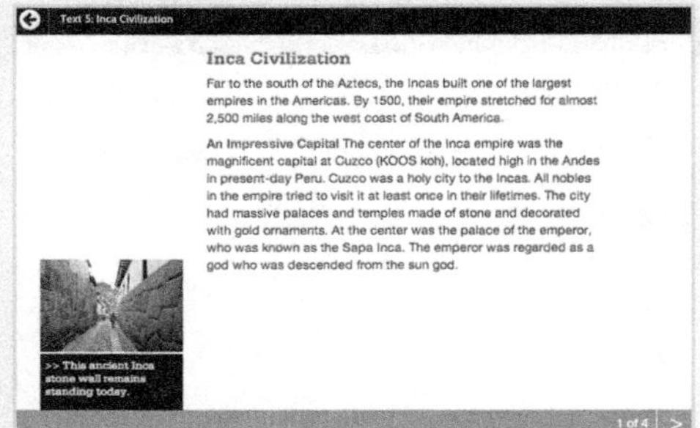

Text 5: Inca Civilization
Inca Civilization
Far to the south of the Aztecs, the Incas built one of the largest empires in the Americas. By 1500, their empire stretched for almost 2,500 miles along the west coast of South America.
An Impressive Capital The center of the Inca empire was the magnificent capital at Cuzco (KOOS koh), located high in the Andes in present-day Peru. Cuzco was a holy city to the Incas. All nobles in the empire tried to visit it at least once in their lifetimes. The city had massive palaces and temples made of stone and decorated with gold ornaments. At the center was the palace of the emperor, who was known as the Sapa Inca. The emperor was regarded as a god who was descended from the sun god.
>> This ancient Inca stone wall remains standing today.
1 of 4

Compare and Contrast where the Incas and the Aztecs lived and how they utilized their environments. *(The Aztecs settled around a lake. They built causeways, canals, and chinampas to farm and get around. The Incas built terraces with stone walls to farm in the mountains. They also built bridges and roads to travel through different regions.)*

Determine Relevance Why is it relevant to know about the physical characteristics of the region in which a civilization lived? *(The characteristics can explain what resources people had, how they used these resources, and how the resources shaped their way of life.)*

DIGITAL TEXT 6

Early North American Societies

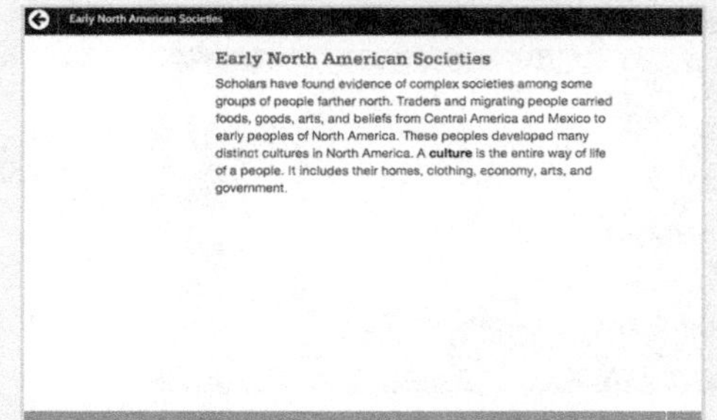

Early North American Societies
Early North American Societies
Scholars have found evidence of complex societies among some groups of people farther north. Traders and migrating people carried foods, goods, arts, and beliefs from Central America and Mexico to early peoples of North America. These peoples developed many distinct cultures in North America. A **culture** is the entire way of life of a people. It includes their homes, clothing, economy, arts, and government.
1 of 5

DIGITAL TEXT 7

Culture and the Physical Geography of North America

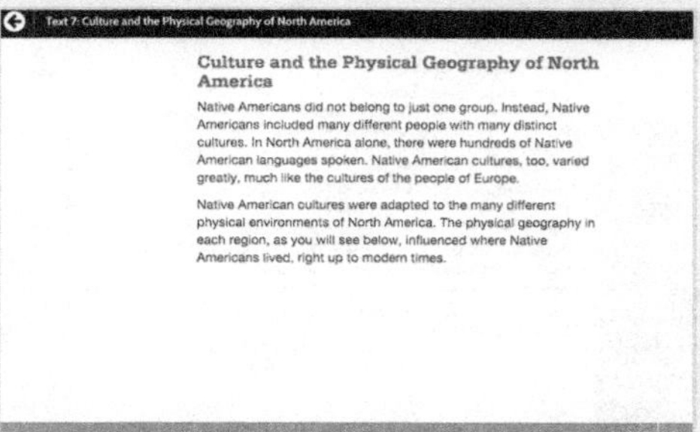

Text 7: Culture and the Physical Geography of North America
Culture and the Physical Geography of North America
Native Americans did not belong to just one group. Instead, Native Americans included many different people with many distinct cultures. In North America alone, there were hundreds of Native American languages spoken. Native American cultures, too, varied greatly, much like the cultures of the people of Europe.
Native American cultures were adapted to the many different physical environments of North America. The physical geography in each region, as you will see below, influenced where Native Americans lived, right up to modern times.
1 of 12

INTERACTIVE MAP

Native American Culture Regions of North America

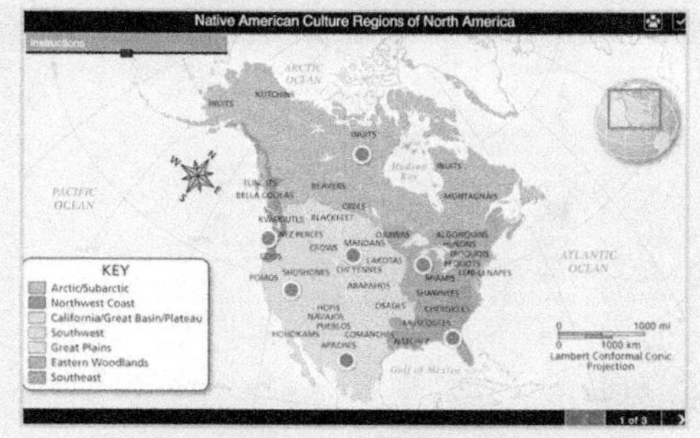

Objective 3: **Identify the human and physical characteristics of regions.**

Quick Instruction

Interactive Map: Native American Culture Regions of North America Project the map and click through the hotspots. Introduce the map activity by telling students that early North American societies were divided into different culture regions. The physical characteristics of these environments influenced the cultures that called each region home. Prompt students to compare these regions in terms of human characteristics.

ACTIVE CLASSROOM

Ask students to use the *Write 1-Get 3* strategy to describe four ways culture regions shaped early North American societies. *(Culture regions determined food, clothing, shelter, settlement patterns, artwork, and religious ceremonies.)*

Analyze Maps What physical characteristics of the environment led North America to be divided into different culture regions? *(Temperature; rainfall; geography; available natural resources)*

ELL Use the ELL activity described in the ELL chart.

Further Instruction

Go through the Interactive Reading Notepad questions for *Early North American Societies and Culture* and *Physical Characteristics of North America* with the class, including the graphic organizer asking students to explain how each Native American culture adapted to the climate and resources in the area.

Identify Central Issues How did the physical environment determine which Native American groups were nomadic and which groups lived in permanent or semi-permanent settlements? *(Native Americans built more permanent settlements in areas with sufficient food and natural resources throughout the year. When there were not enough resources to survive in one place, groups had to move.)*

Support Ideas with Evidence The Hohokams built irrigation ditches, while the Mount Builders did not use irrigation at all. How does this evidence show that the groups lived in different culture regions? *(The Mound Builders lived in a wetter climate than the Hohokams, evidenced by the fact that they did not need to irrigate their crops.)*

The Early Americas

DIGITAL TEXT 8

Religion

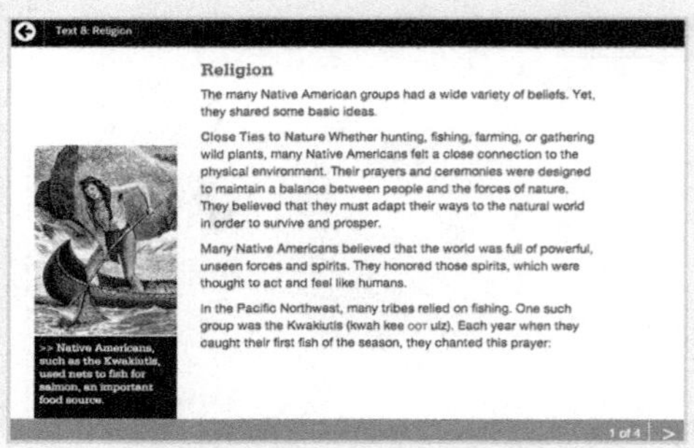

DIGITAL TEXT 9

The Iroquois League

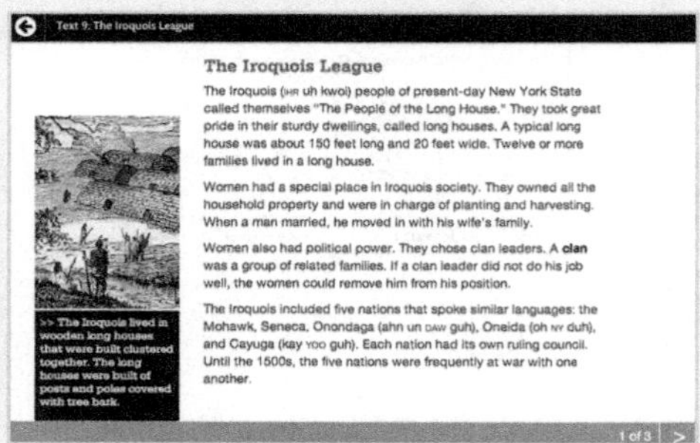

INTERACTIVE GALLERY

Housing Adaptations Based on Environment

Objective 4: Analyze how physical characteristics influenced population distribution and settlement patterns.

Quick Instruction

Remind students that the physical characteristics of regions shaped where people lived and what their lives were like. This includes people's religious practices and housing. It also includes their social and political structures, as with the Iroquois in present-day New York.

Interactive Gallery: Housing Adaptations Based on Environment Project the images. Look at each image individually and then the collection as a whole. Remind students that the human characteristics of each region were different. Native American groups lived in different types of dwellings depending on where they lived.

ACTIVE CLASSROOM

Create a quick copy of one compelling image from the Native American housing adaptations interactive gallery. Label the different features of the dwelling and explain how these features suited the environment in which the dwelling was used.

Analyze Images Ask students to describe the materials used to make the houses in the image gallery. Why was there such wide variety in materials used? *(Houses were made out of snow, clay, trees, and skins. They varied depending on what material were available, whether they needed to be portable, and whether they kept people warm or cool.)*

Further Instruction

Go through the Interactive Reading Notepad questions for *Religion* and *The Iroquios Confederacy* with the class. To extend the lesson, have students go through the additional resource Geography: Population and Settlements.

Remind students that Native American cultures, beliefs, and social structures were shaped by the environments in which people lived.

Draw Conclusions What conclusions about the human characteristics of Iroquois culture and society can you draw based on the fact that they lived in long houses? *(Long houses were built of trees, meaning Iroquois lived in wooded areas. Long houses are sturdy, meaning the Iroquois were not nomadic.)*

Identify Cause and Effect How did the physical environment affect Native American religious practices? *(Native Americans relied on the environment to survive. Ceremonies honored aspects of nature needed for survival, such as rain, fish, and corn.)*

SYNTHESIZE

DIGITAL ACTIVITY

Adapting to the Environment

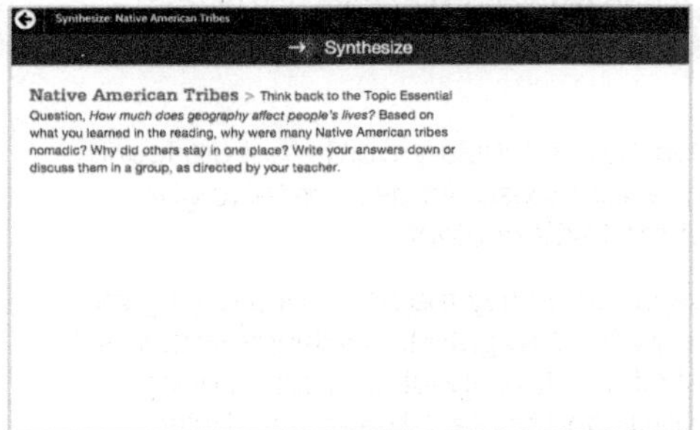

Have students use the Think-Pair-Share strategy to answer the questions in the Adapting to the Environment activity. Poll the class on which culture region that would most want to live in and then discuss why.

Have partners think about the following question. How do people adapt to the physical environments in which they live? Ask students to come up with examples from the lesson, and from their own lives.

DEMONSTRATE

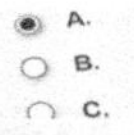

DIGITAL QUIZ

Lesson Quiz and Class Discussion Board

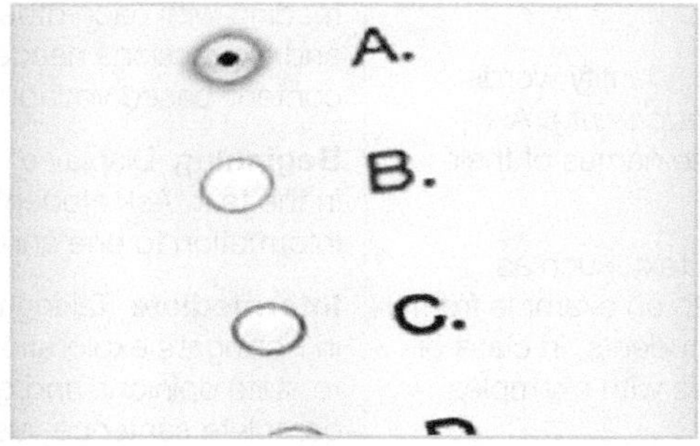

Assign the online Lesson Quiz for this lesson if you haven't already done so. Students will be offered automatic remediation or enrichment based on their score.

Pose these questions to the class on the Discussion Board:

In *The Early Americas*, you read about the first civilizations and cultures of the Americas and how these populations were influenced by the physical characteristics of different regions.

Hypothesize Following the arrival of Europeans to North America, Native American groups were steadily pushed off their land. How do you think relocating to new culture regions impacted Native American traditions? *(Native Americans were forced to adapt their traditions to new physical environments.)*

Pose and Answer Questions What is an additional question that you have about the physical and human characteristics of the early Americas? Write down your question and a possible response.

Topic Inquiry

Have students continue their investigations for the Topic Inquiry.

Early Europe, Africa, and Asia

Supporting English Language Learners

Use with Digital Text 3, **African Cultures and Technologies.**

Speaking

Have students read the section *Ways of Life in Africa*. Encourage students to draw on their own prior experiences to understand the meanings of sentences in the reading.

Beginning Have students, in class or working in pairs, identify words in the subsection that name family members (e.g., *grandparent*). Ask students to draw on their own experience and share the names of their relatives that correspond to these categories.

Intermediate Select one or more key words from the text, such as *extended, loyalty,* or *cooperation*. Provide students with an example from your life that illustrates one of these words. Then ask students, in class or working in pairs, to explain the meanings of other words with examples from their lives.

Advanced In class or working in pairs, have students draw on their own experience of family relationships to make sense of African family structures. Have them compare their own families with African families.

Advanced High Invite students to think about their experiences of family or religion. Invite them to share with the class, or with each other in pairs, how their prior experiences compare and contrast with the information in the reading.

Use with Digital Text 5, **Europe's Renaissance.**

Speaking

Have students read the sections *Portuguese Voyages* and *Further Exploration*, working in pairs. Have students share information from the reading with each other using a range of vocabulary from key words and expressions needed for basic communication to more abstract and content-based vocabulary.

Beginning Display a list of several key vocabulary words that are found in the text. Ask students to choose from these words in order to give information to one another about the text's content.

Intermediate Taking turns, have students say the name of a key figure in Portugal's exploration (e.g., Henry the Navigator). Challenge students to state opinions and give factual information about the person using complete sentences using key words and content-based vocabulary.

Advanced Have students identify three key events during the 1400s that relate to Portugal's exploration. Have students to use transitional words and phrases as they give information about these events in chronological order in extended spoken responses

Advanced High Ask students to infer key themes and concepts from the text. Have each student use abstract and content-based vocabulary to present information about these themes and concepts.

D Differentiate Instruction

Use the Differentiated Instruction notes throughout the lesson plan to support the varied skill sets, levels of readiness, and interests in the mixed-ability classroom.

Challenge These notes include suggestions for expanding the activity for advanced students.

On-Level These notes include suggestions for modifying the activity to address different interests or learning styles.

Extra Support These notes include ideas for providing more scaffolding or reading spuport.

Special Needs These notes provide ideas for adapting instruction to support the needs of various special needs students.

NOTES

PEARSON realize
www.PearsonRealize.com

Go online to access additional resources including:
Primary Sources • Biographies • Supreme Court cases • 21st Century Skill Tutorials • Maps • Graphic Organizers.

Objectives

Objective 1: Describe how Europe changed in the Middle Ages, including through technological innovations.

Objective 2: Describe patterns of trade and technological innovations in the Muslim world, Africa, and East Asia.

Objective 3: Identify the impact of technological innovations on Renaissance Europe.

LESSON 2 ORGANIZER	PACING: APPROX. 1 PERIOD, .5 BLOCKS		RESOURCES	
	OBJECTIVES	PACING	Online	Print
Connect				
DIGITAL START UP ACTIVITY **The World is a Smaller Place**		5 min.	●	
Investigate				
DIGITAL TEXT 1 **Europe in the Middle Ages**	Objective 1	10 min.	●	●
DIGITAL TEXT 2 **The Middle East**	Objective 2	10 min.	●	●
DIGITAL TEXT 3 **African Cultures and Technologies**		10 min.	●	●
INTERACTIVE ILLUSTRATION **How an Astrolabe Works**		10 min.	●	
DIGITAL TEXT 4 **Chinese Trade and Technology**	Objective 2	10 min.	●	●
DIGITAL TEXT 5 **Europe's Renaissance**	Objective 3	10 min.	●	●
3-D MODEL **Seafaring Technologies**		10 min.	●	
Synthesize				
DIGITAL ACTIVITY **Technology and Exploration**		5 min.	●	
Demonstrate				
DIGITAL QUIZ **Lesson Quiz and Class Discussion Board**		10 min.	●	

Early Europe, Africa, and Asia

CONNECT

DIGITAL START UP ACTIVITY

The World is a Smaller Place

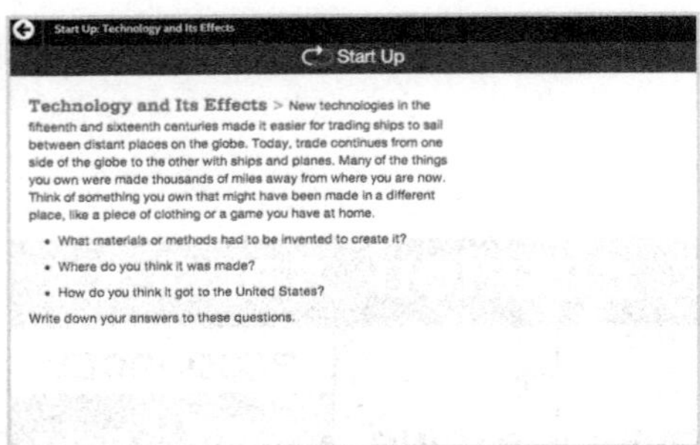

Project the Start Up Activity As students settle in and get ready, ask them to pick an object in the classroom and write a few sentences answering the questions. Then have them discuss their answers with another student, either in class or through a chat or blog space.

Discuss Was your object made in the United States or in a different country? What materials and methods had to be invented to create your object? Has this object improved your life, and if so, how? *(Answers will vary but should mention that many everyday products travel long distances, as innovations continue to make the world smaller and easier.)*

Aa Vocabulary Development: Use the Interactive Reading Notepad to preview the Key Terms and Academic Vocabulary in this lesson with students.

FLIP IT!

Assign the Flipped Video for this lesson.

STUDENT EDITION PRINT PAGES: 21–32

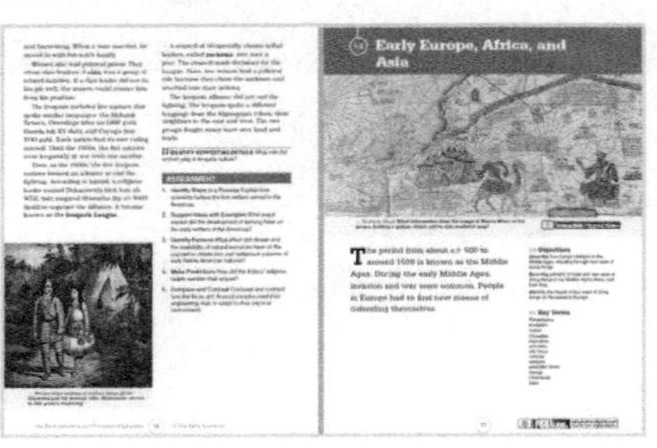

INVESTIGATE

DIGITAL TEXT 1

Europe in the Middle Ages

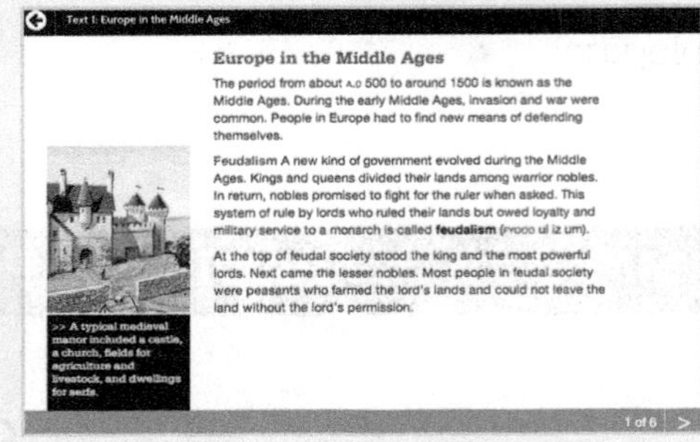

Objective 1: Describe how Europe changed in the Middle Ages, including through technological innovations.

Quick Instruction

Project the image of the mariner's magnetic compass on the whiteboard. Explain that the needle of a magnetic compass points north. Tell students that technological innovations,especially in sailing and navigation, led to changes in Europe and around the world.

D Differentiate: Extra Support Have students draw the four cardinal directions. Explain that before the magnetic compass, people found north by looking at the sun or stars. Ask students why someone navigating a ship would want to locate north.

Draw Conclusions Ask students why they think the development of the magnetic compass was a significant innovation. *(It improved navigation, letting ships travel greater distances. It helped ships determine their direction more accurately.)*

Further Instruction

Go through the Interactive Reading Notepad questions and discuss the answers with the class.

Identify Central Issues Ask students to name three examples of technological innovations that took place in the Middle Ages and explain how they impacted the daily lives of Europeans. *(New methods enabled farmers to produce more food. New sailing skills developed. The magnetic compass and the astrolabe helped sailors travel farther from land.)*

Identify Cause and Effect What factors caused Europeans to travel greater distances outside Europe? *(Demand for trade; the Crusades; technological innovations)*

Make Predictions Make a prediction about how growing trade in the Middle East will impact life in Europe. *(Demand for Middle Eastern goods will continue to grow, prompting more travel and exploration.)*

www.PearsonRealize.com
Access your Digital Lesson

DIGITAL TEXT 2

The Middle East

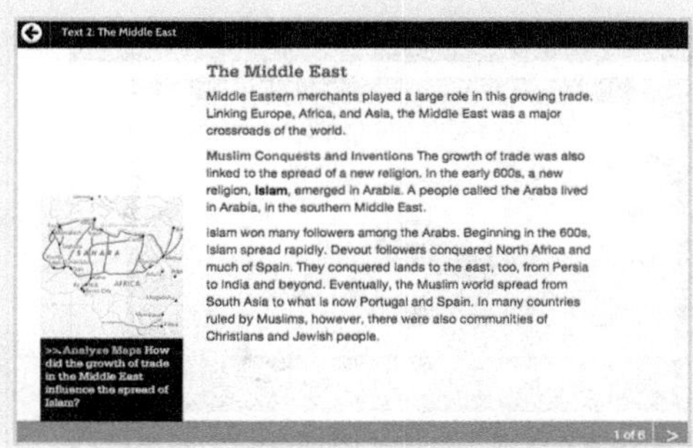

DIGITAL TEXT 3

African Cultures and Technologies

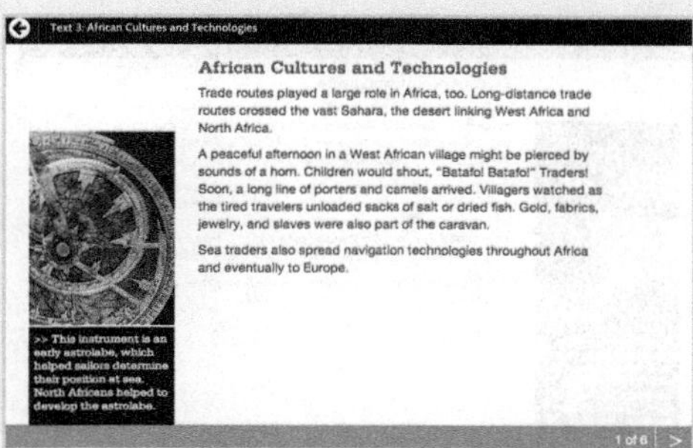

INTERACTIVE ILLUSTRATION

How an Astrolabe Works

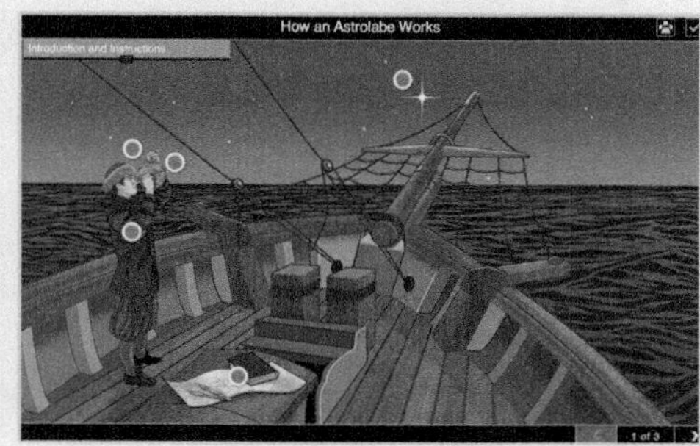

Objective 2: **Describe patterns of trade and technological innovations in the Muslim world, Africa, and East Asia.**

Quick Instruction

Project the image of the astrolabe on the whiteboard. Explain that technological innovations in sailing and navigation allowed Europeans to travel to the Middle East, Africa, and China. Many technologies we use today were developed in these regions. These innovations spread around the world by merchants, traders, sailors, and other travelers.

Interactive Illustration: How an Astrolabe Works Project the interactive activity on the whiteboard and click through the hotspots. Look at each image individually to make sure students understand the components of the astrolabe.

Summarize Have students explain in their own words how an astrolabe works. *(It measures a ship's location in relation to the sun, moon, planets, or stars. The angle between the horizon and the object in the sky corresponds to the ship's latitude.)*

Draw Conclusions How did the astrolabe enable explorers to find new trade routes? *(It let ships travel further from land without getting lost.)*

ACTIVE CLASSROOM

Pair students and have them use the Audio Tour strategy to go through the activity. Have the first student describe each part of the illustration and the second student explain its significance. *(The alidade aligns with a distant object to measure the angle between the object in the sky and the horizon; the mater and rete also measure this angle; a latitude table gives the latitude based on this angle and the date.)*

ELL Use the ELL activity described in the ELL chart.

Further Instruction

Go through the Interactive Reading Notepad questions for *The Middle East, and African Cultures and Technology*, including the graphic organizer summarizing how Muslim groups created an exchange of cultures between the Middle East, Europe, and Asia. To extend the lesson, have students go through the primary source "Travels," by Ibn Battuta.

Be sure that students understand the patterns of trade and technological innovations that impacted the Middle East, Africa, and China. Discuss the technologies that emerged out of each region and how they impacted life around the world.

Early Europe, Africa, and Asia

DIGITAL TEXT 4

Chinese Trade and Technology

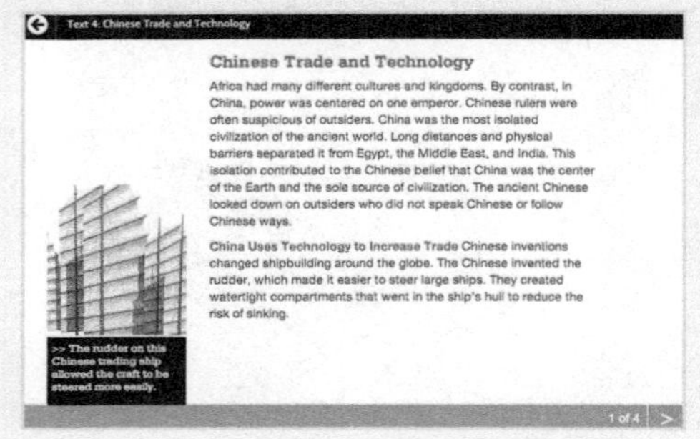

Objective 2: **Describe patterns of trade and technological innovations in the Muslim world, Africa, and East Asia.**

Quick Instruction

Project the image of the Chinese cargo ship on the whiteboard. Explain that technological innovations in sailing and navigation allowed Europeans to travel to China.

Identify Central Issues How did technological innovations give rise to new trade routes? *(Technological innovations enabled explorers to travel greater distances, opening up new trade routes connecting Asia, Africa, Europe, and the Middle East.)*

Further Instruction

Go through the Interactive Notepad questions for *Chinese Trade and Technology.*

Discuss Prompt students to discuss any parallels they see between concurrent technological innovations in China and other regions of the world.

DIGITAL TEXT 5

Europe's Renaissance

Objective 3: **Identify the impact of technological innovations on the Renaissance.**

Quick Instruction

Remind students that technological innovations changed European society and increased the contact Europeans had with other cultures. The Renaissance was a burst of learning and technological innovation in Europe that led to greater exploration and trade.

3-D Model: Seafaring Technologies Project the interactivity on the whiteboard and scroll to animate the image for the students. Click to the second screen to reveal the hotspots. Look at each image individually to make sure students understand the different aspects of navigation technology on the ship.

> **ACTIVE CLASSROOM**
>
> Pair students together. Have the first student describe each part of the 3-D Model and the second explain its significance.

ELL Use the ELL activity described in the ELL chart.

Further Instruction

Go through the Interactive Reading Notepad questions for *Europe's Renaissance* with the class. Have students complete the additional resource Elements of Culture.

3-D MODEL

Seafaring Technologies

Support Ideas with Examples What improvements in sailing occurred during the Renaissance, and how did these innovations impact Europe? *(The development of the caravel, in addition to previous inventions like the astrolabe and magnetic compass, enabled Europeans to travel farther and more accurately. Instruction in navigation and shipbuilding also allowed sailors to travel greater distances, opening up new routes for trade.)*

Infer Ask students why they think the Renaissance led to the first European voyages to the Americas. *(Increased interest in exploration and in finding new trade routes led Europeans to cross the Atlantic in search of a new route to Asia.)*

SYNTHESIZE

DIGITAL ACTIVITY

Technology and Exploration

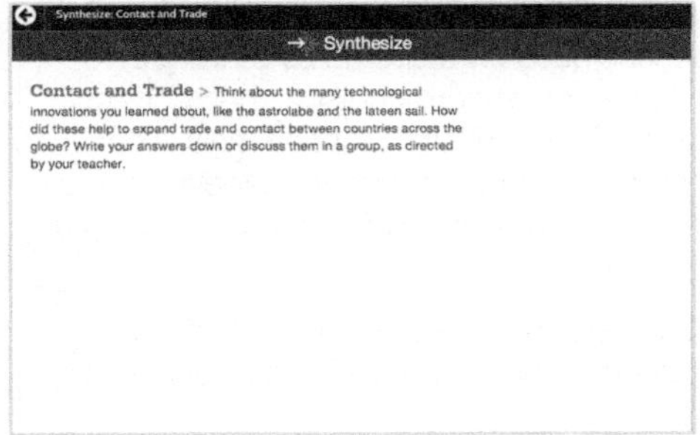

Have students select an innovation discussed in the lesson and answer the questions in the Technology and Exploration Activity. Have students share their findings with the class, ensuring a variety of innovations are covered.

At the beginning of this lesson, students considered how the world became a smaller place. Ask students how the technological innovations they learned about in this lesson made the world smaller. Have students share their answers with the class.

DEMONSTRATE

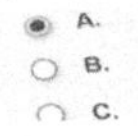

DIGITAL QUIZ

Lesson Quiz and Class Discussion Board

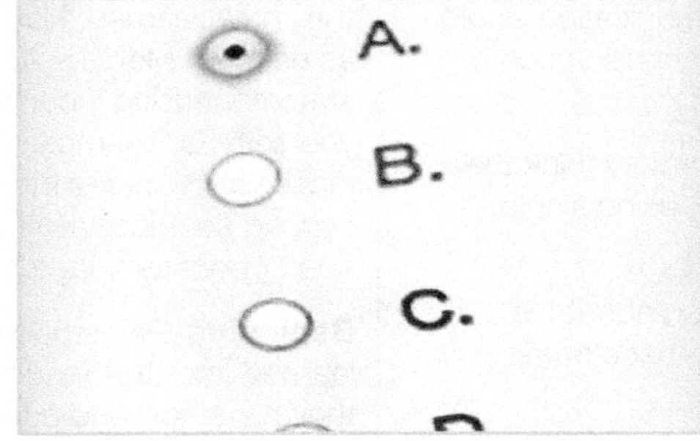

Assign the online Lesson Quiz for this lesson if you haven't already done so. Students will be offered automatic remediation or enrichment based on their score.

Pose these questions to the class on the Discussion Board:

In *Early Europe, Africa, and Asia*, you read about culture and society in early Europe, the Middle East, Africa, and China, and considered technological innovations that changed life around the globe.

Draw Conclusions How did technological innovations lead to greater contact among people in early Europe, Africa, and Asia? *(Improvements in navigation led to voyages of exploration and trade that increased contact among people from different continents.)*

Compare How were the effects of technological innovations in Europe, Asia, Africa, and the Middle East different from the innovations of Native American peoples that you read about in the previous lesson? *(The effects of technological innovations in Europe, Asia, and Africa, unlike those in the Americas, included improvements in navigation. Partly as a result, they spread much more widely among different cultures than innovations in the Americas did.)*

Topic Inquiry

Have students continue their investigations for the Topic Inquiry.

European Exploration in the Americas

Supporting English Language Learners

Use with Digital Text 2, **The Voyages of Columbus.**

Speaking

Review the definition of an opinion. Then have students read the section titled *The Impact of Columbus's Voyages*. Prompt students, in class or working in pairs, to express opinions ranging from communicating single words and short phrases to participating in extended discussions on a variety of social and grade-appropriate academic topics.

Beginning Ask students to state an opinion on whether they think the impact of Columbus's voyages was positive or negative, using single words or short phrases.

Intermediate Invite students to share aloud their opinion about the impact of Columbus's voyages. Provide them with a sentence frame such as: I think that Columbus's voyages _____ because _____.

Advanced Ask students: In your opinion, did the positive impact of Columbus's voyages on Native Americans outweigh their negative impact, or was the opposite true? Have students give reasons for their responses.

Advanced High Pair students that have differing opinions about the impact of Columbus's voyages. Give them time to have an extended discussion of their viewpoints using factual details and persuasive language.

Use with Digital Text 4, **The Columbian Exchange.**

Learning

Have students read the first paragraph in the section *Modifying Environments*. Working in small groups or pairs, have student explain what they have learned. Have students monitor and correct their own speech as needed. Model self-corrective techniques for students by making a statement using incorrect grammar, and poor word choices, then correct yourself. For example, you might say, "Europeans brought animals. The place wasn't never the same after that." Point out the grammar error in the second sentence. Ask students to rephrase your statement using accurate and correct language.

Beginning Pair students. Have each student state one thing that they learned from this reading. Ask students to take turns thinking about what they have said and correcting any mistakes.

Intermediate Ask partners to take turns making statements about the reading. Ask students to identify ways that they could improve their statements, then ask them to rephrase their statement with those improvements.

Advanced In pairs, ask students to take turns making a statement about the reading. Ask students to reflect on what they've said and to rephrase their statement using more academic language and sentences with more than one clause.

Advanced High Invite students, individually or in small groups, to make a statement about the reading using everyday language. Then have students identify ways that academic language differs from everyday language and apply those differences to their statement, rephrasing it using academic language.

D Differentiate Instruction

Use the Differentiated Instruction notes throughout the lesson plan to support the varied skill sets, levels of readiness, and interests in the mixed-ability classroom.

Challenge These notes include suggestions for expanding the activity for advanced students.

On-Level These notes include suggestions for modifying the activity to address different interests or learning styles.

Extra Support These notes include ideas for providing more scaffolding or reading spupport.

Special Needs These notes provide ideas for adapting instruction to support the needs of various special needs students.

NOTES

Go online to access additional resources including: Primary Sources • Biographies • Supreme Court cases • 21st Century Skill Tutorials • Maps • Graphic Organizers.

PEARSON realize™ www.PearsonRealize.com

Objectives

Objective 1: Identify reasons for European exploration of the Americas.

Objective 2: Describe the results of European exploration in the Americas.

Objective 3: Evaluate how exchanges between Europeans and Native Americans modified the physical environment.

LESSON 3 ORGANIZER	PACING: APPROX. 1 PERIOD, .5 BLOCKS			
			RESOURCES	
	OBJECTIVES	PACING	Online	Print
Connect				
DIGITAL START UP ACTIVITY **The Desire to See New Places**		5 min.	●	
Investigate				
DIGITAL TEXT 1 **Early Contact with the Americas**	Objective 1	10 min.	●	●
DIGITAL TEXT 2 **The Voyages of Columbus**		10 min.	●	●
INTERACTIVE CHART **Reasons to Explore**		10 min.	●	
DIGITAL TEXT 3 **Other Spanish Exploration**	Objective 2	10 min.	●	●
DIGITAL TEXT 4 **The Columbian Exchange**	Objective 3	10 min.	●	●
INTERACTIVE MAP **The Columbian Exchange**		10 min.	●	
Synthesize				
DIGITAL ACTIVITY **Exploring the New World**		5 min.	●	
Demonstrate				
DIGITAL QUIZ **Lesson Quiz and Class Discussion Board**		10 min.	●	

Topic 1 Lesson 3

European Exploration in the Americas

CONNECT

DIGITAL START UP ACTIVITY

The Desire to See New Places

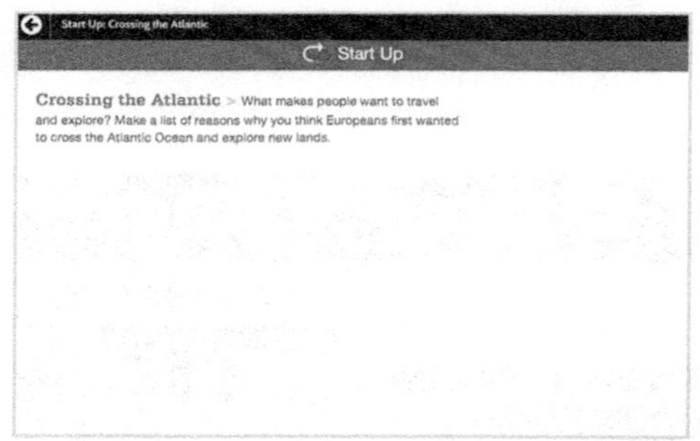

Start Up: Crossing the Atlantic
Start Up
Crossing the Atlantic > What makes people want to travel and explore? Make a list of reasons why you think Europeans first wanted to cross the Atlantic Ocean and explore new lands.

Project the Start Up Activity Ask students to generate their lists as they enter and get settled. Then have them answer the questions alone or in pairs, in class or through a chat or blog space.

Discuss Why did kings and queens want to pay for expensive voyages across the seas? What did they hope to gain? *(Land, wealth, power, knowledge)* Travel in those days was long and filled with dangers. What would make people want to take such risks? *(Curiosity, excitement, desire for wealth or prestige)* What benefits did Europeans expect to gain by traveling? What do you think they found? *(New trade routes; unfamiliar land)*

Aa Vocabulary Development: Use the Interactive Reading Notepad to preview the Key Terms and Academic Vocabulary in this lesson with students.

FLIP IT!

Assign the Flipped Video for this lesson.

STUDENT EDITION PRINT PAGES: 33–40

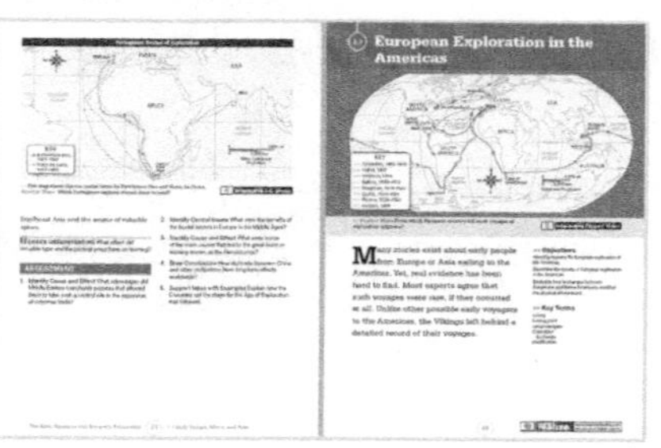

INVESTIGATE

DIGITAL TEXT 1

Early Contact with the Americas

DIGITAL TEXT 2

The Voyages of Columbus

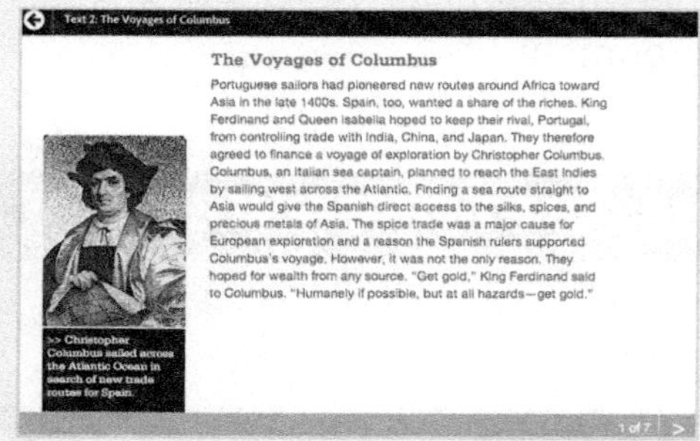

Text 2: The Voyages of Columbus
The Voyages of Columbus
Portuguese sailors had pioneered new routes around Africa toward Asia in the late 1400s. Spain, too, wanted a share of the riches. King Ferdinand and Queen Isabella hoped to keep their rival, Portugal, from controlling trade with India, China, and Japan. They therefore agreed to finance a voyage of exploration by Christopher Columbus. Columbus, an Italian sea captain, planned to reach the East Indies by sailing west across the Atlantic. Finding a sea route straight to Asia would give the Spanish direct access to the silks, spices, and precious metals of Asia. The spice trade was a major cause for European exploration and a reason the Spanish rulers supported Columbus's voyage. However, it was not the only reason. They hoped for wealth from any source. "Get gold," King Ferdinand said to Columbus. "Humanely if possible, but at all hazards—get gold."
>> Christopher Columbus sailed across the Atlantic Ocean in search of new trade routes for Spain.
1 of 7

Objective 1: **Identify reasons for European exploration of the Americas.**

Quick Instruction

Interactive Chart: Reasons to Explore Project the image of the interactive chart on the whiteboard and discuss the reasons for European exploration with students. Explain that Europeans did not know America existed until Columbus traveled west searching for a new trade route to Asia.

ACTIVE CLASSROOM

List the following reasons on the board: land, colonies, riches, religion, personal glory, empire. Have students use the Rank It strategy to rank the reasons for European exploration from strongest to weakest. Ask students to justify their ranking decision and then share their rankings and justifications with a partner. Poll the class to see if there is agreement on the ranking.

Summarize Have students explain in their own words why they think Europeans traveled to North America and continued exploring the continent once they arrived. *(Europeans were looking for land, wealth, and new trade opportunities. They wanted to convert Native Americans to Christianity and spread European empires.)*

ELL Use the ELL activity described in the ELL chart.

Further Instruction

Go through the Interactive Reading Notepad questions for *Early Contact with the Americas* and *The Voyages of Columbus* and discuss the answers with the class. Make sure students understand why Europeans began exploring the Americas and why Columbus's voyage marked a decisive change in history.

PEARSON realize™ www.PearsonRealize.com Access your Digital Lesson

INTERACTIVE CHART

Reasons to Explore

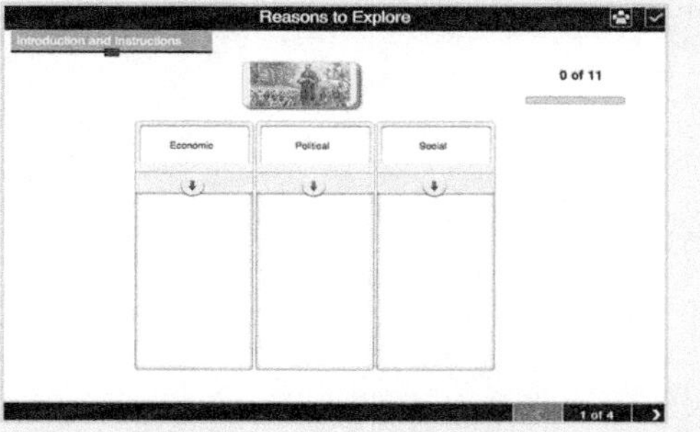

Cite Evidence What evidence does the text give to explain why Ferdinand and Isabella supported Columbus's voyage? *(Spain wanted a share of the riches in Africa and Asia. Ferdinand and Isabella wanted Columbus to increase Spain's access to the spice trade. They also wanted Columbus to get gold.)*

Evaluate Arguments Columbus is often described as "discovering" America. Why is this statement inaccurate? *(People were already living in the Americas when Columbus arrived. Other travelers from Europe and Asia had also set foot in North America before him.)*

DIGITAL TEXT 3

Other Spanish Exploration

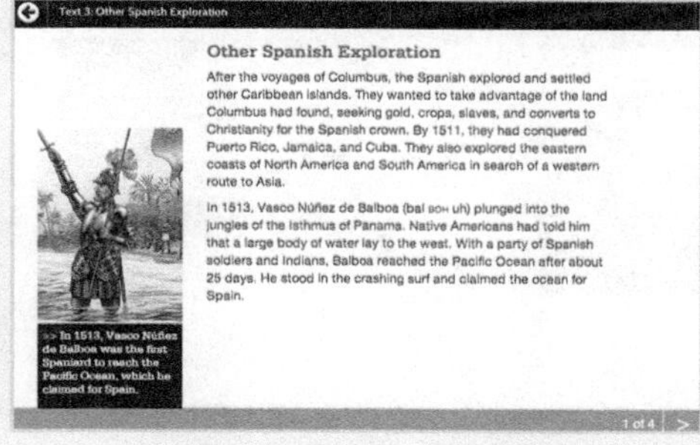

Objective 2: **Describe the results of European exploration in the Americas.**

Quick Instruction

Project the image of Vasco Núñez de Balboa on the whiteboard. Explain that following Columbus, the Spanish exploration moved into North America. Meanwhile, Ferdinand Magellan, Balboa, and others explored the Caribbean and the Pacific.

Infer Why do you think explorers began to explore North America? *(To claim land for Spain; to find new trade routes; because they were curious about the land and people; because they hoped for wealth and fame)*

Hypothesize What difficulties do you think these explorers faced? *(Bad weather and storms; lack of food and water; conflict with Native Americans; disease; getting lost)*

D Differentiate: Extra Support Have students locate the following places on a map or globe: Spain, the Atlantic Ocean, the Caribbean, Panama, North America, the Pacific Ocean, Asia. Have students use the map to trace the voyages of European explorers as they read.

Further Instruction

Go through the Interactive Reading Notepad questions and discuss the answers with the class. As students review the voyages discussed in the lesson, be sure they also consider the impact of these voyages in both Europe and the Americas. To extend the lesson, have students go through the additional resource What is Human Geography: Geography.

Infer What does Magellan's death in a battle with local people of the Philippine islands suggest was one result of European exploration? *(Hostile contact with people who lived in the areas that Europeans were exploring)*

Identify Cause and Effect How did European discoveries in the Americas affect the Spanish empire? *(These discoveries expanded the Spanish to include new territory, opened up new trade routes to Asia, and brought riches to Spain.)*

European Exploration in the Americas

DIGITAL TEXT 4

The Columbian Exchange

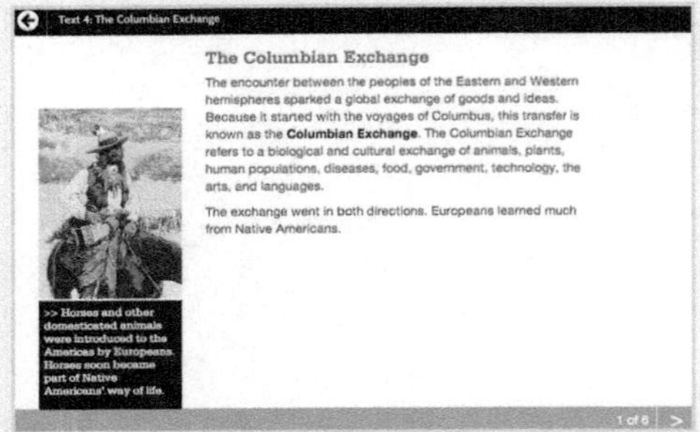

INTERACTIVE MAP

The Columbian Exchange

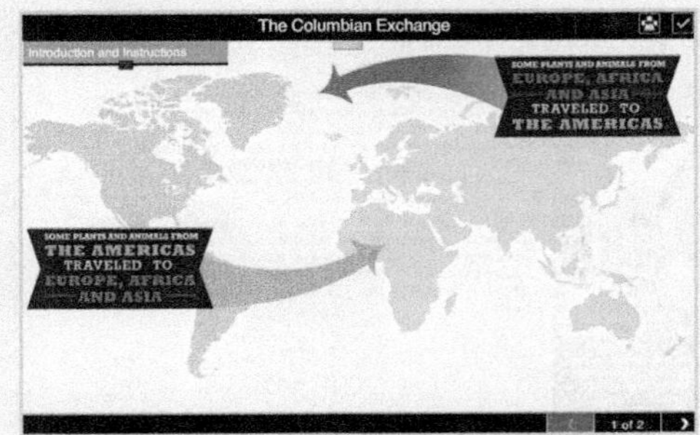

Objective 3: Evaluate the consequences of human modification of the physical environment that resulted from exchange between Europeans and Native Americans.

Quick Instruction

European exploration brought Europeans and Native Americans in contact with one another. This led to a global exchange of goods and ideas that modified cultures on both sides of the Atlantic. It also modified the physical environment of the Americas, with both positive and negative results.

Interactive Map: The Columbian Exchange Project the Interactive Activity on the whiteboard. Use the slider to show the movement of goods from west to east. Point out that this exchange brought new goods from Europe, Africa, and Asia to the Americas, and spread goods from the Americas in turn. Add that it also spread language, skills, ideas, and even disease.

Use Context Clues Have students define what they think a "global exchange" means. *(The swap of goods and ideas back and forth from different places around the globe)*

Identify Central Issues Have students explain why the Columbian Exchange had both positive and negative consequences. *(Some of the new goods, skills, and ideas that were spread made life better for people. The introduction of new species and new ways of modifying the environment was not always as beneficial. The spread of diseases killed millions.)*

ELL Use the ELL activity described in the ELL chart.

ACTIVE CLASSROOM

Have students use the Wallpaper strategy to draw a key piece of information about the Columbian Exchange. Have students post their drawings and look at what others have created, jotting down ideas as they occur.

Further Instruction

Go through the Interactive Reading Notepad questions and use the graphic organizer to list positive and negative consequences of the Columbian Exchange for Native Americans and for Europeans.

Support Ideas with Examples Give an example of how the Columbian Exchange modified the physical environment of the Americas. *(Farming; mining; the introduction of new crops and animals)*

SYNTHESIZE

DIGITAL ACTIVITY

Exploring the New World

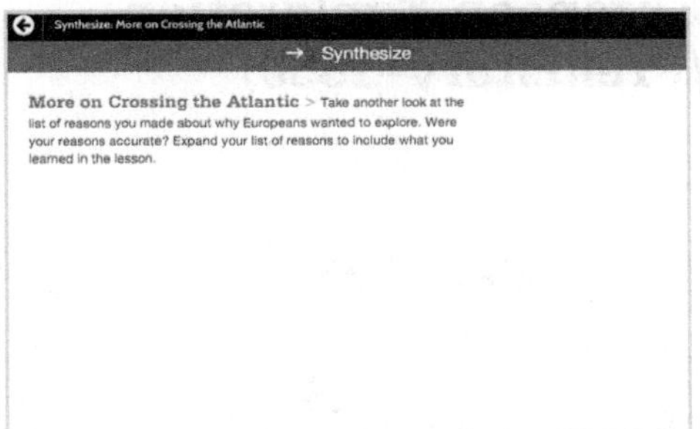

Ask students to recall the list they made in the Digital Start Up Activity considering reasons Europeans wanted to explore. Have them address the consequences of these reasons as they answer the questions in the Exploring the New World activity. Ask students to write down their answers, and then share their findings with a partner.

Have partners think about the final question. Were the overall consequences of European exploration in the Americas positive or negative? Have partners share their answers with the class, explaining their reasoning.

DEMONSTRATE

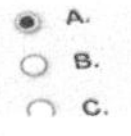

DIGITAL QUIZ

Lesson Quiz and Class Discussion Board

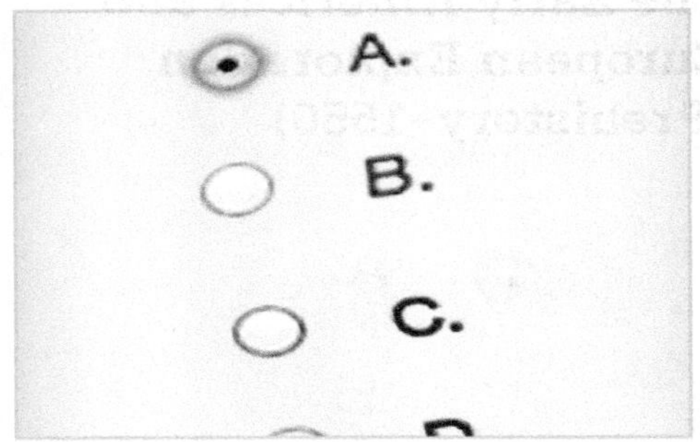

Assign the online Lesson Quiz for this lesson if you haven't already done so. Students will be offered automatic remediation or enrichment based on their score.

Pose these questions to the class on the Discussion Board:

In *European Exploration of the Americas*, you read about the reasons Europeans explored the Americas and the consequences of that exploration.

Support a Point of View with Evidence Why is Columbus's voyage to the Americas considered a "turning point" in world history? *(His voyage led to sustained contact among peoples of all continents in the world for the first time, to the Columbian Exchange, and to the European colonization of the Americas.)*

Make Predictions How would European exploration continue to affect Native Americans and the physical environment of the New World after the period discussed in this lesson? *(European diseases would kill many Native Americans, and European colonization would displace them from their homelands. The physical environment would be affected by European colonization, agricultural practices, and the Columbian Exchange.)*

Topic Inquiry

Have students continue their investigations for the Topic Inquiry.

PEARSON realize™ www.PearsonRealize.com Access your Digital Lesson

The Early Americas and European Exploration (Prehistory–1550)

SYNTHESIZE

DIGITAL ACTIVITY

Reflect on the Essential Question and Topic

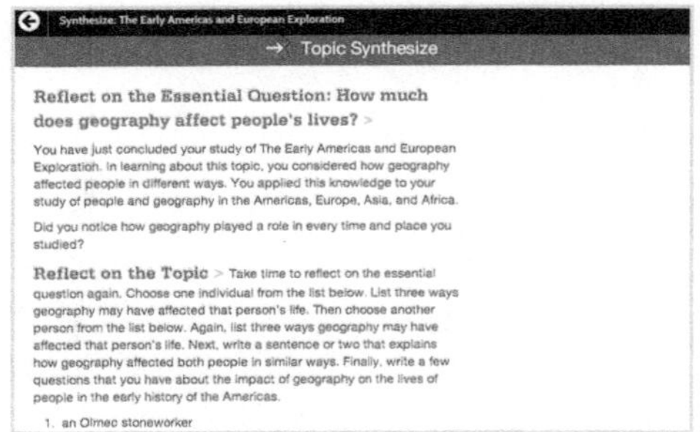

First, ask students to reconsider the Essential Question for the Topic: How much does geography affect people's lives? Remind students that geography includes the land, climate, environment, resources, and other features of a region.

Have students pick two of the individuals listed in the activity. Ask, "How do you think geography influenced their lives?" Ask them to give at least three examples supporting their position. Discuss their answers as a class or ask students to post their answers on the Class Discussion board.

Next ask students to reflect on the Topic as a whole and jot down one to three questions they've thought about during the Topic. Share these examples if they need help getting started:

- How are people affected by the geography of where they live?
- What motivates someone to move to a faraway place?
- How do people impact the physical environment in which they live, positively and negatively?

DEMONSTRATE

DIGITAL TOPIC REVIEW AND ASSESSMENT

The Early Americas and European Exploration (Prehistory–1550)

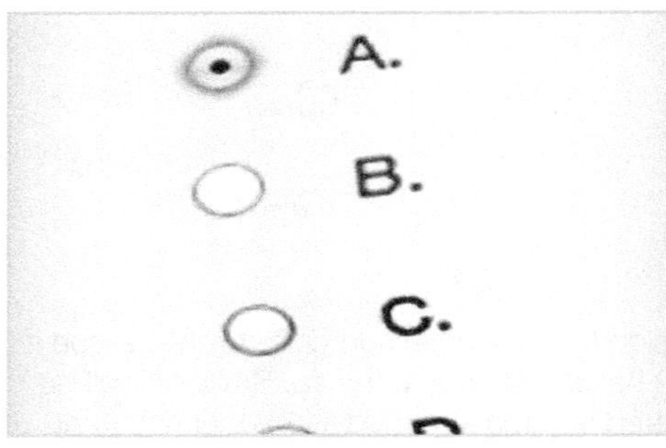

Students can prepare for the Topic Test by answering the questions in the Topic Review and Assessment online or the Assessment questions in the Print Student text. They can also prepare by reviewing their answers to the Interactive Reading Notepad questions or reviewing their notes in the Reading and Notetaking Study Guide.

DIGITAL TOPIC TEST

The Early Americas and European Exploration (Prehistory–1550)

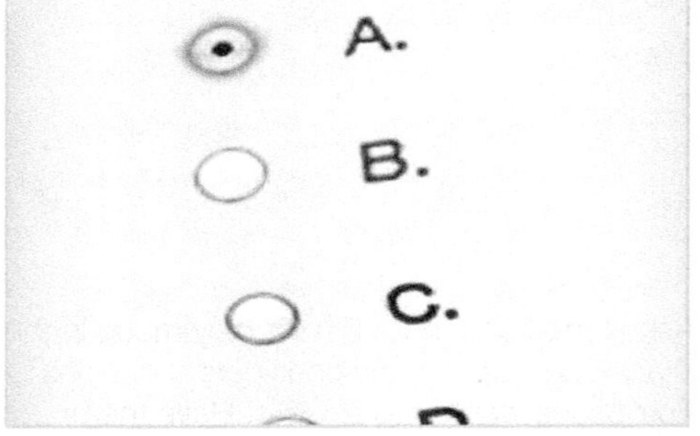

TOPIC TEST

Assign the Topic Test to assess students' understanding of topic content.

BENCHMARK TESTS

Assign these benchmark tests as you complete the relevant topics to monitor student progress toward mastering the course content and as preparation for the End-of-Course Test.

Benchmark Test 1: Topics 1–2

Benchmark Test 2: Topics 3–4

Benchmark Test 3: Topics 5–6

Benchmark Test 4: Topics 7–9

Benchmark Test 5: Topics 10–12

Benchmark Test 6: Topics 13–14

Benchmark Test 7: Topics 15–17

PEARSON realize www.PearsonRealize.com Access your Digital Lesson

European Colonization of North America (1500–1750)

TOPIC 2 ORGANIZER	PACING: APPROX. 10 PERIODS, 5 BLOCKS
	PACING
Connect	1 period
MY STORY VIDEO **John Smith, Jamestown, and the Roots of America**	10 min.
DIGITAL ESSENTIAL QUESTION ACTIVITY **Why Do People Move?**	10 min.
DIGITAL OVERVIEW ACTIVITY **European Colonization of North America**	10 min.
TOPIC INQUIRY: PROJECT-BASED LEARNING **Publish an ePortfolio of Colonial Data**	20 min.
Investigate	3–7 periods
TOPIC INQUIRY: PROJECT-BASED LEARNING **Publish an ePortfolio of Colonial Data**	Ongoing
LESSON 1 Spanish Colonization and New Spain	30–40 min.
LESSON 2 The First French, Dutch, and English Colonies	30–40 min.
LESSON 3 The New England Colonies	30–40 min.
LESSON 4 The Middle Colonies	30–40 min.
LESSON 5 The Southern Colonies	30–40 min.
LESSON 6 Colonial Society	30–40 min.
LESSON 7 Colonial Trade and Government	30–40 min.
Synthesize	1 period
DIGITAL ACTIVITY **Reflect on the Essential Question and Topic**	10 min.
TOPIC INQUIRY: PROJECT-BASED LEARNING **Publish an ePortfolio of Colonial Data**	20 min.
Demonstrate	1–2 periods
DIGITAL TOPIC REVIEW AND ASSESSMENT **European Colonization of North America**	10 min.
TOPIC INQUIRY: PROJECT-BASED LEARNING **Publish an ePortfolio of Colonial Data**	20 min.

TOPIC INQUIRY: PROJECT-BASED LEARNING

Publish an ePortfolio of Colonial Data

In this Topic Inquiry, students create and publish an e-Portfolio with data on the geography and economy of the 13 English colonies in North America. They will use the data they collect to create visual representations of social studies information, including thematic maps, graphs, charts, models, and databases to go in their portfolios. Learning about the geography, economy, and population of the colonies will contribute to students' understanding of the Topic Essential Question: Why do people move?

STEP 1: CONNECT

Develop Questions and Plan the Investigation

Read the Project Launch

Explain to students that in this project, they will be collecting data about the English colonies in North America and publishing that data in an e-Portfolio. Have students read the Project Launch and review the fictional proclamation issued by King George II.

Suggestion: To provide extra support, have students restate the proclamation in their own words. Make sure they understand that they are being asked to investigate and organize facts about the colonies.

Discuss

Have students discuss the proclamation as a class or in small groups. Ask students what facts about the colonies might be relevant to this investigation, such as geography, climate, physical features, natural resources, and economic activities.

Suggestion: Students can work together in pairs or small groups to brainstorm what areas their investigation should cover.

Resources

- Project Launch
- Rubric for an e-Portfolio
- Need-to-Know Questions
- Project Contract
- Student Instructions

PROFESSIONAL DEVELOPMENT

Project-Based Learning

Be sure to view the Project-Based Learning Professional Development resources in the online course.

STEP 2: INVESTIGATE

Apply Disciplinary Concepts and Tools

Identify Needed Information and Conduct Research

Teams will identify information they need to investigate, and research the physical characteristics of the environment in the three colonial regions and how they influenced population distribution and economic activities.

Create a Team Database and Compile Information

Teams will create a database to store their research that is well organized, easy to use, and include sections for all the information gathered.

Suggestion: The database may be electronic or hard copy. Regardless of format, students should develop an organizational system using folders, files, notes, and other methods to keep track of information.

Create Visual Representations of Data (Thematic Maps, Graphs, Charts, and Models)

Teams will create visual representations of their data to present information about the physical features, resources, economies, population, and settlement patterns of the colonies.

Write and Edit Introduction, Captions, and Explanatory Materials

Teams will write and edit material to accompany their visuals. They should have an introduction to their portfolio and provide captions to all images. Students may also wish to include additional explanatory comments to accompany their visual representations.

Resources

- Need-to-Know Questions
- Project Tracker
- Information Organizer

STEP 3: SYNTHESIZE

Evaluate Sources and Use Evidence to Formulate Conclusions

Build Your e-Portfolio or Book

Have students work as a team to put together their e-Portfolio. Portfolios should include visual information, explanatory materials, and any other relevant visual, audio, or written materials gathered during research.

Suggestion: If your class has limited access to the Internet, you could supply materials for students to make a physical binder or book to present their visuals and accompanying materials.

Write Your Conclusions

Have teams write a conclusion section for their portfolios in which they summarize the reasons for the differences among the colonies. Students should consider the physical environment, population distribution, settlement patterns, and economic activities of each region.

Suggestion: Have teams include at least one conclusion and one additional question that they have.

Resources

- Plan Your Book

STEP 4: DEMONSTRATE

Communicate Conclusions and Take Informed Action

Present Your e-Portfolio

Have students present their e-Portfolios to the class or an invited audience. To help students structure their presentations, give them a time limit and have them use a clock to monitor their delivery.

Suggestion: As an extension, have students use the data they collected about the environment, population, and economy of the colonies to draw conclusions about why immigrants moved to each region.

Resources

- Give an Effective Presentation
- Self Assessment

INTRODUCTION

European Colonization of North America (1500–1750)

Following Columbus's first voyages, European empires began exploring the Americas. Spain, France, the Netherlands, France, and England wanted to expand their empires, find faster trade routes to Asia, and generate wealth. They established colonies where they could farm, trade, and exploit the region's many natural resources. Over time, England founded 13 colonies, divided into three regions: New England, the Middle Colonies, and the Southern Colonies. As the colonies grew, they developed their own unique cultures, political structures, and ways of life.

CONNECT

MY STORY VIDEO

John Smith, Jamestown, and the Roots of America

Watch a video about the exploits of John Smith in North America.

Check Understanding What was John Smith's goal in Virginia? *(settling a colony and making money for the Virginia Company)*

Assess Credibility What about John Smith's story of being rescued from his Native American captors would have made it less questionable? *(The story of his rescue is not based on reliable evidence. Historians debate whether it even happened or, if it did, the reason for his rescue.)*

DIGITAL ESSENTIAL QUESTION ACTIVITY

Why Do People Move?

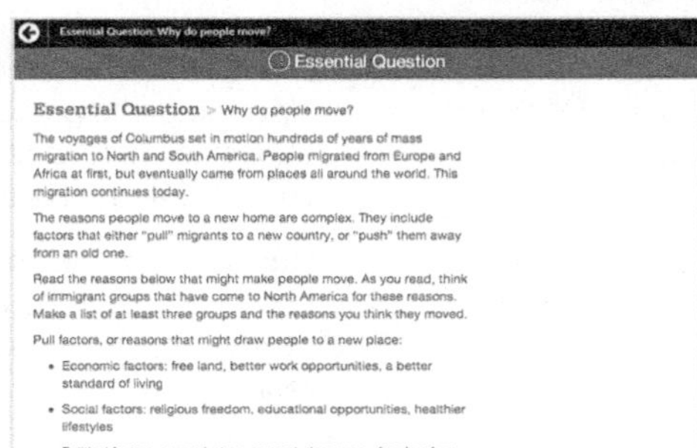

Ask students to think about the Topic Essential Question: Why do people move? People move because they are drawn to certain places (pull factors), and because they want to leave other places behind (push factors). What factors lead people to establish a new home?

If students have not already done so, ask them to think about the questions in the activity. Then go over the answers as a class.

Support a Point of View with Evidence What push or pull factors do you think have the strongest influence on whether people move? Explain your reasoning. *(People move because of economic push factors such as poverty and economic pull factors such as the search for better job opportunities. People also need to be able to meet their basic needs.)*

Identify Central Issues What pull factors do you think drew early settlers to the colonies? *(Land, opportunities to generate wealth, religious freedom, freedom from oppression, and a chance for adventure)*

DIGITAL OVERVIEW ACTIVITY

European Colonization of North America

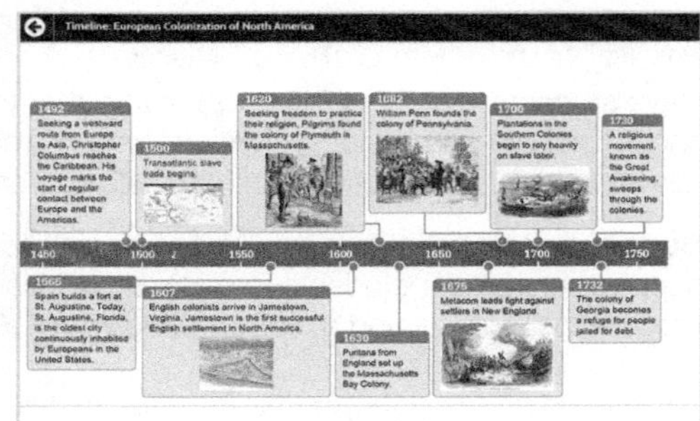

Display the timeline showing key events in the history of European colonization of North America. This timeline will help provide a framework in which students can place the events they learn about while working on this topic.

Analyze Information Based on the timeline, what reasons led European settlers to move to the Americas? *(Religious freedom, economic gain, seeking refuge, and an interest in exploration)*

Draw Conclusions What conclusion can you draw from the knowledge that Metacom led a fight against New England settlers? *(European colonization led to conflicts between Europeans and Native Americans.)*

Topic Inquiry

Launch the Topic Inquiry with students after introducing the topic.

PEARSON realize™ www.PearsonRealize.com Access your Digital Lesson

Spanish Colonization and New Spain

Supporting English Language Learners

Use with Digital Text 4, **The Social Order in New Spain.**

Learning

Read the section titled *Different Social Classes*, or invite volunteers to do so. Tell students that they will be writing about what they've learning and checking their writing to improve it. Tell them that they will need to write complete sentences or paragraphs. Write the following words on the board: "Four social classes in Spanish colony." Ask students what is wrong with this statement. *(It is not a sentence because it lacks a verb, and* colony *should be plural.)* Explain to students that they will be monitoring and correcting their own writing, with your help.

Beginning Have students write a single sentence describing something that they learned from the reading. Ask them to look closely at their sentence and find ways to improve it. Invite them to ask for help as needed.

Intermediate Ask students to write a few sentences describing the creoles. Then ask them to revise their sentences to improve their grammar and to incorporate academic language.

Advanced Have students write a full paragraph about the Spanish colonial social structure. Ask them to check their paragraphs to make sure that they include a clear topic statement and supporting details and to correct any style or grammar errors. Then ask them to revise their paragraphs.

Advanced High Ask students to write a paragraph that compares and contrasts the Creoles and the Mestizos. Have them share their writing with a partner, offer and receive feedback, and revise their paragraph accordingly.

Use with Digital Text 5, **The Transatlantic Slave Trade.**

Speaking

Have students read the text under this heading, including the subheadings. Give students time to gather their thoughts about the transatlantic slave trade, then have them form small groups or pairs. Tell students that they will be expressing ideas by speaking about what they have read. Students should express ideas ranging from communicating single words and short phrases to participating in extended discussions.

Beginning Display a word web with *Bartolomé de Las Casas* written in the center. Ask students to say words and phrases that describe Las Casas and his impact on slave trade in the Americas. Add their responses to the word web.

Intermediate Ask students to express an idea about Bartolomé de Las Casas and his contribution to slave trade in the Americas. Have students' partners ask each of them a follow up question about their ideas, and have students respond orally.

Advanced In pairs or in small groups, have students give a short expressing their ideas about the Atlantic slave trade.. Have students' partners ask each of them a follow up question about their ideas, and have students respond orally.

Advanced High Ask pairs of students to have extended discussions of their ideas about the emergence of the transatlantic slave trade (e.g., what might have happened if Las Casas had not made his suggestion). If appropriate, have them conduct their discussion for the class.

D Differentiate Instruction

Use the Differentiated Instruction notes throughout the lesson plan to support the varied skill sets, levels of readiness, and interests in the mixed-ability classroom.

Challenge These notes include suggestions for expanding the activity for advanced students.

On-Level These notes include suggestions for modifying the activity to address different interests or learning styles.

Extra Support These notes include ideas for providing more scaffolding or reading spuport.

Special Needs These notes provide ideas for adapting instruction to support the needs of various special needs students.

NOTES

Topic 2 Lesson 1

Spanish Colonization and New Spain

Objectives

Objective 1: Describe how conquistadors defeated two Native American empires.

Objective 2: Explain why Spain settled its colonies.

Objective 3: Explain the causes and effects of the transatlantic slave trade.

LESSON 1 ORGANIZER — PACING: APPROX. 1 PERIOD, .5 BLOCKS	OBJECTIVES	PACING	RESOURCES Online	RESOURCES Print
Connect				
DIGITAL START UP ACTIVITY **Álvar Núñez Cabeza de Vaca**		5 min.	●	
Investigate				
DIGITAL TEXT 1 **Conquistadors Arrive in the Americas**	Objective 1	10 min.	●	●
DIGITAL TEXT 2 **Exploring Lands to the North**	Objective 2	10 min.	●	●
DIGITAL TEXT 3 **The Colonization of New Spain**		10 min.	●	●
DIGITAL TEXT 4 **Social Order in New Spain**		10 min.	●	●
INTERACTIVE MAP **Spanish Explorers and Settlements in North America**		10 min.	●	
INTERACTIVE CHART **Social Classes in New Spain**		10 min.	●	
DIGITAL TEXT 5 **Transatlantic Slave Trade**	Objective 3	10 min.	●	●
Synthesize				
DIGITAL ACTIVITY **Interaction in the Americas**		5 min.	●	
Demonstrate				
DIGITAL QUIZ **Lesson Quiz and Class Discussion Board**		10 min.	●	

Go online to access additional resources including: Primary Sources • Biographies • Supreme Court cases • 21st Century Skill Tutorials • Maps • Graphic Organizers.

CONNECT

DIGITAL START UP ACTIVITY

Álvar Núñez Cabeza de Vaca

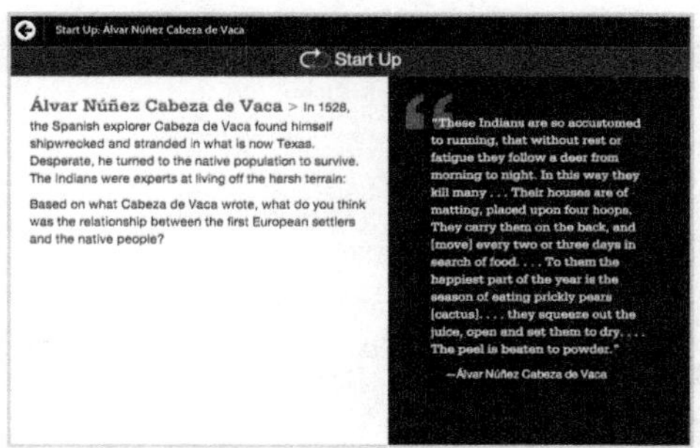

Project the Start Up Activity Ask students to read the quote as they enter and get settled. Have them discuss the quote with another student and then write a few sentences explaining their opinion.

Discuss Based on what he wrote, what opinion do you think Cabeza de Vaca had of the Indians he met? *(He admired their skills; he thought they were very different; he thought they were resourceful but also led simple lives.)*

Tell students that in this lesson they will be learning about the reasons the Spanish settled in North America, the causes and effects of colonization, and the development of the transatlantic slave trade.

Aa Vocabulary Development: Use the Interactive Reading Notepad to preview the Key Terms and Academic Vocabulary in this lesson with students.

FLIP IT!

Assign the Flipped Video for this lesson.

STUDENT EDITION PRINT PAGES: 46–55

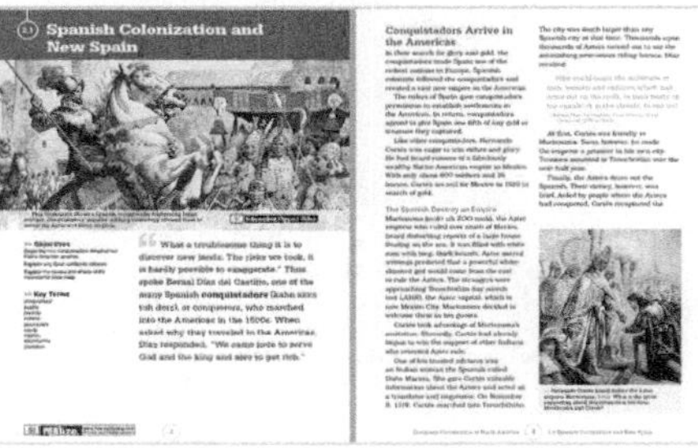

INVESTIGATE

DIGITAL TEXT 1

Conquistadors Arrive in the Americas

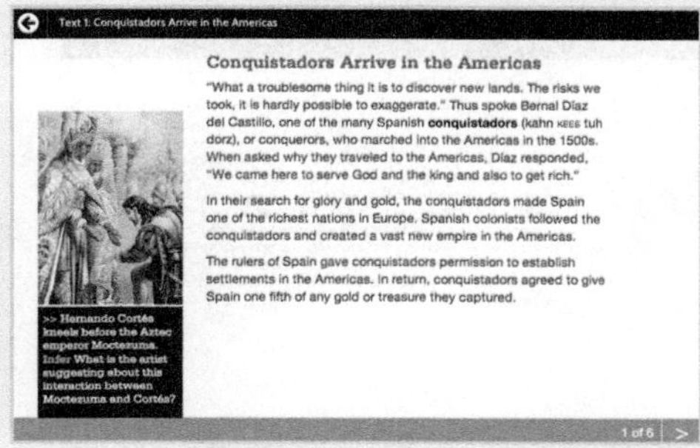

Objective 1: Describe how conquistadors defeated two Native American empires.

Quick Instruction

Project the image of the Francisco Pizarro on the whiteboard. Explain that the conquistadors were conquerors who established the first Spanish settlements in the Americas. Identify reasons for colonization of North America such as their quest to find gold and spread the Spanish empire. Point out that had defeated two Native American empires: the Aztecs and the Incas.

Draw Conclusions Ask students why they think the conquistadors were able to defeat two major empires, citing examples from the image to support their views. *(They had substantial resources including swords, horses, and armor and were well trained in fighting.)*

D Differentiate: Extra Support Tell students that *conquistador* is the Spanish word for conqueror. A conqueror is someone who conquers, or takes control of, a place and its people. Have students draw on these definitions to explain what they think happened when the conquistadors encountered Native American empires.

Further Instruction

Go through the Interactive Reading Notepad questions and discuss the answers with the class, including the graphic organizer on the factors that influenced Spanish military success over the Aztecs and Incas.

Compare Points of View How did Spain view the defeat of the Aztecs and the Incas? How did the Aztecs and Incas view the same events? *(The Spanish viewed the defeat of the empires as a victory. The Native Americans viewed it as a tragedy.)*

Identify Cause and Effect How did the Spanish defeat of Native American empires lead to the development of Spanish colonies? *(Spain was able to take over Native American lands and create new settlements under Spanish rule, which led to colonies.)*

Draw Conclusions What were the reasons the conquistadors came to the Americas? *(They hoped for gold and glory for Spain and wanted to serve the king.)*

Spanish Colonization and New Spain

DIGITAL TEXT 2

Exploring Lands to the North

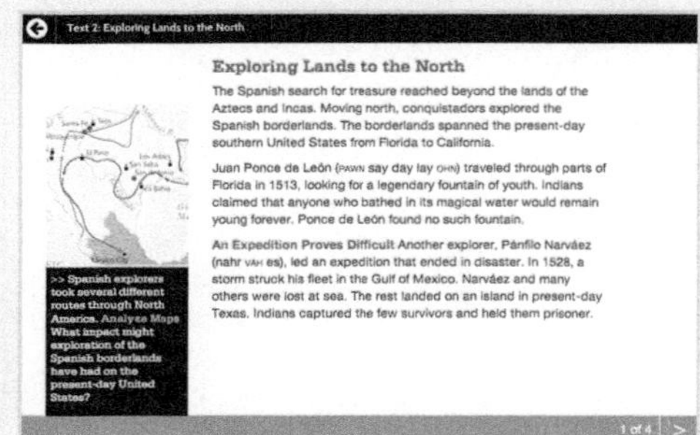

Text 2: Exploring Lands to the North
Exploring Lands to the North
The Spanish search for treasure reached beyond the lands of the Aztecs and Incas. Moving north, conquistadors explored the Spanish borderlands. The borderlands spanned the present-day southern United States from Florida to California.
Juan Ponce de León (PAWN say day lay OHN) traveled through parts of Florida in 1513, looking for a legendary fountain of youth. Indians claimed that anyone who bathed in its magical water would remain young forever. Ponce de León found no such fountain.
An Expedition Proves Difficult Another explorer, Pánfilo Narváez (nahr VAH es), led an expedition that ended in disaster. In 1528, a storm struck his fleet in the Gulf of Mexico. Narváez and many others were lost at sea. The rest landed on an island in present-day Texas. Indians captured the few survivors and held them prisoner.
>> Spanish explorers took several different routes through North America. Analyze Maps What impact might exploration of the Spanish borderlands have had on the present-day United States?
1 of 4

DIGITAL TEXT 3

The Colonization of New Spain

Text 3. The Colonization of New Spain
The Colonization of New Spain
The conquistadors set up colonies in many parts of the Americas. Spain had many causes for colonization, or setting up colonies. One was the search for wealth: settlements provided bases from which expeditions could set out in search of gold. Settlements could also created wealth through farming and trade. A second important cause of settlement was to spread Christianity by converting native peoples. A third cause was to satisfy a thirst for adventure and exploration. Sometimes, historians summarize the Spanish exploration and settlement of the Americas as motivated by "Gold, God, and Glory." Thousands of Spanish immigrants moved to Spanish settlements looking for opportunities the colonies offered, especially farming.
1 of 6

DIGITAL TEXT 4

Social Order in New Spain

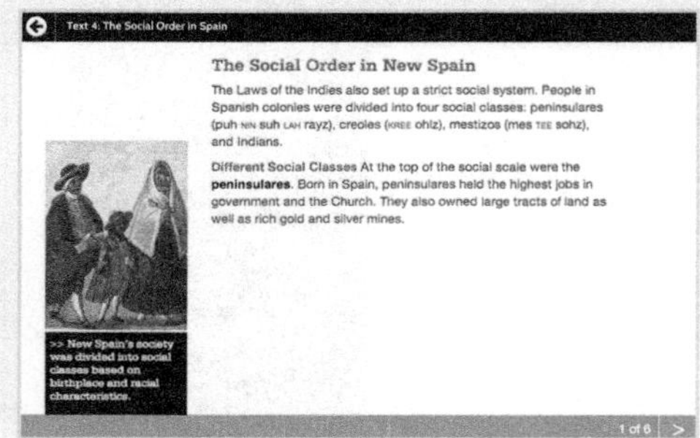

Text 4: The Social Order in Spain
The Social Order in New Spain
The Laws of the Indies also set up a strict social system. People in Spanish colonies were divided into four social classes: peninsulares (puh NIN suh LAH rayz), creoles (KREE ohlz), mestizos (mes TEE sohz), and Indians.
Different Social Classes At the top of the social scale were the peninsulares. Born in Spain, peninsulares held the highest jobs in government and the Church. They also owned large tracts of land as well as rich gold and silver mines.
>> New Spain's society was divided into social classes based on birthplace and racial characteristics.
1 of 6

Objective 2: Explain why Spain settled its colonies.

Quick Instruction

Interactive Map: Spanish Explorers and Settlements Project the map on the whiteboard. Explain that Spanish explorers traveled throughout the southeastern and southwestern United States, establishing settlements. Tell students that in this lesson, they will learn about the reasons for Spanish colonization of North America.

Interactive Chart: Social Classes in New Spain Project the Interactive Chart on the whiteboard. Explain that Spanish colonies were settlements that included different racial and ethnic groups. Identify ethnic groups that settled in the colonies and explain their reasons for immigration. These colonies developed their own social systems and methods of organization.

Generate Explanations Point out that the text identifies the founding of St. Augustine in Florida as the beginning of the era of colonization in the present-day United States, which ended when the United States declared independence in 1776. Ask students to explain why historians refer to this period as the era of colonization. *(During this period, the United States did not yet exist as a nation, but was instead part of colonies belonging to European nations.)*

Identify Cause and Effect As students read Texts 2 through 4, ask them to identify both the causes and the effects of colonization by the Spanish. *(Causes: desire for adventure; desire for more land; interest in searching for riches. Effects: Spanish settlement in the Americas, the spread of Spanish customs and ways of making a living, the spread of Christianity, loss of land and culture for Indians, development of a social system based on people's backgrounds.)*

ACTIVE CLASSROOM

Have students use the Quick Write activity and take 30 seconds to write what they know about the reasons for Spanish colonization of North America. Then have students write down an additional question they have about Spanish exploration and settlements that they hope to learn in this lesson.

ACTIVE CLASSROOM

Have students use a Rank It activity to better understand the class system in New Spain. Ask students to rank the classes according to which had the most significant impact. Ask students to provide a justification for the ranking decisions they made.

ELL Use the ELL activity described in the ELL chart.

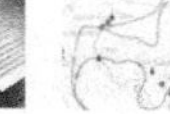

INTERACTIVE MAP

Spanish Explorers and Settlements in North America

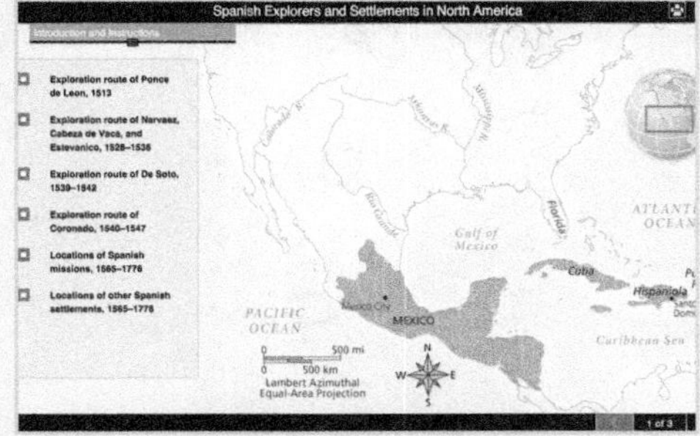

INTERACTIVE CHART

Social Classes in New Spain

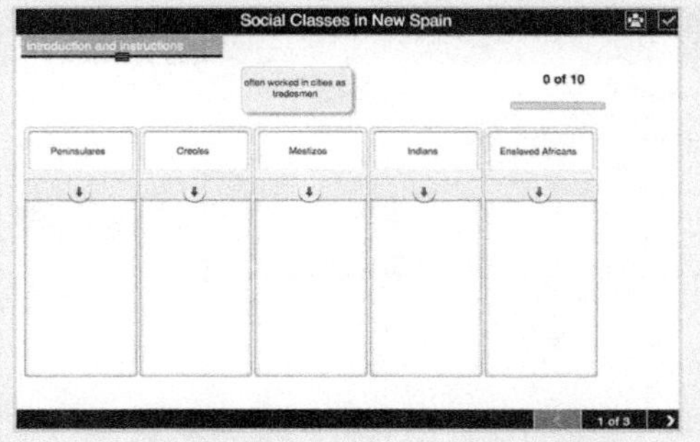

DIGITAL TEXT 5

Transatlantic Slave Trade

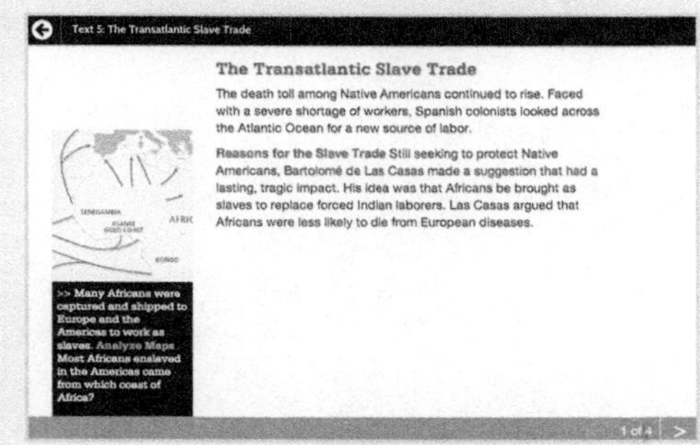

Further Instruction

Go through the Interactive Reading Notepad questions for *Discovering Lands to the North*, *The Colonization of New Spain*, and *Social Order in New Spain* with the class. To extend the lesson, have students go through the primary source *The Destruction of the Indies*, by Las Casas and the additional resource Introducing Physical Geography: Geography.

Be sure students understand the causes and the effects of the Spanish colonization of North America. The Spanish settled in what is now the United States because they wanted to spread Christianity, gain wealth, and satisfy a thirst for adventure. These settlers developed the first colonies in New Spain, with devastating effects on Native American communities.

Draw Conclusions Ask students why they think the Spanish colonies established such a rigid social system. *(To maintain divisions among racial and ethnic groups within the colonies; to ensure the Spanish maintained power over other groups)*

Generate Explanations Most Spanish colonizers were not explorers. What reasons besides adventure prompted Spaniards to settle in the New World? *(Missionaries wanted to convert Native Americans to Christianity; others sought wealth through farming and trade.)*

Objective 3: **Explain the causes and effects of the transatlantic slave trade.**

Quick Instruction

Project the map of the transatlantic slave trade on the white board to help illustrate the reasons for the development of the transatlantic slave trade. Have students study the map and explain where enslaved Africans were taken. Project the bar graph showing the approximate number of enslaved Africans involved in the transatlantic slave trade. Explain that the number of enslaved Africans necessary to sustain the colonies increased as the Spanish colonies grew. Also, the death toll of Native Americans working to support the colonies continued to rise, which further increased the need for enslaved Africans. Together these factors led to the growth of the transatlantic slave trade.

Summarize Ask students to explain the *transatlantic slave trade* in their own words. *(Africans were captured in Africa, transported across the Atlantic, and sold as slaves in the Americas.)*

Draw Conclusions Why did the deaths of Native Americans to European diseases contribute to the development of the transatlantic slave trade? *(Enslaved Africans were used as a new labor source.)*

ELL Use the ELL activity described in the ELL chart.

Spanish Colonization and New Spain

Further Instruction

Go through the Interactive Reading Notepad questions with the class. Review the reasons Las Casas gave for bringing Africans to the Americas. Be sure students understand how the need for labor in European colonies led to the development of the transatlantic slave trade.

Discuss the effects of this development. Emphasize the significant role the development of the transatlantic slave trade played in shaping the early colonies. The slave trade would continue to grow as more Europeans established colonies in North America.

Generate Explanations Explain the reasons for the development of the transatlantic slave trade. *(Because of the high death toll among Native Americans, the Spanish needed new sources of labor for their colonies. They began bringing enslaved Africans to the Americas.)*

Identify Cause and Effect How did the history of slavery in Africa affect the development of the transatlantic slave trade? *(Slavery already existed in Africa. Africans began selling enslaved people to Europeans, who brought them to the Americas.)*

Draw Conclusions How did the growth of European colonization in the Americas contribute to the development of the transatlantic slave trade? *(The growth of colonies increased the need for labor. Europeans relied on slave labor in the colonies, especially on sugar plantations.)*

SYNTHESIZE

DIGITAL ACTIVITY

Interaction in the Americas

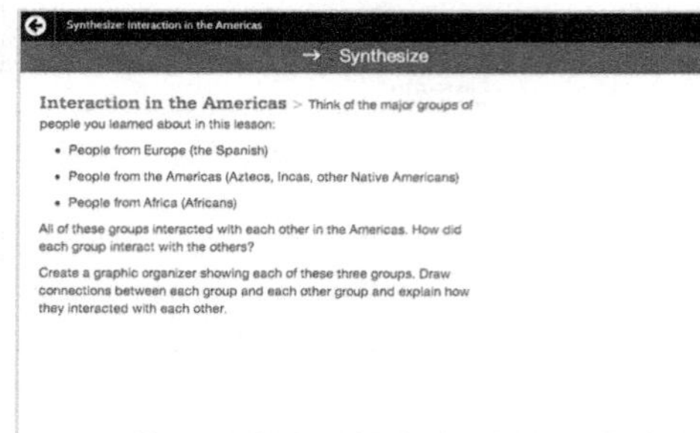

Synthesize: Interaction in the Americas

→ Synthesize

Interaction in the Americas > Think of the major groups of people you learned about in this lesson:

- People from Europe (the Spanish)
- People from the Americas (Aztecs, Incas, other Native Americans)
- People from Africa (Africans)

All of these groups interacted with each other in the Americas. How did each group interact with the others?

Create a graphic organizer showing each of these three groups. Draw connections between each group and each other group and explain how they interacted with each other.

Have students create a graphic organizer to complete the Interaction in the Americas activity. Ask them to write a few sentences explaining the connections among each group in their graphic organizer, then share their answers with a partner.

Discuss Have partners think about the following question: What were the effects of colonization on Europeans, Native Americans, and Africans? Have students discuss their answers with the class.

DEMONSTRATE

DIGITAL QUIZ

Lesson Quiz and Class Discussion Board

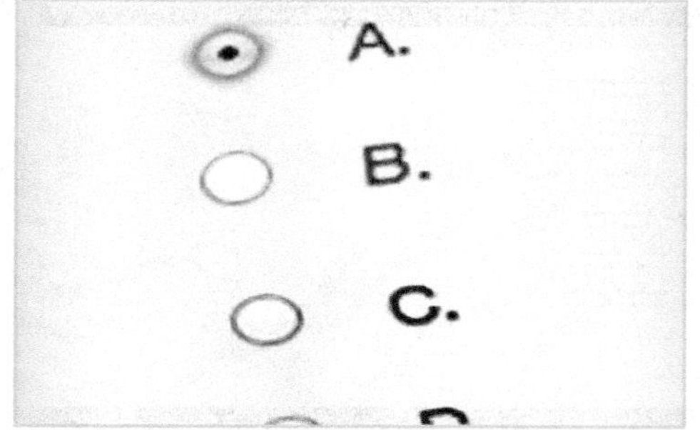

Assign the online Lesson Quiz for this lesson if you haven't already done so. Students will be offered automatic remediation or enrichment based on their score.

Pose these questions to the class on the Discussion Board:

In *Spanish Colonization and New Spain*, you read about the beginning of the era of colonization, the causes and effects of the Spanish colonization of North America, the reasons racial and ethnic groups first settled in the present-day United States, and the reasons for the development of the transatlantic slave trade.

Contrast The growth of colonies in the Americas brought different racial and ethnic groups across the Atlantic. Contrast their reasons for settling in the present-day United States. *(The Spanish came voluntarily to convert Native Americans, generate wealth, and expand Spain's empire. Africans were brought against their will to work on plantations as slaves.)*

Make Generalizations Make a generalization about the effect of colonization on Native Americans. *(Colonization had negative effects on most Native Americans. Many people were brutally conquered, forced to work for Europeans, and killed.)*

Topic Inquiry

Have students continue their investigations for the Topic Inquiry.

The First French, Dutch, and English Colonies

Supporting English Language Learners

Use with Digital Text 3, **The Dutch Establish New Netherland.**

Speaking
Have students read the section titled, *European Settlement Affects Native Americans*. Prompt students to express their feelings about the reading that range from communicating single words and short phrases to participating in extended discussions.

Beginning Display a list of feeling words along with this sentence frame: I feel _____. Based on their reading, ask students to choose an appropriate feeling word and to read the completed sentence aloud.

Intermediate In pairs or in groups, ask students to share their feelings about the effects of European settlement on Native Americans, speaking in complete sentences.

Advanced Have students identify the effects of European settlement on North Americans that they feel is most tragic. In pairs or in groups, ask them to share aloud both the effect and how they feel about it, using academic language as appropriate.

Advanced High In pairs or in groups, ask students to engage in an extended discussion, expressing their feelings about the effects of European settlement on Native Americans.

Use with Digital Text 4, **Roanoke and Jamestown.**

Learning
Have students read the text.Use strategic learning techniques such as concept mapping. Display a blank Venn diagram, and explain to students that they will be using it to help them learn new vocabulary.

Beginning Label the Venn diagram circles with the words *Roanoke* and *Jamestown*. Also display new words from the text that fit each part of the diagram. Ask students to match the words to their proper places on the diagram.

Intermediate Have students copy the Venn diagram circles and label them with the words *Roanoke* and *Jamestown*. Invite students to write vocabulary from the text in each part of the diagram. Circulate to check their responses.

Advanced Ask pairs of students to draw, label, and complete a Venn diagram that compares and contrasts the Roanoke and Jamestown colonies. Encourage them to use as much new vocabulary from the text as possible.

Advanced High Have students independently design, draw, label, and complete a Venn diagram that compares and contrasts terms from the reading for each colony. Have them present and explain their diagrams in small groups or in front of the class.

D Differentiate Instruction

Use the Differentiated Instruction notes throughout the lesson plan to support the varied skill sets, levels of readiness, and interests in the mixed-ability classroom.

Challenge These notes include suggestions for expanding the activity for advanced students.

On-Level These notes include suggestions for modifying the activity to address different interests or learning styles.

Extra Support These notes include ideas for providing more scaffolding or reading spuport.

Special Needs These notes provide ideas for adapting instruction to support the needs of various special needs students.

NOTES

The First French, Dutch, and English Colonies

Objectives

Objective 1: Explain why Europeans explored North America's coast.

Objective 2: Identify the reasons for French and Dutch colonization in North America.

Objective 3: Identify the reasons for English colonization.

Objective 4: Explain how Virginia began a tradition of representative government.

Objective 5: Describe how different groups in Jamestown interacted with the environment.

LESSON 2 ORGANIZER — **PACING: APPROX. 1 PERIOD, .5 BLOCKS**

	OBJECTIVES	PACING	RESOURCES Online	RESOURCES Print
Connect				
DIGITAL START UP ACTIVITY **How Will You Survive?**		5 min.	●	
Investigate				
DIGITAL TEXT 1 **European Rivalries**	Objective 1	10 min.	●	●
DIGITAL TEXT 2 **New France is Colonized**	Objective 2	10 min.	●	●
DIGITAL TEXT 3 **The Dutch Establish New Netherland**	Objective 2	10 min.	●	●
INTERACTIVE MAP **Lands Controlled by Colonial Powers, 1660**	Objective 2	10 min.	●	
DIGITAL TEXT 4 **Roanoke and Jamestown**	Objective 3	10 min.	●	●
INTERACTIVE GALLERY **Arrival and Early Years at Jamestown**	Objective 3	10 min.	●	
DIGITAL TEXT 5 **An Improved Form of Government**	Objective 4	10 min.	●	●
DIGITAL TEXT 6 **The Jamestown Colony Grows**	Objective 5	10 min.	●	●
Synthesize				
DIGITAL ACTIVITY **Surviving a New World**		5 min.	●	
Demonstrate				
DIGITAL QUIZ **Lesson Quiz and Class Discussion Board**		10 min.	●	

Go online to access additional resources including:
Primary Sources • Biographies • Supreme Court cases • 21st Century Skill Tutorials • Maps • Graphic Organizers.

CONNECT

DIGITAL START UP ACTIVITY

How Will You Survive?

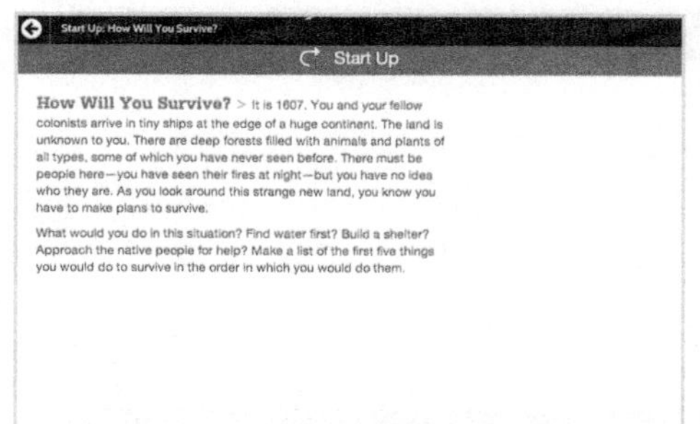

Project the Start Up Activity Have students read the scenario and generate their lists as they enter and get settled. Ask students to discuss their choices with a partner. Then poll the class to see what activities appear most on the lists.

Discuss What would you do in this situation? Make a list of the first five things you would do to survive, in the order in which you would do them. *(Answers should include "find food and water" and "build shelter".)*

Tell students that in this lesson they will be learning about the first European colonists in North America.

Aa Vocabulary Development: Use the Interactive Reading Notepad to preview the Key Terms and Academic Vocabulary in this lesson with students.

FLIP IT!

Assign the Flipped Video for this lesson.

STUDENT EDITION PRINT PAGES: 56–68

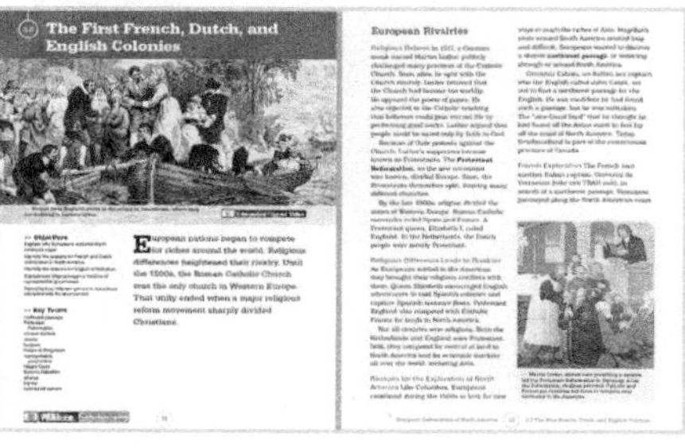

INVESTIGATE

DIGITAL TEXT 1

European Rivalries

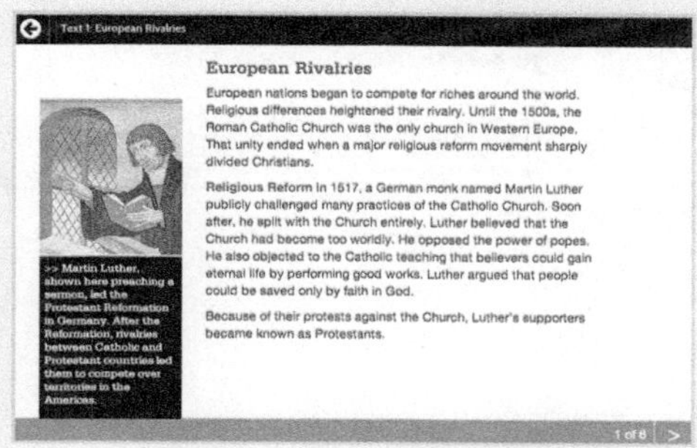

Objective 1: Explain why Europeans explored North America's coast.

Quick Instruction

Tell the class that they will be identifying reasons for European exploration of North America. Project the map on the whiteboard. Explain that one reason Europeans explored North America was to search for a northwest passage. Europeans hoped to find a waterway through or around North America that would provide a route to Asia.

Analyze Maps Ask students to describe the regions each European powers explored.

Make Predictions How will exploration of North America lead Europeans to establish colonies? *(Explorers will learn about the land and geography of North Americas, which will lead rulers to see the potential for profit in the region.)*

Further Instruction

Go through the Interactive Reading Notepad questions and discuss the answers with the class. To extend the lesson, have students complete the additional resource Geography: Mapping Earth.

Generate Explanations Identify reasons for European exploration of North America. *(European explorers were looking for a northwest passage, or a shorter route to Asia. Also, different European nations were competing to claim and control land in North America.)*

Draw Conclusions What motivated explorers to look for new travel routes around the globe? What does this suggest about the reasons for European colonization of North America? *(Explorers wanted to reach Asia because they wanted wealth from Asian trade. This suggests rulers and colonists were also looking for wealth when they established North American colonies.)*

The First French, Dutch, and English Colonies

DIGITAL TEXT 2

New France is Colonized

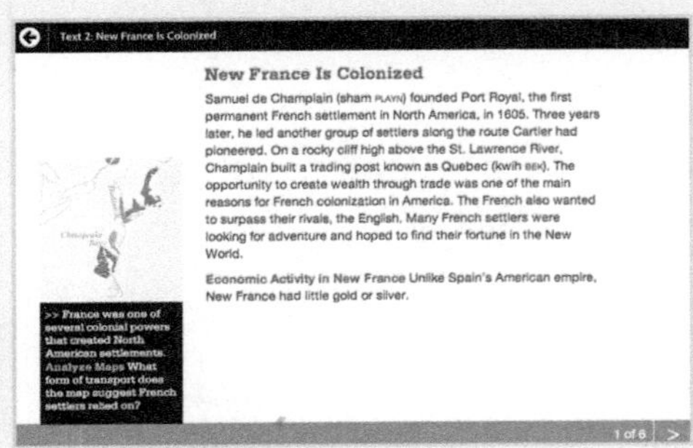

DIGITAL TEXT 3

The Dutch Establish New Netherland

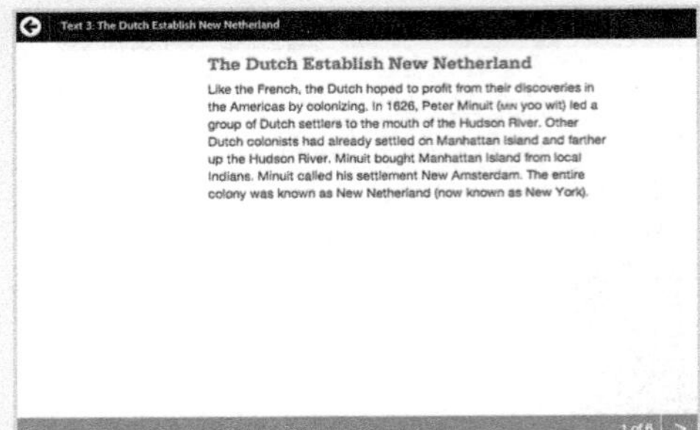

INTERACTIVE MAP

Lands Controlled by Colonial Powers, 1660

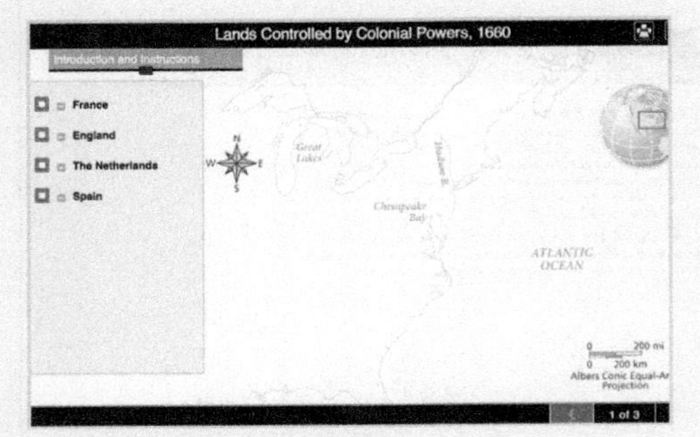

Objective 2: **Identify the reasons for French and Dutch colonization in North America.**

Quick Instruction

Interactive Map: Lands Controlled by Colonial Powers, 1660 Project the map on the whiteboard. Click through the layers showing the land controlled by each European power. Identify the reasons for European colonization of North America: spreading Christianity, gaining wealth, and expanding empire.

Analyze Maps Have students review the map and identify European reasons for colonization of North America. Ask how the physical characteristics of the environment influenced the economic activities of the early colonial powers. *(Resources determined exports and trade; waterways impacted how goods and wealth traveled from the colonies to Europe)*

ACTIVE CLASSROOM

Divide students into groups and use the Walking Tour activity to pick key passages from the lessons that describe the reasons for French and Dutch colonization in North America. Have groups post their passages on individual pages around the room, then tour the passages and then summarize each one.

ELL Use the ELL activity described in the ELL chart.

Further Instruction

Go through the Interactive Reading Notepad questions for *New France is Colonized* and *The Dutch Establish New Netherland* with the class. Have students begin completing the graphic organizer to take notes about the English, Dutch, and French colonies. Be sure students understand the causes of colonization, particularly the reasons for European colonization of North America.

Compare and Contrast French and Dutch immigrants and their reasons for colonization. *(Compare—both sought profit, especially from the fur trade. Contrast—the French also prioritized missionaries; the Dutch established a port colony while the French built smaller settlements inland.)*

Draw Conclusions Describe the effects of colonization, using examples from Dutch and French colonization. *(A fur trade developed and led to a network of trade routes in the interior of North America. French control over the continent's interior gave them a strategic advantage over the Spanish and English. Colonization brought enslaved Africans to North America. Trade rivalries developed between the French and the Dutch over the fur trade. Both sought alliances with Native Americans. The fur trade nearly wiped out beaver populations. European diseases killed thousands of Native Americans. Missionaries brought Christianity to Native Americans.)*

Identify Central Issues Have students describe the places of importance where French and Dutch colonists settled. Ask what geographic factors compelled them to choose these locations. *(French colonists settled along the St. Lawrence and Mississippi Rivers, using the waterways for transportation and trade; they also settled in wooded areas to be close to fishing, trapping, and trade. The Dutch created a port at New Amsterdam in the mouth of the Hudson River. They transported goods along the Hudson and were close to the Atlantic to send furs to the Netherlands.)*

DIGITAL TEXT 4

Roanoke and Jamestown

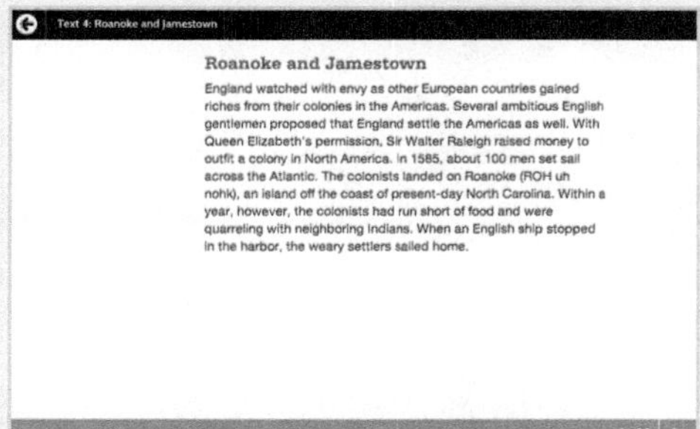

INTERACTIVE GALLERY

Arrival and Early Years at Jamestown

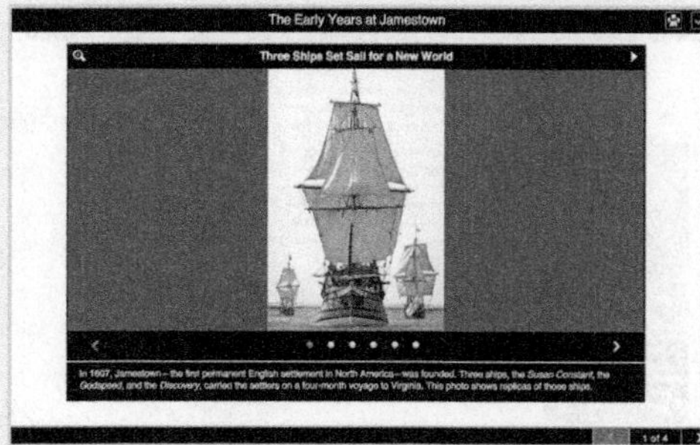

DIGITAL TEXT 5

An Improved Form of Government

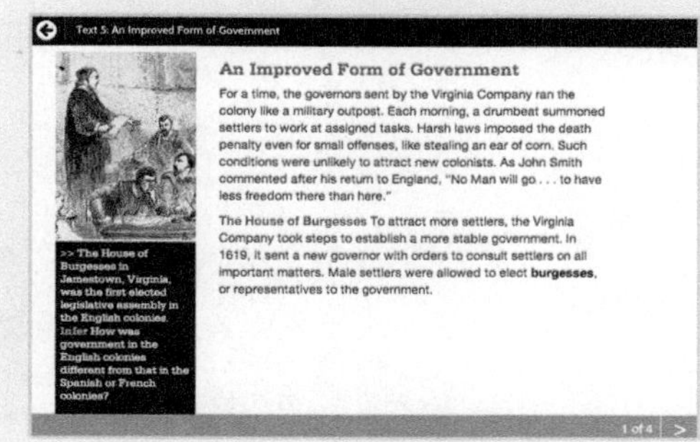

Text 5: An Improved Form of Government
An Improved Form of Government
For a time, the governors sent by the Virginia Company ran the colony like a military outpost. Each morning, a drumbeat summoned settlers to work at assigned tasks. Harsh laws imposed the death penalty even for small offenses, like stealing an ear of corn. Such conditions were unlikely to attract new colonists. As John Smith commented after his return to England, "No Man will go . . . to have less freedom there than here."
The House of Burgesses To attract more settlers, the Virginia Company took steps to establish a more stable government. In 1619, it sent a new governor with orders to consult settlers on all important matters. Male settlers were allowed to elect burgesses, or representatives to the government.
>> The House of Burgesses in Jamestown, Virginia, was the first elected legislative assembly in the English colonies. Infer How was government in the English colonies different from that in the Spanish or French colonies?
1 of 4

Objective 3: **Identify reasons for English colonization.**

Quick Instruction

Interactive Gallery: Arrival and Early Years at Jamestown Project the Interactive Gallery on the white board. Look at each image individually and then the collection as a whole. Discuss students' reactions to the images. Ask what they think it would have been like to be part of the Jamestown settlement.

Summarize Ask students to explain why 1607 is a significant year in American history. *(It marks the founding of Jamestown, the first successful English settlement in North America.)*

Identify Central Issues Why did settlers want to build a colony in Jamestown, Virginia? *(They were looking for wealth and a passage to Asia, and wanted to claim the land for England.)*

ACTIVE CLASSROOM

Have students complete a See-Think-Wonder activity using the Interactive Gallery. Ask students to pair with a partner and ask: What do you see? What does that make you think? What are you wondering about now that you've seen this? Once each partner has answered the questions about the images, ask them to share their insights with the class.

ELL Use the ELL activity described in the ELL chart.

Further Instruction

Go through the Interactive Reading Notepad questions with the class and have students continue completing the graphic organizer to take notes about English, Dutch, and French colonies.

Summarize How did the physical characteristics of the environment influence where the Jamestown colonists settled? *(They wanted somewhere secure, and their location in the Chesapeake Bay along the James River made it difficult for the Spanish to find and fire upon them.)*

Identify Cause and Effect How did the physical characteristics of the Chesapeake Bay influence the Jamestown Colony and its economic activities? *(Jamestown was swampy; the unhealthy water and mosquitoes spread disease. However, it had fertile land for growing tobacco, which the colonists sold to England.)*

Compare and Contrast Describe how different immigrant groups, such as the Dutch colonists in New Netherland and the English colonists in Virginia, interacted with the environment in North America during the 17th century. *(The Dutch in New Netherland interacted with the environment mainly through trade. Their fur trade with Native Americans nearly wiped out the beaver population of the Iroquois lands. The English in Virginia interacted with the environment mainly by relying on it for food—first by hunting, fishing, and raiding nearby Indians, later increasingly through farming tobacco and other crops.)*

Objective 4: **Explain how Virginia began a tradition of representative government.**

Quick Instruction

Project the image of the Magna Carta on the white board. Explain that the Magna Carta, or Great Charter, was a document from 1215 listing the rights of British nobles that couldn't be taken away by the king. Point out its influence on the U.S. system of government. Explain that the Virginia Company established a government in Jamestown that drew on the Magna Carta in order to set up a representative government in the English colonies.

Use Context Clues Ask students to define the term *representative government* and explain why the growth of representative government during the colonial period was an improvement over the colony's previous government. *(In a representative government, voters elect representatives to make laws for them. It was an improvement over Virginia's previous government, which gave people less of a voice.)*

D Differentiate: Challenge Have students read selections from the Magna Carta and identify passages that they think influenced the development of representative government in the United States, citing examples to support their reasoning.

Further Instruction

Go through the Interactive Reading Notepad questions with the class and have students continue completing the graphic organizer to take notes about English, Dutch, and French

The First French, Dutch, and English Colonies

colonies. Be sure that students understand the reasons for the new institution that developed in Virginia during this time: the House of Burgesses.

Generate Explanations Explain the reasons for the growth of representative government during the colonial period. How was the House of Burgesses important to its development? *(The Virginia Company wanted to create a more stable government to attract settlers. It established the House of Burgesses, the first representative government in the colonies.)*

Draw Conclusions How did the Magna Carta influence the development of representative government in Virginia? *(The House of Burgesses called Virginia's charter the "Great Charter" after the Magna Carta. Both documents said that subjects have rights and that all people are subject to the law.)*

Identify Cause and Effect Name an important effect the Jamestown Colony had on the U.S. system of government. *(Established representative government; affirmed that citizens have political rights; said all people are subject to the law)*

DIGITAL TEXT 6

The Jamestown Colony Grows

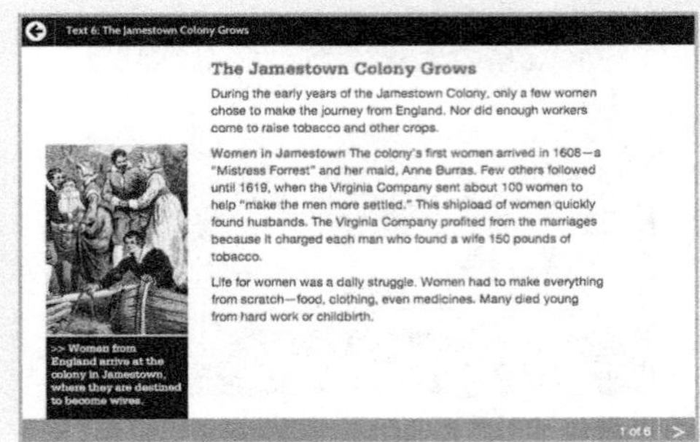

Objective 5: Describe how different groups in Jamestown interacted with the environment.

Quick Instruction

Project the infographic of the ethnic origins of colonial settlers. Explain that ethnic groups had different reasons for immigrating. Jamestown was initially populated by white men looking to make money in the colonies. Small numbers of women came to the colony to marry and work. Enslaved Africans were brought to work on tobacco plantations.

Analyze Data Ask students how the ethnic origins of colonial settlers changed over time, and why. *(More Africans arrived in the colonies as tobacco plantations grew.)*

Further Instruction

Go through the Interactive Reading Notepad questions with the class and have students finish the graphic organizer to take notes about English, Dutch, and French colonies.

Compare and Contrast Ask students to consider what they have learned in this lesson so far. Have them identify different ethnic groups that settled in the present-day United States and explain their reasons for immigration. *(Dutch settlers came mainly to take advantage of trade opportunities. English settlers in Virginia first came seeking gold and trade routes and later came to profit from raising tobacco. Africans came to Virginia to work on plantations because they were forced to do so by slave traders.)*

Support Ideas with Examples Give examples of how different immigrant groups, such as enslaved Africans and English settlers, interacted with the environment in Jamestown. *(Enslaved Africans had to work on plantations growing tobacco; English women used available resources to make what they needed from scratch; English male settlers worked to establish farms and pushed further inland, taking over more land.)*

SYNTHESIZE

DIGITAL ACTIVITY

Surviving a New World

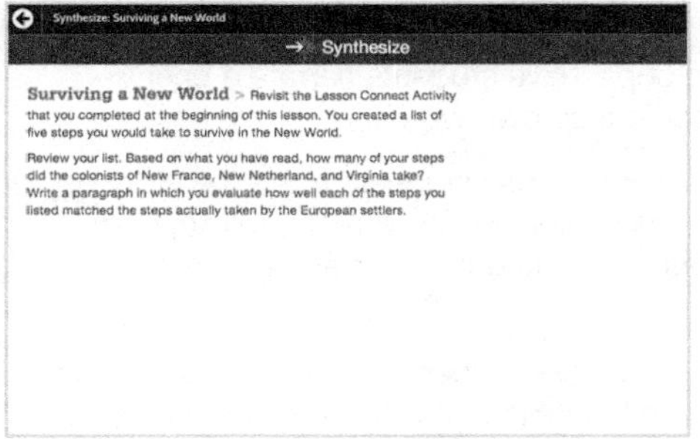

Ask students to recall the list they made for the Digital Start Up Activity at the beginning of this lesson. Have them write a paragraph evaluating their list in light of what they learned about the early colonists.

Discuss Ask students if they would change any of their responses now that they have learned more about the early colonies.

Have students think about the following question: How did geographic factors and the physical characteristics of the environment affect the growth of the early colonies? Discuss students' answers with the class.

DEMONSTRATE

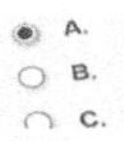

DIGITAL QUIZ

Lesson Quiz and Class Discussion Board

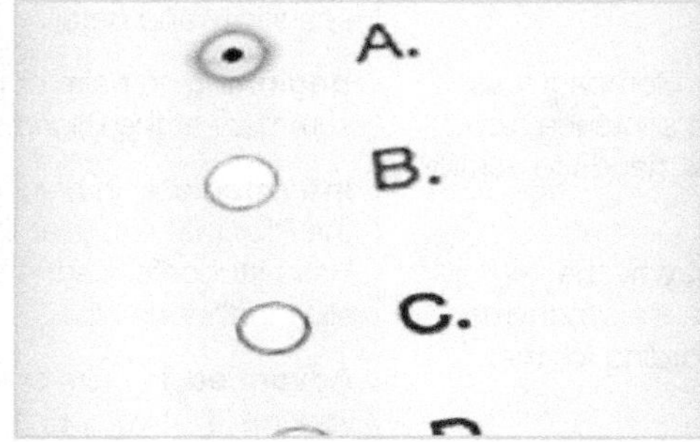

Assign the online Lesson Quiz for this lesson if you haven't already done so. Students will be offered automatic remediation or enrichment based on their score.

Pose these questions to the class on the Discussion Board:

You have read about the development of early European colonies in the Americas, including the reasons for colonization, the impact of the physical environment on the colonies, the racial and ethnic groups that immigrated, and the growth of new institutions.

Identify Central Issues Name at least one political, social, economic, and religious reason for the establishment of French, Dutch, and English colonies. *(political: expansion of European empires; social: arrival of women in Jamestown made the colony feel settled; economic: wealth from farming and trade; religious: missionaries spread Christianity)*

Compare and Contrast France and England's economic reasons for establishing colonies. *(Compare: Both hoped to gain wealth. Contrast: France gained wealth through the fur trade; England gained wealth through tobacco plantations.)*

Topic Inquiry

Have students continue their investigations for the Topic Inquiry.

The New England Colonies

Supporting English Language Learners

Use with Digital Text 2, **Plymouth Colony.**

Learning

Read with students, or have students read the section titled, *A New Pledge to Govern the Colony*. Then define the term *Mayflower Compact*, modeling nonverbal cues, synonyms, and circumlocution.

Beginning Display this sentence frame: The Mayflower Compact was important because _____. Ask students to complete the sentence aloud. Encourage them to use circumlocution, and to raise their hands to ask for help as needed.

Intermediate Ask students to make a statement about why the Mayflower Compact was important. Encourage them to use synonyms and circumlocution if they cannot think of the precise wording for their ideas.

Advanced Ask students about the Mayflower Compact and its significance. Encourage extended responses that push the limits of students' vocabulary. Remind them to use gestures, synonyms, and circumlocution to help them express their thoughts.

Advanced High Tell students to speak about the Mayflower Compact as if they were addressing students at a lower grade level, using gestures and other nonverbal cues as appropriate. Encourage them to use synonyms and circumlocution in place of vocabulary that students at a lower grade level might not understand.

Use with Digital Text 3, **Overcoming Hardships in Plymouth.**

Speaking

Have students read the text. Explain that this text tells the story of the Pilgrims' first year in Plymouth. Prompt students to narrate with increasing specificity and detail.

Beginning In pairs or in small groups, have students narrate a brief summary of the Pilgrims' first year in their own words.

Intermediate In pairs or in small groups, ask students to tell the story of the Pilgrims' first year in about three sentences (beginning, middle, end). Have students' partners ask questions during their narration in order to elicit further detail.

Advanced In pairs or in small groups, ask students to tell the story of the Pilgrims' first year. Encourage them to include descriptive details in their narrative.

Advanced High In pairs or in small groups, have students suppose they must tell the story of the Pilgrims' first year to someone who knows nothing about it. Encourage them to narrate that story, providing plenty of detail so that their listener fully understands.

D Differentiate Instruction

Use the Differentiated Instruction notes throughout the lesson plan to support the varied skill sets, levels of readiness, and interests in the mixed-ability classroom.

Challenge These notes include suggestions for expanding the activity for advanced students.

On-Level These notes include suggestions for modifying the activity to address different interests or learning styles.

Extra Support These notes include ideas for providing more scaffolding or reading spuport.

Special Needs These notes provide ideas for adapting instruction to support the needs of various special needs students.

NOTES

Objectives

Objective 1: Explain how the desire for religious freedom led to the settlement of the New England colonies.

Objective 2: Identify the significance of the Mayflower Compact.

Objective 3: Describe how conflicts over religion and politics were resolved in colonial New England.

Objective 4: Identify reasons for conflict between settlers and Native Americans.

Objective 5: Describe the daily life and the economy in the New England colonies.

LESSON 3 ORGANIZER — PACING: APPROX. 1 PERIOD, .5 BLOCKS	OBJECTIVES	PACING	RESOURCES Online	RESOURCES Print
Connect				
DIGITAL START UP ACTIVITY **The First Thanksgiving**		5 min.	●	
Investigate				
DIGITAL TEXT 1 **Seeking Religious Freedom**	Objective 1	10 min.	●	●
DIGITAL TEXT 2; DIGITAL TEXT 3 **The Plymouth Colony; Overcoming Hardships in Plymouth**	Objective 2	20 min.	●	●
3-D MODEL **Plymouth Plantation**		10 min.	●	
DIGITAL TEXT 4; DIGITAL TEXT 5 **Forming Massachusetts Bay Colony; New Colonies Form Over Religious Differences**	Objective 3	20 min.	●	●
INTERACTIVE CHART **Thomas Hooker**		10 min.	●	
DIGITAL TEXT 6 **War Erupts Between Puritans and Native Americans**	Objective 4	10 min.	●	●
DIGITAL TEXT 7 **The Towns of New England**	Objective 5	10 min.	●	●
INTERACTIVE MAP **The New England Colonies**		10 min.	●	
Synthesize				
DIGITAL ACTIVITY **Challenges of Being a Colonist**		5 min.	●	
Demonstrate				
DIGITAL QUIZ **Lesson Quiz and Class Discussion Board**		10 min.	●	

The New England Colonies

CONNECT

DIGITAL START UP ACTIVITY

The First Thanksgiving

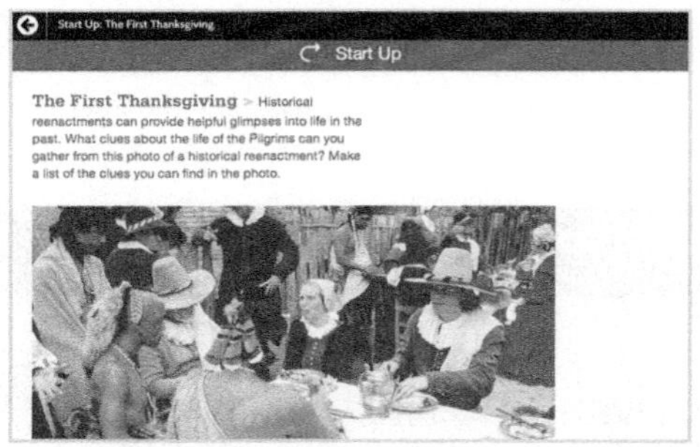

Project the Start Up Activity Ask students to answer the questions as they enter and get settled. Then have them share their ideas with another student, either in class or through a chat or blog space.

Discuss Prompt students to consider if this is an accurate image of early Pilgrims' lives. What difficulties might they have had to overcome when they first arrived to North America? *(Building shelter, finding adequate food and water, growing crops, etc.)*

Tell students they will be learning about life in some of the early North American colonies.

Aa Vocabulary Development: Use the Interactive Reading Notepad to preview Key Terms and Academic Vocabulary in the lesson with students.

FLIP IT!

Assign the Flipped Video for this lesson.

STUDENT EDITION PRINT PAGES: 69–82

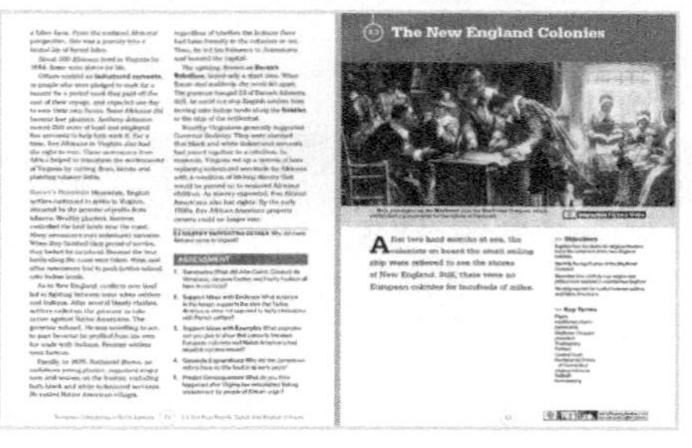

INVESTIGATE

DIGITAL TEXT 1

Seeking Religious Freedom

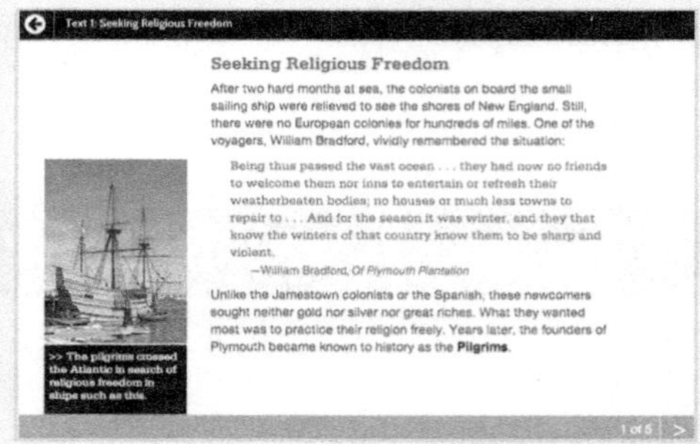

Objective 1: Explain how the desire for religious freedom led to the settlement of the New England Colonies.

Quick Instruction

Project the lesson on the whiteboard. Tell students that Pilgrims and other religious groups were put on trial for violating religious restrictions in England. Explain that Pilgrims were one religious group that settled in the United States. Religion was an important factor in motivating immigration to the colonies.

Use Context Clues Read the section titled "The Pilgrims." Based on context clues in this section, predict how the Pilgrims' circumstances would be a cause of colonization. *(Persecution would cause the Pilgrims to start a new colony to seek religious freedom.)*

Generate Explanations Ask students why they think religion motivated many people to immigrate to the colonies. *(People probably wanted an opportunity to create a new life in which they were free to worship as they pleased.)*

D Differentiate: Extra Support As students discuss the image, have them focus their attention on the individual characters and setting of the image before asking them to discuss the image as a whole.

Further Instruction

Go through the Interactive Reading Notepad questions and discuss the answers with the class.

Identify Central Issues What reasons led the Separatists to establish a colony in North America? *(They wanted to leave the Church of England, escape religious persecution, and preserve their culture.)*

Express Problems Clearly Ask students to describe the problems in Europe that motivated religious groups to immigrate to the colonies. *(European rulers established churches and persecuted people with other beliefs. Those who did not follow the established church had to worship in secret and were imprisoned or even killed if they were caught.)*

Identify Cause and Effect How do you think the arrival of Quakers, Puritans, and other religious groups will affect religious freedom in the colonies? *(There will probably be more religious freedom and a greater openness to different religions in the colonies.)*

DIGITAL TEXT 2

The Plymouth Colony

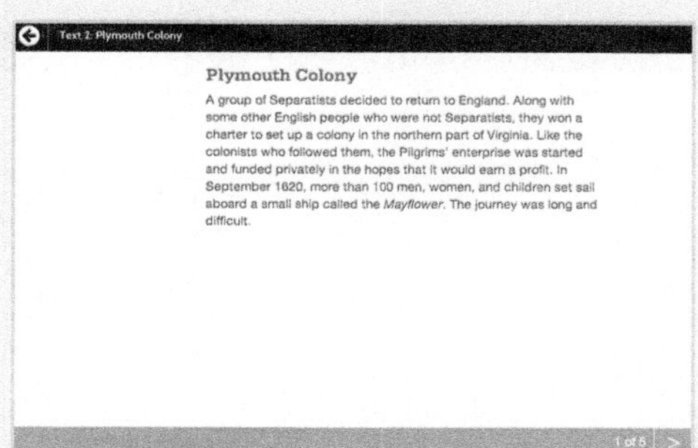

DIGITAL TEXT 3

Overcoming Hardships in Plymouth

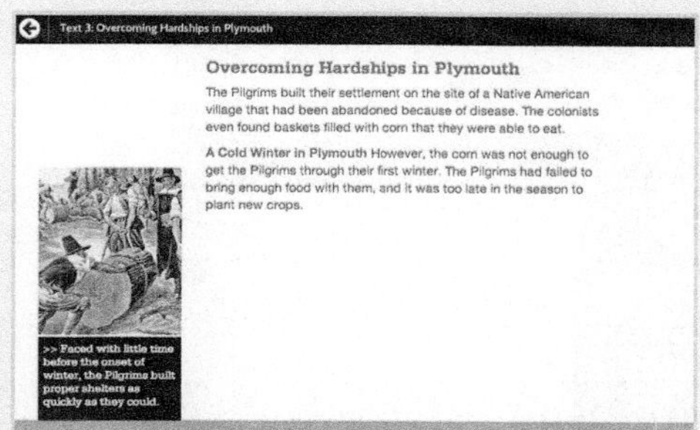

3-D MODEL

Plymouth Plantation

Objective 2: Identify the significance of the Mayflower Compact.

Quick Instruction

The Separatists won a charter from England to set up a colony in Virginia. Describe the Pilgrims' religious motivation for migration to America. *(The Pilgrims migrated to America seeking religious freedom.)* Explain the significance of 1620, the year the Pilgrims arrived in present-day Massachusetts, signed the Mayflower Compact, and established a new colony with its own representative government based on the principle of religious freedom. The Mayflower Compact created a representative government for the colony.

3D Model: Plymouth Plantation Project the 3-D Model on the whiteboard and move the cursor to explore the image of Plymouth Plantation. Discuss how the physical characteristics of the environment influenced the colony.

Express Ideas Clearly How did religion and virtue contribute to the growth of representative government in the North American colonies? *(The Pilgrims expected their elected representatives to show the same religious values and virtue as the citizens they represented and to make decisions for the common good, such as protecting religious freedom. The protection of religious freedom gave the representatives more legitimacy in the eyes of the citizens. This strengthened the institution of representative government.)*

ACTIVE CLASSROOM

Have students use the See-Think-Wonder strategy as they look at the 3-D model of Plymouth Plantation. Ask: What do you see? What does it make you think? What are you wondering about now that you've seen this? Call on students to share their insights with the class.

ELL Use the ELL activity described in the ELL chart.

Further Instruction

Go through the Interactive Reading Notepad questions for *The Plymouth Colony* and *Overcoming Hardships in Plymouth* with the class. Assign the Primary Source: Mayflower Compact.

Interpret Explain how the Mayflower Compact contributed to the growth of representative government in the colonies. *(The Mayflower Compact set a precedent of representative government in the colonies. The people agreed to form a government of elected representatives who would in turn make laws for the greater good.)*

Identify Central Issues Why was the year 1620 significant for the development of religious freedom in the United States? *(1620 was the year the Pilgrims established the Mayflower Compact. The Mayflower Compact established the new representative government's role in protecting religious freedom.)*

The New England Colonies

DIGITAL TEXT 4
Forming Massachusetts Bay Colony

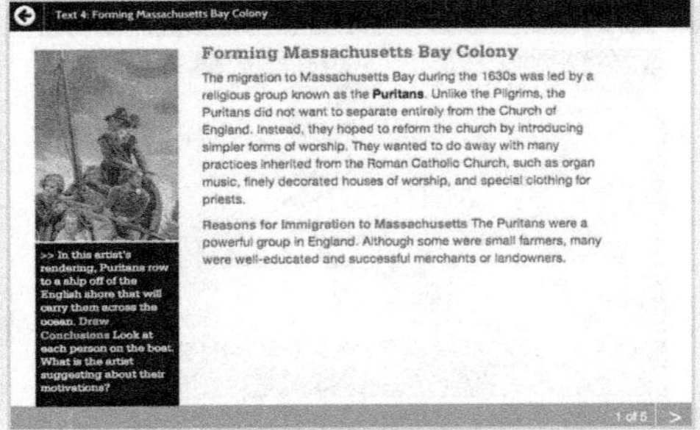

DIGITAL TEXT 5
New Colonies Form Over Religious Differences

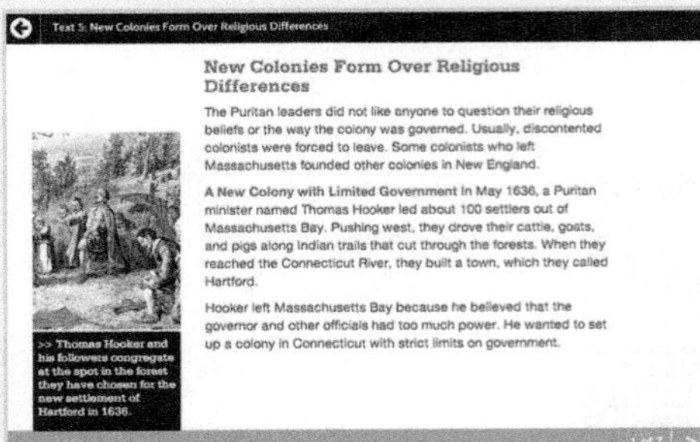

INTERACTIVE CHART
Thomas Hooker

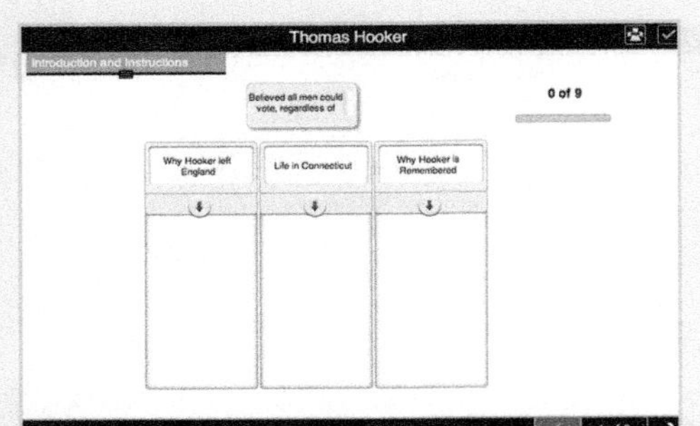

Objective 3: **Describe how conflicts over religion and politics were resolved in colonial New England.**

Quick Instruction

The Puritans established a new government in Massachusetts that did not tolerate religious dissent. Those who questioned the Puritans' policies or beliefs were forced to leave. As a result, other colonies were formed.

Interactive Chart: Thomas Hooker Project the Interactive Chart on the whiteboard and read through the tiles. Explain that Thomas Hooker was a Puritan who left Massachusetts Bay Colony to found a new colony based on principles of self-government.

Compare and Contrast the reasons for immigration of different religious groups, such as the Pilgrims and Puritans. *(Compare: conflicts with the Church of England; search for religious freedom. Contrast: Puritans wanted to reform the Church instead of separate from it.)*

ACTIVE CLASSROOM

Break students into groups and use Circle Write strategy to answer the question: What influence did Thomas Hooker have on the development of self-government in colonial America? Have students write as much as they can for one minute and then switch with the person on their right. Have the next person improve or elaborate on the response. Continue switching until the paper returns to the first person. Have groups share the best responses with the class.

Further Instruction

Go through the Interactive Reading Notepad questions for *Forming Massachusetts Bay Colony* and *New Colonies Form Over Religious Differences* with the class. Have students complete the graphic organizer to summarize why each group left Massachusetts Bay Colony and what happened as a result.

Generate Explanations What relationship did the Fundamental Orders of Connecticut have with the growth of representative government? *(The Fundamental Orders of Connecticut expanded the vote to include all male property owners, not just church members, and limited the governor's power. The limitations on the governor's power and increased political participation strengthened the idea of representative government in the colonies.)*

Summarize How did the founding a new colony in Rhode Island resolve conflicts between people from various religious groups? *(In Massachusetts, the government supported a particular church and non-Puritans were unable to openly practice their faith. By leaving Massachusetts with his followers, Williams resolved conflicts over religion there. Freedom of religion in Rhode Island allowed for the peaceful resolution of conflicts between people from different religious groups.)*

DIGITAL TEXT 6

War Erupts Between Puritans and Native Americans

Objective 4: **Identify reasons for conflict between settlers and Native Americans.**

Quick Instruction

Project the image of colonists and Native Americans fighting on the whiteboard. Explain that conflicts broke out as settlements spread and colonists took over more Native American land. These conflicts would not be resolved for centuries.

Identify Central Issues How did the physical characteristics of the environment contribute to conflict between colonists and Native Americans? *(Population growth strained natural resources. Competition for scarce resources led to hostilities.)*

Further Instruction

Go through the Interactive Reading Notepad questions with the class. Make sure students understand how competition for land and resources led to hostilities between colonists and Native Americans.

Draw Conclusions Ask students how they think the physical characteristics of the environment influenced settlement patterns and economic activity in New England in the 17th century. *(Colonists probably wanted to settle where they had access to natural resources like water and good farmland. These environmental characteristics in turn encouraged specific industries such as farming, fishing, and shipping.)*

DIGITAL TEXT 7

The Towns of New England

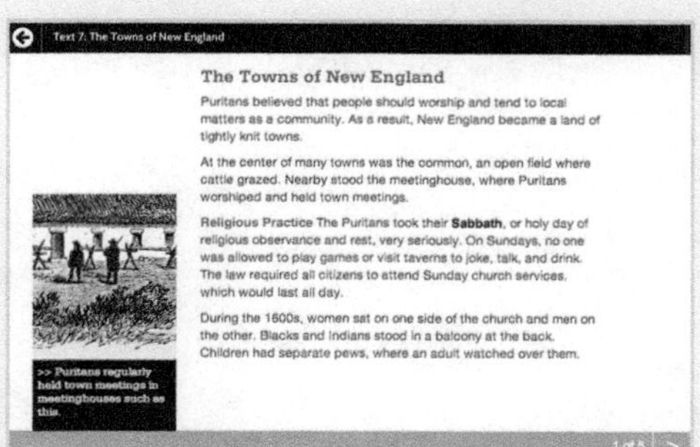

Objective 5: **Describe the daily life and the economy in the New England Colonies.**

Quick Instruction

Puritans established close-knit towns and villages. People gathered together for town meetings and religious services. They modified the environment to cultivate food and resources and to grow their economy. The culture, values, and traditions of this religious group had a lasting impact on American national identity.

Interactive Map: The New England Colonies Project the Interactive Map. Describe how the physical characteristics of the environment influenced economic activities in the colonies: forests for timber and furs; oceans and rivers for fishing and whaling; and land for meat, dairy, and crops. Colonists made a living by farming, fishing, logging, shipbuilding, whaling, and trading.

> **ACTIVE CLASSROOM**
>
> Have students use the Plus/Minus/Interesting strategy to record their reactions to the ways people modified the physical environment for economic purposes in the New England Colonies. Ask: 1. What are the positive ideas about this? 2. What are the negative ideas about this? 3. What is interesting about this? Have students share their responses with the class.

INTERACTIVE MAP

The New England Colonies

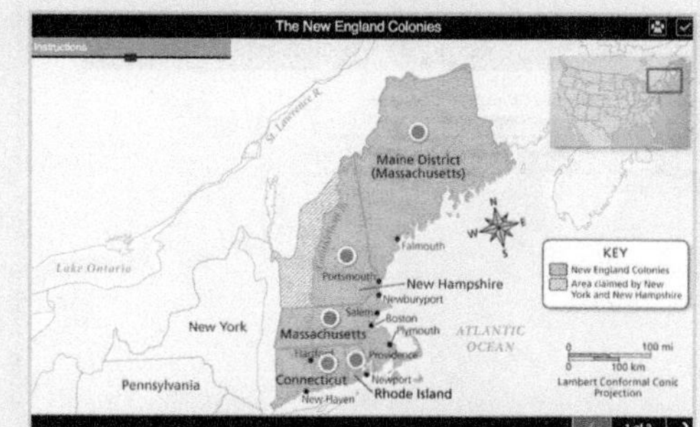

Further Instruction

Go through the Interactive Reading Notepad questions with the class. Be sure students understand the religious practices, form of government, and economic activities of the Puritans.

Compare and Contrast the physical characteristics of the New England Colonies. How did these characteristics contribute to economic differences within the region? *(Connecticut had land for farming and for meat and dairy production. Maine, Massachusetts, and Rhode Island had thick forests and long coastlines with access to the ocean's resources. New Hampshire also had forests and water. These colonies relied on fishing, shipbuilding, and trade.)*

Identify Central Issues What economic factors promoted growth in the New England Colonies? *(Colonists fished and farmed, but they generated the most wealth through shipbuilding, whaling, ironworking, timber exports, and the fur trade.)*

Interpret What were some of the most important effects of colonization in New England? *(Colonization led to the development of representative self-government and religious freedom in New England, and to the development of industries such as shipbuilding and ironworking.)*

The New England Colonies

SYNTHESIZE

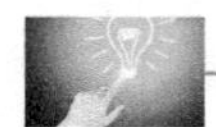

DIGITAL ACTIVITY

Challenges of Being a Colonist

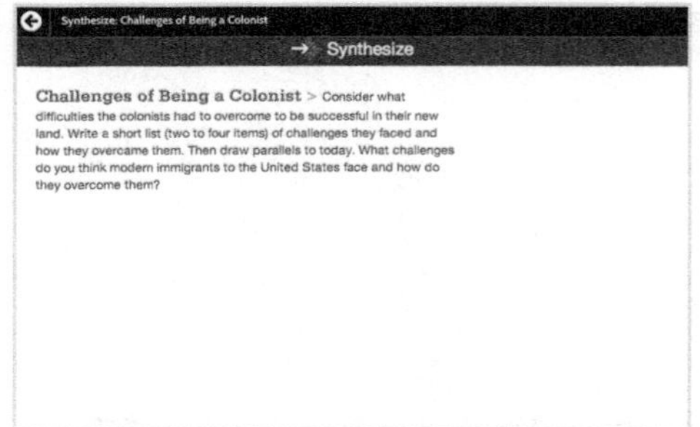

Have students complete the Challenges of Being a Colonist activity. Ask students to share their lists with a partner, and then work together to brainstorm parallels between the colonial period and today. Discuss reasons for immigration and the religious, economic, political, and social differences one might encounter in a new land.

Discuss Have students think about the following question. How did physical characteristics of the environment influence where people settled in the New England Colonies and what their lives were like? Discuss students' answers with the class.

DEMONSTRATE

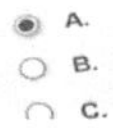

DIGITAL QUIZ

Lesson Quiz and Class Discussion Board

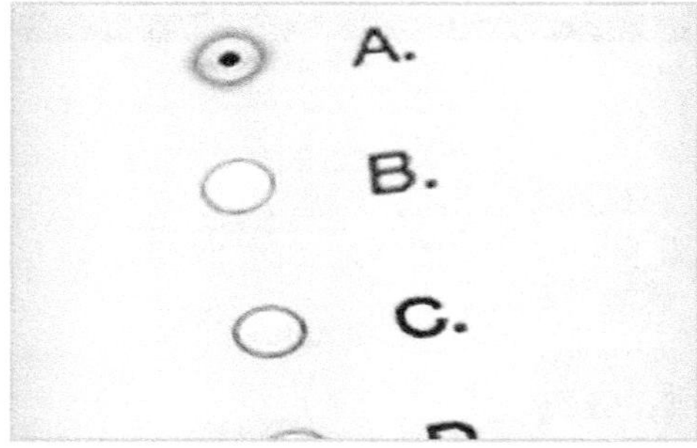

Assign the online Lesson Quiz for this lesson if you haven't already done so. Students will be offered automatic remediation or enrichment based on their score.

Pose these questions to the class on the Discussion Board:

In *The New England Colonies*, you read about the economy, politics, and society of the New England Colonies. Many colonists came to New England seeking religious freedom as well as economic gain. The colonies they established contributed to the rise of representative government and religious freedom in the United States.

Identify Central Issues What new institutions developed in the colonies during this period, and why? *(Representative governments such as the Fundamental Orders of Connecticut and the General Court developed to give colonists a greater say in governance. New religious communities also spread in Massachusetts, Connecticut, and Rhode Island to account for different and dissenting beliefs.)*

Support Ideas with Examples Name three significant individuals who shaped the New England Colonies and explain their impact. *(William Bradford: led Plymouth for 36 years; Squanto: helped the Pilgrims learn to farm and fish; John Winthrop: led Massachusetts Bay Colony; Thomas Hooker: founded Connecticut and the Fundamental Orders of Connecticut; Roger Williams: founded Rhode Island and spread religious tolerance; Anne Hutchinson: became a symbol for religious freedom)*

Topic Inquiry

Have students continue their investigations for the Topic Inquiry.

The Middle Colonies

Supporting English Language Learners

Use with Digital Text 2, **New Jersey Forms Out of New York.**

Learning

Have students read the text. Point out the use of the related words *proprietary* and *proprietors* in the section titled *A Proprietary Colony and Free Enterprise*. Prompt students to internalize new basic language in speaking activities that build concept and language attainment.

Beginning Display this sentence and have students read it after you: The owner of the land was wealthy. Ask students which word is a synonym of *proprietor*. Have students reread the sentence with *proprietor* in place of *owner*. Then have students write a sentence of their own using the word *proprietor*.

Intermediate Discuss the use of *proprietors* in the section. Ask students to use the word (singular or plural form) aloud in an original written sentence about the colonial era. In pairs or in small groups, invite students to use the word *proprietor* in a spoken sentence.

Advanced Have students discuss what makes a colony proprietary. Ask: What other things can be proprietary? Encourage students to use the word *proprietary* in written responses, then have them discuss their responses in pairs or small groups, again using the word *proprietary*.

Advanced High Point out the noun *proprietors* and the adjective *proprietary* in the text. Discuss the words' similarities and differences. Have students use both words to write a paragraph about the colonial era. Then, in pairs or in small groups, have students use the words *proprietors* and *proprietary* to discuss colonial America and the United States today.

Use with Digital Text 3, **Pennsylvania Becomes a Colony.**

Speaking

Have students read the text up to the section titled *Pennsylvania Expands*. Point out the image of William Penn's landing and read the caption. Encourage students to include specificity and detail in their descriptions of the image.

Beginning In pairs or in small groups, have students describe the image in their own words.

Intermediate In pairs or in small groups, ask students to say two sentences describing what they see in the image. The first sentence can be general, but the second should focus on details.

Advanced Ask pairs of students to describe specific parts of the image.

Advanced High In pairs or in small groups, ask students to describe the image in full detail, including all significant parts of the image.

D Differentiate Instruction

Use the Differentiated Instruction notes throughout the lesson plan to support the varied skill sets, levels of readiness, and interests in the mixed-ability classroom.

Challenge These notes include suggestions for expanding the activity for advanced students.

On-Level These notes include suggestions for modifying the activity to address different interests or learning styles.

Extra Support These notes include ideas for providing more scaffolding or reading spuport.

Special Needs These notes provide ideas for adapting instruction to support the needs of various special needs students.

NOTES

The Middle Colonies

Objectives

Objective 1: Explain the reasons for the establishment of the colonies of New York and New Jersey.

Objective 2: Explain the reasons for the establishment of the colonies of Pennsylvania and Delaware.

Objective 3: Describe the economy of the Middle Colonies, including the relationship between the economy and the physical environment.

LESSON 4 ORGANIZER — **PACING: APPROX. 1 PERIOD, .5 BLOCKS**

	OBJECTIVES	PACING	RESOURCES: Online	RESOURCES: Print
Connect				
DIGITAL START UP ACTIVITY **Your City**		5 min.	●	
Investigate				
DIGITAL TEXT 1 **A Dutch Colony Becomes English**	Objective 1	10 min.	●	●
DIGITAL TEXT 2 **New Jersey Forms Out of New York**	Objective 1	10 min.	●	●
DIGITAL TEXT 3 **Pennsylvania Becomes a Colony**	Objective 2	10 min.	●	●
INTERACTIVE GALLERY **The Middle Colonies**	Objective 2	10 min.	●	
DIGITAL TEXT 4 **Daily Life in the Middle Colonies**	Objective 3	10 min.	●	●
INTERACTIVE GALLERY **The Economy of the Middle Colonies**	Objective 3	10 min.	●	
Synthesize				
DIGITAL ACTIVITY **Why Do People Move?**		5 min.	●	
Demonstrate				
DIGITAL QUIZ **Lesson Quiz and Class Discussion Board**		10 min.	●	

PEARSON realize™
www.PearsonRealize.com

Go online to access additional resources including:
Primary Sources • Biographies • Supreme Court cases • 21st Century Skill Tutorials • Maps • Graphic Organizers.

CONNECT

DIGITAL START UP ACTIVITY

Your City

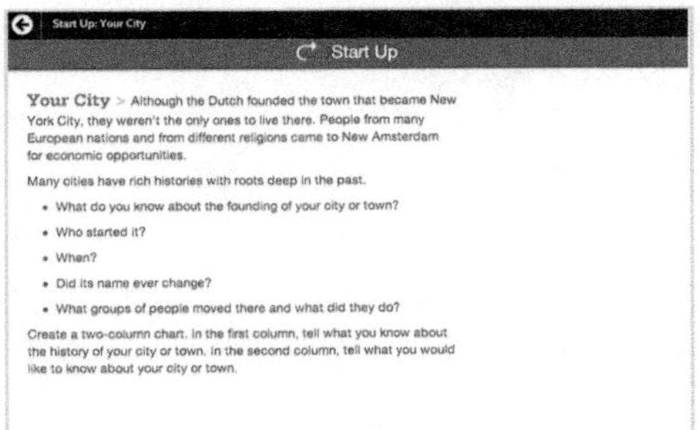

Project the Start Up Activity Ask students to fill in their chart as they enter and get settled. Have students share what they know about the history of their city or town's human and physical characteristics, either in class or through a chat or blog space.

Discuss What do you know about the founding of your city or town? Who started it? When? Did its name ever change? What groups of people moved there and what did they do? *(Answers should address what students know about the history of their city or town, including its physical and human characteristics.)*

Aa Vocabulary Development: Use the Interactive Reading Notepad to preview the Key Terms and Academic Vocabulary in the lesson with students.

FLIP IT!

Assign the Flipped Video for this lesson.

STUDENT EDITION PRINT PAGES: 83–91

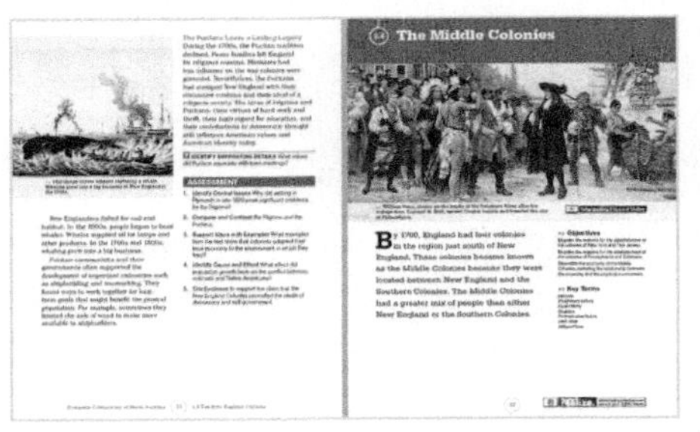

INVESTIGATE

DIGITAL TEXT 1

A Dutch Colony Becomes English

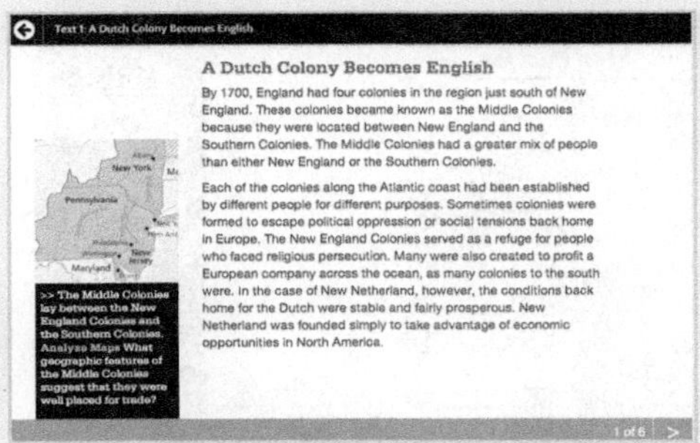

DIGITAL TEXT 2

New Jersey Forms Out of New York

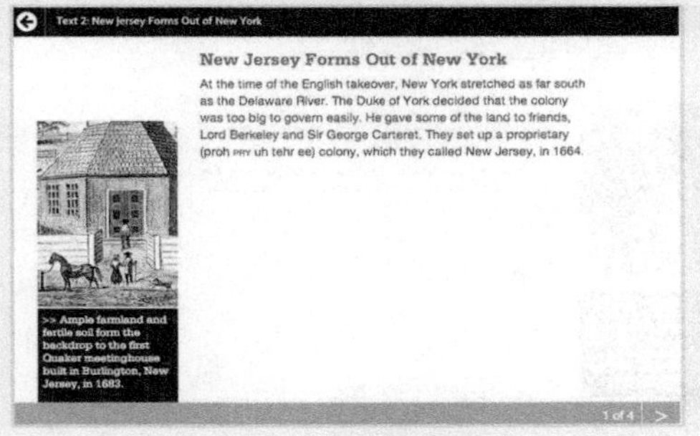

Objective 1: Explain the reasons for the establishment of the colonies of New York and New Jersey.

Quick Instruction

Project the map of the Middle Colonies on the whiteboard. Dutch Protestants founded New Amsterdam to make money from the fur trade. England then took over the colony and renamed it New York. New York industry and New Jersey farmland attracted immigrants in search of peace, prosperity, and religious freedom.

Identify Central Issues What were the political and economic reasons the Dutch and English colonized North America? *(The Dutch and English colonized North America to expand their empires and to make money, especially from trade.)*

Summarize What were the characteristics and benefits of the free-enterprise systemin New Jersey during the 18th century? *(Under the free enterprise system, New Jersey colonists could take advantage of available resources and build businesses with minimal government interference.)*

ELL Use the ELL activity described in the ELL chart.

Further Instruction

Go through the Interactive Reading Notepad questions for *A Dutch Colony Becomes English* and *New Jersey Forms Out of New York* and discuss the answers with the class. Discuss the political, economic, religious, and social reasons for the establishment of New York and New Jersey.

Summarize What ethnic and religious groups settled in New York? Why did many religious groups choose to settle in New York during the 17th century? *(In New Amsterdam and then New York, there were Dutch Protestants, Roman Catholics, French Protestants, Jews, and others. Generally speaking, people enjoyed freedom of worship.)*

Distinguish For what economic reasons was the colony of New Jersey established? *(New Jersey was founded as a proprietary colony, in which economic control was in the hands of a few private individuals who preferred the economy to run with little interference from local government.)*

The Middle Colonies

DIGITAL TEXT 3

Pennsylvania Becomes a Colony

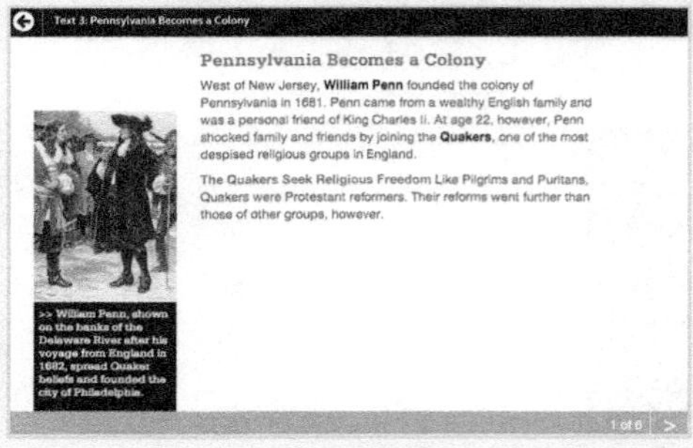

INTERACTIVE GALLERY

The Middle Colonies

Objective 2: Explain the reasons for the establishment of the colonies of Pennsylvania and Delaware.

Quick Instruction

A Quaker named William Penn founded Pennsylvania as a haven for people of different religions. Protestants, Catholics, and Jews settled in the colony. Later, immigrants from England, Scotland, the Netherlands, France, and Germany arrived along with persecuted religious groups such as the Amish and Mennonites. Enslaved Africans were also brought to work as laborers.

Interactive Gallery: The Middle Colonies Project the Interactive Gallery and click through the images. Discuss the contributions of different ethnic groups that immigrated to Pennsylvania, including the English, Scotch-Irish, German, and Dutch. Ask how the arrival of these groups have contributed to America's identity.

Compare What ethnic groups settled Pennsylvania in the 17th and 18th centuries, and what were their reasons for immigration? How did these ethnic groups contribute to the development of our national identity? *(English, Scotch-Irish, German, and Dutch immigrants came to escape persecution as well as for economic gain. The ethnically diverse population of Pennsylvania contributed to the development of a national identity based on ethnic diversity.)*

ACTIVE CLASSROOM

Have students use the Conversation strategy and imagine they are having a conversation with William Penn. Have students write down a question they would ask William Penn, what Penn would say to them, and what they would say in response.

D Differentiate: Extra Support Remind students that persecuted means punished for one's beliefs. Have students explain why persecuted religious groups like the Quakers moved to Pennsylvania.

ELL Use the ELL activity described in the ELL chart.

Further Instruction

Go through the Interactive Reading Notepad questions with the class. Be sure students understand how Pennsylvania developed self-government and religious freedom.

Generate Explanations Explain the role of William Penn in the development of self-government in colonial America. *(He proposed a constitution for Pennsylvania and a General Assembly with increased powers.)*

Compare the political, economic, social, and religious reasons for the establishment of Pennsylvania as a colony with the political, economic, and religious reasons for the establishment of other English colonies? *(Like Roger Williams in Rhode Island, William Penn wanted to establish a colony in which religious freedom was encouraged. As in Rhode Island, Penn had a social goal of harmony among people of different faiths. As in New York and New Jersey, Pennsylvania's political roots were as a proprietary, but as in New England and Virginia, Penn established self-government in Pennsylvania. Like other colonies, Pennsylvania's economic reasons for establishment were to generate a profit for its private funders.)*

www.PearsonRealize.com
Access your Digital Lesson

DIGITAL TEXT 4

Daily Life in the Middle Colonies

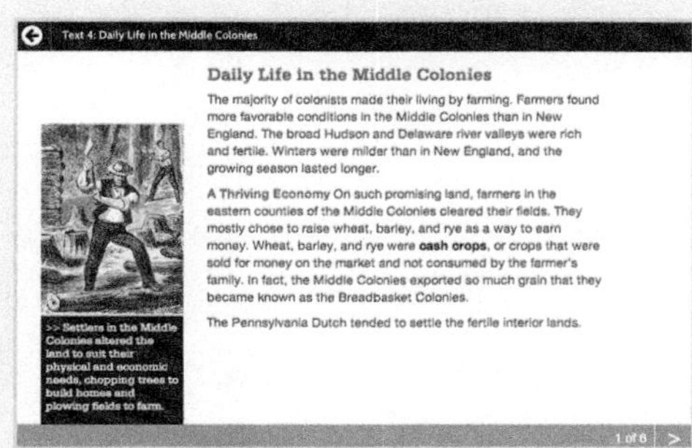

Text 4: Daily Life in the Middle Colonies
Daily Life in the Middle Colonies
The majority of colonists made their living by farming. Farmers found more favorable conditions in the Middle Colonies than in New England. The broad Hudson and Delaware river valleys were rich and fertile. Winters were milder than in New England, and the growing season lasted longer.
A Thriving Economy On such promising land, farmers in the eastern counties of the Middle Colonies cleared their fields. They mostly chose to raise wheat, barley, and rye as a way to earn money. Wheat, barley, and rye were cash crops, or crops that were sold for money on the market and not consumed by the farmer's family. In fact, the Middle Colonies exported so much grain that they became known as the Breadbasket Colonies.
The Pennsylvania Dutch tended to settle the fertile interior lands.
>> Settlers in the Middle Colonies altered the land to suit their physical and economic needs, chopping trees to build homes and plowing fields to farm.
1 of 6

INTERACTIVE GALLERY

The Economy of the Middle Colonies

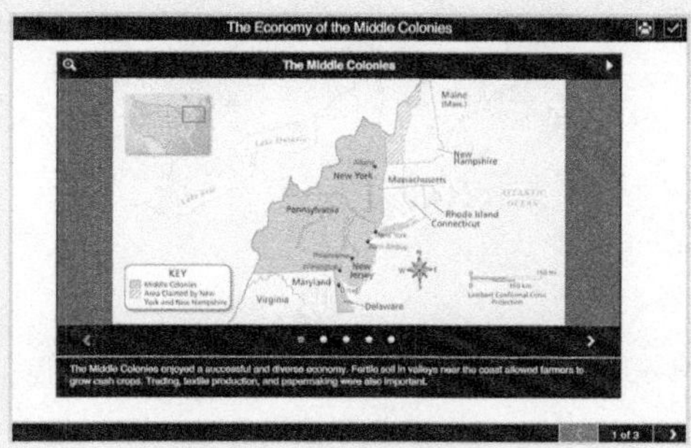

Objective 3: **Describe the economy of the Middle Colonies, including the relationship between the economy and the physical environment.**

Quick Instruction

Interactive Gallery: The Economy of the Middle Colonies Project the Interactive Map. Explicitly point out the economic reasons for the establishment of the Middle Colonies. Have students identify the major economic activities of the region: farming, trade, textile production, and paper-making. Discuss the aspects of the physical environment that made agriculture and trade central to the economy, emphasizing fertile land for livestock and crops.

ACTIVE CLASSROOM

Have students use the A Closer Look strategy to examine the Interactive Map. Project the map and assign New York, New Jersey, Pennsylvania, and Delaware the numbers 1 through 4. Have students count off one through four and then look closely at the corresponding colony. Have them explain what they see and what they learned as a result from their focus on this part of the map. Collect insights for each colony.

Make Predictions Have students make a prediction about how fertile farmland will impact the Middle Colonies. *(The colonies will do well economically; more immigrants will settle there; the colonies will expand; there may be conflict as settlers encroach on Native American lands.)*

Further Instruction

Go through the Interactive Reading Notepad questions with the class.

Compare and Contrast the physical characteristics of the Middle Colonies and New England. How did differences in the physical environment contribute to economic differences between the two regions? *(Land along the Hudson and Delaware Rivers was fertile. Winters were milder and the growing season longer than in New England. These characteristics made farmland better in the Middle Colonies. Farms were big enough to let colonists develop an economy based on cash crops. They also raised livestock to sell.)*

Identify Patterns How did the physical environment influence population distribution and settlement patterns in the Middle Colonies? *(People settled on fertile land for farming. They also lived in areas along the Delaware River with iron deposits. Many people settled in cities and towns close to harbors and waterways for transportation. Others moved inland to clear forests and settle the backcountry.)*

Cite Evidence How did immigrants interact with the environment when they settled the backcountry in the 18th century? *(They cleared forests and relied on natural resources to survive. They used knots from pine trees as candles, made wooden dishes from logs, gathered honey, and hunted animals for food.)*

The Middle Colonies

SYNTHESIZE

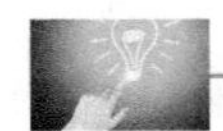

DIGITAL ACTIVITY

Why Do People Move?

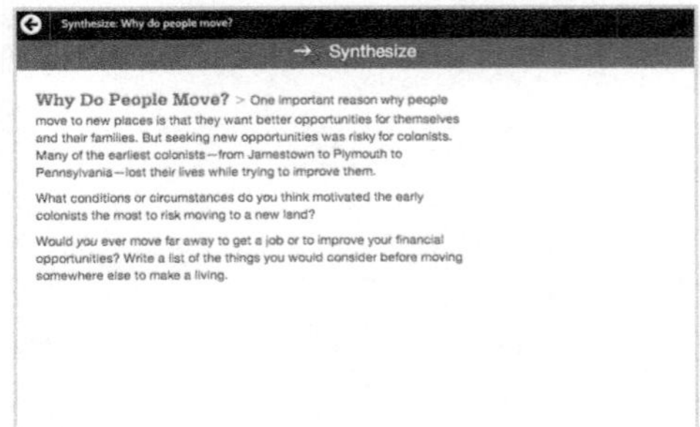

Have students complete the Why Do People Move activity. Ask students to answer the questions and then share their lists with a partner. Discuss the religious, social, economic, and political motivations that prompted immigrants to move to the colonies. Ask students which of those motivations apply to immigrants today.

Discuss Have students think about the following question. How did the physical characteristics of the environment influence economic activities in the Middle Colonies? Discuss students' answers with the class.

DEMONSTRATE

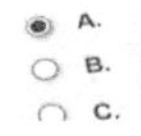

DIGITAL QUIZ

Lesson Quiz and Class Discussion Board

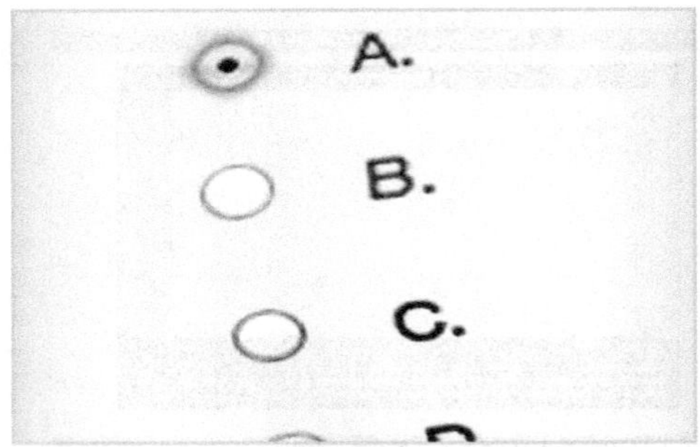

Assign the online Lesson Quiz for this lesson if you haven't already done so. Students will be offered automatic remediation or enrichment based on their score.

Pose these questions to the class on the Discussion Board:

In *The Middle Colonies*, you read about the economy, politics, and society of the Middle Colonies. New York, New Jersey, Pennsylvania, and Delaware were founded by people of different religions and ethnicities seeking economic opportunities and religious freedom. They contributed to the growth of self-government and religious freedom, and to the development of our national identity.

Draw Conclusions What reasons led to the establishment of the Middle Colonies? *New York was founded by the Dutch as New Netherland, mainly to pursue trade. New Jersey was founded by private proprietors to make a profit from its fertile land. Pennsylvania was founded for religious freedom and its fertile land, forests, and minerals. Delaware was founded because its settlers want to be free of the control of Pennsylvania.)*

Identify Cause and Effect How did the desire for religious freedom affect the development of the Middle Colonies? *(Different religious groups settled in the region. Persecuted groups were attracted to Pennsylvania because of its religious freedom, and they contributed to the colony's growth. Later, the English made Pennsylvania turn away Catholics and Jews. New Netherland had freedom of religion as well, before it became New York.)*

Topic Inquiry

Have students continue their investigations for the Topic Inquiry.

PEARSON realize™ www.PearsonRealize.com Access your Digital Lesson

The Southern Colonies

Supporting English Language Learners

Use with Digital Text 1, **Lord Baltimore's Colony.**

Learning

Have students read the text. Then point out the term *Act of Toleration* and discuss its meaning. Prompt students to internalize new basic language in writing activities that build concept and language attainment.

Beginning Have students write a sentence using the word *toleration*. Invite them to ask for help if they are having difficulty. After they have written one sentence, ask them to write a second sentence that uses the word.

Intermediate Ask students to write a brief paragraph using the word *toleration* correctly at least twice.

Advanced Display the words *toleration, tolerance,* and *tolerate*, and discuss their meanings. Ask students to use each of the words at least twice to write original paragraphs about religious freedom.

Advanced High Display the words *toleration, tolerance, tolerant,* and *tolerate*, and discuss their meanings. Have students write a brief essay using each of the words at least twice to compare and contrast colonists' tolerance toward people with different religions and their attitudes toward Native Americans.

Use with Digital Text 3, **Two Regions Develop Differently.**

Speaking

Have students read the section titled *Tidewater Plantations on the Coast*. In pairs, ask students to explain how Tidewater plantations operated. Encourage students to use as much specificity and detail and detail as possible.

Beginning Have students explain verbally, in their own words, why plantations tended to develop along the coast.

Intermediate Ask students to use details from the text to explain verbally how Tidewater plantations operated.

Advanced Ask students to provide facts from the text to explain the economy of tidewater plantations in detail and with specificity.

Advanced High Ask students to provide facts from the text to explain the economy of tidewater plantations in detail and with specificity and to provide details of how the economy of these plantations differed from farming in other parts of the colonies.

D Differentiate Instruction

Use the Differentiated Instruction notes throughout the lesson plan to support the varied skill sets, levels of readiness, and interests in the mixed-ability classroom.

Challenge These notes include suggestions for expanding the activity for advanced students.

On-Level These notes include suggestions for modifying the activity to address different interests or learning styles.

Extra Support These notes include ideas for providing more scaffolding or reading spupport.

Special Needs These notes provide ideas for adapting instruction to support the needs of various special needs students.

NOTES

Topic 2 Lesson 5

The Southern Colonies

Objectives

Objective 1: Explain the reasons for the establishment of Maryland.

Objective 2: Explain the reasons for the establishment of the Carolinas and Georgia.

Objective 3: Describe the relationship between different environments, different settlement patterns, and different economic systems in the Southern Colonies.

Objective 4: Explain the development of the slave trade and the spread of slavery in the Southern Colonies.

LESSON 5 ORGANIZER — **PACING: APPROX. 1 PERIOD, .5 BLOCKS**

	OBJECTIVES	PACING	RESOURCES Online	RESOURCES Print
Connect				
DIGITAL START UP ACTIVITY **Challenges for Settlers**		5 min.	●	
Investigate				
DIGITAL TEXT 1 **Lord Baltimore's Colony**	Objective 1	10 min.	●	●
DIGITAL TEXT 2 **Settlement in the Carolinas and Georgia**	Objective 2	10 min.	●	●
INTERACTIVE MAP **Comparing the Thirteen Colonies**		10 min.	●	
DIGITAL TEXT 3 **Two Regions Develop Differently**	Objective 3	10 min.	●	●
INTERACTIVE ILLUSTRATION **A Southern Colonial Plantation**		10 min.	●	
DIGITAL TEXT 4 **The Slave Trade Expands**	Objective 4	10 min.	●	●
Synthesize				
DIGITAL ACTIVITY **The Tidewater and the Backcountry**		5 min.	●	
Demonstrate				
DIGITAL QUIZ **Lesson Quiz and Class Discussion Board**		10 min.	●	

CONNECT

DIGITAL START UP ACTIVITY

Challenges for Settlers

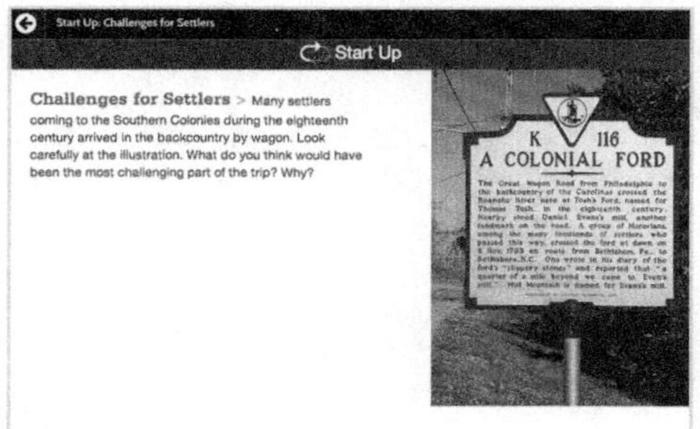

Project the Start Up Activity Ask students to answer the questions as they enter and get settled. Then have them share their ideas with another student, either in class or through a chat or blog space.

Discuss Prompt students to think of some challenges associated with moving over a great distance in the eighteenth century. Encourage them to compare the challenges settlers faced with moving to a new home in a different state today.

Tell students that in this lesson they will be learning about the history of the Southern Colonies.

Aa Vocabulary Development: Use the Interactive Reading Notepad to preview the Key Terms and Academic Vocabulary in this lesson with students.

FLIP IT!

Assign the Flipped Video for this lesson.

STUDENT EDITION PRINT PAGES: 92–100

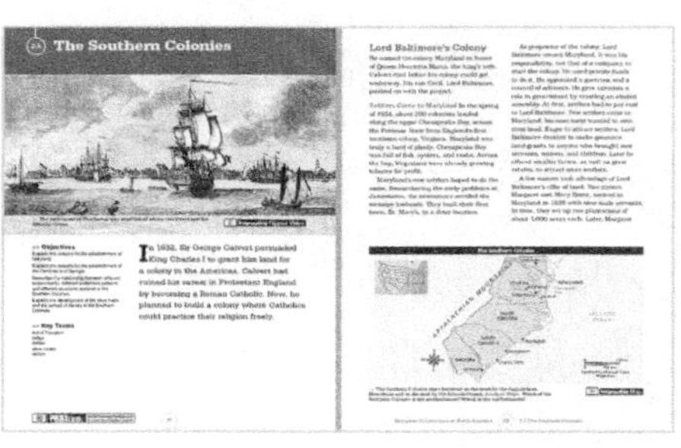

INVESTIGATE

DIGITAL TEXT 1

Lord Baltimore's Colony

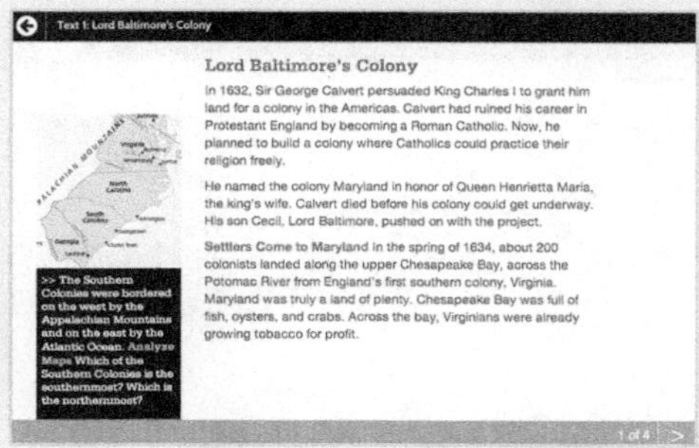
Text 1: Lord Baltimore's Colony

Lord Baltimore's Colony

In 1632, Sir George Calvert persuaded King Charles I to grant him land for a colony in the Americas. Calvert had ruined his career in Protestant England by becoming a Roman Catholic. Now, he planned to build a colony where Catholics could practice their religion freely.

He named the colony Maryland in honor of Queen Henrietta Maria, the king's wife. Calvert died before his colony could get underway. His son Cecil, Lord Baltimore, pushed on with the project.

Settlers Come to Maryland In the spring of 1634, about 200 colonists landed along the upper Chesapeake Bay, across the Potomac River from England's first southern colony, Virginia. Maryland was truly a land of plenty. Chesapeake Bay was full of fish, oysters, and crabs. Across the bay, Virginians were already growing tobacco for profit.

>> The Southern Colonies were bordered on the west by the Appalachian Mountains and on the east by the Atlantic Ocean. **Analyze Maps** Which of the Southern Colonies is the southernmost? Which is the northernmost?

1 of 4

Objective 1: Explain the reasons for the establishment of Maryland.

Quick Instruction

Project the map of the Southern Colonies on the whiteboard. Explain that Maryland was founded by Catholics who wanted to worship freely and hoped to benefit from the fertile land available in the South.

Draw Conclusions Sir George Calvert was a Roman Catholic in Protestant England. Why do you think he requested a land grant to build the colony of Maryland? *(To establish a place where Catholics could worship freely)*

Generate Explanations What were the religious and political reasons for the establishment of Maryland? *(Religious freedom; economic gain from tobacco and natural resources)*

Infer How did Lord Baltimore, proprietor of Maryland, encourage immigrants to settle in the colony? Why do you think he promoted these policies? *(By offering generous land grants and welcoming both Protestants and Catholics; he probably hoped the colony would grow in order to generate wealth)*

ELL Use the ELL activity described in the ELL chart.

Further Instruction

Go through the Interactive Reading Notepad questions and discuss the answers with the class. Be sure students understand the political, social, economic, and religious reasons Maryland was colonized.

Identify Patterns How did the Act of Toleration contribute to the development of religious freedom in the United States? What were the limitations of the act? *(It ensured religious freedom for all Christians, whether Protestant or Catholic; it was limited to Christians and did not grant religious freedom to Jews.)*

Identify Central Issues How did immigrants interact with the environment in Maryland? How did the physical characteristics of the environment influence their settlement patterns and economic activities? *(Immigrants took advantage of the fertile land to build farms and plantations, where they made money from tobacco. They used the Chesapeake Bay for fish, oysters, and crabs, but they avoided building towns in swampy lowlands.)*

Support Ideas with Evidence What evidence suggests that Lord Baltimore contributed to the growth of representative government during the colonial period? *(Although he appointed a governor and a council, he also created an elected assembly. This gave colonists representation in government and a greater say in the colony's affairs.)*

The Southern Colonies

DIGITAL TEXT 2

Settlement in the Carolinas and Georgia

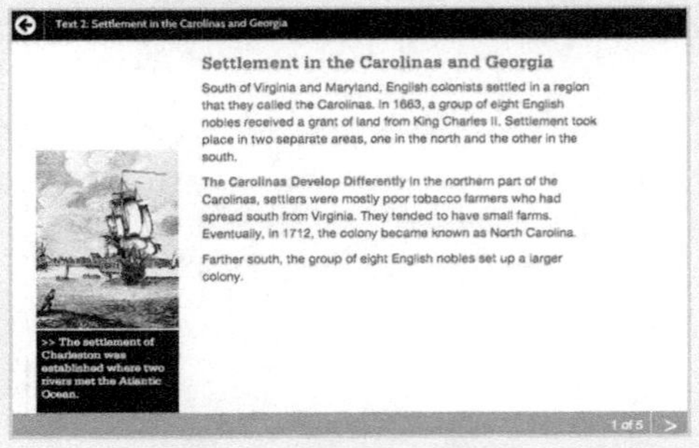

INTERACTIVE MAP

Comparing the Thirteen Colonies

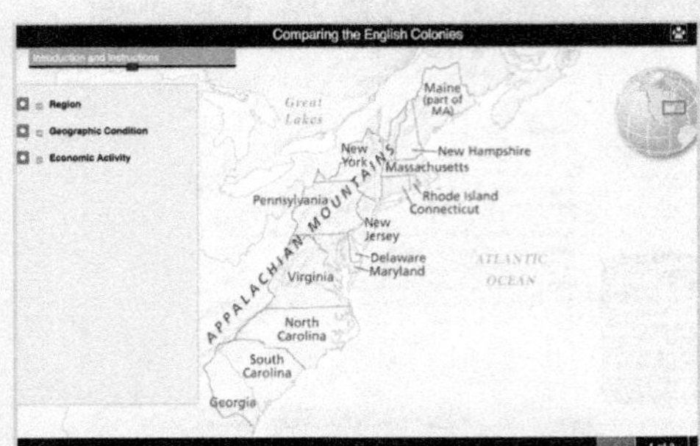

Objective 2: Explain the reasons for the establishment of the Carolinas and Georgia.

Quick Instruction

English settlers from the Caribbean and others immigrants from Europe came to in the Carolinas to grow tobacco, rice, and indigo. Further south, Georgia was founded as a colony where debtors who owed money could restart their lives.

Interactive Map: Comparing the Thirteen Colonies Project the interactive map and click through the layers. Have students locate the three important regions: New England, the Middle Colonies, and the Southern Colonies. Prompt students to consider how the physical characteristics of each region influenced economic activity.

Identify Central Issues How did different immigrant groups interact with the environment in the Carolinas? *(Immigrants came to the Carolinas to farm. They built settlements near rivers and used swampy coastal areas to grow rice.)*

D Differentiate: Extra Support Remind students of the characteristics that define the U.S. free-enterprise system, such as limited government interference with business. Have students reread the last paragraph in the section on Georgia and explain what government decision enabled the colony to grow.

ACTIVE CLASSROOM

Have students use the Quick Write strategy and take 30 seconds to write what they know about Georgia and the Carolinas. Have students share their conclusions with partners or with the class.

Further Instruction

Go through the Interactive Reading Notepad questions with the class.

Compare the human characteristics of Georgia and the Carolinas. Ask students who populated these regions and how they used the land. *(Georgia was founded by a social reformer and populated by debtors. Initially, farms were small and slavery was prohibited. The Carolinas were populated by poor tobacco farmers and European immigrants. They had small farms as well as larger rice and indigo plantations.)*

Compare the economic, political, and social reasons for the establishment of the Carolinas and Georgia with the economic, political, and social reasons for the establishment of other English colonies. *(The Carolinas, like other proprietary colonies, were established to make money for their proprietors. Georgia was established as a haven for debtors, while Pennsylvania and the New England colonies were founded as havens for people facing religious persecution. While New York was established to secure English control over a former Dutch colony, Georgia was established to protect other English colonies from Spanish Florida.)*

Identify Cause and Effect Ask students to give an example of how a free-enterprise system caused the colony of Georgia to grow. *(The government's decision not to limit farm size or slavery brought more people to the region.)*

DIGITAL TEXT 3

Two Regions Develop Differently

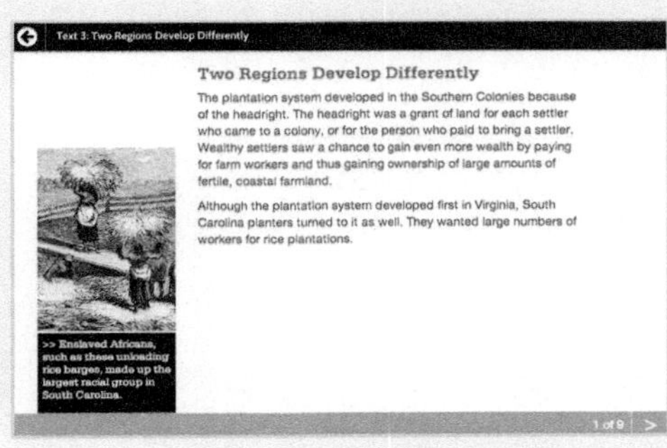

INTERACTIVE ILLUSTRATION

A Southern Colonial Plantation

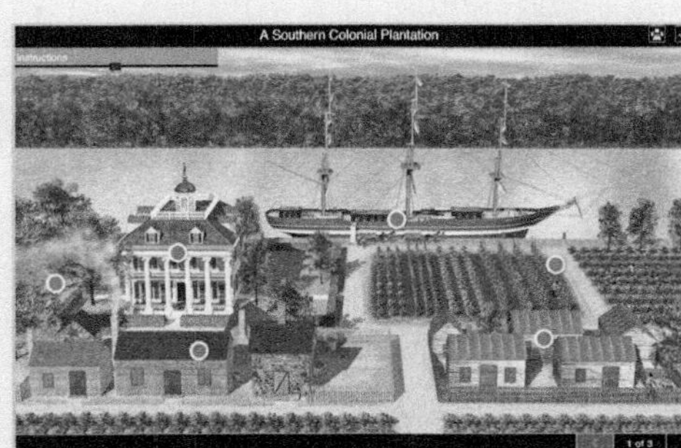

Objective 3: Describe the relationship between different environments, different settlement patterns, and different economic systems in the Southern Colonies.

Quick Instruction

Two regions of the Southern colonies developed different farming systems during the 17th century, or 1600s, and the 18th century, or 1700s. Prompt students to note the relationship between the physical characteristics of the environment of each region and the differences in settlement patterns and population distribution between the two regions. Enslaved Africans labored on plantations in the Tidewater region, clustered near the ocean and rivers. Farther inland, immigrants tended smaller, self-sufficient farms scattered across the backcountry, mainly in valleys.

Interactive Illustration: Plantations of the Southern Colonies Project the interactive illustration and click through the hotspots. Review the reasons for the development of the plantation system and the ways this contributed to the spread of slavery.

Analyze Images What does the image of the Great House suggest about life in some parts of the colonial South? *(Plantation owners were often wealthy and lived in luxurious homes overlooking their property. They were served by enslaved Africans.)*

Generate Explanations Explain why the plantation system and slave labor spread across the Southern Colonies. *(The plantation system and slave labor spread because of the headright, or a grant of land for each settler. Wealthy white settlers could gain wealth by purchasing enslaved Africans and thereby gaining more land. They relied on slave labor from Africa because few white settlers were willing to do the heavy work. Colonists found that the most profitable way to raise crops such as tobacco or rice was on large plantations.)*

ACTIVE CLASSROOM

Have students use the See-Wonder-Think strategy with the images in the interactive gallery. Pair students and have them select an image in the gallery. Ask: What do you see? What does that make you think? What are you wondering about now that you've seen this? Share insights with the class.

ELL Use the ELL activity described in the ELL chart.

Further Instruction

Go through the Interactive Reading Notepad questions with the class and complete the graphic organizer comparing and contrasting the Tidewater and backcountry areas of the Southern Colonies.

Identify Cause and Effect Identify the causes and effects of economic differences between the Tidewater and the backcountry. *(The causes of the differences were that the Tidewater had fertile land and good water transportation access that favored the development of plantation agriculture, while the more remote backcountry was better suited to small farmers raising crops and animals for their own needs. The effects of the differences included the spread of slavery and a rich planter class in the Tidewater and greater equality and democracy in the backcountry.)*

Draw Conclusions How did different immigrant groups interact with the environment in the colonies during the 18th century, or 1700s? *(Enslaved Africans used farming skills they had brought from Africa to grow rice on Tidewater plantations. Scotch-Irish immigrants to the backcountry cleared forests and grew crops such as wheat or raised cattle or pigs on the cleared land.)*

The Southern Colonies

DIGITAL TEXT 4

The Slave Trade Expands

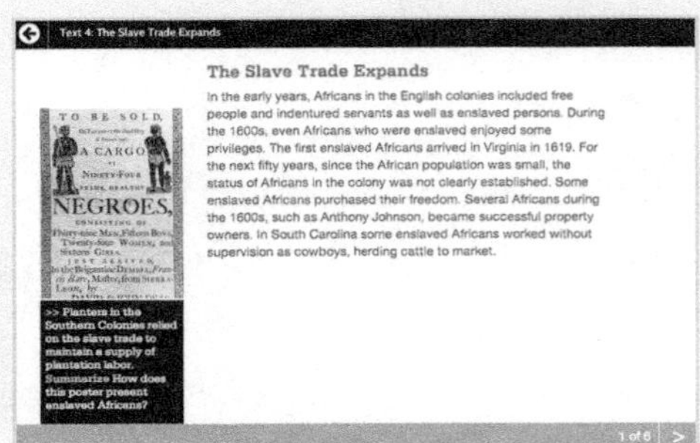

Objective 4: Explain the development of the slave trade and the spread of slavery in the Southern Colonies.

Quick Instruction

Project the image of the slave ship. Have students discuss their reactions. Explain that the Middle Passage referred to the journey that slave-trading ships made from Africa to the colonies and identify selected racial groups that subsequently settled in the United States.

Identify Central Issues How did the plantation system relate to the spread of slavery? *(Planters wanted enslaved Africans to work on their plantations, which created demand for the transatlantic slave trade.)*

Further Instruction

Go through the Interactive Reading Notepad questions with the class. Be sure students understand how the development of the plantation system connected to the transatlantic slave trade and the spread of slavery. Explain that Africans were identified by white colonists as a racial group, and that Africans were settled in the English colonies against their will. That is, the reason why Africans immigrated is that they were forced into slavery and brought to the colonies in chains to work on plantations. Assign the primary source *The Interesting Narrative of the Life of Olaudah Equiano*, by Olaudah Equiano.

Generate Explanations Explain the reasons for the spread of slavery. *(As plantations grew, plantation owners brought more enslaved Africans to work their fields. Racism and the demand for free labor enabled this practice to spread.)*

Infer In the early 1600s, some Africans were servants rather than slaves. Others were able to purchase their freedom. Why do you think these policies changed? *(Enslaved Africans became increasingly necessary to the economy. The spread of slavery meant owners did not want Africans to become free.)*

PEARSON realize™ www.PearsonRealize.com Access your Digital Lesson

SYNTHESIZE

DIGITAL ACTIVITY

The Tidewater and the Backcountry

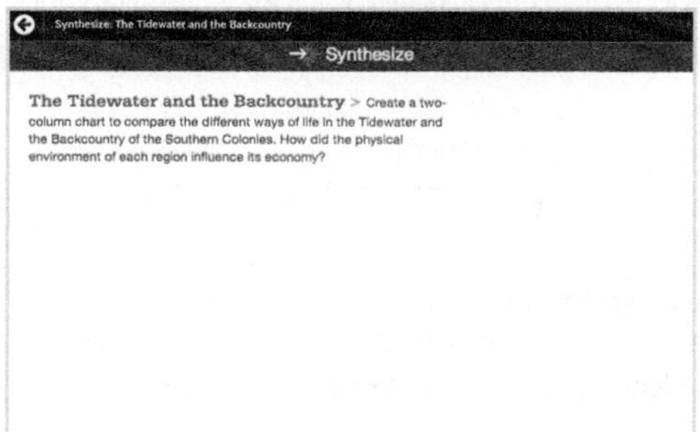

Have students complete *The Tidewater and the Backcountry* activity. Ask students to create a chart and then work with a partner to answer the question. Discuss the physical characteristics of both environments, as well as their economies.

Have students think about the following question. How did the physical characteristics of the environment influence economic activities in the Southern Colonies? Discuss students' answers with the class.

DEMONSTRATE

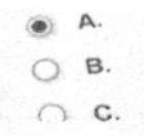

DIGITAL QUIZ

Lesson Quiz and Class Discussion Board

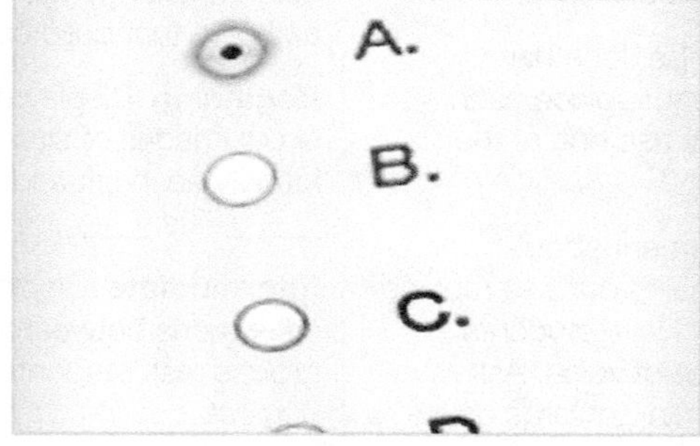

Assign the online Lesson Quiz for this lesson if you haven't already done so. Students will be offered automatic remediation or enrichment based on their score.

Pose these questions to the class on the Discussion Board:

In *The Southern Colonies*, you read about the economy, politics, and society of the Southern Colonies. The growth of the plantation system led to the development of the transatlantic slave trade and the spread of slavery across the South.

Draw Conclusions Why were the Southern Colonies founded? *(Virginia: for gold and trade routes but was later settled mainly to grow tobacco and other crops. Maryland: to promote religious freedom for Catholics and for tobacco cultivation. North Carolina: for profit as a proprietary colony for tobacco farmers spreading south from Virginia. South Carolina: as a proprietary colony for plantation agriculture. Georgia: as a refuge for debtors and to defend the English colonies from Spanish Florida.)*

Compare and Contrast Why did the plantation system develop in the South rather than in the other English colonies? *(The physical environment of the South lent itself to large plantations. Rich soil in low-lying areas was especially ideal for growing rice, which could not grow in the climate or soil further north.)*

Topic Inquiry

Have students continue their investigations for the Topic Inquiry.

Colonial Society

Supporting English Language Learners

Use with Digital Text 3, **A New Religious Movement.**

Speaking

Have students read the section titled, *Enthusiastic Preachers*. Discuss whether Jonathan Edwards likely used informal (casual, conversational) language or formal (elaborate, complex) language in his sermons.

Beginning Display a list of informal words that describe Jonathan Edwards. Work with students in pairs or small groups to replace each word with a more formal synonym. Have each student use one of the formal words in a spoken sentence.

Intermediate Express a one-sentence informal statement about Jonathan Edwards. Work with students in pairs or small groups to replace each part of the sentence with more formal language. Have students practice saying the formal statement using proper tone of voice. Ask students to add a sentence of their own about Jonathan Edwards using formal language.

Advanced In pairs or in small groups, ask students to make a brief statement, including a few sentences in formal language, about Jonathan Edwards. Remind them to speak as if they were addressing a principal or the president, not a friend, and to use a more formal posture and tone of voice as well.

Advanced High In pairs or in small groups, ask students to give a brief speech, using formal language, about Jonathan Edwards and his influence on colonial society. Review the posture, gestures, and tone of voice appropriate to a speech.

Use with Digital Text 5, **A New World of Ideas.**

Learning

Read aloud the introduction to the text. Point out the word *logic* and define it. Discuss why it is important. Prompt students to internalize new academic language by using and reusing it in meaningful ways in speaking activities that build concept and language attainment.

Beginning Display the following: logical ≠ illogical. Explain, act out, or show images of situations that are either logical or illogical. Have students identify each situation by completing this sentence aloud: That is not _____; it is _____.

Intermediate Display the following: logical ≠ illogical. Discuss the differences between the words' meanings and spellings. In pairs or in small groups, ask students to make statements using the terms *logical* and *illogical*.

Advanced Place students in pairs. Ask each student to make at least two statements contrasting the terms *logic* and *superstition* from the text.

Advanced High In pairs or in small groups, ask students to use academic language to discuss the differences between logic and superstition.

D Differentiate Instruction

Use the Differentiated Instruction notes throughout the lesson plan to support the varied skill sets, levels of readiness, and interests in the mixed-ability classroom.

Challenge These notes include suggestions for expanding the activity for advanced students.

On-Level These notes include suggestions for modifying the activity to address different interests or learning styles.

Extra Support These notes include ideas for providing more scaffolding or reading spuport.

Special Needs These notes provide ideas for adapting instruction to support the needs of various special needs students.

NOTES

Objectives

Objective 1: Outline the structure of colonial society.

Objective 2: Describe colonial art,music, and literature, and the impact of ideas on colonial society.

Objective 3: Describe the causes of the Great Awakening and its effects on colonial society.

Objective 4: Explain the growth of educational institutions.

LESSON 6 ORGANIZER	PACING: APPROX. 1 PERIOD, .5 BLOCKS		RESOURCES	
	OBJECTIVES	PACING	Online	Print
Connect				
DIGITAL START UP ACTIVITY **Predictions About Colonial Life**		5 min.	●	
Investigate				
DIGITAL TEXT 1 **Society in Colonial Times**	Objective 1	10 min.	●	●
DIGITAL TEXT 2 **Colonial Art, Literature, and Music**	Objective 2	10 min.	●	●
DIGITAL TEXT 5 **A New World of Ideas**	Objective 2	10 min.	●	●
INTERACTIVE GALLERY **The Arts in Colonial America**	Objective 2	10 min.	●	
DIGITAL TEXT 3 **A New Religious Movement**	Objective 3	10 min.	●	●
DIGITAL TEXT 4 **Colonial Schools and Colleges**	Objective 4	10 min.	●	●
INTERACTIVE CHART **Education in the Colonies**	Objective 4	10 min.	●	
Synthesize				
DIGITAL ACTIVITY **Checking Your Predictions**		5 min.	●	
Demonstrate				
DIGITAL QUIZ **Lesson Quiz and Class Discussion Board**		10 min.	●	

Colonial Society

CONNECT

DIGITAL START UP ACTIVITY

Predictions About Colonial Life

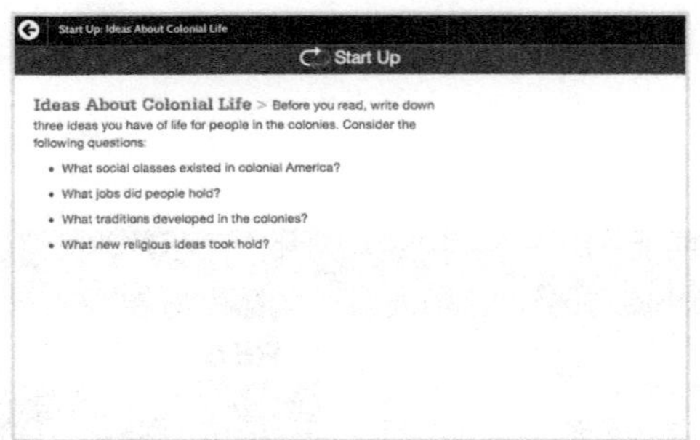

Project the Start Up Activity Have students read the questions as they enter and get settled, and then predict what colonial life was like. Have students share their predictions in class or through a chat or blog space.

Discuss What social classes existed in colonial America? What jobs did people hold? What new religious ideas took hold? *(Upper, middle, and lower classes; planters, merchants, ministers, lawyers, officials, craftsworkers, tradespeople, farmhands, servants, maids, cooks, nurses the Great Awakening developed new religious ideas.)*

Tell students that in this lesson they will learn about colonial life, including art, music, and literature, the influence of religions, and the contributions of various groups to American culture and society.

Aa Vocabulary Development: Use the Interactive Reading Notepad to preview the Key Terms and Academic Vocabulary in the lesson with students.

FLIP IT!

Assign the Flipped Video for this lesson.

STUDENT EDITION PRINT PAGES: 101–111

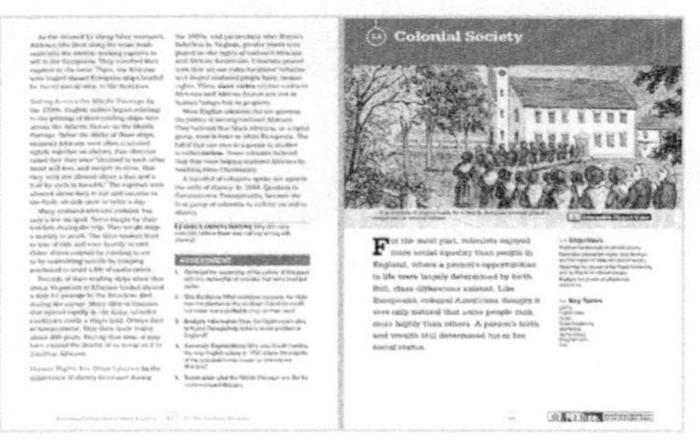

INVESTIGATE

DIGITAL TEXT 1

Society in Colonial Times

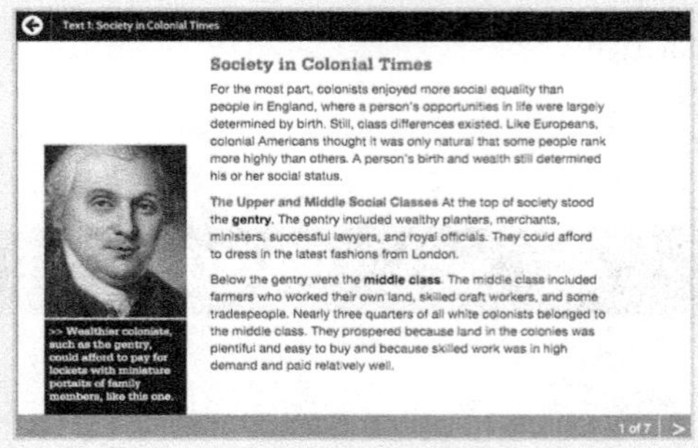

Objective 1: Outline the structure of colonial society.

Quick Instruction

Project the images of the colonial gentry and workers and have students to describe what they see. Discuss the differences between the two images. Ask what evidence suggests one image is of the gentry and one is of the middle class.

Distinguish between the gentry and the middle class. *(Gentry—upper class, including wealthy planters, merchants, ministers, successful lawyers, and royal officials. Middle class—not quite as wealthy, included farmers who owned land, skilled crafts workers, and some tradespeople. Many colonists were middle-class.)*

Support Ideas with Evidence Identify the social and economic contributions of women to colonial society. *(Women ran the home and contributed by cooking, milking cows, watching children, and making necessary goods; they worked in the fields in the backcountry; they got jobs as maids, cooks, nurses, midwives; they learned crafts and trades.)*

Further Instruction

Go through the Interactive Reading Notepad questions with the class and complete the graphic organizer about the various classes that made up colonial society. Discuss how each class contributed to the colonies. Be sure students also understand the contributions of women and African Americans.

Infer Why do you think indentured servants agreed to work without wages? *(They wanted to earn passage to the colonies. They hoped that after their service, they would be able to own land and become more successful.)*

Draw Conclusions Describe the contributions of enslaved Africans to colonial society. *(Enslaved Africans developed new languages such as Gullah, brought their skills to farming, building, and crafts, and contributed to new customs and traditions in the colonies.)*

www.PearsonRealize.com
Access your Digital Lesson

DIGITAL TEXT 2

Colonial Art, Literature, and Music

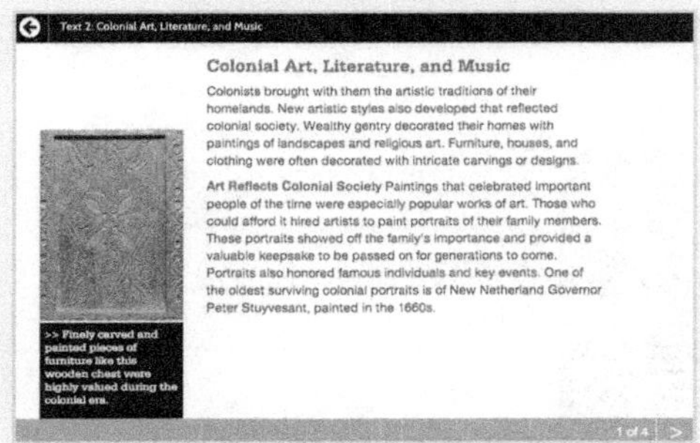

DIGITAL TEXT 5

A New World of Ideas

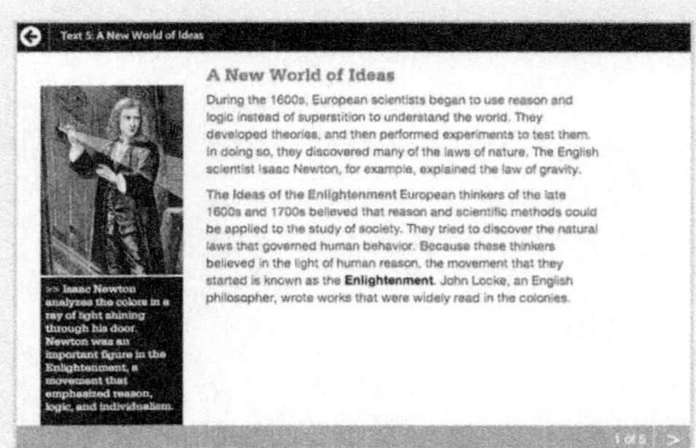

INTERACTIVE GALLERY

The Arts in Colonial America

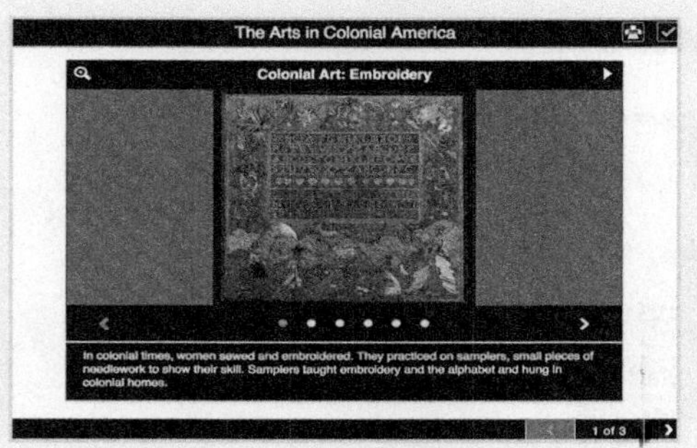

Objective 2: Describe colonial art, music, and literature, and the impact of ideas on colonial society.

Quick Instruction

Project the image of Isaac Newton. Explain that the Enlightenment was a movement of the late 1600s and early 1700s in which European thinkers tried to understand society through reason and science. This movement spread to the colonies to influence daily life in the United States. Colonists also looked to European traditions in art, music, and literature, all of which significantly impacted colonial society. However, certain subsequent developments in those areas were unique to American culture.

Interactive Gallery: Art, Music, and Literature in Colonial America Project the interactive gallery and view the images. Explicitly note the way in which art, music, and literature were reflections of American society in colonial times.

Analyze Images How does the image of Newton illustrate the principles of the Enlightenment? *(Newton is using reason and logic to examine the light, studying the physical laws of the world around him. He is trying to make discoveries based on observation and experimentation.)*

ACTIVE CLASSROOM

Have students use the Sticky Notes strategy and spend five minutes jotting down their responses to this question on sticky notes: What are examples of American, art, music, and literature that reflected society in the colonial era? Ask students to pair up and share their responses. Then have partners discuss why their examples are significant to the creation of a unique American culture.

Draw Conclusions What were the connections between music and religious life in the colonies? *(Music was played in churches. Spirituals and hymns were popular both in and outside church.)*

D Differentiate: Extra Support Point out that *to enlighten* means to provide greater knowledge or understanding. Ask students what how they think the Enlightenment affected society, based on this definition.

ELL Use the ELL activity described in the ELL chart.

Further Instruction

Go through the Interactive Reading Notepad questions with the class. Discuss the new ideas that developed out of the Enlightenment and how these ideas impacted colonial society.

Draw Conclusions How were miniature paintings an example of American art that reflected colonial society? *(The paintings celebrated people and events important to the colonies, for example the founders of colonies. They also affirmed the importance of the family being painted. This suggested prosperity and permanence in the colonies.)*

Support Ideas with Examples What examples show that Benjamin Franklin's scientific discoveries influenced daily life in the colonies? *(Bifocal glasses helped people see, a new kind of iron stove heated houses better, and lightning rods protected buildings during storms. Paved streets made travel easier, fire companies made communities safer, and lending libraries made books and knowledge more available.)*

Draw Conclusions What factors likely contributed to the growth of colonial newspapers during this period? *(Newspapers developed as the colonies grew. People probably wanted to read about what was happening in their communities. The Enlightenment may have led readers to be more curious about understanding society. The emphasis on learning may have made them interested in reading about important events.)*

Colonial Society

DIGITAL TEXT 3

A New Religious Movement

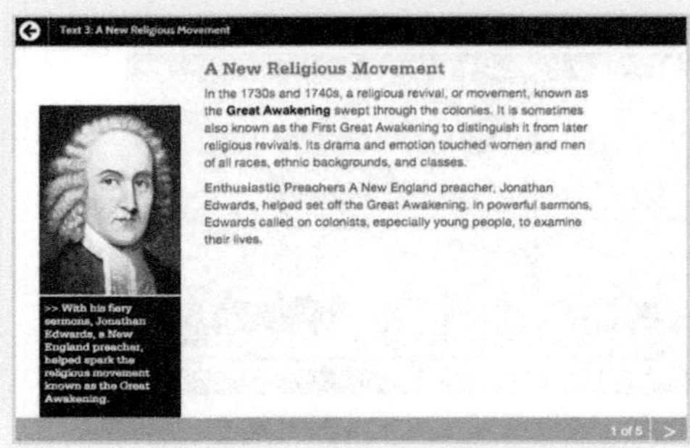

Objective 3: **Describe the impact of the Great Awakening on colonial society.**

Quick Instruction

Project the image of George Whitefield. Explain that Whitefield was an English minister who helped spread a religious movement known as the Great Awakening through the colonies. Point out to students that the Great Awakening was a social movement and discuss its impact on colonial society.

Identify Cause and Effect What were the causes of the Great Awakening? What impact did it have on colonial society? *(Causes—new, powerful preachers inspired colonists. Impact—some religions expanded; new churches grew; people began thinking about religious tolerance and self-rule.)*

Identify Central Issues How did ideas about religion and virtue put forward in the Great Awakening contribute to the growth of representative government in the American colonies? *(Church members controlling their parishes made people think about the importance of self-rule. Preachers also encouraged a spirit of independence. People began believing they could apply the virtues used to run their churches to the running of their government.)*

ELL Use the ELL activity described in the ELL chart.

Further Instruction

Go through the Interactive Reading Notepad questions with the class.

Draw Conclusions How did the Great Awakening contribute to the development of religious freedom in the United States? *(Many new churches sprung up. Colonists had to encounter and become tolerant of people of different faiths.)*

Hypothesize Among the religious influences that led to the Great Awakening as a social movement were the powerful sermons of preachers such as Whitefield and the idea that individuals could shape their own life in parishes without relying on authorities. What impact might this attitude have had on colonists? *(The idea that people could define their own religious life and run their own parishes led to a spirit of independence and a willingness to challenge authorities outside the religious realm.)*

DIGITAL TEXT 4

Colonial Schools and Colleges

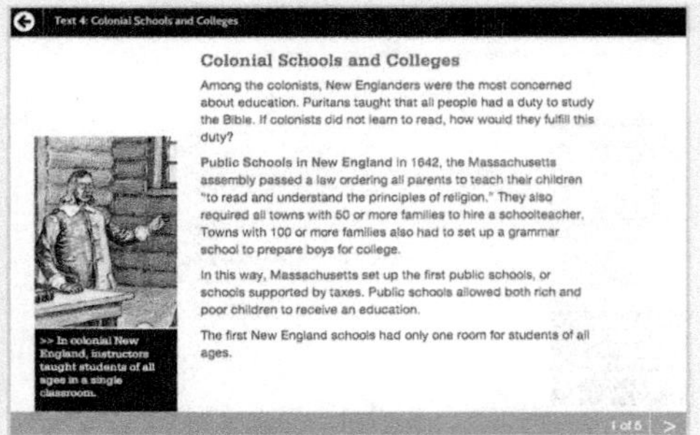

Objective 4: **Explain the growth of educational institutions.**

Quick Instruction

Educational institutions varied by region. New England established the first public schools. The Middle and Southern Colonies had private schools and tutors. Throughout the colonies, boys learned skills through apprenticeships. Enslaved Africans were denied formal educations.

Interactive Chart: Education in the Colonies Project the interactive chart and highlight the regional differences in educational institutions.

Generate Explanations Explain the reasons for the growth of institutions such as public schools during the colonial period. *(Massachusetts Puritans wanted children to learn to read in order to study the Bible. They required towns to hire schoolteachers and set up grammar schools. These were the first public schools that were supported by taxes and open to students regardless of social class.)*

ACTIVE CLASSROOM

Have students use the If Images Could Talk strategy and look at the image in the lesson of a woman educating a child. Ask: What do you think the teacher and the pupil would say if they could talk? What's your evidence?

INTERACTIVE CHART

Education in the Colonies

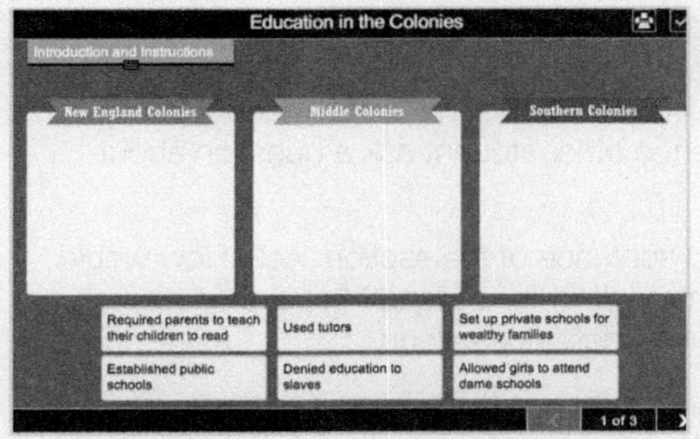

Further Instruction

Go through the Interactive Reading Notepad questions with the class and use the graphic organizer to sum up how formal education developed in different regions of the colonies. Be sure students understand why educational institutions grew during the colonial period.

Generate Explanations Explain the reasons for the growth of colleges and universities during the colonial period. *(To promote European culture and to educate future ministers; colleges later expanded to teach additional areas of study to men)*

Draw Conclusions Why didn't all children go to school in the colonial era? *(Public schools were not widespread and many children could not afford private schools or tutors. Some families lived too far from schools to send their children. Some students worked or served as apprentices instead of attending school. Enslaved African Americans were not allowed to go to school.)*

Cite Evidence How did women contribute to American society through dame schools? *(Women ran dame schools to educate girls, who were not accepted to New England schools. They taught girls reading, writing, and other skills.)*

SYNTHESIZE

DIGITAL ACTIVITY

Checking Your Predictions

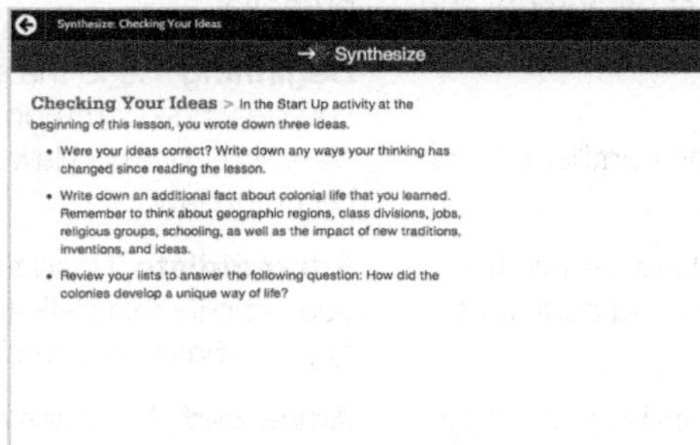

Synthesize: Checking Your Ideas
Synthesize
Checking Your Ideas > In the Start Up activity at the beginning of this lesson, you wrote down three ideas.
Were your ideas correct? Write down any ways your thinking has changed since reading the lesson.
Write down an additional fact about colonial life that you learned. Remember to think about geographic regions, class divisions, jobs, religious groups, schooling, as well as the impact of new traditions, inventions, and ideas.
Review your lists to answer the following question: How did the colonies develop a unique way of life?

Have students complete the Checking Your Predictions activity. Have students review the predictions they made at the beginning of the lesson and then answer the questions. Have students discuss the final question with a partner and share their insights with the class.

Discuss Have students think about the following questions. What were unique aspects of American culture during the colonial era? How are these aspects similar to or different from American culture today? Discuss students' answers with the class.

DEMONSTRATE

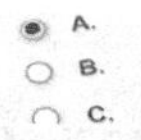

DIGITAL QUIZ

Lesson Quiz and Class Discussion Board

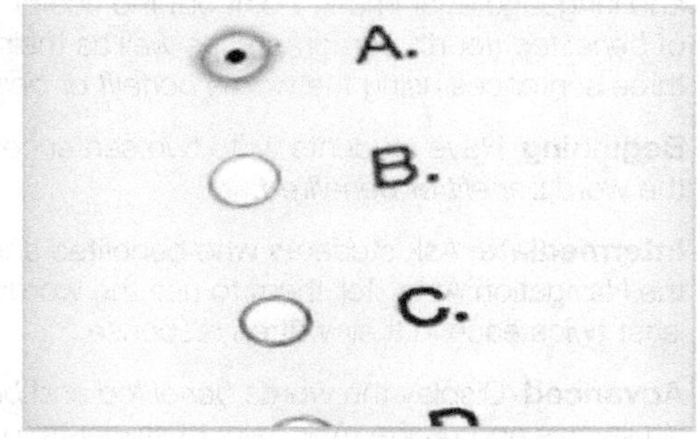

Assign the online Lesson Quiz for this lesson if you haven't already done so. Students will be offered automatic remediation or enrichment based on their score.

Pose these questions to the class on the Discussion Board:

In *Colonial Society*, you read about unique aspects of American society in the colonial era. Colonists developed art, music, and literature that reflected society at the time. Science and religion brought important changes as well.

Identify Cause and Effect How did the Great Awakening impact colonial society? *(New churches developed; ideas about democracy and self-governing spread; people thought about self-improvement and social reform.)*

Summarize What new institutions developed during the colonial era? *(Churches; public schools; colleges and universities; cultural institutions such as theaters and newspapers also developed for entertainment and information)*

Topic Inquiry

Have students continue their investigations for the Topic Inquiry.

Topic 2 Lesson 7

Colonial Trade and Government

Supporting English Language Learners

Use with Digital Text 1, **Mercantilism and the English Colonies.**

Learning

Have students read the text. Discuss the meaning of mercantilism. Prompt students to internalize new language in writing activities that build concept and language attainment. Point out the use of *benefit* (first paragraph) and of *benefited* (fourth paragraph), as well as their meanings. Model two or three sentences using the words *benefit* or *benefited*.

Beginning Have students write two sentences about mercantilism using the word *benefit* or *benefited*.

Intermediate Ask students who benefited and who did not benefit from the Navigation Acts. Tell them to use the words *benefited* and *benefit* at least twice each in their written response.

Advanced Display the words *benefited* and *beneficial*, and discuss their similarities and usage. Ask pairs of students to write a paragraph about mercantilism that uses both words at least twice.

Advanced High Display the words *benefited*, *beneficial*, and *beneficiary*, and discuss their similarities and usage. Have students write at least two paragraphs that describe mercantilism and uses each of the three words at least twice.

Use with Digital Text 3, **Foundations of Representative Government.**

Speaking

Have students read the section *William Blackstone and Common Law*. Encourage students to adapt spoken language appropriately for informal purposes.

Beginning Read the second sentence of the section. Ask: How would you describe common law to a friend? In pairs, have one student briefly describe common law and have the other student ask a question about common law.

Intermediate Read the second sentence of the section. Ask: How would you simplify this definition of common law for a friend? In pairs or in small groups, have students offer informal definitions aloud.

Advanced Ask pairs of students to discuss the meaning and use of common law. Encourage them to use informal, everyday language with each other. Ask: How was your language different from that of the text?

Advanced High In pairs, have students give a brief presentation about common law to an imaginary group of younger students. Encourage them to use informal, accessible language during their talk.

D Differentiate Instruction

Use the Differentiated Instruction notes throughout the lesson plan to support the varied skill sets, levels of readiness, and interests in the mixed-ability classroom.

Challenge These notes include suggestions for expanding the activity for advanced students.

On-Level These notes include suggestions for modifying the activity to address different interests or learning styles.

Extra Support These notes include ideas for providing more scaffolding or reading spuport.

Special Needs These notes provide ideas for adapting instruction to support the needs of various special needs students.

NOTES

Go online to access additional resources including: Primary Sources • Biographies • Supreme Court cases • 21st Century Skill Tutorials • Maps • Graphic Organizers.

PEARSON realize www.PearsonRealize.com

Objectives

Objective 1: Explain the development of mercantilism and colonists' response to it.

Objective 2: Outline the relationship of the slave trade to other kinds of trade.

Objective 3: Describe the development of governments and legal systems in the colonies.

LESSON 7 ORGANIZER	PACING: APPROX. 1 PERIOD, .5 BLOCKS			
			RESOURCES	
	OBJECTIVES	PACING	Online	Print
Connect				
DIGITAL START UP ACTIVITY **William Blackstone**		5 min.	●	
Investigate				
DIGITAL TEXT 1 **Mercantilism and the English Colonies**	Objective 1	10 min.	●	●
DIGITAL TEXT 2 **Trading Across the Atlantic**	Objective 2	10 min.	●	●
INTERACTIVE MAP **The Triangular Trade**		10 min.	●	
DIGITAL TEXT 3 **Foundations of Representative Government**	Objective 3	10 min.	●	●
INTERACTIVE CHART **Influences on Colonial Government**		10 min.	●	
Synthesize				
DIGITAL ACTIVITY **Government Traditions**		5 min.	●	
Demonstrate				
DIGITAL QUIZ **Lesson Quiz and Class Discussion Board**		10 min.	●	

Colonial Trade and Government

CONNECT

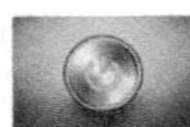

DIGITAL START UP ACTIVITY

William Blackstone

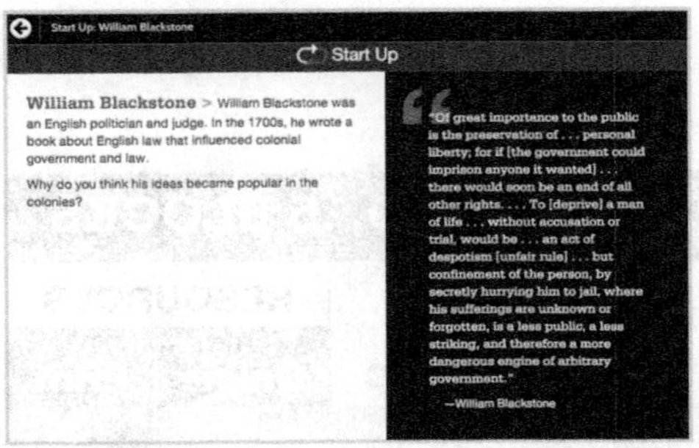

Project the Start Up Activity Have students read the quote and answer the question as they enter and get settled. Ask students to paraphrase Blackstone's main points and discuss their answers with a partner.

Discuss Why do you think Blackstone's ideas became popular in the colonies? *(He emphasized liberty and justice, especially the right to a fair trial. He was critical of unfair and arbitrary government, a feeling colonists also shared.)*

Tell students that in this lesson they will be learning about the government and economy of the 13 English colonies. This period saw the growth of triangular trade and the development of representative government in the colonies.

Aa Vocabulary Development: Use the Interactive Reading Notepad to preview the Key Terms and the Academic Vocabulary in this lesson with students.

FLIP IT!

Assign the Flipped Video for this lesson.

STUDENT EDITION PRINT PAGES: 112–116

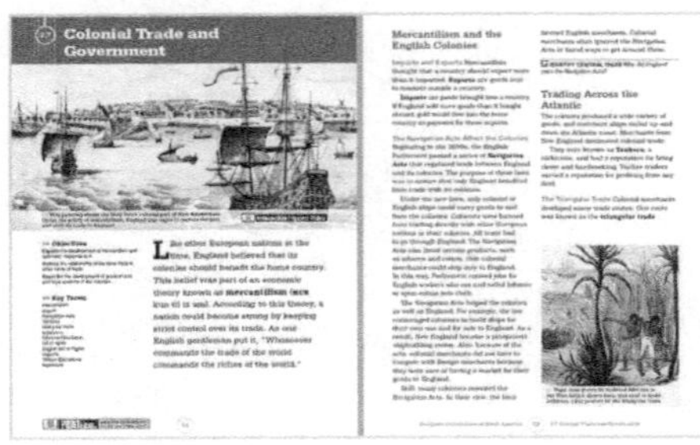

INVESTIGATE

DIGITAL TEXT 1

Mercantilism and the English Colonies

Objective 1: Explain the development of mercantilism and colonists' response to it.

Quick Instruction

Project the image of colonial shipbuilding and discuss industries such as shipbuilding that were strong in the colonies. Explain that mercantilism is an economic theory that says a nation becomes strong by controlling its trade. According to this theory, England believed it should benefit from colonial trade.

Make Predictions Make a prediction about why mercantilism will be one of the causes of the American Revolution. *(Colonists will not want England controlling their trade and making money off their labor.)*

D Differentiate: Extra Support Explain to students that when nations trade, they both buy and sell goods. Exports are goods that are sent out of a country. Imports are goods that are brought into a country. Ask students to come up with an example of an import and an export, from the colonial period or the present day.

ELL Use the ELL activity described in the ELL chart.

Further Instruction

Go through the Interactive Reading Notepad questions with the class and complete the graphic organizer to take notes about the Navigation Acts. Ask students why colonists disliked the Navigation Acts. Be sure students understand why mercantilism and mercantilist policies like the Navigation Acts would become causes of the American Revolution.

Hypothesize Ask students how they think many colonists felt about their trade benefiting England. *(They were probably not happy with this arrangement. They would have wanted to benefit from their trade.)*

Infer What does mercantilism suggest about England's attitude toward its colonies? *(England saw the colonies mainly as a source of wealth for the mother country.)*

DIGITAL TEXT 2

Trading Across the Atlantic

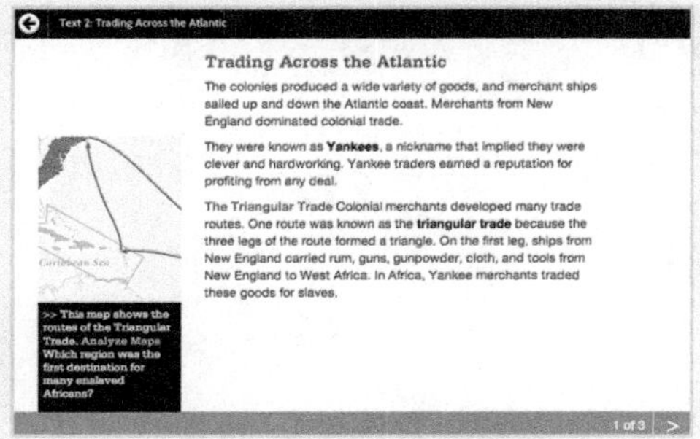

Objective 2: **Outline the relationship of the slave trade to other kinds of trade.**

Quick Instruction

Colonists in New England, the Middle Colonies, and the Southern Colonies traded with Africa and the Caribbean. These trade routes are known as the triangular trade because together they formed a triangle.

Interactive Map: Triangular Trade Project the map on the whiteboard and explore the regions. Have students use the map to describe the trade routes in their own words.

Identify Patterns How did the triangular trade connect to the development of the transatlantic slave trade? *(The transatlantic slave trade was one leg of the triangular trade. Traders sold rum to buy enslaved Africans, who were brought via the slave trade to work on sugar plantations in the Caribbean. The sugar was sold to the North American colonies and made into rum, which was used to buy more slaves.)*

ACTIVE CLASSROOM

Have students use the Connect Two strategy. List the following words for students to copy: merchants, triangular trade, slaves, molasses, Yankees, gunpowder, profits, Middle Passage, transatlantic slave trade, rum, and Navigation Acts. Read the list of words with students. Ask students to choose two words they think might belong together and state the reason. During the reading, have students look for evidence to support or refute their connections.

INTERACTIVE MAP

The Triangular Trade

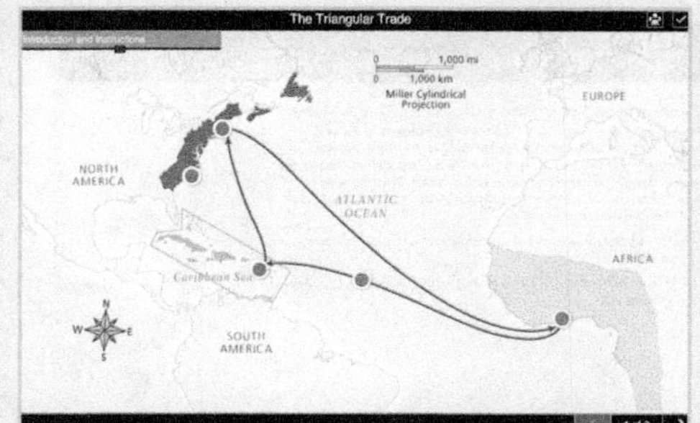

Further Instruction

Go through the Interactive Reading Notepad questions with the class. Be sure students understand the routes of the triangular trade and how it contributed to the development of the transatlantic slave trade.

Identify Central Issues How did the triangular trade benefit both England and the colonies economically? *(The colonies made money from selling rum and enslaved Africans, and from the plantations where enslaved Africans worked. Although traders disregarded the Navigation Acts, England benefited from the economic success of the colonies. England also bought rice, silk, indigo, and tobacco from the Southern Colonies.)*

Identify Cause and Effect Identify an effect of colonization on each group: colonial merchants, the English, and Africans. *(Colonial merchants became wealthy from the triangular trade; the English generated wealth and received new goods such as rice and tobacco; Africans were enslaved and brought to plantations.)*

DIGITAL TEXT 3

Foundations of Representative Government

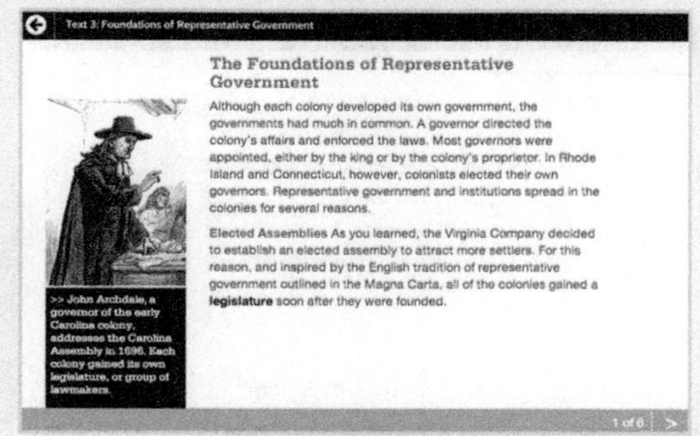

Objective 3: **Describe the development of governments and legal systems in the colonies.**

Quick Instruction

Interactive Chart: Influences on Colonial Government Project the interactive chart on the whiteboard and have students read through the tiles about the three documents. Explain that historic documents such as the English Bill of Rights strongly influenced the development of representative government during the colonial period.

Summarize What government institutions emerged during the colonial period? *(Colonies legislatures emerged and many had elected assemblies. Colonies also had governors and judges.)*

ACTIVE CLASSROOM

Have students use the Write 1-Get 3 strategy to answer the question: What were four key characteristics of colonial government? Have students take a piece of paper and fold it into quarters. Students write down one response in the first box and then go around the room asking to hear other responses. When students think a response is correct, they write it in their boxes until they have three more responses on the page. Have students share responses with the class.

ELL Use the ELL activity described in the ELL chart.

Colonial Trade and Government

INTERACTIVE CHART

Influences on Colonial Government

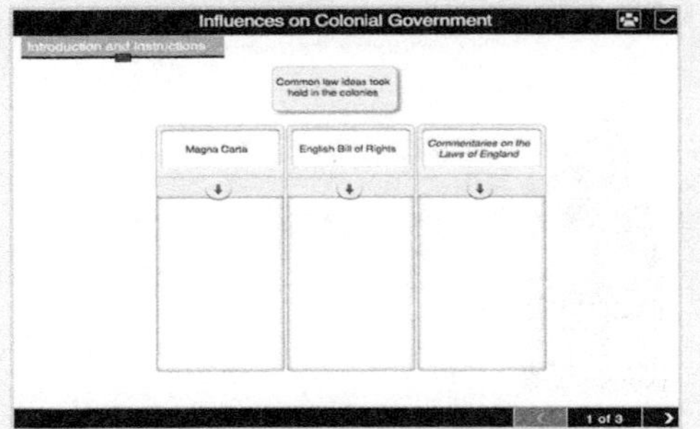

Further Instruction

Go through the Interactive Reading Notepad questions with the class. Review the Commentaries on the Laws of England, the Magna Carta, and the English Bill of Rights. Discuss how and why these documents influenced colonial government. Assign the Primary Source: The English Bill of Rights.

Identify Patterns What ideas from the English Bill of Rights have influenced the U.S. system of government? *(Individuals have rights that the government must protect; those accused of a crime have the right to a trial by jury; rulers cannot raise taxes or an army without approval from a separate legislative body.)*

Draw Conclusions How did William Blackstone contribute to the development of self-government in colonial America? *(Blackstone viewed individuals as free agents capable of controlling themselves, and therefore capable of governing themselves.)*

Cite Evidence Explain the reasons for the growth of representative government and institutions during the colonial period. *(The idea of representative government was enshrined in the Magna Carta, and colonists cherished this and other English democratic traditions. Representative government was strengthened as a result of England's Glorious Revolution in 1688 and its Bill of Rights, which gave more rights and powers to parliament and which also strengthened the position of colonial legislatures.)*

SYNTHESIZE

DIGITAL ACTIVITY

Government Traditions

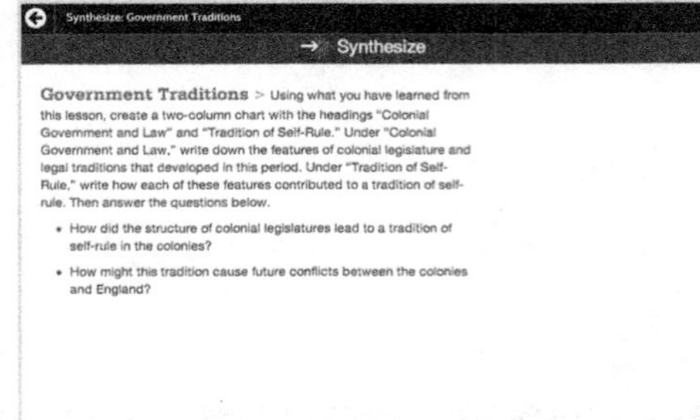

Have students complete the Government Traditions activity. Have students fill in their charts and then answer the questions. Ask students to make a prediction about how the growth of representative government in the colonies will affect relations with England.

Discuss Have students think about the following question: How were the colonies setting themselves up to be economically and politically independent from England? Discuss students' answers with the class.

DEMONSTRATE

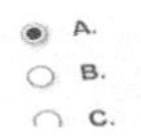

DIGITAL QUIZ

Lesson Quiz and Class Discussion Board

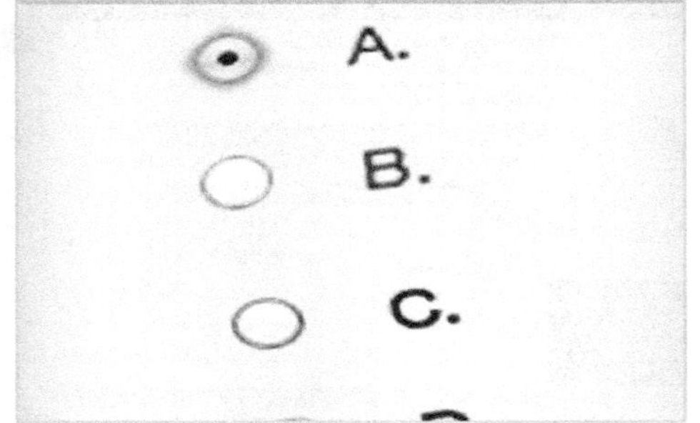

Assign the online Lesson Quiz for this lesson if you haven't already done so. Students will be offered automatic remediation or enrichment based on their score.

Pose these questions to the class on the Discussion Board:

In *Colonial Trade and Government*, you read about the economy and government of the colonies. Mercantilism led to a brisk trade between the colonies and England, while additional trade routes developed to include Africa and the Caribbean. At the same time, colonial government was laying the foundations for self-rule.

Identify Cause and Effect What economic factors caused the colonies to prosper? How might this prosperity affect relations with England? *(Farming, resources, and the triangular trade generated wealth; England might have expected a greater share of the profits from the colonies than colonists wanted to give.)*

Formulate Questions What is a question you have about the development of self-government in the colonies? *(What factors led the U.S. government to extend greater freedoms to those whose rights were limited in the colonies?)*

Topic Inquiry

Have students continue their investigations for the Topic Inquiry.

www.PearsonRealize.com
Access your Digital Lesson

European Colonization of North America (1500–1750)

SYNTHESIZE

DIGITAL ACTIVITY

Reflect on the Essential Question and Topic

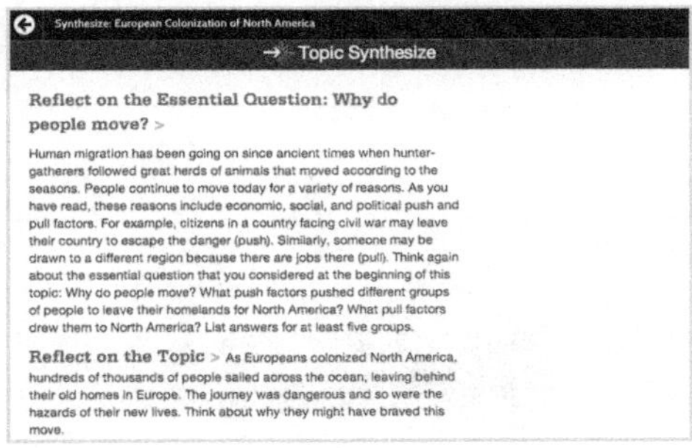

First ask students to reconsider the Topic Essential Question: Why do people move? Remind students that people move because different political, economic, and social factors "push" them from one place and "pull" them to another.

Have students list the push and pull factors that compelled at least five different groups of people to move to North America. Ask: Do you think colonists who moved to North America were able to build the lives they'd imagined when they decided to move? Ask them to consider different groups of colonists and give evidence for support. Discuss their answers as a class or ask students to post their answers on the Class Discussion board.

Next ask students to reflect on the topic as a whole and think of someone they know, or know of, who moved from one place to another. Have students write down why they think this person moved and three additional questions they have about this person's motivations. Have students consider the following motivators if they need help getting started:

- political reasons
- economic reasons
- social reasons
- personal reasons

You may ask students to share their questions and answers on the Class Discussion Board.

Topic Inquiry

Have students complete Step 3 of the Topic Inquiry.

DEMONSTRATE

DIGITAL TOPIC REVIEW AND ASSESSMENT

European Colonization of North America (1500–1750)

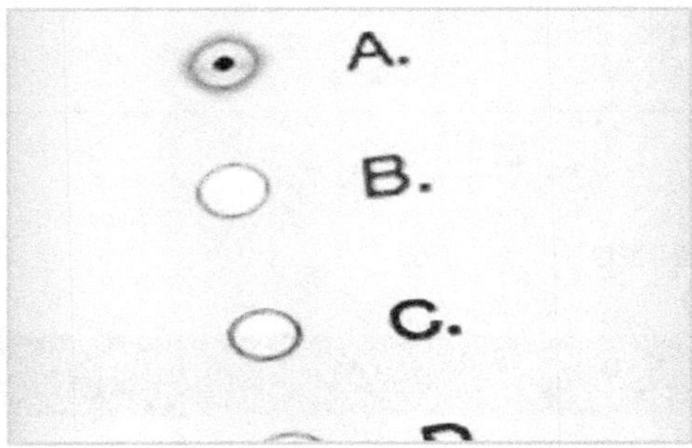

Students can prepare for the Topic Test by answering the questions in the Topic Review and Assessment online or the Assessment questions in the Print Student text. They can also prepare by reviewing their answers to the Interactive Reading Notepad questions or reviewing their notes in the Reading and Notetaking Study Guide.

DIGITAL TOPIC TEST

European Colonization of North America (1500–1750)

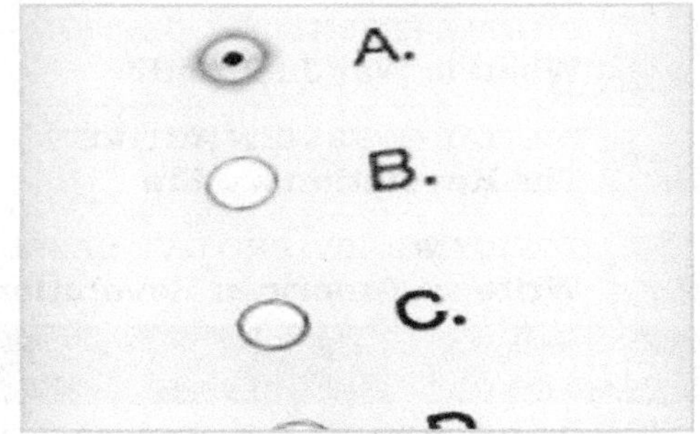

TOPIC TEST

Assign the Topic Test to assess students' understanding of topic content.

BENCHMARK TESTS

Assign these benchmark tests as you complete the relevant topics to monitor student progress toward mastering the course content and as preparation for the End-of-Course Test.

Benchmark Test 1: Topics 1–2

Benchmark Test 2: Topics 3–4

Benchmark Test 3: Topics 5–6

Benchmark Test 4: Topics 7–9

Benchmark Test 5: Topics 10–12

Benchmark Test 6: Topics 13–14

Benchmark Test 7: Topics 15–17

The Revolutionary Era (1750–1783)

TOPIC 3 ORGANIZER	PACING: APPROX. 8 PERIODS, 4 BLOCKS
	PACING
Connect	1 period
MY STORY VIDEO **Benjamin Franklin and the Fight for Independence**	10 min.
DIGITAL ESSENTIAL QUESTION ACTIVITY **When is War Justified?**	10 min.
DIGITAL OVERVIEW ACTIVITY **The Revolutionary Era**	10 min.
TOPIC INQUIRY: PROJECT-BASED LEARNING **Write an American Revolution Blog**	20 min.
Investigate	2–5 periods
TOPIC INQUIRY: PROJECT-BASED LEARNING **Write an American Revolution Blog**	Ongoing
LESSON 1 The French and Indian War	30–40 min.
LESSON 2 Tensions with Britain	30–40 min.
LESSON 3 Taking Up Arms	30–40 min.
LESSON 4 Declaring Independence	30–40 min.
LESSON 5 Winning Independence	30–40 min.
Synthesize	1 period
DIGITAL ACTIVITY **Reflect on the Essential Question and Topic**	10 min.
TOPIC INQUIRY: PROJECT-BASED LEARNING **Write an American Revolution Blog**	20 min.
Demonstrate	1–2 periods
DIGITAL TOPIC REVIEW AND ASSESSMENT **The Revolutionary Era**	10 min.
TOPIC INQUIRY: PROJECT-BASED LEARNING **Write an American Revolution Blog**	20 min.

TOPIC INQUIRY: PROJECT-BASED LEARNING

Write an American Revolution Blog

In this Topic Inquiry, students create, publish, and present an American Revolution blog. The blog will document their decision-making process as they consider whether they would have sided with Britain, the Patriots, or remained neutral during the Revolutionary War if they lived in the Chesapeake Bay in 1776. Learning about how colonists decided which side to support will contribute to students' understanding of the Topic Essential Question: When is war justified?

STEP 1: CONNECT
Develop Questions and Plan the Investigation

Read the Project Launch

Explain to students that in this project, they will be deciding whether they would have supported the British, the Patriots, or remained neutral if they lived in the Chesapeake Bay in 1776. Explain that they will need to create a written presentation of social studies material in the form of a blog. Have students read the Project Launch and review the fictional request from Commander George Washington.

Suggestion: To provide extra support, ask students which side Washington chose. Remind them that not all colonists supported the Patriots. Make sure they understand they are being asked to research how Chesapeake Bay colonists chose sides and will use this information to make their own decision.

Plan the Investigation

Form students into groups. Have them sign the *Project Contract*. Ask the groups to discuss the five steps of the decision-making process. Have students begin their *Need to Know Questions* to form a list of research questions. They may want to consider geography, location, economy, religion, political allegiances, and other social and historical factors that impacted colonists' decisions.

Suggestion: You may assign students their groups, or let students choose. Groups may then select their three subgroups, or you can assign them.

Resources

- Project Launch
- Project Contract
- Rubric for a Written Blog and Group Presentation
- Student Instructions

PROFESSIONAL DEVELOPMENT

Project-Based Learning
Be sure to view the Project-Based Learning Professional Development resources in the online course.

STEP 2: INVESTIGATE
Apply Disciplinary Concepts and Tools

Gathering Sources for Research on the Chesapeake Bay

Groups will work together to identify the information they need to investigate the Chesapeake Bay in 1776.

Suggestion: Students can conduct their research online, but should also remember to consult the readings for this topic.

Investigate Factors Influencing the Decision

Groups will break into three subgroups to address the steps in the decision-making process. Group 1 will identify the situation, Group 2 will identify options, and Group 3 will predict consequences.

Suggestion: If groups get stuck, remind them to review the information they have already gathered from the readings and their research on the region and then generate questions relevant to their step in the decision-making process.

Write and Edit Your Subgroup's Blog Post

Each subgroup will write and edit its own blog post presenting the information gathered as part of the decision-making process. Blog posts should be well organized, stay on topic, and include maps, images, and quotes. Work with students to make sure that they use social studies terminology, standard grammar, spelling, sentence structure, punctuation, and proper citation of sources.

Suggestion: Review how to incorporate research into written material, including proper formatting for citing sources.

Resources

- Work in Teams
- Project Tracker
- Search for Information on the Internet
- Make Decisions
- Information Organizer
- Need to Know Questions
- Model Blog

TOPIC INQUIRY: PROJECT-BASED LEARNING

Write an American Revolution Blog *(continued)*

STEP 3: SYNTHESIZE

Evaluate Sources and Use Evidence to Formulate Conclusions

Build Your Group Blog

Have groups come together to build their blogs. Blogs should incorporate each subgroup's blog post and use both images and text.

Suggestion: If your class has limited access to the Internet, you could supply materials for students to make a physical binder or book to present their posts.

Write Your Conclusions

Have students use their group's blogs to make their own decision about which side they would have taken during the American Revolution. Students should use the prompts to explain the reasons for their decision.

Suggestion: Poll the class to see whether students arrived at different conclusions, and what factors most influenced their decision-making process.

Resources

- Getting Started with WordPress Tutoral

STEP 4: DEMONSTRATE

Communicate Conclusions and Take Informed Action

Present Your Blog

Have students present their blogs to the class or an invited audience. To help students structure their presentations and ensure equal participation, have them divide the presentation among group members.

Suggestion: If your classroom is not equipped to view the blog during the presentation, have students pass around hard copies of their posts for audience members to see.

Reflect on the Project

Have groups meet to go over what went well and what did not so they can be more effective in the future. Students will then complete the Team/Peer Assessment individually.

Suggestion: As an extension, have students use the information they gathered about the Chesapeake Bay to consider how the region was affected by the war.

Heading

- Give an Effective Presentation
- Team/Peer Assessment

INTRODUCTION

The Revolutionary Era (1750–1783)

By the mid-1700s, European powers were fighting to grow their empires in North America. War broke out—the French and Indian War—between Britain, France, and several Native American tribes. The British won, but victory came at a cost. To pay for the war, Parliament imposed new taxes on the colonies, and widespread protests broke out. The American Revolution was not only a fight to break from Britain. It was also a fight for a radically new society and an experimental form of government: democratic republicanism.

CONNECT

MY STORY VIDEO

Benjamin Franklin and the Fight for Independence

Watch a video about the life and accomplishments of Benjamin Franklin.

Check Understanding What key role did Benjamin Franklin play during the American Revolution. *(A diplomat to France, he helped persuade the French to support the American side.)*

Draw Conclusions Why has Franklin been called an 18th century version of a Renaissance man? *(Like leading Renaissance thinkers, Franklin was interested in all aspects of human endeavor. He was conducted experiments, he was an inventor and a writer, and he was deeply involved in the intellectual life of the American colonies.)*

FLIP IT!

Assign the My Story video.

DIGITAL ESSENTIAL QUESTION ACTIVITY

When is War Justified?

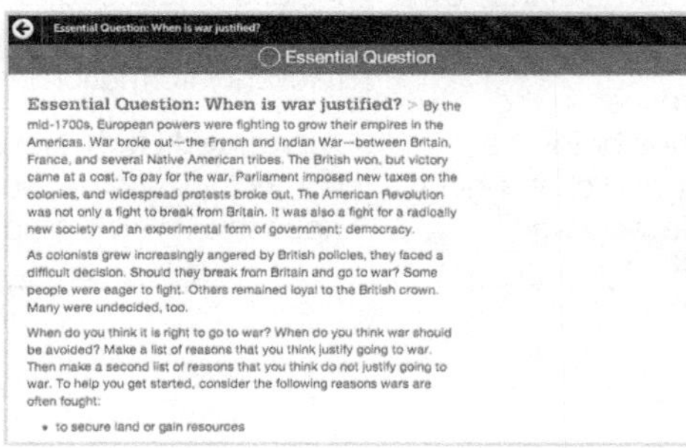

Ask students to think about the Essential Question for this topic: When is war justified? Not all colonists supported the American Revolution. Were the colonists right to go to war?

If students have not already done so, ask them to think about the questions in the activity. Then go over the answers as a class.

Generate Explanations Explain why some colonists might not have thought war with Britain was justified. *(They were loyal to Britain; they hoped the conflict could be solved without war; they did not agree with the reasons for the war.)*

Make Predictions What reasons do you think the colonists will give for going to war? *(To stand up for political ideals; to protect their way of life; to reject British policies; to develop their own government)*

DIGITAL OVERVIEW ACTIVITY

The Revolutionary Era

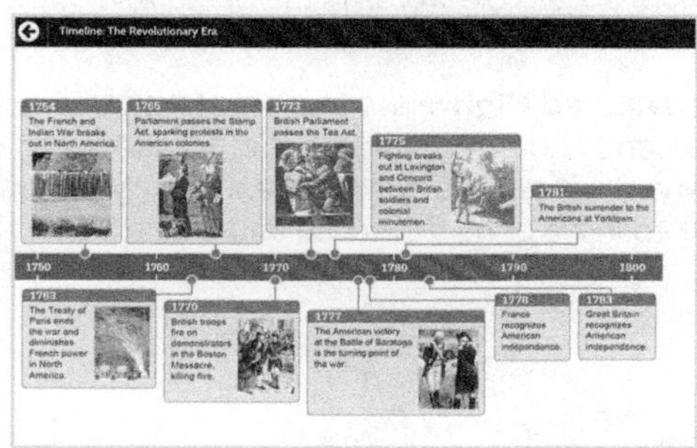

Display the timeline showing key events of the revolutionary era. This timeline will help provide a framework in which students can place the events they learn about during this topic.

Analyze Information Based on the timeline, what major issues between Britain and the colonies were causes of the American Revolution? *(the Stamp Act and the Boston Massacre)*

Identify Cause and Effect How do you think the British victory in the French and Indian War contributed to the causes of the American Revolution? *(Colonists might not have liked Britain gaining power in the region; Britain may have sought money from the colonies to pay for the war; Britain may have imposed policies about land and settlement in new territories that colonists did not like.)*

Topic Inquiry

Launch the Topic Inquiry with students after introducing the topic.

The French and Indian War

Supporting English Language Learners

Use with Digital Text 3, **A Meeting in Albany.**

Learning

Have students read the first paragraph of the text. Use accessible language to help students learn new and essential language. Use accessible language to define the words *delegates*, *cement*, and *alliance*, as used in this paragraph.

Beginning Have students reread the paragraph. Working in groups of three, have each student use his or her own words explain the meaning of one of the three words that you have defined.

Intermediate Have students write their own sentence using each of the three words that you have defined.

Advanced Working in pairs, have students read the second paragraph of this section. Ask students to take turns identifying words in the paragraph that are new to them. Based on the context provided by the more accessible words in the paragraph, have students define in their own words the new words that they have identified.

Advanced High Have students take turns reading sentences in the second and third paragraphs of the reading in small groups or for the whole class. Have each student identify at least one new and challenging word in his or her sentence and define it using accessible language.

Use with Digital Text 5, **Quebec and New France Fall.**

Speaking

Read the text orally, or invite volunteers to do so in order to reinforce concept attainment. Then display the timeline and read its content together, encouraging students to respond orally to the information presented.

Beginning Ask: When does Britain declare war on France? Display this sentence to support their response: Britain declares war in the year _____. As students answer aloud, have them point to the information on the timeline.

Intermediate Ask: What happens in the French and Indian War during the year 1755? Have students read aloud the appropriate entry on the timeline and restate it aloud in their own words.

Advanced Ask: Do the British negotiate with the Iroquois and Ohio Indians before or after more British troops are sent to North America? Have students answer aloud and explain their response by pointing to relevant information on the timeline.

Advanced High Have students read aloud the timeline entries in chronological order and then restate them in their own words. Ask: How does this timeline help you to better understand the war?

D Differentiate Instruction

Use the Differentiated Instruction notes throughout the lesson plan to support the varied skill sets, levels of readiness, and interests in the mixed-ability classroom.

Challenge These notes include suggestions for expanding the activity for advanced students.

On-Level These notes include suggestions for modifying the activity to address different interests or learning styles.

Extra Support These notes include ideas for providing more scaffolding or reading spupport.

Special Needs These notes provide ideas for adapting instruction to support the needs of various special needs students.

NOTES

Go online to access additional resources including: Primary Sources • Biographies • Supreme Court cases • 21st Century Skill Tutorials • Maps • Graphic Organizers.

PEARSON realize www.PearsonRealize.com

Objectives

Objective 1: Explain how the rivalry between Britain and France and conflict over the Ohio Valley led to the French and Indian War in North America.

Objective 2: Identify how mistakes and lack of unity led to British defeats early in the war.

Objective 3: Summarize how the tide of the war turned in Britain's favor.

Objective 4: Explain how the British won the war.

Objective 5: Describe the power shift that occurred after the war.

LESSON 1 ORGANIZER	PACING: APPROX. 1 PERIOD, .5 BLOCKS		RESOURCES	
	OBJECTIVES	PACING	Online	Print
Connect				
DIGITAL START UP ACTIVITY **Causes of the French and Indian War**		5 min.	●	
Investigate				
DIGITAL TEXT 1 **Europeans Fight Over North American Land**	Objective 1	10 min.	●	●
DIGITAL TEXT 2 **The French and Indian War Begins in the Ohio Valley**	Objective 1	10 min.	●	●
DIGITAL TEXT 3 **A Meeting in Albany**	Objective 2	10 min.	●	●
DIGITAL TEXT 4 **British Defeats in the Ohio Valley**	Objective 2	10 min.	●	●
INTERACTIVE MAP **Major Battles of the French and Indian War**	Objective 2	10 min.	●	
DIGITAL TEXT 5 **Quebec and New France Fall**	Objectives 3, 4, 5	10 min.	●	●
INTERACTIVE CHART **Effects of the French and Indian War**	Objectives 3, 4, 5	10 min.	●	
Synthesize				
DIGITAL ACTIVITY **Effects of the French and Indian War**		5 min.	●	
Demonstrate				
DIGITAL QUIZ **Lesson Quiz and Class Discussion Board**		10 min.	●	

The French and Indian War

CONNECT

DIGITAL START UP ACTIVITY

Causes of the French and Indian War

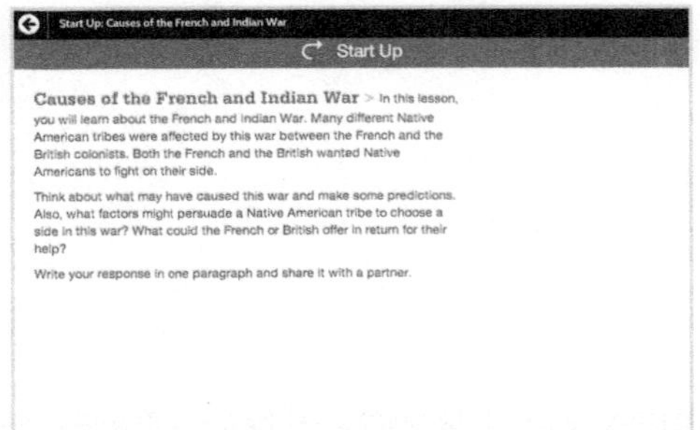

Project the Start Up Activity As they enter and get settled, ask students to look at the maps. Then have them discuss their answers with another student, either in class or through a chat or blog space.

Locate places of importance on the map with students.

Discuss Based on this map, why do you think war broke out between France and Britain? *(The empires were close to one another and fought over territory.)* What do you predict will happen to the Native American tribes in the region? *(They look like they will be caught in the middle and forced to take sides.)*

Tell students that in this lesson they will learn how physical and human geographic factors affected the French and Indian War.

Aa Vocabulary Development: Use the Interactive Reading Notepad to preview the Key Terms and Academic Vocabulary in the lesson with students.

FLIP IT!

Assign the Flipped Video for this lesson.

STUDENT EDITION PRINT PAGES: 122–129

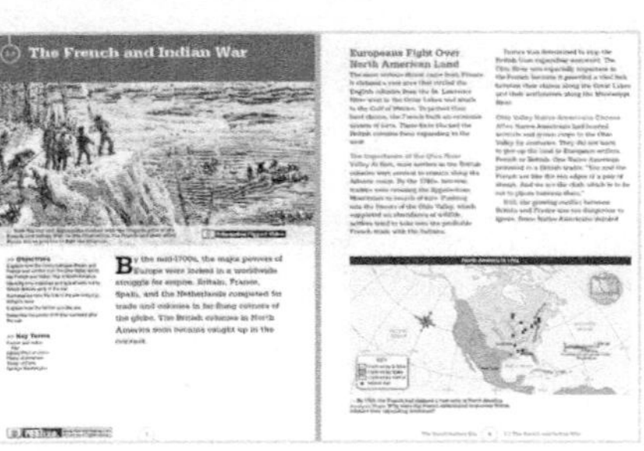

INVESTIGATE

DIGITAL TEXT 1

Europeans Fight Over North American Land

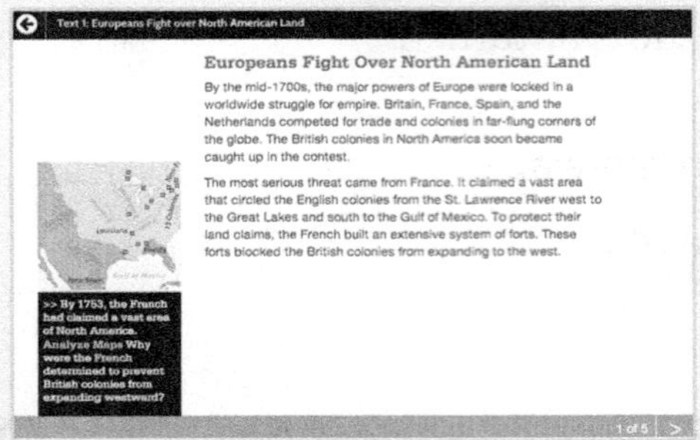

DIGITAL TEXT 2

The French and Indian War Begins in the Ohio Valley

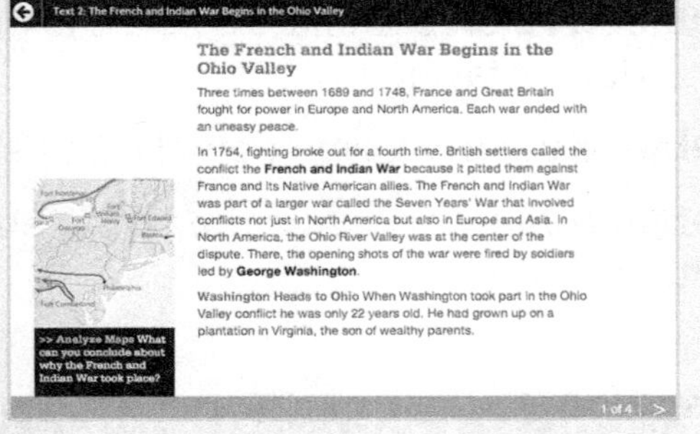

Objective 1: Explain how the rivalry between Britain and France and conflict over the Ohio Valley led to the French and Indian War in North America.

Quick Instruction

Project the map of North America. Have students identify the European powers in North America and their territories. Ask students to locate the Ohio River Valley and discuss its strategic importance.

Analyze Maps Why do you think France wanted to maintain its hold over the Ohio River Valley? *(It wanted to control the fur trade in the region. It also used the river to connect settlements in the region.)*

D Differentiate: Extra Support Have students copy the map and highlight the Ohio River. Ask what areas it connects. Discuss the different ways settlers relied on rivers, including for water, fishing, trapping, and transportation.

Further Instruction

Go through the Interactive Reading Notepad questions for *Europeans Fight Over North American Land* and *The French and Indian War Begins in the Ohio Valley* and discuss the answers with the class, including the graphic organizer noting the alliances and reasons they were formed. Be sure students understand how conflicts over land and resources led fighting to break out.

Compare and Contrast French and British settlements in North America. *(France—claimed lands west of the St. Lawrence River; built forts for protection; were mostly trappers and traders; many adopted Native American ways. Britain—settled primarily along the coast; began pushing west of the Appalachian Mountains; cleared forests for farms; many ignored Native American's rights.)*

Draw Conclusions Why did fighting break out in the Ohio Valley? *(Britain wanted to expand westward. France wanted to limit British expansion into its territories. Native Americans did not want to give up their land.)*

Identify Cause and Effect How did the physical geography of the Ohio Valley affect the early stages of the French and Indian War? How did people interact with the environment? *(Both sides could hide in the woods. The woods also made it possible to sneak up on the enemy. This led the British and French to build forts for protection along rivers in the region.)*

www.PearsonRealize.com
Access your Digital Lesson

DIGITAL TEXT 3

A Meeting in Albany

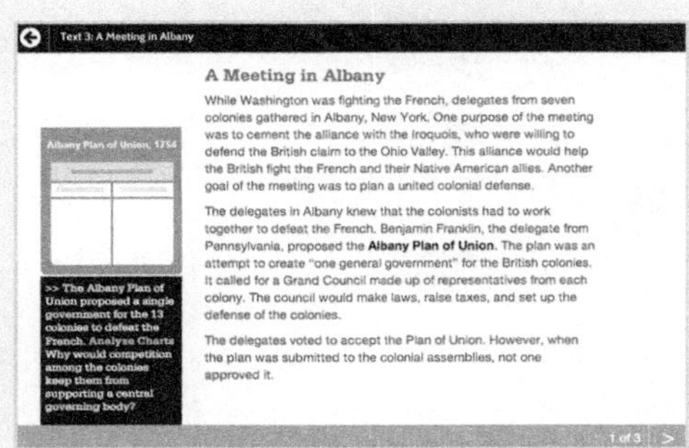

DIGITAL TEXT 4

British Defeats in the Ohio Valley

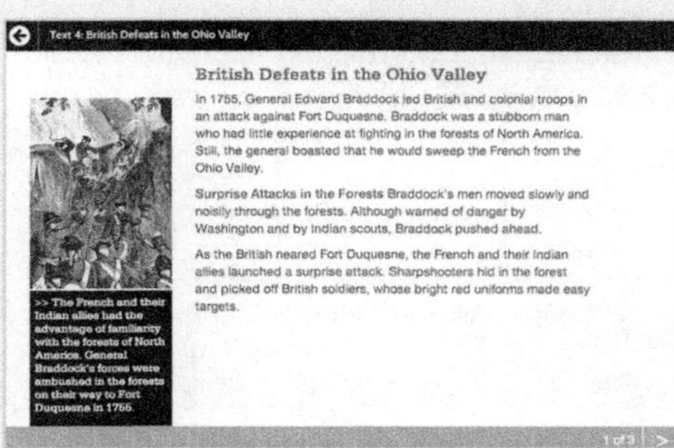

INTERACTIVE MAP

Major Battles of the French and Indian War

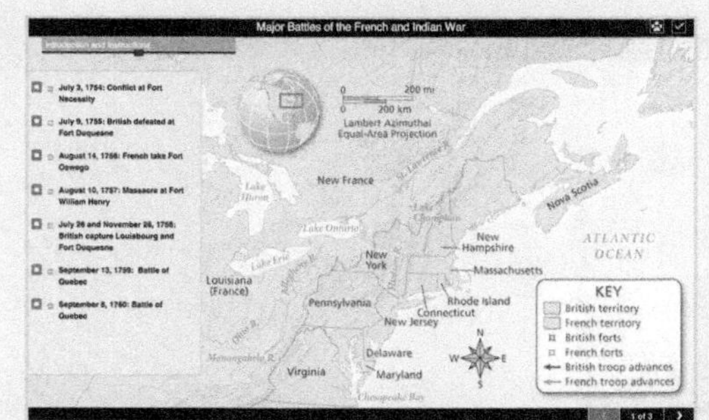

Objective 2: **Identify how mistakes and lack of unity led to British defeats early in the war.**

Quick Instruction

Interactive Map: Major Battles of the French and Indian War Project the map and click through the layers. Ask students how the physical geography of the frontier affected the major battles of the war.

Sequence Events Ask students to give the chronology of events described in the interactive map. *(Washington marched to Great Meadows and was defeated at Fort Necessity; General Braddock was defeated at Fort Duquesne; France captured Fort Oswego; British troops were attacked by Native Americans while fleeing Fort William Henry; Britain captured Louisbourg; France burned Fort Duquesne; Britain captured the fort and renamed it Fort Pitt; Britain captured Quebec; France surrendered.)*

ELL Use the ELL activity described in the ELL chart.

ACTIVE CLASSROOM

Have students use the Cartoon It strategy to draw one compelling image from the texts on a piece of paper. Have students turn their drawing into a political cartoon that illustrates a key concept or main idea. Students can hang their cartoons in the classroom or scan them to a class blog.

Further Instruction

Go through the Interactive Reading Notepad questions for *A Meeting in Albany* and *British Defeats in the Ohio Valley* with the class.

Be sure students understand the reasons for British defeats early in the war. In addition to addressing the physical geographic factors that shaped the war, remind students of the human geographic factors that contributed to British losses, including the lack of British unity and experience with the land in which they fought.

Generate Explanations Explain why British losses strained Britain's alliance with the Iroquois. *(The Iroquois wanted Britain's protection from France and faced further danger from enemy tribes after Britain's early losses.)*

Draw Conclusions Why were the Great Lakes of strategic importance in the war? *(They provided access to areas for trapping and trading in the frontier, allowed for transportation via ships, and connected to rivers used for travel, transportation, and trade.)*

Cite Evidence What evidence suggests British soldiers were unprepared for fighting in the forests of North America? *(The soldiers moved slowly and noisily through the forests so the enemy could track them. Their bright red uniforms made them clear targets.)*

The French and Indian War

DIGITAL TEXT 5

Quebec and New France Fall

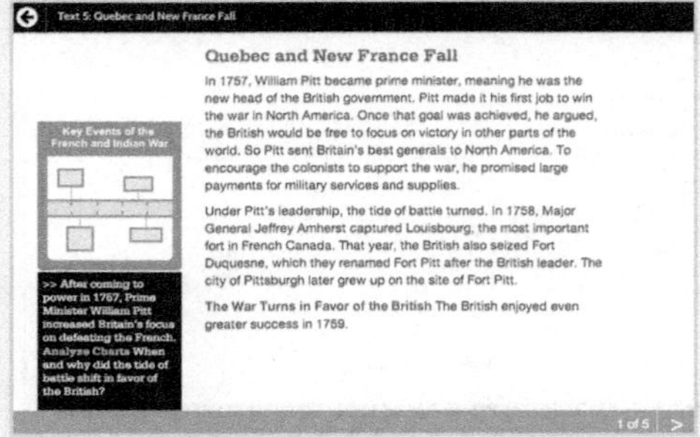

INTERACTIVE CHART

Effects of the French and Indian War

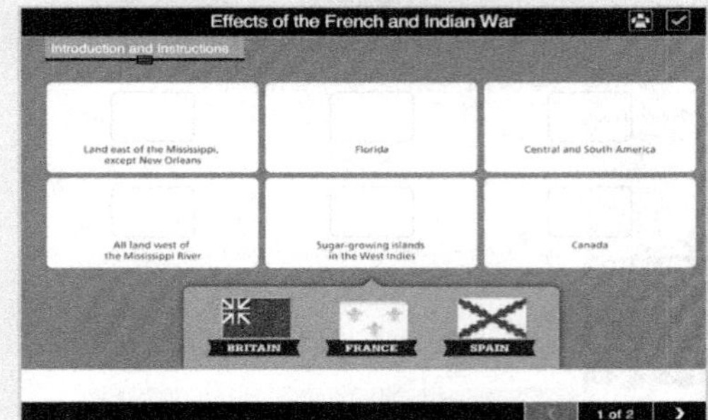

Objectives 3: Summarize how the tide of the war turned in Britain's favor; 4: Explain how the British won the war; 5: Describe the power shift that occurred after the war.

Quick Instruction

Britain won the war when it captured Quebec, a major center of New France. Britain took advantage of the physical geography of the city to launch a surprise attack. Britain's victory shifted the balance of power among European empires in North America.

Interactive Chart: Effects of the French and Indian War Project the interactive chart on the whiteboard and have students read through the table and the flags. Ask students to explain how land in North America was divided after the war.

ACTIVE CLASSROOM

Have students use the Act It Out strategy to explore the fall of Quebec. Project the image of James Wolfe on the whiteboard. Divide students into two groups representing Montcalm's and Wolfe's soldiers and have them bring to life what happened before, during, and after this image. Have students write a short script describing what the soldiers are thinking. Then have them act out their scene.

Summarize What physical geographic features of Quebec did the British exploit to capture the city? *(They took advantage of the river to approach by water. Then they climbed the steep cliff, which the French were not expecting.)*

ELL Use the ELL activity described in the ELL chart.

Further Instruction

Go through the Interactive Reading Notepad questions with the class.

Evaluate Arguments The author writes, "The fall of Quebec sealed the fate of New France." Do you think this is a reasonable claim? Why or why not? *(Yes; Quebec was important to the defense of New France and supplied forts up the St. Lawrence River. Without control over this area, France could not hope to win.)*

Make Generalizations Make a generalization about the power shift in North America following the French and Indian War. *(Britain increased its power and territory over France and Spain.)*

SYNTHESIZE

DIGITAL ACTIVITY

Effects of the French and Indian War

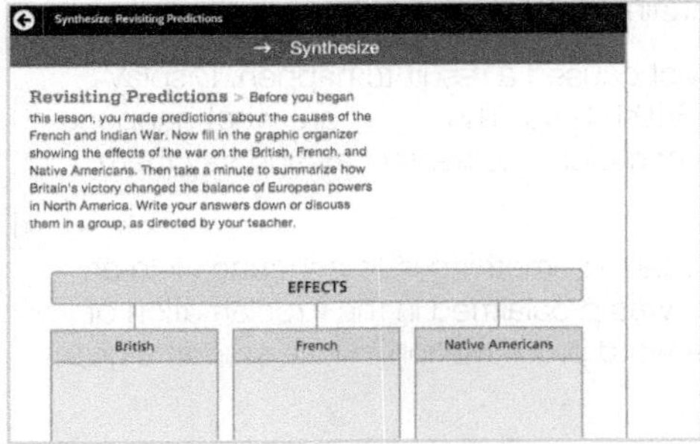

Have students use the Think-Pair-Share Strategy to make predictions about the effects of the French and Indian War in the digital activity. Allow students to work alone or in groups to complete the chart, and then write down or discuss their answers with the class.

Discuss Have students think about the following question. How will Britain's victory affect the colonization of North America? Have students give examples supporting their claims.

DEMONSTRATE

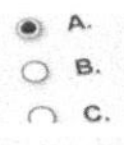

DIGITAL QUIZ

Lesson Quiz and Class Discussion Board

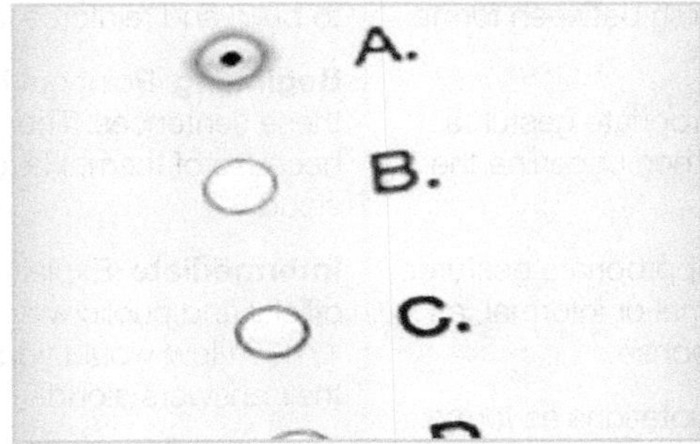

Assign the online Lesson Quiz for this lesson if you haven't already done so. Students will be offered automatic remediation or enrichment based on their score.

Pose these questions to the class on the Discussion Board:

In *The French and Indian War Begins in the Ohio Valley*, you read about the causes, effects, and major events of the French and Indian War, and how these outcomes were influenced by the geography of the region.

Compare and Contrast the physical geographic factors of North America that helped and hindered British soldiers during the war. *(Hindered—soldiers were unfamiliar with fighting in North American forests. They dressed and walked through the woods in ways that made them easy targets. Helped—they used the St. Lawrence River and the cliff on which Quebec is built to their advantage when launching a surprise attack against the city.)*

Identify Central Ideas How did the fighting between Britain and France over the North American frontier impact Native Americans tribes in the region? *(Tribes like the Iroquois were forced to choose sides between the British and the French and became involved in the fighting. The expansion of European colonial powers in the frontier region also threatened Native American lands.)*

Topic Inquiry

Have students continue their investigations for the Topic Inquiry.

Tensions with Britain

Supporting English Language Learners

Use with Digital Text 4, **The Stamp Act Provokes Resistance.**

Learning

Read aloud the section titled, *Resistance to the Stamp Act* or invite volunteers to do so. Point out the section's two quotations (at the end of the first and third paragraphs) to help students distinguish between formal and informal English.

Beginning Read aloud the two quotations, using appropriate gestures and tone of voice. Identify each as formal or informal. Then underline the formal and informal language in each.

Intermediate Read aloud the two quotations, using appropriate gestures and tone of voice. Ask students to identify each as formal or informal, as well as to identify specific words that support their response.

Advanced Ask students to identify each of the two quotations as formal or informal. Then have them read the quotations aloud, using appropriate gestures and tone of voice. Ask how paying attention to gestures and tone can help to identify formal and informal language.

Advanced High Ask students to identify each quotation as formal or informal. Have them read aloud the quotations and then add to them, choosing language that is similar in tone. Ask how they knew whether the language they chose was formal or informal.

Use with Digital Text 7, **The Boston Massacre.**

Speaking

Display the chart titled, *The Rising Tide of Conflict*. Read aloud each of the events, or invite volunteers to do so. Encourage students to respond orally to build and reinforce language attainment.

Beginning Point out how each act caused a result to happen. Display these sentences: The _____ are British laws. The _____ are what happens because of them. Have students complete the sentences and say them aloud.

Intermediate Explain that to proclaim something is to announce it in an official and public way. Ask: What was proclaimed in the Proclamation of 1763? How would you define the word proclamation? Have students give their answers aloud.

Advanced Explain that a tide is the rise or fall of the sea. Ask: What does the title of the chart mean? How else could the same idea be expressed? Have students give their answers aloud.

Advanced High Ask: What did it mean when colonists staged violent protests against the Stamp Act? How is staging a violent protest like and unlike staging a play? Have students give their answers aloud.

D Differentiate Instruction

Use the Differentiated Instruction notes throughout the lesson plan to support the varied skill sets, levels of readiness, and interests in the mixed-ability classroom.

Challenge These notes include suggestions for expanding the activity for advanced students.

On-Level These notes include suggestions for modifying the activity to address different interests or learning styles.

Extra Support These notes include ideas for providing more scaffolding or reading spupport.

Special Needs These notes provide ideas for adapting instruction to support the needs of various special needs students.

NOTES

PEARSON realize™ www.PearsonRealize.com

Go online to access additional resources including:
Primary Sources • Biographies • Supreme Court cases • 21st Century Skill Tutorials • Maps • Graphic Organizers.

Objectives

Objective 1: Describe conflicts in the west after the French and Indian War.

Objective 2: Explain how Britain attempted to ease tensions with the Proclamation of 1763.

Objective 3: Explain why colonists opposed new British taxes such as the Stamp Act.

Objective 4: Describe new colonial leaders who emerged as conflicts with Britain escalated.

Objective 5: Summarize the significance of the Boston Massacre.

LESSON 2 ORGANIZER	PACING: APPROX. 1 PERIOD, .5 BLOCKS		RESOURCES	
	OBJECTIVES	**PACING**	**Online**	**Print**
Connect				
DIGITAL START UP ACTIVITY **The Rights of the Colonists**		5 min.	●	
Investigate				
DIGITAL TEXT 1 **Conflict Over Land**	Objective 1	10 min.	●	●
DIGITAL TEXT 2 **The Proclamation of 1763 Creates Tensions**	Objective 2	10 min.	●	●
DIGITAL TEXT 3 **Mercantilism and Taxation Cause Resentment**	Objective 3	10 min.	●	●
DIGITAL TEXT 4 **The Stamp Act Provokes Resistance**		10 min.	●	●
DIGITAL TEXT 5 **The Townshend Acts Spark Rebellion**		10 min.	●	●
INTERACTIVE CHART **Crisis on the Frontier**		10 min.	●	
DIGITAL TEXT 6 **Colonists Provide Leadership in the Struggle With Britain**	Objective 4	10 min.	●	●
INTERACTIVE GALLERY **Important People of the American Revolution**		10 min.	●	
DIGITAL TEXT 7 **The Boston Massacre**	Objective 5	10 min.	●	●
Synthesize				
DIGITAL ACTIVITY **Causes of the American Revolution**		5 min.	●	
Demonstrate				
DIGITAL QUIZ **Lesson Quiz and Class Discussion Board**		10 min.	●	

Tensions with Britain

CONNECT

DIGITAL START UP ACTIVITY

The Rights of the Colonists

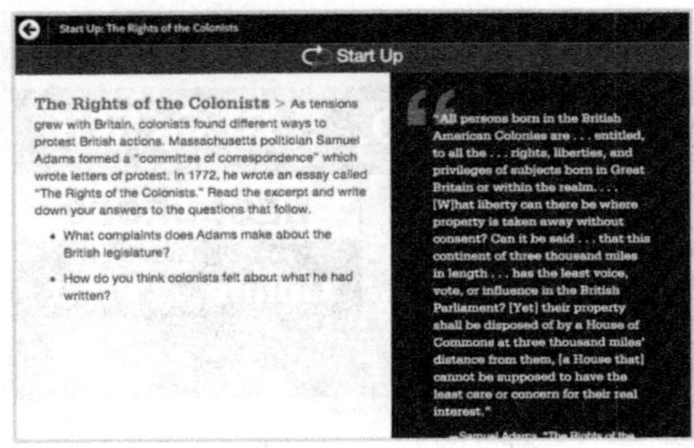

Discuss What complaints does Adams make about the British legislature? *(Property is taken without consent; colonists have no say in British Parliament; Parliament is too removed from the colonies to care about them.)* How do you think colonists felt about what he had written? *(Many colonists probably agreed and felt more strongly anti-British; some colonists probably felt Adams was being disloyal.)*

Tell students that in this lesson they will analyze causes of the American Revolution and learn about the roles significant individuals played during this time.

Aa Vocabulary Development: Use the Interactive Reading Notepad to preview the Key Terms and Academic Vocabulary in this lesson with students.

FLIP IT!

Assign the Flipped Video for this lesson.

STUDENT EDITION PRINT PAGES: 130–140

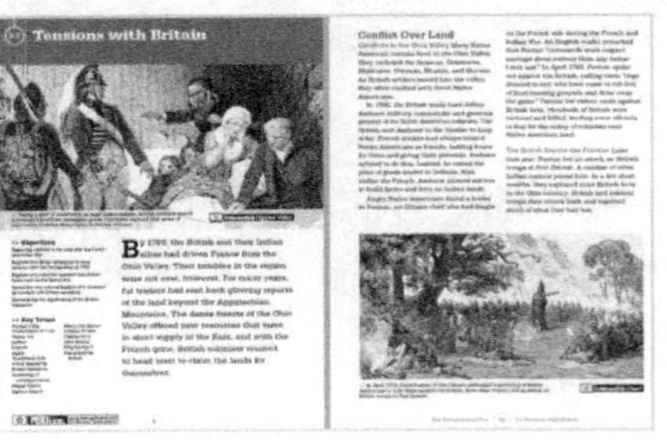

INVESTIGATE

DIGITAL TEXT 1

Conflict Over Land

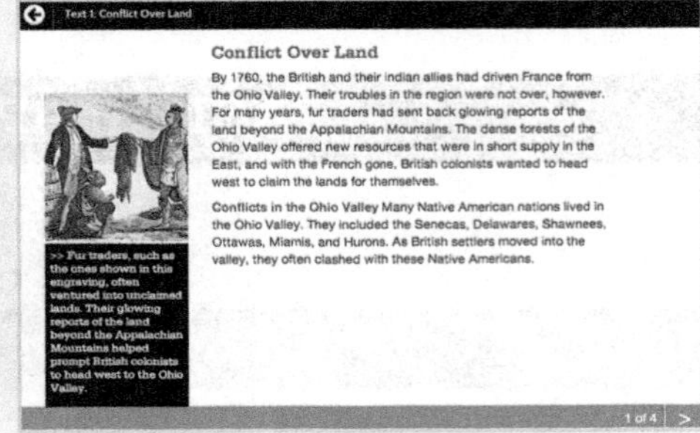

Objective 1: Describe conflicts in the West after the French and Indian War.

Quick Instruction

Project the image of Chief Pontiac. After the French and Indian War, British settlers began heading west to the Ohio Valley. This led to clashes with Native American tribes along the frontier. Ask students to locate the Ohio Valley and explain why conflict erupted in this area.

Hypothesize Why do you think British settlers wanted to move west into the Ohio Valley? *(Exploit new resources; claim land that used to belong to the French)*

Compare and Contrast how French and British settlers interacted with Native Americans in the Ohio Valley. *(French traders treated Native Americans as friends. They held feasts and exchanged gifts. British settlers clashed with Native Americans. They raised prices and cleared land.)*

Further Instruction

Go through the Interactive Reading Notepad questions and discuss the answers with the class. Remind students that the British victory in the French and Indian War meant Britain claimed lands along the frontier that used to belong to the French. Conflicts with Native Americans led to the Proclamation of 1763, which was one of the causes of the American Revolution.

Draw Conclusions How did the Treaty of Paris impact Native Americans on the frontier? *(Native Americans could not turn to the French for help against the encroaching British, because the French no longer had power in the region.)*

Make Predictions Make a prediction about how Pontiac's War and other conflicts between colonists and Native Americans will contribute to the Revolutionary War. *(Colonists may not like British policies regarding Native American tribes and land claims. They may want to make their own decisions about settlements.)*

DIGITAL TEXT 2

The Proclamation of 1763 Creates Tensions

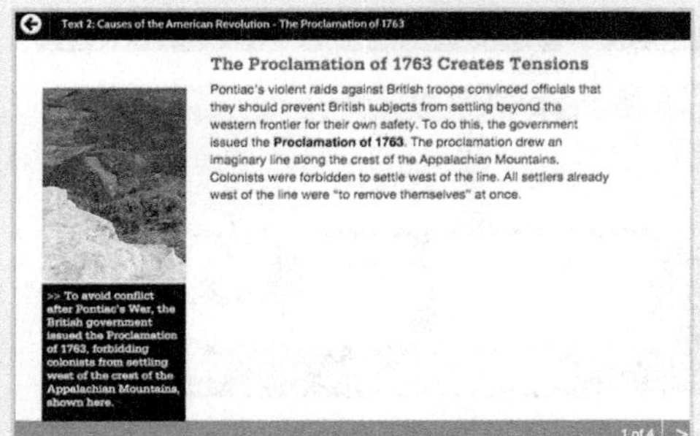

Text 2: Causes of the American Revolution - The Proclamation of 1763
The Proclamation of 1763 Creates Tensions
Pontiac's violent raids against British troops convinced officials that they should prevent British subjects from settling beyond the western frontier for their own safety. To do this, the government issued the Proclamation of 1763. The proclamation drew an imaginary line along the crest of the Appalachian Mountains. Colonists were forbidden to settle west of the line. All settlers already west of the line were "to remove themselves" at once.
>> To avoid conflict after Pontiac's War, the British government issued the Proclamation of 1763, forbidding colonists from settling west of the crest of the Appalachian Mountains, shown here.
1 of 4

Objective 2: Explain how Britain attempted to ease tensions with the Proclamation of 1763.

Quick Instruction

Project the map showing migration west of the Proclamation Line. Explain that colonists were not allowed to settle west of this line.

Sequence Events Explain why Pontiac's War led to the Proclamation of 1763. *(British officials were worried about the safety of settlers and the protection of Native Americans. Pontiac's War led the government to decide that settlers should not provoke conflicts by moving too far west.)*

Analyze Information How did the Proclamation of 1763 contribute to the outbreak of the American Revolution? *(It made colonists angry with the British government for restricting their settlements and keeping land from them. It also made them not want to pay for British policies they had not approved.)*

D Differentiate: Extra Support Explain that a proclamation is an official announcement. The Proclamation of 1763 was an official announcement that created a new rule for settlers.

Further Instruction

Go through the Interactive Reading Notepad questions and discuss the answers with the class. Be sure students analyze how the Proclamation of 1763 was one of the causes of the American Revolution.

Summarize What did the Proclamation of 1763 declare? *(It made an imaginary line along the Appalachian Mountains beyond which colonists could not settle; it created four new spaces for colonists to settle in what used to be Spanish and French territories. These four spaces included Quebec, East Florida, West Florida, and Granada.)*

Determine Point of View What did many colonists think of the Proclamation of 1763, and why? *(They were angered by the Proclamation. They didn't think the British government had the power to tell them where to settle. They thought they had a right to the land and weren't concerned about Native American's rights. They also did not want to pay for the British troops brought over to enforce the rule.)*

DIGITAL TEXT 3

Mercantilism and Taxation Cause Resentment

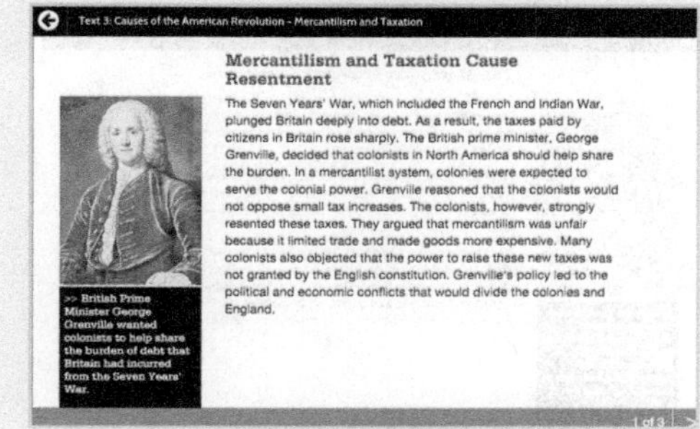

Text 3: Causes of the American Revolution - Mercantilism and Taxation
Mercantilism and Taxation Cause Resentment
The Seven Years' War, which included the French and Indian War, plunged Britain deeply into debt. As a result, the taxes paid by citizens in Britain rose sharply. The British prime minister, George Grenville, decided that colonists in North America should help share the burden. In a mercantilist system, colonies were expected to serve the colonial power. Grenville reasoned that the colonists would not oppose small tax increases. The colonists, however, strongly resented these taxes. They argued that mercantilism was unfair because it limited trade and made goods more expensive. Many colonists also objected that the power to raise these new taxes was not granted by the English constitution. Grenville's policy led to the political and economic conflicts that would divide the colonies and England.
>> British Prime Minister George Grenville wanted colonists to help share the burden of debt that Britain had incurred from the Seven Years' War.
1 of 3

Objective 3: Explain why colonists opposed new British taxes such as the Stamp Act.

Quick Instruction

Interactive Chart: Crisis on the Frontier Project the interactive chart and have students read through the tiles. Explain that there were other causes of the American Revolution in addition to the Proclamation of 1763. Economic policies following the French and Indian War, mercantilism, the Stamp Act, and the lack of representation in Parliament all led to unrest.

Generate Explanations Explain how British economic policies following the French and Indian War were among the causes of the American Revolution. *(Britain raised taxes to pay for its troops and debts from the French and Indian War. Colonists resented paying new taxes without their consent or representation in Parliament.)*

ACTIVE CLASSROOM

List the following policies on the board: Proclamation of 1763, Sugar Act, Stamp Act, Townshend Acts. Have students use the Rank It strategy to rank the policies from most to least influential in causing the American Revolution, providing justifications for their decisions. Poll the class to see if students agree.

ELL Use the ELL activity described in the ELL chart.

Tensions with Britain

DIGITAL TEXT 4

The Stamp Act Provokes Resistance

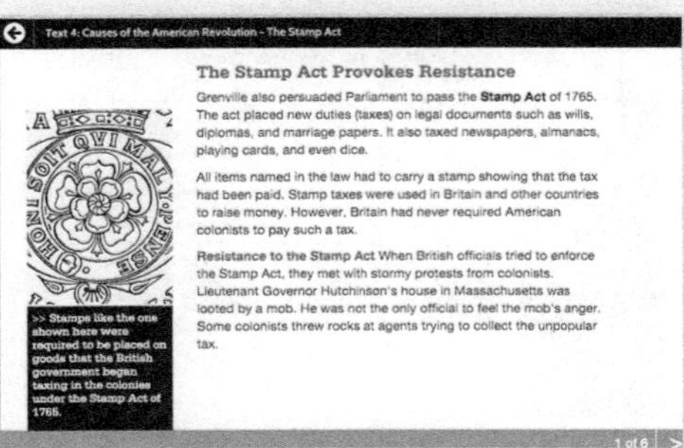

DIGITAL TEXT 5

The Townshend Acts Spark Rebellion

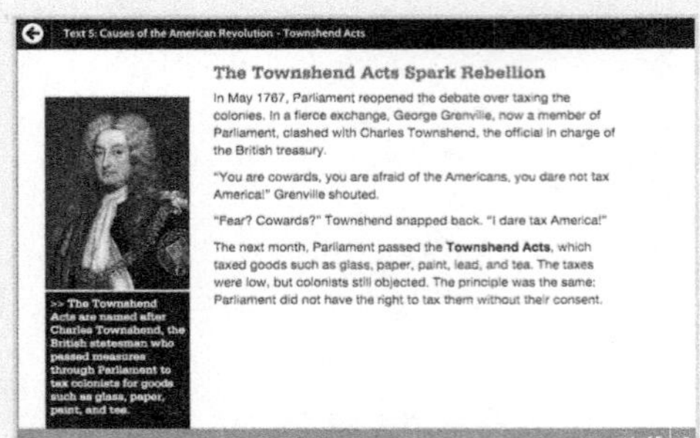

INTERACTIVE CHART

Crisis on the Frontier

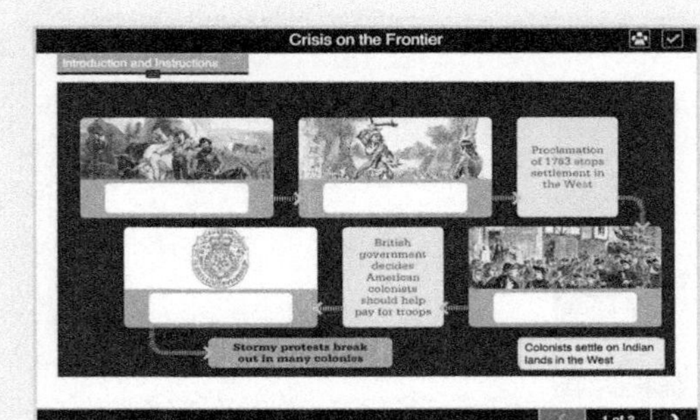

Further Instruction

Go through the Interactive Reading Notepad questions with the class. Assign the additional resource Economics Basics: Core Concepts.

Support Ideas with Evidence What evidence suggests that a free-enterprise system of economics will develop in the new nation? Why did colonists want minimal government intrusion? *(The colonists wanted a free-enterprise system to contribute to economic growth. They hoped to limit government intrusion so that the market, not the government, would determine costs. They looked to a different economic model because they thought British taxes were overly restrictive and limited growth.)*

Cite Evidence that the Stamp Act was an important cause of the American Revolution. *(It united colonists, prompted colonists to send petitions to King George III and Parliament, and led colonists to boycott British goods.)*

Draw Conclusions Why was the lack of representation in Parliament one of the causes of the American Revolution? *(Colonists thought only they or their representatives should be able to impose taxes. They fought to not pay taxes with which they disagreed.)*

PEARSON realize™ **www.PearsonRealize.com** Access your Digital Lesson

DIGITAL TEXT 6

Colonists Provide Leadership in the Struggle With Britain

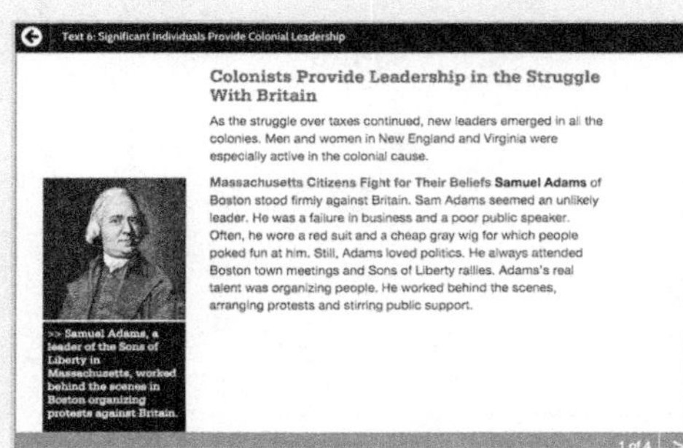

INTERACTIVE GALLERY

Important People of the American Revolution

DIGITAL TEXT 7

The Boston Massacre

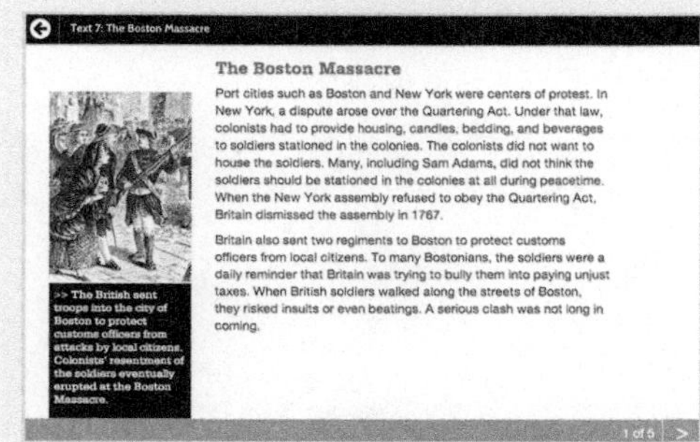

Objective 4: **Describe new colonial leaders who emerged as conflicts with Britain escalated.**

Quick Instruction

Interactive Gallery: Important People of the American Revolution Project the interactive gallery and have students look at the images individually and as a whole. Explain that new leaders emerged to fight for colonists' rights.

Draw Conclusions Ask students how they think significant individuals like those discussed in the gallery shaped colonists' attitudes toward Britain. *(The individuals probably led colonists to feel more strongly against the British and to take action against the crown.)*

ACTIVE CLASSROOM

Have students use the Conversations with History Strategy and suppose they are having a conversation with one of the people in the interactive gallery. Have students select one of the significant individuals and write down a question they would like to ask, what that person would say to them, and what they would say in response.

Further Instruction

Go through the Interactive Reading Notepad questions with the class, including the graphic organizer that sums up the contributions of each colonial leader and how he or she helped the American cause. Be sure students understand the roles played by Mercy Otis Warren, Abigail Adams, Samuel Adams, John Adams, and Patrick Henry in the early stages of the American Revolution. To extend the lesson, assign the primary source readings *Remember the Ladies* (Abigail Adams) and *Give Me Liberty or Give Me Death* (Patrick Henry).

Compare the roles played by Mercy Otis Warren and Abigail Adams leading up to the American Revolution. *(Both used writing to rally colonists against the British and called for women's rights.)*

Summarize How did Samuel Adams contribute to the revolutionary cause? *(He attended meetings and rallies, organized colonists, arranged protests, and generated support for the colonists' cause.)*

Evaluate Arguments What did Patrick Henry mean when he cried, "If this be treason, make the most of it"? What do you think listeners thought of this speech? *(If the colonists were going to be treasonous, they should commit to it and turn against Britain. His comments probably shocked some but encouraged others to fight.)*

Objective 5: **Summarize the significance of the Boston Massacre.**

Quick Instruction

Project the engraving of the Boston Massacre by Paul Revere on the whiteboard. Explain that the Boston Massacre was a violent attack that took place when British soldiers fired into a crowd outside the Boston customs house.

Analyze Images How does Revere's engraving present the events of the massacre? How might this have influenced popular opinion? *(The engraving shows well-organized British soldiers firing into an unarmed crowd. This probably made colonists feel the British were violent, tyrannical, and treating them unfairly.)*

Identify Cause and Effect Name one cause and one effect of the Boston Massacre. *(Cause—colonists were angered by the presence of British soldiers; Effect—anti-British feeling spread among the colonies)*

ELL Use the ELL activity described in the ELL chart.

Further Instruction

Go through the Interactive Reading Notepad questions and discuss the answers with the class. Ask students why the Boston Massacre was an important event in the steps leading up to the American Revolution.

Draw Conclusions Why do you think Crispus Attucks's death played such a significant role in the American Revolution? *(Attucks was one of the first to die in the Boston Massacre. This probably made him an important symbol of the American cause.)*

Tensions with Britain

Identify Patterns How did the actions of King George III shape relations between Britain and the colonies following the massacre? *(Many acts that angered the colonists were ended, including the Townshend Acts and the Quartering Act, but the king still kept the tax on tea. Although relations improved, the change was not permanent.)*

SYNTHESIZE

DIGITAL ACTIVITY

Causes of the American Revolution

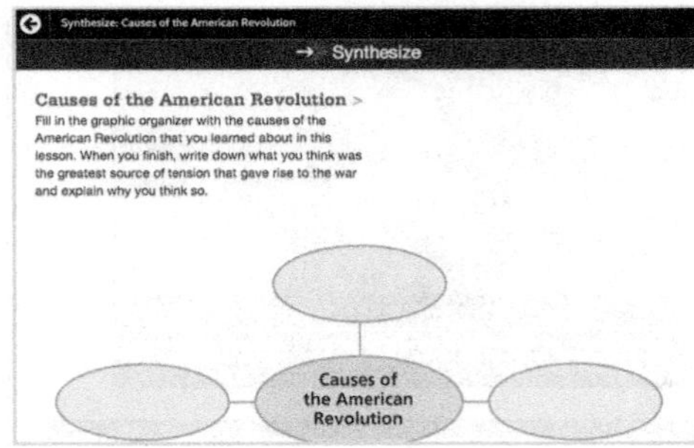

Have students fill in the graphic organizer with the causes of the American Revolution. Then have students write down or discuss with a partner the greatest sources of tension, explaining their reasoning.

Have students think about the following question: What were the colonists' political, economic, and social grievances against Britain, and why did these grievances ultimately lead to war? Have students give examples from the text.

DEMONSTRATE

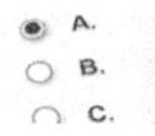

DIGITAL QUIZ

Lesson Quiz and Class Discussion Board

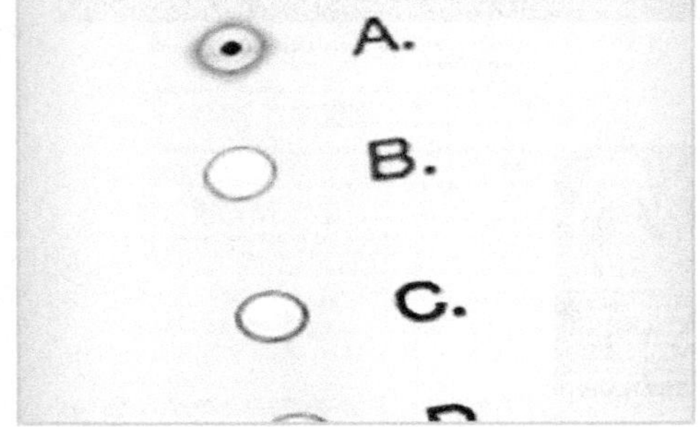

Assign the online Lesson Quiz for this lesson if you haven't already done so. Students will be offered automatic remediation or enrichment based on their score.

Pose these questions to the class on the Discussion Board:

In *Tensions with Britain*, you read about the multiple causes leading to conflicts between the colonists and Britain as well as the significant individuals who led the colonists' cause.

Hypothesize Explain how colonists' anger over the lack of representation may have been expressed in the Declaration of Independence. *(The Declaration of Independence expressed the colonists' desire for a representative government that would defend their rights.)*

Compare and Contrast mercantilism and a free-enterprise system. Which economic policy did colonists favor, and why? *(Mercantilism says that colonies exist to generate wealth for the colonial power. A free-enterprise system is based on minimal government intrusion and lets the market, not the government, set prices. Colonists felt that Britain's mercantilist policies were unfair because they limited trade, increased prices, and led to excessive taxes. Colonists favored a free-enterprise system because it led to economic growth.)*

Topic Inquiry

Have students continue their investigations for the Topic Inquiry.

PEARSON realize™ www.PearsonRealize.com Access your Digital Lesson

Taking Up Arms

Supporting English Language Learners

Use with Digital Text 3, **The Battles of Lexington and Concord.**

Reading

Read aloud the first paragraph of the section's introduction, or invite volunteers to do so. Prompt students to focus on the specific sounds they hear as the introduction is read aloud. Then direct students' attention to specific words and focus on both the relationship between the sounds and corresponding letters in given words.

Beginning Display the word *Massachusetts*. Sound out the syllables, highlighting the corresponding letters as you do so. Then have students sound out the syllables as you highlight the corresponding letters.

Intermediate Display the word *Massachusetts*. As you sound out the word's syllables, have students identify the corresponding groups of letters.

Advanced Display the word *massacre*. As you sound out the word's syllables, have students identify the corresponding groups of letters. Discuss the relationship between the letters *cre* and the sound they represent. Challenge pairs of students to find other words ending with *-cre*.

Advanced High Display the words *minutemen* and *minute*. As you sound out the word's syllables, have students identify the corresponding groups of letters. Ask: In what other way can minute be pronounced? How do you know which way to pronounce it?

Use with Digital Text 4, **The Fighting Continues.**

Learning

Read aloud the section titled, *Vermont Rebels Gain a Route to Canada*, or invite volunteers to do so. Point out the quotation, "Come out, you old rat!" Identify the speaker and his intended audience in order for students to demonstrate increasing knowledge of when to use formal or informal English.

Beginning Explain the meaning of the words *old rat*. Ask: Is this informal or formal language? Help students complete this sentence with a word or phrase: Allen called the commander "old rat" because _____.

Intermediate Ask students to explain the meaning of the quotation and identify it as formal or informal English. Then have them state why Allen would have used such language to call the British commander.

Advanced Have students explain the meaning of the quotation and identify it as formal or informal English. Ask: How do you think the British commander's soldiers addressed him? His wife? His children? Why?

Advanced High Have students identify the quotation as formal or informal English. Then ask them to list other people who might have addressed the British commander and to rank them according to how formally they might have spoken with him. Have pairs of students compare their lists.

D Differentiate Instruction

Use the Differentiated Instruction notes throughout the lesson plan to support the varied skill sets, levels of readiness, and interests in the mixed-ability classroom.

Challenge These notes include suggestions for expanding the activity for advanced students.

On-Level These notes include suggestions for modifying the activity to address different interests or learning styles.

Extra Support These notes include ideas for providing more scaffolding or reading spupport.

Special Needs These notes provide ideas for adapting instruction to support the needs of various special needs students.

NOTES

Topic 3 Lesson 3

Taking Up Arms

Objectives

Objective 1: Explain how a dispute over tea led to further tension between the colonists and Great Britain.

Objective 2: Describe ways that the British Parliament punished the colonists for the Boston Tea Party.

Objective 3: Explain how fighting broke out in Massachusetts, including battles in Lexington and Concord and Bunker Hill.

Objective 4: Explain actions the First and Second Continental Congress enacted to address the crisis with Britain.

Objective 5: Describe the advantages and disadvantages of Britain and the colonists as the war began.

LESSON 3 ORGANIZER	PACING: APPROX. 1 PERIOD, .5 BLOCKS		RESOURCES	
	OBJECTIVES	PACING	Online	Print
Connect				
DIGITAL START UP ACTIVITY **Civil Disobedience in the Colonies**		5 min.	●	
Investigate				
DIGITAL TEXT 1 **The Boston Tea Party**	Objective 1	10 min.	●	●
DIGITAL TEXT 2 **King George III Strikes Back at Boston**	Objective 2	10 min.	●	●
DIGITAL TEXT 3 **The Battles of Lexington and Concord**	Objective 3	10 min.	●	●
DIGITAL TEXT 4 **The Fighting Continues**	Objective 4	10 min.	●	●
DIGITAL TEXT 5 **Opposing Sides at War**	Objective 5	10 min.	●	●
DIGITAL TEXT 6 **The War Comes to Boston**		10 min.	●	●
INTERACTIVE CHART **Advantages and Disadvantages of the British and Colonists**		10 min.	●	
Synthesize				
DIGITAL ACTIVITY **From Protests to War**		5 min.	●	
Demonstrate				
DIGITAL QUIZ **Lesson Quiz and Class Discussion Board**		10 min.	●	

Go online to access additional resources including:
Primary Sources • Biographies • Supreme Court cases • 21st Century Skill Tutorials • Maps • Graphic Organizers.

CONNECT

DIGITAL START UP ACTIVITY

Civil Disobedience in the Colonies

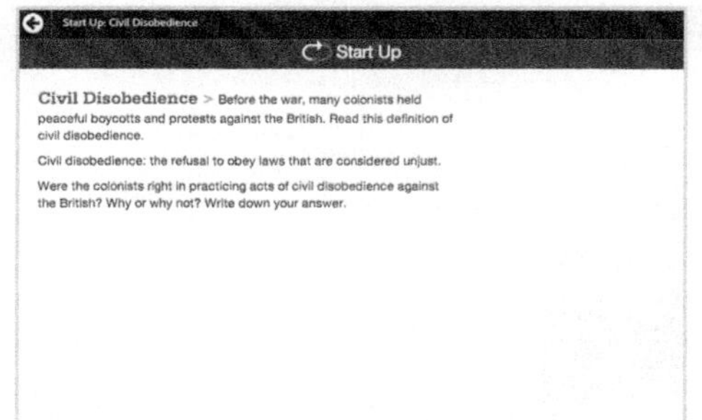

Project the Start Up Activity Ask students to read the definition of civil disobedience as they enter and get settled. Then have them write down their answers and share them with another student, either in class or through a chat or blog space.

Discuss Were the colonists right to practice acts of civil disobedience against the British? Why or why not? *(Answers will vary but should explain why students do or do not think the colonists were right.)*

Tell students that in this lesson they will learn about the causes of the American Revolution, the outbreak of war at the Battles of Lexington and Concord, and the roles of significant individuals who advanced the American cause.

Aa Vocabulary Development: Use the Interactive Reading Notepad to preview the Key Terms and Academic Vocabulary in this lesson with students.

FLIP IT!

Assign the Flipped Video for this lesson.

STUDENT EDITION PRINT PAGES: 141–152

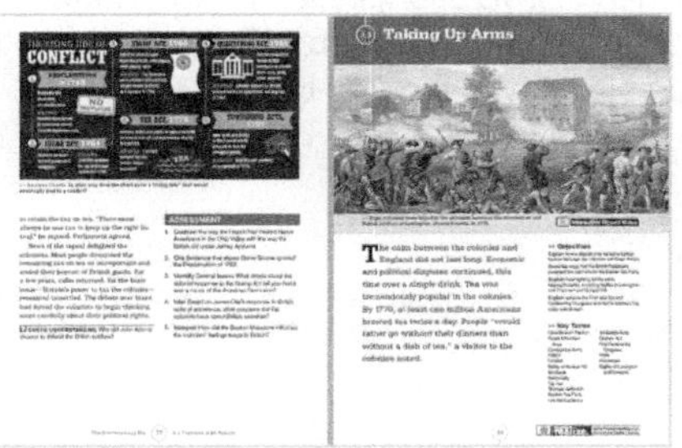

INVESTIGATE

DIGITAL TEXT 1

The Boston Tea Party

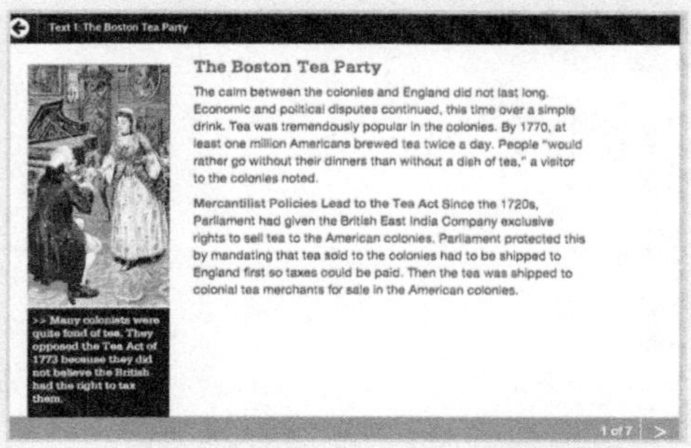

Objective 1: Explain how a dispute over tea led to further tension between the colonists and Great Britain.

Quick Instruction

Colonists opposed taxes on tea because they did not think Britain had the right to tax them. They launched a protest in Boston Harbor known as the Boston Tea Party.

Interactive Illustration: Boston Tea Party Project the interactive illustration and click through the images. Have students explain in their own words the sequence of events leading up to the Boston Tea Party, identifying the location of each incident.

Express Problems Clearly What were the reasons for the civil disobedience of the Boston Tea Party? What might be the impact of the Tea Party? *(Colonists objected to British taxes on tea and the Tea Act. They dumped tea into the harbor when British ships carrying the tea would not leave the harbor without unloading it. The colonists may end up being punished for their actions.)*

ACTIVE CLASSROOM

Have students use the Graffiti Concepts Strategy to create a visual image and/or phrase that represents the concept of civil disobedience. Ask students to post their "graffiti" on the board or on chart paper. Have students look at the visuals and discuss similarities and differences in the responses as a group.

D Differentiate: Extra Support Review the definition of civil disobedience: the nonviolent refusal to obey laws. Explain that boycotting British tea and dumping it into the harbor were acts of civil disobedience. Ask students to come up with other examples of civil disobedience.

Further Instruction

Go through the Interactive Reading Notepad questions and discuss the answers with the class. Review the reasons for and impact of the Boston Tea Party.

Support Ideas with Examples What examples show that Samuel Adams played a significant role in instigating the Boston Tea Party? *(Adams organized the gathering at the Old South Meeting House. He wanted the governor to allow ships in the harbor to leave without unloading their tea. When the governor refused, Adams declared the meeting could do no more. This seemed to be a signal for colonists to go to the harbor, suggesting he had a role in planning what was going to happen.)*

Identify Central Issues How did British economic policies following the French and Indian War, such as mercantilism, contribute to the Boston Tea Party? *(Due to mercantilist policies that generated wealth for Britain, colonists paid taxes on tea and were cut out of the tea trade. Colonists resisted these policies, and this resistance led to the Boston Tea Party.)*

Taking Up Arms

DIGITAL TEXT 2

King George III Strikes Back at Boston

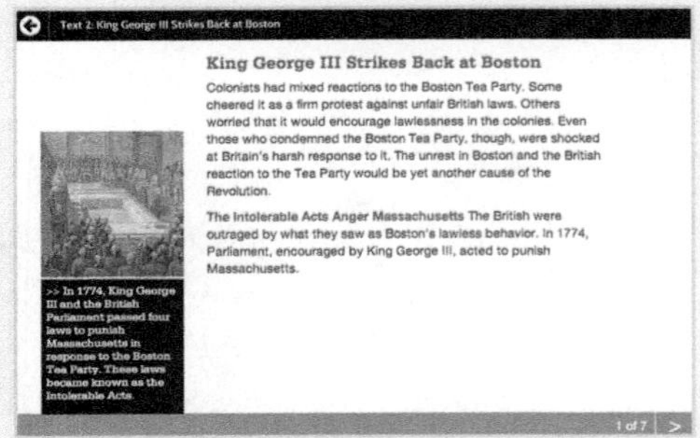

Text 2: King George III Strikes Back at Boston
King George III Strikes Back at Boston
Colonists had mixed reactions to the Boston Tea Party. Some cheered it as a firm protest against unfair British laws. Others worried that it would encourage lawlessness in the colonies. Even those who condemned the Boston Tea Party, though, were shocked at Britain's harsh response to it. The unrest in Boston and the British reaction to the Tea Party would be yet another cause of the Revolution.
The Intolerable Acts Anger Massachusetts The British were outraged by what they saw as Boston's lawless behavior. In 1774, Parliament, encouraged by King George III, acted to punish Massachusetts.
>> In 1774, King George III and the British Parliament passed four laws to punish Massachusetts in response to the Boston Tea Party. These laws became known as the Intolerable Acts.
1 of 7 >

Objective 2: **Describe ways that the British Parliament punished the colonists for the Boston Tea Party.**

Quick Instruction

Project the image of the British warships in Boston Harbor. Explain that King George III of England was outraged by the Boston Tea Party and acted with Parliament to punish the colonists.

Summarize What were the Intolerable Acts, and why were they a cause of the American Revolution? *(The Intolerable Acts closed Boston's port, limited Massachusetts town meetings, allowed officials to be tried outside the state, and imposed a new Quartering Act. These laws angered the colonists, furthering their desire for independence.)*

Further Instruction

Go through the Interactive Reading Notepad questions with the class, including the graphic organizer on the Intolerable Acts. As students read, have them take notes about each act and why the colonists opposed it. Be sure students understand how the Intolerable Acts contributed to the Revolution.

Cite Evidence that Thomas Jefferson strongly opposed the Intolerable Acts. (See the heading *The Intolerable Acts Draw Other Colonies into the Struggle* for assistance with this answer.) *(Thomas Jefferson suggested that a day be set aside to mark the shame of the Intolerable Acts.)*

Draw Conclusions How did the physical geography of Boston lead the city to suffer as a result of the Intolerable Acts? *(Boston was a port city. When Parliament shut down the port, the city's economy declined.)*

Generate Explanations Explain why the extension of Quebec strained relations between the colonists and Parliament. *(Parliament gave land that some American colonists had already claimed to French Canada. These colonists did not want Parliament making decisions about their settlements.)*

DIGITAL TEXT 3

The Battles of Lexington and Concord

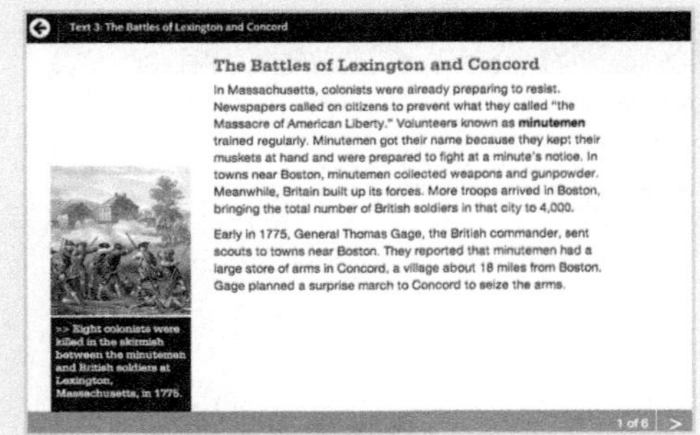

Objective 3: **Explain how fighting broke out in Massachusetts, including the Battles of Lexington and Concord and Bunker Hill.**

Quick Instruction

Analyze Maps Project the map showing the initial battles of the American Revolution. Have students locate Lexington and Concord and explain their importance. *(They were where the first battles of the American Revolution occurred.)*

Sequence Events leading up to the Battles of Lexington and Concord. *(Minutemen collected weapons; British troops marched to Concord to get the weapons; colonists signaled the arrival of the British; the minutemen confronted the British in Lexington; a shot was fired; the British advanced to Concord where colonial troops met them; more fighting broke out.)*

ELL Use the ELL activity described in the ELL chart.

Further Instruction

Go through the Interactive Reading Notepad questions with the class. Discuss the issues surrounding the important early events of the American Revolution, including the Battles of Lexington and Concord. Be sure students understand why the war began.

Infer What can you infer about the minutemen based on the fighting at Lexington and Concord? *(They were organized, because they were able to signal each other using lamps hung from the Old North Church. That they had been collecting weapons and were prepared to fight suggests they expected a battle to break out.)*

Draw Conclusions How did the physical geography of New England affect the Battles of Lexington and Concord? Why did the colonists have an advantage in this location? *(Colonists could signal each other across the river in Boston and prepare to meet the British in Lexington. At Concord, colonists hid in the woods to fire at the British and then took cover behind the trees.)*

DIGITAL TEXT 4

The Fighting Continues

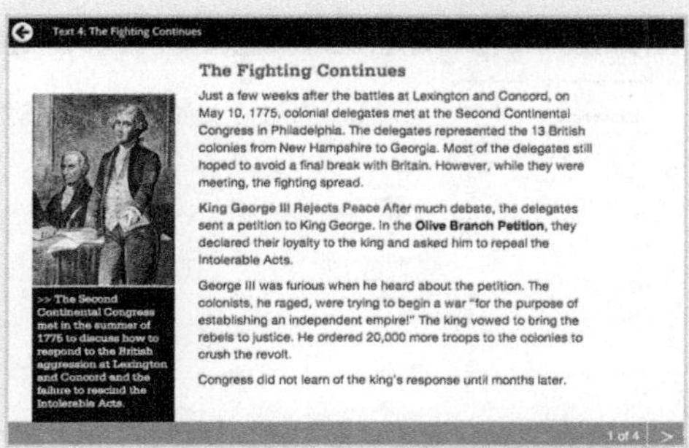

The Fighting Continues

Just a few weeks after the battles at Lexington and Concord, on May 10, 1775, colonial delegates met at the Second Continental Congress in Philadelphia. The delegates represented the 13 British colonies from New Hampshire to Georgia. Most of the delegates still hoped to avoid a final break with Britain. However, while they were meeting, the fighting spread.

King George III Rejects Peace After much debate, the delegates sent a petition to King George. In the **Olive Branch Petition**, they declared their loyalty to the king and asked him to repeal the Intolerable Acts.

George III was furious when he heard about the petition. The colonists, he raged, were trying to begin a war "for the purpose of establishing an independent empire!" The king vowed to bring the rebels to justice. He ordered 20,000 more troops to the colonies to crush the revolt.

Congress did not learn of the king's response until months later.

>> The Second Continental Congress met in the summer of 1775 to discuss how to respond to the British aggression at Lexington and Concord and the failure to rescind the Intolerable Acts.

Objective 4: **Explain actions the First and Second Continental Congress enacted to address the crisis with Britain.**

Quick Instruction

Project the image of George Washington. Explain that Washington played an important role by leading the Continental Army. Washington was appointed by the Second Continental Congress, which formed to address the growing crisis.

Draw Conclusions What do you think the appointment of Washington as commander of the Continental Army signaled to Britain? *(The colonists were putting together an army and were serious about seeking independence.)*

ELL Use the ELL activity described in the ELL chart.

Further Instruction

Go through the Interactive Reading Notepad questions with the class. Be sure students understand the significant roles King George III and George Washington played in the early stages of the war.

Determine Point of View What did King George III think about the colonists' desire for independence? How do you know? *(He thought the rebellion was unacceptable. He was angry that the colonists were trying to establish independence. This is evident by his rejection of the Olive Branch Petition and his decision to send troops to end the revolt.)*

Summarize Why was Vermont so important in the early battles of the war? *(The seizure of Fort Ticonderoga in Vermont gave the Green Mountain Boys a supply of cannons and gunpowder as well as strategic access to routes into Canada.)*

Evaluate Arguments Do you agree with John Adams and Samuel Adams that war could not be avoided? Explain your reasoning. *(Yes; since the king rejected the Olive Branch Petition and sent more troops to the colonies, there was nothing the colonists could do to maintain the peace.)*

Taking Up Arms

DIGITAL TEXT 5

Opposing Sides at War

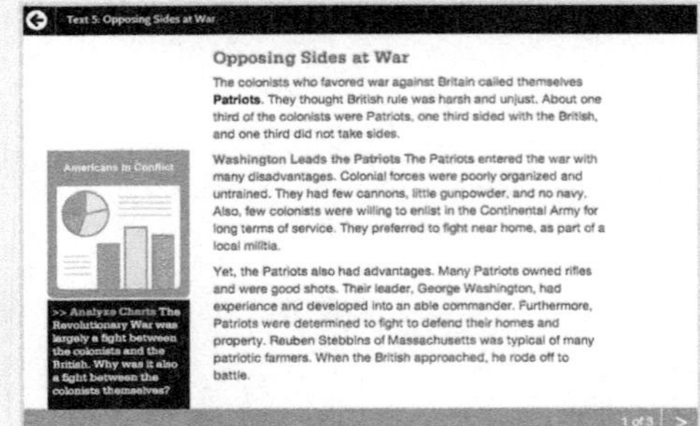

INTERACTIVE CHART

Advantages and Disadvantages of the British and Colonists

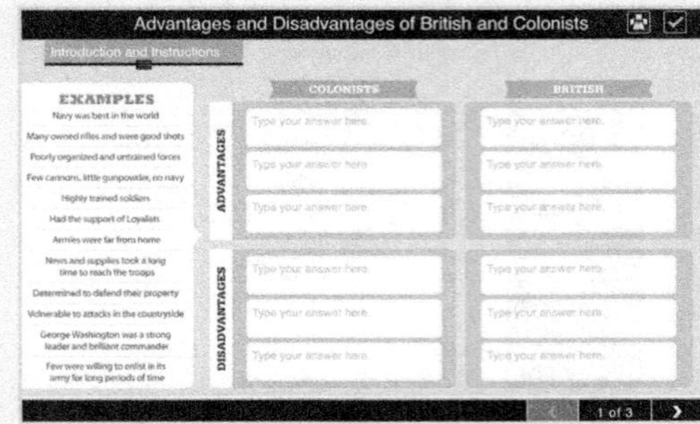

DIGITAL TEXT 6

The War Comes to Boston

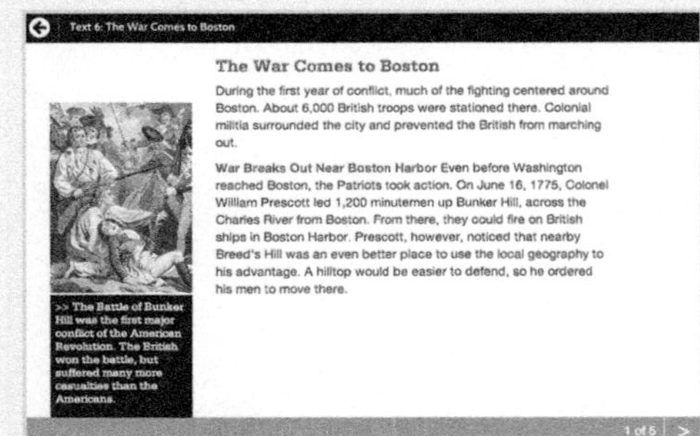

Objective 5: Describe the advantages and disadvantages of Britain and the colonists as the war began.

Quick Instruction

Not all colonists wanted independence. Patriots favored war. Loyalists supported Britain. Other colonists did not take sides. There were more Patriots in the New England colonies, which was where most of the fighting centered in the first year of the war.

Interactive Chart: Advantages and Disadvantages of the British and Colonists Project the interactive chart and have students read through the possible answers. Ask students which side they think had the greatest advantages going into the war, using the chart to support their reasoning.

Identify Cause and Effect How did the physical geography of Boston impact the Battle of Bunker Hill? *(Patriots used the high elevation of the hill to fire down on British ships in the harbor. The British traveled by river and then pushed up the hills. Although the British won, this vulnerable approach left many of their soldiers wounded or dead.)*

Identify Central Issues What factors caused Patriots to fight for independence? *(They opposed British policies; they thought British rule was harsh and unjust; they wanted to defend their homes and properties.)*

ACTIVE CLASSROOM

Divide students into groups and have them use the PMI Strategy to consider the importance of the Battle of Bunker Hill. Have groups create a three-column organizer with the headings Plus/Minus/Interesting. Have groups use the organizer to record their responses to the questions: What were the positive outcomes of the Battle of Bunker Hill for the Patriots? What were the negative outcomes? What is interesting about this battle?

Further Instruction

Go through the Interactive Reading Notepad questions and discuss the answers with the class.

Draw Conclusions How did Washington serve to unite the colonists following the Battle of Bunker Hill? *(He got soldiers from different colonies to work together and form a trained army.)*

Make a Prediction about how colonists will respond to King George III's blockade. *(They will probably be even more angered. They may have to find ways around the blockade. This could help them come together and form a more organized army.)*

SYNTHESIZE

DIGITAL ACTIVITY

From Protests to War

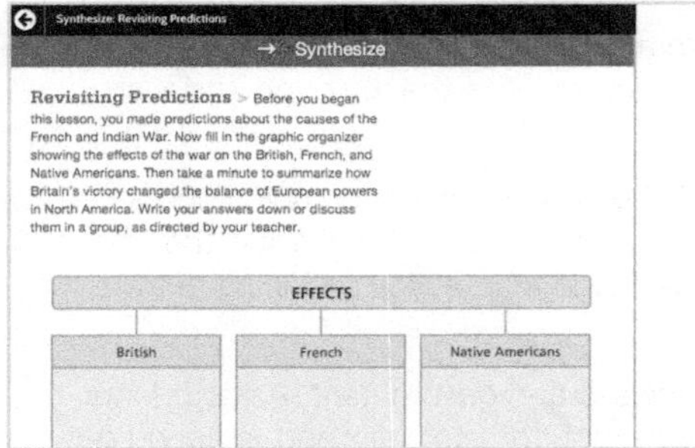

Have students create a timeline of dates, people, and events from the lesson, using the sample timeline to get started. Have students choose one event on their timeline and write down its significance. Discuss with the class what events students chose.

Discuss Have students think about the following question: What were the major causes of the American Revolution? Have students consider the political, economic, and social reasons the colonists went to war.

DEMONSTRATE

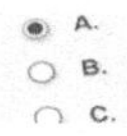

DIGITAL QUIZ

Lesson Quiz and Class Discussion Board

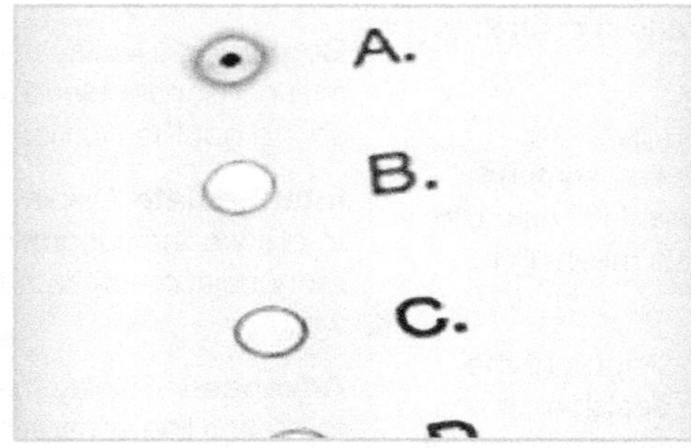

Assign the online Lesson Quiz for this lesson if you haven't already done so. Students will be offered automatic remediation or enrichment based on their score.

Pose these questions to the class on the Discussion Board:

In *Taking Up Arms*, you read about the causes of the American Revolution, the location and importance of major early battles, and the roles of significant individuals as fighting broke out.

Identify Patterns Why do you think King George III and Parliament passed increasingly strict measures against the colonists? Do you think this approach was successful, from the point of view of the British? *(They wanted the colonists to serve Britain and hoped stronger punishments would end the revolt; this approach was not successful because it led many colonists to favor independence.)*

Support a Point of View with Evidence The Declaration of Independence details why the colonists chose to "dissolve the political bands" that tied them to Britain. Name one British political or economic policy and explain why it caused the colonists to make this declaration. *(The Quartering Act—colonists resented having troops in the colonies during peacetime, did not want the troops enforcing British taxes, and felt that hosting the troops was an imposition and another tax.)*

Topic Inquiry

Have students continue their investigations for the Topic Inquiry.

Declaring Independence

Supporting English Language Learners

Use with Digital Text 2, **Choosing Independence.**

Learning

Read aloud the first paragraph of the section titled, *Drafting the Declaration of Independence*. Explain the terms *literal* and *figurative* in order to help students add the ability to analyze sayings and expressions in context to their repertoire of learning strategies.

Beginning Have students act out the verb *face* and complete this sentence: I face the _____. Then display the paragraph's first sentence. Have students face a sign with the question "What will we do?" Ask: Did the delegates really do this? Guide students to a figurative meaning for *faced*.

Intermediate Display the paragraph's first sentence and highlight the word *faced*. Ask: Are the delegates physically facing the decision? If not, what are they doing? Have students write new sentences that replace the word *faced* with a synonymous word or phrase.

Advanced Display the paragraph, and highlight the phrase *no turning back*. Ask students to explain the phrase and determine whether it is literal or figurative. Have them communicate the same idea using other language.

Advanced High Display the paragraph, and highlight the phrases *no turning back* and *fell into British hands*. Discuss the literal and figurative meanings of these expressions. Ask: Which meanings are appropriate for this paragraph? Why do you think figurative expressions were used?

Use with Digital Text 3, **The Declaration of Independence.**

Reading

Read aloud the first page of the text, or invite volunteers to do so. Review the concept of decoding, or sounding out, unknown words when reading.

Beginning Display the words *birth* and *with*. Have students underline the final consonant blend in each. Together, practice the *th* sound and then sound out the words.

Intermediate Display the words *followed* and *endowed*. Ask students to draw a line separating each verb's root from its suffix. Review the pronunciation of the suffix, and have students practice sounding out the words.

Advanced Display the words *happiness* and *government*. Ask students to draw a line separating each word's root from its suffix and to sound out the words. Have pairs of students think of other words with these same suffixes and practice pronouncing them.

Advanced High Display the words *inalienable* and *independence*. Ask students to draw lines separating each word's prefix, root, and suffix. Have them sound out the words. Then ask: What other words share these word parts? How can your prior knowledge help you pronounce them?

D Differentiate Instruction

Use the Differentiated Instruction notes throughout the lesson plan to support the varied skill sets, levels of readiness, and interests in the mixed-ability classroom.

Challenge These notes include suggestions for expanding the activity for advanced students.

On-Level These notes include suggestions for modifying the activity to address different interests or learning styles.

Extra Support These notes include ideas for providing more scaffolding or reading spupport.

Special Needs These notes provide ideas for adapting instruction to support the needs of various special needs students.

NOTES

PEARSON realize™ www.PearsonRealize.com

Go online to access additional resources including: Primary Sources • Biographies • Supreme Court cases • 21st Century Skill Tutorials • Maps • Graphic Organizers.

Objectives

Objective 1: Describe the impact of Thomas Paine's pamphlet, *Common Sense*.

Objective 2: Explain the steps Congress took to declare independence.

Objective 3: Summarize the main ideas of the Declaration of Independence.

LESSON 4 ORGANIZER	PACING: APPROX. 1 PERIOD, .5 BLOCKS			
			RESOURCES	
	OBJECTIVES	PACING	Online	Print
Connect				
DIGITAL START UP ACTIVITY **Why He Fought**		5 min.	●	
Investigate				
DIGITAL TEXT 1 **Thomas Paine's *Common Sense***	Objective 1	10 min.	●	●
INTERACTIVE GALLERY **Thomas Paine's *Common Sense***		10 min.	●	
DIGITAL TEXT 2 **Choosing Independence**	Objective 2	10 min.	●	●
DIGITAL TEXT 3 **The Declaration of Independence**	Objective 3	10 min.	●	●
INTERACTIVE GALLERY **Interactive Declaration of Independence**		10 min.	●	
Synthesize				
DIGITAL ACTIVITY **Reasons for Going to War**		5 min.	●	
Demonstrate				
DIGITAL QUIZ **Lesson Quiz and Class Discussion Board**		10 min.	●	

Declaring Independence

CONNECT

DIGITAL START UP ACTIVITY

Why He Fought

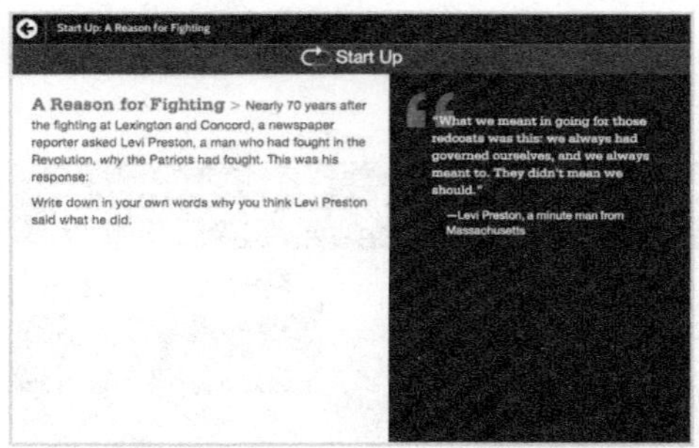

Project the Start Up Activity Ask students to read the quote as they enter and get settled. Have them discuss with partners what Preston said and then write down in their own words why they think he said it.

Discuss Write down in your own words why you think Levi Preston said what he did. *(Answers should address Preston's desire for self-government.)*

Tell students that in this lesson they will be learning about the roles significant individuals played during the American Revolution, the contributions of the Founding Fathers, and the drafting and adoption of the Declaration of Independence.

Aa Vocabulary Development: Use the Interactive Reading Notepad to preview the Key Terms and Academic Vocabulary in this lesson with students.

FLIP IT!

Assign the Flipped Video for this lesson.

STUDENT EDITION PRINT PAGES: 153–157

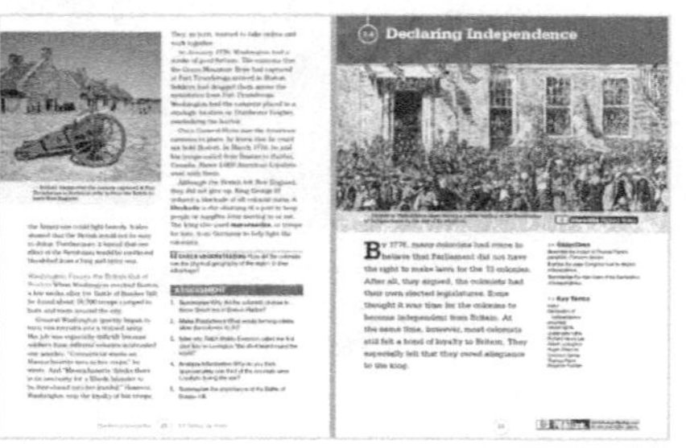

INVESTIGATE

DIGITAL TEXT 1

Thomas Paine's Common Sense

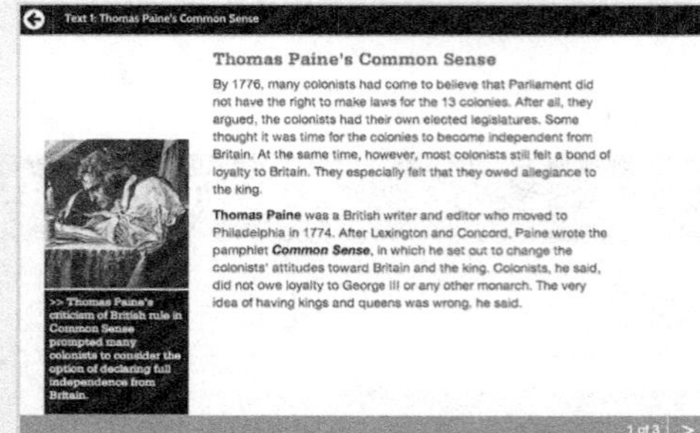

Text 1: Thomas Paine's Common Sense
Thomas Paine's Common Sense
By 1776, many colonists had come to believe that Parliament did not have the right to make laws for the 13 colonies. After all, they argued, the colonists had their own elected legislatures. Some thought it was time for the colonies to become independent from Britain. At the same time, however, most colonists still felt a bond of loyalty to Britain. They especially felt that they owed allegiance to the king.
Thomas Paine was a British writer and editor who moved to Philadelphia in 1774. After Lexington and Concord, Paine wrote the pamphlet ***Common Sense***, in which he set out to change the colonists' attitudes toward Britain and the king. Colonists, he said, did not owe loyalty to George III or any other monarch. The very idea of having kings and queens was wrong, he said.
>> Thomas Paine's criticism of British rule in Common Sense prompted many colonists to consider the option of declaring full independence from Britain.
1 of 3

INTERACTIVE GALLERY

Thomas Paine's Common Sense

Objective 1: Describe the impact of Thomas Paine's pamphlet *Common Sense*.

Quick Instruction

Born in England, Thomas Paine moved to the colonies in 1774. He played a significant role in inspiring the American Revolution. His influential pamphlet *Common Sense* encouraged the colonists to declare independence.

Interactive Gallery: Thomas Paine's *Common Sense* Project the interactive gallery and click through the images. Ask students to explain Paine's vision of government. Discuss why it seemed radical at the time.

Paraphrase Have students read the quote from *Common Sense* in the lesson and restate it in their own words. *(The king does little, and most of what he does do makes the nation worse. An honest man is worth more than a king.)*

ACTIVE CLASSROOM

Have students use the Make Headlines Strategy to write a headline that captures the most important aspect of Paine's *Common Sense* that should be remembered. Have students share their headlines with a partner to review.

Further Instruction

Go through the Interactive Reading Notepad questions and discuss the answers with the class. To extend the lesson, assign the primary source *Common Sense* (Thomas Paine) and the biography of Thomas Paine.

Be sure students understand the main ideas put forth in *Common Sense* and the important role Paine played in the American Revolution. Paine's assertions that the colonists did not owe loyalty to Britain and could form their own representative government prompted many to consider independence.

Draw Conclusions How did Thomas Paine influence the Declaration of Independence? *(Paine helped inspire the change from monarchy to a new, independent government. His pamphlets compelled the colonists to identify natural rights held by all people and to list their grievances against the king.)*

Determine Point of View Why did Paine think the colonists should declare independence? *(Britain wasn't looking out for the colonists' best interests; Parliament didn't have the right to make laws for the colonies; colonists didn't owe allegiance to the crown.)*

DIGITAL TEXT 2

Choosing Independence

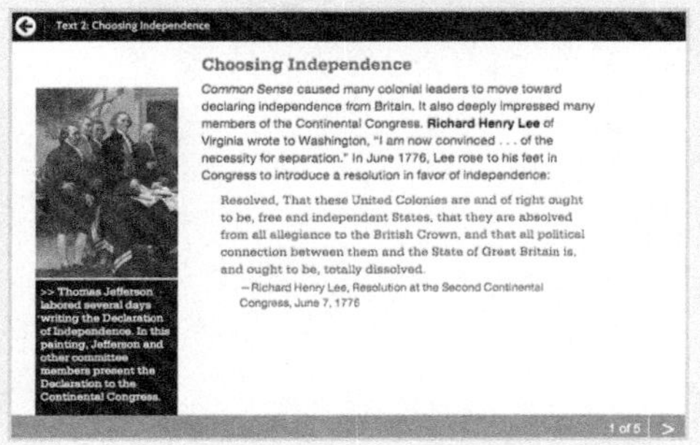

Objective 2: **Explain the steps the Congress took to declare independence.**

Quick Instruction

Project the image of the Declaration of Independence. Explain the significance of 1776, the year when the declaration was adopted, and the year some consider to be the birth of the United States. Review the factors that caused the colonies to declare independence from Britain.

Identify Steps in a Process Why was the adoption of the Declaration of Independence an important event in the American Revolution and a necessary step in the process of achieving independence? *(It made the separation from Britain public and official.)*

Determine Point of View How do you think Loyalists and those who did not take sides in the war felt about the decision to declare independence? *(They probably opposed the declaration. Loyalists may have been afraid of being targeted by Patriots and concerned about the direction the country was headed. Some may have fled the colonies.)*

D Differentiate: Challenge Have students select one of the founders such as John Adams, Benjamin Franklin, or Thomas Jefferson and research his contributions to the Declaration of Independence. Have students use the information they gather to write a short speech from that person's perspective convincing other colonists to support independence. Students may deliver their speeches to the class.

ELL Use the ELL activity described in the ELL chart.

Further Instruction

Go through the Interactive Reading Notepad questions and discuss the answers with the class. To extend the lesson, assign the primary sources *Virginia Declaration of Rights* and *Virginia Statute for Religious Freedom* (Thomas Jefferson) as well as the biography of Benjamin Franklin.

Generate Explanations Why was it risky for the colonies to declare independence? Why do you think the Continental Congress decided to take this risk? *(Britain would consider the colonists traitors and punish them if they lost the war. The Congress felt independence was worth the potential costs.)*

Identify Steps in a Process How did Thomas Jefferson, John Adams, and Benjamin Franklin contribute to the process of separating from Britain? *(They served on the committee charged with telling the world the colonies were separating from Britain. Jefferson drafted the Declaration of Independence, which the other delegates then approved.)*

Predict Consequences Make a prediction about what the effects of signing the Declaration of Independence will be. *(Both sides will intensify the war effort. Other countries will decide whether to recognize the new nation or side with Britain.)*

DIGITAL TEXT 3

The Declaration of Independence

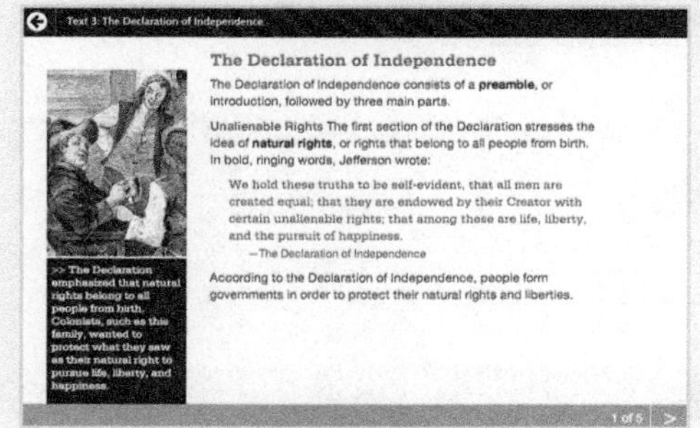

Objective 3: **Summarize the main ideas of the Declaration of Independence.**

Quick Instruction

Interactive Gallery: Interactive Declaration of Independence Project the interactive gallery and click through the hotspots. Review the sections of the Declaration: the Preamble, the discussion of natural rights, the list of grievances, and the assertion of independence.

Identify Central Issues Why was it so radical for the Declaration of Independence to assert that government requires the "consent of the governed"? *(This was a new idea. It asserted the right of the people to protect their rights and freedoms by overthrowing unjust governments.)*

Generate Explanations Define unalienable rights, give an example of one, and explain what makes it unalienable. *(Unalienable rights are rights that cannot be taken away, such as life, liberty, and the pursuit of happiness. They are unalienable because these rights cannot be taken away by governments.)*

Declaring Independence

INTERACTIVE GALLERY

Interactive Declaration of Independence

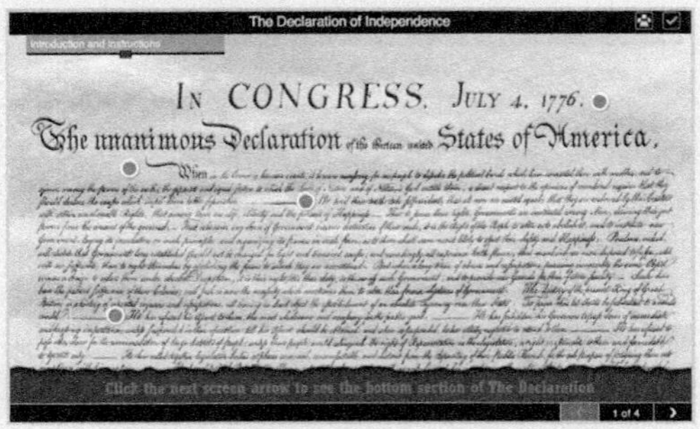

ACTIVE CLASSROOM

Have students use the Walking Tour Strategy to consider the issues surrounding the Declaration of Independence. Divide students into three groups and assign each group a section from the text: *Unalienable Rights*, *Colonial Grievances*, and *Independence*. Have groups post passages from their section around the room. Have students tour the room and discuss each passage, then summarize what they learned.

ELL Use the ELL activity described in the ELL chart.

Further Instruction

Go through the Interactive Reading Notepad questions with the class, including the graphic organizer on the content of the three main parts of the Declaration, and discuss the answers. Assign the primary source The U.S. Declaration of Independence.

Evaluate Arguments What grievances does the Declaration list against Britain? Do you think this list makes a compelling case for independence? Explain your reasoning. *(King George III disbanded colonial legislatures, sent troops to the colonies in peacetime, limited trade, imposed taxes without the people's consent, and did not correct these injustices after the colonists expressed their discontent. Yes; the colonists had many legitimate complaints and sufficiently showed the king's rule to be unfair.)*

Support Ideas with Examples Give one example of how the founders modeled civic virtue for the nation. Why was this an important contribution to the early United States? *(They put forward ideas about natural rights, liberty, and democracy that are foundational to the U.S. government. They modeled how leadership derived from the consent of the governed. They worked to protect rights and meet people's needs.)*

SYNTHESIZE

DIGITAL ACTIVITY

Reasons for Going to War

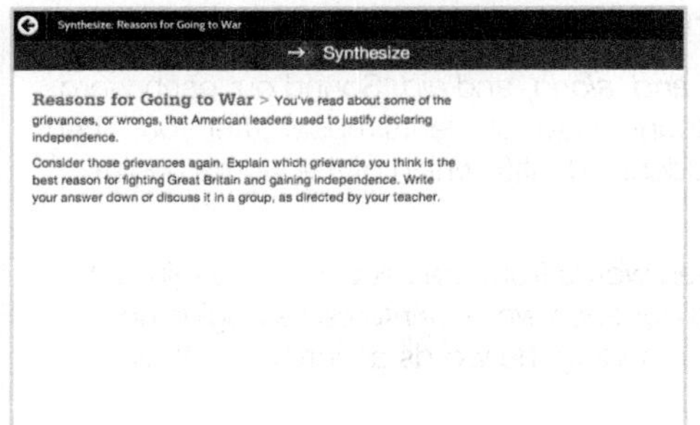

Have students work alone or in groups to list the grievances American leaders used to justify declaring independence. Ask students to explain which grievance they think most justified going to war. Have students write their answers or discuss them with the class.

Have students think about the following question: How did significant individuals advance the cause of freedom during the American Revolution? Ask students to consider what central ideas these individuals imparted.

DEMONSTRATE

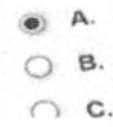

DIGITAL QUIZ

Lesson Quiz and Class Discussion Board

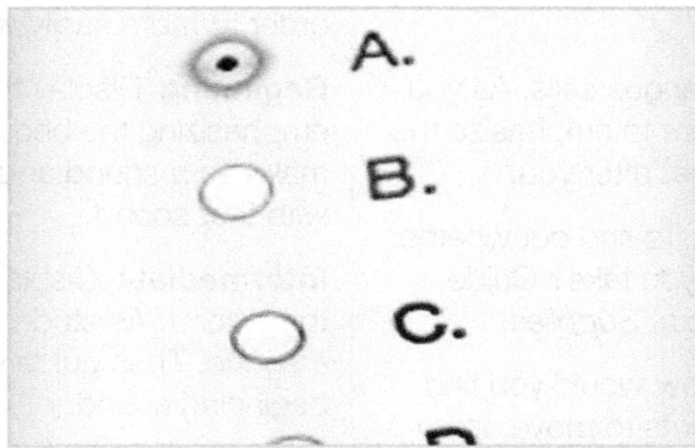

Assign the online Lesson Quiz for this lesson if you haven't already done so. Students will be offered automatic remediation or enrichment based on their score.

Pose these questions to the class on the Discussion Board:

In *Declaring Independence*, you read about the issues surrounding the Declaration of Independence, the significant individuals who shaped the document, and the main ideas it imparts.

Identify Author's Purpose What was the purpose for writing the Declaration of Independence? Did it fulfill what its authors set out to achieve? *(The authors wanted to write a formal declaration asserting independence from Britain. They listed their reasons for independence and put forward new ideas about government. This fulfilled their intention to justify their decision and tell other nations of their plan.)*

Summarize What ideas about government and rights were expressed in the Declaration of Independence? *(People have unalienable rights; government comes from the consent of the governed; people have the right to overthrow a government and create a new one if it fails to protect their rights.)*

Identify Patterns How did important historical documents like the Magna Carta, English Bill of Rights, and *Common Sense* lead the colonists to choose independence? *(These documents put forward ideas about natural rights that led colonists to seek a new government to better protect their liberties.)*

Topic Inquiry

Have students continue their investigations for the Topic Inquiry.

Winning Independence

Supporting English Language Learners

Use with Digital Text 1, **Early Challenges for the Continental Army.**

Reading

Display the chart titled, *Continental vs. British forces*, and explain its purpose in order for students to better recognize directionality of English reading both left-to-right and top-to-bottom.

Beginning Read the chart's title and the content of various cells. As you do so, have students underline the text with their fingers to emphasize the left-to-right aspect of reading English. Have them repeat after you.

Intermediate Discuss the structure of the chart. Ask: To find out whether the forces' supplies are compared, what steps would you take? Guide students to read down the first column until they arrive at *Supplies*.

Advanced Discuss the structure of the chart. Ask: How would you find out about the quality of American forces? Guide students to move down the *Continental* column, to move across the *Quality of forces* row, and to read the information in the intersecting cell.

Advanced High Ask: What is a common-sense way of reading this chart? Once students come up with a logical order (e.g., title, row and column headings, factual content), have them read the chart aloud in this way.

Use with Digital Text 9, **Explaining the American Victory.**

Listening

Read aloud the section titled, *Assistance from Allies*, enunciating each word. Encourage students to focus their attention on specific sounds in order to more easily distinguish between them.

Beginning Display the words *and, along,* and *aid*. Sound out each word, emphasizing the beginning *a* sound. Have students repeat after you. Then make an *a* sound and have students identify which of the words begins with that sound.

Intermediate Display the seven words from the section that begin with the letter *a*. As students sound out each word, reinforce its beginning *a* sound. Then guide students in sorting the words according to their beginning sound.

Advanced Ask pairs of students to locate and list seven different words from the section that begin with the letter *a*. Have them sound out the words together and then sort them according to their beginning sound.

Advanced High Ask students to locate and list words from the section that contain the letter *a* (in any position). Have them sound out the words and then sort them according to their *a* sound (words with more than one *a* may sort into more than one category).

D Differentiate Instruction

Use the Differentiated Instruction notes throughout the lesson plan to support the varied skill sets, levels of readiness, and interests in the mixed-ability classroom.

Challenge These notes include suggestions for expanding the activity for advanced students.

On-Level These notes include suggestions for modifying the activity to address different interests or learning styles.

Extra Support These notes include ideas for providing more scaffolding or reading spuport.

Special Needs These notes provide ideas for adapting instruction to support the needs of various special needs students.

NOTES

PEARSON realize™ www.PearsonRealize.com

Go online to access additional resources including: Primary Sources • Biographies • Supreme Court cases • 21st Century Skill Tutorials • Maps • Graphic Organizers.

Objectives

Objective 1: Describe the war in the middle states, including how the battles at Trenton and Saratoga marked turning points.

Objective 2: Describe the roles of women and African Americans in the war.

Objective 3: Explain how the war was fought on the western frontier and at sea.

Objective 4: Describe the war in the south, including the American victory at Yorktown.

Objective 5: Summarize the reasons why the Americans won the war.

LESSON 5 ORGANIZER	PACING: APPROX. 1 PERIOD, .5 BLOCKS		RESOURCES	
	OBJECTIVES	PACING	Online	Print
Connect				
DIGITAL START UP ACTIVITY **Young People in the War**		5 min.	●	
Investigate				
DIGITAL TEXT 1; DIGITAL TEXT 2; DIGITAL TEXT 3 **Early Challenges for the Continental Army; The Tide Turns for the Americans; Winter at Valley Forge**	Objective 1	30 min.	●	●
DIGITAL TEXT 4; DIGITAL TEXT 5 **Women Contribute to the War Effort; African Americans in the War**	Objective 2	20 min.	●	●
INTERACTIVE GALLERY **Notable People of the American Revolution**	Objective 2	10 min.	●	
DIGITAL TEXT 6 **Native Americans and the Spanish Choose Sides**	Objective 3	10 min.	●	●
DIGITAL TEXT 7; DIGITAL TEXT 8 **Fighting for Independence in the Southern Colonies and at Sea; A Decisive Win Brings the War to a Close**	Objectives 3, 4	20 min.	●	●
DIGITAL TEXT 9 **Explaining the American Victory**	Objective 5	10 min.	●	●
INTERACTIVE TIMELINE **Foreign Aid Plays a Role**	Objective 5	10 min.	●	
Synthesize				
DIGITAL ACTIVITY **Choosing Sides in Time of War**		5 min.	●	
Demonstrate				
DIGITAL QUIZ **Lesson Quiz and Class Discussion Board**		10 min.	●	

Winning Independence

CONNECT

DIGITAL START UP ACTIVITY

Young People in the War

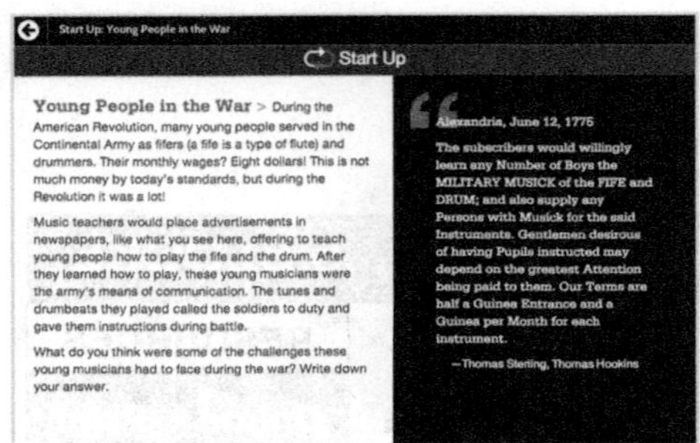

Project the Start Up Activity. Ask students to read the quote as they enter and get settled and then write down their answers to the question. Have them share their thoughts with another student, either in class or through a chat or blog space.

Discuss What do you think were some of the challenges these young musicians had to face during the war? *(Traveling long distances; missing home; hunger and fatigue; danger from battle)*

Tell students that in this lesson they will be learning about the important events of the American Revolution and the contributions of significant individuals to the war.

Aa Vocabulary Development: Use the Interactive Reading Notepad to preview the Key Terms and Academic Vocabulary in the lesson with students.

FLIP IT!

Assign the Flipped Video for this lesson.

STUDENT EDITION PRINT PAGES: 158–172

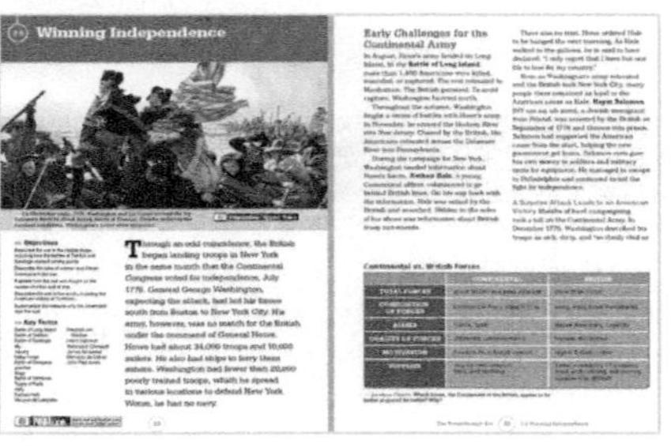

INVESTIGATE

DIGITAL TEXT 1

Early Challenges for the Continental Army

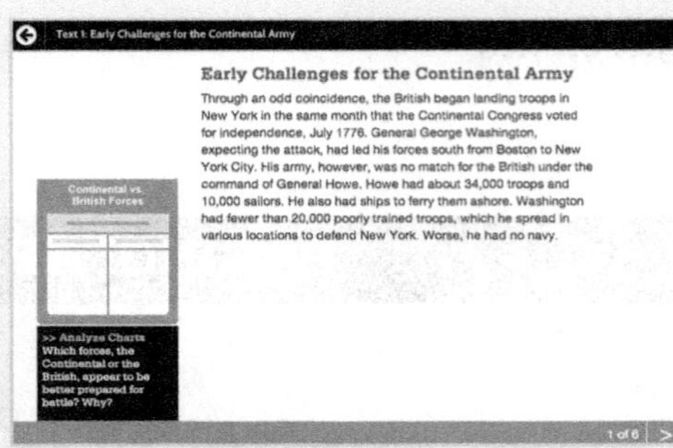

Objective 1: Describe the war in the Middle States, including how the Battles of Trenton and Saratoga marked turning points.

Quick Instruction

Project the chart comparing Continental and British forces. Explain that while the British were more prepared for battle, General George Washington led the Continental Army to surprising victories in the Middle States.

Identify Patterns Describe the effects of physical geographic factors on the Battles of Long Island, Trenton, and Saratoga. *(Battle of Long Island—the water surrounding New York was a disadvantage to the Americans. Howe used ships to ferry soldiers to New York, but Washington had no navy; Battle of Trenton—the British did not expect Washington to cross the Delaware River at night, which let the Americans make a surprise attack; Battle of Saratoga—Patriots used the woods to slow the British by cutting down trees to block the route.)*

Test Conclusions What evidence will you look for to help you conclude that the Battles of Trenton and Saratoga marked turning points in the war? *(Evidence that the Americans struggled, won these battles, and then met with more success)*

ELL Use the ELL activity described in the ELL chart.

Further Instruction

Go through the Interactive Reading Notepad questions and discuss the answers with the class. To extend the lesson, assign the biographies of Haym Salomon and the Marquis de Lafayette.

DIGITAL TEXT 2

The Tide Turns for the Americans

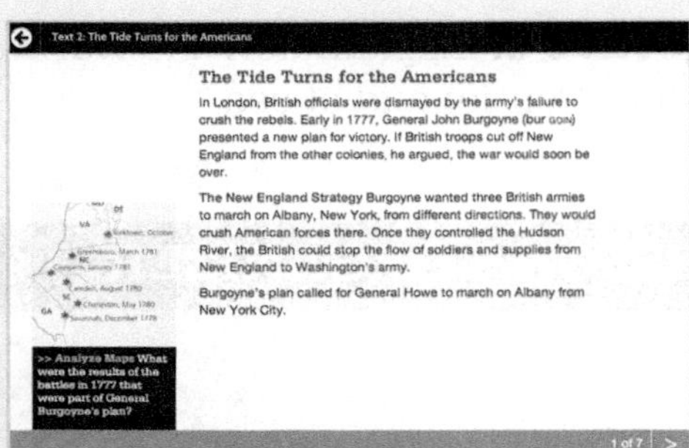

Text 2: The Tide Turns for the Americans
The Tide Turns for the Americans
In London, British officials were dismayed by the army's failure to crush the rebels. Early in 1777, General John Burgoyne (bur GOIN) presented a new plan for victory. If British troops cut off New England from the other colonies, he argued, the war would soon be over.
The New England Strategy Burgoyne wanted three British armies to march on Albany, New York, from different directions. They would crush American forces there. Once they controlled the Hudson River, the British could stop the flow of soldiers and supplies from New England to Washington's army.
Burgoyne's plan called for General Howe to march on Albany from New York City.
>> Analyze Maps What were the results of the battles in 1777 that were part of General Burgoyne's plan?
1 of 7

Generate Explanations What important role did Haym Salomon play in the revolution? Why do you think he is still remembered today? *(He is remembered for his loyalty and sacrifice. He helped the government get loans to pay for the war and donated money to the military. He was captured by the British but escaped and continued supporting the American cause.)*

Infer What inferences can you make about the Continental Army based on the events at Valley Forge? Give evidence supporting your claims. *(The army did not have enough money or supplies, as soldiers did not have enough warm clothes or even shoes to survive the winter. The army was well supported by many in the nation, as Patriots sent needed supplies.)*

DIGITAL TEXT 3

Winter at Valley Forge

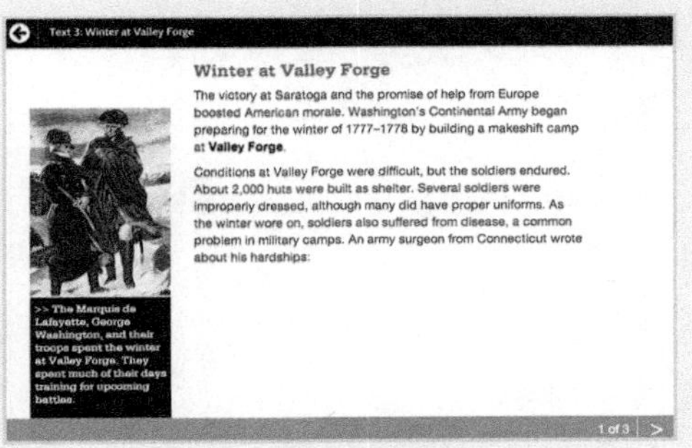

DIGITAL TEXT 4

Women Contribute to the War Effort

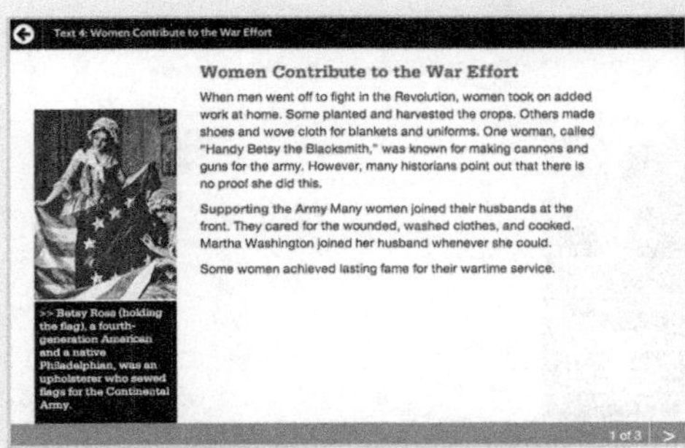

DIGITAL TEXT 5

African Americans in the War

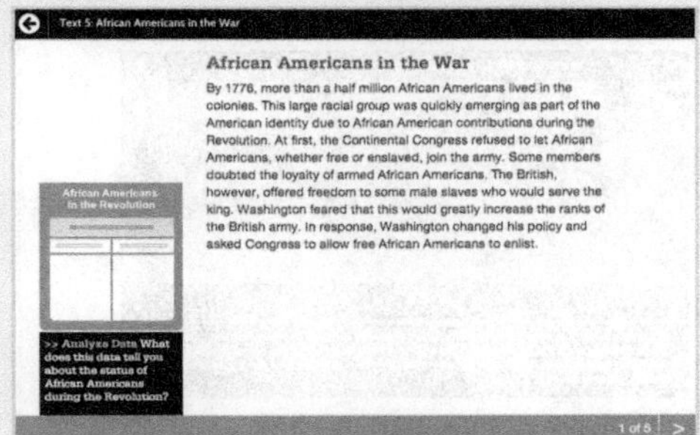

Objective 2: **Describe the roles of women and African Americans in the war.**

Quick Instruction

Interactive Gallery: Notable People of the American Revolution Project the interactive gallery and click through the images. Explain that women and people of various racial groups made important contributions during the revolution.

Draw Conclusions Based on the experiences of Deborah Sampson, Sybil Ludington, and Mary Ludwig Hays, how do you think the American Revolution changed life for women in America? *(Women faced many dangers. Some took on roles that were previously held by men.)*

> **ACTIVE CLASSROOM**
>
> Have students use the Sticky Notes Strategy and take 3 minutes to jot down their ideas about how the contributions of women, African Americans, and other racial groups to the war effort shaped the nation's early identity. Have students post their stickies on a wall. Sort and discuss their observations as a group.

D Differentiate: Extra Support Have students write the contributions that women and African Americans made during the war on their stickies. Ask students to pick one contribution and consider an effect it had on American society.

Further Instruction

Go through the Interactive Reading Notepad questions and discuss the answers with the class. To extend the lesson, assign the biographies of Wentworth Cheswell and James Armistead.

Compare and Contrast the reasons some African Americans supported the British and others supported the Patriots. *(Compare—both sides hoped the war would result in their freedom. Contrast—Britain offered freedom to some African American soldiers. Other African Americans hoped a Patriot victory would end slavery.)*

Compare the contributions of James Armistead and Wentworth Cheswell to the American Revolution. *(Armistead—Patriot spy who helped achieve an American victory at Yorktown; Cheswell—issued warnings when the British were advancing toward Lexington and Concord and enlisted to fight at Saratoga)*

Summarize What economic and social contributions did women make to the war effort? *(Economic—planting and harvesting; making supplies like shoes, blankets, and uniforms; making cannons; Social—caring for wounded soldiers; demonstrating patriotism by sewing flags; speaking out about women's rights)*

Winning Independence

INTERACTIVE GALLERY

Notable People of the American Revolution

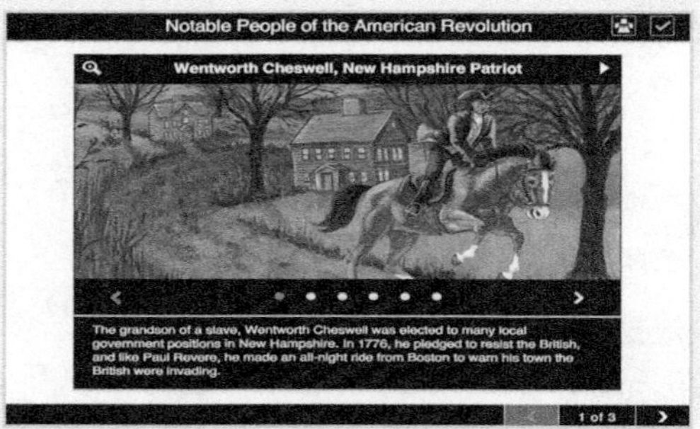

Notable People of the American Revolution
Wentworth Cheswell, New Hampshire Patriot
The grandson of a slave, Wentworth Cheswell was elected to many local government positions in New Hampshire. In 1776, he pledged to resist the British, and like Paul Revere, he made an all-night ride from Boston to warn his town the British were invading.
1 of 3

DIGITAL TEXT 6

Native Americans and the Spanish Choose Sides

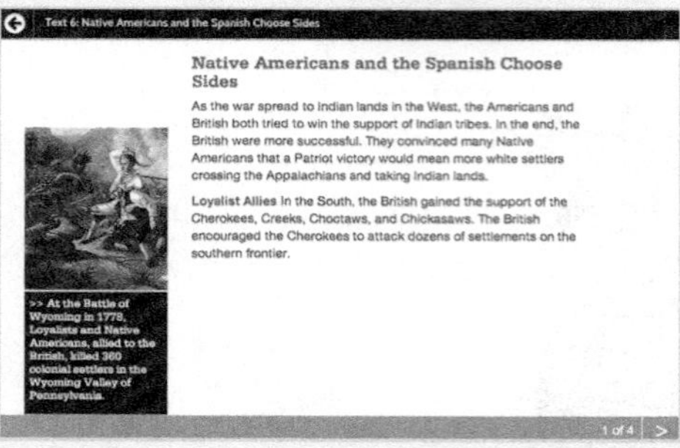

Text 6: Native Americans and the Spanish Choose Sides
Native Americans and the Spanish Choose Sides
As the war spread to Indian lands in the West, the Americans and British both tried to win the support of Indian tribes. In the end, the British were more successful. They convinced many Native Americans that a Patriot victory would mean more white settlers crossing the Appalachians and taking Indian lands.
Loyalist Allies In the South, the British gained the support of the Cherokees, Creeks, Choctaws, and Chickasaws. The British encouraged the Cherokees to attack dozens of settlements on the southern frontier.
>> At the Battle of Wyoming in 1778, Loyalists and Native Americans, allied to the British, killed 360 colonial settlers in the Wyoming Valley of Pennsylvania.
1 of 4

Objective 3: Explain how the war was fought on the western frontier and at sea.

Quick Instruction

Project the map titled, *The War in the West*. Explain that many Native American tribes such as the Iroquois hoped a British victory would keep colonists from spreading west. Other tribes in the Ohio Valley sided with the Patriots.

Draw Conclusions Why were the West and Southwest important regions during the American Revolution, even though the British colonies were in the East? *(The fighting spread from the eastern colonies. Major battles took place along the frontier and in Native American territories.)*

Further Instruction

Go through the Interactive Reading Notepad questions with the class. Be sure students understand that some Native American tribes and Spanish officials contributed to American independence by providing the Patriots with soldiers and supplies. To extend the lesson, assign the biography of Bernardo de Gálvez.

Generate Explanations How did George Rogers Clark use the physical geography of the frontier to help defeat the British? *(He spread his troops through the woods to make it look like there were more Americans than there really were. Without the trees, the British commander would have known Clark's numbers were small. Instead, the commander surrendered.)*

Summarize How did Bernardo de Gálvez help the Patriots in the Southwest? *(He supplied medicine, cloth, muskets, and gunpowder to the Americans, seized British forts, and drove the British from West Florida.)*

DIGITAL TEXT 7

Fighting for Independence in the Southern Colonies and at Sea

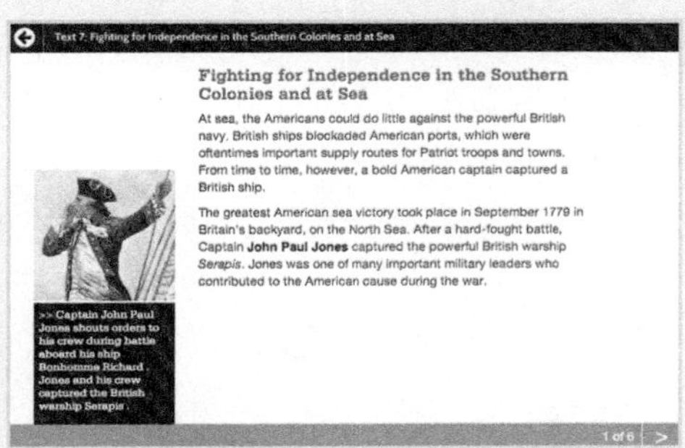

Objectives 3: Explain how the war was fought on the western frontier and at sea; 4: Describe the war in the South, including the American victory at Yorktown.

Quick Instruction

Project the map of the Battle of Yorktown. Ask students how the physical geography of the bay led to an American victory at Yorktown. Explain that American victories in the South led to the British defeat and the Treaty of Paris.

Draw Conclusions How did American military leaders use their knowledge of the physical geography of the southern region to defeat the British there? *(They knew where to advance and how to seize advantageous locations, putting the British at a disadvantage. They also knew how to use different geographic features, like woods or swamps, to hide from the enemy.)*

Further Instruction

Go through the Interactive Reading Notepad questions with the class, including the graphic organizer on the tactics used by commanders to win victories against the British in the South. Be sure students understand how the physical geography of the region affected the outcome of the war.

DIGITAL TEXT 8

A Decisive Win Brings the War to a Close

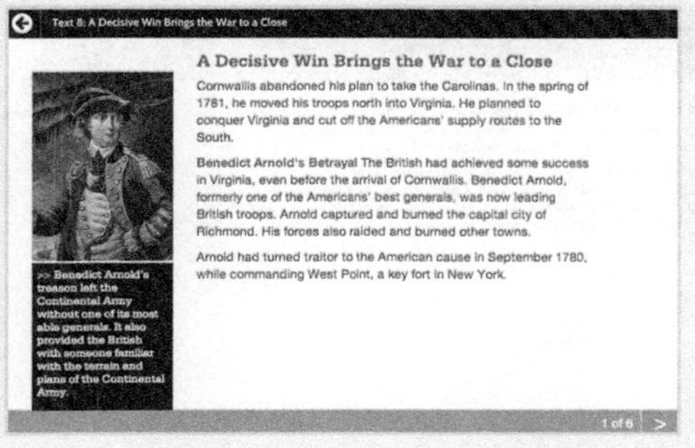

Generate Explanations Explain the events surrounding the Battle of Yorktown. How did the Americans win? What was the effect of this victory? *(Cornwallis had been raiding American towns in an effort to capture Virginia and cut off supply routes to the South. Then Cornwallis retreated to the Yorktown peninsula, mistakenly thinking he could receive supplies from the British there. Washington's soldiers, Lafayette's soldiers, and the French naval fleet trapped Cornwallis on the peninsula, where he could not escape or get supplies. Cornwallis was under siege until he surrendered. The defeat led to the Treaty of Paris.)*

Identify Cause and Effect What was the result of the Treaty of Paris? *(Britain recognized the United States as an independent nation.)*

DIGITAL TEXT 9

Explaining the American Victory

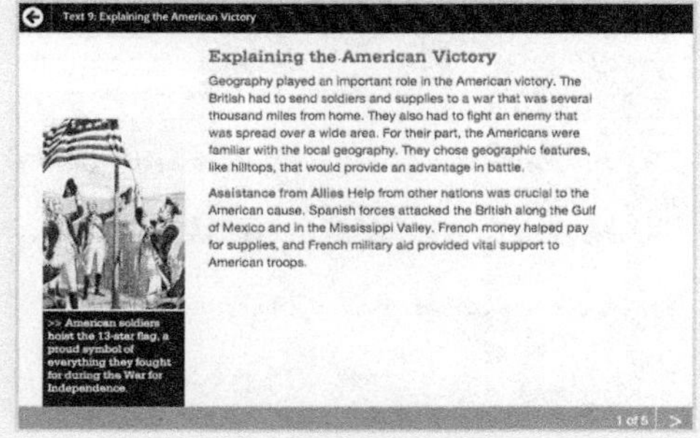

Text 9: Explaining the American Victory
Explaining the American Victory
Geography played an important role in the American victory. The British had to send soldiers and supplies to a war that was several thousand miles from home. They also had to fight an enemy that was spread over a wide area. For their part, the Americans were familiar with the local geography. They chose geographic features, like hilltops, that would provide an advantage in battle.
Assistance from Allies Help from other nations was crucial to the American cause. Spanish forces attacked the British along the Gulf of Mexico and in the Mississippi Valley. French money helped pay for supplies, and French military aid provided vital support to American troops.
>> American soldiers hoist the 13-star flag, a proud symbol of everything they fought for during the War for Independence.
1 of 5

Objective 5: Summarize the reasons why the Americans won the war.

Quick Instruction

Remind students of the advantages Britain held at the outset of war, which they learned about in the *Continental vs. British forces* chart from earlier in the lesson. Explain that there are several reasons Americans won: the physical geography of the North American region, assistance from allies, the contributions of people of various racial groups, and the efforts of General Washington and other significant military leaders.

Interactive Timeline: Foreign Aid Plays a Role Project the interactive chart and click through the tiles. Discuss the ways that aid from France helped the Patriots win the war.

Draw Conclusions What effect do you think foreign aid had on the way Americans felt about the war, and why? *(It probably improved morale and inspired Americans to keep fighting because other nations believed in their cause and recognized their autonomy.)*

ACTIVE CLASSROOM

Have students use the Conversation with History Strategy to suppose they are having a conversation with George Washington after the American victory. Have students write down a question they would ask about the war or its immediate aftermath, then what Washington would say to them, and what they would say in response.

Winning Independence

INTERACTIVE TIMELINE

Foreign Aid Plays a Role

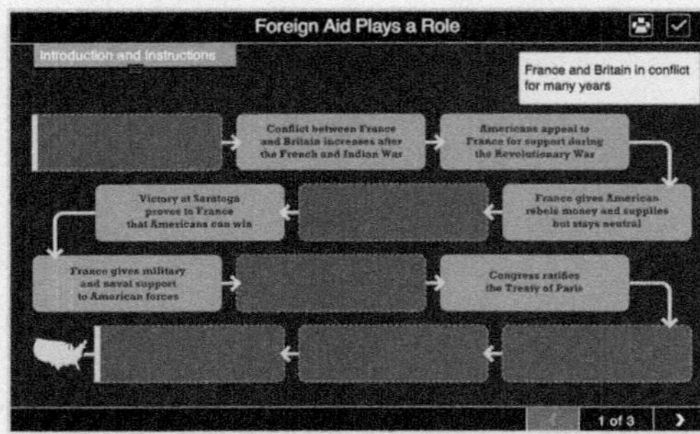

ELL Use the ELL activity described in the ELL chart.

Further Instruction

Go through the Interactive Reading Notepad questions and discuss the answers with the class. Be sure students can explain the reasons America won the war.

Hypothesize Why was George Washington such an important figure in the American Revolution? What do you think might have happened in the war had he not been in command? *(He trained troops to fight and led the Americans to victory with his skilled leadership. Without his leadership, the Patriots might not have been as successful against the British.)*

Summarize How did people of various racial and social groups contribute to American independence and the American identity? *(People of different racial and social groups fought together for the common cause of freedom and independence. This sense of unity became part of the national identity.)*

Identify Cause and Effect What physical geographic factors of the United States impacted the war? What was their effect? *(Distance across the Atlantic—made it hard for Britain to send troops and supplies; large and spread out area—made it difficult for Britain to target soldiers; rivers, woods, and hills—Americans knew the terrain and could use these features to sneak up on, hide from, or attack the enemy.)*

SYNTHESIZE

DIGITAL ACTIVITY

Choosing Sides in Time of War

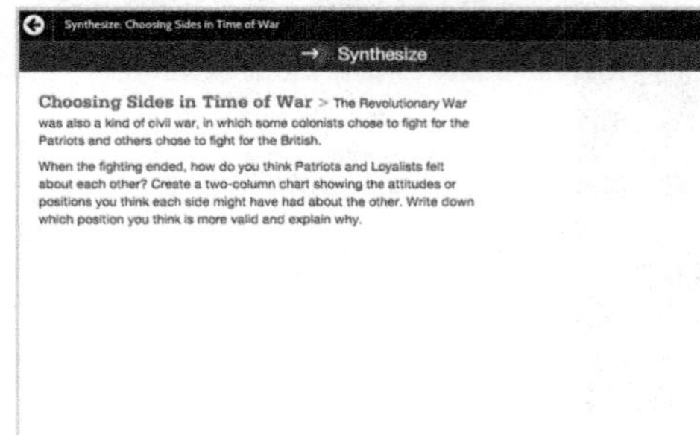

Synthesize: Choosing Sides in Time of War
Synthesize
Choosing Sides in Time of War > The Revolutionary War was also a kind of civil war, in which some colonists chose to fight for the Patriots and others chose to fight for the British.
When the fighting ended, how do you think Patriots and Loyalists felt about each other? Create a two-column chart showing the attitudes or positions you think each side might have had about the other. Write down which position you think is more valid and explain why.

Have students work alone or in groups to create the chart with columns labeled *Patriots* and *Loyalists*. Have students write down which position they think is most valid and why, or have students discuss their views as a class.

Discuss Have students think about the following question: What difficulties do you think Patriots and Loyalists faced working together in the new nation following the war? Have students discuss their views as a class.

DEMONSTRATE

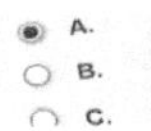

DIGITAL QUIZ

Lesson Quiz and Class Discussion Board

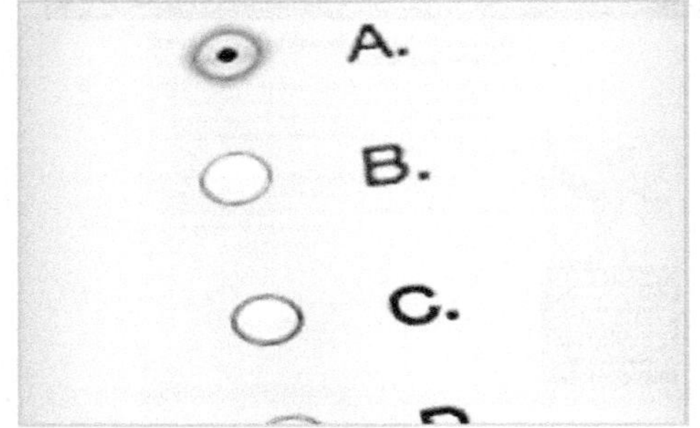

Assign the online Lesson Quiz for this lesson if you haven't already done so. Students will be offered automatic remediation or enrichment based on their score.

Pose these questions to the class on the Discussion Board:

In *Winning Independence*, you read about how both military leaders and ordinary people won the war for the Americans.

Draw Conclusions How was the Continental Army able to overcome its disadvantages in order to win the war? *(Strong leadership from figures like General Washington; the help of many Patriots, including women, African Americans, and other racial groups; help from allies such as the French, Spanish, and some Native American tribes; knowledge of local geography, which helped Americans against a larger and better trained army)*

Make Predictions What do you think is going to be the first major task the new country will have to take on? *(Developing a federal government)*

Topic Inquiry

Have students continue their investigations for the Topic Inquiry.

PEARSON realize™ www.PearsonRealize.com Access your Digital Lesson

The Revolutionary Era (1750–1783)

SYNTHESIZE

DIGITAL ACTIVITY

Reflect on the Essential Question and Topic

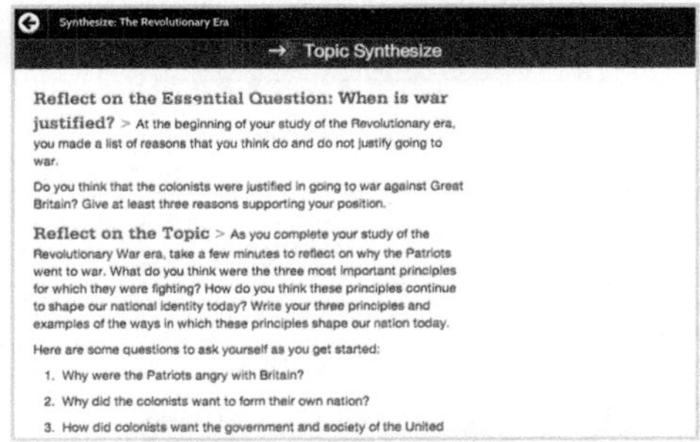

First ask students to reconsider the Essential Question for the topic: When is war justified? Remind students of the lists they made at the beginning of the lesson. For example, justifications may include:

- to secure land or gain resources
- to stand up for ideas
- to defend against aggressors
- to help other allies
- to protect a way of life

Ask students: Do you think the colonists were justified in going to war against Britain? Ask them to give at least three reasons to support their position. Discuss their answers as a class or ask students to post their answers on the Class Discussion Board.

Next ask students to reflect on the topic as a whole and consider why the Patriots went to war. Ask students to write down the three most important principles for which the Patriots were fighting, and how these principles continue to shape our national identity today. Ask these questions if students need help getting started:

- Why were the Patriots angry with Britain?
- Why did the colonists want to form their own nation?
- How did colonists want the government and society of the United States to differ from Britain?

You may ask students to share their questions and answers on the Class Discussion Board.

Topic Inquiry

Have students complete Step 3 of the Topic Inquiry.

DEMONSTRATE

DIGITAL TOPIC REVIEW AND ASSESSMENT

The Revolutionary Era (1750–1783)

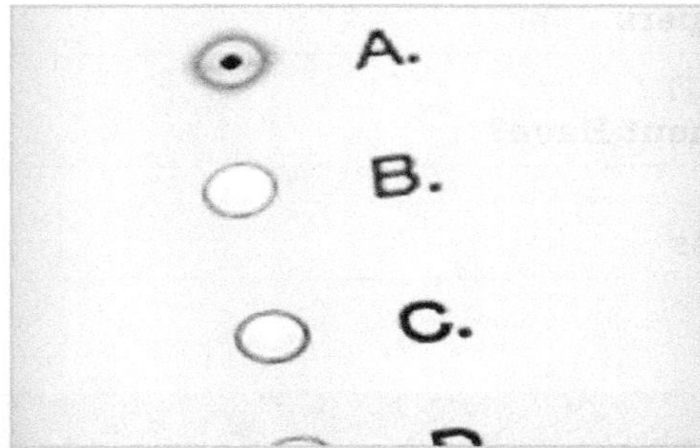

Students can prepare for the Topic Test by answering the questions in the Topic Review and Assessment online or the Assessment questions in the Print Student text. They can also prepare by reviewing their answers to the Interactive Reading Notepad questions or reviewing their notes in the Reading and Notetaking Study Guide.

DIGITAL TOPIC TEST

The Revolutionary Era (1750–1783)

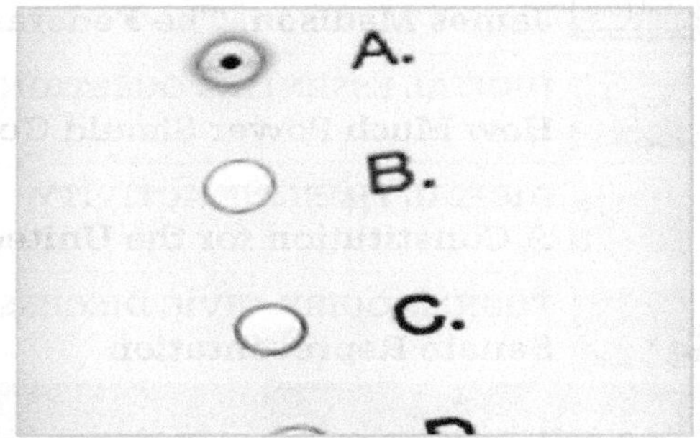

TOPIC TEST

Assign the Topic Test to assess students' understanding of topic content.

BENCHMARK TESTS

Assign these benchmark tests as you complete the relevant topics to monitor student progress toward mastering the course content and as preparation for the End-of-Course Test.

Benchmark Test 1: Topics 1–2

Benchmark Test 2: Topics 3–4

Benchmark Test 3: Topics 5–6

Benchmark Test 4: Topics 7–9

Benchmark Test 5: Topics 10–12

Benchmark Test 6: Topics 13–14

Benchmark Test 7: Topics 15–17

A Constitution for the United States (1776–Present)

TOPIC 4 ORGANIZER	PACING: APPROX. 10 PERIODS, 5 BLOCKS
	PACING
Connect	**1 period**
MY STORY VIDEO **James Madison, The Federalist Papers**	10 min.
DIGITAL ESSENTIAL QUESTION ACTIVITY **How Much Power Should Government Have?**	10 min.
DIGITAL TIMELINE ACTIVITY **A Constitution for the United States**	10 min.
TOPIC INQUIRY: CIVIC DISCUSSION **Senate Representation**	20 min.
Investigate	**3–7 periods**
TOPIC INQUIRY: CIVIC DISCUSSION **Senate Representation**	Ongoing
LESSON 1 A Weak Confederation	30–40 min.
LESSON 2 Drafting a Constitution	30–40 min.
LESSON 3 Ideas That Influenced the Constitution	30–40 min.
LESSON 4 Federalists, Antifederalists and the Bill of Rights	30–40 min.
LESSON 5 Understanding the Constitution	30–40 min.
LESSON 6 Amending the Constitution	30–40 min.
LESSON 7 Citizens' Rights and Responsibilities	30–40 min.
Synthesize	**1 period**
DIGITAL ACTIVITY **Reflect on the Essential Question and Topic**	10 min.
TOPIC INQUIRY: CIVIC DISCUSSION **Senate Representation**	20 min.
Demonstrate	**1–2 periods**
DIGITAL TOPIC REVIEW AND ASSESSMENT **A Constitution for the United States**	10 min.
TOPIC INQUIRY: CIVIC DISCUSSION **Senate Representation**	20 min.

 TOPIC INQUIRY: CIVIC DISCUSSION

Senate Representation

In this Topic Inquiry, students work in teams to examine different perspectives on this issue by analyzing several sources, arguing both sides of a Yes/No question, then developing and discussing their own point of view on the question: **Should representation in the United States Senate be based on population?**

STEP 1: CONNECT

Develop Questions and Plan the Investigation

Launch the Civic Discussion

Divide the class into groups of four students. Students can access the materials they'll need in the online course or you can distribute copies to each student. Read the main question and introduction with the students.

Have students complete Step 1 by reading the Discussion Launch and filling in Step 1 of the Information Organizer. The Discussion Launch provides YES and NO arguments on the main question. Students should extract and paraphrase the arguments from the reading in Step 1 of their Information Organizers.

Next, students share within their groups the arguments and evidence they found to support the YES and NO positions. The group needs to agree on the major YES and NO points and each student should note those points in their Information Organizer.

Resources

- Student Instructions
- Information Organizer
- Discussion Launch

PROFESSIONAL DEVELOPMENT

Civic Discussion

Be sure to view the Civic Discussion Professional Development resources in the online course.

STEP 2: INVESTIGATE

Apply Disciplinary Concepts and Tools

Examine Sources and Perspectives

Students will examine sources with the goal of extracting information and perspectives on the main question. They analyze each source and describe the author's perspective on the main question and key evidence the author provides to support that viewpoint in Information Organizer Step 2.

Ask students to keep in mind:

- **Author/Creator:** Who created the source? An individual? Group? Government agency?
- **Audience:** For whom was the source created?
- **Date/Place:** Is there any information that reveals where and when the source was created?
- **Purpose:** Why was the source created? Discuss with students the importance of this question in identifying bias.
- **Relevance:** How does the source support one argument or another?

Suggestion: Reading the source documents and filling in Step 2 of the Information Organizer could be assigned as homework.

Resources

- Student Instructions
- Information Organizer
- Source documents

 TOPIC INQUIRY: CIVIC DISCUSSION

Senate Representation *(continued)*

STEP 3: SYNTHESIZE
Use Evidence to Formulate Conclusions

Formulate Compelling Arguments with Evidence
Now students will apply perspectives and evidence they extracted from the sources to think more deeply about the main question by first arguing one side of the issue, then the other. In this way students become more prepared to formulate an evidence-based conclusion on their own.

Within each student group, assign half of the students to take the position of YES on the main question and the others to take the position of NO. Students will work with their partners to identify the strongest arguments and evidence to support their assigned YES or NO position.

Present Yes/No Positions
Within each group, those assigned the YES position share arguments and evidence first. As the YES students speak, those assigned NO should listen carefully, take notes to fill in the rest of the Compelling Arguments Chart (Step 3 in Information Organizer) and ask clarifying questions.

When the YES side is finished, students assigned the NO position present while those assigned YES should listen, take notes, and ask clarifying questions. Examples of clarifyin questions are:

- I think you just said [x]. Am I understanding you correctly?
- Can you tell me more about [x]?
- Can you repeat [x]? I am not sure I understand, yet.

Suggestion: You may want to set a 5 minute time limit for each side to present. Provide a two-minute warning so that students make their most compelling arguments within the time frame.

Switch Sides
The students will switch sides to argue the opposite point of view. To prepare to present the other position, partners who first argued YES will use the notes they took during the NO side's presentation, plus add any additional arguments and evidence from the reading and sources. The same for students who first argued the NO position.

STEP 4: DEMONSTRATE
Communicate Conclusions and Take Informed Action

Individual Points of View
Now the students will have the opportunity to discuss the main question from their own points of view. To help students prepare for this discussion, have them reflect on the YES/NO discussions they have participated in thus far and fill in Step 4 of their Information Organizers.

After all of the students have shared their points of view, each group should list points of agreement, filling the last portion of Step 4 on their Information Organizers.

Reflect on the Discussion
Ask students to reflect on the civic discussion thinking about:

- The value of having to argue both the YES and NO positions.
- If their individual views changed over the course of the discussion and why.
- What they learned from participating in the discussion.

Resources
- Student Instructions
- Information Organizer

INTRODUCTION

A Constitution for the United States (1776–Present)

After the Revolutionary War, Americans began the hard work of constructing a new government. First, they needed a new constitution. Drafting the United States Constitution was a challenging task. There were disagreements over the size and scope of the new federal government relative to the individual states in the republic.There were also debates over the best ways to safeguard the liberties for which Americans had fought so dearly. However, after continued debate and compromises, a new, politically united nation took form.

CONNECT

MY STORY VIDEO

James Madison, The Federalist Papers

Watch a video that introduces students to one of the most important political thinkers in U.S. history.

Identify Central Issues Why did Madison, Hamilton, and Jay write the Federalist Papers? (To explain political ideas and promote the ratification of the new Constitution.)

Cite Evidence Explain why Madison was so important in creating the new U.S. government. (Possible answers: He explained political ideas such as checks and balances, was important in debate at Constitutional Convention, helped ensure ratification, served as Secretary of State and then President.)

DIGITAL ESSENTIAL QUESTION ACTIVITY

How Much Power Should Government Have?

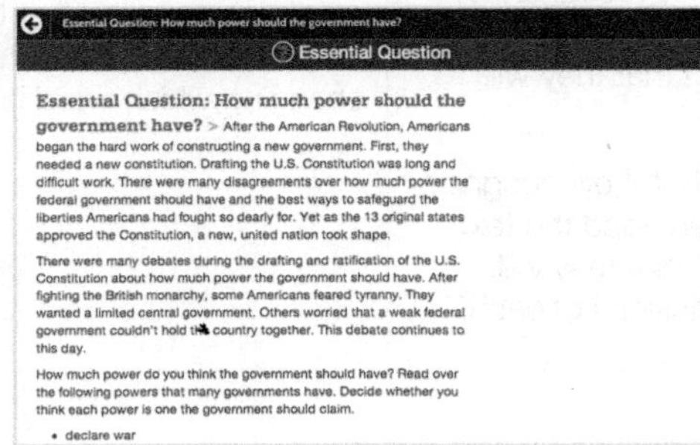

Ask students to think about the Essential Question for this Topic: How much power should government have? Americans disagreed about how much power the federal government of the new nation should have and how that power should be shared with the states.

If students have not already done so, ask them to read the list of government powers and decide which ones they think governments should claim. Have students share their reasoning with the class.

Hypothesize Why do you think Americans disagreed about how much power the government should have following the American Revolution? *(Americans had just fought a war against a government they thought was too powerful. Many people worried about tyranny. Others argued that the government needed enough powers to function effectively.)*

Identify Central issues What powers from the list do you think are the most important for a government to have? Why? *(Answers will vary.)*

Evaluate Arguments Give an argument for limiting government powers. *(Preventing tyranny; protecting individual rights and freedoms; creating a balance of power)*

DIGITAL TIMELINE ACTIVITY

A Constitution for the United States

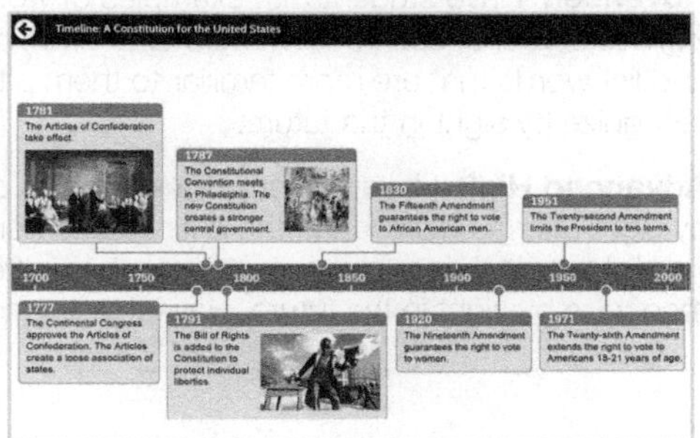

Display the timeline showing the major events surrounding the creation and ratification of the United States Constitution. During this Topic students will learn about these events and many more, but this timeline will provide a framework for placing the events about which they will learn.

Identify Steps in a Process What document came before the United States Constitution? *(The Articles of Confederation)*

Draw Conclusions How has the United States Constitution changed since its ratification in 1787, and why? *(New amendments have been added to expand individual rights and protect liberties.)*

Topic Inquiry

Launch the Topic Inquiry with students after introducing the Topic.

Topic 4 Lesson 1

A Weak Confederation

Supporting English Language Learners

Use with Digital Text 2, **The Articles of Confederation.**

Reading

Before they begin reading, have students make a list of words in a selection of the text that the recognize by sight. Then have them read a selection from the text and list new words that they have learned to recognize to develop basic sight vocabulary used routinely in written classroom materials.

Beginning Have each student make a list of words that he or she recognizes by sight in the first two paragraphs. Then have students read those paragraphs, helping them as needed with words they do not recognize. Finally, have them add new words to their list of words that they will recognize by sight in the future.

Intermediate Have each student make a list of words that he or she recognizes by sight in the first four paragraphs. Then have students read those paragraphs. Finally, have them list new words that are more familiar to them after reading that they will recognize by sight in the future.

Advanced Have students list examples of words that they recognize by sight after a brief scan of the entire text. Then have them read the text and list words that are more familiar to them after reading that they will recognize by sight in the future.

Advanced High Have students list examples of words that they recognize by sight after a brief scan of the entire text. Then have them read the text and list words that are more familiar to them after reading that they will recognize by sight in the future. Have them write brief definitions of each.

Use with Digital Text 4, **An Orderly Expansion.**

Listening

Read aloud the text using proper intonation. Explain that people tend to stress certain words and syllables when speaking or reading aloud.

Beginning Display these words from the text: *important, govern, established*. Say each word with correct intonation, and have students repeat after you. Ask students to underline each word's stressed syllable.

Intermediate Display these words from the text: *important, govern, established*. Say each word with correct intonation, and have students repeat after you. Ask students to underline each word's stressed syllable. Then, in pairs or small groups, have them read the first paragraph, paying special attention to their intonation of these words.

Advanced Read aloud the first sentence of the text, emphasizing the word *did*. Have students identify the stressed word. Ask: Why did I emphasize the word did? What extra meaning did I give the sentence?

Advanced High Read aloud the first sentence of the text twice: emphasize *did* the first time, and *important* the second time. Have students identify the stressed word in each version. Ask: How does changing which word is emphasized affect the sentence's meaning?

D Differentiate Instruction

Use the Differentiated Instruction notes throughout the lesson plan to support the varied skill sets, levels of readiness, and interests in the mixed-ability classroom.

Challenge These notes include suggestions for expanding the activity for advanced students.

On-Level These notes include suggestions for modifying the activity to address different interests or learning styles.

Extra Support These notes include ideas for providing more scaffolding or reading spupport.

Special Needs These notes provide ideas for adapting instruction to support the needs of various special needs students.

NOTES

PEARSON realize www.PearsonRealize.com

Go online to access additional resources including: Primary Sources • Biographies • Supreme Court cases • 21st Century Skill Tutorials • Maps • Graphic Organizers.

Objectives

Objective 1: Explain why state governments wrote constitutions.

Objective 2: Identify the strengths and weaknesses of the Articles of Confederation.

Objective 3: Describe the process the Articles created for admitting new states.

Objective 4: Explain why many Americans called for changes to the Articles.

Objective 5: Summarize Shays' Rebellion and how it influenced leaders to change the Articles of Confederation.

LESSON 1 ORGANIZER	PACING: APPROX. 1 PERIOD,.5 BLOCKS			
			RESOURCES	
	OBJECTIVES	PACING	Online	Print
Connect				
DIGITAL START UP ACTIVITY **Thinking About Government Power**		5 min.	●	
Investigate				
DIGITAL TEXT 1 **Each State Creates a Constitution**	Objective 1	10 min.	●	●
DIGITAL TEXT 2 **The Articles of Confederation**	Objectives 2, 3	10 min.	●	●
INTERACTIVE MAP **Claims to Western Lands**		10 min.	●	
DIGITAL TEXT 3 **Weaknesses of the Confederation**		10 min.	●	●
INTERACTIVE CHART **Problems and Effects of the Articles of Confederation**		10 min.	●	
DIGITAL TEXT 4 **An Orderly Expansion**	Objective 3	10 min.	●	●
DIGITAL TEXT 5 **Economic Problems Lead to Change**	Objectives 4, 5	10 min.	●	●
Synthesize				
DIGITAL ACTIVITY **Debating the Power of a Government**		5 min.	●	
Demonstrate				
DIGITAL QUIZ **Lesson Quiz and Class Discussion Board**		10 min.	●	

A Weak Confederation

CONNECT

DIGITAL START UP ACTIVITY

Thinking About Government Power

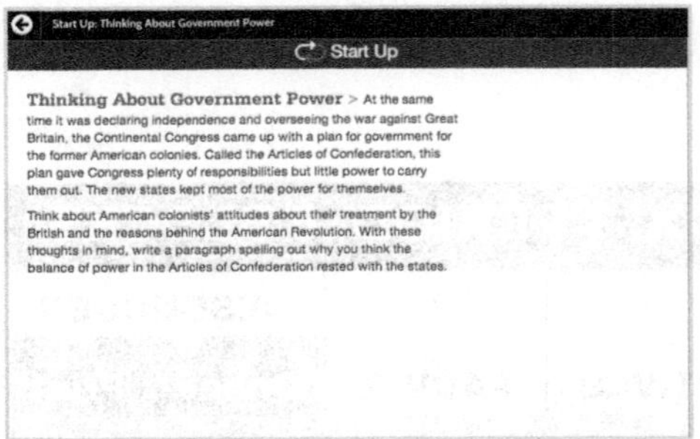

Project the Start Up Activity Ask students to read the instructions and write a brief paragraph about why the balance of power in the Articles of Confederation rested with the states.

Discuss Think about the reasons for the American Revolution. Why were many people reluctant to give up the powers of the states? *(They had just fought a war against a government they thought was tyrannical. They did not want the federal government to be too strong.)*

Tell students that in this lesson they will be learning about the issues surrounding the writing of the Articles of Confederation.

Aa Vocabulary Development: Use the Interactive Reading Notepad to preview the Key Terms and Academic Vocabulary in this lesson with students.

FLIP IT!

Assign the Flipped Video for this lesson.

STUDENT EDITION PRINT PAGES: 178–184

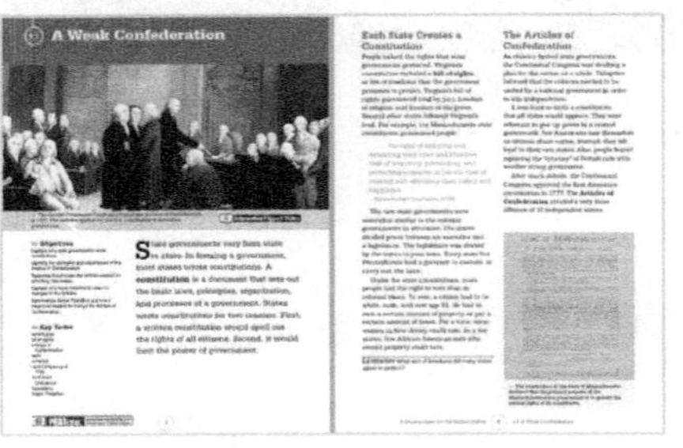

INVESTIGATE

DIGITAL TEXT 1

Each State Creates a Constitution

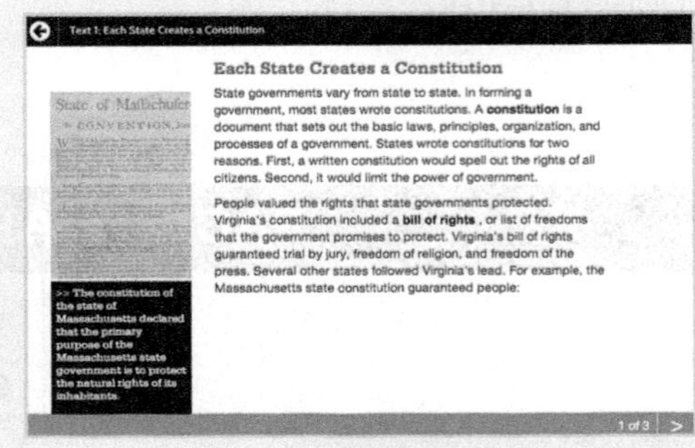

Objective 1: Explain why state governments wrote constitutions.

Quick Instruction

Display the image of the Massachusetts state constitution. States wrote constitutions to enumerate citizens' rights and limit government powers. Discuss why the creation of state constitutions was an important issue surrounding the American Revolution.

Generate Explanations Explain why states needed to create their own constitutions. *(To establish their own governments and protect citizens' rights)*

Further Instruction

Go through the Interactive Reading Notepad questions and discuss the answers with the class. Be sure students understand how state constitutions were structured.

As each state wrote its own constitution, the Continental Congress wrote a constitution for the national government, which they called the Articles of Confederation.

Summarize Reread the excerpt from the Massachusetts Constitution of 1780. What rights did the state guarantee? *(Life, liberty, property, safety, and happiness)*

Hypothesize Why do you think the new nation will decide to draft a national constitution in addition to each state constitution? *(There will need to be a federal government to unite and oversee the different states. That government will require its own written constitution.)*

Identify Patterns How do you think state constitutions will influence the Articles of Confederation drafted by the Continental Congress? *(They may establish some of the rights and liberties discussed in the Articles; the Articles will have to discuss how to balance federal and state power, as laid out in the state constitutions.)*

DIGITAL TEXT 2

The Articles of Confederation

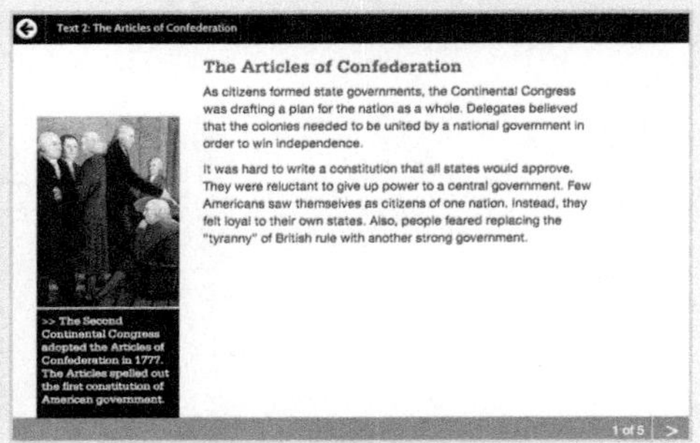

INTERACTIVE MAP

Claims to Western Lands

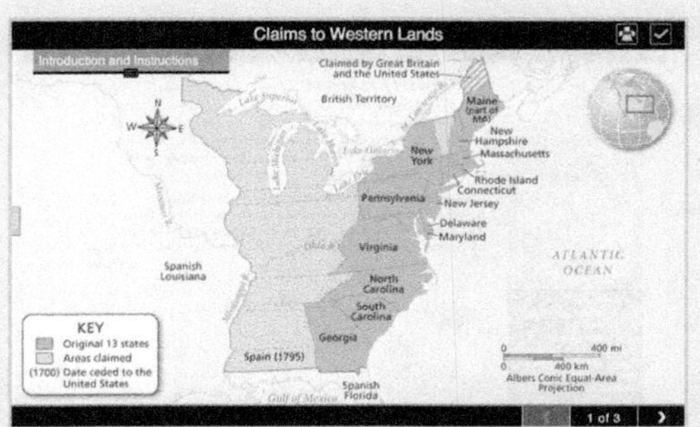

DIGITAL TEXT 3

Weaknesses of the Confederation

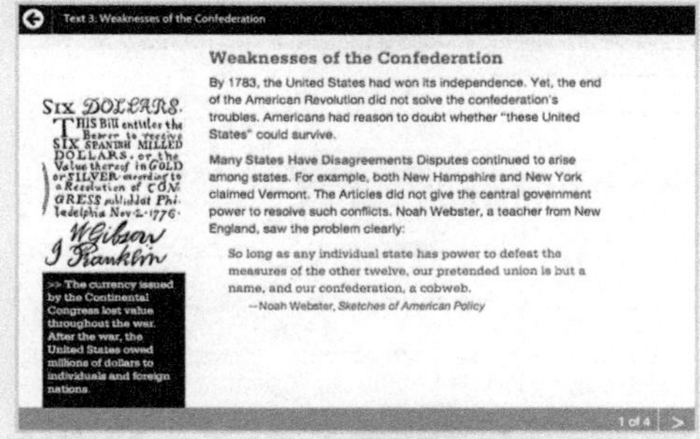

Objectives 2: **Identify the strengths and weaknesses of the Articles of Confederation; 3: Describe the process the Articles created for admitting new states.**

Quick Instruction

Generate Explanations Why was writing the Articles of Confederation an important event of the American Revolution? *(The Articles of Confederation formalized a loose alliance of states in order for them to act together to win independence.)*

Interactive Chart: Problems and Effects of the Articles of Confederation Next, project the interactive chart on the whiteboard. Explain that the procedure for expanding the United States was just one problem the Articles had to address. Have students read through the problems of the Articles and summarize the weaknesses of the document.

Interactive Map: Claims to Western Lands Project the interactive map on the whiteboard and move the slider. One issue surrounding the Articles of Confederation was who controlled western lands. Why do you think state claims to western lands created a problem for the Articles of Confederation? *(The Articles did not have the authority to resolve disputes between states over land ownership.)*

ACTIVE CLASSROOM

Have students use the PMI Strategy to summarize the strengths and weaknesses of the Articles of Confederation. Divide students into groups and have them create a three-column organizer with headings Plus/Minus/Interesting to record their answers to the following questions: What are the positive aspects about the Articles of Confederation? What are its negative aspects? What is interesting about this document?

ACTIVE CLASSROOM

Using the map as their reference, ask students to Make Headlines that summarizes what the map shows about the resolution of disputes among the states over claims to lands west of the Appalachian Mountains, and how those resolutions led to the passage of the Articles of Confederation.

ELL Use the ELL activity described in the ELL chart.

Further Instruction

Go through the Interactive Reading Notepad questions and discuss the answers with the class. Assign the Primary Source: Articles of Confederation.

Summarize the strengths of the Articles of Confederation. *(It let states make their own decisions, limited federal power, granted the states equal representation, and gave the government necessary powers to declare war, coin money, operate post offices, and sign treaties.)*

Summarize the weaknesses of the Articles of Confederation. *(The Congress's powers were limited; laws had to be approved and enforced by the states; there was no president; the Congress couldn't regulate trade or issue taxes; there was no court system; central government couldn't resolve disputes between states.)*

Topic 4 Lesson 1

A Weak Confederation

INTERACTIVE CHART

Problems and Effects of the Articles of Confederation

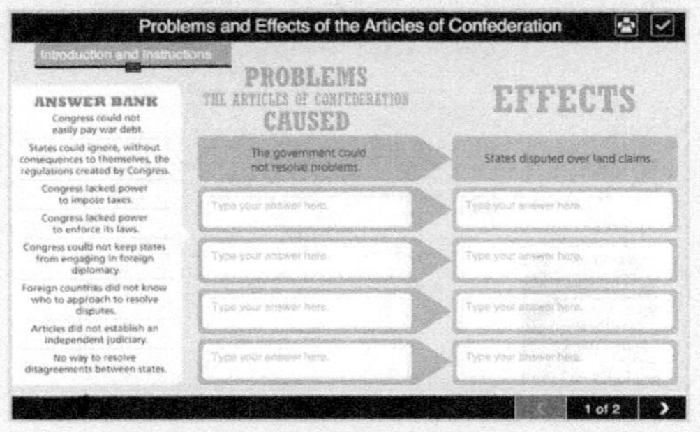

DIGITAL TEXT 4

An Orderly Expansion

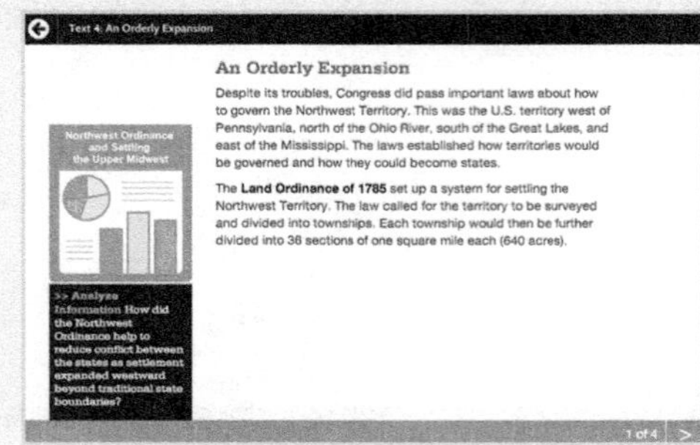

Identify Central Issues Why was the value of U.S. currency so low following the Revolution? How did the weaknesses of the Articles of Confederation contribute to this issue? *(During the Revolution, the Congress printed paper money that wasn't backed by silver or gold, which made the currency almost worthless. States therefore began printing their own money. There was not a strong central government to establish a valuable currency consistent across states.)*

Objective 3: **Describe the process the Articles created for admitting new states.**

Quick Instruction

Project the chart on the whiteboard. Remind students that one weakness of the Articles of Confederation was that it didn't grant the federal government enough authority to regulate disputes between states over land. Explain how the Northwest Ordinance established principles and procedures for the orderly expansion of the United States.

Draw Conclusions Why did the nation need a land ordinance for the Northwest Territory? Why weren't the Articles of Confederation sufficient to oversee the orderly expansion of the United States? *(The Articles of Confederation didn't account for how to resolve disputes among states over land in the territories. The nation needed to establish rules for expansion and settlement of new areas.)*

ELL Use the ELL activity described in the ELL chart.

D Differentiate: Extra Support Explain that an ordinance is an authoritative order. Have students locate the Northwest Territory on a map and state in their own words what authoritative order the Northwest Ordinance made.

Further Instruction

Go through the Interactive Reading Notepad questions and discuss the answers with the class. Assign the Primary Source: Northwest Ordinance. Be sure students can explain how the Northwest Ordinance established principles and procedures for the orderly the expansion of the United States.

Generate Explanations Explain how the Northwest Ordinance established principles and procedures for the orderly expansion of the United States. *(It established a government in the Northwest Territory and allowed the region to be further divided into separate territories. It established the principle that settlers in U.S. territories had basic rights, including the rights to freedom of religion, trial by jury, and basic government functions. It also established the principle and procedures by which new territories could become states. These regulations allowed for orderly expansion.)*

Identify Steps in a Process List the procedures territories had to undergo to become states, as established by the Land Ordinance of 1785 and the Northwest Ordinance. *(Territories were surveyed, then divided into townships. Townships were divided into smaller sections and sold to settlers. Territories had to amass a population over 60,000. Then territories could ask Congress to be admitted as a state.)*

Contrast Why was the Northwest Ordinance more successful than the Articles of Confederation in establishing principles for orderly expansion? *(It established the principle that new territories could become states and set up procedures territories could follow to become states, which the Articles otherwise did not have the authority to direct.)*

DIGITAL TEXT 5

Economic Problems Lead to Change

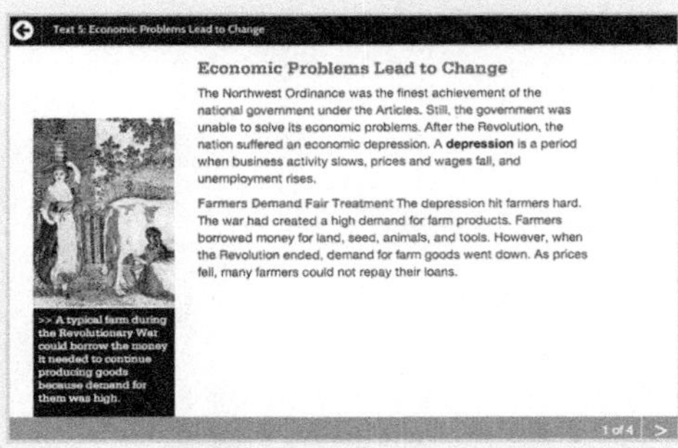

Text 5: Economic Problems Lead to Change
Economic Problems Lead to Change
The Northwest Ordinance was the finest achievement of the national government under the Articles. Still, the government was unable to solve its economic problems. After the Revolution, the nation suffered an economic depression. A **depression** is a period when business activity slows, prices and wages fall, and unemployment rises.
Farmers Demand Fair Treatment The depression hit farmers hard. The war had created a high demand for farm products. Farmers borrowed money for land, seed, animals, and tools. However, when the Revolution ended, demand for farm goods went down. As prices fell, many farmers could not repay their loans.
>> A typical farm during the Revolutionary War could borrow the money it needed to continue producing goods because demand for them was high.
1 of 4

Objectives 4: **Explain why many Americans called for changes in the Articles; 5: Summarize Shays' Rebellion and how it influenced leaders to change the Articles of Confederation.**

Quick Instruction

Project the image of the Massachusetts state militia on the whiteboard. Remind students that the country was in serious debt following the American Revolution. Economic problems caused anger in the new nation and convinced leaders the Articles of Confederation were too weak to provide useful governance. These problems were some of the causes of the creation of the Constitution.

Identify Central Issues How did the weakness of the federal government under the Articles of Confederation impact the economy of the new nation? *(The weaknesses of the Articles meant the federal government did not have the authority to tax. The nation also lacked a strong and stable single currency. This made it difficult to pay off debt and revive the economy.)*

Further Instruction

Go through the Interactive Reading Notepad questions and discuss the answers with the class. Be sure students understand why the Articles of Confederation needed to be replaced.

Recognizing the weaknesses of the Articles of Confederation, the nation's leaders met in Philadelphia in 1787 to begin drafting the United States Constitution. These weaknesses were the main causes for the creation of the Constitution.

Identify Cause and Effect Identify the causes and effects of Shay's Rebellion. *(Causes—A depression following the war meant farmers could not repay their debts. Effects—Leaders decided the Articles of Confederation had to be revised.)*

Evaluate Arguments Why did Washington call the new government "limping?" What does this quote suggest about the Articles of Confederation? *(He is describing the inability of the government to take strong steps to move the country forward. He therefore suggests the Articles of Confederation are too weak.)*

A Weak Confederation

SYNTHESIZE

DIGITAL ACTIVITY

Debating the Power of a Government

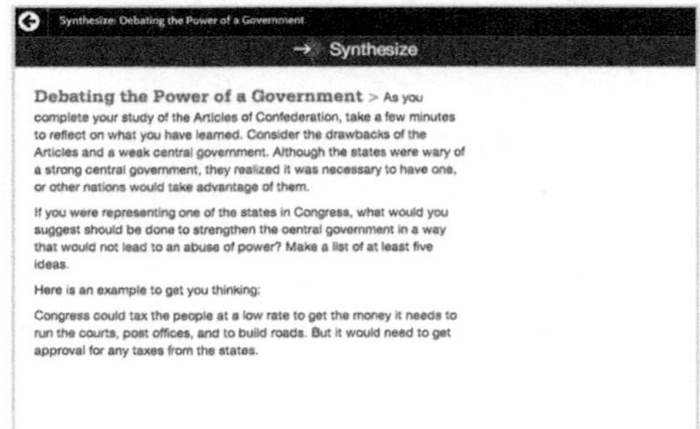

Have students make a list of five ways the early nation could have strengthened the central government without leading to abuses of power. Poll the class to see if students agree on possible solutions.

Have the class consider the following questions: What powers should the federal government have? What federal powers should be limited? Have students generate two lists.

Discuss Have students review their paragraphs from the beginning of the lesson. Ask if they would change anything now that they have learned more about the Articles of Confederation.

DEMONSTRATE

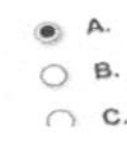

DIGITAL QUIZ

Lesson Quiz and Class Discussion Board

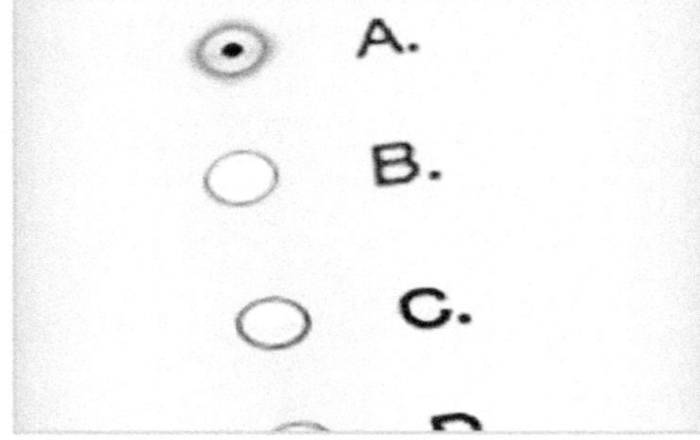

Assign the online Lesson Quiz for this lesson if you haven't already done so. Students will be offered automatic remediation or enrichment based on their score.

Pose these questions to the class on the Discussion Board:

In *A Weak Confederation* you read about the strengths and weaknesses of the Articles of Confederation and how the Northwest Ordinance contributed to the orderly expansion of the United States.

Draw Conclusions Why do you think many colonists wanted a weak federal government, as evidenced by the Articles of Confederation? *(They were wary of centralized power after the Revolution.)*

Make Predictions Name one change you think the United States Constitution would make to strengthen the federal government following the Articles of Confederation, and why. *(It would give the federal government the power to levy taxes in order to generate revenue for the nation to pay off its debts.)*

Topic Inquiry

Have students continue their investigations for the Topic Inquiry.

PEARSON realize™ www.PearsonRealize.com Access your Digital Lesson

Drafting a Constitution

Supporting English Language Learners

Use with Digital Text 1, **A Historic Convention.**

Listening
Read aloud the text, or invite volunteers to do so. As you read, have students follow along and pay special attention to your pronunciation. Prompt students to recognize elements in newly acquired vocabulary, such as long and short vowels.

Beginning Display these words from the text: *revise, describe, debate*. Point out the "long vowel-consonant-silent e" pattern. Then say each word on the list, emphasizing the long vowel sound, and have students repeat after you.

Intermediate Review the "long vowel-consonant-silent e" pattern, and display examples from the text. Then create another list of words from the text that have the spelling but not the sound pattern (e.g., private, representative, delegate). Have students practice reading both lists of words.

Advanced Display a list of words from the text that mixes "long vowel-consonant-silent e" words and exceptions to that rule. Ask students to pronounce the words and sort them into a two-column chart based on their sound pattern.

Advanced High Review that some words have a long vowel while others do not. Have students search the text for words of both types, sort them into a two-column chart, and compare their chart with a partner's.

Use with Digital Text 5, **The Convention Comes to a Conclusion.**

Reading
Distribute the following linguistically accommodated version of the quote from Benjamin Franklin to students, as appropriate according to their level:

"I don't know if any other meeting could make a better Constitution. . . . I wish that every member of this meeting who has problems with this Constitution would do the same as I am doing. That is to see that you might be wrong this time and . . . vote for this Constitution."

Beginning Have students read the linguistically accommodated version of the quote and help them understand words and phrases in this version that are too difficult for them. Have them look at the version of the quote in the student text. Ask them to briefly state the meaning of the quote.

Intermediate Have students read the linguistically accommodated version of the quote and then the version of the quote in the student text, helping them with words and phrases they do not understand. Ask them to explain the meaning of the quote.

Advanced Have students read the version of the quote in the student text, helping them with words and phrases they do not understand. Have them explain the meaning of the quote.

Advanced High Pre-teach a few challenging words from the text as a whole (e.g., *infallibility, instrument, endorsed*). Have students read the version of the quote in the student text, then have them briefly explain their understanding of its meaning and Franklin's reasons for making this statement in writing or in a class discussion.

D Differentiate Instruction

Use the Differentiated Instruction notes throughout the lesson plan to support the varied skill sets, levels of readiness, and interests in the mixed-ability classroom.

Challenge These notes include suggestions for expanding the activity for advanced students.

On-Level These notes include suggestions for modifying the activity to address different interests or learning styles.

Extra Support These notes include ideas for providing more scaffolding or reading spupport.

Special Needs These notes provide ideas for adapting instruction to support the needs of various special needs students.

NOTES

Topic 4 Lesson 2

Drafting a Constitution

Objectives

Objective 1: Identify the leaders of the Constitutional Convention.

Objective 2: Compare the main differences between the two rival plans for the new Constitution.

Objective 3: Summarize compromises the delegates had to reach before the Constitution could be signed.

LESSON 2 ORGANIZER	PACING: APPROX. 1 PERIOD,.5 BLOCKS			
			RESOURCES	
	OBJECTIVES	PACING	Online	Print
Connect				
DIGITAL START UP ACTIVITY **Compromise in Government**		5 min.	●	
Investigate				
DIGITAL TEXT 1 **A Historic Convention**	Objective 1	10 min.	●	●
DIGITAL TEXT 2 **Disagreements Over a New Government**	Objective 2	10 min.	●	●
INTERACTIVE GALLERY **Delegates of the Constitutional Convention**	Objective 2	10 min.	●	
DIGITAL TEXT 3 **The Great Compromise**	Objective 3	10 min.	●	●
INTERACTIVE CHART **The Great Compromise**	Objective 3	10 min.	●	
DIGITAL TEXT 4 **The Three-Fifths Compromise**	Objective 3	10 min.	●	●
DIGITAL TEXT 5 **The Convention Comes to a Conclusion**	Objective 3	10 min.	●	●
Synthesize				
DIGITAL ACTIVITY **Compromise in Government**		5 min.	●	
Demonstrate				
DIGITAL QUIZ **Lesson Quiz and Class Discussion Board**		10 min.	●	

Go online to access additional resources including:
Primary Sources • Biographies • Supreme Court cases • 21st Century Skill Tutorials • Maps • Graphic Organizers.

CONNECT

DIGITAL START UP ACTIVITY

Compromise in Government

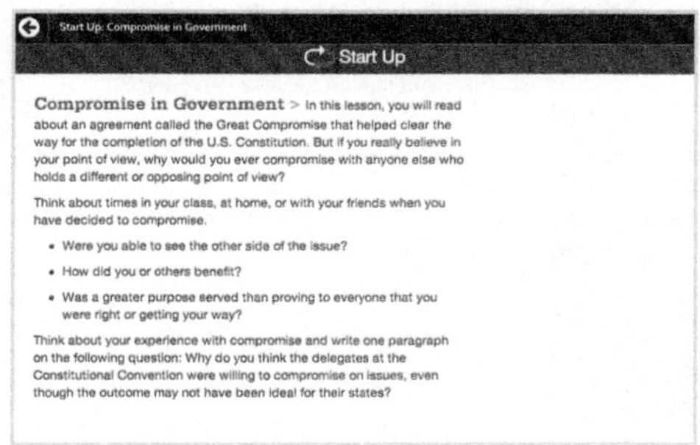

Project the Start Up Activity Ask students to review the activity as they enter and get settled. Then have students write their paragraphs and share them with each other either in class or through a blog space.

Discuss Prompt students to think about the primary need for compromise during the Convention, especially in regards to the question of the size and scope of a new federal government relative to the states.

Tell students that in this lesson they will be learning about the issues of the Constitutional Convention and the writing of the United States Constitution.

Aa Vocabulary Development: Use the Interactive Reading Notepad to preview the Key Terms and Academic Vocabulary in this lesson with students.

FLIP IT!

Assign the Flipped Video for this lesson.

STUDENT EDITION PRINT PAGES: 185–190

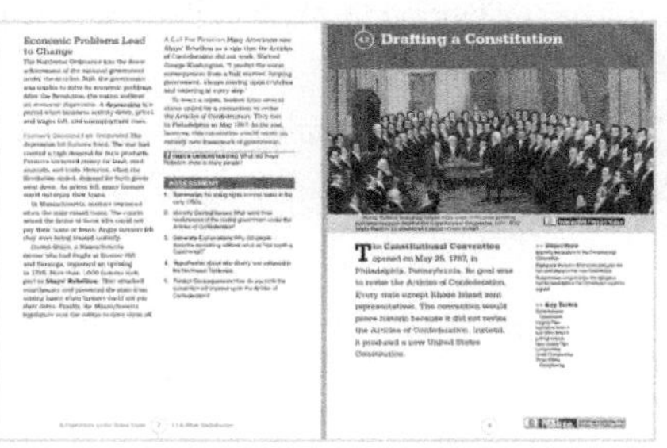

INVESTIGATE

DIGITAL TEXT 1

A Historic Convention

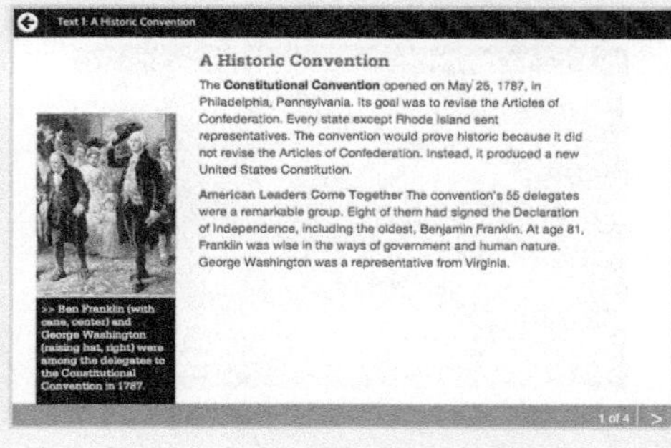

Objective 1: Identify the leaders of the Constitutional Convention.

Quick Instruction

Project the image of Franklin and Washington at the Constitutional Convention. Explain that 1787 is a significant date in U.S. history. It is the year delegates gathered in Philadelphia to write the United States Constitution.

Make Predictions Name one issue you predict will come up in the Constitutional Convention as delegates meet to revise the Articles of Confederation. *(State vs. federal power; the structure of the new government; balance of power among states)*

ELL Use the ELL activity described in the ELL chart.

Further Instruction

Go through the Interactive Reading Notepad questions and discuss the answers with the class. Be sure students can identify key leaders of the Constitutional Convention, including Washington, Franklin, and Madison. These leaders are some of the nation's founders. They will help negotiate important compromises at the Convention to bring about peaceful solutions.

Summarize What was the significance of the year 1787 and the location Philadelphia, Pennsylvania? *(Delegates met at the Constitutional Convention in Philadelphia in 1787 to write the Untied States Constitution.)*

Compare and Contrast Benjamin Franklin and James Madison. How did both of these founders contribute to the convention? *(Contrast—Franklin was 81 and Madison only 36; Franklin had more experience in government while Madison was quiet and shy. Compare—Both had ideas about how to structure the new government; both modeled civic virtue for the new nation.)*

Identify Cause and Effect How did the weaknesses of the Articles of Confederation cause the Constitution to be created? *(The nation needed a new federal government stronger than the one under the Articles.)*

Drafting a Constitution

DIGITAL TEXT 2

Disagreements Over a New Government

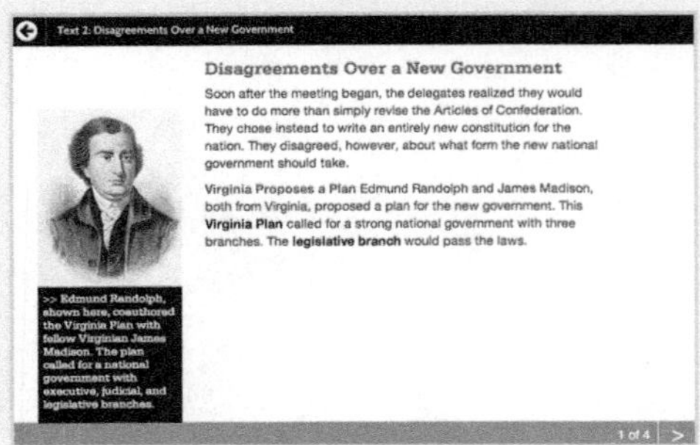

INTERACTIVE GALLERY

Delegates of the Constitutional Convention

DIGITAL TEXT 3

The Great Compromise

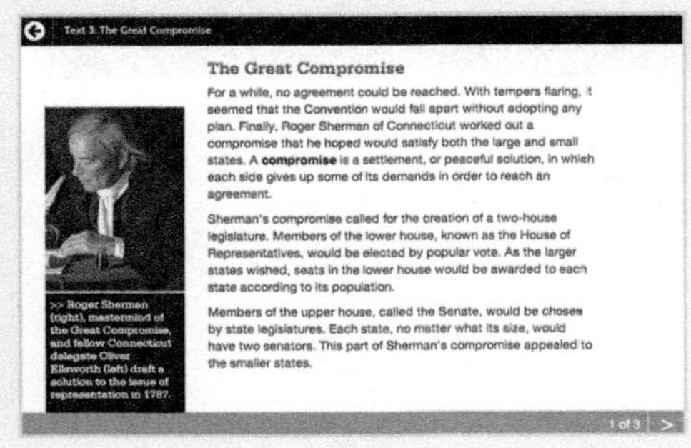

Objective 2: **Compare the main differences between two rival plans for the new Constitution.**

Quick Instruction

Interactive Gallery: Delegates of the Constitutional Convention Project the interactive gallery on the whiteboard and click through the images.

Analyze Images Look at the image of George Washington. How did Washington model civic virtue at the Constitutional Convention? *(He continued to serve the nation instead of retiring; he was a respected leader; he served as president of the Convention.)*

Summarize As you look through the gallery, name one issue that came up for the delegates during the creation of the Constitution. *(How much power small versus large states should have; how the federal government should be structured; how the states should be represented in the federal government.)*

ACTIVE CLASSROOM

Have students use the Walking Tour Strategy to analyze the issues of the Constitutional Convention of 1787. Divide the class into two groups. Have one group post passages from *Virginia Proposes a Plan* on one side of the room. Have the other group post passages from *New Jersey Disagrees* on the other side of the room. Have groups tour the room and discuss the passages, summarizing the different plans.

Further Instruction

Go through the Interactive Reading Notepad questions and discuss the answers with the class. Be sure students can summarize the Virginia and New Jersey plans and understand why the delegates disagreed.

Evaluate Arguments Why did the delegates decide they needed to create a new constitution? *(They didn't think the Articles of Confederation could be sufficiently revised.)*

Compare Points of View How did small states view the Virginia Plan, and why? Why was this difference of opinion such an important issue facing the Convention? *(Small states opposed the Virginia Plan because it awarded delegates to the legislature based on population, giving more power to larger states. The issue needed to be solved because delegates would not be able to create a new government without agreeing on representation.)*

Make Predictions How do you think the delegates would compromise on the Virginia and New Jersey plans to arrive at a peaceful solution? *(They would create two legislative branches, one with seats awarded by population and one with equal representation.)*

Objective 3: **Summarize compromises the delegates had to reach before the Constitution could be signed.**

Quick Instruction

Interactive Chart: The Great Compromise Project the interactive chart on the whiteboard and read through the columns. Review the opposing views put forth in the Virginia and New Jersey plans. Discuss why representation was an issue at the Constitutional Convention of 1787.

Analyze Information Analyze the issues that led to the Great Compromise, and explain how the Great Compromise resulted in a peaceful solution. *(Small states did not want to be outvoted by large states, and large states wanted representation proportional to their population. The Great Compromise resolved this issue by creating a bicameral legislature, with seats in the House of Representatives awarded by population and seats in the Senate set at two per state. This compromise satisfied both larger and smaller states.)*

D Differentiate: Extra Support Explain that *bi-* means two and *cameral* refers to judicial or legislative chambers. Have students use these definitions to explain the meaning of *bicameral legislature*.

ELL Use the ELL activity described in the ELL chart.

INTERACTIVE CHART

The Great Compromise

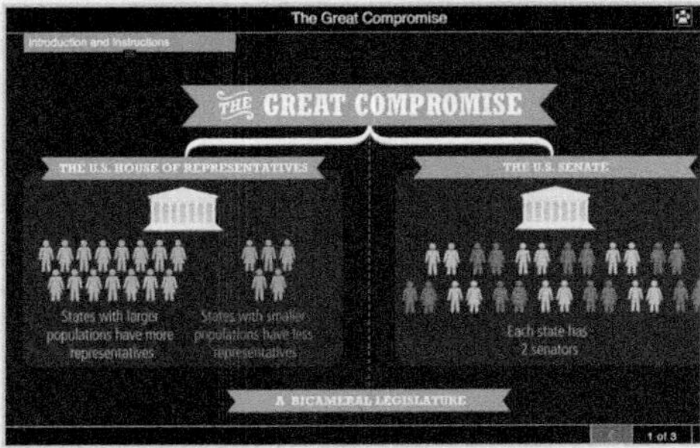

DIGITAL TEXT 4

The Three-Fifths Compromise

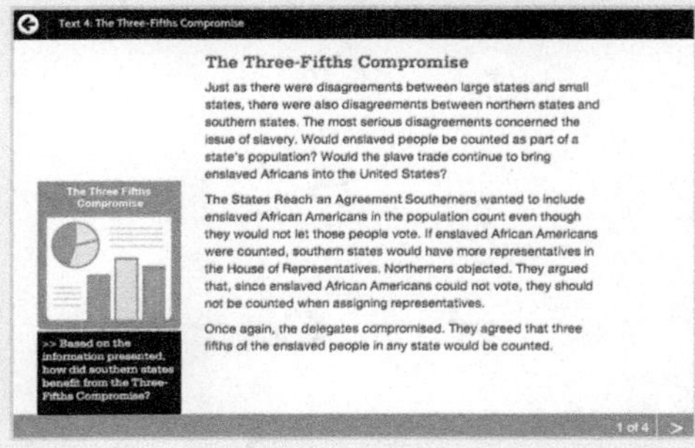

Text 4: The Three-Fifths Compromise
The Three-Fifths Compromise
Just as there were disagreements between large states and small states, there were also disagreements between northern states and southern states. The most serious disagreements concerned the issue of slavery. Would enslaved people be counted as part of a state's population? Would the slave trade continue to bring enslaved Africans into the United States?
The States Reach an Agreement Southerners wanted to include enslaved African Americans in the population count even though they would not let those people vote. If enslaved African Americans were counted, southern states would have more representatives in the House of Representatives. Northerners objected. They argued that, since enslaved African Americans could not vote, they should not be counted when assigning representatives.
Once again, the delegates compromised. They agreed that three fifths of the enslaved people in any state would be counted.
The Three Fifths Compromise
>> Based on the information presented, how did southern states benefit from the Three-Fifths Compromise?
1 of 4

DIGITAL TEXT 5

The Convention Comes to a Conclusion

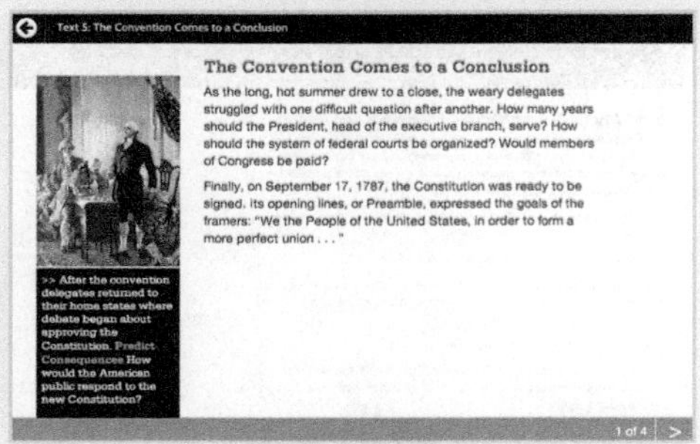

Text 5: The Convention Comes to a Conclusion
The Convention Comes to a Conclusion
As the long, hot summer drew to a close, the weary delegates struggled with one difficult question after another. How many years should the President, head of the executive branch, serve? How should the system of federal courts be organized? Would members of Congress be paid?
Finally, on September 17, 1787, the Constitution was ready to be signed. Its opening lines, or Preamble, expressed the goals of the framers: "We the People of the United States, in order to form a more perfect union . . ."
>> After the convention delegates returned to their home states where debate began about approving the Constitution. Predict Consequences How would the American public respond to the new Constitution?
1 of 4

Further Instruction

Go through the Interactive Reading Notepad questions and discuss the answers with the class. Be sure students can analyze the issues of the Constitutional Convention, including the Great Compromise and the Three-Fifths Compromise, and can summarize how these compromises resulted in a peaceful solution. After the delegates sign the Constitution, it will still need to be ratified by the states.

Interpret Analyze the issues surrounding the Three-Fifths Compromise. *(Northern and southern states disagreed over how to count enslaved African Americans when calculating the number of representatives to the House. Northern states did not think enslaved African Americans should be counted, while southern states wanted them counted. The compromise counted three-fifths of the enslaved population.)*

Identify Cause and Effect What was the main effect of the creation of the Constitution? *(It led to a process by which states had to decide whether to approve it.)*

Topic 4 Lesson 2

Drafting a Constitution

SYNTHESIZE

DIGITAL ACTIVITY

Compromise in Government

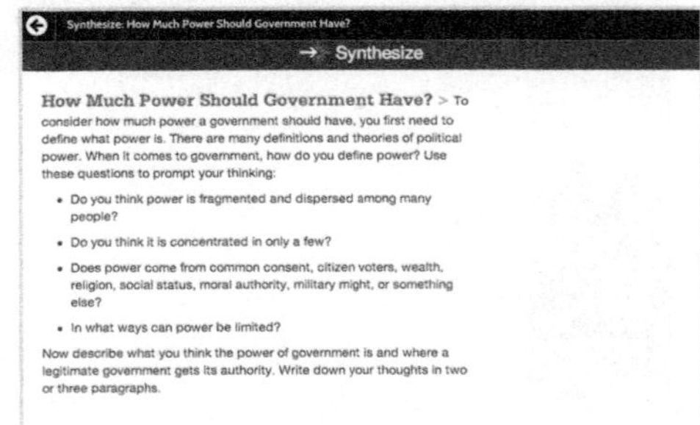

Discuss with students their definitions of power. Then have them write down their thoughts about where legitimate government gets its authority. Have students share their ideas with a a partner.

Have partners consider the following question. According to the United States Constitution, where does the federal government get its authority? Have pairs share their answers with the class.

Discuss Ask students why they think the founders divided the government into different branches. Discuss how the structure they came up with affects the power of the government.

DEMONSTRATE

DIGITAL QUIZ

Lesson Quiz and Class Discussion Board

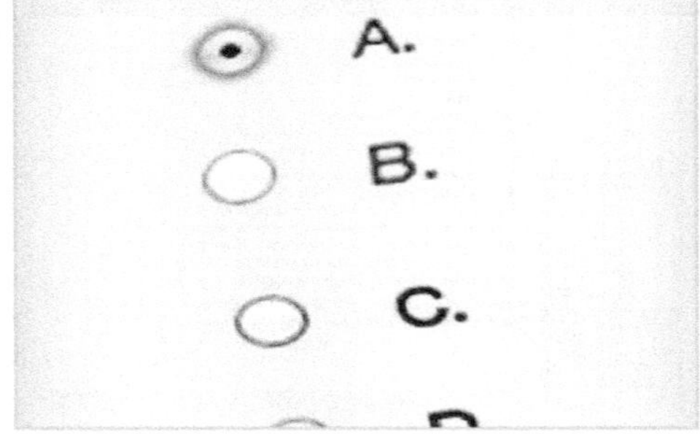

Assign the online Lesson Quiz for this lesson if you haven't already done so. Students will be offered automatic remediation or enrichment based on their score.

Pose these questions to the class on the Discussion Board:

In *Drafting a Constitution* you read about the issues surrounding the Constitutional Convention of 1787 and the compromises delegates made in writing the United States Constitution.

Draw Conclusions Why was compromise necessary for the creation of the Constitution? *(States disagreed over representation in the new government. Delegates needed to compromise over how to represent both large and small states in the legislature.)*

Hypothesize Do you think the Three-Fifths Compromise offered a genuine solution to the issue of representation? Did it result in a peaceful resolution? Explain your reasoning. *(No, it was not a solution because slavery continued to be an issue in the nation. The peaceful resolution was temporary, as the issue eventually led to the Civil War.)*

Topic Inquiry

Have students continue their investigations for the Topic Inquiry.

Ideas That Influenced the Constitution

Supporting English Language Learners

Use with Digital Text 2, **English Influences.**

Reading

Have students read the first two paragraphs of the text. Explain that students will be learning vocabulary used routinely in written classroom materials.

Beginning Display the first sentence, and underline the word *examples*. Demonstrate its meaning by naming familiar categories and showing examples of them (e.g., books, pencils). Ask: What are some examples of rights included in the Constitution? Have them use the word *examples* in a sentence.

Intermediate Help students find the meanings of the words *examples*, *valued*, and *consulting* using context clues. Have use each of these words in a sentence.

Advanced Have students read the entire text under this heading. Then have them write an original paragraph that uses the words *examples*, *extended*, *influenced*, and *affirmed*.

Advanced High Display the first sentence of the text's last paragraph, and underline the word *further*. Explain that *farther* refers to physical distance, while *further* usually refers to something abstract. Discuss how this meaning is exemplified in the text.

Use with Digital Text 3, **America Draws on Its Own Traditions.**

Listening

Read the following instructions to students: "Listen to my instructions not only so that you know what to do, but also so that you learn new language structures. Not only does this text review material you learned earlier, but it also introduces new material. While reading the text, note both the colonial traditions and the other influences that shaped the thinking of the Constitutions framers." Help students learn new language structuresby focusing on the "not only . . . but also" structure and the "both . . . and" structure in your instructions.

Beginning Make sure that students understand these two structures. Ask them what it means when you say not only to do this but also to do that, or when you say "both this and that."

Intermediate Make sure students understand the two structures in your instructions. Working in pairs or in small groups, have each student create a sentence using one of these structures and take turns listening to one another's sentences.

Advanced Have students, in pairs or small groups, create their own sentences using the "not only . . . but also" and the "both . . . and" structures and take turns listening to one another's sentences.

Advanced High Explain to students the concept of the compound sentence, and that the "not only . . . but also" structure can be used to write a compound sentence, as in your instructions. Working in pairs, have students create their own compound sentences and take turns listening to one another's sentences.

D Differentiate Instruction

Use the Differentiated Instruction notes throughout the lesson plan to support the varied skill sets, levels of readiness, and interests in the mixed-ability classroom.

Challenge These notes include suggestions for expanding the activity for advanced students.

On-Level These notes include suggestions for modifying the activity to address different interests or learning styles.

Extra Support These notes include ideas for providing more scaffolding or reading spuport.

Special Needs These notes provide ideas for adapting instruction to support the needs of various special needs students.

NOTES

Ideas That Influenced the Constitution

Objectives

Objective 1: Identify what American leaders learned about government from studying ancient Rome.

Objective 2: Summarize the traditions of freedom that Americans inherited from England and from their own colonial past.

Objective 3: Describe how the Enlightenment ideas shaped the development of the Constitution.

LESSON 3 ORGANIZER	PACING: APPROX. 1 PERIOD, .5 BLOCKS		RESOURCES	
	OBJECTIVES	PACING	Online	Print
Connect				
DIGITAL START UP ACTIVITY **How to Form a Government**		5 min.	●	
Investigate				
DIGITAL TEXT 1 **Principles from the Roman Republic**	Objective 1	10 min.	●	●
DIGITAL TEXT 2 **English Influences**	Objectives 2, 3	10 min.	●	●
DIGITAL TEXT 3 **America Draws on its Own Traditions**		10 min.	●	●
INTERACTIVE TIMELINE **Influences on the Constitution**		10 min.	●	
INTERACTIVE GALLERY **Two Treatises of Government**		10 min.	●	
Synthesize				
DIGITAL ACTIVITY **Ideas That Influenced the Constitution**		5 min.	●	
Demonstrate				
DIGITAL QUIZ **Lesson Quiz and Class Discussion Board**		10 min.	●	

CONNECT

DIGITAL START UP ACTIVITY

How to Form a Government

Project the Start Up Activity Ask students to read about Madison and Jefferson as they enter and get settled. Have each student brainstorm topics and then share ideas with another student, either in class or through a blog space.

Discuss If you were James Madison, what topics do you think you would want to read about before you formed a new government? *(Different structures of government; forms of government throughout history; liberty and natural rights)* Why? *(I would want to learn about other models of government that could provide useful examples and think about the values and principles I wanted the new government to uphold.)*

Aa Vocabulary Development: Use the Interactive Reading Notepad to preview the Key Terms and Academic Vocabulary in this lesson with students.

FLIP IT!

Assign the Flipped Video for this lesson.

STUDENT EDITION PRINT PAGES: 168–171

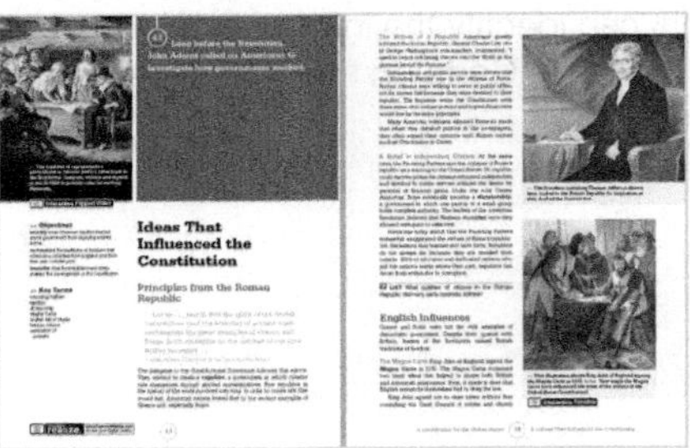

INVESTIGATE

DIGITAL TEXT 1

Principles from the Roman Republic

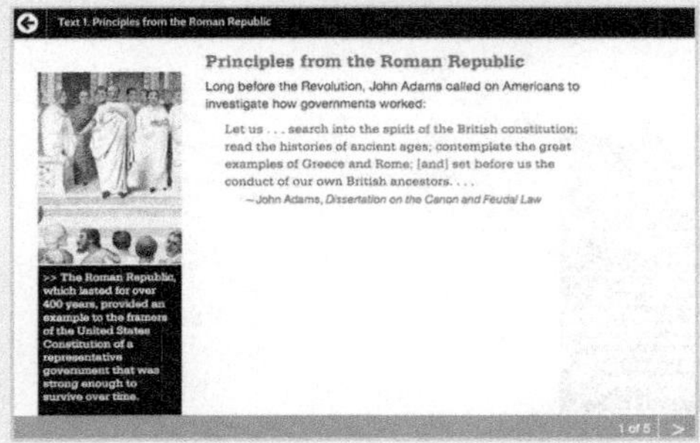

Objective 1: Identify what American leaders learned about government from studying ancient Rome.

Quick Instruction

Project the image of the Roman Republic. Define republic as a government in which citizens rule themselves through elected representatives. Explain that the founders looked to ancient Rome as an example for how to create a lasting republic.

Draw Conclusions How did the formation of a republic stand to address colonial grievances? *(The colonists objected to the king's tyranny. The founders sought to limit tyranny by having citizens rule through elected representatives.)*

Further Instruction

Go through the Interactive Reading Notepad questions and discuss the answers with the class. Be sure students understand how the founders drew on the principles and civic virtues of the Roman Republic when creating the United States Constitution. To extend the lesson, assign Government and Civics: Democracy, Monarchy, and Republic.

Identify Patterns Identify two civic virtues of Rome that the founders drew on and evaluate how they impacted the creation of the United States Constitution. *(Independence and public service: both virtues are found in the Constitution. In order for self-government to work, citizens must be independent-minded and serve the country for the greater good.)*

Evaluate Arguments How did John Adams propose to address colonial grievances in the United States Constitution? Why do you think this was a successful approach? *(He suggested looking to previous examples from ancient civilizations and the British. This was successful because it gave the founders ideas for how to structure the new government and let them learn from history the shortcomings they hoped to avoid.)*

Identify Bias What evidence from the texts shows the founders had a biased view of Rome as a model of civic virtue? *("Historians today admit that the founders somewhat exaggerated the virtues of Rome's republic.")*

Ideas That Influenced the Constitution

DIGITAL TEXT 2

English Influences

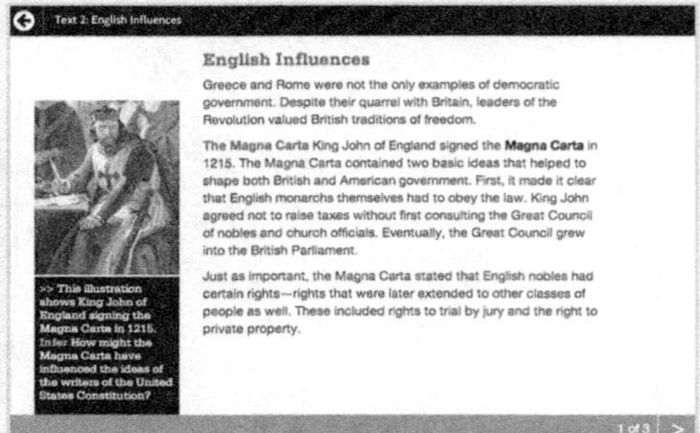

DIGITAL TEXT 3

America Draws on its Own Traditions

INTERACTIVE TIMELINE

Influences on the Constitution

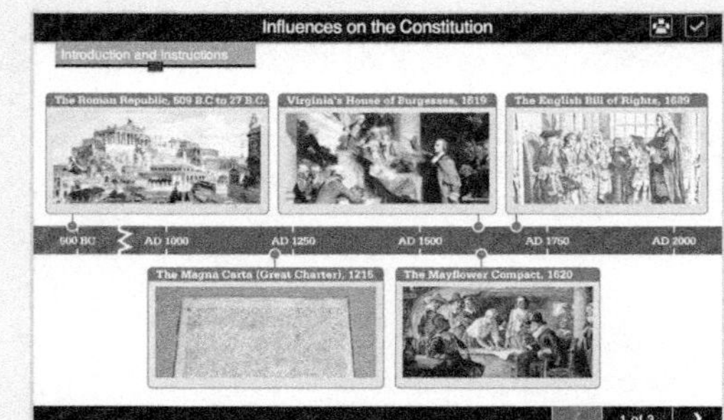

Objectives 2: Summarize the traditions of freedom that Americans inherited from England and from their own colonial past; 3: Describe how Enlightenment ideas shaped the development of the Constitution.

Quick Instruction

The U.S. system of government was influenced by ideas from historic documents including the Magna Carta and English Bill of Rights. It was also influenced by colonial history. Virginia's House of Burgesses and the Mayflower Compact were important to the growth of representative self-government in the early United States.

Interactive Timeline: Influences on the Constitution Project the interactive timeline and discuss each point on the timeline with students. What ideas did the Magna Carta give the founders about how to set up the U.S. system of government? *(The rule of law and the idea that citizens have the right to fair treatment under the law)*

Interactive Gallery: Two Treatises of Government Project the interactive gallery and click through the images. Discuss the example and how it reflects a free-enterprise system.

Identify Central Issues What views of property rights are reflected in Locke's treatise? *(Property is private and acquired through labor; people can use their property but not hoard it.)* How did those views in turn contribute to the development of a free-enterprise system in the new nation? *(The idea of private property was equated with the rights of private business owners to run their businesses with as little interference from the government as possible, which is essential to the development of a free-enterprise system.)*

ACTIVE CLASSROOM

Have students use the Sticky Notes Strategy and spend 3 minutes jotting down their response to the following questions: "What ideas from historic documents influenced the United States Constitution? How did these ideas address colonial grievances listed in the Declaration of Independence?" Ask students to share their responses with a partner.

ACTIVE CLASSROOM

Have students use the Wallpaper Strategy to review the passages on Locke and Montesquieu. Have students design a piece of "wallpaper" that encapsulates an idea from those thinkers that influenced the development of self-government in America. Have students post their wallpaper around the classroom and walk through the gallery, jotting down ideas.

D Differentiate: Challenge Challenge students to select an Enlightenment thinker not discussed in the lesson whose ideas influenced the U.S. system of government, such as Voltaire, Beccaria, or Wollstonecraft. Have students compile a list of important quotes from their thinker and write a few sentences explaining each quote and its impact on the United States.

ELL Use the ELL activity described in the ELL chart.

Further Instruction

Go through the Interactive Reading Notepad questions and discuss the answers with the class. Assign the Primary Sources: Iroquois Confederation and Magna Carta. Be sure students can identify the influence of ideas from the Magna Carta on the U.S. system of government.

INTERACTIVE GALLERY

Two Treatises of Government

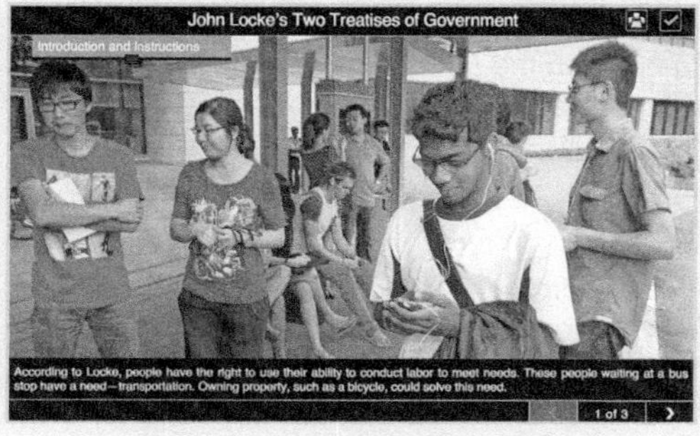

Draw Conclusions How did the Virginia House of Burgesses contribute to the growth of representative government? *(It was the first elected legislative assembly and established the tradition of representative government in America.)*

Identify Patterns What ideas from the Mayflower Compact influenced the U.S. system of government? How did these ideas contribute to the growth of representative government in the United States? *(It showed that people could rule themselves. It was also an example of how to write out the powers and limits of government. It established the tradition of self-government in the United States.)*

Cite Evidence that the United States Constitution explicitly addressed colonial grievances listed in the Declaration of Independence. *(The colonists felt the king put military power above civilians, so they made an elected leader, the President, head of the military. The colonists also felt the judges followed the king, so they established an independent court system.)*

SYNTHESIZE

DIGITAL ACTIVITY

Ideas That Influenced the Constitution

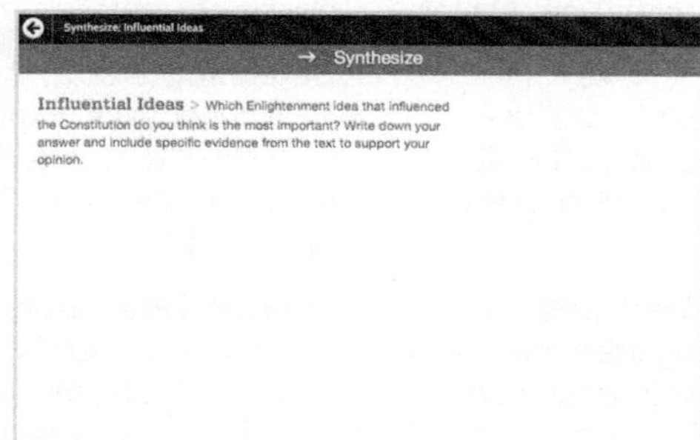

Have students generate a list of influential Enlightenment ideas and then pick the one they think was the most important in influencing the Constitution. Poll the class to see whether students agree. Call on students to support their ideas with evidence.

Have students consider the following question. Why did the Framers of the United States Constitution look to models from the past when creating a new government? Have students give examples for support.

Discuss Have students review the topics they came up with at the beginning of the lesson that they thought James Madison would want to consider. Ask if they would change or add to their response now that they have learned more about the ideas that influenced the Constitution.

DEMONSTRATE

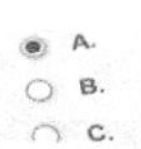

DIGITAL QUIZ

Lesson Quiz and Class Discussion Board

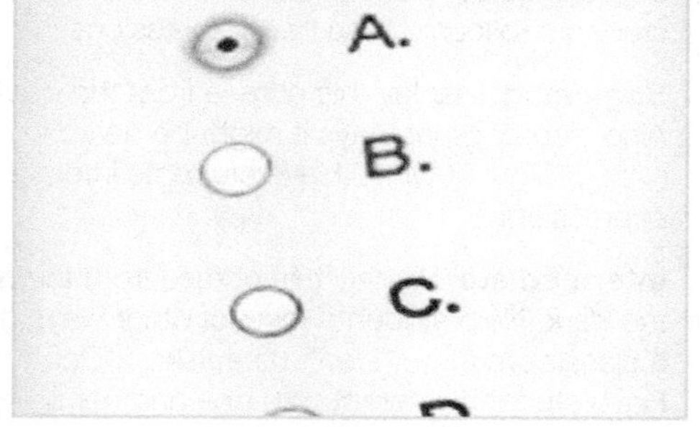

Assign the online Lesson Quiz for this lesson if you haven't already done so. Students will be offered automatic remediation or enrichment based on their score.

Pose these questions to the class on the Discussion Board:

In *Ideas that Influenced the Constitution* you read about the ideas from historic documents,significant individuals, and the colonies that influenced the U.S. system of government.

Identify Patterns What colonial grievances do you think the Framers most wanted to address in the Constitution? What ideas did they draw on to find a solution? *(They wanted government to protect people's rights without becoming too powerful. They drew on Enlightenment thinkers to come up with a separation of powers to guard against tyranny. They also learned from historic documents to write out citizens' rights and government powers.)*

Draw Conclusions How did the Constitution build upon on a tradition of self-government in the colonies? *(The Constitution extended the scope and reach of the representative governments established in the colonies, for example the House of Burgesses and the Mayflower Compact, to apply to the nation.)*

Topic Inquiry

Have students continue their investigations for the Topic Inquiry.

Federalists, Antifederalists and the Bill of Rights

Supporting English Language Learners

Use with Digital Text 3, **The Ratification Process.**

Listening

Working in groups of three, have students take turns reading aloud the paragraphs in the section titled *The Debate in New England*. Point out the sayings used in the quotation by the Federalist farmer as you prompt students to learn these new expressions.

Beginning Display this phrase from the quotation: *Don't be in a hurry*. Also display other ways it might be heard in a classroom (e.g., "Don't rush." "Slow down."). Have students interact with another using these expressions.

Intermediate Display this phrase from the quotation: *Don't take a leap in the dark*. Help students think of other ways of expressing the same idea in a classroom (e.g., "Don't take risks." "Don't do something dangerous."). Have students interact with one another using one of the expressions.

Advanced Display this phrase from the quotation: *Gather fruit when it is ripe*. Ask students, working in pairs, to take turns stating the meaning of this expression in their own words. Have students interact with one another using one of the expressions.

Advanced High Display this phrase from the quotation: *Don't take a leap in the dark*. Also display this phrase: *Don't take a leap in the dark*. Have pairs of students explain the meanings of these expressions and how they contrast with one another. Then have students interact with one another using these expressions.

Use with Digital Text 4, **New Amendments.**

Reading

Read aloud the text, or invite volunteers to do so. Prompt students to comprehend English language structures used routinely in written classroom materials.

Beginning Display these phrases from the text: *10 amendments, 12 amendments*. Explain that a cardinal, or simple, number shows the quantity of a noun and comes before it. Have students complete and read this sentence: The Bill of Rights has _____ amendments, but _____ were proposed.

Intermediate Display these phrases from the text: *first election, Third Amendment*. Explain that ordinal numbers show the order of nouns and come before them. Display the ordinal numbers through tenth, placing each before *amendment*. Have students read the list.

Advanced Make sure that students understand how cardinal and ordinal numbers work with nouns. Then draw their attention to the last sentence in the second-to-last paragraph in this text, beginning "It was only after . . ." Explain that the first phrase in the sentence sets a condition related to timing. The second phrase in the sentence, beginning "that . . ." is true only if the condition set in the first phrase is true.

Advanced High Make sure that students understand how cardinal and ordinal numbers work with nouns. Then draw their attention to the last sentence in the second-to-last paragraph in this text, beginning "It was only after . . ." Explain that the first phrase in the sentence sets a condition related to timing. The second phrase in the sentence, beginning "that . . ." is true only if the condition set in the first phrase is true. Have students create their own complex sentences using this structure.

D Differentiate Instruction

Use the Differentiated Instruction notes throughout the lesson plan to support the varied skill sets, levels of readiness, and interests in the mixed-ability classroom.

Challenge These notes include suggestions for expanding the activity for advanced students.

On-Level These notes include suggestions for modifying the activity to address different interests or learning styles.

Extra Support These notes include ideas for providing more scaffolding or reading spuport.

Special Needs These notes provide ideas for adapting instruction to support the needs of various special needs students.

NOTES

PEARSON realize
www.PearsonRealize.com

Go online to access additional resources including:
Primary Sources • Biographies • Supreme Court cases • 21st Century Skill Tutorials • Maps • Graphic Organizers.

Objectives

Objective 1: Identify the key issues in the constitutional debate.

Objective 2: Explain how the Constitution was finally ratified.

Objective 3: Describe how the Bill of Rights was added to the Constitution.

LESSON 4 ORGANIZER	OBJECTIVES	PACING	RESOURCES: Online	RESOURCES: Print
Connect				
DIGITAL START UP ACTIVITY **List Your Rights**		5 min.	●	
Investigate				
DIGITAL TEXT 1 **The Federalists and the Antifederalists**	Objective 1	10 min.	●	●
INTERACTIVE CHART **Federalists Versus Antifederalists**	Objective 1	10 min.	●	
DIGITAL TEXT 2 **A Bill of Rights**	Objective 1	10 min.	●	●
DIGITAL TEXT 3 **The Ratification Process**	Objective 2	10 min.	●	●
DIGITAL TEXT 4 **New Amendments**	Objective 3	10 min.	●	●
INTERACTIVE MAP **Ratification of the Constitution**	Objective 3	10 min.	●	
Synthesize				
DIGITAL ACTIVITY **List Your Rights**		5 min.	●	
Demonstrate				
DIGITAL QUIZ **Lesson Quiz and Class Discussion Board**		10 min.	●	

PACING: APPROX. 1 PERIOD, .5 BLOCKS

Federalists, Antifederalists and the Bill of Rights

CONNECT

DIGITAL START UP ACTIVITY

List Your Rights

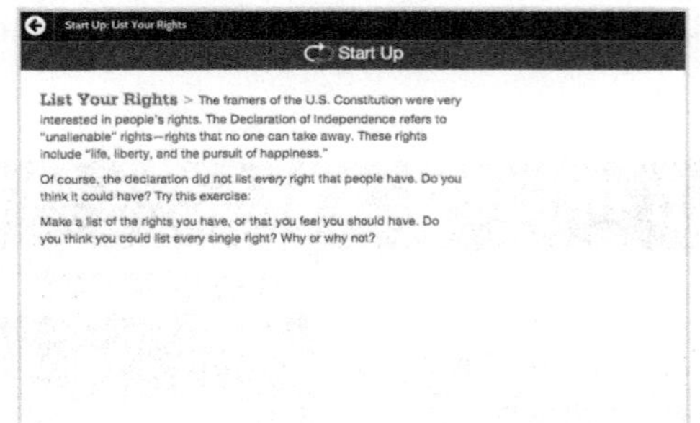

Start Up: List Your Rights
Start Up
List Your Rights > The framers of the U.S. Constitution were very interested in people's rights. The Declaration of Independence refers to "unalienable" rights—rights that no one can take away. These rights include "life, liberty, and the pursuit of happiness."
Of course, the declaration did not list every right that people have. Do you think it could have? Try this exercise:
Make a list of the rights you have, or that you feel you should have. Do you think you could list every single right? Why or why not?

Project the Start Up Activity Ask students to read about the rights listed in the Declaration of Independence and then make a list of the rights they have, or feel they should have. Have students share their lists with another student, either in class or through a blog space.

Discuss Make a list of the rights you have, or that you feel you should have. *(Life, liberty, property, safety, free speech, freedom of movement)* Do you think you could list every single right? Why or why not? *(I probably couldn't list every right because there are so many; I could because rights can be clearly spelled out.)*

Aa Vocabulary Development: Use the Interactive Reading Notepad to preview the Key Terms and Academic Vocabulary in this lesson with students.

FLIP IT!

Assign the Flipped Video for this lesson.

STUDENT EDITION PRINT PAGES: 197–202

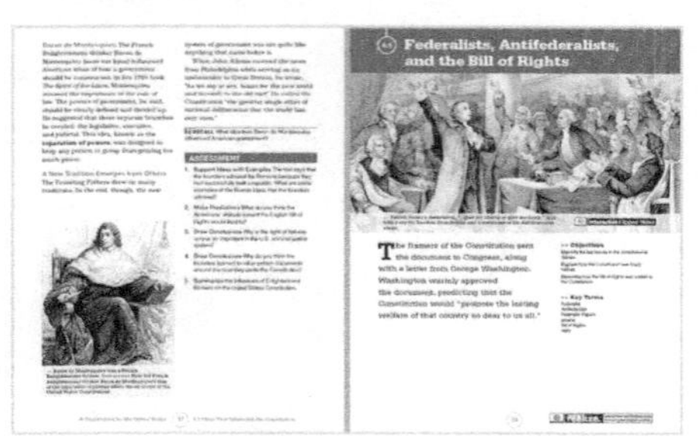

INVESTIGATE

DIGITAL TEXT 1

The Federalists and the Antifederalists

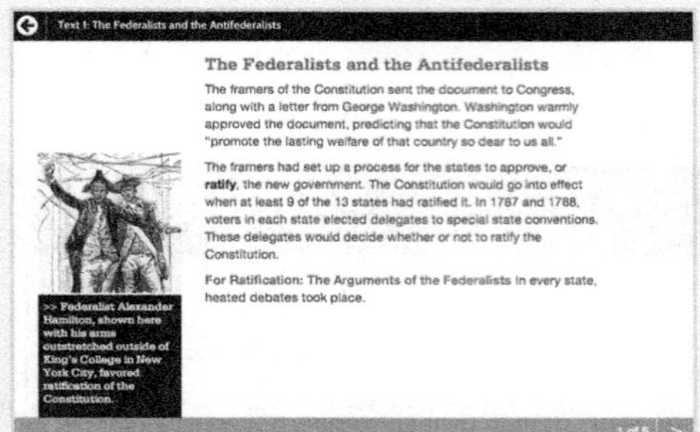

Text 1: The Federalists and the Antifederalists
The Federalists and the Antifederalists
The framers of the Constitution sent the document to Congress, along with a letter from George Washington. Washington warmly approved the document, predicting that the Constitution would "promote the lasting welfare of that country so dear to us all."
The framers had set up a process for the states to approve, or ratify, the new government. The Constitution would go into effect when at least 9 of the 13 states had ratified it. In 1787 and 1788, voters in each state elected delegates to special state conventions. These delegates would decide whether or not to ratify the Constitution.
For Ratification: The Arguments of the Federalists In every state, heated debates took place.
>> Federalist Alexander Hamilton, shown here with his arms outstretched outside of King's College in New York City, favored ratification of the Constitution.
1 of 5

INTERACTIVE CHART

Federalists Versus Antifederalists

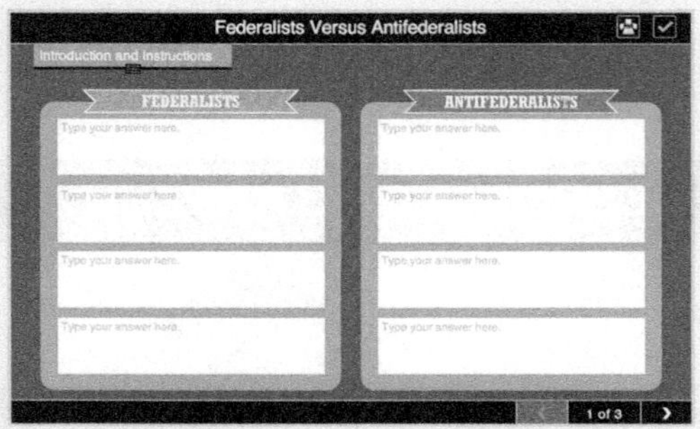

Objective 1: Identify the key issues in the constitutional debate.

Quick Instruction

Interactive Chart: Federalists Versus Antifederalists Project the interactive chart and read through the columns. Remind students that after the Framers signed the Constitution, it had to be ratified by at least nine states to take effect. Supporters of the Constitution called themselves Federalists. Opponents were Antifederalists.

Analyze Information Analyze the arguments of the Federalists and Antifederalists for and against ratification. *(Federalists argued that the Constitution gives the federal government the authority necessary to govern while protecting states' rights. Federalists believed that a strong federal government was needed to perform crucial functions, and that the Constitution provided this while preserving the rights of the states. Antifederalists argued that the Constitution makes the federal government too strong compared to the states and gives the President too much power. Antifederalists were opposed to a strong federal government and believed that most functions of government could best be handled by the states.)*

ACTIVE CLASSROOM

Have students Take a Stand on the balance of power between the federal government and the states. Ask: Who was right, the Federalists or the Antifederalists? Have students move to opposite sides of the room according to their views. Each group writes a justification of their opinion and presents its statement to the other side. Groups may then craft rebuttals.

D Differentiate: Extra Support The word federal refers to the national government. It describes a government formed by the union of states. This should help students remember that Federalists supported the Constitution because they supported the federal government. Antifederalists were against (anti–) a strong federal government.

Further Instruction

Go through the Interactive Reading Notepad questions and discuss the answers with the class. Assign the Primary Sources: Antifederalist positions/papers and *The Federalist (#1, 9, 10, 14, 39, 51, 78)*. Be sure students are able to analyze the arguments for and against ratification.

Evaluate Arguments Analyze the arguments of Patrick Henry against ratification. What is he arguing in his speech, and why? *(He is arguing the Constitution gives too much power to the President. After fighting for independence, he is worried the President could become tyrannical, like a king.)*

DIGITAL TEXT 2

A Bill of Rights

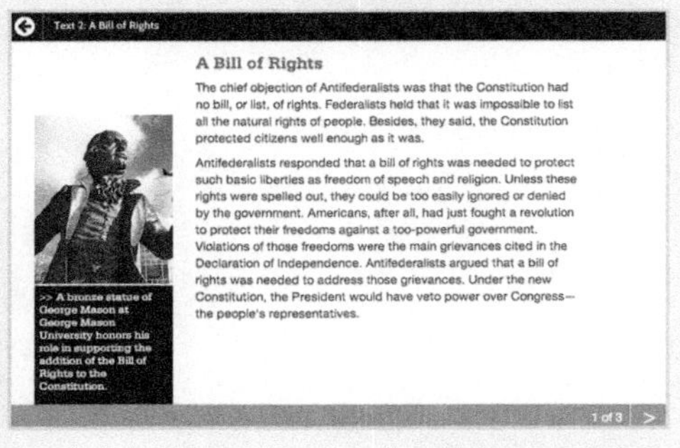

Text 2: A Bill of Rights
A Bill of Rights
The chief objection of Antifederalists was that the Constitution had no bill, or list, of rights. Federalists held that it was impossible to list all the natural rights of people. Besides, they said, the Constitution protected citizens well enough as it was.
Antifederalists responded that a bill of rights was needed to protect such basic liberties as freedom of speech and religion. Unless these rights were spelled out, they could be too easily ignored or denied by the government. Americans, after all, had just fought a revolution to protect their freedoms against a too-powerful government. Violations of those freedoms were the main grievances cited in the Declaration of Independence. Antifederalists argued that a bill of rights was needed to address those grievances. Under the new Constitution, the President would have veto power over Congress—the people's representatives.
>> A bronze statue of George Mason at George Mason University honors his role in supporting the addition of the Bill of Rights to the Constitution.
1 of 3

Draw Conclusions How have ideas from the *Federalist Papers* influenced the U.S. system of government? *(The papers defend the Constitution and discuss the benefits of and reasons for the U.S. system of government.)* How did Antifederalist writings influence the U.S. system of government? *(Writings such as George Mason's "Objections to This Constitution of Government" supported the Bill of Rights.)*

Contrast Analyze the Antifederalist arguments of George Mason and the arguments of Federalists like Alexander Hamilton and James Madison regarding ratification. Contrast the Antifederalist arguments with the arguments of the Federalists. *(Mason supported a bill of rights to protect citizens from presidential power. Hamilton and Madison thought people's natural rights were too many to list. They argued the Constitution protected citizens without the need for a bill.)*

DIGITAL TEXT 3

The Ratification Process

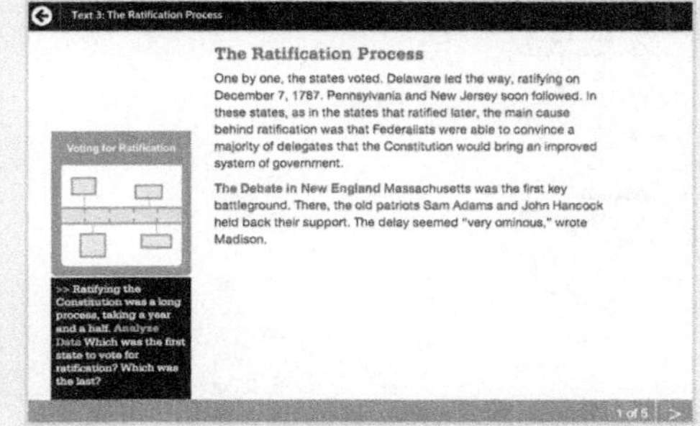

Text 3: The Ratification Process
The Ratification Process
One by one, the states voted. Delaware led the way, ratifying on December 7, 1787. Pennsylvania and New Jersey soon followed. In these states, as in the states that ratified later, the main cause behind ratification was that Federalists were able to convince a majority of delegates that the Constitution would bring an improved system of government.
The Debate in New England Massachusetts was the first key battleground. There, the old patriots Sam Adams and John Hancock held back their support. The delay seemed "very ominous," wrote Madison.
Voting for Ratification
>> Ratifying the Constitution was a long process, taking a year and a half. Analyze Data Which was the first state to vote for ratification? Which was the last?
1 of 5

Objective 2: **Explain how the Constitution was finally ratified.**

Quick Instruction

Project the political cartoon and ask students to describe the image. Identify the creation and ratification of the Constitution as a major event in U.S. history. Explain that debates occurred between Federalists and Antifederalists throughout all 13 states. Discuss the causes and effects of the creation and ratification of the Constitution, including how disagreements over whether or not to ratify the Constitution threatened the unity of the new nation.

Identify Central Issues Why did Patrick Henry and George Mason oppose ratification? *(They thought the Constitution gave the federal government too much power. Mason wanted to include a bill of rights to protect citizens.)*

ELL Use the ELL activity described in the ELL chart.

Further Instruction

Go through the Interactive Reading Notepad questions and discuss the answers with the class. To extend the lesson, assign the biographies of Alexander Hamilton, James Madison, and George Mason. Discuss the opposing viewpoints of these prominent Federalists and Antifederalists and their reasons for and against ratification.

Determine Point of View What did Federalists mean by the saying "gather fruit when it is ripe"? What does this phrase suggest about their view of the Constitution? How was it an argument for ratification? *(They meant the Constitution was ready to be passed, or "ripe." The country wouldn't benefit from waiting. This suggests they thought the Constitution, while not necessarily perfect, was the best government for the nation and should pass without delay.)*

Support Ideas with Evidence What major change finally convinced many states to vote for ratification? How do you know? *(Federalists promised to include a bill of rights. Virginia then ratified the Constitution, followed by New York, North Carolina, and Rhode Island. This suggests it was the Bill of Rights that finally swayed public opinion.)*

Generate Explanations Explain how the Bill of Rights addressed the grievances the colonists had fought for in the American Revolution. *(It safeguarded rights that colonists felt had been trampled on by the British monarchy.)*

Federalists, Antifederalists and the Bill of Rights

DIGITAL TEXT 4

New Amendments

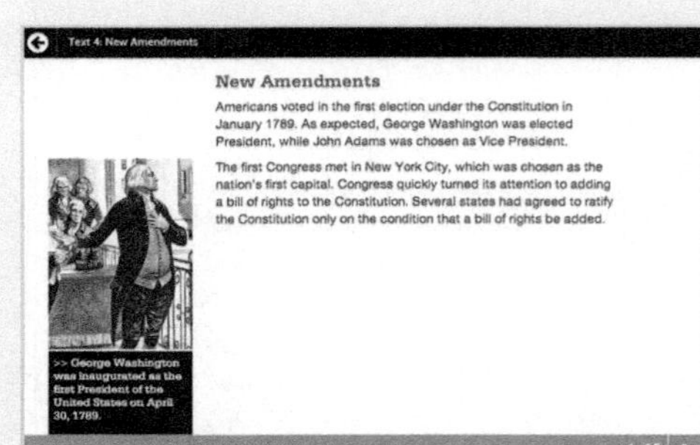

INTERACTIVE MAP

Ratification of the Constitution

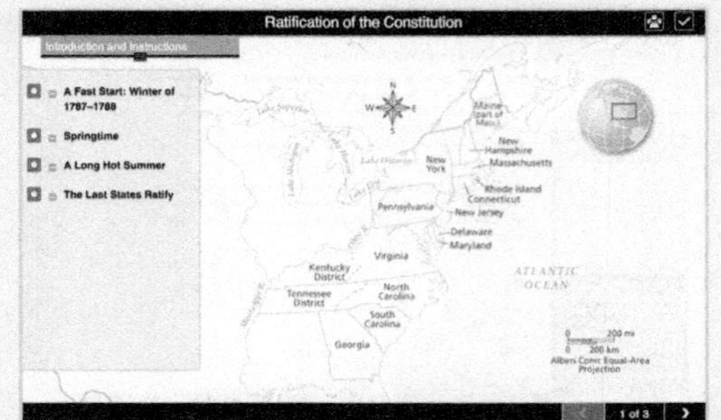

Objective 3: **Describe how the Bill of Rights was added to the Constitution.**

Quick Instruction

Interactive Map: Ratification of the Constitution Project the interactive map and click through the layers to see the ratification process. Remind students that Virginia and New York, two large and influential states, did not ratify the Constitution until the Federalists promised to include a bill of rights.

Analyze Maps Look at the map and compare the sizes of different states. Why do you think Rhode Island ratified the Constitution by such a narrow margin? What arguments do you think Rhode Island Antifederalists may have made against ratification? *(Rhode Island is a small state. Antifederalists may have worried that the power the Constitution gives the federal government would allow large states to dominate smaller states.)*

ACTIVE CLASSROOM

Have groups of two or three students write three newspaper headlines that track the ratification process for the nation's new Constitution. Each headline should summarize a key event in the ratification process. Have students share their headlines and ask for feedback.

ELL Use the ELL activity described in the ELL chart.

Further Instruction

Go through the Interactive Reading Notepad questions and discuss the answers with the class. Be sure students understand how the Bill of Rights addressed colonists' grievances listed in the Declaration of Independence and caused states to ratify the Constitution.

Cite Evidence Name an amendment included in the Bill of Rights that reflects individual rights and explain how it addressed colonial grievances. *(Third Amendment—government cannot quarter troops in citzens' homes without their consent. This addressed the colonists' grievance in the Declaration of Independence that the king forced them to quarter troops in their homes. The Sixth and Seventh Amendments guarantee trial by jury, a right the king suspended.)*

Support Ideas with Examples Give an example of how the United States Constitution reflects the principle of individual rights. *(It gives every citizen equal rights under the law; the Bill of Rights lists rights all people have.)*

Determine Point of View Do you think the inclusion of the Bill of Rights satisfied the concerns of Antifederalists like George Mason and Patrick Henry? Explain your reasoning. *(Mason had called for a bill of rights, so was probably satisfied with the inclusion. Other Antifederalists may have been glad to see a bill of rights but still might have had reservations about federal power.)*

PEARSON realize™ www.PearsonRealize.com Access your Digital Lesson

SYNTHESIZE

DIGITAL ACTIVITY

List Your Rights

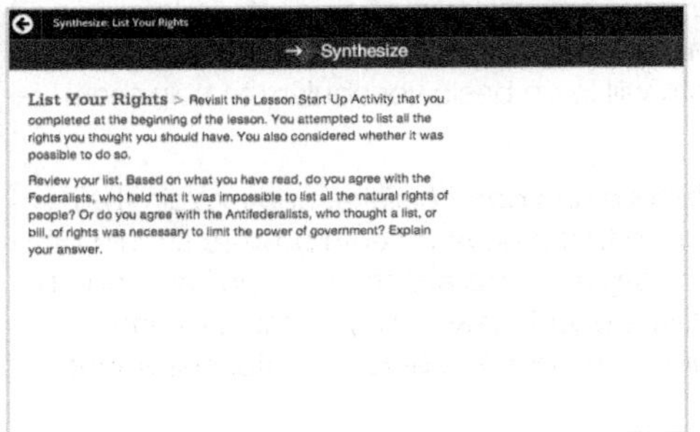

Have students review the lists they made at the beginning of the lesson and their thoughts about the possibility of listing all their natural rights. Ask whether they would like to revise their answers based on what they have learned. Discuss whether they agree with the Federalists or Antifederalists regarding the necessity of a bill of rights.

Have students consider the following question. How have both Federalist and Antifederalist ideas continued to influence the U.S. system of government today? Have students discuss their answers with the class.

Discuss Ask students whose arguments they agree with more, those of the Federalists or Antifederalists. Ask them to provide examples for support.

DEMONSTRATE

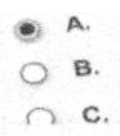

DIGITAL QUIZ

Lesson Quiz and Class Discussion Board

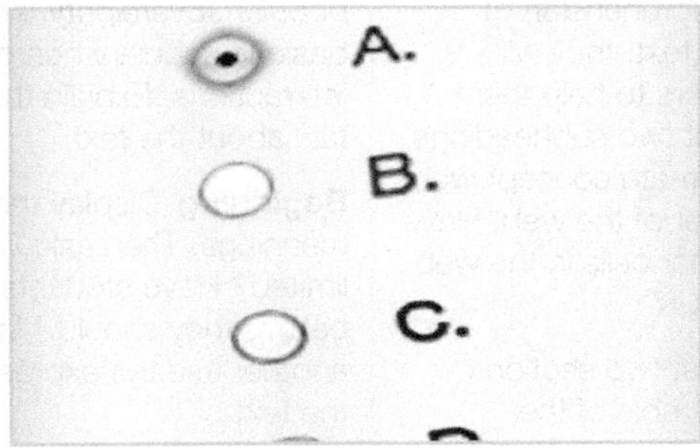

Assign the online Lesson Quiz for this lesson if you haven't already done so. Students will be offered automatic remediation or enrichment based on their score.

Pose these questions to the class on the Discussion Board:

In *Federalists, Antifederalists, and the Bill of Rights* you read about the arguments of Federalists and Antifederalists surrounding ratification and the ways the Bill of Rights addressed colonial grievances.

Evaluate Arguments Do you agree with the Federalists that the United States Constitution reflects the principle of limited government, or do you side with Antifederalist arguments that the Constitution gives federal government dangerous power? Explain your reasoning. *(I think the Constitution reflects the principles of limited government because it creates separate branches of government to limit the power of each branch, and because it lists citizen's rights to prevent government from becoming tyrannical.)*

Topic Inquiry

Have students continue their investigations for the Topic Inquiry.

Understanding the Constitution

Supporting English Language Learners

Use with Digital Text 1, **The Preamble, the Articles, and the Amendments.**

Reading

Use prereading supports such as pretaught topic-related vocabulary, graphic organizers, and other activities to enhance comprehension of written text. Explain to students that before reading the text, they will learn some new vocabulary and create graphic organizers to help them comprehend the material. Display the text's title and first two subheadings. Explain both using simpler vocabulary. Have students create concept web graphic organizers, with the word *preamble* at the center of the web. Have them write words and phrases from the preamble in other cells in the web, along with definitions of those terms in their own words.

Beginning Have students read the introduction and first two sections and fill in their graphic organizers. Ask: What is the Preamble of the Constitution?

Intermediate Have students read the text and fill in their graphic organizers. Ask: What is domestic tranquillity?

Advanced Have students read the text, fill in their graphic organizers, and look up in a dictionary any words that are unfamiliar and not clear from the context. Ask: What is the purpose of the Preamble?

Advanced High Have students read the text and fill in their graphic organizers. In pairs or for the whole class, have them take turns explaining the different terms in the Preamble, and the relationship of the Preamble to the rest of the Constitution.

Use with Digital Text 2, **Seven Basic Principles.**

Listening

Have students read the introduction and the first two subheads of the text. Circulate to make sure that they understand key terms such as *popular sovereignty*, and *limited government*. Prompt students to learn basic vocabulary heard by listening during classroom instruction and interactions. Explain that students will learn basic vocabulary to help them talk about the text.

Beginning Display the words *believe* and *don't believe*, and explain their meanings. Then ask: Do you believe that a governments powers should be limited? Have students answer by saying, "I believe they should" or "I don't believe they should." In pairs, have students take turns listening to one another use the expressions *believe* and *don't believe* in sentences about the text.

Intermediate Display these terms: *agree, disagree*. Explain the meanings of these terms and model sentences using them. Ask: Popular sovereignty is not really important. Do you agree or disagree? Then have each student respond with a sentence of his or her own using one of these terms. Have them take turns, working in pairs, listening to each other's sentences.

Advanced Display these terms: *fact, opinion*. Explain the meanings of these terms and model sentences using them. Then have each student create two sentences of his or her own, each one of these terms. Have them take turns, working in pairs, listening to each other's sentences.

Advanced High Display these terms: *suppose, supposing, assume, assuming*. Explain the meanings of these terms.Then ask questions that use these terms, such as: Assuming a government has no separation of powers, can it have a system of checks and balances? Suppose you had to get rid of one of the seven principles. Which would it be, and why? Working in pairs, have students take turns listening to each other's responses to your questions, which should use these terms.

D Differentiate Instruction

Use the Differentiated Instruction notes throughout the lesson plan to support the varied skill sets, levels of readiness, and interests in the mixed-ability classroom.

Challenge These notes include suggestions for expanding the activity for advanced students.

On-Level These notes include suggestions for modifying the activity to address different interests or learning styles.

Extra Support These notes include ideas for providing more scaffolding or reading spuport.

Special Needs These notes provide ideas for adapting instruction to support the needs of various special needs students.

NOTES

PEARSON realize www.PearsonRealize.com

Go online to access additional resources including: Primary Sources • Biographies • Supreme Court cases • 21st Century Skill Tutorials • Maps • Graphic Organizers.

Objectives

Objective 1: Explain the basic goals of the Constitution as defined by the Preamble.

Objective 2: Identify the framework of government that the Constitution established.

Objective 3: Summarize the seven basic principles of American government.

Objective 4: Identify the powers and duties of the legislative branch, executive branch, and judicial branch of the American government.

Objective 5: Describe the services that state and local governments provide.

LESSON 5 ORGANIZER	PACING: APPROX. 1 PERIOD, .5 BLOCKS			
			RESOURCES	
	OBJECTIVES	PACING	Online	Print
Connect				
DIGITAL START UP ACTIVITY **Your Government, Your Welfare**		5 min.	●	
Investigate				
DIGITAL TEXT 1 **The Preamble, the Articles, and the Amendments**	Objective 1	10 min.	●	●
DIGITAL TEXT 6 **Preventing Abuse of Power**	Objective 2	10 min.	●	●
DIGITAL TEXT 2 **Seven Basic Principles**	Objective 3	10 min.	●	●
INTERACTIVE CHART **The Federal System**		10 min.	●	
DIGITAL TEXTS 3, 4, 5 **The Legislative Branch: Congress; The Executive Branch: the President; the Judicial Branch: the Courts**	Objective 4	30 min.	●	●
INTERACTIVE GALLERY **The U.S. Congress**		10 min.	●	
DIGITAL TEXT 7 **State Government**	Objective 5	10 min.	●	●
DIGITAL TEXT 8 **The Responsibilities of Local Government**		10 min.	●	●
Synthesize				
DIGITAL ACTIVITY **Goals and Principles of the Constitution**		5 min.	●	
Demonstrate				
DIGITAL QUIZ **Lesson Quiz and Class Discussion Board**		10 min.	●	

Understanding the Constitution

CONNECT

DIGITAL START UP ACTIVITY

Your Government, Your Welfare

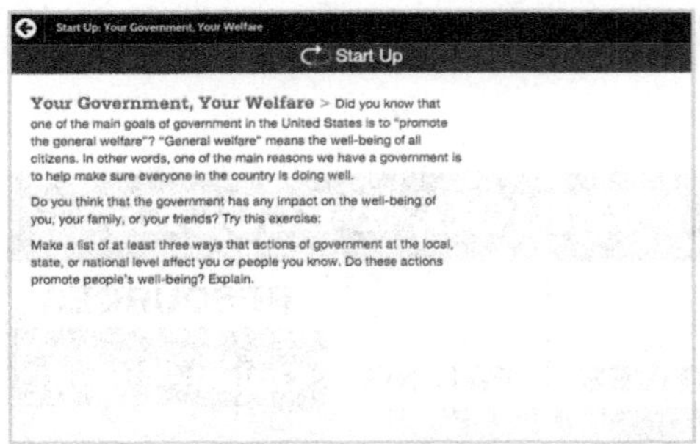

Project the Start Up Activity Ask students to read the definition of "general welfare" and list at least three actions the government takes. Have each student share his or her list with another student, either in class or through a blog space, and have them discuss how these actions affect their lives.

Discuss Do these actions promote people's well-being? *(Answers will vary; students should explain how the actions they listed affect themselves or people they know.)*

Tell students that in this lesson they will be learning about the principles reflected in the United States Constitution.

Aa Vocabulary Development: Use the Interactive Reading Notepad to preview the Key Terms and Academic Vocabulary in this lesson with students.

FLIP IT!

Assign the Flipped Video for this lesson.

STUDENT EDITION PRINT PAGES: 203–218

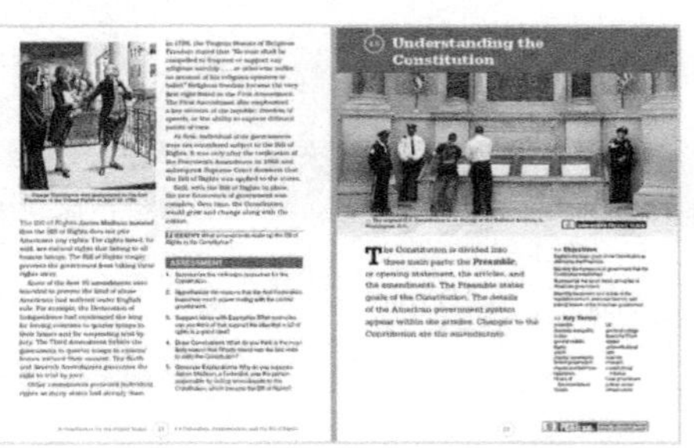

INVESTIGATE

DIGITAL TEXT 1

The Preamble, the Articles, and the Amendments

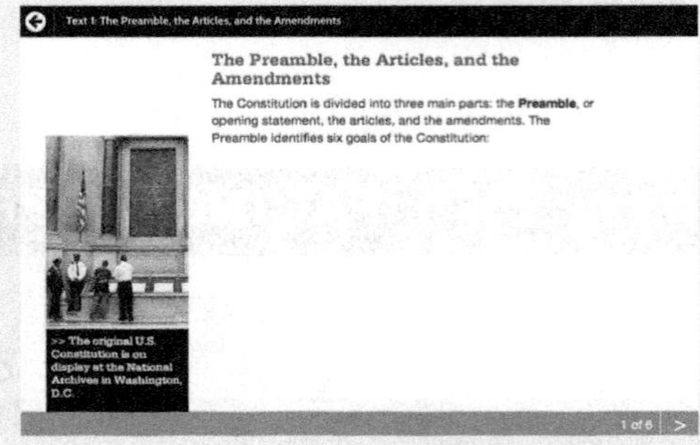

Objective 1: Explain the basic goals of the Constitution as defined by the Preamble.

Quick Instruction

Project the image of the Constitution on the whiteboard. The Constitution begins with an introductory Preamble. It is followed by 7 sections, or articles, and 27 amendments. Read the Preamble aloud with the class.

Draw Conclusions How does the Constitution's intention to form "a more perfect union"reflect the principle of federalism? *(The intention is to join the states into a union in which power is shared between the federal government and the states.)*

D Differentiate: Extra Support Review the definition of federalism, a system government in which power is shared between the federal government and the states. Remind students of the reasons Federalists supported federalism. Why did they think this system would make a more perfect union?

ELL Use the ELL activity described in the ELL chart.

Further Instruction

Go through the Interactive Reading Notepad questions and discuss the answers with the class. Assign the Primary Source: The United States Constitution.

The Constitution reflects a number of principles that are central to democracy and balance the power of the government with the rights of individuals.

Cite Evidence that the American justice system is based on the principle of individual rights. *(T"he American justice system requires that the law be applied fairly to every American.")*

Analyze Information How does Article VI of the United States Constitution reflect the principle of federalism? *(It addresses how power is shared between the federal government and the states. State laws may not conflict with federal laws.)*

Hypothesize Review the goals of the Constitution. Name one way you think adopting the Constitution affected the early republic. *(It made the republic more stable and united; it gave the federal government more power to lead the nation.)*

DIGITAL TEXT 6

Preventing Abuse of Power

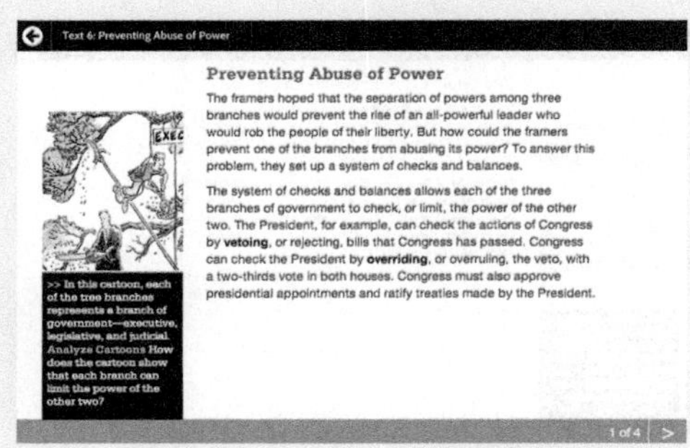

DIGITAL TEXT 2

Seven Basic Principles

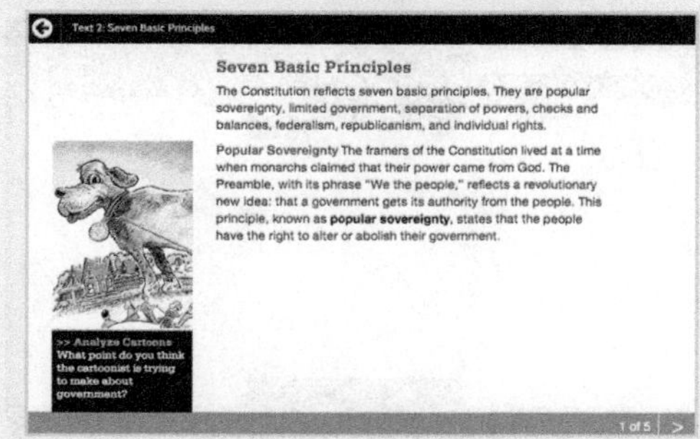

Objective 2: Identify the framework of government that the Constitution established.

Quick Instruction

Project the image of Governor Jan Brewer on the whiteboard. Explain that the separation of powers and system of checks and balances are principles designed to prevent abuse of power. They reflect the principle of limited government put forth in the United States Constitution.

Evaluate Arguments How does the Constitution reflect the principle of separation of powers? What are the reasons for this system? *(The Constitution divides the government into three branches: legislative, executive, and judicial. Each branch can limit the power over the others so that the government does not become too powerful.)*

Further Instruction

Go through the Interactive Reading Notepad questions and discuss the answers with the class. Discuss how the system of checks and balances prevents abuses of power.

Support an Idea with Examples Give an example of how the system of checks and balances reflects the principle of limited government. *(Examples—the President can veto Congress's bills; Congress can override the President's veto; the Supreme Court can declare laws unconstitutional. Each example provides a limit to restrict the power of one branch of government.)*

Draw Conclusions How does the principle of limited government reflected in the Constitution show how the Constitution supports individual rights? *(The Constitution limits government power to ensure the government does not trample individual rights.)*

Objective 3: Summarize the seven basic principles of American government.

Quick Instruction

Interactive Chart: The Federal System
Project the interactive chart and read through the state, national, and concurrent powers outlined in the Constitution. Analyze and discuss how these powers reflect the principle of federalism in the Constitution. To extend the lesson, assign Government and Civics: Rights of the Individual, Process of Naturalization, and Freedom.

Analyze Information Name the seven principles reflected in the United States Constitution and analyze how the Constitution reflects each of them. *(Popular sovereignty: The Constitution's language and content reflect the principle that the government gets its power from the people. Limited government: The Constitution states that government has only the powers granted by the Constitution. Separation of powers: the Constitution divides government into three branches. Checks and balances: The Constitution gives each branch the power to limit the others. Federalism: The Constitution divides power between the federal government and the states. Republicanism: The Constitution creates a system in which citizens elect representatives. Individual rights: The Constitution's Bill of Rights protects the individual rights of citizens.)*

Understanding the Constitution

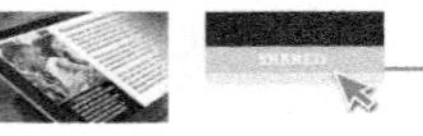

INTERACTIVE CHART

The Federal System

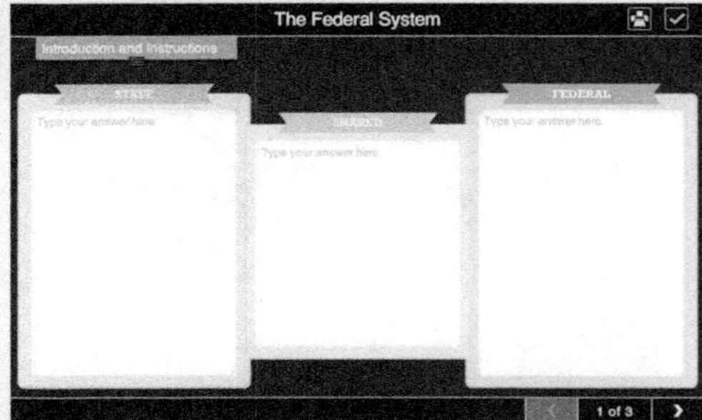

DIGITAL TEXT 3

The Legislative Branch: Congress

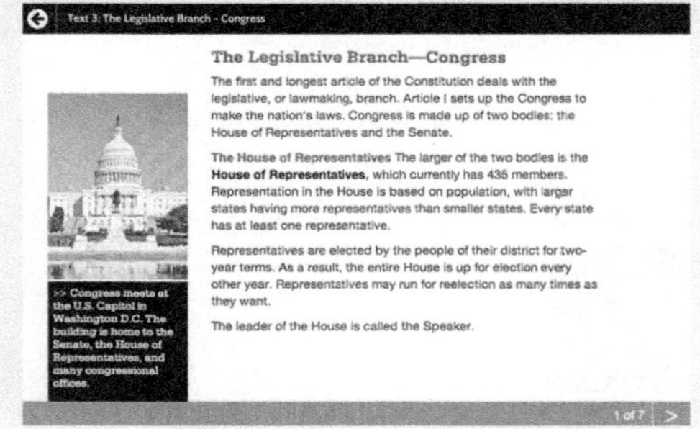

ELL Use the ELL activity described in the ELL chart.

ACTIVE CLASSROOM

Have students select one of the seven principles reflected in the United States Constitution and use the Word Wall Strategy to create a visual image of their principle along with with a definition. Ask students to post their words on the board and look at the various responses. Discuss similarities and differences in the responses as a group.

Further Instruction

Go through the Interactive Reading Notepad questions and discuss the answers with the class. Be sure students understand the principles reflected in the United States Constitution.

Identify Central Issues Why was the principle of popular sovereignty reflected in the United States Constitution such a revolutionary idea at the time? *(Under the principle of popular sovereignty, government gets its authority from the people and can be changed or overthrown. This was a new idea at a time when governments were led by monarchs who claimed that their power came from God, not from citizens.)*

Generate Explanations What caused the Framers to create a Constitution that reflected the principle of limited government? *(They wanted to place limits on the government because the Framers felt the British monarchy had too much power over them when they were colonies.)*

Identify Cause and Effect How does the separation of powers affect the principle of checks and balances reflected in the United States Constitution? *(The separation of powers makes it possible to have a system of checks and balances. The government is divided into three branches. Each has the power to limit the actions of the others.)*

Objective 4: **Identify the powers and duties of the legislative branch, executive branch, and judicial branch of the U.S. government.**

Quick Instruction

Interactive Gallery: the U.S. Congress Project the interactive gallery on the whiteboard and click through the images. Remind students that the Great Compromise divided Congress into two parts: the House of Representatives and the Senate.

Analyze Information How does the Seventeenth Amendment reflect the principle of popular sovereignty? *(It lets people elect senators directly.)*

ACTIVE CLASSROOM

Have students break into groups and use the Circle Write Strategy to answer the question: How does the United States Constitution reflect the principle of republicanism? Have students write as much as they can for 1 minute, then switch with the person on their right. The next person tries to improve or elaborate on the response. Continue to switch until the paper comes back to the first person. The group then shares the best response with the class.

www.PearsonRealize.com
Access your Digital Lesson

INTERACTIVE GALLERY

The U.S. Congress

The U.S. Congress
The House of Representatives
The House of Representatives is one of the two chambers of Congress. It is usually called the House, or the lower house. Members are called representatives. Representation in the House is based on population.
1 of 3

DIGITAL TEXT 4

The Executive Branch: the President

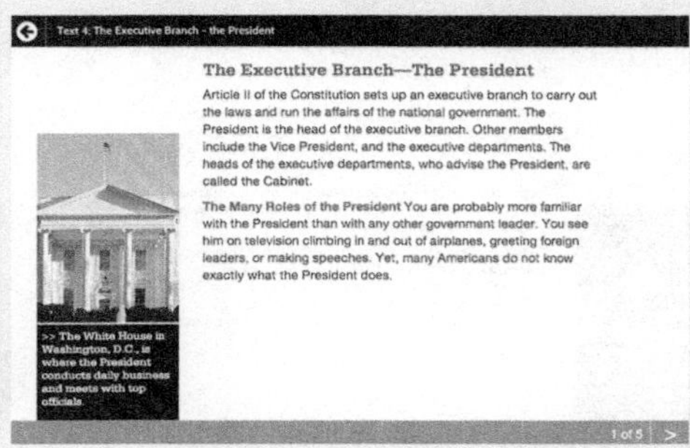

Text 4: The Executive Branch - the President
The Executive Branch—The President
Article II of the Constitution sets up an executive branch to carry out the laws and run the affairs of the national government. The President is the head of the executive branch. Other members include the Vice President, and the executive departments. The heads of the executive departments, who advise the President, are called the Cabinet.
The Many Roles of the President You are probably more familiar with the President than with any other government leader. You see him on television climbing in and out of airplanes, greeting foreign leaders, or making speeches. Yet, many Americans do not know exactly what the President does.
>> The White House in Washington, D.C., is where the President conducts daily business and meets with top officials
1 of 5

DIGITAL TEXT 5

The Judicial Branch: the Courts

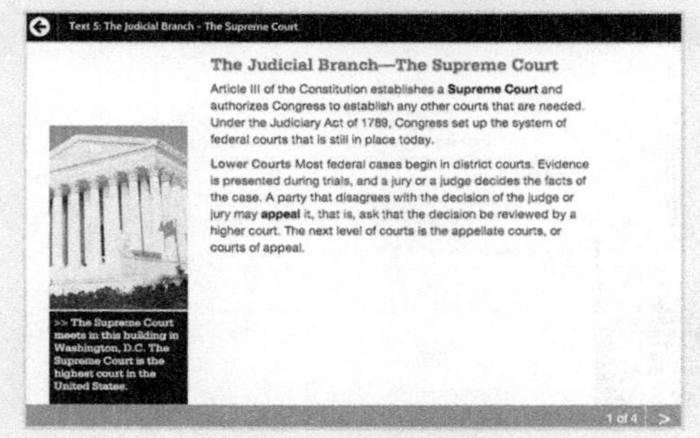

Text 5: The Judicial Branch - The Supreme Court
The Judicial Branch—The Supreme Court
Article III of the Constitution establishes a Supreme Court and authorizes Congress to establish any other courts that are needed. Under the Judiciary Act of 1789, Congress set up the system of federal courts that is still in place today.
Lower Courts Most federal cases begin in district courts. Evidence is presented during trials, and a jury or a judge decides the facts of the case. A party that disagrees with the decision of the judge or jury may appeal it, that is, ask that the decision be reviewed by a higher court. The next level of courts is the appellate courts, or courts of appeal.
>> The Supreme Court meets in this building in Washington, D.C. The Supreme Court is the highest court in the United States.
1 of 4

Further Instruction

Go through the Interactive Reading Notepad questions and discuss the answers with the class. Be sure students understand how the separation of powers creates a system of checks and balances to limit government power and protect individual rights.

Compare and Contrast What is the elastic clause and why is this an issue over which political parties have differing points of view to this day? *(The elastic clause gives Congress the power to make laws that are "necessary and proper." Parties disagree over how broadly or narrowly the clause should be interpreted and how much it should limit government power. Some think the clause gives Congress powers not explicitly mentioned in the Constitution. Others think the clause should not stretch government powers too greatly.)*

Evaluate Arguments Do you think the electoral college reflects the principle of popular sovereignty? Explain your reasoning. *(No, because it doesn't put the power for electing the President directly in the hands of the people. It gives that authority to electorates instead.)*

Identify Central Issues Identify the origin of judicial review. How does this power reflect the principle of checks and balances? *(The Supreme Court has argued that this power is implicit in the Constitution. It was first asserted in the Supreme Court case* Marbury v. Madison *(1803). It grants the Court authority to declare acts of Congress or the President unconstitutional. This puts a check on the powers of the legislative and executive branches.)*

Understanding the Constitution

DIGITAL TEXT 7

State Government

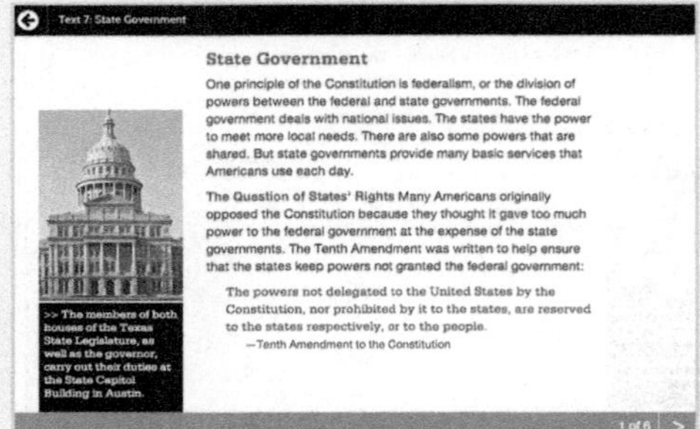

Text 7: State Government
State Government
One principle of the Constitution is federalism, or the division of powers between the federal and state governments. The federal government deals with national issues. The states have the power to meet more local needs. There are also some powers that are shared. But state governments provide many basic services that Americans use each day.
The Question of States' Rights Many Americans originally opposed the Constitution because they thought it gave too much power to the federal government at the expense of the state governments. The Tenth Amendment was written to help ensure that the states keep powers not granted the federal government:
The powers not delegated to the United States by the Constitution, nor prohibited by it to the states, are reserved to the states respectively, or to the people.
—Tenth Amendment to the Constitution
>> The members of both houses of the Texas State Legislature, as well as the governor, carry out their duties at the State Capitol Building in Austin.
1 of 6

DIGITAL TEXT 8

The Responsibilities of Local Government

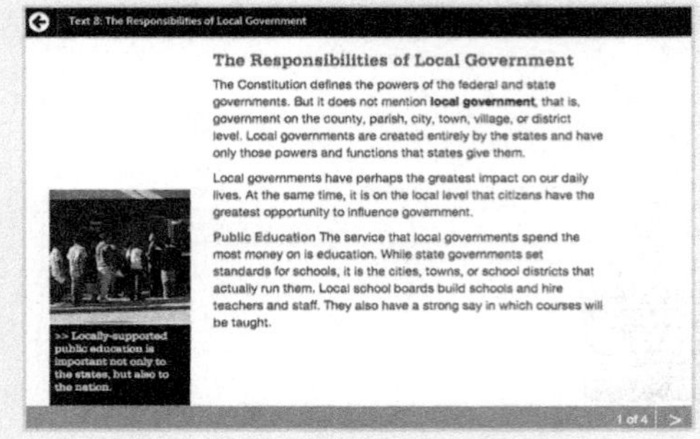

Text 8: The Responsibilities of Local Government
The Responsibilities of Local Government
The Constitution defines the powers of the federal and state governments. But it does not mention local government, that is, government on the county, parish, city, town, village, or district level. Local governments are created entirely by the states and have only those powers and functions that states give them.
Local governments have perhaps the greatest impact on our daily lives. At the same time, it is on the local level that citizens have the greatest opportunity to influence government.
Public Education The service that local governments spend the most money on is education. While state governments set standards for schools, it is the cities, towns, or school districts that actually run them. Local school boards build schools and hire teachers and staff. They also have a strong say in which courses will be taught.
>> Locally-supported public education is important not only to the states, but also to the nation.
1 of 4

Objective 5: **Describe the services that state and local governments provide.**

Quick Instruction

Project the image of the Texas State Capitol on the whiteboard. Remind students that the United States Constitution reflects the principle of federalism, in which power is shared between the national and state governments. States create local governments to serve cities, towns, and other local communities.

Hypothesize How do you think the principle of federalism serves the general welfare of the states? *(It lets state governments retain the power to meet their citizens' needs.)*

Generate Explanations Explain how local governments reflect the principle of popular sovereignty. *(Citizens have the opportunity to influence their local government.)*

Further Instruction

Go through the Interactive Reading Notepad questions and discuss the answers with the class. Discuss the services both state and local governments provide. Be sure students understand how power is shared on the national, state, and local level, and how this division reflects the principles of federalism and republicanism described in the United States Constitution.

Support Ideas With Examples Use the example of public education to explain how, in a federalist system, power is shared among national, state, and local governments. *(Because states have certain powers under federalism, education is primarily a state concern rather than a federal one. States set school standards, and local governments run the schools.)*

Identify Patterns How do state and local governments reflect the principle of limited government? *(State governments have their own constitutions, which limit the powers of state government and protect individual liberties. Local governments have only the power granted them by the states and must conform to state constitutions.)*

Draw Conclusions How do state and local governments reflect the principle of republicanism? *(The people have popular sovereignty and elect legislators and council or board members to represent them in state and local governments.)*

SYNTHESIZE

DIGITAL ACTIVITY

Goals and Principles of the Constitution

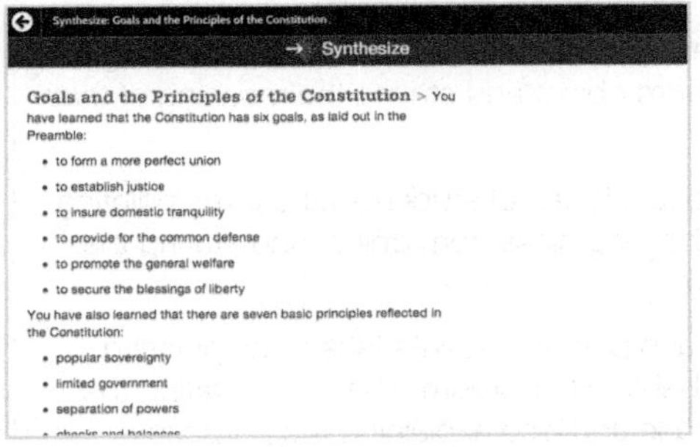

Have students review the lists of goals and principles. Explain how the goal of securing the blessings of liberty is supported by the principle of individual rights. Have students choose one item from each list and explain how they relate. Call on students to share their explanations, making sure to cover a variety of items on the lists.

Have students consider the following question. How do the goals and principles reflected in the Constitution promote their general welfare and well-being? Have students discuss their answers with the class, providing examples to support their reasoning.

Discuss Ask students which goals and principles reflected in the Constitution they think have the greatest impact on their daily lives and why, providing examples for support.

DEMONSTRATE

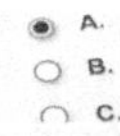

DIGITAL QUIZ

Lesson Quiz and Class Discussion Board

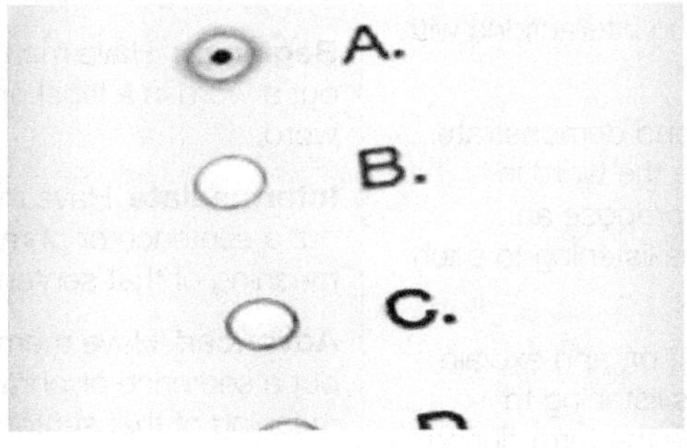

Assign the online Lesson Quiz for this lesson if you haven't already done so. Students will be offered automatic remediation or enrichment based on their score.

Pose these questions to the class on the Discussion Board:

In *Understanding the Constitution*,you read about the principles reflected in the United States Constitution and the powers granted to national, state, and local governments.

Evaluate Arguments Explain the debate over the Tenth Amendment and the elastic clause. What are the different points of view of policial parties on contemporary issues connected with the elastic clause? With whom do you agree, and why? *(The Tenth Amendment grants states rights not explicitly granted to the national government. The elastic clause gives the federal government powers not explicitly stated in the Constitution. Some people think powers not given to the federal government belong to the states, while others think the federal government can assume those powers based on the elastic clause. Student answers should give reasons for their point of view.)*

Identify Central Issues The United States Constitution has endured for hundreds of years. What aspects of the document do you think have enabled it to last? *(The Constitution promotes stability and continuity by sharing power among different branches and levels of government. It is also clear about what powers government has and what individual rights belong to the people, while remaining flexible enough to allow for interpretation and historical change.)*

Topic Inquiry

Have students continue their investigations for the Topic Inquiry Discussion.

Amending the Constitution

Supporting English Language Learners

Use with Digital Text 1, **Constitutional Amendment.**

Listening

Have students read the text. Circulate to make sure that they understand difficult passages. Tell them that they willl earn academic vocabulary heard during classroom instruction. Summarize the main ideas together to encourage students to learn academic vocabulary during interactions with others.

Beginning Display the academic vocabulary *identify*, and demonstrate its meaning by identifying objects in the classroom. Use the word in classroom instruction, saying: Identify the two ways to propose an amendment. Have students, working in pairs, take turns listening to each other's responses to your prompt.

Intermediate Display the academic vocabulary *consist of*, and explain its meaning. Have students, working in pairs, take turns listening to each other tell what everyday items consist of. Then use the term during classroom instruction by saying: What steps does the amendment process consist of? Have students take turns listening to each other use the words *consist of* in their responses.

Advanced Display the academic vocabulary *evaluate*. Discuss its meaning and identify synonyms for it. Use the word in classroom instruction by saying: Evaluate how well the amendment process works. Encourage students, working in pairs, take turns listening to their partner evaluate the ease of amending the Constitution when necessary, as well as protection against too much change.

Advanced High Display the academic vocabulary *draw conclusions*, and discuss its meaning. Demonstrate how the word order changes in a question by asking: What conclusions can you draw about the amendment process? After students, working in pairs, take turns listening to a partner's response, have them use the term in classroom interaction by creating an additional question for a partner to answer.

Use with Digital Text 2, **The Bill of Rights.**

Reading

Have students circulate around the classroom in pairs to look at labels and other forms of writing on objects around the room. Have students derive the meaning of this environmental print.

Beginning Have members of each pair of students take turns pointing out a word in a label or a classroom object and stating the meaning of that word.

Intermediate Have members of each pair of students take turns pointing out a sentence or phrase in a label or a classroom object and stating the meaning of that sentence or phrase.

Advanced Have members of each pair of students take turns pointing out a sentence or phrase in a label or a classroom object and stating the meaning of that sentence or phrase and also explaining the purpose or significance of the label or object.

Advanced High Have pairs of students discuss the meaning and significance of labels and objects in the classroom with writing, and have them compare and contrast those objects.

D Differentiate Instruction

Use the Differentiated Instruction notes throughout the lesson plan to support the varied skill sets, levels of readiness, and interests in the mixed-ability classroom.

Challenge These notes include suggestions for expanding the activity for advanced students.

On-Level These notes include suggestions for modifying the activity to address different interests or learning styles.

Extra Support These notes include ideas for providing more scaffolding or reading spupport.

Special Needs These notes provide ideas for adapting instruction to support the needs of various special needs students.

NOTES

PEARSON realize™ www.PearsonRealize.com

Go online to access additional resources including: Primary Sources • Biographies • Supreme Court cases • 21st Century Skill Tutorials • Maps • Graphic Organizers.

Objectives

Objective 1: Explain how the Constitution can be amended.

Objective 2: Identify the rights that the Bill of Rights protects.

Objective 3: Summarize how later amendments expanded democratic rights.

LESSON 6 ORGANIZER	PACING: APPROX. 1 PERIOD, .5 BLOCKS		RESOURCES	
	OBJECTIVES	PACING	Online	Print
Connect				
DIGITAL START UP ACTIVITY **First Amendment Rights**		5 min.	●	
Investigate				
DIGITAL TEXT 1 **Constitutional Amendment**	Objective 1	10 min.	●	●
INTERACTIVE CHART **Methods of Amending the Constitution**	Objective 1	10 min.	●	
DIGITAL TEXT 2 **The Bill of Rights**	Objective 2	10 min.	●	●
INTERACTIVE GALLERY **The First Amendment**	Objective 2	10 min.	●	
DIGITAL TEXT 3 **Additional Amendments**	Objective 3	10 min.	●	●
Synthesize				
DIGITAL ACTIVITY **Understanding the Bill of Rights**		5 min.	●	
Demonstrate				
DIGITAL QUIZ **Lesson Quiz and Class Discussion Board**		10 min.	●	

Amending the Constitution

CONNECT

DIGITAL START UP ACTIVITY

First Amendment Rights

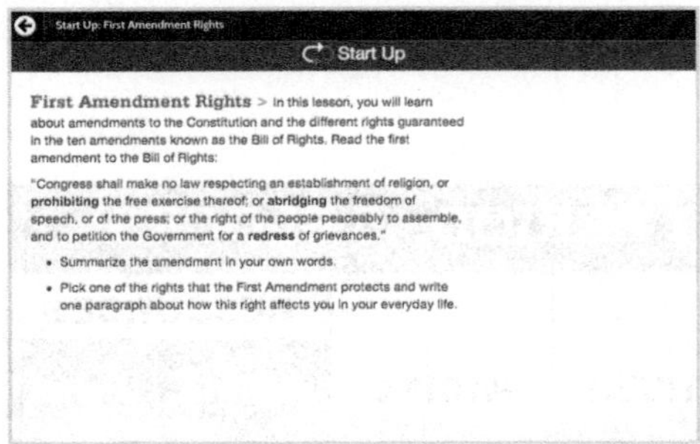

Start Up: First Amendment Rights
Start Up
First Amendment Rights > In this lesson, you will learn about amendments to the Constitution and the different rights guaranteed in the ten amendments known as the Bill of Rights. Read the first amendment to the Bill of Rights:
"Congress shall make no law respecting an establishment of religion, or prohibiting the free exercise thereof; or abridging the freedom of speech, or of the press; or the right of the people peaceably to assemble, and to petition the Government for a redress of grievances."
• Summarize the amendment in your own words.
• Pick one of the rights that the First Amendment protects and write one paragraph about how this right affects you in your everyday life.

Project the Start Up Activity Ask students to read the First Amendment as they enter and get settled and then write a paragraph about how one of the rights listed in the amendment affects their everyday lives.

Discuss Summarize the amendment in your own words. *(Congress cannot make laws that keep people from practicing their religion, speaking freely, assembling, or petitioning the government.)* Pick one of the rights that the First Amendment protects and write one paragraph about how this right affects you in your everyday life. *(Answers will vary but should focus on freedom of religion, freedom of speech, the right to assembly, or the right to petition.)*

Aa Vocabulary Development: Use the Interactive Reading Notepad to preview the Key Terms and Academic Vocabulary in this lesson with students.

FLIP IT!

Assign the Flipped Video for this lesson.

STUDENT EDITION PRINT PAGES: 219–223

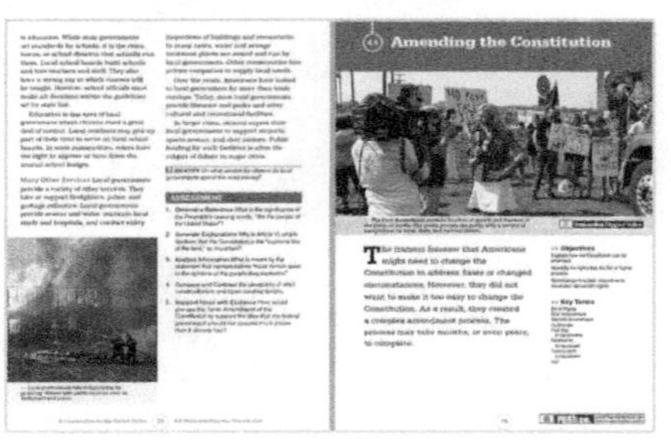

INVESTIGATE

DIGITAL TEXT 1

Constitutional Amendment

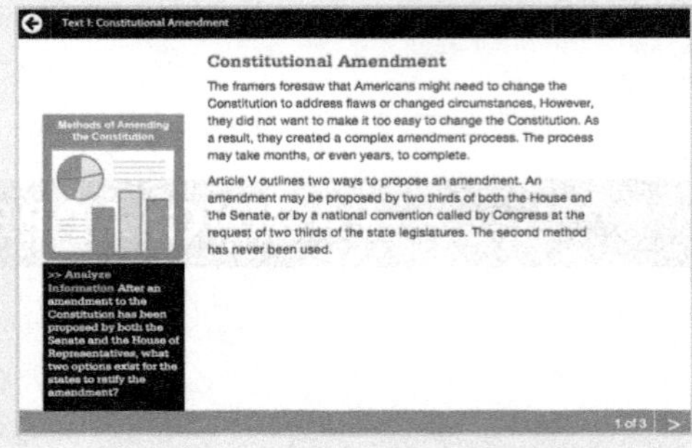

Text 1: Constitutional Amendment
Constitutional Amendment
The framers foresaw that Americans might need to change the Constitution to address flaws or changed circumstances. However, they did not want to make it too easy to change the Constitution. As a result, they created a complex amendment process. The process may take months, or even years, to complete.
Article V outlines two ways to propose an amendment. An amendment may be proposed by two thirds of both the House and the Senate, or by a national convention called by Congress at the request of two thirds of the state legislatures. The second method has never been used.
Methods of Amending the Constitution
>> Analyze Information After an amendment to the Constitution has been proposed by both the Senate and the House of Representatives, what two options exist for the states to ratify the amendment?
1 of 3

INTERACTIVE CHART

Methods of Amending the Constitution

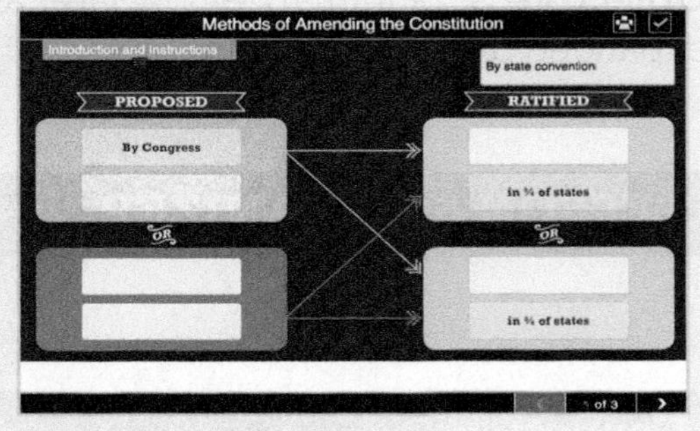

Objective 1: **Explain how to amend the Constitution.**

Quick Instruction

Interactive Chart: Methods of Amending the Constitution Project the interactive chart on the whiteboard and have students read through the graphic. Walk through the process for proposing and ratifying amendments to the United States Constitution.

Summarize the process for amending the United States Constitution. *(Amendments can be proposed by two thirds of the House and Senate, or by national convention. Amendments can be ratified by three fourths of the state legislatures or by special conventions in three fourths of the states.)*

ACTIVE CLASSROOM

Have students divide into groups and use the Sequence It Strategy to explore the process of amending the Constitution. Give each student a piece of paper with a single step in the amendment process. Have students form lines showing the correct order for proposing and ratifying amendments.

ELL Use the ELL activity described in the ELL chart.

Further Instruction

Go through the Interactive Reading Notepad questions and discuss the answers with the class. Be sure students can summarize the purposes and process of amending the United States Constitution.

Identify Central Issues What is the purpose of amending the United States Constitution? *(To change the Constitution to address flaws or new circumstances)*

Determine Point of View Why did the Framers make the process of amending the United States Constitution so involved? *(They wanted to make it difficult to change the Constitution to ensure the document would endure regardless of who was in power.)*

Identify Steps in a Process Summarize the process taken to ratify most of the amendments to the United States Constitution. *(The amendment is passed by two thirds of both the House and Senate and ratified by three fourths of the state legislatures.)*

DIGITAL TEXT 2

The Bill of Rights

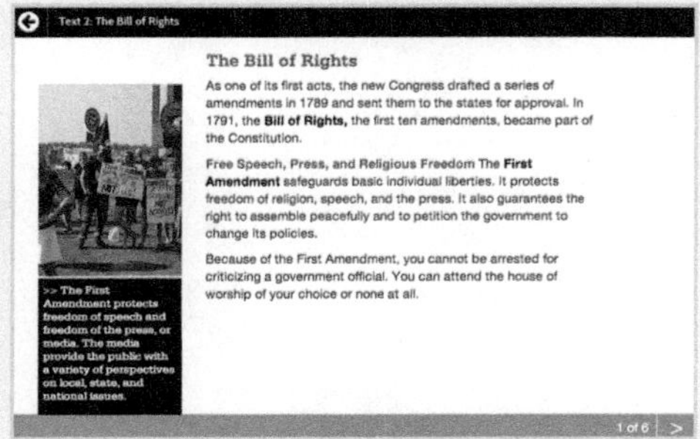

INTERACTIVE GALLERY

The First Amendment

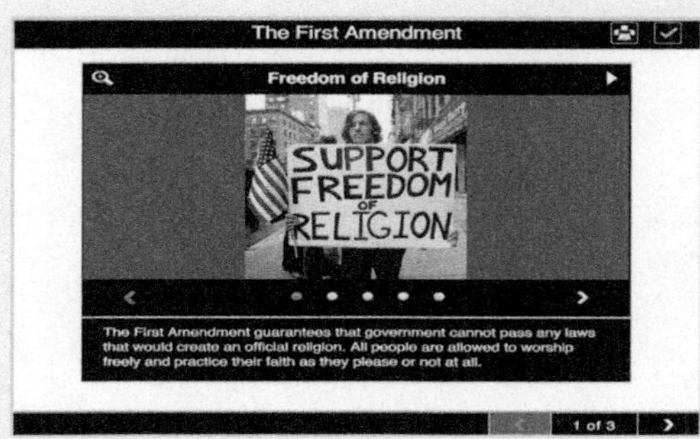

Objective 2: **Identify the rights that the Bill of Rights protects.**

Quick Instruction

The first 10 amendments are called the Bill of Rights. These amendments protect important rights and freedoms that continue to shape the American way of life.

Interactive Gallery: the First Amendment Project the interactive gallery and click through the images. Have students read through the rights guaranteed by the First Amendment.

Summarize the rights guaranteed in the Bill of Rights. *(Free speech, freedom of the press, religious freedom, right to bear arms, freedom from the requirement to house troops, protection against unlawful searches, rights to a fair trial and trial by jury, protection against self-incrimination, protection from cruel or unusual punishment, rights not specifically listed in the Constitution, states' rights not granted to the federal government)*

Make Generalizations Make a generalization about how the passage of the First Amendment shaped the development of religious freedom in the United States. *(It built on colonial traditions of religious freedom and guaranteed religious freedom by law throughout the United States.)*

ACTIVE CLASSROOM

Have students use the Sticky Notes Strategy and spend 3 minutes jotting down their response to the following questions: "Why is free speech important in a constitutional republic?" Have students post their Sticky Notes on the board or on chart paper. Ask them to look at the various responses and then discuss the similarities and differences in the responses as a group. *(Responses should state that free speech is important to a republic because it allows citizens to take part freely in political life.)*

ELL Use the ELL activity described in the ELL chart.

Further Instruction

Go through the Interactive Reading Notepad questions and discuss the answers with the class.

Identify Central Issues Describe the importance of a free press, or free media, in a constitutional republic. *(Free press and media help citizens remain informed and able to make decisions about government.)*

Compare Points of View Identify different points of view on the Second Amendment. Why does this amendment remain controversial today? *(People disagree over how to interpret the wording of the amendment. Some think it guarantees individuals the right to bear arms. Others think it means states have the right to maintain militias.)*

Draw Conclusions Analyze the impact that the guarantee of religious freedom in the First Amendment has had on the American way of life. *(It has led to religious diversity and allowed Americans to worship as they choose.)*

Amending the Constitution

DIGITAL TEXT 3

Additional Amendments

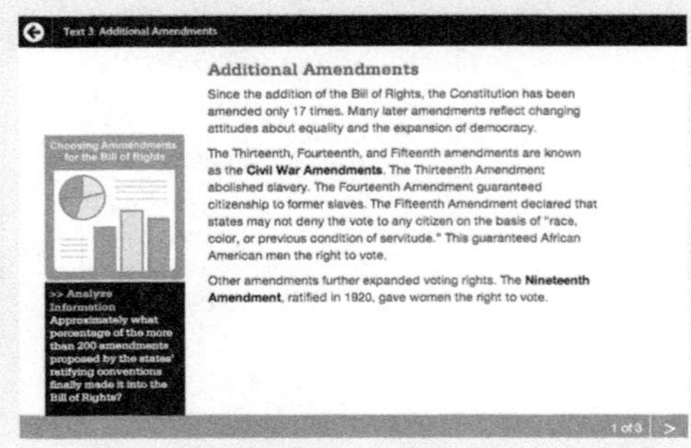

Objective 3: **Summarize how later amendments expanded democratic rights.**

Quick Instruction

Project the graph on the whiteboard and remind students of the process for ratifying an amendment. Discuss how the ratification of amendments in addition to the Bill of Rights has affected the United States Constitution and the American way of life.

Cite Evidence from the text that summarizes the purpose for amending the Constitution beyond the Bill of Rights. *("Many later amendments reflect changing attitudes about equality and the expansion of democracy.")*

D Differentiate: Challenge students to select one of the amendments discussed in this lesson and research its ratification process. Have students prepare a short report in which they present the purpose of the amendment, the process of ratification, and the debates surrounding its approval.

Further Instruction

Go through the Interactive Reading Notepad questions and discuss the answers with the class. Be sure students understand the purposes of the amendments listed and how they changed the Constitution.

Make Generalizations Make a generalization about the purpose for the Thirteenth, Fourteenth, and Fifteenth Amendments of the United States Constitution. *(These amendments expanded rights for African Americans following the Civil War.)*

Support Ideas With Examples Give an example that shows how amending the United States Constitution has made the country more equal. *(The Nineteenth Amendment gave women the right to vote.)*

SYNTHESIZE

DIGITAL ACTIVITY

Understanding the Bill of Rights

Synthesize: Understanding the Bill of Rights

→ Synthesize

Understanding the Bill of Rights > Fill in the chart with the amendments you learned about in this lesson. Include each amendment's number and the protection it offers, adding rows as needed. Then, think about why each amendment is necessary. Fill in the third column with reasons why each amendment was added.

BILL OF RIGHTS		
Amendment	Protection	Reason

Have students fill in the chart with each amendment they learned about the lesson, the protection(s) it offers, and its purpose(s). Have students share their charts with a partner to compare responses.

Have partners review their charts and consider the following questions: Why have these amendments been added to the Constitution? How have they expanded rights and freedoms in the United States? Have partners share their answers with the class.

Discuss Have students review the paragraphs they wrote about the First Amendment. Ask students to pick a different amendment from their chart and write a paragraph explaining how it affects them in their everyday lives. Ask why they think the amendment they chose is important to the American way of life.

DEMONSTRATE

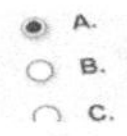

DIGITAL QUIZ

Lesson Quiz and Class Discussion Board

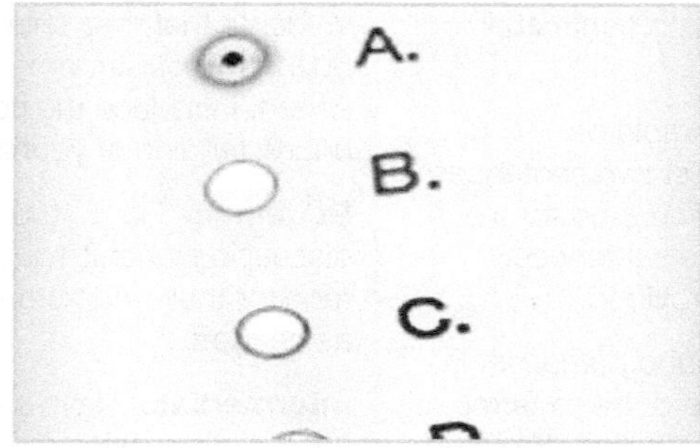

Assign the online Lesson Quiz for this lesson if you haven't already done so. Students will be offered automatic remediation or enrichment based on their score.

Pose these questions to the class on the Discussion Board:

In *Amending the Constitution* you read about the purposes and process of amending the United States Constitution and the rights guaranteed by important amendments.

Draw Conclusions How does the process of amending the United States Constitution affect the balance of power between the federal government and the states? *(The states serve as a check on federal power by limiting Congress's ability to change the Constitution at will.)*

Identify Central Issues How does the Bill of Rights reflect the principle of individual rights in the United States Constitution? *(Nearly all of the rights guaranteed in the Bill of Rights, such as the right to free speech, freedom of religion, and the right to a fair trial, are all rights held by individuals. They apply equally to all Americans.)*

Topic Inquiry

Have students continue their investigations for the Topic Inquiry Discussion.

Citizens' Rights and Responsibilities

Supporting English Language Learners

Use with Digital Text 2, **Citizenship and Democratic Values.**

Reading
Display the two images that accompany the text as visual support as students read grade-appropriate content area text. Ask students to describe what they see. Explain that they will also be using contextual support to read the text

Beginning Use the definition of *civic virtue* and the example of Cincinnatus as contextual support for the ideas in the first two sentences of the text. Use the community projects image as visual support for the ideas presented in the text. Then have students read the sentences, relying on the visual and contextual support you have provided.

Intermediate Point out the boldface terms *civic virtue* and *patriotism* in the text. Discuss how the images illustrate the meanings of these terms and how the surrounding sentences provide contextual support. Provide time for students to read the text in light of this visual and contextual support.

Advanced Display key terms from the text, such as *sacrifice*, *responsibility*, *civic virtue*, and *patriotism*. Ask pairs of students to explore their meanings using the visual support of the photographs and the contextual support of the surrounding text. Then have students read the text, referencing the images and context as needed for further visual support.

Advanced High Display key terms from the text, such as *sacrifice*, *responsibility*, *civic virtue*, and *patriotism*. Ask students to read the text independently and use the visual support of the images and the contextual support of the surrounding text to understand these terms as they are encountered.

Use with Digital Text 3, **Responsible Citizenship.**

Listening
Tell students that you will be instructing them in the key concepts of this text and asking them to work with one another on these concepts. Tell students that they should monitor their understanding of spoken language during this classroom discussion and interaction. Review the meaning of *citizen*. Introduce the concept *responsible.* Remind them to monitor their understanding of your instruction and to ask for help as needed.

Beginning Have students, working in small groups, listen to one another discussing what it could mean to be a responsible citizen. Remind them to monitor their understanding of their partners' language and to ask for help as needed.

Intermediate Have students. working in small groups, listen to one another discussing examples of responsible citizenship. Remind them to monitor their understanding of their partners' language and to ask for help as needed.

Advanced Have students. working in small groups, listen to one another's response to the question, "Why are responsible citizens important in a democracy?" Remind them to monitor their understanding of their partners' language and to ask for help as needed.

Advanced High Have students. working in small groups, listen to one another's response to the question, "What are the dangers to a democracy if citizens are not responsible?" Remind them to monitor their understanding of their partners' language and to ask for help as needed.

D Differentiate Instruction

Use the Differentiated Instruction notes throughout the lesson plan to support the varied skill sets, levels of readiness, and interests in the mixed-ability classroom.

Challenge These notes include suggestions for expanding the activity for advanced students.

On-Level These notes include suggestions for modifying the activity to address different interests or learning styles.

Extra Support These notes include ideas for providing more scaffolding or reading spuport.

Special Needs These notes provide ideas for adapting instruction to support the needs of various special needs students.

NOTES

PEARSON realize™
www.PearsonRealize.com

Go online to access additional resources including:
Primary Sources • Biographies • Supreme Court cases • 21st Century Skill Tutorials • Maps • Graphic Organizers.

Objectives

Objective 1: Summarize what makes a person a citizen of the United States.

Objective 2: Identify how Americans can develop democratic values.

Objective 3: Describe the responsibilities of citizenship.

LESSON 7 ORGANIZER — **PACING: APPROX. 1 PERIOD, .5 BLOCKS**

	OBJECTIVES	PACING	RESOURCES Online	RESOURCES Print
Connect				
DIGITAL START UP ACTIVITY **How to Be a Responsible Citizen**		5 min.	●	
Investigate				
DIGITAL TEXT 1 **American Citizenship**	Objective 1	10 min.	●	●
DIGITAL TEXT 2 **Citizenship and Democratic Values**	Objective 2	10 min.	●	●
INTERACTIVE CHART **Civic Responsibility**	Objective 2	10 min.	●	
DIGITAL TEXT 3 **Responsible Citizenship**	Objective 3	10 min.	●	●
INTERACTIVE CHART **Voting Responsibly**	Objective 3	10 min.	●	
Synthesize				
DIGITAL ACTIVITY **Are You a Responsible Citizen?**		5 min.	●	
Demonstrate				
DIGITAL QUIZ **Lesson Quiz and Class Discussion Board**		10 min.	●	

Citizens' Rights and Responsibilities

CONNECT

DIGITAL START UP ACTIVITY

How to Be a Responsible Citizen

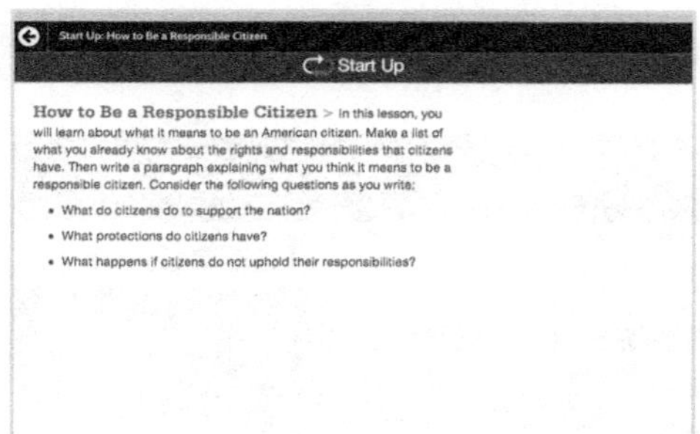

Project the Start Up Activity Ask students to make a list of citizens' rights and responsibilities and then write a paragraph on what it means to be a responsible citizen.

Discuss What do citizens do to support the nation? *(Vote, accept responsibility for their behavior, support their families, obey rules, obey laws, stay informed on public issues, serve on juries)* What protections do citizens' have? *(Rights guaranteed by the Constitution)* What happens if citizens do not uphold their responsibilities? *(Democracy may suffer if citizens do not take responsibility, stay informed, vote, and serve their communities. Citizens may also be fined or imprisoned for disobeying laws.)*

Aa Vocabulary Development Use the Interactive Reading Notepad to preview the Key Terms and Academic Vocabulary in this lesson with students.

FLIP IT!

Assign the Flipped Video for this lesson.

STUDENT EDITION PRINT PAGES: 224–229

INVESTIGATE

DIGITAL TEXT 1

American Citizenship

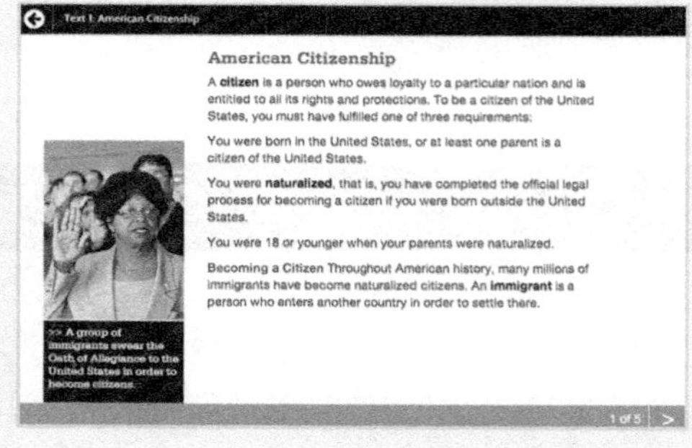

Objective 1: Summarize what makes a person a citizen of the United States.

Quick Instruction

Project the photo of American immigrants taking the oath of citizenship on the whiteboard and define the term *citizen*: a person who owes loyalty to a particular nation and is entitled to all of its rights and protections. Explain that some citizens are born in the United States and others are naturalized, or are born elsewhere and later admitted as citizens.

Summarize some of the rights of citizens of the United States. *(Citizens of the United States enjoy rights to free speech, free worship, and the freedom to vote.)*

D Differentiate: Extra Support Review the three different ways people can become American citizens. Ask students to think of a citizen they know and explain how that person became a citizen.

Further Instruction

Go through the Interactive Reading Notepad questions and discuss the answers with the class. To extend the lesson, assign Government and Civics: U.S. Citizenship According to the Constitution. Make sure students understand the criteria and process by which immigrants become naturalized citizens of the United States.

Identify Steps in a Process Explain the process for becoming a naturalized citizen of the United States. *(Immigrants submit paperwork and attend interviews to become resident aliens. After five years, applicants take a test to show they meet the criteria. They are interviewed about their reasons for wanting to become a citizen. Lastly, they appear before a judge to take an oath.)*

Support Ideas with Examples Give an example of how the rights and responsibilities of U.S. citizens reflect our national identify. *(The right and the responsibility to vote reflect American values such as independence, liberty, and self-governance.)*

PEARSON realize™ **www.PearsonRealize.com** Access your Digital Lesson

DIGITAL TEXT 2

Citizenship and Democratic Values

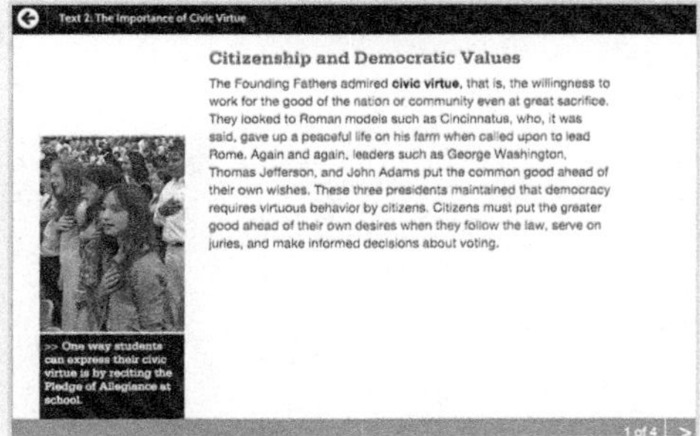

INTERACTIVE CHART

Civic Responsibility

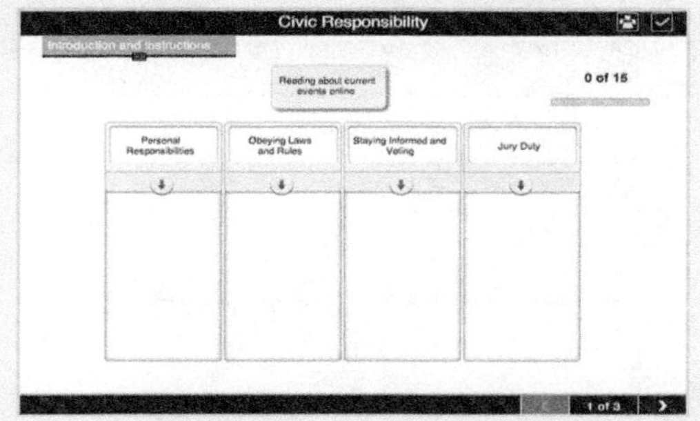

DIGITAL TEXT 3

Responsible Citizenship

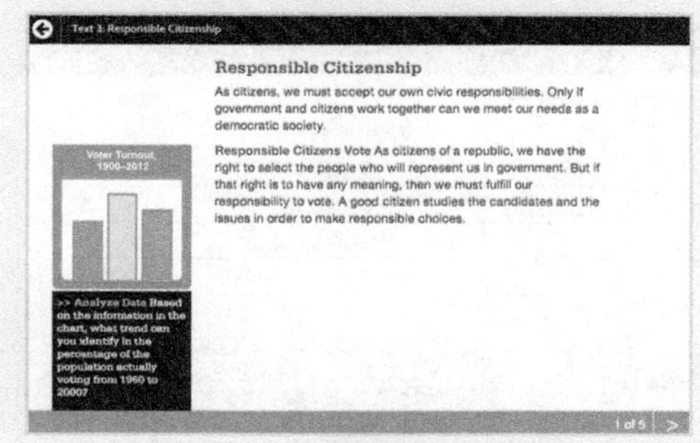

Objective 2: **Identify how Americans can develop democratic values.**

Quick Instruction

Examples of responsible citizenship are both public and private. Being a responsible citizen involves taking responsibility for yourself and thinking about the needs of others.

Interactive Chart: Civic Responsibility Project the interactive chart on the whiteboard and read through the tiles. Ask students to think of additional examples of responsible citizenship that they practice in their everyday lives.

Support Ideas With Examples Give an example of when you have accepted responsibility for your behavior. Explain why accepting personal responsibility for one's behavior is important in a democracy. *(Example—drinking a soft drink and recycling the can instead of littering. It is important to take personal responsibility because, in a democracy, individuals are expected to look out for themselves and one another.)*

ACTIVE CLASSROOM

Have students use the Write 1-Get 3 Strategy to answer the question: What are four key characteristics of responsible citizenship? Have students fold a piece of paper into quarters and write down one response. Ask students to go around the room asking to hear other responses. When they think an answer is correct, they write it in their boxes until they have three more responses on their page. Have students share responses with the class.

ELL Use the ELL activity described in the ELL chart.

Further Instruction

Go through the Interactive Reading Notepad questions and discuss the answers with the class. To extend the lesson, assign Government and Civics: Respect for the Rights of Others. Be sure students can explain the importance of personal responsibilities, such as accepting responsibility for one's behavior and supporting one's family. Ask why it is important for people to take responsibility for supporting their families. *(Families depend on one another.)*

Generate Explanations Identify at least three characteristics of responsible citizenship and explain why these qualities are necessary in a democracy. *(Honesty, compassion, patriotism, courage, responsibility, respect; serving others and working for the good of the community are neccessary for citizens to help make a democracy run.)*

Summarize What is civic virtue, and how did the founders model this behavior for the nation? *(Willingness to work for the greater good; the founders put the good of the country ahead of their own personal wishes.)*

Objective 3: **Describe the responsibilities of citizenship.**

Quick Instruction

Citizens have responsibilities to help democracy work. Citizens serve the nation, help others, follow laws, and participate in self-government.

Interactive Chart: Civic Responsibility: Voting Project the interactive chart and have students read through the tiles. Discuss why voting is an example of responsible citizenship.

Apply Concepts Identify the examples of responsible citizenship described in the text and explain how you fulfill at least one of these responsibilities. *(Voting, obeying laws, obeying rules, defending the nation, serving on juries, participating in one's community, staying informed on public issues. Sample answers may include following rules at home and at school, volunteering, or reading the news.)*

ACTIVE CLASSROOM

Post passages from the reading around the room. Have students use the Walking Tour Strategy to tour the room and discuss each passage. Have students identify examples of responsible citizenship and summarize their importance. Ask what examples of responsible citizenship students practice in their own lives.

ELL Use the ELL activity described in the ELL chart.

Citizens' Rights and Responsibilities

INTERACTIVE CHART

Voting Responsibly

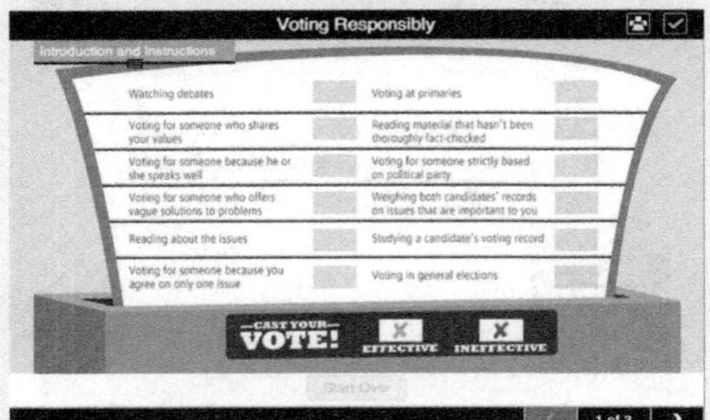

Further Instruction

Go through the Interactive Reading Notepad questions and discuss the answers with the class. Ask students to identify examples of responsible citizenship. Be sure they understand why civic responsibility is necessary in a democratic society.

Generate Explanations Why is staying informed on public issues an important part of responsible citizenship? *(Citizens must be educated about society, political candidates, and political issues in order to make good decisions about whom to vote for and what government policies to support.)*

Compare and Contrast What is the difference between a rule and a law? Why is it important to obey both? *(Contrast—A law is a rule imposed by the nation. A rule is not enforced by the government. Compare—Both keep people safe, help communities live together, and keep people accountable.)*

Summarize What is jury duty, and how does this service help the nation? *(Jury duty is the responsibility to serve on juries. Defendants have the right to a trial by jury. Responsible citizens must serve on juries to ensure that defendants have their rights fulfilled.)*

SYNTHESIZE

DIGITAL ACTIVITY

Are You a Responsible Citizen?

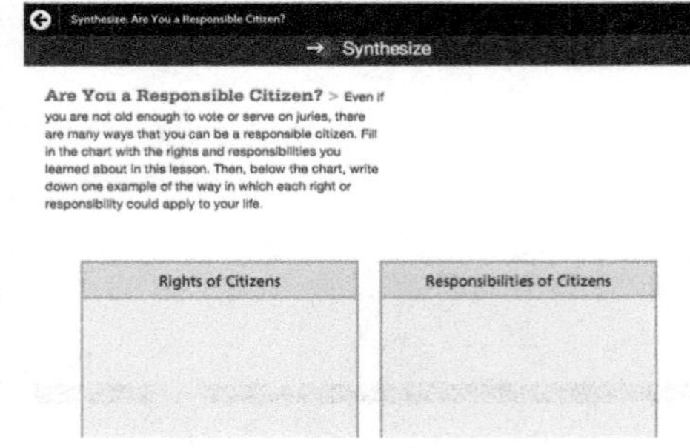

Have students fill in the chart with the rights and responsibilities they learned about in this lesson. Then have them write down an example of how each right or responsibility applies to their lives. Have students share their lists with the class and generate ideas for how to practice responsible citizenship.

Have students review their charts and consider the following question: How do the rights and responsibilities they listed reflect our national identity? Discuss answers with the class.

Discuss Have students consider examples of responsible citizenship and come up with one additional way they can exercise civic responsibility in their everyday lives. Ask how their additional example can improve their lives or their communities.

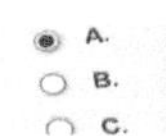

DEMONSTRATE

DIGITAL QUIZ

Lesson Quiz and Class Discussion Board

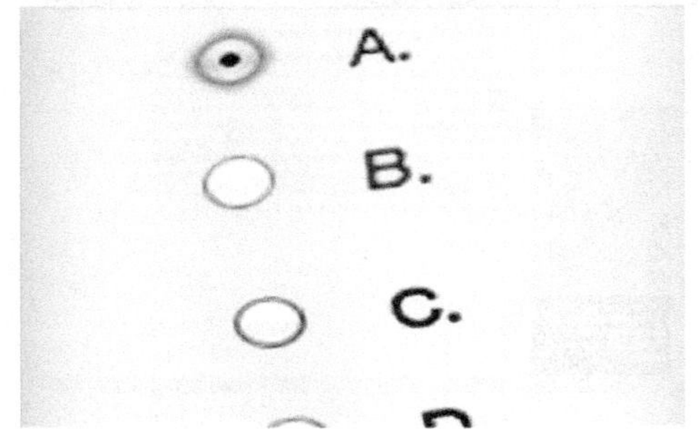

Assign the online Lesson Quiz for this lesson if you haven't already done so. Students will be offered automatic remediation or enrichment based on their score.

Pose these questions to the class on the Discussion Board:

In *Citizens' Rights and Responsibilities* you read about examples of responsible citizenship that reflect our national identity.

Support Ideas With Examples Give an example of how education can help you become a responsible citizen. *(It can teach me to obey rules and help me stay informed on public issues.)*

Draw Conclusions In what ways does democracy depend on responsible citizens? *(Democracy requires that citizens work together to govern themselves. Citizens must stay informed, vote for representatives, and serve the public good.)*

Have students continue their investigations for the Topic Inquiry Discussion.

PEARSON realize™ www.PearsonRealize.com Access your Digital Lesson

A Constitution for the United States (1776–Present)

SYNTHESIZE

DIGITAL ACTIVITY

Reflect on the Essential Question and Topic

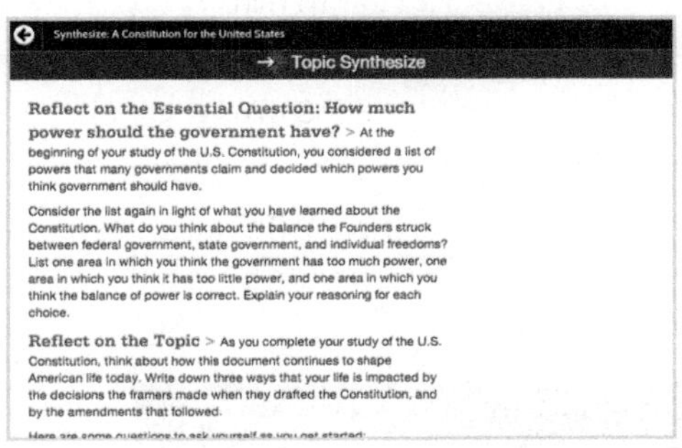

First ask students to reconsider the Essential Question for this Topic: How much power should the government have? Remind students of the government powers they considered at the start of this Topic, for example:

- declare war
- build and maintain roads
- help people meet basic needs
- regulate corporations
- impose taxes
- make and enforce laws
- fund schools, libraries, and research centers
- control natural resources
- control the economy
- maintain relations with other nations

Ask students, "Do you think the United States Constitution gives the government the right amount of power?" Ask them to list one area in which they think the government has too much power, one area in which it has too little, and one area in which they think the balance of power is correct. Discuss their answers as a class or ask students to post their answers on the Class Discussion Board.

Next ask students to reflect on the Topic as a whole and write down three ways their lives are impacted by the Constitution and its amendments. Have students consider the following questions to help them get started:

1. What freedoms do you have that the Constitution guarantees?
2. What government resources or public facilities do you regularly use?
3. How might life be different without the protections of the Constitution?

Have students complete Step 3 of the Topic Inquiry.

DEMONSTRATE

DIGITAL TOPIC REVIEW AND ASSESSMENT

A Constitution for the United States (1776–Present)

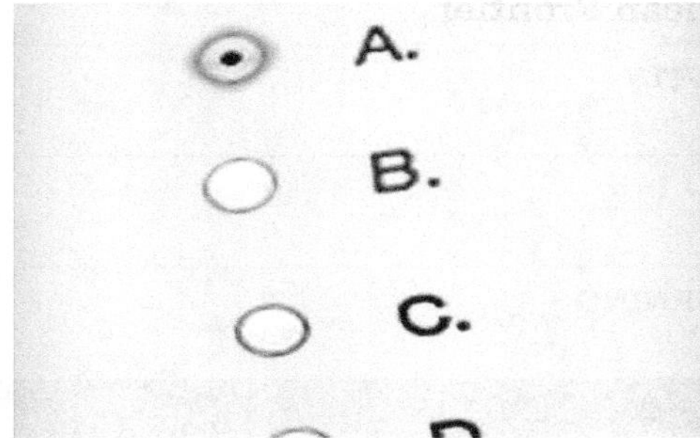

Students can prepare for the Topic Test by answering the questions in the Topic Review and Assessment online or the Assessment questions in the Print Student text. They can also prepare by reviewing their answers to the Interactive Reading Notepad questions or reviewing their notes in the Reading and Notetaking Study Guide.

DIGITAL TOPIC TEST

A Constitution for the United States (1776–Present)

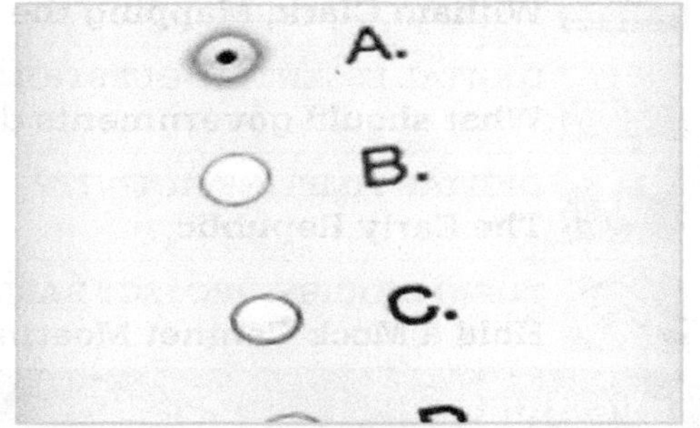

TOPIC TEST

Assign the Topic Test to assess students' understanding of topic content.

BENCHMARK TESTS

Assign these benchmark tests as you complete the relevant topics to monitor student progress toward mastering the course content and as preparation for the End-of-Course Test.

Benchmark Test 1: Topics 1–2

Benchmark Test 2: Topics 3–4

Benchmark Test 3: Topics 5–6

Benchmark Test 4: Topics 7–9

Benchmark Test 5: Topics 10–12

Benchmark Test 6: Topics 13–14

Benchmark Test 7: Topics 15–17

PEARSON realize™ www.PearsonRealize.com Access your Digital Lesson

The Early Republic (1789–1825)

TOPIC 5 ORGANIZER	PACING: APPROX. 9 PERIODS, 4.5 BLOCKS
	PACING
Connect	**1 period**
MY STORY VIDEO **William Clark, Mapping the American Frontier**	10 min.
DIGITAL ESSENTIAL QUESTION ACTIVITY **What should governments do?**	10 min.
DIGITAL TIMELINE ACTIVITY **The Early Republic**	10 min.
TOPIC INQUIRY: PROJECT-BASED LEARNING **Hold a Mock Cabinet Meeting**	
Investigate	**3–6 periods**
TOPIC INQUIRY: PROJECT-BASED LEARNING **Hold a Mock Cabinet Meeting**	Ongoing
LESSON 1 Washington's Presidency	30–40 min.
LESSON 2 The Origin of Political Parties	30–40 min.
LESSON 3 John Adams's Presidency	30–40 min.
LESSON 4 Jefferson's Presidency	30–40 min.
LESSON 5 Madison and the War of 1812	30–40 min.
LESSON 6 Monroe's Presidency	30–40 min.
Synthesize	**1 period**
DIGITAL ACTIVITY **Reflect on the Essential Question and Topic**	10 min.
TOPIC INQUIRY: PROJECT-BASED LEARNING **Hold a Mock Cabinet Meeting**	20 min.
Demonstrate	**1–2 periods**
DIGITAL TOPIC REVIEW AND ASSESSMENT **The Early Republic (1789–1825)**	10 min.
TOPIC INQUIRY: PROJECT-BASED LEARNING **Hold a Mock Cabinet Meeting**	20 min.

PEARSON realize™ www.PearsonRealize.com Access your Digital Lesson

TOPIC INQUIRY: PROJECT-BASED LEARNING

Hold a Mock Cabinet Meeting

In this Topic Inquiry, students work in teams to research the relationships between the United States, Britain, and France in the late eighteenth century. Each student will then solve the problem of how best to respond to the war between Britain and France in 1793 as if he or she were an advisor to one of President Washington's Cabinet members. Solving this problem will contribute to students' understanding of the Topic Essential Question: What should governments do?

STEP 1: CONNECT

Develop Questions and Plan the Investigation

Launch the Project and Generate Questions

Display the request for a Cabinet meeting from President Washington. Tell students they will need to research, write, and perform a mock Cabinet meeting to decide what position the United States should take in the war between Britain and France.

Plan the Investigation

Form students into teams. Have each team review the Skills Tutorials, *Work in Teams* and *Solve Problems*, read and sign the *Project Contract*, and complete the *Need-to-Know Questions* document.

Suggestion: Include students with varied skill levels on each team and ensure the group's responsibilities are evenly distributed.

Walk students through the problem-solving process:

1. Identifying the problem that requires a solution
2. Gathering information to help them decide how to solve it
3. Identifying the available options
4. Predicting the consequences of each option and weighing the advantages and disadvantages of each
5. Choosing and implementing a solution
6. Evaluating the effectiveness of the solution

Resources

- Project Launch
- Student Instructions
- Skills Tutorial, *Work in Teams*
- Project Contract
- Need-to-Know Questions
- Skills Tutorial, *Solve Problems*

PROFESSIONAL DEVELOPMENT

Project-Based Learning

Be sure to view the Project-Based Learning Professional Development resources in the online course.

STEP 2: INVESTIGATE

Apply Disciplinary Concepts and Tools

Gathering Sources for Research on the American Response to the War Between Britain and France

Groups should document the responsibilities of each member and the overall work of the team on the Project Tracker. To guide their research, each subgroup has been provided with a list of viable sources from which to choose as they answer the questions they've created and complete the Information Organizer.

Investigate Factors Influencing the Solution to the Problem

Each subgroup will then research political, economic, and social issues from the late eighteenth century that must influence their decision on a solution to the problem and identify the best options available given that information.

Write and Edit Your Subgroup's Position Paper

Each subgroup should now write the position paper they will use defend their position during the cabinet meeting. Remind students to provide supporting evidence for their position, and encourage them to offer positive, constructive feedback of each other's work.

- Project Tracker
- Information Organizer

TOPIC INQUIRY: PROJECT-BASED LEARNING

Hold a Mock Cabinet Meeting *(continued)*

STEP 3: SYNTHESIZE

Evaluate Sources and Use Evidence to Formulate Conclusions

Hold the Mock Cabinet Meeting to Solve the Problem

Have subgroups come back together to present their position in the mock cabinet meeting. Encourage students to follow the problem-solving process outlined above and in the Student Instructions.

STEP 4: DEMONSTRATE

Communicate Conclusions and Take Informed Action

Summarize the Cabinet's Solution

Have students write an individual summary of the group's solution.

Reflect on the Project

Have students hold a team meeting to reflect on what they have learned and what, if anything, they would have done differently. Each group member should complete a Team/Peer Assessment.

- Team/Peer Assessment

INTRODUCTION

The Early Republic (1789–1825)

After the War of Independence was finally over, Americans debated the role government should play in the life of its citizens. The new government found itself challenged by foreign affairs and another war with Britain, even as the country expanded in size following the Louisiana Purchase. The United States strengthened its presence on the world stage and expanded its influence in newly independent Latin American countries with the Monroe Doctrine.

CONNECT

NBC LEARN 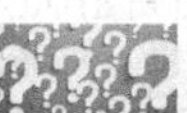 

MY STORY VIDEO

William Clark, Mapping the American Frontier

Watch a video about the Lewis and Clark expedition.

Check Understanding What did President Jefferson ask Lewis and Clark to do? *(explore and map the lands west of the Mississippi that had been purchased in 1803 from France)*

Support a Point of View with Evidence Why was the help provided by Native Americans essential to Lewis and Clark? *(The Native Americans knew the lands that Lewis and Clark wanted to explore. They provided them with information about the terrain and supplied guides to lead them on their journey west.)*

DIGITAL ESSENTIAL QUESTION ACTIVITY

What should governments do?

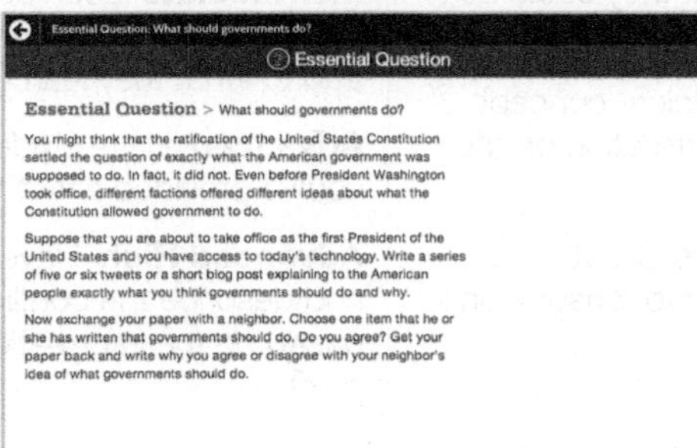

Ask students to think about the Essential Question for this Topic: What should governments do? Americans disagreed over what the Constitution allowed federal and state governments to do.

If students have not already done so, ask them to write five or six tweets or a blog post explaining what they think governments should do and why. Have students share their ideas with a partner and discuss whether they agree or disagree.

Evaluate Arguments Give an argument for and an argument against a strong central government that can perform many functions. *(For—government needs the authority to regulate the economy, make and enforce laws, and keep the country running. Against—a strong government that can do many things can also take power away from the people and interfere with individual rights.)*

Identify Central issues Select an example from your tweets or blog post and explain why it is necessary for government to do. Suppose you are trying to convince someone who disagrees. *(Answers will vary.)*

DIGITAL TIMELINE ACTIVITY

The Early Republic

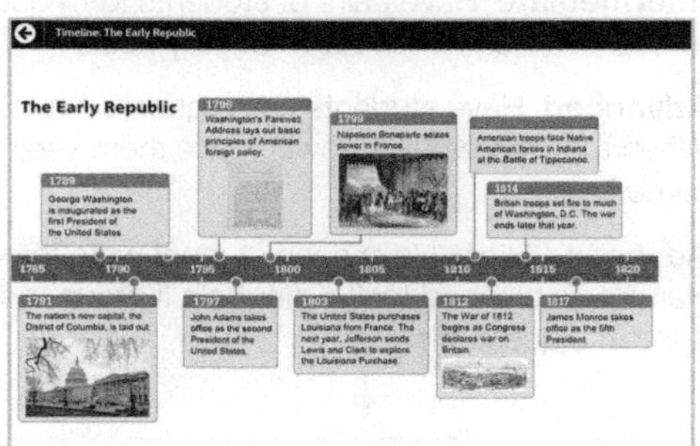

Display the timeline showing the major events of the early Republic. During this Topic students will learn about all of these events and many more, but this timeline will provide a framework into which they can place the events they learn about.

Summarize Identify two major events that happened in the early Republic. *(The Louisiana Purchase; the War of 1812)*

Draw Conclusions How do you think the presidencies of Washington and Adams shaped the authority of the central government? Explain your reasoning. *(The authority probably expanded, because Jefferson wanted to reduce the power of the federal government when he came into office.)*

Launch the Topic Inquiry with students after introducing the Topic.

Washington's Presidency

Supporting English Language Learners

Use with Digital Text 3, **Creating a Stable Economy.**

Listening

Put students in groups of varied English language proficiency levels to provide support as they seek clarification of spoken language during classroom instruction and interactions. Explain that many northerners supported Hamilton's planned tariff, since there were many manufacturers in the North who would benefit if the tariff raised the prices of imported goods. These might otherwise be cheaper than their own products. Explain that many southerners opposed the tariff because for them it would mean higher prices.

Beginning Next, display these sentence frames: *I do not understand ___* and *Can you explain ___ again?* Encourage students to seek clarification using thse frames.

Intermediate Have pairs of students form questions that they could ask to seek clarification about what they hear.

Advanced Have students ask a question to clarify an unclear concept. When they receive an answer, have them seek further clarification on the same topic.

Advanced High Have each student write three questions about Hamilton's planned tariff. Offer help if group members cannot answer one another's questions.

Use with Digital Text 5, **Americans React to the French Revolution.**

Reading

Have students read the introduction and the content under the first two sub-headings. Offer support as needed. Now, remind them of the historical context. Americans had recently won independence from Britain during their own revolution. Direct their attention to the painting of the fire in the streets of Paris. Tell them that they will be using this visual and contextual support to enhance and confirm their understanding.

Beginning Ask students how the American Revolution might affect how Americans viewed the French Revolution. Then ask students to look at the painting and state how American's recent past and events like the one shown in the painting might result in the different reactions mentioned in the text.

Intermediate Look at the painting and ask students to describe what they see. Then ask how the painting and the information you've provided add to what they learned when they read the text.

Advanced Have students explain how the painting and the information you've provided affect their understanding of the content of the text.

Advanced High Have students describe what they see in the painting and describe the conflicting feelings that many Americans may have felt based on the information you've provided and the visual evidence from the painting.

D Differentiate Instruction

Use the Differentiated Instruction notes throughout the lesson plan to support the varied skill sets, levels of readiness, and interests in the mixed-ability classroom.

Challenge These notes include suggestions for expanding the activity for advanced students.

On-Level These notes include suggestions for modifying the activity to address different interests or learning styles.

Extra Support These notes include ideas for providing more scaffolding or reading spuport.

Special Needs These notes provide ideas for adapting instruction to support the needs of various special needs students.

NOTES

PEARSON realize
www.PearsonRealize.com

Go online to access additional resources including:
Primary Sources • Biographies • Supreme Court cases • 21st Century Skill Tutorials • Maps • Graphic Organizers.

Objectives

Objective 1: Describe the steps Washington took to set up the government of the new republic.

Objective 2: Explain how Hamilton aimed to create a stable economic system.

Objective 3: Describe arguments around Hamilton's tax plan and the causes and effects of the Whiskey Rebellion.

Objective 4: Explain Washington's foreign policy, including the goal of neutrality and the impact of his Farewell Address.

LESSON 1 ORGANIZER	PACING: APPROX. 1 PERIOD .5 BLOCKS			
	OBJECTIVES	PACING	Online	Print
Connect				
DIGITAL START UP ACTIVITY **A President Takes Office**		5 min.	●	
Investigate				
DIGITAL TEXT 1 **The First American Presidency**	Objective 1	10 min.	●	●
DIGITAL TEXT 2 **Alexander Hamilton and the National Debt**	Objective 2	10 min.	●	●
DIGITAL TEXT 3 **Creating a Stable Economy**	Objective 3	10 min.	●	●
DIGITAL TEXT 4 **Taxation Sparks the Whiskey Rebellion**		10 min.	●	●
INTERACTIVE CHART **A Controversial Tax**		10 min.	●	
DIGITAL TEXT 5 **Americans React to the French Revolution**	Objective 4	10 min.	●	●
DIGITAL TEXT 6 **Washington Defends Neutrality**		10 min.	●	●
INTERACTIVE MAP **Foreign Affairs Under Washington**		10 min.	●	
Synthesize				
DIGITAL ACTIVITY **The Challenge of Neutrality**		5 min.	●	
Demonstrate				
DIGITAL QUIZ **Lesson Quiz and Class Discussion Board**		10 min.	●	

Washington's Presidency

CONNECT

DIGITAL START UP ACTIVITY

A President Takes Office

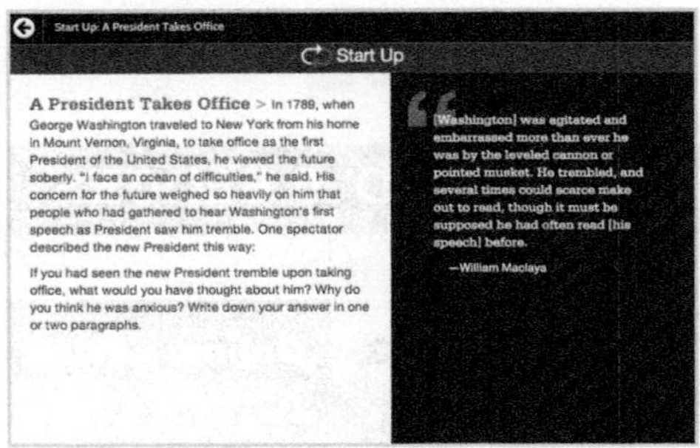

Project the Start Up Activity Ask students to read the quote by Washington and write about his reasons for anxiety as they enter and get settled. Have students share their paragraphs with a partner, either in class or through a blog space.

Discuss If you had seen the new President tremble upon taking office, what would you have thought about him? *(I might have thought he was nervous and wondered about his preparedness to lead the new nation.)* What reasons do you think he had for anxiety? *(As the first President of the United States, he knew there would be difficulties upholding the new government.)*

Aa Vocabulary Development: Use the Interactive Reading Notepad to preview the Key Terms and Academic Vocabulary in this lesson with students.

FLIP IT!

Assign the Flipped Video for this lesson.

STUDENT EDITION PRINT PAGES: 234–244

INVESTIGATE

DIGITAL TEXT 1

The First American Presidency

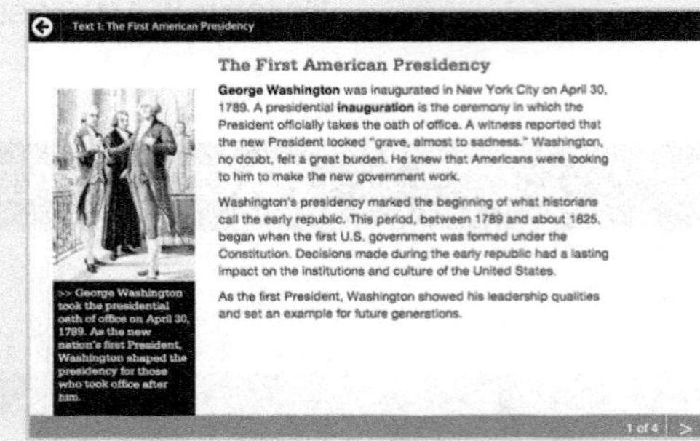

Objective 1: Describe the steps Washington took to set up the government of the new Republic.

Quick Instruction

Project the image of George Washington on the whiteboard. Point out to students that the Constitution was a direct cause of the early Republic's formation. Identify the early Republic as a major era in U.S. history between 1789 and about 1825. Note that the causes of this period were the adoption of the U.S. Constitution and that its effects included the moulding of democratic institutions and practices that have had a lasting impact on the United States. Washington's leadership qualities would set the tone for future presidencies in the early Republic. His important political contributions included choosing strong leaders for his Cabinet and naming the first Chief Justice of the Supreme Court.

Analyze Information How did Washington's actions reflect his leadership qualities? *(Washington was a smart leader who chose well-known, influential, and effective Cabinet members to advise him. The actions that he took set precedents for the federal government. These precedents created a framework for a stable system of government that has lasted to this day.)*

Further Instruction

Go through the Interactive Reading Notepad questions and discuss the answers with the class. Be sure students understand how the leadership qualities of George Washington affected the early Republic and continue to impact the nation today. Explain that one effect of the early Republic on subsequent American history was the establishment of the Supreme Court as outlined in the Constitution.

Summarize Note that one of the major domestic problems the new nation faced was setting up a court system. Describe how Congress addressed this problem. *(Congress passed the Judiciary Act of 1789, which called for the Supreme Court to have one Chief Justice and five Associate Justices. It also created a system of district and circuit courts.)*

Draw Conclusions What precedents did Washington set during his presidency? How did these actions help define the authority of the central government? *(He did not run for three terms and appointed well-known leaders to his Cabinet. These actions limited the power of the President, helped establish a structure for the executive branch, and ensured multiple perspectives would be heard within the government.)*

PEARSON realize™ www.PearsonRealize.com Access your Digital Lesson

DIGITAL TEXT 2

Alexander Hamilton and the National Debt

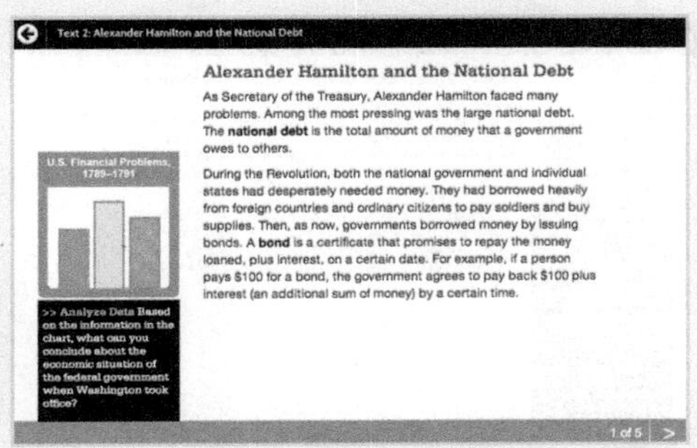

Text 2: Alexander Hamilton and the National Debt
Alexander Hamilton and the National Debt
As Secretary of the Treasury, Alexander Hamilton faced many problems. Among the most pressing was the large national debt. The national debt is the total amount of money that a government owes to others.
During the Revolution, both the national government and individual states had desperately needed money. They had borrowed heavily from foreign countries and ordinary citizens to pay soldiers and buy supplies. Then, as now, governments borrowed money by issuing bonds. A bond is a certificate that promises to repay the money loaned, plus interest, on a certain date. For example, if a person pays $100 for a bond, the government agrees to pay back $100 plus interest (an additional sum of money) by a certain time.
U.S. Financial Problems, 1789–1791
>> Analyze Data Based on the information in the chart, what can you conclude about the economic situation of the federal government when Washington took office?
1 of 5

DIGITAL TEXT 3

Creating a Stable Economy

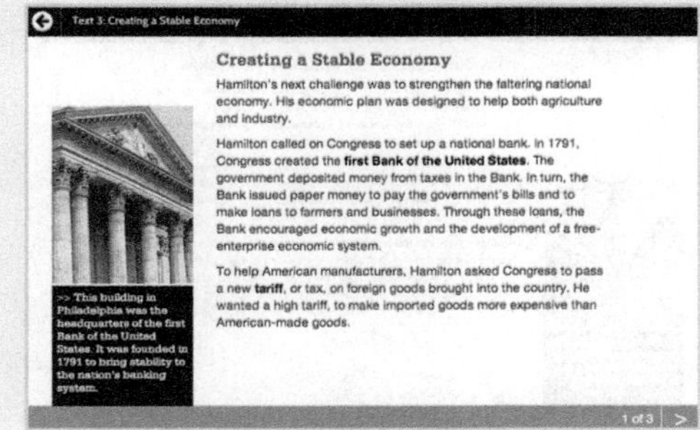

Text 3: Creating a Stable Economy
Creating a Stable Economy
Hamilton's next challenge was to strengthen the faltering national economy. His economic plan was designed to help both agriculture and industry.
Hamilton called on Congress to set up a national bank. In 1791, Congress created the first Bank of the United States. The government deposited money from taxes in the Bank. In turn, the Bank issued paper money to pay the government's bills and to make loans to farmers and businesses. Through these loans, the Bank encouraged economic growth and the development of a free-enterprise economic system.
To help American manufacturers, Hamilton asked Congress to pass a new tariff, or tax, on foreign goods brought into the country. He wanted a high tariff, to make imported goods more expensive than American-made goods.
>> This building in Philadelphia was the headquarters of the first Bank of the United States. It was founded in 1791 to bring stability to the nation's banking system.
1 of 3

Objective 2: **Explain how Hamilton aimed to create a stable economic system.**

Quick Instruction

Project the image of the chart on the whiteboard and discuss the major economic problems facing the early Republic. Ask students what factors they think caused the early Republic to be in debt.

Support Ideas With Examples Describe how Alexander Hamilton's helped resolve one of the major domestic problems faced by the leaders of the new Republic: creating a stable economy. *(He created a plan to repay debts by passing a tariff and issuing bonds.)*

D Differentiate: Extra Support To help students understand the economic problems facing the new republic, such as creating a stable economic system, review the definitions of the following terms: national debt, bond, loan, interest, and tariff.

Further Instruction

Go through the Interactive Reading Notepad questions and discuss the answers with the class. Be sure students understand how leaders of the United States proposed to solve the economic problems facing the new nation.

Although southern and northern states compromised on repaying state debts, arguments regarding taxation continued. Alexander Hamilton for example argued in favor of a tax on imports that would raise money to pay off the government's debts.

Compare Points of View Compare the views of political leaders Hamilton and Madison on how to stabilize the economy. *(Hamilton thought the United States should repay its debts in full by passing a tariff, buying up bonds, and issuing new bonds. Madison opposed paying off the government's old bonds because it rewarded speculators.)*

Infer Describe the contributions of Alexander Hamilton's that show his leadership qualities as an appointed leader. *(He convinced Congress to support much of his plan to pay off the national debt and was also willing to compromise with those who disagreed with him.)*

Draw Conclusions Why was repaying state debts a major domestic problem facing leaders of the new nation? *(The states disagreed over the repayment of state debts. Most southern states had already paid off their debts. They argued that repaying state debts unfairly helped northern states that hadn't repaid what they owed.)*

Objective 3: **Describe arguments around Hamilton's tax plan and the causes and effects of the Whiskey Rebellion.**

Quick Instruction

Interactive Chart: A Controversial Tax Project the interactive chart on the whiteboard and have students read through the barrels. Summarize the arguments for and against taxation.

Summarize the arguments regarding taxation. Why did northerners and southerners disagree over Hamilton's proposal to impose a protective tariff? *(For—the tariff would increase support for domestic goods. Against—people would have to pay more for imported goods. Northerners supported the tariff to protect their factories. Southerners opposed it because they bought more imported goods.)*

ELL Use the ELL activity described in the ELL chart.

ACTIVE CLASSROOM

Group students to use the PMI Strategy and create a three-column chart with headings Plus/Minus/Interesting to record responses to the following questions: What are the positive ideas about taxation in the new Republic? What are the negative ideas about this? What is interesting about this issue? Have groups compare responses.

Topic 5 Lesson 1

Washington's Presidency

DIGITAL TEXT 4

Taxation Sparks the Whiskey Rebellion

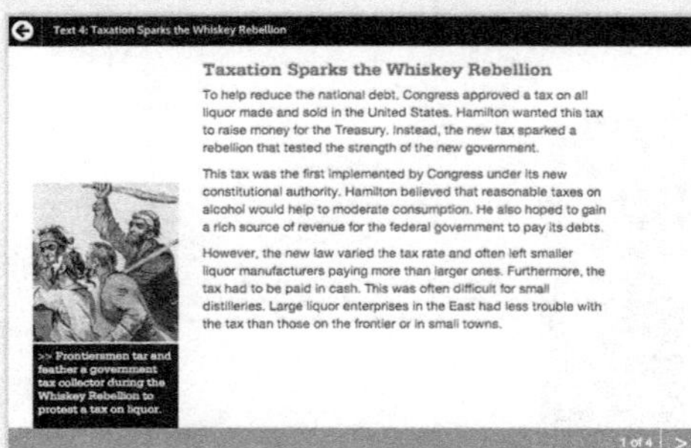

INTERACTIVE CHART

A Controversial Tax

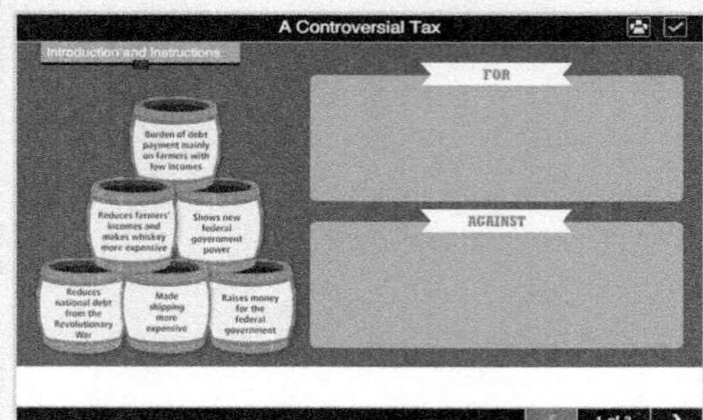

DIGITAL TEXT 5

Americans React to the French Revolution

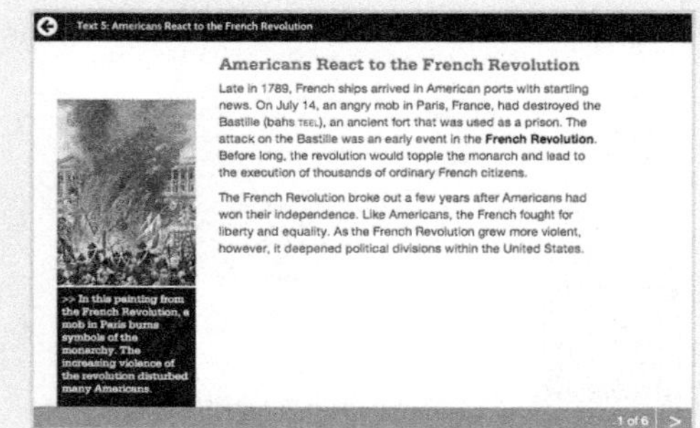

Further Instruction

Go through the Interactive Reading Notepad questions and discuss the answers with the class. Review the arguments regarding the creation of a banking system. Be sure students understand how disagreements over taxation led to rebellion.

Generate Explanations What major domestic problem did Hamilton's tax proposals address, and how did taxation contribute to the development of a free-enterprise system of economics? *(The government faced a debt crisis and needed to find a form of taxation that allowed it to pay off lenders, because attracting lenders is key to financing government in a free-enterprise system.)*

Draw Conclusions What arguments against taxation emerged during the Whiskey Rebellion? *(Taxes on alcohol that were unequal and had to be paid in cash unfairly burdened small distilleries, farmers, and those in frontier towns.)*

Identify Patterns How did Washington's contribution as a military leader during the Whiskey Rebellion address the early Republic's need to define the authority of the central government? *(Washington was swift to call up the militia to end the rebellion, but he showed mercy against protestors. This helped establish the government's authority to enforce laws prevent violence in the new nation without becoming tyrannical.)*

Objective 4: **Explain Washington's foreign policy, including the goal of neutrality and the impact of his Farewell Address.**

Quick Instruction

Interactive Map: Foreign Affairs Under Washington Project the interactive map on the whiteboard and click through the icons. In what areas was U.S. national security threatened by conflicts between Britain and France? *(The West Indies, the Great Lakes, the eastern coast)* Point out to students that one important effect of the formation of the early Republic was the ability of the United States to have a single, coherent foreign policy.

Hypothesize Identify the foreign policies of President Washington. What do you think was one effect of Washington's foreign policy? *(Washington aimed to maintain American neutrality in the face of European conflicts. His policies enabled the United States to stay out of foreign wars.)*

Generate Explanations Explain the impact of Washington's Farewell Address. *(Washington urged the country to stay away from foreign alliances that would lead America to become involved in European issues. His advice guided American foreign policy for many years.)*

DIGITAL TEXT 6

Washington Defends Neutrality

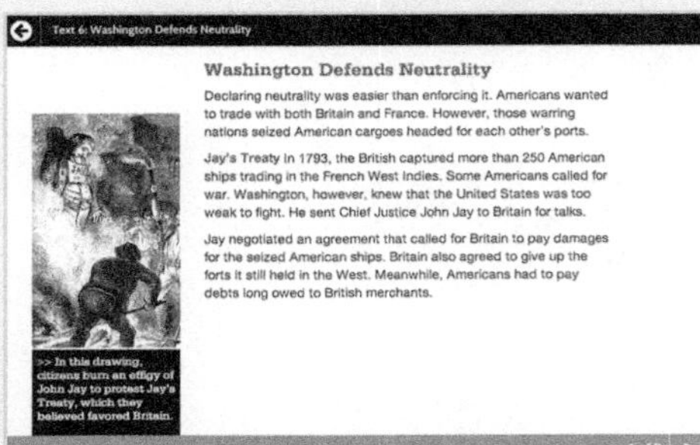

ACTIVE CLASSROOM

Have students Take a Stand on whether or not they agree with Washington's position of neutrality. Ask students to divide into two groups based on their answer and move to separate areas of the classroom. Have students compare their reasons for answering yes or no. Then have a representative present and defend each group's point of view.

ELL Use the ELL activity described in the ELL chart.

Further Instruction

Go through the Interactive Reading Notepad questions and discuss the answers with the class. Be sure students understand how Washington's leadership and his foreign policy helped the United States overcome domestic problems, including national security.

Evaluate Arguments Do you think Washington's foreign policy regarding the French Revolution was effective? Why or why not? *(Yes; in choosing not to take sides in the European wars following the Revolution, he kept the United States from being attacked by Britain and drawn into another war.)*

INTERACTIVE MAP

Foreign Affairs Under Washington

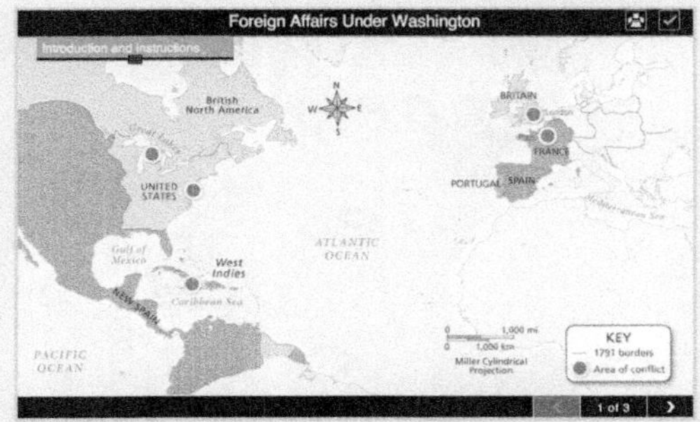

Identify Central Issues What difficulties did Washington face maintaining national security in his second term? Describe the foreign policy that he developed in response to these problems. *(Washington's foreign policy was to maintain American neutrality in the conflict between Britain and France. However, American trading ships were caught in the middle of this conflict. After Britain seized ships trading with France, Washington had John Jay negotiate a treaty with Britain to pay for damages and give up its forts. In exchange, America paid off its debts to Britain.)*

Washington's Presidency

SYNTHESIZE

DIGITAL ACTIVITY

The Challenge of Neutrality

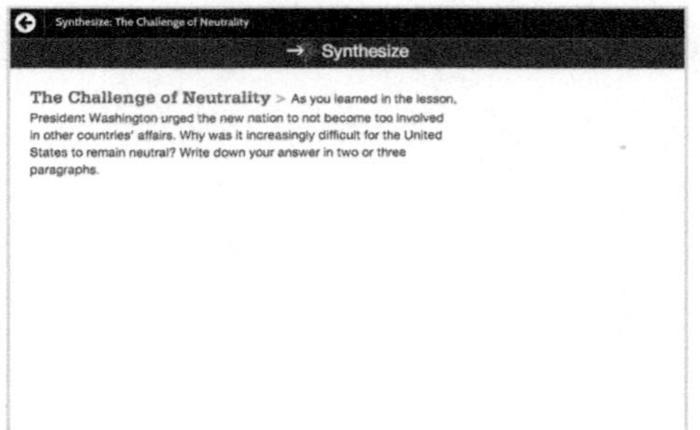

Have students write two to three paragraphs answering the questions about U.S. neutrality during George Washington's presidency and today. Discuss the answers as a class.

Have students review their answers and consider the following question. How did U.S. foreign policy under George Washington respond to issues facing the new Republic? Have students share their answers with the class.

Discuss Have students review the quote by Washington they read at the beginning of the lesson. Ask students to describe the major domestic problems Washington faced during his presidency and explain how he addressed these issues. Ask if they would revise their answers now that they have learned more about his leadership qualities.

DEMONSTRATE

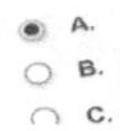

DIGITAL QUIZ

Lesson Quiz and Class Discussion Board

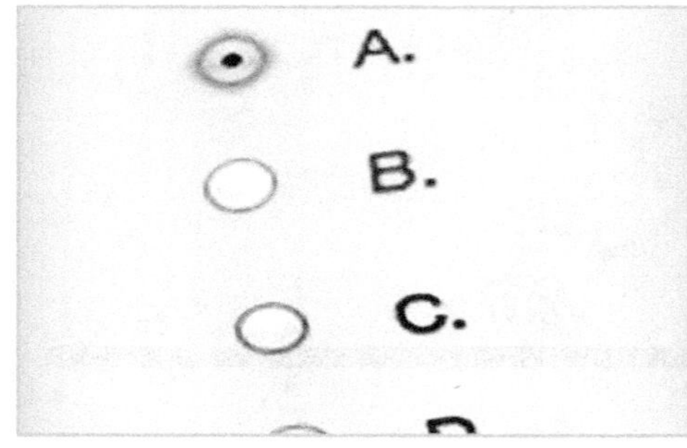

Assign the online Lesson Quiz for this lesson if you haven't already done so. Students will be offered automatic remediation or enrichment based on their score.

Pose these questions to the class on the Discussion Board:

In *Washington's Presidency* you read about George Washington's leadership and the major foreign and domestic problems he faced during his presidency.

Identify Patterns Describe how George Washington helped define the authority of the central government during his presidency. *(He limited his presidency to twp terms, appointed well-known leaders to Cabinet positions, and appointed the first Chief Justice of the Supreme Court. He also showed that the government was prepared to enforce laws during the Whiskey Rebellion.)*

Identify Central Issues Describe one of the major problems Washington faced as president and explain how it was addressed. *(Answers will vary but should explain responses to economic instability; the uncertain authority of the central government; foreign challenges; the need for taxation and creation of a banking system; the creation of a Cabinet and court system;or the difficulty of maintaining neutrality following the French Revolution)*

Topic Inquiry

Have students continue their investigations for the Topic Inquiry.

The Origin of Political Parties

Supporting English Language Learners

Use with Digital Text 1, **Americans Divide Over Politics.**

Listening
Read aloud the first page of the text or invite volunteers to do so. Display the accompanying image of George Washington on horseback as a means of using visual support to enhance and confirm understanding of increasingly complex and elaborated spoken language.

Beginning Ask students to describe the image using words or phrases. Use the visual support of the image to enhance and confirm students' understanding of the text. Ask: Do the Americans seem united or divided? Who are they all looking at?

Intermediate Ask students to describe the image. Use the visual support of the image to enhance and confirm students' understanding of the text. Ask: Did Washington want Americans to be united or divided? How does the image show national unity?

Advanced Ask students to describe the image. Have pairs of students use the visual support of the image to enhance and confirm their understanding of the text by answering this question: How does the image reflect the beginning of Washington's presidency when there were no political parties?

Advanced High Have pairs of students describe the image. Then have them use the visual support of the image to enhance and confirm their understanding of the text. Ask them to discuss how this image reflects Washington's ideas, as well as how another image reflecting the emergence of political parties might look.

Use with Digital Text 3, **New Political Parties Take Shape.**

Reading
Have students read the section titled *Newspapers Influence Public Opinion* and view the print of men reading newspapers. Have them use visual and contextual support to develop vocabulary needed to comprehend increasingly challenging language. You may wish to organize the class into groups by reading level.

Beginning Display basic words from the section (e.g., *newspapers*, *common people*, *read*). When students have read the section and viewed the print, help them find visual and context clues that suggest the meanings of these words.

Intermediate Display high-frequency academic vocabulary from the section (e.g., *demand*, *influence*). When students have read the section and viewed the print, help them find visual and context clues that suggest the meanings of these words.

Advanced Display more challenging academic vocabulary from the section (e.g., *rivalry*, *counterattacks*). When students have read the section and viewed the print, help them find visual and context clues that suggest the meanings of these words.

Advanced High Display more challenging academic vocabulary from the section (e.g., *rivalry*, *counterattacks*). Using visual and context clues, have students write their own sentences using these words to show their comprehension.

D Differentiate Instruction

Use the Differentiated Instruction notes throughout the lesson plan to support the varied skill sets, levels of readiness, and interests in the mixed-ability classroom.

Challenge These notes include suggestions for expanding the activity for advanced students.

On-Level These notes include suggestions for modifying the activity to address different interests or learning styles.

Extra Support These notes include ideas for providing more scaffolding or reading spuport.

Special Needs These notes provide ideas for adapting instruction to support the needs of various special needs students.

NOTES

The Origin of Political Parties

Objectives

Objective 1: Contrast the views of Hamilton and Jefferson.

Objective 2: Explain the origin of political parties in the early republic.

Objective 3: Describe how the election of 1796 increased political tensions.

LESSON 2 ORGANIZER	PACING: APPROX. 1 PERIOD .5 BLOCKS			
			RESOURCES	
	OBJECTIVES	PACING	Online	Print
Connect				
DIGITAL START UP ACTIVITY **New Political Parties**		5 min.	●	
Investigate				
DIGITAL TEXT 1 **Americans Divide Over Politics**	Objective 1	10 min.	●	●
DIGITAL TEXT 2 **Disagreements on Important Issues**	Objective 2	10 min.	●	●
INTERACTIVE GALLERY **Early American Leaders**		10 min.	●	
DIGITAL TEXT 3 **New Political Parties Take Shape**	Objective 3	10 min.	●	●
INTERACTIVE CHART **Federalists Versus Republicans**		10 min.	●	
Synthesize				
DIGITAL ACTIVITY **Reasons for Political Parties**		5 min.	●	
Demonstrate				
DIGITAL QUIZ **Lesson Quiz and Class Discussion Board**		10 min.	●	

Go online to access additional resources including: Primary Sources • Biographies • Supreme Court cases • 21st Century Skill Tutorials • Maps • Graphic Organizers.

CONNECT

DIGITAL START UP ACTIVITY

New Political Parties

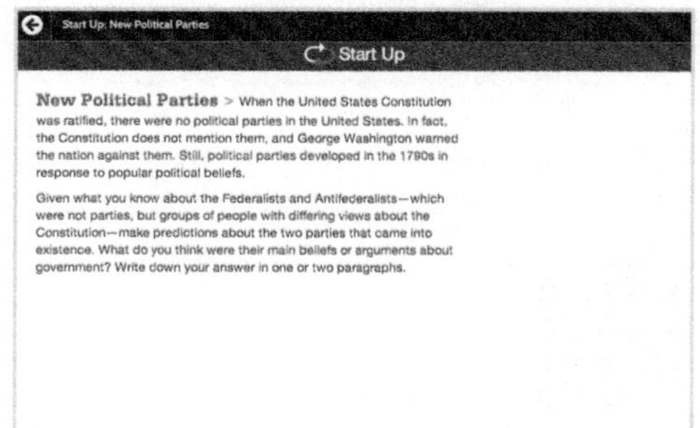

Project the Start Up Activity As students enter and get settled, ask them to read the activity and make a prediction about the political parties that would develop in the 1790s. Have students share their predictions with a partner, either in class or through a blog space.

Discuss Given what you know about the Federalists and Antifederalists, make predictions about the two parties that came into existence. What do you think were their main beliefs or arguments about government? *(Federalists and Antifederalists disagreed over how much power the federal government should have. One political party will favor a stronger central government and the other will favor more power for the states.)*

Aa Vocabulary Development: Use the Interactive Reading Notepad to preview the Key Terms and Academic Vocabulary in this lesson with students.

FLIP IT!

Assign the Flipped Video for this lesson.

STUDENT EDITION PRINT
Pages: 245–250

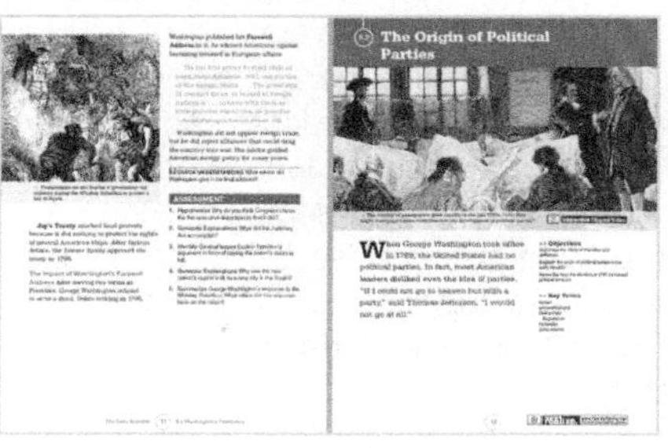

INVESTIGATE

DIGITAL TEXT 1

Americans Divide Over Politics

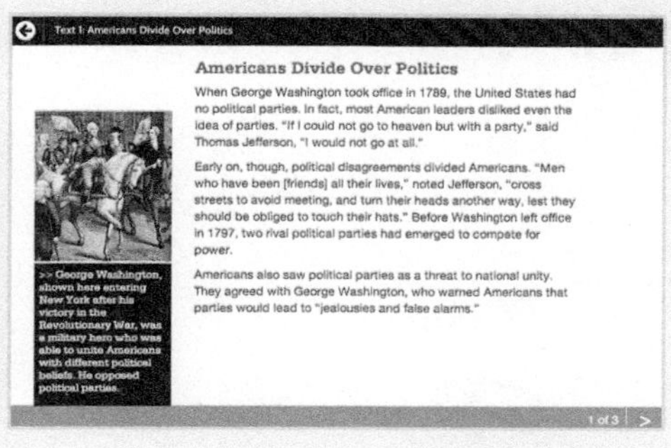

Objective 1: Contrast the views of Hamilton and Jefferson.

Quick Instruction

Project the image of Washington with his supporters on the whiteboard. Explain that when Washington was elected, America had no political parties. By the time he left office, two rival parties had emerged.

Make Predictions Why do you think American political parties would originate during the 1790s? *(Leaders would disagree over political issues. Opposing groups would seek to organize support, creating party divisions.)*

ELL Use the ELL activity described in the ELL chart.

Further Instruction

Go through the Interactive Reading Notepad questions and discuss the answers with the class. To extend the lesson, assign the Primary Source: Declaration of the Rights of Man. Be sure students understand how disagreements between Hamilton and Jefferson contributed to the origin of American political parties.

Evaluate Arguments Why did George Washington oppose the development of American political parties? Do you agree? Explain your reasoning. *(Washington saw political parties as a threat to national unity; answers should explain whether students agree or disagree.)*

Identify Cause and Effect What issues caused factions to develop in the early Republic? *(Hamilton and Jefferson disagreed over how to improve the nation's economy, who should control government, and whether to support Britain or France.)*

DIGITAL TEXT 2

Disagreements on Important Issues

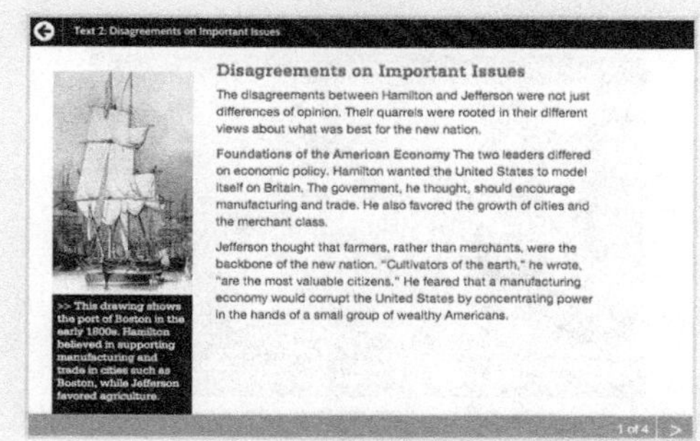

Objective 2: Explain the origin of political parties in the early Republic.

Quick Instruction

Early American leaders disagreed over domestic problems and foreign policy. These disagreements contributed to the development of American political parties in the 1790s.

Interactive Gallery: Early American Leaders Project the image of the interactive gallery on the whiteboard and click through the images. Briefly summarize the political views of each.

Evaluate Arguments How would James Madison explain the origin of American political parties? Explain whether you agree with his reasoning. *(Madison thought parties arose naturally out of political differences. Sample Answer—agree; when people disagree over political issues, they group together with those who share their views in order to work together toward their common goal.)*

ACTIVE CLASSROOM

Pair students to use the Conversations With History Strategy to imagine a conversation between two early American leaders covered in the lesson. The leaders should be from two different political parties. Write down what one of the leaders would say about an important historical issue facing the nation, whether domestic or foreign. Then write down what the other leader would say in response. Have pairs share their dialogues for the class.

The Origin of Political Parties

INTERACTIVE GALLERY

Early American Leaders

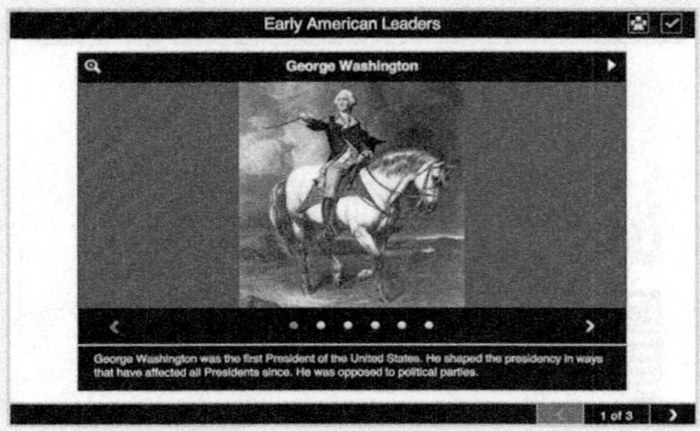

D Differentiate: Extra Support Help students complete the Conversations With History activity by having them write down the contrasting views of Hamilton and Jefferson on the power of the federal government. Ask why these two leaders disagreed over how strong central government should be.

Further Instruction

Go through the Interactive Reading Notepad questions and discuss the answers with the class. Be sure students understand the differences of opinion that led to the development of American political parties.

Compare and Contrast the views of the Federalist Party and the Democratic Republican Party on at least three different historical issues. *(Federalist Party—supported manufacturing and trade, a strong federal government, and favored Britain; Democratic Republican Party—supported small farmers, limited federal government, and favored France.)*

Summarize the arguments for and against the Bank of the United States. *(For—the Constitution gave Congress the power to carry out its duties in the elastic clause. The government needed a bank to collect taxes and pay bills. Against—the Constitution did not explicitly give Congress the power to create a bank, and the elastic clause should not be extended to include powers not explicitly mentioned elsewhere. A national bank gave the government too much power.)*

Draw Conclusions How do you think disagreements between Jefferson and Hamilton on historical issues contributed to the origin of American political parties? *(Politicians and the American public divided according to the leader with whom they most agreed. Political parties arose out of these divisions.)*

DIGITAL TEXT 3

New Political Parties Take Shape

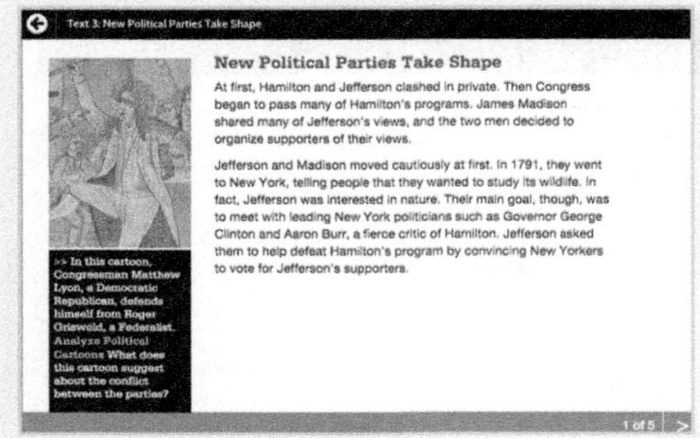
Text 3: New Political Parties Take Shape

New Political Parties Take Shape

At first, Hamilton and Jefferson clashed in private. Then Congress began to pass many of Hamilton's programs. James Madison shared many of Jefferson's views, and the two men decided to organize supporters of their views.

Jefferson and Madison moved cautiously at first. In 1791, they went to New York, telling people that they wanted to study its wildlife. In fact, Jefferson was interested in nature. Their main goal, though, was to meet with leading New York politicians such as Governor George Clinton and Aaron Burr, a fierce critic of Hamilton. Jefferson asked them to help defeat Hamilton's program by convincing New Yorkers to vote for Jefferson's supporters.

>> In this cartoon, Congressman Matthew Lyon, a Democratic Republican, defends himself from Roger Griswold, a Federalist. Analyze Political Cartoons What does this cartoon suggest about the conflict between the parties?

1 of 5

Objective 3: Describe how the election of 1796 increased political tensions.

Quick Instruction

Interactive Chart: Federalists Versus Republicans Project the interactive chart on the whiteboard and read through the tiles. Discuss how the two political parties originated and their different points of view regarding important historical issues. Tell students that by the end of this lesson they should be able to explain the origin of American political parties.

Summarize How did the Democratic Republican Party originate? *(In 1791, Jefferson and Madison met with New York politicians to organize on behalf of Jefferson and his supporters. They hoped to defeat Hamilton's programs.)*

Summarize How did the Federalist Party originate? *(Alexander Hamilton attracted like-minded supporters, such as northern merchants and manufacturers, who believed in a strong Federal government.)*

ACTIVE CLASSROOM

Have students pretend they are starting a newspaper during the election of 1796 and pick which political party their newspaper will support. Have students use the Make Headlines Strategy to write a headline that capture their party's perspective on an important historical issue and convinces readers to support their view. Have students share their headlines with the class.

INTERACTIVE CHART

Federalists Versus Republicans

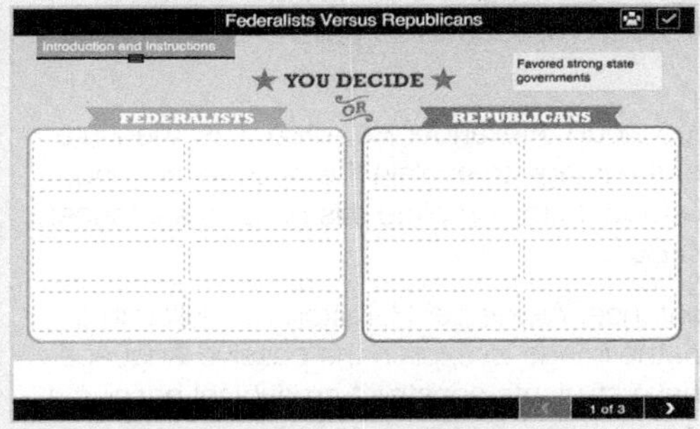

ELL Use the ELL activity described in the ELL chart.

Further Instruction

Go through the Interactive Reading Notepad questions and discuss the answers with the class.

Generate Explanations Explain the role newspapers played in the origin of American political parties. *(Newspapers sided with different parties, influencing public opinion and convincing people to side with one party or the other.)*

Hypothesize How do you think the election of 1796 contributed to the development of American political parties? *(A Federalist, John Adams, became President. A Democratic Republican, Jefferson, became Vice President. Divisions between the two men probably increased political rivalries, causing each party to strengthen its position.)*

SYNTHESIZE

DIGITAL ACTIVITY

Reasons for Political Parties

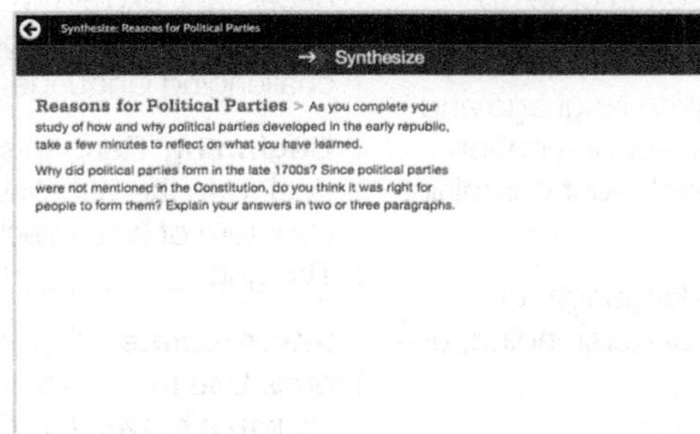

Have students write two to three paragraphs explaining the origin of American political parties and whether they think it was right for parties to form. Discuss the answers as a class.

Have students review their answers and consider the following question. How have American political parties developed and changed since their origin in the 1790s? Have students share their answers with the class.

Discuss Have students review the predictions they made at the beginning of the lesson. Ask students whether they would change their predictions about the two political parties and their points of view now that they have learned more about the origin and development of the party system.

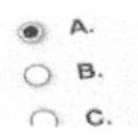

DEMONSTRATE

DIGITAL QUIZ

Lesson Quiz and Class Discussion Board

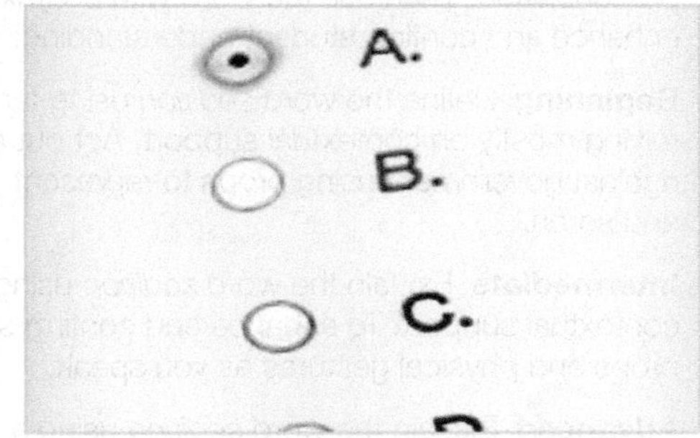

Assign the online Lesson Quiz for this lesson if you haven't already done so. Students will be offered automatic remediation or enrichment based on their score.

Pose these questions to the class on the Discussion Board:

In *The Origin of Political Parties*, you read about the origin and development of American political parties and their different points of view on historical issues.

Identify Central Issues How did the disagreement between political parties over a national banking system reflect a deeper disagreement over federal power? *(The parties disagreed over how much power the federal government should have. The controversy over a national bank was part of this deeper disagreement.)*

Make Predictions What do you think would be an effect of the development of American political parties in the early Republic? *(Sample response: Parties would come to dominate politics in the republic.)*

Topic Inquiry

Have students continue their investigations for the Topic Inquiry.

John Adams's Presidency

Supporting English Language Learners

Use with Digital Text 2, **The Alien and Sedition Acts.**

Listening

Display the word *sedition*, and have students practice its spelling and pronunciation. Then use the word with contextual support in order to enhance and confirm student understanding.

Beginning Define the word *sedition* using familiar spoken language and relying mostly on contextual support. Act out a physical act of rebellion against government using props to represent government, your complaint, and so on.

Intermediate Explain the word *sedition* using spoken language and contextual support. To enhance and confirm students' understanding, use props and physical gestures as you speak.

Advanced Explain the word *sedition* using a more complex spoken language that could be understood without contextual support. To enhance and confirm students' understanding, accompany your words with appropriate gestures and facial expressions.

Advanced High Explain the word *sedition* using a more complex and elaborate spoken language that is not linguistically accommodated in any way. Encourage students to ask questions in order to enhance and confirm their understanding of the topic.

Use with Digital Text 3, **An Important Presidential Election.**

Reading

Display the image of the Hamilton-Burr duel on the second screen. If necessary, explain what a duel is. Use visual and contextual support to develop grasp of language structures needed to comprehend increasingly challenging language

Beginning Read this sentence aloud: Alexander Hamilton was killed in a duel. Use the visual support of the image to explain the passive language structure of *was killed*. Guide students to complete this passive sentence: The gun __________ by Aaron Burr.

Intermediate Display this sentence: Alexander Hamilton was killed in a duel. Use the visual support of the image to explain the passive language structure of *was killed*. Then have students construct an original passive sentence based on the image.

Advanced Point out the passive language structure of *was killed* in the first paragraph of the section *The Federalist Era Comes to a Close*. With students, rewrite the sentence with an active construction. Then ask pairs of students to write an original passive sentence based on the image.

Advanced High Point out the passive language structure of *was killed* in the first paragraph of the section *The Federalist Era Comes to a Close*. Ask pairs of students to rewrite the sentence with an active construction, and then to write an original set of active and passive sentences based on the image.

D Differentiate Instruction

Use the Differentiated Instruction notes throughout the lesson plan to support the varied skill sets, levels of readiness, and interests in the mixed-ability classroom.

Challenge These notes include suggestions for expanding the activity for advanced students.

On-Level These notes include suggestions for modifying the activity to address different interests or learning styles.

Extra Support These notes include ideas for providing more scaffolding or reading spupport.

Special Needs These notes provide ideas for adapting instruction to support the needs of various special needs students.

NOTES

Go online to access additional resources including: Primary Sources • Biographies • Supreme Court cases • 21st Century Skill Tutorials • Maps • Graphic Organizers.

PEARSON realize™ www.PearsonRealize.com

Objectives

Objective 1: Explain Adams's foreign policy.

Objective 2: Describe the controversy over the Alien and Sedition Acts.

Objective 3: Explain why Congress decided the election of 1800 and how that election set a precedent.

LESSON 3 ORGANIZER	PACING: APPROX. 1 PERIOD, .5 BLOCKS		RESOURCES	
	OBJECTIVES	PACING	Online	Print
Connect				
DIGITAL START UP ACTIVITY **The Nation's Second President**		5 min.	●	
Investigate				
DIGITAL TEXT 1 **Escalating Conflict With France**	Objective 1	10 min.	●	●
INTERACTIVE TIMELINE **Relations With France**	Objective 1	10 min.	●	
DIGITAL TEXT 2 **The Alien and Sedition Acts**	Objective 2	10 min.	●	●
INTERACTIVE CHART **Hamilton, Adams, or Jefferson?**	Objective 2	10 min.	●	
DIGITAL TEXT 3 **An Important Presidential Election**	Objective 3	10 min.	●	●
Synthesize				
DIGITAL ACTIVITY **An Elected President's Decision**		5 min.	●	
Demonstrate				
DIGITAL QUIZ **Lesson Quiz and Class Discussion Board**		10 min.	●	

John Adams's Presidency

CONNECT

DIGITAL START UP ACTIVITY

The Nation's Second President

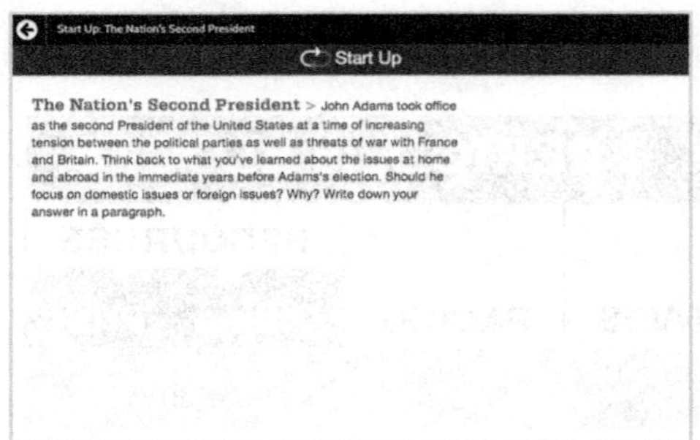

Project the Start Up Activity Have students read the activity and write their paragraphs as they enter and get settled. Have students share their arguments with a partner, either in class or through a blog space.

Discuss Think back to what you've learned about the issues at home and abroad in the immediate years before Adams's election. Should Adams focus on domestic issues or foreign issues? Why? *(If domestic, should mention: the economy, national security, and defining the authority of the central government; if foreign, should mention: the French Revolution, wars between Britain and France, and the Jay Treaty.)*

Aa Vocabulary Development: Use the Interactive Reading Notepad to preview the Key Terms and Academic Vocabulary in this lesson with students.

FLIP IT!

Assign the Flipped Video for this lesson.

STUDENT EDITION PRINT PAGES: 251–255

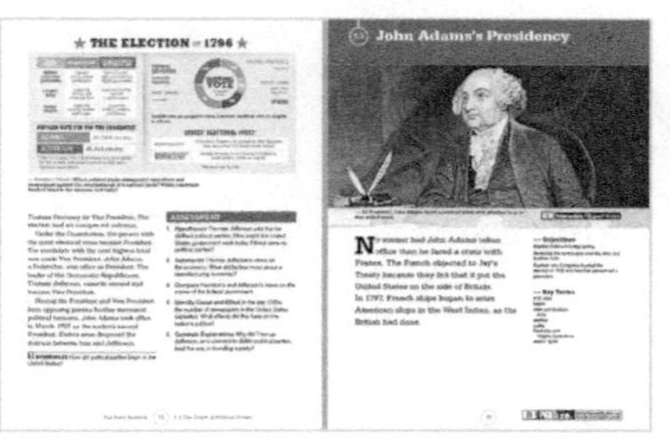

INVESTIGATE

DIGITAL TEXT 1

Escalating Conflict With France

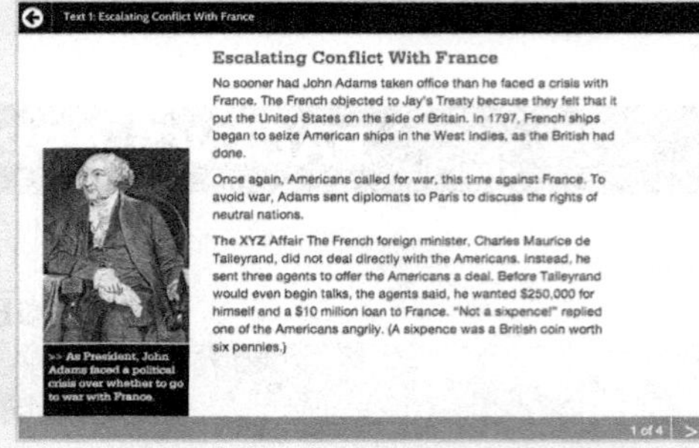

INTERACTIVE TIMELINE

Relations With France

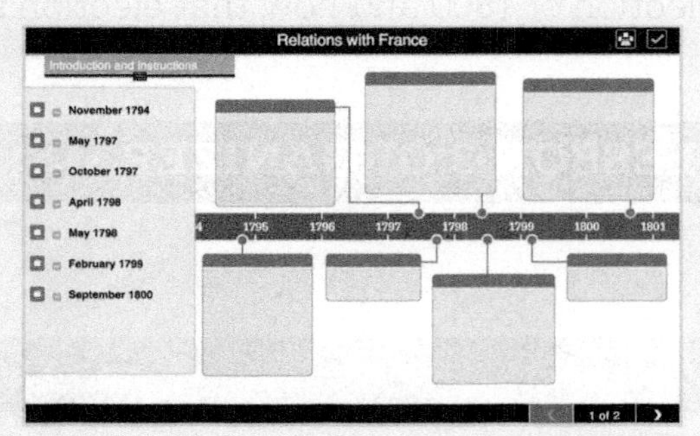

Objective 1: Explain Adams's foreign policy.

Quick Instruction

Interactive Timeline: Relations With France Project the interactive timeline and click through the events. Discuss why relations with France deteriorated as a result of the Jay Treaty and the XYZ affair. Ask how the Treaty of Mortefontaine affected the two nations.

Support Ideas With Evidence Describe Adam's foreign policy and explain what it revealed about his leadership qualities. *(Adams's policy was to maintain American neutrality and to avoid war with France both by strengthening the American military to make the country less of an easy target and by pursuing negotiations for peace with France. This policy showed leadership because it kept the United States out of a dangerous war even though public opinion, especially within Adam's party, supported war with France.)*

ACTIVE CLASSROOM

Pair students to use the See-Wonder-Think Strategy to analyze the political cartoon. Ask: What do you see? What does that make you think? What are you wondering about now that you've seen this? Then ask students what they think about Adams's foreign policy in light of public opinion toward the French. Have students share their insights with the class.

Further Instruction

Go through the Interactive Reading Notepad questions and discuss the answers with the class.

Compare Points of View Identify the different points of view of the Federalists and the Democratic Republicans regarding Adams's foreign policy with France. *(Federalists—wanted war with France to weaken the Democratic Republicans and strengthen the military; they supported Britain. Democratic Republicans—did not want war with France because they saw France as an ally.)*

Cite Evidence Cite evidence that shows how Adams's decision to strengthen the navy helped define the authority of the central government. *(Adam's actions helped confirm the role of the federal government as the guardian of national security.)*

Identify Cause and Effect Identify one cause and one effect of the XYZ affair on domestic or foreign policy. *(Cause—Adams sent diplomats to France because French ships had seized American ships in the West Indies, even though the United States had declared neutrality. Effects—Americans called for war against France; Adams strengthened the navy; Adams again sent diplomats to negotiate with France to end the conflict with the United States)*

DIGITAL TEXT 2

The Alien and Sedition Acts

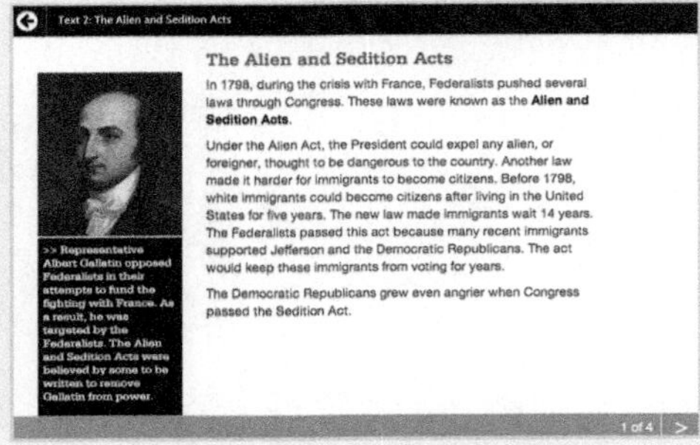

INTERACTIVE CHART

Hamilton, Adams, or Jefferson?

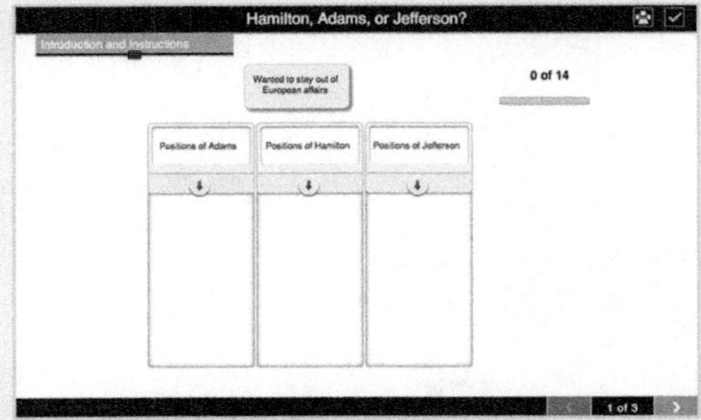

Objective 2: **Describe the controversy over the Alien and Sedition Acts.**

Quick Instruction

Interactive Chart: Hamilton, Adams, or Jefferson? Project the image of the interactive chart and click through the tiles. Identify the views on domestic and foreign policies held by Hamilton, Adams, and Jefferson.

Compare and Contrast How did Adams's foreign policy differ from the approaches favored by Hamilton and Jefferson? *(Adams—did not want war with France or Britain and sent diplomats to negotiate with France. Hamilton—pressured Adams to go to war with France. Jefferson—supported France against Britain.)*

ACTIVE CLASSROOM

Have students use the Sticky Notes Strategy and take 3 minutes to compare and contrast the different points of view of the Federalists and the Democratic Republicans on the Alien and Sedition Acts, citing evidence for support. Have students share their responses with a partner.

D Differentiate: Extra Support Review the definitions of alien—foreigner—and sedition—stirring up rebellion against a government. Have students summarize both the Alien Acts and the Sedition Act in their own words.

ELL Use the ELL activity described in the ELL chart.

Further Instruction

Go through the Interactive Reading Notepad questions and discuss the answers with the class. Be sure students understand the causes of the Alien and Sedition Acts and their effects on the early Republic.

Draw Conclusions Describe how the Kentucky and Virginia resolutions challenged the authority of the central government. *(The resolutions said the states had the right to judge whether laws were constitutional and disobey federal laws they deemed unconstitutional. This gave states powers not listed in Constitution.)*

Evaluate Arguments How might Federalists have argued that the Alien and Sedition Acts were necessary for maintaining national security? Do you agree? Explain. *(In order to keep the nation safe, any immigrants thought to be dangerous had to be expelled. It was also a matter of security to keep citizens from causing rebellion. Students should give reasons why they agree or disagree.)*

Identify Cause and Effect How did the Alien and Sedition Acts affect the development of political parties in the late 1700s and early 1800s? *(The acts were aimed to weaken the Democratic Republican Party. They made it harder for immigrants, many of whom supported the Democratic Republicans, to become voting citizens. They also caused Democratic Republicans to be fined or jailed for expression opinions against the government.)*

John Adams's Presidency

DIGITAL TEXT 3

An Important Presidential Election

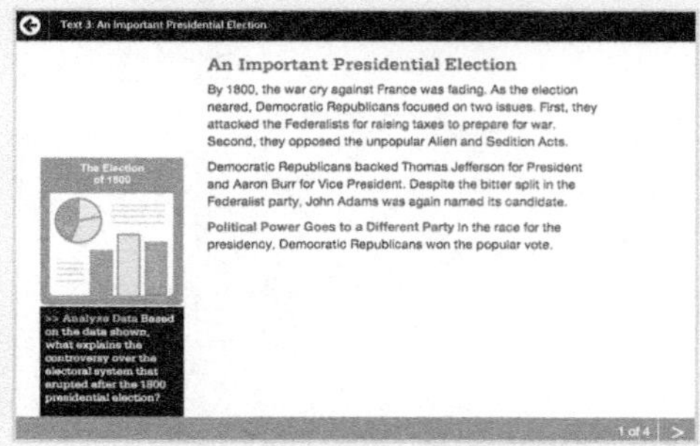

Objective 3: **Explain why Congress decided the election of 1800 and how that election set a precedent.**

Quick Instruction

Project the graphs on the whiteboard and review how the electoral college votes for president. Explain that at the time, the college did not vote separately for President and Vice President.

Identify Central Issues Why did Adams's foreign policy cause a split in the Federalist Party? *(Many Federalists such as Hamilton wanted war with France. They opposed Adams's position of neutrality.)*

ELL Use the ELL activity described in the ELL chart.

Further Instruction

Go through the Interactive Reading Notepad questions and discuss the answers with the class.

Generate Explanations Explain how the election of 1800 affected the development of American political parties. *(The Federalists lost the election as well as several seats in Congress, weakening the party. Democratic Republicans came into power, although many Federalist economic programs remained in place.)*

Make Predictions Name one change you think will result from the election of 1800. Explain your reasoning. *(With Jefferson and the Democratic Republican Party in power, economic policies would be more likely to favor agriculture and the common people over manufacturing and the elite.)*

Draw Conclusions How did the 1800 election set a precedent? *(The election set the precedent that Presidents who failed to win reelection would peacefully and willingly leave office and that the office would pass in an orderly way to the new President.)*

SYNTHESIZE

DIGITAL ACTIVITY

An Elected President's Decision

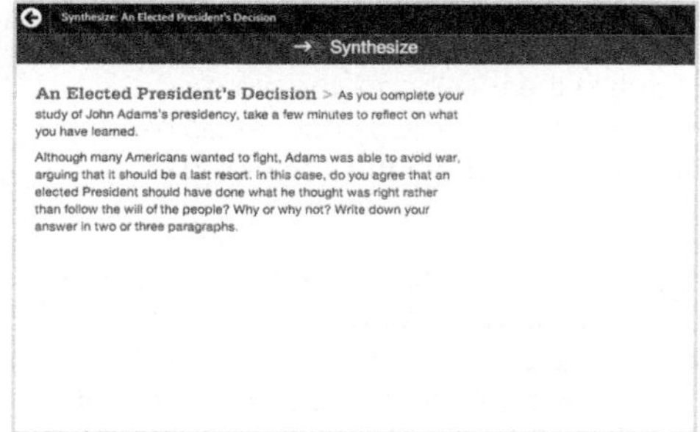

Have students write two to three paragraphs explaining whether they agree or disagree with Adams's decision to avoid war when many Americans wanted to fight. Discuss the answers as a class.

Have students review their answers and consider the following question. How did John Adams's foreign policy affect the early Republic? Have students share their answers in small groups or with the class.

Discuss Have students review the paragraphs they wrote at the beginning of the lesson about whether they thought Adams should focus on domestic or foreign issues during his presidency. Ask students whether they would change their answer now that they have learned about the domestic and foreign problems he faced.

DEMONSTRATE

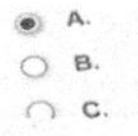

DIGITAL QUIZ

Lesson Quiz and Class Discussion Board

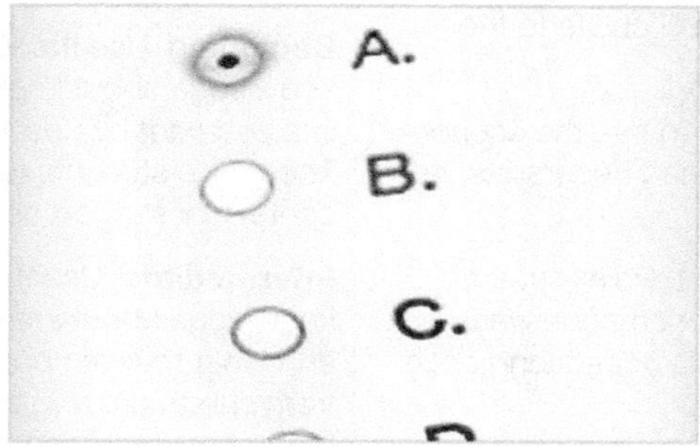

Assign the online Lesson Quiz for this lesson if you haven't already done so. Students will be offered automatic remediation or enrichment based on their score.

Pose these questions to the class on the Discussion Board:

In *John Adams's Presidency*, you read about Adams's leadership, the foreign and domestic problems he faced, and the development of political parties during his presidency.

Identify Patterns How did Adams's foreign policy show continuity and change compared to Washington's foreign policy? *(His foreign policy showed continuity in his effort to maintain U.S. neutrality toward both Britain and France. His foreign policy showed change in his effort to strengthen the nation's defenses and to fight off French attacks.)*

Support Ideas With Examples Why do you think Adams failed to win reelection in 1800? Explain your reasoning. *(Answers should mention Adams's policies that alienated members of both parties.)*

Topic Inquiry

Have students continue their investigations for the Topic Inquiry.

Jefferson's Presidency

Supporting English Language Learners

Use with Digital Text 1, **Jefferson Redefines Government.**

Listening

Use linguistic support to enhance and confirm student understanding of increasingly complex and elaborated spoken language. You may want to group students by language level. Ask students to listen carefully to the following statement about the content in this text, then circulate to the different groups:

"Jefferson brought change to government. He wanted to free the economy from government intrusion. Although his changes alarmed Federalists, he left many Federalist policies in place."

Beginning Repeat the first sentence of your statement. Point out that *brought* is the past tense of *bring*, or a way to say that someone was bringing something in the past. Make sure that students understand each part of the sentence, and the sentence as a whole.

Intermediate Repeat the second sentence of your statement. Point out that to free one thing from a second thing means to take the second thing away so that the first thing is free, or able to do what it wants. Make sure that students understand each part of the sentence, and the sentence as a whole.

Advanced Repeat the third sentence of your statement. Point out that the clause beginning with *although* is a dependent clause, and that a dependent clause beginning with *although* suggests that the idea in the dependent clause is one that would not lead you to expect the idea in the independent clause. Make sure that students understand each part of the sentence, and the sentence as a whole.

Advanced High Repeat the third sentence of your statement. Point out that the clause beginning with *although* is a dependent clause. Have students create their own sentences with dependent clauses and take turns listening to one another's sentences.

Use with Digital Text 5, **American Shipping Faces Challenges.**

Reading

Use the image depicting impressment at the end of the text as a form of visual and contextual support to develop the background knowledge to comprehend the text. Ask students to describe what they see.

Beginning Use the visual support of the image to provide background knowledge about impressment. Explain the meaningof the word *impressment* by describing the image, using physical gestures as needed. Then have students read the final paragraph of the text, providing contextual support as needed.

Intermediate Use the visual support of the image to provide background knowledge about impressment. Identify the various persons in the image and what they are doing.E xplain how the concept of impressment differs from enlistment and the draft. Then have students read the final paragraph of the text, providing contextual support as needed.

Advanced Develop background knowledge by asking students to share what they know about enlisting in and being drafted into the military. Use the visual support of the image to help students understand how the process of impressment is different. Have students read the section titled "Caught Between Britain and France," providing contextual support as needed.

Advanced High Develop background knowledge by asking students how the image might remind them of kidnapping, slavery, or an arrest. Have students read the section titled "Caught Between Britain and France," relying on context as needed to clarify meanings. Then ask students to explain why impressment posed such a challenge to the United States.

D Differentiate Instruction

Use the Differentiated Instruction notes throughout the lesson plan to support the varied skill sets, levels of readiness, and interests in the mixed-ability classroom.

Challenge These notes include suggestions for expanding the activity for advanced students.

On-Level These notes include suggestions for modifying the activity to address different interests or learning styles.

Extra Support These notes include ideas for providing more scaffolding or reading spuport.

Special Needs These notes provide ideas for adapting instruction to support the needs of various special needs students.

NOTES

PEARSON realize www.PearsonRealize.com — **Go online to access additional resources including:** Primary Sources • Biographies • Supreme Court cases • 21st Century Skill Tutorials • Maps • Graphic Organizers.

Objectives

Objective 1: Explain why Jefferson acted to limit the size of the federal government.

Objective 2: Describe the significance and effects of *Marbury* v. *Madison*.

Objective 3: Identify the causes and effects of the Louisiana Purchase.

Objective 4: Describe the discoveries of Lewis, Clark, and Pike.

Objective 5: Explain Jefferson's foreign policy, including conflict with the Barbary States, threats to U.S.neutrality, and the Embargo Act.

LESSON 4 ORGANIZER	PACING: APPROX. 1 PERIOD, .5 BLOCKS			
			RESOURCES	
	OBJECTIVES	PACING	Online	Print
Connect				
DIGITAL START UP ACTIVITY **Understanding Judicial Review**		5 min.	●	
Investigate				
DIGITAL TEXT 1 **Jefferson Redefines Government**	Objective 1	10 min.	●	●
DIGITAL TEXT 2 **Landmark Supreme Court Cases**	Objective 2	10 min.	●	●
DIGITAL TEXT 3 **The Louisiana Purchase**	Objective 3	10 min.	●	●
DIGITAL TEXT 4 **Exploring the Louisiana Territory**	Objective 4	10 min.	●	●
INTERACTIVE MAP **Expansion and Exploration**		10 min.	●	
DIGITAL TEXT 5 **American Shipping Faces Challenges**	Objective 5	10 min.	●	●
DIGITAL TEXT 6 **A Painful Embargo**		10 min.	●	●
INTERACTIVE CHART **Jefferson's Goals and Policies**		10 min.	●	
Synthesize				
DIGITAL ACTIVITY **The Impact of Judicial Review**		5 min.	●	
Demonstrate				
DIGITAL QUIZ **Lesson Quiz and Class Discussion Board**		10 min.	●	

Topic 5 Lesson 4

Jefferson's Presidency

CONNECT

DIGITAL START UP ACTIVITY

Understanding Judicial Review

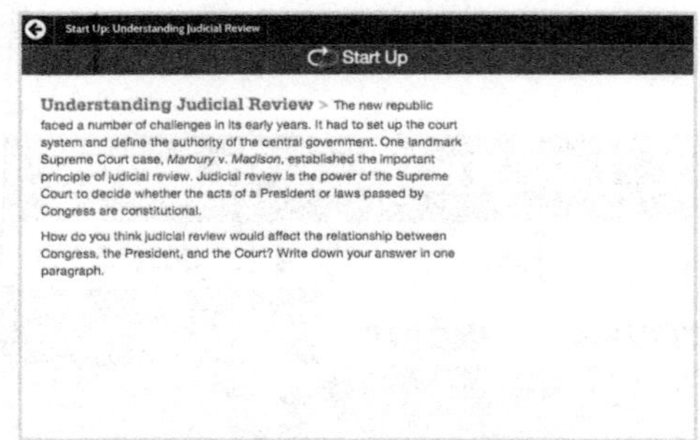

Start Up: Understanding Judicial Review
Start Up
Understanding Judicial Review > The new republic faced a number of challenges in its early years. It had to set up the court system and define the authority of the central government. One landmark Supreme Court case, *Marbury* v. *Madison*, established the important principle of judicial review. Judicial review is the power of the Supreme Court to decide whether the acts of a President or laws passed by Congress are constitutional.
How do you think judicial review would affect the relationship between Congress, the President, and the Court? Write down your answer in one paragraph.

Project the Start Up Activity Have students read the definition of judicial review and answer the question as they enter and get settled. Have students share their answers with a partner, either in class or through a blog space.

Discuss How do you think judicial review would affect the relationship between Congress, the President, and the Court? *(Allowing the Court to strike down laws and actions as unconstitutional would give the Court more authority to check the power of Congress and the President.)*

Tell students that in this lesson they will be learnihg about the Louisiana Purchase of 1803 and the landmark Supreme Court case *Marbury* v. *Madison*.

Aa Vocabulary Development: Use the Interactive Reading Notepad to preview the Key Terms and Academic Vocabulary in this lesson with students.

FLIP IT!

Assign the Flipped Video for this lesson.

STUDENT EDITION PRINT PAGES: 256–269

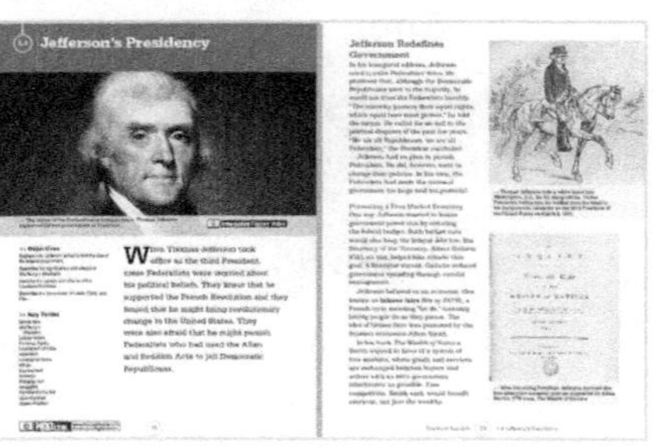

INVESTIGATE

DIGITAL TEXT 1

Jefferson Redefines Government

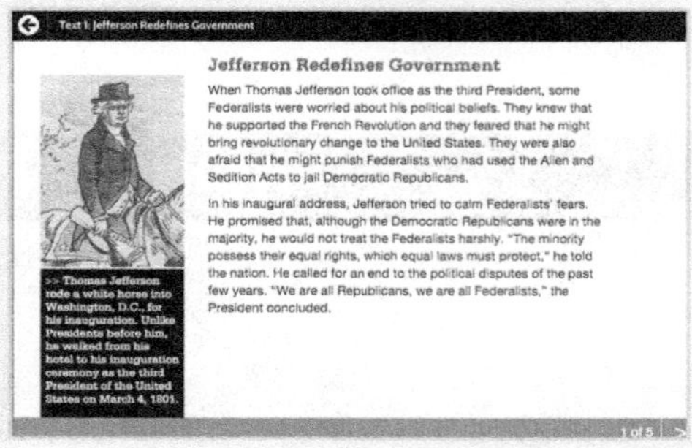

Objective 1: Explain why Jefferson acted to limit the size of the federal government.

Quick Instruction

Project the image of Thomas Jefferson on the whiteboard and remind students of his political views as a Democratic Republican. Explain that afree-enterprise system is an economic system in which goods and services are exchanged with minimal government interference.

Draw Conclusions How did Jefferson's policies contribute to the development of a free-enterprise system in the new nation? *(Jefferson's policies limited the economic role of the central government. This promoted a free-enterprise system, which involves minimal government intrusion in the economy.)*

D Differentiate: Extra Support Explain that an enterprise is a business or company. Ask students to recall the mercantalist economic system exercised by the British to gain wealth from the American colonies. Discuss how a free-enterprise system differs.

ELL Use the ELL activity described in the ELL chart.

Further Instruction

Go through the Interactive Reading Notepad questions and discuss the answers with the class. Be sure students can explain why a free-enterprise system of economics with minimal government intrusion developed in the new nation.

Support Ideas with Examples Give at least three examples of how Jefferson redefined the authority of the central government following Adams's presidency. *(To reduce the authority of the central government, Jefferson cut the federal budget, decreased the size of government departments, reduced the army and navy, repealed the Whiskey Tax, allowed the Sedition Act to expire, overturned the Alien Act, and promoted a free-enterprise system of economics.)*

Compare and Contrast a free-enterprise system with the economic system favored by Federalists. Why did Jefferson favor a laissez-faire policy? *(A free-enterprise system involves minimal government intrusion. The Federalists wanted a stronger central government that promoted trade and manufacturing. Jefferson favored a laissez-faire approach to reduce government interference.)*

Draw Conclusions How did Jefferson try create a stable economic system in the new Republic? *(He reduced the federal budget and the federal debt and continued to pay off state debts. He also promoted economic competition through a free-enterprise system.)*

DIGITAL TEXT 2

Landmark Supreme Court Cases

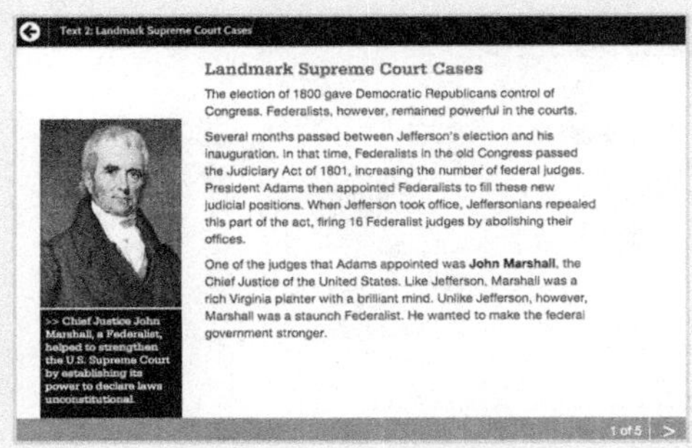

Text 2: Landmark Supreme Court Cases
Landmark Supreme Court Cases
The election of 1800 gave Democratic Republicans control of Congress. Federalists, however, remained powerful in the courts.
Several months passed between Jefferson's election and his inauguration. In that time, Federalists in the old Congress passed the Judiciary Act of 1801, increasing the number of federal judges. President Adams then appointed Federalists to fill these new judicial positions. When Jefferson took office, Jeffersonians repealed this part of the act, firing 16 Federalist judges by abolishing their offices.
One of the judges that Adams appointed was John Marshall, the Chief Justice of the United States. Like Jefferson, Marshall was a rich Virginia planter with a brilliant mind. Unlike Jefferson, however, Marshall was a staunch Federalist. He wanted to make the federal government stronger.
>> Chief Justice John Marshall, a Federalist, helped to strengthen the U.S. Supreme Court by establishing its power to declare laws unconstitutional.
1 of 5

Objective 2: **Describe the significance and effects of *Marbury* v. *Madison*.**

Quick Instruction

Project the image of Chief Justice John Marshall on the whiteboard. Marshall was an appointed official who showed leadership by strengthening the powers of the Supreme Court.

Summarize the issues, the decision, and the significance of *Marbury* v. *Madison*. *(Chief Justice John Marshall ruled that the Judiciary Act was unconstitutional because it gave the Supreme Court power that had not been granted by the Constitution. Congress had to amend the act. This established the principle of judicial review and strengthened the power of the Court'.)*

Further Instruction

Go through the Interactive Reading Notepad questions and discuss the answers with the class. Assign the Supreme Court Case: *Marbury* v. *Madison*. Have students summarize the issues, decisions, and significance of this landmark case.

Support Ideas With Evidence Describe the leadership qualities of John Marshall as an appointed leader, providing evidence for support. *(Marshall was a savvy leader who found a way to strengthen the Supreme Court, and therefore constitutional checks and balances, by declaring the law that required the Court to hear Marbury's case as unconstitutional.)*

Identify Central Issues Identify the origin of judicial review. *(In* Marbury *v.* Madison*, the Supreme Court rejected a law that it considered unconstitutional.)*

Identify Cause and Effect What were the congressional and presidential responses to judicial review during Jefferson's presidency and how did they affect the court's power? *(Congress amended the part of the Judiciary Act ruled unconstitutional. By accepting the Court's ruling and changing the law, Congress affirmed and upheld the Court's power. Jefferson asserted the power of the President to resist some court orders, but he ultimately accepted the process of judicial review.)*

DIGITAL TEXT 3

The Louisiana Purchase

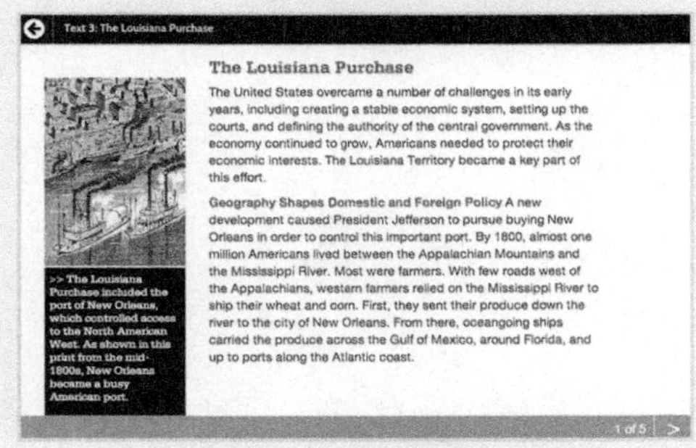

Text 3: The Louisiana Purchase
The Louisiana Purchase
The United States overcame a number of challenges in its early years, including creating a stable economic system, setting up the courts, and defining the authority of the central government. As the economy continued to grow, Americans needed to protect their economic interests. The Louisiana Territory became a key part of this effort.
Geography Shapes Domestic and Foreign Policy A new development caused President Jefferson to pursue buying New Orleans in order to control this important port. By 1800, almost one million Americans lived between the Appalachian Mountains and the Mississippi River. Most were farmers. With few roads west of the Appalachians, western farmers relied on the Mississippi River to ship their wheat and corn. First, they sent their produce down the river to the city of New Orleans. From there, oceangoing ships carried the produce across the Gulf of Mexico, around Florida, and up to ports along the Atlantic coast.
>> The Louisiana Purchase included the port of New Orleans, which controlled access to the North American West. As shown in this print from the mid-1800s, New Orleans became a busy American port.
1 of 5

Objective 3: **Identify the causes and effects of the Louisiana Purchase.**

Quick Instruction

Project the map of the Louisiana Purchase on the whiteboard. Identify the areas acquired through the Louisiana Purchase.

Generate Explanations Explain the significance of the following date: 1803. *(In the year 1803, the United States acquired the Louisiana Purchase, which doubled the size of the United States.)*

Analyze Maps How did the physical geography of the United States affect the decision to purchase the Louisiana Territory? *(Farmers between the Appalachian Mountains and the Mississippi River shipped wheat and corn down the Mississippi to New Orleans and then to Atlantic ports. Purchasing the territory allowed the United States to control this shipping route.)*

Further Instruction

Go through the Interactive Reading Notepad questions and discuss the answers with the class. Be sure students can explain the significance of the Louisiana Purchase and identify the areas acquired to form the United States.

Summarize Describe the contributions of James Monroe to the expansion of the United States *(Along with Robert Livingston, he negotiated with the French to buy Louisiana.)*

Jefferson's Presidency

Draw Conclusions How did the Louisiana Purchase enable leaders of the new Republic to maintain national security? *(The purchase allowed the United States to control the Mississippi, keeping France from building an empire in North America.)*

Identify Cause and Effect What factors caused Jefferson to purchase the Louisiana Territory? What were the effects of this purchase on the early Republic? *(Causes—Napoleon wanted to sell North American territory; Jefferson wanted to control the Mississippi and the port at New Orleans. Effects—the United States doubled its area and controlled lands west of the Mississippi.)*

DIGITAL TEXT 4

Exploring the Louisiana Territory

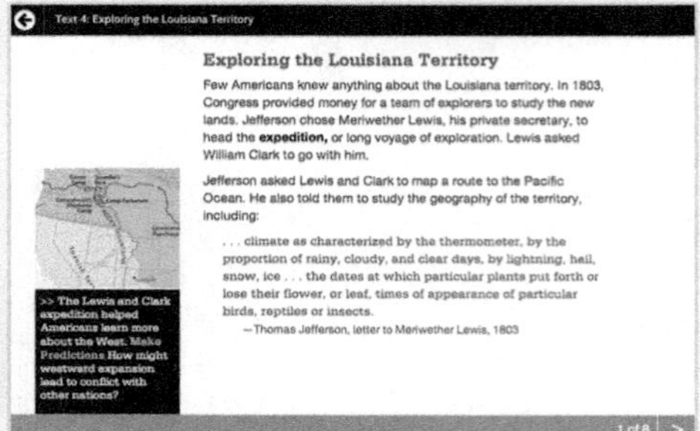

Text 4: Exploring the Louisiana Territory

Exploring the Louisiana Territory

Few Americans knew anything about the Louisiana territory. In 1803, Congress provided money for a team of explorers to study the new lands. Jefferson chose Meriwether Lewis, his private secretary, to head the **expedition,** or long voyage of exploration. Lewis asked William Clark to go with him.

Jefferson asked Lewis and Clark to map a route to the Pacific Ocean. He also told them to study the geography of the territory, including:

> . . . climate as characterized by the thermometer, by the proportion of rainy, cloudy, and clear days, by lightning, hail, snow, ice . . . the dates at which particular plants put forth or lose their flower, or leaf, times of appearance of particular birds, reptiles or insects.
>
> —Thomas Jefferson, letter to Meriwether Lewis, 1803

>> The Lewis and Clark expedition helped Americans learn more about the West. Make Predictions How might westward expansion lead to conflict with other nations?

1 of 8

Objective 4: Describe the discoveries of Lewis, Clark, and Pike.

Quick Instruction

Interactive Map: Expansion and Exploration Project the interactive map on the whiteboard and click through the layers. Identify the areas of the Louisiana Purchase explored by Lewis, Clark, and Pike.

Draw Conclusions How did Lewis and Clark's expedition impact U.S. expansion? *(They traveled through areas such as Oregon that were later acquired to form the United States.)*

ACTIVE CLASSROOM

Pair students to use the Audio Tour Strategy to locate places of importance in the United States during the 19th century. Have the first student give the second a verbal tour of the interactive map and the routes it shows. Have the second student explain the significance of the routes and what the map means.

INTERACTIVE MAP

Expansion and Exploration

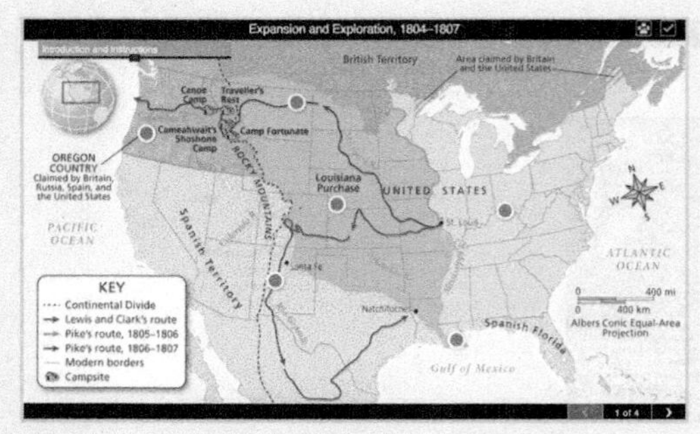

Further Instruction

Go through the Interactive Reading Notepad questions and discuss the answers with the class.

Identify Cause and Effect Identify the effects of Lewis, Clark, and Pike's expeditions on the early Republic. *(Lewis and Clark brought back useful information about the geography of the Louisiana Territory, met Native American groups, and claimed the Oregon Country for the United States. Pike expanded American knowledge about the Southwest.)*

Identify Steps in a Process How did Louisiana gain statehood? *(Settlers moved to the region around the Mississippi River and New Orleans. When the territory had enough U.S. citizens, settlers applied for statehood.)*

DIGITAL TEXT 5

American Shipping Faces Challenges

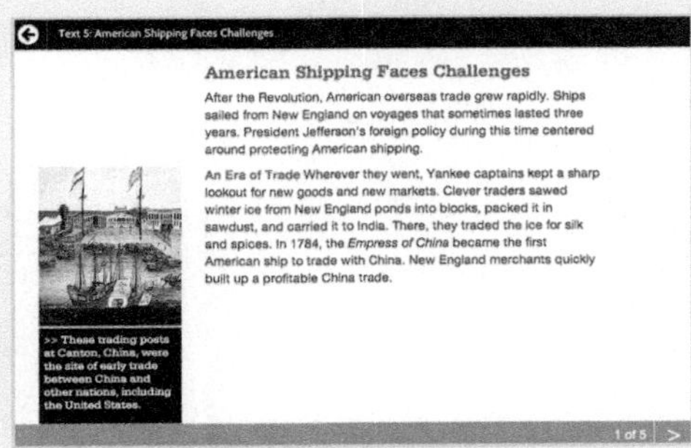

DIGITAL TEXT 6

A Painful Embargo

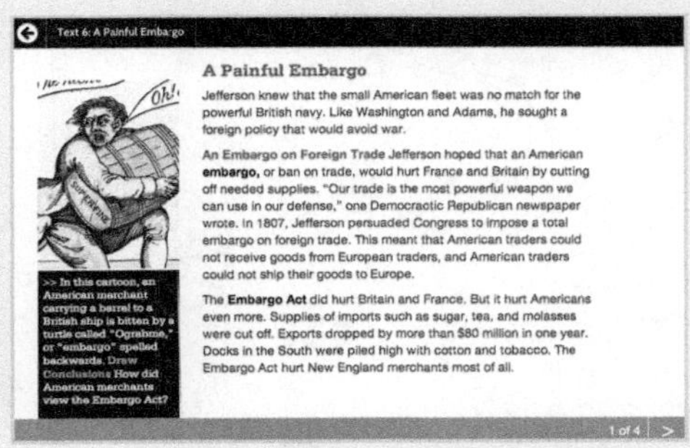

INTERACTIVE CHART

Jefferson's Goals and Policies

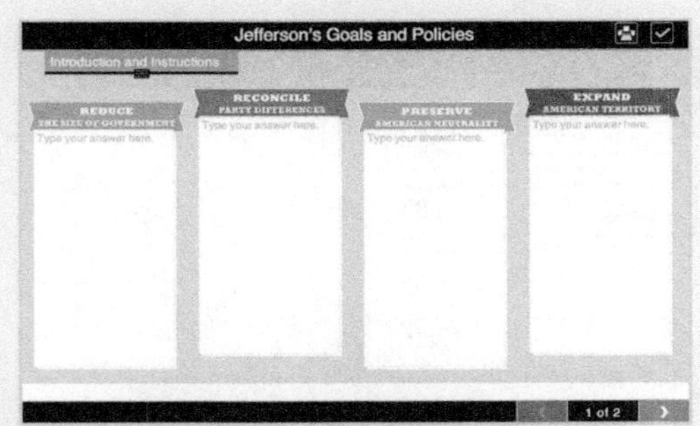

Objective 5: **Explain Jefferson's foreign policy, including conflict with the Barbary States, threats to U.S. neutrality, and the Embargo Act.**

Quick Instruction

Interactive Chart: Jefferson's Goals and Policies Project the interactive chart on the whiteboard and read through Jefferson's goals and policies. Ask students to describe how Jefferson addressed domestic problems such as creating a stable economic system, maintaining national security, and defining the authority of the central government.

Identify Cause and Effect Give an example of how the acquisition of new areas through the Louisiana Purchase affected the U.S. economy. *(Traders bought and sold furs from Native Americans in the region.)*

ACTIVE CLASSROOM

Have students Take a Stand on the following question: Were Jefferson's efforts to maintain national security and create a stable economic system during his presidency successful? Ask students to talk with each other to compare their reasons for answering yes or no, providing examples for support.

ELL Use the ELL activity described in the ELL chart.

Further Instruction

Go through the Interactive Reading Notepad questions and discuss the answers with the class.

The United States would not be able to remain neutral in the conflict between Britain and France. Fighting with Native Americans in the Ohio Valley eventually drew the Untied States into war with Britain.

Summarize Describe Jefferson's foreign policy. *(Jefferson tried to avoid war and protect American shipping abroad. He ordered the navy to blockade the port of Tripoli and launched a surprise attack to keep Tripoli from interfering with American ships. Rather than go to war with Britain and France, he imposed an embargo on trade.)*

Evaluate Arguments Do you think Jefferson's Embargo Act reflected a free-enterprise system of economics? Why or why not? *(No; the Embargo Act reflected government intervention rather than a free-enterprise system.)*

Compare Points of View Identify the different points of view of both Democratic Republicans and Federalists toward the Embargo Act. *(Democratic Republicans generally supported the Embargo as a means to punish Britain and France. Federalists were generally against the Embargo, because they felt it would hurt the American economy to not trade with two significant countries.)*

Jefferson's Presidency

SYNTHESIZE

DIGITAL ACTIVITY

The Impact of Judicial Review

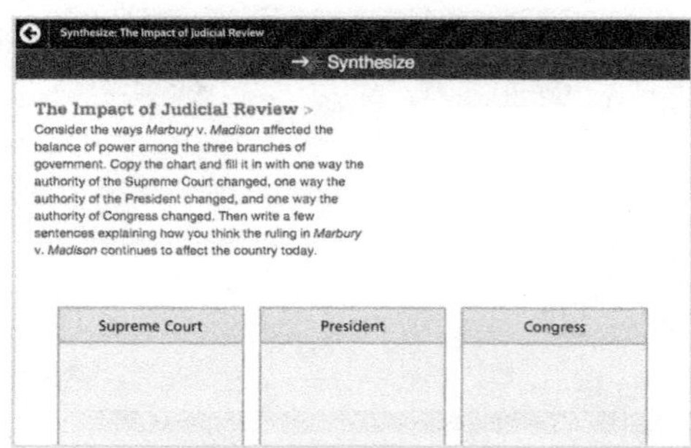

Have students fill in the chart with the ways *Marbury* v. *Madison* affected the three branches of government and explain how the ruling affects the country today. Have students compare their charts with a partner.

Have partners review their charts and consider the following question. How did the landmark case *Marbury* v. *Madison* reflect the principle of checks and balances? Have partners share their answers with the class.

Discuss Have students review the predictions they made at the beginning of the lesson about how judicial review would affect the relationship between Congress, the President, and the Court. Ask students whether they would change their answer now that they have learned more about the significance of judicial review and the responses of Congress and the President.

DEMONSTRATE

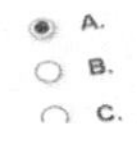

DIGITAL QUIZ

Lesson Quiz and Class Discussion Board

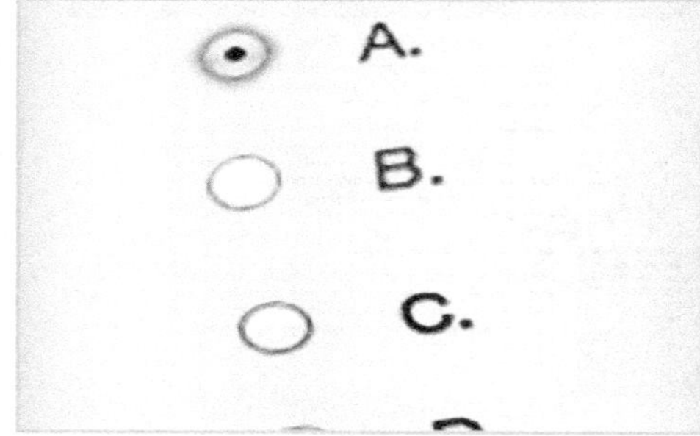

Assign the online Lesson Quiz for this lesson if you haven't already done so. Students will be offered automatic remediation or enrichment based on their score.

Pose these questions to the class on the Discussion Board:

In *Jefferson's Presidency*, you read about the significance of the Louisiana Purchase and the landmark Supreme Court case *Marbury* v. *Madison*.

Identify Central Issues What areas acquired through the Louisiana Purchase allowed the United States to better maintain its national security, and why? *(Control of the Mississippi River and its mouth, including the port of New Orleans, gave the United States better control of its national security since these waterways were vital for settlers in the lands west of the Appalachian Mountains, and any foreign power controlling them could threaten those settlers.)*

Draw Conclusions Why is *Marbury* v. *Madison* considered such a significant Supreme Court case? *(The case established the power of judicial review for the Supreme Court, that is the power to review the constitutionality of laws passed by Congress.)*

Support Ideas with Examples Give an example of Jefferson's use of the authority of the central government during his presidency. *(Possible responses include the Louisiana Purchase and the Embargo Act.)*

Topic Inquiry

Have students continue their investigations for the Topic Inquiry.

PEARSON realize™ www.PearsonRealize.com Access your Digital Lesson

Madison and the War of 1812

Supporting English Language Learners

Use with Digital Text 2, **The Causes of the War of 1812.**

Reading

Introduce the text by reading and discussing the title and subheadings in order to model using support from peers and teachers to read grade-appropriate content area text and to develop vocabulary needed to comprehend increasingly challenging language.

Beginning Pre-teach key words from the introductory paragraphs to help students read grade-appropriate content area text and develop vocabulary needed to read and comprehend increasingly challenging language. Then echo read the paragraphs under "War Is Declared" with students. Encourage them to ask you the meanings of additional words after the reading.

Intermediate Pre-teach key words from the text to help students read grade-appropriate content area text and develop vocabulary needed to comprehend increasingly challenging language. Then have students read the text in small groups, assisting one another with additional word meanings and pronunciation as needed.

Advanced Have pairs of students read the text, paragraph by paragraph. Encourage them to develop vocabulary needed to comprehend increasingly challenging language by asking each other to clarify word meanings as they read, as well as asking you or their partner for help with pronunciation.

Advanced High Have students read grade-appropriate content area text independently. As they read, encourage them to make note of unfamiliar words. Then they can develop vocabulary needed to comprehend increasingly challenging language.Encourage students who have mastered vocaulary to help their peers.

Use with Digital Text 5, **The War's Conclusion.**

Listening

Reference the last paragraph of the section titled *Untrained Armies Fall in Washington*. Have students listen to a recording of "The Star-Spangled Banner" to build and reinforce concept attainment. Remind students that "The Star-Spangled Banner"is the U.S. national anthem and was inspired by the War of 1812.

Beginning Play a recording of "The Star-Spangled Banner."Then display key vocabulary from the anthem (e.g., *star-spangled banner, land of the free, home of the brave*) Explain their meanings in order to build and reinforce concept and language attainment.

Intermediate Play a recording of "The Star-Spangled Banner." Then display the lyrics. Explain the meanings of key words and phrases, and encourage students to ask for additional clarification in order to build and reinforce concept and language attainment.

Advanced Play a recording of "The Star-Spangled Banner." Then assign one or two different lines from the anthem to pairs of students. Ask them to restate the lines in their own words and explain the lines' significance in order to build and reinforce concept and language attainment. Have pairs share their work.

Advanced High Play a recording of "The Star-Spangled Banner." Then assign one or two different lines from the anthem to pairs of students. Ask them to restate the lines in their own words and explain the lines' significance in order to build and reinforce concept and language attainment. Have pairs share their work.

D Differentiate Instruction

Use the Differentiated Instruction notes throughout the lesson plan to support the varied skill sets, levels of readiness, and interests in the mixed-ability classroom.

Challenge These notes include suggestions for expanding the activity for advanced students.

On-Level These notes include suggestions for modifying the activity to address different interests or learning styles.

Extra Support These notes include ideas for providing more scaffolding or reading spuport.

Special Needs These notes provide ideas for adapting instruction to support the needs of various special needs students.

NOTES

Madison and the War of 1812

Objectives

Objective 1: Explain the reasons for conflict between white settlers and Native Americans during the early 1800s.

Objective 2: Identify the causes of the War of 1812.

Objective 3: Explain the challenges that the United States faced in preparing for war.

Objective 4: Describe the important events and effects of the War of 1812.

LESSON 5 ORGANIZER	PACING: APPROX. 1 PERIOD, .5 BLOCKS			
			RESOURCES	
	OBJECTIVES	PACING	Online	Print
Connect				
DIGITAL START UP ACTIVITY **Making Predictions About the War of 1812**		5 min.	●	
Investigate				
DIGITAL TEXT 1 **Conflict in Ohio**	Objective 1	10 min.	●	●
INTERACTIVE MAP **Indian Lands Lost by 1810**		10 min.	●	
DIGITAL TEXT 2 **The Causes of the War of 1812**	Objective 2	10 min.	●	●
DIGITAL TEXT 3 **Early Events in the War of 1812**	Objective 3	10 min.	●	●
DIGITAL TEXT 4 **The War in Canada**	Objective 4	10 min.	●	●
DIGITAL TEXT 5 **The War's Conclusion**		10 min.	●	●
INTERACTIVE MAP **The War of 1812**		10 min.	●	
DIGITAL TEXT 6 **The Impact of the War of 1812**		10 min.	●	●
Synthesize				
DIGITAL ACTIVITY **Causes and Effects of the War of 1812**		5 min.	●	
Demonstrate				
DIGITAL QUIZ **Lesson Quiz and Class Discussion Board**		10 min.	●	

Go online to access additional resources including: Primary Sources • Biographies • Supreme Court cases • 21st Century Skill Tutorials • Maps • Graphic Organizers.

CONNECT

DIGITAL START UP ACTIVITY

Making Predictions About the War of 1812

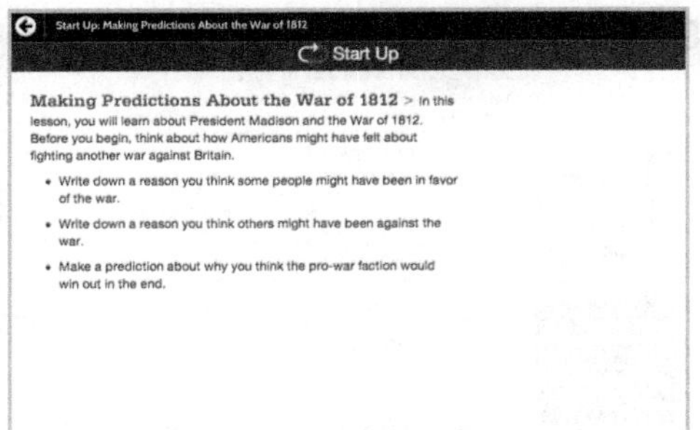

Project the Start Up Activity Have students read the activity and predict who supported the war, who was against war, and why the pro-war faction won out. Have students share their predictions with a partner, either in class or through a blog space.

Discuss Write why some people might have been in favor of the war. *(Nationalism; anger toward the British)* Write down why others might have been against the war. *(Favored neutrality; disagreed with the reasons for fighting; feared the war's impact on the economy; questioned whether the U.S. military was strong enough to win)* Predict the pro-war faction won out in the end. *(More Americans favored war.)*

Vocabulary Development: Use the Interactive Reading Notepad to preview the Key Terms and Academic Vocabulary in this lesson with students.

FLIP IT!

Assign the Flipped Video for this lesson.

STUDENT EDITION PRINT PAGES 270–281

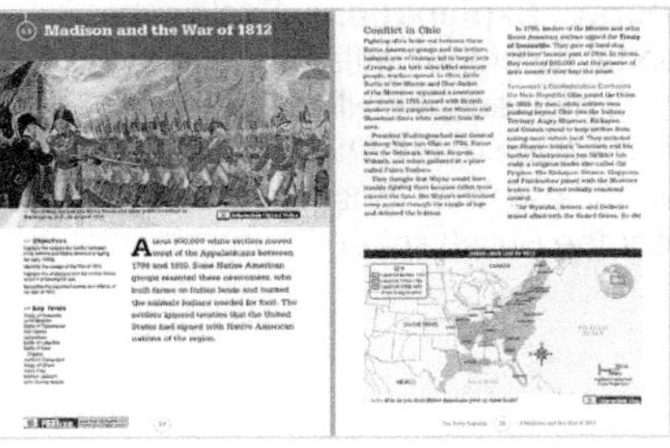

INVESTIGATE

DIGITAL TEXT 1

Conflict in Ohio

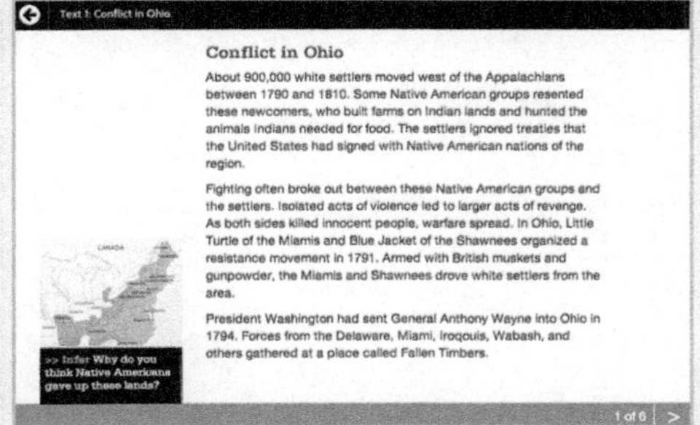

INTERACTIVE MAP

Indian Lands Lost by 1810

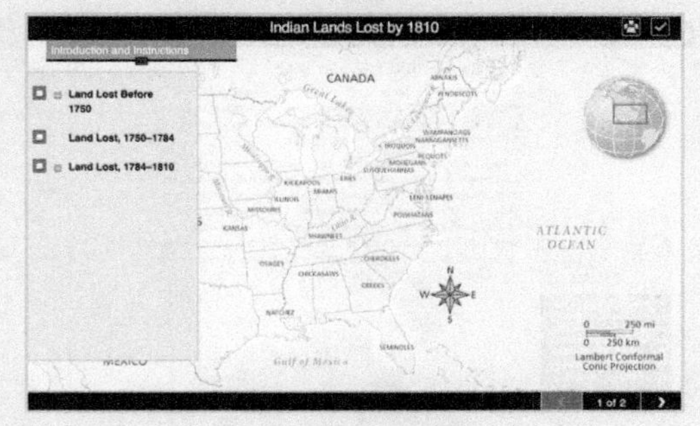

Objective 1: Explain the reasons for conflict between white settlers and Native Americans during the early 1800s.

Quick Instruction

Interactive Map: Indian Lands Lost by 1810 Project the interactive map and click through the squares. Have students locate the area of Ohio on the map and discuss its importance.

Make Predictions How will conflicts in Ohio help to causes of the War of 1812? *(The British will fuel Native American attacks on U.S. settlements, drawing the United States into war with Britain.)*

ACTIVE CLASSROOM

Divide students into groups and give them pieces of paper listing important events from the lesson, including: settlers move past the Appalachians, Little Turtle and Blue Jacket organize a resistance movement, Battle of Fallen Timbers, Treaty of Greenville, Tecumseh forms a confederation, Prophetstown is built, Battle of Tippecanoe. You may use more or fewer events depending on the size of the groups. Have groups use the Sequence It Strategy to put the lists in order.

Further Instruction

Go through the Interactive Reading Notepad questions and discuss the answers with the class. Be sure students understand why fighting broke out in Ohio and why this was a cause of the War of 1812.

Identify Central Issues Why did leaders of the new Republic have difficulty maintaining national security along the frontier? *(Fighting broke out when white settlers moved west of the Appalachian Mountains, taking over land where Native American groups lived.)*

Infer How do you think human geographic factors contributed to the fighting between Native American groups and white settlers along the frontier? *(The white settlers and Native American groups had different cultures and ways of life. They were competing over land and resources.)*

Madison and the War of 1812

DIGITAL TEXT 2

The Causes of the War of 1812

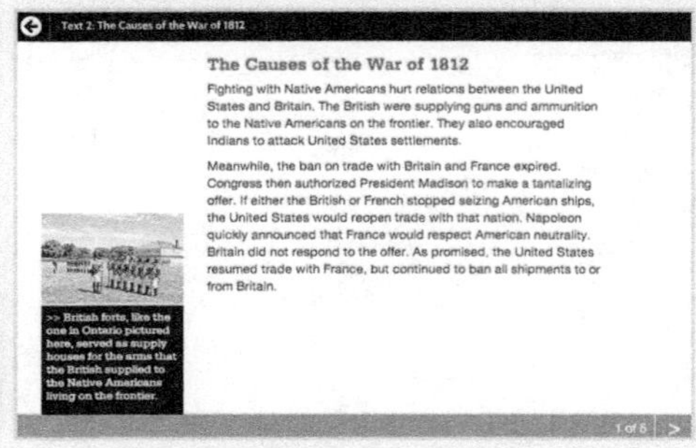

DIGITAL TEXT 3

Early Events in the War of 1812

Objective 2: **Identify the causes of the War of 1812.**

Quick Instruction

Project the image of Henry Clay on the whiteboard. Define the War Hawks as southern and western members of Congress who pushed for war with Britain.

Compare Points of View What were the causes the War Hawks gave for engaging in the War of 1812? Why did some Americans not think these causes justified going to war? *(Nationalism and defending American rights; punishing Britain for seizing American ships; conquering Canada and Florida; bringing safety to the frontier. New Englanders feared the British would attack their seaports. Others thought the war was only to increase U.S. territory and power.)*

D Differentiate: Extra Support Explain that a hawk is a large bird of prey. Ask students why they think a hawk also refers to a person who aggressively pushes for war.

ELL Use the ELL activity described in the ELL chart.

Further Instruction

Go through the Interactive Reading Notepad questions and discuss the answers with the class. Be sure students can explain the causes of the War of 1812.

Cite Evidence from the text to explain the causes of the War of 1812? *(Britain was seizing American ships, blockading ports, and arming Native Americans to fight white settlers on the frontier.)*

Identify Steps in a Process Identify James Madison's foreign policy and how it was connected to the causes of the War of 1812. *(Madison offered to reopen trade with Britain if Britain stopped seizing ships. When Britain refused, he continued to ban shipments to and from Britain. After the British blockaded American ports and continued to impress American sailors, Madison declared war.)*

Objective 3: **Explain the challenges the United States faced in preparing for war.**

Quick Instruction

Project the image of the U.S.S. *Constitution* and the HMS *Guerriere*. Explain that Britain had a much stronger navy than the United States. The major domestic problems faced by the new Republic included building a military and maintaining national security.

Identify Cause and Effect Why didn't the new Republic have a strong military? *(Jefferson had reduced defense spending. As a result the army was small, ill-equipped, and untrained.)*

Further Instruction

Go through the Interactive Reading Notepad questions and discuss the answers with the class. Be sure students understand why building a military and maintaining national security were major domestic problems for the new Republic.

Summarize How did the United States go about building a military at the start of the War of 1812? *(Congress paid volunteers in cash and land.)*

Generate Explanations Explain the importance of the battle between the U.S.S. *Constitution* and the HMS *Guerriere*. *(The United States did not have a strong navy. Nevertheless, the* Constitution *was able to defeat the British ship.)*

DIGITAL TEXT 4

The War in Canada

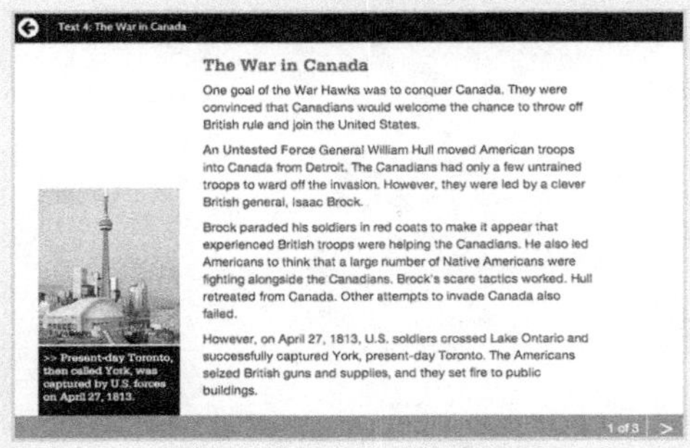

DIGITAL TEXT 5

The War's Conclusion

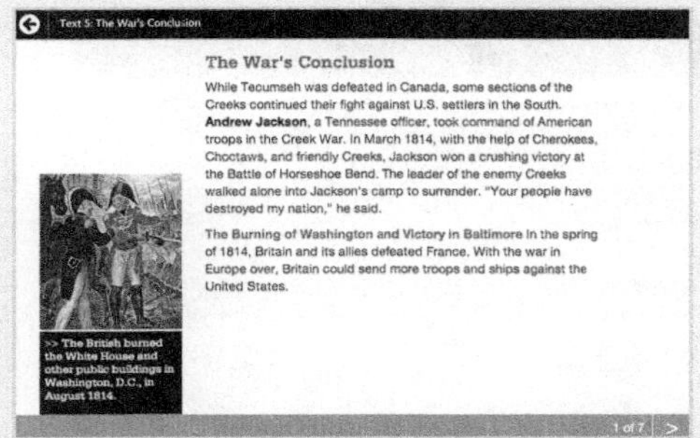

INTERACTIVE MAP

The War of 1812

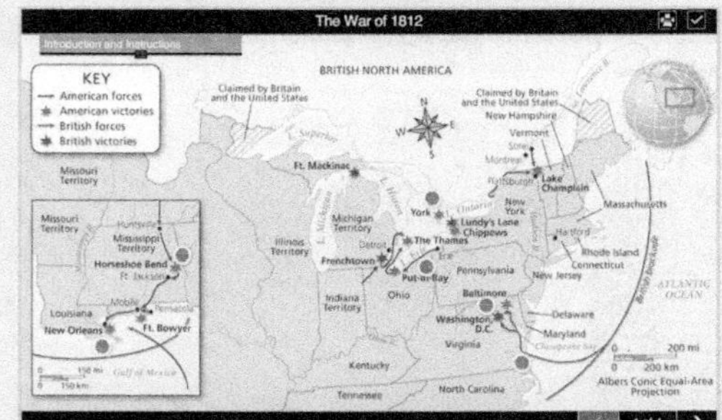

Objective 4: **Describe the important events and effects of the War of 1812.**

Quick Instruction

Interactive Map: The War of 1812 Project the interactive map on the whiteboard and click through the red circles.

Analyze Maps Why was the Battle of Lake Erie such an important event in the War of 1812? *(It ensured that the United States would retain its lands along the Great Lakes, letting the Americans use the waterways for transportation and to control surrounding lands.)*

ACTIVE CLASSROOM

Divide the interactive map into four numbered quadrants. Have students count off one to four and then use the A Closer Look Strategy to look at the part of the image in their quadrant. Have them tell you what they see and what they learned about the important events of the War of 1812 as a result of their focus. Have students share their insights with the class.

ELL Use the ELL activity described in the ELL chart.

Further Instruction

Go through the Interactive Reading Notepad questions and discuss the answers with the class. Be sure students can explain the important events of the War of 1812, such as the Battle of Lake Erie, the burning of Washington, victory in Baltimore, and the Battle of New Orleans, as well as the war's effects on the early Republic.

Identify Cause and Effect Explain the effects of the War of 1812. *(The war hurt the economy of New England and led to opposition to the war by Federalists there. U.S. success in the war in turn permanently weakened the Federalist Party. The ability to resist Britain at war may have earned the United States greater respect. Another effect of the war was to strengthen the American national identity.)*

Madison and the War of 1812

DIGITAL TEXT 6

The Impact of the War of 1812

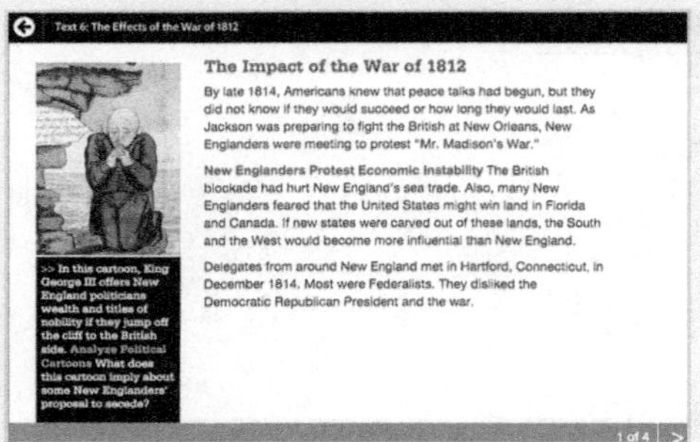

Text 6: The Effects of the War of 1812
The Impact of the War of 1812
By late 1814, Americans knew that peace talks had begun, but they did not know if they would succeed or how long they would last. As Jackson was preparing to fight the British at New Orleans, New Englanders were meeting to protest "Mr. Madison's War."
New Englanders Protest Economic Instability The British blockade had hurt New England's sea trade. Also, many New Englanders feared that the United States might win land in Florida and Canada. If new states were carved out of these lands, the South and the West would become more influential than New England.
Delegates from around New England met in Hartford, Connecticut, in December 1814. Most were Federalists. They disliked the Democratic Republican President and the war.
>> In this cartoon, King George III offers New England politicians wealth and titles of nobility if they jump off the cliff to the British side. Analyze Political Cartoons What does this cartoon imply about some New Englanders' proposal to secede?

Identify Cause and Effect What was the effect of the War of 1812 on Native Americans? How did the war resolve the conflicts between white settlers and Native American groups? *(The war was devastating for Native American groups. With Tecumseh's defeat, the Indian confederation fell apart. The Creeks also lost to Jackson in the Battle of Horseshoe Bend.)*

SYNTHESIZE

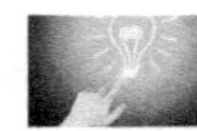

DIGITAL ACTIVITY

Causes and Effects of the War of 1812

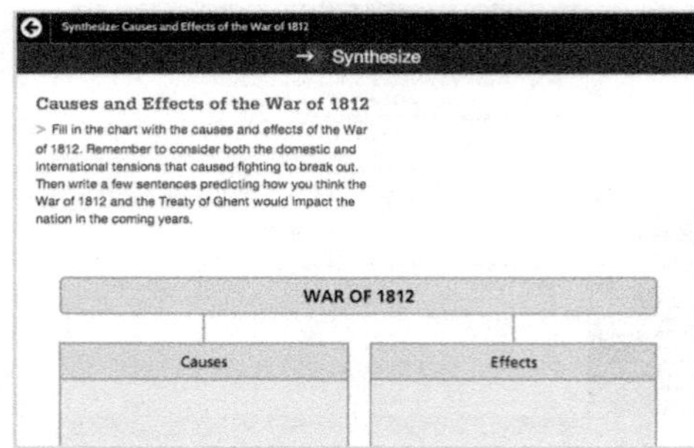

Synthesize: Causes and Effects of the War of 1812
Synthesize
Causes and Effects of the War of 1812
> Fill in the chart with the causes and effects of the War of 1812. Remember to consider both the domestic and international tensions that caused fighting to break out. Then write a few sentences predicting how you think the War of 1812 and the Treaty of Ghent would impact the nation in the coming years.
WAR OF 1812
Causes
Effects

Have students fill in the chart with the causes and effects of the War of 1812 and make a prediction about how the war and the Treaty of Ghent would affect the nation. Have students compare their charts with a partner.

Have partners review their charts and consider the following question. What were the benefits and drawbacks of Madison's foreign policy with regard to Britain? Have partners share their answers with the class.

Discuss Have students review the predictions they made at the beginning of the lesson about why the pro-war faction would win out and consider whether they agree with faction's arguments for war. Ask students whether they would change their answer now that they have learned more about the causes and effects of the War of 1812.

DEMONSTRATE

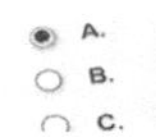

DIGITAL QUIZ

Lesson Quiz and Class Discussion Board

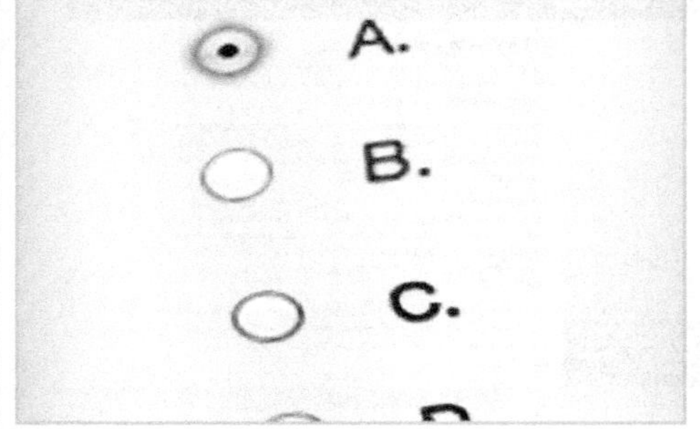

Assign the online Lesson Quiz for this lesson if you haven't already done so. Students will be offered automatic remediation or enrichment based on their score.

Pose these questions to the class on the Discussion Board:

In *Madison and the War of 1812*, you read about the causes, effects, and important events of Madison's foreign policy and the War of 1812.

Evaluate Arguments Based on the effects of the War of 1812, do you think it was worth it for the United States to go to war? Explain your reasoning. *(Sample answers: Yes, the war forced Britain to respect the sovereignty of the United States. No, nothing significant was gained, and it would have been better to negotiate over the issues.)*

Generate Explanations Why did the United States and Britain go to war in 1812? *(Britain was attacking American shipping and kidnapping American sailors. Meanwhile, American War Hawks wanted to punish Britain and conquer its colony, Canada. In response, President Madison asked Congress to declare war.)*

Topic Inquiry

Have students continue their investigations for the Topic Inquiry.

PEARSON realize™ www.PearsonRealize.com Access your Digital Lesson

Monroe's Presidency

Supporting English Language Learners

Use with Digital Text 4, **Latin America Wins Independence.**

Listening

Orally highlight language used in the text that pertains to Mexico's relationship with and struggle for independence from Spain in order to prompt students to understand the general meaning of spoken language in which topics are unfamiliar.

Beginning Using basic spoken language, tell students about the relative locations of Spain and Mexico. Then have students show that they understand the general meaning of your words in a phrase or sentence.

Intermediate Using spoken language, summarize the section titled *Mexico Gains Independence*. Then ask students to show that they understand the general meaning of your words by restating your main idea.

Advanced Using spoken language, paraphrase the section titled *Mexico Gains Independence*. Then ask students to show that they understand the general meaning of your words by summarizing what you said.

Advanced High Using spoken language, describe the life of Miguel Hidalgo (using details that are unfamiliar to students and not provided in the text). Ask students to show that they understand the general meaning of your words by summarizing what you said.

Use with Digital Text 6, **The Monroe Doctrine.**

Reading

Review the word *doctrine* to prepare students for reading and comprehending the text. Prompt students to use support from peers and teachers to enhance and confirm understanding.

Beginning Echo read the paragraph that defines the Monroe Doctrine and have students complete this sentence: The Monroe Doctrine said that the United States would not _____. Add details to, or ask questions about, students' responses in order to enhance and confirm their understanding of the paragraph.

Intermediate Read aloud the paragraph that defines the Monroe Doctrine and the following paragraph,or invite volunteers to do so. Ask students to define the Monroe Doctrine. Add details to, or ask questions about, students' responses in order to enhance and confirm their understanding of the paragraphs.

Advanced Have pairs of students read the paragraph that defines the Monroe Doctrine and the following paragraph, and discuss the meaning of the Monroe Doctrine. Encourage them to respond to, add to, and ask questions about each other's statements in order to enhance and confirm their understanding of the paragraphs.

Advanced High Have students independently read the text. With a partner, have them define the Monroe Doctrine and describe its influence on world events. Encourage students to ask questions and build on each other's statements in order to enhance and confirm their understanding of the text.

D Differentiate Instruction

Use the Differentiated Instruction notes throughout the lesson plan to support the varied skill sets, levels of readiness, and interests in the mixed-ability classroom.

Challenge These notes include suggestions for expanding the activity for advanced students.

On-Level These notes include suggestions for modifying the activity to address different interests or learning styles.

Extra Support These notes include ideas for providing more scaffolding or reading spupport.

Special Needs These notes provide ideas for adapting instruction to support the needs of various special needs students.

NOTES

Monroe's Presidency

Objectives

Objective 1: Explain the significance of regional differences during the Era of Good Feelings.

Objective 2: Identify different points of view on tariffs.

Objective 3: Explain how the Supreme Court under John Marshall expanded federal power.

Objective 4: Describe the impact of revolution in Latin America.

Objective 5: Explain U.S. foreign policy under Monroe, including the Monroe Doctrine and policies toward Florida.

LESSON 6 ORGANIZER	PACING: APPROX. 1 PERIOD, .5 BLOCKS		RESOURCES	
	OBJECTIVES	PACING	Online	Print
Connect				
DIGITAL START UP ACTIVITY **The Era of Good Feelings**		5 min.	●	
Investigate				
DIGITAL TEXT 1 **Sectionalism in the Era of Good Feelings**	Objective 1	10 min.	●	●
DIGITAL TEXT 2 **Creating a Stable Economy After the War**	Objective 2	10 min.	●	●
INTERACTIVE CHART **The Beginnings of Sectionalism**		10 min.	●	
DIGITAL TEXT 3 **Supreme Court Decisions Expand Federal Power**	Objective 3	10 min.	●	●
INTERACTIVE GALLERY **The Expansion of Federal Power**		10 min.	●	
DIGITAL TEXT 4 **Latin America Wins Independence**	Objective 4	10 min.	●	●
DIGITAL TEXT 5 **Gaining Florida**	Objective 5	10 min.	●	●
DIGITAL TEXT 6 **The Monroe Doctrine**		10 min.	●	●
Synthesize				
DIGITAL ACTIVITY **The Legacy of President Monroe**		5 min.	●	
Demonstrate				
DIGITAL QUIZ **Lesson Quiz and Class Discussion Board**		10 min.	●	

Go online to access additional resources including: Primary Sources • Biographies • Supreme Court cases • 21st Century Skill Tutorials • Maps • Graphic Organizers.

CONNECT

DIGITAL START UP ACTIVITY

The Era of Good Feelings

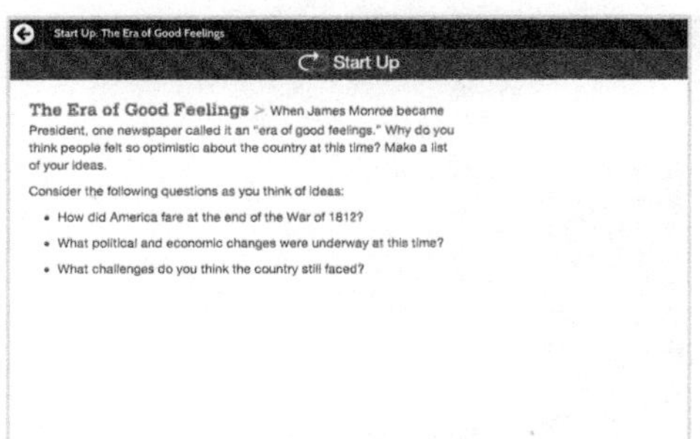

Project the Start Up Activity Have students read the questions and make a list of why they think people felt optimistic about the country following the War of 1812.

Discuss How did America fare at the end of the War of 1812? *(Americans were patriotic. Its borders were preserved. Industry grew as a result of the war.)* What political and economic changes were underway at this time? *(Decline of the Federalists; feelings of national unity; economic growth followed by instability)* What challenges do you think the country still faced? *(Divisions between North and South; the unresolved question of slavery; economic instabilities)*

Aa Vocabulary Development: Use the Interactive Reading Notepad to preview the Key Terms and Academic Vocabulary in this lesson with students.

FLIP IT!

Assign the Flipped Video for this lesson.

STUDENT EDITION PRINT PAGES: 282–294

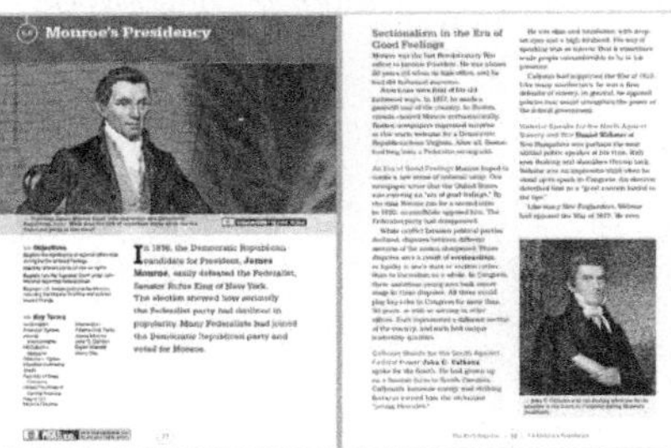

INVESTIGATE

DIGITAL TEXT 1

Sectionalism in the Era of Good Feelings

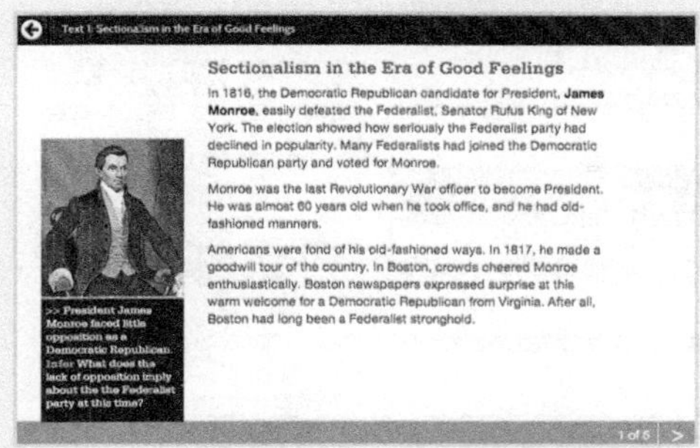

Sectionalism in the Era of Good Feelings

In 1816, the Democratic Republican candidate for President, **James Monroe**, easily defeated the Federalist, Senator Rufus King of New York. The election showed how seriously the Federalist party had declined in popularity. Many Federalists had joined the Democratic Republican party and voted for Monroe.

Monroe was the last Revolutionary War officer to become President. He was almost 60 years old when he took office, and he had old-fashioned manners.

Americans were fond of his old-fashioned ways. In 1817, he made a goodwill tour of the country. In Boston, crowds cheered Monroe enthusiastically. Boston newspapers expressed surprise at this warm welcome for a Democratic Republican from Virginia. After all, Boston had long been a Federalist stronghold.

Objective 1: Explain the significance of regional differences during the Era of Good Feelings.

Quick Instruction

Project the image of James Monroe. Monroe was a Democratic Republican who hoped to create a sense of national unity after the war.

Identify Central issues How did James Monroe contribute to feelings of national unity after the war? What caused a rift in this harmony? *(Monroe was popular and completed a goodwill tour after his election. However, the rise of sectionalism sharpened divisions within the country.)*

D Differentiate: Extra Support Help students understand the causes of sectionalism by having them locate the different regions of the early Republic on a map: North (the present-day Northeast), South, and West (the present-day Midwest). Explain that each of these regions was known as a section. Ask students to identify at least one way in which the sections differed.

Further Instruction

Go through the Interactive Reading Notepad questions and discuss the answers with the class.

Identify Cause and Effect Explain what sectionalism is and identify its causes. *(Sectionalism is loyalty to one's region or section rather than to the nation. The causes of sectionalism include differences in the culture and economies of the regions. These differences led people to emphasize differences between the regions and identify with their sections.)*

Compare and Contrast the leadership qualities of Calhoun, Webster, and Clay. On what points did they disagree? *(Calhoun—energetic and intense speaker from the South; supported slavery and states' rights. Webster—skilled public speaker from the North; against the War of 1812 and slavery, favored more powerful federal government. Clay—known as a charming speaker from the West; favored war and an active federal government.)*

Make Generalizations Identify the economic differences between the North and South. *(The North's economy was based on manufacturing and trade. The southern economy was agrarian.)*

Monroe's Presidency

DIGITAL TEXT 2

Creating a Stable Economy After the War

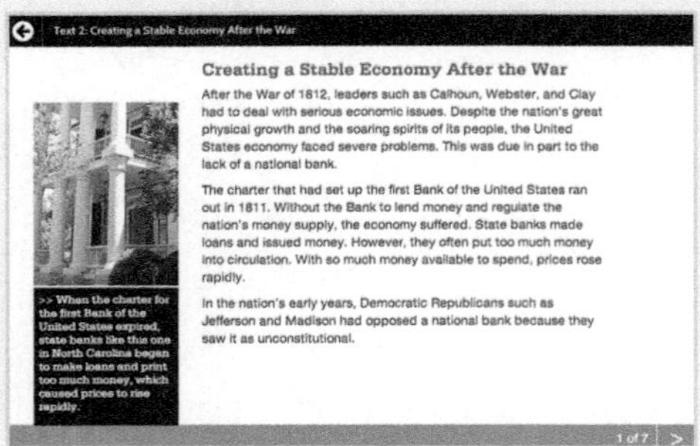

INTERACTIVE CHART

The Beginnings of Sectionalism

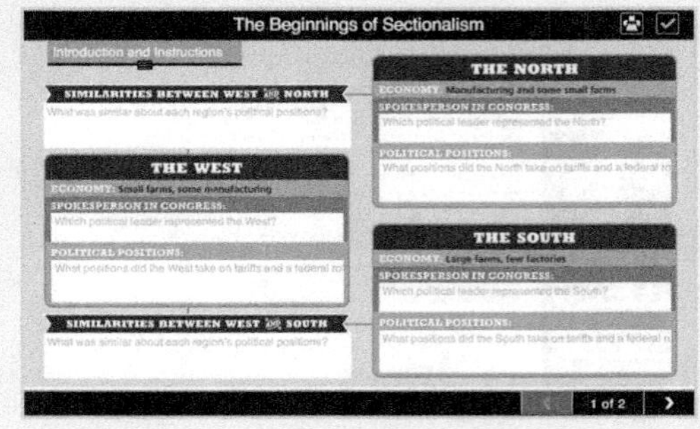

DIGITAL TEXT 3

Supreme Court Decisions Expand Federal Power

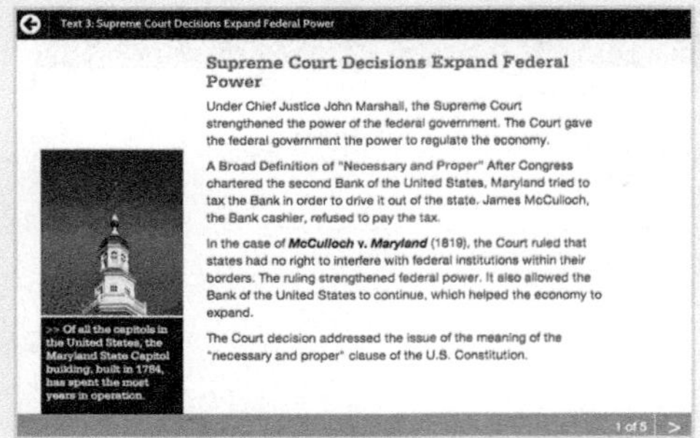

Objective 2: **Identify different points of view on tariffs.**

Quick Instruction

Interactive Chart: The Beginnings of Sectionalism Project the interactive chart and read through the tiles. Have students describe how each leader wanted to approach the major domestic problems faced by the new Republic, including creating a stable economic system and defining the authority of the central government.

Compare and Contrast Analyze the impact of the Tariff of 1816 on sections of the United States, that is, on the North, West, and South. *(North—benefited from the tariff as goods produced by northern factories became cheaper than imported goods. The North could sell more. South and West—had to pay more for imported goods or buy more expensive northern goods.)*

ACTIVE CLASSROOM

Have students use the Write 1-Get 3 Strategy to answer the question: What are four key areas in which sectional leaders disagreed? Have students take a piece of paper and fold it into quarters. Students write down one response in the first box and then go around the room asking to hear other responses. When students think a response is correct, they write it in one of their boxes until they have three more responses on their pages. Have students share their responses with the class.

Further Instruction

Go through the Interactive Reading Notepad questions and discuss the answers with the class.

Summarize Summarize Henry Clay's arguments for protective tariffs. Why did he think tariffs were a good compromise to appeal to different sections of the United States? *(Clay believed tariffs would help the economies of the North, South, and West. He argued that high tariffs would give northerners the money to buy farm products from the South and West. In addition, Congress could use money raised from tariffs for internal improvements to help farmers in these regions.)*

Compare Points of View Explain the arguments for and against the banking system. Why did Democratic Republicans change their point of view on the Bank of the United States? *(For—A central bank could lend money and regulate the money supply to keep prices from rising. Against—Democratic Republicans initially argued a national bank was unconstitutional and gave the federal government too much power. Later they decided a central bank was necessary to create a stable economy.)*

Objective 3: **Explain how the Supreme Court under John Marshall expanded federal power.**

Quick Instruction

Interactive Gallery: The Expansion of Federal Power Project the interactive gallery and click through the images.

Generate Explanations Summarize the decision of the Supreme Court in *McCulloch* v. *Maryland* as well as the issues behind the decision and its significance. *(The issues were whether a national bank was constitutional and whether a state could regulate an arm of the federal government. The Court interpreted the necessary and proper clause of the Constitution to mean Congress had the power to charter a national bank. This increased the authority of the federal government.)*

Summarize the issues behind the landmark case *Gibbons* v. *Ogden*. What was the court's decision and the significance of this decision? *(A steamboat company wanted to retain a monopoly on interstate travel granted by New York State. The Court ruled that only the federal government has the power to regulate interstate commerce. This increased federal power over the states and helped the economy by creating a unified nationwide market.)*

INTERACTIVE GALLERY

The Expansion of Federal Power

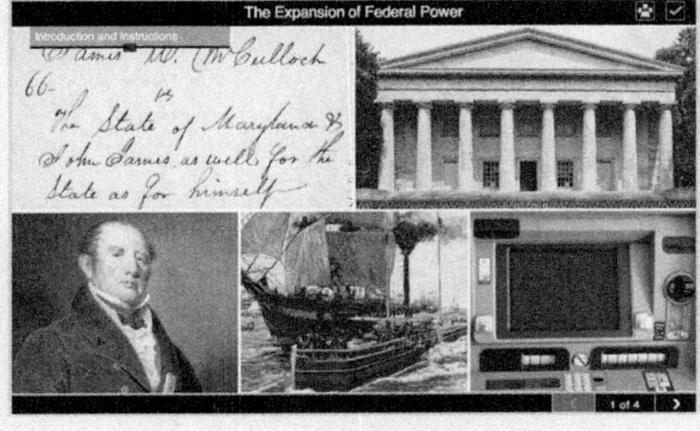

ACTIVE CLASSROOM

Have students Take a Stand on the significance of *McCulloch* v. *Maryland*. Was this expansion of federal power relative to the states constitutional? Have students divide into two groups based on their answer and move to separate areas of the classroom. Have students compare their reasons for answering yes or no. Then ask a representative from each side to share and defend the group's point of view.

Further Instruction

Go through the Interactive Reading Notepad questions and discuss the answers with the class. To extend the lesson, assign the Supreme Court cases *McCulloch* v. *Maryland* and *Gibbons* v. *Ogden*. Be sure students can summarize the issues, decisions, and significance of both landmark cases.

Draw Conclusions Why was the Court's ruling in *McCulloch* v. *Maryland* controversial? *(The Court took a loose-constructionist view of the Constitution, deciding the necessary and proper clause gave Congress the power to charter the Bank. Some people argued the Court should take a strict-constructionist view and grant Congress only those powers stated in the Constitution.)*

Support Ideas With Examples Give an example of how John Marshall's leadership defined the authority of the central government. *(Granting Congress powers through the necessary and proper clause and giving the federal government sole power to regulate interstate commerce strengthened the central government. Government could take actions not stated in the Constitution and oversee state activities.)*

DIGITAL TEXT 4

Latin America Wins Independence

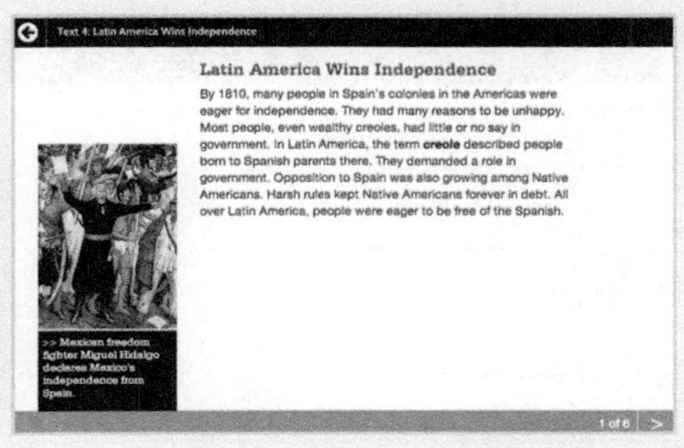

Objective 4: **Identify the impact of revolution in Latin America.**

Quick Instruction

Project the map of new nations in Latin America. Have students identify the new nations formed by revolutions.

Make Predictions How do you think revolutions in Latin America would impact Monroe's foreign policy? *(He would have to decide on a foreign policy toward the new nations.)*

ELL Use the ELL activity described in the ELL chart.

Further Instruction

Go through the Interactive Reading Notepad questions and discuss the answers with the class. Discuss the impact of revolutions in Latin American on U.S.foreign policy.

Compare and Contrast America's Revolutionary War to the revolutionary movements in Latin America. *(Compare—As in the United States, colonies fought for independence from European powers. Contrast—The U.S. colonies united to form a single country; the United States adopted and maintained a democratic government while many Latin American countries did not; not all of the revolutions in Latin America were violent.)*

Hypothesize How do you think revolutions in Latin American affected the United States? *(Monroe had to develop his foreign policy toward the new nations; Americans may have been glad to see other colonies rebelling against European powers and establishing their own governments.)*

DIGITAL TEXT 5

Gaining Florida

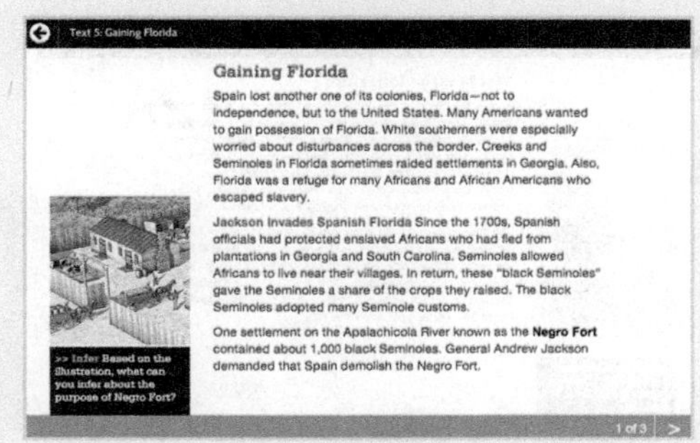

Objective 5: **Explain U.S. foreign policy under Monroe, including policies toward Florida and the Monroe Doctrine.**

Quick Instruction

Project the image of Monroe with his cabinet. Explain that Monroe created a new foreign policy regarding Latin America that has affected that region ever since.

Generate Explanations Explain the Monroe Doctrine and its impact. *(The Doctrine stated that the United States would not interfere with European nations or their colonies, but that the United States would oppose new European attempts to colonize the Americas. The Doctrine kept Europe from intervening in the newly independent republics in the Americas, affirming their independence.)*

ELL Use the ELL activity described in the ELL chart.

Further Instruction

Go through the Interactive Reading Notepad questions and discuss the answers with the class. Be sure students can identify Monroe's foreign policy, including the Monroe Doctrine.

Identify Cause and Effect How did Monroe's foreign policy toward Spain lead to the acquisition of new territory? *(The United States invaded Florida and then negotiated its purchase from Spain.)*

Monroe's Presidency

DIGITAL TEXT 6

The Monroe Doctrine

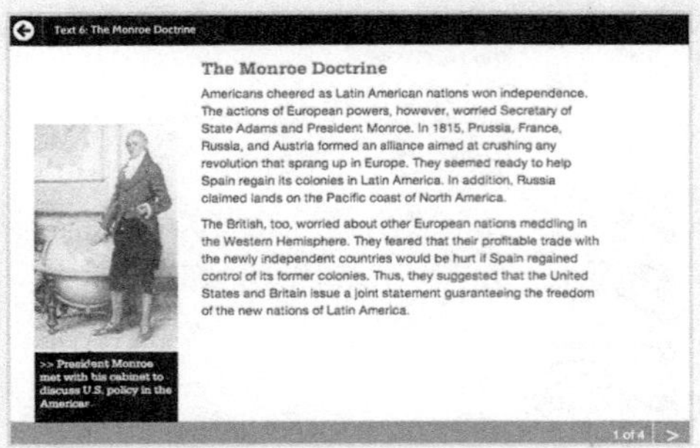

Determine Point of View Why was Monroe's statement about foreign policy toward Latin America an important historical contribution? *(European powers were crushing revolutions and seemed intent on claiming land in the Americas. Monroe aimed to keep European powers from reclaiming the former colonies. The Monroe Doctrine helped achieve this goal. It was also an important contribution because it helped shape U.S. foreign policy for more than 100 years.)*

Determine Author's Purpose Why do you think the author calls the Monroe Doctrine "bold"? Explain your reasoning. *(The author sees the doctrine as bold because the United States was still young and small in population compared to the European powers. Defying those powers was a bold step.)*

SYNTHESIZE

DIGITAL ACTIVITY

The Legacy of President Monroe

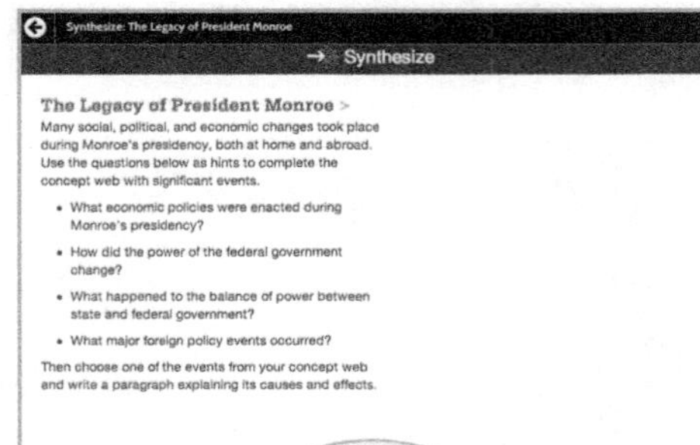

Have students complete the concept web with the significant events that took place during Monroe's presidency. Have students compare their concept webs with a partner.

Have partners review their webs and consider the following question. What domestic and foreign problems did Monroe face during his presidency, and how did he address them? Have partners share their answers with the class.

Discuss Have students review the lists they made at the beginning of the lesson about the Era of Good Feelings. Ask students whether they think this era persisted throughout Monroe's presidency, explaining why or why not.

DEMONSTRATE

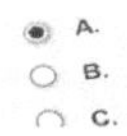

DIGITAL QUIZ

Lesson Quiz and Class Discussion Board

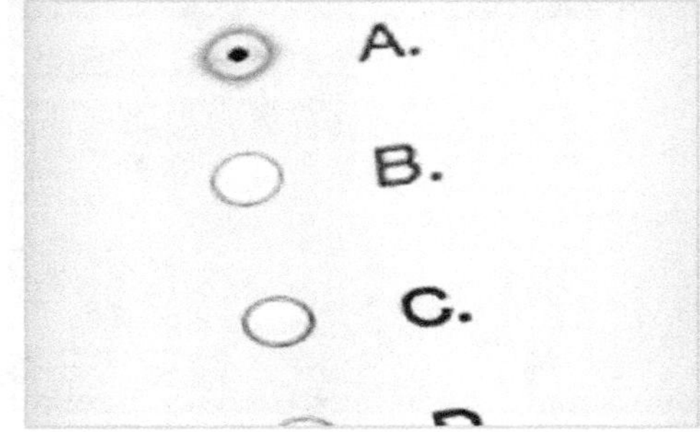

Assign the online Lesson Quiz for this lesson if you haven't already done so. Students will be offered automatic remediation or enrichment based on their score.

Pose these questions to the class on the Discussion Board:

In *Monroe's Presidency*, you read about major domestic problems and foreign policies during Monroe's presidency.

Identify Cause and Effect In what ways did the War of 1812 cause economic change in the nation? *(The war kept British goods out of the country, which contributed to the growth of American industry until the war's end, when cheaper British goods flooded the market. Foreign competition caused New England businesses to fail. This led Congress to pass protective tariffs, which angered southerners and westerners. Economic problems convinced leaders who had initially opposed a national bank that a bank was necessary.)*

Draw Conclusions How did events during Monroe's presidency define the authority of the central government? Give examples for support. *(The central government strengthened through the Supreme Court's rulings in* McCulloch v. Maryland *and* Gibbons v. Ogden *and the creation of a national bank.)*

Topic Inquiry

Have students continue their investigations for the Topic Inquiry.

The Early Republic (1789–1825)

SYNTHESIZE

DIGITAL ACTIVITY

Reflect on the Essential Question and Topic

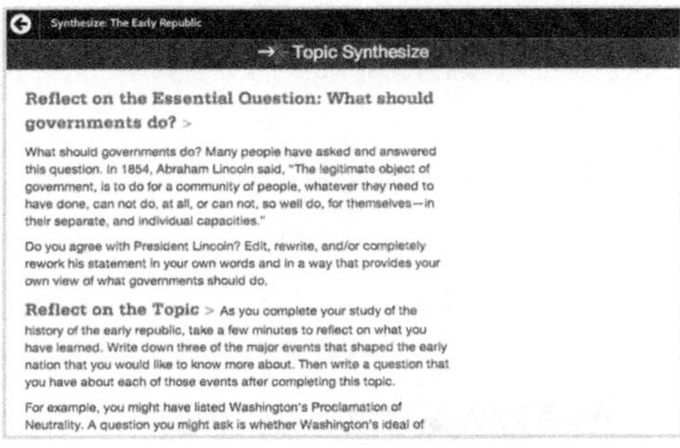

Synthesize: The Early Republic

→ Topic Synthesize

Reflect on the Essential Question: What should governments do? >

What should governments do? Many people have asked and answered this question. In 1854, Abraham Lincoln said, "The legitimate object of government, is to do for a community of people, whatever they need to have done, can not do, at all, or can not, so well do, for themselves—in their separate, and individual capacities."

Do you agree with President Lincoln? Edit, rewrite, and/or completely rework his statement in your own words and in a way that provides your own view of what governments should do.

Reflect on the Topic > As you complete your study of the history of the early republic, take a few minutes to reflect on what you have learned. Write down three of the major events that shaped the early nation that you would like to know more about. Then write a question that you have about each of those events after completing this topic.

For example, you might have listed Washington's Proclamation of Neutrality. A question you might ask is whether Washington's ideal of

First ask students to reconsider the Essential Question for this Topic: What should governments do? Have students read the quote by Lincoln and consider whether they agree or disagree. Have students edit, rewrite, or completely rework his statement in their own words to provide their own view of what governments should do.

Ask students, "Do you think the U.S. government does what governments should do?" Have students review their statements about what governments should do and give an example of how the U.S. government does or does not fulfill this obligation. Discuss their statements and examples as a class or ask students to post their answers on the Class Discussion Board.

Next ask students to reflect on the Topic as a whole and write down three major events that shaped the early nation and a question about each. Have students consider the following event and question to help them get started:

1. Washington's Proclamation of Neutrality
2. Does Washington's proclamation still make sense in today's world?

Topic Inquiry

Have students complete Step 3 of the Topic Inquiry.

DEMONSTRATE

DIGITAL TOPIC REVIEW AND ASSESSMENT

The Early Republic (1789–1825)

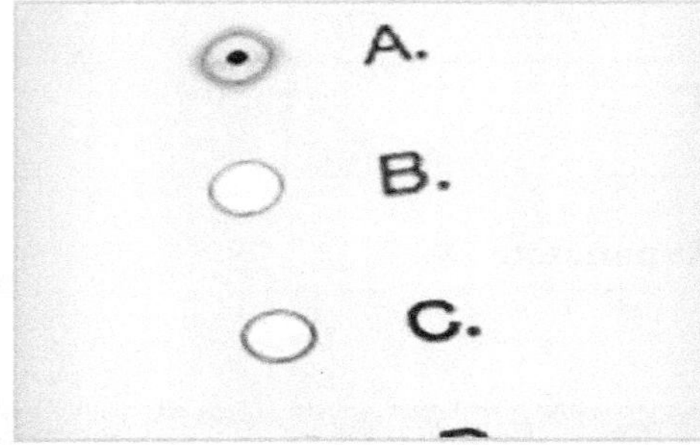

Students can prepare for the Topic Test by answering the questions in the Topic Review and Assessment online or the Assessment questions in the Print Student text. They can also prepare by reviewing their answers to the Interactive Reading Notepad questions or reviewing their notes in the Reading and Notetaking Study Guide.

DIGITAL TOPIC TEST

The Early Republic (1789–1825)

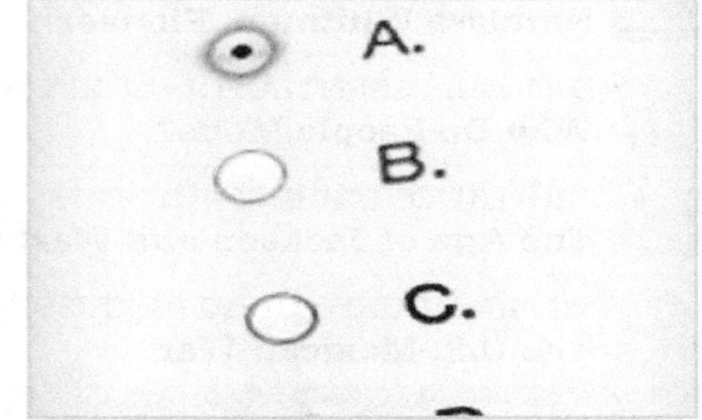

TOPIC TEST

Assign the Topic Test to assess students' understanding of topic content.

BENCHMARK TESTS

Assign these benchmark tests as you complete the relevant topics to monitor student progress toward mastering the course content and as preparation for the End-of-Course Test.

Benchmark Test 1: Topics 1–2

Benchmark Test 2: Topics 3–4

Benchmark Test 3: Topics 5–6

Benchmark Test 4: Topics 7–9

Benchmark Test 5: Topics 10–12

Benchmark Test 6: Topics 13–14

Benchmark Test 7: Topics 15–17

Topic 6

The Age of Jackson and Westward Expansion (1824–1860)

TOPIC 6 ORGANIZER	PACING: APPROX. 10 PERIODS, 5 BLOCKS
	PACING
Connect	1 period
MY STORY VIDEO **Narcissa Whitman, Pioneer**	10 min.
DIGITAL ESSENTIAL QUESTION ACTIVITY **Why Do People Move?**	10 min.
DIGITAL OVERVIEW ACTIVITY **The Age of Jackson and Westward Expansion**	10 min.
TOPIC INQUIRY: CIVIC DISCUSSION **The U.S.-Mexican-War**	20 min.
Investigate	3–7 periods
TOPIC INQUIRY: CIVIC DISCUSSION **The U.S.-Mexican-War**	Ongoing
LESSON 1 Jackson Wins the Presidency	30–40 min.
LESSON 2 Political Conflict and Economic Crisis	30–40 min.
LESSON 3 Native Americans on the Frontier	30–40 min.
LESSON 4 Westward Movement	30–40 min.
LESSON 5 Settling Oregon Country	30–40 min.
LESSON 6 Independence for Texas	30–40 min.
LESSON 7 Manifest Destiny in California and the Southwest	30–40 min.
Synthesize	1 period
DIGITAL ESSENTIAL QUESTION ACTIVITY **Why do people move?**	10 min.
TOPIC INQUIRY: CIVIC DISCUSSION **The U.S.-Mexican-War**	20 min.
Demonstrate	1–2 periods
DIGITAL TOPIC REVIEW AND ASSESSMENT **The Age of Jackson and Westward Expansion (1824–1860)**	10 min.
TOPIC INQUIRY: CIVIC DISCUSSION **The U.S.-Mexican-War**	20 min.

TOPIC INQUIRY: CIVIC DISCUSSION

The U.S.-Mexican-War

In this Topic Inquiry, students work in teams to examine different perspectives on this issue by analyzing several sources, arguing both sides of a Yes/No question, then developing and discussing their own point of view on the question: **Was the U.S.-Mexican War justified?**

STEP 1: CONNECT

Develop Questions and Plan the Investigation

Launch the Civic Discussion

Divide the class into groups of four students. Students can access the materials they'll need in the online course or you can distribute copies to each student. Read the main question and introduction with the students.

Have students complete Step 1 by reading the Discussion Launch and filling in Step 1 of the Information Organizer. The Discussion Launch provides YES and NO arguments on the main question. Students should extract and paraphrase the arguments from the reading in Step 1 of their Information Organizers.

Next, students share within their groups the arguments and evidence they found to support the YES and NO positions. The group needs to agree on the major YES and NO points and each student should note those points in their Information Organizer.

Resources

- Student Instructions
- Information Organizer
- Discussion Launch

PROFESSIONAL DEVELOPMENT

Civic Discussion

Be sure to view the Civic Discussion Professional Development resources in the online course.

STEP 2: INVESTIGATE

Apply Disciplinary Concepts and Tools

Examine Sources and Perspectives

Students will examine sources with the goal of extracting information and perspectives on the main question. They analyze each source and describe the author's perspective on the main question and key evidence the author provides to support that viewpoint in Information Organizer Step 2.

Ask students to keep in mind:

- **Author/Creator:** Who created the source? An individual? Group? Government agency?
- **Audience:** For whom was the source created?
- **Date/Place:** Is there any information that reveals where and when the source was created?
- **Purpose:** Why was the source created? Discuss with students the importance of this question in identifying bias.
- **Relevance:** How does the source support one argument or another?

Suggestion: Reading the source documents and filling in Step 2 of the Information Organizer could be assigned as homework.

Resources

- Student Instructions
- Information Organizer
- Source documents

TOPIC INQUIRY: CIVIC DISCUSSION

The U.S.-Mexican-War *(continued)*

STEP 3: SYNTHESIZE
Use Evidence
to Formulate Conclusions

Formulate Compelling Arguments with Evidence

Now students will apply perspectives and evidence they extracted from the sources to think more deeply about the main question by first arguing one side of the issue, then the other. In this way students become more prepared to formulate an evidence-based conclusion on their own.

Within each student group, assign half of the students to take the position of YES on the main question and the others to take the position of NO. Students will work with their partners to identify the strongest arguments and evidence to support their assigned YES or NO position.

Present Yes/No Positions

Within each group, those assigned the YES position share arguments and evidence first. As the YES students speak, those assigned NO should listen carefully, take notes to fill in the rest of the Compelling Arguments Chart (Step 3 in Information Organizer) and ask clarifying questions.

When the YES side is finished, students assigned the NO position present while those assigned YES should listen, take notes, and ask clarifying questions. Examples of clarifyin questions are:

- I think you just said [x]. Am I understanding you correctly?
- Can you tell me more about [x]?
- Can you repeat [x]? I am not sure I understand, yet.

Suggestion: You may want to set a 5 minute time limit for each side to present. Provide a two-minute warning so that students make their most compelling arguments within the time frame.

Switch Sides

The students will switch sides to argue the opposite point of view. To prepare to present the other position, partners who first argued YES will use the notes they took during the NO side's presentation, plus add any additional arguments and evidence from the reading and sources. The same for students who first argued the NO position.

STEP 4: DEMONSTRATE
Communicate Conclusions
and Take Informed Action

Individual Points of View

Now the students will have the opportunity to discuss the main question from their own points of view. To help students prepare for this discussion, have them reflect on the YES/NO discussions they have participated in thus far and fill in Step 4 of their Information Organizers.

After all of the students have shared their points of view, each group should list points of agreement, filling the last portion of Step 4 on their Information Organizers.

Reflect on the Discussion

Ask students to reflect on the civic discussion thinking about:

- The value of having to argue both the YES and NO positions.
- If their individual views changed over the course of the discussion and why.
- What they learned from participating in the discussion.

Resources

- Student Instructions
- Information Organizer

INTRODUCTION

The Age of Jackson and Westward Expansion (1824–1860)

The early 1800s was an era of growth for the United States. As the United States grew in size, so too did the number of people who could participate in government.

- As more states were added to the Union, changes were made to the voting process and many more Americans could vote than ever before.
- Although democratization was beneficial to some Americans, others remained without a voice in government.
- While westward expansion was a boon for the American economy and a great opportunity for pioneers, the process was devastating to Native Americans whose homeland was being encroached upon.

CONNECT

MY STORY VIDEO

Narcissa Whitman, Pioneer

Now let's watch a video that tells the story of one pioneer who took part in westward expansion. It begins to explore what life was like during their journeys and reasons why Americans began moving westward.

Infer What type of person do you think would have been willing to move to the frontier in the 1800s? *(Adventurous, daring, brave, bold, courageous, fearless, a loner, gutsy)*

Identify Central Issues What kind of difficulties do you think were encountered by pioneers as they traveled West? *(Dangerous river crossings, animal attacks, diseases, hunger/thirst, broken wagons, uncomfortable sleeping arrangements, untrustworthy travel companions, uncertain encounters with Native Americans, inclement weather, desert crossings, runaway horses)*

Hypothesize Would you have been willing to make the trek? Why or why not? *(Although it sounds like it would be a very exciting experience, I don't enjoy camping or living in the outdoors and would be unwilling to travel in this manner.)*

DIGITAL ESSENTIAL QUESTION ACTIVITY

Why Do People Move?

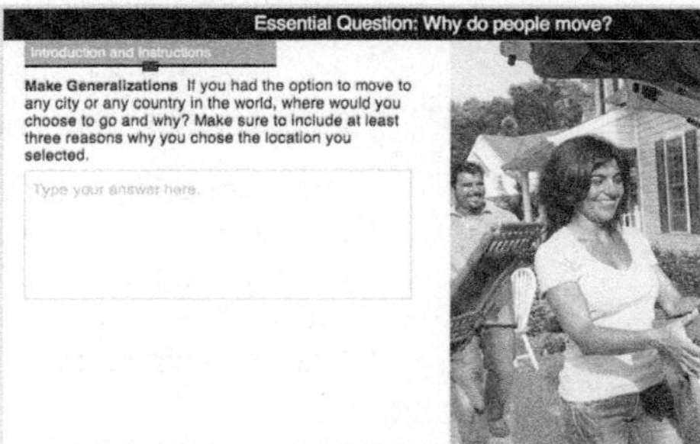

Look at the Essential Question for this Topic: Why do people move? People have moved from place to place since the dawn of time for economic, social, political, or environmental reasons.

Ask students to complete the short answer question for the Essential Question activity. Then review their responses.

Categorize Which of the reasons would be categorized as push factors and which as pull factors? *(Push: few job opportunities, overcrowding, insufficient housing, desire to live in a foreign country; Pull: a specific job opportunity, warm climate, family/friends live there)*

Identify Central Issues Why might someone move to the United States from another country? *(Political persecution/unrest, lack of jobs, better education, democratic freedom, family, better climate)*

D Differentiate: Challenge Which factor—economic, social, political, or environmental—do you think most often causes someone to move? Why do you think this is the case? *(Economic, because people move for a job or better financial opportunities. Or: Political, because many people move due to political unrest in their homeland.)*

DIGITAL OVERVIEW ACTIVITY

The Age of Jackson and Westward Expansion

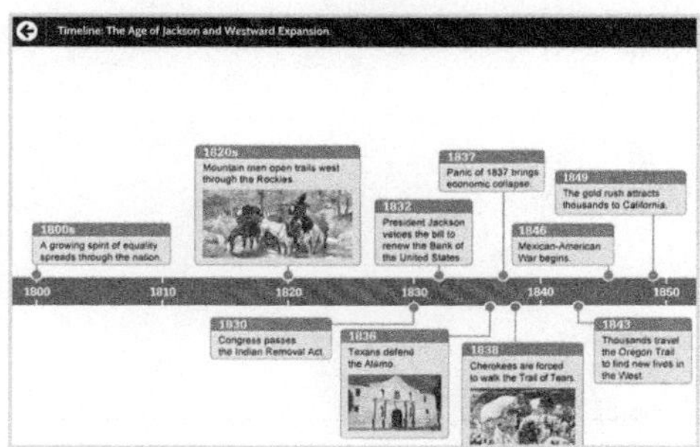

Let's look at a timeline showing the major turning points in *The Age of Jackson and Westward Expansion*. During this Topic, we'll learn about all of these events and many more. This timeline will provide a framework to place the events about which we will learn.

Use Context Clues Which items in the timeline give examples of the Topic title, *Westward Expansion*? *(Mountain men open trails west through the Rockies, the gold rush attracts thousands to California, thousands travel the Oregon Trail to find new lives in the West.)*

Identify Cause and Effect What two events do you think are linked? *(President Jackson vetoes the bill to renew the Bank of the United States and the Panic of 1837 brings economic collapse; Congress passes the Indian Removal Act and Cherokees are forced to walk the Trail of Tears.)*

Topic Inquiry

Launch the Topic Inquiry with students after introducing the topic.

Jackson Wins the Presidency

Supporting English Language Learners

Use with Digital Text 1, **Democracy Expands.**

Listening

Recall the meaning of the term *social class* with students. Prompt students to understand the meaning of spoken language in a range of situations.

Beginning Use familiar vocabulary and language structures to speak about power and voting rights in America and Europe. Have students express the general meaning of what you said by completing this sentence: White men had _____ power and voting rights in America than in Europe.

Intermediate Use familiar vocabulary and language structures to speak about the differences in social class between America and Europe. Have students express the general meaning of what you said in a sentence.

Advanced Use familiar, yet challenging, vocabulary and language structures to speak about the differences in social class between America and Europe. Ask: What is the general meaning of what I said?

Advanced High Combine challenging and unfamiliar vocabulary and language structures to speak about the differences in social class between America and Europe. Ask: What is the general meaning of what I said?

Use with Digital Text 5, **The Spoils System.**

Reading

Review the purpose of before-noun placement of an adjective in English. Support students and encourage them to use support from peers to identify when nouns can be used as adjectives. Recognizing this will prevent confusion while reading and develop their grasp of this and other language structures.

Beginning Have pairs of students work together to determine definitions for noun and adjective. Then display the phrase *government jobs*. Explain how the noun *government* acts as an adjective. Support students in grasping the noun-as-adjective language structure by helping them complete this sentence: Government jobs are jobs in _____.

Intermediate Have pairs of students work together to determine definitions for noun and adjective. Then display the phrases *government employees* and *government jobs*. Explain how the noun *government* acts as an adjective. Support students in grasping the noun-as-adjective language structure by helping them to form other phrases using *government* as an adjective.

Advanced Display the phrase *spoils system*. Explain how the noun *spoils* acts as an adjective. Then have pairs of students support each other as they search the text for three other examples of the noun-as-adjective language structure and explain their meanings.

Advanced High Display the phrases *spoils system* and *government jobs*. Explain how the nouns *spoils* and *government* act as adjectives. Then have students support each other as they write original sentences about the spoils system or Andrew Jackson that include the noun-as-adjective language structure.

D Differentiate Instruction

Use the Differentiated Instruction notes throughout the lesson plan to support the varied skill sets, levels of readiness, and interests in the mixed-ability classroom.

Challenge These notes include suggestions for expanding the activity for advanced students.

On-Level These notes include suggestions for modifying the activity to address different interests or learning styles.

Extra Support These notes include ideas for providing more scaffolding or reading spuport.

Special Needs These notes provide ideas for adapting instruction to support the needs of various special needs students.

NOTES

PEARSON realize
www.PearsonRealize.com

Go online to access additional resources including: Primary Sources • Biographies • Supreme Court cases • 21st Century Skill Tutorials • Maps • Graphic Organizers.

Objectives

Objective 1: Describe who gained suffrage by the 1820s.

Objective 2: Identify compromises made after the 1824 election, including the roles of Henry Clay and John Quincy Adams.

Objective 3: Explain the origin and development of new political parties under John Quincy Adams.

Objective 4: Describe the causes and effects of Jacksonian democracy and the impact of the election of Andrew Jackson.

Objective 5: Explain the spoils system.

LESSON 1 ORGANIZER	PACING: APPROX. 1 PERIOD, .5 BLOCKS			
			RESOURCES	
	OBJECTIVES	PACING	Online	Print
Connect				
DIGITAL START UP ACTIVITY **Jackson's Story**		5 min.	●	
Investigate				
DIGITAL TEXT 1 **Democracy Expands**	Objective 1	10 min.	●	●
INTERACTIVE TIMELINE **Changing Voting Rights in Early America**		10 min.	●	
DIGITAL TEXT 2 **The Election of 1824 Leads to a "Bargain"**	Objective 2	10 min.	●	●
DIGITAL TEXT 3 **The Presidency of John Quincy Adams**	Objective 3	10 min.	●	●
INTERACTIVE CHART **Political Parties in the Age of Jackson**		10 min.	●	
DIGITAL TEXT 4 **Jacksonian Democracy**	Objective 4	10 min.	●	●
INTERACTIVE CHART **Causes and Effects of Jacksonian Democracy**		10 min.	●	
DIGITAL TEXT 5 **The Spoils System**	Objective 5	10 min.	●	●
Synthesize				
DIGITAL ACTIVITY **Americans and Their Government**		5 min.	●	
Demonstrate				
DIGITAL QUIZ **Lesson Quiz and Class Discussion Board**		10 min.	●	

Jackson Wins the Presidency

CONNECT

DIGITAL START UP ACTIVITY

Jackson's Story

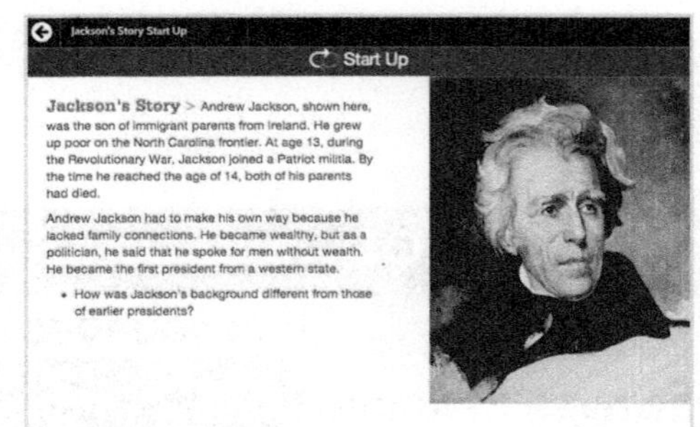

Project the Start Up Activity Ask students to answer the questions as they enter and get settled. You may have them share their ideas with another student or post them to the class discussion board.

Discuss What does Andrew Jackson's life suggest about America during the Age of Jackson? *(It suggests that people could get ahead without money or family connections; or it suggests that white people enjoyed advantages while people from other races suffered.)* How did Jackson's background influence his political positions? *(He spoke out for white men who were, like himself, from poor backgrounds.)*

Aa Vocabulary Development: Use the Interactive Reading Notepad to preview the Key Terms and Academic Vocabulary in this lesson with students.

FLIP IT!

Assign the Flipped Video for this lesson.

STUDENT EDITION PRINT PAGES: 302–312

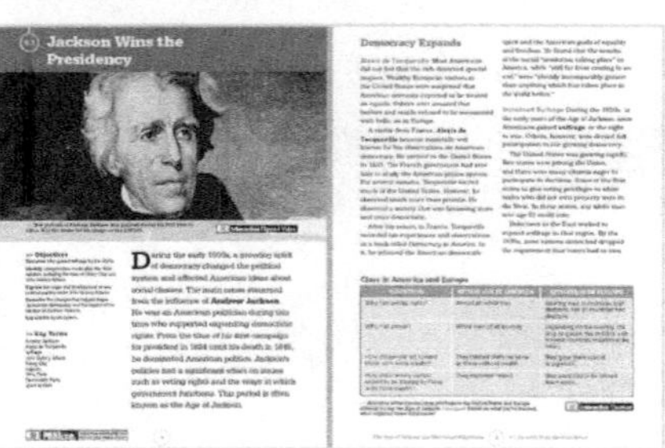

INVESTIGATE

DIGITAL TEXT 1

Democracy Expands

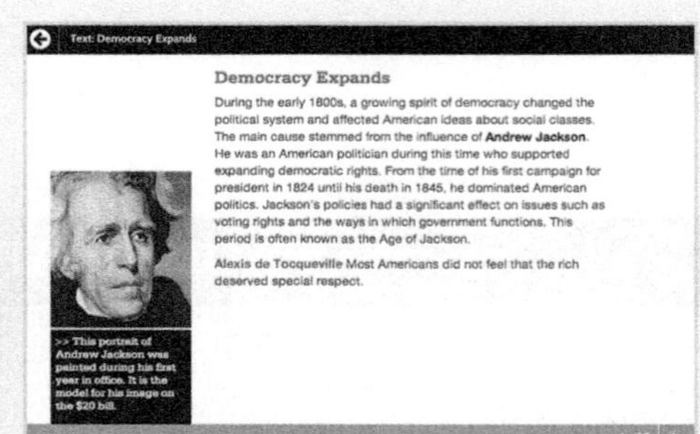

INTERACTIVE TIMELINE

Changing Voting Rights in Early America

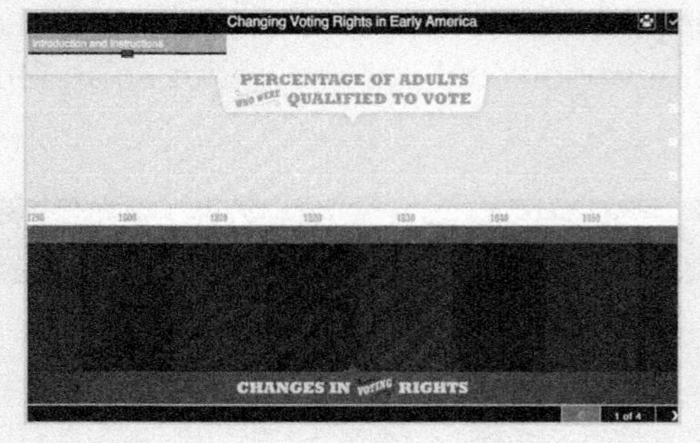

Objective 1: Describe who gained suffrage by the 1820s.

Quick Instruction

Interactive Timeline: Changing Voting Rights in America Project the interactive timeline. Discuss changes in voting rights and percentages of the population who were qualified to vote with students. During the age of Jackson, did the number of states with property qualifications for voting increase or decrease? Why? *(The number of states with property qualifications decreased. Some states removed the property qualifications and new states without property qualifications joined the United States.)*

Compare and Contrast How did the change in voting rights affect poor white men compared to free African American men? How did this change affect enslaved African Americans compared to free African Americans? *(Even though most white men had won suffrage, free African American men lost the right to vote in many states. Enslaved African Americans were not affected by this change because they had no political rights and could not vote in any state.)*

ACTIVE CLASSROOM

Have students Make Headlines. Ask students to suppose they are investigative journalists who have uncovered information about voting rights over the previous few decades. Ask: If you were to write a headline about voting rights in this time frame, what would that headline be? Have students pass their headlines to a partner for revision suggestions.

ELL Use the ELL activity described in the ELL chart.

D Differentiate: Extra Support Ask students to think carefully about what the bars above the timeline represent. Ask them to explain this relationship in their own words. Then ask them to think of ways that changes listed below the timeline could lead to changes in the height of the bars above the timeline.

Further Instruction

Integrate Information What concern does de Tocqueville suggest when he writes "It remains to be shown. . .," and how do these concerns reflect de Tocqueville's frame of reference? Cite evidence to support your response. *(His use of expressions such as "superior to the laws," "passions," and "unbounded authority" suggest that unlimited democracy could result in arbitrary or unjust government.)*

DIGITAL TEXT 2

The Election of 1824 Leads to a "Bargain"

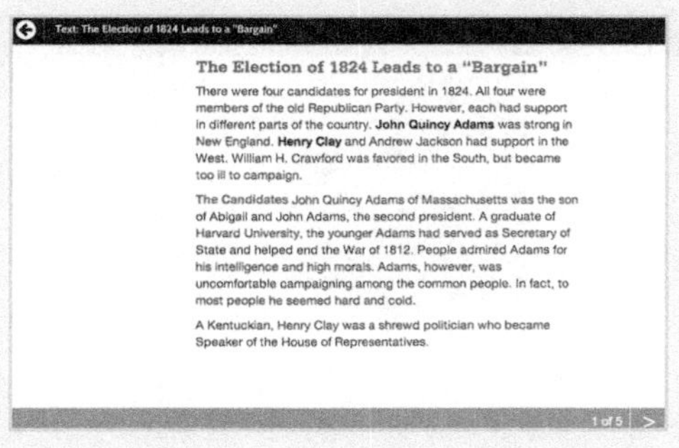

Objective 2: **Identify compromises made after the 1824 election, including the roles of Henry Clay and John Quincy Adams.**

Quick Instruction

In 1824, politicians had different positions, but they all belonged to the same party. There were four candidates for President, and none of them won a majority of electoral votes.

Interpret Review the image showing the constitutional process that led to the House of Representatives deciding who won 1824 presidential election. Ask students how the vote in the House was connected to the popular vote. *(In states that had a popular vote, it determined the electoral vote. The three candidates with the most electoral votes then faced a vote in the House of Representatives. However, that vote had no direct relation to the popular vote.)*

Summarize What were the roles of John Quincy Adams and Henry Clay in the congressional compromise that decided the election of 1824, and what were the effects of that compromise? *(Henry Clay urged his supporters in the House of Representatives to vote for John Quincy Adams. As a result, Adams won the election.)*

Further Instruction

Identify Cause and Effect Under what provision was the election of 1824 decided? *(It was based on the provision of the Constitution, which states that the House is to decide presidential elections when there is no one who wins the majority of electoral votes.)*

DIGITAL TEXT 3

The Presidency of John Quincy Adams

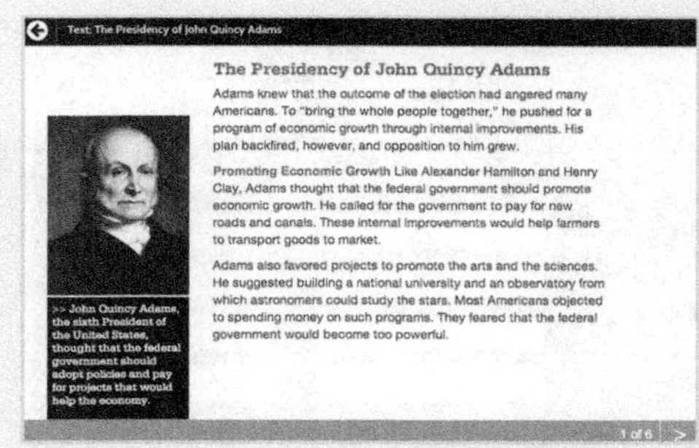

Objective 3: **Explain the origin and development of new political parties under John Quincy Adams.**

Quick Instruction

Interactive Chart: Political Parties in the Age of Jackson Project the interactive chart. Ask students to consider not only which goals each party had, but also how those goals were related to one another and how they reflected the interests of each party's supporters.

Explain to students that differences between Jackson's supporters and the supporters of Adams and Clay gave rise to new American political parties during the presidency of John Quincy Adams. Explain that some of those differences were regional.

Contrast Ask student to explain the point of view of each party on the following important historic issues: the role of the federal government and tariffs? *Whigs supported a strong and active federal government; Democrats wanted a limited federal government. Whigs supported tariffs; Democrats opposed them.)*

ACTIVE CLASSROOM

Conduct a Take a Stand activity. Ask students to take a stand on the following question: During the Age of Jackson, would you have been a Whig or a Democrat?

- Ask students to divide into two groups based on their answer and move to separate areas of the classroom.
- Ask a representative from each side to present and defend the group's point of view.

INTERACTIVE CHART

Political Parties in the Age of Jackson

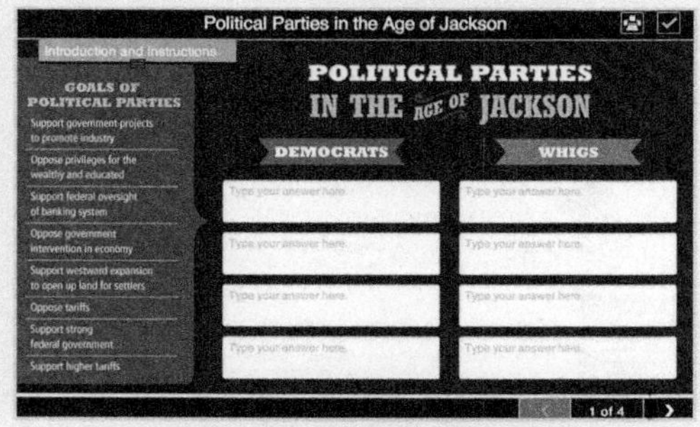

Further Instruction

Identify Cause and Effect Explain the reasons for the origin and development of political parties during the presidency of John Quincy Adams. *(Jackson's supporters were angry that Adams had won the presidency even though Jackson had won more votes. Jackson's supporters differed from Adams's supporters over whether the government should have a role in the economy. Jackson's supporters opposed high tariffs and called for more political power for ordinary white men. Adams's supporters wanted the federal government to promote business and oversee banks.)*

Distinguish What role did regional interests play in the formation of political parties? *(The businesspeople who supported the Whigs and their policies of economic development were concentrated in the Northeast. Support from small farmers and workers, who backed small-government policies, gave the Democrats more influence in the South and West.)*

Jackson Wins the Presidency

DIGITAL TEXT 4

Jacksonian Democracy

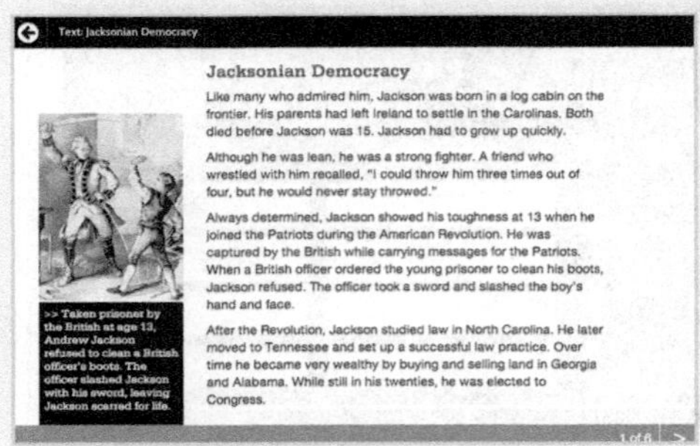

Text: Jacksonian Democracy

Jacksonian Democracy

Like many who admired him, Jackson was born in a log cabin on the frontier. His parents had left Ireland to settle in the Carolinas. Both died before Jackson was 15. Jackson had to grow up quickly.

Although he was lean, he was a strong fighter. A friend who wrestled with him recalled, "I could throw him three times out of four, but he would never stay throwed."

Always determined, Jackson showed his toughness at 13 when he joined the Patriots during the American Revolution. He was captured by the British while carrying messages for the Patriots. When a British officer ordered the young prisoner to clean his boots, Jackson refused. The officer took a sword and slashed the boy's hand and face.

After the Revolution, Jackson studied law in North Carolina. He later moved to Tennessee and set up a successful law practice. Over time he became very wealthy by buying and selling land in Georgia and Alabama. While still in his twenties, he was elected to Congress.

>> Taken prisoner by the British at age 13, Andrew Jackson refused to clean a British officer's boots. The officer slashed Jackson with his sword, leaving Jackson scarred for life.

1 of 6

Objective 4: **Describe the causes and effects of Jacksonian democracy and the impact of the election of Andrew Jackson.**

Quick Instruction

Interactive Chart: Causes and Effects of Jacksonian Democracy Project the interactive chart. Ask students to think about each of the changes listed. Explicitly identify the Jackson era as a major era in U.S. history. Ask them not only to identify which changes are causes and which are effects, but also how each cause helped shape the Jackson era and how conditions during this era led to each effect.

Identify Cause and Effect After filling in the causes of the Jackson era, pick one cause and describe how that change helped shape this era. *(When white men without property gained the vote, the government became more democratic and paid more attention to ordinary people.)*

Identify Steps in a Process After filling in the effects of the Jackson era, pick one effect and describe how conditions during this era led to that effect. *(Andrew Jackson promised to help ordinary Americans. He did not think that government jobs required special qualifications, so he rewarded his supporters with government jobs.)*

INTERACTIVE CHART

Causes and Effects of Jacksonian Democracy

ACTIVE CLASSROOM

Conduct a Sequence It activity. For a key sequence of events that explain an effect of the Jackson era, give small groups of students pieces of paper and have them put the list in order.

Further Instruction

Identify Cause and Effect Explain how the impact of Andrew Jackson's election was connected to expanded suffrage? *(Jackson's Democratic Party introduced political campaigns that appealed to common people and their concerns. These campaigns motivated white men to vote and to get involved in the political process.)*

Support Ideas with Examples Describe some examples of contributions of Andrew Jackson to his country. *(He won a victory over the British and brought ordinary people into politics. However, his contributions were not all positive. For example, he took land away from Native Americans.)*

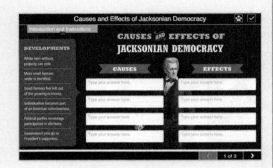

DIGITAL TEXT 5

The Spoils System

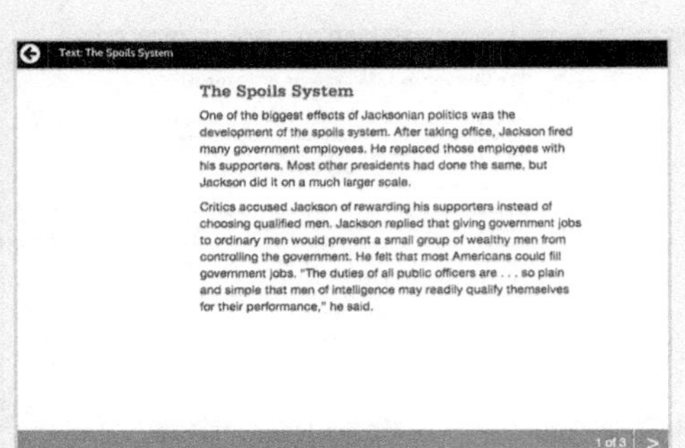

Text: The Spoils System

The Spoils System

One of the biggest effects of Jacksonian politics was the development of the spoils system. After taking office, Jackson fired many government employees. He replaced those employees with his supporters. Most other presidents had done the same, but Jackson did it on a much larger scale.

Critics accused Jackson of rewarding his supporters instead of choosing qualified men. Jackson replied that giving government jobs to ordinary men would prevent a small group of wealthy men from controlling the government. He felt that most Americans could fill government jobs. "The duties of all public officers are . . . so plain and simple that men of intelligence may readily qualify themselves for their performance," he said.

1 of 3

Objective 5: **Explain the spoils system.**

Quick Instruction

Identify Central Issues How were Jackson's political views connected with his support for the spoils system? *(Jackson believed that people with wealth, education, and connections did not deserve privilege. In his view, that meant that educated and well-connected people had no more right to government jobs than the ordinary people who supported him. Jackson believed in a powerful presidency and felt that it was his right to give his supporters jobs if he chose.)*

ELL Use the ELL activity described in the ELL chart.

Further Instruction

Draw Conclusions Explain to students that some would argue that it is wrong to give political supporters government jobs. These people would argue that only the best-qualified people should hold government jobs, regardless of their political beliefs. Others would argue that elected officials need supporters working for them in order to carry out their policies, since even the best-qualified opponent might try to undermine those policies. If time permits, ask students their opinion on this question. *(Answers will vary.)*

PEARSON realize™ **www.PearsonRealize.com** Access your Digital Lesson

SYNTHESIZE

DIGITAL ACTIVITY

Americans and Their Government

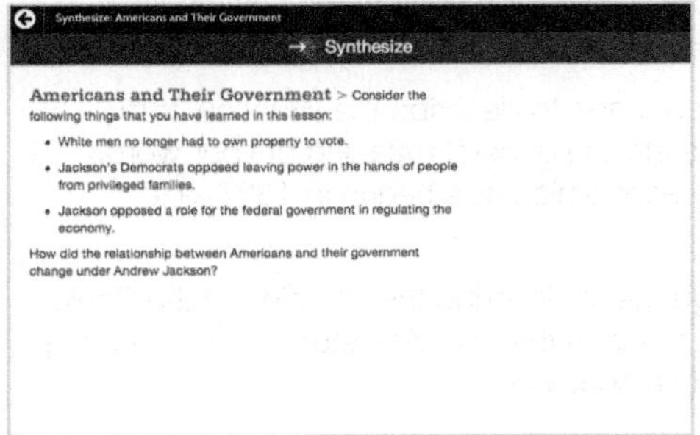

Ask students to think about each of the facts listed about citizenship and government in the Jackson era.

Discuss Ask students to think about how the relationship between Americans and their government changed under Andrew Jackson. How was that relationship connected to national identity?

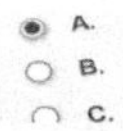

DEMONSTRATE

DIGITAL QUIZ

Lesson Quiz and Class Discussion Board

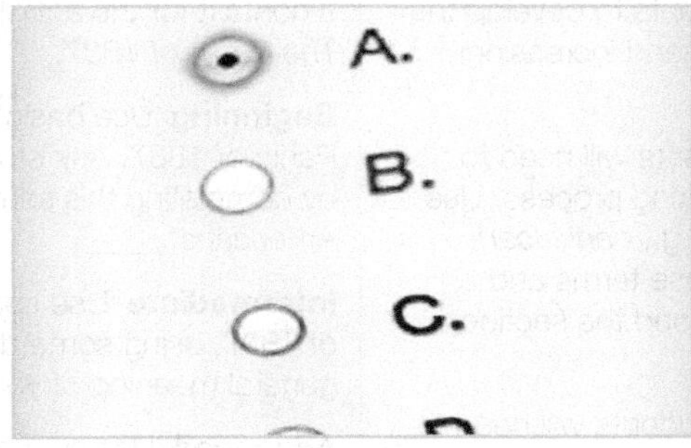

Assign the online Lesson Quiz for this lesson if you haven't already done so. Students will be offered automatic remediation or enrichment based on their score.

Pose these questions to the class on the Discussion Board:

Predict Consequences What kinds of conflicts might develop over the exclusion of some Americans from the country's democratic system? *(When an American is excluded from the democratic system, government representation and justice are lost for that person, leading to conflicts over such things as land, rights, and the benefits of being a citizen.)*

Identify Patterns What does the expansion of suffrage during this period suggest about the right to suffrage in later periods of American history? *(The expansion of suffrage suggests that even more people might be granted suffrage later in American history.)*

Topic Inquiry

Have students continue their investigations for the Topic Inquiry.

Political Conflict and Economic Crisis

Supporting English Language Learners

Use with Digital Text 2, **The Bank War.**

Reading

Prepare students for reading the text by discussing its title and headings. Encourage students to predict what background knowledge they might need in order to understand this reading. Prompt students to develop the necessary background knowledge in order to comprehend increasingly challenging language.

Beginning Develop the background knowledge students will need to comprehend the text's language by acting out the banking process. Use vocabulary from the text as you explain your actions (e.g., *bank, loan, borrow, lend*). Then have pairs of students discuss these terms and anything else they know about banking. Finally, read aloud the section titled *A Controversial Bank* as students follow along.

Intermediate Develop the background knowledge students will need to comprehend the text's language by explaining the banking process. Use vocabulary from the text to increase students' familiarity with these words. Then have pairs of students discuss what they know about banking. Finally, read aloud the text, or invite volunteers to do so.

Advanced Ask volunteers to share with their peers what they already know about banks. As they speak, record key words that will help students as they read the text. Review this vocabulary, and then have pairs of students read the text together.

Advanced High Ask volunteers to share with their peers what they already know about banks. Provide additional support by adding details about how a central bank is like and unlike a neighborhood bank. Then invite students to read the text independently.

Use with Digital Text 3, **Economic Crisis and Political Changes.**

Listening

Prompt students to understand the general meaning of spoken language ranging from situations in which contexts are familiar to unfamiliar. Provide a context for the activity by reading aloud (or revisiting) the section titled *The Panic of 1837*.

Beginning Use basic spoken language to describe the situation of the Panic of 1837. Ask students to state the general meaning of your words by completing this sentence: An economic crisis began in 1837, and Americans _____.

Intermediate Use spoken language to describe the situation of the Panic of 1837, using some details not found in the text. Ask students to state the general meaning of your words in a sentence.

Advanced Use spoken language to explain the word *depression* in the contexts of both the Panic of 1837 and the Great Depression. Ask students to state the general meaning of your words in a sentence or two.

Advanced High Use spoken language to explain the word *depression* in both familiar and unfamiliar contexts (e.g., economic and psychological). After you compare and contrast the meanings of depression in these contexts, ask students to state the general meaning of your words in a sentence or two.

D Differentiate Instruction

Use the Differentiated Instruction notes throughout the lesson plan to support the varied skill sets, levels of readiness, and interests in the mixed-ability classroom.

Challenge These notes include suggestions for expanding the activity for advanced students.

On-Level These notes include suggestions for modifying the activity to address different interests or learning styles.

Extra Support These notes include ideas for providing more scaffolding or reading spuport.

Special Needs These notes provide ideas for adapting instruction to support the needs of various special needs students.

NOTES

PEARSON realize
www.PearsonRealize.com

Go online to access additional resources including:
Primary Sources • Biographies • Supreme Court cases • 21st Century Skill Tutorials • Maps • Graphic Organizers.

Objectives

Objective 1: Explain the issues of nullification and states' rights.

Objective 2: Summarize arguments regarding the banking system.

Objective 3: Identify the economic problems Martin Van Buren faced.

Objective 4: Describe the election campaigns of 1840.

LESSON 2 ORGANIZER — PACING: APPROX. 1 PERIOD, .5 BLOCKS			RESOURCES	
	OBJECTIVES	PACING	Online	Print
Connect				
DIGITAL START UP ACTIVITY **What Do I Need to Know?**		5 min.	●	
Investigate				
DIGITAL TEXT 1 **A Conflict Over States Rights**	Objective 1	10 min.	●	●
INTERACTIVE MAP **Tariffs and Trade**		10 min.	●	
DIGITAL TEXT 2 **The Bank War**	Objective 2	10 min.	●	●
INTERACTIVE CHART **Disagreements Over the Bank**		10 min.	●	
DIGITAL TEXT 3 **Economic Crisis and Political Changes**	Objectives 3, 4	10 min.	●	●
INTERACTIVE TIMELINE **Choosing a Presidential Candidate**		10 min.	●	
Synthesize				
DIGITAL ACTIVITY **Discuss Need-to-Know Questions**		5 min.	●	
Demonstrate				
DIGITAL QUIZ **Lesson Quiz and Class Discussion Board**		10 min.	●	

Topic 6 Lesson 2

Political Conflict and Economic Crisis

CONNECT

DIGITAL START UP ACTIVITY

What Do I Need to Know?

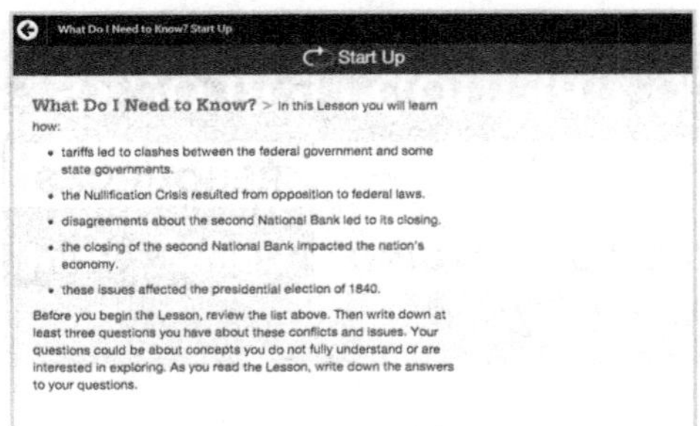

Project the Start Up Activity Ask students to read the list and make a list of questions as they get settled.

Discuss To help students make their list of questions ask: What do you already know about this material? What terms do you not understand? What concepts would you like more information about?

Tell students that in this lesson they will be learning about the differences between political parties, geographic regions, and individual states during the presidency of Andrew Jackson.

Aa Vocabulary Development: Use the Interactive Reading Notepad to preview the Key Terms and Academic Vocabulary in this lesson with students.

FLIP IT!

Assign the Flipped Video for this lesson.

STUDENT EDITION PRINT PAGES: 313–322

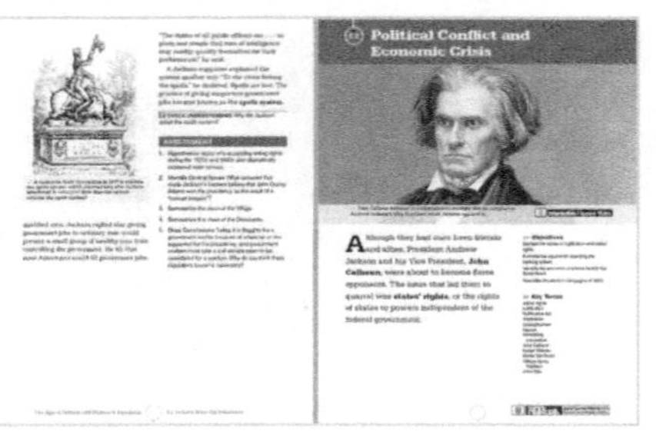

INVESTIGATE

DIGITAL TEXT 1

A Conflict Over States Rights

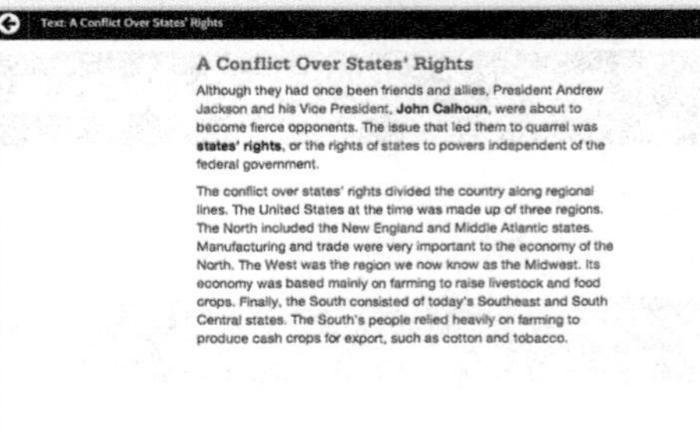

INTERACTIVE MAP

Tariffs and Trade

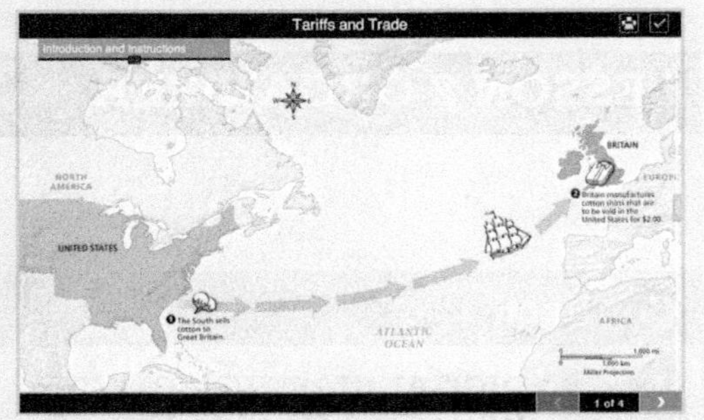

Objective 1: Explain the issues of nullification and states' rights.

Quick Instruction

Remind students that at this time period the United States reached as far west as Missouri. The North, South, and West (today's Midwest) were regions of importance in the United States during the nineteenth century. Each region had very different economies and political traditions. These regional differences laid the foundation for the Nullification Crisis.

Interactive Map: Tariffs and Trade Project the interactive map. Go over steps one and two of the activity with the students. Move the slider from right to left, stopping to review each step of the diagram.

Summarize How did the economies of different regions in the United States differ? *(The North's economy was based on manufacturing and trade. The South's economy was based on agriculture, while the West's featured both agriculture and livestock.)*

Apply Concepts Describe the issue of states' rights and explain the connection between that issue and John C. Calhoun's arguments for nullification. *(The issue of states' rights is a debate about how political power should be split between the federal and state governments. Calhoun believed that states had the right to nullify, or cancel, a federal law if they felt it was unconstitutional. Calhoun supported stronger states' rights.)*

ACTIVE CLASSROOM

Have students complete a Jigsaw activity. Divide the class into four groups. Using the primary source on nullification, instruct two groups to read the speech by Calhoun, and two other groups to read the speech by Webster. Use the Jigsaw Strategy to help students identify different points of view of political parties and interest groups on the issue of nullification.

Further Instruction

Tariff policies impacted sections of the United States differently during the Tariff of 1828 crisis. Politicians representing different parts of the nation took part in the conflict and the resulting compromise. The argument caused southern politician John C. Calhoun to call for nullification of the federal law. Northern politician Daniel Webster argued for the tariff. In an attempt to compromise and diffuse the crisis, Henry Clay proposed a lower tariff, which Congress passed.

Contrast Have students use the Think-Pair-Share Strategy to summarize different arguments regarding protective tariffs. *(Many people in the North argued for the tariff, which assisted the economy of the North by helping northern manufacturers to sell more goods. Many people in the South argued against the tariff, which hurt the economy of the South because it caused goods to be more expensive there and reduced the amount of southern cotton that Britain bought.)*

Compare and Contrast Compare the impact of the tariff of 1828 and Henry Clay's compromise tariff. *(The tariff of 1828 raised the cost of imported goods, leading to the threat of nullification from South Carolina.)*

DIGITAL TEXT 2

The Bank War

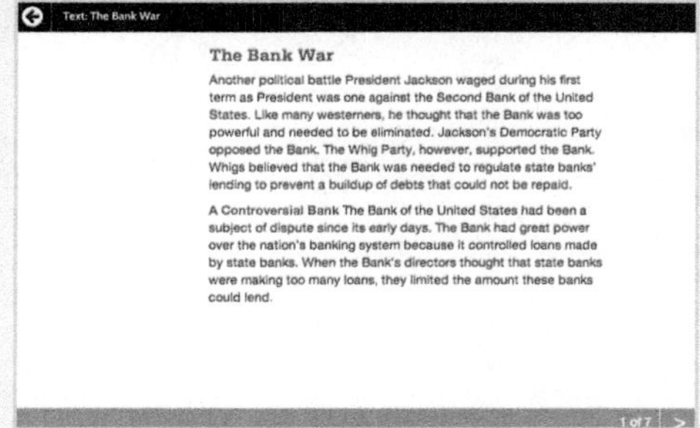

Objective 2: **Summarize arguments regarding the banking system.**

Quick Instruction

The first Bank of the United States closed in 1811. The second National Bank was opened in 1816 to help manage the nation's ailing economy and the debt from the War of 1812. The Bank's broad reach into the economy and occasional mismanagement made President Andrew Jackson its greatest opponent. He and other leading Democrats disagreed with the Whigs over the role of the banking system.

Interactive Chart: Disagreements Over the Bank Project the interactive chart. Have students drag a view on the Bank into its correct position based on the party that supported it.

Summarize Summarize arguments regarding the banking system. *(Supporters of the Bank believed it was needed to regulate state banks' lending and to prevent a buildup of debts that could not be repaid. Opponents thought the Bank was undemocratic, unconstitutional, and had too much power over the economy.)*

ACTIVE CLASSROOM

Have students complete a Quick Write activity to answer the question, Why did President Jackson want to change the nation's banking system?

INTERACTIVE CHART

Disagreements Over the Bank

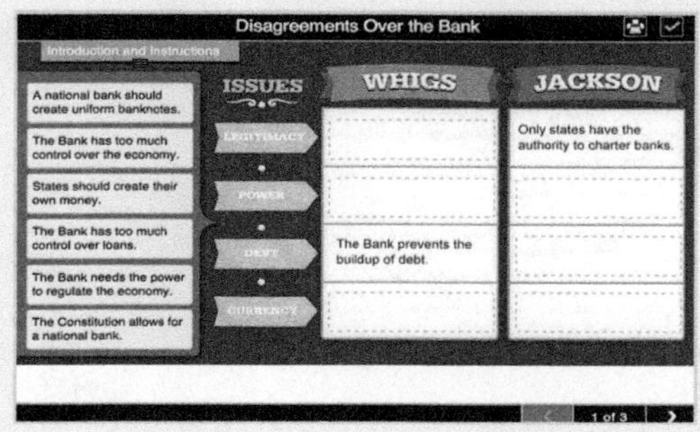

D Differentiate: Challenge Have students split into teams of two. Conduct a series of debates on the advantages and disadvantages of the second National Bank.

ELL Use the ELL activity described in the ELL chart.

Further Instruction

Go through the Interactive Reading Notepad questions and discuss the answers with the class.

Identify Central Issues Why did the second National Bank close? *(Jackson vetoed the Bank's charter. After he was reelected, Jackson ordered the Secretary of the Treasury to stop funding the Bank.)*

Summarize What were the effects of the Bank's closing on the financial system? *(States regulated their own banking systems. Individual banks produced their own money and sometimes failed.)*

DIGITAL TEXT 3

Economic Crisis and Political Changes

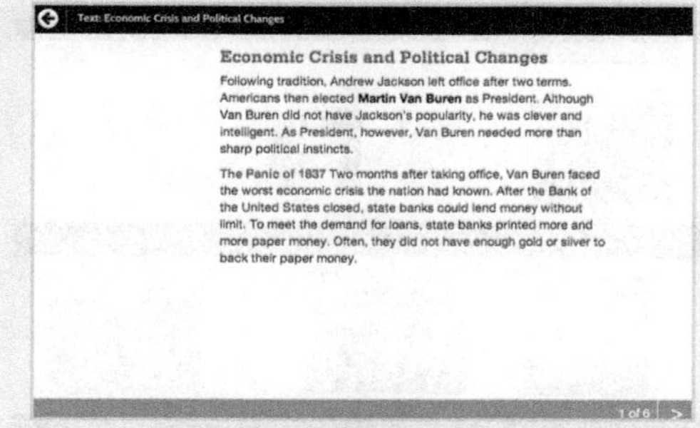

Objectives 3: **List the economic problems Martin Van Buren faced;** 4: **Describe the campaigns of 1840.**

Quick Instruction

Interactive Timeline: Choosing a Presidential Candidate Project the timeline. Have students explain how the nomination process changed over time. Then ask: Did the nominating process become more democratic with each change? Why or why not? *(The nominating of presidential candidates by party leaders or early caucuses did not make the process more democratic because it continued to be dominated by a few powerful people. The move to use conventions and then primaries did make the process more democratic because it involved many more members of the public.)*

ACTIVE CLASSROOM

Have groups of students Take a Stand on the following question: Was Martin Van Buren to blame for the economic depression during his presidency?

- Ask students to divide into two groups based on their answer and move to separate areas of the classroom.
- Ask students to talk with each other to compare their reasons for answering yes or no.
- Ask a representative from each side to present and defend the group's point of view.

Political Conflict and Economic Crisis

INTERACTIVE TIMELINE

Choosing a Presidential Candidate

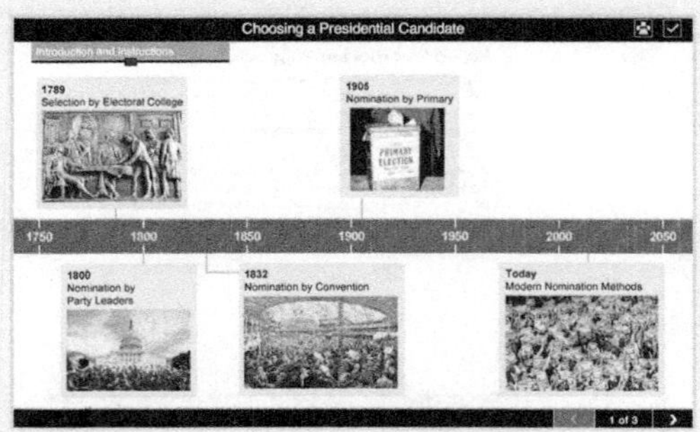

ELL Use the ELL activity described in the ELL chart.

Further Instruction

In the Panic of 1837, about 600 banks closed. This crisis turned into a full-blown depression that would have an impact on the economy of the entire United States and the reelection hopes of Martin Van Buren.

Hypothesize What strategy did the Whigs use to win the election of 1840? Would this strategy work today? *(They portrayed Harrison as a man of the people who came from humble roots. The strategy could work today because people want to relate to those they elect to office.)*

SYNTHESIZE

DIGITAL ACTIVITY

Discuss Need-to-Know Questions

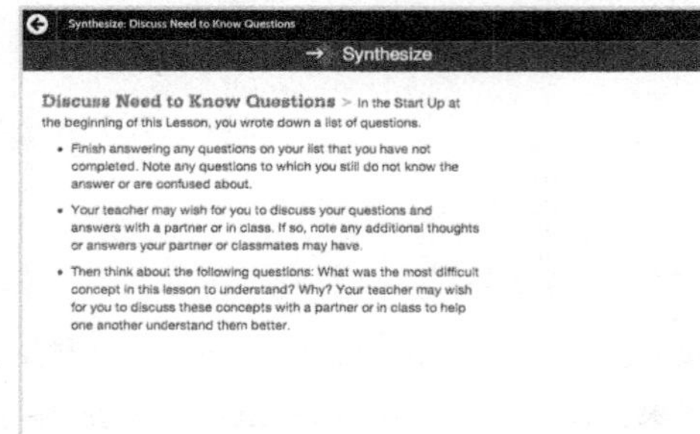

Synthesize: Discuss Need to Know Questions
Synthesize
Discuss Need to Know Questions > In the Start Up at the beginning of this Lesson, you wrote down a list of questions.
Finish answering any questions on your list that you have not completed. Note any questions to which you still do not know the answer or are confused about.
Your teacher may wish for you to discuss your questions and answers with a partner or in class. If so, note any additional thoughts or answers your partner or classmates may have.
Then think about the following questions: What was the most difficult concept in this lesson to understand? Why? Your teacher may wish for you to discuss these concepts with a partner or in class to help one another understand them better.

During the Jackson era, the issues raised by the Tariff of 1828 and the arguments over the role of the second National Bank both raised questions about government's role in the economy.

Have students go over their Need-to-Know Questions with each other and then as a class. Then ask the question below.

Discuss How did President Jackson's view of the federal government's role in the economy change from the Nullification Crisis to the Bank war? *(President Jackson supported the right of federal laws over state laws in the Nullification Crisis, but during the Bank war he supported state banks over federal banks.)*

DEMONSTRATE

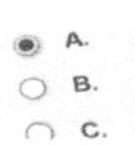

DIGITAL QUIZ

Lesson Quiz and Class Discussion Board

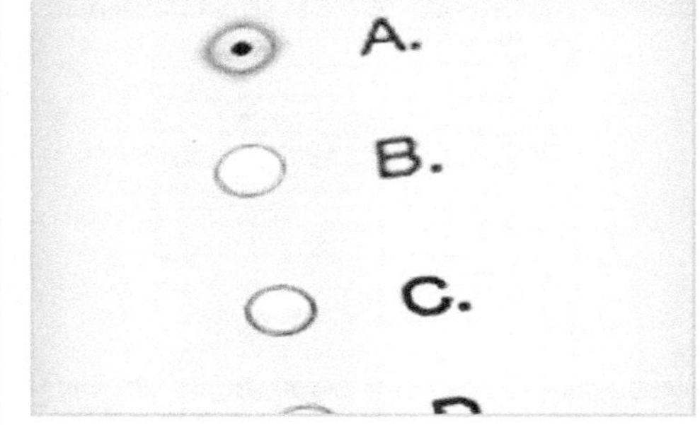

Assign the online Lesson Quiz for this lesson if you haven't already done so. Students will be offered automatic remediation or enrichment based on their score.

Pose these questions to the class on the Discussion Board:

Summarize What were the effects of the conflicts and compromises in this lesson? *(The effects of these conflicts and compromises were mixed. Tariffs and the threat of nullification divided the nation, but a compromise over the tariff resolved the issue, even though tensions remained. The Bank War, however, did not end with a compromise, which had negative effects on the nation.)*

Generate Explanations How are issues of states' rights versus federal rights still apparent today? *(Americans continue to weigh whether the federal government has the right to assert laws and enact programs that some people feel should be handled at the state level.)*

Topic Inquiry

Have students continue their investigations for the Topic Inquiry.

Native Americans on the Frontier

Supporting English Language Learners

Use with Digital Text 2, **Indian Removal.**

Listening

Familiarize students with the text's topic by reviewing or summarizing its content. Prompt students to understand the main points of spoken language ranging from situations in which topics are familiar to those in which they are unfamiliar.

Beginning Use basic spoken language to paraphrase the content of the introductory paragraph. Help students to understand your main points by having them answer these questions: What did the government want Native Americans to do? Did Native Americans sell their land?

Intermediate Use spoken language to paraphrase the content of the introductory paragraph. Have students demonstrate their understanding of what you said by stating three of your main points.

Advanced Use spoken language to give additional details about the case *Cherokee Nation* v. *Georgia* (1831), which should be a somewhat familiar topic because it is briefly mentioned in the text. Have pairs of students demonstrate their understanding of what you said by listing your main points.

Advanced High Use spoken language to tell about one of the groups affected by the Indian Removal Act (e.g., Ottawa or Potawatomi). Provide information about their way of life, both past and present. Have pairs of students demonstrate their understanding of what you said by discussing your main points.

Use with Digital Text 3, **Southern Native Americans on the Trail of Tears.**

Reading

Introduce the text by reading its title and subheadings and by predicting its content. Explain that you will be using a shared reading strategy to read part of the text together. Prompt students to demonstrate comprehension of increasingly complex English as they participate in the shared reading.

Beginning After you read aloud the introductory paragraph once, highlight words familiar to students. Then invite them to participate in a second reading of the paragraph by reading the highlighted words they encountered. Ask: Why did Native American leaders feel forced to sign new treaties?

Intermediate After you read aloud the section titled *The Chickasaw* once, invite students to participate in a second reading by saying the final clause or phrase of each sentence. Ask: Did the U.S. government pay the Chickasaw for their land? When?

Advanced After you read aloud the section titled *The Cherokee* once, invite students to participate in a second reading with you by reading every other sentence. During and after the reading, ask questions so students can demonstrate their comprehension.

Advanced High After you read aloud the section titled *The Cherokee* once, invite students to participate in a second reading by reading the entire section with you. During and after the reading, ask challenging questions so students can demonstrate their comprehension.

D Differentiate Instruction

Use the Differentiated Instruction notes throughout the lesson plan to support the varied skill sets, levels of readiness, and interests in the mixed-ability classroom.

Challenge These notes include suggestions for expanding the activity for advanced students.

On-Level These notes include suggestions for modifying the activity to address different interests or learning styles.

Extra Support These notes include ideas for providing more scaffolding or reading spuport.

Special Needs These notes provide ideas for adapting instruction to support the needs of various special needs students.

NOTES

Native Americans on the Frontier

Objectives

Objective 1: Describe the cultures of Native Americans between the Appalachians and Mississippi.

Objective 2: Explain the conflict over land occupied by Native Americans between the Appalachians and Mississippi.

Objective 3: Discuss the forced removal of Native Americans.

LESSON 3 ORGANIZER	PACING: APPROX. 1 PERIOD, .5 BLOCKS		RESOURCES	
	OBJECTIVES	PACING	Online	Print
Connect				
DIGITAL START UP ACTIVITY **Black Hawk and the Removal of His People**		5 min.	●	
Investigate				
DIGITAL TEXT 1 **Native Americans on the Frontier**	Objectives 1, 2	10 min.	●	●
INTERACTIVE MAP **Selected Native American Groups, 1820**	Objectives 1, 2	10 min.	●	
DIGITAL TEXT 2 **Indian Removal**	Objectives 2, 3	10 min.	●	●
DIGITAL TEXT 3 **Southern Native Americans on the Trail of Tears**	Objective 3	10 min.	●	●
INTERACTIVE MAP **The Trail of Tears**	Objective 3	10 min.	●	
Synthesize				
DIGITAL ACTIVITY **Why Did Native Americans Move?**		5 min.	●	
Demonstrate				
DIGITAL QUIZ **Lesson Quiz and Class Discussion Board**		10 min.	●	

PEARSON realize™
www.PearsonRealize.com

Go online to access additional resources including: Primary Sources • Biographies • Supreme Court cases • 21st Century Skill Tutorials • Maps • Graphic Organizers.

CONNECT

DIGITAL START UP ACTIVITY

Black Hawk and the Removal of His People

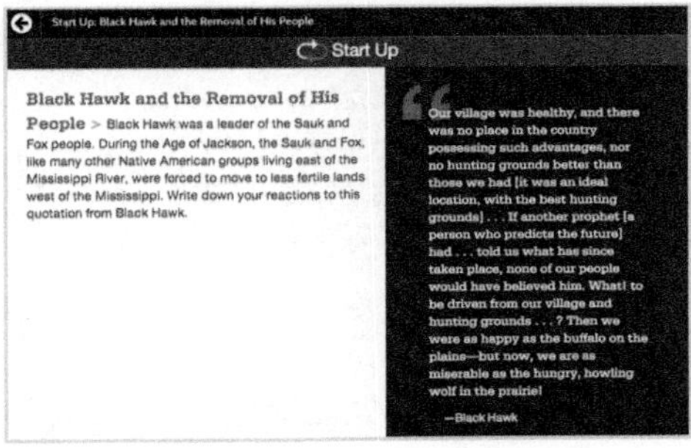

Project the Start Up Activity Ask students to read the excerpt from Black Hawk's autobiography and answer the questions as they enter and get settled.

Discuss How does Black Hawk feel about his people's movement to a new home? Cite evidence from the text. *(He feels shocked—"none of our people would have believed him"—and unhappy—"miserable as the hungry, howling wolf.")* What effects might this kind of move have had on a Native American tribe and its social development, that is, on its life as a tribe? *(The tribe might have lost faith in its traditional culture and might have had to adapt to living as a minority group in a larger nation.)*

Aa Vocabulary Development: Use the Interactive Reading Notepad to preview the Key Terms and Academic Vocabulary in this lesson with students.

FLIP IT!

Assign the Flipped Video for this lesson.

STUDENT EDITION PRINT PAGES: 323–330

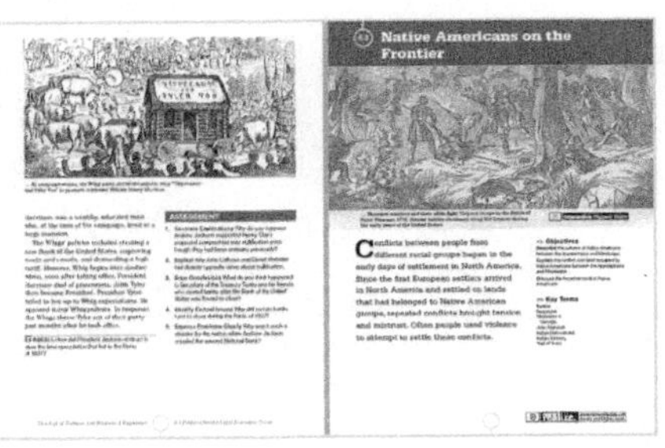

INVESTIGATE

DIGITAL TEXT 1

Native Americans on the Frontier

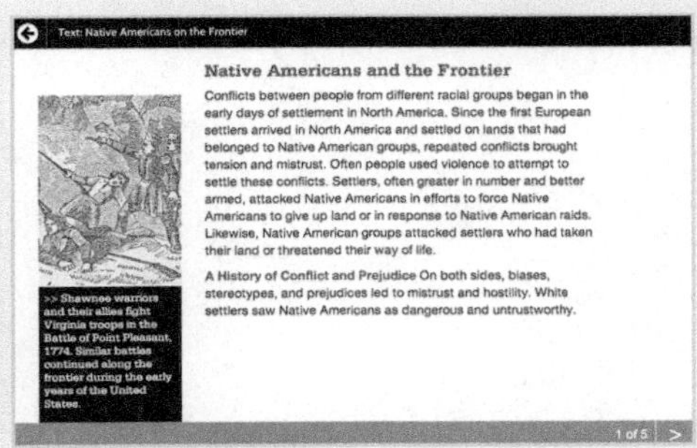

Text: Native Americans on the Frontier
Native Americans and the Frontier
Conflicts between people from different racial groups began in the early days of settlement in North America. Since the first European settlers arrived in North America and settled on lands that had belonged to Native American groups, repeated conflicts brought tension and mistrust. Often people used violence to attempt to settle these conflicts. Settlers, often greater in number and better armed, attacked Native Americans in efforts to force Native Americans to give up land or in response to Native American raids. Likewise, Native American groups attacked settlers who had taken their land or threatened their way of life.
A History of Conflict and Prejudice On both sides, biases, stereotypes, and prejudices led to mistrust and hostility. White settlers saw Native Americans as dangerous and untrustworthy.
>> Shawnee warriors and their allies fight Virginia troops in the Battle of Point Pleasant, 1774. Similar battles continued along the frontier during the early years of the United States.
1 of 5

INTERACTIVE MAP

Selected Native American Groups, 1820

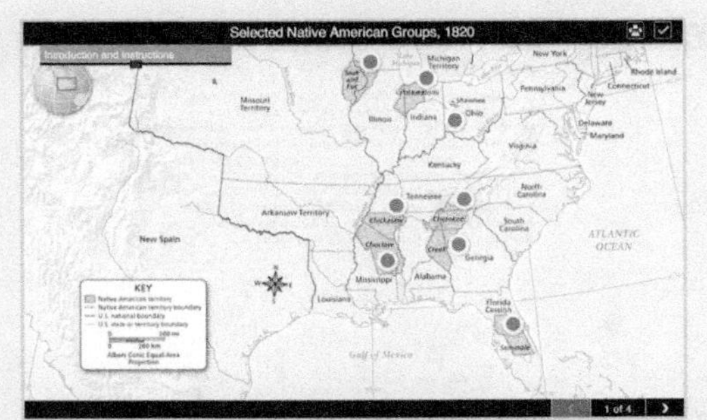

Objectives 1: Describe the culture of Native Americans in the Southeast; 2: Explain the conflict over land occupied by Native Americans in the Southeast.

Quick Instruction

There was a long history of hostility between Native Americans on the frontier and white settlers who wanted Native Americans' land. During the Revolutionary War and the War of 1812, many Native Americans sided with the British. Later, tribes tried to win favor from the United States. None of these strategies ended the conflict with white settlers.

Interactive Map: Selected Native American Groups, 1820 Project the interactive map. Explain that the map shows Native American groups living on the frontier east of the Mississippi River in the early 1800s. Select the hot spots on the map to learn more about each of the Native American groups shown. Considering the locations of these groups.What do you think might happen as white settlers move into the areas around them? *(They would be forced, one by one, to give up their land to settlers.)*

ACTIVE CLASSROOM

Have students complete a Graffiti Concepts activity. Ask students to reflect on the similarities and differences between the Native American groups shown on the interactive map. Have them create a visual image or set of phrases that represents those similarities and differences.

Ask students to post their "graffiti" on the board or on chart paper and them to look at all the various responses.Then, discuss similarities and differences in the responses as a group.

D Differentiate: Extra Support Ask students why relations on the frontier were tense between Native Americans and whites. Have them cite examples from the text to support their answer.

Further Instruction

Cite Evidence Did Native American groups present a national security threat—or a threat to the safety of the nation—to the leaders of the newly formed United States? Cite evidence from the reading. *(Some groups presented a national security threat because they sided with the British during the Revolutionary War and the War of 1812.)*

Identify Cause and Effect Why did some Native Americans side with the British? *(They feared that, unless they sought British help, white American settlers would take their land.)*

Native Americans on the Frontier

DIGITAL TEXT 2

Indian Removal

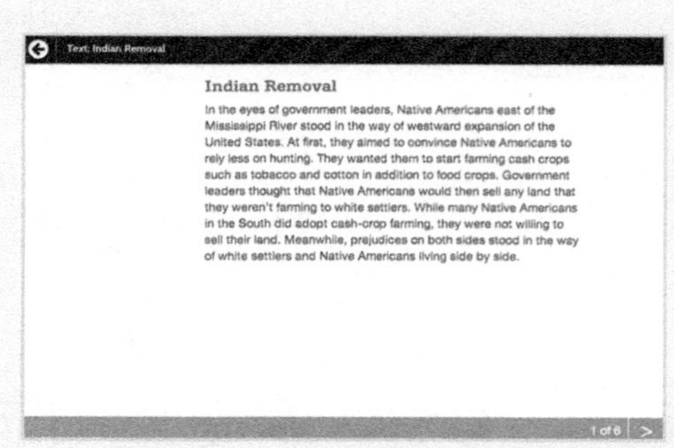

Text: Indian Removal
Indian Removal
In the eyes of government leaders, Native Americans east of the Mississippi River stood in the way of westward expansion of the United States. At first, they aimed to convince Native Americans to rely less on hunting. They wanted them to start farming cash crops such as tobacco and cotton in addition to food crops. Government leaders thought that Native Americans would then sell any land that they weren't farming to white settlers. While many Native Americans in the South did adopt cash-crop farming, they were not willing to sell their land. Meanwhile, prejudices on both sides stood in the way of white settlers and Native Americans living side by side.
1 of 6

Objectives 2: **Explain the conflict over land occupied by Native Americans in the Southeast; 3: Discuss the forced removal of Native Americans.**

Quick Instruction

In the years leading up to the Jackson era, more and more white settlers moved across the Appalachians into the Old Northwest (Ohio, Michigan, Indiana, Illinois, Wisconsin, Minnesota, and Iowa) and the Old Southwest (Alabama, Mississippi, Tennessee, Kentucky, Missouri, Arkansas, and Louisiana). The westward movement of these settlers increased tensions with Native Americans living in the area. Many settlers wanted the Native Americans' land. Meanwhile, the U.S. Supreme Court's *Worcester* v. *Georgia* decision made it illegal for states to take Native American land on their own. Andrew Jackson's government came up with a federal plan to move the Native Americans out of settlers' way.

Identify Cause and Effect How did the *Worcester* v. *Georgia* decision and the Indian Removal Act lead to the removal and resettlement of Native American groups such as the Cherokee from their homelands? *(The* Worcester v. Georgia *decision made it more difficult for states to clear Native American land for white settlement and made Indian removal a federal issue. However, since President Jackson ignored the ruling, the Cherokee lost any protection it provided. The Indian Removal Act provided the federal government with a legal framework for removing Native Americans from their lands and resettling them on lands west of the Mississippi River.)*

Contrast How do you see President Jackson's views on states' right differ between his response to the *Worcester* v. *Georgia* decision and his stance during the Nullification Crisis? *(President Jackson supported states' rights in the* Worcester v. Georgia *decision, but he supported the idea of a stronger federal government during the Nullification Crisis.)*

ELL Use the ELL activity described in the ELL chart.

Further Instruction

Summarize What effect did the Indian Removal Act have on the human geography of contemporary times? *(Many Native American tribes, including the Choctaw, Chickasaw, Cherokee, and Seminole, were forced to move west of the Mississippi. Therefore, in modern times few Native Americans live east of the Mississippi River.)*

Make Predictions Would the Indian Removal Act resolve conflicts between people from different racial groups in the early United States? *(Yes, offering new homelands to Native Americans so that they would leave the land desired by white settlers would resolve the conflict. No, Native Americans did not want to leave their homelands.)*

DIGITAL TEXT 3

Southern Native Americans on the Trail of Tears

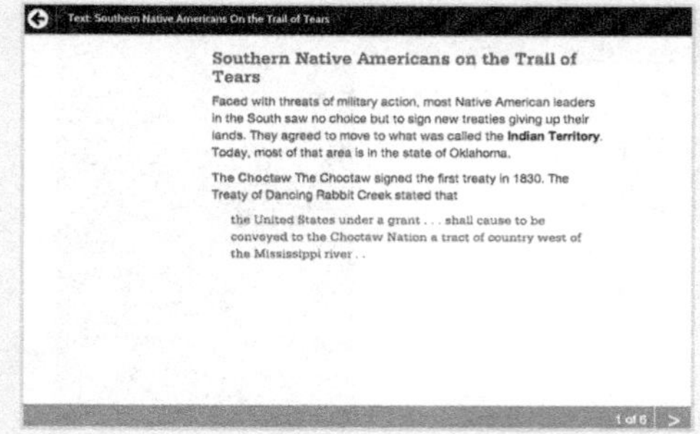

Objective 3: **Discuss the forced removal of Native Americans.**

Quick Instruction

The Trail of Tears was a series of forced migrations during the Age of Jackson. Faced with threats of U.S. military action, the Cherokee and other Native American groups in the present-day Southeast moved to lands west of the Mississippi. Their movement is known as the Trail of Tears because of the suffering they faced during their journeys.

Interactive Map: The Trail of Tears Project the interactive map. Explain that each map shows a different aspect of the Trail of Tears, including the original homelands of each Native American group affected, the routes they took to their new territories, and those new territories. Select the different maps to explore the Trail of Tears in detail.

INTERACTIVE MAP

The Trail of Tears

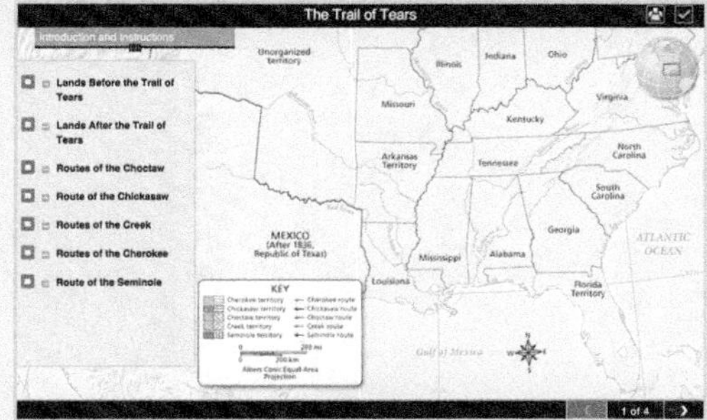

ACTIVE CLASSROOM

Use a Circle Write activity. Break students into small groups and ask them to consider this question:

At the end of the Trail of Tears, southern Native American groups were settled in a region later called Indian Territory and now part of Oklahoma. Based on what you've learned, why do you think that this region was chosen for them? *(This was an area where white settlers did not yet want to live. The land in the Indian Territory may not have been as good for farming.)*

Have students write as much as they can for 1 minute then switch with the person on their right. The next person tries to improve or elaborate the response where the other person left off. Continue to switch until the paper comes back to the first person. The group then decides which is the best response and shares that with the larger group.

ELL Use the ELL activity described in the ELL chart.

Further Instruction

Identify Cause and Effect What were the reasons for the removal and resettlement of the Cherokee in the march which became known as the Trail of Tears? *(The Cherokee resisted resettlement. In 1838, President Martin Van Buren forced the Cherokee, who had not made agreements with North Carolina, to move. The United States Army forced more than 15,000 Cherokee to march westward. In the winter of 1838–39, they went to Indian Territory, patrolled by 7,000 soldiers. The Cherokee trekked hundreds of miles over a period of several months. Thousands perished during the march that became known as the Trail of Tears.)*

Infer What does the history of the Trail of Tears indicate about the resolution of conflict between whites and Native Americans during the Jackson era? *(The conflict between whites and some Native American tribes was temporarily resolved, though not to the Native American's advantage.)*

Native Americans on the Frontier

SYNTHESIZE

DIGITAL ACTIVITY

Why Did Native Americans Move?

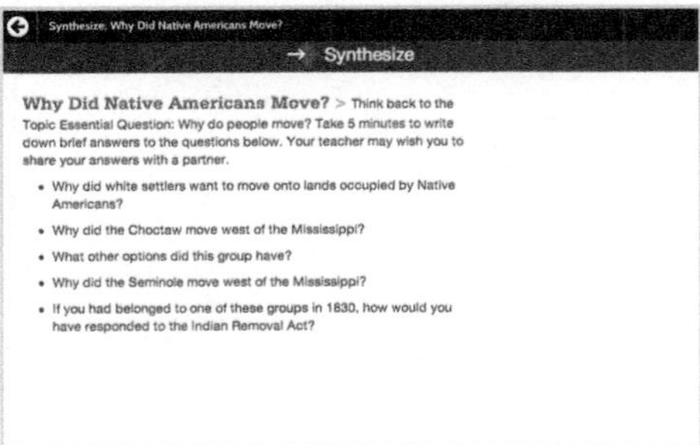

Ask students to think about each of the questions about the reasons why Native Americans moved during the Jackson era.

Discuss Why did the Cherokee move? *(The United States military rounded them up and forced them to move.)* How have these questions changed your thinking about the Topic Essential Question: Why do people move? *(Answers should show an awareness that migration can be voluntary or involuntary. Some students may not have previously considered forced migration such as how it occurred with the Indian Removal Act.)*

DEMONSTRATE

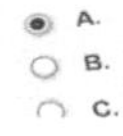

DIGITAL QUIZ

Lesson Quiz and Class Discussion Board

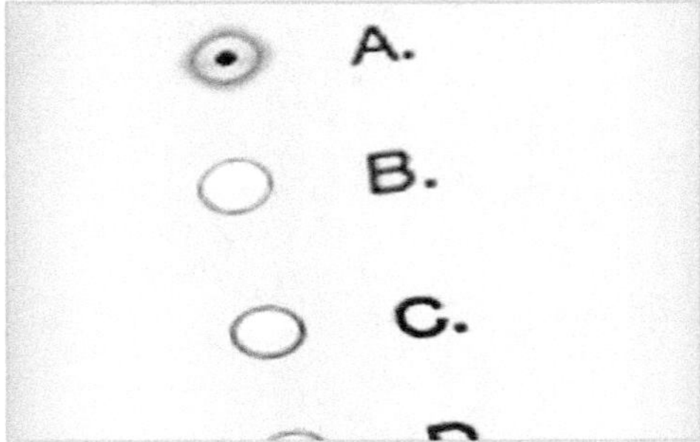

Assign the online Lesson Quiz for this lesson if you haven't already done so. Students will be offered automatic remediation or enrichment based on their score.

Pose these questions to the class on the Discussion Board:

In *Native Americans on the Frontier*, you read about the conflicts between white settlers and Native Americans, which eventually led to the forced removal of Native Americans west of the Mississippi River.

Draw Conclusions How did the relationship between Native Americans and the United States government change during the Jackson era?

Identify Patterns By the 1850s, most members of every major group of Southeastern Native Americans had been relocated to new lands in the Indian Territory west of the Mississippi. Think about the ongoing westward movement of settlers. What do you think would happen at a later date to the Native Americans in Indian Territory?

Topic Inquiry

Have students continue their investigations for the Topic Inquiry.

Westward Movement

Supporting English Language Learners

Use with Digital Text 1, **Heading Into the West.**

Listening

Read aloud the first two paragraphs of the reading *Heading Into the West* or invite a volunteer to read the passage aloud. Then prompt students to understand the main points of spoken language by completing the following tasks:

Beginning Have students work in pairs to the complete the following sentence: Settlers traveled west because they wanted _____.

Intermediate Ask students to orally name some places from which travelers often came. Then ask them to orally name some places travelers often settled. Model correct pronunciation of unfamiliar place names for students as needed.

Advanced Organize students into small groups. Have them take turns orally summarizing the passage. Direct students to restate one main point from the speaker's summary to show their understanding.

Advanced High Have students write a sentence or two that restates the main idea of the first paragraph in their own words. Then direct them to write a few sentences explaining how the details given in the second paragraph support the main idea of the first paragraph.

Use with Digital Text 4, **Canals Connect the Country.**

Reading

Have students read silently the information under the heading *An Instant Success*. After students complete the reading, use the following activities to demonstrate their comprehension of increasingly complex English by retelling or summarizing material.

Beginning Draw a Main Idea and Details graphic organizer on the board. Add the details "lowered costs of shipping," "made New York City more important," and "encouraged more canal building" to the details boxes. Then have students reread the passage and provide a main idea to summarize the details by completing the sentence starter: The Erie Canal _____.

Intermediate Have students work in small groups. Tell students to take turns rereading each sentence of the passage silently and then retelling its meaning aloud. Then direct groups to work together to write three sentences summarizing the entire passage.

Advanced Have students reread the passage and write a few sentences to summarize the effects of the opening of the Erie Canal. Have some students volunteer to retell how the canal affected both people in the West and in New York City.

Advanced High Have students reread the passage and write a short paragraph retelling the effects of the Erie Canal from the perspective of a person who shipped goods from Buffalo to New York City. The paragraph should tell how the opening of the canal changed the speed and cost of sending goods.

D Differentiate Instruction

Use the Differentiated Instruction notes throughout the lesson plan to support the varied skill sets, levels of readiness, and interests in the mixed-ability classroom.

Challenge These notes include suggestions for expanding the activity for advanced students.

On-Level These notes include suggestions for modifying the activity to address different interests or learning styles.

Extra Support These notes include ideas for providing more scaffolding or reading spupport.

Special Needs These notes provide ideas for adapting instruction to support the needs of various special needs students.

NOTES

Westward Movement

Objectives

Objective 1: Describe how settlers traveled west.

Objective 2: List the steps Americans took to improve their roads.

Objective 3: Explain how steamboats and canals improved transportation for Americans.

LESSON 4 ORGANIZER		PACING: APPROX. 1 PERIOD, .5 BLOCKS	RESOURCES	
	OBJECTIVES	PACING	Online	Print
Connect				
DIGITAL START UP ACTIVITY **Heading Into the West**		5 min.	●	
Investigate				
DIGITAL TEXT 1 **Heading Into the West**	Objective 1	10 min.	●	●
DIGITAL TEXT 2 **Building Better Roads**	Objective 2	10 min.	●	●
INTERACTIVE GALLERY **New Transportation Methods**		10 min.	●	
DIGITAL TEXT 3 **The Age of Steam**	Objective 3	10 min.	●	●
DIGITAL TEXT 4 **Canals Connect the Country**		10 min.	●	●
INTERACTIVE MAP **The Erie Canal**		10 min.	●	
Synthesize				
DIGITAL ACTIVITY **What Route to Take**		5 min.	●	
Demonstrate				
DIGITAL QUIZ **Lesson Quiz and Class Discussion Board**		10 min.	●	

CONNECT

DIGITAL START UP ACTIVITY

Heading Into the West

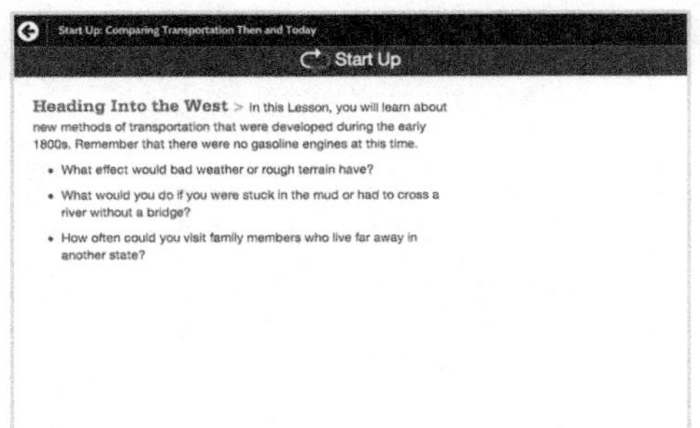

Project the Start-Up Activity as students get settled. Have students brainstorm the types of transportation available in the 1800s and how different their lives would be without modern transportation. Then have students partner to answer one of the Connect questions. Have them share with the class or on the Class Discussion Board.

Express Problems Clearly Ask students what impact transportation in the 1800s would have on the question they selected to answer. How would it affect their day-to-day lives? *(Travel would be difficult and slow, and simple tasks would take longer.)*

Infer If the main form of transportation is a horse-drawn wagon, what would solve the problem of bad terrain? *(Developing a way to build roads through or bridges over these obstacles.)*

Aa Vocabulary Development: Use the Interactive Reading Notepad to preview the Key Terms and Academic Vocabulary in this lesson with students.

FLIP IT!

Assign the Flipped Video for this lesson.

STUDENT EDITION PRINT PAGES: 331–336

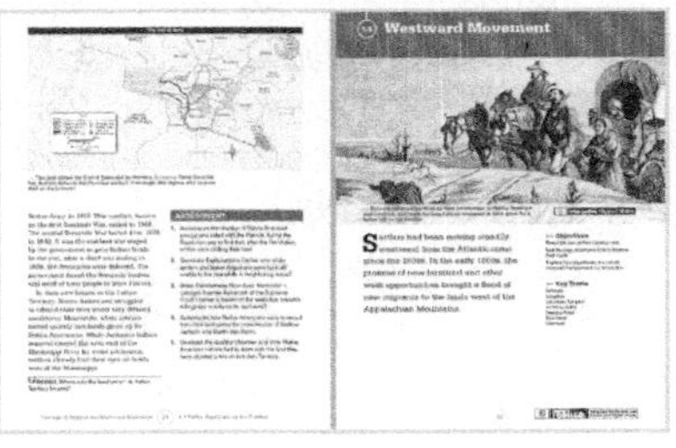

INVESTIGATE

DIGITAL TEXT 1

Heading Into the West

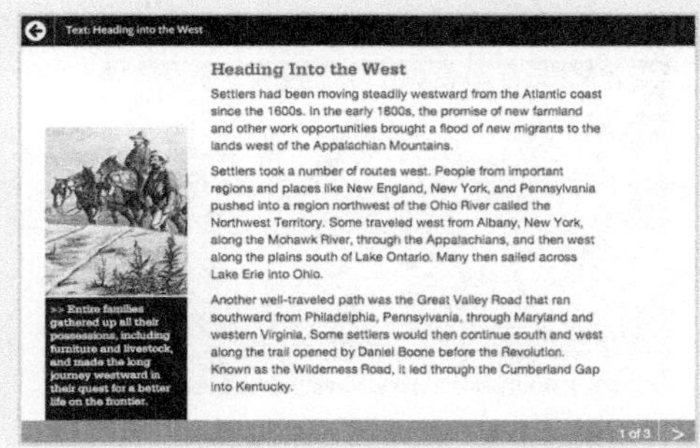

Objective 1: Describe how settlers traveled west.

Quick Instruction

While people had been exploring the land west of the original colonies for almost two centuries, the number of people looking to settle that land greatly increased in the early 1800s. The difficulties involved in large numbers of people traveling through this wild terrain created a need for new technologies and methods of transportation.

Generate Explanations Project the *New States, 1792–1819* map. Ask students to reflect on some reasons why the states formed in the order they did. Give students an appropriate amount of time to formulate a response. Ask students to pair up or turn to an assigned partner. Have them discuss their responses. *(Settlers came at different times and from different directions. They explored and settled in more easily accessible land first. Populations weren't large enough to apply for statehood.)*

D Differentiate: On-Level The title of this reading is *Heading Into the West*. Ask students to locate where the West was in the United States of the early 1800s. *(The West was the areas just slightly west and southwest of the original colonies.)* Are these areas what we consider the West today? *(No, they are areas that now make up the regions we call the Midwest and the South.)*

ELL Use the ELL activity described in the ELL chart.

Further Instruction

Project and discuss the Interactive Reading Notepad graphic organizer about the major routes available to settlers. Review the routes with the class and fill in the graphic organizer on the whiteboard as you go. Discuss whether these major routes were the only ways possible for people to travel at the time.

Draw Conclusions What do you think caused Americans to move westward? *(The availability of land in the West, overcrowded towns and cities in the East, desire to start anew, zest for adventure)*

Westward Movement

DIGITAL TEXT 2

Building Better Roads

Text: Building Better Roads

Building Better Roads

Settlers faced difficult journeys as they traveled to the West. Many roads were narrow dirt trails, barely wide enough for a single wagon. Trails often plunged through muddy swamps. Tree stumps stuck up in the road and often broke the wagon axles of careless travelers. The nation badly needed better roads.

Paying Tolls In the United States, as in Europe, private companies built gravel and stone roads. To pay for these roads, the companies collected tolls from travelers. At various points along the road, a pike, or pole, blocked the road. After a wagon driver had paid a toll, the pike keeper turned the pole aside to let the wagon pass. As a result, these toll roads were called **turnpikes**.

Probably the best road in the United States was the **Lancaster Turnpike**. Built in the 1790s by a private company, the road linked Philadelphia and Lancaster, Pennsylvania.

1 of 3

INTERACTIVE GALLERY

New Transportation Methods

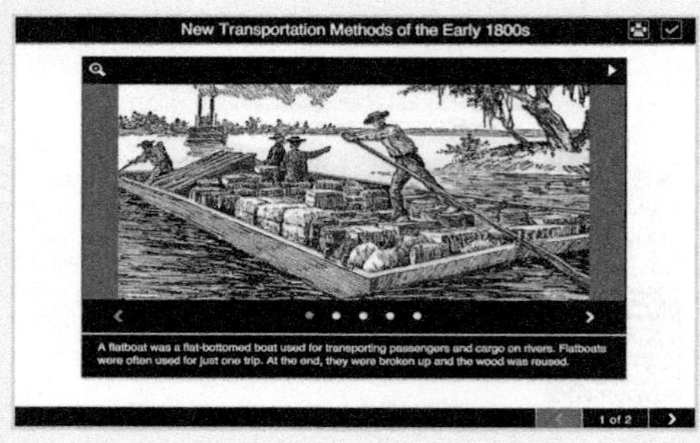

New Transportation Methods of the Early 1800s
A flatboat was a flat-bottomed boat used for transporting passengers and cargo on rivers. Flatboats were often used for just one trip. At the end, they were broken up and the wood was reused.
1 of 2

DIGITIAL TEXT 3

The Age of Steam

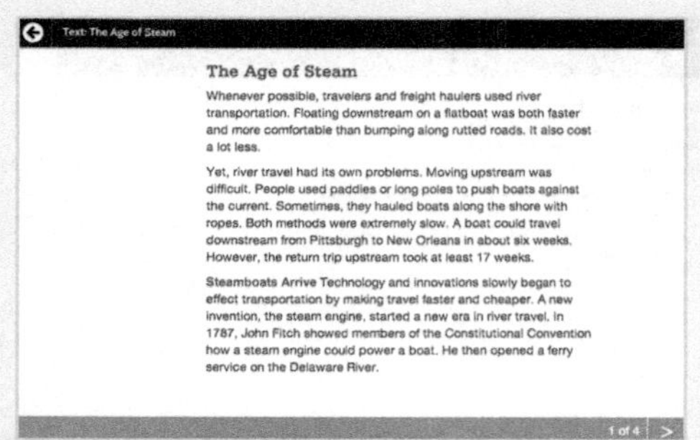

Text: The Age of Steam

The Age of Steam

Whenever possible, travelers and freight haulers used river transportation. Floating downstream on a flatboat was both faster and more comfortable than bumping along rutted roads. It also cost a lot less.

Yet, river travel had its own problems. Moving upstream was difficult. People used paddles or long poles to push boats against the current. Sometimes, they hauled boats along the shore with ropes. Both methods were extremely slow. A boat could travel downstream from Pittsburgh to New Orleans in about six weeks. However, the return trip upstream took at least 17 weeks.

Steamboats Arrive Technology and innovations slowly began to effect transportation by making travel faster and cheaper. A new invention, the steam engine, started a new era in river travel. In 1787, John Fitch showed members of the Constitutional Convention how a steam engine could power a boat. He then opened a ferry service on the Delaware River.

1 of 4

Objective 2: **List the steps Americans took to improve their roads.**

Quick Instruction

Interactive Gallery: New Transportation Methods Project the interactive gallery. Click through each image and ask for student volunteers to read the caption aloud. Ask students to explain the specific problems that each of these transportation methods were designed to address. *(Flatboats could be used in shallow rivers. Gravel roads were smoother and less muddy than dirt roads. Corduroy roads allowed easier travel over marshes and swampy ground. Turnpikes collected money that paid for building the roads.)*

Predict Consequences How did technological innovations, such as improved roads,affect western migration? *(Better roads meant faster and easier travel, so more people and goods could be moved.)*

ACTIVE CLASSROOM

Use the See-Think-Wonder Strategy to have pairs of students analyze the images in the gallery and share their insights with the class.

D Differentiate: Challenge How were the construction and upkeep of state and federal roads funded? *(Through state and federal taxes)* Did building the National Road in western states, such as Illinois, have a positive consequence for a taxpayer in New England? *(Yes, because products made or grown in Illinois could be transported to New England more easily and less expensively.)*

Further Instruction

Infer One thing we take for granted today is paved roads. If drivers and their passengers get annoyed when they drive through a pothole today, think about what it must have been like to travel on unpaved roads everywhere you went. Ask students to think about the types of dangers travelers would have faced when traveling on roads in the early 1800s. *(Travelers faced mud, ruts, uneven paths, dangerous slopes, vegetation, and lack of markings.)*

Support Ideas with Evidence Did building a toll road have positive consequences for both the private owner and the traveler? Explain your reasoning. *(Yes, the owner would benefit because the cost of the road and its upkeep would eventually be surpassed by the income received in tolls. The traveler would benefit because the time saved and the ease of travel would be worth the expense of the toll.)*

Objective 3: **Explain how steamboats and canals improved transportation for Americans.**

Quick Instruction

The United States has a vast network of rivers and other bodies of water that connect cities and regions. They are extremely useful for getting people and goods from one place to another. Like the nineteenth century system of roads, however, travel along rivers was slow and dangerous—that is, until the advent of the steam engine.

Interactive Map: The Erie Canal Project the interactive map and click through the hotspots. Review the lock system so that students understand how it worked and how important the locks were to the success of a canal. Explicitly describe the Erie Canal as a positive consequence of human modification of the physical environment. Prompt students to analyze its impact on the growth and development of the United States. *(Expanding trade networks, access to new markets, growth of towns and cities)*

Analyze Information Ask students to explain the consequences of technological innovations, such as the steamboat. *(Steamboats made travel along rivers faster. This gave merchants and farmers a cheap way to move their goods and revolutionized travel in the West. The stump-puller helped speed the digging of the Erie Canal.)*

www.PearsonRealize.com
Access your Digital Lesson

DIGITAL TEXT 4

Canals Connect the Country

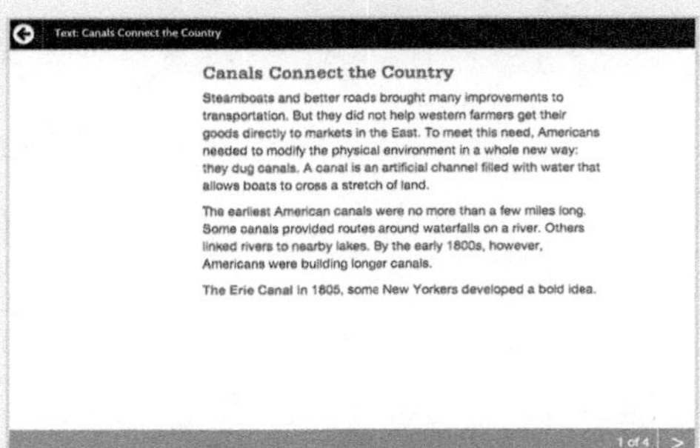

Summarize What impact did transportation systems such as the Erie Canal have on the growth and development of the United States? *(The Erie Canal significantly decreased the cost of shipping and encouraged the continued economic growth and development of New York City.)*

ACTIVE CLASSROOM

Using the Sequence It Strategy, ask students to recreate the steps in the locks system described in the first hotspot of the interactive map. Encourage small groups to act out the sequence and to use hand or body motions to indicate the rising and lowering water at different stages in the process.

ELL Use the ELL activity described in the ELL chart.

Further Instruction

Draw Conclusions Why do you think Fulton's steamboat company succeeded when Fitch's did not? *(Because of Americans' interest in moving around the country, the timing of Fulton's steamboat may have been more advantageous.)*

INTERACTIVE MAP

The Erie Canal

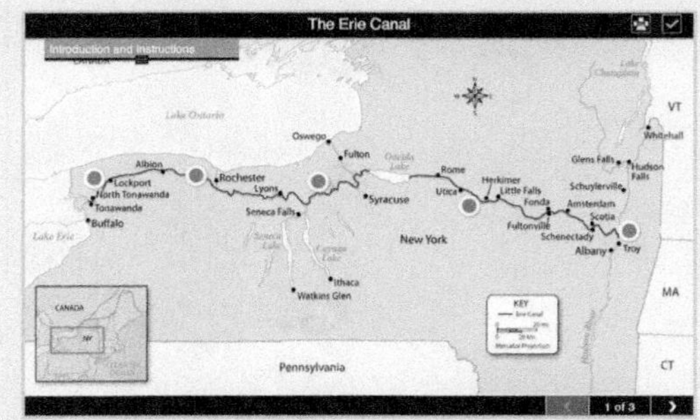

Support a Point of View With Evidence Do you agree with Thomas Jefferson's belief that building the Erie Canal was "little short of madness" for the time? Why or why not? *(Considering the lack of technology and the amount of back-breaking labor building the canal would take, I agree with Jefferson that the building of the canal was something unimaginable for the time.)*

Westward Movement

SYNTHESIZE

DIGITAL ACTIVITY

What Route to Take

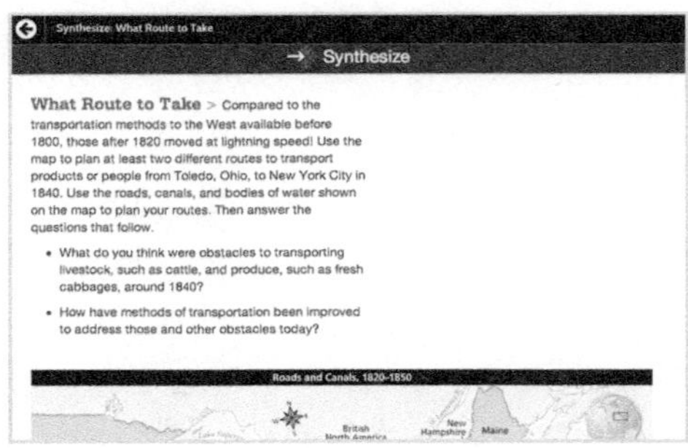

Synthesize: What Route to Take
→ Synthesize
What Route to Take > Compared to the transportation methods to the West available before 1800, those after 1820 moved at lightning speed! Use the map to plan at least two different routes to transport products or people from Toledo, Ohio, to New York City in 1840. Use the roads, canals, and bodies of water shown on the map to plan your routes. Then answer the questions that follow.
• What do you think were obstacles to transporting livestock, such as cattle, and produce, such as fresh cabbages, around 1840?
• How have methods of transportation been improved to address those and other obstacles today?
Roads and Canals, 1820–1850

Tell students that by the mid-1800s Americans had a variety of routes to transport goods and people. For many, choosing a route depended on what was being transported. Project the What Route to Take activity and have students work in pairs to determine which route they think would be the best to use for the different items. Then ask the following questions:

Draw Conclusions What do you think were obstacles in transporting livestock and produce in the 1800s? *(Some possible obstacles included the cost and storage of feed for livestock, keeping livestock alive during a long trip, keeping livestock safe from injury, keeping produce fresh enough to sell at the final destination, and keeping vermin away from produce.)*

Support Ideas With Examples How have methods of transportation been improved to address those and other obstacles today? *(Today, we have faster methods of transportation to reduce feed costs, boxcar and trucks designed for livestock's comfort and safety, refrigeration methods to keep produce fresh, and sanitation methods to prevent infestation.)*

DEMONSTRATE

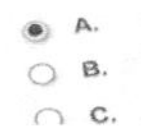

DIGITAL QUIZ

Lesson Quiz and Class Discussion Board

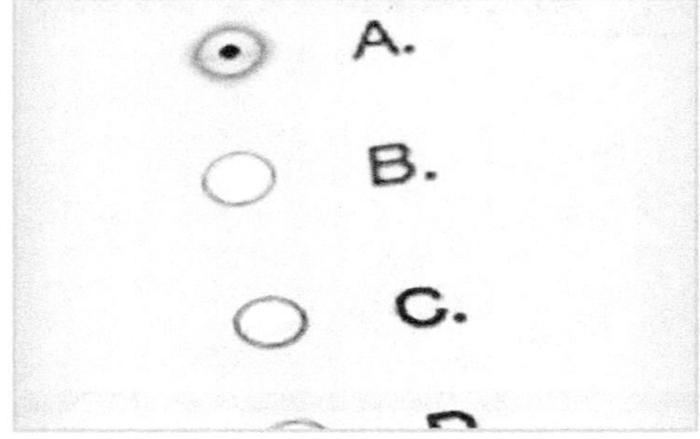

Assign the online Lesson Quiz for this lesson if you haven't already done so. Students will be offered automatic remediation or enrichment based on their score.

Pose these questions to the class on the Discussion Board:

You read about a variety of new transportation methods that developed to allow faster and more efficient movement around the United States. Although trade was one of the driving forces behind these innovations, another was the desire of many Americans to move westward.

Make Predictions What new method of transportation do you think will be developed in a later period that will be the most influential in the American quest to move even farther westward? *(The railroad)*

Draw Conclusions How will westward migration affect the growth and development of the United States? *(Americans and immigrants from around the globe will take advantage of new opportunities and will settle in areas on the frontier. The nation will grow in population and size as territories are absorbed into the United States.)*

Topic Inquiry

Have students continue their investigations for the Topic Inquiry.

PEARSON realize www.PearsonRealize.com Access your Digital Lesson

Settling Oregon Country

Supporting English Language Learners

Use with Digital Text 2, **The Far West Fur Trade.**

Reading

Explain to students that they will demonstrate reading comprehension by reading from the text and referring back to it in order to respond to questions.

Beginning Have students read the first three paragraphs of the text silently. Then read aloud the passage while students follow along. After each paragraph, have students respond to one of these questions: Who traveled to Oregon to buy furs? Who caught animals for their fur? What is one interesting detail about a mountain man's appearance?

Intermediate Ask for volunteers to read aloud the first three paragraphs of the text. Then have students respond to these questions: What route might a fur trader take after leaving New England? What did a mountain man look like?

Advanced Have pairs of students read the section titled *The Fur Trade*. Then have them respond to these questions: What two main things happened at a rendezvous? What are two reasons why the fur trade died out?

Advanced High Ask students to independently read the section titled *The Fur Trade*. Have them respond to these questions on paper: What happened at a rendezvous? Why did the fur trade die out? What did some mountain men do after that? Provide time for students to discuss their answers with a partner.

Use with Digital Text 3, **The Oregon Trail**

Listening

Prompt students to understand the main points of spoken language by rereading or reviewing the text in order to gain more familiarity with it.

Beginning Use basic spoken language to describe typical daily events in a wagon train. Have students demonstrate their understanding of what you said by restating your main points. Ask: What did people do in the morning? At noon? In the evening?

Intermediate Use spoken language to describe (with some detail) the typical daily events in a wagon train. Have students demonstrate their understanding of what you said by restating your main points.

Advanced Use spoken language to describe the costs and benefits of traveling on the Oregon Trail, using details from both the text and other sources. Have students demonstrate their understanding of what you said by restating your main points.

Advanced High Use spoken language to describe the Oregon Trail in the context of its current use as a National Historic Trail. Provide details about things that visitors can do and see along the trail. Then have students demonstrate their understanding of what you said by restating your main points.

D Differentiate Instruction

Use the Differentiated Instruction notes throughout the lesson plan to support the varied skill sets, levels of readiness, and interests in the mixed-ability classroom.

Challenge These notes include suggestions for expanding the activity for advanced students.

On-Level These notes include suggestions for modifying the activity to address different interests or learning styles.

Extra Support These notes include ideas for providing more scaffolding or reading spuport.

Special Needs These notes provide ideas for adapting instruction to support the needs of various special needs students.

NOTES

Topic 6 Lesson 5

Settling Oregon Country

Objectives

Objective 1: Explain the appeal of Oregon and the Far West.

Objective 2: Summarize how mountain men helped explore the Far West.

Objective 3: Describe the role missionaries played in Oregon.

Objective 4: Identify the hardships faced on wagon trains to the West.

LESSON 5 ORGANIZER	PACING: APPROX. 1 PERIOD, .5 BLOCKS		RESOURCES	
	OBJECTIVES	PACING	Online	Print
Connect				
DIGITAL START UP ACTIVITY **Who Is a Pioneer?**		5 min.	●	
Investigate				
DIGITAL TEXT 1 **In Search of New Territory**	Objective 1	10 min.	●	●
INTERACTIVE GALLERY **Oregon Country**		10 min.	●	
DIGITAL TEXT 2 **The Far West Fur Trade**	Objective 2	10 min.	●	●
DIGITAL TEXT 3 **The Oregon Trail**	Objectives 3, 4	10 min.	●	●
INTERACTIVE MAP **The Oregon Trail**		10 min.	●	
3-D MODEL **The Covered Wagon**		10 min.	●	
Synthesize				
DIGITAL ACTIVITY **Pioneering Success**		5 min.	●	
Demonstrate				
DIGITAL QUIZ **Lesson Quiz and Class Discussion Board**		10 min.	●	

Go online to access additional resources including:
Primary Sources • Biographies • Supreme Court cases • 21st Century Skill Tutorials • Maps • Graphic Organizers.

CONNECT

DIGITAL START UP ACTIVITY

Who Is a Pioneer?

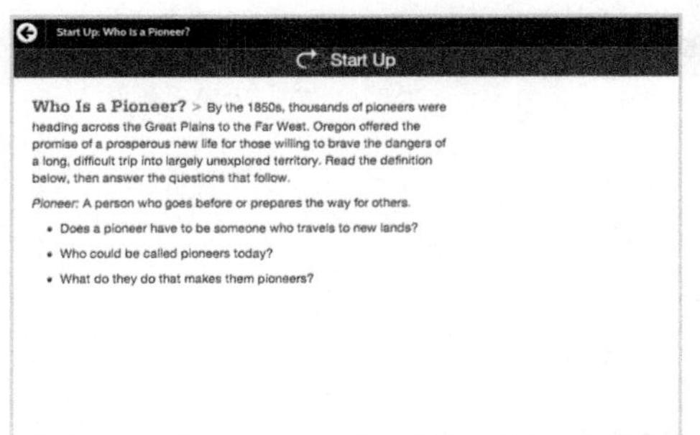

Project the Start Up activity as students enter and get settled. Have students brainstorm what it means to be a pioneer, and how exploring new territory can be defined. Then have them share their ideas with the class by answering these questions or ask students to post their responses online on the Class Discussion Board.

Discuss If a pioneer is an explorer, what are some personality traits that make someone a good pioneer? *(Answers could include curiosity about the unknown, bravery or fearlessness, willingness to keep going in the face of danger or uncertainty.)*

Tell students that in this lesson they will be learning about Oregon and the Far West.

Aa Vocabulary Development: Use the Interactive Reading Notepad to preview the Key Terms and Academic Vocabulary in this lesson with students.

FLIP IT!

Assign the Flipped Video for this lesson.

STUDENT EDITION PRINT PAGES: 337–343

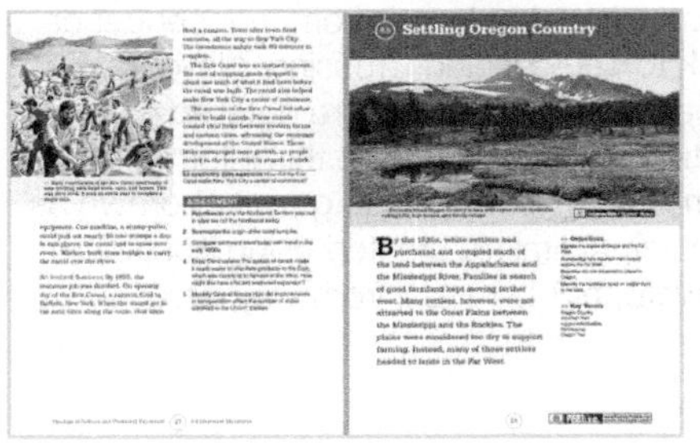

INVESTIGATE

DIGITAL TEXT 1

In Search of New Territory

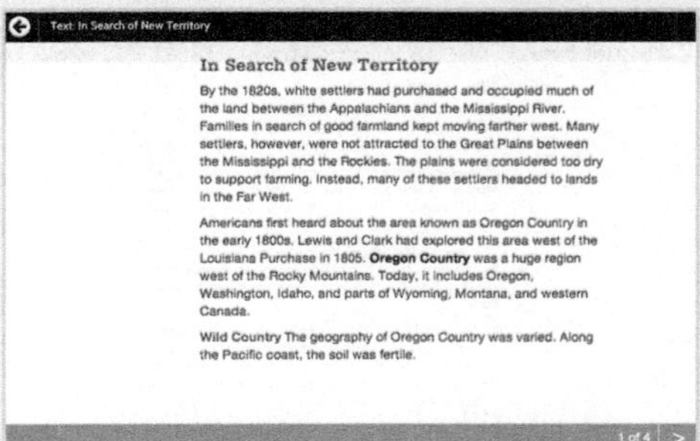

INTERACTIVE GALLERY

Oregon Country

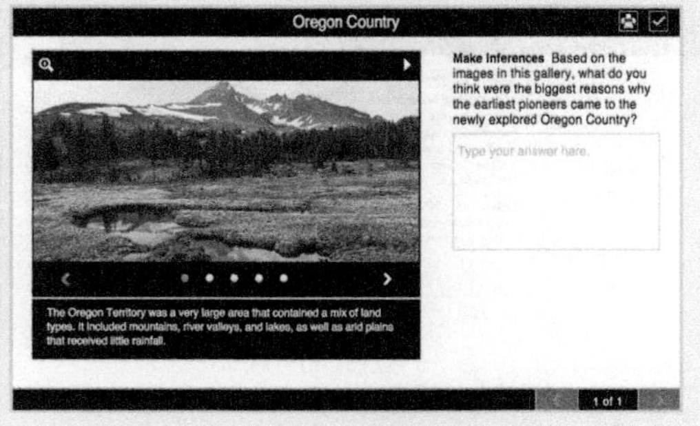

Objective 1: **Explain the appeal of Oregon and the Far West.**

Quick Instruction

By the early 1800s, the population of the United States had moved westward as far as the Mississippi River. The plains in the middle of the continent, acquired from the Louisiana Purchase, were less hospitable for farming, which meant that explorers kept pushing westward across the Rocky Mountains and to the Pacific coast. The territory they founded, Oregon Country, was fertile and varied, but several countries wanted to lay claim to the area.

Interactive Gallery: Oregon Country Project the interactive gallery and click through the images. Discuss the features of Oregon Country that made it different from the eastern United States. *(Taller mountains, fur-bearing wildlife like beavers, open space for raising cattle, arid plains)*

ACTIVE CLASSROOM

Conduct a Think-Pair-Share activity. Project "The United States in 1830" map on the board. Ask the students to reflect on this question:

Oregon Territory is on the opposite side of the continent from the rest of the United States. Why would the United States have wanted to claim land so far away from the other states? *(Much of the land closer to the other states was considered too dry for farming. Oregon Territory also had access to resources like fur trapping and a more direct trade route to China and the Far East.)*

Ask students to pair up or turn to an assigned partner. Have them discuss their responses.

D Differentiate: On-Level The last section of the text is titled *Nations Compete*. Why would countries like Spain and Great Britain want to lay claim to Oregon Country? *(The area had resources like furs and farmland. Oregon Country was also next to territory they already possessed, Mexico and Canada.)*

Further Instruction

Make Inferences Why would trading happen at a military outpost, such as Fort Astoria? *(In largely unexplored land, military forts and bases were the safest places to buy and sell supplies and goods.)*

Settling Oregon Country

DIGITAL TEXT 2

The Far West Fur Trade

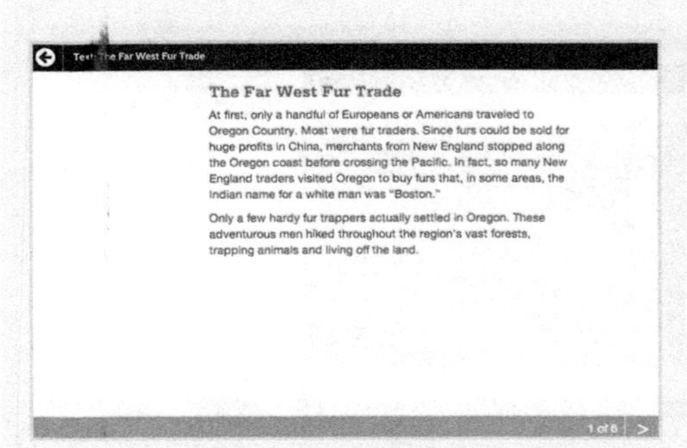

Text: The Far West Fur Trade

The Far West Fur Trade

At first, only a handful of Europeans or Americans traveled to Oregon Country. Most were fur traders. Since furs could be sold for huge profits in China, merchants from New England stopped along the Oregon coast before crossing the Pacific. In fact, so many New England traders visited Oregon to buy furs that, in some areas, the Indian name for a white man was "Boston."

Only a few hardy fur trappers actually settled in Oregon. These adventurous men hiked throughout the region's vast forests, trapping animals and living off the land.

1 of 6

DIGITAL TEXT 3

The Oregon Trail

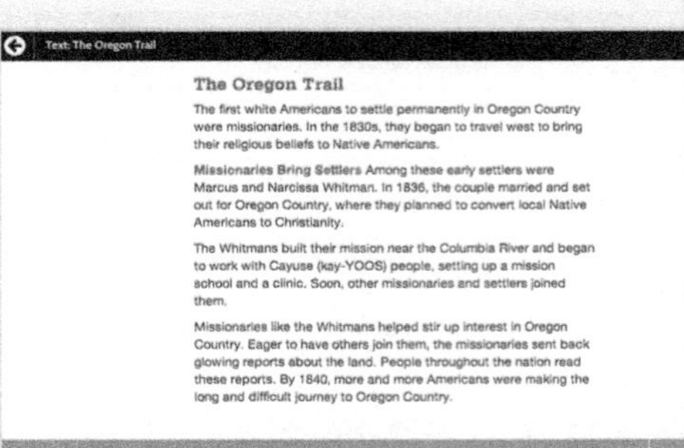

Text: The Oregon Trail

The Oregon Trail

The first white Americans to settle permanently in Oregon Country were missionaries. In the 1830s, they began to travel west to bring their religious beliefs to Native Americans.

Missionaries Bring Settlers Among these early settlers were Marcus and Narcissa Whitman. In 1836, the couple married and set out for Oregon Country, where they planned to convert local Native Americans to Christianity.

The Whitmans built their mission near the Columbia River and began to work with Cayuse (kay-YOOS) people, setting up a mission school and a clinic. Soon, other missionaries and settlers joined them.

Missionaries like the Whitmans helped stir up interest in Oregon Country. Eager to have others join them, the missionaries sent back glowing reports about the land. People throughout the nation read these reports. By 1840, more and more Americans were making the long and difficult journey to Oregon Country.

1 of 6

INTERACTIVE MAP

The Oregon Trail

Objective 2: Summarize how mountain men helped explore the Far West.

Quick Instruction

Some of the first people to come west to Oregon Country were fur traders, who supplied a successful trade of furs as far away as China. These trappers were known as *mountain men*, and they lived and worked individually in harsh conditions in the wild. Gathering once a year at a celebration called a rendezvous, they would compete, party, and sell their wares. When the fur trade eventually fell off, many of these mountain men found new work as explorers and guides, helping others find their way through the rough terrain of Oregon.

Infer Why would mountain men choose to endure the harsh lifestyle of a trapper? *(They were independent and self-sufficient. They sought a life that promised adventure and a good income.)*

ELL Use the ELL activity described in the ELL chart.

Further Instruction

Hypothesize After the fur trade stopped being so successful, why did people keep coming to Oregon Country? *(The wilderness lifestyle still appealed to people. There were also other opportunities for work, such as farming or raising cattle.)*

Objectives 3: Describe the role missionaries played in Oregon; 4: Identify the hardships faced on wagon trains to the West.

Quick Instruction

The first permanent settlers in Oregon were missionaries like Marcus and Narcissa Whitman. They worked to convert the local Native Americans, set up clinics, and encouraged others to come west. Large groups of families looking to relocate in the west would join together in wagon trains. They would leave Missouri in early spring, struggling across 2,000 miles of plains and mountains to try and beat the winter snows. The way was long and difficult, but over the years thousands made it through to the other side of the continent.

Interactive Map: The Oregon Trail Project the interactive map and click through the hotspots. Review the kinds of hazards and obstacles faced by settlers traveling along the Trail, so that students can understand the determination of people trying to start a new life in the West. Ask students to explain why the Oregon Trail followed the route it did, rather than coming across farther to the north. *(The trail followed the course of several passes and rivers, such as the Snake River, through the Rocky Mountains. Getting wagons across a different part of the mountains would probably have been much more difficult.)*

3-D Model: The Covered Wagon Project the 3-D Model and click through the screens. Work with students to complete the Traveling Then and Now chart and answer the questions that follow.

Identify Cause and Effect Why did the work of missionaries increase the flow of settlers into Oregon Country? *(Missionaries sent word back to people living in the East about how good it was in the new territory. They inspired others to come and help with their mission.)*

ACTIVE CLASSROOM

Conduct a Write 1 Get 3 activity. Ask: What specific problems did the pioneers face as they traveled westward? *(They had to leave their old lives behind. The journey was very long. Weather, food, and hostile locals were all potential threats. Once they arrived, they would have to build everything themselves.)*

Have students take a piece of paper and fold it into quarters, write down one response in the first box, and then go around room asking to hear other responses. If students think a response is correct, write it in one of the boxes until there are three more responses on the page. Share responses with class.

D Differentiate: Challenge Ask students to focus on a smaller portion of the Oregon Trail, such as the length from Independence Rock to Three Island Crossing. Have them research and create a more detailed map of the trail. They can present this information in a format of their choice (e.g., hand-drawn as a poster, digital art created using illustration software, a 3-D model from clay, etc.).

3-D MODEL

The Covered Wagon

ELL Use the ELL activity described in the ELL chart.

Further Instruction

Make Inferences Why would Narcissa Whitman have wanted to be one of the first pioneer women across the Rocky Mountains? *(She was a strong believer in the pioneer spirit and felt it was her duty to travel west as a missionary.)*

Infer Why did settlers travel overland along the Oregon Trail instead of by ship? *(Buying a wagon and carrying all their supplies and belongings was less expensive and faster than buying passage on a boat. Settlers also had more control over when and where they went once they reached the new territory.)*

SYNTHESIZE

DIGITAL ACTIVITY

Pioneering Success

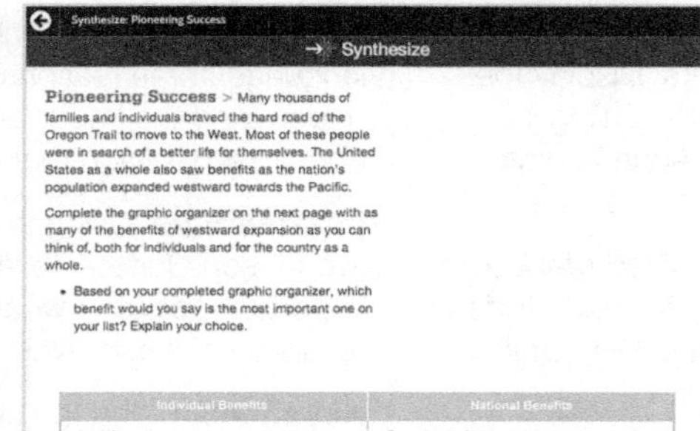

Synthesize: Pioneering Success
Synthesize
Pioneering Success > Many thousands of families and individuals braved the hard road of the Oregon Trail to move to the West. Most of these people were in search of a better life for themselves. The United States as a whole also saw benefits as the nation's population expanded westward towards the Pacific.
Complete the graphic organizer on the next page with as many of the benefits of westward expansion as you can think of, both for individuals and for the country as a whole.
• Based on your completed graphic organizer, which benefit would you say is the most important one on your list? Explain your choice.
Individual Benefits
National Benefits

Tell the students that by the mid-1800s, a large number of Americans and others had resettled in Oregon Country. There were a number of reasons why they all chose to make the move westward. Project the Individual Benefits vs. National Benefits graphic organizer and have students work in pairs to determine what sorts of benefits came out of the settlement of Oregon Country. Then ask the following questions.

Draw Conclusions How did the westward movement of people along the Oregon Trail benefit both individuals and the United States as a whole? *(Individuals benefited the most by taking the opportunity to make a better life for themselves. The country benefited by becoming larger, with more access to resources and international trade.)*

DEMONSTRATE

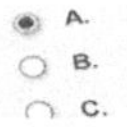

DIGITAL QUIZ

Lesson Quiz and Class Discussion Board

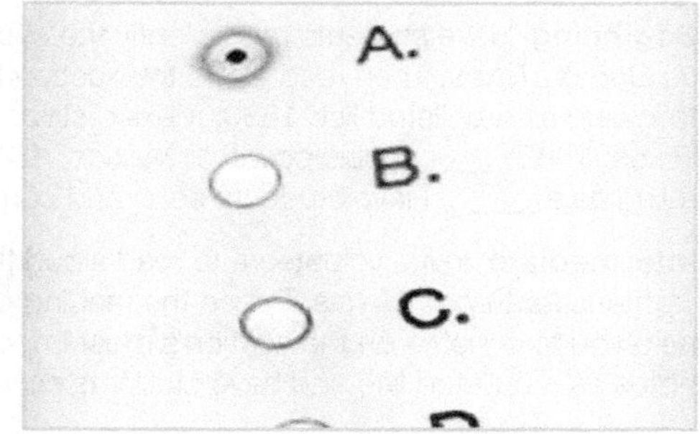

Assign the online Lesson Quiz for this lesson if you haven't already done so. Students will be offered automatic remediation or enrichment based on their score.

Pose these questions to the class on the Discussion Board:

In *Oregon Country*, you read about the people who originally traveled westward to populate the new territory, what they found when they got there, and the troubles they endured while getting there. People traveled west for a variety of reasons, looking to build better and often more independent lives for themselves.

Draw Conclusions How will westward migration along the Oregon Trail affect the growth and development of the United States?

Infer What do mountain men and migrating settlers tell us about the developing personality of the American people?

Topic Inquiry

Have students continue their investigations for the Topic Inquiry.

Independence for Texas

Supporting English Language Learners

Use with Digital Text 2, **Conflict With the Mexican Government.**

Reading

Explain that students will be taking notes in order to demonstrate their comprehension of a text.

Beginning Have students read silently the section titled *Mexico Tightens Its Grip on Texas*. Then read aloud the section for students. Display the following as a bulleted list: 1830: Mexico stops _____ from settling in Texas; 1833: _____ gains power in Mexico; 1835: Santa Anna begins ruling as a _____. Have students copy and complete the notes.

Intermediate Invite volunteers to read aloud the section titled *Mexico Tightens Its Grip on Texas*. Pause the reading periodically to have students help you take notes on the section's most important points. Display the notes as a bulleted list, and have students copy them.

Advanced Have pairs of students read the section titled *Mexico Tightens Its Grip on Texas*. Explain that after every paragraph, they should stop and take notes on the most important points they have just read. Encourage them to organize their notes as a bulleted list with a heading.

Advanced High Have students independently read the text. Explain that as they read, they should pause to take notes on the most important points they encounter. Encourage them to organize their notes using the same title and subheadings as the text.

Use with Digital Text 4, **The Republic of Texas Is Born.**

Learning Strategies Listening

Review the meanings of annex and annexation in preparation for the activities.

Beginning Using the chart as a reference, explain (in basic spoken language) three reasons for the Texas annexation. To help students understand the important points of what you said, ask a literal question about each reason that students can answer with a word or phrase.

Intermediate Using the chart as a reference, explain (in spoken language) five reasons for the Texas annexation. To help students understand the important points of what you said, ask a literal question about each reason. Then ask: Which of these reasons is most important, and why?

Advanced Using the chart as a reference, explain (in spoken language) the reasons for and against the Texas annexation. Then have pairs of students discuss the important points of each side of the argument.

Advanced High Compare and contrast some basic facts about the familiar topic of the Texas annexation and the unfamiliar topic of the Hawaii annexation (e.g., reasons for it, support of inhabitants, date in history). Then have pairs of students discuss the important points you made.

D Differentiate Instruction

Use the Differentiated Instruction notes throughout the lesson plan to support the varied skill sets, levels of readiness, and interests in the mixed-ability classroom.

Challenge These notes include suggestions for expanding the activity for advanced students.

On-Level These notes include suggestions for modifying the activity to address different interests or learning styles.

Extra Support These notes include ideas for providing more scaffolding or reading spupport.

Special Needs These notes provide ideas for adapting instruction to support the needs of various special needs students.

NOTES

PEARSON realize™ www.PearsonRealize.com

Go online to access additional resources including:
Primary Sources • Biographies • Supreme Court cases • 21st Century Skill Tutorials • Maps • Graphic Organizers.

Objectives

Objective 1: Summarize the cooperation and conflict between American settlers in Texas and the Mexican government.

Objective 2: Explain how Texas gained independence.

Objective 3: Describe how the events at the Alamo affected Texans.

Objective 4: Identify the challenges faced by the Lone Star Republic.

LESSON 6 ORGANIZER — PACING: APPROX. 1 PERIOD, .5 BLOCKS	OBJECTIVES	PACING	RESOURCES: Online	RESOURCES: Print
Connect				
DIGITAL START UP ACTIVITY **I Wish to See Texas Free**		5 min.	●	
Investigate				
DIGITAL TEXT 1 **Americans Colonize Mexican Texas**	Objective 1	10 min.	●	●
INTERACTIVE MAP **The Settlement of Texas**	Objective 1	10 min.	●	
DIGITAL TEXT 2 **Conflict With the Mexican Government**	Objective 2	10 min.	●	●
DIGITAL TEXT 3 **Independence for Texas**	Objective 3	10 min.	●	●
INTERACTIVE GALLERY **The Defenders of the Alamo**	Objective 3	10 min.	●	
DIGITAL TEXT 4 **The Republic of Texas Is Born**	Objective 4	10 min.	●	●
INTERACTIVE TIMELINE **Texas: From Settlement to Statehood**	Objective 4	10 min.	●	
Synthesize				
DIGITAL ACTIVITY **Republic of Texas Cause-and-Effect Relationships**		5 min.	●	
Demonstrate				
DIGITAL QUIZ **Lesson Quiz and Class Discussion Board**		10 min.	●	

Independence for Texas

CONNECT

DIGITAL START UP ACTIVITY

I Wish to See Texas Free

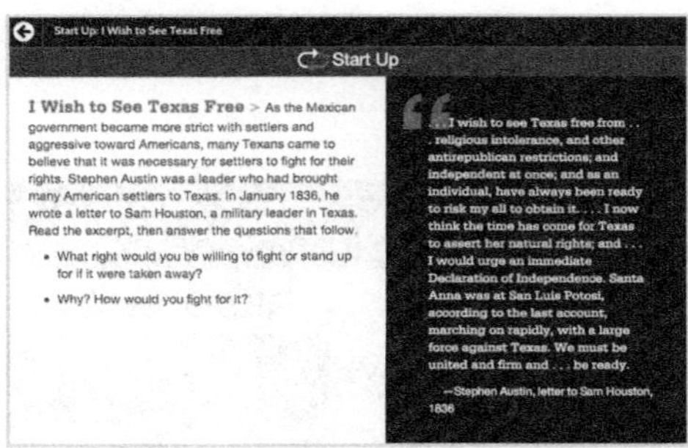

Project the Start Up Activity Ask students to read the quote and answer the questions as they enter and get settled. Have students share their answers with a partner, either in class or through a blog space.

Tell students that in this lesson they will be learning about how Texas became an independent republic and later a part of the United States.

Aa Vocabulary Development: Use the Interactive Reading Notepad to preview the Key Terms and Academic Vocabulary in this lesson with students.

FLIP IT!

Assign the Flipped Video for this lesson.

STUDENT EDITION PRINT PAGES: 344–350

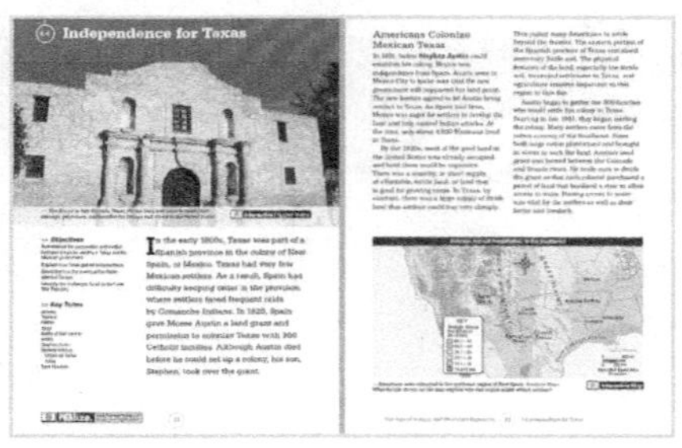

INVESTIGATE

DIGITAL TEXT 1

Americans Colonize Mexican Texas

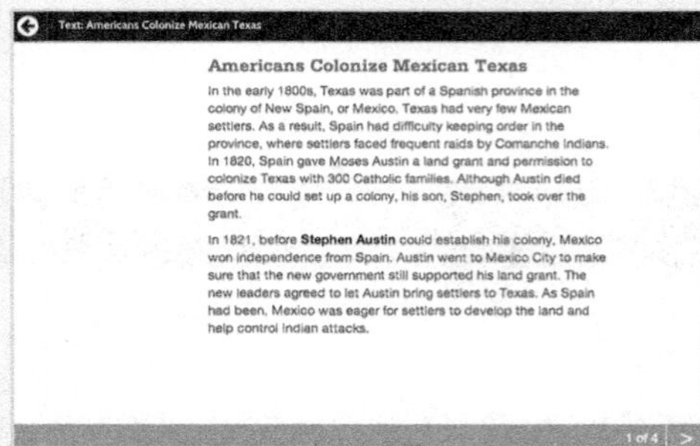

INTERACTIVE MAP

The Settlement of Texas

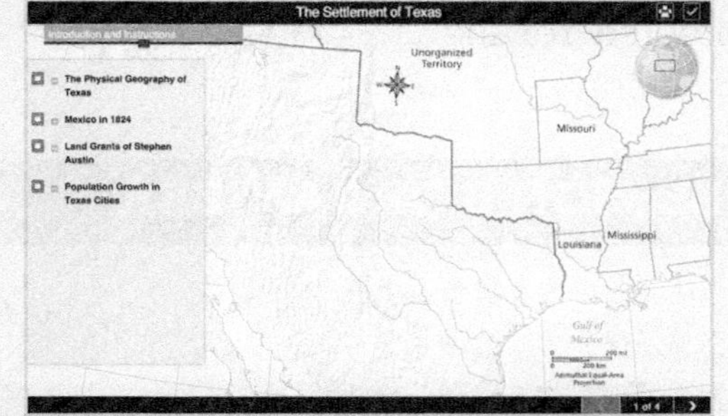

Objective 1: Summarize the cooperation and conflict between American settlers in Texas and the Mexican government.

Quick Instruction

Interactive Map: The Settlement of Texas Project the interactive map on the whiteboard and click through the topics. Show students the region that was once part of Mexico and then became Texas. Ask students to describe the physical geography of Texas as shown on the map. Discuss how physical characteristics of the environment likely affected settlement patterns in the area.

Analyze Maps Click on the "Physical geography of Texas" layer. Ask students where they think Americans first settled in Texas, and why. *(Along rivers and near the Gulf of Mexico, where there was fertile soil for farming and waterways for transportation)*

Summarize Describe the physical characteristics of the environment that pushed people from the United States and pulled them to Mexican Texas. *(The best land in the United States was already taken, and land was expensive. Texas had large amounts of cheap, fertile land for farming.)*

ACTIVE CLASSROOM

Have students suppose they are Stephen Austin and are trying to bring settlers to Texas. Have students use the Make Headlines activity to make a headline that captures the reasons for moving to Texas. Have students share their headlines with the class and discuss the most compelling arguments.

Further Instruction

Go through the Interactive Reading Notepad questions and discuss the answers with the class. Be sure students understand the physical and human geographic factors that shaped the early settlement of Texas.

Cite Evidence City evidence that explains why Mexico welcomed American settlers in Texas. *("Mexico was eager for settlers to develop the land and help control Indian attacks.")*

Cite Evidence Why does the physical geography of Texas remain important today? *(Increased settlement in Texas is due in part to the fertile soil that continues to ensure significant agricultural production.)*

Summarize Where was Austin's land grant? How did he divide the land to help ensure the success of the colony? *(His land grant was between the Colorado and Brazos rivers. He divided the land so colonists could access water. This decision was successful because his colony grew and more settlers came.)*

DIGITAL TEXT 2

Conflict With the Mexican Government

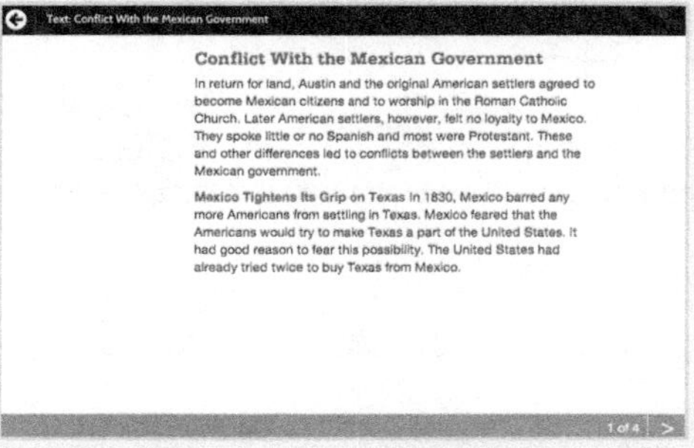

Text: Conflict With the Mexican Government

Conflict With the Mexican Government

In return for land, Austin and the original American settlers agreed to become Mexican citizens and to worship in the Roman Catholic Church. Later American settlers, however, felt no loyalty to Mexico. They spoke little or no Spanish and most were Protestant. These and other differences led to conflicts between the settlers and the Mexican government.

Mexico Tightens Its Grip on Texas In 1830, Mexico barred any more Americans from settling in Texas. Mexico feared that the Americans would try to make Texas a part of the United States. It had good reason to fear this possibility. The United States had already tried twice to buy Texas from Mexico.

1 of 4 >

Objective 2: **Explain how Texas gained independence.**

Quick Instruction

Project the image of German settlers on the whiteboard. Review the reasons settlers were drawn to Mexican Texas, including land for farming.

Identify Cause and Effect How did westward expansion cause conflict with the Mexican government? *(As more American settlers came to Texas, the Mexican government worried about losing the region to the United States. Later settlers were not loyal toward Mexico. They were Protestant, did not speak Spanish, and many supported slavery. To assert its authority, Mexico began to enforce laws that had long been ignored, including a law that banned slavery in the region. Many American settlers relied on enslaved workers to grow cotton. Settlers' anger grew when Mexico sent troops to enforce its will.)*

D Differentiate: Extra Support Review the definition of the key term *dictator* : a ruler with absolute power and authority. Ask students to consider what made Santa Anna a dictator. If they had settled in Texas during this time, would they have rebelled against his rule?

ELL Use the ELL activity described in the ELL chart.

Further Instruction

Go through the Interactive Reading Notepad questions and discuss the answers with the class.

Summarize Where was the first clash between Texan settlers and Mexican troops? Why did this clash occur? *(Gonzales, Texas. Texans wanted independence from Mexico; Tejanos wanted to overthrow Santa Anna.)*

Hypothesize Why do you think Texan settlers chose to go to war with Mexico instead of migrating to another region where they would be free of Santa Anna's rule? *(The settlers benefited from Texas's geography. They had fertile land and successful farms, which they did not want to leave.)*

DIGITAL TEXT 3

Independence for Texas

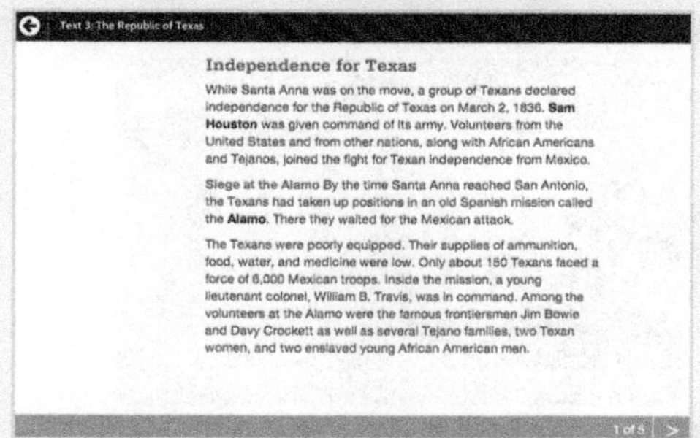

Text 3: The Republic of Texas

Independence for Texas

While Santa Anna was on the move, a group of Texans declared independence for the Republic of Texas on March 2, 1836. **Sam Houston** was given command of its army. Volunteers from the United States and from other nations, along with African Americans and Tejanos, joined the fight for Texan independence from Mexico.

Siege at the Alamo By the time Santa Anna reached San Antonio, the Texans had taken up positions in an old Spanish mission called the **Alamo**. There they waited for the Mexican attack.

The Texans were poorly equipped. Their supplies of ammunition, food, water, and medicine were low. Only about 150 Texans faced a force of 6,000 Mexican troops. Inside the mission, a young lieutenant colonel, William B. Travis, was in command. Among the volunteers at the Alamo were the famous frontiersmen Jim Bowie and Davy Crockett as well as several Tejano families, two Texan women, and two enslaved young African American men.

1 of 5 >

Objective 3: **Describe how the events at the Alamo affected Texans.**

Quick Instruction

Interactive Gallery: Defenders of the Alamo Project the interactive gallery on the whiteboard and click through the images.

Analyze Images Look at the image of the Alamo compound. How did the physical geography of the region influence the events of the siege? *(The land was flat and open, making the mission the best place for the Texans to shield themselves from Santa Anna's attack. With no other natural barriers, the Mexicans could approach the mission and bombard it until they broke through. Once they broke through, there was no way for the Texans to hide or escape.)*

ACTIVE CLASSROOM

Have students use the Conversations With History Strategy and suppose they are having a conversation with William B. Travis about the siege of the Alamo. Have them write down a question they would ask, what Travis would say, and what they would say in response.

Independence for Texas

INTERACTIVE GALLERY

The Defenders of the Alamo

The Defenders of the Alamo
The Alamo
Built by the Spanish in 1724, this building was part of the mission of San Antonio de Valero for 70 years. It later housed Spanish troops who nicknamed it the Alamo. It went on to play a major role in Texas history.
1 of 3

Further Instruction

Go through the Interactive Reading Notepad questions and discuss the answers with the class. Be sure students understand the factors that influenced the siege of the Alamo and its significance.

Sequence Events Describe the siege of the Alamo. *(Texans waited for Santa Anna's attack from inside an old Spanish mission, the Alamo. The Texans were not equipped to hold off the attack by thousands of Mexican troops. They lasted 12 days as the Mexicans bombarded the mission. Finally, the attackers broke through the mission walls and defeated the Texans inside.)*

DIGITAL TEXT 4

The Republic of Texas Is Born

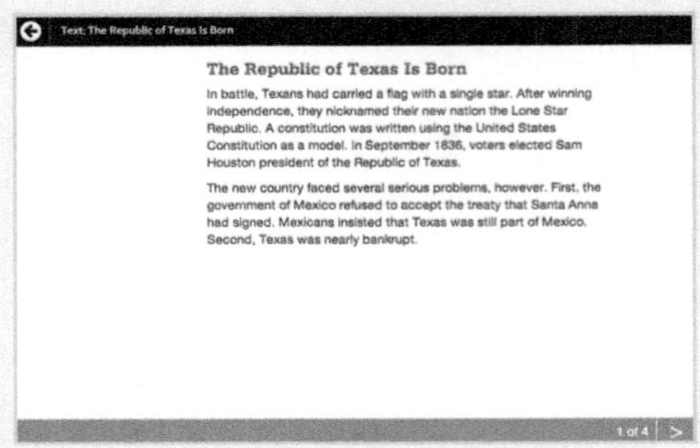

Text: The Republic of Texas Is Born

The Republic of Texas Is Born

In battle, Texans had carried a flag with a single star. After winning independence, they nicknamed their new nation the Lone Star Republic. A constitution was written using the United States Constitution as a model. In September 1836, voters elected Sam Houston president of the Republic of Texas.

The new country faced several serious problems, however. First, the government of Mexico refused to accept the treaty that Santa Anna had signed. Mexicans insisted that Texas was still part of Mexico. Second, Texas was nearly bankrupt.

1 of 4

Objective 4: **Identify the challenges faced by the Lone Star Republic.**

Quick Instruction

Interactive Timeline: From Settlement to Statehood Project the interactive timeline on the whiteboard and have students read the event tiles. Ask students to state in their own words the events that led Texas to achieve independence.

Draw Conclusions How did the physical geography of Texas helped the republic grow? *(The Texan government attracted new settlers with the promise of cheap and plentiful land to farm.)*

ACTIVE CLASSROOM

Have students use the Circle Write activity to write about how they think the annexation of Texas will affect the United States politically, economically, and socially. Students break into groups and write as much as they can for 1 minute, then switch with the person on their right. The next person tries to improve or elaborate on the response. Students continue to switch until the paper comes back to the first person. Have groups share the response they think is the best.

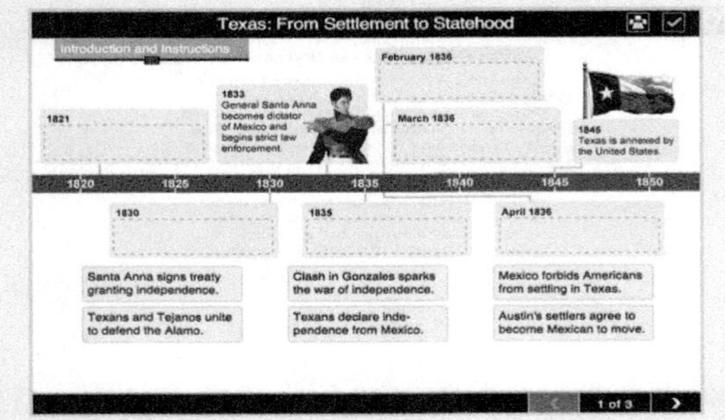

INTERACTIVE TIMELINE

Texas: From Settlement to Statehood

ELL Use the ELL activity described in the ELL chart.

Further Instruction

Go through the Interactive Reading Notepad questions and discuss the answers with the class.

Compare Points of View What were the arguments within the United States for and against annexing Texas? *(Because many Texans owned slaves, southerners favored annexation as a way to add another slave state to the Union. Northerners opposed annexation for this same reason. President Jackson also feared war with Mexico.)*

Make Predictions How do you think the geography of Texas might affect future relations with Mexico? *(Because they share a border, they will also share resources, such as water. They may have closer economic ties as a result; there will likely be tensions, too.)*

SYNTHESIZE

DIGITAL ACTIVITY

Republic of Texas Cause-and-Effect Relationships

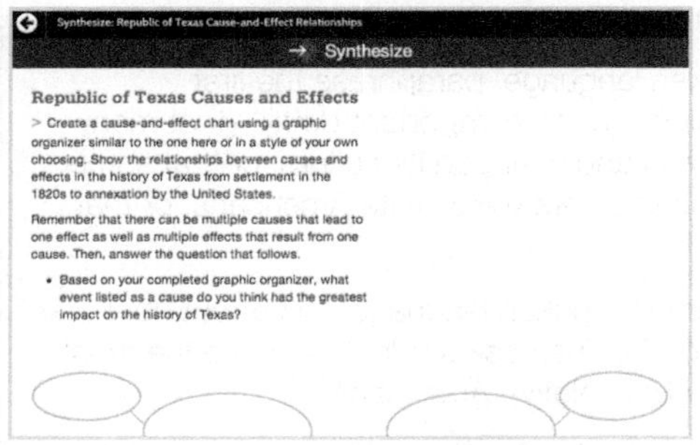

Have students review the events leading up to the annexation of Texas and fill in the chart.

Discuss Ask students to think about the important events leading up to the annexation of Texas. What geographic factors led to westward expansion into Texas? What were the effects of this expansion?

DEMONSTRATE

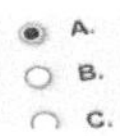

DIGITAL QUIZ

Lesson Quiz and Class Discussion Board

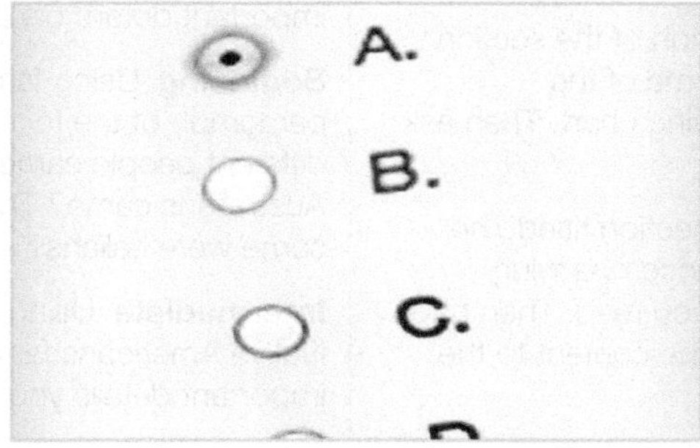

Assign the online Lesson Quiz for this lesson if you haven't already done so. Students will be offered automatic remediation or enrichment based on their score.

Pose these questions to the class on the Discussion Board:

Predict Consequences How will the annexation of Texas contribute to tensions over slavery in the United States?

Support Ideas With Examples What political, economic, social, and geographic factors led to the expansion of the United States? Give examples to support your view.

Topic Inquiry

Have students continue their investigations for the Topic Inquiry.

Manifest Destiny in California and the Southwest

Supporting English Language Learners

Use with Digital Text 2, **Manifest Destiny.**

Reading

Explain to students that using techniques to increase comprehension will help them to read silently for longer periods of time.

Beginning With students, echo read the first paragraph of the section titled *The Roots of Manifest Destiny*. Point out how some of the paragraph's information is repeated in the accompanying chart. Then ask students to silently read the same paragraph.

Intermediate Read aloud the first paragraph of the section titled *The Roots of Manifest Destiny*, modeling how to use the accompanying chart's "Social" column to support and confirm what you read. Then have students silently read the next paragraph and match the content to the chart's "Economic" column.

Advanced Display the chart titled *The Roots of Manifest Destiny* and read its content. Then ask students to silently read the section titled *The Roots of Manifest Destiny*, referring to the chart periodically to support and confirm what they are reading.

Advanced High With students, examine and discuss the three visual aids that accompany the text. Then have students silently read the text. Encourage them to refer to the visual aids as appropriate in order to increase their interest and understanding of the text.

Use with Digital Text 5, **The Effects of Migration to California.**

Listening

Introduce your speaking topic by locating California on a map and reviewing the term *gold rush*. Prompt students to understand the important details of spoken language.

Beginning Using familiar spoken language, paraphrase the first paragraph of the text. Ask: Which is a more important detail—that many different people came to California and changed its culture, or that some Australians came? That most newcomers were white Americans, or that some were Italians?

Intermediate Using mostly familiar spoken language, talk about how Native Americans fared in California. Then ask students to state the most important details you provided about Native Americans.

Advanced Using a mix of familiar and unfamiliar spoken language, talk about how Native Americans and African Americans fared in California. Then ask students to state the most important details you provided about each group.

Advanced High Using spoken language that is not linguistically accommodating and includes both familiar and unfamiliar vocabulary, talk about what Mexicans, Native Americans, Chinese, and African Americans faced in California. Challenge students to recall the most important details you provided about each group.

D Differentiate Instruction

Use the Differentiated Instruction notes throughout the lesson plan to support the varied skill sets, levels of readiness, and interests in the mixed-ability classroom.

Challenge These notes include suggestions for expanding the activity for advanced students.

On-Level These notes include suggestions for modifying the activity to address different interests or learning styles.

Extra Support These notes include ideas for providing more scaffolding or reading spuport.

Special Needs These notes provide ideas for adapting instruction to support the needs of various special needs students.

NOTES

Objectives

Objective 1: Describe life for the Spanish and Native Americans on the missions and ranches of California and New Mexico.

Objective 2: Analyze the relationship between the concept of Manifest Destiny and the westward growth of the nation.

Objective 3: List the causes and effects of the Mexican-American War.

Objective 4: Explain why the Mormons moved to Utah.

Objective 5: Describe how the gold rush affected California.

LESSON 7 ORGANIZER	PACING: APPROX. 1 PERIOD, .5 BLOCKS			
			RESOURCES	
	OBJECTIVES	PACING	Online	Print
Connect				
DIGITAL START UP ACTIVITY **We Are a Restless People**		5 min.	●	
Investigate				
DIGITAL TEXT 1 **New Mexico Territory and California**	Objective 1	10 min.	●	●
DIGITAL TEXT 2 **Manifest Destiny**	Objective 2	10 min.	●	●
INTERACTIVE MAP **The Growth of the West to 1860**		10 min.	●	
DIGITAL TEXT 3 **The Mexican-American War**	Objective 3	10 min.	●	●
DIGITAL TEXT 4 **Settling the Mexican Cession**	Objectives 3, 4, 5	10 min.	●	●
DIGITAL TEXT 5 **The Effects of Migration to California**	Objective 5	10 min.	●	●
INTERACTIVE GALLERY **The People of California**		10 min.	●	
Synthesize				
DIGITAL ACTIVITY **Expansion of the United States**		5 min.	●	
Demonstrate				
DIGITAL QUIZ **Lesson Quiz and Class Discussion Board**		10 min.	●	

Manifest Destiny in California and the Southwest

CONNECT

DIGITAL START UP ACTIVITY

We Are a Restless People

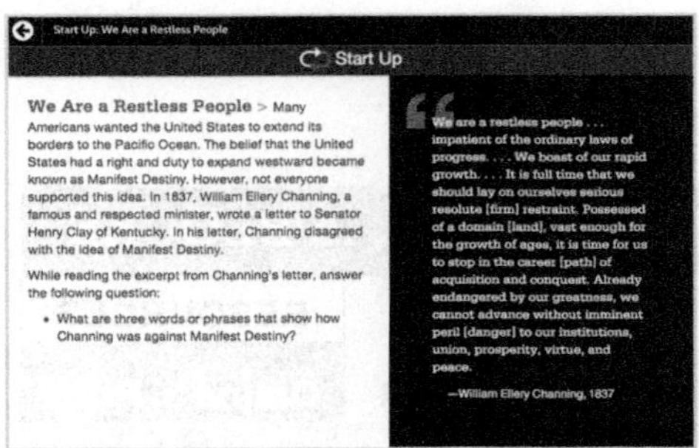

Project the Start Up activity consisting of a quotation on Manifest Destiny while the students enter and get settled. Ask students to read the quotation and answer the question. Then have them share their ideas with another student, either in-class or through an online chat or blog space.

Discuss Why was Channing against Manifest Destiny? *(He believed the rapid growth would have a negative impact on the institutions and prosperity of the Union.)*

Tell students that they will be learning about the idea of Manifest Destiny, the causes and effects of the Mexican-American War, why the Mormons moved to Utah, and events in California.

Aa Vocabulary Development: Use the Interactive Reading Notepad to preview the Key Terms and Academic Vocabulary in this lesson with students.

FLIP IT!

Assign the Flipped Video for this lesson.

STUDENT EDITION PRINT PAGES: 351–362

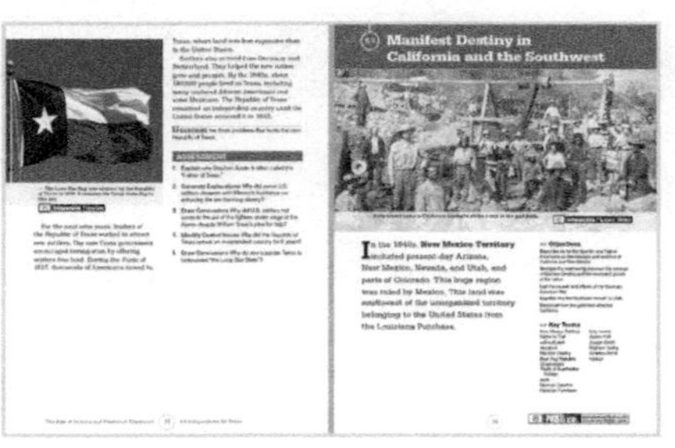

INVESTIGATE

DIGITAL TEXT 1

New Mexico Territory and California

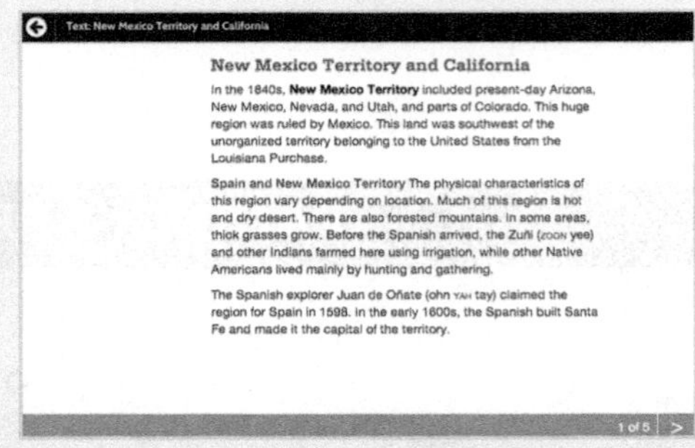

Text: New Mexico Territory and California
New Mexico Territory and California
In the 1840s, New Mexico Territory included present-day Arizona, New Mexico, Nevada, and Utah, and parts of Colorado. This huge region was ruled by Mexico. This land was southwest of the unorganized territory belonging to the United States from the Louisiana Purchase.
Spain and New Mexico Territory The physical characteristics of this region vary depending on location. Much of this region is hot and dry desert. There are also forested mountains. In some areas, thick grasses grow. Before the Spanish arrived, the Zuñi (ZOON yee) and other Indians farmed here using irrigation, while other Native Americans lived mainly by hunting and gathering.
The Spanish explorer Juan de Oñate (ohn YAH tay) claimed the region for Spain in 1598. In the early 1600s, the Spanish built Santa Fe and made it the capital of the territory.
1 of 5

Objective 1: Describe life for the Spanish and Native Americans on the missions and ranches of California and New Mexico.

Quick Instruction

The parts of the country that we now know as California and the Southwest were part of Spain and then Mexico before they were added to the United States. Spain and Mexico established settlements along the Pacific Coast, including missions and ranches, where people of Spanish descent and Native Americans lived and worked together.

Analyze Images Project the image of Native Americans working on a Spanish mission from the reading. Ask students: How may this image reflect or differ from the reality of life on the missions? *(This image shows work that may have been done by Native Americans to help the mission function, including making rope and baskets. It does not show how hard life could be for Native Americans.)*

Summarize How did life change for Native Americans on California missions and ranches? *(Native Americans had lived in their own communities before the Spanish built their settlements. After, they lived with the Spanish on the missions and ranches. They were forced to give up their culture and did most of the work to keep the settlements functioning.)*

Further Instruction

Have students locate the different types of settlements and their locations on the regional map "Spanish Territory in North America, 1820" from the reading. Then have students answer the question below.

Compare and Contrast How did the physical geography of the New Mexico territory compare to much of the rest of the United States? *(Much of this region has a hotter, drier climate than most of the rest of the United States. Agriculture was difficult in much of this region. Before the Spanish arrived, the Zuñi (ZOON yee) and other Indians farmed here using irrigation, while other Native Americans lived mainly by hunting and gathering).* What physical characteristics of the environment attracted settlers to New Mexico and increased its population? *(Natural resources attracted settlers.)*

Draw Conclusions Ask students who was moving to California and the Southwest in the early 1800s. Have students explain the reasons these early settlers moved there. *(Spaniards moved to California and parts of the Southwest, like Santa Fe, to establish settlements and trading posts in their territory. Roman Catholic missionaries moved to convert the Native Americans. Some Americans also traveled to the Southwest.)*

DIGITAL TEXT 2

Manifest Destiny

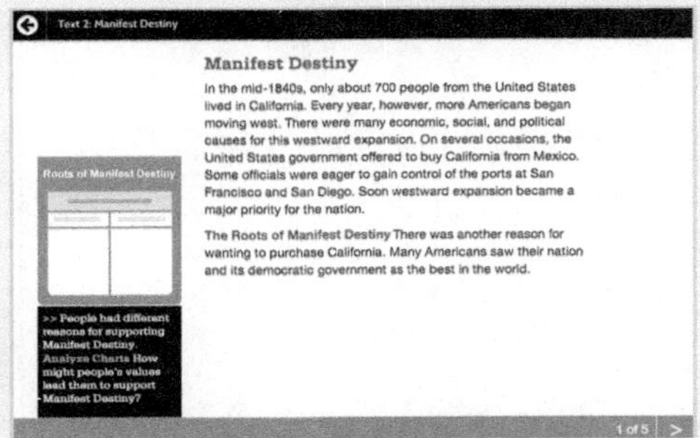

Objective 2: **Analyze the relationship between the concept of Manifest Destiny and the westward growth of the nation.**

Quick Instruction

Remind students that in the 1840s the United States reached as far west as the lands of the Louisiana Purchase. By this time many Americans were eager to expand the country even farther west, prompted in part by the idea of Manifest Destiny. Have students discuss the political, economic and social roots of Manifest Destiny and encourage them to identify the relationship between Manifest Destiny and westward expansion.

Interactive Map: The Growth of the West to 1860 Project the interactive map and click on the hotspots. Prompt students to connect reasons for population distribution and settlement patterns with the physical characteristics of the region.

> **ACTIVE CLASSROOM**
>
> Conduct a Ranking Strategy activity. Ask students to rank what they think are the most important causes of westward expansion presented in the interactive map and have them explain their rationale for ranking the reasons the way they did.

INTERACTIVE MAP

The Growth of the West to 1860

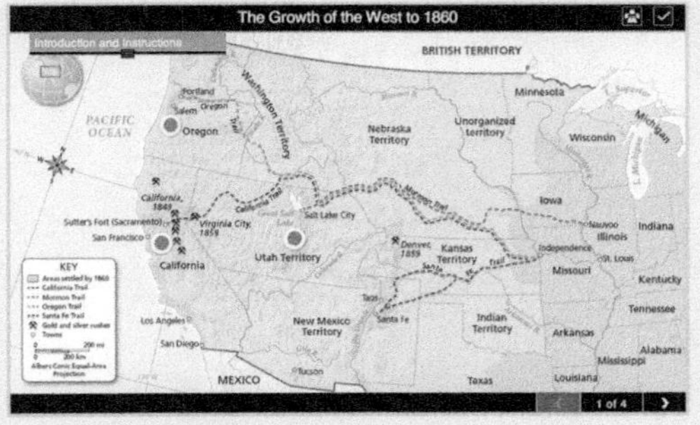

D Differentiate: Extra Support Have each group of students rank the items in order of importance for one of the three categories listed in the "Roots of Manifest Destiny" table (political, economic, and social roots).

ELL Use the ELL activity described in the ELL chart.

Further Instruction

Americans who supported Manifest Destiny helped elect Polk as President in 1844. He ushered in the next era of westward expansion. Ask students to point out on a map which parts of the country were added under President Polk. *(The Oregon territory, which is now the states Oregon, Washington, and Idaho)*

Evaluate Impact Ask students how Manifest Destiny was related to the growth of the nation under President Polk. *(Polk was elected because he supported Manifest Destiny. He pushed to acquire new lands from Britain.)*

DIGITAL TEXT 3

The Mexican-American War

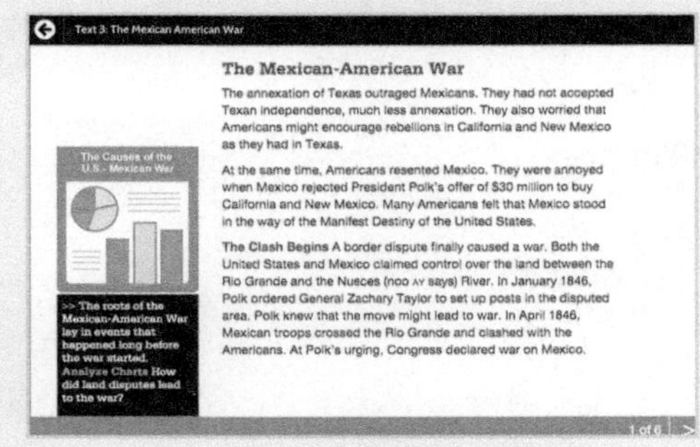

Objective 3: **List the causes and results of the U.S.-Mexican War.**

Quick Instruction

The U.S.-Mexican War was a turning point in growth of the United States. This war caused by a border dispute and the annexation of Texas, was fought over a vast territory from the heart of Mexico to northern California. With the lands gained from this war and the Gadsden Purchase, many Americans felt that their dream of Manifest Destiny had been fulfilled.

Identify Central Issues What were the effects of the U.S.-Mexican War? What was the impact of the U.S.-Mexican War on the growth of the United States? *(Because the United States won the U.S.-Mexican War, Mexico ceded California and the Southwest to the United States. The United States was also able to keep Texas and buy the lands of the Gadsden Purchase. These additions to the U.S. greatly expanded the western part of the country.)*

Further Instruction

The U.S.-Mexican War was the result of disputes and clashes between the United States and its neighbor Mexico. Ask the questions below before the Quick Instruction to understand the causes and details of the U.S.-Mexican War.

Manifest Destiny in California and the Southwest

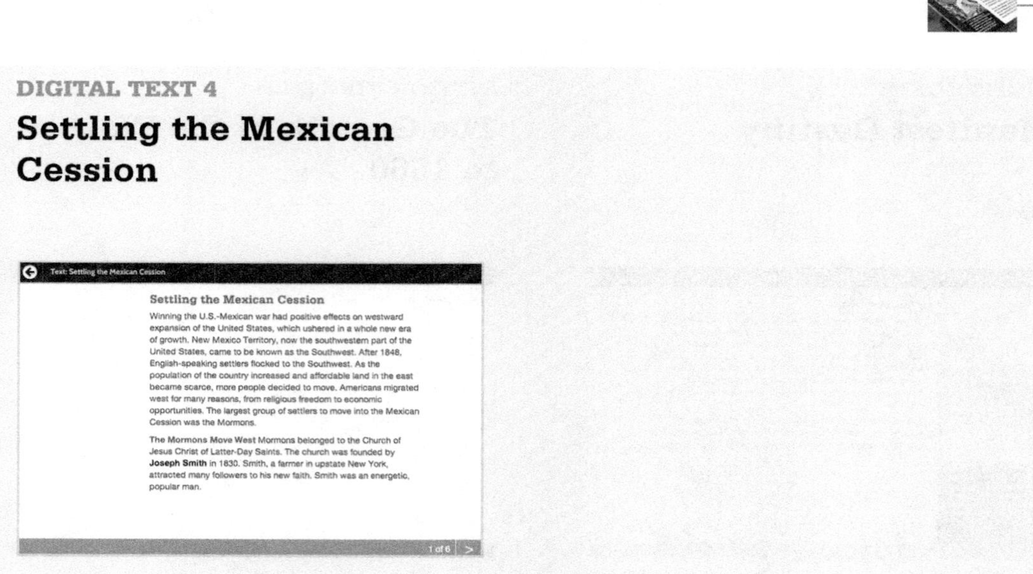

DIGITAL TEXT 4

Settling the Mexican Cession

Text: Settling the Mexican Cession

Settling the Mexican Cession

Winning the U.S.-Mexican war had positive effects on westward expansion of the United States, which ushered in a whole new era of growth. New Mexico Territory, now the southwestern part of the United States, came to be known as the Southwest. After 1848, English-speaking settlers flocked to the Southwest. As the population of the country increased and affordable land in the east became scarce, more people decided to move. Americans migrated west for many reasons, from religious freedom to economic opportunities. The largest group of settlers to move into the Mexican Cession was the Mormons.

The Mormons Move West Mormons belonged to the Church of Jesus Christ of Latter-Day Saints. The church was founded by **Joseph Smith** in 1830. Smith, a farmer in upstate New York, attracted many followers to his new faith. Smith was an energetic, popular man.

1 of 6 >

Summarize What were the causes of the U.S.-Mexican War? *(Causes included the annexation of Texas, disputes over territory, Manifest Destiny, and clashes between Mexican and American troops in disputed lands.)*

Analyze Sequence Have students record in sequential order the key events of the U.S.-Mexican War. *(The United States and Mexican armies clashed in the disputed territory in April 1846. After crossing into Mexico, American General Taylor clashed with Mexican General Santa Anna at the Battle of Buena Vista in February 1847. American General Scott sailed to Veracruz, Mexico in 1847. American General Kearny captured Santa Fe and San Diego in 1847. In 1847 General Scott reached Mexico City and was able to overtake it. In 1848 the Mexican government moved to make peace with the United States.)*

Objectives 3: List the causes and results of the U.S.-Mexican War; 4: Explain why the Mormons moved to Utah; 5: Describe how the gold rush affected California.

Quick Instruction

Once the lands of the Mexican Cession became part of the United States, Americans began to flock to the West. Early settlers came for a variety of reasons from economic opportunities provided by the gold rush to religious freedom. The physical characteristics of the environment impacted those who moved to the West and why they moved there. Immigrants came from all over the world for the economic opportunities in California. Others came to establish a new life based on farming in Utah.

Generate Explanations Ask students to compare how physical and human characteristics differed in places across the West. How were different parts of this region shaped by the people who moved there? *(Some parts of the West had good farmland while other parts had valuable resources, such as gold. People who came to the West to farm and establish lives for their families created different economies and cultures from people who came from around the world to make money mining, and then often move onwards. People who came west for religious purposes helped establish communities based on their values.)*

Further Instruction

Show and discuss the Reading Support graphic organizer about why people moved to California and Utah. Help fill in the answers by asking: Which ethnic and religious groups settled in Utah and California? Why did they move to these regions? *(Mormons moved to Utah for religious freedom. Many different ethnic groups came to California for the economic opportunities of the Gold Rush.)*

Apply Concepts What effect did human geographic factors have on the Mormon settlement of Utah? *(Mormon leader Brigham Young chose an isolated valley between the Rocky Mountains hoping the Mormons would be safe from persecution there. Young planned an irrigation system to bring water to farms. He also drew up plans for a large city, called Salt Lake City, to be built in the desert. Waves of Mormon settlers came and the settlement quickly grew.)*

DIGITAL TEXT 5

The Effects of Migration to California

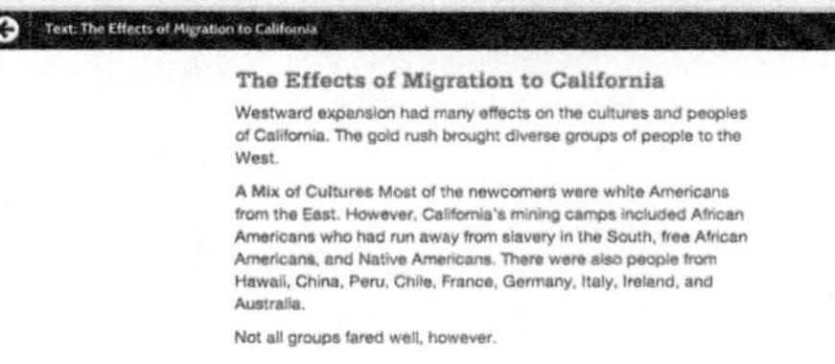

Text: The Effects of Migration to California
The Effects of Migration to California
Westward expansion had many effects on the cultures and peoples of California. The gold rush brought diverse groups of people to the West.
A Mix of Cultures Most of the newcomers were white Americans from the East. However, California's mining camps included African Americans who had run away from slavery in the South, free African Americans, and Native Americans. There were also people from Hawaii, China, Peru, Chile, France, Germany, Italy, Ireland, and Australia.
Not all groups fared well, however.
1 of 4

INTERACTIVE GALLERY

The People of California

Objective 5: **Describe how the Gold Rush affected California.**

Quick Instruction

Remind students that before the Gold Rush, the population of California consisted mainly of Native Americans and people of Spanish descent. With the Gold Rush, California went through dramatic changes in its population, economy, and politics.

Interactive Gallery: The People of California Project the gallery and go over each of the images with the students.

Summarize Describe the effect of the Gold Rush and this era of western expansion on Native Americans and Mexicans living in California. *(During the 1850s and 1860s, many Mexicans and Native Americans lost their land. In 1850, about 100,000 Native Americans lived in California, but by the 1870s, the state's Native American population had dropped to 17,000.)*

ACTIVE CLASSROOM

Have students use the Group Spokesperson Strategy to answer the following question: Did the opportunities provided by the Gold Rush outweigh the hardships people faced? Explain your answer with specific examples. *(For many people the opportunities provided by the Gold Rush outweighed the hardships faced. White immigrants from the United States and Europe were able to work in the mines or in other businesses, though most miners did not become rich. African Americans faced discrimination, but were able to live in a state that did not allow slavery.)*

Draw Conclusions How did the physical characteristics of the environment influence settlement patterns and population distribution in the West? *(The population of the California increased during this time, but the distribution of the population remained patchy. Locations that had gold attracted settlers. People also moved to areas with farmland.)*

ELL Use the ELL activity described in the ELL chart.

Further Instruction

Distinguish Identify one racial group that migrated to California. Explain their reasons for moving there, *(African Americans came to California to escape slavery in other parts of the United States, make money running businesses, and work in the mining industry.)*

Summarize How did different immigrant groups, such as the Chinese, interact with the environment in California? *(Chinese Americans shaped the environment by draining swamplands and digging irrigation systems to turn dry land into fertile farmland.)*

Manifest Destiny in California and the Southwest

SYNTHESIZE

DIGITAL ACTIVITY

Expansion of the United States

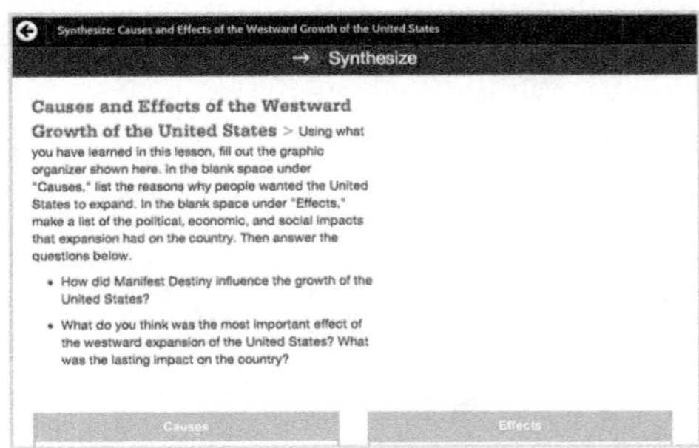

While today we picture the United States reaching from the Atlantic to the Pacific Ocean, in 1803 the nation only reached as far as the lands of the Louisiana Purchase. Many factors and major events led to the rapid growth of the country in the 1840s and 1850s. This expansion changed our nation forever.

Discuss Have partners think about the following question. What were the causes and effects of the westward growth of the United States? Ask partners to share their answers with the class.

DEMONSTRATE

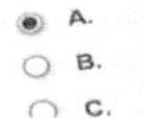

DIGITAL QUIZ

Lesson Quiz and Class Discussion Board

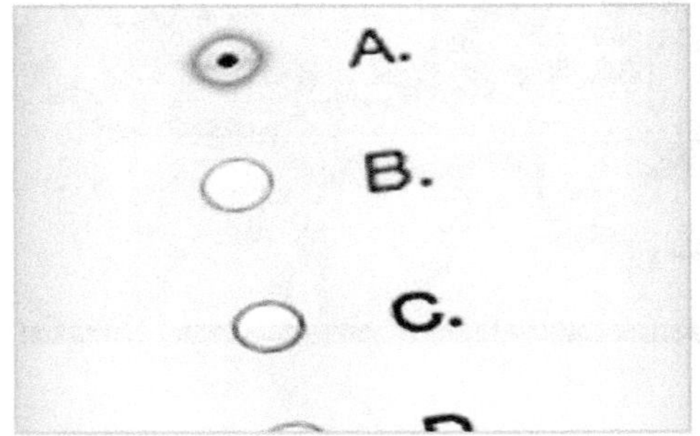

Assign the online Lesson Quiz for this lesson if you haven't already done so. Students will be offered automatic remediation or enrichment based on their score.

Pose these questions to the class on the Discussion Board:

In *California and the Southwest*, you read about the many factors that led to the growth of the United States in a short period of time.

Apply Concepts How did Manifest Destiny influence the westward growth of the United States? *(Americans who supported Manifest Destiny were more supportive of events that led to the growth of the country, such as the Mexican-American War.)*

Topic Inquiry

Have students continue their investigations for the Topic Inquiry.

PEARSON realize
www.PearsonRealize.com
Access your Digital Lesson

The Age of Jackson and Westward Expansion (1824–1860)

SYNTHESIZE

DIGITAL ESSENTIAL QUESTION ACTIVITY

Why do people move?

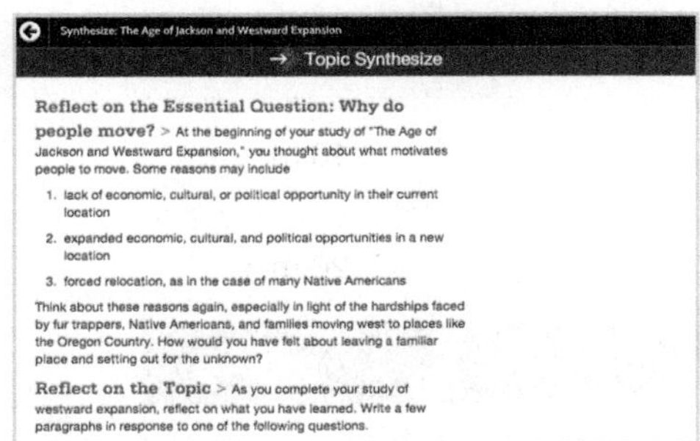

First, ask students to reconsider the Essential Question for the topic: Why do people move? Remind students of the reasons they considered at the beginning of the topic. For example: lack of economic, cultural, or political opportunity in their current location; expanded economic, cultural, and political opportunities in a new location; forced relocation, as in the case of many Native Americans.

Ask students, "What factors led many settlers to leave their homes and find a new home further west?"

Next, ask students to reflect on the topic as a whole and write down 1-3 questions they've thought about during the topic.

Prompt students to identify the specific push and pull factors that encouraged westward migration across the country. Ask students to work in small groups as they write a response to one of the following questions: Why did people leave their homes during this time period? What economic, cultural, or political opportunities were unavailable where they previously lived? Why did people choose to move westward to Oregon Country? Why were many Native Americans forced to move westward?

Topic Inquiry

Have students complete Step 3 of the Topic Inquiry.

DEMONSTRATE

DIGITAL TOPIC REVIEW AND ASSESSMENT

The Age of Jackson and Westward Expansion (1824–1860)

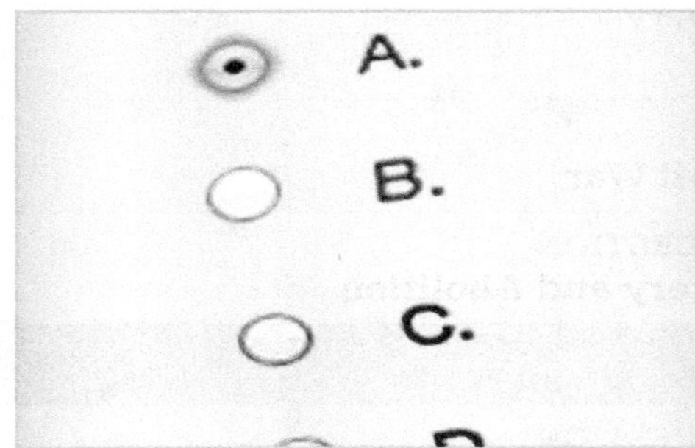

Students can prepare for the Topic Test by answering the questions in the Topic Review and Assessment online or the Assessment questions in the Print Student text. They can also prepare by reviewing their answers to the Interactive Reading Notepad questions or reviewing their notes in the Reading and Notetaking Study Guide.

DIGITAL TOPIC TEST

The Age of Jackson and Westward Expansion (1824–1860)

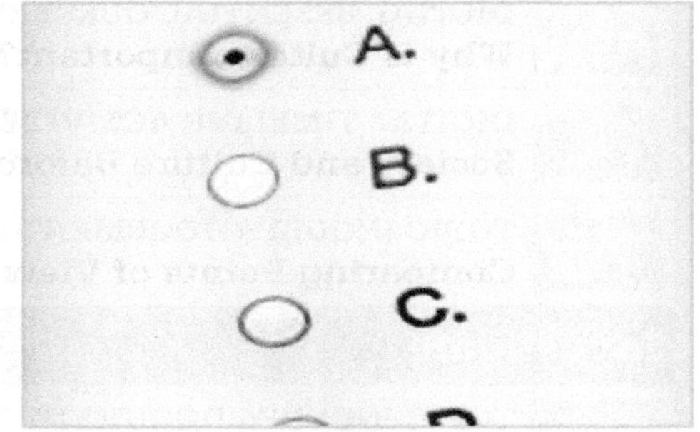

TOPIC TEST

Assign the Topic Test to assess students' understanding of topic content.

BENCHMARK TESTS

Assign these benchmark tests as you complete the relevant topics to monitor student progress toward mastering the course content and as preparation for the End-of-Course Test.

Benchmark Test 1: Topics 1–2

Benchmark Test 2: Topics 3–4

Benchmark Test 3: Topics 5–6

Benchmark Test 4: Topics 7–9

Benchmark Test 5: Topics 10–12

Benchmark Test 6: Topics 13–14

Benchmark Test 7: Topics 15–17

Topic 7

Society and Culture Before the Civil War (1820–1860)

TOPIC 7 ORGANIZER	PACING: APPROX. 9 PERIODS, 4.5 BLOCKS
	PACING
Connect	1 period
MY STORY VIDEO **Lucy Larcom, Weaving Opportunity**	10 min.
DIGITAL ESSENTIAL QUESTION ACTIVITY **Why is Culture Important?**	10 min.
DIGITAL TIMELINE ACTIVITY **Society and Culture Before the Civil War**	10 min.
TOPIC INQUIRY: DOCUMENT-BASED QUESTION **Comparing Points of View on Slavery and Abolition**	20 min.
Investigate	3–6 periods
TOPIC INQUIRY: DOCUMENT-BASED QUESTION **Comparing Points of View on Slavery and Abolition**	Ongoing
LESSON 1 The Industrial Revolution and Life in the North	30–40 min.
LESSON 2 King Cotton and Life in the South	30–40 min.
LESSON 3 Reform Movements	30–40 min.
LESSON 4 Abolitionism	30–40 min.
LESSON 5 Women's Rights	30–40 min.
LESSON 6 Arts and Literature	30–40 min.
Synthesize	1 period
DIGITAL ACTIVITY **Reflect on the Essential Question and Topic**	10 min.
TOPIC INQUIRY: DOCUMENT-BASED QUESTION **Comparing Points of View on Slavery and Abolition**	20 min.
Demonstrate	1–2 periods
DIGITAL TOPIC REVIEW AND ASSESSMENT **Society and Culture Before the Civil War**	10 min.
TOPIC INQUIRY: DOCUMENT-BASED QUESTION **Comparing Points of View on Slavery and Abolition**	20 min.

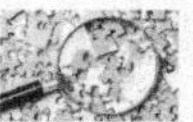

TOPIC INQUIRY: DOCUMENT-BASED QUESTION

Comparing Points of View on Slavery and Abolition

In this Topic Inquiry, students will examine primary source documents to answer the following question: What points of view did people have toward slavery and abolition? Developing a deeper understanding of these points of view, the people that held them, and the reasons for their disagreement will contribute to students' understanding of the Essential Question: Why is culture important?

STEP 1: CONNECT

Develop Questions and Plan the Investigation

Read Aloud

Divide students into pairs or small groups and have them take turns reading the speech and the poem aloud. Tell students that to answer the document-based question, they will be examining images, speeches, and lectures from pro and antislavery points of view.

Suggestion: You may want to let students read the speech and the poem to themselves beforehand. Provide a physical or online dictionary so they can look up any words they don't understand before reading aloud.

Discuss

Discuss as a class the points of view and frames of reference of the speech and the poem. Ask students to identify the point of view of each source based on the historical context surrounding the events each source discusses. Remind students that slavery and abolition were issues that divided the country in the years before the Civil War. Explain to students that this historical context shaped the frames of reference of each author and that frames of reference are the ways people think about events based on their experience and background. Discuss as a class the bias in the speech and the poem. Remind students that bias can mean prejudice. It can also mean a particular point of view. Discuss how the bias in each source reflects its author's point of view, calling on students to cite evidence for support.

Suggestion: If students are having difficulty identifying bias, have them begin rereading from the beginning of each piece. Have them stop after each line and ask themselves what the author is saying, how the author is saying it, why the author is expressing this view, and whether the piece simply states facts or whether it expresses a particular point of view, or bias.

STEP 2: INVESTIGATE

Apply Disciplinary Concepts and Tools

Analyze the Documents

Students will work individually to examine six documents and consider the different points of view they express. To guide their thinking, ask them to identify the point of view of each document based on its historical context, the frame of reference of each document's creator or author, and the bias present in each document, and then have students explain how they identified these characteristics.

Suggestion: Remind students to look up any words or phrases they do not understand. Students struggling to comprehend the documents may want to write a brief summary of each.

Check Your Understanding

Students will work individually to answer the multiple choice and short answer questions attached to each document. Answering the questions will help students identify areas in which their comprehension may be struggling. Students should review the documents as needed and correct their mistakes.

Suggestion: You may want to check students' answers for comprehension, or have students swap with a partner to check each other's work.

PROFESSIONAL DEVELOPMENT

Document-Based Question

Be sure to view the Document-Based Question Professional Development resources in the online course.

TOPIC INQUIRY: DOCUMENT-BASED QUESTION

Comparing Points of View on Slavery and Abolition *(continued)*

STEP 3: SYNTHESIZE

Evaluate Sources and Use Evidence to Formulate Conclusions

Write Your Essay

Students will use the documents to write essays on the following topic: What points of view did people have toward slavery and abolition? Remind students that they are being asked to think more deeply about the different points of view, frames of reference, and biases, and the ways people presented and justified their positions. Students should use their two charts to help them write their first draft.

Suggestion: Review the requirements for the essay. Students must use and mention at least four specific examples from the documents, two for each side of the argument. Essays should be clearly organized and free of errors.

STEP 4: DEMONSTRATE

Communicate Conclusions and Take Informed Action

Digital Topic Review and Assessment

Society and Culture Before the Civil War Students can prepare for the Topic Test by reviewing their notes for each lesson. Use the Test Bank to create your own Topic Test.

Digital Topic Test and Test Bank

TEKS Mastery Test Students can take a cumulative TEKS Mastery Test online to monitor their progress toward mastering the TEKS for this course and as preparation for the End-of-Course test.

Print Test

End-of-Course Practice Test You may want to assign the End-of-Course Practice Test found in the print Student text.

Topic Inquiry

Have students submit their essays.

INTRODUCTION

Society and Culture Before the Civil War (1820–1860)

American culture and society changed dramatically before the Civil War. New technological inventions led to industrialization and urbanization in the North. Cotton production soared in the South, bringing wealth to the region but also spreading slavery. Economic, religious, and political changes gave rise to social changes as reformers sought to improve society, end slavery, and increase women's rights. A changing society also gave rise to uniquely American forms of cultural expression.

CONNECT

MY STORY VIDEO

Lucy Larcom, Weaving Opportunity

Watch a video about Lucy Larcom, a worker in an early 19th century Lowell textile mill.

Check Understanding Where did many of the workers in the early textile mills come from? *(farms)*

Determine Point of View What may have accounted for the change in Lucy Larcom's view of mill work? *(Once she had grown accustomed to mill work, the novelty of it wore off. She grew to dislike the constant noise, and refused to become a slave to machines. The tedium of the labor and the need constantly to service the machines no doubt accounted for her change in view.)*

DIGITAL ESSENTIAL QUESTION ACTIVITY

Why is Culture Important?

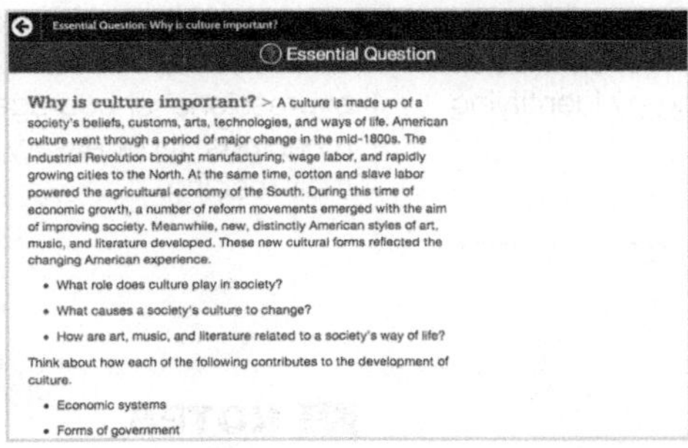

Ask students to think about the Essential Question for this topic: Why is culture important? Changes to American culture in the early 1800s impacted the nation and the American way of life.

If students have not already done so, ask them to read the list and think about how each factor contributes to the development of culture. Have students answer the questions and share their ideas with a partner.

Identify Cause and Effect What factors caused America's culture to change in the early 1800s?

Draw Conclusions How is the economy related to culture? Why would changes to the economy have a cultural impact?

DIGITAL TIMELINE ACTIVITY

Society and Culture Before the Civil War

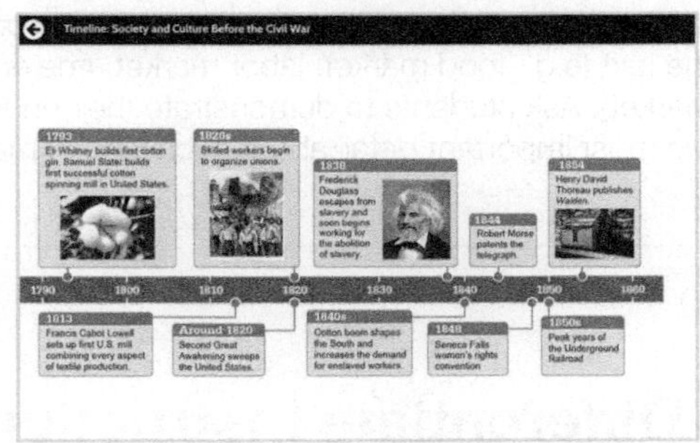

Display the timeline showing the major events before the Civil War. During this topic students will learn about all of these events and many more, but this timeline will provide a framework into which they can place the events they learn about.

Summarize Name at least two major reforms that occurred during this time. *(education; treatment for the mentally ill; women's rights; antislavery movement)*

Make Predictions How do you think the Second Great Awakening would shape American culture in the 1800s? *(It would increase religious feelings and inspire social reform.)*

Topic Inquiry

Launch the Topic Inquiry with students after introducing the topic.

Topic 7 Lesson 1

The Industrial Revolution and Life in the North

Supporting English Language Learners

Use with Digital Text 2, **Factories Come to America.**

Listening
Understand the important details of spoken language like the meaning of the word credit using the familiar context of credit cards.

Beginning Use basic spoken language to paraphrase the first paragraph of the text. Then help students to understand the important details of what you said by having them complete these sentences: *During the Industrial Revolution, the banking system was _____. People could get _____ to help them start businesses.*

Intermediate Use spoken language to paraphrase the first two paragraphs of the text. Then ask students to demonstrate their understanding by identifying the most important details from what you said.

Advanced Use spoken language to explain how supply and demand influenced business and investing, using the text as a reference. Ask students to demonstrate their understanding by identifying the most important details from what you said.

Advanced High Use spoken language to discuss markets in contexts that range from familiar to unfamiliar and may or may not be included in the text (e.g., food market, labor market, free enterprise market, stock market). Ask students to demonstrate their understanding by identifying the most important detail about each kind of market.

Use with Digital Text 5, **New Technologies.**

Reading
Tell students that if they read for comprehension rather than for speed, they will be able to read silently for longer periods of time.

Beginning Read aloud the first paragraph of the section titled *Farm Machines*, and explain any difficult words or phrases. Then ask students to silently read each sentence in the paragraph twice: once to decode individual words, and once to understand how the words fit together.

Intermediate Ask students to silently read the section titled *Farm Machines*. Encourage them to pause and reread any sentences they do not understand. Explain that they do not need to understand every word, but they should comprehend the general meaning of each sentence before moving on.

Advanced Ask students to silently read the section titled *A New Communications System, the Telegraph*. Encourage them to pause after each paragraph and identify its main idea, rereading it if necessary before moving on.

Advanced High Provide students with a dictionary, and ask them to silently read the text. When they encounter unfamiliar words or expressions, encourage them first to use context clues to determine their meanings. If necessary, they can also use the dictionary before resuming their reading.

D Differentiate Instruction

Use the Differentiated Instruction notes throughout the lesson plan to support the varied skill sets, levels of readiness, and interests in the mixed-ability classroom.

Challenge These notes include suggestions for expanding the activity for advanced students.

On-Level These notes include suggestions for modifying the activity to address different interests or learning styles.

Extra Support These notes include ideas for providing more scaffolding or reading spupport.

Special Needs These notes provide ideas for adapting instruction to support the needs of various special needs students.

NOTES

PEARSON realize
www.PearsonRealize.com

Go online to access additional resources including:
Primary Sources • Biographies • Supreme Court cases • 21st Century Skill Tutorials • Maps • Graphic Organizers.

Objectives

Objective 1: Identify the Industrial Revolution and explain its effects.

Objective 2: Explain the impact of the Industrial Revolution on cities.

Objective 3: Describe how technological change affected the economy of the North.

Objective 4: Identify the impact of the Industrial Revolution on working conditions, social class, and daily life.

Objective 5: Describe the impact of immigration and attitudes toward immigrants and African Americans in the North.

LESSON 1 ORGANIZER — **PACING: APPROX. 1 PERIOD, .5 BLOCKS**

	OBJECTIVES	PACING	RESOURCES Online	RESOURCES Print
Connect				
DIGITAL START UP ACTIVITY **A Model Factory Town**		5 min.	●	
Investigate				
DIGITAL TEXT 1 **The Industrial Revolution Begins**	Objective 1	10 min.	●	●
DIGITAL TEXT 2 **Factories Come to America**	Objective 1	10 min.	●	●
3-D MODEL **Nineteenth-Century Textile Mill**	Objective 1	10 min.	●	
DIGITAL TEXT 3 **Daily Life in Factory Towns**	Objective 2	10 min.	●	●
DIGITAL TEXT 4 **Cities Expand**	Objective 2	10 min.	●	●
DIGITAL TEXT 5 **New Technologies**	Objective 3	10 min.	●	●
INTERACTIVE TIMELINE **New Inventions Improve Life**	Objective 3	10 min.	●	
DIGITAL TEXT 6 **The Age of Steam Power**	Objective 3	10 min.	●	●
INTERACTIVE GALLERY **The Steam Locomotive**	Objective 3	10 min.	●	
DIGITAL TEXT 7 **Workers Respond to Challenges**	Objective 4	10 min.	●	●
DIGITAL TEXT 8 **Ethnic Minorities in the North**	Objective 5	10 min.	●	●
Synthesize				
DIGITAL ACTIVITY **A New Revolution**		5 min.	●	
Demonstrate				
DIGITAL QUIZ **Lesson Quiz and Class Discussion Board**		10 min.	●	

The Industrial Revolution and Life in the North

CONNECT

DIGITAL START UP ACTIVITY

A Model Factory Town

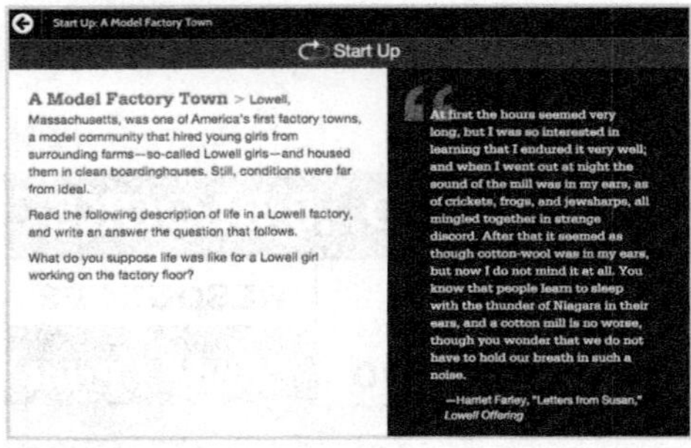

Project the Start Up Activity Ask students to read the quote and answer the questions as they enter and get settled. Have students share their answers with a partner, either in class or through a blog space.

Discuss What do you suppose life was like for a Lowell girl working on the factory floor? *(The girls worked long hours doing difficult, repetitive work, but it was exciting to learn new skills, meet other girls, and work outside the home.)*

Tell students that in this lesson they will be learning about the Industrial Revolution in the North and thetechnological innovations that changed life in the United States.

Aa Vocabulary Development: Use the Interactive Reading Notepad to preview the Key Terms and Academic Vocabulary in this lesson with students.

FLIP IT!

Assign the Flipped Video for this lesson.

STUDENT EDITION PRINT PAGES: 368–388

INVESTIGATE

DIGITAL TEXT 1

The Industrial Revolution Begins

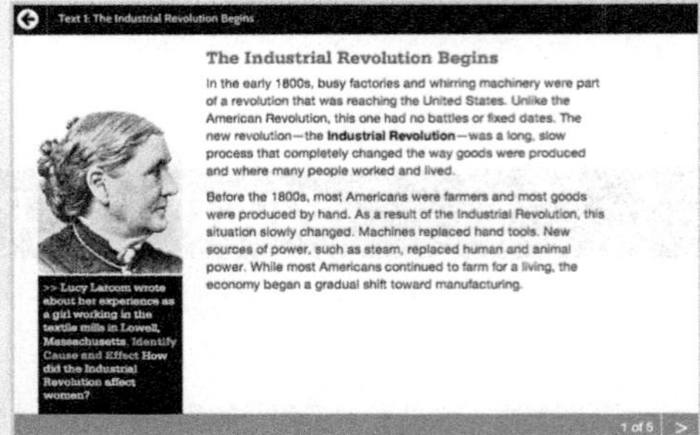

DIGITAL TEXT 2

Factories Come to America

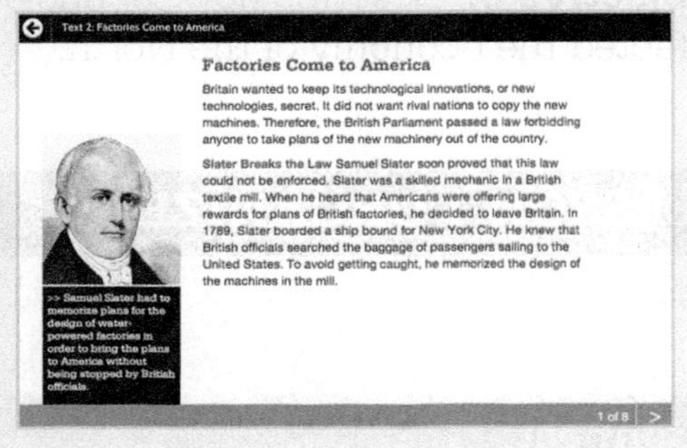

Objective 1: Identify the Industrial Revolution and explain its effects.

Quick Instruction

The Industrial Revolution began in Britain and soon spread, along with its factories, to the United States. Americans learned to rely on the physical characteristics of the environment, such as running water, to provide fuel for factories in the early nineteenth century, or 1800s. At the beginning of industrialization, factories were built to take advantage of water power. Factors, such as increased supply, lower costs, and growing demand, brought about rapid industrialization. Inventions, such as the textile mill, the spinning jenny, and the cotton gin, allowed producers to meet the growing demand.

3-D Model: Nineteenth-Century Textile Mill Project the 3-D model of the textile mill on the whiteboard and click through the images. Have students look at the wheel. Ask what environmental feature the textile mills were dependent on. *(rivers)*

Identify Cause and Effect How did new technologies change the way goods were manufactured in the United States and elsewhere? *(Spinning jennies and power looms allowed workers to produce much more cloth than they could by hand in both the United States and Britain.)*

ELL Use the ELL activity described in the ELL chart.

ACTIVE CLASSROOM

Ask students to write brief explanations for the reasons for the increase in factories. Have students use the Write 1-Get 3 Activity and fold a piece of paper into quarters. Students write down one response in the first box and then go around asking to hear other responses. When students think a response is correct, they write it in their boxes until they have three more responses. Have students share their responses with the class.

Further Instruction

Go through the Interactive Reading Notepad questions and discuss the answers with the class. To extend the lesson, assign 21st Century Skills: Create Databases.

Generate Explanations Explain the effects of scientific and technological innovations such as the use of interchangeable parts. How did such technological innovations bring about economic growth? *(Interchangeable parts increased efficiency and saved time and money. Instead of making parts specific to each individual item, machine-made parts were identical and could be used interchangeably. This contributed to the increase in factories, which could produce the parts faster and more cheaply than small workshops. Other technological innovations, such as the steam engine, further increased efficiency and production. Because factories could sell more goods, workers and factory owners made more money and could buy more goods. This increase in supply and demand brought economic growth.)*

3-D MODEL

Nineteenth-Century Textile Mill

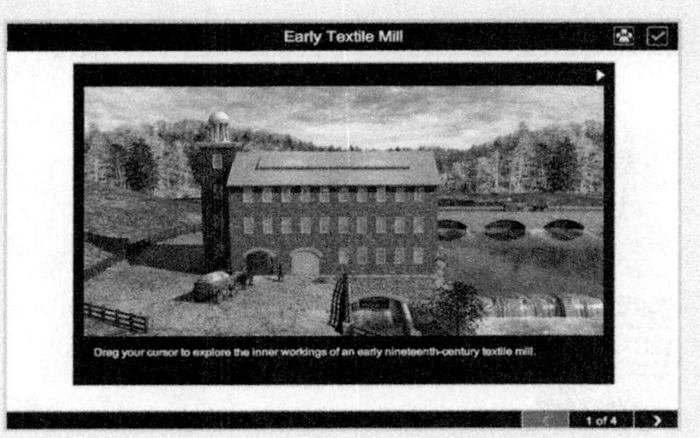

Identify Patterns What economic changes did the War of 1812 cause in the nation, and how did these changes contribute to the Industrial Revolution? *(The British blockade during the war forced Americans to build more factories to manufacture their own goods.)*

Draw Conclusions Describe the characteristics of the free enterprise system in the nineteenth century. What were the benefits of this system on the U.S. economy? *(Characteristics—few restrictions on trade or business growth; access to credit for bank loans; low taxes. Benefits—people were more easily able to finance new mills and factories; competition spurred economic growth.)*

DIGITAL TEXT 3

Daily Life in Factory Towns

Objective 2: Explain the impact of the Industrial Revolution on cities.

Quick Instruction

Project the infographic on urban industrial growth on the whiteboard. Have students consider the population growth in northern cities and explain the reasons for the increase in urbanization.

Identify Cause and Effect Identify the economic factors that brought about rapid urbanization in the nineteenth century. *(Factories increased profits, which led investors to build even more factories. These factories attracted more workers from farms who were seeking jobs and money. Cities developed and expanded around the factories as more people came to work in industries.)*

Further Instruction

Go through the Interactive Reading Notepad questions and discuss the answers with the class.

Summarize Identify the economic contributions of women to American society during the Industrial Revolution. *(Women such as the Lowell girls worked in the mills, providing labor, making products, and earning wages for their families.)*

DIGITAL TEXT 4

Cities Expand

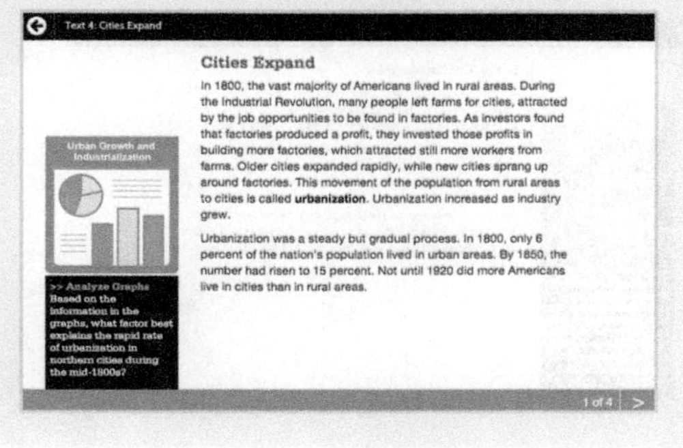

Support Ideas with Examples Using Lowell, Massachusetts, as an example, identify how industrialization changed life in the United States. *(More people moved to cities and worked in factories, including children and girls. Mill workers put in long hours year-round, in conditions that worsened as industrialization progressed. More family members began working outside of the home to earn money. This affected women's roles, as many women took paying jobs. Women who could afford it, however, stayed home.)*

Compare and Contrast Describe the positive and negative consequences of human modification of the physical environment through urbanization. *(Positive—cities offered work opportunities and new attractions and entertainment. Negative—the streets overflowed with garbage and untreated sewage; contaminated water spread disease; coal used to power industries and homes polluted the air and caused health problems.)*

The Industrial Revolution and Life in the North

DIGITAL TEXT 5

New Technologies

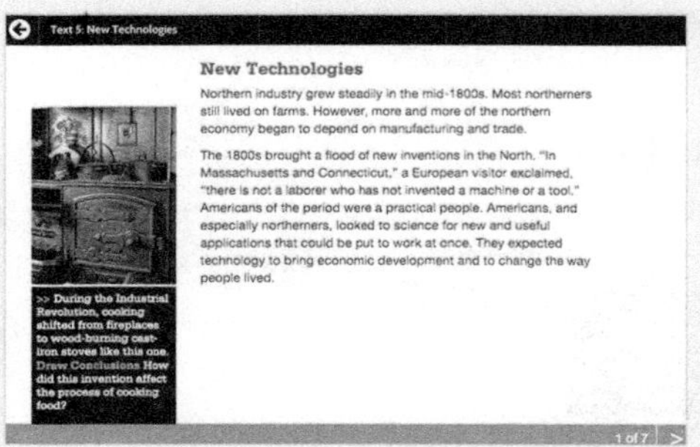

INTERACTIVE TIMELINE

New Inventions Improve Life

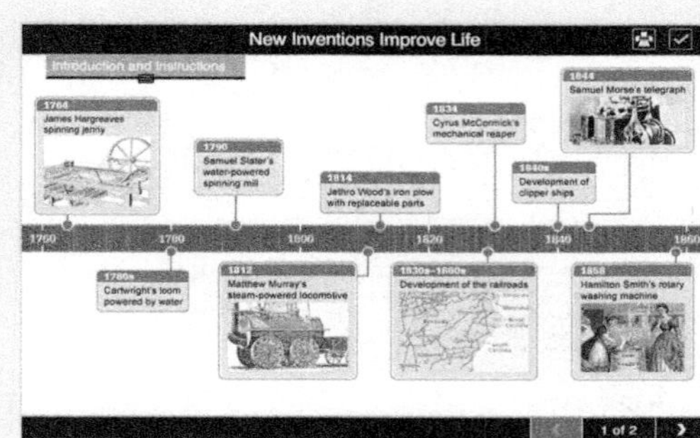

DIGITAL TEXT 6

The Age of Steam Power

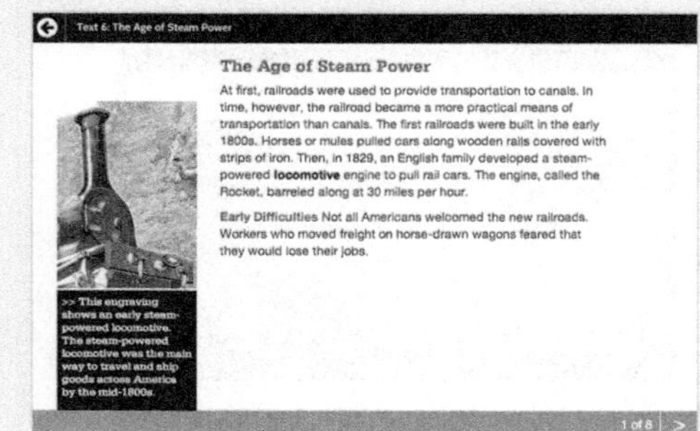

Objective 3: **Describe how technological change affected the economy of the North.**

Quick Instruction

Interactive Timeline: New Inventions Improve Life Project the interactive timeline on the whiteboard and click through the events. Have students pick two scientific discoveries, explain their effects, and compare how they influenced daily life in the nineteenth century, or the 1800s, then have them pick two technological innovations, explain their effects, and compare how they influenced daily life in the same period.

Generate Explanations Explain the impact of communications systems such as the telegraph. How did they affect the growth, development, and urbanization of the United States? *(The telegraph contributed to the growth and development of the United States by connecting farmers and business people with different markets, increasing business opportunities and economic growth and encouraging the development of new regions. It contributed to urbanization, as business people located in cities with good telegraph services.)* How did technological innovations such as the telegraph, the railroad, and steamships change the way goods were marketed nationally and internationally? *(Goods could now be marketed to distant customers, including customers in other countries.)*

Compare How was the locomotive an improvement over earlier railroad systems? *(The first railroads were pulled by horses or mules. The steam-powered locomotive engine pulled cars much faster. As engineering improved, locomotive railroads became safer and faster than previous forms of transportation.)*

ACTIVE CLASSROOM

Have students imagine they are advertising one of the new technological innovations of the Industrial Revolution and use the Make Headlines Activity to capture the importance of the device and the impact it will have.

ACTIVE CLASSROOM

Project a visual image from the steam locomotive and divide it into four numbered quadrants. Have students count off 1 to 4. Then have them look closely at the part of the image in their quadrant. Have them tell you what they see and what they learned as a result of their focus on this part of the image. Collect insights for each quadrant.

ELL Use the ELL activity described in the ELL chart.

Further Instruction

Go through the Interactive Reading Notepad questions and discuss the answers with the class. Be sure students can give examples of how technological innovations brought about economic growth. To extend the lesson, assign Personal Finance: Budgeting.

INTERACTIVE GALLERY

The Steam Locomotive

Support Ideas with Examples Give three examples of how the free enterprise system benefited Americans during the Industrial Revolution. *(mass production lowered prices; standard of living increased; wages increased)*

Identify Cause and Effect What was the impact of transportation systems on the urbanization of the United States? *(Railroads connected cities across the United States, allowing people to migrate more easily to urban centers. Factories and businesses grew in cities with good rail connections, which further encouraged more people to move to these areas.)*

DIGITAL TEXT 7

Workers Respond to Challenges

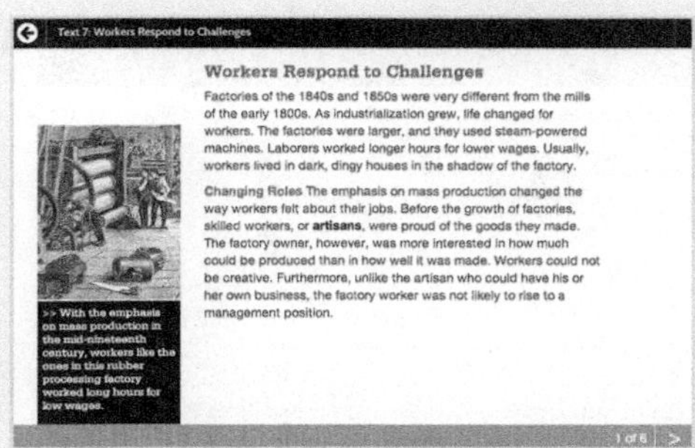

Objective 4: **Identify the impact of the Industrial Revolution on working conditions, social class, and daily life.**

Quick Instruction

Analyze Images Project the image of the factory and have students describe the working conditions visible in the image. Explain that this is an example of how industrialization changed life in the United States. Why do you think a labor reform movement developed in the United States? *(As a result of industrialization, laborers worked long hours at dangerous jobs for low wages. They organized to improve their hours, pay, and working conditions.)*

D Differentiate: Extra Support To understand the reasons for conflicts over labor, have students answer the following question from the point of view of a factory worker. What kinds of practices would you want the factory owner to follow? Now have them answer from the factory owner's point of view. What practices would you want to follow instead? Have students consider the different perspectives to understand how the interests of workers and owners differed.

Further Instruction

Go through the Interactive Reading Notepad questions and discuss the answers with the class.

Evaluate Arguments Evaluate the impact of the labor reform movement. Was it successful? Provide evidence to support your view. *(The movement did not completely transform working conditions, but it did meet with some success. Government employees won a ten-hour workday, strikes became legal, and some skilled workers won better pay.)*

Summarize Based on material in this text and preceding texts, what are some examples of how industrialization changed life in the United States? *(New jobs were available in factories; people moved from farms to cities; more goods were available more cheaply; people worked long hours in factories; family life became oriented around factory work.)*

Identify Cause and Effect How did urbanization lead to conflicts between people of different social classes? *(Urban working conditions created divisions between skilled and unskilled labor and between workers, managers, and business owners. These divisions did not exist when most people were farmers. The different classes lived together in the cities, but they often had different interests and conflicting views. These differences led to conflicts such as strikes.)*

The Industrial Revolution and Life in the North

DIGITAL TEXT 8

Ethnic Minorities in the North

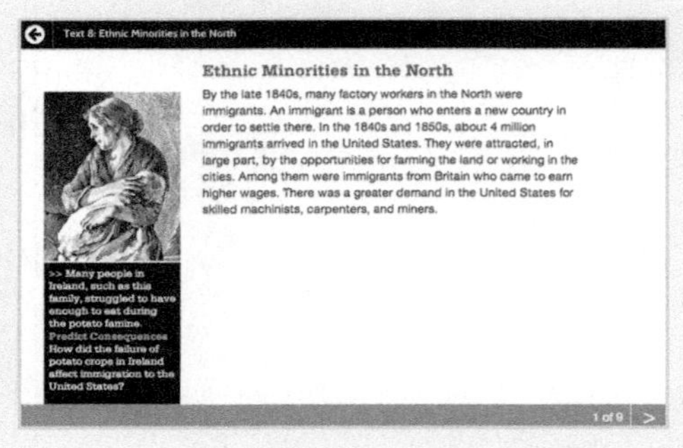

Text 8: Ethnic Minorities in the North
Ethnic Minorities in the North
By the late 1840s, many factory workers in the North were immigrants. An immigrant is a person who enters a new country in order to settle there. In the 1840s and 1850s, about 4 million immigrants arrived in the United States. They were attracted, in large part, by the opportunities for farming the land or working in the cities. Among them were immigrants from Britain who came to earn higher wages. There was a greater demand in the United States for skilled machinists, carpenters, and miners.
>> Many people in Ireland, such as this family, struggled to have enough to eat during the potato famine.
Predict Consequences How did the failure of potato crops in Ireland affect immigration to the United States?
1 of 9

Objective 5: **Describe the impact of immigration and attitudes toward immigrants and African Americans in the North.**

Quick Instruction

Project the photo of immigrants on the whiteboard and review the reasons industrialization drew people to northern cities, including immigrants.

Identify Central Issues Identify three ethnic groups that settled in the United States during this time and explain their reasons for immigration. *(British—higher wages; Irish—freedom from hunger and British rule; Germans—fertile land, a better life, democracy)*

Further Instruction

Go through the Interactive Reading Notepad questions and discuss the answers with the class.

Identify Cause and Effect How did urbanization lead to conflicts over differences in religion? *(Most Americans during the early 1800s were Protestant, but many immigrants were Catholic or Jewish. Many immigrants came to cities, which grew increasingly diverse. Not all Americans tolerated people of different religions. This lack of tolerance led to conflict between members of the different religions.)*

Make Predictions How do you think conflicts between various ethnic groups would be resolved? *(Americans would grow more tolerant as diversity increased; immigrants would adapt to American culture.)*

SYNTHESIZE

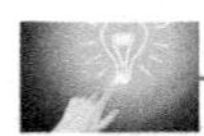

DIGITAL ACTIVITY

A New Revolution

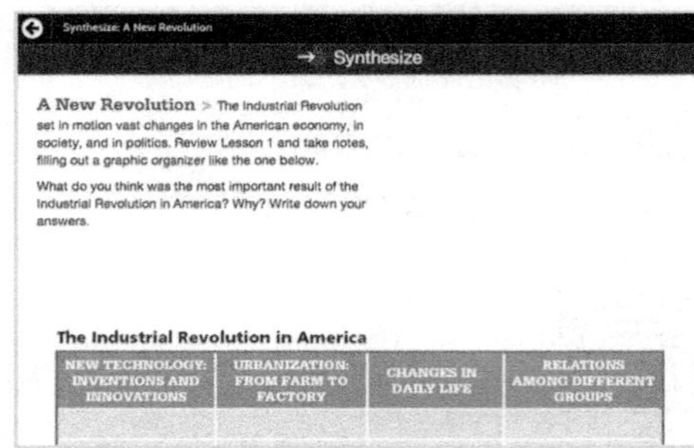

Synthesize: A New Revolution
→ Synthesize
A New Revolution > The Industrial Revolution set in motion vast changes in the American economy, in society, and in politics. Review Lesson 1 and take notes, filling out a graphic organizer like the one below.
What do you think was the most important result of the Industrial Revolution in America? Why? Write down your answers.
The Industrial Revolution in America
NEW TECHNOLOGY: INVENTIONS AND INNOVATIONS
URBANIZATION: FROM FARM TO FACTORY
CHANGES IN DAILY LIFE
RELATIONS AMONG DIFFERENT GROUPS

Have students complete the graphic organizer and explain what they think was the most important result of the Industrial Revolution, providing evidence for support.

Discuss Ask students to review the quote from the beginning of the lesson and decide whether they think Susan's view of factory life was typical for Americans working in industry. Discuss what it was like for women, immigrants, African Americans, and skilled and unskilled laborers to work in factories as America became more urban and industrial.

DEMONSTRATE

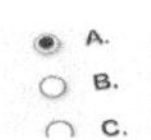

DIGITAL QUIZ

Lesson Quiz and Class Discussion Board

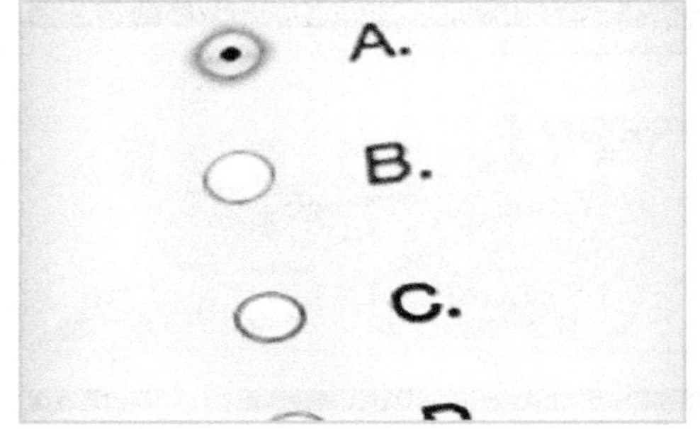

Assign the online Lesson Quiz for this lesson if you haven't already done so. Students will be offered automatic remediation or enrichment based on their score.

Pose these questions to the class on the Discussion Board:

Draw Conclusions How do you think the Industrial Revolution contributed to economic differences among different regions of the United States? Explain your reasoning.

Identify Cause and Effect How did the factory system contribute to rapid industrialization? What were the effects of this innovation on the United States?

Topic Inquiry

Have students continue their investigations for the Topic Inquiry.

King Cotton and Life in the South

Supporting English Language Learners

Use with Digital Text 4, **Southern African Americans.**

Reading
Explain to students that they will be employing basic reading skills and English comprehension to locate the answers to questions provided to them beforehand.

Beginning Provide students with a list titled *Jobs of African Americans*. On the list, include some from the text's third paragraph and some not. Have students read the paragraph and demonstrate English comprehension by circling the jobs on the list that are also mentioned in the paragraph.

Intermediate Display these questions: What are two ways an African American obtained freedom? In what trades did African Americans work? Ask pairs of students to read the second and third paragraphs of the text. Then have them demonstrate English comprehension by answering the questions.

Advanced Display these questions: Why was there tension between white slave owners and free African Americans? What difficulties did free African Americans face? Ask pairs of students to read the section titled Free African Americans and demonstrate English comprehension by answering the questions.

Advanced High Provide students with a blank Venn diagram. Then ask them to read the text and demonstrate English comprehension by comparing and contrasting the work and working conditions of free and enslaved African Americans.

Use with Digital Text 5, **Slavery in the South.**

Listening
Before the activity, review the term implicit idea and provide a simple example in increasingly complex spoken language (e.g., the implicit idea in saying you are hungry is that you want to eat).

Beginning Use basic spoken language to paraphrase the first two sentences of the section titled *Hard Work*. Ask: Which idea is implicit in what I said—that enslaved workers usually worked less than 16 hours per day, worked more than 16 hours per day, or worked alongside their owners?

Intermediate Use spoken language to paraphrase the first paragraph of the section titled *Hard Work*. Ask students to identify implicit ideas about the duration and intensity of enslaved workers' workdays.

Advanced Use spoken language to paraphrase the section titled *Slave Codes*. Ask: What did slave codes forbid enslaved African Americans to do? What does this information imply about what free people could do?

Advanced High Use spoken language to paraphrase the section titled *Slave Codes*. Ask pairs of students to discuss these questions: What does this information about slave codes imply about what free people could do? What does it imply about the value given to education?

D Differentiate Instruction

Use the Differentiated Instruction notes throughout the lesson plan to support the varied skill sets, levels of readiness, and interests in the mixed-ability classroom.

Challenge These notes include suggestions for expanding the activity for advanced students.

On-Level These notes include suggestions for modifying the activity to address different interests or learning styles.

Extra Support These notes include ideas for providing more scaffolding or reading spuport.

Special Needs These notes provide ideas for adapting instruction to support the needs of various special needs students.

NOTES

Topic 7 Lesson 2

King Cotton and Life in the South

Objectives

Objective 1: Identify how the development of the cotton gin affected the South.

Objective 2: Describe the agricultural economy of the South.

Objective 3: Describe southern society.

Objective 4: Compare the economic, social, and political conditions of free and enslaved African Americans.

Objective 5: Explain the impact of slavery.

LESSON 2 ORGANIZER	PACING: APPROX. 1 PERIOD, .5 BLOCKS			
			RESOURCES	
	OBJECTIVES	PACING	Online	Print
Connect				
DIGITAL START UP ACTIVITY **The Price of Freedom**		5 min.	●	
Investigate				
DIGITAL TEXT 1 **The Cotton Kingdom**	Objective 1	10 min.	●	●
3-D MODEL **The Cotton Gin**		10 min.	●	
DIGITAL TEXT 2 **Reliance on Agriculture**	Objective 2	10 min.	●	●
DIGITAL TEXT 3 **Southern Whites**	Objective 3	10 min.	●	●
DIGITAL TEXT 4 **Southern African Americans**	Objective 4	10 min.	●	●
INTERACTIVE CHART **Different Ways of Life in the South**		10 min.	●	
DIGITAL TEXT 5 **Slavery in the South**	Objective 5	10 min.	●	●
INTERACTIVE CHART **Lives of Free and Enslaved African Americans**		10 min.	●	
DIGITAL TEXT 6 **Resisting Slavery**		10 min.	●	●
Synthesize				
DIGITAL ACTIVITY **Cotton is King**		5 min.	●	
Demonstrate				
DIGITAL QUIZ **Lesson Quiz and Class Discussion Board**		10 min.	●	

Go online to access additional resources including: Primary Sources • Biographies • Supreme Court cases • 21st Century Skill Tutorials • Maps • Graphic Organizers.

CONNECT

DIGITAL START UP ACTIVITY

The Price of Freedom

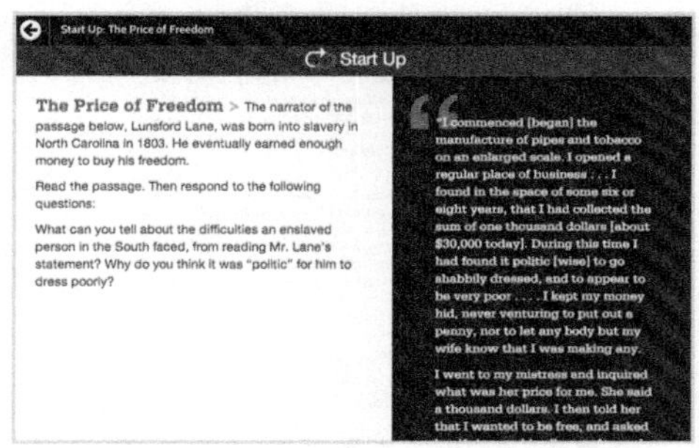

Project the Start Up Activity Ask students to read the quote and answer the questions as they enter and get settled. Have students share their answers with a partner, either in class or through a blog space.

Discuss What can you tell about the difficulties an enslaved person in the South faced from reading Mr. Lane's statement? Why do you think it was "politic" for him to dress poorly? *(Lane had to make sure no one would suspect that he was making money and successfully running a business. He did not want anyone to think he was preparing to buy his freedom.)*

Tell students that in this lesson they will be learning about the economic and social characteristics of life in the South.

Aa Vocabulary Development: Use the Interactive Reading Notepad to preview the Key Terms and Academic Vocabulary in this lesson with students.

FLIP IT!

Assign the Flipped Video for this lesson.

STUDENT EDITION PRINT PAGES: 389–400

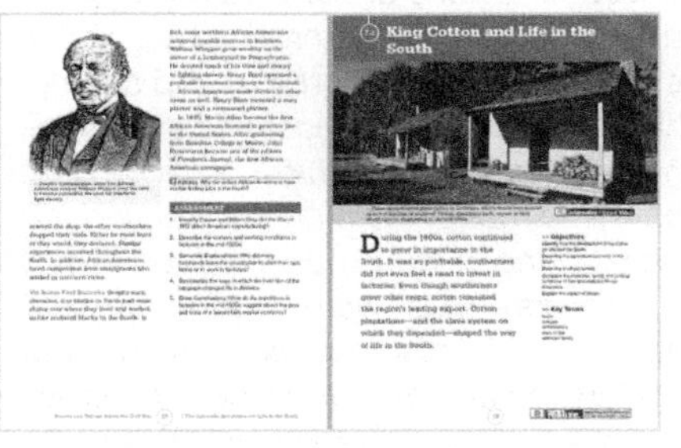

INVESTIGATE

DIGITAL TEXT 1

The Cotton Kingdom

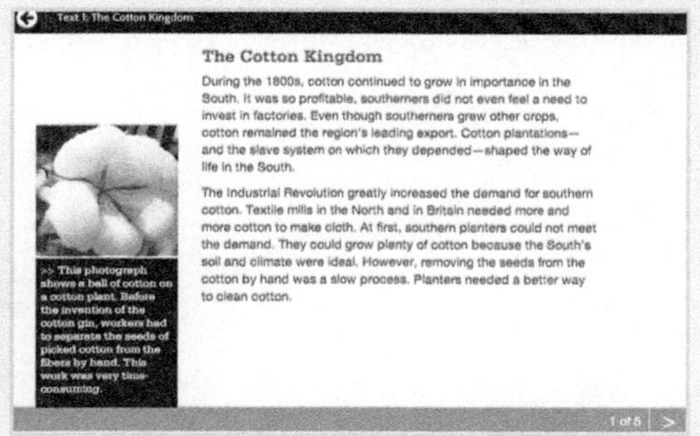

3-D MODEL

The Cotton Gin

Objective 1: **Identify how the development of the cotton gin affected the South.**

Quick Instruction

3-D Model: The Cotton Gin Project the 3-D model of the cotton gin on the whiteboard and click through the images. Remind students how factories changed the economy in the North. Ask how they think the cotton gin affected the economy in South.

ACTIVE CLASSROOM

Have students use the Quick Write Strategy and take 30 seconds to write what they already know about the southern economy. Then have students discuss in groups or as a class how they think the rise of the cotton kingdom will impact the southern economy and way of life.

D Differentiate: Extra Support Ask students what they think is meant by the term "Cotton Kingdom." Discuss why this term describes the South in the 1800s.

Further Instruction

Go through the Interactive Reading Notepad questions and discuss the answers with the class. Be sure students explain the effects of technological developments such as the cotton gin on the economic development of the South.

Make Generalizations Describe the economic differences between the North and South. *(The North was more industrialized and made profits from factories and manufacturing. The South was more agricultural. Wealthy southerners made so much money on cotton that they did not see a need to invest in factories.)*

Generate Explanations Explain how the cotton gin impacted economic development in both the North and South. *(South—Because the gin could clean cotton much faster than individuals could, planters began making huge profits off cotton. Agriculture spread and profits increased. North—used southern cotton to make cloth, bringing profits to the textile mills.)*

Cite Evidence that the cotton gin contributed to the rise of slavery and the plantation system. *("The huge demand for cotton, the efficiency offered by cotton gins, and southern planters' reliance on slave labor led to the growth of large plantations, each with many enslaved workers.")*

King Cotton and Life in the South

DIGITAL TEXT 2

Reliance on Agriculture

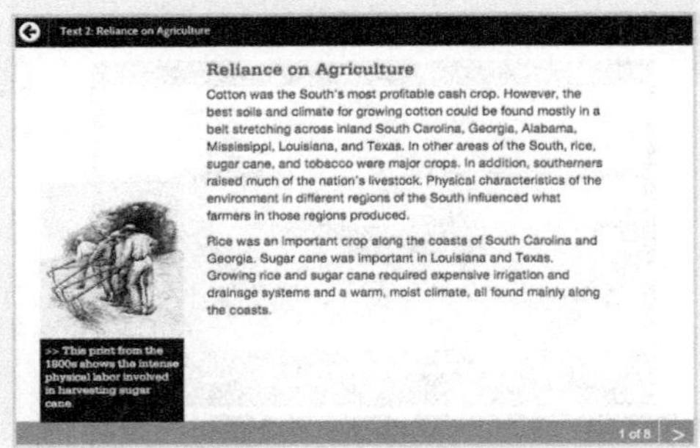

Text 2: Reliance on Agriculture
Reliance on Agriculture
Cotton was the South's most profitable cash crop. However, the best soils and climate for growing cotton could be found mostly in a belt stretching across inland South Carolina, Georgia, Alabama, Mississippi, Louisiana, and Texas. In other areas of the South, rice, sugar cane, and tobacco were major crops. In addition, southerners raised much of the nation's livestock. Physical characteristics of the environment in different regions of the South influenced what farmers in those regions produced.
Rice was an important crop along the coasts of South Carolina and Georgia. Sugar cane was important in Louisiana and Texas. Growing rice and sugar cane required expensive irrigation and drainage systems and a warm, moist climate, all found mainly along the coasts.
>> This print from the 1800s shows the intense physical labor involved in harvesting sugar cane.
1 of 8

Objective 2: Describe the agricultural economy of the South.

Quick Instruction

Analyze Graphs Project the infographic on cotton cultivation. Have students study the graphs and draw a conclusion about the agricultural economy of the South and the development of slavery.

Summarize Identify the key economic differences between the North and the South. *(The North relied more and more on industry and commerce. The South remained dependent on agriculture.)*

Compare and Contrast industry in the North and South. *(North—more urban, with large and diverse industries. Manufactured tools and goods made from metal and cloth. South—less industrial. The only industries served farms, by milling flour and manufacturing railroad equipment and machinery.)*

Further Instruction

Go through the Interactive Reading Notepad questions and discuss the answers with the class.

Identify Cause and Effect Identify the causes and effects of economic differences between the North and South. *(Causes—planters had invested their money in land and in enslaved African Americans to work the plantations. Because they had come to rely on those investments and made a good income from them, they saw little reason to invest in industry. Demand for factory goods was also low, as enslaved African Americans could not purchase them. By contrast, northern investors gained profits from investing in industry, and technological innovations and urban growth spurred growth in the North's industrial economy. Effects—poor southerners on small farms had fewer opportunities than northerners to find work outside farming; the South became dependent on northern and European industries; Southerners borrowed money from northern banks.)*

Draw Conclusions How did the economic differences between the North and South lead to divisions within the nation? *(The South was largely dependent on the North for capital and for industrial goods. Many southerners were proud of the cotton economy and resented their dependence on the northern economy.)*

Summarize What physical characteristics of the environment influenced economic activities in the South? *(The South had a warm climate and rich soil for growing cotton and tobacco. Along the coast, irrigation and drainage systems and a warm, moist climate supported rice and sugar cane. Land unsuitable for crops was used for livestock.)*

DIGITAL TEXT 3

Southern Whites

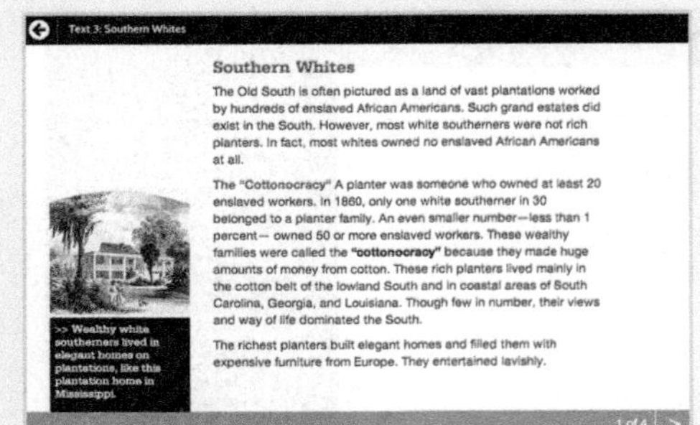

Text 3: Southern Whites
Southern Whites
The Old South is often pictured as a land of vast plantations worked by hundreds of enslaved African Americans. Such grand estates did exist in the South. However, most white southerners were not rich planters. In fact, most whites owned no enslaved African Americans at all.
The "Cottonocracy" A planter was someone who owned at least 20 enslaved workers. In 1860, only one white southerner in 30 belonged to a planter family. An even smaller number—less than 1 percent— owned 50 or more enslaved workers. These wealthy families were called the "cottonocracy" because they made huge amounts of money from cotton. These rich planters lived mainly in the cotton belt of the lowland South and in coastal areas of South Carolina, Georgia, and Louisiana. Though few in number, their views and way of life dominated the South.
The richest planters built elegant homes and filled them with expensive furniture from Europe. They entertained lavishly.
>> Wealthy white southerners lived in elegant homes on plantations, like this plantation home in Mississippi.
1 of 4

Objective 3: Describe southern society.

Quick Instruction

Project the images of the wealthy plantation family and the poor southern family on the whiteboard. Although the Old South is known for its grand estates, most white southerners were not wealthy planters and did not own enslaved African Americans.

Draw Conclusions How did the physical characteristics of the South influence human characteristics such as social classes in different parts of the region? *(Wealthy planters lived in the lowland and coastal areas that were best for growing cotton. Small farmers were in most parts of the South, but there were fewer in the cotton belt and coastal regions. Poor farmers lived in hilly regions north and west of the cotton belt, where the land was not suitable for cotton production and generated little wealth.)*

Further Instruction

Go through the Interactive Reading Notepad questions and discuss the answers with the class. Be sure students understand the social and economic characteristics of life for whites in the South.

Compare regions of the United States in terms of human characteristics by comparing the characteristics of northern and southern whites. *(Northerners—most whites were small farmers; the wealthiest were capitalists who made money from investing in industry; many worked in industries and lived in cities. Southerners—most were small farmers; the wealthiest were planters who made money from farming and from the labor of enslaved African Americans; few lived in cities.)*

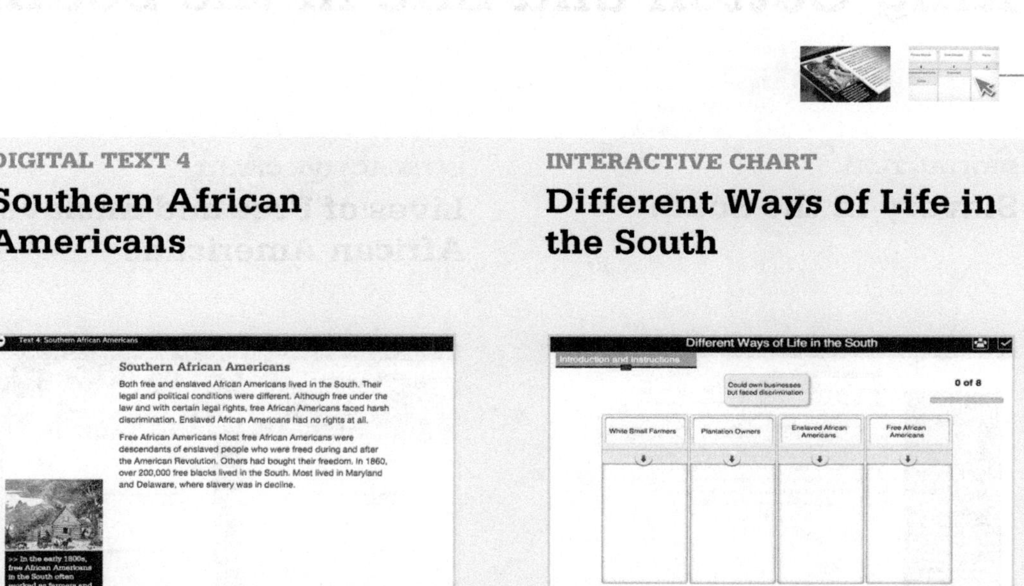

DIGITAL TEXT 4

Southern African Americans

INTERACTIVE CHART

Different Ways of Life in the South

Summarize How did the upland South differ economically and socially, in terms of its human characteristics, from the lowland cotton region? *(The cotton region was wealthier and dominated the South. This was where the richest planters of the cottonocracy lived. Poor farmers lived in the upland South. Many did not own their land.)*

Objective 4: **Compare the economic and social conditions of free and enslaved African Americans.**

Quick Instruction

Interactive Chart: Different Ways of Life in the South Project the interactive chart on the whiteboard and have students read through the tiles. Compare the social and economic factors that influenced life for free and enslaved African Americans.

Support Ideas with Examples How did southern laws limit opportunities for free African Americans? *(They made life harder by prohibiting African Americans from voting or traveling. Many free African Americans moved to reduce the risk of being kidnapped and enslaved.)*

ACTIVE CLASSROOM

Have students use the Conversations with History Activity to suppose they are talking with African American inventors Norbert Rillieux or Henry Blair. Have them write down a question they would ask, what the person would say, and what they would say in response.

ELL Use the ELL activity described in the ELL chart.

Further Instruction

Both free and enslaved African Americans lived in the southern United States, but the effects of economic and social factors differed between these populations. While free African Americans faced brutal discrimination and limitations under the law, they enjoyed some rights, including the ability to own and operate businesses. On the other hand, enslaved African Americans had no rights.

As students read the text, have them compare the economic and social circumstances of enslaved and free African Americans.

Compare the family lives of free and enslaved African Americans. *(The families of enslaved African Americans could be broken up by their owners. All family members were forced to work long hours on the plantations. Free African Americans faced discrimination but were not forced to separate.)*

Determine Point of View Why did white slave owners fear the presence of free African Americans in the South? *(White owners feared they might encourage enslaved African Americans to seek freedom; they countered the slave owners' attempts to justify slavery.)*

Summarize Describe the economic contributions of free and enslaved African Americans. *(Enslaved African Americans worked on plantations, generating wealth for white owners and for the southern economy. Free African Americans owned and operated businesses, worked as farmers, developed skills and trades, and invented devices that improved southern life.)*

King Cotton and Life in the South

DIGITAL TEXT 5

Slavery in the South

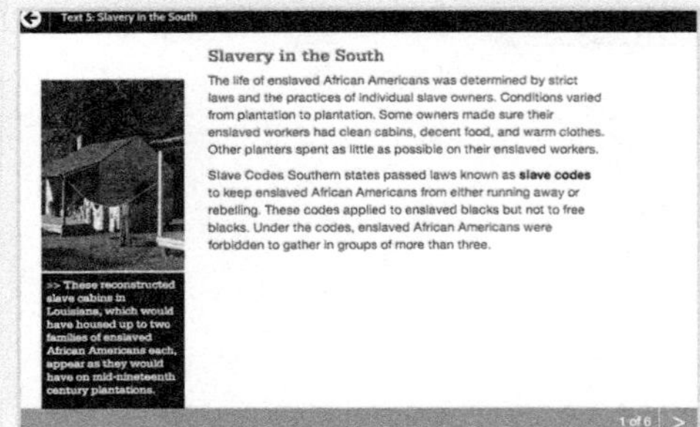

Text 5: Slavery in the South
Slavery in the South
The life of enslaved African Americans was determined by strict laws and the practices of individual slave owners. Conditions varied from plantation to plantation. Some owners made sure their enslaved workers had clean cabins, decent food, and warm clothes. Other planters spent as little as possible on their enslaved workers.
Slave Codes Southern states passed laws known as slave codes to keep enslaved African Americans from either running away or rebelling. These codes applied to enslaved blacks but not to free blacks. Under the codes, enslaved African Americans were forbidden to gather in groups of more than three.
>> These reconstructed slave cabins in Louisiana, which would have housed up to two families of enslaved African Americans each, appear as they would have on mid-nineteenth century plantations.
1 of 6

Objective 5: **Explain the impact of slavery.**

Quick Instruction

Interactive Chart: Lives of Free and Enslaved African Americans Project the interactive chart on the whiteboard and read the columns. Have students fill in the graphic organizer.

Summarize Why were enslaved African Americans kept illiterate? *(Owners thought it would be harder for enslaved African Americans to escape slavery if they couldn't read and write, because they wouldn't be able to read maps or train schedules.)*

ACTIVE CLASSROOM

Ask students, "Why is Nat Turner important?" Have students use the Sticky Notes Activity and spend three minutes jotting down questions, comments, or observations about Turner and his revolt. Sort the stickies and discuss the questions as a group.

ELL Use the ELL activity described in the ELL chart.

INTERACTIVE CHART

Lives of Free and Enslaved African Americans

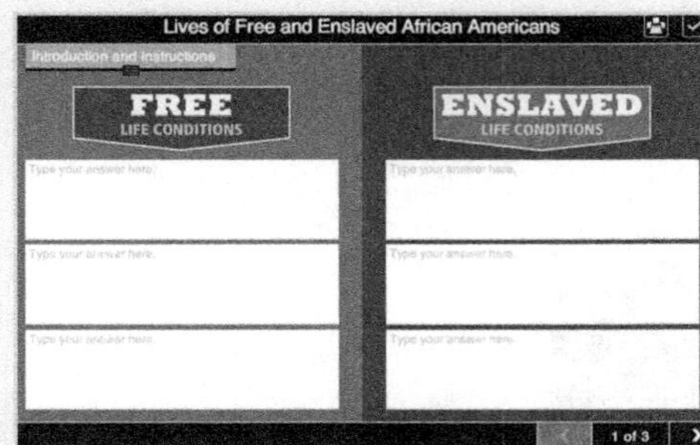

Further Instruction

Go through the Interactive Reading Notepad questions and discuss the answers with the class.

Identify Cause and Effect What were the slave codes? What were the effects of these laws? *(The laws prohibited enslaved African Americans from gathering in large groups, leaving their owner's land without permission, owning guns, and learning to read and write. These laws made it harder for African Americans to run away or rebel.)*

DIGITAL TEXT 6

Resisting Slavery

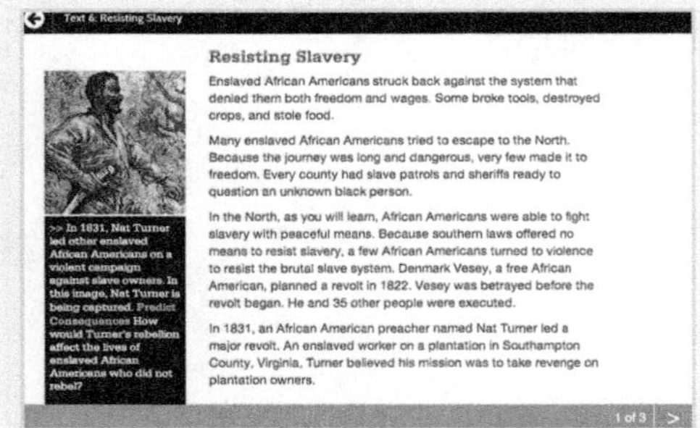

Draw Conclusions Why did religion play such an important role in the lives of enslaved African Americans? *(Religion provided hope. It offered inspiring examples of other groups escaping slavery and allowed enslaved African Americans to sing about freedom in ways that were acceptable to slave owners.)*

Identify Patterns Identify the ways in which enslaved African Americans resisted slavery. *(They resisted the plantation system by breaking tools, destroying crops, and stealing food. Some tried to escape to the North. Nat Turner led a major revolt.)*

SYNTHESIZE

DIGITAL ACTIVITY

Cotton is King

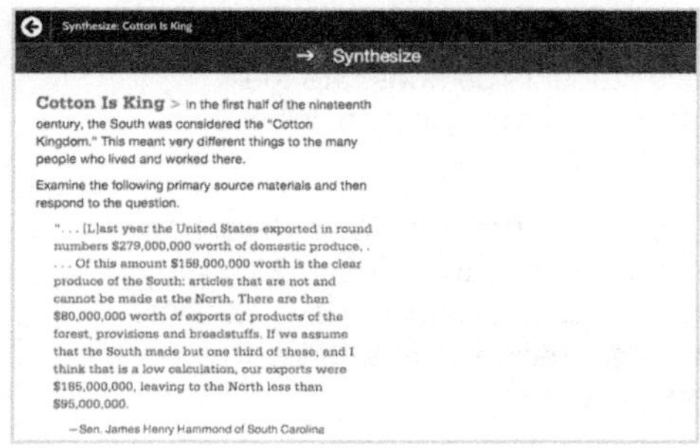

Have students examine the primary sources and answer the question.

Discuss Ask students to review the quote from the beginning of the lesson. Now that they have learned more about life in the South, have them explain the ways in which Lane's experience was and was not typical. Discuss what life in the Cotton Kingdom was like for poor and wealthy southern whites, free African Americans, and enslaved African Americans.

DEMONSTRATE

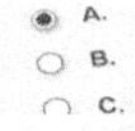

DIGITAL QUIZ

Lesson Quiz and Class Discussion Board

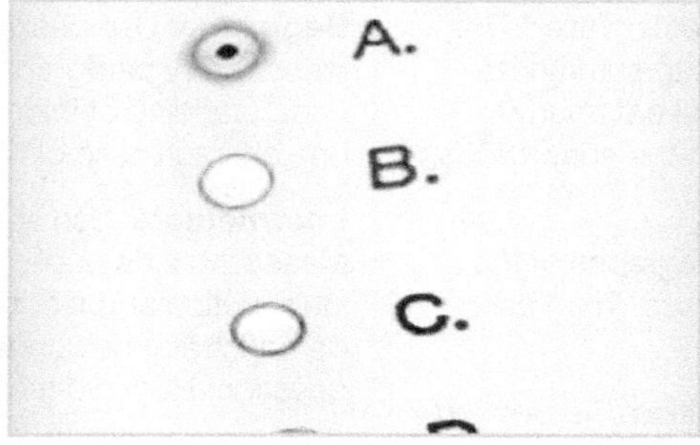

Assign the online Lesson Quiz for this lesson if you haven't already done so. Students will be offered automatic remediation or enrichment based on their score.

Pose these questions to the class on the Discussion Board:

Compare and Contrast Why did slavery develop in the South? Why do you think slavery was less extensive in the North?

Identify Cause and Effect How did slavery impact the economy and society of the South?

Analyze Information Was slavery solely a southern institution, as it is sometimes considered, or did the North contribute to its spread? Explain your reasoning.

Topic Inquiry

Have students continue their investigations for the Topic Inquiry.

Reform Movements

Supporting English Language Learners

Use with Digital Text 1, **An Era of Reform.**

Reading

Recall that when we summarize text, we identify the most important details and restate them in our own words.

Beginning Echo read the first two paragraphs of the section titled *The Second Great Awakening and Its Causes*. Ask students to summarize them by completing these sentences: During the colonial era, many Protestants believed their _____ was already decided. In the early 1800s, the idea of _____ became popular.

Intermediate Invite volunteers to read the first two paragraphs of the section titled *The Second Great Awakening and Its Causes*. Then ask students to summarize each paragraph in a sentence.

Advanced Invite pairs of students to read the section titled *The Second Great Awakening and Its Causes*. Then have them discuss these questions: What are the four or five most important pieces of information? How can you use them to create a summary of the section?

Advanced High Ask students to independently read the text and write a written summary of it. Encourage them to use the text's title and subheadings to help them organize their summary.

Use with Digital Text 3, **The Impact of Educational Reform.**

Listening

Explain to students that you will be speaking about education and educational reform in the 1800s. Discuss the meaning of *reform*.

Beginning Use basic spoken language to paraphrase the text's introductory paragraphs. Then have students demonstrate their understanding of information by answering this question: What was one characteristic of Massachusetts public schools?

Intermediate Use spoken language to explain with some detail how Massachusetts public schools changed during the 1800s, using the introduction and first section of the text as a reference. Have students demonstrate their understanding of information by answering this question: How did teacher training improve?

Advanced Use somewhat complex spoken language to paraphrase the section titled *Education Reform Gives Rise to Public Schools*. Have pairs of students demonstrate their understanding of information by answering this question: How and why did Horace Mann improve Massachusetts public schools?

Advanced High Use complex spoken language to paraphrase the section titled *Education Reform Gives Rise to Public Schools*. Have students demonstrate their understanding of information by writing a response to this question and discussing it with a partner: How were public schools alike and different in New York and Massachusetts?

D Differentiate Instruction

Use the Differentiated Instruction notes throughout the lesson plan to support the varied skill sets, levels of readiness, and interests in the mixed-ability classroom.

Challenge These notes include suggestions for expanding the activity for advanced students.

On-Level These notes include suggestions for modifying the activity to address different interests or learning styles.

Extra Support These notes include ideas for providing more scaffolding or reading spuport.

Special Needs These notes provide ideas for adapting instruction to support the needs of various special needs students.

NOTES

PEARSON realize™ www.PearsonRealize.com

Go online to access additional resources including: Primary Sources • Biographies • Supreme Court cases • 21st Century Skill Tutorials • Maps • Graphic Organizers.

Objectives

Objective 1: Explain how political and religious trends, including the Second Great Awakening, inspired reform movements.

Objective 2: Describe the impact of movements for temperance and for the reform of mental health care and prisons.

Objective 3: Explain the impact of movements for the reform of education and care for the disabled.

LESSON 3 ORGANIZER	PACING: APPROX. 1 PERIOD, .5 BLOCKS		RESOURCES	
	OBJECTIVES	PACING	Online	Print
Connect				
DIGITAL START UP ACTIVITY **Religious Movements and Social Reform**		5 min.	●	
Investigate				
DIGITAL TEXT 1 **An Era of Reform**	Objective 1	10 min.	●	●
DIGITAL TEXT 2 **Social Reform Movements**	Objective 2	10 min.	●	●
DIGITAL TEXT 3 **The Impact of Educational Reform**	Objective 3	10 min.	●	●
INTERACTIVE GALLERY **Changes in American Schools**	Objective 3	10 min.	●	
Synthesize				
DIGITAL ACTIVITY **The Impact of Social Reform**		5 min.	●	
Demonstrate				
DIGITAL QUIZ **Lesson Quiz and Class Discussion Board**		10 min.	●	

Reform Movements

CONNECT

DIGITAL START UP ACTIVITY

Religious Movements and Social Reform

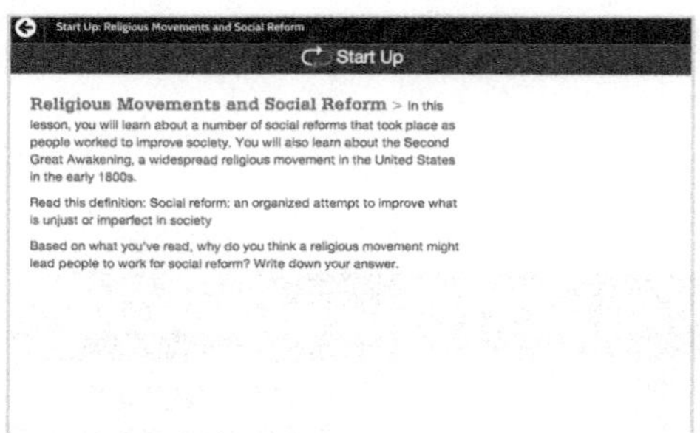

Project the Start Up Activity Ask students to read the definition and answer the question as they enter and get settled. Have students share their answers with a partner, either in class or through a blog space.

Discuss Based on what you've read, why do you think a religious movement might lead people to work for social reform? *(Religious teachings might emphasize moral action, helping others in need, or making the world a better place.)*

Tell students that in this lesson they will be learning about the causes and effects of reform movements inspired by the Second Great Awakening.

Aa Vocabulary Development: Use the Interactive Reading Notepad to preview the Key Terms and Academic Vocabulary in this Lesson with students.

FLIP IT!

Assign the Flipped Video for this lesson.

STUDENT EDITION PRINT PAGES: 401–406

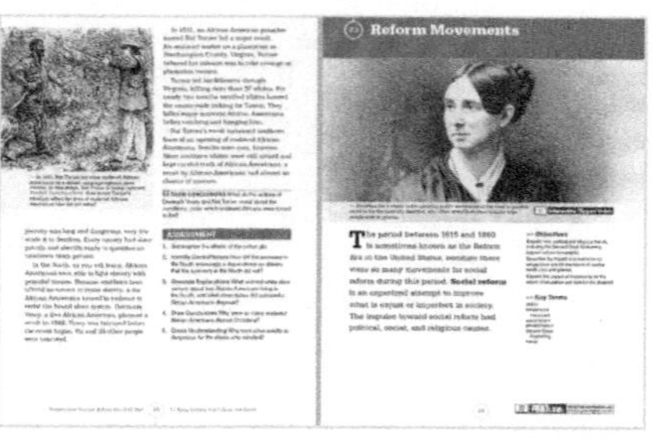

INVESTIGATE

DIGITAL TEXT 1

An Era of Reform

Text 1: An Era of Reform

An Era of Reform

The period between 1815 and 1860 is sometimes known as the Reform Era in the United States, because there were so many movements for social reform during this period. **Social reform** is an organized attempt to improve what is unjust or imperfect in society. The impulse toward social reform had political, social, and religious causes.

Political Ideals Lead to Reform As you have read, during the Jacksonian era, politics was becoming more democratic. More people could vote and take part in government than ever before.

The Reform Movement

>> Analyze Charts Based on the information in the chart, how did the reform movement reflect American culture in the early 1800s?

1 of 5

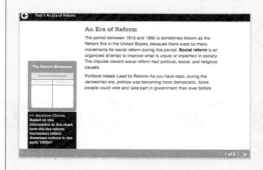

Objective 1: Explain how political and religious trends, including the Second Great Awakening, inspired reform movements.

Quick Instruction

Analyze Charts Explain to students that the period from 1815 to 1860 is sometimes known as the Reform Era. Project the chart on the whiteboard and ask how the reform movements of the nineteenth century were rooted in American cultural and political ideals.

Identify Cause and Effect Describe the causes of the Reform Era. *(Democratic ideals led to a desire to correct injustices. Industrialization and urbanization had brought hardships and challenges, and there was a need to address these. Finally, a religious movement called the Second Great Awakening aroused a desire for moral action, including helping society.)*

D Differentiate: On-Level Point out to students that a religious revival movement known as the Second Great Awakening swept the United States during the early 1800s. Ask: What were the causes of this religious revival movement? *(the spread of belief that people's fates relied on their use of their free will and their good actions rather than predestination)*

ELL Use the ELL activity described in the ELL chart.

Further Instruction

Go through the Interactive Reading Notepad questions and discuss the answers with the class.

Connect How did people of various religious groups, especially those who believed in free will, contribute to our national identity? *(By convincing people that they could be saved by their actions, preachers of free promoted practical engagement in society contributed the idea of improving society to our national identity.)*

Draw Conclusions What were the effects of the Second Great Awakening, and how did it have a religious influence on social movements? *(It encouraged the development of social reform movements because it taught that people had a religious and moral calling to improve society and reform the world.)*

DIGITAL TEXT 2

Social Reform Movements

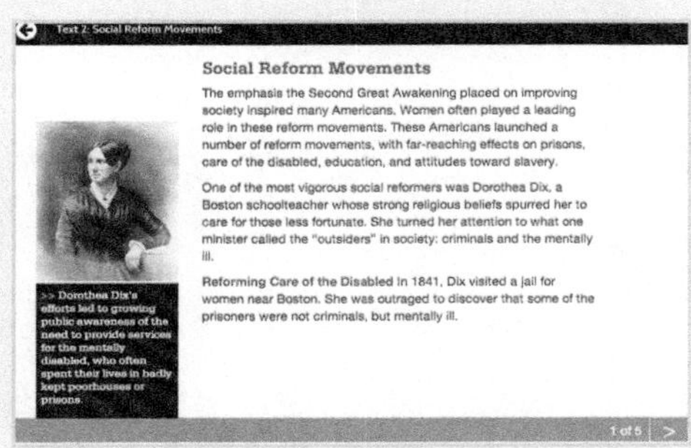

Text 2: Social Reform Movements
Social Reform Movements
The emphasis the Second Great Awakening placed on improving society inspired many Americans. Women often played a leading role in these reform movements. These Americans launched a number of reform movements, with far-reaching effects on prisons, care of the disabled, education, and attitudes toward slavery.
One of the most vigorous social reformers was Dorothea Dix, a Boston schoolteacher whose strong religious beliefs spurred her to care for those less fortunate. She turned her attention to what one minister called the "outsiders" in society: criminals and the mentally ill.
Reforming Care of the Disabled In 1841, Dix visited a jail for women near Boston. She was outraged to discover that some of the prisoners were not criminals, but mentally ill.
>> Dorothea Dix's efforts led to growing public awareness of the need to provide services for the mentally disabled, who often spent their lives in badly kept poorhouses or prisons.
1 of 5

DIGITAL TEXT 3

The Impact of Educational Reform

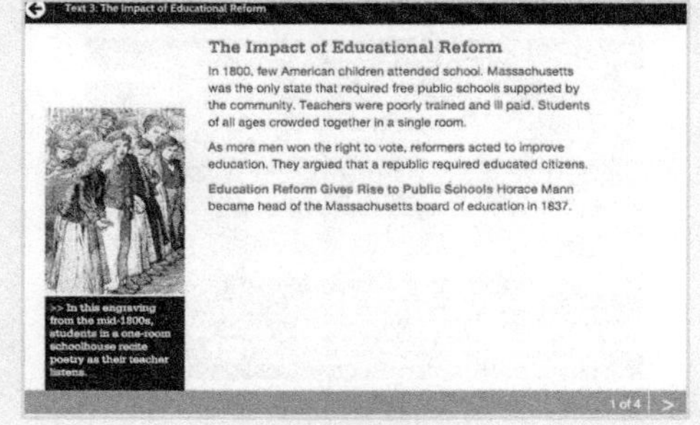

Text 3: The Impact of Educational Reform
The Impact of Educational Reform
In 1800, few American children attended school. Massachusetts was the only state that required free public schools supported by the community. Teachers were poorly trained and ill paid. Students of all ages crowded together in a single room.
As more men won the right to vote, reformers acted to improve education. They argued that a republic required educated citizens.
Education Reform Gives Rise to Public Schools Horace Mann became head of the Massachusetts board of education in 1837.
>> In this engraving from the mid-1800s, students in a one-room schoolhouse recite poetry as their teacher listens.
1 of 4

Objective 2: **Describe the impact of movements for temperance and for the reform of mental health care and prisons.**

Quick Instruction

Project the political cartoon on the whiteboard and have students describe what they see. Ask what values reformers hoped to instill in American society.

Analyze Cartoons How do you think religious beliefs shaped the values outlined in the cartoon? How did these values contribute to our national identity? *(Religious beliefs emphasized morality and proper living. Many Americans believed individuals should pursue goodness and knowledge and live moral lives. These values have come to shape American identity.)*

Identify Cause and Effect What were some of the effects of reform movements? *(Social reform movements led to important reforms in prisons, the care of the disabled, and also led to the temperance movement, which sought to limit alcohol consumption.)*

Further Instruction

Go through the Interactive Reading Notepad questions and discuss the answers with the class.

Summarize How did the social contributions of women affect American society? What was the impact of reform movements they led on care of the disabled? *(They worked to publicize ills and push for remedies. For example, Dorothea Dix visited jails, poorhouses, and hospitals and wrote reports about what she saw. These reports convinced legislators to fund a new mental hospital. By traveling the country and raising awareness about treatment facilities, she improved care and changed the way people viewed the mentally ill.)*

Support a Point of View with Evidence Evaluate the impact of the prison reforms of the nineteenth century. What were the effects of these reforms? Do you think these reforms were successful? Support your point of view with evidence from the text. *(Prison reform was successful because it improved conditions. Some states built less crowded prisons, cruel punishments were banned, and minor crimes received shorter sentences. States also moved away from treating debtors as criminals.)*

Draw Conclusions Why do you think women were leaders in the temperance movement? Evaluate the impact of temperance reform. *(Women and children were negatively affected by men's alcohol abuse. Women therefore fought to limit or abolish drinking. As a result, nine states banned the sale of alcohol.)*

Objective 3: **Explain the impact of movements for the reform of education and care for the disabled.**

Quick Instruction

Interactive Gallery: Changes in American Schools Project the interactive gallery and click through the images. Discuss how education in the 1800s differed from education today. Have students fill in the Interactive Chart: The Reform Movement.

Identify Central Issues Why did Americans call for education reform? *(As voting rights expanded, Americans argued that citizens needed to be better educated in order to serve the nation. Few children attended school at the time, and most states did not have public education. Teachers were poorly trained, and schools were overcrowded.)*

ACTIVE CLASSROOM

Use a Quick Draw strategy. Pair students for a short period (typically 30 seconds) in which to share what they know about school reform by writing with symbols or drawings.

Reform Movements

INTERACTIVE GALLERY

Changes in American Schools

ACTIVE CLASSROOM

Have students pick one of the reforms they have learned about and use the Wallpaper Strategy to design a piece of wallpaper encapsulating key issues related to the reform. Have students post their wallpaper and take a gallery walk around the room, noting what others have written or illustrated. Have students jot down ideas and then discuss the reforms as a class.

Further Instruction

Go through the Interactive Reading Notepad questions and discuss the answers with the class.

Identify Cause and Effect Evaluate the impact of educational reform. *(States built new schools, extended the school year, raised teachers' pay, and provided better training for teachers. Public education spread as states established free elementary schools supported by taxes.)*

Summarize How did Horace Mann's efforts affect the public school system? *(Massachusetts already had public schools but Mann expanded the system. As head of the Massachusetts Board of Education, he convinced legislators to provide more funding for education. Massachusetts became a model for other states.)*

Cite Evidence Describe the ways in which the Second Great Awakening contributed to education reform. How did people of various religious groups contribute to American education? *(Horace Mann believed education reform would help citizens become better Christians. Samuel Gridley Howe was inspired by the movement to improve education. He founded the first American school for the blind. Prudence Crandall was a Quaker whose religious beliefs inspired her to begin a school for African American girls.)*

SYNTHESIZE

DIGITAL ACTIVITY

The Impact of Social Reform

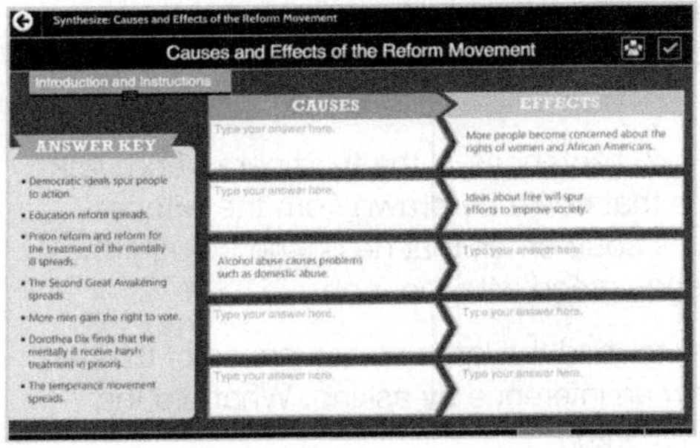

Have students fill in the chart and answer the questions. Have students discuss with a partner the reforms they think were the most important, and why.

Discuss Ask students what they think has been the lasting impact of the Reform Era. Have them review their charts and discuss the ways in which social reforms shaped the nation in the 1800s, giving examples for support. Ask how these reforms influence American society today.

DEMONSTRATE

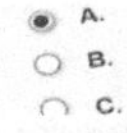

DIGITAL QUIZ

Lesson Quiz and Class Discussion Board

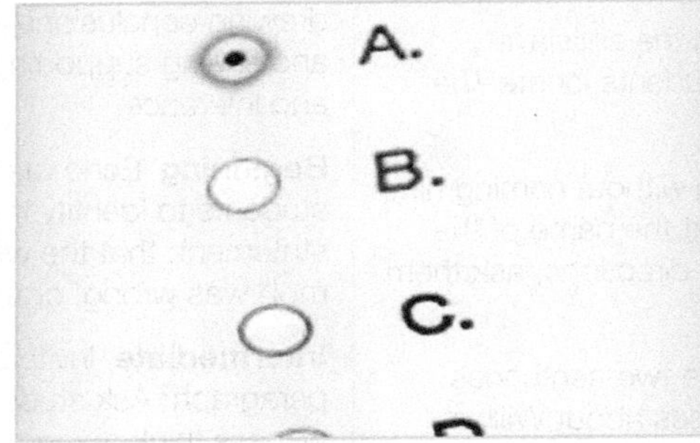

Assign the online Lesson Quiz for this lesson if you haven't already done so. Students will be offered automatic remediation or enrichment based on their score.

Pose these questions to the class on the Discussion Board:

Identify Central Issues How did the Second Great Awakening affect the American way of life?

Support Ideas with Examples How did women contribute to reform movements in the 1800s? Cite examples for support.

Topic Inquiry

Have students continue their investigations for the Topic Inquiry.

Abolitionism

Supporting English Language Learners

Use with Digital Text 2, **Abolition Gains Momentum.**

Listening

Explain that students will be following your directions in order to demonstrate their listening comprehension of spoken English.

Beginning Give the following spoken directions: Find the antislavery newspaper started by William Lloyd Garrison. After students locate *The Liberator*, discuss the strategies they used to find it.

Intermediate Describe the life of Frederick Douglass without naming him. Give the following spoken directions: Locate in the text the name of the person I described. After students have followed your directions, ask them to suggest adjectives that describe Douglass.

Advanced Give the following spoken directions: Write two sentences about Frederick Douglass, and then write two sentences about William Lloyd Garrison. After students have done so, provide time for them to share their work with a partner.

Advanced High Give the following spoken directions (in reverse order): Write two sentences contrasting Frederick Douglass and William Lloyd Garrison after you write two sentences comparing them. After students have done so, provide time for them to share their work with a partner.

Use with Digital Text 3, **Abolition Faces Opposition.**

Reading

Explain that students will demonstrate English comprehension and expand reading skills such as predicting, making connections between ideas, drawing conclusions and inferences from the text and graphic sources, and finding supporting text evidence. Review the meanings of conclusion and inference.

Beginning Echo read the last two sentences of the third paragraph. Ask students to identify the inference that could be drawn from the witness' statement: that the witness was a southerner, that he or she thought the mob was wrong, or that he or she agreed with the mob.

Intermediate Invite a volunteer to read the last two sentences of the third paragraph. Ask students to draw an inference by asking: What did the witness think about the mob's actions?

Advanced Discuss how anti-abolitionists tended to use violence against abolitionists, yet they also accused abolitionists of preaching violence. Ask: What conclusions can you draw about the fairness of those who opposed abolitionism?

Advanced High Ask pairs of students to draw conclusions by discussing this question: How much opposition to abolitionism do you think was based on racism, and how much was based on other factors, such as economy and culture? Encourage students to reference the text as needed.

Differentiate Instruction

Use the Differentiated Instruction notes throughout the lesson plan to support the varied skill sets, levels of readiness, and interests in the mixed-ability classroom.

Challenge These notes include suggestions for expanding the activity for advanced students.

On-Level These notes include suggestions for modifying the activity to address different interests or learning styles.

Extra Support These notes include ideas for providing more scaffolding or reading spupport.

Special Needs These notes provide ideas for adapting instruction to support the needs of various special needs students.

NOTES

PEARSON realize™ www.PearsonRealize.com

Go online to access additional resources including: Primary Sources • Biographies • Supreme Court cases • 21st Century Skill Tutorials • Maps • Graphic Organizers.

Objectives

Objective 1: Describe the historical development of the abolitionist movement.

Objective 2: Explain the roles of Frederick Douglass and others in the abolitionist movement.

Objective 3: Identify the Underground Railroad and the role that civil disobedience played in it.

Objective 4: Describe the different points of view of interest groups on abolition.

LESSON 4 ORGANIZER	PACING: APPROX. 1 PERIOD, .5 BLOCKS		RESOURCES	
	OBJECTIVES	PACING	Online	Print
Connect				
DIGITAL START UP ACTIVITY **The Antislavery Movement**		5 min.	●	
Investigate				
DIGITAL TEXT 1 **Early Opposition to Slavery**	Objective 1	10 min.	●	●
DIGITAL TEXT 2 **Abolitionism Gains Momentum**	Objectives 2, 3	10 min.	●	●
INTERACTIVE MAP **The Underground Railroad**		10 min.	●	
DIGITAL TEXT 3 **Abolitionism Faces Opposition**	Objective 4	10 min.	●	●
INTERACTIVE CHART **Opposing Views on Slavery**		10 min.	●	
Synthesize				
DIGITAL ACTIVITY **The Contributions of Abolitionist Leaders**		5 min.	●	
Demonstrate				
DIGITAL QUIZ **Lesson Quiz and Class Discussion Board**		10 min.	●	

Abolitionism

CONNECT

DIGITAL START UP ACTIVITY

The Antislavery Movement

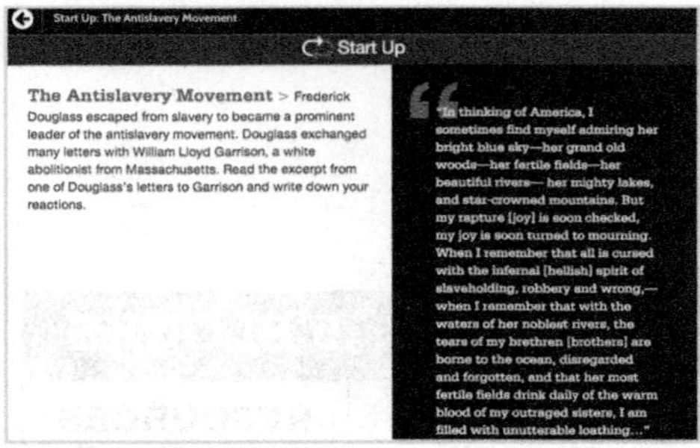

Project the Start Up Activity Ask students to read the excerpt and write down their reactions as they enter and get settled. Have students share their answers with a partner, either in class or through a blog space.

Tell students that in this lesson they will be learning about the development and impact of the abolitionist movement.

Aa Vocabulary Development: Use the Interactive Reading Notepad to preview the Key Terms and Academic Vocabulary in this lesson with students.

FLIP IT!

Assign the Flipped Video for this lesson.

STUDENT EDITION PRINT PAGES: 407–412

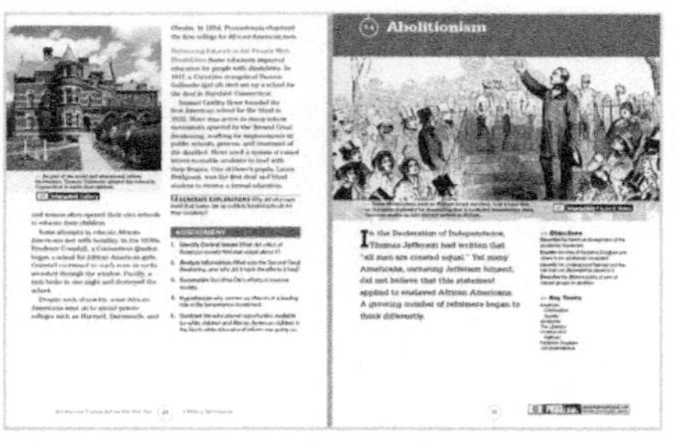

INVESTIGATE

DIGITAL TEXT 1

Early Opposition to Slavery

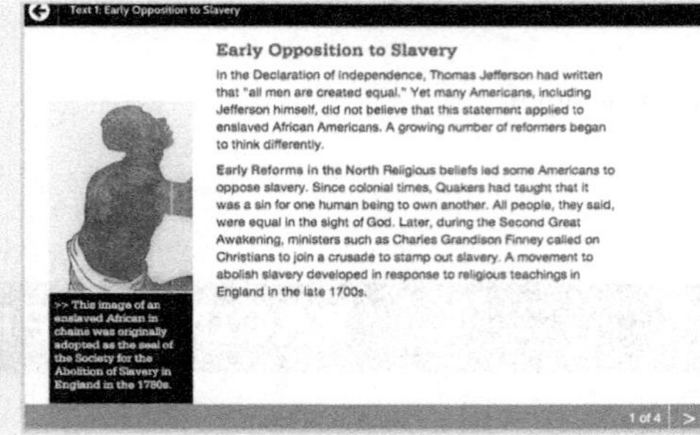

Objective 1: Describe the historical development of the abolitionist movement.

Quick Instruction

Project the antislavery medallion. The abolitionist movement began as an increasing number of northerners came to oppose slavery.

Identify Central Issues What steps did northern states take to end slavery? How effective were these efforts? Explain your reasoning. *(The northern states gradually abolished slavery. This had little impact in the South, though, where there were almost a million enslaved African Americans and little support for abolition.)*

Further Instruction

Go through the Interactive Reading Notepad questions and discuss the answers with the class.

Compare the impact of slavery on the economy and societyof the North and South. Explain the reasons for these differences. *(North—the economy was largely industrial and not dependent on slavery. South—the economy was largely based on slavery, as enslaved African Americans labored on the cotton plantations that generated the region's wealth.)*

Summarize Describe the American Colonization Society and its historical impact. *(The society established an independent colony in Liberia for freed Africans and African Americans. A few thousand African Americans moved there but most wanted to stay in their homeland in America.)*

Make a Generalization Identify how some religious groups viewed slavery, citing evidence for support. *(Some religious groups opposed slavery and wanted to abolish it—"Quakers had taught that it was a sin for one human being to own another"; "during the Second Great Awakening, ministers ... called on Christians to join a crusade to stamp out slavery.")*

DIGITAL TEXT 2

Abolitionism Gains Momentum

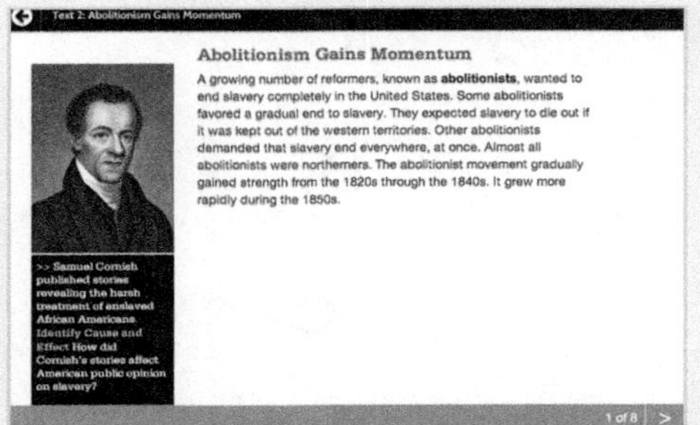

Objectives 2: **Explain the roles of Frederick Douglass and others in the abolitionist movement; 3: Identify the Underground Railroad and the role that civil disobedience played in it.**

Quick Instruction

Interactive Map: The Underground Railroad Project the interactive map on the whiteboard and click on the red circles. Have students discuss the impact of the Underground Railroad, citing evidence for support.

Generate Explanations Why did participants in the Underground Railroad choose to engage in civil disobedience, and what was the impact of that civil disobedience? *(It was illegal to help enslaved African Americans to escape. Abolitionists who helped fugitives engaged in civil disobedience against laws they felt were unjust because they saw it as the best way to free people from slavery. The impact of their civil disobedience was to free a number of African Americans from slavery.)*

D Differentiate: Extra Support Explain to students that *abolish* means to formally put an end to something. Ask what abolitionists were trying to end. Have students discuss the ways abolitionists spread their message.

INTERACTIVE MAP

The Underground Railroad

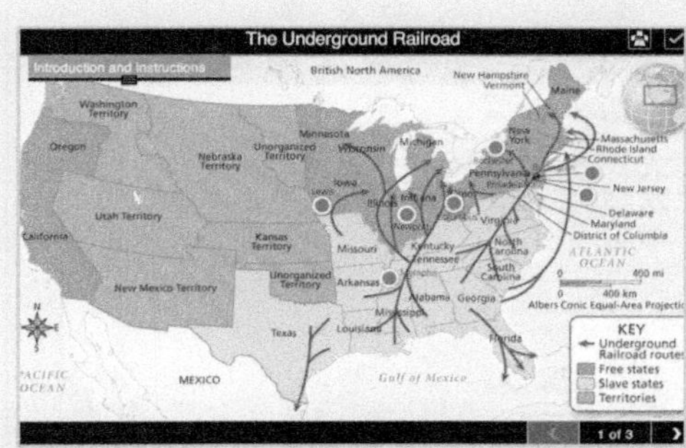

ACTIVE CLASSROOM

Have students work in pairs to develop a poster combining visuals with text to describe the historical development of the abolitionist movement. If time permits, students may present their posters to the rest of the class.

Further Instruction

Go through the Interactive Reading Notepad questions and discuss the answers with the class.

Summarize Describe the contributions of social leaders such as Frederick Douglass, William Lloyd Garrison, and the Grimké sisters. *(Douglass was the best-known African American abolitionist. He gave lectures in the United States and Britain about slavery and freedom and published an antislavery newspaper to promote the abolitionist cause. Garrison was an outspoken abolitionist who called for an immediate end to slavery. He published an influential antislavery newspaper and founded the New England AntiSlavery society. The Grimké sisters spoke out against slavery. Their public lectures also influenced the women's rights movement.)*

Draw Conclusions Evaluate the impact of the abolitionist movement. *(The abolitionist movement spread opposition to slavery, especially in the North. It succeeded in winning freedom for a number of African Americans, for example through the Underground Railroad. It also increased tensions between the North and the South.)*

DIGITAL TEXT 3

Abolitionism Faces Opposition

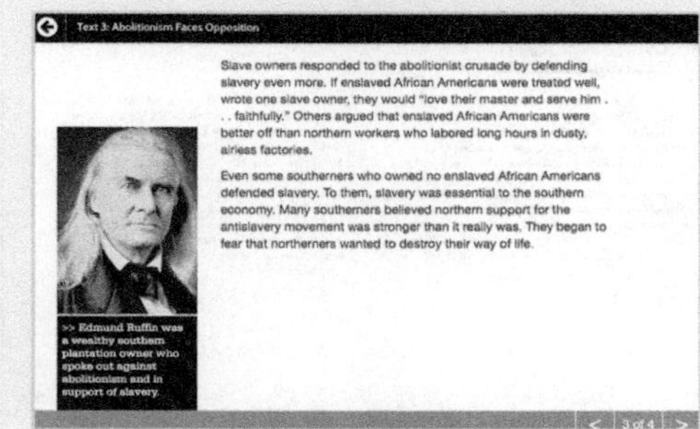

Objective 4: **Describe the different points of view of interest groups on abolition.**

Quick Instruction

Interactive Chart: Opposing Views on Slavery Project the interactive chart on the whiteboard and have students fill in the graphic organizer.

Analyze Images Identify the different points of view on slavery presented in the political cartoon. Based on the image, evaluate the impact of the abolitionist movement on national unity. *(Northerners opposed slavery and southerners supported it; disagreements over slavery and the growing push for abolition was tearing the nation apart.)*

ACTIVE CLASSROOM

Pair students to use the See-Think-Wonder Activity as they study the political cartoon. Ask: What do you see? What does that make you think about? What are you wondering about now that you've seen this? Have partners share their insights with the class.

ELL Use the ELL activity described in the ELL chart.

Abolitionism

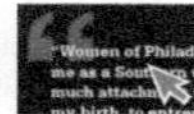

INTERACTIVE CHART

Opposing Views on Slavery

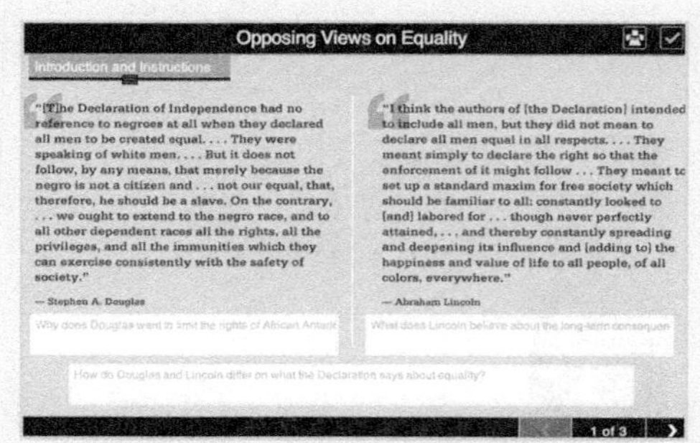

Further Instruction

Go through the Interactive Reading Notepad questions and discuss the answers with the class.

Compare and Contrast Identify the different points of views of northern interest groups on slavery. What were the reasons for these opposing viewpoints? *(Some northerners were abolitionists, but not all. Abolitionists opposed slavery because they felt that it was morally wrong. Those who depended on cotton for their livelihood, including mill owners, bankers, and merchants, supported slavery as acceptable and necessary. Some workers also feared abolition would cause African Americans north to come north and compete for their jobs.)*

Identify Central Issues The North and South increasingly had different points of view over slavery. How did social and economic factors contribute to these divisions? *(Economic—the South was more economically dependent on slavery than the North. Social—southerners feared that an attack on slavery was an attack on their way of life.)*

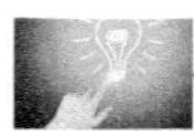

SYNTHESIZE

DIGITAL ACTIVITY

The Contributions of Abolitionist Leaders

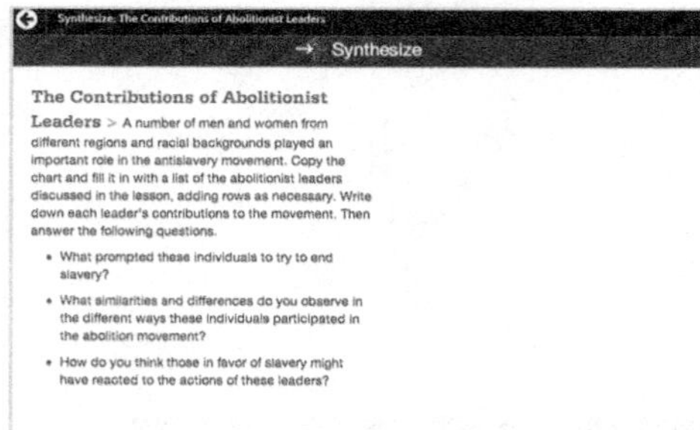

Have students fill in the chart and answer the questions. Have students share their charts with a partner and discuss how these abolitionist leaders contributed to the movement.

Discuss Remind students of the excerpt they read at the start of the lesson. Ask how they think passages like the one from Douglass's letter affected the abolitionist movement. Discuss how leaders like Douglass have contributed to our national identity.

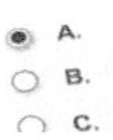

DEMONSTRATE

DIGITAL QUIZ

Lesson Quiz and Class Discussion Board

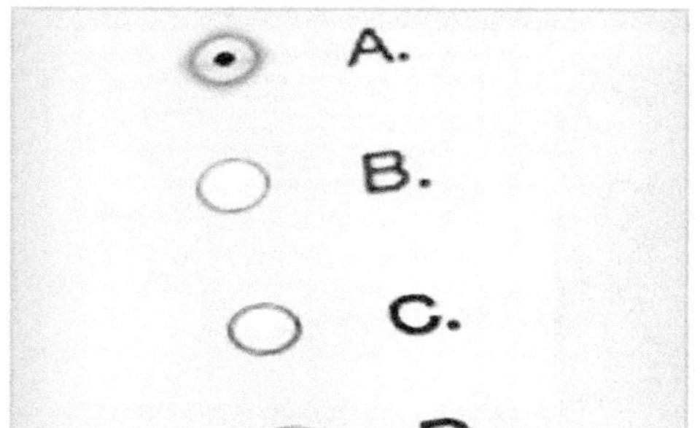

Assign the online Lesson Quiz for this lesson if you haven't already done so. Students will be offered automatic remediation or enrichment based on their score.

Pose these questions to the class on the Discussion Board:

Identify Central Issues What do you think were the most important factors that led to the development of the abolitionist movement? Explain your reasoning.

Make Predictions What factors do you think would cause the abolitionist movement to gain strength leading up to the Civil War?

Support Ideas with Examples How did women contribute to the abolitionist movement? Provide examples for support.

Topic Inquiry

Have students continue their investigations for the Topic Inquiry.

PEARSON realize www.PearsonRealize.com Access your Digital Lesson

Women's Rights

Supporting English Language Learners

Use with Digital Text 1, **Early Calls for Women's Rights.**

Reading

Discuss how authors' beliefs and opinions often influence the way they write about a subject, and how employing analytical skills such as evaluating written information and performing critical analyses can help a reader expand his or her reading skills.

Beginning Read this sentence from the text: Truth was a spellbinding speaker. Ask students to demonstrate English comprehension with this question: Based on this sentence, do you think the author has a positive or negative view of Sojourner Truth?

Intermediate Review the section about Sojourner Truth. Ask students to demonstrate English comprehension with this question: What opinion of Sojourner Truth do you think the author has?

Advanced Review the section about Sojourner Truth. Ask pairs of students to demonstrate English comprehension by answering these questions: What opinion of Sojourner Truth do you think the author has? Would someone who did not respect Sojourner Truth have written about her in the same way? If not, what might that person have said?

Advanced High Review the text as needed. Ask pairs of students to demonstrate English comprehension by answering these questions: Do you think the author sides with or against these women? Do you think the author gives a fair, unbiased view of the topic? Locate specific passages that support your views.

Use with Digital Text 3, **Women Gain New Opportunities.**

Listening

Prepare students for the activity by brainstorming strategies they can use to help them comprehend the key points of a spoken message (e.g., jotting down or memorizing words or phrases, retelling, or summarizing).

Beginning Pair students and have one student in each pair read aloud the first two sentences of the quotation by Elizabeth Cady Stanton. Then have the other student retell the meaning of the sentences. Have each pair work together to refine the retelling for clarity.

Intermediate Pair students and have one student in each pair read aloud the first two sentences of the quotation by Elizabeth Cady Stanton. Then have the other student summarize the sentences into one main idea. Have each pair work together to refine the summary for clarity.

Advanced Pair students and have one student in each pair read aloud the entire quotation by Elizabeth Cady Stanton. Have the other student retell the details of the quotation. Then have the pairs work together to create a summary based on the retelling.

Advanced High Read aloud the entire quotation by Elizabeth Cady Stanton. Have students create both a retelling and also a summary of the quote. Have volunteers share their summaries and retellings with the class.

D Differentiate Instruction

Use the Differentiated Instruction notes throughout the lesson plan to support the varied skill sets, levels of readiness, and interests in the mixed-ability classroom.

Challenge These notes include suggestions for expanding the activity for advanced students.

On-Level These notes include suggestions for modifying the activity to address different interests or learning styles.

Extra Support These notes include ideas for providing more scaffolding or reading spuport.

Special Needs These notes provide ideas for adapting instruction to support the needs of various special needs students.

NOTES

Topic 7 Lesson 5

Women's Rights

Objectives

Objective 1: Describe the origins of the women's rights movement.

Objective 2: Explain the impact of the Seneca Falls Convention, including the roles of Elizabeth Cady Stanton and Susan B. Anthony.

Objective 3: Describe the impact of the women's rights movement on opportunities for women.

LESSON 5 ORGANIZER		PACING: APPROX. 1 PERIOD, .5 BLOCKS		
			RESOURCES	
	OBJECTIVES	PACING	Online	Print
Connect				
DIGITAL START UP ACTIVITY **The Struggle for Equal Rights**		5 min.	●	
Investigate				
DIGITAL TEXT 1 **Early Calls for Women's Rights**	Objective 1	10 min.	●	●
INTERACTIVE TIMELINE **The Early Women's Rights Movement**		10 min.	●	
DIGITAL TEXT 2 **A Women's Movement Organizes**	Objective 2	10 min.	●	●
DIGITAL TEXT 3 **Women Gain New Opportunities**	Objective 3	10 min.	●	●
INTERACTIVE GALLERY **New Opportunities for Women**		10 min.	●	
Synthesize				
DIGITAL ACTIVITY **Contributions of Women Leaders**		5 min.	●	
Demonstrate				
DIGITAL QUIZ **Lesson Quiz and Class Discussion Board**		10 min.	●	

Go online to access additional resources including: Primary Sources • Biographies • Supreme Court cases • 21st Century Skill Tutorials • Maps • Graphic Organizers.

CONNECT

DIGITAL START UP ACTIVITY

The Struggle for Equal Rights

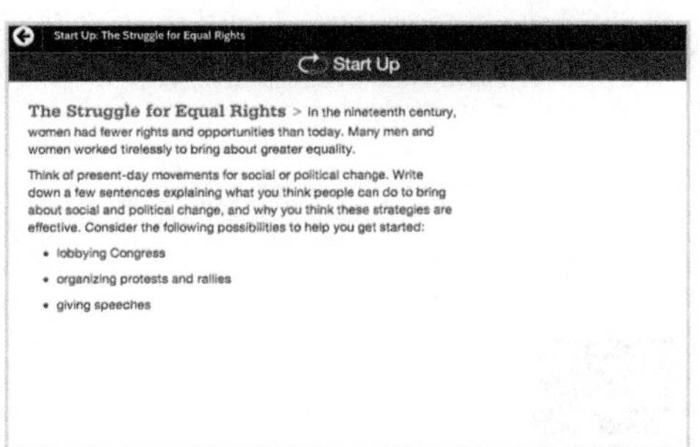

Start Up: The Struggle for Equal Rights
Start Up
The Struggle for Equal Rights > In the nineteenth century, women had fewer rights and opportunities than today. Many men and women worked tirelessly to bring about greater equality.
Think of present-day movements for social or political change. Write down a few sentences explaining what you think people can do to bring about social and political change, and why you think these strategies are effective. Consider the following possibilities to help you get started:
• lobbying Congress
• organizing protests and rallies
• giving speeches

Project the Start Up Activity Ask students to review the strategies and write down their thoughts as they enter and get settled. Have students share their responses with a partner, either in class or through a blog space.

Tell students that in this lesson they will be learning about the causes and effects of the women's rights movement.

Aa Vocabulary Development: Use the Interactive Reading Notepad to preview the Key Terms and Academic Vocabulary in this lesson with students.

FLIP IT!

Assign the Flipped Video for this lesson.

STUDENT EDITION PRINT PAGES: 413–418

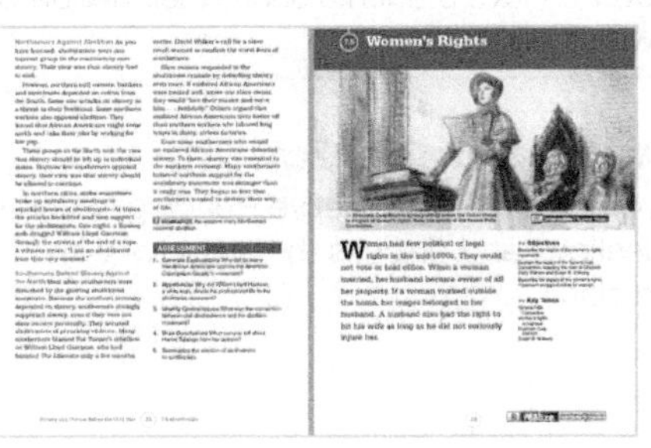

INVESTIGATE

DIGITAL TEXT 1

Early Calls for Women's Rights

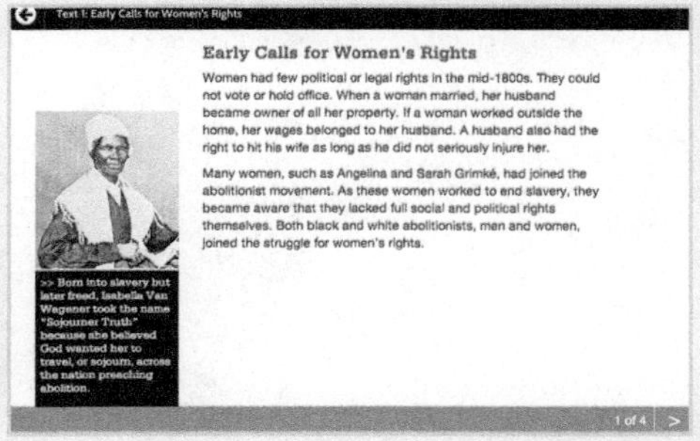

INTERACTIVE TIMELINE

The Early Women's Rights Movement

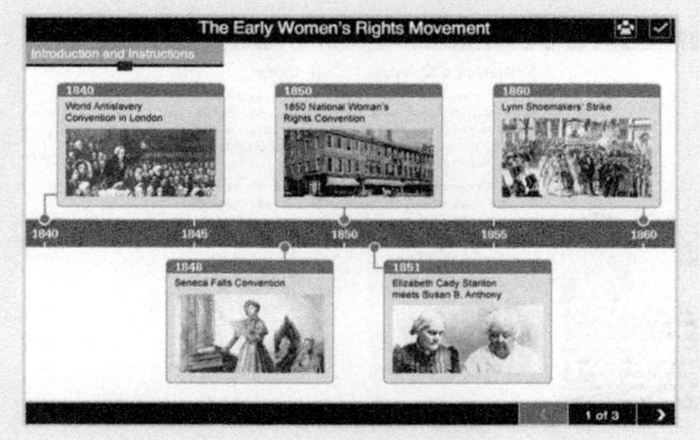

Objective 1: Describe the origins of the women's rights movement.

Quick Instruction

Interactive Timeline: The Early Women's Rights Movement Project the interactive timeline and click through the events.

Summarize Describe the contributions of Elizabeth Cady Stanton to the women's rights movement as a social leader. *(She was an active leader of the movement. When she was not allowed to actively participate in the World Antislavery Convention in London because she was a woman, she began working for women's rights.)*

ACTIVE CLASSROOM

Have students use the Conversation with History Activity and suppose they are having a conversation with Elizabeth Cady Stanton after she has returned from the World Antislavery Convention in London. Have students write down a question they'd like to ask, what they think Stanton would say, and what they would say in response.

ELL Use the ELL activity described in the ELL chart.

Further Instruction

Go through the Interactive Reading Notepad questions and discuss the answers with the class. To extend the lesson, assign Primary Sources: Ain't I a Woman (Sojourner Truth).

Paraphrase Review the quote by Sojourner Truth. What was she arguing? How did her argument support the cause of women's rights? *(Truth challenged the idea that women were inferior by pointing to her experiences under slavery, where she worked as hard as men.)*

Draw Conclusions How was the women's rights movement connected to the abolitionist movement? *(While fighting for social and political rights for African Americans, women in the abolitionist movement became increasingly aware that their rights were limited as well.)*

Women's Rights

DIGITAL TEXT 2

A Women's Movement Organizes

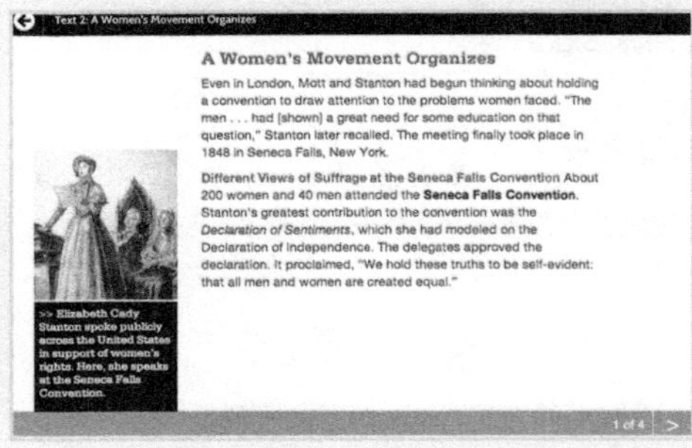

DIGITAL TEXT 3

Women Gain New Opportunities

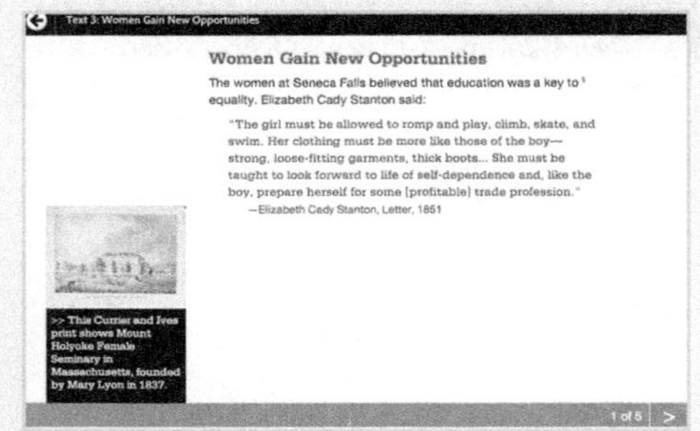

Objective 2: Explain the impact of the Seneca Falls Convention, including the roles of Elizabeth Cady Stanton and Susan B. Anthony.

Quick Instruction

Analyze Images Display the images of Elizabeth Cady Stanton and Susan B. Anthony. Describe the contributions of these two significant social leaders. *(Both women were key leaders of the women's rights movement and both were influential in promoting women's rights.)*

Summarize Describe the contributions of Elizabeth Cady Stanton and Susan B. Anthony to the women's rights movement. *(Elizabeth Cady Stanton helped organize the Seneca Falls Convention, which launched the women's rights movement. She also drafted the* Declaration of Sentiments, *which spelled out the movement's goals, for the convention. Anthony traveled the country speaking to audiences and convincing them that women deserved equal rights, especially the right to vote.)*

D Differentiate: Extra Support Explain to students that sentiments are views or feelings. Ask them what views they think the *Declaration of Sentiments* expressed and how they know.

ELL Use the ELL activity described in the ELL chart.

Further Instruction

Go through the Interactive Reading Notepad questions and discuss the answers with the class. To extend the lesson, assign the Primary Source: Seneca Falls Declaration of Sentiments and Resolutions.

Compare and Contrast Identify the political contributions of women to American society through the women's rights movement. *(Women involved in the women's rights movement contributed to American society the idea that women deserved equal rights, including the right to an education, the right to equality of opportunity in employment, and the right to vote.)*

Summarize What was the Seneca Falls Convention and why did it play such an important role in the women's rights movement? *(It was a major convention designed to draw attention to the problems women faced. It laid out demands for equality and began the organized campaign for women's rights.)*

Objective 3: Describe the impact of the women's rights movement on opportunities for women.

Quick Instruction

Interactive Gallery: New Opportunities for Women Project the interactive gallery on the whiteboard and click through the images. Discuss the impact of the women's rights movement on education, employment, suffrage, and property rights.

Identify Cause and Effect Evaluate the impact of the early women's rights movement. *(The early women's rights movement emphasized education to give women greater opportunities outside the home. It led women like Emma Willard and Mary Lyon to open schools and colleges for girls. This led to increased educational opportunities for women and, as a further result, to increased career opportunities.)*

ACTIVE CLASSROOM

Have students imagine they are a reporter covering the Seneca Falls Convention and use the Make Headlines Activity to write a headline that captures this significant event. Have students share their headline with the class.

Further Instruction

Go through the Interactive Reading Notepad questions and discuss the answers with the class.

INTERACTIVE GALLERY

New Opportunities for Women

Compare and Contrast Identify the different points of view of interest groups on the contemporary issue of paid maternity leave. With whom do you agree, and why? *(For—groups like the National Organization for Women believe women should be paid during maternity leave to receive support during time away from their job. Against—groups like the Independent Women's Forum worry that requiring paid maternity leave might make employers not want to hire women.)*

Support Ideas with Examples Give at least three examples of how women contributed to American society through the gains during women's rights movement. *(Emma Willard—opened a high school for girls; Mary Lyon—founded Mt. Holyoke college for women; Elizabeth Blackwell—became the first women in the United States to earn a medical degree; Maria Mitchell—astronomer; Sarah Josepha Hale—magazine editor; Antoinette Blackwell—first U.S. woman ordained a minister.)*

SYNTHESIZE

DIGITAL ACTIVITY

Contributions of Women Leaders

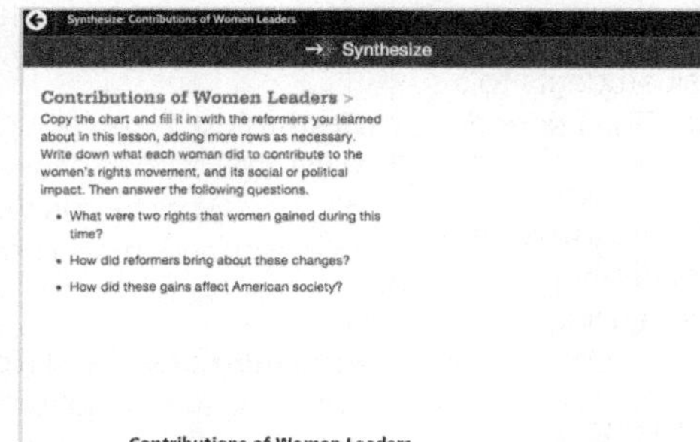

Synthesize
Contributions of Women Leaders
Copy the chart and fill it in with the reformers you learned about in this lesson, adding more rows as necessary. Write down what each woman did to contribute to the women's rights movement, and its social or political impact. Then answer the following questions.
What were two rights that women gained during this time?
How did reformers bring about these changes?
How did these gains affect American society?

Have students fill in the chart and answer the questions. Have students share their charts with a partner and discuss the major changes these leaders brought about.

Discuss Have students review what they wrote at the beginning of the lesson about effective strategies for bringing about social and political change. Ask if they would change or add to their answers now that they have read more about the women's rights movement. Have students discuss what strategies leaders of the women's rights movement used to bring about change, citing examples for support.

DEMONSTRATE

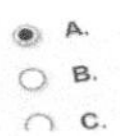

DIGITAL QUIZ

Lesson Quiz and Class Discussion Board

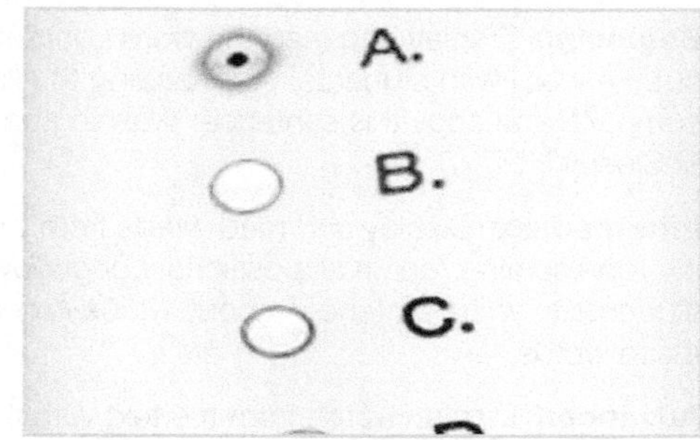

Assign the online Lesson Quiz for this lesson if you haven't already done so. Students will be offered automatic remediation or enrichment based on their score.

Pose these questions to the class on the Discussion Board:

Identify Central Issues How did the women's right movement affect American society in the 1800s? How do you think the movement's impact continues to influence American society today?

Evaluate Arguments Why do you think many of the ideas advanced by reformers such as Stanton and Anthony were considered so revolutionary at the time?

Topic Inquiry

Have students continue their investigations for the Topic Inquiry.

Arts and Literature

Supporting English Language Learners

Use with Digital Text 2, **A New Nation Finds a Voice.**

Writing

Explain that students will be learning the relationships between the sounds and letters of *ow*.

Beginning Display and read the word *Longfellow* from the text. Sound out the word with students, emphasizing the final /oe/. Ask students to complete and copy this sentence: Washington Irving wrote"The Legend of Sleepy Holl__."

Intermediate Display and read words from the text that have the letters *ow* representing /oe/ in all positions: *Longfellow, known, own*. Ask students to write sentences about 1800s American literature using these words.

Advanced Display words from the text with the final letters *ow* representing either /oe/ or /ow/: *Longfellow, hollow, how, now*. Ask pairs of students to brainstorm and sort other words ending with *ow*. Then have them write sentences about 1800s American literature with three of the words.

Advanced High Review that *ow* can represent either /oe/ or /ow/. Then say the following words while students write them: *Longfellow, however, own, brown, now, hollow*. Have students write a paragraph about 1800s American literature that uses at least three words containing *ow* (using the words above or others).

Use with Digital Text 3, **The Development of Transcendentalism.**

Listening

Review with students that some questions require a factual answer and others request an opinion. Explain that students will demonstrate listening comprehension of spoken English by responding to questions that ask for a factual answer about the text and questions that requestan opinion.

Beginning Read aloud to students the section *Henry David Thoreau and Civil Disobedience.* Ask: What did Thoreau believe each person must decide? What words would you use to describe Thoreau? Have students brainstorm words to complete this sentence: I think Thoreau was a(n) _____ person.

Intermediate Read aloud to students the sections about Emerson and Thoreau. Ask: What are the main ideas of Emerson and Thoreau? Which man's works are you more interested in reading? Why?

Advanced Read aloud to students the section *Henry David Thoreau and Civil Disobedience.* Ask: Do you agree with Thoreau that every person can and should decide for himself or herself what is right and wrong? Why or why not? How do you know what is right and wrong? Have small groups discuss their responses.

Advanced High In small groups have students read the text aloud. Then have each group consider these questions:: Do you agree that the most important truths in life cannot be understood by thinking about them? Why or why not? What do you think are the most important truths? Have students write down their responses to these questions before discussing them with the group.

D Differentiate Instruction

Use the Differentiated Instruction notes throughout the lesson plan to support the varied skill sets, levels of readiness, and interests in the mixed-ability classroom.

Challenge These notes include suggestions for expanding the activity for advanced students.

On-Level These notes include suggestions for modifying the activity to address different interests or learning styles.

Extra Support These notes include ideas for providing more scaffolding or reading spuport.

Special Needs These notes provide ideas for adapting instruction to support the needs of various special needs students.

NOTES

Go online to access additional resources including: Primary Sources • Biographies • Supreme Court cases • 21st Century Skill Tutorials • Maps • Graphic Organizers.

PEARSON realize www.PearsonRealize.com

Objectives

Objective 1: Describe American painting in the early to mid-1800s, including the Hudson River School and the work of John James Audubon.

Objective 2: Analyze American literature and music during the early to mid-1800s.

Objective 3: Describe transcendentalism.

LESSON 6 ORGANIZER — **PACING: APPROX. 1 PERIOD, .5 BLOCKS**

	OBJECTIVES	PACING	RESOURCES: Online	RESOURCES: Print
Connect				
DIGITAL START UP ACTIVITY **The Hudson Valley School**		5 min.	●	
Investigate				
DIGITAL TEXT 1 **A New American Art Style**	Objective 1	10 min.	●	●
INTERACTIVE GALLERY **Painting America**	Objective 1	10 min.	●	
DIGITAL TEXT 2 **A New Nation Finds a Voice**	Objective 2	10 min.	●	●
INTERACTIVE MAP **Early American Music and Literature**	Objective 2	10 min.	●	
DIGITAL TEXT 3 **The Development of Transcendentalism**	Objective 3	10 min.	●	●
Synthesize				
DIGITAL ACTIVITY **Themes of American Art, Music, and Literature in the 1800s**		5 min.	●	
Demonstrate				
DIGITAL QUIZ **Lesson Quiz and Class Discussion Board**		10 min.	●	

Arts and Literature

CONNECT

DIGITAL START UP ACTIVITY

The Hudson Valley School

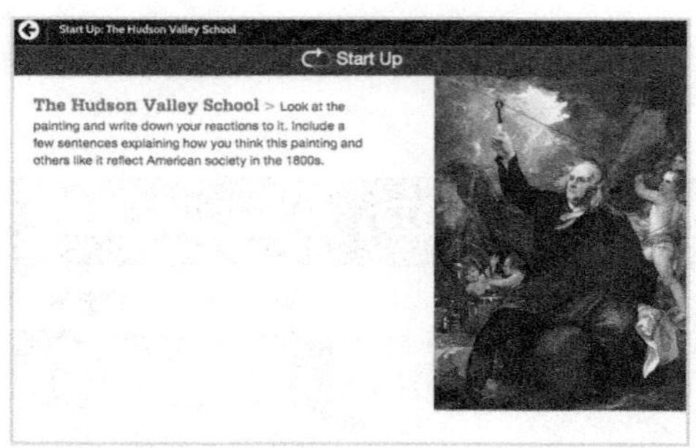

Start Up: The Hudson Valley School
Start Up
The Hudson Valley School > Look at the painting and write down your reactions to it. Include a few sentences explaining how you think this painting and others like it reflect American society in the 1800s.

Project the Start Up Activity Ask students to look at the painting and respond to the prompt as they enter and get settled. Have students share their responses with a partner, either in class or through a blog space.

Discuss How do you think this painting and others like it reflect American society in the 1800s? *(The paintings depict a romantic view of life in America. They show American landscapes, scenes from American history, important American figures, and ordinary Americans hard at work.)*

Tell students that in this lesson they will be learning about developments in art, music, and literature in the early 1800s.

Aa Vocabulary Development: Use the Interactive Reading Notepad to preview the Key Terms and Academic Vocabulary in this lesson with students.

FLIP IT!

Assign the Flipped Video for this lesson.

STUDENT EDITION PRINT PAGES: 419–425

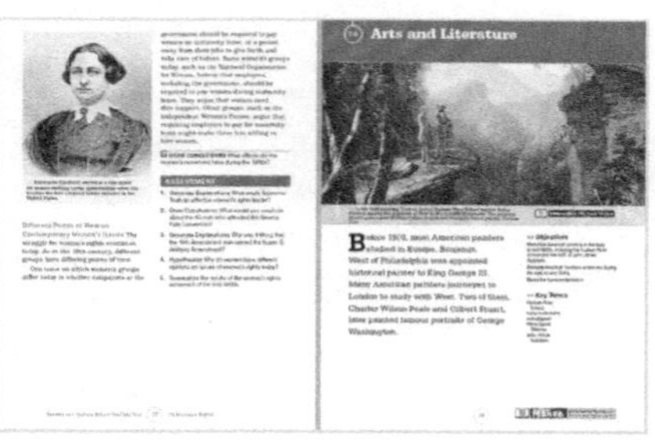

INVESTIGATE

DIGITAL TEXT 1

A New American Art Style

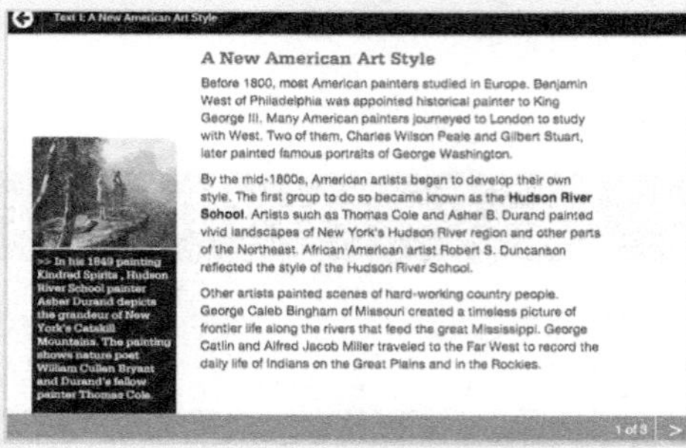

INTERACTIVE GALLERY

Painting America

Objective 1: Describe American painting in the early to mid-1800s, including the Hudson River School and the work of John James Audubon.

Quick Instruction

Interactive Gallery: Painting America Project the interactive gallery and click through the images. Identify the Hudson River School as the first group to develop a uniquely American style of painting. Have students look through the images and describe the work of the Hudson River School artists. Discuss how the Hudson River School reflected American society in the early 1800s.

Hypothesize Why do you think art styles that were unique to American culture developed at this time? How did these art styles reflect American society during this period? *(Artists were moving away from European influences and interested in reflecting American themes. Artists were interested in the landscapes, wildlife, and people that made up the country. The approach of the Hudson River School reflected American society in the early 1800s, because like many Americans at the time, these artists were motivated by patriotism and optimism.)*

ACTIVE CLASSROOM

Project the painting *Kindred Spirits* and use a whiteboard tool to divide it into four numbered sections: the mountains, the valley, the cliffs, and the figures. Have students count off 1 through 4 and use the A Closer Look Strategy to examine the part of the image in their section. Have students tell what they see and what they learned as a result of their focus on this part of the image. Have students share their insights and discuss the image as a whole.

Further Instruction

Go through the Interactive Reading Notepad questions and discuss the answers with the class.

Analyze Images Have students examine Audubon's painting of the turtle doves and describe his work. How were his paintings unique to American culture as developments in art? How did they reflect American society in the early 1800s? *(The painting is extremely detailed and lifelike. It shows the birds in their natural habitat. Audubon's work displayed the breadth and diversity of American wildlife as Americans were discovering more about different regions of the country during the early 1800s.)*

Compare and Contrast In what ways did fine arts in the early 1800s reflect both continuity and change in the American way of life? Why do you think these were important subjects for the artists? *(Continuity—landscape paintings showed the timelessness of the geography; paintings of Americans on farms showed traditional patterns of work and daily life. Change—paintings showing the frontier depicted the nation's expansion and the changes brought by westward movement. In capturing American society at the time, painters were showing the nation's permanence as well as its growth.)*

DIGITAL TEXT 2

A New Nation Finds a Voice

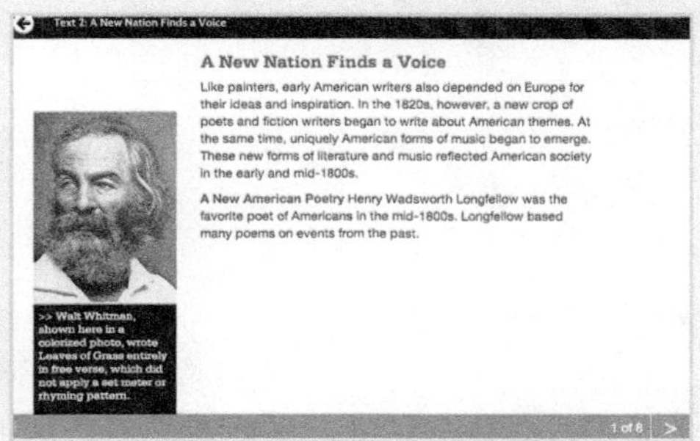

Objective 2: Analyze American literature and music during the early to mid-1800s.

Quick Instruction

Interactive Map: Early American Music and Literature Project the interactive map and click on the locations. Discuss how the nation's geography, diversity, and expansion influenced developments in art, music, and literature.

Draw Conclusions Describe developments in literature during the early 1800s that were unique to American culture. *(Whitman wrote about the common people of America and celebrated democracy. He wrote about the diversity of the country and its vast geography. Writers such as Longfellow, Irving, and Hawthorne wrote about themes from American history and expressed a uniquely American identity during the early 1800s.)*

ACTIVE CLASSROOM

Have students use the Write 1-Get 3 activity to answer the question "Who are key American writers of the 1800s and what was their contribution to the development of American literature?"Have students fold a piece of paper into quarters, write down a response in the first box, and go around room asking to hear other responses. When students think a response is correct, have them write it in one of their boxes until they have three more responses on the page. Have students share responses with class.

INTERACTIVE MAP

Early American Music and Literature

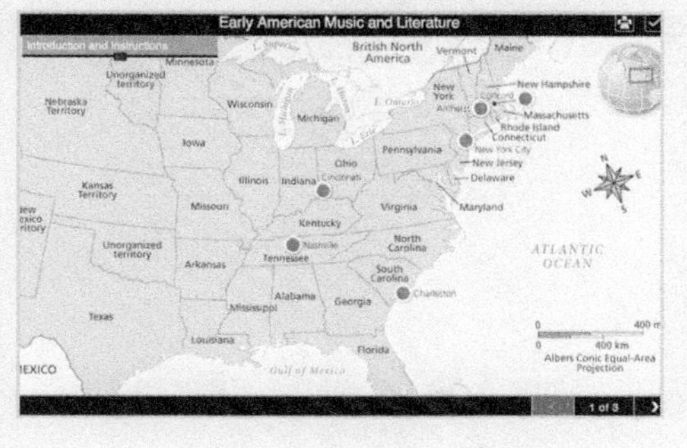

ELL Use the ELL activity described in the ELL chart.

Further Instruction

Discuss answers to the Interactive Reading Notepad questions with the class. Be sure students can describe this era's developments in literature and music.

Support Ideas with Examples Give three examples of American literature of the 1800s that are unique to American culture and explain how each reflected society during this time. *(The Deerslayer and The Last of the Mohicans (Cooper) idealized frontier life. The Sketch Book (Irving) described the richness of America's past. Moby-Dick (Melville) described American whaling. The Scarlett Letter (Hawthorne) wrestled with the legacy of Puritan ideals. Clotel (Brown) described slavery and the Underground Railroad. Women writers like Sedgwick and Fern showed women who gained wealth, and the hardships of widows.)*

Identify Patterns What developments did American music undergo in the 1800s that were unique to American culture? How did these forms of music reflect society at the time? *(New American musical styles emerged as different groups came into contact with one another. They reflected American perspectives and the rise of a new middle class. African American spirituals and work songs merged European and African traditions to create uniquely American musical forms that gave rise to later forms such as blues, jazz, country, and rock.)*

Arts and Literature

DIGITAL TEXT 3

The Development of Transcendentalism

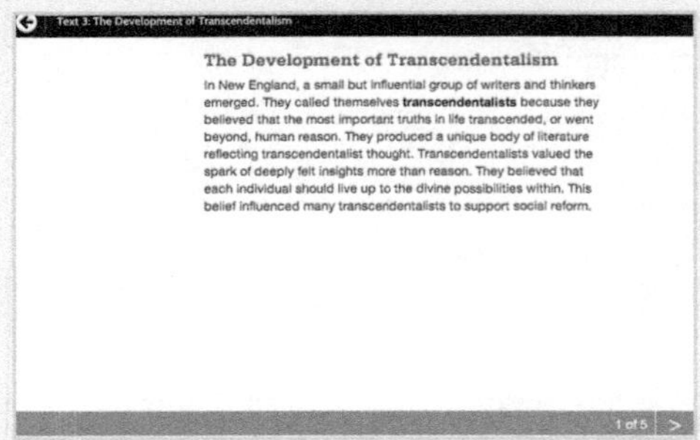

Text 3: The Development of Transcendentalism
The Development of Transcendentalism
In New England, a small but influential group of writers and thinkers emerged. They called themselves transcendentalists because they believed that the most important truths in life transcended, or went beyond, human reason. They produced a unique body of literature reflecting transcendentalist thought. Transcendentalists valued the spark of deeply felt insights more than reason. They believed that each individual should live up to the divine possibilities within. This belief influenced many transcendentalists to support social reform.
1 of 5

Objective 3: **Describe transcendentalism.**

Quick Instruction

Analyze Images Display the photograph of Ralph Waldo Emerson lecturing at the Summer School of Philosophy. Explain that he, and his contemporary Henry David Thoreau, were beacons of the Transcendentalist movement in literature and thought. What can you conclude about Emerson's popularity and influence based on this image and its caption? *(Emerson was a skilled lecturer and was quite popular, given the size and breadth of his audience. His thinking likely influenced most of the students and others who listened to him speak.)*

Context Clues Define *transcendentalism*. How was it unique to American culture? *(It was a movement of New England writers and thinkers who believed in nature, divinity, and the human spirit. Transcentalists produced a unique body of literature reflecting transcentdalist thought. It was unique to American culture in its emphasis on individualism.)*

D Differentiate: Extra Support Remind students that *transcend* means "to go beyond." Have students reread the first paragraph of the text and explain in their own words what they think the transcendentalists were trying to "go beyond."

ELL Use the ELL activity described in the ELL chart.

Further Instruction

Go through the Interactive Reading Notepad questions and discuss the answers with the class.

Infer Why do you think transcendentalism developed in America during this time? *(Transcendentalists were reacting to industrialization and urbanization. They were also responding to the spirit of social reform that arose in the 1800s and the spread of slavery.)*

Generate Explanations Explain how Emerson and the transcendentalists reflected American society in the 1800s. *(Emerson emphasized distinctly American values such as self-reliance and individualism. Transcendentalists also prioritized social reform, a popular movement at this time.)*

Identify Cause and Effect Explain why Henry David Thoreau engaged in civil disobedience by refusing to pay taxes. Analyze what impact you think his act of civil disobedience had, citing evidence for support. *(Thoreau did not want to pay taxes to support the U.S.-Mexican War because he believed the war was wrong. This act had a strong influence. Many Americans read his essay explaining the importance of civil disobedience. Future leaders such as Mohandas Gandhi and Martin Luther King, Jr., drew on his ideas during their struggles for justice.)*

SYNTHESIZE

DIGITAL ACTIVITY

Themes of American Art, Music, and Literature in the 1800s

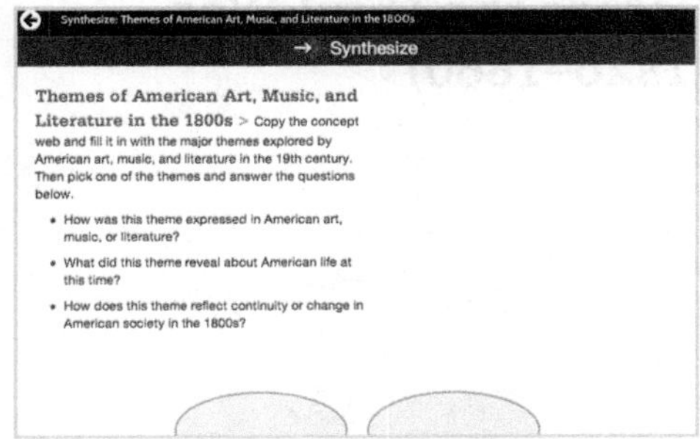

Have students fill in the concept web and answer the questions. Have students share their webs with a partner and discuss their responses.

Discuss Have students review their concept webs and the examples of American art, music, and literature they read about in this lesson. Ask students what themes they think are particular to the time in which the artwork was created and what themes they think continue to influence American art, music, and literature today.

DEMONSTRATE

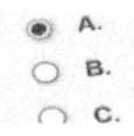

DIGITAL QUIZ

Lesson Quiz and Class Discussion Board

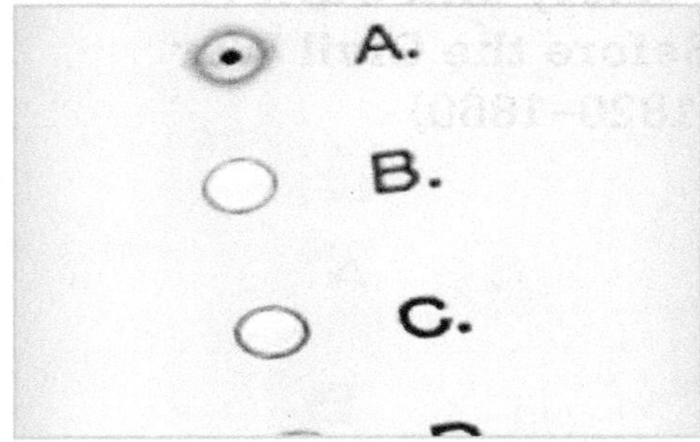

Assign the online Lesson Quiz for this lesson if you haven't already done so. Students will be offered automatic remediation or enrichment based on their score.

Pose these questions to the class on the Discussion Board:

Summarize In what ways did America develop its own unique cultural traditions in the nineteenth century? Give examples to support your views.

Draw Conclusions How do you think the development of American art, music, and literature in the 1800s helped form an American national identity at this time?

Topic Inquiry

Have students continue their investigations for the Topic Inquiry.

PEARSON realize www.PearsonRealize.com Access your Digital Lesson

Society and Culture Before the Civil War (1820–1860)

SYNTHESIZE

DIGITAL ACTIVITY

Reflect on the Essential Question and Topic

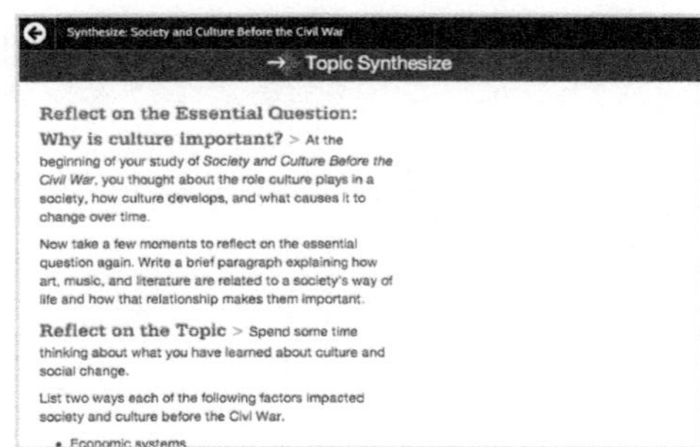

First ask students to reconsider the Essential Question for this topic: Why is culture important? Have students make a list of three or four historical processes they learned about that changed American society, and then answer the questions.

Ask students, "How did American culture reflect these historical changes?" Have students give examples from the topic. Discuss their responses as a class or ask students to post their answers on the Class Discussion Board.

Next ask students to reflect on the topic as a whole and fill in the chart. Give students the following examples of changes in society to help them get started:

1. industrialization
2. urbanization
3. technological innovations
4. westward expansion
5. the spread of slavery

Topic Inquiry

Have students complete Step 3 of the Topic Inquiry.

DEMONSTRATE

DIGITAL TOPIC REVIEW AND ASSESSMENT

Society and Culture Before the Civil War (1820–1860)

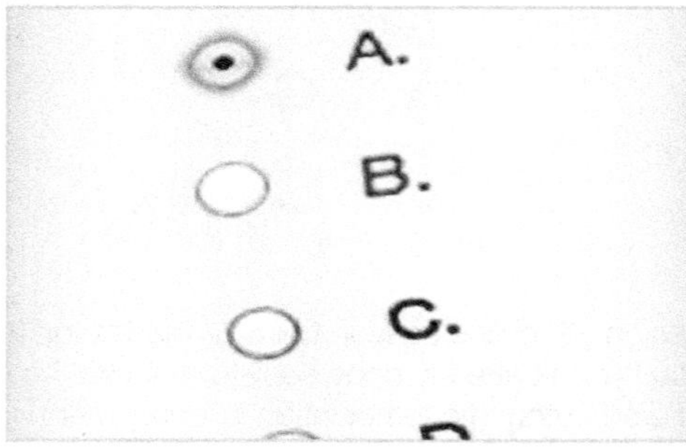

Students can prepare for the Topic Test by answering the questions in the Topic Review and Assessment online or the Assessment questions in the Print Student text. They can also prepare by reviewing their answers to the Interactive Reading Notepad questions or reviewing their notes in the Reading and Notetaking Study Guide.

DIGITAL TOPIC TEST

Society and Culture Before the Civil War (1820–1860)

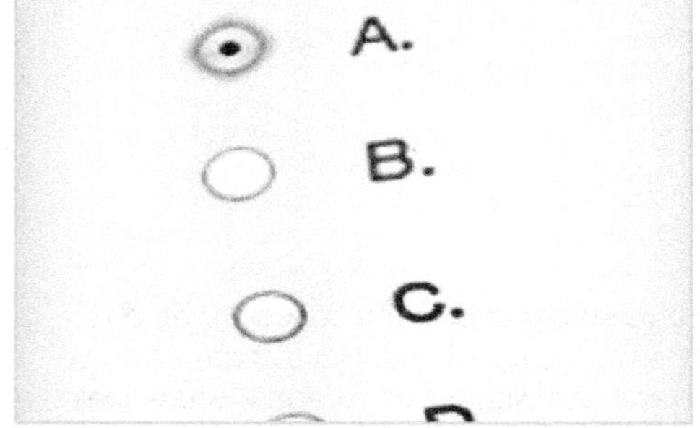

TOPIC TEST

Assign the Topic Test to assess students' understanding of topic content.

BENCHMARK TESTS

Assign these benchmark tests as you complete the relevant topics to monitor student progress toward mastering the course content and as preparation for the End-of-Course Test.

Benchmark Test 1: Topics 1–2

Benchmark Test 2: Topics 3–4

Benchmark Test 3: Topics 5–6

Benchmark Test 4: Topics 7–9

Benchmark Test 5: Topics 10–12

Benchmark Test 6: Topics 13–14

Benchmark Test 7: Topics 15–17

Sectionalism and Civil War

TOPIC 8 ORGANIZER — PACING: APPROX. 9 PERIODS, 4.5 BLOCKS	PACING
Connect	1 period
MY STORY VIDEO **Robert E. Lee, The Marble Man**	10 min.
DIGITAL ESSENTIAL QUESTION ACTIVITY **When is War Justified?**	10 min.
DIGITAL OVERVIEW ACTIVITY **Sectionalism and Civil War**	10 min.
TOPIC INQUIRY: PROJECT-BASED LEARNING **Build a Website on the Impact of the Civil War**	20 min.
Investigate	3–6 periods
TOPIC INQUIRY: PROJECT-BASED LEARNING **Build a Website on the Impact of the Civil War**	Ongoing
LESSON 1 Conflicts and Compromises	30–40 min.
LESSON 2 Growing Tensions	30–40 min.
LESSON 3 Division and the Outbreak of War	30–40 min.
LESSON 4 The Course of War	30–40 min.
LESSON 5 Emancipation and Life in Wartime	30–40 min.
LESSON 6 The War's End	30–40 min.
Synthesize	1 period
DIGITAL ACTIVITY **Reflect on the Essential Question and Topic**	10 min.
TOPIC INQUIRY: PROJECT-BASED LEARNING **Build a Website on the Impact of the Civil War**	20 min.
Demonstrate	1–2 periods
DIGITAL TOPIC REVIEW AND ASSESSMENT **Sectionalism and Civil War**	10 min.
TOPIC INQUIRY: PROJECT-BASED LEARNING **Build a Website on the Impact of the Civil War**	20 min.

TOPIC INQUIRY: PROJECT-BASED LEARNING

Build a Website on the Impact of the Civil War

In this Topic Inquiry students work together to build a website that promotes a fictitious museum display about the economic, social, and political impact of the Civil War. Learning how civil war impacts a country will contribute to students' understanding of the Topic Essential Question: When is war justified?

STEP 1: CONNECT

Develop Questions and Plan the Investigation

Launch the Project and Generate Questions

Review with students the *Project Launch* document, the letter from the fictitious Valley and Forest Museum. Ensure students understand that their project is to create a website to promote an exhibit, *The Impact of the Civil War in Numbers*, at the museum. In creating the website they will be transferring statistical and written information into visual representations, such as maps and charts, that will generate interest in and be representative of the museum exhibit. The website should include content related to the economic, social, and political impact of the Civil War.

Suggestion: Ensure that students can differentiate among economic, social, and political impacts. Review the examples of each. Hold a class discussion about how the three can overlap.

Prepare the Investigation

Organize the class into teams, if appropriate, and have students sign the *Project Contract.* Have students prepare by beginning the *Need-to-Know Questions* while keeping the Guiding Question in mind: In what ways did the Civil War affect the lives of Americans economically, socially, and politically?

Suggestion: Consider having students consider the points of view of various types of Americans during the Civil War. For example, How would the war most likely affect a young person in the North? A child in the South? A recent immigrant to New York? And so on.

Resources

- Student Instructions
- Project Launch
- Rubric for a Website on the Impact of the Civil War
- The Project Contract
- Need-to-Know Questions

STEP 2: INVESTIGATE

Apply Disciplinary Concepts and Tools

Research Written and Statistical Information on the Impact of the Civil War

Students will now commence their research. Begin by directing students to review the relevant *Skills Tutorials.* Remind students to keep track of their work in the *Project Tracker* as they continue to use the *Need-to-Know Questions* to guide their work. Explain that students should locate more information than they will need to complete their project. That way, they will be able to choose the statistics that are most compelling, complementary, and suitable for presenting through a variety of visual means.

Suggestion: Review applicable Internet use rules before students commence their research.

Determine How to Present Information and Statistics

Having acquired a variety of statistics about the economic, social, and political impact of the Civil War, students must now decide how to present the information. Ask students to identify the strengths and weaknesses of a variety of visual representations of quantitative information, such as different kinds of graphs, charts, tables, and maps. Assist students in effectively transferring information between different media: from written media to visual media and from statistical media to the written and visual media. Guide students in presenting factual and quantitative information visually and also in presenting quantitative information in a descriptive text.

Suggestion: Remind students that their website is being created to entice people to visit a museum exhibit, so their representations should both be accurate and visually enticing.

Resources

- Search for Information on the Internet
- Evaluate Web Sites
- Analyze Data and Models
- Identify Evidence
- Interpret Sources
- Project Tracker
- Need-to-Know Questions
- Information Organizer

PROFESSIONAL DEVELOPMENT

Project-Based Learning

Be sure to view the Project-Based Learning Professional Development resources in the online course.

STEP 3: SYNTHESIZE

Evaluate Sources and Use Evidence to Formulate Conclusions

Select Digital Tools and Software and Create Your Visual Representations

In this step, students use a variety of digital tools to create their visual representations. A wide variety of tools are listed and suggested in the *Student Instructions.*

Suggestion: Encourage students to expand their skill sets by using digital tools that are new to them.

Create Your Website

Students create their websites using WordPress. Encourage students to include more than just their visual representations on their websites. They should include titles, captions, and information about the museum exhibit.

Revise Your Website

Review students' websites and allow them time to revise them. Encourage them to ensure that their website answers the Guiding Question: In what ways did the Civil War affect the lives of Americans economically, socially, and politically?

Suggestion: Point out to students that, like writing an essay, constructing a website requires the basic steps of planning, creating, and revising. Explain how that oftentimes revising can end up being the most time-consuming—and important—step in making anything.

Resources

- Project Tracker

STEP 4: DEMONSTRATE

Communicate Conclusions and Take Informed Action

Present Your Website

Have students prepare their website presentations and then watch the team presentations. Limit their presentation time. To help the teams structure their time, set up a clock in the back of the room, and alert them when they have only a few minutes left.

Reflect on the Project

Conclude by reviewing the project and eliciting students' answers to these questions: What went well? What did not go so well? What are three lasting lessons you have learned from this project?

Suggestion: As an extension activity, have students learn some basics about search engine optimization (SEO), or the process of building websites that appear in Internet search engine results. How would they revise their websites to help them reach a wider audience on the Internet?

Resources

- Give an Effective Presentation

INTRODUCTION

Society and Culture Before the Civil War (1820–1860)

The United States was divided by the Civil War, but the divisions had been part of American life for decades. The obvious distinction between free states and slave states was but one. The country was also divided geographically, into the North and the South. Economically, the interests of rural southerners and urban northerners regarding questions of tariffs, for example, were opposite. Social divides existed, too.Interstate and interregional travel was still rare and difficult, and truly knowing the people of a different state or region was the exception rather than the rule. All of these divisions had led to conflict and compromise. Soon, they would lead to war.

CONNECT

MY STORY VIDEO

Robert E. Lee, The Marble Man

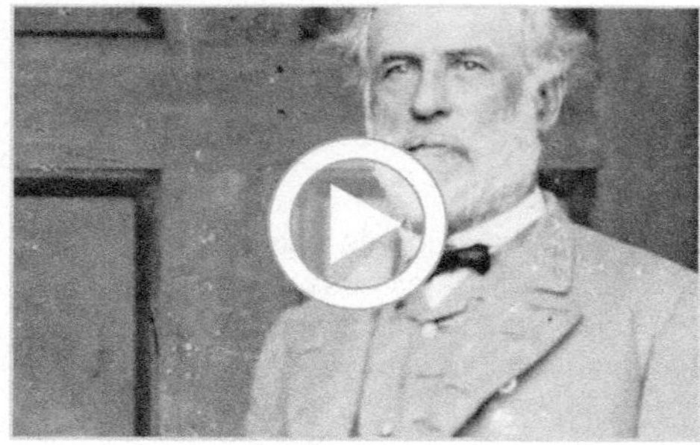

Watch a video about Robert E. Lee's leadership at the Battle of Chancellorsville.

Check Understanding How was Robert E. Lee able to win victory at Chancellorsville? *(His risky decision to divide his forces resulted in a major victory for the South. However, the Confederate side suffered many casualties, among them General Stonewall Jackson.)*

Determine Point of View When the Civil War broke out, Robert E. Lee was offered command of the Union forces, but he chose to fight for the South. Why do you think he made that decision? *(A native Virginian, his desire to defend his home state from Union attack no doubt overruled his desire to see the Union be kept intact.)*

FLIP IT!

Assign the My Story Video

DIGITAL ESSENTIAL QUESTION ACTIVITY

When is War Justified?

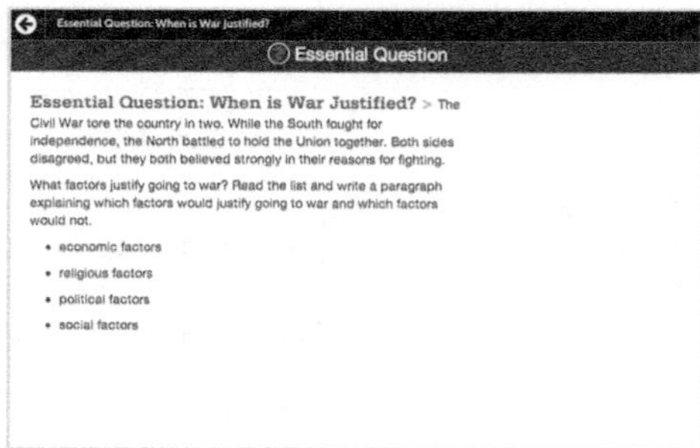

Ask students to think about the Essential Question for this topic: When is war justified?

Have students consider the types of factors that can divide a people: economic, political, religious, and social. Discuss which factors would justify going to war and which factors would not.

Interpret Invite a student to define a *civil* war. (A war between the citizens of the same country) Ask whether they think a civil war is ever more or less justified than a war between countries. (War against one's fellow citizens would be more difficult to justify because of the shared citizenship and cultural traits.)

Express Ideas Clearly Ask students if they think wars are generally caused by one event or factor or by several. (Wars are more likely to be caused by several factors because human relationships are complex, and more than one factor might be needed to convince people that such a deadly choice as war is justified.)

DIGITAL OVERVIEW ACTIVITY

Sectionalism and Civil War

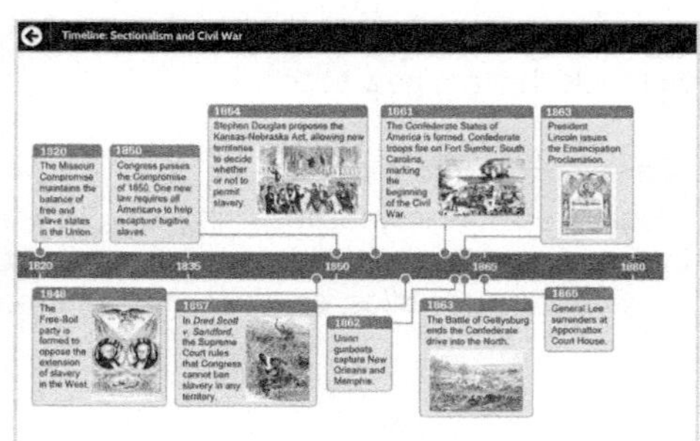

Point out that the first event in the timeline takes place more than 40 years—nearly half a century—before the beginning of the Civil War. Tell students that this reflects the fact that the Civil War did not come up "out of nowhere." It was an event long feared—and long predicted—that was the result of deep, old divisions in American society.As they learn about the Civil War, encourage students to think of it not so much as an event but as an effect, one that resulted from several causes.

Infer Ask students what all of the entries on the timeline before the Civil War have in common. (They are all concerned with slavery.) What can students infer from this? (That divisions over slavery were a major cause of the Civil War.)

Topic Inquiry

Launch the Topic Inquiry with students after introducing the Topic.

PEARSON realize™ www.PearsonRealize.com Access your Digital Lesson

Conflicts and Compromises

Supporting English Language Learners

Use with Digital Text 4, **California Reignites the Slavery Debate.**

Listening

Explain to students that they will demonstrate listening comprehension of what you say through collaboration with peers.

Beginning Read the following sentences to students, then have pairs of students collaborate to explain in their own words what the sentences mean: *Calhoun insisted that slavery be allowed in the western territories. In addition, he demanded that fugitives, or African Americans who had fled slavery, be returned to their owners.*

Intermediate Orally ask students the following questions about Calhoun and Webster. In groups, have them restate the questions in their own words and then answer the questions: 1) Which man viewed slavery as evil? 2) Which man wanted to legalize slavery in the western territories? 3) Which man supported the return of fugitive slaves?

Advanced Read aloud Daniel Webster's speech excerpt from the text. Then have pairs of students demonstrate listening comprehension by collaborating to restate the excerpt into more familiar language.

Advanced High Compare and contrast the positions of Calhoun and Webster. Have pairs of students play the roles of Calhoun and Webster, state their positions in the slavery debate, and work to reach a compromise.

Use with Digital Text 6, **A Book Sways the North Against Slavery.**

Writing

Review the plot and popularity of *Uncle Tom's Cabin* in preparation for the activity. Prompt students to write using newly acquired basic vocabulary from the reading.

Beginning Explain the meanings of the basic vocabulary *bought,whipped,* and *refused*. Have students complete and write down this summary of *Uncle Tom's Cabin*: Simon Legree _____ a slave named Uncle Tom. Tom _____ to tell him where two runaway slaves were, so Legree _____ him.

Intermediate Discuss the meanings of the descriptive words *kindness,piety,* and *brutal*. Ask students to suggest sentences about Uncle Tom or Simon Legree using this newly acquired basic vocabulary. Record their suggestions, and have students write them down.

Advanced Discuss the meanings of the words *novel, injustice, appeal, printing,* and *translated*. Have pairs of students write an advertisement for *Uncle Tom's Cabin* that uses this newly acquired basic vocabulary.

Advanced High Discuss the meanings of the words *objected, claimed, firsthand, moral,* and *political*. Have students use this newly acquired basic vocabulary to write a paragraph explaining the importance of *Uncle Tom's Cabin*. Provide time for students to share their paragraph with a partner.

D Differentiate Instruction

Use the Differentiated Instruction notes throughout the lesson plan to support the varied skill sets, levels of readiness, and interests in the mixed-ability classroom.

Challenge These notes include suggestions for expanding the activity for advanced students.

On-Level These notes include suggestions for modifying the activity to address different interests or learning styles.

Extra Support These notes include ideas for providing more scaffolding or reading spupport.

Special Needs These notes provide ideas for adapting instruction to support the needs of various special needs students.

NOTES

Topic 8 Lesson 1

Conflicts and Compromises

Objectives

Objective 1: Describe how the Missouri Compromise affected slavery.

Objective 2: Explain why conflict arose over the issue of slavery in western territories.

Objective 3: Identify why the Free-Soil party was founded.

Objective 4: Explain how the Compromise of 1850 tried to resolve the issue of slavery.

Objective 5: Summarize how Uncle Tom's Cabin affected attitudes toward slavery.

LESSON 1 ORGANIZER — **PACING: APPROX. 1 PERIOD, .5 BLOCKS**

	OBJECTIVES	PACING	RESOURCES Online	RESOURCES Print
Connect				
DIGITAL START UP ACTIVITY **The Impact of Slavery**		5 min.	●	
Investigate				
DIGITAL TEXT 1 **Henry Clay's Missouri Compromise**	Objective 1	10 min.	●	●
DIGITAL TEXT 2 **Western Expansion Heightens Tension Over Slavery**	Objective 2	10 min.	●	●
DIGITAL TEXT 3 **The Free-Soil Party Opposes Slavery in the West**	Objective 3	10 min.	●	●
DIGITAL TEXT 4 **California Reignites the Slavery Debate**	Objective 4	10 min.	●	●
DIGITAL TEXT 5 **Congress Reaches a Compromise**	Objective 4	10 min.	●	●
INTERACTIVE CARTOON **The Fugitive Slave Act**	Objective 4	10 min.	●	
DIGITAL TEXT 6 **A Book Sways the North Against Slavery**	Objective 5	10 min.	●	●
INTERACTIVE GALLERY ***Uncle Tom's Cabin***	Objective 5	10 min.	●	
Synthesize				
DIGITAL ACTIVITY **Conflicts and Compromises Prior to the Civil War**		5 min.	●	
Demonstrate				
DIGITAL QUIZ **Lesson Quiz and Class Discussion Board**		10 min.	●	

PEARSON realize www.PearsonRealize.com

Go online to access additional resources including: Primary Sources • Biographies • Supreme Court cases • 21st Century Skill Tutorials • Maps • Graphic Organizers.

CONNECT

DIGITAL START UP ACTIVITY

The Impact of Slavery

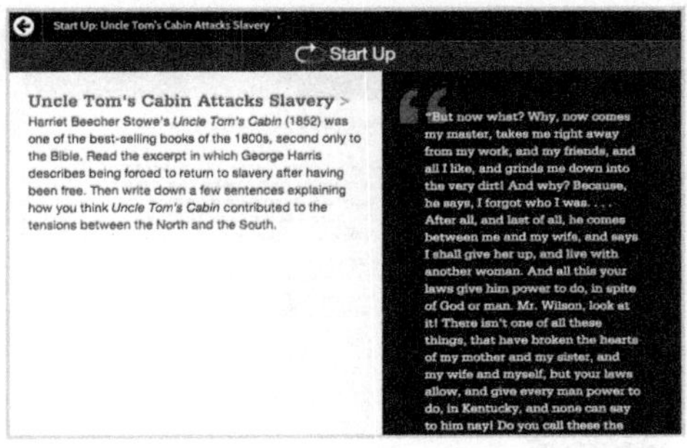

Project the Start Up Activity Ask students to read and respond to the excerpt as they enter and get settled. Then have students share their ideas in small groups.

Interpret What does George Harris say his master does? *(Takes him away from his work, his friends, and all that he likes; makes him give up his wife and live with another woman)* What does Harris suggest about the laws of Kentucky and the nation? *(The laws should not allow people like his master to treat other people in this way.)* How does this excerpt and the book *Uncle Tom's Cabin* show sectionalism and slavery as causes of the Civil War? *(It shows why some people opposed slavery and were willing to fight to end slavery and win liberty.)*

Aa Vocabulary Development: Use the Interactive Reading Notepad to preview the Key Terms and Academic Vocabulary in this lesson with students.

FLIP IT!

Assign the Flipped Video for this lesson.

STUDENT EDITION PRINT PAGES: 430–438

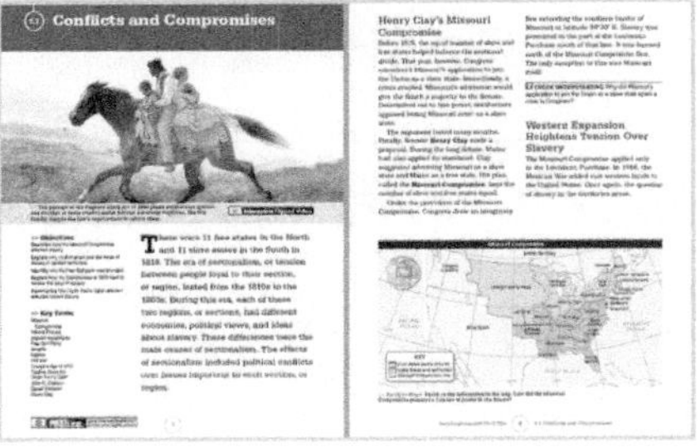

INVESTIGATE

DIGITAL TEXT 1

Henry Clay's Missouri Compromise

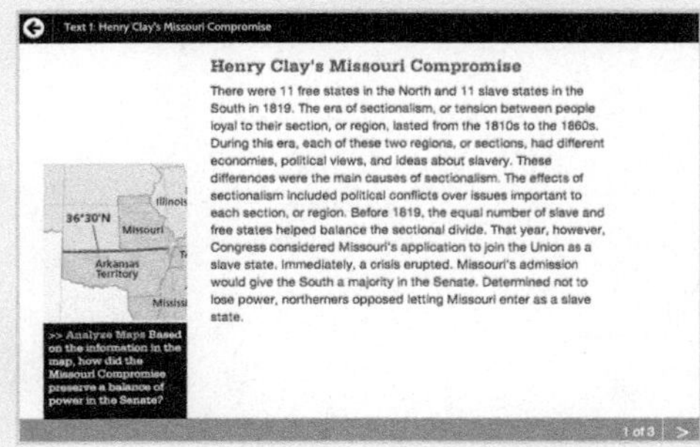

Objective 1: Describe how the Missouri Compromise affected slavery.

Quick Instruction

Analyze Maps Project the map showing the geographic distribution of free and slave states prior to the Missouri Compromise. Challenge students to consider what would happen to the balance of free and slave states if Missouri were admitted as a state.

Explain that in this lesson, students will explore the provisions of the Missouri Compromise, the role of Henry Clay, and the manner by which the Missouri Compromise provided a peaceful, if temporary, resolution to the challenges of sectionalism and slavery.

Summarize What role did Henry Clay play in achieving congressional compromise before the Civil War? *(Henry Clay determined that the United States could admit two states, one free and one slave, to maintain the balance of power between free and slave states, thereby avoiding wider conflict. He proposed his compromise in Congress, where it was passed and made law.)*

Further Instruction

Go through the Interactive Reading Notepad questions and discuss the answers with the class.

Invite students to define the term *compromise*. Guide students to understand that a compromise attempts to find a peaceful resolution to a conflict by ensuring that the parties to a conflict each give up and get something that they want.

Recall What were the main provisions of the Missouri Compromise? *(The Missouri Compromise admitted Missouri as a slave state and Maine as a free state. It also drew an imaginary line across the southern border of Missouri. In the Louisiana Purchase territories, slavery was illegal north of this line and legal south of this line.)*

Identify Central Issues Describe how sectionalism and slavery caused the core conflict that the Missouri Compromise attempted to address. How did that compromise provide a temporary, peaceful resolution to the conflict? *(Slavery had become a sectional issue in the United States, whereby people in southern states tended to support the spread of slavery and people in northern states tended to oppose the spread of slavery. When Missouri asked to become a state, Congress was divided sectionally over whether to admit Missouri as a free or slave state, since either decision would give more political power to one section or another. The Missouri Compromise provided a peaceful resolution to the immediate conflict by admitting two states, one free and one slave, to prevent either section from gaining more power.)*

Conflicts and Compromises

DIGITAL TEXT 2

Western Expansion Heightens Tension Over Slavery

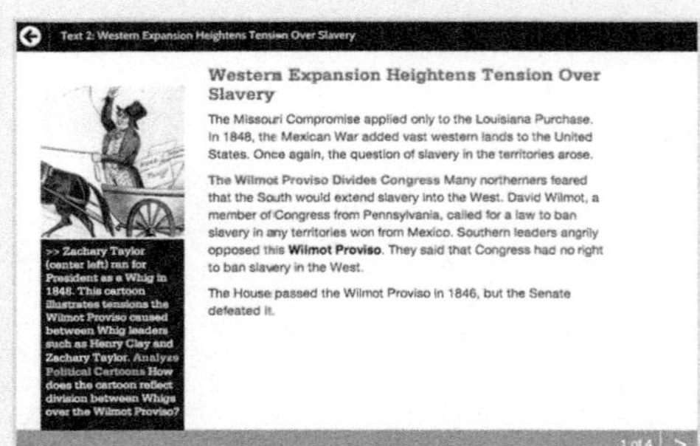

Objective 2: Explain why conflict arose over the issue of slavery in western territories.

Quick Instruction

Prompt students to understand that the Missouri Compromise provided a guideline for slavery in the Louisiana Purchase territory, but it did not solve the question of future states or of future territories. Be sure students understand that the sectional debate over slavery originated as a conflict between northern and southern sections of the nation. However, as the nation expanded west, the sectional debate expanded, too. Each section wanted to enlarge their influence and prevent the other from gaining more influence.

Distinguish What was a primary cause of sectionalism? *(The issue of slavery and property rights continued to divide Americans across regional lines. There were many perspectives on the issue, but generally speaking, entire states felt one way or the other. These differences prompted debate over the status of western territories.)*

Infer What effect would sectionalism have on congressional conflicts over territorial gains? *(Congressional leaders from the South would likely want to allow slavery in new territories, while congressional leaders from the north would likely want to ban slavery in new territories.)*

D Differentiate: Extra Support Explain that the root of *popular* comes from the Latin for "people," and the root of *sovereignty* comes from the Latin for "authority" or "rule." Together, *popular sovereignty* means "rule by the people." Applied to the question of slavery in territories, the phrase was used to mean that the people of the territory would decide for themselves whether to allow slavery.

Further Instruction

Analyze Cartoons Project the political cartoon on the Wilmot Proviso. Congressional leaders attemped to add the proviso to many other bills. However, the proviso failed to be adopted each time. Why is the proviso portrayed as a stumbling block in the cartoon? *(Congressional leaders kept adding the proviso to other bills, making it more difficult for Zachary Taylor to win the presidential election and for the Whigs to pass their other policy items.)*

Make Predictions What impact would slavery have on the acquisition of new territories? What challenge would it pose? *(The nation would have to decide whether to allow slavery in these territories.)*

Explain What were the provisions of the Wilmot Proviso? Why did sectionalism prevent the proviso from being adopted? *(The Wilmot Proviso would have made slavery illegal in territories gained from Mexico. This would have upset the balance between free and slave territories and states. Southern congressional leaders refused to pass the proviso in order to preserve the balance between slave and free sections of the nation.)*

DIGITAL TEXT 3

The Free-Soil Party Opposes Slavery in the West

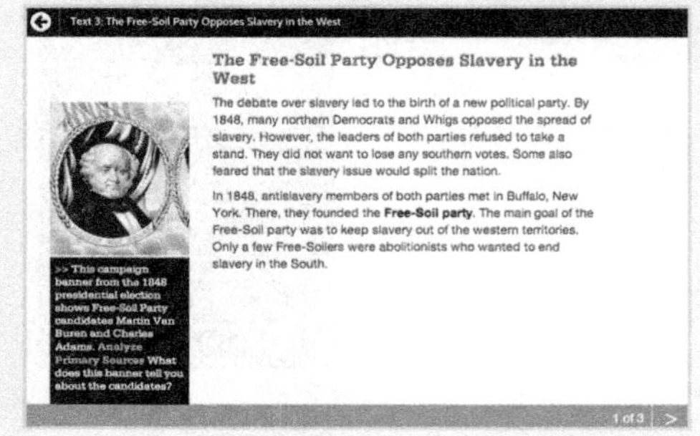

Text 3: The Free-Soil Party Opposes Slavery in the West
The Free-Soil Party Opposes Slavery in the West
The debate over slavery led to the birth of a new political party. By 1848, many northern Democrats and Whigs opposed the spread of slavery. However, the leaders of both parties refused to take a stand. They did not want to lose any southern votes. Some also feared that the slavery issue would split the nation.
In 1848, antislavery members of both parties met in Buffalo, New York. There, they founded the Free-Soil party. The main goal of the Free-Soil party was to keep slavery out of the western territories. Only a few Free-Soilers were abolitionists who wanted to end slavery in the South.
>> This campaign banner from the 1848 presidential election shows Free-Soil Party candidates Martin Van Buren and Charles Adams. Analyze Primary Sources What does this banner tell you about the candidates?
1 of 3 >

Objective 3: Identify why the Free-Soil Party was founded.

Quick Instruction

Analyze Images Project the image of a Free-Soil Party campaign banner. Prompt students to discuss what ideas they think the Free-Soil Party represented. Explain that this lesson contrasts the point of view of the Free-Soil Party with other political parties on the historical issue of slavery.

Categorize Draw a three-column chart with the headings *Whig, Democratic,* and *Free-Soil.* List each party's 1848 presidential candidate beneath each heading. Then, list each candidate's point of view on the important historical issues of slavery. *(Whig: Zachary Taylor, did not take an official stance on slavery but was assumed to support slavery as a slave owner; Democratic: Lewis Cass, supported popular sovereignty; Free-Soil: Martin Van Buren, wanted to ban slavery in Mexican Cession)*

Further Instruction

Go through the Interactive Reading Notepad questions and discuss the answers with the class.

Compare Points of View Given the effects of sectionalism, why might voters have been unlikely to support Lewis Cass for president? *(Slavery was a major issue of the election, and the nation was divided largely on sectional lines. Popular sovereignty did not ensure either a balance between sections or a clear victory for either. Because popular sovereignty left the question of slavery to occupants of a territory, it was kind of risky. Neither those who supported slavery nor those who opposed it could not be sure that popular sovereignty would protect their interests. Therefore, both sides of the debate were less likely to support Cass, who promoted popular sovereignty.)*

DIGITAL TEXT 4

California Reignites the Slavery Debate

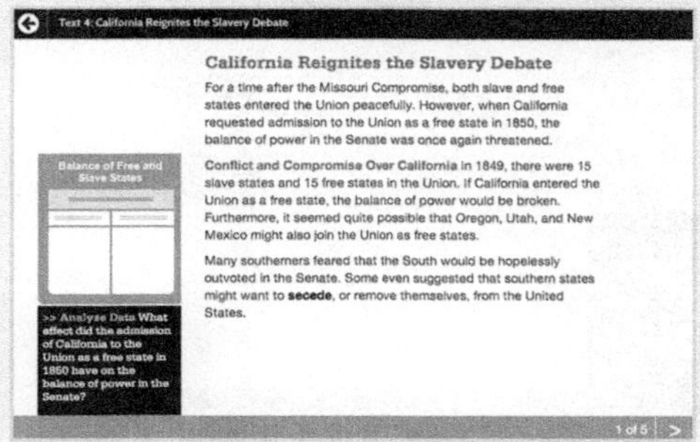

Text 4: California Reignites the Slavery Debate
California Reignites the Slavery Debate
For a time after the Missouri Compromise, both slave and free states entered the Union peacefully. However, when California requested admission to the Union as a free state in 1850, the balance of power in the Senate was once again threatened.
Conflict and Compromise Over California In 1849, there were 15 slave states and 15 free states in the Union. If California entered the Union as a free state, the balance of power would be broken. Furthermore, it seemed quite possible that Oregon, Utah, and New Mexico might also join the Union as free states.
Many southerners feared that the South would be hopelessly outvoted in the Senate. Some even suggested that southern states might want to secede, or remove themselves, from the United States.
Balance of Free and Slave States
>> Analyze Data What effect did the admission of California to the Union as a free state in 1850 have on the balance of power in the Senate?
1 of 5

Objective 4: **Explain how the Compromise of 1850 tried to resolve the issue of slavery.**

Quick Instruction

Prompt students to understand the roles of Henry Clay, John C. Calhoun, and Daniel Webster in compromising to achieve a peaceful resolution to the conflict between different sections of the nation. Be sure that students understand that secession, or the withdrawal of some states from the nation, was proposed prior to the Civil War. Clay, Calhoun, and Webster, in their ways, sought to prevent violent conflict and secession.

Interactive Cartoon: The Fugitive Slave Act Project the cartoon. Roll over the hotspots to reveal details about the cartoon and discuss them with students. How does this cartoon illustrate that tensions regarding the issue of slavery were rising? *(The cartoon shows the violence that surrounds the issue of slavery and the Fugitive Slave Act. People were willing to kill to recover escaped slaves, and others were willing to kill to help escaped slaves. The conflict was not just about ideas but about people's lives.)*

Compare and Contrast Summarize the roles played by John C. Calhoun, Henry Clay, and Daniel Webster in the congressional conflict over California's statehood. What did their approaches have in common, and how did they differ? *(Calhoun remained adamant that slavery must be allowed in the western territories and that northern states must be required to return fugitive slaves. He insisted that these demands be met to prevent secession. Webster opposed both of Calhoun's demands, but he believed it was more important to preserve the union, so he agreed to support southern demands that northerners be required to return escaped slaves. Clay proposed the Compromise of 1850 to partially meet Calhoun's demands by allowing the extension of slavery in some parts of the western territories while prohibiting it in others. The Compromise of 1850 also included a strict fugitive slave law.)*

DIGITAL TEXT 5

Congress Reaches a Compromise

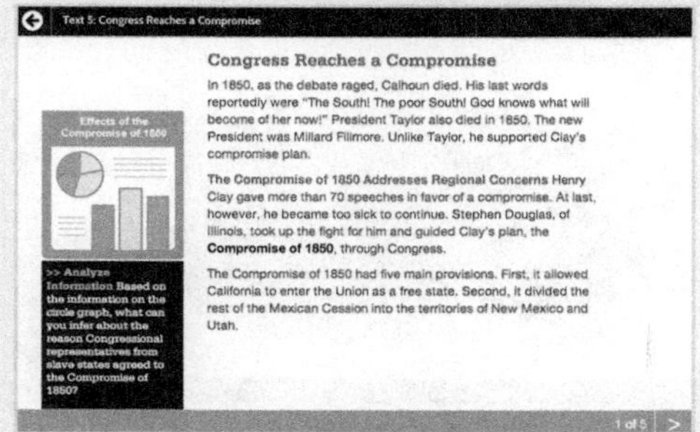

Text 5: Congress Reaches a Compromise
Congress Reaches a Compromise
In 1850, as the debate raged, Calhoun died. His last words reportedly were "The South! The poor South! God knows what will become of her now!" President Taylor also died in 1850. The new President was Millard Fillmore. Unlike Taylor, he supported Clay's compromise plan.
The Compromise of 1850 Addresses Regional Concerns Henry Clay gave more than 70 speeches in favor of a compromise. At last, however, he became too sick to continue. Stephen Douglas, of Illinois, took up the fight for him and guided Clay's plan, the Compromise of 1850, through Congress.
The Compromise of 1850 had five main provisions. First, it allowed California to enter the Union as a free state. Second, it divided the rest of the Mexican Cession into the territories of New Mexico and Utah.
Effects of the Compromise of 1850
>> Analyze Information Based on the information on the circle graph, what can you infer about the reason Congressional representatives from slave states agreed to the Compromise of 1850?
1 of 5

ACTIVE CLASSROOM

Ask the following questions using the Circle Write Strategy: Why did people in the north, even those who did not necessarily support a ban on slavery, oppose the Fugitive Slave Act? Why did it make so many people angry? If students struggle with the questions, you may wish to model a Think Aloud: "Hmm, let me think how I would feel. If I had lived in the North, and Congress told me that I had to capture escaped slaves, whether I agreed with slavery or not, and help return them to the South, would I want to do that?"

ELL Use the ELL activity described in the ELL chart.

Topic 8 Lesson 1

Conflicts and Compromises

INTERACTIVE CARTOON

The Fugitive Slave Act

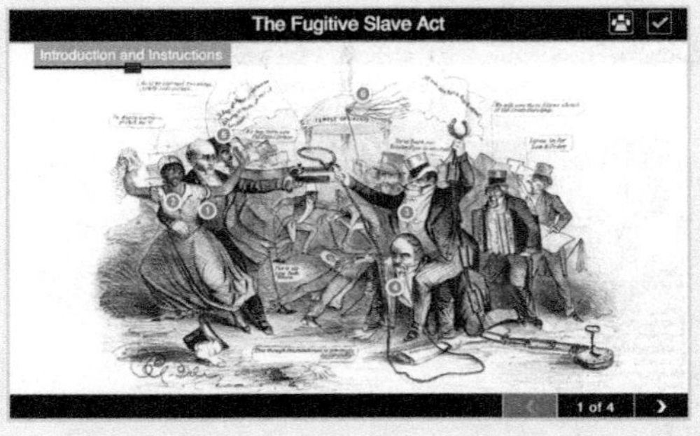

Further Instruction

Draw Conclusions Do you think the provisions of the Compromise of 1850 provided for a peaceful resolution to the conflict over slavery? Explain your reasoning. *(Like the Missouri Compromise, I think it provided a temporary peaceful resolution. States did not secede and engage in armed conflict right away, but the Fugitive Slave Act resulted in violence. Also, it did not resolve the fundamental debate over slavery in the nation, which would lead to violence eventually.)*

DIGITAL TEXT 6

A Book Sways the North Against Slavery

Objective 5: **Summarize how *Uncle Tom's Cabin* affected attitudes toward slavery.**

Quick Instruction

Interactive Gallery: *Uncle Tom's Cabin* Project the slideshow. Look at each image and source individually and discuss its meaning. Then, evaluate the collection as a whole and discuss its historical significance. Prompt students to explore how the images demonstrate the divisive nature of sectionalism and slavery in the United States leading up to the Civil War.

Summarize How did *Uncle Tom's Cabin* impact perceptions of slavery in the North? *(The publication of the novel only fueled opinions against slavery. Before the novel's publication, some northerners may have had little or no contact with people who had been enslaved. Stowe's novel made slavery and its consequences more real and personal.)*

ACTIVE CLASSROOM

Use the Conversation With History Strategy to help students engage with the gallery. Organize students into small groups, and ask each person in the group to write and answer a question to the author of *Uncle Tom's Cabin*, Harriet Beecher Stowe.

ELL Use the ELL activity described in the ELL chart.

INTERACTIVE GALLERY

Uncle Tom's Cabin

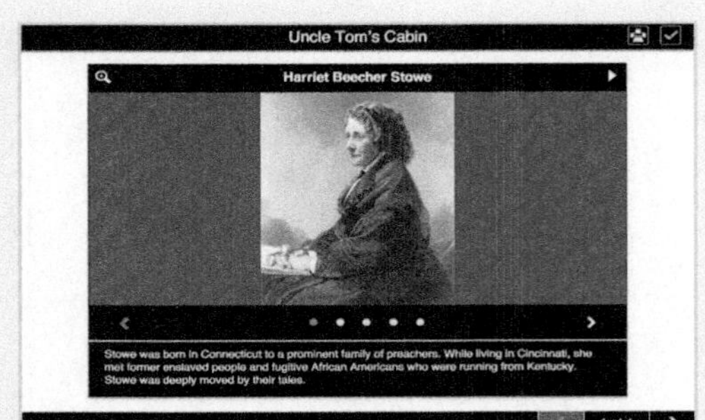

Further Instruction

Determine Author's Purpose What did Harriet Beecher Stowe hope to convey about the effects of slavery on people in the South? *(Stowe hoped to convey the cruelty and hardship of slavery by showing how badly Tom and other enslaved persons were treated by their owners.)*

SYNTHESIZE

DIGITAL ACTIVITY

Conflicts and Compromises Prior to the Civil War

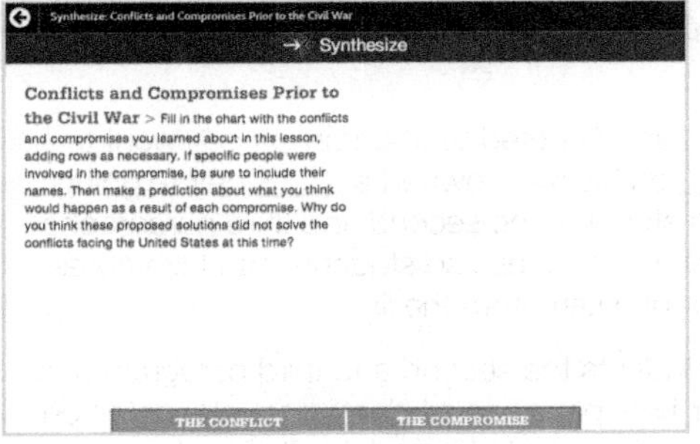

Synthesize: Conflicts and Compromises Prior to the Civil War
→ Synthesize
Conflicts and Compromises Prior to the Civil War > Fill in the chart with the conflicts and compromises you learned about in this lesson, adding rows as necessary. If specific people were involved in the compromise, be sure to include their names. Then make a prediction about what you think would happen as a result of each compromise. Why do you think these proposed solutions did not solve the conflicts facing the United States at this time?
THE CONFLICT
THE COMPROMISE

Ask students to review the lesson to identify key congressional conflicts that existed prior to the Civil War. Have them record these conflicts. Then, have them identify and record congressional compromises that attempted to find peaceful resolutions to these conflicts. Circulate the room to keep students on task. Ensure that students identify sectionalism and the expansion of slavery as two key conflicts and the Missouri Compromise and the Compromise of 1850 as two key compromises.

Instruct small groups to discuss how each compromise provided a peaceful resolution to a congressional conflict. Then, challenge each group to answer the question: Why do you think these proposed solutions did not solve the conflicts facing the United States at this time?

Discuss Call on each group to share ideas. Have groups record their responses to post on the class blog. Finally, tell each group to predict how sectionalism and slavery will incite the nation to war, despite attempts at compromise.

DEMONSTRATE

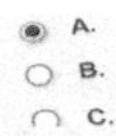

DIGITAL QUIZ

Lesson Quiz and Class Discussion Board

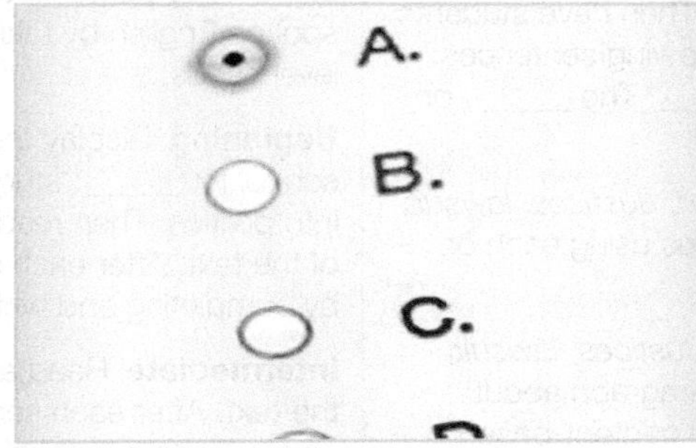

Assign the online Lesson Quiz for this lesson if you haven't already done so. Students will be offered automatic remediation or enrichment based on their score.

Pose these questions to the class on the Discussion Board:

In *Conflicts and Compromises*, you read about congressional conflicts driven by sectionalism and slavery that existed before the Civil War. You also learned about the roles played by legislators such as Henry Clay, John C. Calhoun, and Daniel Webster in attempting to achieve compromises. Finally, you examined two compromises that resulted in peaceful resolutions to congressional conflicts over the expansion of slavery into new states and territories. The Missouri Compromise and the Compromise of 1850 each provided temporary solutions to deep-rooted problems.

Compare Points of View Why did Clay and Webster oppose the expansion of slavery? Why did Calhoun fight so hard to promote the expansion of slavery? What incentive did all three leaders have to reach a compromise?

Make Decisions Clay and Webster decided that preserving the union was more important than restricting slavery. Do you agree that the provisions of the Compromise of 1850 were necessary? Why or why not?

Topic Inquiry

Have students continue their investigations for the Topic Inquiry.

Growing Tensions

Supporting English Language Learners

Use with the Text 4, **The Impact of the Dred Scott Case.**

Writing

Prompt students to write about the Dred Scott case using content-based, grade-level vocabulary pertaining to the legal system.

Beginning Explain the words *case, court,* and *ruling*. Then have students use this content-based vocabulary to complete the following sentences: *Dred Scott* v. *Sanford* was a _____ in the Supreme _____. The _____ , or decision, helped the issue of slavery.

Intermediate Discuss the meanings of *Supreme Court, Justices, lawsuit, ruling,* and *decision*. Then have students write sentences using each of these terms.

Advanced Discuss the meanings of *Supreme Court, Justices, lawsuit, ruling,* and *decision*. Ask pairs of students to write a paragraph about the Dred Scott case that uses at least four of these five content-based vocabulary words.

Advanced High Discuss the meanings of *Supreme Court, Justices, lawsuit, ruling, decision, outlaw,* and *unconstitutional*. Ask students to use this content-based vocabulary to write a mock news article about the Dred Scott case that could have been printed just after the Supreme Court announced its decision.

Use with Digital Text 6, **Abraham Lincoln Leads the Republican Party.**

Listening

Review reasons for taking notes when someone is speaking, and encourage students to include only the main ideas in their notes. Prompt students to demonstrate listening comprehension of increasingly complex spoken English by taking notes commensurate with content and grade-level needs.

Beginning Display these notes as a bulleted list: born in _____ ; went to school for _____ ; studied _____ on his own; owned a _____ before going into politics. Then read aloud to students the second and third paragraphs of the text. After each sentence or two, pause so students can take notes by completing and writing down one item from the list.

Intermediate Read aloud to students the second and third paragraphs of the text. After each sentence or two, pause so students can take notes on what you have just said. Encourage students to organize their notes as a bulleted list.

Advanced Read aloud to students the fourth paragraph of the text.Have students jot down important words and phrases. Afterward, encourage them to fill in any gaps in their notes.

Advanced High Have students take notes as you read aloud the section titled "Lincoln and Douglas Debate Slavery."Afterward, encourage them to fill in any gaps or condense their notes as necessary.

D Differentiate Instruction

Use the Differentiated Instruction notes throughout the lesson plan to support the varied skill sets, levels of readiness, and interests in the mixed-ability classroom.

Challenge These notes include suggestions for expanding the activity for advanced students.

On-Level These notes include suggestions for modifying the activity to address different interests or learning styles.

Extra Support These notes include ideas for providing more scaffolding or reading spuport.

Special Needs These notes provide ideas for adapting instruction to support the needs of various special needs students.

NOTES

Objectives

Objective 1: Identify the goals and outcomes of the Kansas-Nebraska Act.

Objective 2: Summarize the impact of the Dred Scott case on the nation.

Objective 3: Explain why the Republican Party was founded.

Objective 4: Explain the rapid emergence of Abraham Lincoln as a Republican Party leader.

Objective 5: Describe the reaction to John Brown's raid on Harpers Ferry.

LESSON 2 ORGANIZER	PACING: APPROX. 1 PERIOD, .5 BLOCKS		RESOURCES	
	OBJECTIVES	PACING	Online	Print
Connect				
DIGITAL START UP ACTIVITY **Tensions Divide the Nation**		5 min.	●	
Investigate				
DIGITAL TEXT 1 **The Question of Slavery in Kansas and Nebraska**	Objective 1	10 min.	●	●
DIGITAL TEXT 2 **Violent Clashes Over Slavery in Kansas**	Objective 1	10 min.	●	●
DIGITAL TEXT 3 **Violence Over Slavery Breaks Out in the Senate**	Objective 1	10 min.	●	●
INTERACTIVE GALLERY **The Effects of the Kansas-Nebraska Act**	Objective 1	10 min.	●	
DIGITAL TEXT 4 **The Impact of the Dred Scott Case**	Objective 2	10 min.	●	●
INTERACTIVE GALLERY **The Dred Scott Case**	Objective 2	10 min.	●	
DIGITAL TEXT 5 **The Republican Party Challenges Other Parties**	Objective 3	10 min.	●	●
DIGITAL TEXT 6 **Abraham Lincoln Leads the Republican Party**	Objective 4	10 min.	●	●
DIGITAL TEXT 7 **John Brown's Antislavery Campaign**	Objective 5	10 min.	●	●
Synthesize				
DIGITAL ACTIVITY **Tensions Divide the Nation**		5 min.	●	
Demonstrate				
DIGITAL QUIZ **Lesson Quiz and Class Discussion Board**		10 min.	●	

Growing Tensions

CONNECT

DIGITAL START UP ACTIVITY

Tensions Divide the Nation

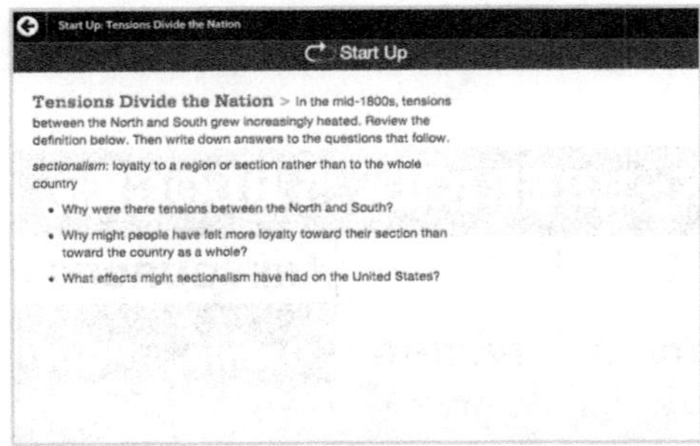

Start Up: Tensions Divide the Nation
Start Up
Tensions Divide the Nation > In the mid-1800s, tensions between the North and South grew increasingly heated. Review the definition below. Then write down answers to the questions that follow.
sectionalism: loyalty to a region or section rather than to the whole country
• Why were there tensions between the North and South?
• Why might people have felt more loyalty toward their section than toward the country as a whole?
• What effects might sectionalism have had on the United States?

Project the Start Up Activity Ask students to answer the questions as they enter and get settled. Then, have them share their ideas in small groups.

Discuss Why might people have felt more loyalty toward their section of the country than the country as a whole? *(Many people in each section probably shared certain ways of life, economic activities, and political views. This likely made them feel closer to their friends, families, neighbors, and communities within their sections.)* How might have sectionalism increased tensions in the United States? *(Sectionalism would have encouraged people to put the interests, politics, and ideas of their own sections above the unity of the nation.)*

Aa Vocabulary Development: Use the Interactive Reading Notepad to preview the Key Terms and Academic Vocabulary in this lesson with students.

FLIP IT!

Assign the Flipped Video for this lesson.

STUDENT EDITION PRINT PAGES: 439–449

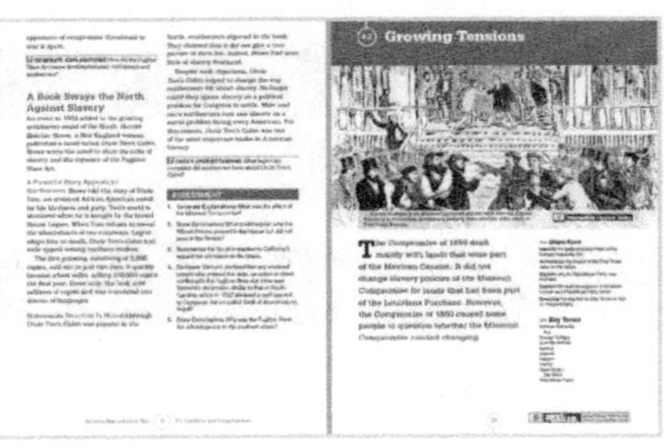

INVESTIGATE

DIGITAL TEXT 1

The Question of Slavery in Kansas and Nebraska

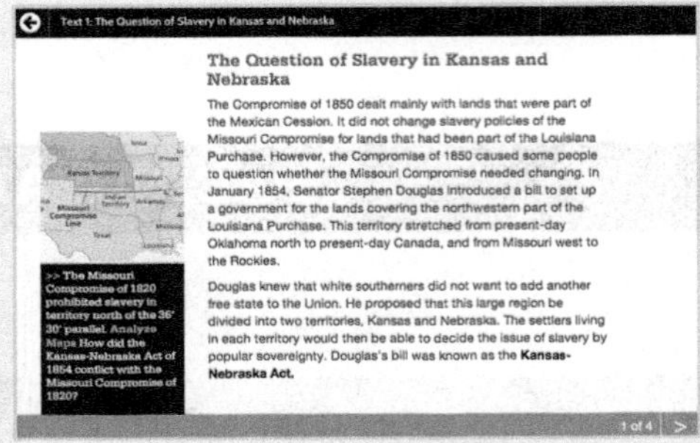

Text 1: The Question of Slavery in Kansas and Nebraska
The Question of Slavery in Kansas and Nebraska
The Compromise of 1850 dealt mainly with lands that were part of the Mexican Cession. It did not change slavery policies of the Missouri Compromise for lands that had been part of the Louisiana Purchase. However, the Compromise of 1850 caused some people to question whether the Missouri Compromise needed changing. In January 1854, Senator Stephen Douglas introduced a bill to set up a government for the lands covering the northwestern part of the Louisiana Purchase. This territory stretched from present-day Oklahoma north to present-day Canada, and from Missouri west to the Rockies.
Douglas knew that white southerners did not want to add another free state to the Union. He proposed that this large region be divided into two territories, Kansas and Nebraska. The settlers living in each territory would then be able to decide the issue of slavery by popular sovereignty. Douglas's bill was known as the Kansas-Nebraska Act.
>> The Missouri Compromise of 1820 prohibited slavery in territory north of the 36° 30' parallel. Analyze Maps How did the Kansas-Nebraska Act of 1854 conflict with the Missouri Compromise of 1820?
1 of 4

Objective 1: Identify the goals and outcomes of the Kansas-Nebraska Act.

Quick Instruction

Interactive Gallery: The Effects of the Kansas-Nebraska Act Project the Interactive gallery and click through the items. Call on a volunteer to define *popular sovereignty*. Explain that the Kansas-Nebraska Act attempted to apply popular sovereignty to western territories. Ask students to consider how popular sovereignty might conflict with the Missouri Compromise. Prompt students to think about the effect the Kansas-Nebraska Act will have on sectionalism in the United States.

Cite Evidence that the effects of the Kansas-Nebraska Act showed the potentially violent outcomes of sectional differences over slavery. *(The Kansas-Nebraska Act's popular sovereignty provision was intended to decide the question of slavery in Kansas through a popular vote. However, pro- and antislavery forces saw it as an opportunity to tip the balance in national politics. They sent settlers to occupy Kansas and sway the vote. Settlers from both sides of the issues clashed, even on the floor of the Senate. The events demonstrated that people for and against slavery were willing to commit acts of violence to defend their positions, increasing the likelihood of war.)*

DIGITAL TEXT 2

Violent Clashes Over Slavery in Kansas

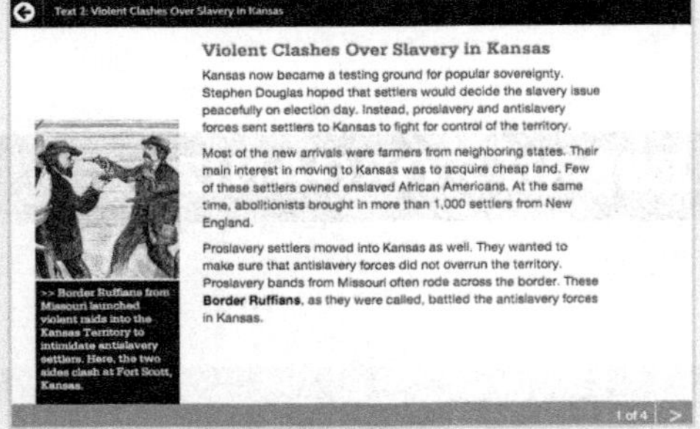

ACTIVE CLASSROOM

Have students Make Headlines for items in the Interactive gallery. Assign each student one of the pictures for which to write a headline. Then, organize students into groups so that each group has a headline for each item. Instruct students to share and revise their headlines. Discuss headlines as a class, or post them to the class blog.

Further Instruction

Begin by asking students to recall previous discussions of popular sovereignty. Draw a T-chart on the white board, and call on volunteers to list pros and cons of popular sovereignty as a solution to sectional debates about slavery. Then, display the map of the Missouri Compromise. Call on students to locate places of importance, such as the Missouri Compromise line and the unorganized territory which would eventually become the Kansas and Nebraska Territories.Point out that the Kansas-Nebraska Act changed the rules established by the Missouri Compromise by allowing citizens, not geographic boundaries, to determine the question of slavery. Explain that this circumstance posed a new precedent.

DIGITAL TEXT 3

Violence Over Slavery Breaks Out in the Senate

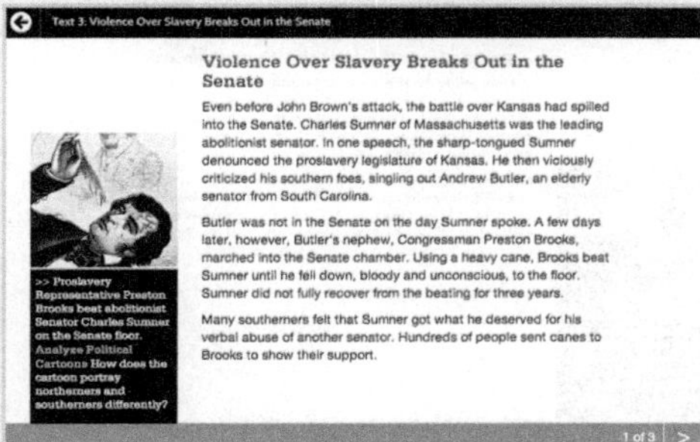

Be sure to point out that the Kansas-Nebraska Act was a major event in U.S. history because it exposed sectionalism and slavery as causes of strife that would lead to the Civil War. The Kansas-Nebraska Act attempted to resolve the sectional debate about slavery and avoid conflict by providing for popular sovereignty in two new territories. However, it led to more argument and violence as both sides of the issue rushed to win control of Kansas. This violence spilled over into the politics of the Senate.

INTERACTIVE GALLERY

The Effects of the Kansas-Nebraska Act

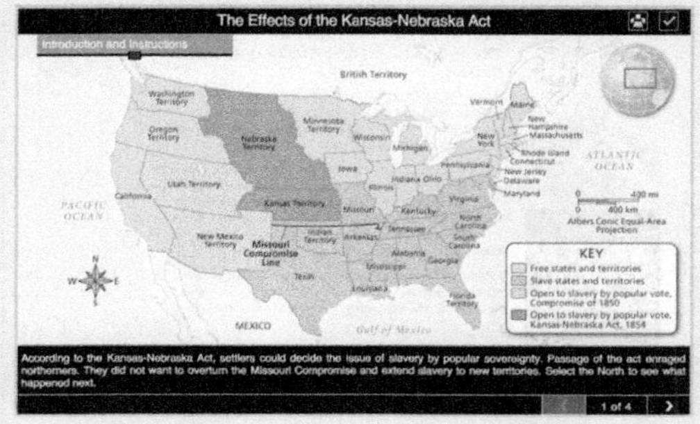

Infer What relationship do you see between the violence that occurred on the Senate floor and the fact that slavery was a cause of the Civil War? *(The fight on the Senate floor shows that Congress was unable to find a political solution to the slavery issue, leaving war as the only alternative.)*

DIGITAL TEXT 4

The Impact of the Dred Scott Case

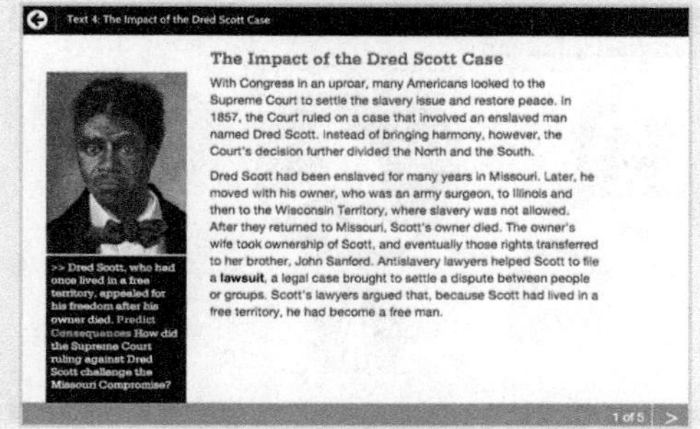

Text 4: The Impact of the Dred Scott Case
The Impact of the Dred Scott Case
With Congress in an uproar, many Americans looked to the Supreme Court to settle the slavery issue and restore peace. In 1857, the Court ruled on a case that involved an enslaved man named Dred Scott. Instead of bringing harmony, however, the Court's decision further divided the North and the South.
Dred Scott had been enslaved for many years in Missouri. Later, he moved with his owner, who was an army surgeon, to Illinois and then to the Wisconsin Territory, where slavery was not allowed. After they returned to Missouri, Scott's owner died. The owner's wife took ownership of Scott, and eventually those rights transferred to her brother, John Sanford. Antislavery lawyers helped Scott to file a lawsuit, a legal case brought to settle a dispute between people or groups. Scott's lawyers argued that, because Scott had lived in a free territory, he had become a free man.
>> Dred Scott, who had once lived in a free territory, appealed for his freedom after his owner died. Predict Consequences How did the Supreme Court ruling against Dred Scott challenge the Missouri Compromise?
1 of 5

Objective 2: Summarize the impact of the Dred Scott case on the nation.

Quick Instruction

Interactive Gallery: The Dred Scott Case Project the Interactive gallery, and click through the items. Have students write a short summary of the issues and decisions in the landmark Supreme Court case *Dred Scott* v. *Sandford*. Then, have them evaluate the impact of the case on African Americans, the slavery debate, southerners, and northerners.

Draw Conclusions What impact did *Dred Scott* v. *Sandford* have on enslaved persons and the abolitionist movement? *(This decision changed the way slavery and enslaved persons were treated in the nation. Enslaved persons could not escape from slave states and hope for protection. Moreover, abolitionists could not count on national laws to prevent the spread of slavery, because Congress could not regulate slavery within states and territories.)*

ACTIVE CLASSROOM

Conduct Write 1-Get 3 about the Dred Scott aase. Ask: What are four ways that the decision in the Dred Scott Case affected the lives of people in the United States? Have students take a piece of paper and fold it into quarters, write down one response in the first box, and then go around room asking to hear other responses. If students think a response is correct, they should write it in one of the boxes until they have three more responses on the page. Have students share the responses they recorded with the class.

Growing Tensions

INTERACTIVE GALLERY

The Dred Scott Case

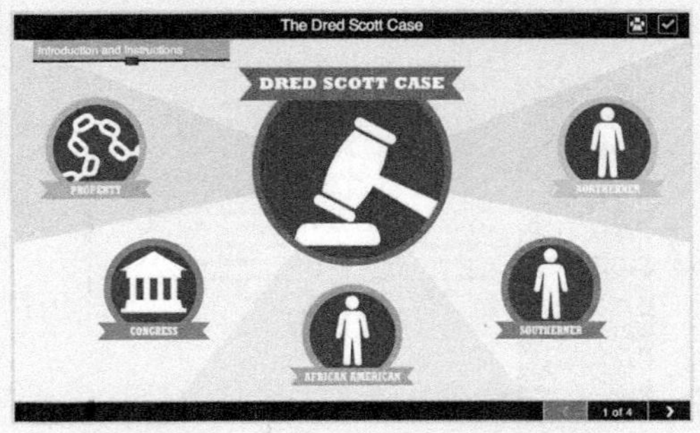

D Differentiate: Extra Support Display a map of the United States at the time of the Dred Scott decision and illustrate the path of Dred Scott's travels *(from Missouri to Illinois to the Wisconsin Territory and then back to Missouri)*, pointing out where the laws of the different states and territories conflicted, leaving the Supreme Court to determine which laws applied to Dred Scott. Ask students: What does this case demonstrate about the challenges of leaving the question of slavery to individual states and territories? Have them discuss their answers in small groups.

ELL Use the ELL activity described in the ELL chart.

Further Instruction

Hypothesize If Dred Scott had left his owners or pursued his lawsuit while he was in Illinois or Wisconsin, do you think this case would have had a different outcome? Why or why not? *(I think the Supreme Court would have made the same ruling because it clearly meant to rule in favor of slavery. The court likely would have ruled that Dred Scott was property when he left Missouri and remained property wherever he went.)*

DIGITAL TEXT 5

The Republican Party Challenges Other Parties

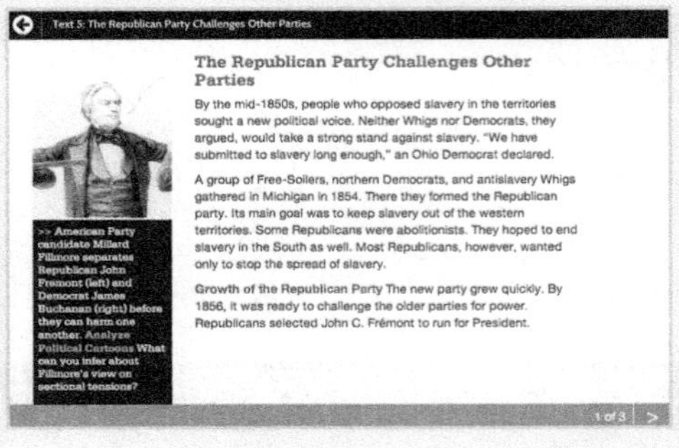

Objective 3: **Explain why the Republican Party was founded.**

Quick Instruction

Analyze Cartoons Display the political cartoon of Fillmore, Fremont, and Buchanan. Point out the political positions of each: Republican John Fremont, who opposed the spread of slavery; Democrat James Buchanan, who supported the spread of slavery; and American pParty candidate Millard Fillmore, who supported the Compromise of 1850. Ask students to explain how the political cartoon shows different points of view of political parties on the issue of slavery.

Further Instruction

Be sure that students understand that not all Republicans were abolitionists. Most Republicans opposed the spread of slavery to the western territories but not the existence of slavery in existing states. They were not trying to outlaw slavery throughout the nation but to contain it in the South. However, proslavery forces considered this stance a threat to their way of life.

Determine Point of View How did the points of view of the Republican and the Democratic Parties differ? How did the point of view of the American Party contrast with both? *(The Republicans opposed the expansion of slavery into western territories, while the Democrats supported the expansion of slavery into western territories. The American Party favored compromise, providing for the expansion of slavery in some territories in order to preserve the United States as a nation.)*

DIGITAL TEXT 6

Abraham Lincoln Leads the Republican Party

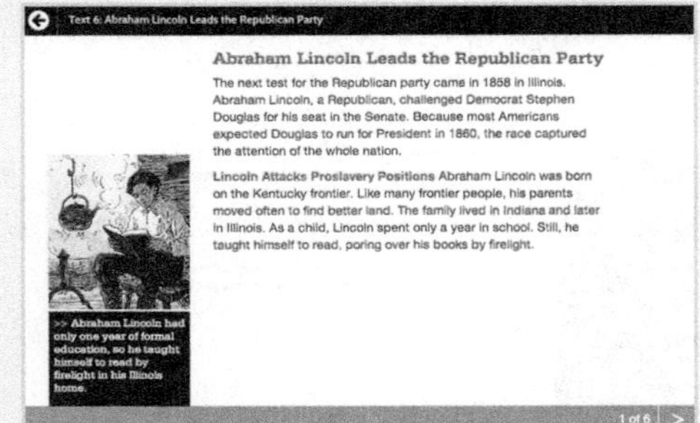

Objective 4: **Explain the rapid emergence of Abraham Lincoln as a Republican Party leader.**

Quick Instruction

Analyze Images Display the image of the Lincoln-Douglas debate and the excerpt from Lincoln's speech at Ottawa in 1858. Prompt students to interpret Lincoln's point of view in the speech. How did Lincoln feel about slavery? *(Lincoln thinks slavery is wrong because African Americans are entitled to the same natural rights as others.)* How did his point of view compare to the Republican point of view of the time? *(His views were perfectly in line with those of the Republican Party.)*

Determine Relevance What made the Lincoln-Douglas debates and their outcome such a major event in U.S. history? *(Because of its focus on the issue of slavery, the debates between Lincoln and Douglas garnered national attention. The debates not only helped elevate Lincoln's stature, preparing him to run for president, but also kept the argument over the expansion of slavery in the national spotlight. The debates themselves made slavery a central issue.)*

ELL Use the ELL activity described in the ELL chart.

DIGITAL TEXT 7

John Brown's Antislavery Campaign

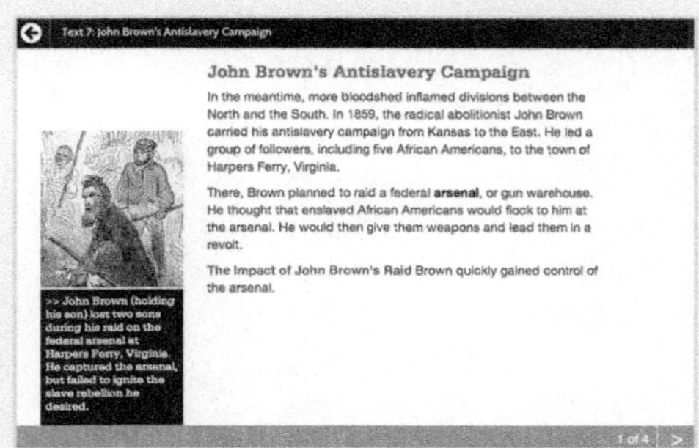

Text 7: John Brown's Antislavery Campaign
John Brown's Antislavery Campaign
In the meantime, more bloodshed inflamed divisions between the North and the South. In 1859, the radical abolitionist John Brown carried his antislavery campaign from Kansas to the East. He led a group of followers, including five African Americans, to the town of Harpers Ferry, Virginia.
There, Brown planned to raid a federal arsenal, or gun warehouse. He thought that enslaved African Americans would flock to him at the arsenal. He would then give them weapons and lead them in a revolt.
The Impact of John Brown's Raid Brown quickly gained control of the arsenal.
>> John Brown (holding his son) lost two sons during his raid on the federal arsenal at Harpers Ferry, Virginia. He captured the arsenal, but failed to ignite the slave rebellion he desired.
1 of 4

Further Instruction

Be sure that students understand Lincoln's personal views about slavery were tempered by his political motivations. Like other politicians of the time, Lincoln strove for compromise. He wanted to maintain the unity of the nation. Though he opposed slavery as a moral and social ill, he did not set out to abolish slavery where it existed throughout the nation. His primary objective as a political candidate was to prevent the spread of slavery.

Connect How did Lincoln's point of view in the debates foreshadow slavery and sectionalism as causes of the Civil War? *(Lincoln stated that he opposed slavery as a moral wrong and that enslaved persons were entitled to the same liberties as other Americans. Although he did not call for the abolition of slavery, these sentiments undermined the very existence of slavery. Such views and the reactions to those views resulted in sectional differences over slavery and highlighted the rift between North and South. Lincoln's point of view made clear that slave and free states could not continue to exist under one nation without eventually deciding the question of slavery for the entire nation.)*

Objective 5: **Describe the reaction to John Brown's raid on Harpers Ferry.**

Quick Instruction

Analyze Images Display the image of John Brown's raid on Harpers Ferry. Ask students to describe what they see. Recall that Brown had also been involved in the events of Bleeding Kansas. Prompt students to think about the causes and effects of the raid, including its lasting cultural legacy as developed in the song "The Battle Hymn of the Republic." Point out that the song "John Brown's Body" and the later poem "The Battle Hymn of the Republic" each celebrated antislavery themes.

Summarize Why was Brown's raid a major event in U.S. history leading up to the Civil War? *(Brown's raid at Harpers Ferry demonstrated that both sides in the sectional debates over slavery were willing to resort to violence.)*

Further Instruction

Display a map showing free and slave states in the United States around 1859. You may wish to use the map of the Missouri Compromise from the first reading in the lesson. Call on students to identify Virginia on the map and to determine whether Virginia was a free or a slave state. Then, point out the location of Harpers Ferry at the very northern tip of Virginia near the border with Maryland. Ask students why they think John Brown might have chosen this location for his raid. Discuss not only the location of the arsenal but also the area's location along the border between free and slave states.

Describe Describe the development of the "The Battle Hymn of the Republic." What makes its writing and message unique to American culture and history? *(The song began as a poem, written by Julia Ward Howe after the start of the Civil War. Howe wrote the poem after she had heard the song "John Brown's Body," which celebrated Brown as a martyr in the fight against slavery. The poem, set to the same tune as "John Brown's Body," became a popular song of the Civil War. It rallied northern troops by celebrating their cause as morally just.)*

Topic 8 Lesson 2

Growing Tensions

SYNTHESIZE

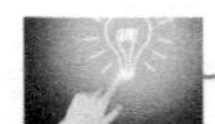

DIGITAL ACTIVITY

Tensions Divide the Nation

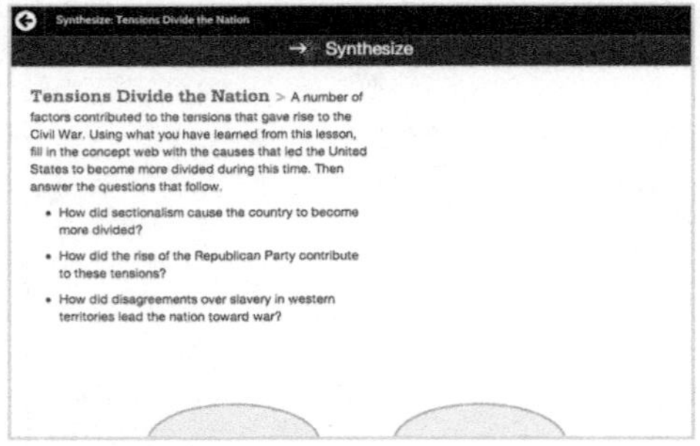

Remind students that this lesson examined the growing tensions in the nation over issues of sectionalism and slavery. Point out that violence broke out on several occasions: in Kansas, at Harpers Ferry, and even in the Senate. Have them work in pairs to complete the concept web and then review the webs as a class.

Organize students into groups to answer the following questions: How did sectionalism cause the country to become more divided? How did the rise of the Republican Party contribute to these tensions? How did disagreements over slavery in western territories lead the nation towards war? Call on each group to share one of their answers with the class.

Discuss Challenge student groups to Rank It by putting the following major events in U.S. history in order from least to most significant impact on leading the nation to war: Bleeding Kansas, Dred Scott case, Lincoln-Douglas debates, Brown's raid on Harpers Ferry. Call on groups to share and explain their rankings.

DEMONSTRATE

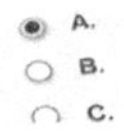

DIGITAL QUIZ

Lesson Quiz and Class Discussion Board

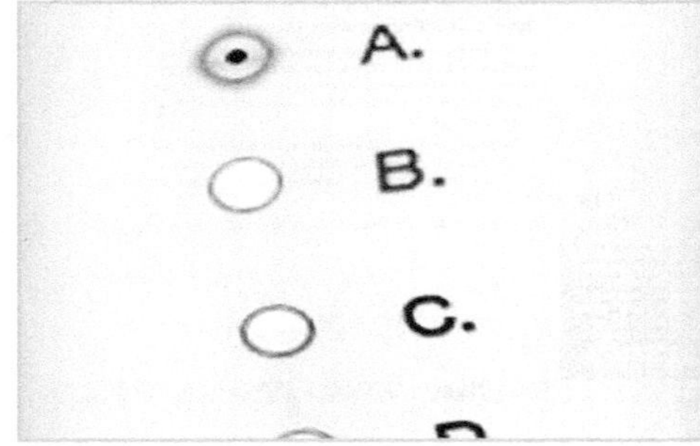

Assign the online Lesson Quiz for this lesson if you haven't already done so. Students will be offered automatic remediation or enrichment based on their score.

Pose these questions to the class on the Discussion Board:

In *Growing Tensions* , you read about the causes and effects of the following major events in U.S. history: the Kansas-Nebraska Act, the landmark Supreme Court case *Dred Scott* v. *Sandford,* the formation of the Republican Party, the Lincoln-Douglas debates, and John Brown's raid on Harpers Ferry.

Predict Consequences Which of these events most clearly elevated slavery as a national issue divisive enough to cause the Civil War? Explain your reasoning.

Synthesize Which of these events most clearly demonstrated the effects of sectionalism in the United States, and foreshadowed how sectional conflict would lead to a national civil war? Explain your reasoning.

Topic Inquiry

Have students continue their investigations for the Topic Inquiry.

Division and the Outbreak of War

Supporting English Language Learners

Use with Digital Text 1, **The Nation Moves Toward Civil War.**

Writing

Introduce the activity by showing where the following states are on a U.S. map: Alabama, Florida, Georgia, Kentucky, Louisiana, Mississippi, Missouri, South Carolina, and Texas. Prompt students to learn to spell these familiar words correctly.

Beginning Review the locations and spellings of Alabama, Florida, and Texas. Then display each word with one or more letters missing and have students complete and write the name. Repeat the activity, increasing the number of blanks in each word.

Intermediate Display two versions of the words *Florida, South Carolina, Kentucky, Georgia,* and *Louisiana*: one spelled correctly and one spelled incorrectly. Have pairs of students work to identify and write down the correct version of each word. Review the answers so students can check and correct their work.

Advanced Review the spelling of all nine states listed above. Then say the states aloud and have students write the words. Review the answers and repeat the activity so students can try to improve their accuracy.

Advanced High Provide students with a blank U.S. map with state boundaries. Say each of the nine states above, and have students try to correctly spell each name on the correct location of the map. Then display a map that students can use to check and correct their work.

Use with Digital Text 4, **Taking Sides.**

Speaking

Pronounce /shə/ and have students repeat after you. Explain that they will practice producing this sound in newly acquired vocabulary in a increasingly comprehensible manner.

Beginning Display *martial law*. Underline *-tia* in *martial*, and explain that it represents /shə/. Sound out each syllable and have students repeat after you. Repeat until students are pronouncing it correctly at regular speed.

Intermediate Display *martial, social,* and *official*. Underline *-tia* or *-cia* in each word, and explain that both letter combinations represent /shə/. Sound out each word, and have students repeat after you. Repeat until students are pronouncing the words correctly at regular speed.

Advanced Display the words *martial, official, population*, and *tension*. Underline *-tia, -cia, -tio,* and *-sio* in each word. Explain that all of these letter combinations represent /shə/. Sound out each word, and have students repeat after you. Repeat until students are pronouncing the words correctly at regular speed.

Advanced High Display the words *martial, especially, sectionalism* , and *tension*. Underline *-tia, -cia, -tio,* and *-sio* in each word. Explain that all of these letter combinations represent /shə/. Also display *decision* and demonstrate the different *-sio* sound in this word. Sound out each word and have students repeat after you.

D Differentiate Instruction

Use the Differentiated Instruction notes throughout the lesson plan to support the varied skill sets, levels of readiness, and interests in the mixed-ability classroom.

Challenge These notes include suggestions for expanding the activity for advanced students.

On-Level These notes include suggestions for modifying the activity to address different interests or learning styles.

Extra Support These notes include ideas for providing more scaffolding or reading spupport.

Special Needs These notes provide ideas for adapting instruction to support the needs of various special needs students.

NOTES

Division and the Outbreak of War

Objectives

Objective 1: Identify how the 1860 election reflected sectional differences.

Objective 2: Explain why southern states seceded from the Union following the election of 1860.

Objective 3: Identify how the Civil War began in 1861.

Objective 4: Describe the strengths and weaknesses of the North and South as the war began.

Objective 5: Identify the leaders of each side in the war.

LESSON 3 ORGANIZER	PACING: APPROX. 1 PERIOD, .5 BLOCKS		RESOURCES	
	OBJECTIVES	PACING	Online	Print
Connect				
DIGITAL START UP ACTIVITY **Divisions Lead to Civil War**		5 min.	●	
Investigate				
DIGITAL TEXT 1 **Abraham Lincoln and the Election of 1860**	Objective 1	10 min.	●	●
DIGITAL TEXT 2 **The Nation Moves Toward Civil War**	Objective 1	10 min.	●	●
DIGITAL TEXT 3 **War Breaks Out**	Objectives 2, 3	10 min.	●	●
DIGITAL TEXT 4 **Taking Sides**	Objectives 2, 3	10 min.	●	●
DIGITAL TEXT 5 **Strengths and Weaknesses of the North and South**	Objective 4	10 min.	●	●
INTERACTIVE CHART **Resources in the North and the South, 1860**	Objective 4	10 min.	●	
DIGITAL TEXT 6 **The Leadership Roles of Lincoln and Davis**	Objective 5	10 min.	●	●
INTERACTIVE CHART **Abraham Lincoln and Jefferson Davis**	Objective 5	10 min.	●	
Synthesize				
DIGITAL ACTIVITY **The North and South at War**		5 min.	●	
Demonstrate				
DIGITAL QUIZ **Lesson Quiz and Class Discussion Board**		10 min.	●	

Go online to access additional resources including:
Primary Sources • Biographies • Supreme Court cases • 21st Century Skill Tutorials • Maps • Graphic Organizers.

CONNECT

DIGITAL START UP ACTIVITY

Divisions Lead to Civil War

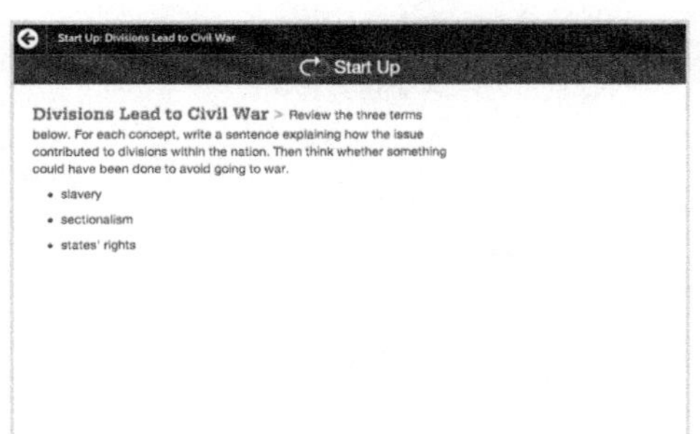

Project the Start Up Activity Ask students to complete the activity as they enter and get settled. Then have them share their ideas with another student.

Discuss How did states' rights contribute to divisions in the nation? *(Southern states and territories considered the question of slavery and other issues to be state concerns. They did not think that the federal government had the right to restrict slavery, and they resented northern attempts to impose such laws.)*

Tell students that this lesson will take a closer look at the causes and effects of the Civil War. They will examine constitutional issues arising over states' rights and the effect of economic differences among various regions of the United States.

Aa Vocabulary Development: Use the Interactive Reading Notepad to preview the Key Terms and Academic Vocabulary in this lesson with students.

FLIP IT!

Assign the Flipped Video for this lesson.

STUDENT EDITION PRINT PAGES: 450–460

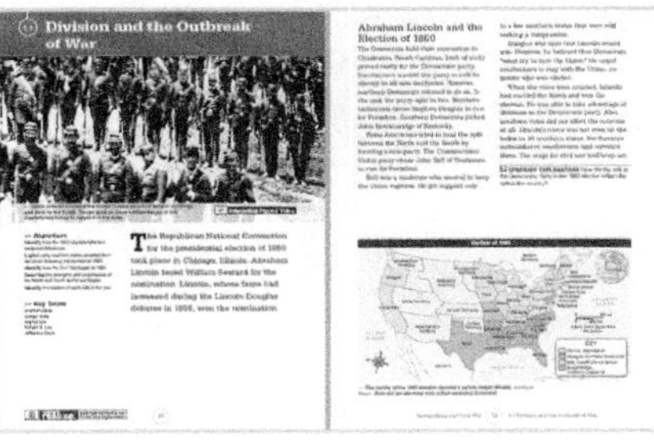

INVESTIGATE

DIGITAL TEXT 1

Abraham Lincoln and the Election of 1860

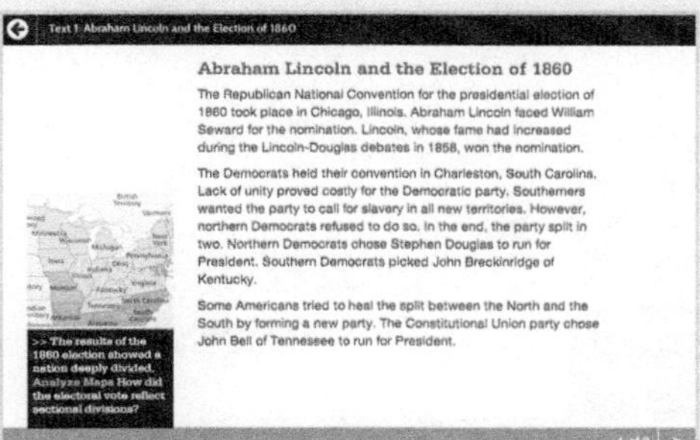

DIGITAL TEXT 2

The Nation Moves Toward Civil War

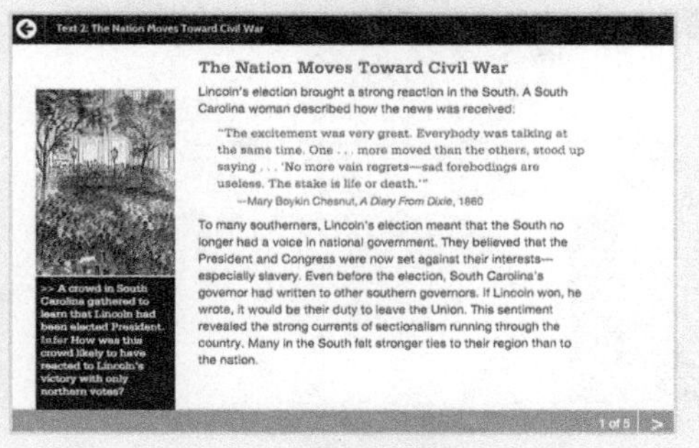

Objective 1: Identify how the 1860 election reflected sectional differences.

Quick Instruction

The outcome of the 1860 election solidified the divisions that already existed in the nation. Lincoln's election inflamed the South and gave southern secessionists a driving motivation to withdraw from the Union. However, the withdrawal itself posed a constitutional issue over states' rights: Were states entitled to leave the Union? The South said yes. Lincoln and the North said no. The disagreement over states' rights was a significant cause of the Civil War.

Connect How did the divisions in the election reflect the intensity of sectionalism as a cause of the Civil War? *(The election made clear that the nation was largely divided sectionally over the issues of slavery and states' rights, with northern support behind Lincoln and southern support against Lincoln and divided among other candidates.)*

D Differentiate: Extra Support Record the names of the presidential candidates and their political parties on the board: Abraham Lincoln (Republican), Stephen Douglas (Northern Democrat), John Breckenridge (Southern Democrat, and John Bell (Constitutional Union). List each candidate's stance on expansion of slavery. Draw a box around the three columns with Douglas, Breckenridge, and John Bell. Above the box, have them write "Split the South." Above Lincoln, have them write "Won the North." If Lincoln took most of the northern vote, and the three other candidates had to share the southern vote, which candidate would get the most votes? *(Lincoln would get the most votes.)*

ELL Use the ELL activity described in the ELL chart.

Further Instruction

Be sure that students understand that Lincoln had solid support in the North, which had a larger population than the South. Meanwhile, citizens in the South split their votes among three candidates. This meant that Lincoln could win the election without a single electoral vote from the South, which he did.

Contrast How does Lincoln's stance on slavery contrast with southern views about states' rights? *(Lincoln's firm position against the expansion of slavery indicates that he would not support states' rights to expand and regulate slavery without federal oversight.)*

Synthesize Explain the connection between sectionalism, slavery, and states' rights as causes of the Civil War. How did the southern response to the 1860 election results demonstrate this connection? *(The nation was divided along sectional lines over the issues of slavery and states' rights. The South rallied around opposition to Lincoln's election, putting its own sectional interests and loyalties over those of the Union.)*

Division and the Outbreak of War

DIGITAL TEXT 3

War Breaks Out

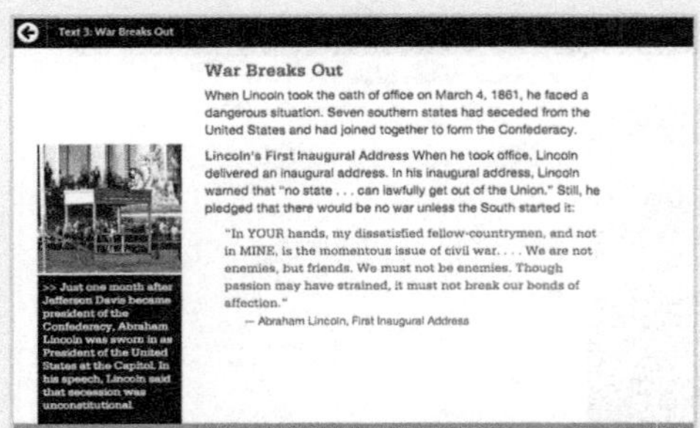

DIGITAL TEXT 4

Taking Sides

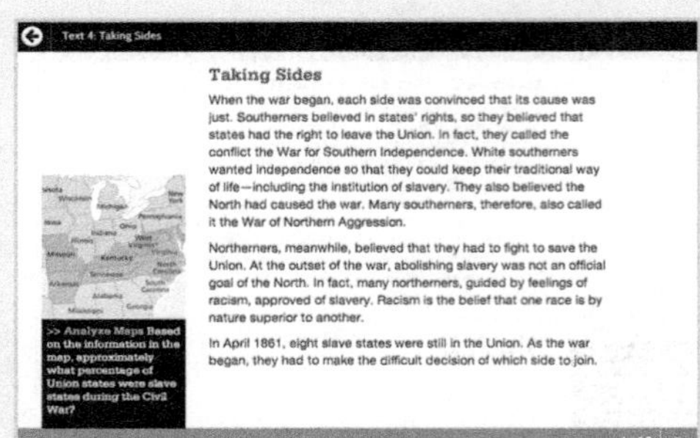

Objectives 2: **Explain why southern states seceded from the Union following the election of 1860; 3: Identify how the Civil War began in 1861.**

Quick Instruction

The Civil War was a major era in U.S. history. Lasting from 1861–1865, it was significant in that it was a lengthy, destructive time for the nation. The Civil War was caused by several interconnected issues that unfolded into armed conflict through a series of events. Southern states left the Union in response to Abraham Lincoln's election. War resulted from the firing on Fort Sumter after debate over the constitutional issue of states' rights to secede created conflicts over federal property.

Contrast How did Lincoln's ideas about the Union in his first inaugural address conflict with Davis's ideas about states' rights in his address? *(Lincoln asserted that the disagreeing parties in the nation must remain friends and stay united for the good of all. The Union was of paramount importance to him. In contrast, Davis asserted that the states must look firt to the preservation of their own rights and interests before considering the wider interests of the Union.)*

Contrast Lincoln's views on government with Davis's views on government from their first inaugural addresses. *(Lincoln stated that government required acquiescence, or the willingness to accept laws whether or not a person agreed with those laws. Davis emphasized that government exists only with the consent of the governed. Since southerners could no longer consent to a government they considered opposed to their interests, they had to break away and form a government to which they could consent. Davis also argued that, under the U.S. Constitution, states had the right to reclaim powers that they had given to the federal government by seceding. Lincoln took the opposite view, that states had no such right.)*

Explain What roles did Abraham Lincoln and Jefferson Davis play in the onset of war? *(Jefferson Davis was elected president of the Confederacy and helped rally people to support the newly formed nation and to find just cause in the southern states' secession. Lincoln, as President of the United States, spoke on behalf of the Union. His ideas regarding slavery as well as states' rights and secession helped bolster opposition to the Union in the South. He also made the decision to engage in war following the firing on Fort Sumter.)*

ELL Use the ELL activity described in the ELL chart.

Further Instruction

Read aloud, or call on a student to read aloud, the excerpt from Lincoln's inaugural address. Prompt students to find examples of where they see Lincoln discussing his ideas about liberty and equality in the speech. Pose questions such as: What does Lincoln mean when he says, "In YOUR hands, my dissatisfied countrymen, and not in MINE, is the momentous issue of civil war?" To whom is he speaking? Instruct students to discuss their ideas with a partner, and call on pairs to share their responses. Then ask students to explain Jefferson Davis's views on liberty and equality. *(For Davis, liberty and equality existed only between white men.)*

Hypothesize Why did the firing on Fort Sumter mark the start of the Civil War? Would the war have happened had the Confederacy not fired on Fort Sumter? Explain. *(The war started at Fort Sumter because the Confederacy fired on a federal fort and seized control of the fort from the Union. This was an overt act of aggression that Lincoln could not disregard without acknowledging secession as a legal path for southern states. I think the war still would have occurred had the firing on Fort Sumter not happened. Violence would have broken out elsewhere.)*

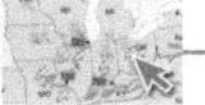

DIGITAL TEXT 5

Strengths and Weaknesses of the North and South

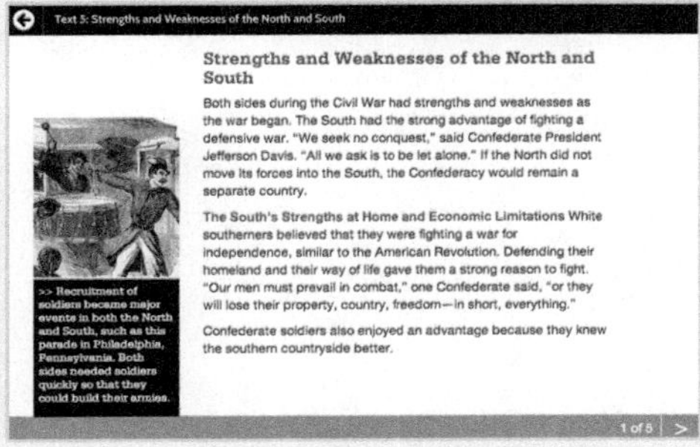

INTERACTIVE CHART

Resources in the North and the South, 1860

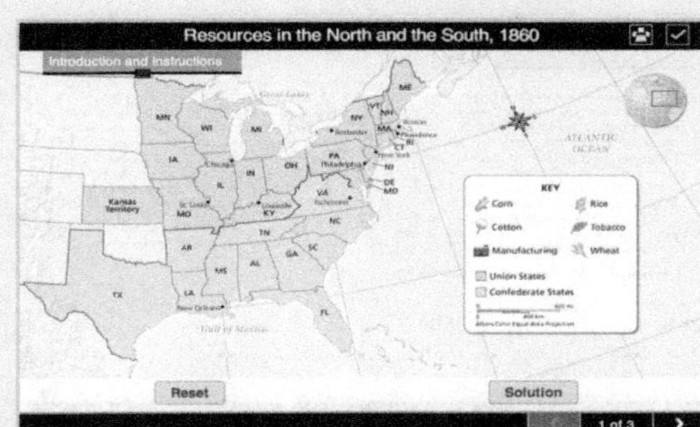

Objective 4: **Describe the strengths and weaknesses of the North and South as the war began.**

Quick Instruction

Interactive Chart: Strengths and Weaknesses in the North and South, 1860 Project the Interactive chart, and drag and drop resources to contrast the economic differences among different regions in the United States. At the time of the Civil War, the northern states were the industrial, financial, and manufacturing center of the United States. The southern states relied heavily on agriculture, and a large percentage of the southern population was enslaved. As the Civil War progressed, the economic differences among different regions in the United States began to have an effect.

Analyze Charts Which region, the North or the South, had the economic advantage going into the war? Why? *(I think the North had the advantage because it had industry, banking, manufacturing, shipping, and agricultural resources. The South had largely agricultural resources, much of which was not food crops, and depended on slave labor.)*

ACTIVE CLASSROOM

Have students review the Interactive chart and Take a Stand on whether the North orSouth was better prepared for war. Instruct students to organize into groups based on their responses and to discuss and defend their reasoning. Repeat the exercise when students have read the first section of the text. Repeat again when they have read the rest of the text. Discuss changes in the vote.

Further Instruction

Display the pie charts from the text, and compare the data with that of the interactive chart. Instruct students to draw concept webs in their notebooks, one for the Union and one for the Confederacy. As they study the charts and complete the text, have them record advantages and resources for each side of the Civil War.

Infer What was the objective of the Union in the Civil War? What was the objective of the Confederacy? Explain which of the two sides had the more difficult task, and why. *(The Union's objective was to bring the Confederacy back into the nation. The Confederacy's objective was to remain independent. I think that the Union had the more difficult challenge because it had to subdue the entire South and force it to comply with federal laws, whereas the Confederacy had to defend its lands and keep the Union out.)*

Synthesize How did the economic differences among different regions in the United States complicate the objectives of the Union and the Confederacy? Explain how economics shifted the advantage. *(The Confederacy had to remain independent, which meant it had to pay for the war and keep its economy going. This would be difficult because many southern states lacked industry, infrastructure, and other economic resources. This shifted the advantage to the Union, which had more money, industry, and infrastructure, such as transportation networks.)*

Hypothesize How would the differences in economics and objectives become manifest in the effects of the Civil War on each region of the country? *(The Union's diversified economy, larger population, and solid infrastructure would allow for the region to remain relatively intact. As an underdog, the Confederacy suffered great losses of land as a result of Union invasion as well as economic and supply difficulties. The Confederacy would be forced to diversify industry in order to survive.)*

Division and the Outbreak of War

DIGITAL TEXT 6

The Leadership Roles of Lincoln and Davis

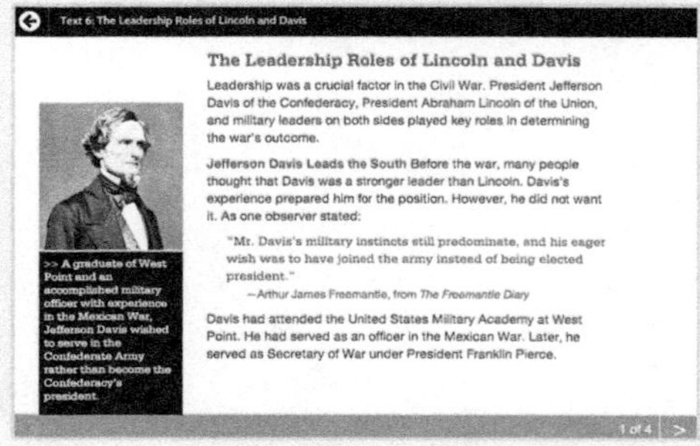

INTERACTIVE CHART

Abraham Lincoln and Jefferson Davis

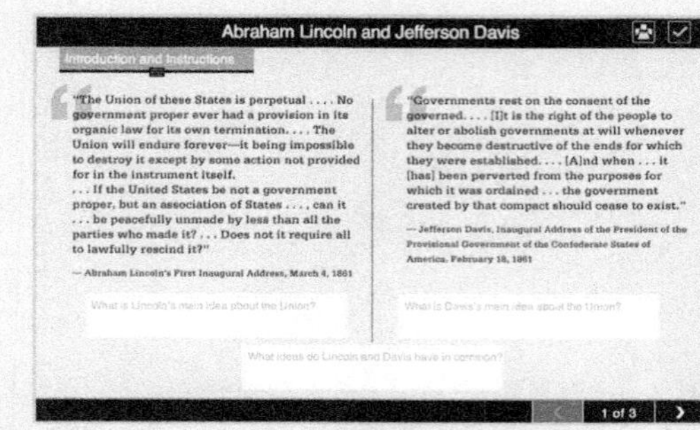

Objective 5: **Identify the leaders of each side in the war.**

Quick Instruction

Interactive Chart: Abraham Lincoln and Jefferson Davis Project the Interactive chart, and call on students to read aloud the excerpts from Lincoln's and Davis's inaugural speeches. Guide students through the Interactive graphic organizer. Point out ideas about liberty, equality, union, and government in Lincoln's Inaugural Address, and highlight key ideas in Davis's address.

Evaluate Sources How do ideas in Lincoln's Inaugural Address reflect his role as President of the United States? How do ideas in Davis's Inaugural Address reflect his role as president of the Confederacy? *(Lincoln's address places the most importance on the necessity of maintaining the Union. He make it clear that he views secession and its causes as contrary to the founding principles of liberty and equality in the United States. He also accuses secessionists of anarchy, undermining the very purpose of government. This reinforces his role as President of the United States, charged with preserving the nation and enforcing its federal laws. Davis emphasizes the importances of states' rights and interests, and makes the liberty of the southern states paramount over national interests. His concepts of liberty also apply only to southern citizens, not to all people. His words reinforce his position as president of the secessionist states, those who dissent from Lincoln's leadership.)*

ACTIVE CLASSROOM

Challenge students to hold a Conversation with Lincoln and Davis. Organize the students into two groups, one for Lincoln and one for Davis. Have them script questions and answers for each. Ask one student from each group to portray Lincoln or Davis and to begin by reading aloud an excerpt from his inaugural address. Then, tell the rest of the students in each group to pose their questions, and have Lincoln and Davis respond.

Further Instruction

Prompt students to consider the qualities of good leadership as they answer the questions below.

Contrast What challenges do you think Jefferson Davis faced in his role as president of the Confederacy that Lincoln did not? What challenges do you think Lincoln faced in his role as President of the United States that Davis did not? *(Davis faced the additional challenge of building a new nation with a new government and structuring that nation's economy while defending its lands and people. Lincoln faced the challenge of rallying the North to fight a war in order to bring the southern states back into the nation.)*

Make Generalizations How did the Civil War reflect the different ideas about liberty and equality expressed in the Inaugural Addresses given by Lincoln and Davis? *(Lincoln expressed the idea that liberty and equality applied to all people and that the actions of the South undermined these principles. Davis expressed the idea that the liberties of the states were paramount and that liberty and equality applied only to recognized citizens.)*

SYNTHESIZE

DIGITAL ACTIVITY

The North and South at War

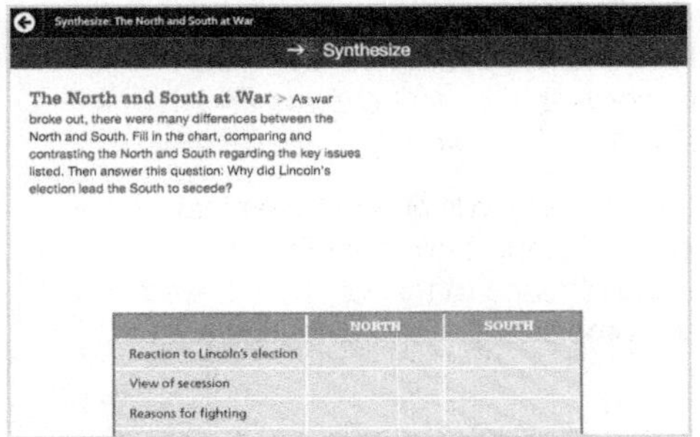

Have students work in pairs to complete the chart in which they compare the North and the South at the onset of the Civil War. Tell them to identify significant economic differences between the two regions. Then, challenge students to write a prediction about how those differences will affect the outcome of the conflict. Share students' responses in class or on a classroom blog.

Discuss Pose the question: Why did Lincoln's election lead the South to secede? Instruct students to write a response in which they use the following terms: *sectionalism, slavery,* and *states' rights.* Have them share and revise their responses in small groups. Ask each group to select the best response to share with the rest of the class. Finally, tell the student groups to answer the following question: Why did secession cause the Civil War to break out in 1861? Again, have them discuss and then share their responses.

DEMONSTRATE

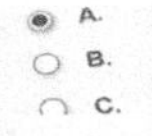

DIGITAL QUIZ

Lesson Quiz and Class Discussion Board

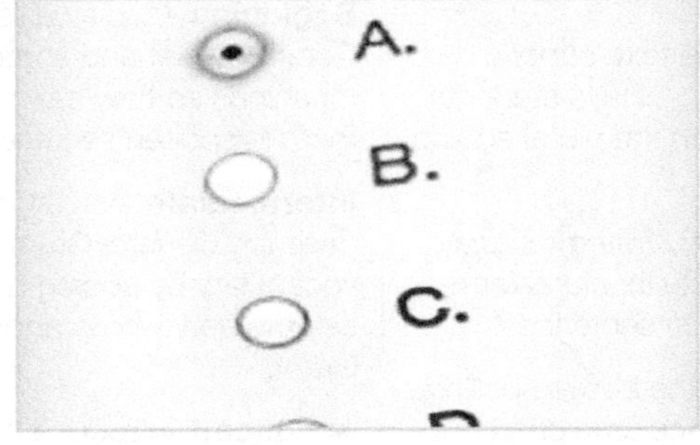

Assign the online Lesson Quiz for this lesson if you haven't already done so. Students will be offered automatic remediation or enrichment based on their score.

Pose these questions to the class on the Discussion Board:

Evaluate Arguments Why did the Confederacy fire on Fort Sumter in 1861? Why did the Union respond by going to war? Evaluate the arguments of both side of the conflict, and explain which you find to be the most just and why.

Analyze Context Lincoln and Davis made their decisions without knowing the full consequences of their actions. Summarize the motivation of both men in their roles as leaders on opposite sides of the conflict. Then, explain whether you think either would have acted differently had they known the costs of the Civil War to come. Consider whether each man could have chosen a different course of action and remained true to his principles.

Topic Inquiry

Have students continue their investigations for the Topic Inquiry.

Topic 8 Lesson 4

The Course of War

Supporting English Language Learners

Use with Digital Text 1, **North and South Adopt Different Strategies.**

Writing
Prompt students to employ English spelling rules. Explain the spelling rule that many words ending in *–y* drop that letter and add *–ies* to become plural.

Beginning Display the following pairs of words from the text: *supply, suppl _____; country, countr _____; factory, factor _____*. Have students write down each pair, completing each second word with the plural ending *–ies*.

Intermediate Display the following words from the text: *strategy, supply, country, factory.* Have students copy each word and write its plural form next to it. Then have them use three of the plural words in sentences.

Advanced Explain that some words are exceptions to the above spelling rule. Have pairs of students sort these words into a two-column chart depending on how their plurals are formed: *supply, boy, tray, country, donkey, essay, strategy, army.* Then have pairs use five of the plurals in written sentences.

Advanced High Explain that some words are exceptions to the above spelling rule. Have students sort these words into a two-column chart depending on how their plurals are formed: *supply, boy, tray, country, donkey, essay, strategy, army.* Ask: What rule can you make to explain which column a *–y* word fits into?

Use with Digital Text 4, **Union Forces Find Success in the West.**

Speaking
Display the image of General Grant to help students learn and use high-frequency English words necessary for identifying and describing people.

Beginning Display a list of high-frequency words, some describing General Grant and some not. Help students internalize the words' meanings so they can choose the words that describe Grant and use them in spoken sentences: General Grant is/looks _____.

Intermediate Ask students to brainstorm words and phrases that describe General Grant in the portrait. Expand their initial English vocabulary by adding new words and phrases to the list. Then have them use the new words and phrases in complete spoken sentences about Grant.

Advanced Introduce new high-frequency English words that might be used to describe General Grant. Have pairs of students use these words, as well as their own, to discuss and describe the portrait of Grant.

Advanced High Place students in pairs, and have them take turns drawing a portrait of General Grant based on their partner's description. Encourage speakers to use specific high-frequency words so their partners know what to draw. Then have partners compare the drawing and original portrait and identify additional details that could have been said.

D Differentiate Instruction

Use the Differentiated Instruction notes throughout the lesson plan to support the varied skill sets, levels of readiness, and interests in the mixed-ability classroom.

Challenge These notes include suggestions for expanding the activity for advanced students.

On-Level These notes include suggestions for modifying the activity to address different interests or learning styles.

Extra Support These notes include ideas for providing more scaffolding or reading spuport.

Special Needs These notes provide ideas for adapting instruction to support the needs of various special needs students.

NOTES

Objectives

Objective 1: Describe the strategies the North and South adopted to win the war.

Objective 2: Explain how early battles dispelled hopes for a quick end to the war.

Objective 3: Identify the victories of the Confederates and the Union in the early years of the war.

LESSON 4 ORGANIZER	PACING: APPROX. 1 PERIOD, .5 BLOCKS		RESOURCES	
	OBJECTIVES	PACING	Online	Print
Connect				
DIGITAL START UP ACTIVITY **A Short War?**		5 min.	●	
Investigate				
DIGITAL TEXT 1 **The Different Strategies of the North and South**	Objective 1	10 min.	●	●
INTERACTIVE MAP **The Union's Strategies to Win the Civil War**	Objective 1	10 min.	●	
DIGITAL TEXT 2 **The Beginnings of a Long War**	Objective 2	10 min.	●	●
DIGITAL TEXT 3 **Confederate Forces Win in the East**	Objective 3	10 min.	●	●
DIGITAL TEXT 4 **Union Forces Find Success in the West**	Objective 3	10 min.	●	●
INTERACTIVE TIMELINE **Early Battles of the Civil War**	Objective 3	10 min.	●	
Synthesize				
DIGITAL ACTIVITY **Visiting Civil War Locations**		5 min.	●	
Demonstrate				
DIGITAL QUIZ **Lesson Quiz and Class Discussion Board**		10 min.	●	

The Course of War

CONNECT

DIGITAL START UP ACTIVITY

A Short War?

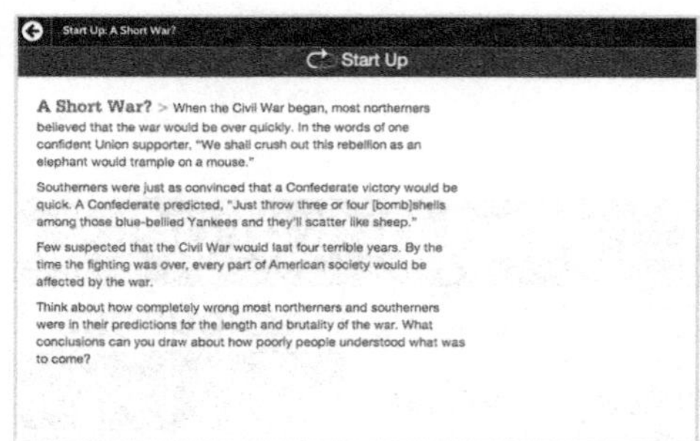

Project the Start Up Activity Tell students to consider the question as they enter and get settled. Ask: What conclusions can you make about how poorly people understood what was to come? *(Neither northerners nor southerners had any real idea of the war they were about to enter into because they had no experience with anything like it.)* Then have them share their conclusions with another student, either in class or through a chat or blog space.

Tell students in this lesson they will be learning about the course of the Civil War. They will learn about each side's strategies and how these strategies played out in dramatic battles in the East and the West.

Aa Vocabulary Development: Use the Interactive Reading Notepad to preview the Key Terms and Academic Vocabulary in the lesson with students.

FLIP IT!

Assign the Flipped Video for this lesson.

STUDENT EDITION PRINT PAGES: 461–467

INVESTIGATE

DIGITAL TEXT 1

The Different Strategies of the North and South

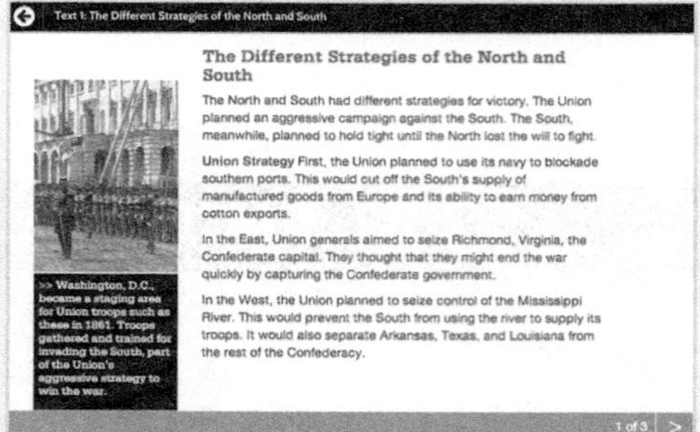

INTERACTIVE MAP

The Union's Strategies to Win the Civil War

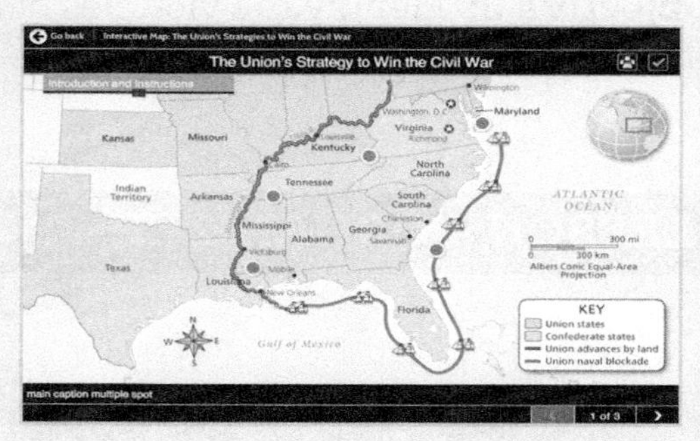

Objective 1: Describe the strategies the North and South adopted to win the war.

Quick Instruction

Interactive Cartoon: The Union's Strategies to Win the Civil War Project the Interactive cartoon and click on the red circles to reveal the Union's strategy to win the Civil War. Ask students what the plan was called. *(The Anaconda Plan)* Why was it called this? *(It was dubbed the Anaconda Plan by the media after the snake that squeezes its victims to death.)* Explain that the plan was developed by Winfield Scott, who was soon replaced by General George McClellan.

ACTIVE CLASSROOM

Have students Make Headlines for each of the strategies used by the North and the South to win the Civil War. These strategies include the North's encirclement and blockading of the South (the Anaconda Plan), its desire to capture Richmond (through the Peninsular Campaign), and the South's defensive strategy. Ask: If you were to write a headline for each of these that captured the most important aspect of it, what would that headline be? Emphasize to students that their headlines could depict a strategy as a whole or aspects of it. Allow them to use subheadings if they would like. Have students pass their headlines to a partner to review.

ELL Use the ELL activity described in the ELL chart.

Further Instruction

Make Generalizations Direct students to make one generalization about the Union strategy for victory in the Civil War and one generalization about the Confederate strategy. *(The Union planned to starve the Confederates into submission (Anaconda Plan) or capture the capital of Richmond and force a surrender. The Confederacy planned to hold out until popular opinion among northerners turned against the war.)*

DIGITAL TEXT 2

The Beginnings of a Long War

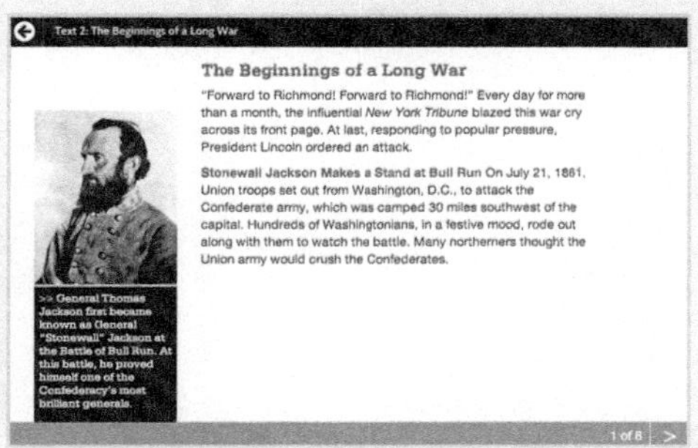

Objective 2: **Explain how early battles dispelled hopes for a quick end to the war.**

Quick Instruction

Ensure students understand that one early battle was the Battle of Bull Run, or what the Confederates called the Battle of Manassas. Invite a student to apply relative chronology by summarizing the next major event in the east, the Peninsular Campaign. *(In March 1862, McClellan led his troops up the Virginia Peninsula toward Richmond. Lee counterattacked and threatened Washington, denying McClellan additional troops and defeating his attempt to capture the Confederate capitol.)* Ask: Who won the battle between the Union ironclad *Monitor* and the Confederate ironclad *Virginia* at Hampton Roads? *(Neither; the battle was a draw.)* Conclude by asking students to explain the Battle of Antietam. What was Lee's goal? Who won the battle? *(In September 1862, General Lee took the offensive and marched his troops north into Maryland, hoping that a southern victory on northern soil would be a great blow to northern morale. General McClellan learned of the plan and attacked Lee's troops near Antietam Creek. Lee ordered his troops back into Virginia. Neither side was a clear winner. However, the North was able to claim victory, since Lee had ordered his forces to withdraw. This increased northern morale.)*

Analyze Images Display the image of Stonewall Jackson. What evidence do you see in the text and image to support the idea Jackson was a significant military leader? *(During the Battle of Manassas (Bull Run), Jackson rallied the Virginia troops on a hilltop. Another officer is said to have cried out "There is Jackson standing like a stone wall! Rally behind the Virginians!" Jackson became known as Stonewall Jackson after the battle concluded.)*

D Differentiate: Extra Support Split students into small groups. One side in a group will represent the Union and the other the Confederacy. Walk the groups through the events described in the lesson. Structure questions to the Union group as follows: the Confederacy did this. What did you do in response? Why? Ask parallel questions of the Confederate group.

Further Instruction

Infer Based on the conclusion of the Battle of Bull Run, what could you infer about the length of the war? *(The Confederates proved they could fight against Union soldiers, which implied the war would not be as quick as many had hoped.)*

Summarize What significant contributions did General George McClellan make to the war effort? *(McClellan transformed the inexperienced recruits of the Army of the Potomac into an army of trained soldiers prepared for battle. He hoped to capture the Confederate capital of Richmond, Virginia but failed. At the Battle of Antietam, he kept Lee from victory on northern soil.)*

Infer What can students infer about the significant political and military leaders mentioned in the lesson? Ask them to list character or leadership qualities of Lincoln, McClellan, Jackson, and Lee. *(Lincoln: thoughtful; McClellan: cautious; Jackson: brave; Lee: intelligent)*

DIGITAL TEXT 3

Confederate Forces Win in the East

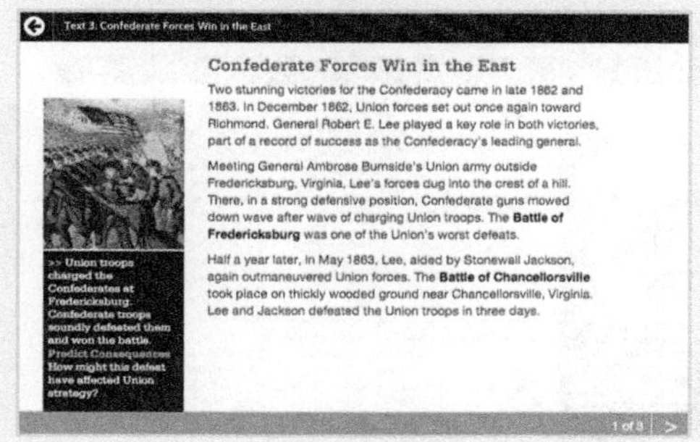

Objective 3: **Identify the victories of the Confederates and the Union in the early years of the war.**

Quick Instruction

Interactive Timeline: Early Battles of the Civil War Display the Interactive timeline. To help students interpret information from the timeline, point out that it covers battles in the early part of the war from April 1861 to May 1863. Remind students that the Union hoped to win by surrounding and splitting the Confederacy and that the Confederacy planned to fight a defensive war while outmaneuvering and defeating Union forces when they could. Discuss each battle with students in order relative to each other, as they apply absolute and relative chronology to sequence these significant events.

Draw Conclusions Review the events at the Battle of Fredericksburg and the Battle of Chancellorsville. Ask: How did the early events of the Civil War show the significance of General Lee's role in the war? *(Despite the confidence of many in the North that they could win the war quickly, Lee's skill as a military leader allowed the Confederate army to win many significant victories and inflict serious damage to the Union army.)*

Summarize Why was the Battle of Shiloh a significant victory for the Union? *(Union forces were able to gain control of the Tennessee river, cutting off one of the Confederate supply lines.)*

Topic 8 Lesson 4

The Course of War

DIGITAL TEXT 4

Union Forces Find Success in the West

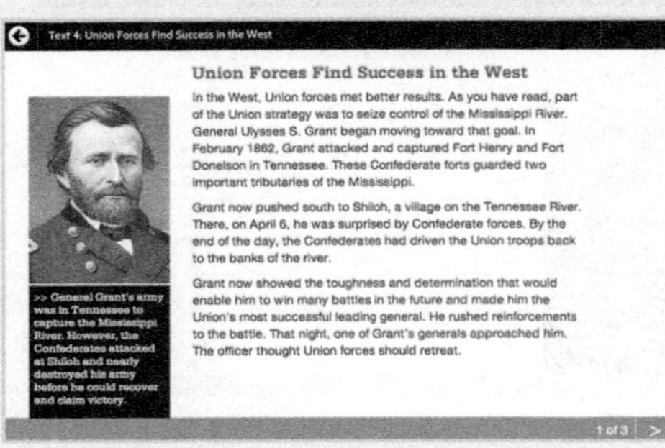

Text 4: Union Forces Find Success in the West
Union Forces Find Success in the West
In the West, Union forces met better results. As you have read, part of the Union strategy was to seize control of the Mississippi River. General Ulysses S. Grant began moving toward that goal. In February 1862, Grant attacked and captured Fort Henry and Fort Donelson in Tennessee. These Confederate forts guarded two important tributaries of the Mississippi.
Grant now pushed south to Shiloh, a village on the Tennessee River. There, on April 6, he was surprised by Confederate forces. By the end of the day, the Confederates had driven the Union troops back to the banks of the river.
Grant now showed the toughness and determination that would enable him to win many battles in the future and made him the Union's most successful leading general. He rushed reinforcements to the battle. That night, one of Grant's generals approached him. The officer thought Union forces should retreat.
>> General Grant's army was in Tennessee to capture the Mississippi River. However, the Confederates attacked at Shiloh and nearly destroyed his army before he could recover and claim victory.
1 of 3

INTERACTIVE TIMELINE

Early Battles of the Civil War

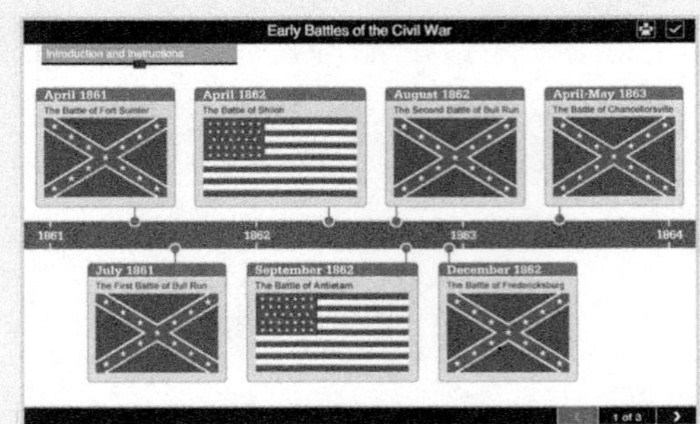

ACTIVE CLASSROOM

Have students apply absolute and relative chronology through the sequencing of significant events by making "Human Order" timelines. Give students pieces of paper and have them write the names of important early battles of the Civil War on each one, along with the date of the battle and a note of who won. Students should then get out of their seats at your signal and arrange themselves in correct chronological order. Consider having multiple groups with identical pieces of paper compete against each other.

ELL Use the ELL activity described in the ELL chart.

Further Instruction

Categorize Challenge students to identify each of the following as a Confederate victory in the East or a Union success in the West: Battle of Fredericksburg *(Confederate victory in the East)*; Battle of Chancellorsville *(Confederate victory in the East)*; Fort Henry and Fort Donelson *(Union success in the West)*; Battle of Shiloh *(Union success in the West)*; New Orleans *(Union success in the West)*; Memphis *(Union success in the West)*.

SYNTHESIZE

DIGITAL ACTIVITY

Visiting Civil War Locations

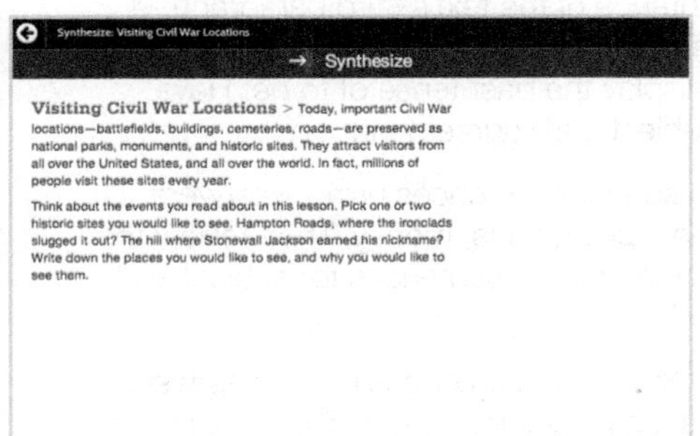

Discuss Discuss as a class the Civil War sites students are interested in visiting. As time allows, go the federal website for each historic site and discuss what the main attractions of the site are.

Make Predictions Now that students have learned about the early course of the Civil War, how might they predict the rest of the war will proceed? *(More devastating battles will occur for both sides before the war reaches its conclusion.)*

DEMONSTRATE

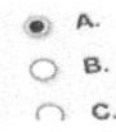

DIGITAL QUIZ

Lesson Quiz and Discussion Board

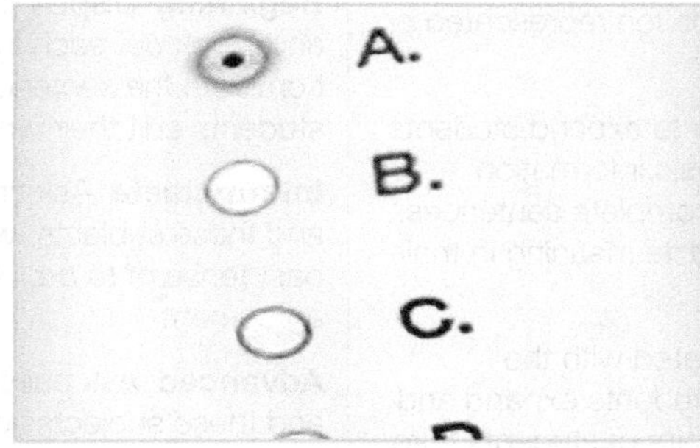

Assign the online Lesson Quiz for this lesson if you haven't already done so. Students will be offered automatic remediation or enrichment based on their score.

Pose these questions to the class on the Discussion Board:

In the *Course of War*, you learned about the early years of the Civil War. The North hoped to win the war quickly by surrounding the Confederacy or capturing Richmond, while the South planned a defensive war that they hoped would outlast the North's will to fight. The first Battle of Bull Run and the failed Peninsular Campaign disproved the notion the war would be short, however. Battles proved horrific.The Battle of Antietam made September 17, 1862 the bloodiest day in American history. Confederate victories in the East were matched by Union successes in the West. 1861 and 1862 proved to be bloody years with no end to the carnage in sight.

Compare and Contrast Do you see the North as having demonstrated any particular advantages at this point? The South?

Make Predictions How might these advantages play out as the war progresses?

Topic Inquiry

Have students continue their investigations for the Topic Inquiry.

Emancipation and Life in Wartime

Supporting English Language Learners

Use with Digital Text 2, **African Americans Fight Heroically for the Union.**

Speaking

Display the picture of 54th Regiment soldiers, and read the corresponding caption. Prompt students to expand and internalize initial English vocabulary by retelling simple stories and basic information represented or supported by pictures.

Beginning Describe what is happening in the picture to expand students' initial English vocabulary. Then have students retell basic information represented by the picture using words, phrases, or complete sentences. Encourage students to include the word *regiment* and its meaning in their retelling.

Intermediate Brainstorm words and phrases associated with the picture, such as *withdraw* and *Fort Wagner*, to help students expand and internalize their initial English vocabulary. Then have pairs of students take turns saying sentences that give basic information about the picture.

Advanced Place students in groups of three. Have each student expand and internalize initial English vocabulary by retelling the beginning, middle, or end of the story of the 54th Regiment. Explain that at least one part of the story should be represented or supported by the picture. Encourage students to use and define the words *recruit*, *withdraw*, and *Medal of Honor* in their retelling.

Advanced High Place students in pairs and have partners take turns adding sentences to an oral retelling of the story of the 54th Regiment. Explain that at least one part of the story should be represented or supported by the picture and that they should aim to expand and internalize their vocabulary by using as many specific details as possible. Encourage students to use and define the words *heroism* and *courage* in their retelling.

Use with Digital Text 6, **War Devastates the Southern Economy.**

Writing

Review subjects and verbs in a sentence in order to prepare students to edit writing for standard grammar and usage.

Beginning Display the last sentence of the text's third paragraph, and block out each instance of *was* or *were*. Have students copy and complete the sentence. Then display the past tense of *to be*. Have students edit their writing for subject-verb agreement.

Intermediate Ask students to suggest sentences using *was/were* and these subjects: war, supplies, plantations, money. Then review the past tense of *to be*. Have students edit the sentences for subject-verb agreement.

Advanced Ask pairs of students to write sentences using *was/were* and these subjects: loss, plantations, supplies, Davis. Then review the past tense of *to be*. Have students edit the sentences for subject-verb agreement. Ask: Are all nouns ending in –*s* plural?

Advanced High Ask students to write sentences using *was/were* and these subjects: Confederacy, plantations, money, the South, Davis. Then review the past tense of *to be*. Have students edit the sentences for subject-verb agreement. Ask: Britain is one thing representing a lot of people, land, and so on. So does it agree with *was* or *were*?

D Differentiate Instruction

Use the Differentiated Instruction notes throughout the lesson plan to support the varied skill sets, levels of readiness, and interests in the mixed-ability classroom.

Challenge These notes include suggestions for expanding the activity for advanced students.

On-Level These notes include suggestions for modifying the activity to address different interests or learning styles.

Extra Support These notes include ideas for providing more scaffolding or reading spupport.

Special Needs These notes provide ideas for adapting instruction to support the needs of various special needs students.

NOTES

PEARSON realize www.PearsonRealize.com

Go online to access additional resources including: Primary Sources • Biographies • Supreme Court cases • 21st Century Skill Tutorials • Maps • Graphic Organizers.

Objectives

Objective 1: Describe the purpose of the Emancipation Proclamation and its effects.

Objective 2: Explain African Americans' contributions to the war effort in the Union army and behind Confederate lines.

Objective 3: Describe conditions for Civil War soldiers.

Objective 4: Explain problems on the home front, including economic issues.

Objective 5: Identify the role women played in the war.

LESSON 5 ORGANIZER — **PACING: APPROX. 1 PERIOD, .5 BLOCKS**

	OBJECTIVES	PACING	RESOURCES Online	RESOURCES Print
Connect				
DIGITAL START UP ACTIVITY **Freedom**		5 min.	●	
Investigate				
DIGITAL TEXT 1 **The Emancipation Proclamation**	Objective 1	10 min.	●	●
DIGITAL TEXT 2 **African Americans Fight Heroically for the Union**	Objective 2	10 min.	●	●
DIGITAL TEXT 3 **Soldiers Face the Horrors of War**	Objective 3	10 min.	●	●
INTERACTIVE GALLERY **The Hardships of Soldiers**	Objective 3	10 min.	●	
INTERACTIVE GALLERY **Photography and the Civil War**	Objective 3	10 min.	●	
DIGITAL TEXT 4 **Political Challenges in the North and South**	Objective 4	10 min.	●	●
DIGITAL TEXT 5 **War Challenges and Fuels the Northern Economy**	Objective 4	10 min.	●	●
DIGITAL TEXT 6 **War Devastates the Southern Economy**	Objective 4	10 min.	●	●
DIGITAL TEXT 7 **Social Contributions of Women to the War Effort**	Objective 5	10 min.	●	●
Synthesize				
DIGITAL ACTIVITY **What Do You Think of the War?**		5 min.	●	
Demonstrate				
DIGITAL QUIZ **Lesson Quiz and Discussion Board**		10 min.	●	

Emancipation and Life in Wartime

CONNECT

DIGITAL START UP ACTIVITY

Freedom

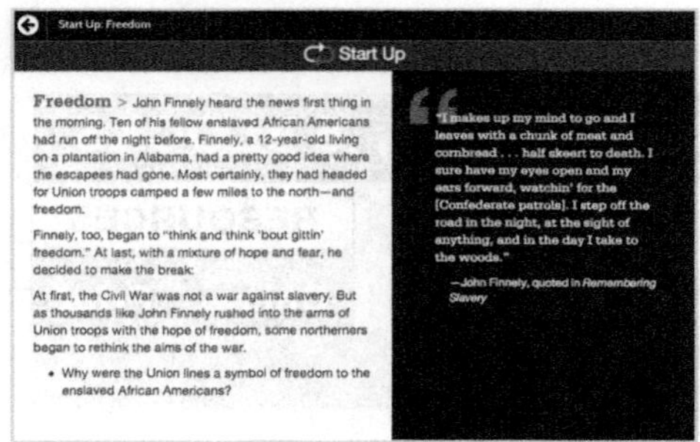

Project the Start Up Activity Tell students to read the story of John Finnely and consider the question as they enter and get settled. Ask: Why were the Union lines a symbol of freedom to the enslaved African Americans? (Slavery was illegal in most of the Union.) Extend the activity by asking students to describe the feelings that Finnely and others in his situation must have felt.

Tell students in this lesson they will be learning about the role of African Americans during the Civil War and the draft in the North and the South and how it was received. They will then turn from the political to the economic and analyze how the war affected the northern and southern economies.

Aa Vocabulary Development: Use the Interactive Reading Notepad to preview the Key Terms and Academic Vocabulary in this lesson with students.

FLIP IT!

Assign the Flipped Video for this lesson.

STUDENT EDITION PRINT PAGES: 468–477

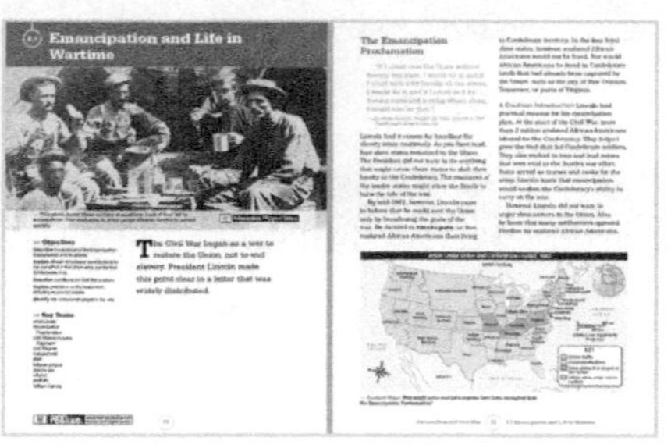

INVESTIGATE

DIGITAL TEXT 1

The Emancipation Proclamation

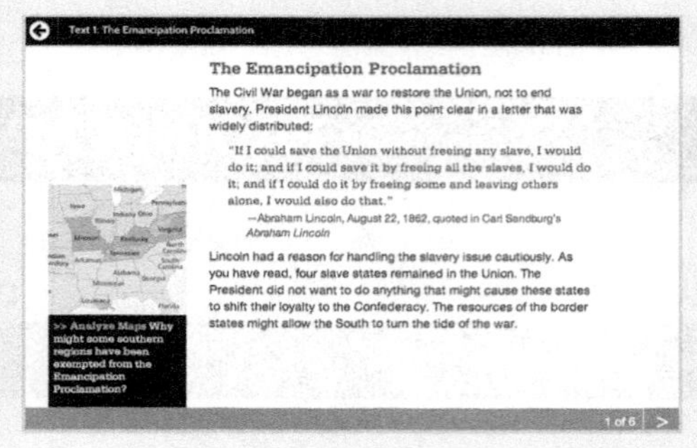

Text 1: The Emancipation Proclamation
The Emancipation Proclamation
The Civil War began as a war to restore the Union, not to end slavery. President Lincoln made this point clear in a letter that was widely distributed:
"If I could save the Union without freeing any slave, I would do it; and if I could save it by freeing all the slaves, I would do it; and if I could do it by freeing some and leaving others alone, I would also do that."
—Abraham Lincoln, August 22, 1862, quoted in Carl Sandburg's Abraham Lincoln
Lincoln had a reason for handling the slavery issue cautiously. As you have read, four slave states remained in the Union. The President did not want to do anything that might cause these states to shift their loyalty to the Confederacy. The resources of the border states might allow the South to turn the tide of the war.
>> Analyze Maps Why might some southern regions have been exempted from the Emancipation Proclamation?
1 of 6

Objective 1: Describe the purpose of the Emancipation Proclamation and its effects.

Quick Instruction

Analyze Images Project the image of the Emancipation Proclamation. Explain that the announcement of the Emancipation Proclamation was one of the significant events of the Civil War. Ask: What was the Emancipation Proclamation? *(Lincoln's declaration freeing slaves in the Confederacy)* When was it issued? *(January 1, 1863)* Discuss with students the political considerations Lincoln took into account before issuing the proclamation. He prioritized saving the Union over abolition, so the proclamation only freed slaves in the Confederacy and not in Union slave states or in any Union-captured territory.

Further Instruction

Compare and Contrast How was the Emancipation Proclamation received in the North? In the South? In Europe? *(In the North it received a mixed reception. Abolitionists and free African Americans received news of it with joy. Many northerners, though, were opposed to the abolition of slavery and were unhappy about the news. In the South it was generally viewed as a fiendish destruction of property. European workers were generally in favor of it.)*

Interpret What was the significance of the announcement of the Emancipation Proclamation? *(The Emancipation Proclamation changed the dynamic of the war and broadened its purpose. It also made it less likely that Britain or any other European country would come to the aid of the South.)*

DIGITAL TEXT 2

African Americans Fight Heroically for the Union

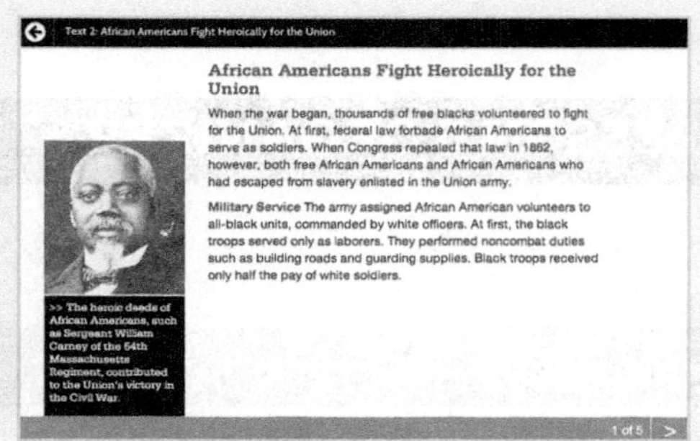

Text 2: African Americans Fight Heroically for the Union
African Americans Fight Heroically for the Union
When the war began, thousands of free blacks volunteered to fight for the Union. At first, federal law forbade African Americans to serve as soldiers. When Congress repealed that law in 1862, however, both free African Americans and African Americans who had escaped from slavery enlisted in the Union army.
Military Service The army assigned African American volunteers to all-black units, commanded by white officers. At first, the black troops served only as laborers. They performed noncombat duties such as building roads and guarding supplies. Black troops received only half the pay of white soldiers.
>> The heroic deeds of African Americans, such as Sergeant William Carney of the 54th Massachusetts Regiment, contributed to the Union's victory in the Civil War.
1 of 5

Objective 2: Explain African Americans' contributions to the war effort in the Union army and behind Confederate lines.

Quick Instruction

Generate Explanations Project the image of William Carney. Ask students to explain the role played by William Carney and the 54th Massachusetts Regiment in the Civil War. *(The courage of the 54th Massachusetts and other regiments helped to win respect for African American soldiers. Sergeant William Carney of the 54th Massachusetts was one of the first African American soldier to win the Congressional Medal of Honor in the Civil War.)* Tell them that Carney was but one of about 200,000 African Americans that had fought for the Union during the Civil War.

Sequence Events The following events are in correct chronological order. Provide them in a random order for students and challenge them to analyze the information by sequencing them correctly.

- Federal law forbids African Americans from serving as soldiers.
- Congress repeals law forbidding African Americans from serving as soldiers.
- African American troops serve only in noncombat roles.
- African American troops serve in combat and fight in major battles.
- All Union soldiers receive equal pay.

Identify Central Issues Conclude by asking students how African Americans' contributed to the Union war effort from behind Confederate line. *(They slowed down their work or refused to work at all, or escaped.)*

D Differentiate: Challenge An interested student can look up the citation for William Carney's Medal of Honor to learn what exactly he did to earn it. The student can then share what he or she learns with other students.

ELL Use the ELL activity described in the ELL chart.

Further Instruction

Summarize Ask students to describe the 54th Massachusetts Regiment. *(The 54th Massachusetts Regiment was an African American unit in the Union army. It led an attack on Fort Wagner near Charleston, South Carolina. Almost half the regiment was killed.)*

Identify Central Issues Have students complete the Biography: William Carney activity at the close of this text.

DIGITAL TEXT 3

Soldiers Face the Horrors of War

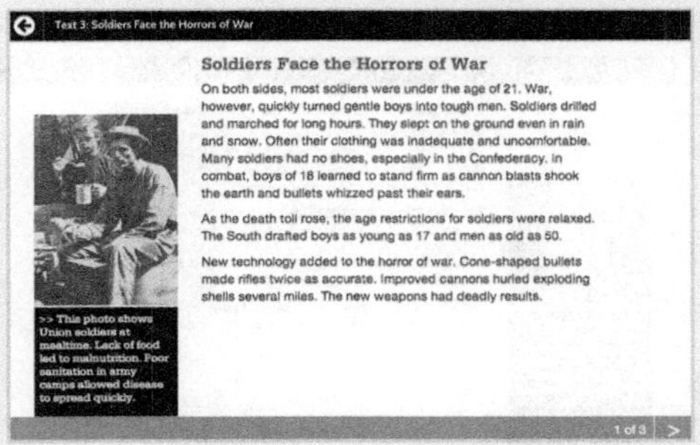

INTERACTIVE GALLERY

The Hardships of Soldiers

Objective 3: Describe conditions for Civil War soldiers.

Quick Instruction

Interactive Gallery: The Hardships of Soldiers Project the interactive gallery. Select the red circles to reveal details about life as a soldier. Before you select each one, ask students what they think it will reveal. Then have them compare what they expected with what they learned. Ask them how might this parallel the experience of the soldiers themselves. *(Many soldiers from the North and South had romantic ideas of what life as a soldier would be like, but the reality was much more harsh.)*

Interactive Gallery: Photography and the Civil War Project the interactive gallery. Click on each photograph to reveal the caption. Emphasize to students that Matthew Brady was a photographer, but that many photographs attributed to him were actually taken by his employees. Work your way through the photographs and invite student comment. Challenge students to identify what aspects of the Civil War the images do not reveal.

ACTIVE CLASSROOM

Have students learn more about the hardships of war by letting them Act It Out. Challenge students to recreate the scene in "The Hardships of Soldiers," or a similar scene. Each student should prepare a brief speech about one aspect of life for soldiers during the Civil War.

ACTIVE CLASSROOM

Have students consider the importance of photography as a way to record the experience of war by having them make Wallpaper. Direct each student to decorate a piece of printer paper with images and/or words that capture what they feel is the most important photograph in the gallery. Post their work in the classroom. Invite individual students to give a verbal tour of the work to classroom visitors.

Further Instruction

Analyze Data Share this fact with students: One out of every seven Union soldiers and one out of every nine Confederate soldiers deserted. Direct students to express these figures as percentages. *(1/7 = 14.3 percent Union desertion rate; 1/9 = 11.1 percent Confederate desertion rate.)*

Infer What can students infer from these rates? *(Possible inferences include that life was difficult for both Union and Confederate soldiers, leading to high desertion rates, and that outside factors—such as proximity to their homes or commitment to the war effort—might be reflected in the desertion rates.)*

Emancipation and Life in Wartime

INTERACTIVE GALLERY

Photography and the Civil War

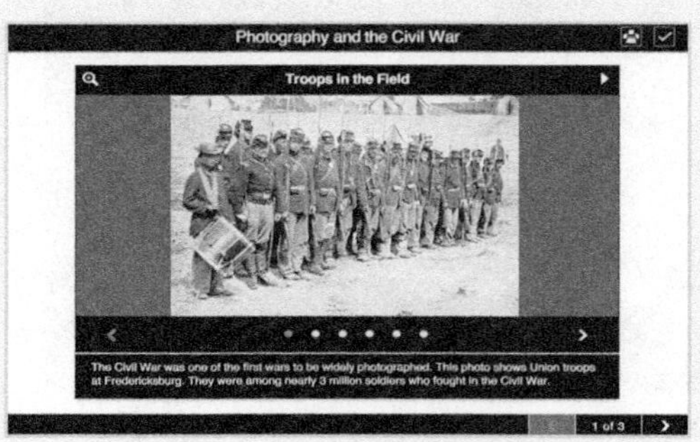

DIGITAL TEXT 4

Political Challenges in the North and South

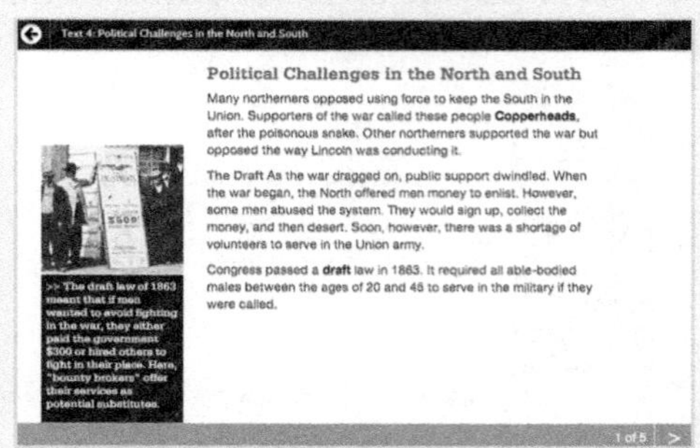

DIGITAL TEXT 5

War Challenges and Fuels the Northern Economy

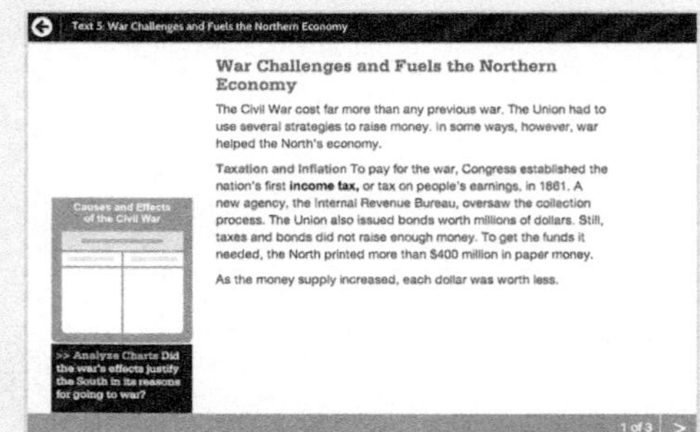

Objective 4: Explain problems on the home front, including economic issues.

Quick Instruction

Analyze Images Project the image of draft riots. Provide context for students by explaining that it is a depiction of a draft riot that took place in New York City during July 1863. Ensure they know that the draft is a law that requires people of a certain age to enlist in the military.Ask students why it led to rioting. *(Opposition to the draft in the North was rooted in opposition to the war itself, its conduct, and the fact that men of means could pay a fee and avoid the draft. Moreover, many white northerners did not want to fight against slavery, the end of which would increase competition for work and lower wages.)*

Generate Explanations Challenge students to use their knowledge of the draft riots to explain the relationship between urbanization and conflicts resulting from differences in political beliefs. *(Urbanization created areas where many people were gathered together. People of different ethnic, racial, and economic backgrounds were mixed. These different groups had different economic interests and political beliefs. For example, recent immigrants were much more likely to oppose the war, abolition, and the draft than others. These differences led to conflict, with rioters attacking free blacks and rich New Yorkers who had paid to avoid serving in the army.)*

Summarize Describe the political and economic effects of the Civil War in the South. *(The South also instituted a draft, excluding wealthy slave owners, and thereby angering some. The Civil War devastated the economy of the South, a result of taxes, inflation from overprinting money, and the dramatic reduction in income from cotton exports caused by the Union blockade.)*

ELL Use the ELL activity described in the ELL chart.

Further Instruction

Distinguish Explain that the conflict over the draft was a political effect of the Civil War in the North. What were some economic effects? *(The creation of an income tax, the printing of paper money, and the inflation that resulted from the increase in the money supply all resulted from the war. However, the wartime demand for farm equipment and clothing, shoes, guns, and other goods helped many northern industries.)*

www.PearsonRealize.com
Access your Digital Lesson

DIGITAL TEXT 6

War Devastates the Southern Economy

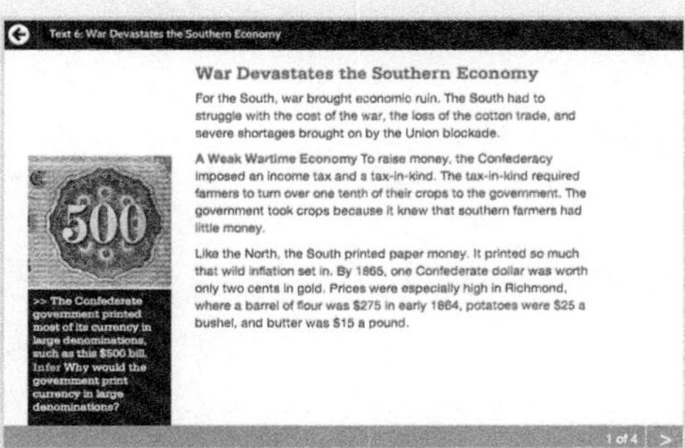

Text 6: War Devastates the Southern Economy

War Devastates the Southern Economy

For the South, war brought economic ruin. The South had to struggle with the cost of the war, the loss of the cotton trade, and severe shortages brought on by the Union blockade.

A Weak Wartime Economy To raise money, the Confederacy imposed an income tax and a tax-in-kind. The tax-in-kind required farmers to turn over one tenth of their crops to the government. The government took crops because it knew that southern farmers had little money.

Like the North, the South printed paper money. It printed so much that wild inflation set in. By 1865, one Confederate dollar was worth only two cents in gold. Prices were especially high in Richmond, where a barrel of flour was $275 in early 1864, potatoes were $25 a bushel, and butter was $15 a pound.

>> The Confederate government printed most of its currency in large denominations, such as this $500 bill. Infer Why would the government print currency in large denominations?

1 of 4 >

Interpret Ask students how the New York City draft riots might be considered an attempt to resolve conflicts between people from various racial groups. *(Northern whites wanted to avoid competing with freed blacks in the labor marketplace. The riots were an attempt to oppose the war and the freeing of enslaved African Americans.)*

DIGITAL TEXT 7

Social Contributions of Women to the War Effort

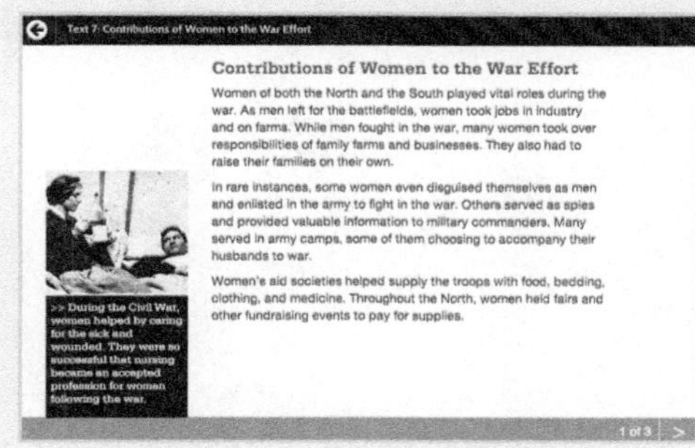

Text 7: Contributions of Women to the War Effort

Contributions of Women to the War Effort

Women of both the North and the South played vital roles during the war. As men left for the battlefields, women took jobs in industry and on farms. While men fought in the war, many women took over responsibilities of family farms and businesses. They also had to raise their families on their own.

In rare instances, some women even disguised themselves as men and enlisted in the army to fight in the war. Others served as spies and provided valuable information to military commanders. Many served in army camps, some of them choosing to accompany their husbands to war.

Women's aid societies helped supply the troops with food, bedding, clothing, and medicine. Throughout the North, women held fairs and other fundraising events to pay for supplies.

>> During the Civil War, women helped by caring for the sick and wounded. They were so successful that nursing became an accepted profession for women following the war.

1 of 3 >

Objective 5: **Identify the role women played in the war.**

Quick Instruction

Summarize Remind students that Matthew Brady took very few photographs of women even though they played a significant role in the Civil War. Challenge students to identify at least three important social contributions of women during the Civil War. *(Taking jobs in industry and on farms; forming aid societies that helped supply the troops with food, bedding, clothing, and medicine; working as nurses; providing comfort to fathers, brothers, sons who served as soldiers)*

Further Instruction

Generate Explanations Tell students that, before the Civil War, nursing was not an acceptable occupation for women. After the war it was. Challenge them to explain why this was so. *(Women were needed to serve as nurses during the war. They proved they were up to the task, and so it became an acceptable occupation.)*

Emancipation and Life in Wartime

SYNTHESIZE

DIGITAL ACTIVITY

What Do You Think of the War?

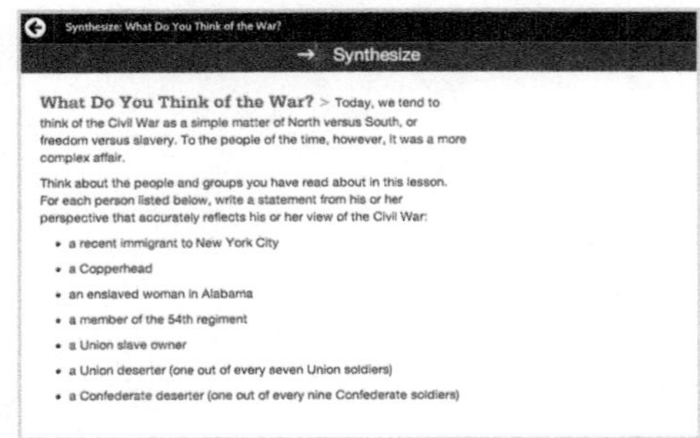

Synthesize: What Do You Think of the War?

→ Synthesize

What Do You Think of the War? > Today, we tend to think of the Civil War as a simple matter of North versus South, or freedom versus slavery. To the people of the time, however, it was a more complex affair.

Think about the people and groups you have read about in this lesson. For each person listed below, write a statement from his or her perspective that accurately reflects his or her view of the Civil War:

- a recent immigrant to New York City
- a Copperhead
- an enslaved woman in Alabama
- a member of the 54th regiment
- a Union slave owner
- a Union deserter (one out of every seven Union soldiers)
- a Confederate deserter (one out of every nine Confederate soldiers)

Focus students on the individuals listed. Begin by making sure they understand who each person was. Encourage them to think from the listed people's points of view. What would each individual have to gain or lose from the Civil War?

Discuss Ask students if they think that the Civil War was the most important or memorable part of these people's lives. *(Given the monumental influence of the war on life in America, it probably was.)*

DEMONSTRATE

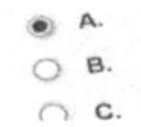

DIGITAL QUIZ

Lesson Quiz and Discussion Board

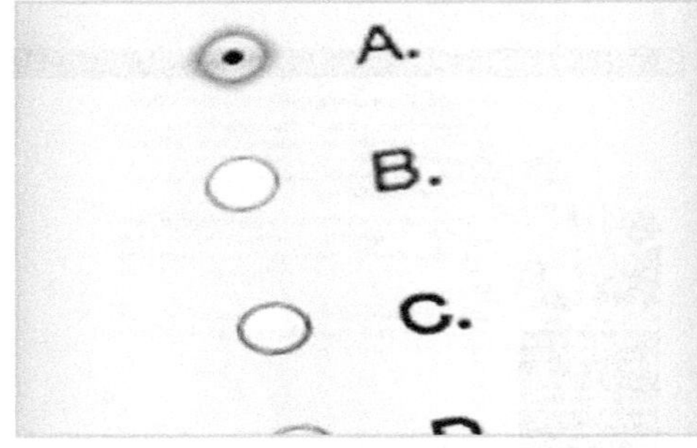

Assign the online Lesson Quiz for this lesson if you haven't already done so. Students will be offered automatic remediation or enrichment based on their score.

Pose these questions to the class on the Discussion Board:

In *Emancipation and Life in Wartime*, you learned about the Emancipation Proclamation and how it changed the course of the Civil War. You also learned about how African Americans served bravely as Union Soldiers. An outstanding example is Sergeant William Carney of the famous 54th Massachusetts Regiment, who won a Congressional Medal of Honor. African American soldiers, like all soldiers during the war, suffered terrible hardships. On the home front, the draft was resented by northerners and southerners alike. Draft riots rocked New York City. The war proved beneficial to many northern industries, even though the economy suffered from inflation. The war devastated the southern economy, which also suffered inflation and the results of the Union blockade. Women in both the North and South made valuable contributions to the war effort. An outstanding example is Union nurse Clara Barton, who later founded the American Red Cross.

Express Ideas Clearly Who is one individual from the Civil War era that you find particularly interesting, heroic, or admirable? Express your views about him or her.

Topic Inquiry

Have students continue their investigations for the Topic Inquiry.

PEARSON realize www.PearsonRealize.com Access your Digital Lesson

The War's End

Supporting English Language Learners

Use with Digital Text 2, **The Battle of Gettysburg.**

Writing

Review the meaning of *pronoun* to prepare students to edit writing for standard grammar and usage of pronoun agreement commensurate with grade-level expectations.

Beginning Have students write these sentences, using pronouns in the blanks: Lee moved his army north. _____ wanted to surprise the Yankees. The Confederates fought hard, but _____ still lost. Then display the subject pronouns. Ask students to edit their writing for pronoun agreement.

Intermediate Display the following sentences: Lee moved his army north. The Confederates fought hard. Ask students to copy each sentence and write a follow-up sentence using a pronoun for the subject. Then display the subject pronouns, and have students edit their writing.

Advanced Ask pairs of students to write a paragraph about Pickett's Charge that uses at least three subject pronouns. Then display the subject pronouns, and have pairs edit their writing. Ask: Which pronoun corresponds to Pickett's Charge: *he* (for *Pickett*) or *it* (for *Charge*)?

Advanced High Ask students to write a paragraph about Pickett's Charge that uses at least three subject and three object pronouns. Then display the subject and object pronouns, and have students edit their writing. Ask: Which pronouns are the same as both a subject and an object?

Use with Digital Text 5, **Contrasting Ideas of Liberty and Union.**

Speaking

Review the concept of contrasting and discuss the vocabulary used to contrast. Prompt students to speak about Abraham Lincoln and Jefferson Davis using routine contrasting words.

Beginning Explain that the word *but* is routine language used to contrast ideas in classroom communication. Have students complete and say this sentence: Lincoln wanted slaves to be free, but Davis wanted _____.

Intermediate Explain that the words *but* and *however* are routine language used to contrast ideas in classroom communication. Have students speak using *but* and *however* to contrast the ideas of Lincoln and Davis.

Advanced Discuss how the terms *however* and *in contrast* are used to differentiate ideas in classroom communication. Have pairs of students speak using these words to contrast the ideas of Lincoln and Davis.

Advanced High Discuss how the vocabulary *by comparison* and *on the other hand* are used to contrast ideas in classroom communication. Have pairs of students use these phrases to respond to each others' statements as they discuss Lincoln and Davis.

D Differentiate Instruction

Use the Differentiated Instruction notes throughout the lesson plan to support the varied skill sets, levels of readiness, and interests in the mixed-ability classroom.

Challenge These notes include suggestions for expanding the activity for advanced students.

On-Level These notes include suggestions for modifying the activity to address different interests or learning styles.

Extra Support These notes include ideas for providing more scaffolding or reading spuport.

Special Needs These notes provide ideas for adapting instruction to support the needs of various special needs students.

NOTES

The War's End

Objectives

Objective 1: Explain why the Union victories at Vicksburg and Gettysburg helped turn the war in the Union's favor.

Objective 2: Describe Grant's plan for ending the war and the war's outcome.

Objective 3: Identify Lincoln's hopes for the Union after his reelection.

Objective 4: Summarize why the Civil War marked a turning point in American history.

LESSON 6 ORGANIZER		PACING: APPROX. 1 PERIOD, .5 BLOCKS		
			RESOURCES	
	OBJECTIVES	PACING	Online	Print
Connect				
DIGITAL START UP ACTIVITY **"He Fights"**		5 min.	●	
Investigate				
DIGITAL TEXT 1 **The Siege of Vicksburg**	Objective 1	10 min.	●	●
INTERACTIVE MAP **The Battle of Vicksburg**	Objective 1	10 min.	●	
DIGITAL TEXT 2 **The Battle of Gettysburg**	Objective 1	10 min.	●	●
3-D MODEL **The Battle at Gettysburg**	Objective 1	10 min.	●	
DIGITAL TEXT 3 **The Gettysburg Address**	Objective 1	10 min.	●	●
DIGITAL TEXT 4 **Union Forces Move Southward**	Objective 2	10 min.	●	●
DIGITAL TEXT 6 **The Confederacy Surrenders at Appomattox**	Objective 2	10 min.	●	●
INTERACTIVE MAP **Key Battles of the Civil War**	Objective 2	10 min.	●	
DIGITAL TEXT 5 **Contrasting Ideas of Liberty and Union**	Objective 3	10 min.	●	●
DIGITAL TEXT 7 **The Nation Begins a New Chapter**	Objective 4	10 min.	●	●
Synthesize				
DIGITAL ACTIVITY **A Turning Point**		5 min.	●	
Demonstrate				
DIGITAL QUIZ **Lesson Quiz and Class Discussion Board**		10 min.	●	

CONNECT

DIGITAL START UP ACTIVITY
"He Fights"

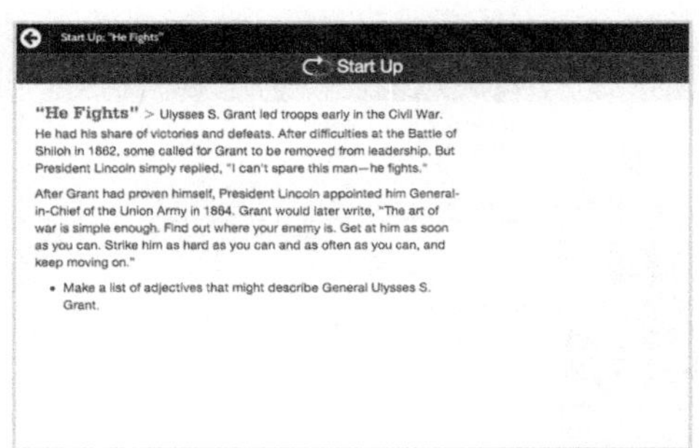

Project the Start Up Activity Ask students to answer the question as they enter and get settled. Then have them share their ideas with another student, either in class or through a chat or blog space.

Discuss Ask students to explain their choices of adjectives used to describe General Grant. What evidence from the text did they use to support their choices? *(Answers will vary, but students should cite specific examples from the text to explain their thinking.)*

Tell students that in this lesson they will be learning how the Battles of Vicksburg and Gettysburg turned the war's outcome in favor of the Union.

Aa Vocabulary Development: Use the Interactive Reading Notepad to preview the Key Terms and Academic Vocabulary in this lesson with students.

FLIP IT!

Assign the Flipped Video for this lesson.

STUDENT EDITION PRINT PAGES: 478–487

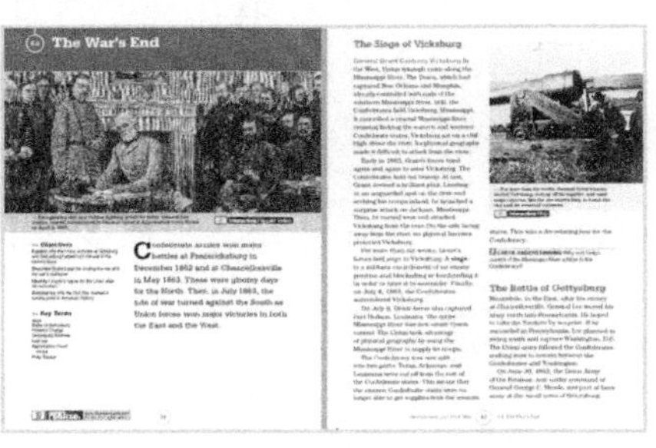

INVESTIGATE

DIGITAL TEXT 1
The Siege of Vicksburg

Text 1: The Siege of Vicksburg

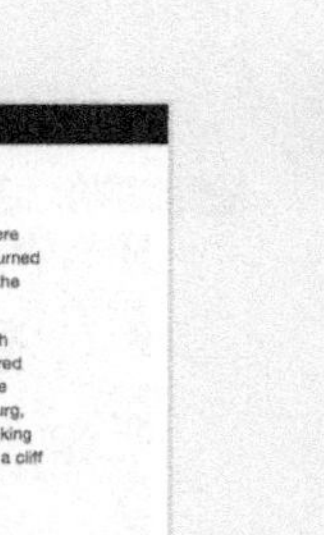

>> For more than six weeks, General Grant's forces circled Vicksburg, cutting off its supplies, and used siege cannons, like the one shown here, to bomb the city until its eventual surrender.

The Siege of Vicksburg

Confederate armies won major battles at Fredericksburg in December 1862 and at Chancellorsville in May 1863. These were gloomy days for the North. Then, in July 1863, the tide of war turned against the South as Union forces won major victories in both the East and the West.

General Grant Captures Vicksburg In the West, Union triumph came along the Mississippi River. The Union, which had captured New Orleans and Memphis, already controlled both ends of the southern Mississippi River. Still, the Confederates held Vicksburg, Mississippi. It controlled a crucial Mississippi River crossing linking the eastern and western Confederate states. Vicksburg sat on a cliff high above the river. Its physical geography made it difficult to attack from the river.

Early in 1863, Grant's forces tried again and again to seize Vicksburg.

1 of 3

INTERACTIVE MAP
The Battle of Vicksburg

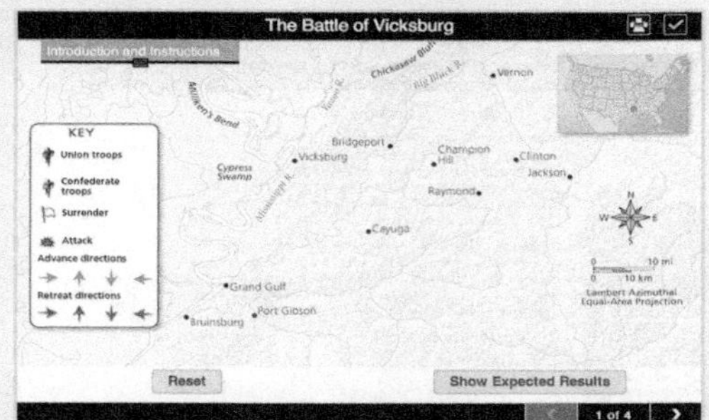

Objective 1: **Explain why the Union victories at Vicksburg and Gettysburg helped turn the war in the Union's favor.**

Quick Instruction

Interactive Map: The Battle of Vicksburg Project the Interactive map. Guide students to use the hints to place icons that will correctly show the outcome of the battle. Ask students how physical geographic factors affected the siege. *(The Confederate soldiers were able to defend the higher ground on the cliffs above the river, so the siege lasted longer than it otherwise would have because Grant's army had to circle around and attack by land.)*

Generate Explanations Ask students to explain the role of Ulysses S. Grant in the Union victory at the Battle of Vicksburg. *(General Grant's leadership led to the Union victory. Grant's forces had tried many times to take Vicksburg. At last, Grant devised a brilliant plan. Marching his troops inland, he launched a surprise attack on Jackson, Mississippi. Then, he turned west and attacked Vicksburg from the rear.)*

3-D Model: The Battle of Gettysburg Project the 3-D model. Explain the significant events of the Battle of Gettysburg using the student perspective near Cemetery Ridge.

Summarize Why was the Union victory at the Battle of Vicksburg a significant event of the Civil War? *(The Union army's victory at Vicksburg, combined with another victory days later, gave the North control of the Mississippi river, effectively splitting the South in two and breaking Confederate military supply lines.)*

ACTIVE CLASSROOM

Imagine that you are having a conversation with one of the soldiers who participated in the Battle of Vicksburg. Write down a question you'd like to ask, and then what that person would say to you, and what you would say in response.

ACTIVE CLASSROOM

Conduct a Circle Write activity. Break students into small groups and ask them to address this question: Why was the Battle of Gettysburg a significant event of the Civil War? Have students write as much as they can for 1 minute and then switch with the person on their right. The next person tries to improve or elaborate the response where the other person left off. Continue to switch until the paper comes back to the first person. The group then decides which is the best composition (or response) and shares that with the larger group.

The War's End

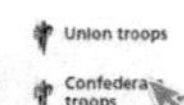

DIGITAL TEXT 2

The Battle of Gettysburg

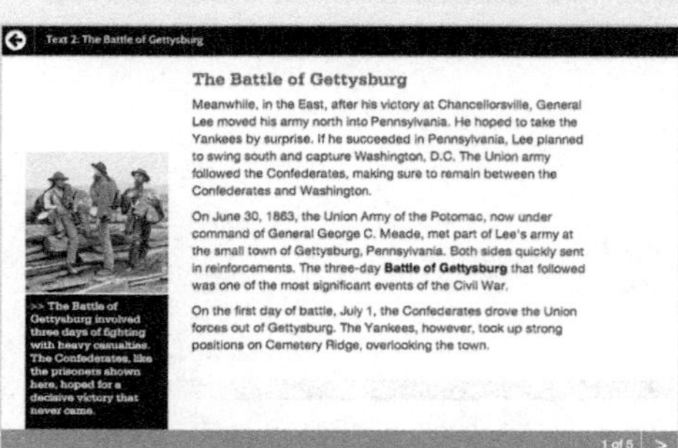

Text 2: The Battle of Gettysburg

The Battle of Gettysburg

Meanwhile, in the East, after his victory at Chancellorsville, General Lee moved his army north into Pennsylvania. He hoped to take the Yankees by surprise. If he succeeded in Pennsylvania, Lee planned to swing south and capture Washington, D.C. The Union army followed the Confederates, making sure to remain between the Confederates and Washington.

On June 30, 1863, the Union Army of the Potomac, now under command of General George C. Meade, met part of Lee's army at the small town of Gettysburg, Pennsylvania. Both sides quickly sent in reinforcements. The three-day **Battle of Gettysburg** that followed was one of the most significant events of the Civil War.

On the first day of battle, July 1, the Confederates drove the Union forces out of Gettysburg. The Yankees, however, took up strong positions on Cemetery Ridge, overlooking the town.

>> The Battle of Gettysburg involved three days of fighting with heavy casualties. The Confederates, like the prisoners shown here, hoped for a decisive victory that never came.

1 of 5

3-D MODEL

The Battle at Gettysburg

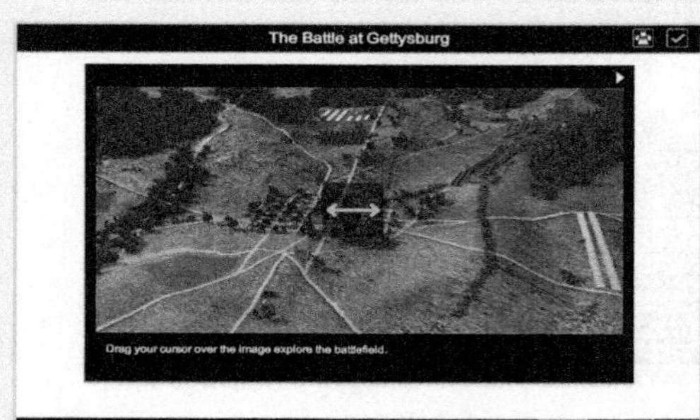

DIGITAL TEXT 3

The Gettysburg Address

Text 3: The Gettysburg Address

The Gettysburg Address

The Battle of Gettysburg left more than 50,000 dead or wounded. On November 19, 1863, there was a ceremony to dedicate a cemetery to the memory of those soldiers who died at Gettysburg. President Lincoln attended the ceremony. He delivered a speech now known as the **Gettysburg Address**. The speech expressed the purpose of the Civil War and exemplified Lincoln's leadership at a time of tremendous crisis. Lincoln said that the Civil War was a test of whether or not a democratic government could survive. This claim implied that the nation's survival depended on the integrity of the Union. He also addressed the theme of equality. He reminded Americans that their nation was founded on the belief that "all men are created equal." Lincoln told the audience:

>> Describing the sacrifices made at the Battle of Gettysburg, President Lincoln proclaimed that, if the war preserved the Union and its principles of liberty and equality, "these dead shall not have died in vain."

1 of 3

ELL Use the ELL activity described in the ELL chart.

Further Instruction

Infer In the Gettysburg Address, President Lincoln shared his ideas about liberty, equality, union, and the government. How did President Lincoln feel about these ideas based on the Gettysburg Address? Cite specific evidence from the Address in your answer. *(In the Gettysburg Address, Lincoln stated "all men are created equal" and that government should serve the people who create it, so it seems he felt strongly about equality and moving towards a country in which everyone would have a say in government. He also said that the war was a test of whether a democratic government could survive. He claimed that if the Union were to survive, then the men who died in the battle had not done so "in vain." This suggests how important he believed the Union was. In addition, he described "a new birth of freedom" in the event of a Union victory, so he believed liberty had a cost.)*

DIGITAL TEXT 4

Union Forces Move Southward

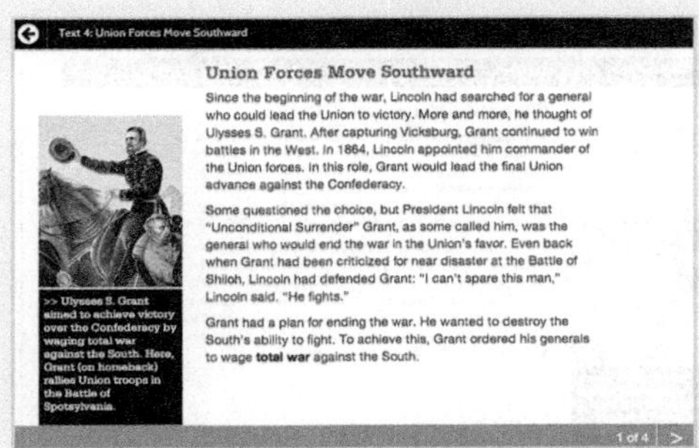

Text 4: Union Forces Move Southward
Union Forces Move Southward
Since the beginning of the war, Lincoln had searched for a general who could lead the Union to victory. More and more, he thought of Ulysses S. Grant. After capturing Vicksburg, Grant continued to win battles in the West. In 1864, Lincoln appointed him commander of the Union forces. In this role, Grant would lead the final Union advance against the Confederacy.
Some questioned the choice, but President Lincoln felt that "Unconditional Surrender" Grant, as some called him, was the general who would end the war in the Union's favor. Even back when Grant had been criticized for near disaster at the Battle of Shiloh, Lincoln had defended Grant: "I can't spare this man," Lincoln said. "He fights."
Grant had a plan for ending the war. He wanted to destroy the South's ability to fight. To achieve this, Grant ordered his generals to wage total war against the South.
>> Ulysses S. Grant aimed to achieve victory over the Confederacy by waging total war against the South. Here, Grant (on horseback) rallies Union troops in the Battle of Spotsylvania.
1 of 4

DIGITAL TEXT 6

The Confederacy Surrenders at Appomattox

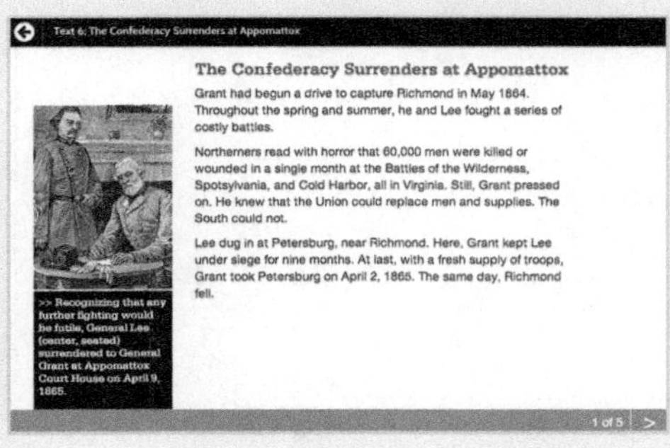

INTERACTIVE MAP

Key Battles of the Civil War

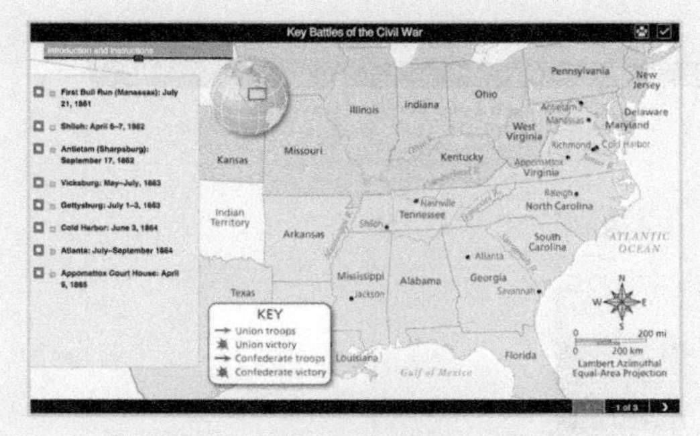

Objective 2: Describe Grant's plan for ending the war and the war's outcome.

Quick Instruction

Interactive Map: Key Battles of the Civil War Project the Interactive map. Guide students through the significant events of the Civil War. Point out how the physical geographic factors of the United States affected this major historical event.The armies were fighting for territory, positioning themselves geographically, and using geographic factors, like rivers and elevated ground, to their advantage in battles.General Grant, in his role as the Union general leading the final advance against the Confederacy, planned to wage total war.

Summarize Ask students to explain Lee's surrender at Appomattox Court House. When did Lee surrender? What terms did General Grant set for the Confederate soldiers? *(Lee surrendered on April 9, 1865. Grant offered generous terms of surrender. Soldiers had to turn over their rifles, but officers could keep their pistols. Soldiers who had horses could keep them. Finally, Grant allowed the Confederate soldiers to return to their homes without fear of being pursued by U.S. authorities.)*

Support Ideas With Evidence What evidence do you see in the text to support the idea that General Grant showed honorable leadership qualities in his respectful treatment of the Confederate army after the surrender at Appomattox? *(Grant allowed former Confederate soldiers to keep their horses and ordered that they be allowed to peacefully return to their homes.)*

ACTIVE CLASSROOM

Consider performing a large-scale Act It Out with students in order to help them understand significant events of the Civil War, including the Battles of Gettysburg and Vicksburg as well as Lee's surrender at Appomattox Court House. Use sidewalk chalk to sketch out a large, rough map of the eastern United States. Have students assume the roles of the major battles of the latter part of the Civil War. Each student should give a very brief oral description—including date and outcome—of his or her battle. Have students speak in chronological order. Consider expanding the activity to have students assume the roles of armies to show large-scale, essential movements, like Sherman's March to the Sea.

Further Instruction

Identify Central Issues Focus students' attention on Grant's plan for ending the war. Ask them what "total war" means. *("Total war" is an all-out war that affects civilians at home and soldiers in combat.)*

Summarize What role did Philip Bazaar play in the Civil War? Why is he considered a hero? *(During the assault on Fort Fisher on January 15, 1865, Philip Bazaar braved terrible fire to deliver important messages between the navy and army.)*

The War's End

DIGITAL TEXT 5

Contrasting Ideas of Liberty and Union

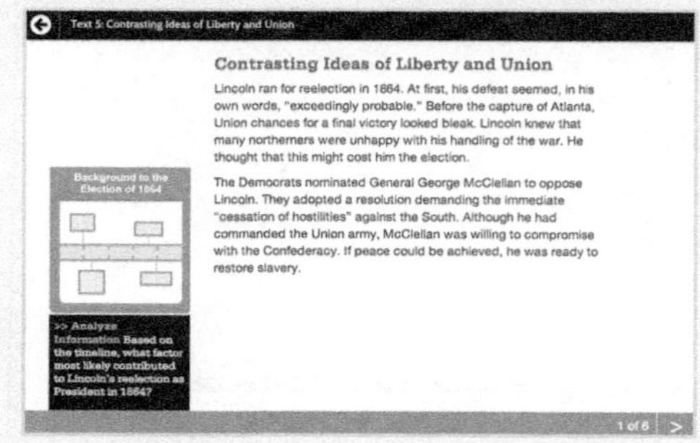

Objective 3: **Identify Lincoln's hopes for the Union after his reelection.**

Quick Instruction

Set the scene for students. 1864: an election year. The Civil War has raged for three years—much longer than anyone really expected—and northerners are unhappy with the President. Lincoln's former head of the army, cautious General George McClellan, is running against him. Lincoln fears defeat. Then, Sherman takes Atlanta, a city that symbolized the power of the South. Lincoln is reelected and expresses his hopes for the future in his Second Inaugural Address. Invite a volunteer to read excerpts from the speech aloud. Then hold a discussion in which you guide the class as they analyze Abraham Lincoln's ideas about liberty, equality, union, and government as contained in his First and Second Inaugural Addresses. Emphasize that, in both speeches, Lincoln stressed the importance of the Union of the states.

Determine Point of View Upon what document was Jefferson Davis arguing for secession from the Union in his Inaugural Address? What specific ideas did he use to support his argument? *(Davis based his arguments on the Declaration of Independence, in which the founders justified independence from Britain based on the consent of the governed. Similar about how the colonies did not want to be ruled by Britain, Davis argued for an independent Confederacy because its member states no longer wanted to be ruled by the United States government.)*

ELL Use the ELL activity described in the ELL chart.

Further Instruction

Contrast Challenge students to contrast the ideas Lincoln expressed about liberty, equality, union, and government in his First and Second Inaugural Addresses with the ideas contained in Jefferson Davis's Inaugural Address. *(While Lincoln emphasized the Union of the states based on the Constitution, Davis emphasized the fact that the Union was created by the consent of individual states and that states had the right to leave that Union and government. While Lincoln's speeches called for equality and liberty for enslaved African Americans, Davis called for the equality and liberty only of southern whites.)*

Infer What do the ideas expressed in Lincoln's and Davis's Inaugural Addresses suggest about the leadership qualities possessed by these elected U.S. leaders? *(In their Inaugural Addresses, both men show the leadership qualities of intelligence, public-speaking ability, dedication, and conviction.)*

DIGITAL TEXT 7

The Nation Begins a New Chapter

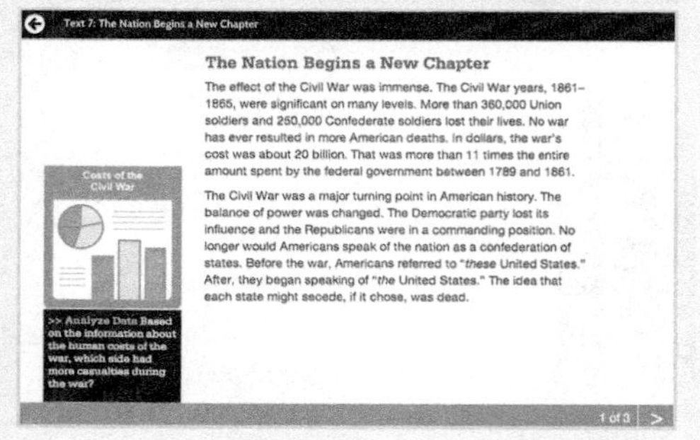

Objective 4: **Summarize why the Civil War marked a turning point in American history.**

Quick Instruction

Sequence Events Share the following list with students and challenge them to identify whether each was an effect of the Civil War.

- Democrats more powerful (before the War)
- Republicans more powerful (after the War)
- country called "these United States" (before the War)
- country called "the United States" (after the War)
- state secession a valid option (before the War)
- state secession unthinkable (after the War)
- slavery allowed (before the War)
- slavery abolished (after the War)

Further Instruction

Analyze Data Display the infographic about the costs of the Civil War. Ask students to explain what this data suggests about the significance of the Civil War to American history. *(The data suggests that the Civil War was significant in its monetary and human costs. It had a major impact on the population of America and the American economy.)*

Use Context Clues Why is it significant that Americans began referring to the country as *the* United States rather than *these* United States after the Civil War? *(Americans began to think of the country as a unified whole rather than a collection of loosely joined states.)*

SYNTHESIZE

DIGITAL ACTIVITY

A Turning Point

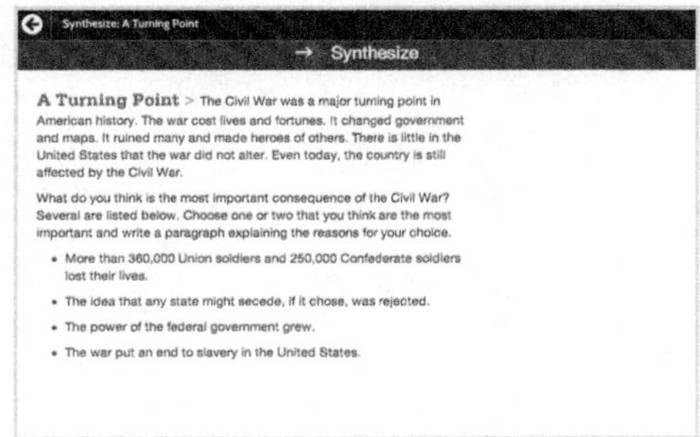

Invite a student to explain why it is important to study the Civil War, which happened so long ago. Guide the class into understanding how the Civil War still affects us today. Everything from the status of African Americans to the power of the federal government was changed by the war.

Encourage students to spend a few minutes pre-writing before they begin their paragraphs. If students feel that all of the consequences of the Civil War were equally important, allow them to express and support that point of view.

Discuss Was the Civil War *the* most important event in American history up to that point in time? Why or why not? Encourage debate in class.

DEMONSTRATE

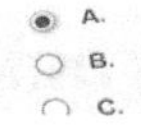

DIGITAL QUIZ

Lesson Quiz and Class Discussion Board

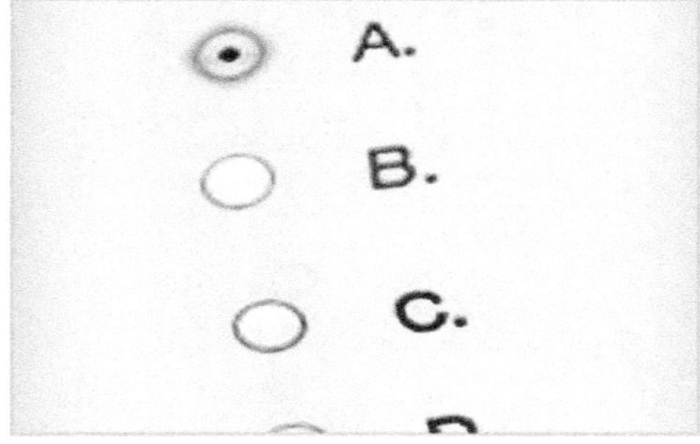

Assign the online Lesson Quiz for this lesson if you haven't already done so. Students will be offered automatic remediation or enrichment based on their score.

Pose these questions to the class on the Discussion Board:

In *The War's End*, you learned about two great battles that changed the course of the war: the Union capture of Vicksburg and the Union victory at Gettysburg. It was at Gettysburg that Lincoln gave his famous address expressing American ideals. Soon after, Union forces moved deep into the South, eventually forcing the Confederacy to surrender at Appomattox Court House. The Civil War was over. It had cost many lives and great amounts of money, and it changed the country in ways that are still apparent today.

Make Generalizations What do you think are the "lessons" of the Civil War for Americans today?

Express Ideas Clearly What aspect of the Civil War do you find most interesting? The military? The politics? Something else? Explain why.

Topic Inquiry

Have students continue their investigations for the Topic Inquiry.

Sectionalism and Civil War

SYNTHESIZE

DIGITAL ACTIVITY

Reflect on the Essential Question and Topic

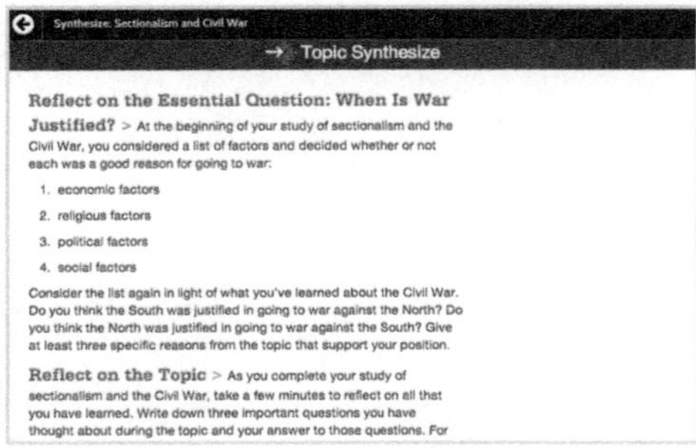

First ask students to reconsider the Essential Question for the Topic: When is war justified? Remind students of the factors that might justify going to war that they considered at the start of the Topic:

- economic factors
- religious factors
- political factors
- social factors

Ask students to reconsider their answers in light of what they've learned about the Civil War. Do they think the South was justified in going to war against the North? Do they think the North was justified in going to war against the South? What factors were involved?

Next ask students to reflect on the Topic as a whole and jot down one to three questions they've developed while learning about the Civil War. Share these examples if students need help getting started:

- Which factor or combination of factors—economic, religious, political, social—led to the Civil War?
- Do you think people of the time thought the war was caused by the same things that historians today would say caused the war?
- How can disagreements rooted in sectionalism be resolved without going to war?

You may ask students to share their questions and answers on the Class Discussion Board.

Topic Inquiry

Have students complete Step 3 of the Topic Inquiry.

DEMONSTRATE

DIGITAL TOPIC REVIEW AND ASSESSMENT

Sectionalism and Civil War

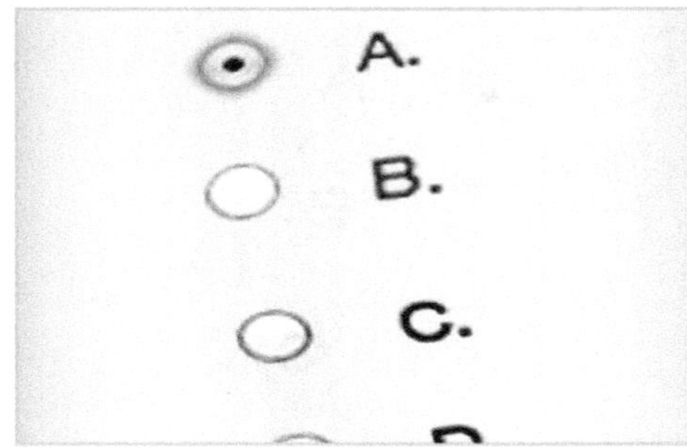

Students can prepare for the Topic Test by answering the questions in the Topic Review and Assessment online or the Assessment questions in the Print Student text. They can also prepare by reviewing their answers to the Interactive Reading Notepad questions or reviewing their notes in the Reading and Notetaking Study Guide.

DIGITAL TOPIC TEST

Sectionalism and Civil War

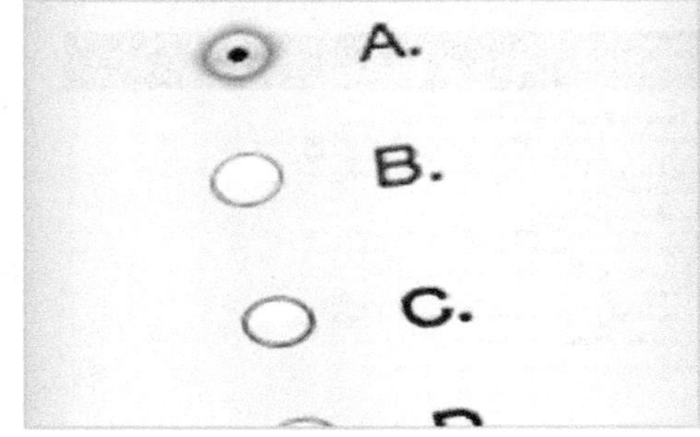

TOPIC TEST

Assign the Topic Test to assess students' understanding of topic content.

BENCHMARK TESTS

Assign these benchmark tests as you complete the relevant topics to monitor student progress toward mastering the course content and as preparation for the End-of-Course Test.

Benchmark Test 1: Topics 1-2

Benchmark Test 2: Topics 3-4

Benchmark Test 3: Topics 5-6

Benchmark Test 4: Topics 7-9

Benchmark Test 5: Topics 10-12

Benchmark Test 6: Topics 13-14

Benchmark Test 7: Topics 15-17

Topic 9

PEARSON realize

www.PearsonRealize.com
Access your Digital Lesson

The Reconstruction Era

TOPIC 9 ORGANIZER	PACING: APPROX. 7 PERIODS, 3.5 BLOCKS
	PACING
Connect	1 period
MY STORY VIDEO **Born into Slavery**	10 min.
DIGITAL ESSENTIAL QUESTION ACTIVITY **How Should We Handle Conflict?**	10 min.
DIGITAL TIMELINE ACTIVITY **The Reconstruction Era**	10 min.
TOPIC INQUIRY: CIVIC DISCUSSION **Ending Reconstruction**	20 min.
Investigate	3–7 periods
TOPIC INQUIRY: CIVIC DISCUSSION **Ending Reconstruction**	Ongoing
LESSON 1 Early Reconstruction	30–40 min.
LESSON 2 Radical Reconstruction	30–40 min.
LESSON 3 Reconstruction and Southern Society	30–40 min.
LESSON 4 The Aftermath of Reconstruction	30–40 min.
Synthesize	1 period
DIGITAL ACTIVITY **Reflect on the Essential Question and Topic**	10 min.
TOPIC INQUIRY: CIVIC DISCUSSION **Ending Reconstruction**	20 min.
Demonstrate	1–2 periods
DIGITAL TOPIC REVIEW AND ASSESSMENT **The Reconstruction Era**	10 min.
TOPIC INQUIRY: CIVIC DISCUSSION **Ending Reconstruction**	20 min.

TOPIC INQUIRY: CIVIC DISCUSSION

Ending Reconstruction

In this Topic Inquiry, students work in teams to examine different perspectives on this issue by analyzing several sources, arguing both sides of a Yes/No question, then developing and discussing their own point of view on the question: **Should the United States have ended Reconstruction in 1877?**

STEP 1: CONNECT

Develop Questions and Plan the Investigation

Launch the Civic Discussion

Divide the class into groups of four students. Students can access the materials they'll need in the online course or you can distribute copies to each student. Read the main question and introduction with the students.

Have students complete Step 1 by reading the Discussion Launch and filling in Step 1 of the Information Organizer. The Discussion Launch provides YES and NO arguments on the main question. Students should extract and paraphrase the arguments from the reading in Step 1 of their Information Organizers.

Next, students share within their groups the arguments and evidence they found to support the YES and NO positions. The group needs to agree on the major YES and NO points and each student should note those points in their Information Organizer.

Resources

- Student Instructions
- Information Organizer
- Discussion Launch

PROFESSIONAL DEVELOPMENT

Civic Discussion

Be sure to view the Civic Discussion Professional Development resources in the online course.

STEP 2: INVESTIGATE

Apply Disciplinary Concepts and Tools

Examine Sources and Perspectives

Students will examine sources with the goal of extracting information and perspectives on the main question. They analyze each source and describe the author's perspective on the main question and key evidence the author provides to support that viewpoint in Information Organizer Step 2.

Ask students to keep in mind:

- **Author/Creator:** Who created the source? An individual? Group? Government agency?
- **Audience:** For whom was the source created?
- **Date/Place:** Is there any information that reveals where and when the source was created?
- **Purpose:** Why was the source created? Discuss with students the importance of this question in identifying bias.
- **Relevance:** How does the source support one argument or another?

Suggestion: Reading the source documents and filling in Step 2 of the Information Organizer could be assigned as homework.

Resources

- Student Instructions
- Information Organizer
- Source documents

STEP 3: SYNTHESIZE

Use Evidence to Formulate Conclusions

Formulate Compelling Arguments with Evidence

Now students will apply perspectives and evidence they extracted from the sources to think more deeply about the main question by first arguing one side of the issue, then the other. In this way students become more prepared to formulate an evidence-based conclusion on their own.

Within each student group, assign half of the students to take the position of YES on the main question and the others to take the position of NO. Students will work with their partners to identify the strongest arguments and evidence to support their assigned YES or NO position.

Present Yes/No Positions

Within each group, those assigned the YES position share arguments and evidence first. As the YES students speak, those assigned NO should listen carefully, take notes to fill in the rest of the Compelling Arguments Chart (Step 3 in Information Organizer) and ask clarifying questions.

When the YES side is finished, students assigned the NO position present while those assigned YES should listen, take notes, and ask clarifying questions. Examples of clarifyin questions are:

- I think you just said [x]. Am I understanding you correctly?
- Can you tell me more about [x]?
- Can you repeat [x]? I am not sure I understand, yet.

Suggestion: You may want to set a 5 minute time limit for each side to present. Provide a two-minute warning so that students make their most compelling arguments within the time frame.

Switch Sides

The students will switch sides to argue the opposite point of view. To prepare to present the other position, partners who first argued YES will use the notes they took during the NO side's presentation, plus add any additional arguments and evidence from the reading and sources. The same for students who first argued the NO position.

STEP 4: DEMONSTRATE

Communicate Conclusions and Take Informed Action

Individual Points of View

Now the students will have the opportunity to discuss the main question from their own points of view. To help students prepare for this discussion, have them reflect on the YES/NO discussions they have participated in thus far and fill in Step 4 of their Information Organizers.

After all of the students have shared their points of view, each group should list points of agreement, filling the last portion of Step 4 on their Information Organizers.

Reflect on the Discussion

Ask students to reflect on the civic discussion thinking about:

- The value of having to argue both the YES and NO positions.
- If their individual views changed over the course of the discussion and why.
- What they learned from participating in the discussion.

Resources

- Student Instructions
- Information Organizer

Topic 9

INTRODUCTION

The Reconstruction Era

Following the Civil War, Congress instituted sweeping political, economic, and social changes in the former Confederate states. During this period of Reconstruction, African Americans gained many rights. They were still, however, denied full equality, especially in the South.

CONNECT

MY STORY VIDEO

Born into Slavery

Watch a video about what it was like to be born into slavery and the changes that came with emancipation.

Check Understanding What was the basis for the descriptions of slavery in this video? *(interviews in the 1930s with formerly enslaved African Americans)*

Assess Credibility How credible a view does the video present of slavery and its aftermath? *(Because the video is based on the recollections of people who endured slavery, their first-hand accounts must be taken as credible, even though the passage of time may have affected their memories.)*

DIGITAL ESSENTIAL QUESTION ACTIVITY

How Should We Handle Conflict?

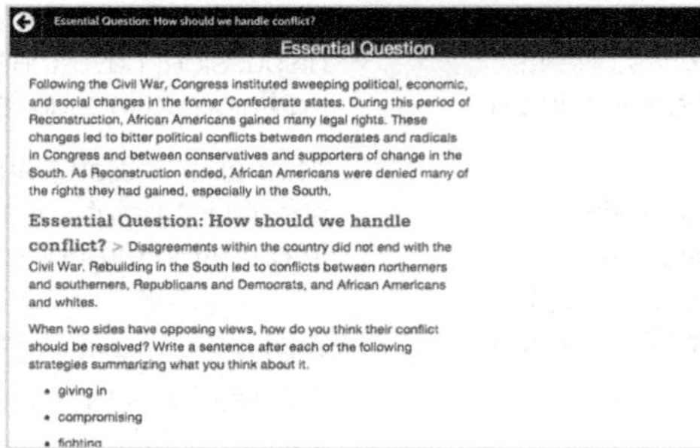

Ask students to think about the Essential Question for this topic: How should we handle conflict? Point out that disagreements continued after the Civil War over how to rebuild the South.

If students have not already done so, ask them to read the list and write a sentence about each strategy. Have students share their ideas with a partner.

Support Ideas with Examples Why do you think Americans continued to face conflicts following the Civil War? Name three areas in which you think conflict occurred and why.

Make Predictions What strategies do you think Americans will use to address conflicts following the Civil War? Explain your reasoning.

DIGITAL TIMELINE ACTIVITY

The Reconstruction Era

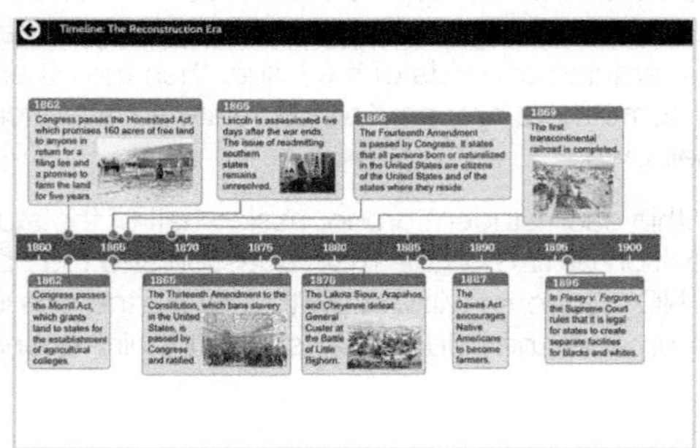

Display the timeline showing the major events of the Reconstruction era. During this topic, students will learn about all of these events and many more, but this timeline will provide a framework into which they can place the events they learn about.

Summarize What three amendments were passed following the Civil War and how did they impact the nation? *(Thirteenth—abolished slavery; Fourteenth—granted African Americans citizenship; Fifteenth—forbade states from denying citizens the right to vote because of race)*

Identify Cause and Effects Based on this timeline, how do you think Lincoln's assassination affected Reconstruction? *(His mild plan was not implemented and Reconstruction became harsher.)*

Topic Inquiry

Launch the Topic Inquiry with students after introducing the topic.

Early Reconstruction

Supporting English Language Learners

Use with Digital Text 2, **The Causes and Effects of Reconstruction.**

Speaking

Prompt students to speak using a variety of grammatical structures such as appositives. Explain that an appositive is a grammatical structure that renames, explains, or identifies a noun next to it.

Beginning Display this sentence: Reconstruction, a time of rebuilding, followed the war. Point out the appositive *a time of rebuilding,* and brainstorm alternatives. Have students say the sentence aloud using one of the alternatives.

Intermediate Read aloud the sentences from the text that include the boldface terms *Wade-Davis Bill* and *Freedmen's Bureau*. Help students to identify the appositive in each. Then have students say additional sentences about the boldface terms that include appositives for them.

Advanced Read aloud the sentences from the text that include the boldface terms *Wade-Davis Bill* and *Freedmen's Bureau*. Ask students to identify the appositive in each. Then have pairs of students say sentences that include appositives for these words: *Lincoln, Reconstruction.*

Advanced High Read aloud the sentences from the text that include the boldface terms *Wade-Davis Bill* and *Freedmen's Bureau*. Ask students to identify the appositive in each. Then have pairs of students discuss Reconstruction using at least two appositives.

Use with Digital Text 4, **President Johnson's Reconstruction Plan.**

Writing

Discuss how editing writing for standard grammar and usage of appropriate verb tenses improves communication and avoids misunderstanding.

Beginning Display these sentences: The Thirteenth Amendment (bans/banned) slavery. Slavery (is/was) still illegal today. Have students choose between each pair of verbs and write down the sentences. Then discuss the present and past tenses, and have students edit their writing for appropriate verb tenses.

Intermediate Display these sentences: The Thirteenth Amendment _____ slavery. Slavery _____ still illegal today. Have students write down and complete the sentences. Then discuss the present and past tenses, and have students edit their writing for appropriate verb tenses.

Advanced Ask pairs of students to write a paragraph about the Thirteenth Amendment that uses the present, past, and future tenses. Then review each tense and answer students' questions. Have pairs edit their writing for appropriate verb tenses.

Advanced High Ask students to write a paragraph about the Thirteenth Amendment that uses the present, past, and future tenses and includes these verbs: approve, forbid, be, overturn. Then review each tense and answer students' questions. Have students edit their writing for appropriate verb tenses.

D Differentiate Instruction

Use the Differentiated Instruction notes throughout the lesson plan to support the varied skill sets, levels of readiness, and interests in the mixed-ability classroom.

Challenge These notes include suggestions for expanding the activity for advanced students.

On-Level These notes include suggestions for modifying the activity to address different interests or learning styles.

Extra Support These notes include ideas for providing more scaffolding or reading spuport.

Special Needs These notes provide ideas for adapting instruction to support the needs of various special needs students.

NOTES

Topic 9 Lesson 1

Early Reconstruction

Objectives

Objective 1: Describe the nation's economic, political, and social problems after the Civil War.

Objective 2: Identify the early steps that were taken during Reconstruction.

Objective 3: Explain how the assassination of Lincoln and the inauguration of a new President led to conflict.

LESSON 1 ORGANIZER — **PACING: APPROX. 1 PERIOD, .5 BLOCKS**

	OBJECTIVES	PACING	RESOURCES Online	RESOURCES Print
Connect				
DIGITAL ACTIVITY **Predicting Postwar Problems**		5 min.	●	
Investigate				
DIGITAL TEXT 1 **Effects of the Civil War**	Objective 1	10 min.	●	●
BEFORE AND AFTER **The Downfall of the Southern Economy**	Objective 1	10 min.	●	
DIGITAL TEXT 2 **The Causes and Effects of Reconstruction**	Objective 2	10 min.	●	●
DIGITAL TEXT 3 **The Assassination of Abraham Lincoln**	Objective 3	10 min.	●	●
DIGITAL TEXT 4 **President Johnson's Reconstruction Plan**	Objective 3	10 min.	●	●
INTERACTIVE GALLERY **Lincoln and Reconstruction**	Objective 3	10 min.	●	
Synthesize				
DIGITAL ACTIVITY **Events that Affected Reconstruction**		5 min.	●	
Demonstrate				
DIGITAL QUIZ **Lesson Quiz and Class Discussion Board**		10 min.	●	

Go online to access additional resources including:
Primary Sources • Biographies • Supreme Court cases • 21st Century Skill Tutorials • Maps • Graphic Organizers.

CONNECT

DIGITAL ACTIVITY

Predicting Postwar Problems

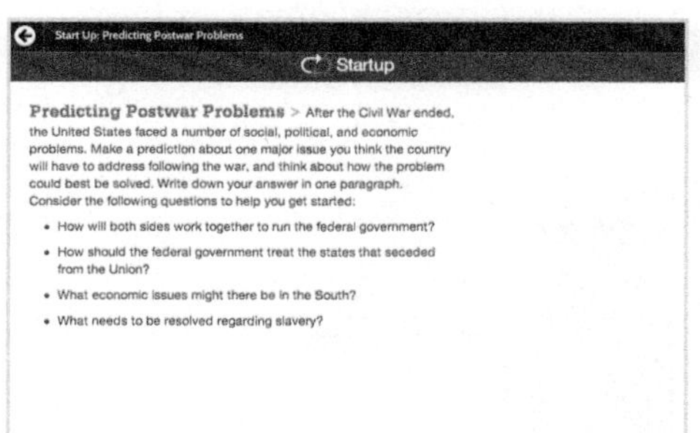

Project the Start Up Activity Ask students to read the questions and make a prediction as they enter.

Discuss How will both sides work together to run the federal government? *(There will be major disagreements; the North will be politically dominant.)* How should the federal government treat the states that seceded from the Union? *(Ensure that the states that seceded are loyal to the Union and will follow its laws outlawing slavery.)* What economic issues might there be in the South? *(losses from the war; lack of industrialization; downturns in agricultural production; the expense of rebuilding)* What needs to be resolved regarding slavery? *(the political and social status of African Americans)*

Aa Vocabulary Development: Use the Interactive Reading Notepad to preview the Key Terms and Academic Vocabulary in this lesson with students.

FLIP IT!

Assign the Flipped Video for this lesson.

STUDENT EDITION PRINT PAGES: 492–498

INVESTIGATE

DIGITAL TEXT 1

Effects of the Civil War

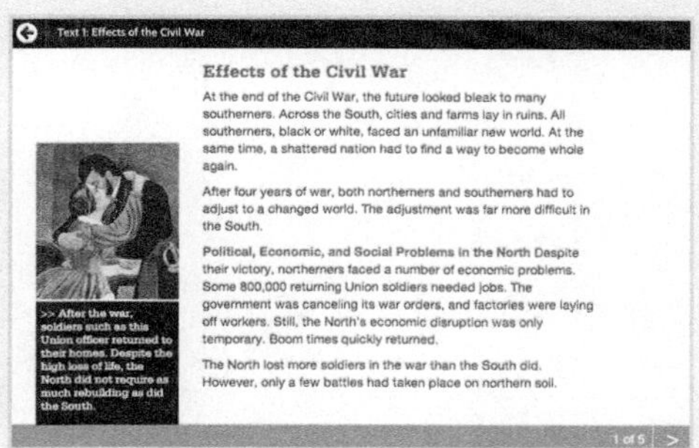

Objective 1: Describe the nation's economic, political, and social problems after the Civil War.

Quick Instruction

Before and After: The Downfall of the Southern Economy Project the Before and After activity and use the slider to show how prices and dollar values changed in the South during the war.

Analyze Graphs Describe the effects of the Civil War on the Confederate dollar. *(the dollar weakened until it was almost worthless)*

ACTIVE CLASSROOM

Have students use the Quick Write Strategy and take 30 seconds to write what they know about the political, social, and economic issues facing the nation as a result of the Civil War.

Further Instruction

Go through the Interactive Reading Notepad questions and discuss the answers with the class.

Compare and Contrast the economic problems faced by the North and South following the Civil War. What caused the economic differences between these two regions? *(North—returning soldiers needed jobs and factories were laying off workers. South—cities and farms lay in ruins, Confederate money was worthless, loans were never repaid, and banks closed. Causes—fighting mostly took place in the South; the North had industries to return to, whereas the South could not rebuild its plantation system)*

BEFORE AND AFTER

The Downfall of the Southern Economy

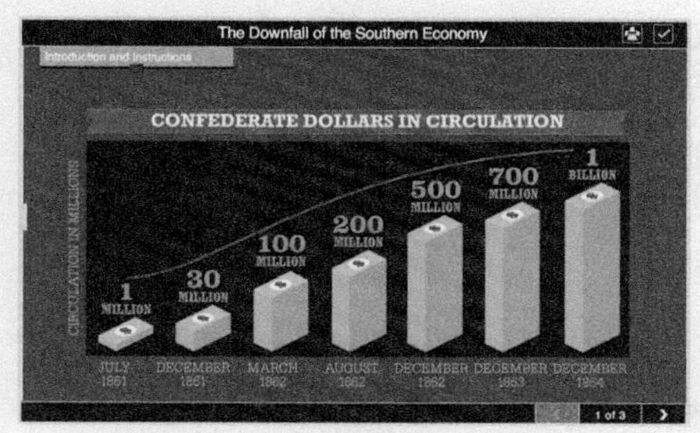

Generate Explanations Explain the social and political problems faced by the South after the war. *(Social—The South had millions of new freedmen but no legal systems to protect them. Political—There was no clear structure for running the state governments. Many Confederates were barred from office and feared African Americans gaining political power.)*

Make Predictions How do you think the economic differences between the North and South will affect Reconstruction? *(They will make it difficult for the South to rebuild; many southerners will resent wealthier and more economically stable northerners dictating Reconstruction polities.)*

Topic 9 Lesson 1

Early Reconstruction

DIGITAL TEXT 2

The Causes and Effects of Reconstruction

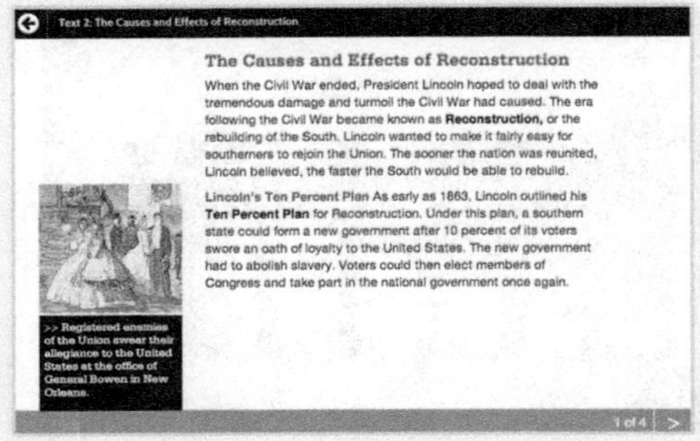

Text 2: The Causes and Effects of Reconstruction
The Causes and Effects of Reconstruction
When the Civil War ended, President Lincoln hoped to deal with the tremendous damage and turmoil the Civil War had caused. The era following the Civil War became known as Reconstruction, or the rebuilding of the South. Lincoln wanted to make it fairly easy for southerners to rejoin the Union. The sooner the nation was reunited, Lincoln believed, the faster the South would be able to rebuild.
Lincoln's Ten Percent Plan As early as 1863, Lincoln outlined his Ten Percent Plan for Reconstruction. Under this plan, a southern state could form a new government after 10 percent of its voters swore an oath of loyalty to the United States. The new government had to abolish slavery. Voters could then elect members of Congress and take part in the national government once again.
>> Registered enemies of the Union swear their allegiance to the United States at the office of General Bowen in New Orleans.
1 of 4

Objective 2: Identify the early steps that were taken during Reconstruction.

Quick Instruction

Project the image of the African American school. Define Reconstruction as the era of rebuilding the South following the Civil War. Explain that the Civil War resulted in extensive damage economically, politically, and socially, which caused there to be a Reconstruction period to repair and heal. Explain that Reconstruction also had many effects, such as building schools like this one for freedmen.

Summarize How did the Freedman's Bureau impact African Americans? *(It provided food and clothing to formerly enslaved people, helped freedmen find jobs, and set up schools for African Americans.)*

D Differentiate: Extra Support Explain that to reconstruct means to rebuild, or to build something again after it has been destroyed. Ask students what was destroyed that needed to be rebuilt after the Civil War. Discuss why they think the term Reconstruction is used to describe this era.

ELL Use the ELL activity described in the ELL chart.

Further Instruction

Go through the Interactive Reading Notepad questions and discuss the answers with the class.

Compare and Contrast the Wade-Davis Bill and Lincoln's Ten Percent Plan and explain how each proposed to address political, economic, and social problems during Reconstruction. What do the differences between these bills reveal about the nation's political problems following the Civil War? *(Ten Percent—proposed that southern states would form new governments and rejoin the Union after 10 percent of voters swore a loyalty oath; required the abolition of slavery; offered amnesty to former Confederates who had not been leaders. Wade Davis—proposed a majority of white men to swear a loyalty oath; prohibited Confederates from voting or holding office. The Wade-Davis Bill was harsher than Lincoln's plan, suggesting many Republicans disagreed with his policies and felt he was being too easy on the South.)*

Cite Evidence Describe Lincoln's leadership qualities following the Civil War, citing evidence for support. *(generous toward the South and concerned about the nation's future after the war—"Lincoln wanted to make it fairly easy for southerners to rejoin the Union. The sooner the nation was reunited, Lincoln believed, the faster the South would be able to rebuild." Willing to stand up to Republicans with whom he disagreed—"Lincoln refused to sign the Wade-Davis Bill because he felt it was too harsh.")*

DIGITAL TEXT 3

The Assassination of Abraham Lincoln

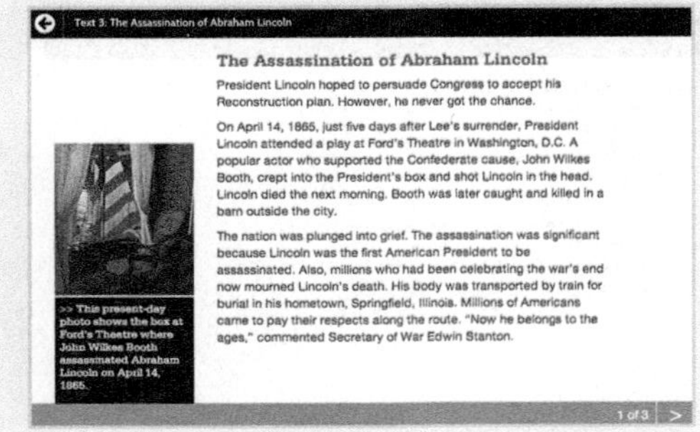

Objective 3: Explain how the assassination of Lincoln and the inauguration of a new President led to conflict.

Quick Instruction

Interactive Gallery: Lincoln and Reconstruction Project the interactive gallery and discuss the images with students.

Generate Explanations Explain the significance of Lincoln's assassination on the course of Reconstruction. *(Lincoln was not able to implement his more moderate Ten Percent Plan. Johnson became President and also took a moderate approach, but Republicans who wanted harsher measures were able to take control.)*

> **ACTIVE CLASSROOM**
>
> Ask students to Take a Stand on the following question: "Were Republicans right to demand harsher measures against the South during Reconstruction?" Ask students to divide into two groups based on their answer and move to separate areas of the room. Ask students to talk with each other to compare their reasons for answering yes or no. Have representatives from each side present and defend the group's point of view.

ELL Use the ELL activity described in the ELL chart.

Further Instruction

Go through the Interactive Reading Notepad questions and discuss the answers with the class.

DIGITAL TEXT 4

President Johnson's Reconstruction Plan

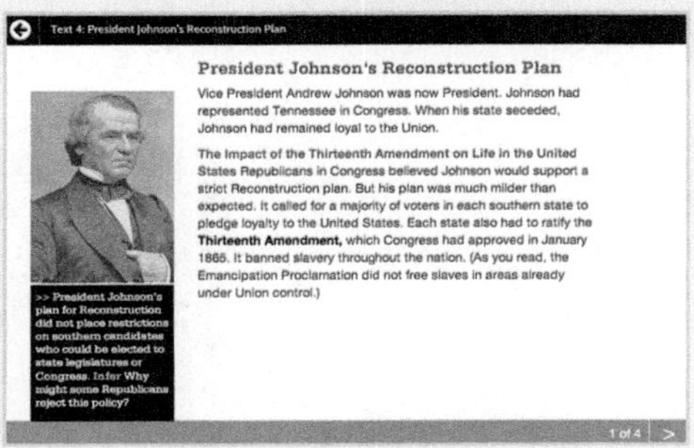

Identify Cause and Effect Describe the impact of the Thirteenth Amendment on life in the United States. *(It banned slavery throughout the nation, overturning previous rulings. This created a new social and economic system in the South. African Americans were hired as workers and many migrated North.)*

INTERACTIVE GALLERY

Lincoln and Reconstruction

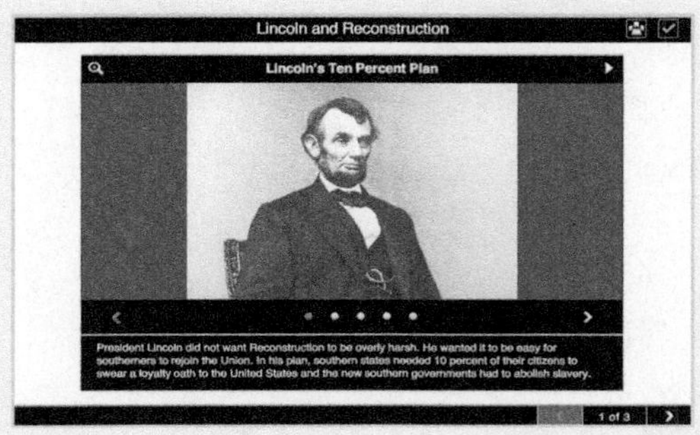

Lincoln and Reconstruction
Lincoln's Ten Percent Plan
President Lincoln did not want Reconstruction to be overly harsh. He wanted it to be easy for southerners to rejoin the Union. In his plan, southern states needed 10 percent of their citizens to swear a loyalty oath to the United States and the new southern governments had to abolish slavery.
1 of 3

Make Predictions Analyze the leadership qualities of Andrew Johnson. How do you think he will fare in the showdown against Republicans? Explain your reasoning. *(Johnson was not as strong a leader as Lincoln. He had not been elected President and was not the leader who won the war. Given that the Republicans are organizing against him, he will probably not be able to prevent Congress from implementing a harsher reconstruction plan.)*

Topic 9 Lesson 1

Early Reconstruction

SYNTHESIZE

DIGITAL ACTIVITY

Events that Affected Reconstruction

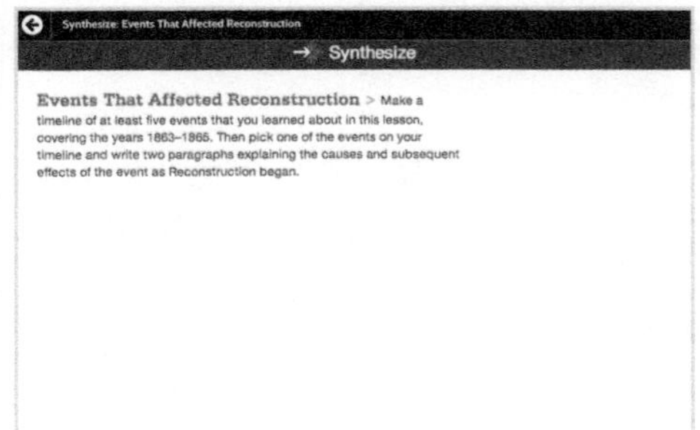

Have students make a timeline and choose one of the events to write about. Have students share their timelines with a partner and discuss their responses.

Discuss Have students review the predictions they made at the beginning of the lesson. Ask how they would revise their answers now that they have learned more about the causes and effects of early Reconstruction.

DEMONSTRATE

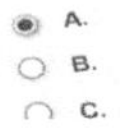

DIGITAL QUIZ

Lesson Quiz and Class Discussion Board

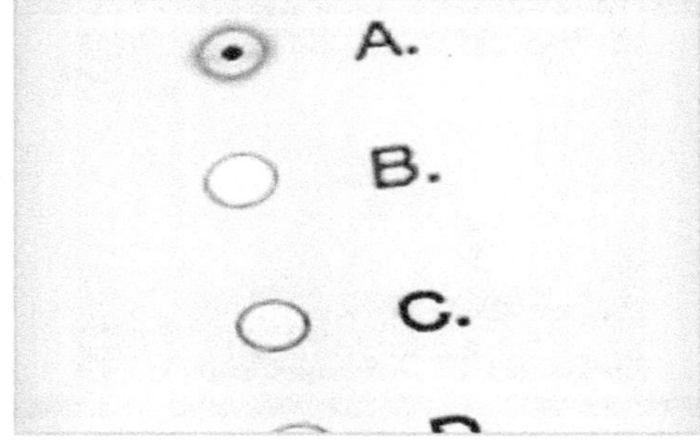

Assign the online Lesson Quiz for this lesson if you haven't already done so. Students will be offered automatic remediation or enrichment based on their score.

Pose these questions to the class on the Discussion Board:

Summarize Describe the causes and effects of Reconstruction.

Compare and Contrast How did Reconstruction impact different groups in the South, including African Americans, poor whites, and former Confederates? Give examples for support.

Topic Inquiry

Have students continue their investigations for the Topic Inquiry.

PEARSON realize™ www.PearsonRealize.com Access your Digital Lesson

Radical Reconstruction

Supporting English Language Learners

Use with Digital Text 1, **Reconstruction Difficulties Persist.**

Writing

Display the first sentence of the text. Prompt students to employ increasingly complex grammatical structures such as using the possessive case. Point out the apostrophe -s in *Johnson's*, and explain the relationship between Johnson and the Reconstruction plan.

Beginning Display this sentence: The South black codes did not allow freedmen to _____. Have students write down the sentence, add an apostrophe -s to employ the possessive case correctly, and fill in the blank with an appropriate word or phrase.

Intermediate Ask students to suggest sentences that use the possessive case (apostrophe –s) correctly using the following words: The South's, Freedmen's. Record students' suggestions, and have students write down the sentences.

Advanced Ask pairs of students to write a paragraph about the challenges of Reconstruction by using the possessive case (apostrophe –s) correctly with these words: Reconstruction's, Tennessee's, Johnson's, protest's. Have pairs read their paragraphs to one another.

Advanced High Ask students to write a paragraph about the challenges of Reconstruction using the possessive case (apostrophe –s) correctly at least three times. Have partners read each other's paragraphs and explain each instance of the possessive case that they encounter.

Use with Digital Text 4, **Political Problems and a New President.**

Speaking

Have students speak using a variety of sentence lengths with increasing accuracy and ease as they acquire more English.Explain that varying sentence length, or using a mix of shorter and longer sentences, can make spoken language more interesting and understandable.

Beginning Display this sentence: The House impeached Johnson. Brainstorm a list of prepositional phrases that could be added to the sentence in order to lengthen it. Ask students to add one of the phrases and say the new sentence aloud.

Intermediate Display this sentence: The House impeached Johnson. Ask students to think of ways that prepositional phrases could be added to the beginning and to the end of this sentence in order to lengthen it. Have students share these sentences aloud.

Advanced Display this sentence: The House impeached Johnson. Have pairs of students practice speaking with a variety of sentence lengths by adding prepositional phrases and independent clauses to the original sentence.

Advanced High Display this sentence: The House impeached Johnson. Ask pairs of students to practice speaking with a variety of sentence lengths by adding a dependent clause to the original sentence, as well as changing the original to a dependent clause and then adding a new independent clause to it.

D Differentiate Instruction

Use the Differentiated Instruction notes throughout the lesson plan to support the varied skill sets, levels of readiness, and interests in the mixed-ability classroom.

Challenge These notes include suggestions for expanding the activity for advanced students.

On-Level These notes include suggestions for modifying the activity to address different interests or learning styles.

Extra Support These notes include ideas for providing more scaffolding or reading spupport.

Special Needs These notes provide ideas for adapting instruction to support the needs of various special needs students.

NOTES

Radical Reconstruction

Objectives

Objective 1: Describe how Congress reacted to the passage of black codes in the South.

Objective 2: Explain how Radical Republicans gained power in Congress.

Objective 3: Identify why President Johnson was impeached.

LESSON 2 ORGANIZER — **PACING: APPROX. 1 PERIOD, .5 BLOCKS**

	OBJECTIVES	PACING	RESOURCES Online	RESOURCES Print
Connect				
DIGITAL START UP ACTIVITY **Causes of Radical Reconstruction**		5 min.	●	
Investigate				
DIGITAL TEXT 1 **Reconstruction Difficulties Persist**	Objective 1	10 min.	●	●
DIGITAL TEXT 2 **Reforms of the Radical Reconstruction Congress**	Objective 2	10 min.	●	●
DIGITAL TEXT 3 **Political and Social Problems During Reconstruction**	Objective 3	10 min.	●	●
INTERACTIVE GALLERY **The Massacre of New Orleans**		10 min.	●	
DIGITAL TEXT 4 **Political Problems and a New President**		10 min.	●	●
Synthesize				
DIGITAL ACTIVITY **The Effects of Radical Republicans in Congress**		5 min.	●	
Demonstrate				
DIGITAL QUIZ **Lesson Quiz and Class Discussion Board**		10 min.	●	

Go online to access additional resources including: Primary Sources • Biographies • Supreme Court cases • 21st Century Skill Tutorials • Maps • Graphic Organizers.

CONNECT

DIGITAL START UP ACTIVITY

Causes of Radical Reconstruction

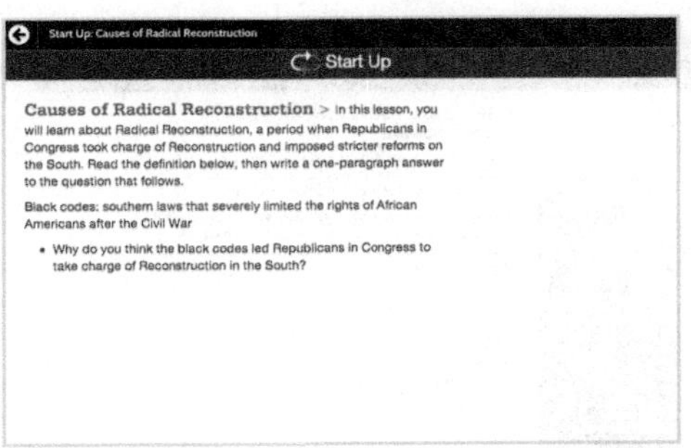

Start Up: Causes of Radical Reconstruction
Start Up
Causes of Radical Reconstruction > In this lesson, you will learn about Radical Reconstruction, a period when Republicans in Congress took charge of Reconstruction and imposed stricter reforms on the South. Read the definition below, then write a one-paragraph answer to the question that follows.
Black codes: southern laws that severely limited the rights of African Americans after the Civil War
• Why do you think the black codes led Republicans in Congress to take charge of Reconstruction in the South?

Project the Start Up Activity. Ask students to read the definition and answer the question as they enter and get settled. Have students share their responses with a partner, either in class or through a blog space.

Discuss Why do you think the black codes led Republicans in Congress to take charge of Reconstruction in the South? *(The Republicans felt the South was trying to preserve their power over African Americans and not make changes to its politics or society.)*

Tell students that in this lesson they will be learning about the Radical Reconstruction and the new legislative reforms of the Radical Reconstruction Congress.

Aa Vocabulary Development: Use the Interactive Reading Notepad to preview the Key Terms and Academic Vocabulary in this lesson with students.

FLIP IT!

Assign the Flipped Video for this lesson.

STUDENT EDITION PRINT PAGES: 499–505

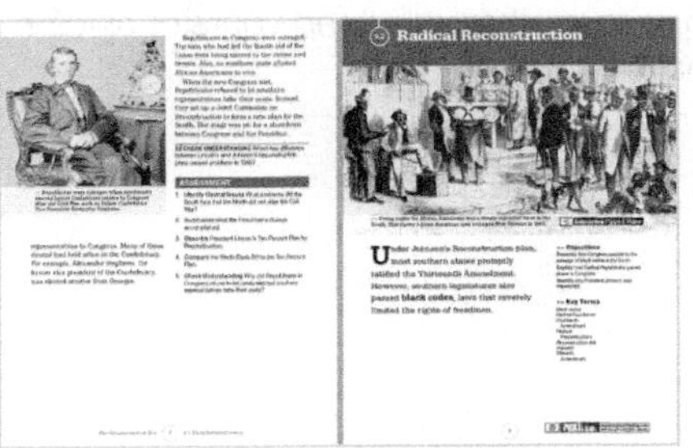

INVESTIGATE

DIGITAL TEXT 1

Reconstruction Difficulties Persist

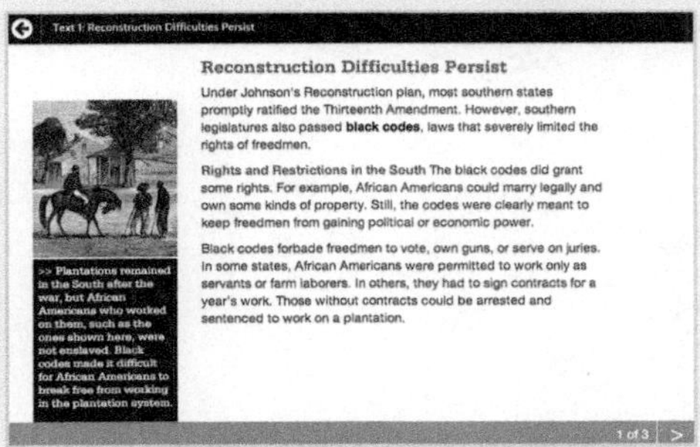

Text 1: Reconstruction Difficulties Persist
Reconstruction Difficulties Persist
Under Johnson's Reconstruction plan, most southern states promptly ratified the Thirteenth Amendment. However, southern legislatures also passed black codes, laws that severely limited the rights of freedmen.
Rights and Restrictions in the South The black codes did grant some rights. For example, African Americans could marry legally and own some kinds of property. Still, the codes were clearly meant to keep freedmen from gaining political or economic power.
Black codes forbade freedmen to vote, own guns, or serve on juries. In some states, African Americans were permitted to work only as servants or farm laborers. In others, they had to sign contracts for a year's work. Those without contracts could be arrested and sentenced to work on a plantation.
>> Plantations remained in the South after the war, but African Americans who worked on them, such as the ones shown here, were not enslaved. Black codes made it difficult for African Americans to break free from working in the plantation system.
1 of 3

Objective 1: Describe how Congress reacted to the passage of black codes in the South.

Quick Instruction

Project the image of African American sharecroppers on the whiteboard. Define the black codes as laws that severely limited the rights of freedmen. Discuss how the black codes impacted African Americans by making it harder to escape the plantation system.

Summarize How did Radical Republicans react to the black codes passed in the South? *(Radical Republicans thought Reconstruction had been too lenient. They believed Reconstruction policies didn't force the South to change its politics, allowing the states to pass unjust laws. Radical Republicans vowed to take control of Reconstruction.)*

ELL Use the ELL activity described in the ELL chart.

Further Instruction

Go through the Interactive Reading Notepad questions and discuss the answers with the class. Be sure students understand the effects of Lincoln's and Johnson's Reconstruction plans and the causes of Radical Reconstruction.

Support Ideas with Examples How did the black codes impact African Americans socially, economically, and politically? Provide examples for support. *(The codes limited freedmen's political power by preventing them from voting or holding public office. In many states the codes limited their economic power by allowing them to work only as servants or farm laborers. They had to sign contracts or be forced to work on a plantation. Socially, the codes kept freedmen from achieving equality.)*

Identify Cause and Effect Describe the social and political problems during Reconstruction that caused Radical Republicans to seek control of Congress. *(Black codes limited the rights of freedmen; violence broke out against African Americans in Memphis and New Orleans; Johnson ignored a report by the Joint Committee on Reconstruction about conditions in the South.)*

Radical Reconstruction

DIGITAL TEXT 2

Reforms of the Radical Reconstruction Congress

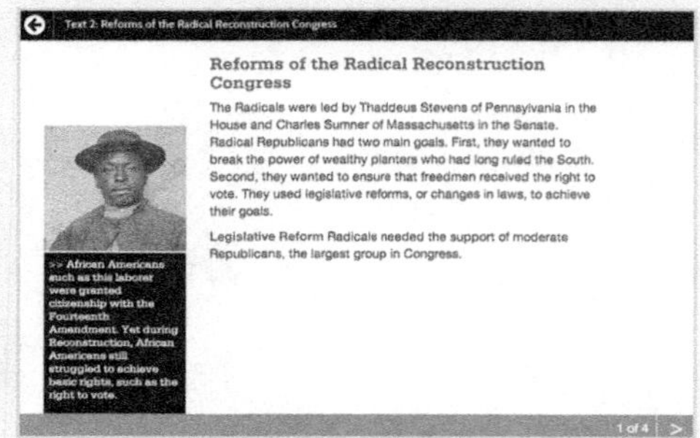

Objective 2: **Explain how Radical Republicans gained power in Congress.**

Quick Instruction

Project the image of the African American laborer. Explain that the Radical Reconstruction Congress passed a number of legislative reforms, including Constitutional amendments, that impacted African Americans during Reconstruction.

Make Generalizations What were the effects of the Radical Reconstruction Congress on Reconstruction? *(Reconstruction became harsher toward the South. The South had to follow more reforms. Legislation passed to ensure greater equality for African Americans.)*

D Differentiate: Extra Support The Radical Reconstruction Congress wanted a tougher approach toward the South. Explain that radical can mean *thorough, different,* or *extreme*. It can also refer to a complete social or political change. Have students give one example of a reform that the Radical Reconstruction Congress passed and explain why it was considered radical.

Further Instruction

Go through the Interactive Reading Notepad questions and discuss the answers with the class.

Draw Conclusions Describe the impact of the Fourteenth Amendment on life in the United States. *(The amendment protected the citizenship of African Americans. It overturned the Dred Scott ruling and made it illegal to deny voting rights to African Americans on the basis of race. However, the amendment did not fully protect the rights of African Americans or change the discrimination African Americans faced until many years later.)*

Evaluate Arguments Evaluate the legislative reform programs of the Radical Reconstruction Congress. Were the Civil Rights Act of 1866 and the Fourteenth Amendment effective? Why or why not? *(the reforms were not effective in combating discrimination and ensuring equality at the time. However, they set an important foundation for African Americans to achieve greater rights as citizens in the future.)*

DIGITAL TEXT 3

Political and Social Problems During Reconstruction

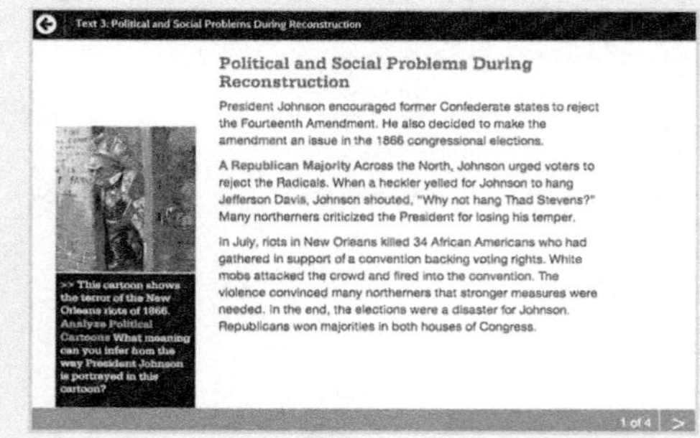

Objective 3: **Identify why President Johnson was impeached.**

Quick Instruction

Interactive Chart: Legislation and Reform During Reconstruction Project the interactive chart and read through the tiles. Have students fill in the chart and discuss their answers.

Interactive Gallery: The Massacre of New Orleans Project the interactive gallery about the Massacre of New Orleans. What political problems does the cartoon depict? *(the failed policies of Reconstruction; disagreements between Johnson and the Radical Republicans; ongoing violence against African Americans in the South)*

ACTIVE CLASSROOM

Ask students to complete a Make Headlines Activity. Have students write a headline that captures a main idea associated with the Massacre of New Orleans. Ask: If you were to write a headline right now that captured the most important aspect of the Massacre of New Orleans, what would that headline be? Pass your headline to a partner for them to review—they can keep yours or ask for theirs back.

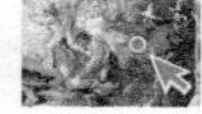

INTERACTIVE GALLERY

The Massacre of New Orleans

DIGITAL TEXT 4

Political Problems and a New President

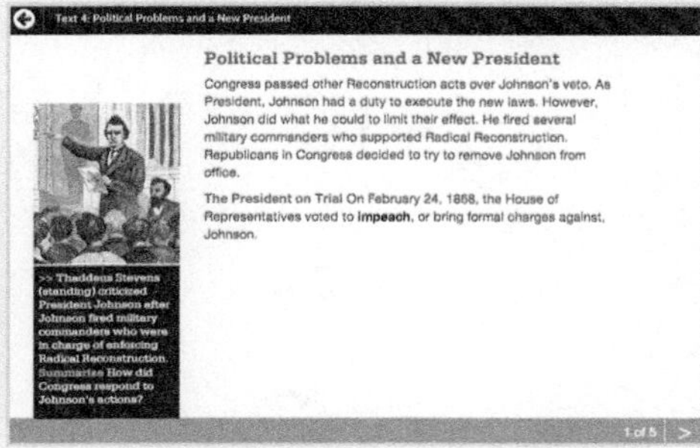

ACTIVE CLASSROOM

Have students use the Sticky Notes Strategy and spend three minutes jotting down their response to this question on sticky notes: "Why did the Radical Reconstruction Congress impose additional legislative reforms on the South?" Ask students to post their sticky notes on the board or on chart paper and look at the various responses. Discuss similarities and differences in the responses as a group.

ELL Use the ELL activity described in the ELL chart.

Further Instruction

Go through the Interactive Reading Notepad questions and discuss the answers with the class.

Compare the impacts of the Fourteenth and Fifteenth Amendments. How were these amendments intended to address social and political problems during Reconstruction? Why were their impacts limited? *(Fourteenth—African Americans were citizens. Fifteenth—citizens could not be denied the right to vote based on race. The amendments were meant to grant social and political equality to African Americans but states found ways around them initially.)*

Summarize What were the Military Reconstruction Acts of 1867 and how did they impact southern whites, northern Republicans, and African Americans? *(The Acts divided southern states into military districts. Southern whites had less power to rule themselves, especially since former Confederates could not vote. African Americans had their right to vote protected by the army. Northern Republicans won state elections because African Americans voted Republican while many southern whites were not allowed to vote or refused in protest.)*

Identify Cause and Effect Describe the causes and effects of political tensions between President Johnson and Congress. *(Causes—Johnson opposed Radical Reconstruction and vetoed the Reconstruction Act. Congress passed other acts over his veto, but Johnson tried to limit their effects. Effects—Johnson fired military commanders who supported Radical Reconstruction, so Republicans tried to impeach him. Republican Ulysses S. Grant easily won the 1868 presidential election.)*

Radical Reconstruction

SYNTHESIZE

DIGITAL ACTIVITY

The Effects of Radical Republicans in Congress

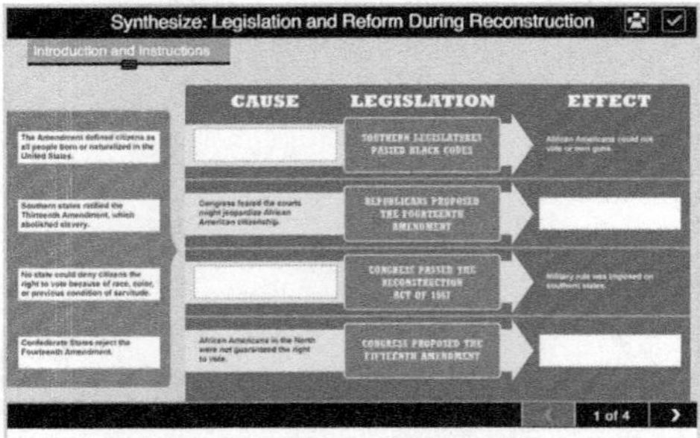

Have students complete the concept web and choose one of the changes to write about. Have students share their webs with a partner and discuss their responses.

Discuss Have students review the answers they wrote at the beginning of the lesson about why the black codes led Republicans to take charge of Reconstruction in the South. Ask how they would revise or add to their answers now that they have learned more about the rise of Radical Reconstruction. Discuss the additional factors that caused the Radical Reconstruction Congress to come to the power and the effects this had on the nation.

DEMONSTRATE

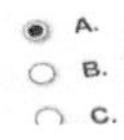

DIGITAL QUIZ

Lesson Quiz and Class Discussion Board

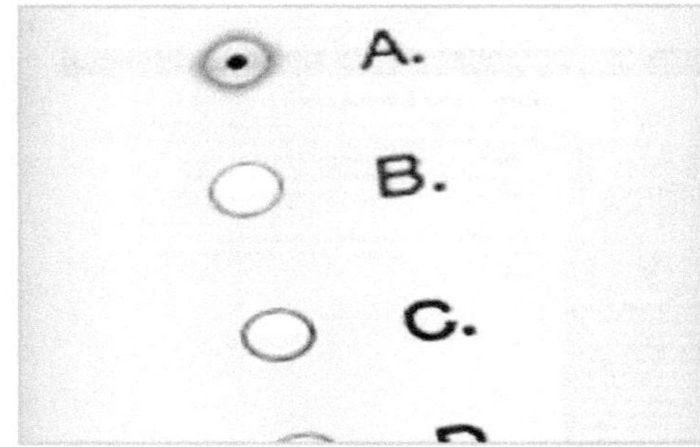

Assign the online Lesson Quiz for this lesson if you haven't already done so. Students will be offered automatic remediation or enrichment based on their score.

Pose these questions to the class on the Discussion Board:

Identify Cause and Effect How did the Fourteenth and Fifteenth Amendments impact the rise of the Republicans in state and federal government?

Evaluate Arguments Do you think Republicans were right to impose harsher Reconstruction policies than President Johnson against the South following the Civil War? Explain your reasoning, providing examples for support.

Topic Inquiry

Have students continue their investigations for the Topic Inquiry.

www.PearsonRealize.com
Access your Digital Lesson

Reconstruction and Southern Society

Supporting English Language Learners

Use with Digital Text 1, **New Political Groups in the South.**

Speaking

Explain that using a variety of sentence types adds clarity and interest to spoken language. Review the four main sentence types (exclamatory, interrogative, imperative, declarative), and prompt students to practice speaking using terms from the text, with the goal of increasing their speaking accuracy and ease.

Beginning Briefly summarize information presented in the text about scalawags. Ask students to say a declarative sentence that borrows information from your summary.

Intermediate Say a declarative sentence about the scalawags, and ask students to say an interrogative sentence that borrows information from it (or has the declarative sentence as its answer). Encourage students to use a rising inflection at the end of their questions.

Advanced Ask: Why might carpetbaggers have moved to the South? Have pairs of students practice using the exclamatory sentence type as they answer this question.

Advanced High Ask pairs of students to discuss what motivated carpetbaggers to move to the South. Encourage each partner to use a variety of sentence types during the discussion by including each type at least once.

Use with Digital Text 3, **Political Problems and Legislative Reform.**

Writing

Display the text's second paragraph, and highlight each sentence in a different color. Point out the variety of sentence lengths. Have students write using a variety of grade-appropriate sentence lengths in increasingly accurate ways.

Beginning Display these sentences: After the war, the South built _____. Taxes also _____. Have students use words or phrases to create sentences of varying lengths and write the sentences down.

Intermediate Ask pairs of students to write about Reconstruction in the South using a variety of grade-appropriate sentence lengths. Have them include a sentence under five words, one between five and nine words, and one of at least ten words (which could consist of two independent clauses).

Advanced Ask pairs of students to write a cohesive paragraph about Reconstruction in the South using a variety of grade-appropriate sentence lengths. Encourage them to include one sentence under five words and one of at least ten words.

Advanced High Ask students to write a cohesive paragraph about Reconstruction in the South using a variety of grade-appropriate sentence lengths. Then have partners read each other's work and discuss not only the variety of sentence lengths, but also how they are distributed within the paragraph.

D Differentiate Instruction

Use the Differentiated Instruction notes throughout the lesson plan to support the varied skill sets, levels of readiness, and interests in the mixed-ability classroom.

Challenge These notes include suggestions for expanding the activity for advanced students.

On-Level These notes include suggestions for modifying the activity to address different interests or learning styles.

Extra Support These notes include ideas for providing more scaffolding or reading spupport.

Special Needs These notes provide ideas for adapting instruction to support the needs of various special needs students.

NOTES

Reconstruction and Southern Society

Objectives

Objective 1: Identify new forces in southern politics.

Objective 2: Describe how southern conservatives resisted Reconstruction.

Objective 3: Analyze the economic, political, and social challenges facing Reconstruction governments.

Objective 4: Explain why sharecropping led to a cycle of poverty.

LESSON 3 ORGANIZER	PACING: APPROX. 1 PERIOD, .5 BLOCKS			
	OBJECTIVES	PACING	RESOURCES Online	RESOURCES Print
Connect				
DIGITAL START UP ACTIVITY **Social, Political, and Economic Challenges in the South**		5 min.	●	
Investigate				
DIGITAL TEXT 1 **New Political Groups in the South**	Objective 1	10 min.	●	●
DIGITAL TEXT 2 **Conservatives Resist Reform**	Objective 2	10 min.	●	●
INTERACTIVE GALLERY **Reconstruction-Era Political Groups**	Objective 2	10 min.	●	
DIGITAL TEXT 3 **Political Problems and Legislative Reform**	Objective 3	10 min.	●	●
DIGITAL TEXT 4 **Economic Problems During Reconstruction**	Objective 4	10 min.	●	●
INTERACTIVE CHART **The Cycle of Poverty**	Objective 4	10 min.	●	
Synthesize				
DIGITAL ACTIVITY **Differing Views of Reconstruction**		5 min.	●	
Demonstrate				
DIGITAL QUIZ **Lesson Quiz and Class Discussion Board**		10 min.	●	

PEARSON realize™ www.PearsonRealize.com

Go online to access additional resources including:
Primary Sources • Biographies • Supreme Court cases • 21st Century Skill Tutorials • Maps • Graphic Organizers.

CONNECT

DIGITAL START UP ACTIVITY

Social, Political, and Economic Challenges in the South

Project the Start Up Activity Ask students to read the activity and write down their responses as they enter and get settled. Have students share their responses with a partner, either in class or through a blog space.

Discuss Write down one social problem, one political problem, and one economic problem that you think the South will continue to face as Reconstruction progresses. *(racial inequality; conflicts with Republicans in power in state and federal governments; the cost of rebuilding.)* Then make a prediction about how you think one of these problems will affect life in the reconstructed states. *(African Americans will face discrimination and violence; southern whites will seek to regain power; the South will diversify its industries in an effort to make the economy grow)*

Aa Vocabulary Development: Use the Interactive Reading Notepad to preview the Key Terms and Academic Vocabulary in this lesson with students.

FLIP IT!

Assign the Flipped Video for this lesson.

STUDENT EDITION PRINT PAGES: 506–512

INVESTIGATE

DIGITAL TEXT 1

New Political Groups in the South

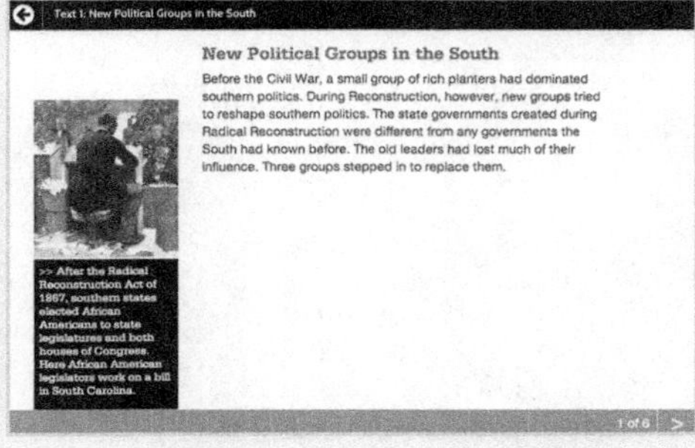

Objective 1: Identify new forces in southern politics.

Quick Instruction

Project the image of Hiram Rhodes Revels, the nation's first African American senator. Discuss the ways in which Revels's election impacted the nation.

Summarize Identify the three new groups that took over southern politics during Reconstruction. *(Scalawags—white southern Republicans, largely businesspeople rebuilding the South. Carpetbaggers—northerners who came to the South for profit, to help freedmen, and because they loved the land. African Americans—voted in large numbers for the first time and were elected to public offices.)*

ELL Use the ELL activity described in the ELL chart.

Further Instruction

Go through the Interactive Reading Notepad questions and discuss the answers with the class. To extend the lesson assign the Biography: Hiram Rhodes Revels.

Compare Points of View Contrast the views of white southern Democrats and white southern Republicans on Reconstruction, citing evidence for support. *(White southern Democrats did not support Reconstruction, as evidenced by their use of the derogatory term scalawags to describe white southern Republicans who did. White southern Democrats thought the scalawags were traitors. White southern Republicans supported Reconstruction because many of them had opposed secession and wanted to forget the war and rebuild.)*

Analyze Information Reread the last paragraph of the text. Evaluate the impact of Hiram Rhodes Revels's election in light of what you learned. *(Revels's election was a significant victory that reflected the social and political changes taking place in the South, but it did not change the fact that African Americans still faced discrimination and had a limited voice in government.)*

Topic 9 Lesson 3

Reconstruction and Southern Society

DIGITAL TEXT 2

Conservatives Resist Reform

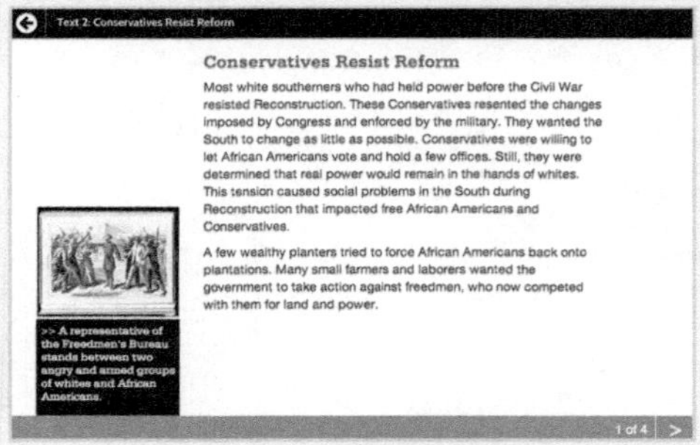

Text 2: Conservatives Resist Reform
Conservatives Resist Reform
Most white southerners who had held power before the Civil War resisted Reconstruction. These Conservatives resented the changes imposed by Congress and enforced by the military. They wanted the South to change as little as possible. Conservatives were willing to let African Americans vote and hold a few offices. Still, they were determined that real power would remain in the hands of whites. This tension caused social problems in the South during Reconstruction that impacted free African Americans and Conservatives.
A few wealthy planters tried to force African Americans back onto plantations. Many small farmers and laborers wanted the government to take action against freedmen, who now competed with them for land and power.
>> A representative of the Freedmen's Bureau stands between two angry and armed groups of whites and African Americans.
1 of 4

INTERACTIVE GALLERY

Reconstruction-Era Political Groups

DIGITAL TEXT 3

Political Problems and Legislative Reform

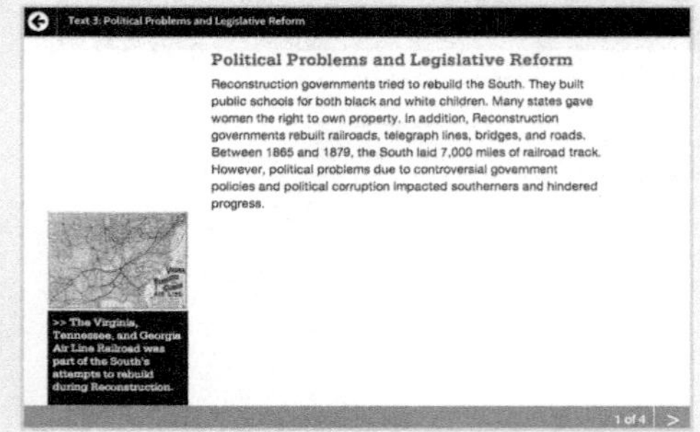

Objective 2: **Describe how southern Conservatives resisted Reconstruction.**

Quick Instruction

Interactive Gallery: Reconstruction-Era Political Groups Project the interactive gallery on the whiteboard and click through the images. Identify the different points of view of Republicans and Democrats on Reconstruction.

Cite Evidence that southern Conservatives opposed Reconstruction, and why. *("These Conservatives resented the changes imposed by Congress and enforced by the military. They wanted the South to change as little as possible.")*

ACTIVE CLASSROOM

Have students use Cartoon It Strategy and create a quick copy of one compelling image from the text or the interactive gallery. Have students turn their image into a political cartoon that illustrates a key concept or main idea about the Reconstruction-era political groups.

D Differentiate: Extra Support Explain to students that the terms Republican and Democratic did not have the same meaning in the 1800s as they do today. Have students review the text and identify the points of view of Republicans and Democrats during Reconstruction.

Further Instruction

Go through the Interactive Reading Notepad questions and discuss the answers with the class.

Draw Conclusions What social, political, and economic factors do you think caused the rise of conservative feelings in the South? *(Social—the strong measures taken by Republicans to change southern society led to resentment. Many southerners saw the Republicans as outsiders. Political—Conservatives wanted to return to a time when they held power. Economic—planters wanted African Americans to work on plantations and small farmers and laborers did not want to compete with African Americans for jobs.)*

Summarize the social and political impact of the Ku Klux Klan on African Americans in the South. *(Klan members terrorized African Americans, making many people afraid to vote.)*

Analyze Information Reread the quotes from the U.S. Senator and African American voters in the text. Based on this evidence, explain the social and political problems that emerged during this portion of Reconstruction and evaluate the impact on southern whites and African Americans. *(Southern whites felt the country belonged to them and did not want to share political power with African Americans. Secret societies like the KKK used violence and fear to keep African Americans and white allies from voting and holding office.)*

Objective 3: **Analyze the economic, political, and social challenges facing Reconstruction governments.**

Quick Instruction

Project the image on the whiteboard and discuss the steps Reconstruction governments took to rebuild the South.

Summarize Give three examples of how Reconstruction governments brought improvements to southern states. *(They built public schools, gave women the right to own property in many states, and rebuilt infrastructure including railroads, telegraph lines, bridges, and railroads.)*

Draw Conclusions What political problems hindered progress of rebuilding in the South? *(There was political corruption within governments and some former Confederates were taxed without representation. Voting rights also remained an issue, particularly for African Americans.)*

Support Ideas with Evidence How did economic differences between the North and South affect attitudes toward Reconstruction? Cite evidence for support. *(Reconstruction raised taxes, creating resentment among southerners. The financial burden caused some landowners to lose their land. Southerners also opposed corruption by Reconstruction governments.)*

ELL Use the ELL activity described in the ELL chart.

Further Instruction

Go through the Interactive Reading Notepad questions and discuss the answers with the class.

Draw Conclusions Identify the legislative reform programs of the reconstructed state governments and evaluate whether they were effective in rebuilding southern states. *(New state constitutions put in place adult male suffrage, took away restrictions for holding office, reinstated elections for public officials, and increased power of the executive branches. These measures allowed the southern states to form new governments but did not lead to changes in the power structure, as states imposed new voting restrictions against African Americans, allowed former Confederates to vote and hold office, and forced African Americans from office.)*

DIGITAL TEXT 4

Economic Problems During Reconstruction

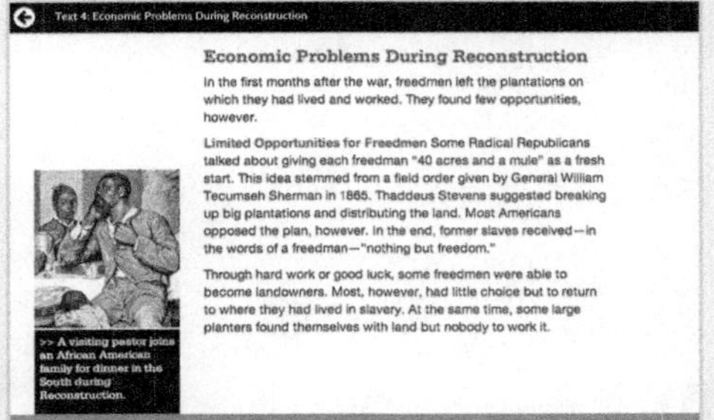

Objective 4: **Explain why sharecropping led to a cycle of poverty.**

Quick Instruction

Interactive Chart: The Cycle of Poverty Project the interactive chart and have students read through the tiles. Discuss the ways in which sharecropping created a cycle of poverty for African Americans and poor whites.

Generate Explanations Explain the economic problems African Americans and poor white southerners faced that led them to become sharecroppers. *(African Americans left plantations after the Civil War but did not have other economic opportunities. Most African Americans and poor whites did not have money to become landowners and so had to rent land as sharecroppers instead.)*

ACTIVE CLASSROOM

Have students use the Write 1-Get 3 Strategy to answer the question: What are 4 key characteristics of sharecropping? Have students take a piece of paper and fold it into quarters, write down 1 response in the first box, and then go around room asking to hear other responses. If they think a response is correct, have them write it in one of their boxes until they have three more responses on their page. Call on students to share their responses with class.

INTERACTIVE CHART

The Cycle of Poverty

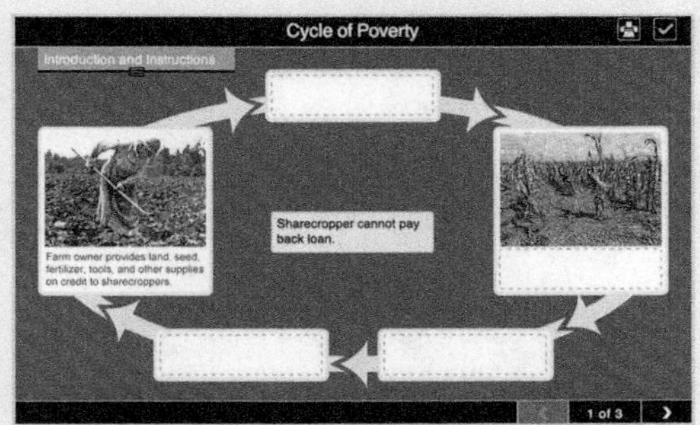

Further Instruction

Go through the Interactive Reading Notepad questions and discuss the answers with the class.

Analyze Information Describe the effects of Reconstruction on economic opportunities for African Americans. Why did one freedman say those who had been enslaved received "nothing but freedom"? *(Reconstruction did not create many new economic opportunities for African Americans. They had little chance to become landowners and work their way out of poverty. The freedman meant that African Americans had received freedom but no additional opportunities or support to help them become self-sufficient.)*

Identify Cause and Effect Describe the positive and negative effects of sharecropping on African Americans. *(They had greater independence and could hope to become landowners, but many instead fell into debt.)*

Reconstruction and Southern Society

SYNTHESIZE

DIGITAL ACTIVITY

Differing Views of Reconstruction

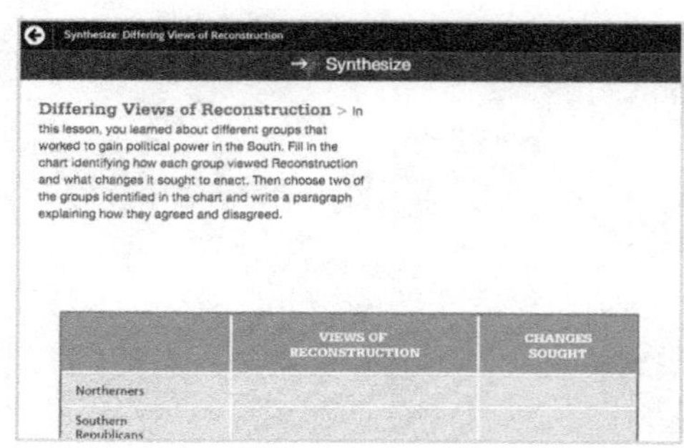

Have students fill in the chart and choose two of the groups to write about. Have students share their charts with a partner and discuss their responses.

Discuss Have students review the predictions they made at the beginning of the lesson about the social, political, and economic problems the South faced as Reconstruction progressed. Ask students how accurate their predictions were and whether they would revise their list of problems now that they have learned more. Have students discuss how the problems they listed were addressed during Reconstruction.

DEMONSTRATE

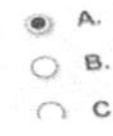

DIGITAL QUIZ

Lesson Quiz and Class Discussion Board

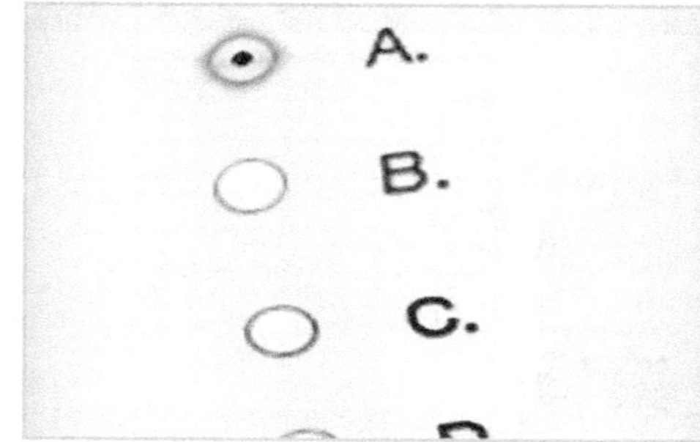

Assign the online Lesson Quiz for this lesson if you haven't already done so. Students will be offered automatic remediation or enrichment based on their score.

Pose these questions to the class on the Discussion Board:

Identify Cause and Effect How did Reconstruction cause the political landscape of the South to change?

Summarize What social, political, and economic problems did African Americans continue to face during Reconstruction?

Topic Inquiry

Have students continue their investigations for the Topic Inquiry.

The Aftermath of Reconstruction

Supporting English Language Learners

Use with Digital Text 1, **Reconstruction Ends.**

Speaking

Explain that using a variety of connecting words can make spoken language easier to follow.

Beginning Display and read aloud the last sentence of the text's second paragraph. Explain how the word *but* shows that the two independent clauses contradict each other. Then have students complete and say this sentence: Tilden won the popular vote, but _____.

Intermediate Display and read aloud the last sentence of the text's second paragraph. Explain that *but* connects contradictory ideas, while *and* suggests agreement. Have students complete and say this sentence two ways: Congress passed the Amnesty Act, but/and _____.

Advanced Explain the use of *however*, both at the beginning and in the middle of sentences. Then have pairs of students discuss the 1876 election using *however* in both the beginning and middle of sentences.

Advanced High Point out the phrase *at the same time* used in the text's third and last paragraphs. Then have students use the phrases, *as well as*, *but*, and *however* in a discussion about the end of Reconstruction. Ask: Can you use *but*, *however*, and *as well as* interchangeably? Why or why not?

Use with Digital Text 3, **The "New South" Moves Toward Industry.**

Writing

Explain that knowing a variety of sentence patterns can help students write original, grammatically correct sentences on any topic.

Beginning Display these sentences: Cotton is important. Cotton is a crop. Explain that *important* and *crop* describe *cotton*. Then have students complete these sentences with descriptive words or phrases and write them down: Henry Grady was _____. James Duke was _____.

Intermediate Display this sentence: Cotton production recovered _____. Ask: What words or phrases could be added to describe how, when, or where cotton production recovered? Have students complete and write down the sentence three different ways.

Advanced Display this sentence: James Duke used new machinery in North Carolina. Point out the subject, verb, object, and adverbial phrase. Then have pairs of students write additional sentences about the "New South" using this sentence pattern.

Advanced High Display this sentence: In the South, textiles gave the economy a boost. Discuss how the phrase in the South could be relocated to the end of the sentence, as well as how the direct and indirect objects might be reversed. Then have students create additional sentences about the "New South" using this sentence pattern and its variations.

D Differentiate Instruction

Use the Differentiated Instruction notes throughout the lesson plan to support the varied skill sets, levels of readiness, and interests in the mixed-ability classroom.

Challenge These notes include suggestions for expanding the activity for advanced students.

On-Level These notes include suggestions for modifying the activity to address different interests or learning styles.

Extra Support These notes include ideas for providing more scaffolding or reading spuport.

Special Needs These notes provide ideas for adapting instruction to support the needs of various special needs students.

NOTES

The Aftermath of Reconstruction

Objectives

Objective 1: Summarize the events that led to the end of Reconstruction.

Objective 2: Explain how the rights of African Americans were restricted in the South after Reconstruction.

Objective 3: Identify industries that flourished in the "New South."

LESSON 4 ORGANIZER	PACING: APPROX. 1 PERIOD, .5 BLOCKS		RESOURCES	
	OBJECTIVES	PACING	Online	Print
Connect				
DIGITAL START UP ACTIVITY **The Rise of Segregation**		5 min.	●	
Investigate				
DIGITAL TEXT 1 **Reconstruction Ends**	Objective 1	10 min.	●	●
DIGITAL TEXT 2 **New Legislation Restricts African American Rights**	Objective 2	10 min.	●	●
INTERACTIVE TIMELINE **Oppression of African Americans**		10 min.	●	
DIGITAL TEXT 3 **The "New South" Moves Toward Industry**	Objective 3	10 min.	●	●
BEFORE AND AFTER **Change in Southern Industry**		10 min.	●	
Synthesize				
DIGITAL ACTIVITY **The Effects of Reconstruction**		5 min.	●	
Demonstrate				
DIGITAL QUIZ **Lesson Quiz and Class Discussion Board**		10 min.	●	

Go online to access additional resources including:
Primary Sources • Biographies • Supreme Court cases • 21st Century Skill Tutorials • Maps • Graphic Organizers.

CONNECT

DIGITAL START UP ACTIVITY

The Rise of Segregation

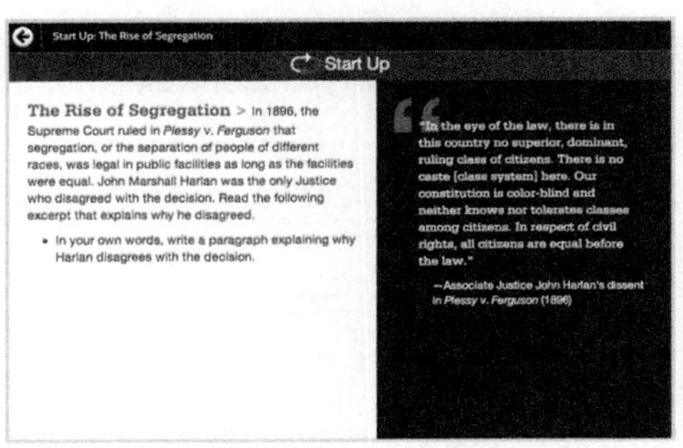

Project the Start Up Activity Ask students to read the quote and write down their response as they enter and get settled. Have students share their responses with a partner, either in class or through a blog space.

Discuss In your own words, write a paragraph explaining why Harlan disagreed with the decision. *(Harlan believed the Constitution applies equally to all citizens. He did not think segregating people based on race was legal because it treated citizens differently under the law.)*

Tell students that in this lesson they will be learning about the political, social, and economic impact of Reconstruction following the end of the Reconstruction Era.

Aa Vocabulary Development: Use the Interactive Reading Notepad to preview the Key Terms and Academic Vocabulary in this lesson with students.

FLIP IT!

Assign the Flipped Video for this lesson.

STUDENT EDITION PRINT PAGES: 513–518

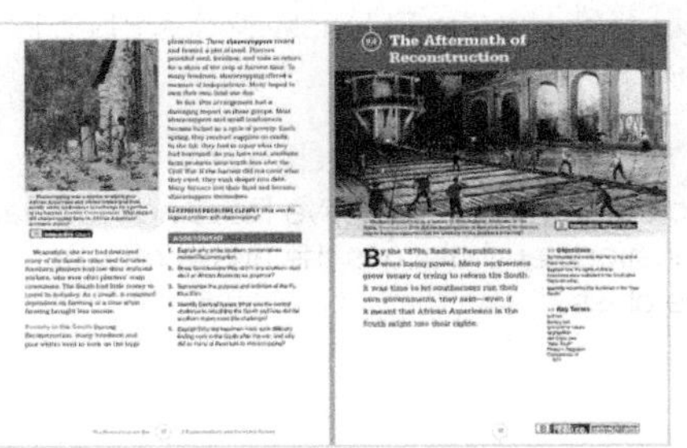

INVESTIGATE

DIGITAL TEXT 1

Reconstruction Ends

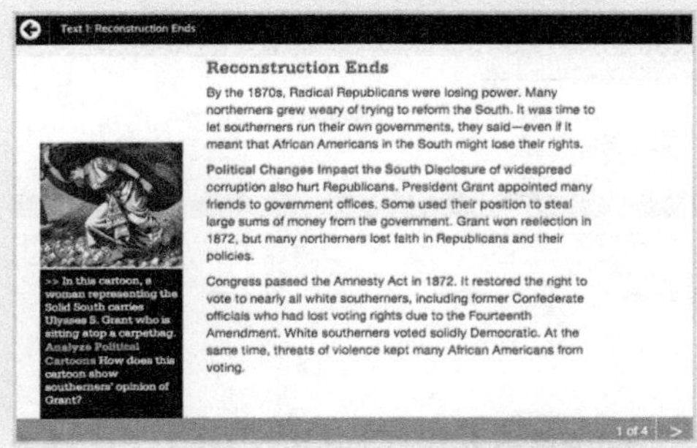

Objective 1: Summarize the events that led to the end of Reconstruction.

Quick Instruction

Project the image of the political cartoon on the whiteboard and have students describe what they see. Ask students to use the cartoon to make a prediction about how attitudes toward Reconstruction will lead to the end of this era.

Summarize What factors caused Reconstruction to end? *(Radical Republicans were losing power; many northerners did not want to keep trying to reform the South; corruption hurt the Republican party; Hayes won the presidential election and agreed to end Reconstruction if the South did not contest his victory.)*

ELL Use the ELL activity described in the ELL chart.

Further Instruction

Go through the Interactive Reading Notepad questions and discuss the answers with the class.

Infer Evaluate the legislative reform programs of the reconstructed state governments and their impact based on the following sentence: "It was time to let southerners run their own governments, they said—even if it meant that African Americans in the South might lose their rights." *(The sentence suggests the legislative reform programs did not have a lasting impact if rights for African Americans were eroded as soon as Reconstruction came to an end.)*

Identify Cause and Effect Explain the causes and effects of the Democratic rise to power in the South. *(Causes—Congress passed the Amnesty Act giving nearly all white southerners the right to vote, and they voted solidly Democratic. Threats of violence kept many African Americans who would have voted Republican from the polls. Effects—Democrats became a powerful bloc and won the popular vote in the presidential election. They agreed to give the disputed election to Hayes in exchange for an end to Reconstruction. The Democratic party became a stronghold in the South and African Americans lost most political rights.)*

Topic 9 Lesson 4

The Aftermath of Reconstruction

DIGITAL TEXT 2

New Legislation Restricts African American Rights

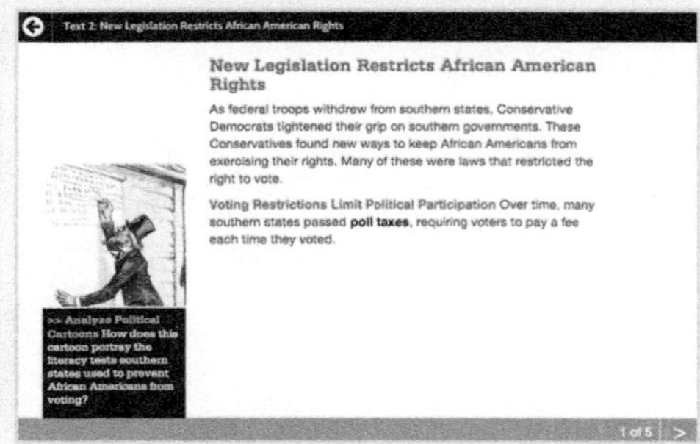

Objective 2: Explain how the rights of African Americans were restricted in the South after Reconstruction.

Quick Instruction

Interactive Timeline: Oppression of African Americans Project the interactive timeline and read through the events. Discuss the political problems that led to the erosion of African American rights.

Support Ideas with Examples Give three examples of new laws passed in the South and explain their impact on African Americans. *(poll taxes—required voters to pay to vote; kept poor people, including many African Americans, from voting. Literacy tests—required voters to read and explain a section of the Constitution; many African Americans had little education and could not pass the tests. Grandfather clauses—if voters had a father or grandfather eligible to vote in 1867, they were exempt from the literacy test; allowed illiterate white voters to vote but not African Americans; Jim Crow laws—instituted segregation.)*

ACTIVE CLASSROOM

Have students take 30 seconds and use the Quick Write Strategy to write down their responses to the quote by George Washington Cable about segregation.

INTERACTIVE TIMELINE

Oppression of African Americans

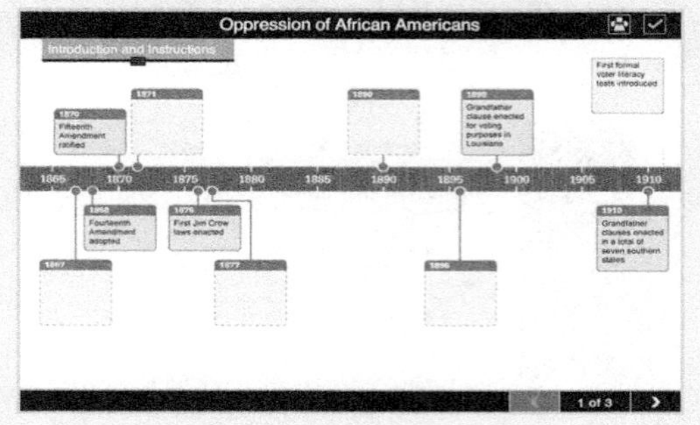

D Differentiate: Extra Support Explain to students that to segregate means to separate or isolate. Have them explain the system of segregation in their own words.

Further Instruction

Go through the Interactive Reading Notepad questions and discuss the answers with the class. To extend the lesson assign the Landmark Supreme Court Case: *Plessy* v. *Ferguson*.

Summarize How did the Plessy case address conflicts between African Americans and southern whites? *(The case legalized segregation, creating separate facilities for African Americans and whites and ensuring discrimination would continue.)*

Draw Conclusions What were the effects of Reconstruction on African Americans' social and political rights? *(African Americans wound up losing many of the rights they had gained in the early years of Reconstruction. Laws kept them from voting and segregation was used to prevent social equality.)*

DIGITAL TEXT 3

The "New South" Moves Toward Industry

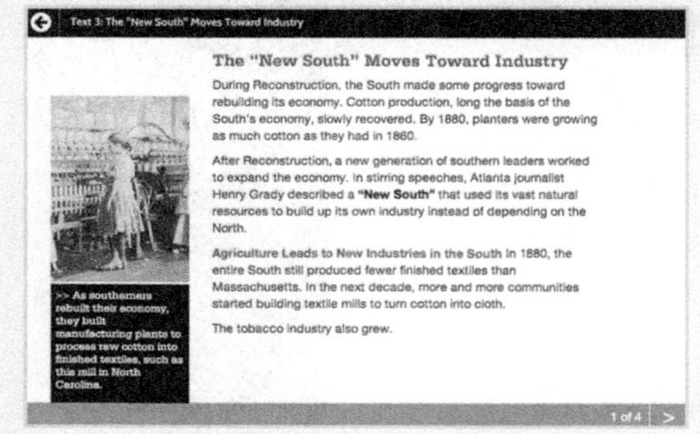

Objective 3: Identify industries that flourished in the "New South."

Quick Instruction

Before and After: Change in Southern Industry Project the interactive activity on the whiteboard and move the slider to show the changes. Have students locate the new southern industries on the map.

Identify Cause and Effect How did the Civil War and Reconstruction cause the South to develop new industries? *(The war destroyed many farms and plantations and ended the plantation system; even when cotton production recovered, southerners wanted to build up southern industry instead of depending on the North.)*

ACTIVE CLASSROOM

Pair students and have them use the See-Think-Wonder Strategy to study the interactive map. Have students use the slider to view both maps. Then ask: What do you see? What does that make you think? What are you wondering about now that you've seen this? Have students share their insights with the class.

ELL Use the ELL activity described in the ELL chart.

Further Instruction

Go through the Interactive Reading Notepad questions and discuss the answers with the class.

BEFORE AND AFTER

Change in Southern Industry

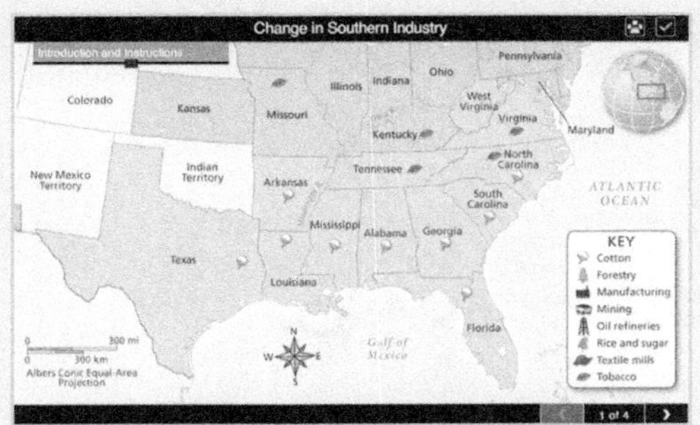

Draw Conclusions How did the physical characteristics of the environment influence economic activities in the South during the nineteenth century? *(The South developed industries based on its natural resources. It grew cotton and tobacco, mined for minerals, and developed industries in oil and steel. The South also built factories to take advantage of its lumber supply.)*

Summarize Describe the positive consequences of human modification of the physical environment on the South. *(Clearing land, using natural resources, and building farms and factories provided jobs and opportunities that helped the economy recover after the war.)*

SYNTHESIZE

DIGITAL ACTIVITY

The Effects of Reconstruction

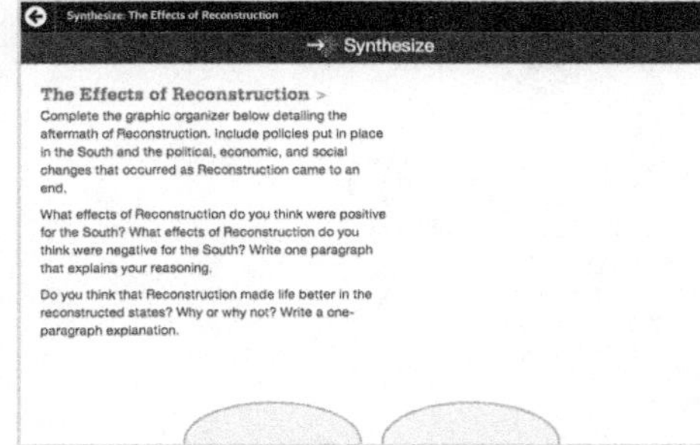

Synthesize: The Effects of Reconstruction
Synthesize
The Effects of Reconstruction
Complete the graphic organizer below detailing the aftermath of Reconstruction. Include policies put in place in the South and the political, economic, and social changes that occurred as Reconstruction came to an end.
What effects of Reconstruction do you think were positive for the South? What effects of Reconstruction do you think were negative for the South? Write one paragraph that explains your reasoning.
Do you think that Reconstruction made life better in the reconstructed states? Why or why not? Write a one-paragraph explanation.

Have students fill in the graphic organizer and answer the questions. Have students share their graphic organizers with a partner and discuss their answers.

Discuss Have students share their views about the overall effectiveness of Reconstruction and the ways it changed life in the South. Ask students to consider the effects of Reconstruction on white southerners and African Americans, and how it impacted relations between the North and South. Remind students to use examples to support their views.

DEMONSTRATE

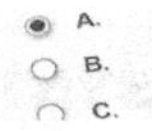

DIGITAL QUIZ

Lesson Quiz and Class Discussion Board

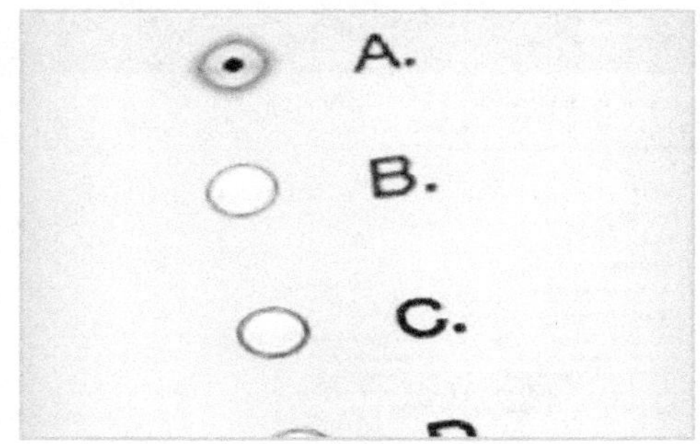

Assign the online Lesson Quiz for this lesson if you haven't already done so. Students will be offered automatic remediation or enrichment based on their score.

Pose these questions to the class on the Discussion Board:

Identify Central Issues Why did Reconstruction come to a close? What were the effects of its ending?

Make Generalizations How did Reconstruction change life for African Americans socially and politically?

Identify Patterns In what ways did a "New South" develop following the Civil War?

Topic Inquiry

Have students continue their investigations for the Topic Inquiry.

The Reconstruction Era

SYNTHESIZE

DIGITAL ACTIVITY

Reflect on the Essential Question and Topic

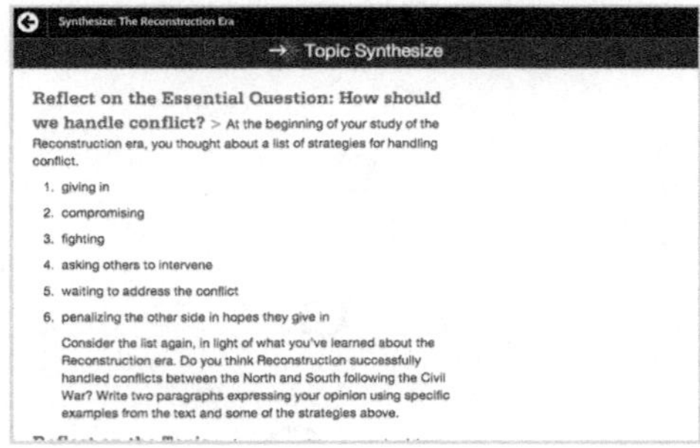

First ask students to reconsider the Essential Question for this topic: How should we handle conflict? Have students consider the list of strategies for handling conflict in light of what they have learned. Then ask students to answer the question using specific examples and at least two of the strategies.

Ask students, "What were the conflicts that arose during Reconstruction? How were they resolved?" Have students give examples from the topic. Discuss their responses as a class or ask students to post their answers on the Class Discussion Board.

Next ask students to reflect on the topic as a whole and write down three important changes that Reconstruction and westward expansion brought, and how each of these changes shaped the nation. Give students the following examples of changes to help them get started:

1. changes in political leadership
2. economic developments
3. new legislation
4. social shifts
5. advancements and setbacks to civil rights
6. population, migration, and settlement patterns

Topic Inquiry

Have students complete Step 3 of the Topic Inquiry.

DEMONSTRATE

DIGITAL TOPIC REVIEW AND ASSESSMENT

The Reconstruction Era

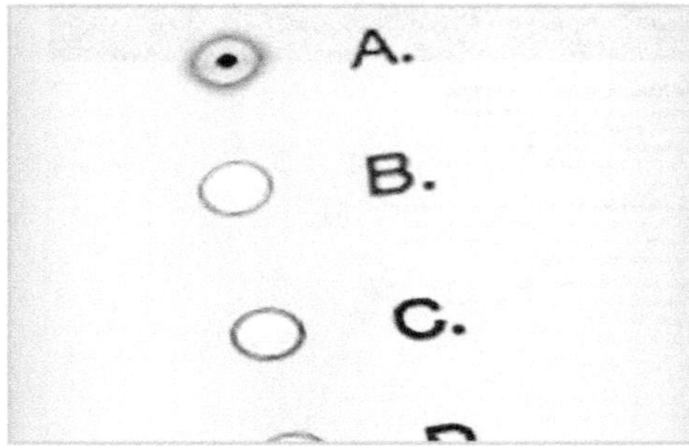

Students can prepare for the Topic Test by answering the questions in the Topic Review and Assessment online or the Assessment questions in the Print Student text. They can also prepare by reviewing their answers to the Interactive Reading Notepad questions or reviewing their notes in the Reading and Notetaking Study Guide.

DIGITAL TOPIC TEST

The Reconstruction Era

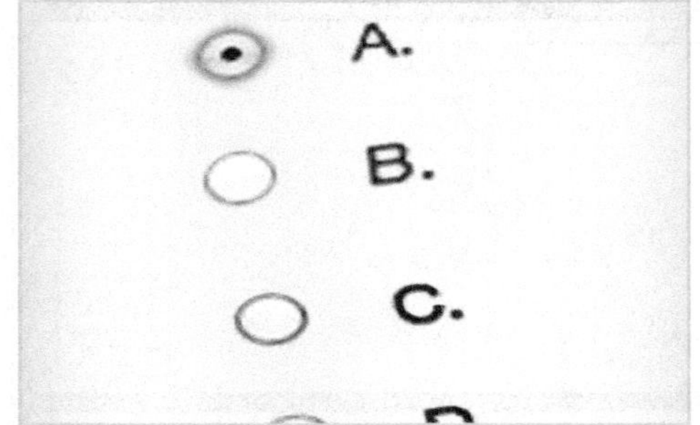

TOPIC TEST

Assign the Topic Test to assess students' understanding of topic content.

BENCHMARK TESTS

Assign these benchmark tests as you complete the relevant topics to monitor student progress toward mastering the course content and as preparation for the End-of-Course Test.

Benchmark Test 1: Topics 1–2

Benchmark Test 2: Topics 3–4

Benchmark Test 3: Topics 5–6

Benchmark Test 4: Topics 7–9

Benchmark Test 5: Topics 10–12

Benchmark Test 6: Topics 13–14

Benchmark Test 7: Topics 15–17

END-OF-COURSE TESTS

Assign End-Of-Course Test 1 or 2 to measure students' progress in mastering the course content.

Industrial and Economic Growth

TOPIC 10 ORGANIZER	PACING: APPROX. 9 PERIODS, 4.5 BLOCKS
	PACING
Connect	1 period
MY STORY VIDEO **The McCormicks, Strike and Violence in Chicago**	10 min.
DIGITAL ESSENTIAL QUESTION ACTIVITY **How Should Resources Be Distributed?**	10 min.
DIGITAL OVERVIEW ACTIVITY **Industrial and Economic Growth**	10 min.
TOPIC INQUIRY: CIVIC DISCUSSION **High-Speed Rail**	20 min.
Investigate	1–3 periods
TOPIC INQUIRY: CIVIC DISCUSSION **High-Speed Rail**	Ongoing
LESSON 1 Mining, Railroads, and the Economy	30–40 min.
LESSON 2 Western Agriculture	30–40 min.
LESSON 3 Hardship for Native Americans	30–40 min.
LESSON 4 Industry and Corporations	30–40 min.
LESSON 5 The Labor Movement	30–40 min.
LESSON 6 New Technologies	30–40 min.
Synthesize	1 period
DIGITAL ACTIVITY **Reflect on the Essential Question and Topic**	10 min.
TOPIC INQUIRY: CIVIC DISCUSSION **High-Speed Rail**	20 min.
Demonstrate	1–2 periods
DIGITAL TOPIC REVIEW AND ASSESSMENT **Industrial and Economic Growth**	10 min.
TOPIC INQUIRY: CIVIC DISCUSSION **High-Speed Rail**	20 min.

TOPIC INQUIRY: CIVIC DISCUSSION

High-Speed Rail

In this Topic Inquiry, students work in teams to examine different perspectives on this issue by analyzing several sources, arguing both sides of a Yes/No question, then developing and discussing their own point of view on the question: **Should America invest in high speed rail?**

STEP 1: CONNECT
Develop Questions and Plan the Investigation

Launch the Civic Discussion

Divide the class into groups of four students. Students can access the materials they'll need in the online course or you can distribute copies to each student. Read the main question and introduction with the students.

Have students complete Step 1 by reading the Discussion Launch and filling in Step 1 of the Information Organizer. The Discussion Launch provides YES and NO arguments on the main question. Students should extract and paraphrase the arguments from the reading in Step 1 of their Information Organizers.

Next, students share within their groups the arguments and evidence they found to support the YES and NO positions. The group needs to agree on the major YES and NO points and each student should note those points in their Information Organizer.

Resources

- Student Instructions
- Information Organizer
- Discussion Launch

STEP 2: INVESTIGATE
Apply Disciplinary Concepts and Tools

Examine Sources and Perspectives

Students will examine sources with the goal of extracting information and perspectives on the main question. They will analyze each source and describe the author's perspective on the main question and key evidence the author provides to support that viewpoint in Step 2 of the Information Organizer.

Ask students to keep in mind:

- **Author/Creator:** Who created the source? An individual? Group? Government agency?
- **Audience:** For whom was the source created?
- **Date/Place:** Is there any information that reveals where and when the source was created?
- **Purpose:** Why was the source created? Discuss with students the importance of this question in identifying bias.
- **Relevance:** How does the source support one argument or another?

Suggestion: Reading the source documents and filling in Step 2 of the Information Organizer could be assigned as homework.

Resources

- Student Instructions
- Information Organizer
- Source documents

PROFESSIONAL DEVELOPMENT

Civic Discussion

Be sure to view the Civic Discussion Professional Development resources in the online course.

STEP 3: SYNTHESIZE

Use Evidence to Formulate Conclusions

Formulate Compelling Arguments with Evidence

Now students will apply perspectives and evidence they extracted from the sources to think more deeply about the main question by first arguing one side of the issue, then the other. In this way students become more prepared to formulate an evidence-based conclusion on their own.

Within each student group, assign half of the students to take the position of YES on the main question and the others to take the position of NO. Students will work with their partners to identify the strongest arguments and evidence to support their assigned YES or NO position.

Present Yes/No Positions

Within each group, those assigned the YES position share arguments and evidence first. As the YES students speak, those assigned NO should listen carefully, take notes to fill in the rest of the Compelling Arguments Chart (Step 3 in Information Organizer) and ask clarifying questions.

When the YES side is finished, students assigned the NO position present while those assigned YES should listen, take notes, and ask clarifying questions. Examples of clarifyin questions are:

- I think you just said [x]. Am I understanding you correctly?
- Can you tell me more about [x]?
- Can you repeat [x]? I am not sure I understand, yet.

Suggestion: You may want to set a 5 minute time limit for each side to present. Provide a two-minute warning so that students make their most compelling arguments within the time frame.

Switch Sides

The students will switch sides to argue the opposite point of view. To prepare to present the other position, partners who first argued YES will use the notes they took during the NO side's presentation, plus add any additional arguments and evidence from the reading and sources. The same for students who first argued the NO position.

STEP 4: DEMONSTRATE

Communicate Conclusions and Take Informed Action

Individual Points of View

Now the students will have the opportunity to discuss the main question from their own points of view. To help students prepare for this discussion, have them reflect on the YES/NO discussions they have participated in thus far and fill in Step 4 of their Information Organizers.

After all of the students have shared their points of view, each group should list points of agreement, filling the last portion of Step 4 on their Information Organizers.

Reflect on the Discussion

Ask students to reflect on the civic discussion thinking about:

- The value of having to argue both the YES and NO positions.
- If their individual views changed over the course of the discussion and why.
- What they learned from participating in the discussion.

Resources

- Student Instructions
- Information Organizer

INTRODUCTION

Industrial and Economic Growth

The late 1800s was a time of enormous industrial growth. Individuals such as Andrew Carnegie and John D. Rockefeller built empires in age of industrialization. Big business took over small factories and changed the face of the American workplace and the relationship between workers and owners. As a result, workers banded together and called for reform, demanding shorter hours, better pay, and safer conditions. However, their requests were slow to be met, with the government and the courts on the side of business owners. In the meantime, innovators were hard at work, submitting thousands of patent requests for their new and often revolutionary ideas.

CONNECT

MY STORY VIDEO

The McCormicks, Strike and Violence in Chicago

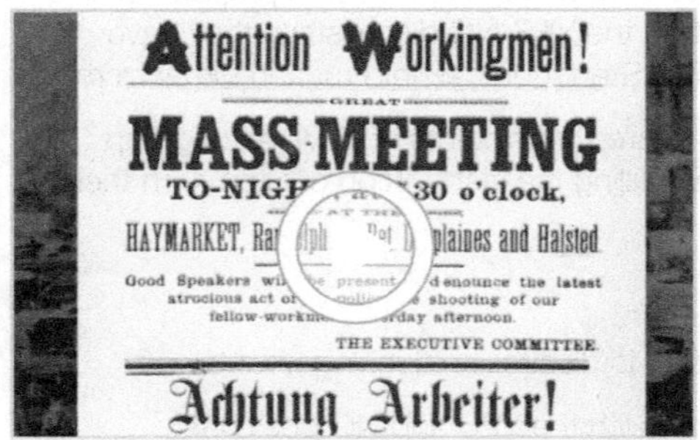

Watch a video about the Haymarket Riot of 1886.

Check Understanding Why did Chicago unions go out on strike against the McCormick Harvester Works in 1886? *(to limit workdays to eight hours)*

Identify Central Issues Why was the strike unsuccessful? *(The violence that broke out was disturbing to many Americans, as was the fear that the strikers were advancing dangerous foreign ideas that were anti-American.)*

DIGITAL ESSENTIAL QUESTION ACTIVITY

How Should Resources Be Distributed?

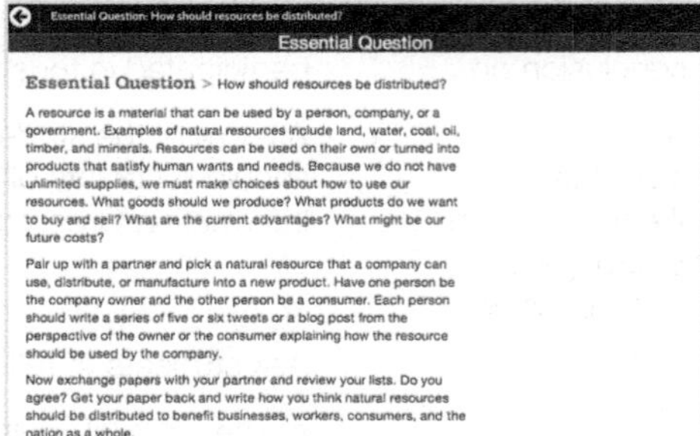

Ask students to think about the Essential Question for this Topic: How should resources be distributed? Resources include raw materials, such as oil and timber, or products made from raw materials, such as gasoline and furniture.

If students have not already done so, have them complete and exchange their writing. Allow students time to construct paragraphs that convey their ideas about how natural resources should be distributed. Invite volunteers to share their work with the class.

Compare Points of View Why would a business owner have a different idea about the distribution of resources than a consumer? Think about the factors that motivate both owners and consumers. *(A business owner is interested in making money from the resources, while a consumer is interested in getting the most resources for his or her money.)*

Evaluate Arguments Have partners exchange their final paragraphs suggesting how resources should be distributed. Then, have them take turns evaluating each other's arguments, explaining why the ideas are workable or not, and suggesting improvements or changes.

DIGITAL OVERVIEW ACTIVITY

Industrial and Economic Growth

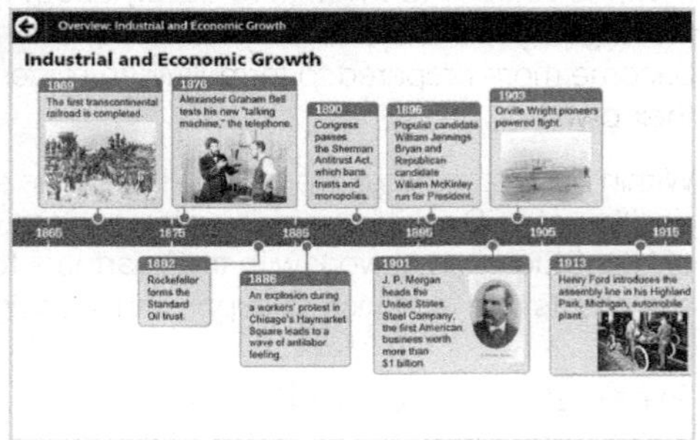

Display the timeline showing the major inventions and advancements of the late 1800s. During this topic students will learn more about these events and many more. This timeline will provide a framework into which they can place the new events they learn about.

Predict Consequences How do you think the completion of the first transcontinental railroad will affect American business and the daily lives of many Americans? *(Connecting two sides of the country will allow businesses to ship products more cheaply and efficiently, opening up national markets for many products. The railroad will also allow Americans to travel long distances more easily than ever before.)*

Topic Inquiry

Launch the Topic Inquiry with students after introducing the topic.

PEARSON realize™ www.PearsonRealize.com Access your Digital Lesson

Mining, Railroads, and the Economy

Supporting English Language Learners

Use with the reading, **The Railroad Encourages Economic Growth**.

Speaking

Explain to students that they can help one another in cooperative learning interactions by sharing verbally what they know about a topic.

Beginning Ask students to share information about the transcontinental railroad. In small groups, have students use these sentence starters as support, sharing what they know from the text about immigrant workers and difficulties of building the railroad: Railroad companies hired _____. Working on a railroad was _____.

Intermediate Ask students to share what they know about transcontinental railroad work. In small groups, have students state a fact corresponding to one of these categories: workers' ethnicities, weather, environment, dangers.

Advanced Ask students to share what they know about the work and working conditions of transcontinental railroad labor. Have pairs of students state an opinion and then support it with a fact from the text.

Advanced High Ask students to share what they know about why the transcontinental railroad was important to the United States. Have pairs of students say what they know about its effects on the country's economy, demographics, communication, and morale, using specific facts from the text to support their claims.

Use with the reading, **Building a National Network of Rails**.

Writing

Display and read aloud the last paragraph of the section Westinghouse Brakes and Pullman Cars. Ask: What if only the first sentence had been included? How do the other sentences add to the description of long-distance travel?

Beginning To fulfill content area writing needs, ask students to describe one way that railroad expansion changed American life. Have them write down this sentence and complete it with a word or phrase: With railroad expansion, people could _____.

Intermediate To fulfill content area writing needs, ask students to describe one way that railroad expansion changed American life. Record students' responses, and then have students write them down.

Advanced To fulfill content area writing needs, ask pairs of students to write a paragraph describing what a railroad network is. Have them include specific details about both its physical and business structures. Then have pairs compare the details included in one another's paragraphs.

Advanced High To fulfill content area writing needs, ask students to write a paragraph describing what the growth of railroads meant for the average American. Have students use specific details from the text to support their claims. Ask partners to compare the details they included in their descriptions.

D Differentiate Instruction

Use the Differentiated Instruction notes throughout the lesson plan to support the varied skill sets, levels of readiness, and interests in the mixed-ability classroom.

Challenge These notes include suggestions for expanding the activity for advanced students.

On-Level These notes include suggestions for modifying the activity to address different interests or learning styles.

Extra Support These notes include ideas for providing more scaffolding or reading spupport.

Special Needs These notes provide ideas for adapting instruction to support the needs of various special needs students.

NOTES

Topic 10 Lesson 1

Mining, Railroads, and the Economy

Objectives

Objective 1: Describe how the boom in gold and silver changed the West.

Objective 2: Identify problems that arose on the mining frontier.

Objective 3: Explain how railroads helped the West develop.

Objective 4: Analyze how railroad services became more efficient over time.

Objective 5: Describe how railroads encouraged economic growth.

LESSON 1 ORGANIZER	PACING: APPROX. 1 PERIOD, .5 BLOCKS			
			RESOURCES	
	OBJECTIVES	PACING	Online	Print
Connect				
DIGITAL START UP ACTIVITY **The Great Miracle**		5 min.	●	
Investigate				
DIGITAL TEXT 1 **Silver and Gold Mining**	Objective 1	10 min.	●	●
INTERACTIVE GALLERY **Boomtowns and Ghost Towns**		10 min.	●	
DIGITAL TEXT 2 **The Costs of Mining**	Objective 2	10 min.	●	●
DIGITAL TEXT 3 **The Railroad Encourages Economic Growth**	Objective 3	10 min.	●	●
INTERACTIVE MAP **The Transcontinental Railroad**		10 min.	●	
DIGITAL TEXT 4 **Building a National Network of Rails**	Objective 4	10 min.	●	●
DIGITAL TEXT 5 **Railroads and Competition**	Objective 5	10 min.	●	●
DIGITAL TEXT 6 **Railroads Build a Nation**		10 min.	●	●
Synthesize				
DIGITAL ACTIVITY **One Cause, Many Effects**		5 min.	●	
Demonstrate				
DIGITAL QUIZ **Lesson Quiz and Class Discussion Board**		10 min.	●	

PEARSON realize™
www.PearsonRealize.com

Go online to access additional resources including:
Primary Sources • Biographies • Supreme Court cases • 21st Century Skill Tutorials • Maps • Graphic Organizers.

CONNECT

DIGITAL START UP ACTIVITY

The Great Miracle

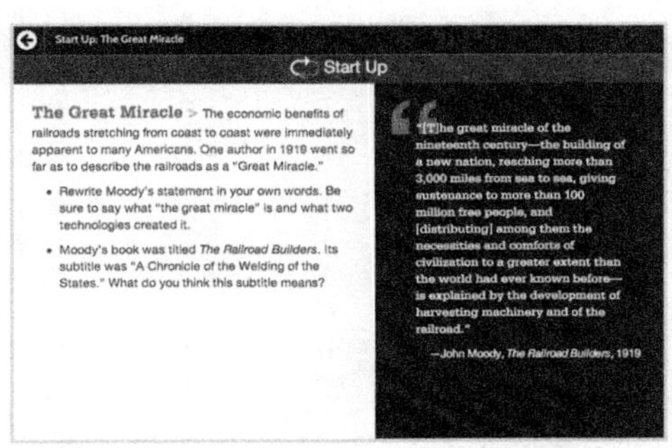

Project the Start Up Activity Ask students to read the quote and answer the questions as they enter and get settled. Have students share their answers with a partner, either in class or through a blog space.

Discuss Rewrite Moody's statement in your own words. Be sure to say what "the great miracle" is and what two technologies created it. *(The great miracle is the United States in the nineteenth century and that harvesting machinery and railroads played such an important role in creating this vast, populous, and advanced nation.)* Moody's book was titled *The Railroad Builders*. Its subtitle was "A Chronicle of the Welding of the States." What do you think this subtitle means? *(It is an account of how the states developed and came together through technology and machinery.)*

Aa Vocabulary Development: Use the Interactive Reading Notepad to preview the Key Terms and Academic Vocabulary in this lesson with students.

FLIP IT!

Assign the Flipped Video for this lesson.

STUDENT EDITION PRINT PAGES: 524–534

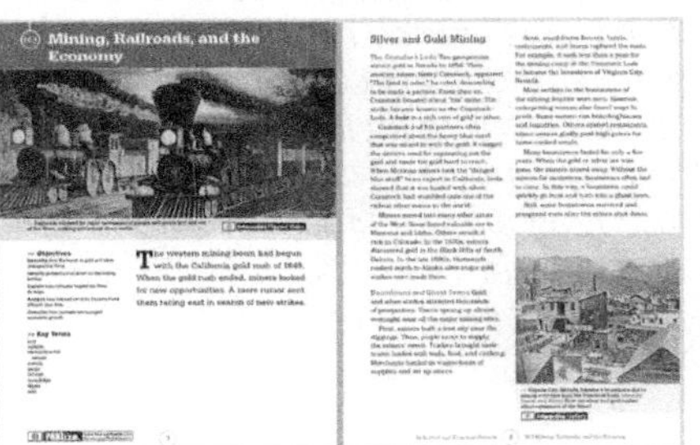

INVESTIGATE

DIGITAL TEXT 1

Silver and Gold Mining

Objective 1: Describe how the boom in gold and silver changed the West.

Quick Instruction

Interactive Gallery: Boomtowns and Ghost Towns Project the interactive gallery on the whiteboard and click through the images. Discuss how western mining shaped the growth and development of the United States.

Draw Conclusions How did physical characteristics of the environment influence economic activities during the nineteenth century? *(Discoveries of gold and silver created a mining boom in the West.)*

ACTIVE CLASSROOM

Have students use the Sticky Notes Strategy and spend three minutes jotting down their ideas about how physical characteristics of the environment influenced economic development and population growth in the West. Have students post their sticky notes on the board or on chart paper and ask students to look at the various responses. Discuss similarities and differences in the responses as a group.

INTERACTIVE GALLERY

Boomtowns and Ghost Towns

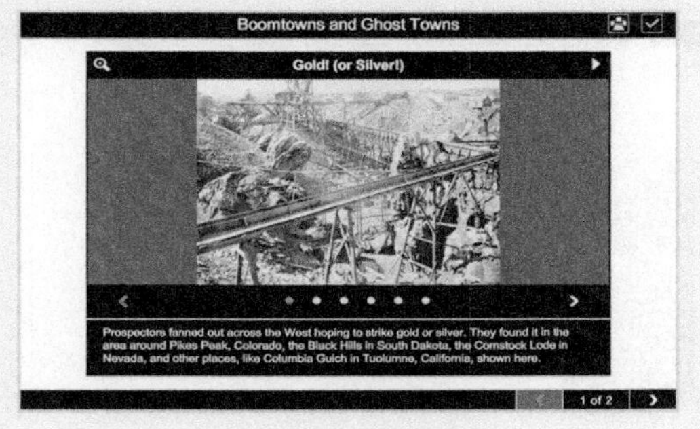

Further Instruction

Go through the Interactive Reading Notepad questions and discuss the answers with the class.

Generate Explanations How did boomtowns contribute to the growth of the United States, despite the fact that many of them turned into ghost towns? *(Boomtowns drew prospectors to mining sites, causing towns to emerge. Not all the boomtowns disappeared when the mine closed. Some miners stayed and found other ways to make a living, creating new towns and cities across the West.)*

Hypothesize Make a hypothesis about how railroads impacted the growth of boomtowns. Explain your reasoning. *(Railroads caused boomtowns to grow because they brought people and goods to mining areas.)*

Mining, Railroads, and the Economy

DIGITAL TEXT 2

The Costs of Mining

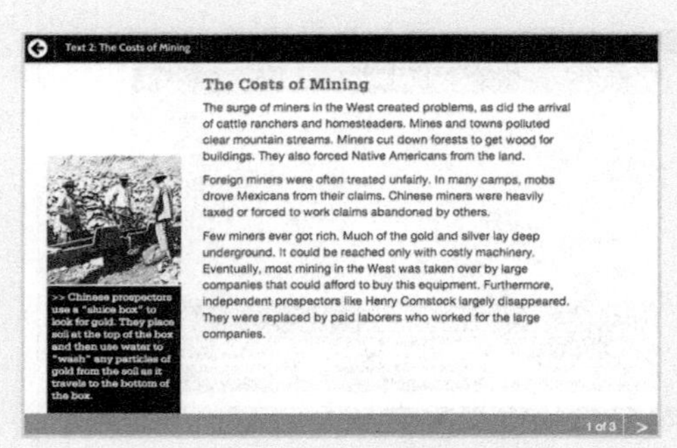

DIGITAL TEXT 3

The Railroad Encourages Economic Growth

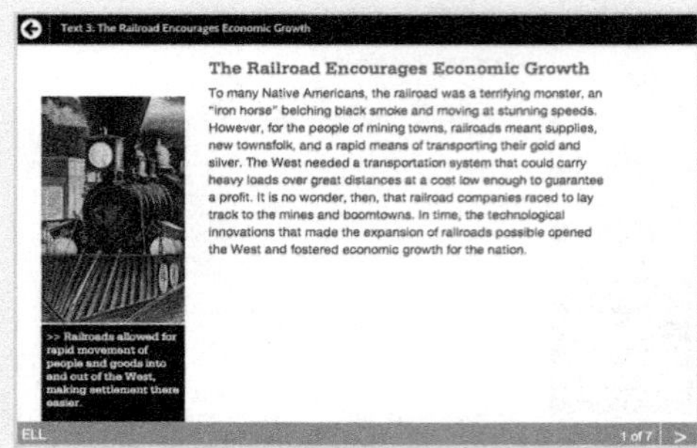

Text 3: The Railroad Encourages Economic Growth
The Railroad Encourages Economic Growth
To many Native Americans, the railroad was a terrifying monster, an "iron horse" belching black smoke and moving at stunning speeds. However, for the people of mining towns, railroads meant supplies, new townsfolk, and a rapid means of transporting their gold and silver. The West needed a transportation system that could carry heavy loads over great distances at a cost low enough to guarantee a profit. It is no wonder, then, that railroad companies raced to lay track to the mines and boomtowns. In time, the technological innovations that made the expansion of railroads possible opened the West and fostered economic growth for the nation.
>> Railroads allowed for rapid movement of people and goods into and out of the West, making settlement there easier.
ELL
1 of 7

INTERACTIVE MAP

The Transcontinental Railroad

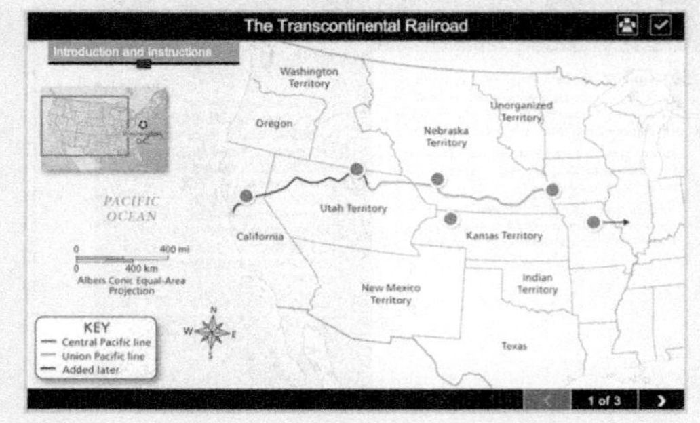

Objective 2: **Identify problems that arose on the mining frontier.**

Quick Instruction

Project the image of the miners on the whiteboard and discuss how physical characteristics of the environment drew immigrants to the West.

Summarize How did mining impact the physical environment in the West? *(mines and towns polluted waterways and miners cut down forests)*

Further Instruction

Go through the Interactive Reading Notepad questions and discuss the answers with the class.

Identify Cause and Effect How did technological innovations in mining influence the mining economy and life for laborers? *(Most of the gold and silver could only be reached by machines, which were very expensive. Mining was taken over by large companies that could afford the equipment. Miners worked for the companies instead of independently.)*

Hypothesize How do you think the physical geography of the West affected law enforcement in the areas? *(Because towns were relatively small and far from other cities, they did not have established governments or law enforcement agencies. The remoteness of the town probably helped give rise to vigilante groups that took the law into their own hands.)*

Objective 3: **Explain how railroads helped the West develop.**

Quick Instruction

Interactive Map: The Transcontinental Railroad Project the interactive map on the whiteboard and click through the hotspots. Ask students why they think the nation wanted to have a transcontinental railroad.

Generate Explanations Explain how transportation systems impacted the growth and development of the United States. *(Railroads allowed people and supplies to move quickly across the country. Towns and cities grew up along the railroad lines, as well as industries. Railroads brought more people west. Western territories grew into states connected across the nation by railroad lines.)*

ACTIVE CLASSROOM

Group students to use the PMI Strategy to fill in a 3-column organizer with the headings Plus/Minus/Interesting. Have student use the organizer to record their responses to the following questions: 1. What were the positive impacts of the railroad in the nineteenth century? 2. What were the negative impacts? 3. What is interesting about this technology?

D Differentiate: Extra Support Explain to students that *trans-* is a prefix that means *across*. Have them use this definition to explain in their own words what the transcontinental railroad was. Help them locate on a map the railroad route and show how it went across the country.

ELL Use the ELL activity described in the ELL chart.

Further Instruction

Go through the Interactive Reading Notepad questions and discuss the answers with the class.

Draw Conclusions How do you think the arrival of railroad lines influenced daily life in the West in the nineteenth century? *(people had access to new goods and supplies and could send their products to new markets; cities and towns developed, many people who lived in more remote areas were connected to the rest of the country)*

Support Ideas with Examples Give an example of how technological innovations in transportation brought about economic growth. *(railroads encouraged towns, cities, and industries to grow; railroads provided jobs and brought immigrants to the United States to lay tracks; workers used specialized tools and explosives to build the railroad, linking parts of the United States so goods and services could travel across the country)*

Identify Cause and Effect Why did the government subsidize the railroads? What were the effects of this policy? *(The government provided financial aid and land grants because it wanted railroad companies to lay new track to connect the nation so the entire country would benefit. As a result, the transcontinental railroad was built, leading to economic development, urbanization, and population growth.)*

DIGITAL TEXT 4

Building a National Network of Rails

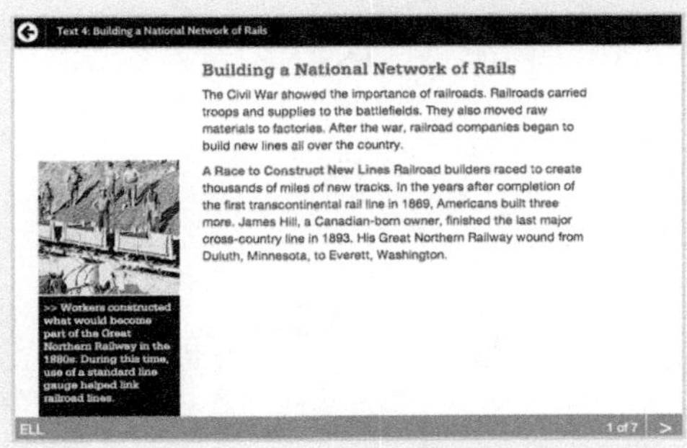

Text 4: Building a National Network of Rails
Building a National Network of Rails
The Civil War showed the importance of railroads. Railroads carried troops and supplies to the battlefields. They also moved raw materials to factories. After the war, railroad companies began to build new lines all over the country.
A Race to Construct New Lines Railroad builders raced to create thousands of miles of new tracks. In the years after completion of the first transcontinental rail line in 1869, Americans built three more. James Hill, a Canadian-born owner, finished the last major cross-country line in 1893. His Great Northern Railway wound from Duluth, Minnesota, to Everett, Washington.
>> Workers constructed what would become part of the Great Northern Railway in the 1880s. During this time, use of a standard line gauge helped link railroad lines.
ELL
1 of 7
>

Objective 4: **Analyze how railroad services became more efficient over time.**

Quick Instruction

Project the image of the railroad workers on the whiteboard. Explain that a railroad network is a system of connected railroad lines. Workers used new technological innovations to build a national network across the country, which had a significant effect on economic growth.

Support Ideas with Evidence Why did the ability to ship goods long distances change the nation's economy? Provide evidence for support. *(Businesses transported raw materials to factories; goods could be shipped across the country at reasonable prices; consumers had greater access to goods; farmers expanded their markets)*

ELL Use the ELL activity described in the ELL chart.

Further Instruction

Go through the Interactive Reading Notepad questions and discuss the answers with the class.

Summarize Select one technological innovation described in this text and explain its impact. *(Westinghouse brakes—air brake that stopped all railroad cars at once. Trains were safer, could have more cars, and could traveled faster. Pullman cars—cars with convertible berths for sleeping and lavatories. Rail travel became more comfortable over long distances.)*

Identify Cause and Effect How did innovations to railroad gauges bring about economic growth? *(Workers standardized gauges by changing the width of railroad tracks in the South. This allowed trains to run on tracks throughout the country, benefiting shippers who needed to transport goods long distances.)*

Make Predictions How do you think consolidation of businesses will impact railroad companies and American consumers? *(Smaller companies will go out of business; larger companies like Vanderbilt's will dominate the industry; prices may rise for consumers, who will no longer have a choice of companies to use.)*

DIGITAL TEXT 5

Railroads and Competition

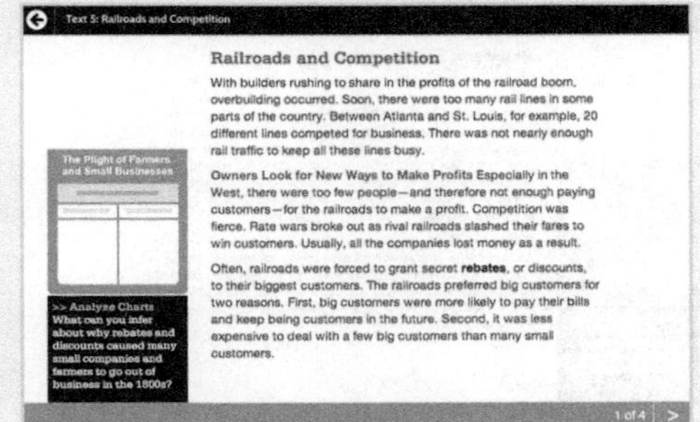

Text 5: Railroads and Competition
Railroads and Competition
With builders rushing to share in the profits of the railroad boom, overbuilding occurred. Soon, there were too many rail lines in some parts of the country. Between Atlanta and St. Louis, for example, 20 different lines competed for business. There was not nearly enough rail traffic to keep all these lines busy.
Owners Look for New Ways to Make Profits Especially in the West, there were too few people—and therefore not enough paying customers—for the railroads to make a profit. Competition was fierce. Rate wars broke out as rival railroads slashed their fares to win customers. Usually, all the companies lost money as a result.
Often, railroads were forced to grant secret rebates, or discounts, to their biggest customers. The railroads preferred big customers for two reasons. First, big customers were more likely to pay their bills and keep being customers in the future. Second, it was less expensive to deal with a few big customers than many small customers.
The Plight of Farmers and Small Businesses
>> Analyze Charts What can you infer about why rebates and discounts caused many small companies and farmers to go out of business in the 1800s?
1 of 4
>

Objective 5: **Describe how railroads encouraged economic growth.**

Quick Instruction

Project on the whiteboard the political cartoon showing congressmen looking like train engines and have students describe what they see. Have students use the cartoon to draw a conclusion about the railroad industry in the late 1800s.

Identify Cause and Effect What factors caused railroad prices to soar? What were the political and economic effects of high prices? *(Causes—Railroads were overbuilding, so that there were too many rail lines and not enough paying customers. Companies offered secret rebates to big customers, but smaller shippers still had to pay full price. Railroad companies ended competition by creating a pool and setting high prices. Effects—Farmers could not afford to ship their products; many farmers became Populists; Congress passed laws regulating railroads, although this did not end abuses.)*

Generate Explanations Explain the Panic of 1893 in your own words. What role did transportation systems play in this economic downturn? *(Railroads had been overextended. When the Philadelphia and Reading Railroad went bankrupt, many people panicked. Railroad companies went out of business, hurting industries that depended on railroads and causing millions of Americans to lose their jobs.)*

Mining, Railroads, and the Economy

DIGITAL TEXT 6

Railroads Build a Nation

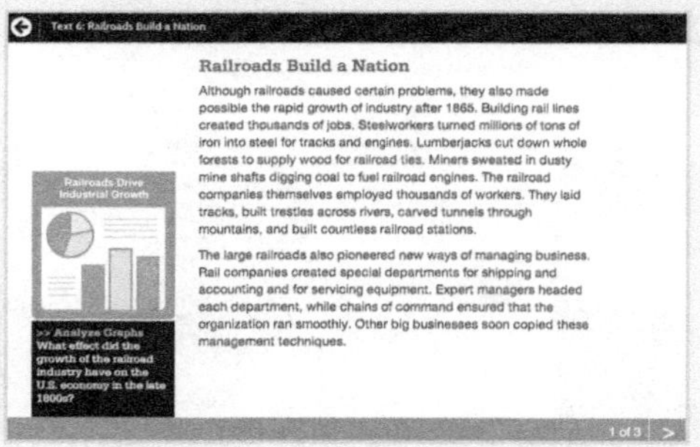

Text 6: Railroads Build a Nation
Railroads Build a Nation
Although railroads caused certain problems, they also made possible the rapid growth of industry after 1865. Building rail lines created thousands of jobs. Steelworkers turned millions of tons of iron into steel for tracks and engines. Lumberjacks cut down whole forests to supply wood for railroad ties. Miners sweated in dusty mine shafts digging coal to fuel railroad engines. The railroad companies themselves employed thousands of workers. They laid tracks, built trestles across rivers, carved tunnels through mountains, and built countless railroad stations.
The large railroads also pioneered new ways of managing business. Rail companies created special departments for shipping and accounting and for servicing equipment. Expert managers headed each department, while chains of command ensured that the organization ran smoothly. Other big businesses soon copied these management techniques.
Railroads Drive Industrial Growth
>> Analyze Graphs What effect did the growth of the railroad industry have on the U.S. economy in the late 1800s?
1 of 3

Further Instruction

Go through the Interactive Reading Notepad questions and discuss the answers with the class.

Identify Central Issues How did railroads cause industry to grow in the nineteenth century? *(Building rail lines created jobs for steelworkers, lumberjacks, miners, and the laborers who laid tracks, built stations, and worked on the lines. Railroad companies also developed business departments and management techniques used by other businesses to run more efficiently.)*

SYNTHESIZE

DIGITAL ACTIVITY

One Cause, Many Effects

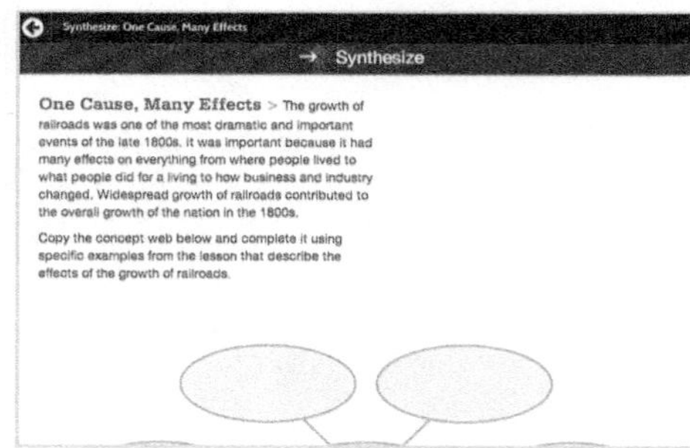

Synthesize: One Cause, Many Effects
Synthesize
One Cause, Many Effects > The growth of railroads was one of the most dramatic and important events of the late 1800s. It was important because it had many effects on everything from where people lived to what people did for a living to how business and industry changed. Widespread growth of railroads contributed to the overall growth of the nation in the 1800s.
Copy the concept web below and complete it using specific examples from the lesson that describe the effects of the growth of railroads.

Have students complete the concept web and then discuss with a partner how the growth of railroads contributed to the overall growth of the nation. Have partners share their ideas with the class.

Discuss Have students review the quote they read at the beginning of the lesson and give examples of how the railroad brought about "the great miracle" of the nineteenth century—the building of the United States. Ask students why railroads were so important to the growth and development of the United States, providing examples for support.

DEMONSTRATE

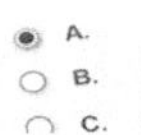

DIGITAL QUIZ

Lesson Quiz and Class Discussion Board

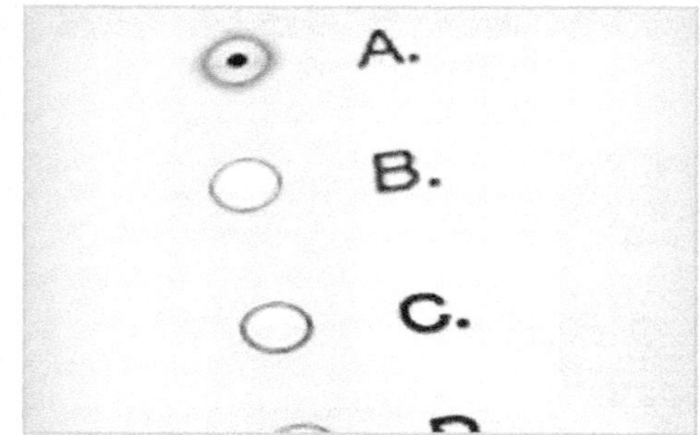

Assign the online Lesson Quiz for this lesson if you haven't already done so. Students will be offered automatic remediation or enrichment based on their score.

Pose these questions to the class on the Discussion Board:

Identify Central Issues What role did mining play in the development of western territories and the growth of the United States? Explain your reasoning.

Draw Conclusions Draw a conclusion about the role of transportation in the development of the United States.

Topic Inquiry

Have students continue their investigations for the Topic Inquiry.

PEARSON realize™ www.PearsonRealize.com Access your Digital Lesson

Western Agriculture

Supporting English Language Learners

Use with the reading, **Effects of the Homestead Act**.

Writing

Point out these connecting words in the text's second paragraph: *but, also, as a result*. Review the purpose of connecting words. Have students write using a variety of grade-appropriate connecting words to combine phrases, clauses, and sentences in increasingly accurate ways.

Beginning Review the difference between *but* and *and*. Then have students write down these sentences, combining their clauses with either *but* or *and* : Many people wanted free land, _____ they did not have money to move west. Many people wanted free land, _____ they used it to set up farms.

Intermediate Display these sentences: Anglos in the Southwest got the best jobs and land. As a result, _____. Ask students to complete and write down the sentences. Have students share their sentences in small groups.

Advanced Ask pairs of students to write a paragraph about settlement in the Southwest using the connecting words *but*, *also*, *as a result*, and one other of their choosing. Then have pairs read one another's paragraphs and identify the fourth connecting word that was used.

Advanced High Ask students to write a paragraph about the effects of the Homestead Act using at least three different connecting words to combine phrases, clauses, and sentences. Have partners read each other's paragraph and identify the connecting words that were used.

Use with the reading, **Farming and the Economy**.

Speaking

Point out the content area boldface words *cooperative* and *wholesale* in the text, and discuss their meanings. Then have students internalize these content area vocabulary words by speaking them in contexts that they understand.

Beginning Display and read aloud these sentences: The farmers were part of a group called a _____. It helped them save money by buying supplies at _____ prices. To help students internalize these content area words, have them complete the sentences with the boldface words and read the sentences aloud.

Intermediate To help students internalize these content area words, ask them to answer the following questions aloud, using complete sentences and at least one of the boldface words: How did the Grangers help farmers save money? How did farmers increase their political influence?

Advanced To help them internalize these content area words, ask pairs of students to discuss the following questions: How does a cooperative work? What might have happened to a farmer who did not join a cooperative? Encourage students to use both boldface words in their discussion.

Advanced High To help them internalize these content area words, have pairs of students play the roles of a Granger (trying to convince a farmer to join a cooperative) and a farmer (asking for more details and expressing concerns). Encourage students to use both boldface words in their discussion.

D Differentiate Instruction

Use the Differentiated Instruction notes throughout the lesson plan to support the varied skill sets, levels of readiness, and interests in the mixed-ability classroom.

Challenge These notes include suggestions for expanding the activity for advanced students.

On-Level These notes include suggestions for modifying the activity to address different interests or learning styles.

Extra Support These notes include ideas for providing more scaffolding or reading spupport.

Special Needs These notes provide ideas for adapting instruction to support the needs of various special needs students.

NOTES

Topic 10 Lesson 2

Western Agriculture

Objectives

Objective 1: Identify the Cattle Kingdom.

Objective 2: Describe cowhands and cow towns during the cattle boom.

Objective 3: Summarize the massive westward migration following the Homestead Act.

Objective 4: Identify challenges western farmers faced and the alliances created to improve their conditions.

Objective 5: Explain why the Populist Party was formed.

LESSON 2 ORGANIZER | **PACING: APPROX. 1 PERIOD, .5 BLOCKS**

	OBJECTIVES	PACING	RESOURCES Online	RESOURCES Print
Connect				
DIGITAL START UP ACTIVITY **Western Settlements and Agriculture**		5 min.	●	
Investigate				
DIGITAL TEXT 1 **A Cattle Kingdom on the Plains**	Objective 1	10 min.	●	●
INTERACTIVE MAP **Cattle Trails**	Objective 1	10 min.	●	
INTERACTIVE GALLERY **Cowhands and their Gear**	Objective 1	10 min.	●	
DIGITAL TEXT 2 **Ranching Impacts Settlement Patterns**	Objective 2	10 min.	●	●
DIGITAL TEXT 3 **The Spread of Farming**	Objective 2	10 min.	●	●
DIGITAL TEXT 4 **Effects of the Homestead Act**	Objective 3	10 min.	●	●
DIGITAL TEXT 5 **Effects of the Morrill Acts**	Objective 3	10 min.	●	●
DIGITAL TEXT 6 **Life on the Plains**	Objective 4	10 min.	●	●
3-D MODEL **Nineteenth-Century Sod House**	Objective 4	10 min.	●	
DIGITAL TEXT 7 **Farming and the Economy**	Objective 4	10 min.	●	●
DIGITAL TEXT 8 **The Rise of the People's Party in the West**	Objective 5	10 min.	●	●
Synthesize				
DIGITAL ACTIVITY **The Effects of the Homestead Act**		5 min.	●	
Demonstrate				
DIGITAL QUIZ **Lesson Quiz and Class Discussion Board**		10 min.	●	

Go online to access additional resources including:
Primary Sources • Biographies • Supreme Court cases • 21st Century Skill Tutorials • Maps • Graphic Organizers.

CONNECT

DIGITAL START UP ACTIVITY

Western Settlements and Agriculture

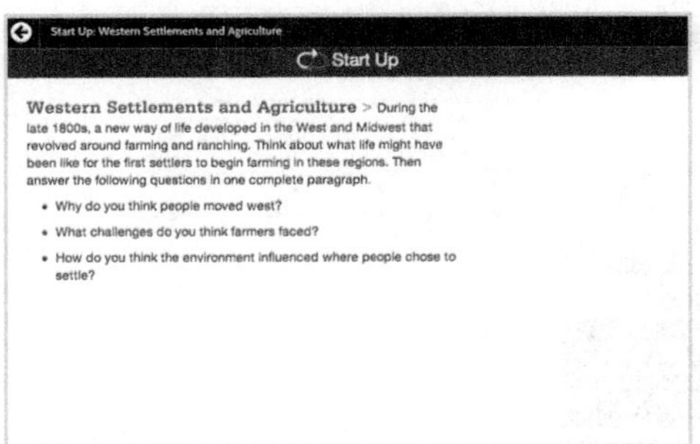

Start Up: Western Settlements and Agriculture
Start Up
Western Settlements and Agriculture > During the late 1800s, a new way of life developed in the West and Midwest that revolved around farming and ranching. Think about what life might have been like for the first settlers to begin farming in these regions. Then answer the following questions in one complete paragraph.
• Why do you think people moved west?
• What challenges do you think farmers faced?
• How do you think the environment influenced where people chose to settle?

Project the Start Up Activity Ask students to read the activity and write down their paragraph as they enter and get settled. Have students share their paragraphs with a partner, either in class or through a blog space.

Discuss Why do you think people moved west? What challenges do you think farmers faced? How do you think the environment influenced where people chose to settle? *(People moved west in search of adventure, opportunity, and land for farming. Farmers faced many challenges, as not all land was suitable for farming. Drought and floods could ruin crops, leaving farmers poor and in debt. In general, people settled where they could find the best farmland and have access to water and other resources.)*

Aa Vocabulary Development: Use the Interactive Reading Notepad to preview the Key Terms and Academic Vocabulary in this lesson with students.

FLIP IT!

Assign the Flipped Video for this lesson.

STUDENT EDITION PRINT PAGES: 535–546

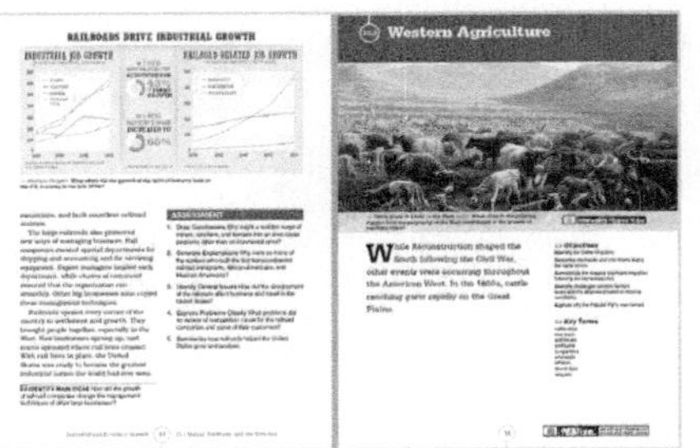

INVESTIGATE

DIGITAL TEXT 1

A Cattle Kingdom on the Plains

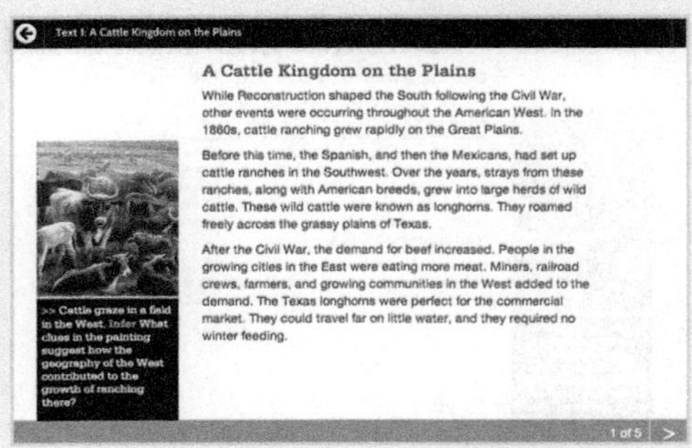

Objective 1: Identify the Cattle Kingdom.

Quick Instruction

Interactive Map: Cattle Trails Project the interactive map and click through the layers. Have students locate where the cattle trails went and explain their purpose.

Summarize Why did cattle ranching spread in the plains? *(Strays from Spanish and Mexican cattle ranches and American breeds grew into large herds of Texas longhorns that grazed on the open grasslands.)*

ACTIVE CLASSROOM

Have students complete a Circle Write Activity. Break into groups. Have students write as much as they can about cattle trails for one minute then switch with the person on their right. The next person tries to improve or elaborate the response where the other person left off. Continue to switch until the paper comes back to the first person. The group then decides which is the best composition (or response) and shares that with the larger group.

ACTIVE CLASSROOM

Have students use the Conversation with History Strategy and imagine they are having a conversation with a former Confederate soldier who has moved to Texas to become a cowhand after the war. Have students write down a question they'd like to ask, what the cowhand would say, and what they would say in response.

INTERACTIVE MAP

Cattle Trails

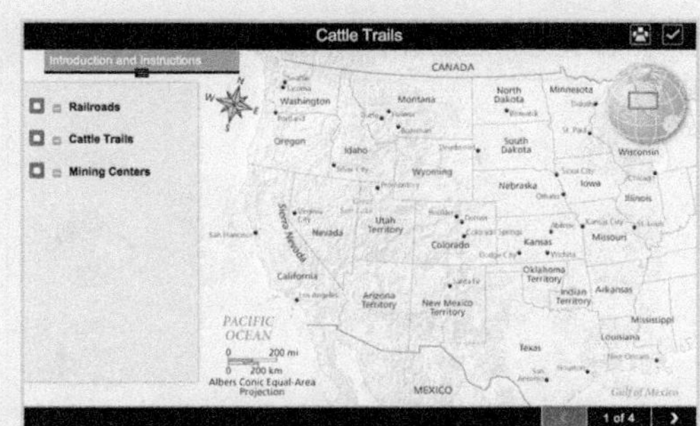

Further Instruction

Go through the Interactive Reading Notepad questions and discuss the answers with the class.

Draw Conclusions How do you think the rise of the cattle industry contributed to westward expansion? *(The cattle industry developed to meet the growing demand for beef from the East. There were jobs available on the ranches, including for Confederate soldiers looking for opportunities after the war. More people were probably drawn west as the industry expanded and it became clear that there was money to be made in the West.)*

Western Agriculture

INTERACTIVE GALLERY

Cowhands and their Gear

Identify Cause and Effect How did physical characteristics of the environment influence life for cowhands? *(Their gear was designed to protect them from the environment, including a wide-brimmed hat for the sun and chaps to protect them from thorny plants. Work on the open plains was difficult. Cattle drives were hot, dirty, and tiring. Cowhands had to be outside in storms and faced dangers on the trails from other animals and natural disasters like grass fires.)*

DIGITAL TEXT 2

Ranching Impacts Settlement Patterns

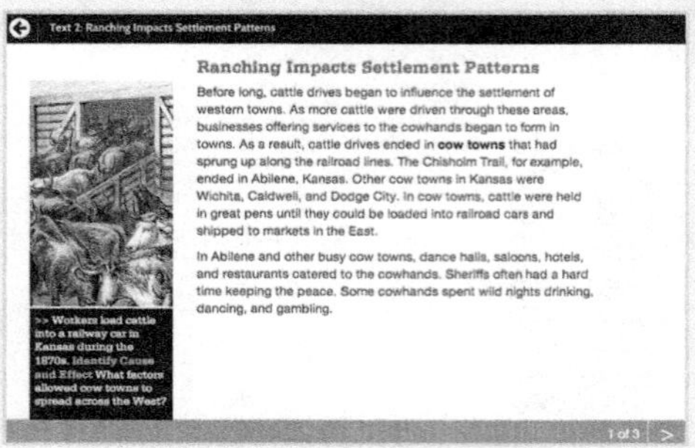

Text 2: Ranching Impacts Settlement Patterns
Ranching Impacts Settlement Patterns
Before long, cattle drives began to influence the settlement of western towns. As more cattle were driven through these areas, businesses offering services to the cowhands began to form in towns. As a result, cattle drives ended in cow towns that had sprung up along the railroad lines. The Chisholm Trail, for example, ended in Abilene, Kansas. Other cow towns in Kansas were Wichita, Caldwell, and Dodge City. In cow towns, cattle were held in great pens until they could be loaded into railroad cars and shipped to markets in the East.
In Abilene and other busy cow towns, dance halls, saloons, hotels, and restaurants catered to the cowhands. Sheriffs often had a hard time keeping the peace. Some cowhands spent wild nights drinking, dancing, and gambling.
>> Workers load cattle into a railway car in Kansas during the 1870s. Identify Cause and Effect What factors allowed cow towns to spread across the West?
1 of 3

Objective 2: **Describe cowhands and cow towns during the cattle boom.**

Quick Instruction

Project the image of the cattle being loaded into a railway car on the whiteboard. Discuss how cattle trails contributed to the growth of towns in the West.

Summarize How did cattle drives influence settlement patterns in the West during the nineteenth century? *(Towns formed along the railroad lines where the cattle drives ended. Businesses developed to cater to the cowhands. More people moved to these thriving communities, causing the towns to grow.)*

Infer How do you think physical characteristics of the environment influenced population distribution in the West in the nineteenth century? What role do you think railroads played in determining how people were distributed across the plains? *(People settled more densely in areas where there were resources for homes, farms, and businesses. More people lived in towns connected by railroad lines. The population would have thinned further away from railroad lines and the towns that grew up around them.)*

DIGITAL TEXT 3

The Spread of Farming

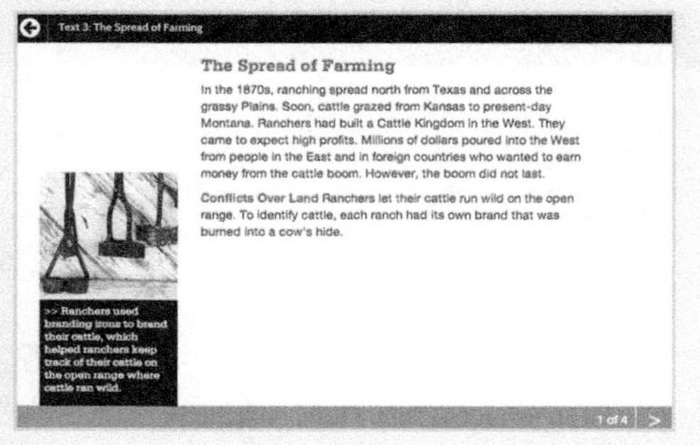

Text 3: The Spread of Farming
The Spread of Farming
In the 1870s, ranching spread north from Texas and across the grassy Plains. Soon, cattle grazed from Kansas to present-day Montana. Ranchers had built a Cattle Kingdom in the West. They came to expect high profits. Millions of dollars poured into the West from people in the East and in foreign countries who wanted to earn money from the cattle boom. However, the boom did not last.
Conflicts Over Land Ranchers let their cattle run wild on the open range. To identify cattle, each ranch had its own brand that was burned into a cow's hide.
>> Ranchers used branding irons to brand their cattle, which helped ranchers keep track of their cattle on the open range where cattle ran wild.
1 of 4

Further Instruction

Go through the Interactive Reading Notepad questions and discuss the answers with the class.

Support Ideas with Examples Give examples that show how changes to the physical environment caused a downturn in the cattle industry. *(Ranchers claimed sheep made grazing lands unusable for cattle. Farmers and railroads encroached on the plains. As people began using barbed wire, the open range was divided into private property, meaning cattle could no longer graze freely. There was not enough land to support all the cattle, and disease, cold winters, hot summers, and droughts killed many herds.)*

DIGITAL TEXT 4

Effects of the Homestead Act

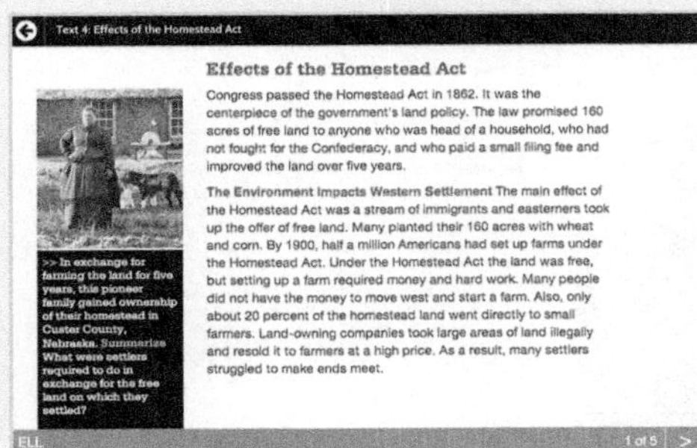

Text 4: Effects of the Homestead Act
Effects of the Homestead Act
Congress passed the Homestead Act in 1862. It was the centerpiece of the government's land policy. The law promised 160 acres of free land to anyone who was head of a household, who had not fought for the Confederacy, and who paid a small filing fee and improved the land over five years.
The Environment Impacts Western Settlement The main effect of the Homestead Act was a stream of immigrants and easterners took up the offer of free land. Many planted their 160 acres with wheat and corn. By 1900, half a million Americans had set up farms under the Homestead Act. Under the Homestead Act the land was free, but setting up a farm required money and hard work. Many people did not have the money to move west and start a farm. Also, only about 20 percent of the homestead land went directly to small farmers. Land-owning companies took large areas of land illegally and resold it to farmers at a high price. As a result, many settlers struggled to make ends meet.
>> In exchange for farming the land for five years, this pioneer family gained ownership of their homestead in Custer County, Nebraska. Summarize What were settlers required to do in exchange for the free land on which they settled?
ELL
1 of 5

Objective 3: Summarize the massive westward migration following the Homestead Act.

Quick Instruction

Project on the whiteboard the image of the pioneer family and have students discuss the environmental and economic factors that drew settlers west.

Draw Conclusions How did physical characteristics of the environment shape economic activities in the West? *(Open land led settlers to move west and build farms. Land-owning companies also made money selling plots of land to farmers. There was often not enough affordable land suitable for farming available, however, which created economic hardships for many homesteaders.)*

ELL Use the ELL activity described in the ELL chart.

DIGITAL TEXT 5

Effects of the Morrill Acts

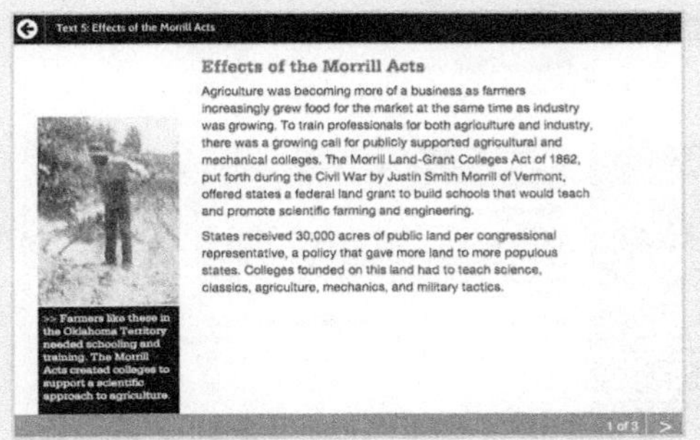

Text 5: Effects of the Morrill Acts
Effects of the Morrill Acts
Agriculture was becoming more of a business as farmers increasingly grew food for the market at the same time as industry was growing. To train professionals for both agriculture and industry, there was a growing call for publicly supported agricultural and mechanical colleges. The Morrill Land-Grant Colleges Act of 1862, put forth during the Civil War by Justin Smith Morrill of Vermont, offered states a federal land grant to build schools that would teach and promote scientific farming and engineering.
States received 30,000 acres of public land per congressional representative, a policy that gave more land to more populous states. Colleges founded on this land had to teach science, classics, agriculture, mechanics, and military tactics.
>> Farmers like these in the Oklahoma Territory needed schooling and training. The Morrill Acts created colleges to support a scientific approach to agriculture.
1 of 3

Further Instruction

Go through the Interactive Reading Notepad questions and discuss the answers with the class.

Identify Cause and Effect Identify the effects of the Homestead Act. *(Millions of settlers moved west to build farms on the free land given by the Homestead Act. This helped settle the region. Much of the land went to large land-owning companies, which illegally resold the land to farmers at a higher price.)*

Identify Cause and Effect Identify the effects of the Morrill Acts. *(States used federal land grants to found agricultural colleges—schools that taught practical skills to help Americans find jobs in an agricultural society. These public schools were more affordable than private colleges and increased access to higher education for many Americans. They also showed that government would support colleges.)*

DIGITAL TEXT 6

Life on the Plains

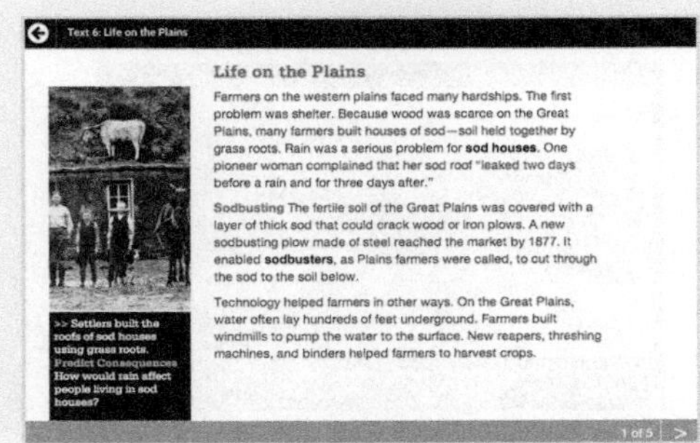

Text 6: Life on the Plains
Life on the Plains
Farmers on the western plains faced many hardships. The first problem was shelter. Because wood was scarce on the Great Plains, many farmers built houses of sod—soil held together by grass roots. Rain was a serious problem for sod houses. One pioneer woman complained that her sod roof "leaked two days before a rain and for three days after."
Sodbusting The fertile soil of the Great Plains was covered with a layer of thick sod that could crack wood or iron plows. A new sodbusting plow made of steel reached the market by 1877. It enabled sodbusters, as Plains farmers were called, to cut through the sod to the soil below.
Technology helped farmers in other ways. On the Great Plains, water often lay hundreds of feet underground. Farmers built windmills to pump the water to the surface. New reapers, threshing machines, and binders helped farmers to harvest crops.
>> Settlers built the roofs of sod houses using grass roots. Predict Consequences How would rain affect people living in sod houses?
1 of 5

Objective 4: Identify challenges western farmers faced and the alliances created to improve their conditions.

Quick Instruction

3-D Model: Nineteenth-Century Sod House Project the 3-D model on the whiteboard and click through the images. Discuss how the physical conditions of the plains environment shaped the features of the sod house.

Summarize How did the physical environment of the plains create difficulties for farmers? *(There was no wood for houses and sod houses leaked in the rain. The dry climate damaged crops and created grass fires. In the summer there were pests that ate the crops, and the winters were extremely cold and snowy.)*

Topic 10 Lesson 2

Western Agriculture

3-D MODEL

Nineteenth-Century Sod House

DIGITAL TEXT 7

Farming and the Economy

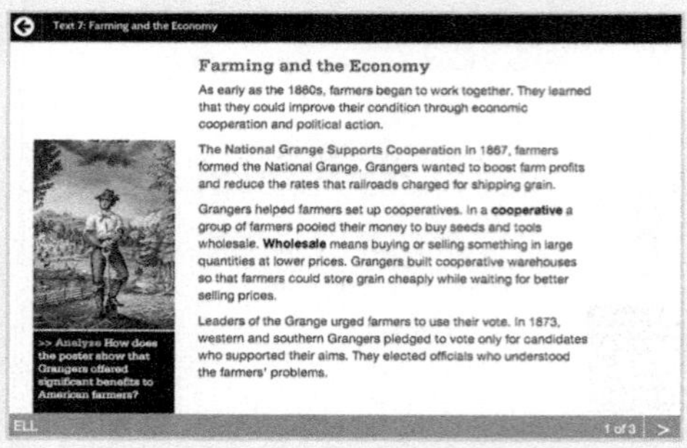

DIGITAL TEXT 8

The Rise of the People's Party in the West

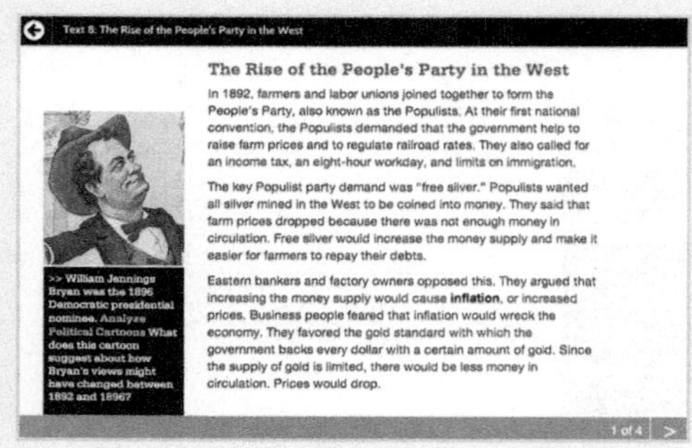

ACTIVE CLASSROOM

Have students use the Cartoon It Strategy and create a copy of one compelling image from these texts on a piece of paper. Have students turn their image into a political cartoon that illustrates a key concept from the lesson. Have students share their cartoons with the class.

ELL Use the ELL activity described in the ELL chart.

Further Instruction

Go through the Interactive Reading Notepad questions and discuss the answers with the class.

Support Ideas with Examples Give three examples of how homesteaders used technology to overcome environmental challenges and improve farming. *(a sodbusting plow made of steel cut through the layer of sod covering the soil; windmills pumped water hundreds of feet underground to the surface; reapers, threshing machines, and binders improved harvests)*

Draw Conclusions How did the physical characteristics of the environment influence economic and social activities for farmers in the Great Plains? *(The open land was used for farming. Homesteaders invested in their land to make their farms productive. They often had lean harvests because of the climate and environment, but many were able to grow huge amounts of wheat and corn to sell. Homesteaders' farms were miles apart, and people looked forward to social events that brought neighbors together.)*

Identify Steps in a Process Describe the steps farmers took to improve their economic conditions. *(They formed alliances such as the National Grange and the Farmers' Alliance to boost profits and reduce the shipping rates railroads charged. Farmers set up cooperatives to buy tools and seeds wholesale and built shared warehouses to store grain cheaply. Farmers also voted for candidates who supported their needs.)*

Objective 5: **Explain why the Populist Party was formed.**

Quick Instruction

Project the political cartoon of William Jennings Bryan on the whiteboard, followed by the political cartoon of William McKinley. Ask students to consider the two images and make a prediction about the major issues involved in the election of 1896.

Summarize Identify the legislative acts the Populist Party wanted to pass. What did they hope would be the effects of these acts? *(Legislation—raise farm prices, regulate railroads, instate an income tax, mandate an eight-hour workday, limit immigration, institute free silver. Effects—improve working conditions for farmers and laborers, boost profits especially for farms in the West, increase the money supply to help farmers repay debts)*

D Differentiate: Extra Support Have students look at the word *populist*. Tell them that *populist* comes from the Latin word *populus*, which means *people.* Explain that the Populist Party aimed to represent ordinary people. Have students choose an issue the Populist Party supported and explain how it represented the interests of common Americans, as opposed to wealthy businesses.

Further Instruction

Go through the Interactive Reading Notepad questions and discuss the answers with the class. To extend the lesson, assign the Primary Source: Preamble to the Platform of the Populist Party.

Compare and Contrast the views of Bryan and McKinley. *(Bryan—young Democrat running on the Populist platform, championed the common people against the rich, wanted to increase the nation's supply of money by coining silver. McKinley—Republican candidate, against free silver, favored by bankers and businesspeople in the East.)*

Identify Cause and Effect What factors caused the Populist Party to gain support? What factors then caused the party to disband? *(Economic difficulties led farmers and labor unions to seek greater government regulation to help workers. A depression helped the party gain support, as more people faced hardships and sought a party that supported ordinary Americans. The party disbanded after McKinley won the election with support from cities in the East. Democrats adopted some populist causes and the economy bounced back, meaning many Americans no longer had the economic concerns that had led them to support the party.)*

SYNTHESIZE

DIGITAL ACTIVITY

The Effects of the Homestead Act

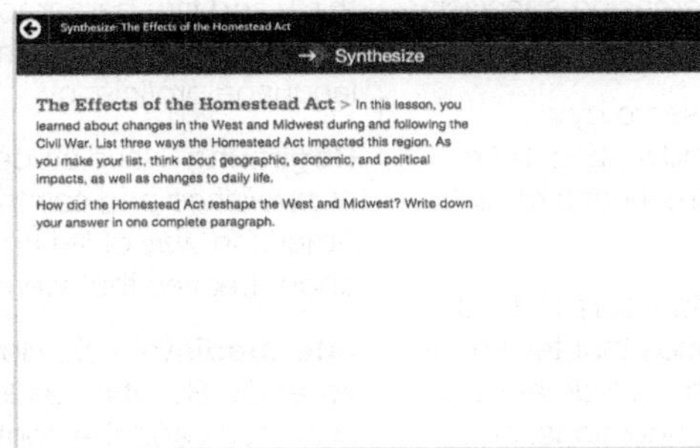

Have students compile a list of effects and then answer the question in a complete paragraph. Have students share their lists with a partner and discuss their answers.

Discuss Have students review the paragraphs they wrote at the beginning of the lesson about life for settlers in the West. Ask if they would revise any of their answers now that they have learned more about how the physical environment of the region influenced economic activities and daily life in the region. Have students discuss what factors, including the Homestead Act, led settlers to build farms in the West despite the challenges and risks.

DEMONSTRATE

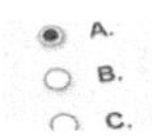

DIGITAL QUIZ

Lesson Quiz and Class Discussion Board

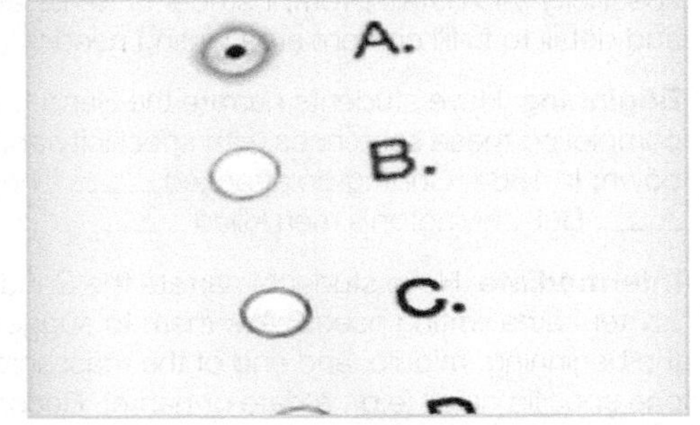

Assign the online Lesson Quiz for this lesson if you haven't already done so. Students will be offered automatic remediation or enrichment based on their score.

Pose these questions to the class on the Discussion Board:

Identify Patterns Trace the economic development of the West from the end of the Civil War through the election of 1896. What role did the physical environment play in shaping the economic activities of the region?

Support Ideas with Evidence What factors influenced settlement patterns and population distribution in the West during the nineteenth century? Provide evidence for support.

Topic Inquiry

Have students continue their investigations for the Topic Inquiry.

Hardship for Native Americans

Supporting English Language Learners

Use with the reading, **Broken Promises**.

Writing

Discuss the elements of a strong written story, including the use of specificity and detail. Prompt students to narrate with increasing specificity and detail to fulfill content area writing needs.

Beginning Have students narrate the Sand Creek Massacre by completing these sentences with specificity and detail and writing them down: In 1864, Chivington attacked ____. The Native Americans raised ____. But Chivington's men killed ____.

Intermediate Have students narrate the Sand Creek Massacre to fulfill content area writing needs. Ask them to suggest sentences that tell about the beginning, middle, and end of the massacre, and that include at least one specific detail (e.g., a date or name). Record their suggestions, and have students write them down.

Advanced Have pairs of students write a narration of the Sand Creek Massacre to fulfill content area writing needs. Encourage them to include at least three specific details about the event. Ask pairs to read one another's narrations and identify the specific details.

Advanced High Ask students to write a narration of the Sand Creek Massacre to fulfill content area writing needs. Have them reread their writing and revise it to increase the specificity and detail in each sentence. Have partners share their narrations and compare the details they included.

Use with the reading, **Calls to Reform Native American Policies**.

Speaking

Point out the grade-level content area vocabulary in the text's second, third, and fifth paragraphs, including *lectured*, *published*, and *policy*. Have students use these terms orally to clarify meanings and to build academic language proficiency.

Beginning Have students complete these sentences with either *lectured* or *published* and say them aloud: Susette La Flesche ____ on the Native American way of life and its destruction. Helen Hunt Jackson ____ a book about treaties that were broken.

Intermediate Ask: How did Helen Hunt Jackson help Native Americans? What did Susette La Flesche do? Have students answer using complete sentences and the content area vocabulary *lectured* and *published* in order to build academic language proficiency.

Advanced Have pairs of students use the content area vocabulary *lectured* and *published* as they discuss these questions: How did reformers such as La Flesche and Jackson make a difference in the lives of Native Americans? How did they change the lives of the rest of the United States?

Advanced High Discuss the grade-level content area vocabulary word *policy*. Have pairs of students use *policy*, along with *lectured* and *published*, to build academic language proficiency as they discuss how reformers such as La Flesche and Jackson helped change Native American policies.

D Differentiate Instruction

Use the Differentiated Instruction notes throughout the lesson plan to support the varied skill sets, levels of readiness, and interests in the mixed-ability classroom.

Challenge These notes include suggestions for expanding the activity for advanced students.

On-Level These notes include suggestions for modifying the activity to address different interests or learning styles.

Extra Support These notes include ideas for providing more scaffolding or reading spupport.

Special Needs These notes provide ideas for adapting instruction to support the needs of various special needs students.

NOTES

Objectives

Objective 1: Describe the life of the Plains Indians and their uses of buffalo.

Objective 2: Summarize promises made to Native Americans.

Objective 3: Explain why the Plains Indian way of life ended.

Objective 4: Identify why reforms in favor of Native Americans failed.

LESSON 3 ORGANIZER	PACING: APPROX. 1 PERIOD, .5 BLOCKS		RESOURCES	
	OBJECTIVES	PACING	Online	Print
Connect				
DIGITAL START UP ACTIVITY **The Basic Needs of Life**		5 min.	●	
Investigate				
DIGITAL TEXT 1 **The Plains Indians**	Objective 1	10 min.	●	●
DIGITAL TEXT 2 **Life on the Plains**		10 min.	●	●
DIGITAL TEXT 3 **Gender Roles in Plains Indian Society**		10 min.	●	●
DIGITAL TEXT 4 **Broken Promises**	Objective 2	10 min.	●	●
DIGITAL TEXT 5 **Conflict in the West Continues**	Objective 3	10 min.	●	●
DIGITAL TEXT 6 **Remembering a Lost Way of Life**		10 min.	●	●
DIGITAL TEXT 7 **Calls to Reform Native American Policies**	Objective 4	10 min.	●	●
INTERACTIVE MAP **Native American Losses, 1850–1890**		10 min.	●	
Synthesize				
DIGITAL ACTIVITY **The Desire for Reform**		5 min.	●	
Demonstrate				
DIGITAL QUIZ **Lesson Quiz and Class Discussion Board**		10 min.	●	

Hardship for Native Americans

CONNECT

DIGITAL START UP ACTIVITY
The Basic Needs of Life

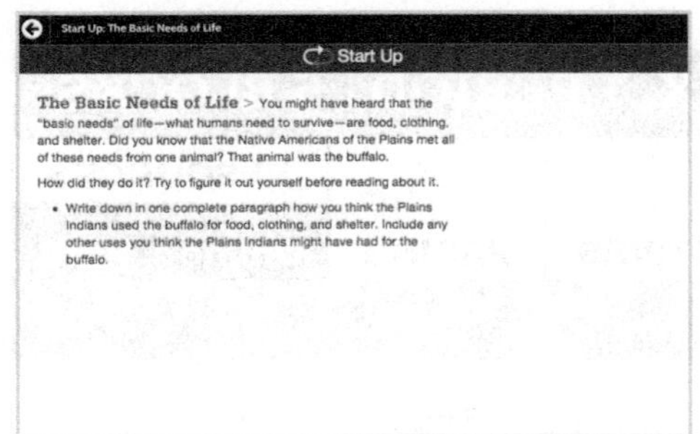

Start Up: The Basic Needs of Life
Start Up
The Basic Needs of Life > You might have heard that the "basic needs" of life—what humans need to survive—are food, clothing, and shelter. Did you know that the Native Americans of the Plains met all of these needs from one animal? That animal was the buffalo.
How did they do it? Try to figure it out yourself before reading about it.
• Write down in one complete paragraph how you think the Plains Indians used the buffalo for food, clothing, and shelter. Include any other uses you think the Plains Indians might have had for the buffalo.

Project the Start Up Activity Ask students to read the activity and write down their paragraph as they enter and get settled. Have students share their paragraphs with a partner, either in class or through a blog space.

Discuss Write down in one complete paragraph how you think the Plains Indians could use the buffalo for food, clothing, and shelter. Include any other uses you think the Plains Indians might have had for the buffalo. *(Plains Indians could use buffalo meat for food, make clothes from skins and sinews, and build shelter out of the hide. Fur could be woven to make blankets and cloth. The buffalo also had value to the Plains Indians as a symbol of their way of life.)*

Aa Vocabulary Development: Use the Interactive Reading Notepad to preview the Key Terms and Academic Vocabulary in this lesson with students.

FLIP IT!

Assign the Flipped Video for this lesson.

STUDENT EDITION PRINT PAGES: 547–556

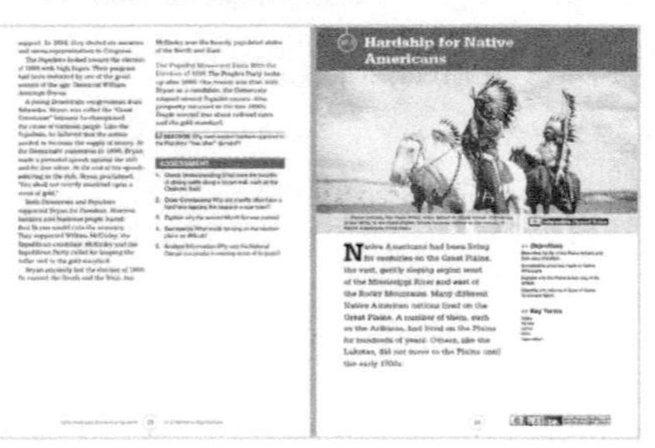

INVESTIGATE

DIGITAL TEXT 1
The Plains Indians

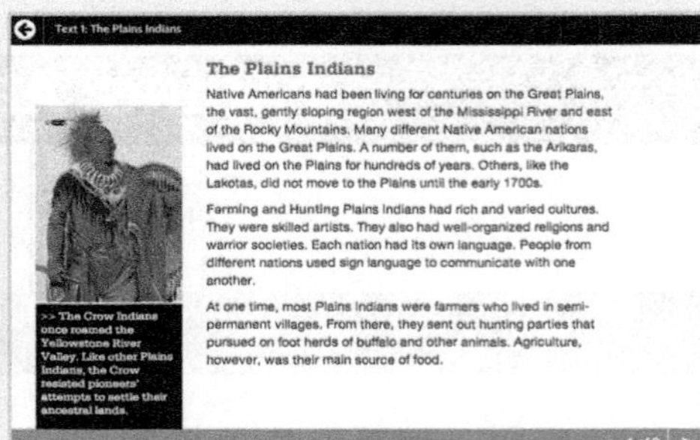

Text 1: The Plains Indians
The Plains Indians
Native Americans had been living for centuries on the Great Plains, the vast, gently sloping region west of the Mississippi River and east of the Rocky Mountains. Many different Native American nations lived on the Great Plains. A number of them, such as the Arikaras, had lived on the Plains for hundreds of years. Others, like the Lakotas, did not move to the Plains until the early 1700s.
Farming and Hunting Plains Indians had rich and varied cultures. They were skilled artists. They also had well-organized religions and warrior societies. Each nation had its own language. People from different nations used sign language to communicate with one another.
At one time, most Plains Indians were farmers who lived in semi-permanent villages. From there, they sent out hunting parties that pursued on foot herds of buffalo and other animals. Agriculture, however, was their main source of food.
>> The Crow Indians once roamed the Yellowstone River Valley. Like other Plains Indians, the Crow resisted pioneers' attempts to settle their ancestral lands.
1 of 3

DIGITAL TEXT 2
Life on the Plains

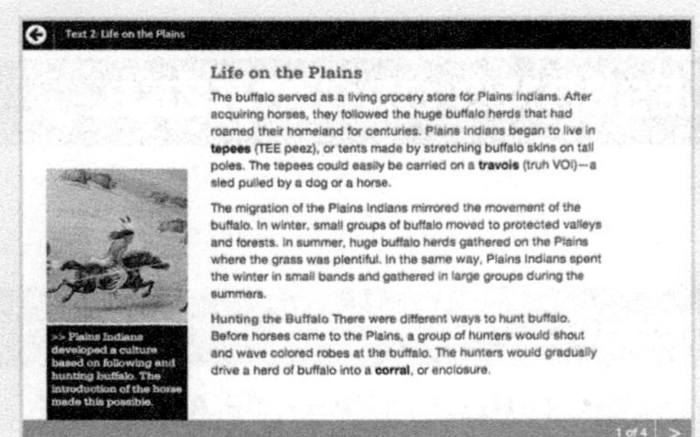

Text 2: Life on the Plains
Life on the Plains
The buffalo served as a living grocery store for Plains Indians. After acquiring horses, they followed the huge buffalo herds that had roamed their homeland for centuries. Plains Indians began to live in tepees (TEE peez), or tents made by stretching buffalo skins on tall poles. The tepees could easily be carried on a travois (truh VOI)—a sled pulled by a dog or a horse.
The migration of the Plains Indians mirrored the movement of the buffalo. In winter, small groups of buffalo moved to protected valleys and forests. In summer, huge buffalo herds gathered on the Plains where the grass was plentiful. In the same way, Plains Indians spent the winter in small bands and gathered in large groups during the summers.
Hunting the Buffalo There were different ways to hunt buffalo. Before horses came to the Plains, a group of hunters would shout and wave colored robes at the buffalo. The hunters would gradually drive a herd of buffalo into a corral, or enclosure.
>> Plains Indians developed a culture based on following and hunting buffalo. The introduction of the horse made this possible.
1 of 4

Objective 1: **Describe the life of the Plains Indians and their uses of buffalo.**

Quick Instruction

Project on the whiteboard the image of the Sioux riding on horseback. Explain that Plains Indians relied on the physical environment of the West. They used horses, introduced by the Spanish, for hunting, traveling, raiding, hauling their possessions, and trading with neighboring tribes.

Summarize Describe how the physical environment shaped life for the Plains Indians. *(They relied on the environment for food, clothing, and shelter. They farmed and hunted, using horses to follow huge buffalo herds from protected valleys and forests to the open plains. They built tepees that could be carried on sleds called travois when they moved.)*

Further Instruction

Go through the Interactive Reading Notepad questions and discuss the answers with the class.

Compare and Contrast Describe the responsibilities of men and women in Plains Indians cultures. *(Women—gathered food, prepared meals, made tepees, raised and took down tepees when traveling, cared for children, made crafts and art. Men—hunted, provided protection against enemies, led religious ceremonies, waged war.)*

DIGITAL TEXT 3

Gender Roles in Plains Indian Society

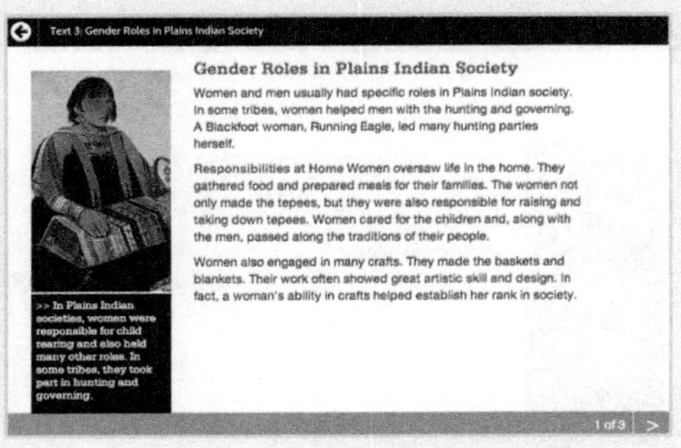

Text 3: Gender Roles in Plains Indian Society
Gender Roles in Plains Indian Society
Women and men usually had specific roles in Plains Indian society. In some tribes, women helped men with the hunting and governing. A Blackfoot woman, Running Eagle, led many hunting parties herself.
Responsibilities at Home Women oversaw life in the home. They gathered food and prepared meals for their families. The women not only made the tepees, but they were also responsible for raising and taking down tepees. Women cared for the children and, along with the men, passed along the traditions of their people.
Women also engaged in many crafts. They made the baskets and blankets. Their work often showed great artistic skill and design. In fact, a woman's ability in crafts helped establish her rank in society.
>> In Plains Indian societies, women were responsible for child rearing and also held many other roles. In some tribes, they took part in hunting and governing.
1 of 3

Make a Prediction about how life for Plains Indians will be affected by white settlers killing off the buffalo. Explain your reasoning. *(The Plains Indians will suffer and lose their way of life. They used the buffalo for food, shelter, and clothing, and following buffalo herds was a major part of their life. Killing the buffalo will leave the Plains Indians without their most important resource.)*

DIGITAL TEXT 4

Broken Promises

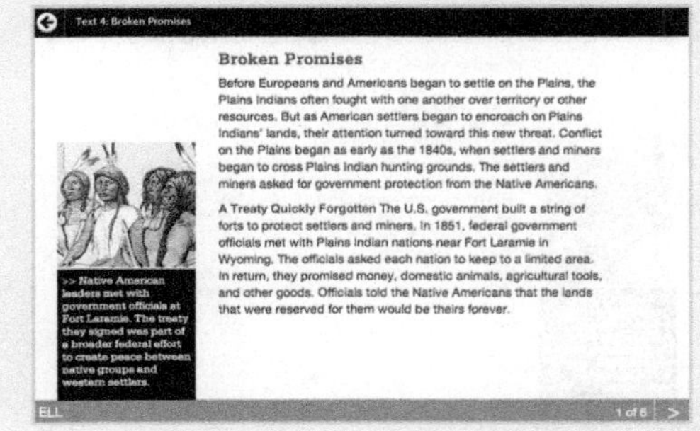

Text 4: Broken Promises
Broken Promises
Before Europeans and Americans began to settle on the Plains, the Plains Indians often fought with one another over territory or other resources. But as American settlers began to encroach on Plains Indians' lands, their attention turned toward this new threat. Conflict on the Plains began as early as the 1840s, when settlers and miners began to cross Plains Indian hunting grounds. The settlers and miners asked for government protection from the Native Americans.
A Treaty Quickly Forgotten The U.S. government built a string of forts to protect settlers and miners. In 1851, federal government officials met with Plains Indian nations near Fort Laramie in Wyoming. The officials asked each nation to keep to a limited area. In return, they promised money, domestic animals, agricultural tools, and other goods. Officials told the Native Americans that the lands that were reserved for them would be theirs forever.
>> Native American leaders met with government officials at Fort Laramie. The treaty they signed was part of a broader federal effort to create peace between native groups and western settlers.
ELL
1 of 6

Objective 2: **Summarize promises made to Native Americans.**

Quick Instruction

Project on the whiteboard the image of Native Americans and government officials meeting at Fort Laramie, where a treaty was signed in 1851. Discuss with students the reasons why a treaty such as this might be broken.

Summarize Summarize the promises made to Native Americans. *(The U.S. government promised Native Americans land that would be theirs permanently if they did not interfere with settlers and miners. The government also promised money, domestic animals, tools, and other goods.)*

D Differentiate: Extra Support Explain to students that a massacre is a tragic event in which a large number of people are violently killed. It implies that those who are killed are innocent, helpless, or unprepared for such a brutal attack. Have students read through the text and locate context clues that explain why several of the conflicts between Native Americans and white settlers are called massacres.

ELL Use the ELL activity described in the ELL chart.

Further Instruction

Go through the Interactive Reading Notepad questions and discuss the answers with the class.

Draw Conclusions How did the discovery of gold affect land treaties with Native Americans? *(The discovery of gold in Colorado caused miners to flock to land belonging to the Cheyenne and Arapaho tribes. Because settlers wanted gold, Native Americans were forced to give up land that had been promised to them.)*

Identify Cause and Effect Explain the effects of the Sand Creek Massacre. *(Plains Indians and U.S. soldiers went to war. In response to the violence, federal officials urged Native Americans to live like white settlers. Native Americans were forced off their lands and onto reservations.)*

Hardship for Native Americans

DIGITAL TEXT 5

Conflict in the West Continues

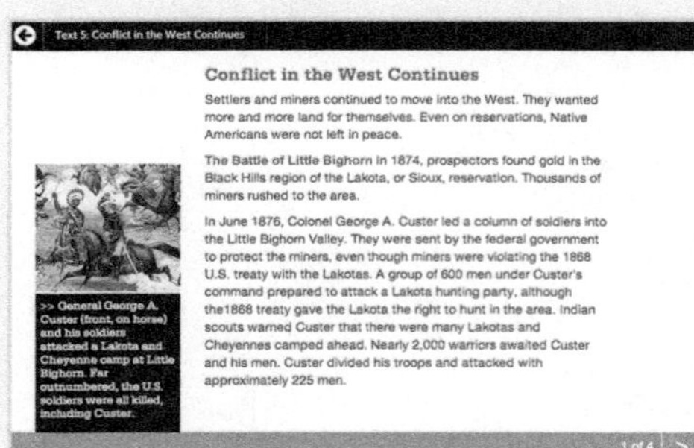

DIGITAL TEXT 6

Remembering a Lost Way of Life

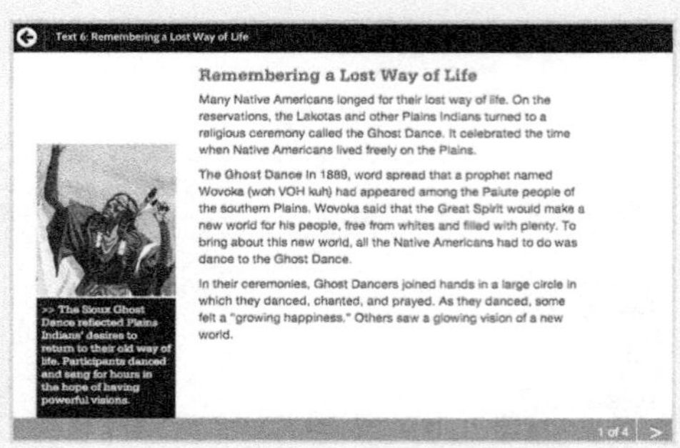

DIGITAL TEXT 7

Calls to Reform Native American Policies

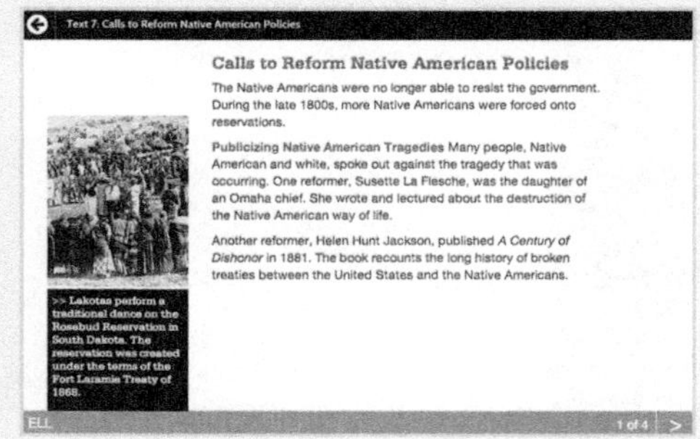

Objective 3: **Explain why the Plains Indian way of life ended.**

Quick Instruction

Project the image of the Battle of Little Bighorn on the whiteboard and have students describe what they see. Discuss the causes and effects of conflicts between white settlers and Native American tribes on the frontier.

Draw Conclusions What factors caused the Plains Indian way of life to end? *(White settlers pushed Native Americans off their land and into reservations; white settlers killed off the buffalo on which Plains Indians depended; the discovery of gold brought more white settlers and miners into the West.)*

Further Instruction

Go through the Interactive Reading Notepad questions and discuss the answers with the class. To extend the lesson, assign the Primary Source: I Will Fight No More Forever (Chief Joseph).

Sequence Events of the Sioux War of 1876. *(Prospectors found gold on the Lakota, or Sioux, reservation; miners rushed to the area; Native Americans fought back; the federal government sent soldiers to protect the miners; Colonel George A. Custer and his men were killed in the Battle of Little Bighorn; the U.S. army fought back and defeated the Lakotas and Cheyenne; Congress threatened to cut off food rations to Native Americans; the Lakotas surrendered territory they had been promised in the Fort Laramie Treaty.)*

Identify Cause and Effect What caused the Paiute people to perform the Ghost Dance? What were the effects of this celebration? *(Causes—the loss of the Native American way of life caused the Paiute to develop a religious ceremony called the Ghost Dance, which promised a new world free from white settlers and the suffering they had caused. Effects—The dance was misinterpreted by white settlers, who thought it was a preparation for war. Police accidentally shot and killed Sitting Bull, claiming he was spreading the Ghost Dance to the Lakotas. His death led to the massacre at Wounded Knee, which ended the Ghost Dance religion.)*

Cite Evidence explaining the significance of Geronimo's surrender. *("It marked the end of formal warfare between Native Americans and whites.")*

Objective 4: **Identify why reforms in favor of Native Americans failed.**

Quick Instruction

Interactive Map: Native American Losses, 1850–1890 Project the interactive map on the whiteboard and click through the layers. Have students use the map to make a generalization about how western expansion impacted Native Americans.

Identify Patterns What factors caused Native Americans to lose lands in the 1800s? *(White settlers moved west seeking land to settle and farm, as well as gold. Government policies did not protect Native American land and resources and many treaties were broken.)*

> **ACTIVE CLASSROOM**
>
> Pair students to use the Audio Tour Strategy to examine the interactive map. Have the first student give the second student a "tour" of the map explaining what it shows. Have the second student give the first an explanation of what the map means.

ELL Use the ELL activity described in the ELL chart.

Further Instruction

Go through the Interactive Reading Notepad questions and discuss the answers with the class.

Support Ideas with Examples Give an example of how Americans called for reforms to the treatment of Native Americans.

INTERACTIVE MAP

Native American Losses, 1850–1890

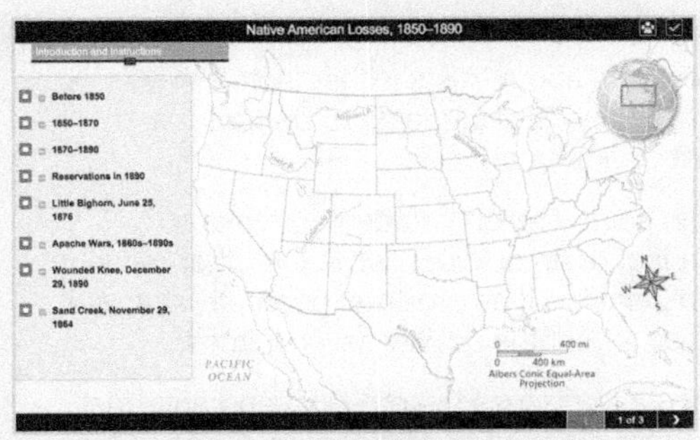

(Reformers spoke out against forcing Native Americans onto reservations. Susette La Flesche wrote and lectured about how Native American ways of life were being destroyed; Helen Hunt Jackson published A Century of Dishonor, *a history of broken treaties between the United States and Native Americans.)*

Generate Explanations Explain the Dawes Act and identify its effects. *(The Dawes Act of 1887 divided tribal lands and gave them to individual families to farm. Instead of forcing Native Americans onto reservations, the act was intended to make them more like American farmers. However, many Native American groups did not want to be restricted to private farms, and much of the land they received was not suitable for farming. They wound up selling their land to whites.)*

SYNTHESIZE

DIGITAL ACTIVITY

The Desire for Reform

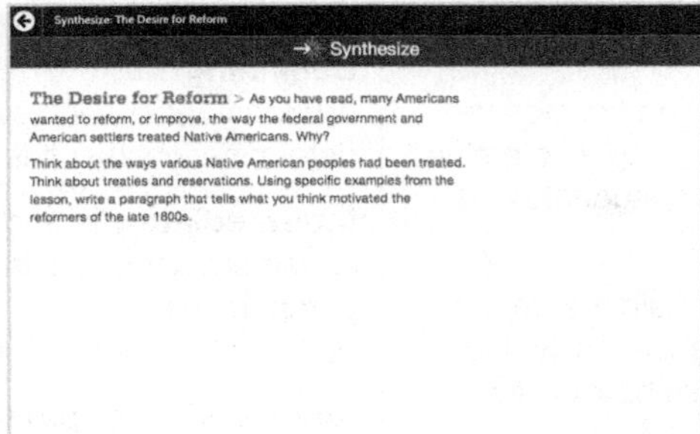

Have students read the activity and write a paragraph using specific examples to tell what motivated the reformers of the late 1800s. Have students share their paragraphs with a partner and discuss their answers. Then have the class discuss why these reforms were not effective.

Discuss Have students review the lesson and discuss the ways life for Native Americans in the Plains changed as a result of westward expansion in the 1800s. Have students give specific examples that show the hardships Native Americans faced. Remind students to consider social, economic, political, and environmental factors.

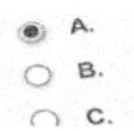

DEMONSTRATE

DIGITAL QUIZ

Lesson Quiz and Class Discussion Board

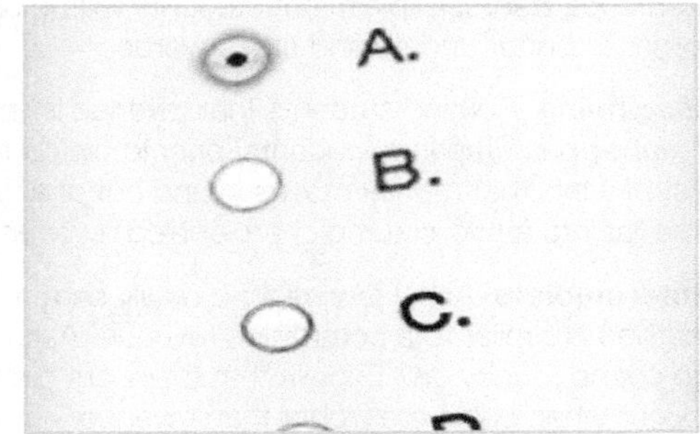

Assign the online Lesson Quiz for this lesson if you haven't already done so. Students will be offered automatic remediation or enrichment based on their score.

Pose these questions to the class on the Discussion Board:

Identify Patterns Why didn't the U.S. government keep its promises to Native Americans?

Evaluate Arguments Evaluate the different ways that the federal government treated Native Americans in the 1800s. What approaches did the government take, and why? What were the different effects?

Topic Inquiry

Have students continue their investigations for the Topic Inquiry.

Industry and Corporations

Supporting English Language Learners

Use with the reading, **The Rise of Corporations and Banks**.

Learning

Point out key vocabulary related to business (e.g., *revenue, costs, profit, bankrupt, debt*). Explain that students will be using prior knowledge in order to better understand these words.

Beginning Remind students that revenue is "money in," and costs are "money out." Tap into students' prior knowledge by displaying a scrambled list of ways that money moves in and out of a family. Have students sort the list into a two-column chart labeled *revenue* and *costs*.

Intermediate Ask: How might a family earn money? Explain that money earned is similar to a company's revenue. Ask: What might a family need to spend money on? Explain that these are costs. Discuss how debts occur when costs are higher than revenue.

Advanced Discuss the following scenarios: collecting revenue, incurring costs, earning a profit, going into debt, declaring bankruptcy. Have pairs use prior knowledge to discuss how a person might experience each of the above.

Advanced High Invite pairs of students to identify two local businesses: one successful, and one struggling. Have pairs use prior knowledge and the vocabulary above to write brief descriptions of each business.

Use with the reading, **The Debate Over Trusts**.

Speaking

Review the definition of *trust*. Explain that students will use listening skills and peer collaboration to demonstrate their understanding of trusts.

Beginning Make several statements about trusts (either facts or opinions). After each statement, ask pairs of students to discuss it and determine whether it is pro-trust or anti-trust.

Intermediate Place students in pairs. Ask one student to make a statement about trusts (either a fact or an opinion), while the other student paraphrases the statement and identifies it as pro-trust or anti-trust. Invite partners to alternate roles as they repeat the activity several times.

Advanced Invite pairs of students to discuss the pro-trust and anti-trust viewpoints. In their discussion, have them address these questions: Which groups or individuals made up each side? What did each side believe? How did each side defend its ideas? Encourage partners to build on each other's comments in order to demonstrate listening comprehension.

Advanced High Invite small groups to debate trusts. Have each group divide into pro-trust and anti-trust camps. Explain that group members should take turns persuading the other side to adopt their position, as well as listen to their opponents' statements and respectfully try to refute them.

D Differentiate Instruction

Use the Differentiated Instruction notes throughout the lesson plan to support the varied skill sets, levels of readiness, and interests in the mixed-ability classroom.

Challenge These notes include suggestions for expanding the activity for advanced students.

On-Level These notes include suggestions for modifying the activity to address different interests or learning styles.

Extra Support These notes include ideas for providing more scaffolding or reading spuport.

Special Needs These notes provide ideas for adapting instruction to support the needs of various special needs students.

NOTES

Objectives

Objective 1: Explain the growth of the steel industry.

Objective 2: Describe the economic contributions of corporations and bankers.

Objective 3: Explain how Rockefeller built a huge oil trust.

Objective 4: Identify arguments for and against trusts and monopolies.

LESSON 4 ORGANIZER — **PACING: APPROX. 1 PERIOD, .5 BLOCKS**

	OBJECTIVES	PACING	RESOURCES Online	RESOURCES Print
Connect				
DIGITAL START UP ACTIVITY **Building an Industry**		5 min.	●	
Investigate				
DIGITAL TEXT 1 **The Steel Industry Expands**	Objective 1	10 min.	●	●
DIGITAL TEXT 2 **Andrew Carnegie Builds an Empire**	Objective 1	10 min.	●	●
DIGITAL TEXT 3 **The Rise of Corporations and Banks**	Objective 2	10 min.	●	●
DIGITAL TEXT 4 **Rockefeller and the Oil Industry**	Objective 3	10 min.	●	●
INTERACTIVE MAP **Railroads and Industry**	Objective 3	10 min.	●	
DIGITAL TEXT 5 **The Debate Over Trusts**	Objective 4	10 min.	●	●
INTERACTIVE CHART **Advantages and Disadvantages of Big Business**	Objective 4	10 min.	●	
Synthesize				
DIGITAL ACTIVITY **Building an Industry**		5 min.	●	
Demonstrate				
DIGITAL QUIZ **Lesson Quiz and Discussion Board**		10 min.	●	

Industry and Corporations

CONNECT

DIGITAL START UP ACTIVITY

Building an Industry

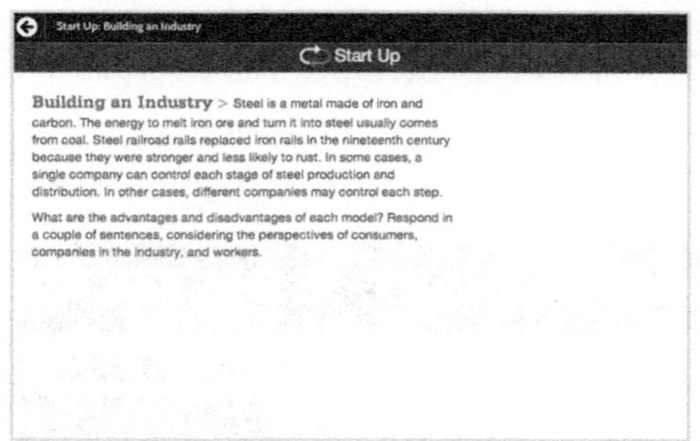

Start Up: Building an Industry
Start Up
Building an Industry > Steel is a metal made of iron and carbon. The energy to melt iron ore and turn it into steel usually comes from coal. Steel railroad rails replaced iron rails in the nineteenth century because they were stronger and less likely to rust. In some cases, a single company can control each stage of steel production and distribution. In other cases, different companies may control each step.
What are the advantages and disadvantages of each model? Respond in a couple of sentences, considering the perspectives of consumers, companies in the industry, and workers.

Project the Start Up Activity Have students read and complete the activity as they enter the classroom.

Discuss A single company can control each stage of steel production and distribution or different companies may control each step. What are the advantages and disadvantages of each model? *(When a single company controls all steps, the consumers, workers, and other companies in the industry lose power and choice. When different companies are involved power and choice are more evenly distributed.)*

Tell students that this lesson examines the role of big business in American economics and politics, and its impact on American lives.

Aa Vocabulary Development: Use the Interactive Reading Notepad to preview the Key Terms and Academic Vocabulary in this lesson with students.

FLIP IT!

Assign the Flipped Video for this lesson.

STUDENT EDITION PRINT PAGES: 557–564

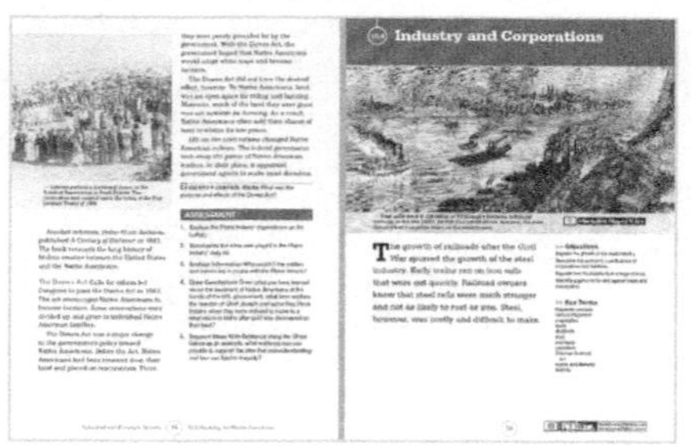

INVESTIGATE

DIGITAL TEXT 1

The Steel Industry Expands

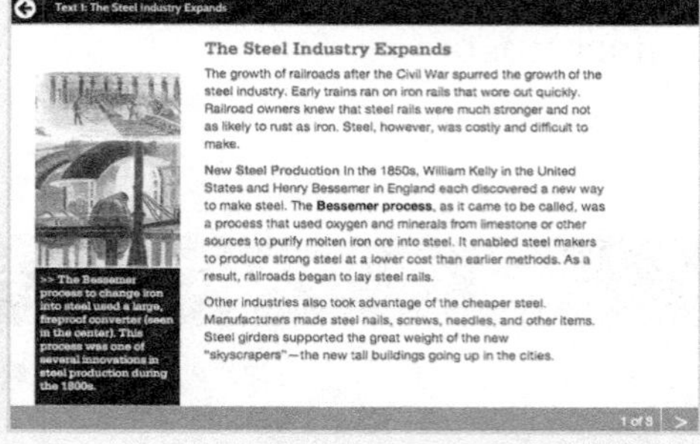

DIGITAL TEXT 2

Andrew Carnegie Builds an Empire

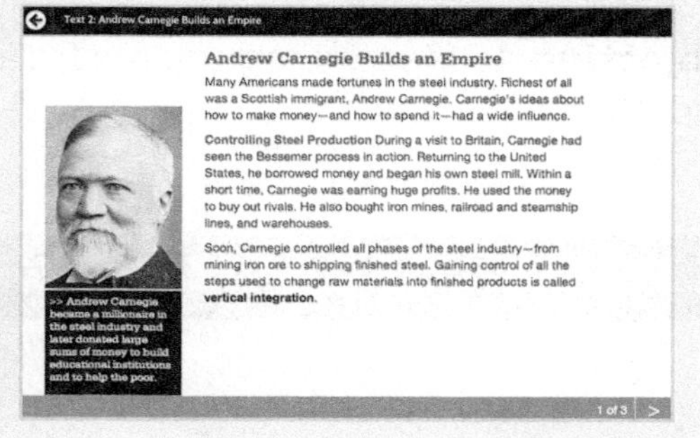

Objective 1: Explain the growth of the steel industry.

Quick Instruction

Display the illustration of the Bessemer process. Then, explain to students that in the 1800s Americans depended on railroads to transport goods across the country. Steel tracks lasted much longer than iron, but steel was extremely expensive to produce until the Bessemer process was invented. Once this quick and inexpensive process became popular, the steel industry rapidly expanded.

Predict Consequences Ask students how they think the expansion of the steel industry affected the economy and the environment. *(The steel industry boosted the economy as steel was employed in railroad tracks and tall buildings, but the industrial waste from steel production was harmful to the environment.)*

Further Instruction

Identify Cause and Effect What initially caused the expansion of the steel industry? *(The invention of the Bessemer process.)* Name three effects of the expansion of the steel industry. *(Possible responses: Longer-lasting railroad tracks, steel towns and economic growth in the Midwest, pollution, an economic boom nationwide)*

Determine Relevance How did the Bessemer process affect the development of skyscrapers? *(Efficient steel production led to steel girders that could support the weight of skyscrapers and elevator shafts.)*

DIGITAL TEXT 3

The Rise of Corporations and Banks

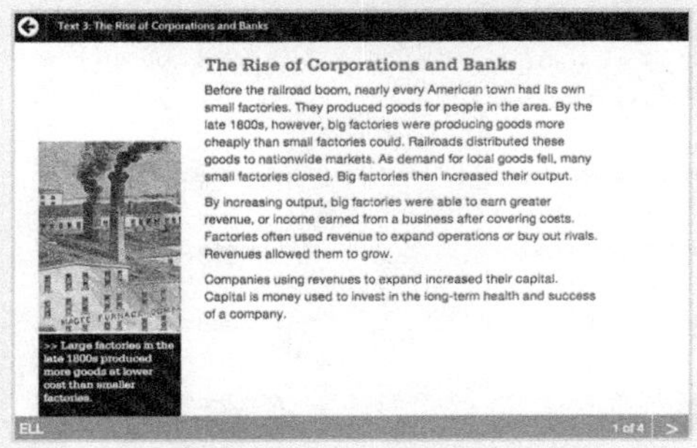

Text 3: The Rise of Corporations and Banks
The Rise of Corporations and Banks
Before the railroad boom, nearly every American town had its own small factories. They produced goods for people in the area. By the late 1800s, however, big factories were producing goods more cheaply than small factories could. Railroads distributed these goods to nationwide markets. As demand for local goods fell, many small factories closed. Big factories then increased their output.
By increasing output, big factories were able to earn greater revenue, or income earned from a business after covering costs. Factories often used revenue to expand operations or buy out rivals. Revenues allowed them to grow.
Companies using revenues to expand increased their capital. Capital is money used to invest in the long-term health and success of a company.
>> Large factories in the late 1800s produced more goods at lower cost than smaller factories.
ELL
1 of 4

Objective 2: **Describe the economic contributions of corporations and bankers.**

Quick Instruction

Display the photograph of the large factory and explain that in the late 1800s, many small factories were replaced by these big businesses. Discuss the essentials of reorganizing a business into a corporation with students: by selling shares, or stock, of the business, owners could obtain more money to invest in the business, which, in turn, made it even bigger. As businesses grew, they also borrowed money from banks. Bankers made huge amounts of money, and businesses benefited from the loans. Prompt students to discuss how the reorganization of business helped owners, investors, and the economy.

Compare and Contrast Ask students to compare and contrast privately owned businesses and corporations. Challenge them to identify benefits and drawbacks of each kind of business organization. *(Possible responses: Private ownership—owner has full control but also takes all the risk. Corporation—company has more financial resources and owners are shielded from risk, but profits and control are shared among stockholders.)*

D Differentiate: Extra Support Provide extra support by creating a glossary of business terms with students. Help students define in their own words business vocabulary, such as *corporation, investor, stock, dividends, capital,* and *revenue.* Guide students through the vocabulary as you explain how these terms are related.

ELL Use the ELL activity described in the ELL chart.

Further Instruction

Generate Explanations How were corporations and banks connected? How did they impact each other? *(Corporations borrowed money from banks, and banks earned interest on the loans. They had a positive effect on each other because their relationship provided corporations with the funding needed to make more money, and the interest corporations paid generated income for the banking industry.)*

DIGITAL TEXT 4

Rockefeller and the Oil Industry

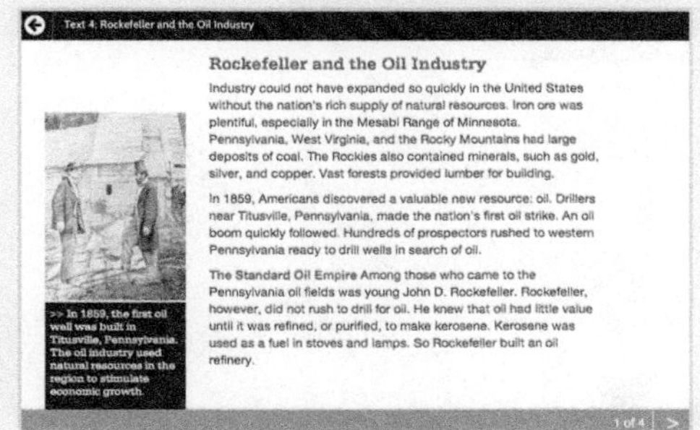

Text 4: Rockefeller and the Oil Industry
Rockefeller and the Oil Industry
Industry could not have expanded so quickly in the United States without the nation's rich supply of natural resources. Iron ore was plentiful, especially in the Mesabi Range of Minnesota. Pennsylvania, West Virginia, and the Rocky Mountains had large deposits of coal. The Rockies also contained minerals, such as gold, silver, and copper. Vast forests provided lumber for building.
In 1859, Americans discovered a valuable new resource: oil. Drillers near Titusville, Pennsylvania, made the nation's first oil strike. An oil boom quickly followed. Hundreds of prospectors rushed to western Pennsylvania ready to drill wells in search of oil.
The Standard Oil Empire Among those who came to the Pennsylvania oil fields was young John D. Rockefeller. Rockefeller, however, did not rush to drill for oil. He knew that oil had little value until it was refined, or purified, to make kerosene. Kerosene was used as a fuel in stoves and lamps. So Rockefeller built an oil refinery.
>> In 1859, the first oil well was built in Titusville, Pennsylvania. The oil industry used natural resources in the region to stimulate economic growth.
1 of 4

Objective 3: **Explain how Rockefeller built a huge oil trust.**

Quick Instruction

Interactive Map: Railroads and Industry
Project the Interactive Map. Before you guide students through the hotspots on the map, point out that railroads transported goods across the country and opened up a national market. Because of the railroads, businesses had access to buyers all over the nation. Then, guide students through each hotspot on the map, discussing the industries such as oil that were impacted by the expansion of the railways.

Support Ideas with Evidence How did Rockefeller feel about competition? *(He believed it was wasteful.)* What did he do to support his belief? *(He did everything he could to eliminate competition, including buying other refineries and creating the Standard Oil trust.)*

ACTIVE CLASSROOM

Use the Audio Tour strategy to further discuss the information in the map. Pair students. Have the first student give the second a verbal "tour" of the map. The first student should clearly explain what the map shows. Then, have the second student explain what the map means.

Industry and Corporations

INTERACTIVE MAP

Railroads and Industry

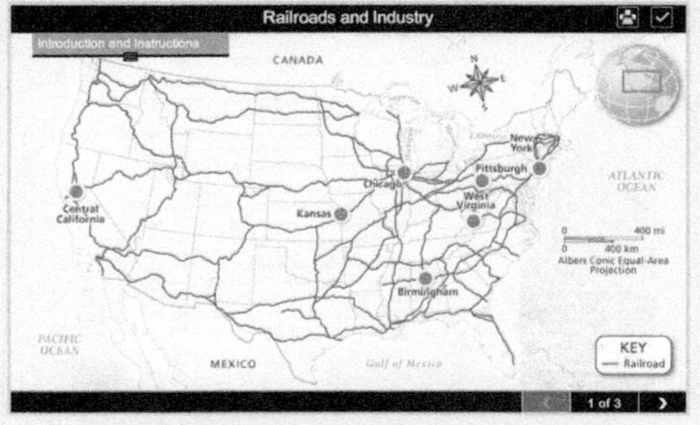

Further Instruction

Generate Explanations Why was Rockefeller more interested in the business of refining oil than he was in drilling for new oil sources? *(Rockefeller understood that crude oil was of little use to consumers before it was refined into usable products, so he invested in refineries, assuming correctly that the flow of crude oil would continue.)*

Connect What is the relationship between the expansion of railways throughout the nation and Rockefeller's ability to establish his business? *(The railroad allowed Rockefeller to access a national customer base from centrally-based refineries, which increased demand and allowed his business to grow exponentially.)*

DIGITAL TEXT 5

The Debate Over Trusts

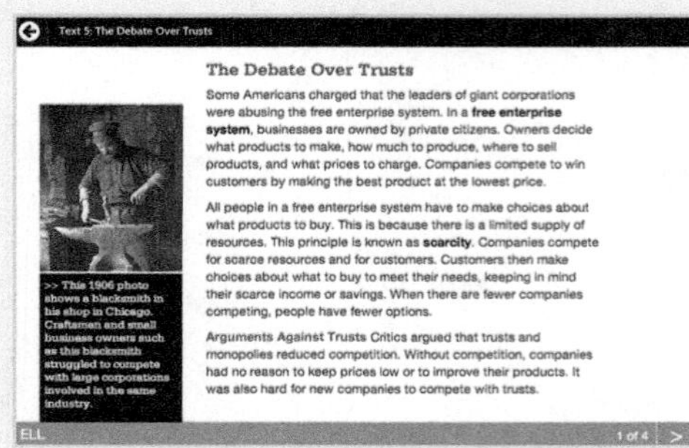
Text 5: The Debate Over Trusts

The Debate Over Trusts

Some Americans charged that the leaders of giant corporations were abusing the free enterprise system. In a **free enterprise system**, businesses are owned by private citizens. Owners decide what products to make, how much to produce, where to sell products, and what prices to charge. Companies compete to win customers by making the best product at the lowest price.

All people in a free enterprise system have to make choices about what products to buy. This is because there is a limited supply of resources. This principle is known as **scarcity**. Companies compete for scarce resources and for customers. Customers then make choices about what to buy to meet their needs, keeping in mind their scarce income or savings. When there are fewer companies competing, people have fewer options.

Arguments Against Trusts Critics argued that trusts and monopolies reduced competition. Without competition, companies had no reason to keep prices low or to improve their products. It was also hard for new companies to compete with trusts.

>> This 1906 photo shows a blacksmith in his shop in Chicago. Craftsmen and small business owners such as this blacksmith struggled to compete with large corporations involved in the same industry.

ELL 1 of 4

Objective 4: **Identify arguments for and against trusts and monopolies.**

Quick Instruction

Interactive Chart: Advantages and Disadvantages of Big Business Project the Interactive Chart. Ask volunteers to explain what a trust is and what a monopoly is, and prompt students to complete the chart. Students could also complete the Short Answer and Multiple Choice questions first and have them transfer that information to the chart in the form of advantages and disadvantages. Make sure that students understand that trusts, or groups of corporations run by the same board of directors, create monopolies, or companies that control almost all of the business in a particular industry.

ACTIVE CLASSROOM

Use the Take a Stand strategy to expand on the debate over trusts. After you complete the Interactive Chart: Advantages and Disadvantages of Big Business, ask students to take a stand on this question: Should trusts be allowed in the American free enterprise system? Yes or no? Ask students to divide into two groups based on their answers and move to separate areas of the room. Then, ask students to discuss their reasons for answering as they did. Finally, have a representative from each side present and defend the group's point of view in an informal debate.

INTERACTIVE CHART

Advantages and Disadvantages of Big Business

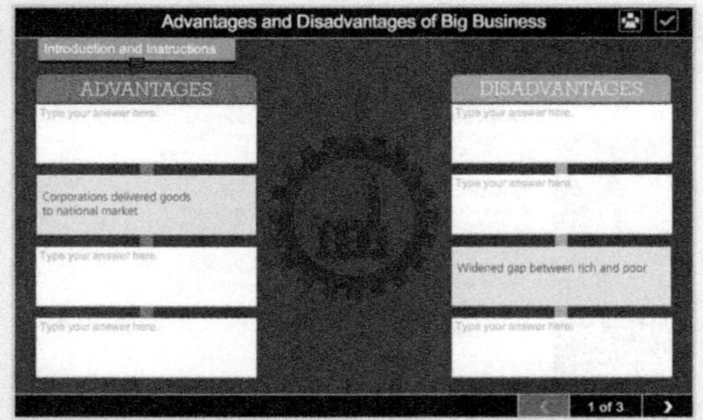

ELL Use the ELL activity described in the ELL chart.

Further Instruction

Identify Central Issues Outline the arguments for and against trusts. *(Those in favor of trusts argued that too much competition ruined businesses and put people out of work. They argued that trusts provided lower prices and higher wages. Those against trusts argued that they eliminated competition, which jeopardized the free enterprise system and eliminated consumer choice. They gave the trusts the power to increase prices without improving products.)*

Evaluate Arguments Identify the strengths and weaknesses of each argument, then choose which argument makes more sense using specific evidence to support your position. *(The argument for trusts was strengthened by the fact that in the presence of trusts the economy was booming. It was weakened by the fact that free enterprise is based on competition, and without competition the businesses were given free rein to govern themselves. Sample answer: The argument against trusts makes sense because trusts gave the corporations all the power in hiring, producing, setting prices, and improving products. Without another choice, the only option consumers had was to purchase whatever the trust sold for whatever price it asked.)*

PEARSON realize

www.PearsonRealize.com
Access your Digital Lesson

SYNTHESIZE

DIGITAL ACTIVITY

Building an Industry

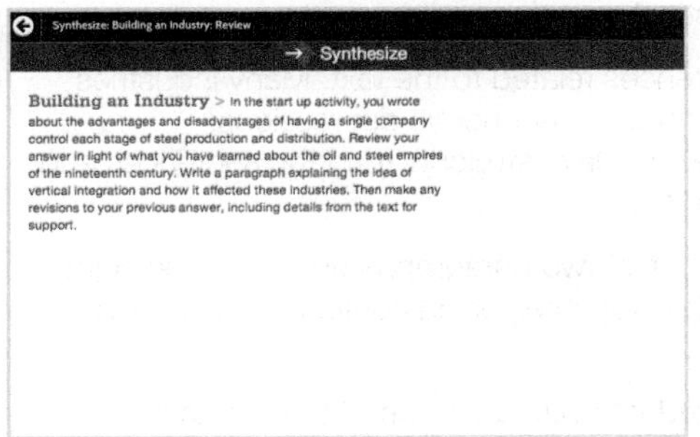

Have students review their answers from the Start Up Activity. Then, have them consider what they have learned and write their revisions. Invite volunteers to share their revisions with the class, noting how their ideas have changed with the knowledge they have gained.

Discuss Review what students have learned about vertical integration, trusts, monopolies, and free enterprise. Ask students to discuss how vertical integration threatens free enterprise and how it is connected with monopolies.

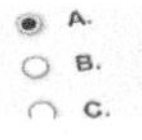

DEMONSTRATE

DIGITAL QUIZ

Lesson Quiz and Discussion Board

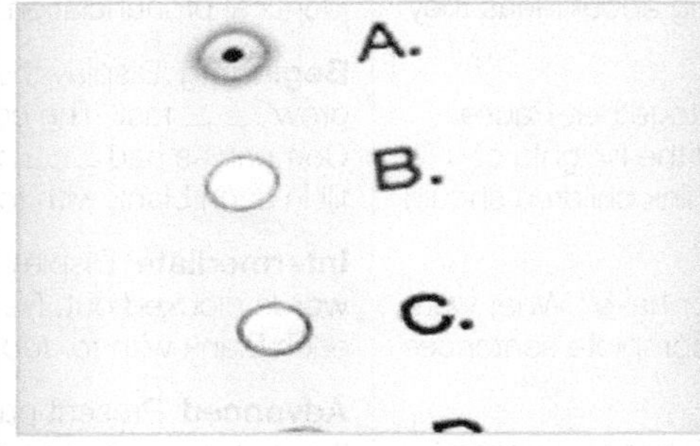

Assign the online Lesson Quiz for this lesson if you haven't already done so. Students will be offered automatic remediation or enrichment based on their score.

In *Industry and Corporations*, you learned about the causes and effects of the expansion of the steel industry. You also learned how privately owned businesses began to reorganize into corporations. These corporations often joined trusts that created monopolies, creating a threat to free enterprise. Key players in big business and banking, such as Rockefeller, Carnegie, and Morgan, were introduced.

Post these questions to the class on the Discussion Board:

Summarize What role did Andrew Carnegie, John D. Rockefeller, and J. P. Morgan play in the economy of the late 1800s?

Hypothesize How would the American economic system be different today if the government did not step in to regulate trusts?

Topic Inquiry

Have students continue their investigations for the Topic Inquiry.

The Labor Movement

Supporting English Language Learners

Use with the reading, **Workers Organize Unions**.

Speaking

With students, brainstorm techniques they can use to express ideas in a clear and effective way. Explain that they will be speaking about ideas they read in the text.

Beginning Reread the first five paragraphs of the text together. Pause periodically to ask close-ended questions, such as: Did the Knights of Labor believe that strikes were a good idea? Did they think children should work more or less?

Intermediate Ask: What goals did the Knights of Labor have? What were the AFL's goals? Encourage students to answer using complete sentences and to revisit the text for information as needed.

Advanced Place students in pairs. Have each partner state the ideas of either the Knights of Labor or the AFL. Encourage partners to revisit the text and ask each other follow-up questions as needed.

Advanced High Ask pairs of students to compare and contrast the ideas, goals, and actions of the Knights of Labor and the AFL. Encourage them to incorporate specific details from the text in their discussion.

Use with the reading, **Labor Faces Challenges**.

Writing

Display these basic sight vocabulary words: to, too, two. Discuss their identical pronunciation and distinct meanings.

Beginning Display these sentences related to the text: Many industries grew ____ fast. The country had ____ economic depressions. Companies had ____ fire workers. Have students read the sentences and fill in each blank with *to, too,* or *two*.

Intermediate Display the text's first two paragraphs with the three sight words blocked out. Read the text together, using context clues to fill in each blank with *to, too,* or *two*.

Advanced Present pairs of students with a version of the text that has every occurrence of *to, too,* and *two* highlighted, with some used incorrectly. Have students read through the text, identify which highlighted words are used correctly, and change those that are incorrect.

Advanced High Present students with a version of the text that has every occurrence of *to*, *too*, and *two* highlighted, with some used incorrectly. Have students read through the text, identify which highlighted words are used correctly, and change those that are incorrect. Have them explain the reason for each correction.

D Differentiate Instruction

Use the Differentiated Instruction notes throughout the lesson plan to support the varied skill sets, levels of readiness, and interests in the mixed-ability classroom.

Challenge These notes include suggestions for expanding the activity for advanced students.

On-Level These notes include suggestions for modifying the activity to address different interests or learning styles.

Extra Support These notes include ideas for providing more scaffolding or reading spuport.

Special Needs These notes provide ideas for adapting instruction to support the needs of various special needs students.

NOTES

PEARSON realize www.PearsonRealize.com

Go online to access additional resources including: Primary Sources • Biographies • Supreme Court cases • 21st Century Skill Tutorials • Maps • Graphic Organizers.

Objectives

Objective 1: Explain how changes in the workplace led to the rise of labor organizations.

Objective 2: Identify the issues that women faced in the workplace during the late 1800s.

Objective 3: Explain the challenges that the labor movement faced during the late 1800s.

LESSON 5 ORGANIZER — **PACING: APPROX. 1 PERIOD, .5 BLOCKS**

	OBJECTIVES	PACING	RESOURCES Online	RESOURCES Print
Connect				
DIGITAL START UP ACTIVITY **Children at Work**		5 min.	●	
Investigate				
DIGITAL TEXT 1 **Changing Working Conditions**	Objective 1	10 min.	●	●
DIGITAL TEXT 2 **Workers Organize Unions**	Objective 1	10 min.	●	●
INTERACTIVE GALLERY **Late 1800s Working Conditions**	Objective 1	10 min.	●	
DIGITAL TEXT 3 **Women in the Workplace**	Objective 2	10 min.	●	●
DIGITAL TEXT 4 **Labor Faces Challenges**	Objective 3	10 min.	●	●
INTERACTIVE TIMELINE **The Labor Movement**	Objective 3	10 min.	●	
Synthesize				
DIGITAL ACTIVITY **A Need for Labor Reform**		5 min.	●	
Demonstrate				
DIGITAL QUIZ **Lesson Quiz and Discussion Board**		10 min.	●	

The Labor Movement

CONNECT

DIGITAL START UP ACTIVITY
Children at Work

Start Up: Children at Work

Start Up

Children at Work > Study the photograph of children posing outside of the Pennsylvania coal mine where they worked. Then respond to the questions below.

- Based on the photo, what do you think it was like to work in industry in the 1800s?
- What difficulties do you think these children faced? Use evidence from the photo for support.
- How do you think the daily lives of many young people in the late 1800s differed from your own?

Project the Start Up Activity Have students study the photograph and answer the questions as they enter the classroom.

Discuss Based on the photo, what do you think it was like to work in industry in the 1800s? *(Possible response: It was difficult, dirty work.)* How do you think the daily lives of many young people in the late 1800s differed from your own? *(Possible response: Young people were expected to work like adults at that time. Today, this is illegal.)*

Tell students that this lesson examines issues workers faced and how changes in the workplace led to the rise of labor organizations in the late 1800s.

Aa Vocabulary Development: Use the Interactive Reading Notepad to preview the Key Terms and Academic Vocabulary in this lesson with students.

FLIP IT!

Assign the Flipped Video for this lesson.

STUDENT EDITION PRINT PAGES: 565–571

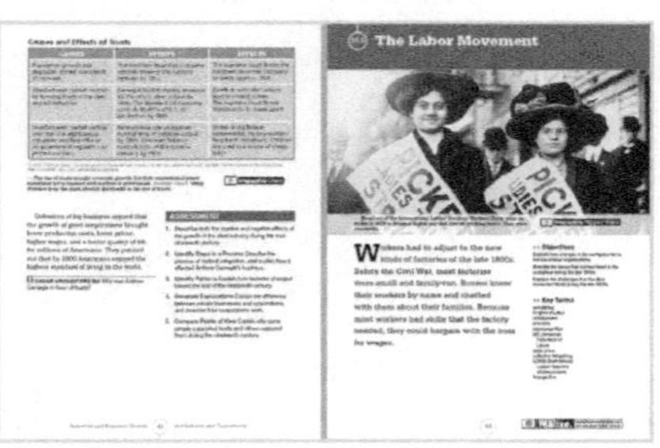

INVESTIGATE

DIGITAL TEXT 1
Changing Working Conditions

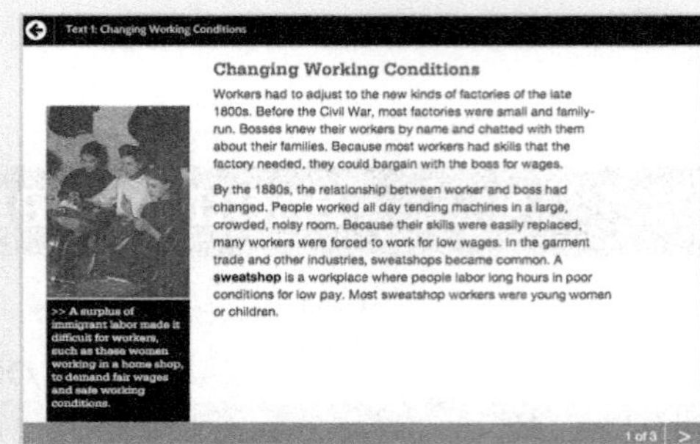

Text 1: Changing Working Conditions

Changing Working Conditions

Workers had to adjust to the new kinds of factories of the late 1800s. Before the Civil War, most factories were small and family-run. Bosses knew their workers by name and chatted with them about their families. Because most workers had skills that the factory needed, they could bargain with the boss for wages.

By the 1880s, the relationship between worker and boss had changed. People worked all day tending machines in a large, crowded, noisy room. Because their skills were easily replaced, many workers were forced to work for low wages. In the garment trade and other industries, sweatshops became common. A **sweatshop** is a workplace where people labor long hours in poor conditions for low pay. Most sweatshop workers were young women or children.

>> A surplus of immigrant labor made it difficult for workers, such as these women working in a home shop, to demand fair wages and safe working conditions.

1 of 3

DIGITAL TEXT 2
Workers Organize Unions

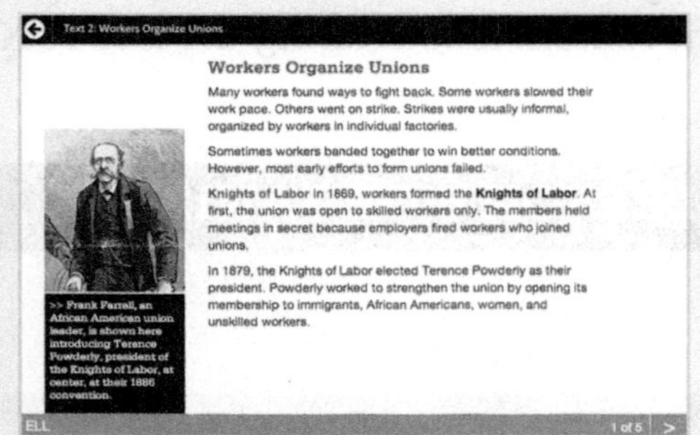

Text 2: Workers Organize Unions

Workers Organize Unions

Many workers found ways to fight back. Some workers slowed their work pace. Others went on strike. Strikes were usually informal, organized by workers in individual factories.

Sometimes workers banded together to win better conditions. However, most early efforts to form unions failed.

Knights of Labor In 1869, workers formed the **Knights of Labor**. At first, the union was open to skilled workers only. The members held meetings in secret because employers fired workers who joined unions.

In 1879, the Knights of Labor elected Terence Powderly as their president. Powderly worked to strengthen the union by opening its membership to immigrants, African Americans, women, and unskilled workers.

>> Frank Farrell, an African American union leader, is shown here introducing Terence Powderly, president of the Knights of Labor, at center, at their 1886 convention.

ELL 1 of 5

Objective 1: Explain how changes in the workplace led to the rise of labor organizations.

Quick Instruction

Interactive Gallery: Late 1800s Working Conditions Display the Interactive Gallery, and discuss the issues raised by each image. Explain to students that in the late 1800s, women outnumbered men in the garment industry. Along with men, women and children worked in unsafe conditions for long hours and little pay. Women formed their own unions with little success, but one woman, Mother Jones, did raise awareness about the working conditions faced by women and children. At last, the tragedy at the Triangle Shirtwaist Factory shed light on the abuses women suffered at the hands of factory management.

Make Generalizations Ask students to describe what they think it would have been like to work in such a place as a young person. *(Possible response: It would have been exhausting and disheartening to have to work so hard and be treated so poorly, especially as a young person who would expect to spend his or her entire life in the same situation.)*

Generate Explanations How did forming unions give workers more power? *(Individual workers were easily replaced, but when they joined together in a strike or negotiation, they could affect the factory's production and could not be replaced as quickly or easily. They formed unions and organized strikes to gain pay increases, shorter workdays, and job safety.)*

ACTIVE CLASSROOM

Use the A Closer Look activity to further investigate the images in the Interactive Gallery. Project and assign numbers to four of the images. Have students count off one to four. Then have them look closely at the image that matches their number, studying the details. Have them tell you what they see and what they learned as a result of their focus on this single image.

ELL Use the ELL activity described in the ELL chart.

Further Instruction

Summarize How did changes in industry in the late 1800s change working conditions? *(Big factories replaced small ones. The big factories relied on machines to do much of the work. The machines created loud, dirty, and often dangerous working conditions. In addition, most workers were unskilled so were easily replaced. They were required to work long hours for little pay.)*

Support Ideas with Examples How can one support the idea that the Haymarket Riots and declining membership in the Knights of Labor are related? *(Although the Knights of Labor did not support the worker strikes in Chicago, much of the blame for the ensuing violence was placed on the labor movement, resulting in declining membership.)*

INTERACTIVE GALLERY

Late 1800s Working Conditions

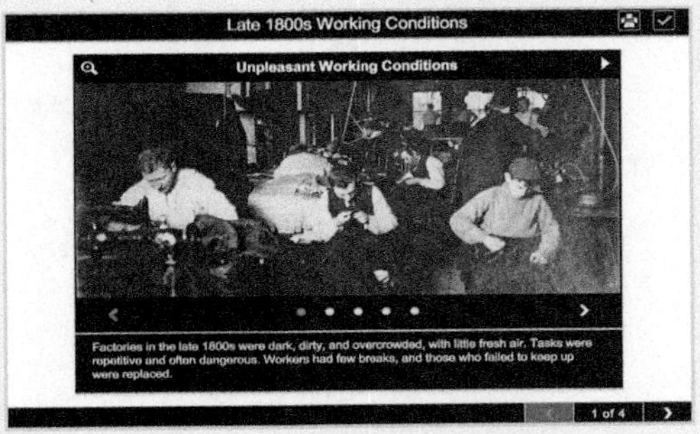

Late 1800s Working Conditions
Unpleasant Working Conditions
Factories in the late 1800s were dark, dirty, and overcrowded, with little fresh air. Tasks were repetitive and often dangerous. Workers had few breaks, and those who failed to keep up were replaced.
1 of 4

Compare and Contrast What two things did the Knights of Labor and the AFL have in common? *(They were both created to improve working conditions.)* What are two ways the Knights of Labor and the AFL differed? *(The Knights of Labor admitted skilled and unskilled workers, while the AFL allowed only skilled workers. The Knights of Labor did not support strikes, while the AFL did.)*

DIGITAL TEXT 3

Women in the Workplace

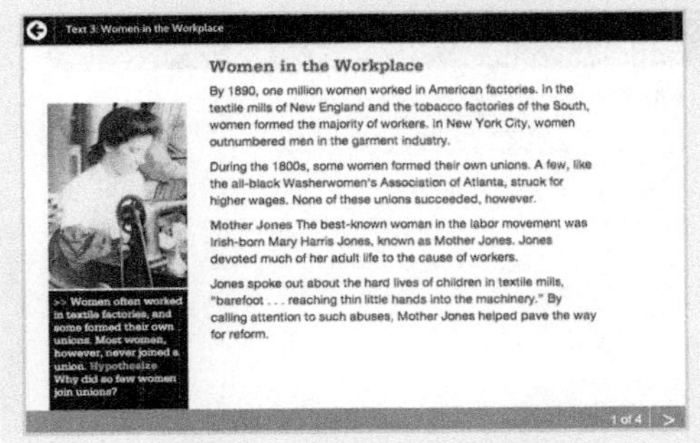
Text 3: Women in the Workplace

Women in the Workplace

By 1890, one million women worked in American factories. In the textile mills of New England and the tobacco factories of the South, women formed the majority of workers. In New York City, women outnumbered men in the garment industry.

During the 1800s, some women formed their own unions. A few, like the all-black Washerwomen's Association of Atlanta, struck for higher wages. None of these unions succeeded, however.

Mother Jones The best-known woman in the labor movement was Irish-born Mary Harris Jones, known as Mother Jones. Jones devoted much of her adult life to the cause of workers.

Jones spoke out about the hard lives of children in textile mills, "barefoot . . . reaching thin little hands into the machinery." By calling attention to such abuses, Mother Jones helped pave the way for reform.

>> Women often worked in textile factories, and some formed their own unions. Most women, however, never joined a union. Hypothesize Why did so few women join unions?

1 of 4

Objective 2: **Identify the issues that women faced in the workplace during the late 1800s.**

Quick Instruction

Connect What relationship did the AFL have with the International Ladies' Garment Workers Union? *(The AFL was made up of trade unions consisting of skilled workers. The ILGWU was a separate trade union, but the two entities worked together.)*

Further Instruction

Emphasize that the tragic Triangle Shirtwaist Factory fire was a turning point in reform. The women who lost their lives would have likely survived had they not been locked in and crammed into the work rooms. As a result of the Triangle Fire, politicians embraced the need for reform that offered workers more protection on the job.

Support Ideas with Examples What example in the text supports the idea that workers had more power acting together than individually? *(Sample answer: The ILGWU led a strike that ended in workers gaining pay increases and shorter hours.)*

DIGITAL TEXT 4

Labor Faces Challenges

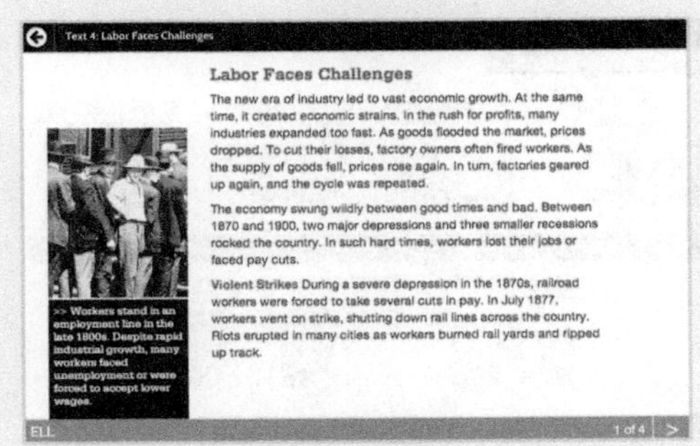
Text 4: Labor Faces Challenges

Labor Faces Challenges

The new era of industry led to vast economic growth. At the same time, it created economic strains. In the rush for profits, many industries expanded too fast. As goods flooded the market, prices dropped. To cut their losses, factory owners often fired workers. As the supply of goods fell, prices rose again. In turn, factories geared up again, and the cycle was repeated.

The economy swung wildly between good times and bad. Between 1870 and 1900, two major depressions and three smaller recessions rocked the country. In such hard times, workers lost their jobs or faced pay cuts.

Violent Strikes During a severe depression in the 1870s, railroad workers were forced to take several cuts in pay. In July 1877, workers went on strike, shutting down rail lines across the country. Riots erupted in many cities as workers burned rail yards and ripped up track.

>> Workers stand in an employment line in the late 1800s. Despite rapid industrial growth, many workers faced unemployment or were forced to accept lower wages.

ELL 1 of 4

Objective 3: **Explain the challenges that the labor movement faced during the late 1800s.**

Quick Instruction

Interactive Timeline: The Labor Movement Display the Interactive Timeline. Guide students through the hotspots and discuss the importance of each event. Explain that even though many people joined unions, the vast majority of unskilled workers did not have the support of a union. After the Triangle Fire, some safety regulations were put in place, but court rulings generally supported factory owners, not workers. Big business discouraged the growth of unions.

ACTIVE CLASSROOM

Use the Conversation with History activity to further investigate the information presented in the timeline. Tell students to choose one of the images from the timeline and to imagine that they are having a conversation with one of the people pictured. Instruct students to write down a question they'd like to ask, then what that person would say to them, and what the students would say in response.

PEARSON realize™ www.PearsonRealize.com Access your Digital Lesson

The Labor Movement

INTERACTIVE TIMELINE

The Labor Movement

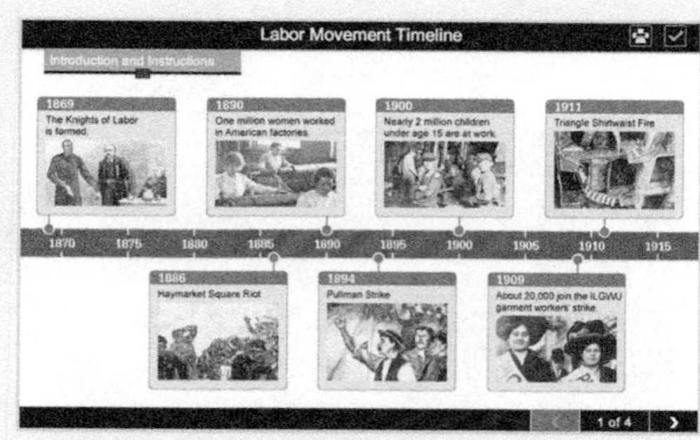

D Differentiate: Extra Support Make sure students understand that the events in the timeline are listed in chronological order, even though they have learned about some of them out of order. Ask students questions to help them sequence events properly: Did the Triangle Fire happen before or after the formation of the ILGWU? Which happened first, the Haymarket Riot or the Pullman Strike?

ELL Use the ELL activity described in the ELL chart.

Further Instruction

Draw Conclusions How might an uncertain economy have increased the potential for violent worker protests? *(The economic swings that led to frequent unemployment and wage cuts likely frustrated desperate workers, which in turn increased the potential for violent strikes.)*

Identify Central Issues Why was the use of the Sherman Antitrust Act in judicial cases against workers such a strong blow to unions? *(The Act was created to stop trusts from limiting free trade, yet federal courts ruled that workers were limiting free trade when they went on strike, which made it clear that the courts were on the side of business owners.)*

SYNTHESIZE

DIGITAL ACTIVITY

A Need for Labor Reform

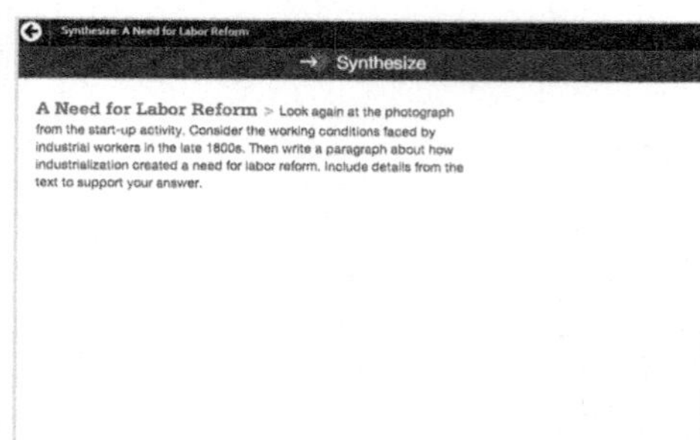

Synthesize: A Need for Labor Reform
Synthesize
A Need for Labor Reform > Look again at the photograph from the start-up activity. Consider the working conditions faced by industrial workers in the late 1800s. Then write a paragraph about how industrialization created a need for labor reform. Include details from the text to support your answer.

Have students review the photograph and their answers from the Start Up Activity. Then, have them consider what they have learned about industrialization and the conditions it created before they write their paragraphs. Tell students to make sure they include specific details from the text to support their ideas.

Discuss What kind of working conditions arose from industrialization? How did these conditions contribute to the need for labor reform?

DEMONSTRATE

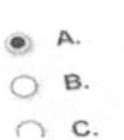

DIGITAL QUIZ

Lesson Quiz and Discussion Board

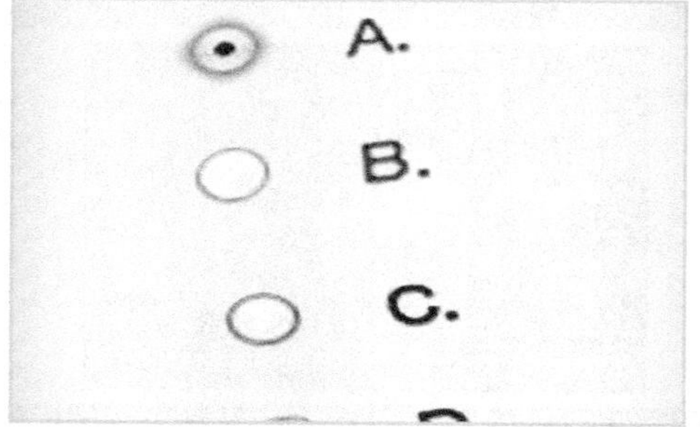

Assign the online Lesson Quiz for this lesson if you haven't already done so. Students will be offered automatic remediation or enrichment based on their score.

In *The Labor Movement*, you learned about the ways industrialization changed the workplace during the late 1800s and created conditions that called for reform. You also learned about the issues women and children faced at work. As workers organized, labor unions faced challenges from business owners and the government.

Pose these questions to the class on the Discussion Board:

Make Generalizations What trends do you see developing in the relationship between labor unions and business owners in the late 1800s and early 1900s?

Compare Points of View How did business owners and workers differ on the issues of workplace safety, increased pay, and shorter workdays?

Topic Inquiry

Have students continue their investigations for the Topic Inquiry.

New Technologies

Supporting English Language Learners

Use with the reading, **Technology in Everyday Life**.

Learning

Display a blank word web with *technology* in the center. Invite students to cite examples of technology in their lives, as well as name other words related to technology. Add their responses to the word web.

Beginning Explain the words *refrigeration* and *spoiled* in the text. Ask: What foods in your home need refrigeration? What happens when food is spoiled? Then have students complete this sentence: _____ keeps food from getting _____.

Intermediate Point out the word *refrigeration*. With students, brainstorm its variants *(refrigerator, refrigerated, refrigerate)*. Use these words to ask students questions about the role of refrigeration in their lives, and have them respond in complete sentences using the above words.

Advanced Point out challenging vocabulary in the paragraph about cameras, such as: *photography, equipment, shutter, developed*. Discuss the words' meanings, and invite students to use the words to compare and contrast their picture-taking experiences with those described in the text.

Advanced High Display challenging content words from the text, such as: *device, refrigeration, spoiled, typewriter, photography, shutter, automatically*. Ask partners to determine the words' meanings and apply them to a discussion about technology in their own lives.

Use with the reading, **Automobile Production**.

Reading

Review the term *suffix*. Then explain that the suffix *–less* means "without" or "not having." Encourage students to listen for the suffix *–less* during the activity.

Beginning Say: The horseless carriage moved with an engine. Ask: Which word ended with the suffix *–less*? What does that word mean? What does the word *useless* mean? Is a horseless carriage useless?

Intermediate Review the meaning of the word *horseless* from the text. Brainstorm a list of other words ending in *–less* (e.g., useless, fearless, wireless, seamless). Ask students questions about the text using these words, and encourage students to repeat these words in their responses.

Advanced Review the meaning of the phrase *horseless carriage* from the text. Then ask pairs of students to brainstorm other *–less* words and use them to discuss the dawn of the automobile age.

Advanced High Display the words *horseless* and *usefulness* from the text, and explain that *–ness* means "a state of being." Ask students to define these two words. Then have pairs of students brainstorm *–less* and *–ness* words and use them to discuss the text.

D Differentiate Instruction

Use the Differentiated Instruction notes throughout the lesson plan to support the varied skill sets, levels of readiness, and interests in the mixed-ability classroom.

Challenge These notes include suggestions for expanding the activity for advanced students.

On-Level These notes include suggestions for modifying the activity to address different interests or learning styles.

Extra Support These notes include ideas for providing more scaffolding or reading spuport.

Special Needs These notes provide ideas for adapting instruction to support the needs of various special needs students.

NOTES

New Technologies

Objectives

Objective 1: Explain how new devices sped up communication during the late 1800s.

Objective 2: Describe how inventions by Thomas Edison and others transformed life for Americans.

Objective 3: Explain how automobiles and airplanes came to transform transportation.

LESSON 6 ORGANIZER	PACING: APPROX. 1 PERIOD, .5 BLOCKS		RESOURCES	
	OBJECTIVES	PACING	Online	Print
Connect				
DIGITAL START UP ACTIVITY **Changes in the Way We Communicate**		5 min.	●	
Investigate				
DIGITAL TEXT 1 **New Communication Technologies**	Objective 1	10 min.	●	●
DIGITAL TEXT 2 **Thomas Edison, American Inventor**	Objective 2	10 min.	●	●
DIGITAL TEXT 3 **Technology in Everyday Life**	Objective 2	10 min.	●	●
INTERACTIVE CHART **Inventions Improve Daily Life**	Objective 2	10 min.	●	
DIGITAL TEXT 4 **Automobile Production**	Objective 3	10 min.	●	●
DIGITAL TEXT 5 **The Wright Brothers Take Flight**	Objective 3	10 min.	●	●
INTERACTIVE TIMELINE **American Inventors That Changed Society**	Objective 3	10 min.	●	
Synthesize				
DIGITAL ACTIVITY **Inventions and Resources**		5 min.	●	
Demonstrate				
DIGITAL QUIZ **Lesson Quiz and Discussion Board**		10 min.	●	

PEARSON realize™ www.PearsonRealize.com

Go online to access additional resources including:
Primary Sources • Biographies • Supreme Court cases • 21st Century Skill Tutorials • Maps • Graphic Organizers.

CONNECT

DIGITAL START UP ACTIVITY

Changes in the Way We Communicate

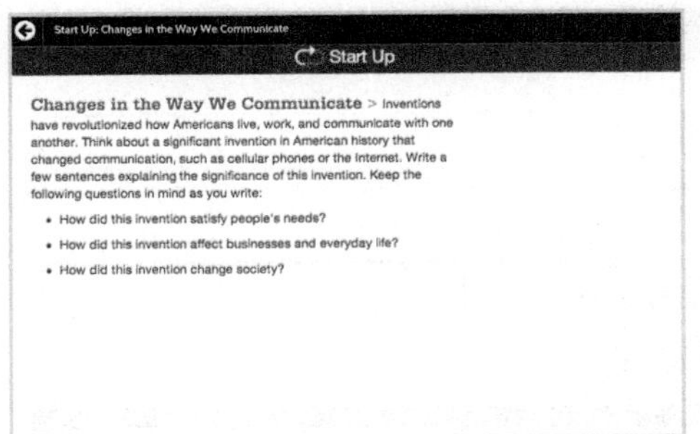

Project the Start Up Activity Have students read and complete the activity as they enter the classroom. Then ask them to share and discuss their sentences with partners if time permits.

Discuss How did this invention satisfy people's needs? How did this invention affect businesses and everyday life? How did this invention change society? *(Students responses should appropriately reflect the impact of their chosen inventions.)*

Tell students that this lesson examines technological innovations of the late 1800s and early 1900s in communication and travel. Students will be introduced to several different inventors and their inventions.

Aa Vocabulary Development: Use the Interactive Reading Notepad to preview the Key Terms and Academic Vocabulary in this lesson with students.

FLIP IT!

Assign the Flipped Video for this lesson.

STUDENT EDITION PRINT PAGES: 572–578

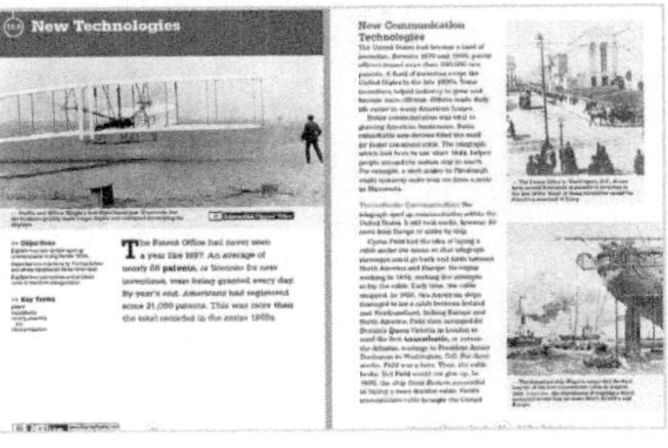

INVESTIGATE

DIGITAL TEXT 1

New Communication Technologies

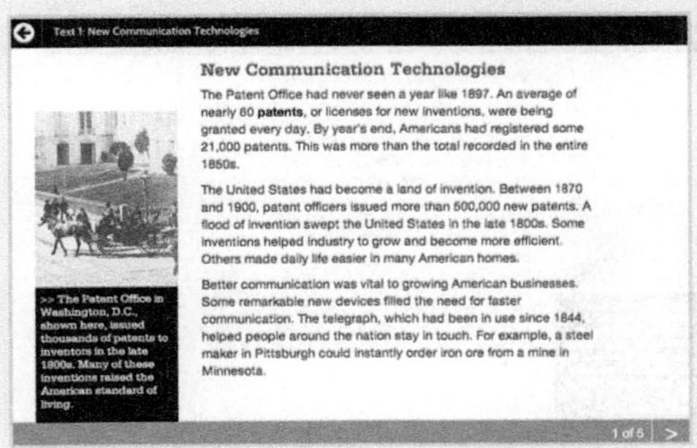
Text 1: New Communication Technologies

New Communication Technologies

The Patent Office had never seen a year like 1897. An average of nearly 60 **patents**, or licenses for new inventions, were being granted every day. By year's end, Americans had registered some 21,000 patents. This was more than the total recorded in the entire 1850s.

The United States had become a land of invention. Between 1870 and 1900, patent officers issued more than 500,000 new patents. A flood of invention swept the United States in the late 1800s. Some inventions helped industry to grow and become more efficient. Others made daily life easier in many American homes.

Better communication was vital to growing American businesses. Some remarkable new devices filled the need for faster communication. The telegraph, which had been in use since 1844, helped people around the nation stay in touch. For example, a steel maker in Pittsburgh could instantly order iron ore from a mine in Minnesota.

>> The Patent Office in Washington, D.C., shown here, issued thousands of patents to inventors in the late 1800s. Many of these inventions raised the American standard of living.

1 of 5

Objective 1: Explain how new devices sped up communication during the late 1800s.

Quick Instruction

Display the illustration of the *Niagara* installing cable in the ocean. Explain that in the late 1800s, Americans relied on the telegraph to communicate messages quickly across the country. However, communication with Europe often took weeks to travel via ship. Cables such as this significantly speeded up communication between North America and Europe. The late 1800s also saw the birth of the telephone, the first device able to transmit voices. People were soon able to have conversations over distance for the first time.

Predict Consequences How do you think the introduction of the telephone impacted the way Americans conducted business? *(The use of the telephone would speed up business transactions, and it would likely make business less personal because people did not have to see each other face to face.)*

D Differentiate: Extra Support Discuss the illustration with students, pointing out that in the late 1800s all information was transferred through cables and wires. There were no satellites or radios to transmit information through the air. As a result, ships had to drop cable all the way across the ocean to connect Europe to North America. Ask students what some of the challenges of laying the cable might be.

Further Instruction

Generate Explanations Why was the telephone perceived as both an amazing invention and a toy? *(It was the first device that allowed people's voices to be transmitted over cables. However, it was somewhat of a novelty because many people hadn't yet thought of its many uses as a communications tool for society as a whole.)*

Connect How did innovations in communication during the late 1800s encourage the development of similar innovations that we use today? *(The benefits from improvements in communication back then encouraged innovators to continue down similar paths to improve what came before them. Today's global community, connected by wireless phones and the Internet, is a result of that process.)*

New Technologies

DIGITAL TEXT 2

Thomas Edison, American Inventor

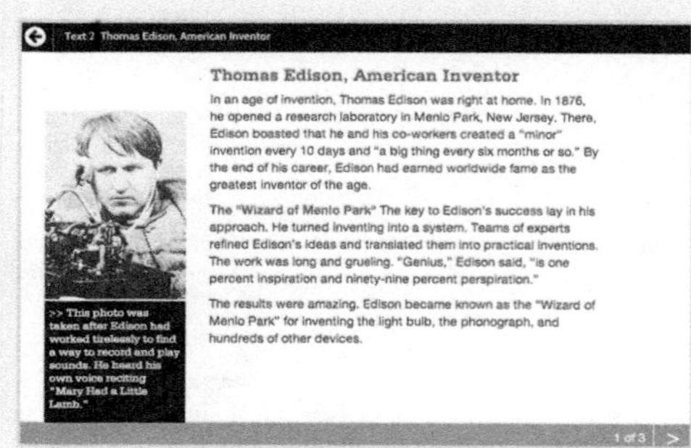

Text 2 Thomas Edison, American Inventor

Thomas Edison, American Inventor

In an age of invention, Thomas Edison was right at home. In 1876, he opened a research laboratory in Menlo Park, New Jersey. There, Edison boasted that he and his co-workers created a "minor" invention every 10 days and "a big thing every six months or so." By the end of his career, Edison had earned worldwide fame as the greatest inventor of the age.

The "Wizard of Menlo Park" The key to Edison's success lay in his approach. He turned inventing into a system. Teams of experts refined Edison's ideas and translated them into practical inventions. The work was long and grueling. "Genius," Edison said, "is one percent inspiration and ninety-nine percent perspiration."

The results were amazing. Edison became known as the "Wizard of Menlo Park" for inventing the light bulb, the phonograph, and hundreds of other devices.

>> This photo was taken after Edison had worked tirelessly to find a way to record and play sounds. He heard his own voice reciting "Mary Had a Little Lamb."

1 of 3

DIGITAL TEXT 3

Technology in Everyday Life

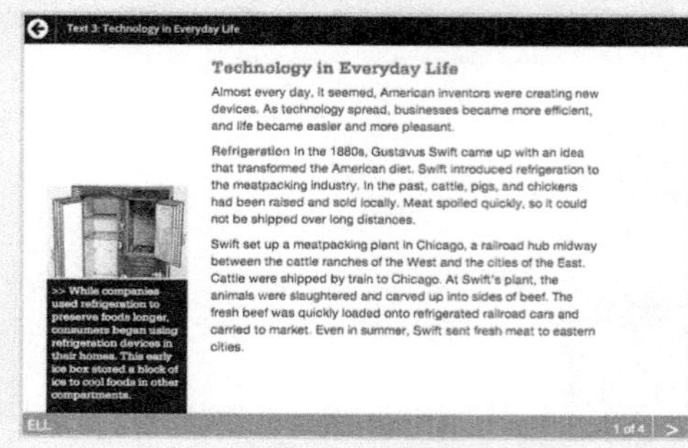

Text 3: Technology in Everyday Life

Technology in Everyday Life

Almost every day, it seemed, American inventors were creating new devices. As technology spread, businesses became more efficient, and life became easier and more pleasant.

Refrigeration In the 1880s, Gustavus Swift came up with an idea that transformed the American diet. Swift introduced refrigeration to the meatpacking industry. In the past, cattle, pigs, and chickens had been raised and sold locally. Meat spoiled quickly, so it could not be shipped over long distances.

Swift set up a meatpacking plant in Chicago, a railroad hub midway between the cattle ranches of the West and the cities of the East. Cattle were shipped by train to Chicago. At Swift's plant, the animals were slaughtered and carved up into sides of beef. The fresh beef was quickly loaded onto refrigerated railroad cars and carried to market. Even in summer, Swift sent fresh meat to eastern cities.

>> While companies used refrigeration to preserve foods longer, consumers began using refrigeration devices in their homes. This early ice box stored a block of ice to cool foods in other compartments.

ELL 1 of 4

INTERACTIVE CHART

Inventions Improve Daily Life

Inventions Improve Daily Life

Introduction and Instructions

	INVENTIONS	IMPROVEMENTS
HOME		
WORK		
COMMUNICATION		
TRAVEL		

1 of 4

Objective 2: **Describe how inventions by Thomas Edison and others transformed life for Americans.**

Quick Instruction

Interactive Chart: Inventions Improve Daily Life Use the Interactive Chart as an introduction to the inventions of the late 1800s. Guide students as they categorize inventions and consider their impact. Ask students what they know about Thomas Edison and explain that he was responsible for inventions including the light bulb, which lit American homes and businesses. Other inventors and inventions, such as refrigeration, also had a large impact on the everyday life of Americans.

Identify Cause and Effect How did refrigeration affect the American diet? *(Refrigeration allowed for the transport via railways of fresh meat across long distances, so many Americans had access to fresh meat that otherwise wouldn't have been available.)*

ACTIVE CLASSROOM

Use the Rank It strategy to further evaluate the impact of inventions in the late 1800s. Ask students to rank inventions according to which had the greatest impact. Have students provide justification for the ranking decisions they made. Then, pair students and instruct them to share their rankings and justifications. End by polling the class to see if there is agreement on the ranking.

ELL Use the ELL activity described in the ELL chart.

Further Instruction

Summarize Post a list of the inventors identified in the text, including Thomas Edison, Gustavus Swift, Christopher Sholes, George Eastman, Elijah McCoy, Granville T. Woods, and Jan Matzeliger. Allow students time to write a one- to two-sentence summary of the contributions of each inventor.

DIGITAL TEXT 4

Automobile Production

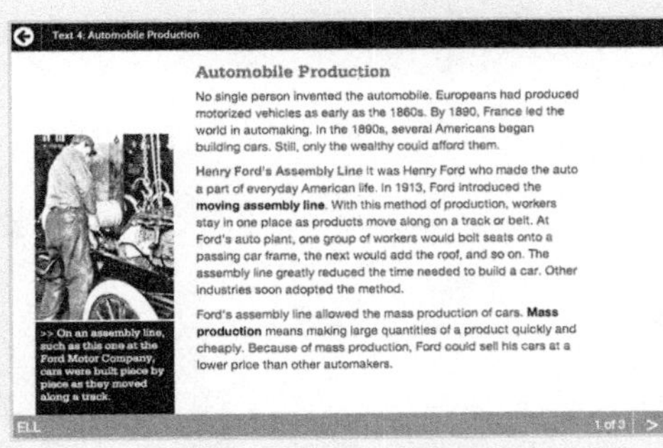

DIGITAL TEXT 5

The Wright Brothers Take Flight

INTERACTIVE TIMELINE

American Inventors That Changed Society

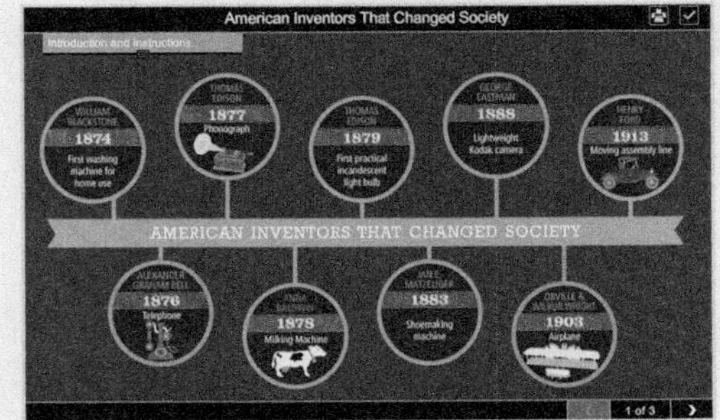

Objective 3: Explain how automobiles and airplanes came to transform transportation.

Quick Instruction

Interactive Timeline: Key Inventions of the Late 1800s Project the Interactive Timeline, and navigate through the events as a class. Lead a class discussion about what life was like before each invention and after. Draw students' attention to the 1913 entry for Henry Ford's moving assembly line. Explain that the invention of this manufacturing process revolutionized the automobile industry, allowing many Americans access to an increasingly affordable automobile. Point out that other advances in transportation were also in the making. Wilbur and Orville Wright experimented with the flying machine and succeeded.

Generate Explanations Why was the military interested in the Wrights' flying machine? *(The military saw the possibilities for using the machine to learn about enemy position and unknown territory.)*

ACTIVE CLASSROOM

Use the My Metaphor activity to challenge students to think about the inventions of the late 1800s. Post this frame on the board: This timeline shows that _____ is (are) like _____ because _____. When students complete the frame, invite them to share and post their metaphors in the classroom.

ELL Use the ELL activity described in the ELL chart.

Further Instruction

Identify Cause and Effect How did Henry Ford's invention of the moving assembly line affect automobile production? *(It made production faster and less expensive.)* How did it affect the use of automobiles? Explain. *(It increased the use of automobiles by reducing the price so more people could afford them.)*

Infer What role did the development of electricity and oil as power sources play in the increasing number of inventions in the late 1800s and early 1900s? *(Power sources such as electricity gave turn-of-the-century innovators more freedom to create new inventions that otherwise wouldn't have been possible.)*

Determine Relevance How did the rise in popularity of the automobile and the invention of the flying machine transform transportation? *(The automobile made travel faster and easier. People could now travel for longer distances and did not need to tend to horses. The flying machine would see early use in the military and mail service and would eventually connect people across continents and oceans.)*

Topic 10 Lesson 6

New Technologies

SYNTHESIZE

DIGITAL ACTIVITY

Inventions and Resources

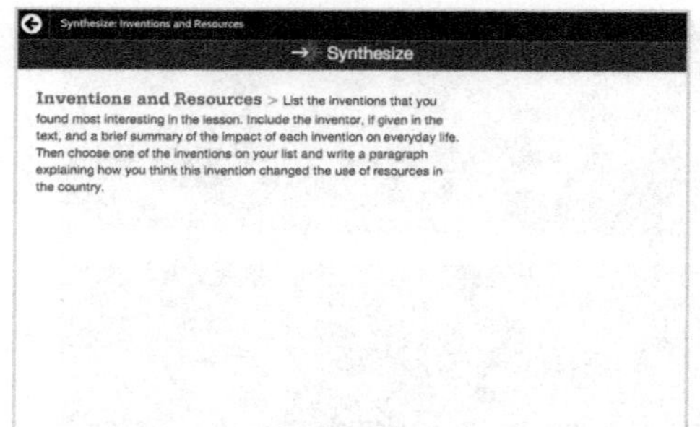

After students make their lists and write their paragraphs, invite volunteers to share their paragraphs with the class, and ask them to emphasize the societal impact of each invention.

Discuss Lead a class discussion about the improvements in daily life students' chosen inventions ushered in. Ask students to consider some of the drawbacks of these new inventions.

DEMONSTRATE

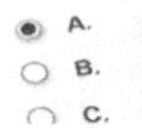

DIGITAL QUIZ

Lesson Quiz and Discussion Board

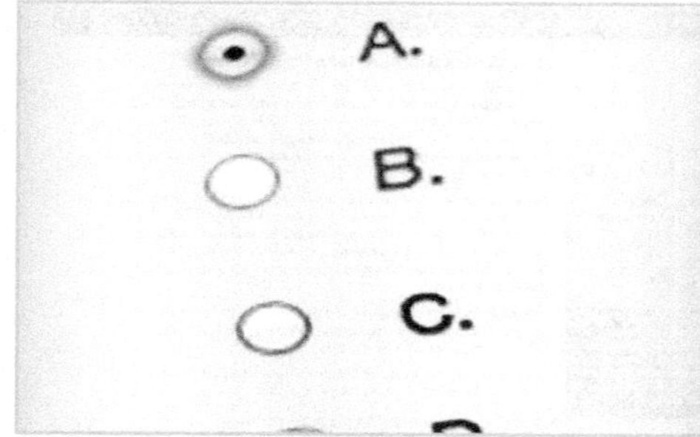

Assign the online Lesson Quiz for this lesson if you haven't already done so. Students will be offered automatic remediation or enrichment based on their score.

In *New Technologies*, you were introduced to several important inventors of the late 1800s and their life-changing inventions. You learned about advances in communication that allowed for instant access to information. You also learned about the mass production of the automobile and the invention of the flying machine, two devices that would transform transportation.

Pose these questions to the class on the Discussion Board:

Make Generalizations The late 1800s were a time of rapid change in the lives of Americans. The inventions in communication, transportation, and other technologies allowed people freedoms they had not yet experienced. How do you think the average American felt about these innovations and the social changes they introduced?

Draw Conclusions Why do you think people failed at first to see the importance of such inventions as the telephone, the automobile, and the airplane?

Topic Inquiry

Have students continue their investigations for the Topic Inquiry.

PEARSON realize™ www.PearsonRealize.com Access your Digital Lesson

Industrial and Economic Growth

SYNTHESIZE

DIGITAL ACTIVITY

Reflect on the Essential Question and Topic

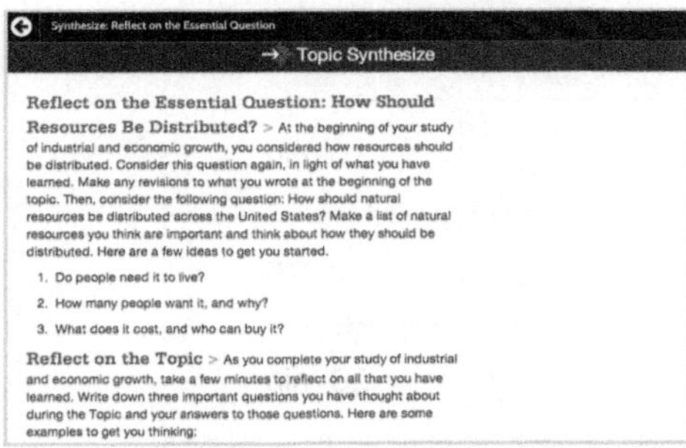

First ask students to reconsider the Essential Question for the topic: How should resources be distributed? Invite students to review their ideas from the start of the topic. As they review their opinions about how resources should be distributed, and the nation as a whole, encourage them to consider the inequality in the distribution of resources from big businesses.

Ask students to consider the question posed in the Synthesize activity and guide them as they list important natural resources, such as

- water
- oil
- timber
- coal

Have students consider the questions from the student activity in light of each of these resources. Then, have them share their ideas with the class.

Next, ask students to reflect on the Topic and jot down three important questions they've considered during their study. Review the sample questions in the student activity.

- What changes did organized labor bring about, and how do those reforms affect the workplace today?
- How did the rise of automobiles impact the railroad industry and transportation?

Finally, ask students to share their questions and answers on the Class Discussion Board.

Topic Inquiry

Have students complete Step 3 of the Topic Inquiry.

DEMONSTRATE

DIGITAL TOPIC REVIEW AND ASSESSMENT

Industrial and Economic Growth

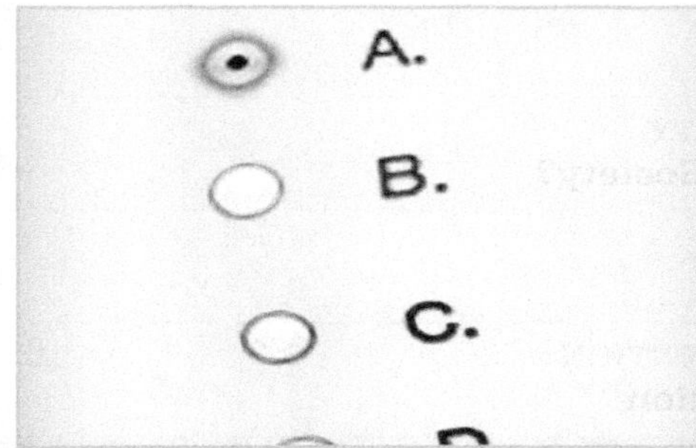

Students can prepare for the Topic Test by answering the questions in the Topic Review and Assessment online or the Assessment questions in the Print Student text. They can also prepare by reviewing their answers to the Interactive Reading Notepad questions or reviewing their notes in the Reading and Notetaking Study Guide.

DIGITAL TOPIC TEST

Industrial and Economic Growth

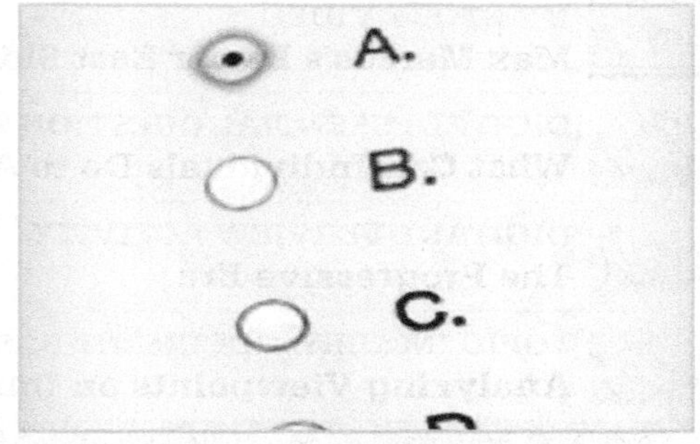

TOPIC TEST

Assign the Topic Test to assess students' understanding of topic content.

BENCHMARK TESTS

Assign these benchmark tests as you complete the relevant topics to monitor student progress toward mastering the course content and as preparation for the End-of-Course Test.

Benchmark Test 1: Topics 1–2

Benchmark Test 2: Topics 3–4

Benchmark Test 3: Topics 5–6

Benchmark Test 4: Topics 7–9

Benchmark Test 5: Topics 10–12

Benchmark Test 6: Topics 13–14

Benchmark Test 7: Topics 15–17

Topic 11

The Progressive Era

TOPIC 11 ORGANIZER	PACING: APPROX. 9 PERIODS, 4.5 BLOCKS
	PACING
Connect	1 period
MY STORY VIDEO **Max Marcus's Lower East Side**	10 min.
DIGITAL ESSENTIAL QUESTION ACTIVITY **What Can Individuals Do to Affect Society?**	10 min.
DIGITAL OVERVIEW ACTIVITY **The Progressive Era**	10 min.
TOPIC INQUIRY: DOCUMENT-BASED QUESTION **Analyzing Viewpoints on Immigration**	20 min.
Investigate	3–6 periods
TOPIC INQUIRY: DOCUMENT-BASED QUESTION **Analyzing Viewpoints on Immigration**	Ongoing
LESSON 1 A New Wave of Immigration	30–40 min.
LESSON 2 Urbanization	30–40 min.
LESSON 3 The Rise of Progressivism	30–40 min.
LESSON 4 The Progressive Presidents	30–40 min.
LESSON 5 Progress and Setbacks for Social Justice	30–40 min.
LESSON 6 A Changing American Culture	30–40 min.
Synthesize	1 period
DIGITAL ACTIVITY **Reflect on the Essential Question and Topic**	10 min.
TOPIC INQUIRY: DOCUMENT-BASED QUESTION **Analyzing Viewpoints on Immigration**	20 min.
Demonstrate	1–2 periods
DIGITAL TOPIC REVIEW AND ASSESSMENT **The Progressive Era**	10 min.
TOPIC INQUIRY: DOCUMENT-BASED QUESTION **Analyzing Viewpoints on Immigration**	20 min.

PEARSON realize www.PearsonRealize.com Access your Digital Lesson

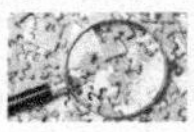

TOPIC INQUIRY: DOCUMENT-BASED QUESTION

Analyzing Viewpoints on Immigration

In this Topic Inquiry, students work independently to analyze documents that express various viewpoints on immigration and write essays in which they respond to the inquiry question, "How did immigration affect immigrants and other Americans around the year 1900?" Learning about immigration will contribute to students' understanding of the Topic Essential Question: **What can individuals do to affect society?**

STEP 1: CONNECT

Develop Questions and Plan the Investigation

Launch the DBQ Writing Activity

Discuss some of the challenges immigrants to America faced around the year 1900 with the class. Display the question students will respond to and tell them to keep it in mind as they embark on this topic inquiry. Make sure students understand they will write an essay in which they share their analyses of several documents pertaining to immigration. Play the video for the class and encourage students to take notes as they watch.

Generate Questions

Pair students and allow them time to share their notes and reflections on the video. Have partners work together to generate their own questions and answer the Questions to Discuss from Step 1B of the *Student Instructions*. Use the questions as a basis for class or partner discussion. As the discussion winds down, explain that students will be working individually to analyze a set of documents. Each student will write his or her own essay based on their analysis of the documents. Consider sharing the Rubric at this point so students can begin considering how their essays will be evaluated.

Suggestion: Allow time for partners to share their ideas and answers with the whole class. Encourage students to record ideas they find original or interesting to discuss in their writing.

Resources

- Project Launch
- Student Instructions
- Ellis Island Video

PROFESSIONAL DEVELOPMENT

Document-Based Question

Be sure to view the Document-Based Question Professional Development resources in the online course.

STEP 2: INVESTIGATE

Apply Disciplinary Concepts and Tools

Analyze the Documents

As students read the documents, they should keep their lists of questions in hand, recording answers as they go. Students might find it helpful to categorize documents based on point of view. For example, they might divide the documents into pro- and anti-immigration or separate the firsthand accounts. Students can use this categorization as a starting point for the organization of their essays.

Suggestion: Remind students to use quotation marks and source information for direct quotations as they take notes.

Check Your Understanding

Students can reconvene with their partners to share and discuss the answers they provided to the questions attached to each document. Partners should share their interpretations of the central ideas of each document, taking time to discuss and resolve any discrepancies in interpretation.

Resources

- Student Instructions
- Document A: Excerpt from the Constitution of the Immigration Restriction League, 1894
- Document B: Excerpt from *The Promised Land* by Mary Antin, 1912
- Document C: Excerpt from *The Biography of a Chinaman* by Lee Chew, 1903
- Document D: Excerpt from The Chinese Exclusion Conference, San Francisco Building Trades Council, in *American Federation of Labor, Some Reasons for Chinese Exclusion,* 1902
- Document E: Excerpt from *Working in a Sweatshop, 1905* by Sadie Frowne, 13 year-old Polish Immigrant, 1905
- Document F: Excerpt from "Is America Too Hospitable?" by Charlotte Perkins Gilman, 1923, in *The Twenties in Contemporary Commentary*

TOPIC INQUIRY: DOCUMENT-BASED QUESTION

Analyzing Viewpoints on Immigration *(continued)*

STEP 3: SYNTHESIZE

Evaluate Sources and Use Evidence to Formulate Conclusions

Write Your Essay

Display the *Rubric for a DBQ Essay* for the class and review the Criteria for an Excellent essay. Post the guiding question (How did immigration affect immgrants and other Americans around the year 1900?) and review the bulleted list in the Student Instructions that guides students through the writing process.

Suggestion: Before writing, students should outline their essays, noting where they will cite each document and the analysis it will support. After students finish writing, they should give themselves time away from the essay and then revisit it to make revisions and edits.

Resources

- Student Instructions
- Rubric for a DBQ Essay

STEP 4: DEMONSTRATE

Communicate Conclusions and Take Informed Action

Reflect on the Project

After students have submitted their essays, lead a class discussion in which students reflect on what they have learned and share the opinions they have formed and the reasoning behind those opinions. Ask students how they predict this new-found understanding of the immigration issue will inform their future study of history or sociology.

Suggestion: As an extension activity, have students research immigration issues in America today and make comparisons to the issues the learned about in the topic inquiry.

Resources

- Student Instructions

INTRODUCTION

The Progressive Era

The early twentieth century was marked by immigration and industrialization, both of which directly contributed to rapid urbanization in America. The boom in city populations and factory work contributed to poor living and working conditions. As a result, people fought for reform. A succession of progressive presidents had differing opinions about how to address social issues, but they were forward thinking and generally supportive of change. At the same time, women fought for suffrage, and temperance became a key social and political issue. Despite all these advances, discrimination was a harsh reality for Americans of color.

CONNECT

MY STORY VIDEO

Max Marcus's Lower East Side

Watch a video about the experiences of the son of immigrants trying to succeed in business in New York City.

Check Understanding What lesson in business did Max Marcus learn? (the need to change with the times)

Hypothesize What were some of the qualities that may have pushed Max Marcus to achieve success in business? (Students may mention the work ethic of immigrants to succeed and make a better life for their families, as well as Max Marcus's ability to understand the fundamentals of meeting customer needs and changing with the times.)

DIGITAL ESSENTIAL QUESTION ACTIVITY

What Can Individuals Do to Affect Society?

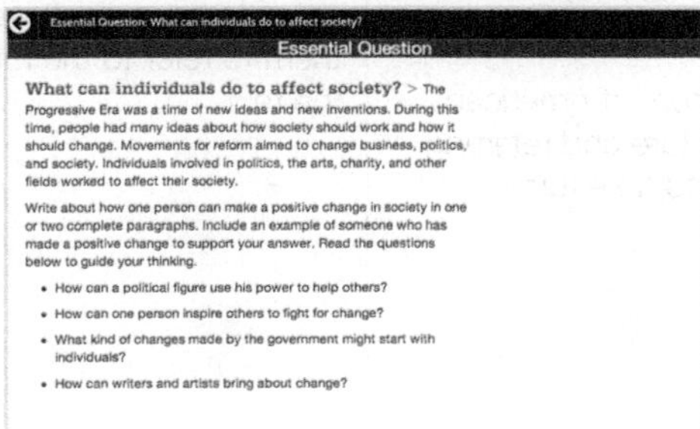

Ask students to think about the Essential Question for this Topic: What can individuals do to affect society? People have the opportunity to impact others in both positive and negative ways.

If students have not already done so, have them consider the questions and choose a person to write about in their paragraphs.

Make Generalizations How is the amount of power a person has in society related to the amount of change he or she can effect? *(Possible response: The more power a person has the more impact he has. For example, a politician would likely have more impact than a factory worker.)*

Identify Cause and Effect What inspired people to fight for change in society? *(Possible responses: injustice, corruption, mistreatment, lack of resources)*

Connect How can the Internet and social media empower people to effect change today? *(Social media gives reformers more power because they are able to reach more people with their messages and generate more popular support.)*

DIGITAL OVERVIEW ACTIVITY

The Progressive Era

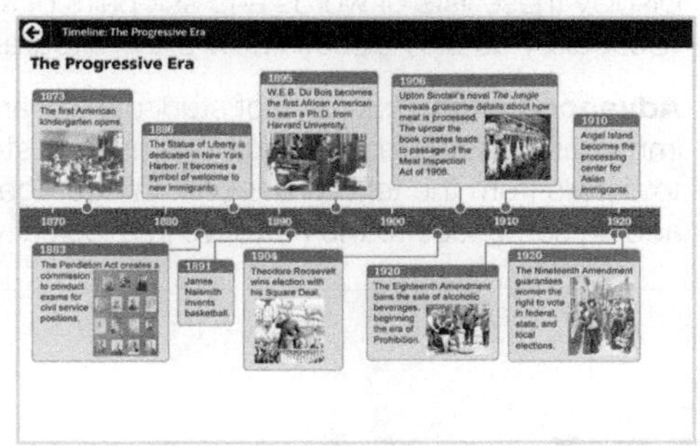

Display the timeline of major events in the Progressive Era. During this topic, students will learn about all these events and many more. This timeline will provide a framework into which students can place the events they learn about as they study the Topic.

Analyze Information What are three key issues covered in this timeline? *(Possible responses: education, immigration, prohibition, suffrage)*

Topic Inquiry

Launch the Topic Inquiry with students after introducing the Topic.

Topic 11 Lesson 1

A New Wave of Immigration

Supporting English Language Learners

Use with the reading, **A Challenging Journey Across an Ocean**.

Learning

Display the three photographs that accompany the text. Explain that these photographs not only help a reader to comprehend the text but also provide support when speaking about it.

Beginning Display these sentences: Immigrants sailed on ships that were _____. The Statue of Liberty made immigrants feel _____. Asian immigrants sailed to _____. Invite students to refer to the photographs as they say the sentences aloud and complete them.

Intermediate Invite students to make statements about each photograph. If necessary, ask questions in order to elicit further detail, such as: What did immigrants endure on the ships? What did the Statue of Liberty mean to immigrants? What was the experience of Asian immigrants?

Advanced Brainstorm words that describe each of the photographs. Display these lists of words and ask pairs of students to use the vocabulary as they discuss how the photographs are connected to the text

Advanced High Ask pairs of students to narrate the story of American immigrants, using the photographs as their story's structure and referring to details from the text as needed. Encourage partners to take turns adding sentences to the narrative in a logical way.

Use with the reading, **The Immigrant Experience in America**.

Reading

Point out some of the ethnicities mentioned in paragraphs four through seven of the text. Ask students to share what they know about them.

Beginning Review the pronunciation of the ethnic names in paragraph five. Highlight the countries associated with them on a map of Europe and Asia. Then echo read the paragraph together.

Intermediate Together, identify the countries associated with the ethnicities in paragraph five. Invite volunteers to find these countries on a map of Europe and Asia. Then reread the paragraph.

Advanced Provide pairs of students with a blank map of Europe and Asia. Invite them to label the map with the countries of those immigrants mentioned in paragraphs four and five. Then have pairs reread the paragraphs together.

Advanced High Provide individual students with a map of Europe and Asia. As they silently reread paragraphs four through seven, encourage them to refer to the map as necessary in order to better understand the text.

D Differentiate Instruction

Use the Differentiated Instruction notes throughout the lesson plan to support the varied skill sets, levels of readiness, and interests in the mixed-ability classroom.

Challenge These notes include suggestions for expanding the activity for advanced students.

On-Level These notes include suggestions for modifying the activity to address different interests or learning styles.

Extra Support These notes include ideas for providing more scaffolding or reading spuport.

Special Needs These notes provide ideas for adapting instruction to support the needs of various special needs students.

NOTES

PEARSON realize™ www.PearsonRealize.com

Go online to access additional resources including: Primary Sources • Biographies • Supreme Court cases • 21st Century Skill Tutorials • Maps • Graphic Organizers.

Objectives

Objective 1: Explain why immigrants made the difficult journey to the United States.

Objective 2: Describe the problems "new immigrants" faced in adapting to life in the United States.

Objective 3: Explain the causes and effects of nativist opposition to immigration.

LESSON 1 ORGANIZER	PACING: APPROX. 1 PERIOD, .5 BLOCKS			
			RESOURCES	
	OBJECTIVES	PACING	Online	Print
Connect				
DIGITAL START UP ACTIVITY **Arriving in America**		5 min.	•	
Investigate				
DIGITAL TEXT 1 **Reasons for Immigration**	Objective 1	10 min.	•	•
DIGITAL TEXT 2 **A Challenging Journey Across an Ocean**	Objective 1	10 min.	•	•
INTERACTIVE CHART **Immigration, 1870–1900**	Objective 1	10 min.	•	
DIGITAL TEXT 3 **The Immigrant Experience in America**	Objective 2	10 min.	•	•
INTERACTIVE CHART **Issues Facing Immigrants**	Objective 2	10 min.	•	
DIGITAL TEXT 4 **Nativist Opposition**	Objective 3	10 min.	•	•
Synthesize				
DIGITAL ACTIVITY **Arriving in America**		5 min.	•	
Demonstrate				
LESSON QUIZ **Lesson Quiz and Class Discussion Board**		10 min.	•	

A New Wave of Immigration

CONNECT

DIGITAL START UP ACTIVITY
Arriving in America

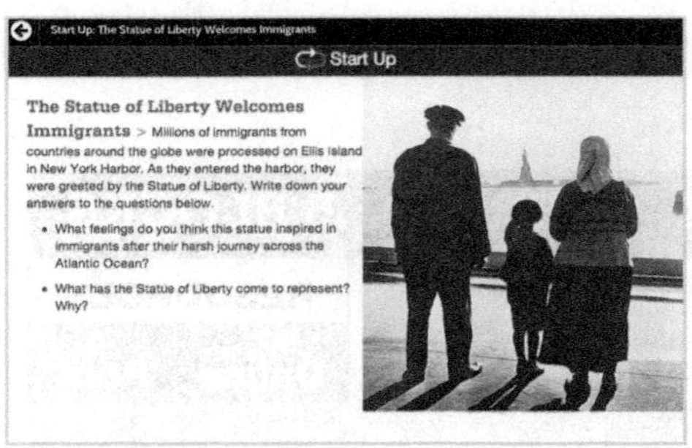

Project the Start Up Activity Tell students to study the image of the Statue of Liberty and to respond to the questions as they enter and get settled. Then, have them share their responses with a classmate.

Discuss The Statue of Liberty was designed by French artist Frédéric Auguste Bartholdi and was given to the United States as a gift from the French people. What do you think most immigrants hoped to do in the United States? *(start new lives, explore opportunities, escape hardship in other countries)*

Tell students that in this lesson they will explore what motivated immigrants in the late 1800s and early 1900s. They will also examine the challenges faced by immigrants.

Aa Vocabulary Development: Use the Interactive Reading Notepad to preview the Key Terms and Academic Vocabulary in this lesson with students.

FLIP IT!

Assign the Flipped Video for this lesson.

STUDENT EDITION PRINT PAGES: 584–590

INVESTIGATE

DIGITAL TEXT 1
Reasons for Immigration

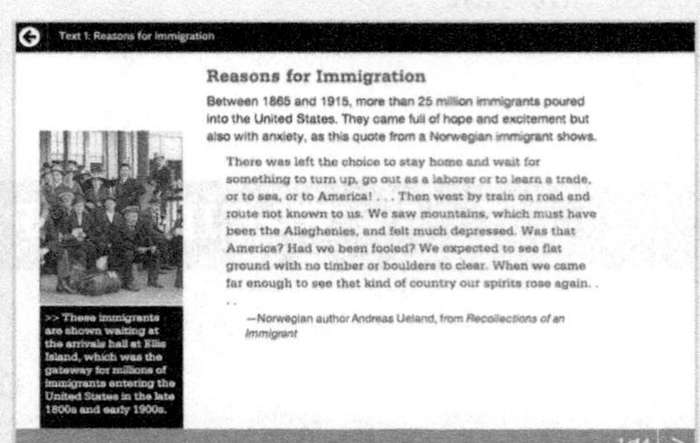

DIGITAL TEXT 2
A Challenging Journey Across an Ocean

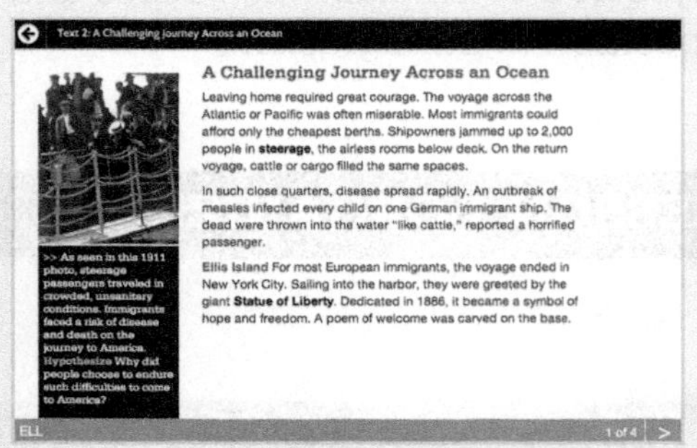

Objective 1: Explain why immigrants made the difficult journey to the United States.

Quick Instruction

Interactive Chart: Immigration, 1870–1910 Project the Interactive Chart showing immigration numbers in the late nineteenth and early twentieth century. From what part of the world did most immigrants come in the late 1800s? *(Northern and Western Europe, including Germany)* From what part of the world did most immigrants come in the early 1900s? *(Southern and Eastern Europe, including Poland, Austria, Spain, and Italy)* From what area did the lowest number of immigrants come from 1870 to 1910? *(Asia)* What does this graph suggest about the population of immigrants in the United States at the turn of the century? *(Most of the population of immigrants were Europeans. A much smaller number of immigrants were of Latin American and Asian origins.)* Why do you think this might have been the case? *(The United States was founded by colonists from European nations who maintained close cultural, political, and economic ties with Europe. This made the United States a likely destination for many people leaving Europe. Also, Americans were more likely to welcome other people from the nations of their own origins.)*

Connect How did push factors and pull factors work together to motivate immigrants? *(Push and pull factors often complemented one another. Push factors motivated people to leave their countries of origin. Pull factors motivated people to come to the United States. Often, one or more pull factors addressed the problem of one or more push factors. For example, the push factor of political and religious persecution was complemented by the pull factor of political and religious freedom.)*

ACTIVE CLASSROOM

Organize students into small groups. Have them use the Circle Write strategy to answer the following questions: (1) What factors that encouraged immigration did people from different regions likely have in common? (2) What factors seem specific to one region? Tell student groups to discuss their final responses and to select one answer to each question to share with the class. You may wish to post all group responses to the class blog or discussion board.

D Differentiate: On Level point out that the numbers on the y-axis represent figures in the thousands. This means that in 1870, about 300,000 (not 300) immigrants came from Northern and Western Europe.

ELL Use the ELL activity described in the ELL chart.

Further Instruction

Be sure that students understand that many immigrants, despite differences in origin and culture, shared similar reasons for coming to the United States. Encourage students to draw T-charts or concept webs in which they list the push and pull factors that motivated immigration. Tell students to draw lines connecting related push and pull factors.

www.PearsonRealize.com
Access your Digital Lesson

INTERACTIVE CHART

Immigration, 1870–1900

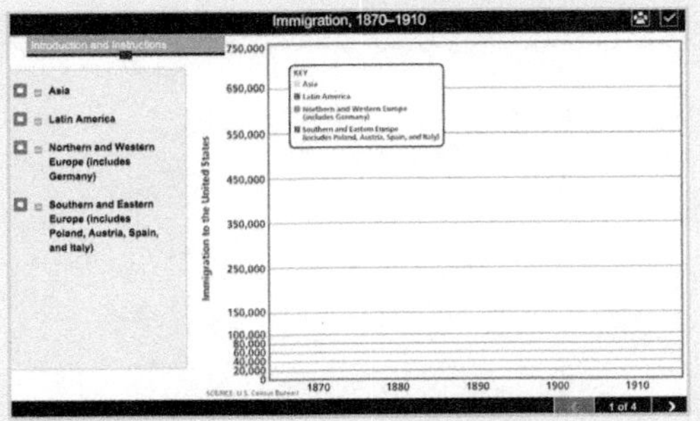

DIGITAL TEXT 3

The Immigrant Experience in America

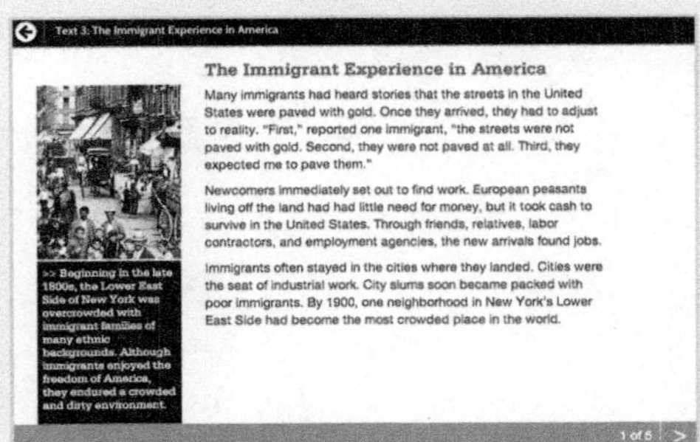

INTERACTIVE CHART

Issues Facing Immigrants

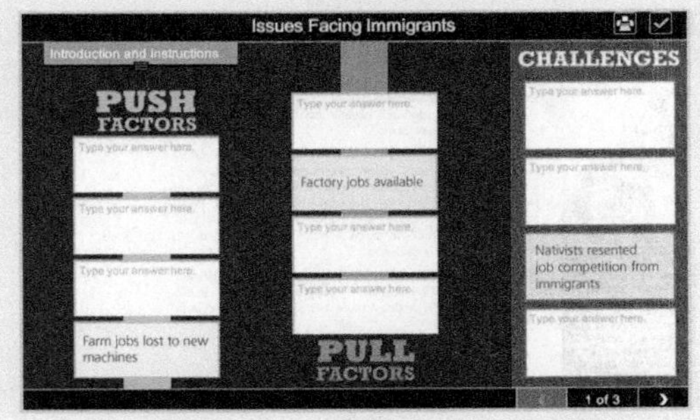

For example, the push factors of land scarcity and economic hardship relate to the pull factors of available land and industrial jobs.

Generate Explanations Would people have immigrated without both push and pull factors? Explain. *(Some people would have immigrated based just on push factors or just on pull factors; however, most people were probably motivated by both. It would not have made sense to many people to go from one place of scarcity to another place of scarcity. Scarcity motivated them to leave one place while the promise of resources attracted them to another.)*

Evaluate Sources Read aloud *The New Colossus* by Emma Lazarus. How does this statement reflect both the push and the pull factors experienced by many immigrants? *(The statement appeals to the push factors that drove many people to immigrate, including poverty and persecution. It also holds up a lamp, the promise of liberty and opportunity, as a pull factor. The statement itself is a pull factor, an appeal to immigrants to come to the United States.)*

Objective 2: **Describe the problems "new immigrants" faced in adapting to life in the United States.**

Quick Instruction

Interactive Chart: Issues Facing Immigrants Project the Interactive Chart. Remind students that immigrants had reasons for leaving their countries of origin, called push factors, as well as reasons for coming to the United States, called pull factors. Often, the reality of the circumstances in the United States did not live up to immigrants' expectations. Many experienced conditions just as difficult as in their homelands. Have students brainstorm about what it might have been like to arrive in the United States as an immigrant from Europe, Latin America, or Asia at the turn of the century. Ask them to list their ideas and share them with the class.

ACTIVE CLASSROOM

Instruct students to use the Sticky Notes strategy to answer the questions that follow the Interactive Chart. Have them jot down their responses to the questions. Then, ask students to share and revise their ideas with partners. Finally, display the sticky notes on the board. Challenge students to find a sticky note with which they agree and one with which they disagree. In class discussion, or on the class discussion board, tell students to share and explain their findings.

ELL Use the ELL activity described in the ELL chart.

Further Instruction

Instruct students to work individually to complete the Interactive Reading Notepad for *The Immigrant Experience in America*. Then, have them compare their responses with a partner. Be sure to explain that many immigrants left one style of life, farming, for another, industrial factory work. Immigrants arrived with different languages and customs. For this reason, they often settled near immigrants with similar backgrounds, resulting in urban areas organized along ethnic lines.

Infer Reread the following: "First," reported one immigrant, "the streets were not paved with gold. Second, they were not paved at all. Third, they expected me to pave them." What does this statement tell you about the expectations of immigrants and the realities of what they found in the United States? *(Many Immigrants hoped to not face the hardships they found in their native countries. They hoped to find jobs, land, and freedom, although some challenges may have been unexpected. They had to struggle for many freedoms.)*

Explain Why did "new immigrants" face more challenges and discrimination in the United States? *(They came from non-English-speaking countries and often had different religious beliefs and customs than a majority of the existing Americans. Language was a major barrier, but differences in religion and ways of life also led to conflict and discrimination.)*

A New Wave of Immigration

DIGITAL TEXT 4

Nativist Opposition

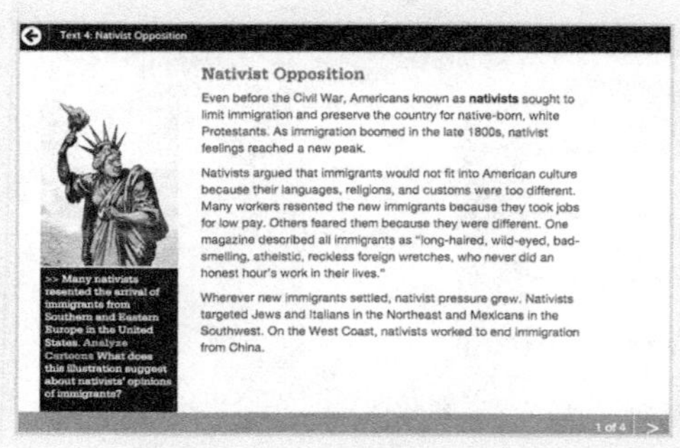

Objective 3: **Explain the causes and effects of nativist opposition to immigration.**

Quick Instruction

Project the political cartoon from the lesson. Prompt students to discuss the meanings behind each of the images in the cartoon, and ask them to predict what they will learn about the experiences of immigrants in the United States based on those images.

Analyze Political Cartoons How does the nativist portrayal of the Statue of Liberty differ from the actual statue? *(Liberty is shown looking angry and unpleasant. She does not appear happy and is holding up her robes as ships drop immigrants on her island. The actual statue appears tranquil and even welcoming. She holds aloft her torch in an inspiring way.)* What did the nativists hope to gain through propaganda like this cartoon? *(They hoped to convince other Americans that immigrants should not be allowed to come to the nation. They hoped to portray the immigrants as useless and as dirtying the nation. They wanted to persuade officials and other Americans to stop immigration.)*

Further Instruction

Draw Conclusions Why were immigrants, especially "new immigrants," often objects of discrimination and persecution? *(They did not speak English, and often, they looked and behaved differently than other Americans and "old immigrants." They formed separate groups within cities and communities, making it easier to blame them for other social and economic problems.)*

Integrate Information What reasons likely motivated immigrants to stay in the United States despite the hardships they encountered when they first arrived? *(Many might have hoped that they could still succeed and work hard enough to build a better life. Some may have decided to stay because their families and friends were there. Others may have remained more afraid of conditions in their home countries. Many likely had to stay to work and earn money before they could even consider returning. The longer they stayed, the harder it might have become for them to leave, especially as they probably had a difficult time saving money.)*

SYNTHESIZE

DIGITAL ACTIVITY

Arriving in America

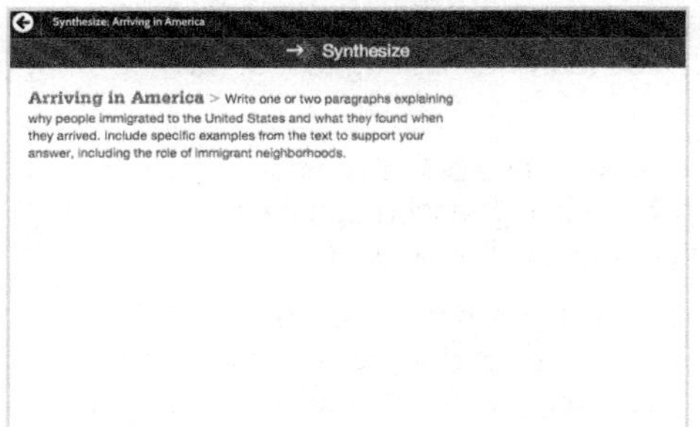

Tell students to use the Think-Pair-Share strategy to generate ideas for their paragraphs. Then, have students work individually to write their responses to the digital activity. Finally, instruct them to share their work and give feedback in small groups.

Discuss What relationship did nativism have with economic issues of the time? *(Nativism was largely a response to difficult economic conditions. Immigrants and other Americans were all competing for the same jobs, land, resources, and services. Differences based on language, race, religion, and ethnicity made it easier for people to get angry and blame each other for economic problems like poverty.)*

DEMONSTRATE

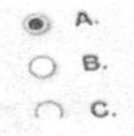

LESSON QUIZ

Lesson Quiz and Class Discussion Board

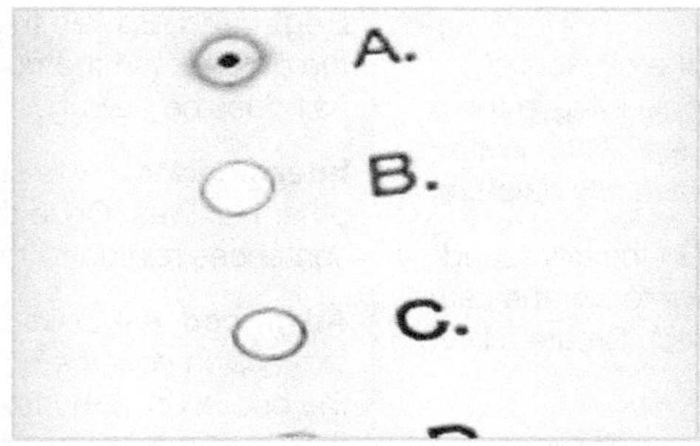

Assign the online Lesson Quiz for this lesson if you haven't already done so. Students will be offered automatic remediation or enrichment based on their score.

Pose these questions to the class on the Discussion Board:

In *A New Wave of Immigration*, you learned about the push and pull factors that brought many immigrants to the United States. You also explored the experiences of immigrants once they had arrived in their new home and the reasons for some challenges they faced.

Make Predictions How might the experiences of individual immigrants motivate them and other sympathetic American citizens to become more active in politics? *(Their experiences might motivate immigrants and other citizens to demand reforms not only to help immigrants but other workers and people facing challenging conditions.)*

Support Ideas with Evidence How did American businesses benefit from immigration to the United States during this period? Cite evidence to support your ideas. *(Sample answer: I think factories, railroads, and similar businesses that needed cheap labor to grow their industries most benefited. They gained a ready and large supply of labor, and could set the terms and wages of employment.)*

Topic Inquiry

Have students continue their investigations for the Topic Inquiry.

Urbanization

Supporting English Language Learners

Use with the reading, **Cities Expand Rapidly**.

Writing

Ask students what they do to improve their English. Explain that learning how to express a thought in more than one way is a good technique for building vocabulary and other language skills.

Beginning Display this sentence: New people living in the city found many kinds of jobs. Ask: Which means the same as people living in the city: bank tellers, immigrants, city dwellers, factory workers? Then invite students to rephrase the original sentence using the phrase *city dwellers*.

Intermediate Display this sentence: New people living in the city found many kinds of jobs. Invite students to suggest other ways to say the same thing (using different vocabulary or grammatical structures). Create a list of these alternatives.

Advanced Invite pairs of students to practice rewording each other's sentences. Have one partner make a statement about African American migration, while the other partner paraphrases it. Then have partners switch roles.

Advanced High Invite students to restate in writing the quotation from *The Good Old Days—They Were Terrible!* Provide them with a thesaurus with which to expand their options. Then ask pairs of students to compare their work.

Use with the reading, **Effects of Rapid Urbanization**.

Reading

Read aloud the text's second paragraph and the quotation from *How the Other Half Lives*. Discuss the meaning of the quotation.

Beginning Explain the expression how the other half lives. Ask: Who is *the other half* in the quotation? Does the writer belong to that half? To what half does he belong?

Intermediate Invite students to make sense of the expression how the other half lives. Once they grasp its meaning, encourage them to use it in sentences related to the text or another familiar subject.

Advanced Ask pairs of students to determine the meaning of the expression *how the other half lives*, as well as discuss how it relates to the quotation in the text. Then have them create an original sentence that uses the expression. Provide time for pairs to say their sentences to one another.

Advanced High Speak briefly to students using the expressions *how the other half lives* and the similar sounding *other half* (i.e., spouse). Provide time for pairs to compare and contrast the expressions' meanings and use them in original sentences.

D Differentiate Instruction

Use the Differentiated Instruction notes throughout the lesson plan to support the varied skill sets, levels of readiness, and interests in the mixed-ability classroom.

Challenge These notes include suggestions for expanding the activity for advanced students.

On-Level These notes include suggestions for modifying the activity to address different interests or learning styles.

Extra Support These notes include ideas for providing more scaffolding or reading spuport.

Special Needs These notes provide ideas for adapting instruction to support the needs of various special needs students.

NOTES

Objectives

Objective 1: Explain why cities grew rapidly in the late 1800s.

Objective 2: Describe the relationship between social class and cities' geographies.

Objective 3: Describe the causes and effects of the settlement house and other urban reform movements.

LESSON 2 ORGANIZER — PACING: APPROX. 1 PERIOD, .5 BLOCKS	OBJECTIVES	PACING	RESOURCES: Online	RESOURCES: Print
Connect				
DIGITAL START UP ACTIVITY **Urban Living in Chicago**		5 min.	●	
Investigate				
DIGITAL TEXT 1 **Cities Expand Rapidly**	Objective 1	10 min.	●	●
DIGITAL TEXT 2 **City Neighborhoods Defined by Status**	Objective 2	10 min.	●	●
INTERACTIVE GRAPH **New York City Changes, 1840 to 1900**	Objective 2	10 min.	●	
DIGITAL TEXT 3 **Effects of Rapid Urbanization**	Objective 3	10 min.	●	●
3-D MODEL **Living in a Tenement**	Objective 3	10 min.	●	
DIGITAL TEXT 4 **The Settlement House Movement**	Objective 3	10 min.	●	●
INTERACTIVE GALLERY **Urban Problems**	Objective 3	10 min.	●	
Synthesize				
DIGITAL ACTIVITY **Urban Life**		5 min.	●	
Demonstrate				
LESSON QUIZ **Lesson Quiz and Class Discussion Board**		10 min.	●	

Urbanization

CONNECT

DIGITAL START UP ACTIVITY

Urban Living in Chicago

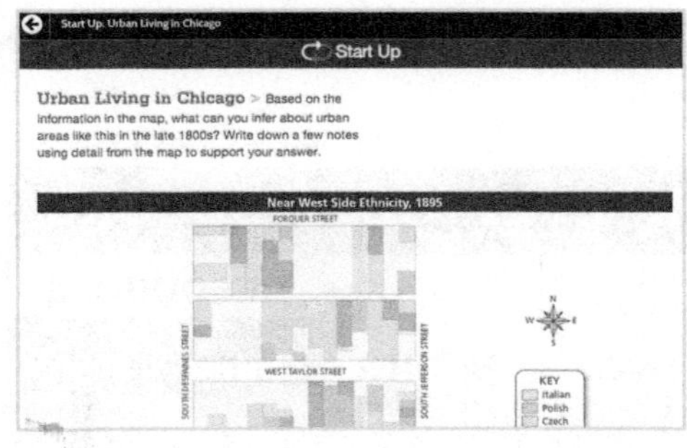

Start Up: Urban Living in Chicago
Start Up
Urban Living in Chicago > Based on the information in the map, what can you infer about urban areas like this in the late 1800s? Write down a few notes using detail from the map to support your answer.
Near West Side Ethnicity, 1895
FORQUER STREET
WEST TAYLOR STREET
SOUTH DESPLAINES STREET
SOUTH JEFFERSON STREET
N
W
E
S
KEY
Italian
Polish
Czech

Project the Start Up Activity Have students work in pairs to study the map and complete the activity as they enter and get settled.

Discuss What effect do you think these ethnic groups may have had on social relations in urban neighborhoods? *(Sample answer: I think many people probably maintained social relations where they shared ways of life. The close proximity of different groups might have led to some interaction but it also might have caused conflict.)*

Tell students that in this lesson they will learn about rapid urbanization in the late 1800s. They also explore the roles status and ethnicity played. Finally, they will investigate living conditions in cities and evaluate the impact of reform movements.

Aa Vocabulary Development: Use the Interactive Reading Notepad to preview the Key Terms and Academic Vocabulary in this lesson with students.

FLIP IT!

Assign the Flipped Video for this lesson.

STUDENT EDITION PRINT PAGES: 591–596

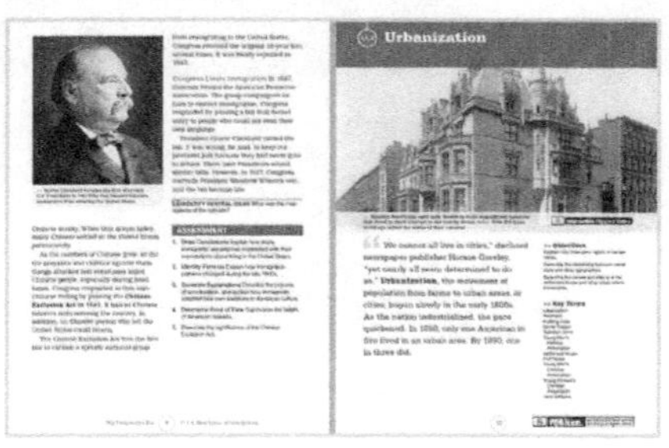

INVESTIGATE

DIGITAL TEXT 1

Cities Expand Rapidly

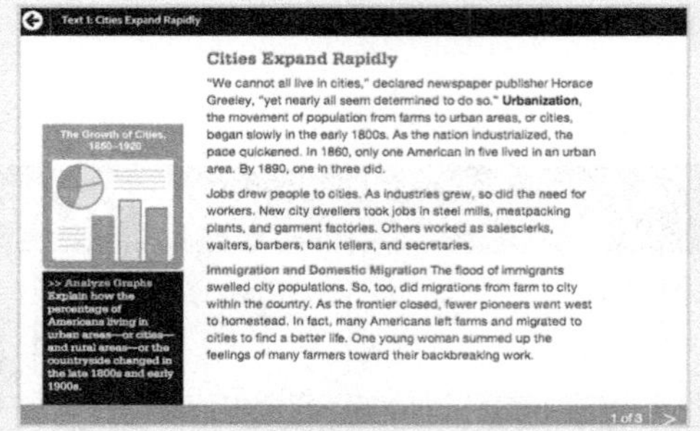

Text 1: Cities Expand Rapidly
Cities Expand Rapidly
"We cannot all live in cities," declared newspaper publisher Horace Greeley, "yet nearly all seem determined to do so." Urbanization, the movement of population from farms to urban areas, or cities, began slowly in the early 1800s. As the nation industrialized, the pace quickened. In 1860, only one American in five lived in an urban area. By 1890, one in three did.
Jobs drew people to cities. As industries grew, so did the need for workers. New city dwellers took jobs in steel mills, meatpacking plants, and garment factories. Others worked as salesclerks, waiters, barbers, bank tellers, and secretaries.
Immigration and Domestic Migration The flood of immigrants swelled city populations. So, too, did migrations from farm to city within the country. As the frontier closed, fewer pioneers went west to homestead. In fact, many Americans left farms and migrated to cities to find a better life. One young woman summed up the feelings of many farmers toward their backbreaking work.
The Growth of Cities, 1850–1920
>> Analyze Graphs Explain how the percentage of Americans living in urban areas—or cities—and rural areas—or the countryside changed in the late 1800s and early 1900s.
1 of 3

Objective 1: Explain why cities grew rapidly in the late 1800s.

Quick Instruction

Before you begin, have students talk in groups about the cities with which they are familiar, either through personal experience or through the media. Ask them to draw a T-chart labeled "Pros" and "Cons." Then, tell them to brainstorm a list of characteristics of cities that might draw people to live in them (pros) and a list of characteristics that might make cities an unpleasant place to live (cons). Share students' ideas as a class. As students move through the text, have them revise their lists.

Infer Re-read the quotation from *The Good Old Days—They Were Terrible!* What does this statement tell you about life on the frontier in the late 1800s? *(Life on the frontier must have been very difficult if the woman was willing to starve in town rather than go back to homesteading. People likely worked hard and faced many challenges, such as a starvation, drought, illness, loneliness or isolation, and conflict with other settlers and American Indians.)*

D Differentiate: Challenge Organize students into pairs or groups. Assign each pair or group one of the following cities in the United States: Boston, New York City, Chicago, San Francisco, New Orleans, and St. Louis. Tell each group to research the population growth for their assigned city from 1860 to 1910. Have them graph the population data of their cities for each decade. Then, ask students to write a summary paragraph in which they analyze their findings and relate the data to the lesson content. Display complete graphs and paragraphs in the classroom or on the class website. You may wish to refer students to relevant online resources, such as http://www.census.gov/.

ELL Use the ELL activity described in the ELL chart.

Further Instruction

Be sure that students understand that cities grew in this period because so many people were coming to the United States to find jobs and start new lives. Though many hoped to own land and farm, most ended up working in factories and other industries in and around cities. Many urban centers began as factory and mill towns that grew up along rivers and other bodies of water and later along railroad lines.

Make Predictions Horace Greeley states that everyone seemed determined to move into the cities. What issues most likely resulted from so many people in relatively small areas? *(Cities grew up very rapidly and likely included many tall buildings as well as cramped and overcrowded living conditions. Streets were probably crowded, and public spaces might not have been designed and built well if they went up too quickly. Sanitation and public health might have become a problem.)*

Generate Explanations What impact did immigration and African American migration likely have on cultural, social, and economic conditions in cities? *(Immigration and African American migration likely contributed to culture diversity and the blending of traditions and ways of life. It also may have contributed to social challenges, such as discrimination and conflict among different groups of people. Economically, the influx of so many people, regardless of their background, likely increased competition for jobs and resources in cities.)*

DIGITAL TEXT 2

City Neighborhoods Defined by Status

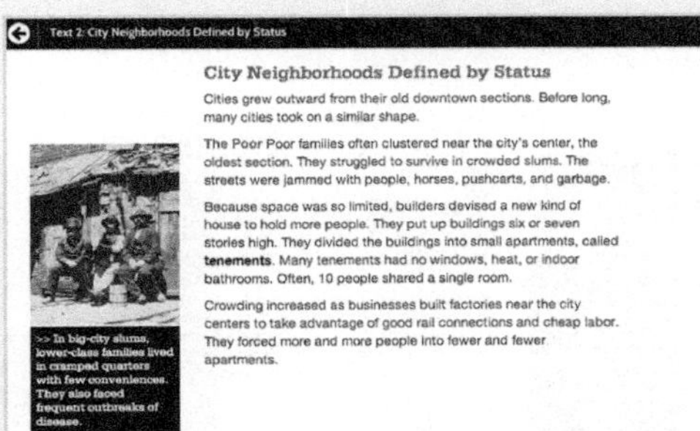

INTERACTIVE GRAPH

New York City Changes, 1840 to 1900

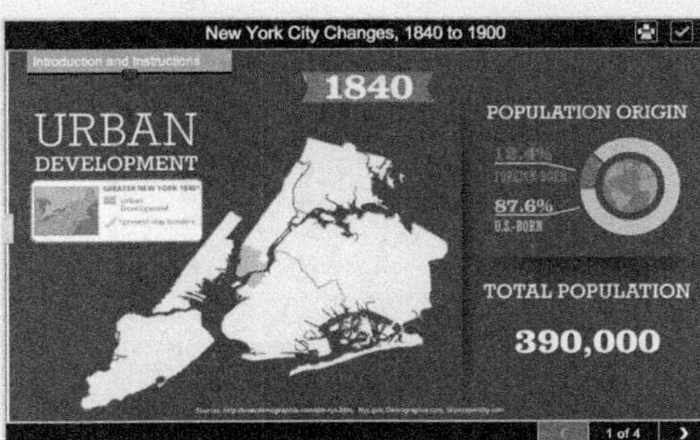

Objective 2: **Describe the relationship between social class and cities' geographies.**

Quick Instruction

Interactive Graph: New York City Changes, 1840 to 1900 Project the Interactive Graph. Ask students to write down what they think is the most important fact in the Interactive Graph and then call on volunteers to explain their decisions. Ask: How does the information shown in the first set of maps and graphs relate to the second? *(The map shows how New York City increased in size, and the graphs show why by providing data on the increase in the city's population and the percentage of that population that grew from immigration.)*

Make Generalizations How would you describe many of the people who moved to cities during this time? *(Many of the people moving to cities were immigrants, African Americans, and others who were looking for work. Many were probably poor or had few resources.)*

ACTIVE CLASSROOM

Organize students into small groups. Assign each group one of the images from the text. Tell students to use the If Images Could Talk strategy to write speech bubbles for the people shown in the photographs. Display their images and bubbles in the class. Have students take a tour of the completed images and jot down responses to share in class discussion.

D Differentiate: On Level To help students understand economic divisions in society, you may wish to draw a pyramid. Divide the pyramid into three tiers: lower status on the bottom; middle status in the middle; upper status on the top. Prompt students to understand that the type of job a person does and the amount of money a person makes often determines his or her economic status.

Further Instruction

Explain that more than 70% of immigrants to the United States during this time arrived in New York City. Many stayed in New York City, which accounts for its rapid growth. Others moved on to other cities in the eastern part of the country, and some even went farther west. Have students work in small groups to complete the Interactive Reading Notepad questions. Then, jigsaw the groups to share and discuss responses. Be sure that students understand that industrialization led to new occupations and the growth of the middle class.

Draw Conclusions Why were many city neighborhoods defined by social status? *(Many people in cities tended to live near others who shared similar cultural backgrounds but also shared similar economic status. For example, poor people tended to live in areas of cities with lower property values, because they could not afford to live in an apartment for which they would pay more rent.)*

Hypothesize Would cities have grown so quickly without industrialization? Why or why not? *(Cities probably would not have grown as quickly. Urban areas have always existed as centers of trade and government, but industrialization encouraged a more rapid expansion of cities. The number of new jobs encouraged migration and immigration, and people often had to live near the places where they worked.)*

Connect How did tenement housing both solve and produce problems? *(Tenement housing provided a solution to housing needs for large numbers of people who moved to cities. However, tenement housing also contributed to problems of overcrowding, public health, waste production, and lack of sanitation.)*

Urbanization

DIGITAL TEXT 3

Effects of Rapid Urbanization

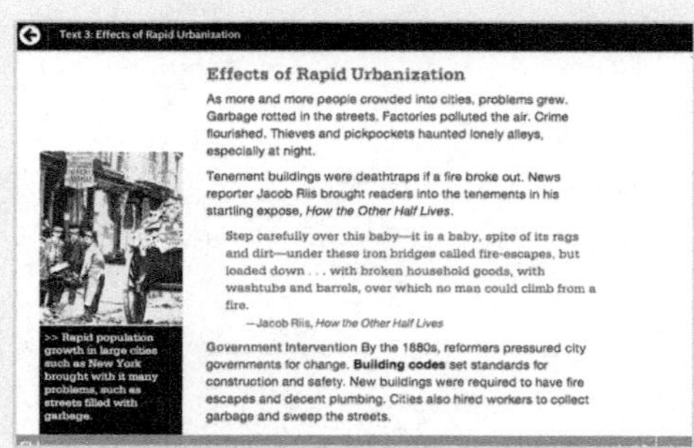
Text 3: Effects of Rapid Urbanization

Effects of Rapid Urbanization

As more and more people crowded into cities, problems grew. Garbage rotted in the streets. Factories polluted the air. Crime flourished. Thieves and pickpockets haunted lonely alleys, especially at night.

Tenement buildings were deathtraps if a fire broke out. News reporter Jacob Riis brought readers into the tenements in his startling expose, *How the Other Half Lives*.

> Step carefully over this baby—it is a baby, spite of its rags and dirt—under these iron bridges called fire-escapes, but loaded down . . . with broken household goods, with washtubs and barrels, over which no man could climb from a fire.
>
> —Jacob Riis, *How the Other Half Lives*

Government Intervention By the 1880s, reformers pressured city governments for change. **Building codes** set standards for construction and safety. New buildings were required to have fire escapes and decent plumbing. Cities also hired workers to collect garbage and sweep the streets.

>> Rapid population growth in large cities such as New York brought with it many problems, such as streets filled with garbage.

3-D MODEL

Living in a Tenement

DIGITAL TEXT 4

The Settlement House Movement

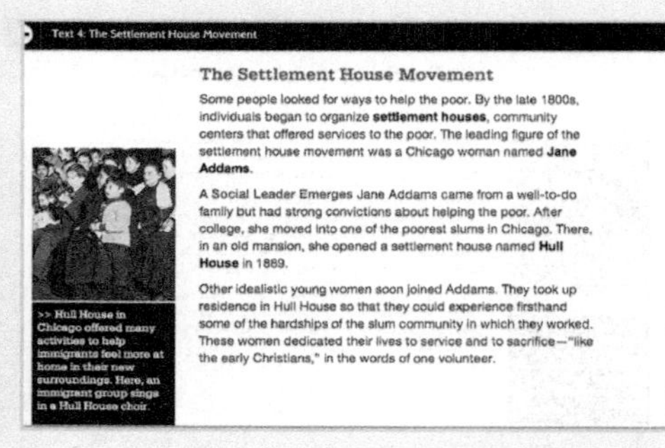
Text 4: The Settlement House Movement

The Settlement House Movement

Some people looked for ways to help the poor. By the late 1800s, individuals began to organize **settlement houses**, community centers that offered services to the poor. The leading figure of the settlement house movement was a Chicago woman named **Jane Addams**.

A Social Leader Emerges Jane Addams came from a well-to-do family but had strong convictions about helping the poor. After college, she moved into one of the poorest slums in Chicago. There, in an old mansion, she opened a settlement house named **Hull House** in 1889.

Other idealistic young women soon joined Addams. They took up residence in Hull House so that they could experience firsthand some of the hardships of the slum community in which they worked. These women dedicated their lives to service and to sacrifice—"like the early Christians," in the words of one volunteer.

>> Hull House in Chicago offered many activities to help immigrants feel more at home in their new surroundings. Here, an immigrant group sings in a Hull House choir.

Objective 3: **Describe the causes and effects of the settlement house and other urban reform movements.**

Quick Instruction

3-D Model: Living in a Tenement Project the 3-D Model. Invite students to take a tour of the tenement house. Have them record notes about each part of the model. Then, ask them to Think-Pair-Share a response to what they observed. What hazards and challenges might result from many people living in close quarters and crowded housing? *(Sanitation, waste disposal, and the spread of illness might pose challenges in overcrowded conditions, and it would be difficult to escape these buildings in a fire. Conflict and crime might also increase with so many people sharing space.)* What benefits did tenement housing likely offer residents? *(Tenements were less expensive than other housing in cities. Families and friends could live together and build communities.)*

ACTIVE CLASSROOM

Organize students into small groups. Have them take turns using the Audio Tour strategy to conduct one another on a tour of the 3-D model tenement. You may wish to record MP3's of the audio tours to post on the class website. When students have finished, ask them to spend a few minutes describing what it would have been like to live in the tenement house.

Interactive Gallery: Urban Problems Project the Interactive Gallery and navigate through the images with students. Prompt students to connect the images with specific reform movements mentioned in the text.

ACTIVE CLASSROOM

Conduct a Make a Headline activity. Have students choose an image in the Interactive Gallery for which they will write a headline. Prompt students to write headlines that capture what they believe is the most important aspect of the image. Have students pass their headlines to a partner for a review and discussion. Encourage volunteers to share their headlines with the class.

ELL Use the ELL activity described in the ELL chart.

Further Instruction

Be sure that students understand the essential point that problems associated with urbanization led city governments to develop services and prompted social reformers to work for other improvements.

Generate Explanations How did the settlement house movement encourage a culture of service and volunteerism? *(The settlement house movement brought together many reformers dedicated to improving the lives of people in need in urban centers and other areas. These like-minded individuals worked not only to assist urban immigrants and the poor but also to win political reform.)*

INTERACTIVE GALLERY

Urban Problems

Urban Problems
Fire Safety
Progressives in New York City fought for the Tenement House Act of 1901, which required every apartment building to have a fire escape, like the ones shown here. This law saved many lives.
1 of 3

Connect What services and benefits of city life today derive from reform efforts and changes made by city governments in the late 1800s? *(Many public services in cities, including fire departments, public water and utilities, public sanitation, police protection, and building regulations, came from this period. Also, private efforts such as community centers, church shelters, and food services started during this time. Many reformers also worked on related political issues, such as workers' rights, fair wages, women's suffrage, and child labor laws.)*

SYNTHESIZE

DIGITAL ACTIVITY

Urban Life

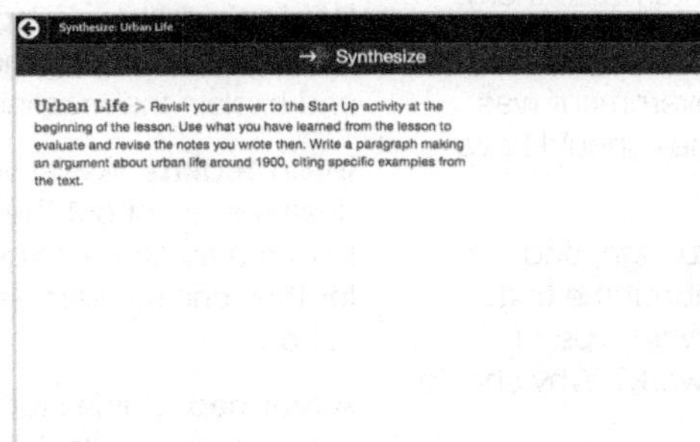

Synthesize: Urban Life
Synthesize
Urban Life > Revisit your answer to the Start Up activity at the beginning of the lesson. Use what you have learned from the lesson to evaluate and revise the notes you wrote then. Write a paragraph making an argument about urban life around 1900, citing specific examples from the text.

Have students discuss their notes in small groups and brainstorm ideas for their paragraphs. Then, tell students to formulate a thesis statement about life in the cities around 1900s. Have them write an introductory paragraph to explain and support their thesis paragraph. If time allows, instruct students to share their paragraphs with a partner and provide feedback.

Discuss Tell students to consider the rapid ways in which the geography, population, and economy of the United States changed in the late 1800s. How might they expect American society to continue to change in the early 1900s? In what ways might industrialization, immigration, and reform movements affect the politics of the United States?

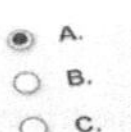

DEMONSTRATE

LESSON QUIZ

Lesson Quiz and Class Discussion Board

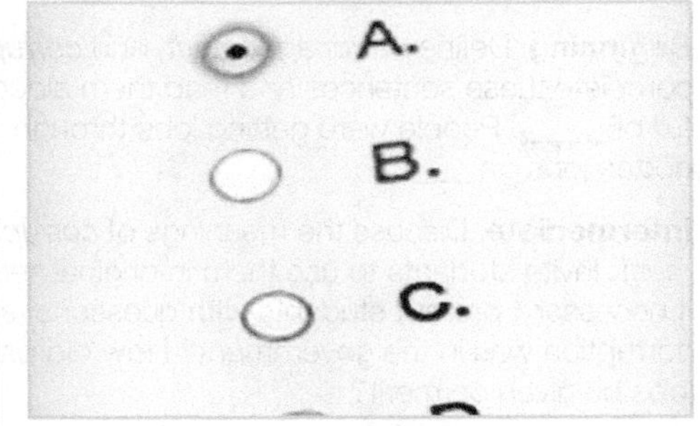

Assign the online Lesson Quiz for this lesson if you haven't already done so. Students will be offered automatic remediation or enrichment based on their score.

Pose these questions to the class on the Discussion Board:

In *Urbanization*, you learned about the rapid population growth and growth of cities in the United States during the late 1800s. You also read about the effects of that growth and explored ways in which city government and reformers responded to challenges in cities.

Solve Problems Several challenges arose as cities, population, and industry grew. Identify two of these problems and propose solutions.

Connect How do the challenges of city life in the late 1800s compare with the challenges of urban life today?

Topic Inquiry

Have students continue their investigations for the Topic Inquiry.

The Rise of Progressivism

Supporting English Language Learners

Use with the reading, **Federal and Local Reform Efforts**.

Learning

Display key content-area vocabulary from the text (e.g., *spoils system*, *patronage*, *merit*, *corruption*, *honest*, *reform*, *investigation*). Explain that using these words when speaking will help students to internalize them.

Beginning Define *patronage*, *merit*, and *corruption*. Invite students to complete these sentences and read them aloud: The government was full of _____. People were getting jobs through _____. They should have gotten jobs on _____.

Intermediate Discuss the meanings of *corruption*, *patronage*, and *merit*. Invite students to use them in original sentences about the text. If necessary, prompt students with questions, such as: What type of corruption was in the government? How did patronage work? Why should jobs be given on merit?

Advanced Discuss the meanings of *corruption*, *reform*, *merit*, and *honest*, as well as their variants (e.g., *corrupt*, *reformed*, *merit* as a verb, *honesty*). Encourage students to use these vocabulary words as you discuss the state of the U.S. government around 1880 together.

Advanced High Have pairs of students analyze the state of the U.S. government around 1880. Provide them with a list of the seven terms above, and have them check off the terms as they use them during their discussion.

Use with the reading, **Progressive Reforms**.

Speaking

Display these words from the text: *primary*, *initiative*, *referendum*, *recall*. Review the meaning of each word with students.

Beginning Using simple words, actions, and gestures, act out the word *recall* without saying the word. Invite students to guess the correct word and explain the reasons for their choice.

Intermediate Assist volunteers in using simple words, actions, and gestures to act out the word *recall* without saying the word. Invite students from the audience to guess the correct word and explain the reasons for their choice. Also ask the actors to explain how they decided what to act out.

Advanced Guide students to create brief skits that use words, actions, and gestures to depict the words *primary*, *initiative*, *referendum*, and *recall*. For added challenge, encourage students to incorporate two or more words into a single skit.

Advanced High Assign the words *primary*, *initiative*, *referendum*, and *recall* to a different pair or small group of students. Invite students to write a skit that illustrates their word. Then have students act out their skits for one another.

D Differentiate Instruction

Use the Differentiated Instruction notes throughout the lesson plan to support the varied skill sets, levels of readiness, and interests in the mixed-ability classroom.

Challenge These notes include suggestions for expanding the activity for advanced students.

On-Level These notes include suggestions for modifying the activity to address different interests or learning styles.

Extra Support These notes include ideas for providing more scaffolding or reading spupport.

Special Needs These notes provide ideas for adapting instruction to support the needs of various special needs students.

NOTES

Objectives

Objective 1: Describe politics during the Gilded Age and efforts at political reform.

Objective 2: Identify efforts to regulate big business.

Objective 3: Explain how the muckrakers inspired reform.

Objective 4: Identify the Progressives and explain their reforms.

LESSON 3 ORGANIZER	PACING: APPROX. 1 PERIOD, .5 BLOCKS			
			RESOURCES	
	OBJECTIVES	PACING	Online	Print
Connect				
DIGITAL START UP ACTIVITY **Determine the Author's Purpose**		5 min.	●	
Investigate				
DIGITAL TEXT 1 **Gilded Age Politics**	Objective 1	10 min.	●	●
DIGITAL TEXT 2 **Federal and Local Reform Efforts**	Objective 2	10 min.	●	●
DIGITAL TEXT 3 **The Power of Big Business**		10 min.	●	●
DIGITAL TEXT 4 **The Muckrakers**	Objective 3	10 min.	●	●
DIGITAL TEXT 5 **Progressive Reforms**	Objective 4	10 min.	●	●
INTERACTIVE TIMELINE **Government Reforms in the Progressive Era**		10 min.	●	
INTERACTIVE CHART **Progressive Political Reforms**		10 min.	●	
Synthesize				
DIGITAL ACTIVITY **Muckrakers**		5 min.	●	
Demonstrate				
LESSON QUIZ **Lesson Quiz and Class Discussion Board**		10 min.	●	

The Rise of Progressivism

CONNECT

DIGITAL START UP ACTIVITY

Determine the Author's Purpose

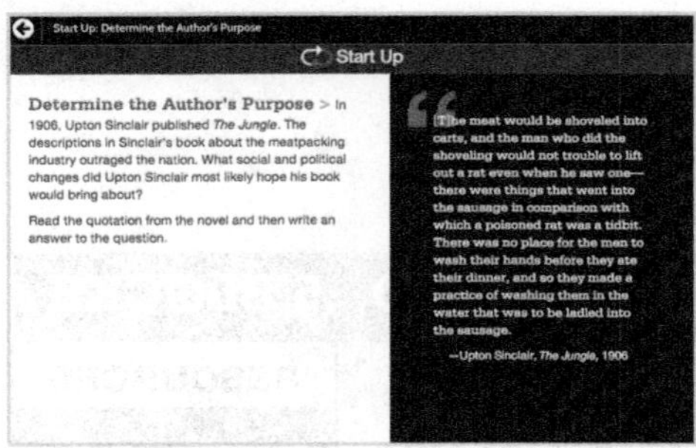

Start Up: Determine the Author's Purpose
Start Up
Determine the Author's Purpose > In 1906, Upton Sinclair published The Jungle. The descriptions in Sinclair's book about the meatpacking industry outraged the nation. What social and political changes did Upton Sinclair most likely hope his book would bring about?
Read the quotation from the novel and then write an answer to the question.
[T]he meat would be shoveled into carts, and the man who did the shoveling would not trouble to lift out a rat even when he saw one—there were things that went into the sausage in comparison with which a poisoned rat was a tidbit. There was no place for the men to wash their hands before they ate their dinner, and so they made a practice of washing them in the water that was to be ladled into the sausage.
—Upton Sinclair, The Jungle, 1906

Project the Start Up Activity Instruct students to read the quote and respond to the question as they enter and get settled. Then, have them share their responses in small groups. Ask groups to identify the most disturbing part of the quote and explain their choice.

Discuss Why would this information outrage the nation? *(People reasonably expected their food to be safe to eat.)*

Tell students that in this lesson, they will explore the reform movements of the late 1800s and early 1900s. They will also learn about the response of big business and government to these reform movements.

Aa Vocabulary Development: Use the Interactive Reading Notepad to preview the Key Terms and Academic Vocabulary in this lesson with students.

FLIP IT!

Assign the Flipped Video for this lesson.

STUDENT EDITION PRINT PAGES: 597–604

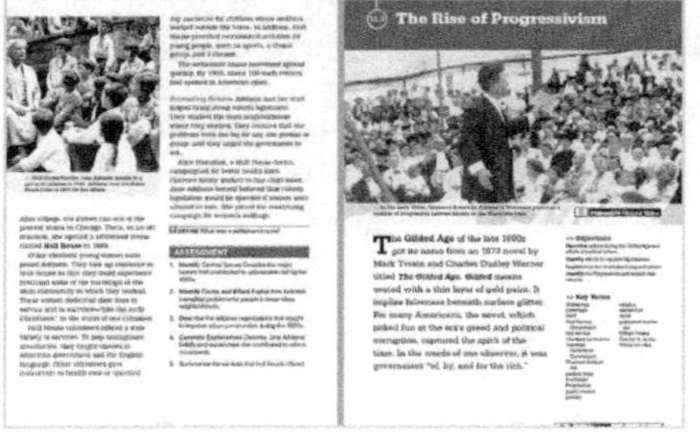

INVESTIGATE

DIGITAL TEXT 1

Gilded Age Politics

Text 1: Gilded Age Politics
Gilded Age Politics
The Gilded Age of the late 1800s got its name from an 1873 novel by Mark Twain and Charles Dudley Warner titled The Gilded Age. Gilded means coated with a thin layer of gold paint. It implies falseness beneath surface glitter. For many Americans, the novel, which poked fun at the era's greed and political corruption, captured the spirit of the time. In the words of one observer, it was government "of, by, and for the rich."
The Gilded Age lasted from the 1870s through the 1890s. During this time, reformers struggled to clean up political corruption. Political power in the Gilded Age was split between the two major parties. Usually, the North and West voted Republican, and the South voted Democratic. Neither party controlled Congress for more than a term or two, although Republicans held the White House for nearly 25 years. However, Presidents generally had less power than Congress during the period.
>> The ornate furnishings in this New York City home were fashionable among the wealthy in the Gilded Age. Many Americans worried about the power the wealthy had gained in business and politics.
1 of 4

Objective 1: Describe politics during the Gilded Age and efforts at political reform.

Quick Instruction

Begin by reading aloud the following quote from Mark Twain's *The Gilded Age: A Tale of Today:* "Unless you can get the ear of a Senator... and persuade him to use his 'influence' in your behalf, you cannot get employment of the most trivial nature in Washington. Mere merit, fitness and capability, are useless baggage to you without 'influence.'" Ask students to jot down what they think this quotation means. Discuss their ideas as a class. Then, tell students to make a prediction for what they will learn about in this text.

Analyze Political Cartoons What do the two political cartoons suggest about Boss Tweed? *(that he had so much money that he was too powerful to be contained by jail or government)* What can you infer from these political cartoons about government in general during the Gilded Age? *(that government, or political power, was not as important as wealth; that wealth made big businessmen and party bosses more powerful than government officials)*

D Differentiate: Extra Support Draw a concept web on the board with *Gilded Age* in the center oval. Have students copy the web. Instruct them to add details to the web as they move through the lesson. Prompt students by drawing attention to the opening lines of the text. Write "greed and political corruption" on the web. Add a spoke from "greed and political corruption" and call attention to related ideas in the text. For example, *bankers, industrialists, and other wealthy men were controlling politics*, *bribery and voter fraud*, and *spoils system*.

Further Instruction

Explain that the word spoils means "booty, or goods captured during war." It comes from an Old French word meaning the same. During the late 1800s, this term became associated with political elections. In the spoils system, politicians who won campaigns were expected to award jobs to their supporters.

Generate Explanations Party bosses liked Boss Tweed were corrupt and broke the law. How did they become so popular among urban populations? *(They gave jobs to people, made loans, and found other ways to help the poor, such as giving food or coal to people in need.)*

Infer What does the popularity of party bosses like Boss Tweed suggest about government? *(People did not feel that government was doing all that it could to provide for them. They were not receiving the jobs and services that they needed through regular means. Political officials failed to meet their needs or act in their interests.)*

DIGITAL TEXT 2

Federal and Local Reform Efforts

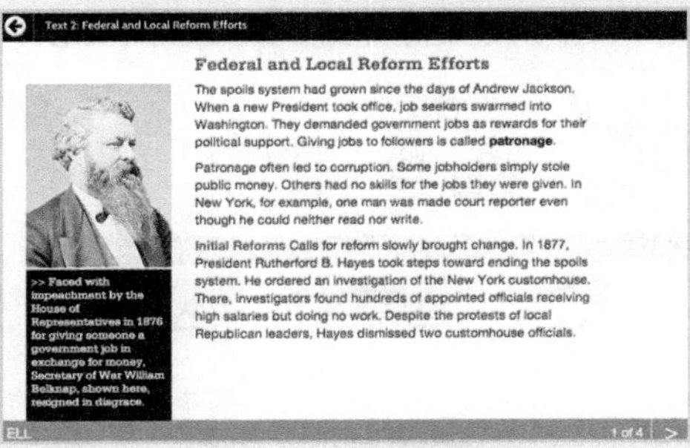

Text 2: Federal and Local Reform Efforts
Federal and Local Reform Efforts
The spoils system had grown since the days of Andrew Jackson. When a new President took office, job seekers swarmed into Washington. They demanded government jobs as rewards for their political support. Giving jobs to followers is called patronage.
Patronage often led to corruption. Some jobholders simply stole public money. Others had no skills for the jobs they were given. In New York, for example, one man was made court reporter even though he could neither read nor write.
Initial Reforms Calls for reform slowly brought change. In 1877, President Rutherford B. Hayes took steps toward ending the spoils system. He ordered an investigation of the New York customhouse. There, investigators found hundreds of appointed officials receiving high salaries but doing no work. Despite the protests of local Republican leaders, Hayes dismissed two customhouse officials.
>> Faced with impeachment by the House of Representatives in 1876 for giving someone a government job in exchange for money, Secretary of War William Belknap, shown here, resigned in disgrace.
ELL
1 of 4

Objective 2: **Identify efforts to regulate big business.**

Quick Instruction

Preview the text by displaying key words: *spoils system, patronage, merit, civil service, interstate commerce, competition, trusts,* and *monopoly*. Tell students to watch for these words as they move through the text. Then, have them work in pairs to write sentences in which they use the words listed to explain the content.

Connect The root word in *patronage* is *patron*. This word means "a protector," and comes from a Latin word that means "father." How does the idea of patronage relate to its root word's meaning? *(Through patronage, political officials act as patrons. They award, or protect and look after, those who support them.)* What notable patrons are named in the text? *(Andrew Jackson, William Belknap)*

Check Understanding Why did competing corporations join together to form trusts? *(It was in their interest to work together to eliminate other competition in order to gain more wealth and power.)*

ELL Use the ELL activity described in the ELL chart.

DIGITAL TEXT 3

The Power of Big Business

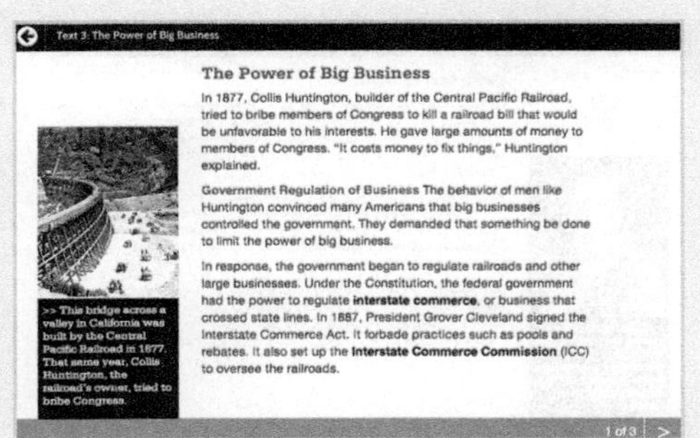

Text 3: The Power of Big Business
The Power of Big Business
In 1877, Collis Huntington, builder of the Central Pacific Railroad, tried to bribe members of Congress to kill a railroad bill that would be unfavorable to his interests. He gave large amounts of money to members of Congress. "It costs money to fix things," Huntington explained.
Government Regulation of Business The behavior of men like Huntington convinced many Americans that big businesses controlled the government. They demanded that something be done to limit the power of big business.
In response, the government began to regulate railroads and other large businesses. Under the Constitution, the federal government had the power to regulate interstate commerce, or business that crossed state lines. In 1887, President Grover Cleveland signed the Interstate Commerce Act. It forbade practices such as pools and rebates. It also set up the Interstate Commerce Commission (ICC) to oversee the railroads.
>> This bridge across a valley in California was built by the Central Pacific Railroad in 1877. That same year, Collis Huntington, the railroad's owner, tried to bribe Congress.
1 of 3

Further Instruction

Point out the circular nature of corruption during this era by drawing a circle. On the circle, write "political officials grant favors to big business," "big business establishes monopolies and accumulates great wealth," and "big business pays political officials for influence." Each element of the cycle reinforces the next. Challenge students to identify ways in which to break the cycle, and have them share their ideas.

Cite Evidence During the Gilded Age, government officials and citizens took steps to address corruption and rein in big business. Cite evidence from the text to support this statement. *(Government passed new laws, including the Sherman Antitrust Act and the Pendleton Act, to reduce and prevent corruption and to limit the power of big business to establish monopolies. Citizens also formed good-government leagues to monitor, to watch for, and to respond to local political corruption. Workers fought against big business through unions.)*

DIGITAL TEXT 4

The Muckrakers

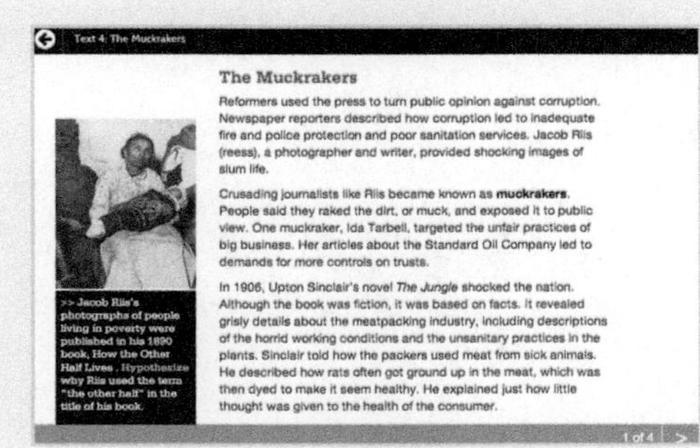

Text 4: The Muckrakers
The Muckrakers
Reformers used the press to turn public opinion against corruption. Newspaper reporters described how corruption led to inadequate fire and police protection and poor sanitation services. Jacob Riis (reess), a photographer and writer, provided shocking images of slum life.
Crusading journalists like Riis became known as muckrakers. People said they raked the dirt, or muck, and exposed it to public view. One muckraker, Ida Tarbell, targeted the unfair practices of big business. Her articles about the Standard Oil Company led to demands for more controls on trusts.
In 1906, Upton Sinclair's novel The Jungle shocked the nation. Although the book was fiction, it was based on facts. It revealed grisly details about the meatpacking industry, including descriptions of the horrid working conditions and the unsanitary practices in the plants. Sinclair told how the packers used meat from sick animals. He described how rats often got ground up in the meat, which was then dyed to make it seem healthy. He explained just how little thought was given to the health of the consumer.
>> Jacob Riis's photographs of people living in poverty were published in his 1890 book, How the Other Half Lives . Hypothesize why Riis used the term "the other half" in the title of his book.
1 of 4

Objective 3: **Explain how the muckrakers inspired reform.**

Quick Instruction

Display the photograph from Jacob Riis as well as the quotes from Upton Sinclair and Lincoln Steffens. Prompt students to consider these primary sources and think about what they suggest about American society in the late 1800s.

Determine Relevance Why are Jacob Riis's photographs and Upton Sinclair's and Lincoln Steffens's stories significant? *(They reveal the reality of living and working conditions in cities. They exposed hardships experienced by many people as well as threats to public health and safety and prompted reform efforts.)*

Further Instruction

When students have completed reading the text, tell them to work in groups to complete the Interactive Reading Notepad. Then, jigsaw the groups, and have them compare and revise their responses. To extend student learning, assign the primary sources *How the Other Half Lives* and *The Jungle*.

The Rise of Progressivism

Hypothesize Would reforms such as the Pure Food and Drug and Meat Inspection Act have happened without muckrakers? Why or why not? *(Without people investigating and exposing conditions in cities and factories, the public would not have been informed and outraged enough to demand change of government. Officials would have felt the pressure needed to enact change.)*

Integrate Information What do you think motivated muckrakers like Jacob Riis to undertake such reform efforts? *(Muckrakers and other reformers were motivated by a sense of concern for their fellow citizens. They wanted to improve the lives of other people, including workers and immigrants, as well as to protect consumers.)*

DIGITAL TEXT 5

Progressive Reforms

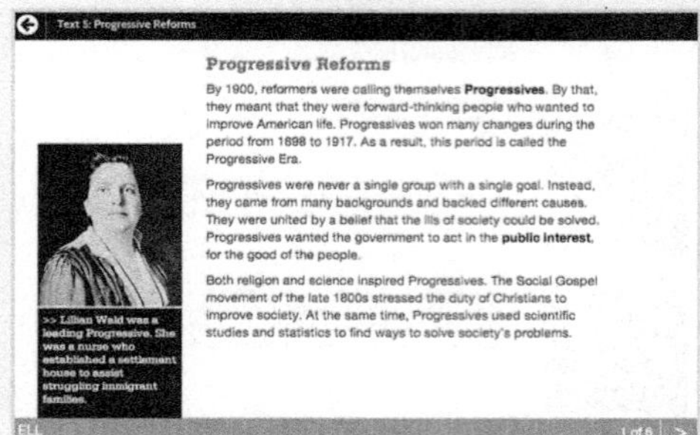

Objective 4: Identify the Progressives and explain their reforms.

Quick Instruction

Interactive Timeline: Government Reforms in the Progressive Era Project the Interactive Timeline and click through the reforms. How did the reforms on the timeline most likely affect citizens' lives? *(Ending the spoils system would have enabled more people to pursue positions in government. The Interstate Commerce and Sherman Antitrust Acts would have increased competition and potentially lowered prices for consumers. Election reforms would have made government more representative and increased participation, giving average citizens more voice in government.)*

ACTIVE CLASSROOM

Conduct a Cartoon It activity. Review examples of political cartoons from the text, then organize students into pairs. Assign each pair one Progressive reform (or reform issue) and have them draw one political cartoon showing the problem and one political cartoon depicting a solution to the problem. Remind students that they can use words in their cartoons, as titles, captions, and thought or speech bubbles. Display completed cartoons in the classroom or on the class blog.

INTERACTIVE TIMELINE

Government Reforms in the Progressive Era

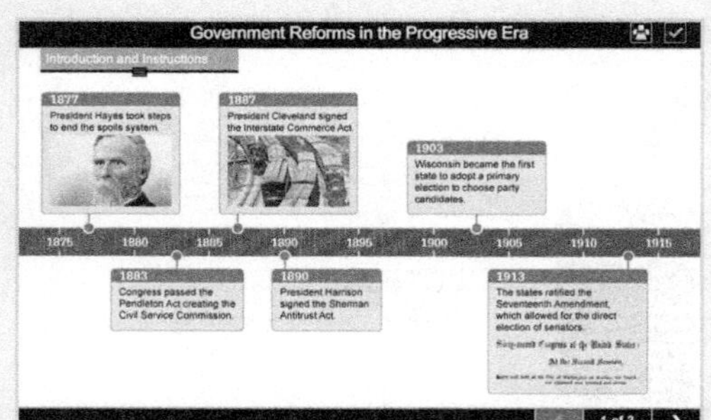

Interactive Chart: Progressive Political Reforms Project the Interactive Chart and guide students to complete the drag and drop activity. Which political reform gave citizens the most influence over the passage of new laws? Why? *(The referendum gave citizens the most influence over new laws because they could vote directly on a bill rather than have an elected representative vote for them.)*

ACTIVE CLASSROOM

Conduct a Word Wall activity. Split students into small groups. Have each group choose one of the terms in the Interactive Chart and create a visual image with a definition. Ask students to post their words on the board or on chart paper and prompt the class to consider the similarities and differences between the visual images.

ELL Use the ELL activity described in the ELL chart.

Further Instruction

Review the instructions for the Interactive Reading Notepad. Have students complete the questions as they move through the lesson. Then, discuss students' responses as a class. Be sure that students understand that the Progressive Era comprised many different reform movements. Some reforms overlapped, and reformers did not always agree. Often, reform groups split over issues of race, gender, and religious ideas. Still, during this time, large numbers of everyday citizens engaged in unprecedented social, economic, and political activity to demand changes that they thought would improve life in the United States.

INTERACTIVE CHART

Progressive Political Reforms

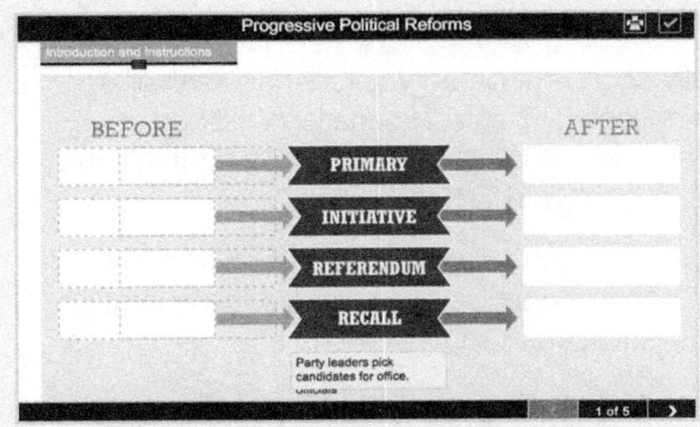

Determine Relevance Why were political reforms like *initiative* and *recall* so important to enacting wider social and economic reforms? *(These political reforms gave citizens more power in government. They increased civil participation and enabled citizens to go around politicians, especially those in the pocket of big business, to pursue changes important to them. They made government, especially local and state government, more answerable to the people.)*

Compare Perspectives What arguments could be made for and against a graduated income tax? *(People against a graduated income tax might argue that different levels of taxation are unfair, as all people have the opportunity to pursue economic opportunities, and taxation is based on a percentage of income. They might argue that it penalizes people for pursuing wealth and better employment and hinders economic growth and incentives. People for the graduated income tax might argue that the same level of taxation is unfair, as a certain percentage of a poor person's income means much more to that person than does the same percentage of a wealthy person's income.)*

SYNTHESIZE

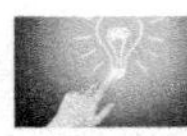

DIGITAL ACTIVITY

Muckrakers

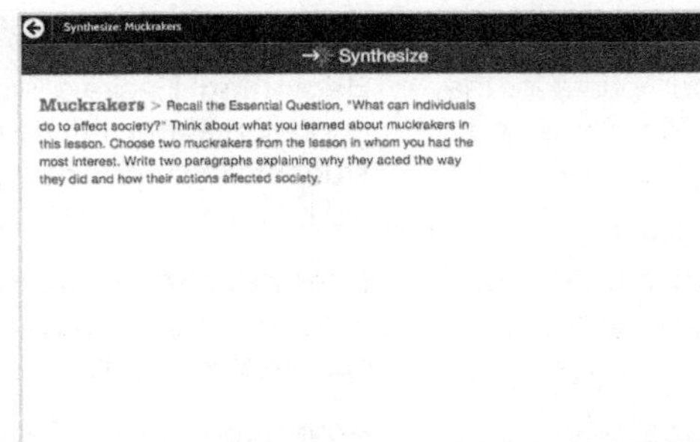

Have students choose two muckrakers about which to write. Then, have them work individually to write a response to the question for each individual. If time allows, ask students to share their responses with a partner.

Discuss Which muckraker had the greatest impact on improving the lives of Americans, and why? Have students state a position and defend their ideas with evidence from the text.

DEMONSTRATE

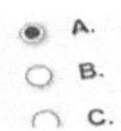

LESSON QUIZ

Lesson Quiz and Class Discussion Board

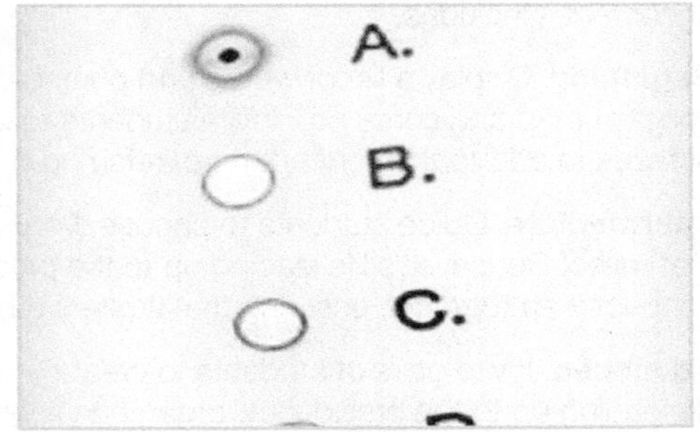

Assign the online Lesson Quiz for this lesson if you haven't already done so. Students will be offered automatic remediation or enrichment based on their score.

Pose these questions to the class on the Discussion Board:

In *The Rise of Progressivism*, you learned about the causes and effects of Progressive reform movements in the late 1800s. You explored problems in government and big businesses during the Gilded Age and examined efforts to correct those problems.

Compare and Contrast What did reform efforts in the late 1800s have in common and how did they differ?

Connect How did the muckrakers influence today's media reporters and citizens?

Topic Inquiry

Have students continue their investigations for the Topic Inquiry.

The Progressive Presidents

Supporting English Language Learners

Use with the reading, **Theodore Roosevelt's Path to the White House**.

Writing

Display the beginning of a concept map by writing "Roosevelt's Early Life" in a center circle. Explain how a concept map is structured and what kind of content it includes.

Beginning Display a list of words and phrases, some appropriate for the concept map and some not. Invite students to identify which words and phrases to add to the concept map, referring to the text as needed.

Intermediate Guide students to choose words and phrases from the text that reflect Roosevelt's life leading up to the presidency. Then review the concept web together, ensuring that it offers a balanced characterization.

Advanced Invite pairs of students to create a concept web of Roosevelt's life leading up to the presidency, organizing it into hierarchical branches where necessary. Then ask students to share information from their web and aggregate their responses onto a class web.

Advanced High Have individual students create a concept web of Roosevelt's life leading up to the presidency, creating hierarchical branches where necessary. Provide time for partners to share and revise their webs. Then display the webs for students to look at.

Use with the reading, **President Taft**.

Speaking

With students, brainstorm why they might restate or summarize what someone else says (e.g., to show they are listening, to make sure they understand what was said, to better remember what was said).

Beginning Recite a linguistically accommodated version of Roosevelt's quotation about Taft (twice if necessary). Then ask questions that guide students in summarizing the statement, such as: Does Roosevelt think Taft will be a good president? Do Roosevelt and Taft think alike?

Intermediate Recite Roosevelt's quotation about Taft (making linguistic accommodations as needed). Then invite students to restate the quotation in their own words. Ask: What is Roosevelt's main point?

Advanced Recite Roosevelt's quotation about Taft from the text (twice if necessary). Then ask pairs of students to paraphrase the quotation and discuss what it means.

Advanced High Recite Roosevelt's quotation about Taft from the text (twice if necessary). Ask students to paraphrase the quotation in writing. Provide time for partners to compare what they wrote down.

D Differentiate Instruction

Use the Differentiated Instruction notes throughout the lesson plan to support the varied skill sets, levels of readiness, and interests in the mixed-ability classroom.

Challenge These notes include suggestions for expanding the activity for advanced students.

On-Level These notes include suggestions for modifying the activity to address different interests or learning styles.

Extra Support These notes include ideas for providing more scaffolding or reading spuport.

Special Needs These notes provide ideas for adapting instruction to support the needs of various special needs students.

NOTES

PEARSON realize™ www.PearsonRealize.com

Go online to access additional resources including: Primary Sources • Biographies • Supreme Court cases • 21st Century Skill Tutorials • Maps • Graphic Organizers.

Objectives

Objective 1: Identify Theodore Roosevelt's reform goals, including the Square Deal.

Objective 2: Compare and contrast William Howard Taft's policies with Theodore Roosevelt's.

Objective 3: Describe reforms under Woodrow Wilson.

LESSON 4 ORGANIZER	PACING: APPROX. 1 PERIOD, .5 BLOCKS		RESOURCES	
	OBJECTIVES	PACING	Online	Print
Connect				
DIGITAL START UP ACTIVITY **"Grim Energy and Resolute Courage"**		5 min.	●	
Investigate				
DIGITAL TEXT 1 **Theodore Roosevelt's Path to the White House**	Objective 1	10 min.	●	●
DIGITAL TEXT 2 **Encouraging Fair Business Practices**	Objective 1	10 min.	●	●
DIGITAL TEXT 3 **The Square Deal**	Objective 1	10 min.	●	●
INTERACTIVE GALLERY **National Land Conservation**	Objective 1	10 min.	●	
DIGITAL TEXT 4 **President Taft**	Objective 2	10 min.	●	●
DIGITAL TEXT 5 **Wilson Wins the Presidency**	Objective 3	10 min.	●	●
INTERACTIVE CHART **Three Presidents' Accomplishments**	Objective 3	10 min.	●	
Synthesize				
DIGITAL ACTIVITY **Progressive Accomplishments**		5 min.	●	
Demonstrate				
LESSON QUIZ **Lesson Quiz and Class Discussion Board**		10 min.	●	

The Progressive Presidents

CONNECT

DIGITAL START UP ACTIVITY

"Grim Energy and Resolute Courage"

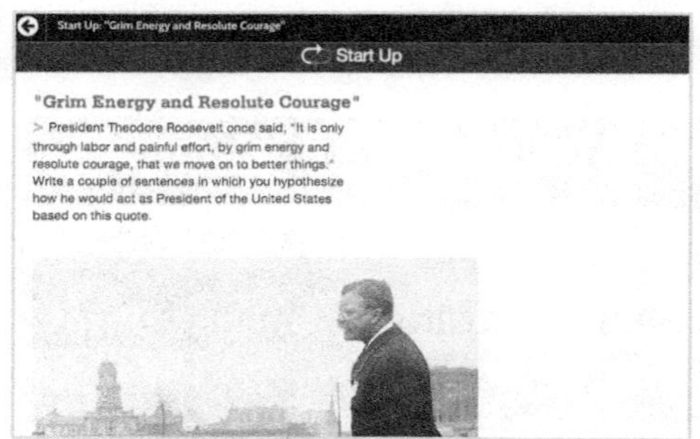
Start Up: "Grim Energy and Resolute Courage"

Start Up

"Grim Energy and Resolute Courage"

> President Theodore Roosevelt once said, "It is only through labor and painful effort, by grim energy and resolute courage, that we move on to better things." Write a couple of sentences in which you hypothesize how he would act as President of the United States based on this quote.

Project the Start Up Activity Instruct students to read and respond to the quote from President Theodore Roosevelt as they get settled. Have them Think-Pair-Share ideas.

Discuss What challenges did President Roosevelt likely face in 1901? *(Roosevelt would have faced many social and economic challenges. Many workers faced difficult working conditions. Women did not have the right to vote. Racial and ethnic groups faced persecution.*

Tell students that in this lesson they will learn about Theodore Roosevelt. They will compare and contrast Roosevelt's policies with those of William Howard Taft and Woodrow Wilson, and will be able to describe what it means to be a Progressive president.

Aa Vocabulary Development: Use the Interactive Reading Notepad to preview the Key Terms and Academic Vocabulary in this lesson with students.

FLIP IT!

Assign the Flipped Video for this lesson.

STUDENT EDITION PRINT PAGES: 605–611

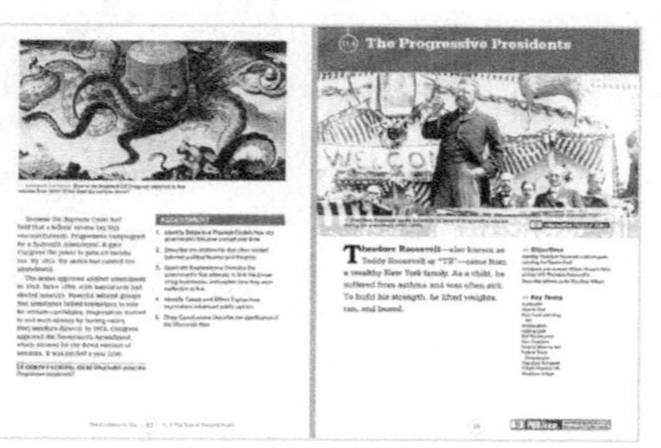

INVESTIGATE

DIGITAL TEXT 1

Theodore Roosevelt's Path to the White House

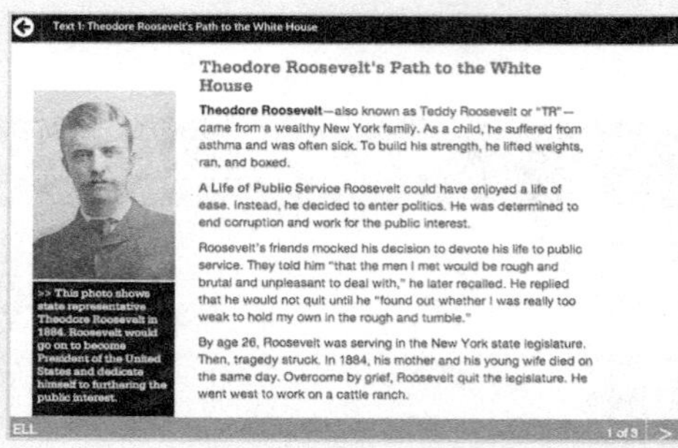
Text 1: Theodore Roosevelt's Path to the White House

Theodore Roosevelt's Path to the White House

Theodore Roosevelt—also known as Teddy Roosevelt or "TR"—came from a wealthy New York family. As a child, he suffered from asthma and was often sick. To build his strength, he lifted weights, ran, and boxed.

A Life of Public Service Roosevelt could have enjoyed a life of ease. Instead, he decided to enter politics. He was determined to end corruption and work for the public interest.

Roosevelt's friends mocked his decision to devote his life to public service. They told him "that the men I met would be rough and brutal and unpleasant to deal with," he later recalled. He replied that he would not quit until he "found out whether I was really too weak to hold my own in the rough and tumble."

By age 26, Roosevelt was serving in the New York state legislature. Then, tragedy struck. In 1884, his mother and his young wife died on the same day. Overcome by grief, Roosevelt quit the legislature. He went west to work on a cattle ranch.

>> This photo shows state representative Theodore Roosevelt in 1884. Roosevelt would go on to become President of the United States and dedicate himself to furthering the public interest.

ELL 1 of 3 >

DIGITAL TEXT 2

Encouraging Fair Business Practices

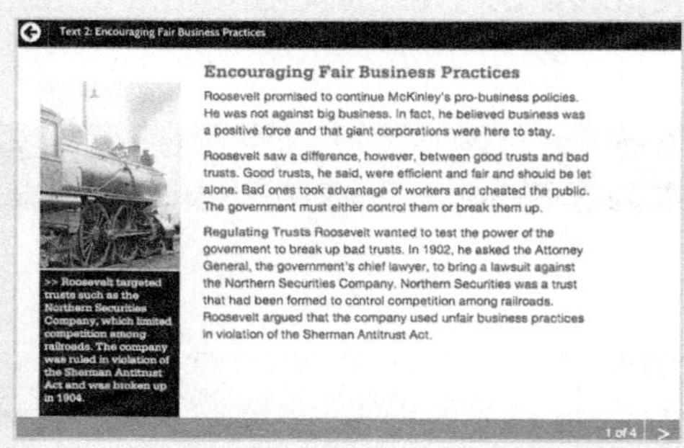
Text 2: Encouraging Fair Business Practices

Encouraging Fair Business Practices

Roosevelt promised to continue McKinley's pro-business policies. He was not against big business. In fact, he believed business was a positive force and that giant corporations were here to stay.

Roosevelt saw a difference, however, between good trusts and bad trusts. Good trusts, he said, were efficient and fair and should be let alone. Bad ones took advantage of workers and cheated the public. The government must either control them or break them up.

Regulating Trusts Roosevelt wanted to test the power of the government to break up bad trusts. In 1902, he asked the Attorney General, the government's chief lawyer, to bring a lawsuit against the Northern Securities Company. Northern Securities was a trust that had been formed to control competition among railroads. Roosevelt argued that the company used unfair business practices in violation of the Sherman Antitrust Act.

>> Roosevelt targeted trusts such as the Northern Securities Company, which limited competition among railroads. The company was ruled in violation of the Sherman Antitrust Act and was broken up in 1904.

1 of 4 >

Objective 1: Identify Theodore Roosevelt's reform goals, including the Square Deal.

Quick Instruction

Interactive Gallery: National Land Conservation Project the Interactive Gallery. Prompt students to describe what they see in the images and to speculate why President Roosevelt would set aside this land. Explain that conservation refers to the protecting of land, water, and other natural resources. Specifically, it means protecting resources for future use and enjoyment. How do President Roosevelt's policies reflect an interest in conservation? *(Roosevelt pushed Congress to start the National Forest Service. Under Roosevelt, the government also set aside about 194,000 acres for national parks. He encouraged lumber companies to plant new trees to replace those that they had cut down.)*

Explain Why did Roosevelt target railroads for regulation? *(Roosevelt considered the railroads and related companies to be bad trusts. They took advantage of workers and cheated the public for their own profit. He wanted to break up the trusts, under the Sherman Antitrust Act, and to end railroad rebates and other abuses. He hoped that these changes would give consumers and workers better economic opportunities.)*

ACTIVE CLASSROOM

Conduct a Conversation with History activity. Organize students into groups to write interview questions and answers for President Theodore Roosevelt about his policies. Tell them to act out their Q&A sessions in a role play. Each student should have a turn playing President Roosevelt, and each should have a turn asking a question. You may wish to record the Q&A skits to post on the class blog.

D Differentiate: Extra Support To help students navigate the text, encourage them to use a concept web or a chart to record notes about President Roosevelt's policies. Draw attention to the subheadings in the text: Regulating Trusts, A Pro-Labor President, Pushing for Regulations, and Resource Conservation. Advise students to use these subheadings in their charts.

ELL Use the ELL activity described in the ELL chart.

DIGITAL TEXT 3

The Square Deal

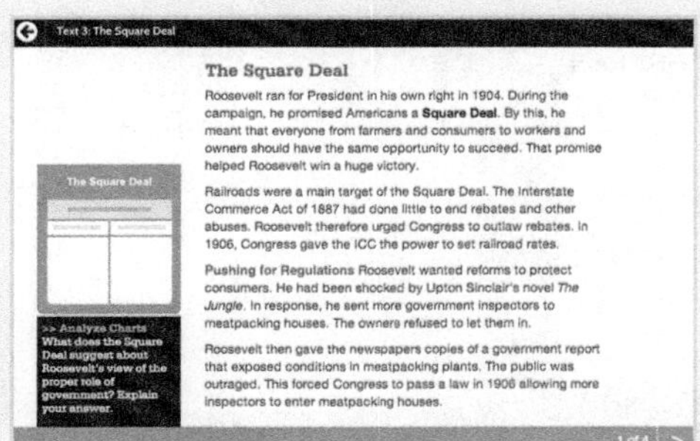

INTERACTIVE GALLERY

National Land Conservation

DIGITAL TEXT 4

President Taft

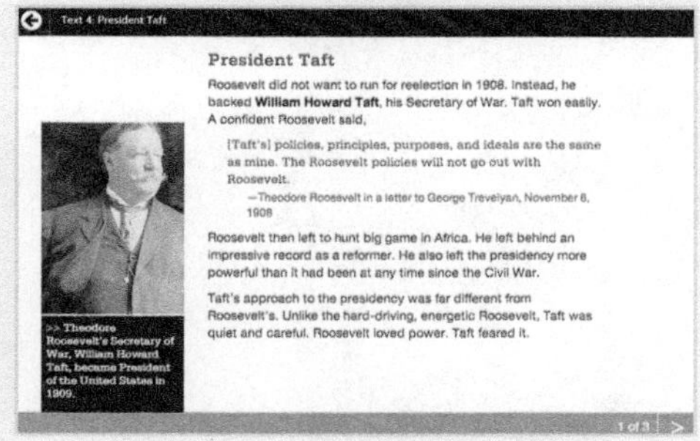

Further Instruction

Analyze Primary Sources What did one newspaper mean when it stated, "Wall Street is paralyzed at the thought that a President of the United States would sink so low as to try to enforce the law"? *(Stock prices plummeted in response to Roosevelt's efforts to break up bad trusts. Investors didn't have faith in the profit-making abilities of companies that didn't break the law.)*

Determine Relevance What was significant about Roosevelt's response to the 1902 Pennsylvania coal miners' strike? *(It was the first time that a president had sided with labor against big business. Roosevelt compelled the mine owners to make a deal with the workers or to face intervention by federal troops.)*

Connect The term *square* can often be used to mean "fair, or honest." In that sense, how were Roosevelt's Square Deal policies square? *(The Interstate Commerce Act tried to make interstate trade and travel, especially on the railroads, more fair for consumers and businesses. Roosevelt urged Congress to pass laws such as the Pure Food and Drug Act to protect consumers. He also supported conservation efforts to effectively manage and protect the environment for future generations.)*

Objective 2: Compare and contrast William Howard Taft's policies with Theodore Roosevelt's.

Quick Instruction

Compare and Contrast How did Taft's policies and methods resemble and differ from Roosevelt's? *(Most of Taft's policies were just as progressive as Roosevelt's. His approach to the presidency, however, was more timid. He was not as aggressive as Roosevelt and did not relish the expansion of presidential power in the way that Roosevelt had. Still, he broke up trusts, supported a graduated income tax, approved new safety codes for mines, and signed into law the eight-hour workday. However, he also took several actions that angered Progressives, including the increase in tariffs and the firing of a high-level Forest Service official.)*

Check Understanding Why did Taft's support of tariffs anger Progressives? *(Progressives believed that raising tariffs would raise prices for consumers. This would largely hurt middle- and lower-class citizens.)*

ELL Use the ELL activity described in the ELL chart.

The Progressive Presidents

Further Instruction

Review the directions for the Interactive Reading Notepad. Tell students to work in pairs to answer the questions. Then, combine pairs into small groups. Have them share and revise their answers.

Connect How did Roosevelt's presidency help Taft not only win office but also pursue Progressive reforms? *(Roosevelt had been a powerful president who not only achieved many Progressive reforms himself but also enjoyed wide popularity and expanded the power of the presidency. Roosevelt also left Taft in a good position to continue pushing for Progressive reforms and to use the power of the presidency to advance his policies.)*

DIGITAL TEXT 5

Wilson Wins the Presidency

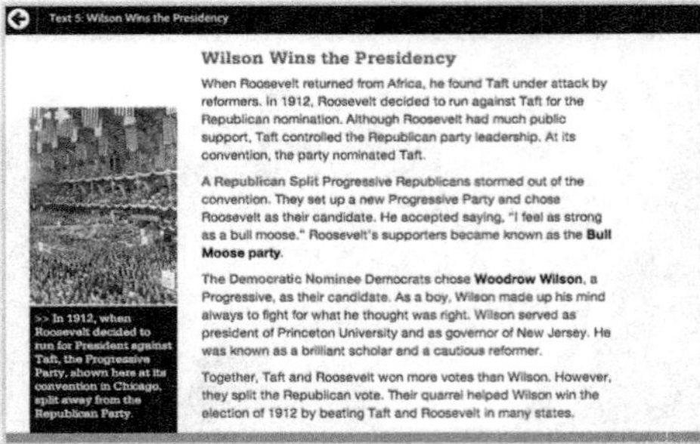

Wilson Wins the Presidency

When Roosevelt returned from Africa, he found Taft under attack by reformers. In 1912, Roosevelt decided to run against Taft for the Republican nomination. Although Roosevelt had much public support, Taft controlled the Republican party leadership. At its convention, the party nominated Taft.

A Republican Split Progressive Republicans stormed out of the convention. They set up a new Progressive Party and chose Roosevelt as their candidate. He accepted saying, "I feel as strong as a bull moose." Roosevelt's supporters became known as the **Bull Moose party**.

The Democratic Nominee Democrats chose **Woodrow Wilson**, a Progressive, as their candidate. As a boy, Wilson made up his mind always to fight for what he thought was right. Wilson served as president of Princeton University and as governor of New Jersey. He was known as a brilliant scholar and a cautious reformer.

Together, Taft and Roosevelt won more votes than Wilson. However, they split the Republican vote. Their quarrel helped Wilson win the election of 1912 by beating Taft and Roosevelt in many states.

>> In 1912, when Roosevelt decided to run for President against Taft, the Progressive Party, shown here at its convention in Chicago, split away from the Republican Party.

Objective 3: Describe reforms under Woodrow Wilson.

Quick Instruction

Interactive Chart: Three Presidents' Accomplishments Project the Interactive Chart. Have students click through the squares in the chart to view the accomplishments of Presidents Roosevelt, Taft, and Wilson. Then, have them work in pairs to answer the questions. Review students' responses as a class.

Evaluate Information Which president had the most Progressive impact, and why? Cite evidence from the chart and the lesson to support your answer. *(Answers will vary. For example, students may cite President Taft for breaking up more trusts than the other two presidents and shepherding passage of the graduated income tax. Taft also proclaimed eleven national monuments and led Congress to establish the Bureau of Mines. Students may cite President Roosevelt for leading the way in Progressive reforms, breaking up trusts, siding with labor in a coal miners' strike, and shepherding the Pure Food and Drug Act through Congress, as well as leading the effort to establish the National Forest Service.)*

ACTIVE CLASSROOM

Organize students into three groups and assign each group a president on which to report. Have each group use the Wallpaper strategy to prepare four to six pieces of wallpaper on the accomplishments and challenges of their assigned president. Display students' wallpaper in the class and take a Wisdom Walk.

INTERACTIVE CHART

Three Presidents' Accomplishments

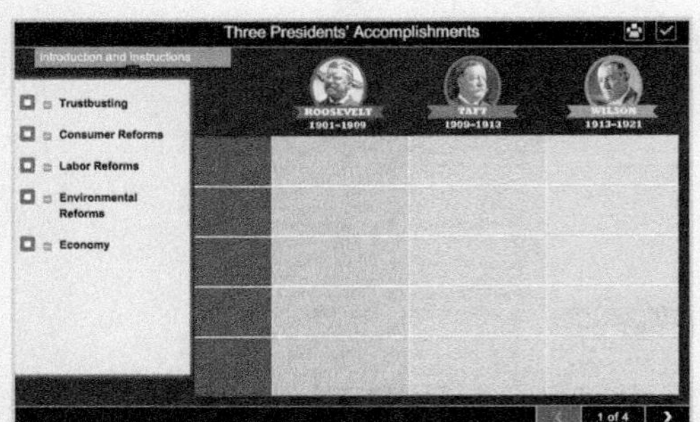

D Differentiate: Challenge Organize students into groups. Assign each group to select an excerpt from Wilson's Inaugural Address on March 4, 2013, or from his First Annual Message, on December 2, 1913. Tell them to research the meaning of the excerpt. Then, have them prepare a delivery of their portion of the speech and present their explanation of its context and importance. Invite students to perform their presentations for the class.

Further Instruction

Generate Explanations Wilson did not win a majority of the votes in the election of 1912. How did he win the presidency? *(The Republican Party and its voters split around Taft and Roosevelt. Even though Taft and Roosevelt combined won more votes than Wilson, neither had enough votes individually to beat him.)*

Summarize What Progressive reforms did Wilson undertake? *(Wilson continued trustbusting policies. In 1914, he signed the Clayton Antitrust Act. He led Congress to form the Federal Trade Commission to regulate competition in commerce. Wilson also persuaded Congress to lower tariffs to encourage competition and lower prices for consumers. Under Wilson, Congress passed the Federal Reserve Act to regulate banking and manage the nation's money supply.)*

Synthesize What impact did the three presidents have on labor in the United States? *(Under each president, labor gained some ground. The eight-hour workday was passed, and laws regulating conditions in factories benefited workers. President Roosevelt sided with workers in a labor strike in Pennsylvania.)*

SYNTHESIZE

DIGITAL ACTIVITY

Progressive Accomplishments

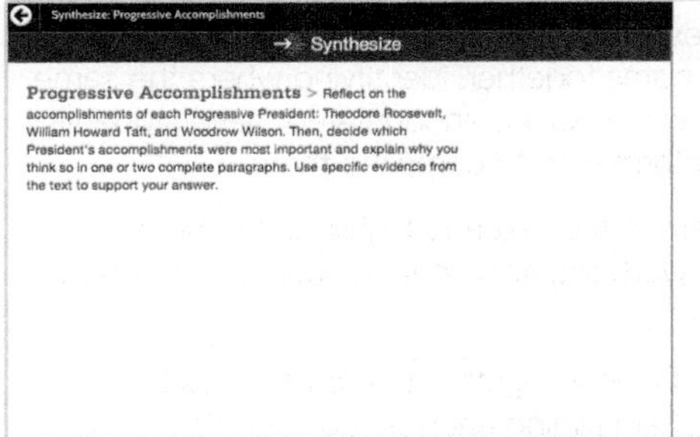

Project the Digital Activity Organize students into pairs to brainstorm ideas and evidence for their responses. Then, give students ten minutes to write their responses to the activity. Have them post their ideas on the class discussion board, and challenge students to read and respond to two other students' writings.

Discuss Why did these three presidents experience success with their Progressive platforms? *(Answers will vary. Students may note that the political, social, and economic climate was primed for reform. Industrialization and urbanization left many people living and working under conditions that demanded change. Wealth disparity and corruption had also grown dramatically, and the media, labor unions, and other organizations exposed these issues. Moreover, large numbers of people were now living in towns and cities. They were concentrated to a degree never before seen, enabling them to engage more actively in politics and to organize for reform.)*

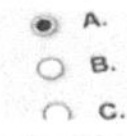

DEMONSTRATE

LESSON QUIZ

Lesson Quiz and Class Discussion Board

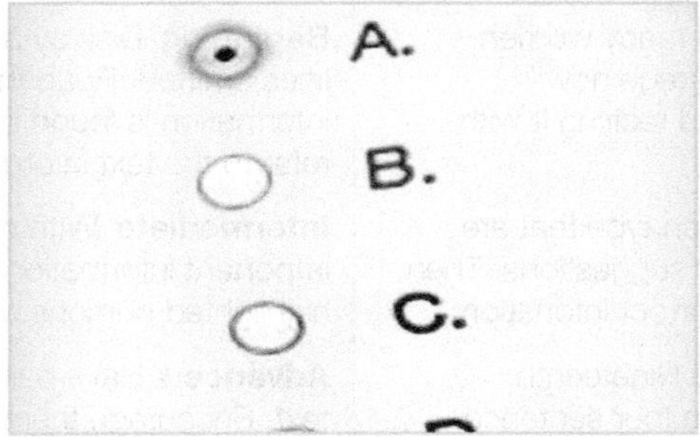

Assign the online Lesson Quiz for this lesson if you haven't already done so. Students will be offered automatic remediation or enrichment based on their score.

Pose these questions to the class on the Discussion Board:

In *The Progressive Presidents*, you explored the accomplishments of the presidencies of Theodore Roosevelt, William Howard Taft, and Woodrow Wilson.

Connect How have the Progressive policies achieved during this period contributed to economic and social norms that exist in the United States today?

Make Predictions President Wilson took office in 1913, on the eve of the outbreak of World War I in Europe. How do you think war would affect the president's attempts at reform?

Topic Inquiry

Have students continue their investigations for the Topic Inquiry.

Progress and Setbacks for Social Justice

Supporting English Language Learners

Use with the reading, **The Nineteenth Amendment**.

Speaking

Review the purpose, intonation, and punctuation of the four types of sentences: declarative, interrogative, imperative, and exclamatory.

Beginning Display the following sentences: What did many women want? They wanted the right to vote. "Let us vote. Suffrage now!" Support students in identifying each sentence type and reciting it with correct intonation.

Intermediate Invite students to say sentences for each type that are related to the text. Use a four-column chart to list their suggestions. Then have students practice reciting the sentences using correct intonation.

Advanced Invite pairs of students to discuss how the Nineteenth Amendment came to be. Provide pairs with a list of the four sentence types, and encourage them to check off each type as they use it in their discussion.

Advanced High Challenge pairs of students to write a dialogue that President Wilson and Alice Paul could have had, using all four sentence types in the process. Then have pairs do a dramatic reading of their dialogue for one another.

Use with the reading, **Fighting for Prohibition**.

Reading

Discuss both the purpose and process of taking notes. Then share with students a simple note-taking method using headings and bulleted lists.

Beginning Display a set of notes with various words, phrases, and/or lines omitted. Read through the notes together, identifying where the same information is found in the text. As blanks are encountered, have students refer to the text in order to find information to complete them.

Intermediate With students, reread the text and highlight the most important information in it. Then work together to take notes based on the highlighted portions of the text.

Advanced Have pairs of students work together to create notes for the text. Encourage them to pause after reading each paragraph, determine its most important information, and add it to their outline. Then invite pairs to compare and contrast the notes they took.

Advanced High Invite individual students to take notes on the text as they silently reread it. Encourage them to use headings and subheadings in order to better organize their notes. Then have partners compare and contrast the notes they took.

D Differentiate Instruction

Use the Differentiated Instruction notes throughout the lesson plan to support the varied skill sets, levels of readiness, and interests in the mixed-ability classroom.

Challenge These notes include suggestions for expanding the activity for advanced students.

On-Level These notes include suggestions for modifying the activity to address different interests or learning styles.

Extra Support These notes include ideas for providing more scaffolding or reading spuport.

Special Needs These notes provide ideas for adapting instruction to support the needs of various special needs students.

NOTES

Objectives

Objective 1: Describe women's efforts to win suffrage and improved opportunities.

Objective 2: Explain the campaign against alcohol.

Objective 3: Describe how African Americans confronted discrimination during the Progressive Era.

Objective 4: Identify the discrimination and hardships faced by Mexican Americans, Asian Americans, and American Indians during the Progressive Era.

LESSON 5 ORGANIZER	PACING: APPROX. 1 PERIOD, .5 BLOCKS			
			RESOURCES	
	OBJECTIVES	PACING	Online	Print
Connect				
DIGITAL START UP ACTIVITY **Addressing Discrimination**		5 min.	●	
Investigate				
DIGITAL TEXT 1 **The Path to Women's Suffrage**	Objective 1	10 min.	●	●
DIGITAL TEXT 2 **The Nineteenth Amendment**		10 min.	●	●
DIGITAL TEXT 3 **New Opportunities Arise**		10 min.	●	●
INTERACTIVE GALLERY **New Opportunities for Women**		10 min.	●	
DIGITAL TEXT 4 **Fighting for Prohibition**	Objective 2	10 min.	●	●
DIGITAL TEXT 5 **African Americans Face Discrimination**	Objective 3	10 min.	●	●
INTERACTIVE TIMELINE **African American Reform Movement, 1895–1915**		10 min.	●	
DIGITAL TEXT 6 **The Mexican-American Experience**	Objective 4	10 min.	●	●
DIGITAL TEXT 7 **Blocking Asian Immigration**		10 min.	●	●
DIGITAL TEXT 8 **Discrimination Against American Indians**		10 min.	●	●
Synthesize				
DIGITAL ACTIVITY **Leaders Fight for Social Change**		5 min.	●	
Demonstrate				
LESSON QUIZ **Lesson Quiz and Class Discussion Board**		10 min.	●	

Progress and Setbacks for Social Justice

CONNECT

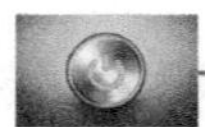

DIGITAL START UP ACTIVITY

Addressing Discrimination

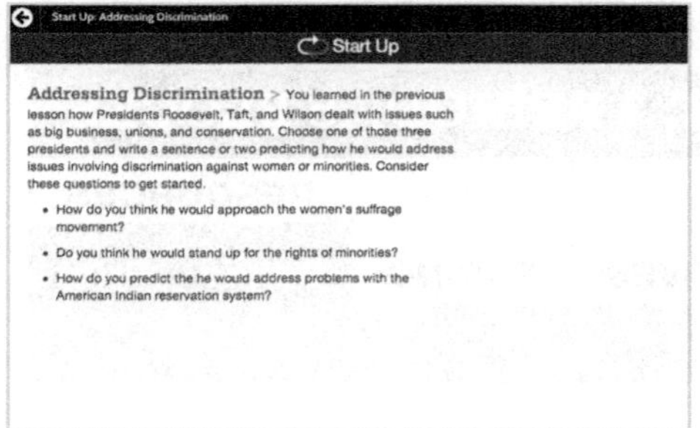

Start Up: Addressing Discrimination
Start Up
Addressing Discrimination > You learned in the previous lesson how Presidents Roosevelt, Taft, and Wilson dealt with issues such as big business, unions, and conservation. Choose one of those three presidents and write a sentence or two predicting how he would address issues involving discrimination against women or minorities. Consider these questions to get started.
• How do you think he would approach the women's suffrage movement?
• Do you think he would stand up for the rights of minorities?
• How do you predict the he would address problems with the American Indian reservation system?

Project the Start Up Activity Ask students to answer the questions as they get settled. Then have them share their ideas with another student.

Discuss If you were denied essential rights, how would you have felt? *(Possible answers: shocked, angered)* What would you have done to address your concerns? *(Possible answers: organize groups of people with similar views; contact political leaders; protest)*

Tell students that in this lesson they will be learning how women and minorities struggled with inequality during the Progressive Era.

Aa Vocabulary Development: Use the Interactive Reading Notepad to preview the Key Terms and Academic Vocabulary in this lesson with students.

FLIP IT!

Assign the Flipped Video for this lesson.

STUDENT EDITION PRINT PAGES: 612–622

INVESTIGATE

DIGITAL TEXT 1

The Path to Women's Suffrage

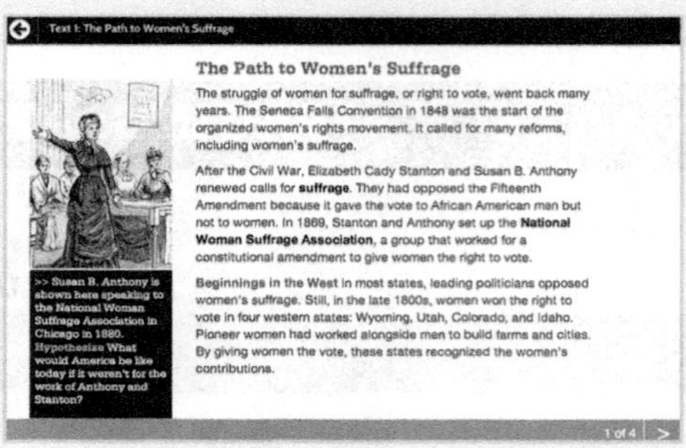

Text 1: The Path to Women's Suffrage
The Path to Women's Suffrage
The struggle of women for suffrage, or right to vote, went back many years. The Seneca Falls Convention in 1848 was the start of the organized women's rights movement. It called for many reforms, including women's suffrage.
After the Civil War, Elizabeth Cady Stanton and Susan B. Anthony renewed calls for suffrage. They had opposed the Fifteenth Amendment because it gave the vote to African American men but not to women. In 1869, Stanton and Anthony set up the National Woman Suffrage Association, a group that worked for a constitutional amendment to give women the right to vote.
Beginnings in the West In most states, leading politicians opposed women's suffrage. Still, in the late 1800s, women won the right to vote in four western states: Wyoming, Utah, Colorado, and Idaho. Pioneer women had worked alongside men to build farms and cities. By giving women the vote, these states recognized the women's contributions.
>> Susan B. Anthony is shown here speaking to the National Woman Suffrage Association in Chicago in 1880. Hypothesize What would America be like today if it weren't for the work of Anthony and Stanton?
1 of 4

DIGITAL TEXT 2

The Nineteenth Amendment

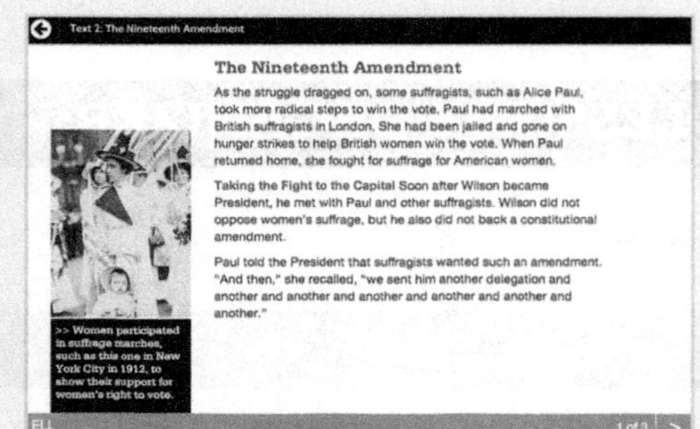

Objective 1: Describe women's efforts to win suffrage and improved opportunities.

Quick Instruction

Interactive Gallery: New Opportunities for Women Project the Interactive Gallery. Click on each image to identify new opportunities in education, work, and political participation of women in American society. Some of the women featured in the interactivity may be familiar to students. Begin by asking students what types of contributions the women shown made. *(Possible answers include education and career opportunities.)* After asking what they know or think they know about each woman individually, follow by revealing her specific contributions.

Summarize What were some of the issues for which these reformers were fighting? *(The issues included expanding career and economic opportunities, to receive equal pay, and to have the right to vote.)*

ACTIVE CLASSROOM

Play a game of Rank It. List the following names of reform leaders on the board: *Susan B. Anthony, Elizabeth Cady Stanton, Carrie Chapman Catt, Alice Paul,* and *Florence Kelley*. Ask students to rank the women based on who had the greatest impact on society and to provide justification for their decisions. Poll the class to see where points of agreement or disagreement occur. Prompt students to defend their positions.

ELL Use the ELL activity described in the ELL chart.

DIGITAL TEXT 3

New Opportunities Arise

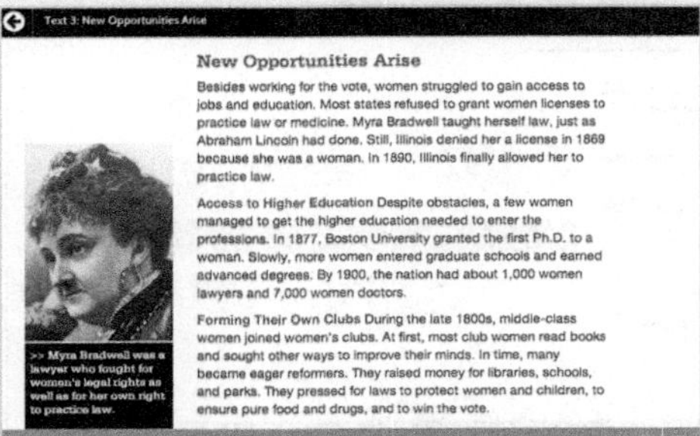

Further Instruction

Determine Relevance How did these women contribute to the success of the women's rights movement during this time? *(Women like Blackwell and Walker helped show that women could make valuable contributions in business and education that were important to all Americans. Their work and accomplishments inspired other American women and girls.)*

Draw Conclusions What impact did the Nineteenth Amendment have on elections in the United States? *(The amendment doubled the number of eligible voters.)*

INTERACTIVE GALLERY

New Opportunities for Women

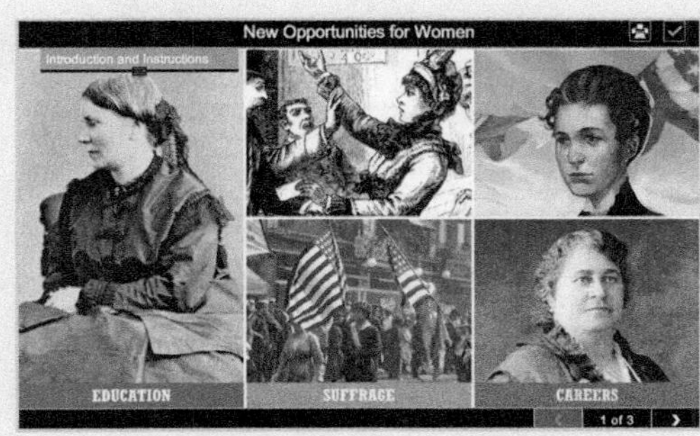

Connect How are the achievements of Susan B. Anthony and Elizabeth Cady Stanton reflected in the United States today? *(Women in the United States vote in elections today. Many American women serve as political leaders in our government and as business leaders of corporations.)*

DIGITAL TEXT 4

Fighting for Prohibition

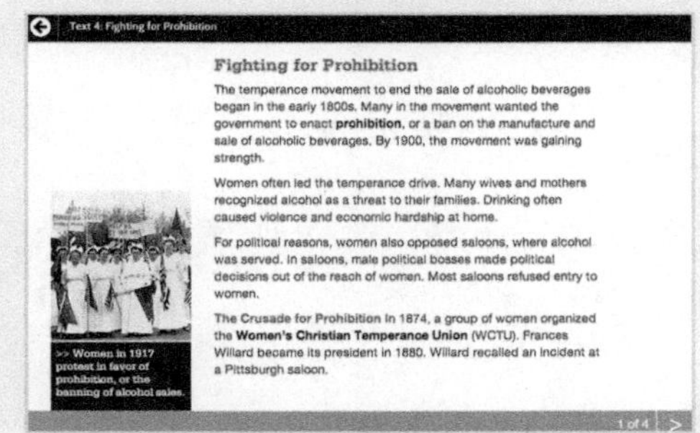

Objective 2: Explain the campaign against alcohol.

Quick Instruction

Explain that many Americans supported the prohibition of alcohol sales for several reasons. Point out that the causes of prohibition were related to social problems that many Americans believed were caused by drinking alcohol, including poverty, unemployment, domestic violence, and poor health.

Infer Why do you think that women played such important roles in leading the fight for Prohibition? *(Many of the social problems caused by alcohol, such as economic hardship, affected women.)*

ELL Use the ELL activity described in the ELL chart.

Further Instruction

Briefly discuss how the growing influence of women in American society affected the temperance and suffrage movements. Point out that many women, like Frances E. Willard, were strong supporters of both movements.

Contrast two different methods that supporters of prohibition used to fight for the cause. *(Some supporters, like members of the WCTU, used their religious beliefs to help them make their arguments for prohibition. Others, like Carrie Nation, were more radical and often used violence to seek the change they were looking for.)*

Progress and Setbacks for Social Justice

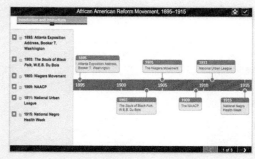

Identify Cause and Effect Why did support for the Temperance Movement gain support after the United States entered World War I in 1917? *(The United States entered World War I in 1917. Many Americans argued that grain used to make liquor should be used instead to feed American soldiers.)*

DIGITAL TEXT 5

African Americans Face Discrimination

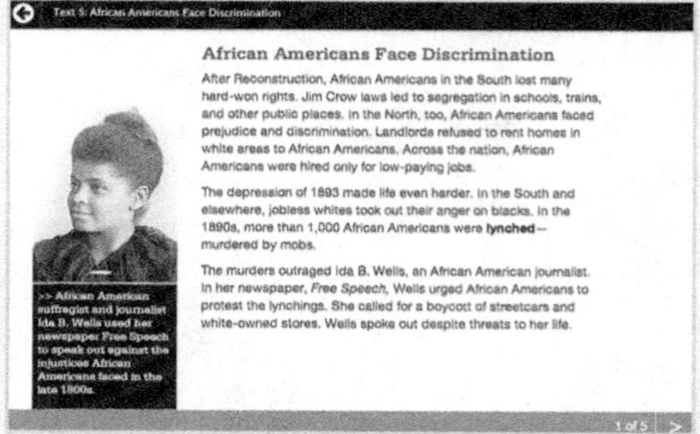

Objective 3: **Describe how African Americans confronted discrimination during the Progressive Era.**

Quick Instruction

Interactive Timeline: African American Reform Movement, 1895–1915 Project the timeline. Tell students that the timeline helps trace the historical development of the civil rights movement for African Americans in the late 19th and early 20th centuries. Review each entry in the timeline, inviting students to explain why or in what way each is significant.

Evaluate Arguments Booker T. Washington urged African Americans to accept segregation in order to work for economic advancement. Do you agree with Washington's thinking? Why or why not? *(Possible answer: I don't agree with Washington. African Americans could never be truly equal as long as they were segregated and not a part of all aspects of American society.)*

ACTIVE CLASSROOM

Direct students to have a Conversation With Booker T. Washington or W.E.B. Du Bois. Tell students that they are going to have a fictional conversation with their chosen individual. Students should write down a question they would like to ask, then what their chosen person would say to the students, and then what the student would say in response.

INTERACTIVE TIMELINE

African American Reform Movement, 1895–1915

D Differentiate: Challenge Encourage students to conduct research on one of the African American organizations in the interactivity. Each student could then share what he or she learns with the rest of the class.

Further Instruction

To extend the discussion, assign the Primary Source: Atlantic Exposition Address, Booker T. Washington.

Infer According to Booker T. Washington, why was education so important to the future of African Americans? *(Washington thought that by getting an education or learning a trade, African Americans could then improve their economic status, which would in turn improve their prospects for political equality.)*

Support Ideas with Examples In your opinion, did the federal government help or hinder African Americans' fight for equality? *(Possible answer: The government hindered the fight for equality. Teddy Roosevelt dishonorably discharged an entire regiment of African American soldiers that was accused of rioting in Texas. Later, President Wilson ordered the segregation of African American and white government workers thinking that it was better for the African American workers to be segregated.)*

PEARSON
realize
www.PearsonRealize.com
Access your Digital Lesson

DIGITAL TEXT 6

The Mexican-American Experience

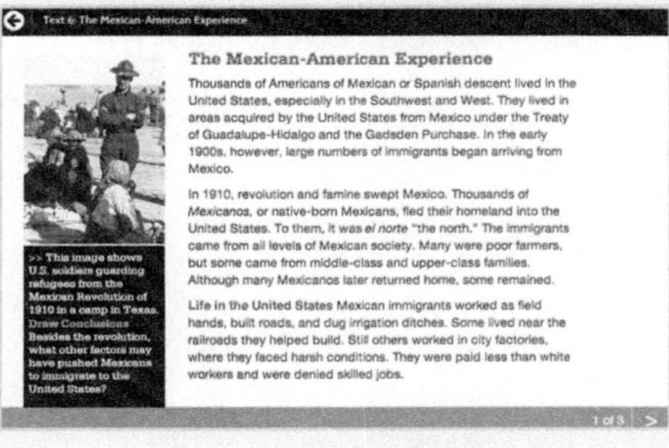
Text 6: The Mexican-American Experience
The Mexican-American Experience
Thousands of Americans of Mexican or Spanish descent lived in the United States, especially in the Southwest and West. They lived in areas acquired by the United States from Mexico under the Treaty of Guadalupe-Hidalgo and the Gadsden Purchase. In the early 1900s, however, large numbers of immigrants began arriving from Mexico.
In 1910, revolution and famine swept Mexico. Thousands of *Mexicanos*, or native-born Mexicans, fled their homeland into the United States. To them, it was *el norte* "the north." The immigrants came from all levels of Mexican society. Many were poor farmers, but some came from middle-class and upper-class families. Although many Mexicanos later returned home, some remained.
Life in the United States Mexican immigrants worked as field hands, built roads, and dug irrigation ditches. Some lived near the railroads they helped build. Still others worked in city factories, where they faced harsh conditions. They were paid less than white workers and were denied skilled jobs.
>> This image shows U.S. soldiers guarding refugees from the Mexican Revolution of 1910 in a camp in Texas. Draw Conclusions Besides the revolution, what other factors may have pushed Mexicans to immigrate to the United States?
1 of 3

DIGITAL TEXT 7

Blocking Asian Immigration

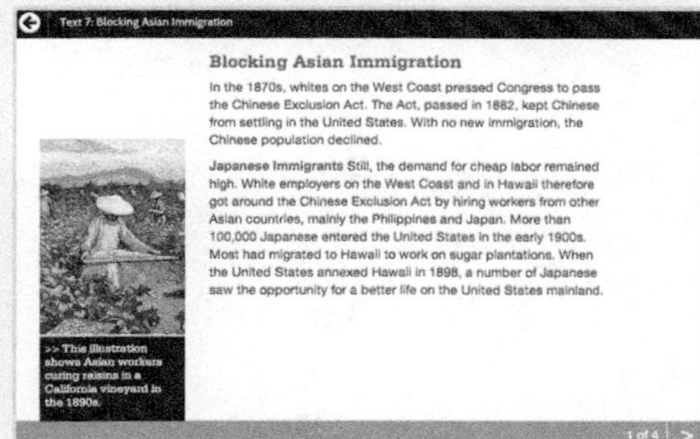
Text 7: Blocking Asian Immigration
Blocking Asian Immigration
In the 1870s, whites on the West Coast pressed Congress to pass the Chinese Exclusion Act. The Act, passed in 1882, kept Chinese from settling in the United States. With no new immigration, the Chinese population declined.
Japanese Immigrants Still, the demand for cheap labor remained high. White employers on the West Coast and in Hawaii therefore got around the Chinese Exclusion Act by hiring workers from other Asian countries, mainly the Philippines and Japan. More than 100,000 Japanese entered the United States in the early 1900s. Most had migrated to Hawaii to work on sugar plantations. When the United States annexed Hawaii in 1898, a number of Japanese saw the opportunity for a better life on the United States mainland.
>> This illustration shows Asian workers curing raisins in a California vineyard in the 1890s.
1 of 4

DIGITAL TEXT 8

Discrimination Against American Indians

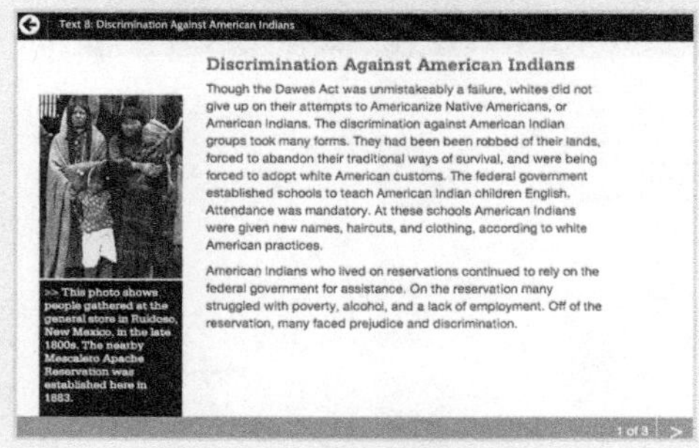
Text 8: Discrimination Against American Indians
Discrimination Against American Indians
Though the Dawes Act was unmistakeably a failure, whites did not give up on their attempts to Americanize Native Americans, or American Indians. The discrimination against American Indian groups took many forms. They had been been robbed of their lands, forced to abandon their traditional ways of survival, and were being forced to adopt white American customs. The federal government established schools to teach American Indian children English. Attendance was mandatory. At these schools American Indians were given new names, haircuts, and clothing, according to white American practices.
American Indians who lived on reservations continued to rely on the federal government for assistance. On the reservation many struggled with poverty, alcohol, and a lack of employment. Off of the reservation, many faced prejudice and discrimination.
>> This photo shows people gathered at the general store in Ruidoso, New Mexico, in the late 1800s. The nearby Mescalero Apache Reservation was established here in 1883.
1 of 3

Objective 4: **Identify the discrimination and hardships faced by Mexican Americans, Asian Americans, and American Indians during the Progressive Era.**

Quick Instruction

Project the image of U.S. soldiers guarding refugees from the Mexican Revolution of 1910. Invite students to offer reasons that may have pushed or pulled Mexicans to immigrate to the United States. *(Many were trying to escape the problems in Mexico. Others were being pulled by more opportunities or better living conditions in the United States.)* Ask students to locate other examples of people from other countries who were immigrating to the United States during the Progressive Era. *(Possible answers include Chinese, Japanese, Filipinos, Koreans.)*

Summarize the ways the federal government and Americans restricted Asian immigration and made life difficult for those who managed to move to the United States. *(Congress passed the Chinese Exclusion Act in 1882 to keep large numbers of Chinese from settling in the United States. American businesses and farmers restricted Asian immigration by bringing diverse groups instead of large numbers of people from one country. Americans made life difficult for Asian immigrants by barring Asians from owning land and forcing all Asian students to attend separate schools.)*

Further Instruction

Begin a discussion of American Indians by inviting students to share what they know of the traditional ways of life for Indians before the end of the Indian Wars.

Support Ideas with Evidence What evidence can you locate that supports the claim that the reservation system for American Indians was failing? *(Indians living on reservations were dependent on the federal government for survival. Many also struggled with poverty, alcohol, and unemployment.)*

Hypothesize Why might many American Indian groups have opposed the Society for American Indians' idea to abolish reservations? *(Many Indians probably didn't want to move into mainstream American society. To them, their homes, traditions, and cultures were tied to the lands where the reservations were established. Abolishing the reservations probably felt to them as though their cultures were being abolished.)*

Progress and Setbacks for Social Justice

SYNTHESIZE

DIGITAL ACTIVITY

Leaders Fight for Social Change

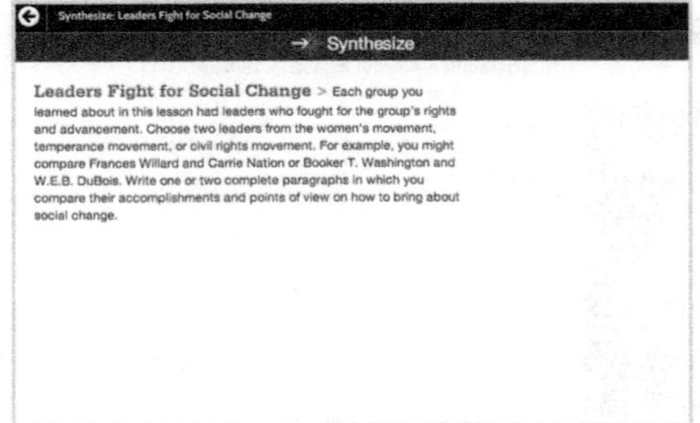

Some students may benefit from a brief prewriting activity to organize their thoughts. Project a table with two column headings: *Accomplishments* and *Views to Bring About Social Change* to help students think about ways in which they can compare their two subjects.

Discuss Which person do you think was most effective at fighting for social change? Use specific examples to support your answer.

DEMONSTRATE

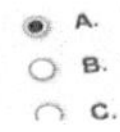

LESSON QUIZ

Lesson Quiz and Class Discussion Board

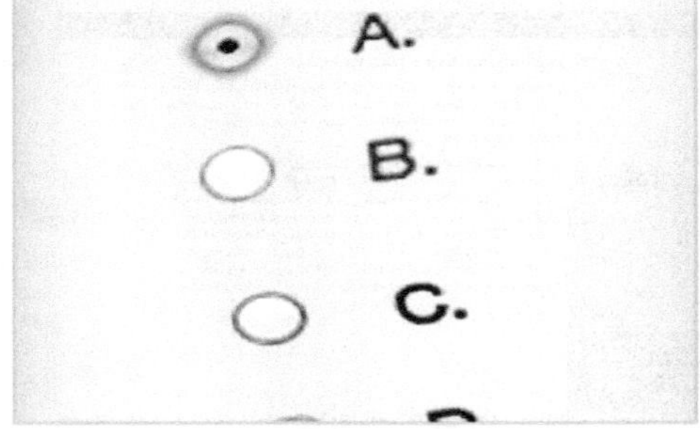

Assign the online Lesson Quiz for this lesson if you haven't already done so. Students will be offered automatic remediation or enrichment based on their score.

Pose these questions to the class on the Discussion Board:

In *Progress and Setbacks for Social Justice*, you read about how social and political leaders in the Progressive Era had different ways of approaching reform. While some preferred patience and perseverance, others took radical action to influence public opinion.

Generate Explanations Why are many of the organizations created during the Progressive Era to advance the political and economic status of minorities still in existence today?

Support Ideas with Examples American women used many methods to expand their rights to participate in the democratic process, including meeting with political leaders and nonviolent protesting. Which method do you think was the most effective? Why? Give examples to support your position.

Topic Inquiry

Have students continue their investigations for the Topic Inquiry.

A Changing American Culture

Supporting English Language Learners

Use with the reading, **News in Print**.

Speaking

Build on prior knowledge by asking students to share their experiences with newspapers. Discuss why they would have been more popular around 1900 than they are now.

Beginning Make simple statements about newspapers based on information in the text. After each statement, invite students to repeat it after you. Then repeat it after them, and have them repeat it a second time. Encourage students to self-correct their speaking according to what they hear you say.

Intermediate Ask students questions about the text, such as: Around 1900, what did newspapers report on? How did publishers compete for readers? After students respond, repeat their answers (with necessary corrections), and allow students to self-correct as they repeat after you.

Advanced Invite pairs of students to discuss newspapers around the year 1900. Encourage students to self-correct their own speaking errors, as well as to enlist their partner's help when necessary.

Advanced High Invite pairs of students to record themselves as they compare and contrast newspapers from around 1900 with those of today. Then have them listen to the recording and identify specific ways to improve their speaking.

Use with the reading, **American Writers and Artists Excel**.

Listening

Display and read a list of the writers mentioned in the text. Explain that students can refer to this list as they take notes on what you say.

Beginning Say two or three sentences about the text, such as: In the late 1800s, some writers wrote about real life. Kate Chopin wrote about life in New Orleans. Repeat the sentences at least once as you give students time to write down key words and phrases they heard.

Intermediate Provide students with partially completed notes for the paragraph about Stephen Crane. Then read aloud the paragraph while students listen for information with which they can finish the notes.

Advanced Read aloud the first few paragraphs two times—once so students to listen to the words and once so they can take notes on the key points you made. Invite students to share and compare their notes.

Advanced High Invite pairs of students to discuss American writers from the late 1800s and take notes on what their partner says. Then ask volunteers to use their notes to summarize their partner's ideas aloud.

D Differentiate Instruction

Use the Differentiated Instruction notes throughout the lesson plan to support the varied skill sets, levels of readiness, and interests in the mixed-ability classroom.

Challenge These notes include suggestions for expanding the activity for advanced students.

On-Level These notes include suggestions for modifying the activity to address different interests or learning styles.

Extra Support These notes include ideas for providing more scaffolding or reading spupport.

Special Needs These notes provide ideas for adapting instruction to support the needs of various special needs students.

NOTES

A Changing American Culture

Objectives

Objective 1: Describe how city life changed during the Progressive Era.

Objective 2: Identify forms of entertainment that Americans enjoyed during this period.

Objective 3: Describe how public education grew during the Progressive Era.

Objective 4: Identify changes in reading habits.

Objective 5: Explain the interest of Progressive Era writers and painters in subjects from everyday life.

LESSON 6 ORGANIZER	PACING: APPROX. 1 PERIOD, .5 BLOCKS			
			RESOURCES	
	OBJECTIVES	PACING	Online	Print
Connect				
DIGITAL START UP ACTIVITY **Life in the Progressive Era**		5 min.	●	
Investigate				
DIGITAL TEXT 1 **Changes and Challenges in City Life**	Objective 1	10 min.	●	●
DIGITAL TEXT 2 **More Americans Play Sports**	Objective 2	10 min.	●	●
DIGITAL TEXT 3 **New Forms of Theater and Music**		10 min.	●	●
INTERACTIVE GALLERY **Leisure Activities at the Turn of the Century**		10 min.	●	
DIGITAL TEXT 4 **More Americans Attend School**	Objective 3	10 min.	●	●
DIGITAL TEXT 5 **News in Print**	Objective 4	10 min.	●	●
DIGITAL TEXT 6 **American Writers and Artists Excel**	Objective 5	10 min.	●	●
INTERACTIVE GALLERY **American Realist Artists**		10 min.	●	
Synthesize				
DIGITAL ACTIVITY **Answer Questions About the Progressive Era**		5 min.	●	
Demonstrate				
LESSON QUIZ **Lesson Quiz and Class Discussion Board**		10 min.	●	

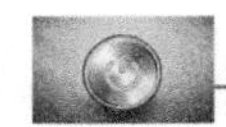

CONNECT

DIGITAL START UP ACTIVITY

Life in the Progressive Era

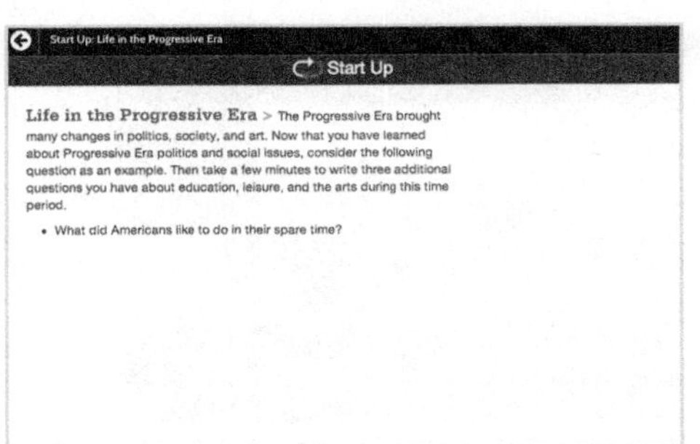

Start Up: Life in the Progressive Era
Start Up
Life in the Progressive Era > The Progressive Era brought many changes in politics, society, and art. Now that you have learned about Progressive Era politics and social issues, consider the following question as an example. Then take a few minutes to write three additional questions you have about education, leisure, and the arts during this time period.
• What did Americans like to do in their spare time?

Project the Start Up Activity Encourage students to discuss their possible questions about Progressive Era education, leisure, and the arts with a partner. Invite them to share their ideas.

Discuss How can something Americans do in their leisure time impact society in a meaningful way? *(Possible answer: A sport or popular art can provide people with a sense of unity.)*

Tell students that they will be learning how American writers and artists portrayed daily life during the Progressive Era.

Aa Vocabulary Development: Use the Interactive Reading Notepad to preview the Key Terms and Academic Vocabulary in this lesson with students.

FLIP IT!

Assign the Flipped Video for this lesson.

STUDENT EDITION PRINT PAGES: 623–632

INVESTIGATE

DIGITAL TEXT 1

Changes and Challenges in City Life

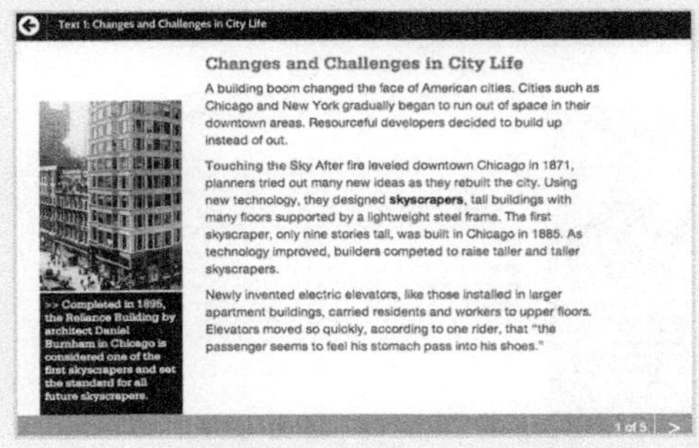

Objective 1: Describe how city life changed during the Progressive Era.

Quick Instruction

Project the image of the electric streetcar. Prompt students to explain how the image represents aspects of city life in late nineteenth century America. *(increasing population, urbanization, congestion, technological innovation)*

Summarize how the development of skyscrapers helped fuel urban growth. *(Skyscrapers increased the amount of space in which people could live and work, which brought more people to urban areas.)*

D Differentiate: Extra Support Pair students to review the text and the interactive activity and to write down ways in which reforms improved the lives of citizens living in urban centers.

Further Instruction

Encourage students to describe aspects of urban areas with which they are familiar. *(Possible responses include tall buildings, crowded streets, museums, buses, subway or elevated trains, large public parks, lots of shopping areas or stores.)* Invite volunteers to discuss how those features affect the lives of the cities' citizens. *(These features of urban life provide most of what people need to live. Transportation, businesses, shopping—even parks and open spaces—allow people to live in cities without having to travel long distances to get what they need. The features provide conveniences.)*

Draw Conclusions Which innovation do you think had the most important impact on daily life in U.S. cities? Support your answer with details from the text. *(Possible answer: The development of mass transit systems like the electric cable car system and the subway had the most important impact on daily life, because they made it possible for large numbers of people to live and work within a large city. Mass transit also helped make suburban life possible by providing a way for people to commute to jobs in the city.)*

Infer Challenge students to explain how department stores were made possible by technology. *(New production technologies allowed businesses to make more goods available to the public at lower prices. Building innovations allowed stores to sell more goods in one location, creating department stores.)*

A Changing American Culture

DIGITAL TEXT 2

More Americans Play Sports

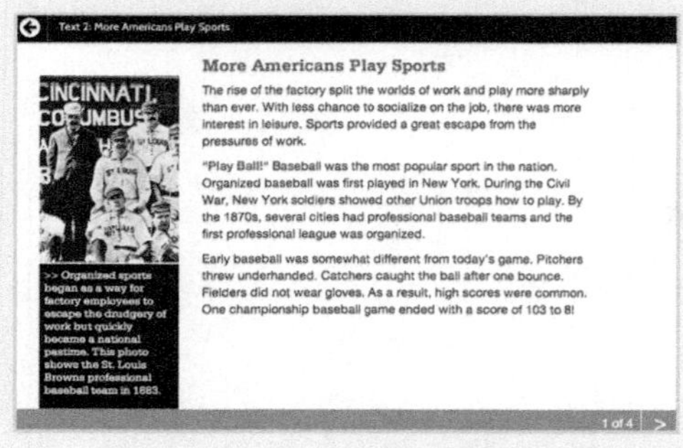

DIGITAL TEXT 3

New Forms of Theater and Music

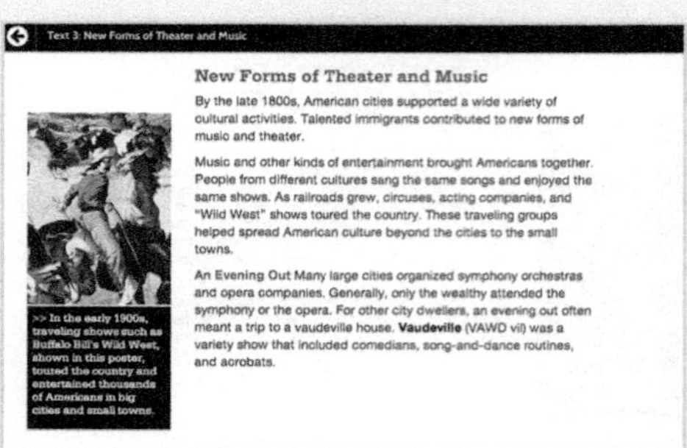

INTERACTIVE GALLERY

Leisure Activities at the Turn of the Century

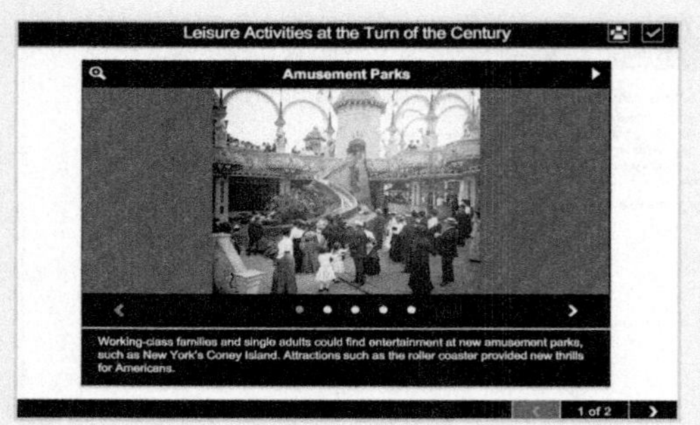

Objective 2: **Identify forms of entertainment that Americans enjoyed during this period.**

Quick Instruction

Interactive Gallery: Leisure Activities at the Turn of the Century Project the Interactive Gallery. As you guide students through the gallery, prompt them to compare and contrast each form of entertainment with a parallel form of entertainment that is popular today.

Compare and Contrast Which forms of entertainment popular during the Progressive Era are still popular today? *(Possible answer: roller coasters and amusement parks; bicycles and cars; movies; and spectator sports such as baseball and football)* What does their lasting popularity suggest about these forms of entertainment? *(People living during the Progressive Era shared many of the same leisure interests as people do today.)*

ACTIVE CLASSROOM

Select 10 to 12 words or phrases you think are important for students to know in digital texts 2 and 3. List the words on the board for students to copy on small pieces of paper. Read the list of words with students. Ask students to "connect two" or choose two words they think might belong together and state the reason, e.g. "I would connect _____ and _____ because...." Students should look for evidence to support or refute their connections in the reading.

Further Instruction

Summarize What were some of the benefits and drawbacks of the increased interest in organized sports in the Progressive Era? *(Sports provided a great escape for American workers from the pressures of their jobs. In addition, many Americans became more active as sports grew in popularity. However, some sports, like football, were very dangerous and caused many injuries and even deaths. Professional sports were also segregated. African Americans for example were not allowed to play professional baseball. This created another area in which African Americans were denied equal opportunities.)*

Draw Conclusions How did Vaudeville reflect the changing American population? *(Vaudeville provided opportunities for people from many ethnic backgrounds, including Irish Americans, Jewish, and American Indian performers.)*

Use Context Clues How did technology help popularize and spread American culture? *(Technological innovations like Edison's phonograph helped create the music recording industry, providing a way for millions of Americans all over the country to hear and experience new American-made music. New transportation technologies like the railroad helped spread American culture beyond the cities to the small towns.)*

DIGITAL TEXT 4

More Americans Attend School

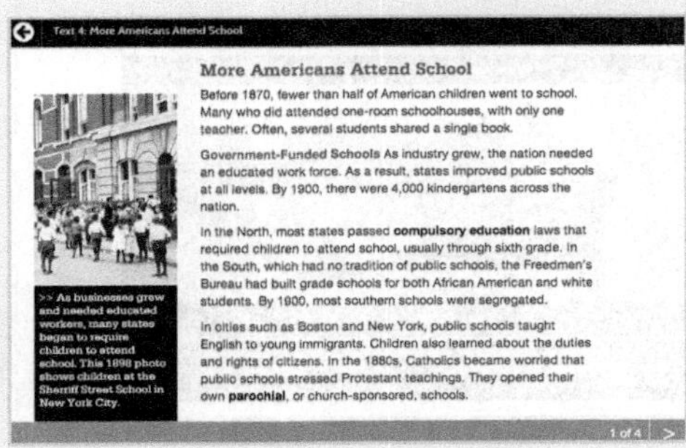
Text 4: More Americans Attend School

More Americans Attend School

Before 1870, fewer than half of American children went to school. Many who did attended one-room schoolhouses, with only one teacher. Often, several students shared a single book.

Government-Funded Schools As industry grew, the nation needed an educated work force. As a result, states improved public schools at all levels. By 1900, there were 4,000 kindergartens across the nation.

In the North, most states passed **compulsory education** laws that required children to attend school, usually through sixth grade. In the South, which had no tradition of public schools, the Freedmen's Bureau had built grade schools for both African American and white students. By 1900, most southern schools were segregated.

In cities such as Boston and New York, public schools taught English to young immigrants. Children also learned about the duties and rights of citizens. In the 1880s, Catholics became worried that public schools stressed Protestant teachings. They opened their own **parochial**, or church-sponsored, schools.

>> As businesses grew and needed educated workers, many states began to require children to attend school. This 1898 photo shows children at the Sherriff Street School in New York City.

1 of 4 >

DIGITAL TEXT 5

News in Print

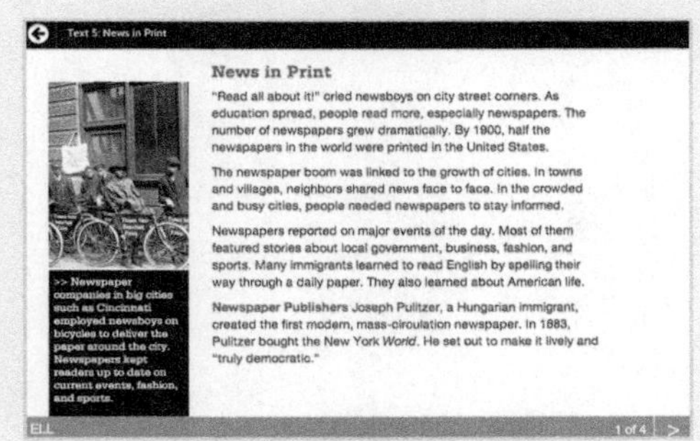
Text 5: News in Print

News in Print

"Read all about it!" cried newsboys on city street corners. As education spread, people read more, especially newspapers. The number of newspapers grew dramatically. By 1900, half the newspapers in the world were printed in the United States.

The newspaper boom was linked to the growth of cities. In towns and villages, neighbors shared news face to face. In the crowded and busy cities, people needed newspapers to stay informed.

Newspapers reported on major events of the day. Most of them featured stories about local government, business, fashion, and sports. Many immigrants learned to read English by spelling their way through a daily paper. They also learned about American life.

Newspaper Publishers Joseph Pulitzer, a Hungarian immigrant, created the first modern, mass-circulation newspaper. In 1883, Pulitzer bought the New York *World*. He set out to make it lively and "truly democratic."

>> Newspaper companies in big cities such as Cincinnati employed newsboys on bicycles to deliver the paper around the city. Newspapers kept readers up to date on current events, fashion, and sports.

ELL 1 of 4 >

Objective 3: **Describe how public education grew during the Progressive Era.**

Quick Instruction

Project the image of the school classroom. Encourage students to use their own experiences to compare and contrast today's classrooms with the one in the image. Emphasize that reading, writing, and arithmetic were the focus of schools in the late 1800s. Invite students to discuss the importance of these three subjects in education today. Ask: What other subjects do schools require today? *(Possible responses: science, computer technologies)*

Generate Explanations Why was there more support for public schools in the northern region of the country than in the South? *(The southern economy was based on agriculture, and industry was not as developed as in the North, so fewer trained or educated workers were necessary at the time.)*

Draw Conclusions How did religious differences contribute to the growth of education during the Progressive Era? *(In the 1880s, Catholics became worried that public schools stressed Protestant teachings. Catholics opened their own parochial, or church-sponsored, schools, providing even more educational opportunities.)*

Further Instruction

Cite Evidence How did the needs of business and industry influence public education in the United States? Cite specific examples from the text. *(As industry grew, the nation needed more educated workers. As a result, states improved public schools at all levels. Some people opened specialized schools to train workers for "shop work." Most public schools in the country created programs to prepare students for jobs in business and in industry.)*

Use Context Clues Based on the information in the reading, what was the primary goal of the Chautauqua Society? *(The primary goal was to provide spiritual guidance and religious education. The society was founded by a Methodist minister for Bible teachers.)*

Objective 4: **Identify changes in reading habits.**

Quick Instruction

Direct students' attention to the image of the newsboys on bicycles. Invite a volunteer to explain what the image might suggest about the availability and the speed with which news was circulated. *(The technology to report and spread news in the 1800s was much more limited than today and would have taken much longer for readers to get the news.)* Ask students to discuss how news is spread today. *(Possible responses include through television, radio, computer, e-mail, texting.)*

Summarize What role did newspapers play in helping immigrants assimilate into American society? *(Many immigrants learned to read and speak English by reading daily newspapers. They also learned about American life.)*

Infer What did Joseph Pulitzer mean when he said he wanted his newspaper, The *World*, to be "truly democratic"? *(Pulitzer was a Hungarian immigrant who created the first modern, mass-circulation newspaper. He wanted his paper to be read by all Americans, not just the wealthy or educated classes. He also lowered prices and added features to appeal to a wider audience.)*

ELL Use the ELL activity described in the ELL chart.

Topic 11 Lesson 6

A Changing American Culture

DIGITAL TEXT 6

American Writers and Artists Excel

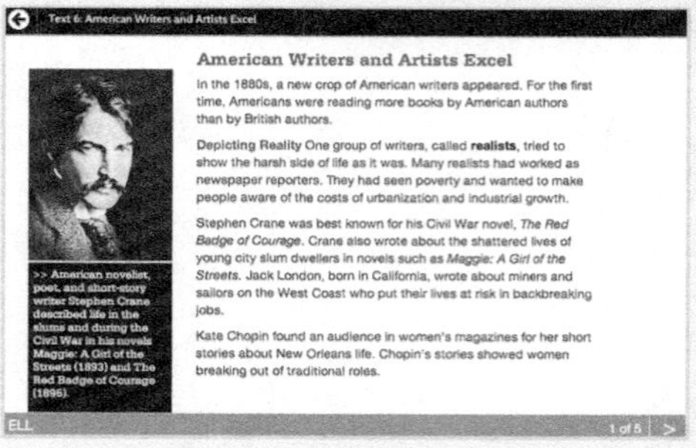

INTERACTIVE GALLERY

American Realist Artists

Further Instruction

Go through the Interactive Reading Notepad questions and use them as a springboard to discuss the reasons that print media gained such wide popularity in the Progressive Era. *(growing numbers of literate Americans; more women readers; printing and distribution innovations)*

Make Generalizations How would you describe the relationship between newspapers and their female readers? *(Newspapers gained a great number of new readers by providing features that appealed to or were important to women. Women's views were better represented in newspapers, yet the newspapers still would not support equal rights for women.)*

Connect Which elements in Horatio Alger's books related to American values of the time? *(Alger's dime novels told of poor boys who became rich and respected through hard work, luck, and honesty. "Rags-to-riches" stories offered the hope that even the poorest person could succeed in the United States. They reflected America as the "land of opportunity.")*

Objective 5: **Explain the interest of Progressive Era writers and painters in subjects from everyday life.**

Quick Instruction

Interactive Gallery: American Realist Artists Project the Interactive Gallery and click through the images. Prompt students to understand the realist artists wanted to present life as it appeared to them.

Support Ideas with Examples What examples support the idea that Mark Twain portrayed real life in his stories? *(Many of Twain's characters used words and accents associated with particular regions of the United States. He also openly addressed issues such as slavery.)*

ACTIVE CLASSROOM

Organize students to create a Circle Write. Break students into groups and provide this question as a writing prompt: How did American writers and artists depict American life? Have students write as much as they can for 1 minute then switch with the person on their right. The next person tries to improve or elaborate the response where the other person left off. Continue to switch until the paper comes back to the first person. The group then decides which is the best composition (or response) and shares that with the larger group.

D Differentiate: Extra Support Pair students to review the text and the interactive activity and write down ways in which American writers and artists depicted American life.

ELL Use the ELL activity described in the ELL chart.

Further Instruction

Prompt students to identify some realist American authors and the titles of their influential works. *(Stephen Crane, Jack London, Kate Chopin, Paul Laurence Dunbar, Mark Twain)*

Draw Conclusions Why did realist authors use local color in their works? *(Using local color helped writers to create more life-like and realistic characters and settings.)*

Infer According to the reading, Henry Tanner, a talented African American artist, moved to Paris to enjoy greater freedom. What might this suggest about the status of African American artists working during the Progressive Era? *(It suggests that even though African Americans had made some progress in gaining some equality, some still thought that they lacked the same opportunities or artistic freedoms as white artists in America or artists in general living in other countries.)*

SYNTHESIZE

DIGITAL ACTIVITY

Answer Questions About the Progressive Era

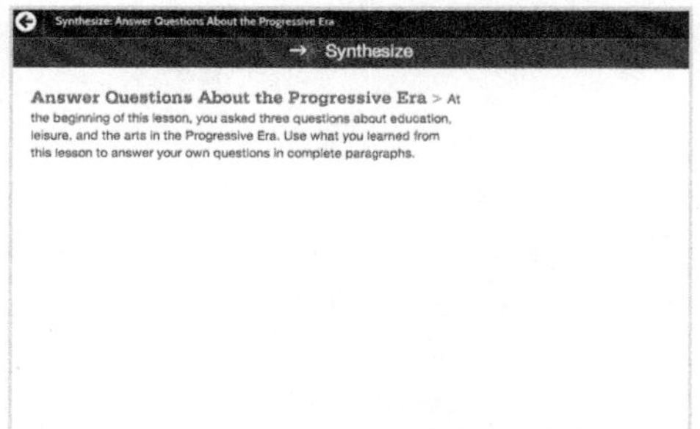

Synthesize: Answer Questions About the Progressive Era
→ Synthesize
Answer Questions About the Progressive Era > At the beginning of this lesson, you asked three questions about education, leisure, and the arts in the Progressive Era. Use what you learned from this lesson to answer your own questions in complete paragraphs.

Discuss Before students begin the activity, lead a brief discussion about the roles of education, leisure, and the arts during the Progressive Era. Then provide opportunities for students to share their questions and answers with the class.

Encourage students to provide constructive feedback on their peer's responses using information learned in the lesson.

DEMONSTRATE

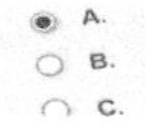

LESSON QUIZ

Lesson Quiz and Class Discussion Board

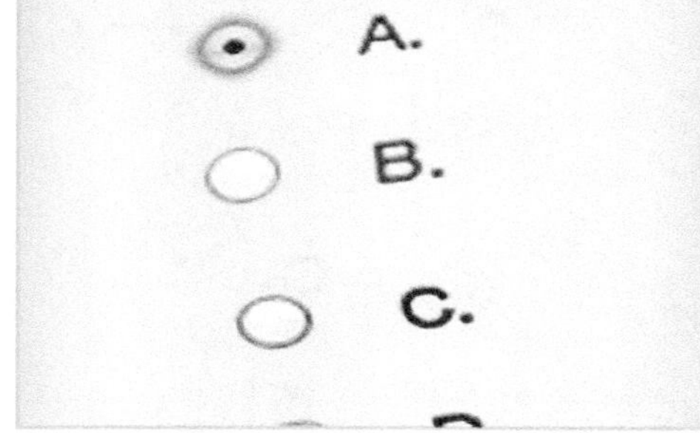

Assign the online Lesson Quiz for this lesson if you haven't already done so. Students will be offered automatic remediation or enrichment based on their score.

In *A Changing American Culture*, students read about how the growth of cities changed America's physical and cultural landscape. At the same time, more Americans gained an education, leisure activities grew, and the arts and literature pushed for social change.

Pose these questions to the class on the Discussion Board:

Compare and Contrast How was American life in the late 1800s most similar to life today? How was it most different?

Apply Concepts Can writers and artists be effective promoters of social reforms? Why or why not?

Topic Inquiry

Have students continue their investigations for the Topic Inquiry.

Topic 11

The Progressive Era

SYNTHESIZE

DIGITAL ACTIVITY

Reflect on the Essential Question and Topic

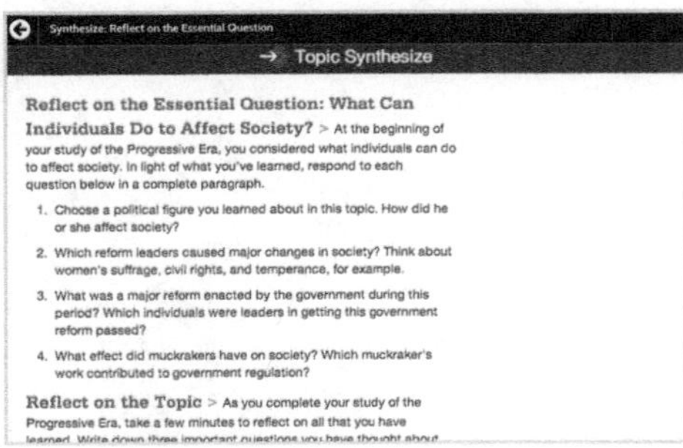

Ask students to reconsider the Essential Question for the Topic: What can individuals do to affect society? Remind students of the possibilities they considered at the start of the Topic. For example, individuals can make changes in

- politics
- the arts
- charity
- community
- business
- education

After students have responded to the questions, ask volunteers to share their writing with the class. Encourage discussion and debate as students share their reflections. Invite students to post their answers on the Class Discussion Board.

Next, ask students to reflect on the Topic as a whole and jot down three questions about the Topic content and the answers to those questions. Review the sample questions and encourage students to share their own questions with the class. Invite students to post their questions and answers on the Class Discussion Board.

Topic Inquiry

Have students complete Step 3 of the Topic Inquiry.

DEMONSTRATE

DIGITAL TOPIC REVIEW AND ASSESSMENT

The Progressive Era

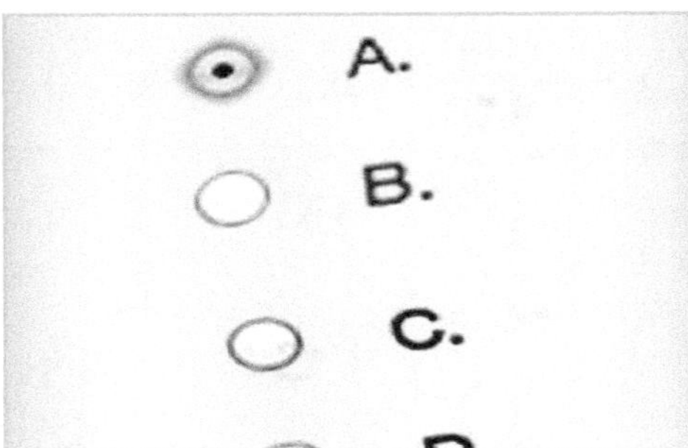

Students can prepare for the Topic Test by answering the questions in the Topic Review and Assessment online or the Assessment questions in the Print Student text. They can also prepare by reviewing their answers to the Interactive Reading Notepad questions or reviewing their notes in the Reading and Notetaking Study Guide.

DIGITAL TOPIC TEST

The Progressive Era

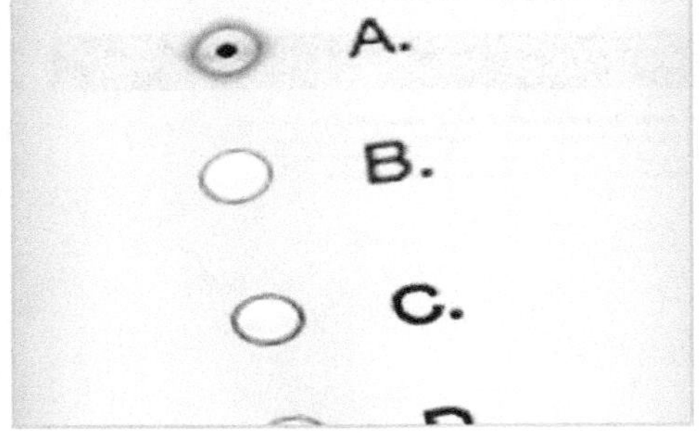

TOPIC TEST

Assign the Topic Test to assess students' understanding of topic content.

BENCHMARK TESTS

Assign these benchmark tests as you complete the relevant topics to monitor student progress toward mastering the course content and as preparation for the End-of-Course Test.

Benchmark Test 1: Topics 1–2
Benchmark Test 2: Topics 3–4
Benchmark Test 3: Topics 5–6
Benchmark Test 4: Topics 7–9
Benchmark Test 5: Topics 10–12
Benchmark Test 6: Topics 13–14
Benchmark Test 7: Topics 15–17

Imperialism and World War I

TOPIC 12 ORGANIZER	PACING: APPROX. 10 PERIODS, 5 BLOCKS
	PACING
Connect	1 period
MY STORY VIDEO **Theodore Roosevelt Pushes for Expansion**	10 min.
DIGITAL ESSENTIAL QUESTION ACTIVITY **What is America's role in the world?**	10 min.
DIGITAL TIMELINE ACTIVITY **Imperialism and World War I**	10 min.
TOPIC INQUIRY: CIVIC DISCUSSION **Annexing Hawaii**	20 min.
Investigate	3–7 periods
TOPIC INQUIRY: CIVIC DISCUSSION **Annexing Hawaii**	Ongoing
LESSON 1 Expansion in the Pacific	30–40 min.
LESSON 2 War and Empire	30–40 min.
LESSON 3 U.S. Power in Latin America	30–40 min.
LESSON 4 A European War	30–40 min.
LESSON 5 Entering the War	30–40 min.
LESSON 6 Winning the War	30–40 min.
LESSON 7 Wilson and Isolationism	30–40 min.
Synthesize	1 period
DIGITAL ACTIVITY **Reflect on the Essential Question and Topic**	10 min.
TOPIC INQUIRY: CIVIC DISCUSSION **Annexing Hawaii**	20 min.
Demonstrate	1–2 periods
DIGITAL TOPIC REVIEW AND ASSESSMENT **Imperialism and World War I**	10 min.
TOPIC INQUIRY: CIVIC DISCUSSION **Annexing Hawaii**	20 min.

TOPIC INQUIRY: CIVIC DISCUSSION

Annexing Hawaii

In this Topic Inquiry, students work in teams to examine different perspectives on this issue by analyzing several sources, arguing both sides of a Yes/No question, then developing and discussing their own point of view on the question: **Should the U.S. have annexed Hawaii?**

STEP 1: CONNECT

Develop Questions and Plan the Investigation

Launch the Civic Discussion

Divide the class into groups of four students. Students can access the materials they'll need in the online course or you can distribute copies to each student. Read the main question and introduction with the students.

Have students complete Step 1 by reading the Discussion Launch and filling in Step 1 of the Information Organizer. The Discussion Launch provides YES and NO arguments on the main question. Students should extract and paraphrase the arguments from the reading in Step 1 of their Information Organizers.

Next, students share within their groups the arguments and evidence they found to support the YES and NO positions. The group needs to agree on the major YES and NO points and each student should note those points in their Information Organizer.

Resources

- Student Instructions
- Information Organizer
- Discussion Launch

PROFESSIONAL DEVELOPMENT

Civic Discussion

Be sure to view the Civic Discussion Professional Development resources in the online course.

STEP 2: INVESTIGATE

Apply Disciplinary Concepts and Tools

Examine Sources and Perspectives

Students will examine sources with the goal of extracting information and perspectives on the main question. They analyze each source and describe the author's perspective on the main question and key evidence the author provides to support that viewpoint in Information Organizer Step 2.

Ask students to keep in mind:

- **Author/Creator:** Who created the source? An individual? Group? Government agency?
- **Audience:** For whom was the source created?
- **Date/Place:** Is there any information that reveals where and when the source was created?
- **Purpose:** Why was the source created? Discuss with students the importance of this question in identifying bias.
- **Relevance:** How does the source support one argument or another?

Suggestion: Reading the source documents and filling in Step 2 of the Information Organizer could be assigned as homework.

Resources

- Student Instructions
- Information Organizer
- Source documents

www.PearsonRealize.com
Access your Digital Lesson

STEP 3: SYNTHESIZE

Use Evidence to Formulate Conclusions

Formulate Compelling Arguments with Evidence

Now students will apply perspectives and evidence they extracted from the sources to think more deeply about the main question by first arguing one side of the issue, then the other. In this way students become more prepared to formulate an evidence-based conclusion on their own.

Within each student group, assign half of the students to take the position of YES on the main question and the others to take the position of NO. Students will work with their partners to identify the strongest arguments and evidence to support their assigned YES or NO position.

Present Yes/No Positions

Within each group, those assigned the YES position share arguments and evidence first. As the YES students speak, those assigned NO should listen carefully, take notes to fill in the rest of the Compelling Arguments Chart (Step 3 in Information Organizer) and ask clarifying questions.

When the YES side is finished, students assigned the NO position present while those assigned YES should listen, take notes, and ask clarifying questions. Examples of clarifyin questions are:

- I think you just said [x]. Am I understanding you correctly?
- Can you tell me more about [x]?
- Can you repeat [x]? I am not sure I understand, yet.

Suggestion: You may want to set a 5 minute time limit for each side to present. Provide a two-minute warning so that students make their most compelling arguments within the time frame.

Switch Sides

The students will switch sides to argue the opposite point of view. To prepare to present the other position, partners who first argued YES will use the notes they took during the NO side's presentation, plus add any additional arguments and evidence from the reading and sources. The same for students who first argued the NO position.

STEP 4: DEMONSTRATE

Communicate Conclusions and Take Informed Action

Individual Points of View

Now the students will have the opportunity to discuss the main question from their own points of view. To help students prepare for this discussion, have them reflect on the YES/NO discussions they have participated in thus far and fill in Step 4 of their Information Organizers.

After all of the students have shared their points of view, each group should list points of agreement, filling the last portion of Step 4 on their Information Organizers.

Reflect on the Discussion

Ask students to reflect on the civic discussion thinking about:

- The value of having to argue both the YES and NO positions.
- If their individual views changed over the course of the discussion and why.
- What they learned from participating in the discussion.

Resources

- Student Instructions
- Information Organizer

INTRODUCTION

Imperialism and World War I

In the late 1800s, the United States became an imperial power with greater political and economic influence abroad. It gained new territories in the Pacific and adopted interventionist policies in Latin America. This increasing involvement in global affairs made it difficult for the United States to remain neutral when war broke out in Europe in 1914. The United States entered World War I in 1917 on the side of the Allies. The Allies united to win the war, but it soon became clear they did not share the same visions for peace. The peace plan that was established had significant problems and many critics.

CONNECT

MY STORY VIDEO

Theodore Roosevelt Pushes for Expansion

Watch a video about the life of Theodore Roosevelt.

Check Understanding How did Roosevelt become President? *(upon the assassination of President McKinley)*

Compare and Contrast What are arguments both for and against Roosevelt's sending of American military forces to Panama in 1903? *(By sending American forces to Panama, Roosevelt was able ultimately to get the Panama Canal built, significantly cutting travel time between the Atlantic and Pacific oceans. The action of interfering in the affairs of other nations, however, angered those who wanted the United States to avoid the imperialistic practices of European nations.)*

DIGITAL ESSENTIAL QUESTION ACTIVITY

What is America's role in the world?

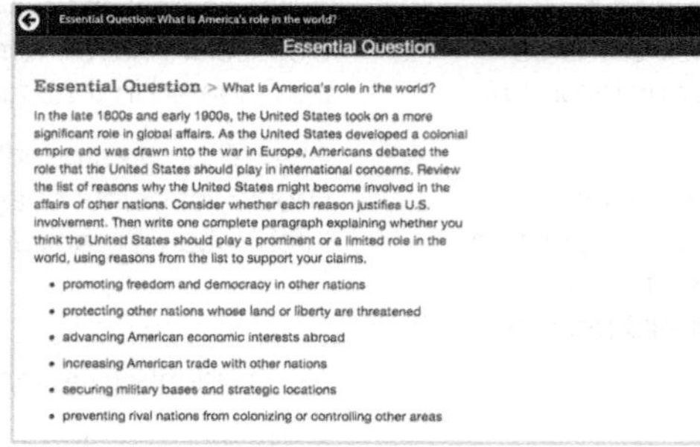

Ask students to think about the Essential Question for this Topic: What is America's role in the world? America's rise as an imperialist power, its involvement in World War I, and its leadership in the peace process changed the country's position in the world.

If students have not already done so, ask them to read the list of reasons why the United States might become involved in the affairs of other nations. Then ask them to write a complete paragraph explaining whether they think the United States should play a prominent or a limited role in the world, using reasons from the list for support.

Identify Cause and Effect What reasons from the list do you think caused the United States to become involved in World War I?

Make Generalizations Make a generalization about how you think America's role in the world changed from the late 1800s to the end of World War I.

DIGITAL TIMELINE ACTIVITY

Imperialism and World War I

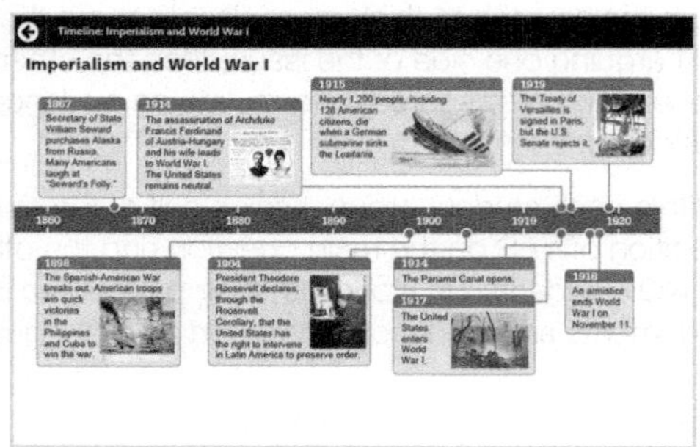

Display the timeline showing the major events related to U.S. imperialism and World War I.

Support Ideas with Examples Give two examples from the timeline that show how the United States expanded its power and influence during this time. *(It purchased Alaska; expanded its influence in the Pacific; opened the Panama Canal; won victories in the Spanish-American War; declared the Roosevelt Corollary; and entered World War I.)*

Identify Cause and Effect How do you think the sinking of the *Lusitania* affected U.S. neutrality during World War I? Provide evidence to support your claim. *(The sinking of the Lusitania by a German submarine made it harder for the United States to remain neutral. In 1917, the United States declared war on Germany.)*

Topic Inquiry

Launch the Topic Inquiry with students after introducing the topic.

PEARSON realize™ www.PearsonRealize.com Access your Digital Lesson

Expansion in the Pacific

Supporting English Language Learners

Use with the reading, **Expansion Leads to Trade with Japan.**

Learning

Read aloud the first four paragraphs of *Expansion Leads to Trade with Japan*. Explain to students that they can request assistance, use non-verbal cues, and convey ideas by defining or describing when they do not know the exact English word.

Beginning Tell students to raise their hand when they hear an unfamiliar word, such as *expansionism*. Pause and say the word slowly and clearly. Elicit a familiar word that is part of this larger word, e.g., expand. Use hand gestures to illustrate *expand*. Explain that expansionism means making the boundaries bigger.

Intermediate Tell students to raise their hand when they do not know the meaning of a word, for example, *isolationism*. Pause and provide a simple definition or use simple words to describe it. After reading, ask: Whose beliefs influenced the policy of isolationism? Why did Presidents follow a policy of isolationism?

Advanced Pause after reading this sentence in the first paragraph: *He had been concerned about forming dangerous alliances with other nations*. Ask partners to discuss what they think *dangerous alliances* means. Have them use other words to define or describe what the expression means.

Advanced High Ask students to take turns retelling the information in the section to less proficient classmates. Encourage them to use simple language in place of words like *alliances, influenced,* and *pressing westward*.

Use with the reading, **The Age of Imperialism.**

Listening

Read aloud the first five paragraphs of *The Age of Imperialism*. Tell students that you will reread different paragraphs so they can answer specific questions about the information in them.

Beginning Read aloud the first paragraph of the text. Pause after the third sentence and ask a fact-based question, such as, Which countries controlled most of Africa and part of Asia?

Intermediate Ask a fact-based question about imperialism. Then read aloud the first paragraph and ask students to listen for the answer. Encourage them to share their answers.

Advanced Read aloud the first paragraph of the text. Ask students to talk about what imperialism is. Have them name imperial nations and the nations they controlled.

Advanced High Read aloud the section titled *Reasons for Imperialism*. Ask partners to name the three main reasons for imperialism. Then have them ask and answer questions explaining the rationale of these reasons.

D Differentiate Instruction

Use the Differentiated Instruction notes throughout the lesson plan to support the varied skill sets, levels of readiness, and interests in the mixed-ability classroom.

Challenge These notes include suggestions for expanding the activity for advanced students.

On-Level These notes include suggestions for modifying the activity to address different interests or learning styles.

Extra Support These notes include ideas for providing more scaffolding or reading spupport.

Special Needs These notes provide ideas for adapting instruction to support the needs of various special needs students.

NOTES

Expansion in the Pacific

Objectives

Objective 1: Explain the early steps the United States took toward expansion in the Pacific.

Objective 2: Identify the meaning of imperialism and explain its causes.

Objective 3: Describe how the United States gained control of American Samoa and Hawaii.

Objective 4: Summarize how Americans protected their trade with China.

LESSON 1 ORGANIZER	PACING: APPROX. 1 PERIOD, .5 BLOCKS			
			RESOURCES	
	OBJECTIVES	PACING	Online	Print
Connect				
DIGITAL START UP ACTIVITY **U.S. Expansion**		5 min.	●	
Investigate				
DIGITAL TEXT 1 **Expansion Leads to Trade With Japan**	Objective 1	10 min.	●	●
DIGITAL TEXT 2 **U.S. Interest in the Pacific**	Objective 1	10 min.	●	●
DIGITAL TEXT 3 **The Age of Imperialism**	Objective 2	10 min.	●	●
DIGITAL TEXT 4 **American Influence in the Pacific**	Objective 3	10 min.	●	●
INTERACTIVE MAP **U.S. Expansion in the Pacific, 1867–1899**	Objective 3	10 min.	●	
DIGITAL TEXT 5 **Competition for Chinese Trade**	Objective 4	10 min.	●	●
INTERACTIVE CHART **U.S. Influence in Foreign Nations**	Objective 4	10 min.	●	
Synthesize				
DIGITAL ACTIVITY **U.S. Involvement in the Pacific**		5 min.	●	
Demonstrate				
DIGITAL QUIZ **Lesson Quiz and Discussion Board**		10 min.	●	

Go online to access additional resources including:
Primary Sources • Biographies • Supreme Court cases • 21st Century Skill Tutorials • Maps • Graphic Organizers.

CONNECT

DIGITAL START UP ACTIVITY

U.S. Expansion

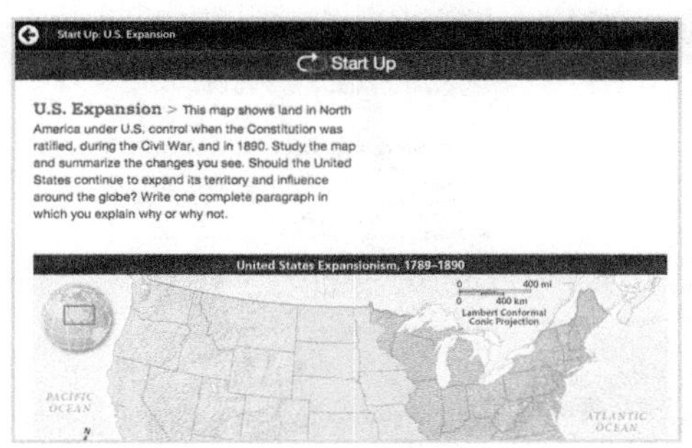

Project the Start Up Activity Ask students to answer the question in the activity as they enter and get settled. Then ask them to share their ideas with partners, either in class or through a chat or blog space.

Discuss Ask volunteers to share their responses to the writing prompt, "Should the United States continue to expand its territory and influence around the globe?" Guide students to develop some general connections between their responses and the economic and political reasons that accounted for U.S. expansion in the Pacific.

Tell students that in this lesson they will be learning about the meaning of imperialism and the reasons for U.S. expansion in the Pacific.

Aa Vocabulary Development: Use the Interactive Reading Notepad to preview the Key Terms and Academic Vocabulary in this lesson with students.

FLIP IT!

Assign the Flipped Video for this lesson.

STUDENT EDITION PRINT PAGES: 638–647

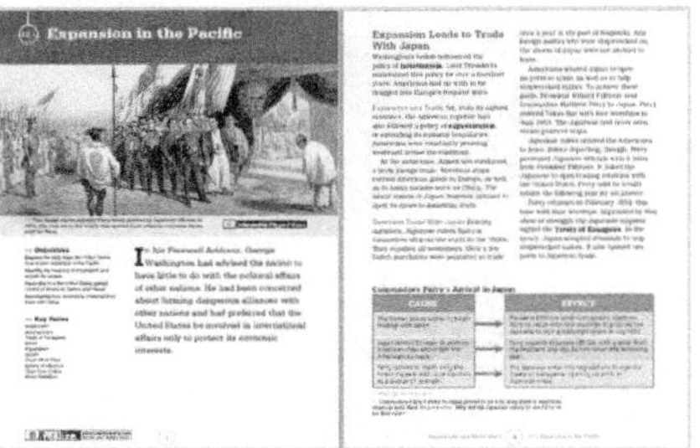

INVESTIGATE

DIGITAL TEXT 1

Expansion Leads to Trade With Japan

DIGITAL TEXT 2

U.S. Interest in the Pacific

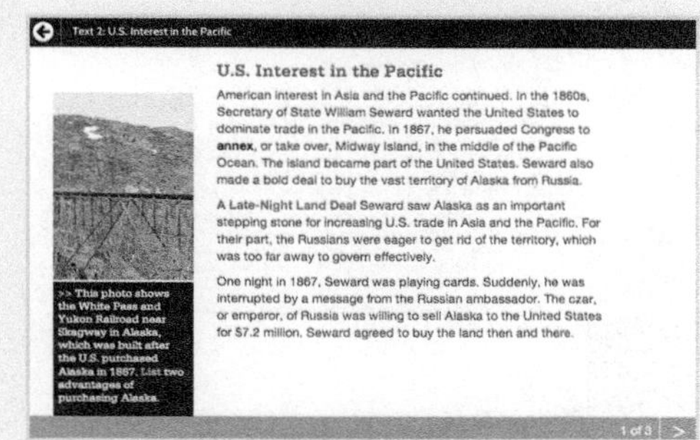

Objective 1: Explain the early steps the United States took toward expansion in the Pacific.

Quick Instruction

Discuss the terms *isolationism* and *expansionism* in the context of the lesson. Point out that though the two policies seem at odds, they worked well together for the United States. By staying out of foreign conflicts, the United States was able to focus on expanding its territory and its foreign trade. Display the illustration of the American ship in Japan and point out that Japan itself followed a strict policy of isolationism until it opened its doors to trade with the United States in 1854.

Hypothesize Why do you think the United States was so interested in expanding trade and territory in the Pacific? *(The Pacific countries offered goods that were not available in Europe or America. Gaining territory in the Pacific would ensure access to these goods.)*

ELL Use the ELL activity described in the ELL chart.

Further Instruction

Analyze Charts Display the chart titled *Commodore Perry's Arrival in Japan*. Ask: Why did President Fillmore send Commodore Perry to Japan? *(Americans wanted to convince Japan to help shipwrecked sailors and open up to trade with the United States.)* What effect did Perry's visit have? *(The United States achieved its goal.)*

Identify Cause and Effect Draw a similar chart for the class and prompt students to explain the causes and effects of Secretary of State Seward's push to annex Midway Island and purchase Alaska. *(Causes: want of proximity to Pacific nations; need for help for U.S. sailors trading in the area. Effects: opened up trade with East Asian and Pacific countries; spurred the Alaska gold rush in the 1890s; ended with Alaska becoming a state in 1959)*

Expansion in the Pacific

DIGITAL TEXT 3
The Age of Imperialism

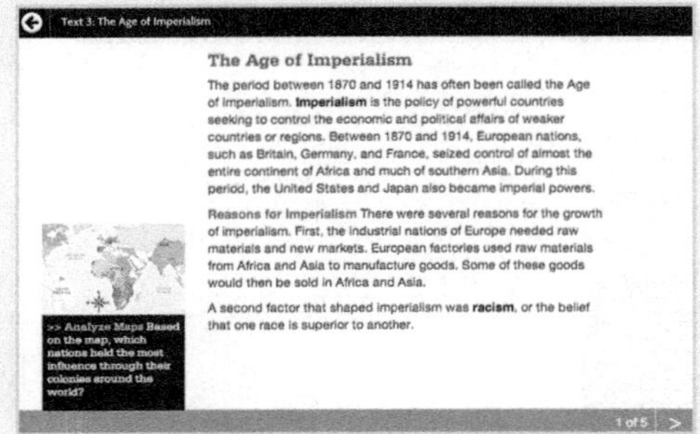

Objective 2: Identify the meaning of imperialism and explain its causes.

Quick Instruction

Analyze Maps Discuss the term *imperialism* with the class as you display the *World Imperialism* map. Prompt students to understand how so few countries were able to exert influence over so many others. What were three main reasons for imperialism? *(Imperialism was driven in part by economic needs for raw materials and new markets in which to sell finished products, competition between countries to acquire those materials and markets, and racism.)*

Generate Explanations What connection exists between racism and imperialism? *(Racism was oftentimes used to justify imperialist policies. Some Europeans thought people living in Asia or Africa were "less civilized" and a European presence in their country was helping others to learn how to live "properly".)*

D Differentiate: Challenge Divide students into small groups and have them discuss why the United States, with its vast supply of natural resources and land, would be interested in becoming an imperialist country. Also, challenge them to discuss how the concepts of isolationism, which the United States had followed for a century, conflicted with imperial aspirations. Invite groups to share their conclusions with the rest of the class.

ELL Use the ELL activity described in the ELL chart.

Further Instruction

Compare How is the policy of expansionism related to imperialism? *(Both policies involve expanding a country's economic influence beyond its own borders.)*

Paraphrase the essential argument pro-imperialist Americans presented. *(U.S. economic production exceeded domestic demand, so the country needed new markets in which to sell its finished goods. Without these markets, pro-imperialists argued, the U.S. economy would collapse. In addition, pro-imperialists believed it was their Christian duty to spread democracy and Christianity to other cultures.)*

DIGITAL TEXT 4
American Influence in the Pacific

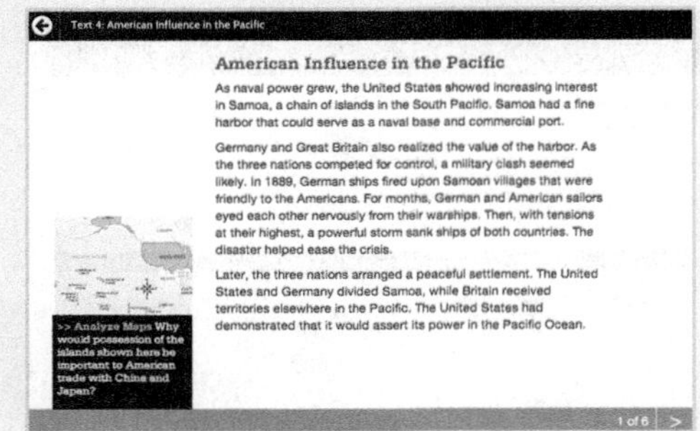

Objective 3: Describe how the United States gained control of American Samoa and Hawaii.

Quick Instruction

Interactive Map: U.S. Expansion in the Pacific, 1867–1899 Project the Interactive Map and navigate the hot spots on the map with students. Discuss the importance of each of the featured acquisitions. Make sure students understand that the United States used force to gain control of both Samoa and Hawaii. Ask: Why would controlling these lands be worth a battle? *(Possible response: The possible financial gain outweighed the cost of battle from the perspective of the American government.)*

Compare and Contrast How was the acquisition of Hawaii different from that of Alaska? *(The United States purchased Alaska in a mutual agreement with Russia. On the other hand, the United States annexed Hawaii using force to dethrone the native government.)* How are the benefits reaped from the acquisition of Alaska and Hawaii similar? *(Both acquisitions gave the United States access to Asia. Both lands provided natural resources that benefited American citizens.)*

PEARSON realize
www.PearsonRealize.com
Access your Digital Lesson

INTERACTIVE MAP

U.S. Expansion in the Pacific, 1867–1899

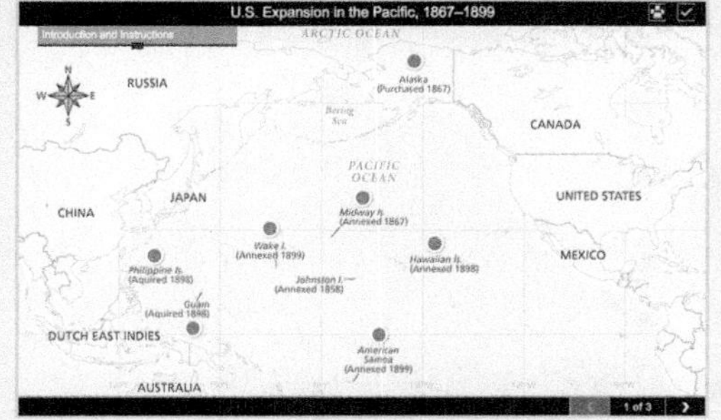

ACTIVE CLASSROOM

Use the Make Headlines activity to further investigate the interactive map. Have students write headlines that capture the importance of the U.S. acquisitions featured in the map. Assign a country, island, or territory to small groups to feature in a headline. Ask: What headline that relates to your area would best capture the most important aspect of its acquisition? When students finish their headlines, group them based on subject. Have groups choose one or two outstanding headlines to share with the class.

Further Instruction

Infer Why were the islands of Samoa so important to control? *(Samoa's location in the South Pacific, along with its established harbor, offered a perfect place for a naval base and port of trade with relatively easy access to east Asia.)*

Generate Explanations How did the shift of power to plantation owners in Hawaii affect the environment? *(Because the land came under control of the plantation owners, they were able to clear forests for agriculture and divert water for irrigation. Also, these westerners introduced new species of plants and animals to Hawaii. In general, the shift of power led to dramatic environmental change on the islands.)*

DIGITAL TEXT 5

Competition for Chinese Trade

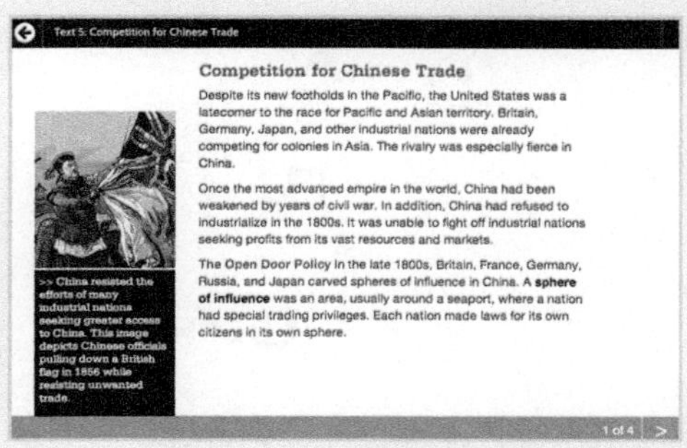

Objective 4: Summarize how Americans protected their trade with China.

Quick Instruction

Interactive Chart: U.S. Influence in Foreign Nations Display the Interactive Chart and prompt students to compare and contrast the relationships America had with each of the nations. If needed, quickly review the events from Digital Texts 1 and 2 to complete the columns for Russia and Japan. Ask students to identify Russia's biggest contribution to U.S. expansion. *(Alaska)*

Summarize What was the purpose of the Open Door Policy? *(Britain, France, Germany, Russia, and Japan each had trading privileges in an area of China called a sphere of influence. Because the United States wanted to gain access to trade with China, Secretary of State John Hay asked the nations with spheres of influence to allow other nations to trade within their spheres. This would open up China to the United States as well as other nations that did not have the power of a sphere of influence there.)*

INTERACTIVE CHART

U.S. Influence in Foreign Nations

ACTIVE CLASSROOM

Use the Sticky Notes strategy to further investigate U.S. influence in foreign nations. Ask students to record questions or comments about U.S. influence on foreign nations on stickies and post them on the wall. Suggest that students consider how U.S. involvement in Russia, Japan, and China affected citizens of these nations and how those citizens felt about U.S. influence. Challenge students to consider how each relationship benefited the countries involved. When students have finished writing, sort and discuss the questions as a group.

Further Instruction

Generate Explanations How did the Open Door Policy relate to U.S. economic interests in Asia? *(If the Chinese government tried to block U.S. trade, the United States could access trade through one of the foreign country's spheres of influence. Therefore, the Open Door Policy guaranteed access to the Chinese market and Chinese raw materials.)*

Identify Central Issues Who were the Boxers and why did they rebel? *(The Boxers were members of a Chinese secret society who resented foreign political and economic influence in China. They rebelled in an effort to expel foreigners from their country.)*

Expansion in the Pacific

SYNTHESIZE

DIGITAL ACTIVITY

U.S. Involvement in the Pacific

After students have completed their graphic organizers, invite them to share their work with partners before responding to the questions. Allow students time to consider their answers based on what they have learned and construct paragraphs in response.

Discuss Lead a class discussion in which students consider the impact of U.S. expansion both on the United States and on the countries of the Pacific. Challenge students to consider this involvement in the context of the global community of today's world.

DEMONSTRATE

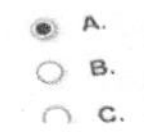

DIGITAL QUIZ

Lesson Quiz and Discussion Board

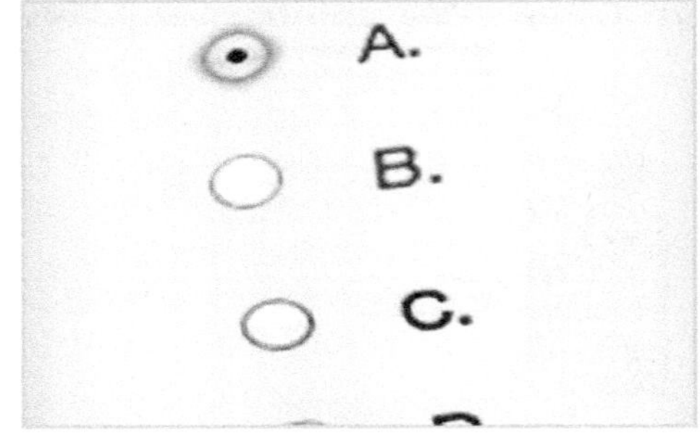

Assign the online Lesson Quiz for this lesson if you haven't already done so. Students will be offered automatic remediation or enrichment based on their score.

In *Expansion in the Pacific*, students learned how the United States expanded its trade and influence in the Pacific by opening trade with Japan, acquiring Alaska, and annexing Hawaii and other Pacific islands. They also learned about U.S. influence in Asia and the efforts the government made to protect its trade interests in the region.

Post these questions to the class on the Discussion Board:

Construct Create a chart in which you list key American figures in the expansion of the United States,including descriptions for Matthew Perry, William Seward, Alfred Mahan, James Cook, and John Hay. Explain how each contributed to American expansion.

Draw Conclusions Why was the United States so eager to expand its economic influence in the late 1800s?

Topic Inquiry

Have students continue their investigations for the Topic Inquiry.

PEARSON realize™ www.PearsonRealize.com Access your Digital Lesson

War and Empire

Supporting English Language Learners

Use with the reading, **The Cuban Revolution.**

Speaking

Have students read *The Cuban Revolution* silently. Answer any questions they have about vocabulary and/or concepts. Then read aloud the last part of the section titled *Americans Are Divided*. Tell students to think about what they read and to form their own opinions about whether they think the United States should have intervened in the Cuban war with Spain.

Beginning Ask partners to use these sentence frames to discuss their ideas and express their opinions: Some Americans thought defending Cuba would be bad for _____. Others wanted to help Cuba fight for _____. I think/don't think the United States should have gotten involved.

Intermediate Ask partners to identify the reasons why some Americans thought the United States should defend Cuba and others didn't agree. Then ask them to take turns telling their partner which opinions they agree with.

Advanced Ask partners to talk about the reasons why the United States considered involvement in the Cuban war with Spain. Encourage them to explain their opinion in a few sentences.

Advanced High Ask partners to talk about the U.S. involvement in the Cuban war with Spain. Ask them whether they think the Cuban rebels were like the Patriots in the American Revolution. Encourage them to support their opinions with facts.

Use with the reading, **War Fever.**

Reading

Read aloud the section titled *Sensational News*. Ask students to follow along in their books to prepare for their own reading of the text.

Beginning Ask partners to take turns reading sentences aloud. Tell them to raise their hand when they come to a word they do not know. Say the word for them and explain the meaning.

Intermediate In small groups, have students take turns reading a paragraph aloud while the others follow along in their book. Answer any questions students have about unfamiliar words or other difficulties with the reading.

Advanced Ask partners to take turns reading a paragraph aloud. Encourage them to check each other's pronunciation. Have them try to work out any questions they have before asking for additional help from classmates or the teacher.

Advanced High Tell students to read the section silently. Have them write down any unfamiliar words or questions they have about the text. Then students get a partner to help answer their queries. If they do not know the answer, they can refer to a dictionary or other reference material.

D Differentiate Instruction

Use the Differentiated Instruction notes throughout the lesson plan to support the varied skill sets, levels of readiness, and interests in the mixed-ability classroom.

Challenge These notes include suggestions for expanding the activity for advanced students.

On-Level These notes include suggestions for modifying the activity to address different interests or learning styles.

Extra Support These notes include ideas for providing more scaffolding or reading spupport.

Special Needs These notes provide ideas for adapting instruction to support the needs of various special needs students.

NOTES

War and Empire

Objectives

Objective 1: Summarize why tensions in Cuba led Americans to call for war with Spain.

Objective 2: Explain how Americans won a quick victory in the Spanish-American War.

Objective 3: Describe how the United States gained and ruled its new empire.

LESSON 2 ORGANIZER	PACING: APPROX. 1 PERIOD, .5 BLOCKS		RESOURCES	
	OBJECTIVES	PACING	Online	Print
Connect				
DIGITAL START UP ACTIVITY **Predicting the Effects of the Spanish-American War**		5 min.	●	
Investigate				
DIGITAL TEXT 1 **The Cuban Revolution**	Objective 1	10 min.	●	●
DIGITAL TEXT 2 **War Fever**	Objective 1	10 min.	●	●
DIGITAL TEXT 3 **The Spanish-American War**	Objective 2	10 min.	●	●
INTERACTIVE MAP **Spanish-American War**	Objective 2	10 min.	●	
DIGITAL TEXT 4 **Becoming a Colonial Power**	Objective 3	10 min.	●	●
INTERACTIVE CHART **Causes and Effects of the Spanish-American War**	Objective 3	10 min.	●	
Synthesize				
DIGITAL ACTIVITY **Returning to the Essential Question**		5 min.	●	
Demonstrate				
DIGITAL QUIZ **Lesson Quiz and Discussion Board**		10 min.	●	

CONNECT

DIGITAL START UP ACTIVITY

Predicting the Effects of the Spanish-American War

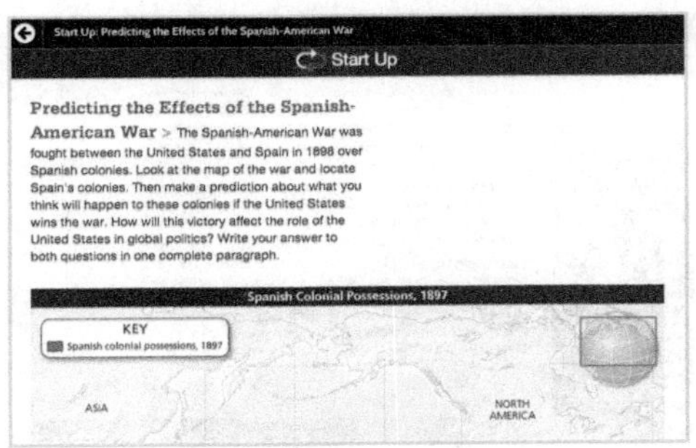

Start Up: Predicting the Effects of the Spanish-American War
Start Up
Predicting the Effects of the Spanish-American War > The Spanish-American War was fought between the United States and Spain in 1898 over Spanish colonies. Look at the map of the war and locate Spain's colonies. Then make a prediction about what you think will happen to these colonies if the United States wins the war. How will this victory affect the role of the United States in global politics? Write your answer to both questions in one complete paragraph.
Spanish Colonial Possessions, 1897
KEY
Spanish colonial possessions, 1897
ASIA
NORTH AMERICA

Project the Start Up Activity Have students study the map and complete the writing as they enter the classroom. Then ask them to share and discuss their ideas with partners.

Discuss Lead a class discussion in which students share their predictions about the outcome of the war and the impact it will have on the U.S. role in global politics.

Tell students that this lesson examines the tensions that led to the Spanish-American War, the American victory, and the way in which the United States gained and ruled its new empire.

Aa Vocabulary Development: Use the Interactive Reading Notepad to preview the Key Terms and Academic Vocabulary in this lesson with students.

FLIP IT!

Assign the Flipped Video for this lesson.

STUDENT EDITION PRINT PAGES: 648–656

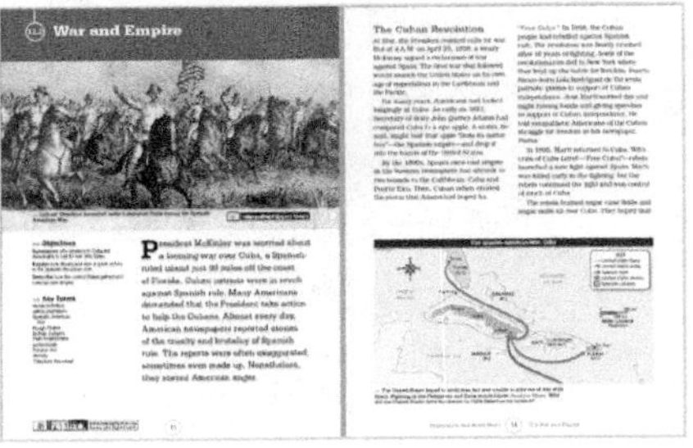

INVESTIGATE

DIGITAL TEXT 1

The Cuban Revolution

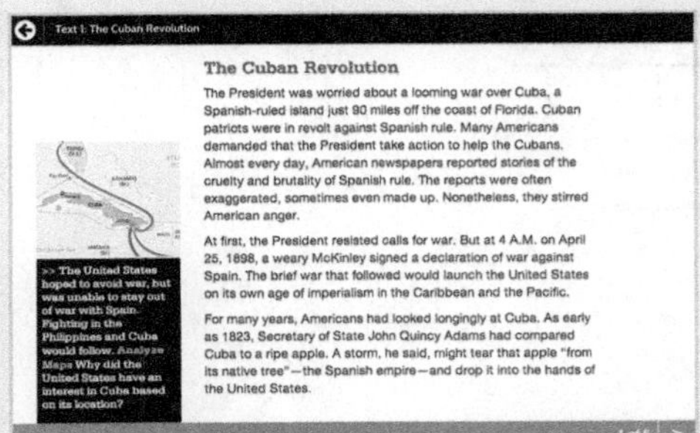

DIGITAL TEXT 2

War Fever

Objective 1: **Summarize why tensions in Cuba led Americans to call for war with Spain.**

Quick Instruction

Analyze Maps Display the map titled *The Spanish-American War: Cuba*. After students study the map and identify why Cuba's location was of interest to the United States, ask: Why would Americans have a vested interested in the outcome of the Cuban Revolution? *(The proximity of Cuba would make it a source of interest for the United States.)* Explain that America had significant financial ties to Cuba, which was a trade partner.

Connect Why did some Americans see similarities between the Cuban Revolution and the American Revolution? *(The Cuban Revolution was a battle against unfair imperial rule, much like the American battle against Britain a century before had been.)*

ELL Use the ELL activity described in the ELL chart.

Further Instruction

Hypothesize How would a change in the Cuban government likely affect the country's relationship with the United States? *(If the United States supported the Cuban rebels, the change in government would likely be beneficial to the relationship. Americans hoped their support would foster a relationship as a strong ally.)*

Draw Conclusions How significant was yellow journalism's influence on public opinion during this time? *(Yellow journalism played a key role in swaying public opinion in favor of Cuban independence and declaring war on Spain. Though the journalism was not based on fact, the reports that the Spanish had blown up an American ship inspired public outrage and eventually influenced the United States to declare war.)*

War and Empire

DIGITAL TEXT 3

The Spanish-American War

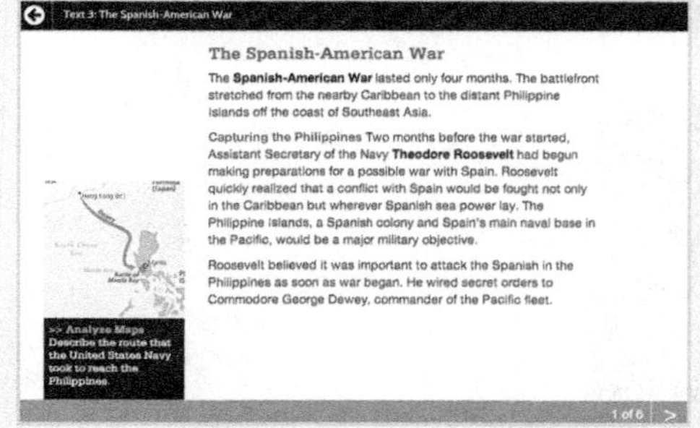

Objective 2: Explain how Americans won a quick victory in the Spanish-American War.

Quick Instruction

Interactive Map: Spanish-American War Project the Interactive Map and navigate through the hot spots, guiding students chronologically and geographically through the key events of the Spanish-American War.

Support a Point of View with Evidence Which decision or battle was the key to winning the Spanish-American War? *(Sample answer: Dewey's surprise attack on Manila solidified American strength and gave them the advantage in the far reaches of the war—the area that should have been most challenging to fight.)*

ACTIVE CLASSROOM

Use the Sequence It strategy to deepen understanding of the events in the Spanish-American War. Display an unordered list of the important sites from the map and the events that took place there. Challenge students to put the list of events in sequential order.

INTERACTIVE MAP

Spanish-American War

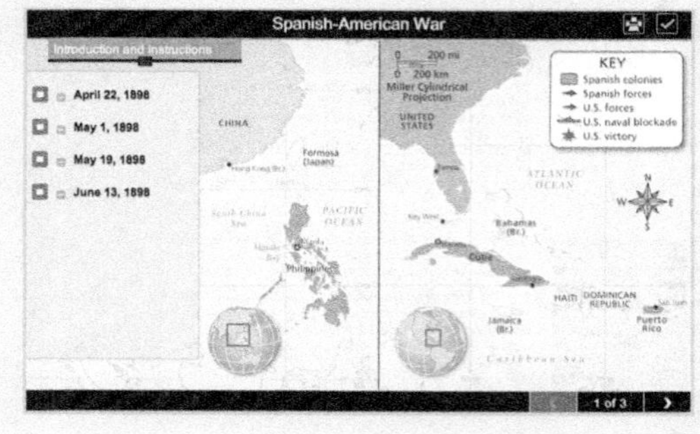

Further Instruction

Draw Conclusions How did Roosevelt's strategy impact the Spanish-American War? *(His plan to attack the Philippines at the very start of the war established American forces in the Pacific, which allowed the United States to take control of that front in the war.)*

Infer How did the United States gain the support of Filipino rebels led by Emilio Aguinaldo? *(The rebels had been fighting for independence from Spain for years, so they believed the United States' forces supported their fight for self-rule as well.)*

DIGITAL TEXT 4

Becoming a Colonial Power

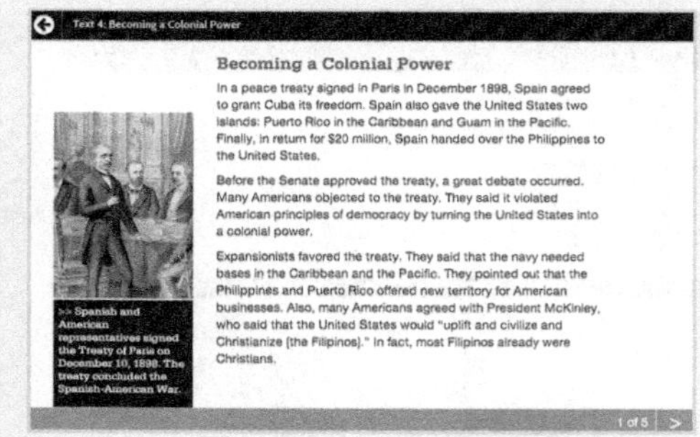

Objective 3: Describe how the United States gained and ruled its new empire.

Quick Instruction

Interactive Chart: Causes and Effects of the Spanish-American War Display the Interactive Chart and work together as a class to pair the causes with their effects. Point out to students that one major effect of the Spanish-American War was the birth of the American empire, which included the Philippines, Guam, Puerto Rico, and the protectorate of Cuba.

Express Problems Clearly Why did the Filipinos revolt against the new U.S. government? *(They had fought alongside the United States against Spain in hopes of achieving independence from outside rule. When the United States took over the role Spain had played before the war, the United States became the enemy ruler of the people of the Philippines. They wanted to rule themselves.)*

PEARSON realize™ www.PearsonRealize.com Access your Digital Lesson

INTERACTIVE CHART

Causes and Effects of the Spanish-American War

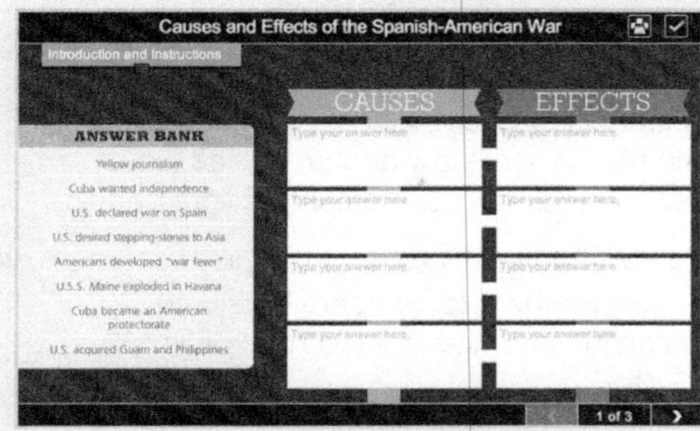

ACTIVE CLASSROOM

Use the PMI strategy to further investigate the causes and effects of the Spanish-American War. Group students. Give each group a three-column organizer with the headings *Plus, Minus,* and *Interesting*. Instruct groups to record their responses to these questions: What are the positive aspects of the United States becoming a colonial power? What are the negative aspects of the United States becoming a colonial power? What is interesting about the United States becoming a colonial power? After groups complete their charts, reconvene as a class to share responses.

D Differentiate: Extra Support Review the concept of imperialism with students. Make sure they understand that the United States is the strong country taking control of a weaker country in the case of the Philippines, Guam, and Puerto Rico. Then, write the word *protectorate* on the board and underline the base *protect.* Point out that the United States aimed to protect its interests in Cuba, not to protect the country of Cuba itself.

Further Instruction

Apply Concepts How could acquiring an empire be seen by some as acting against the democratic ideals upon which the United States was built? *(The essence of democracy lies in a government of the people for the people. By taking control of a country, the United States robbed the citizens of that country of the opportunity to participate in a democratic government.)*

SYNTHESIZE

DIGITAL ACTIVITY

Returning to the Essential Question

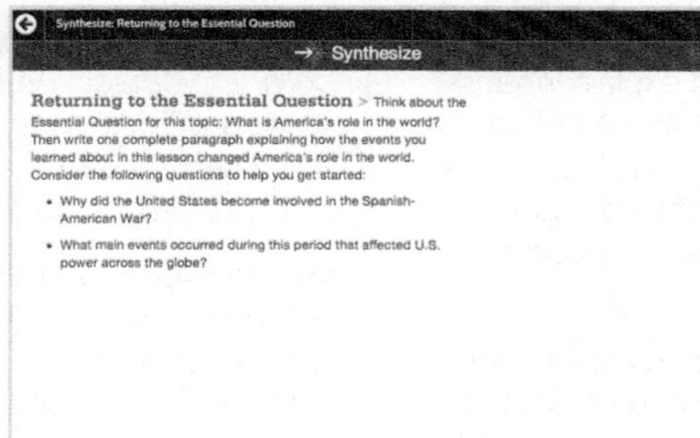

Have students consider the Essential Question for this topic: What is America's role in the world? Prompt students to consider the Essential Question in light of this lesson's content before they begin the Synthesize activity.

Discuss Invite volunteers to share the predictions they made in the Start Up Activity concerning the fate of the colonies and the role of the United States in global affairs.

DEMONSTRATE

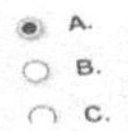

DIGITAL QUIZ

Lesson Quiz and Discussion Board

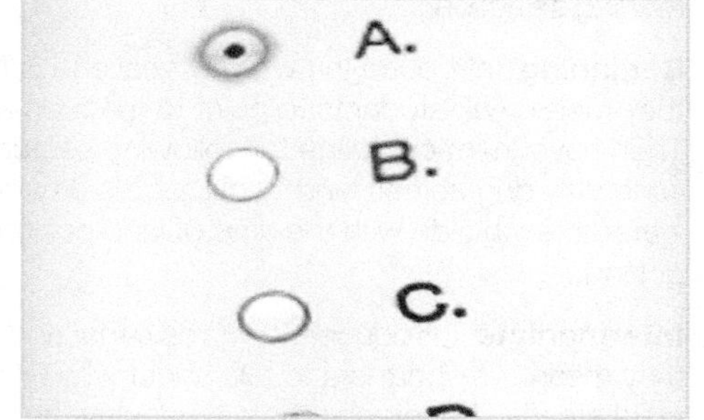

Assign the online Lesson Quiz for this lesson if you haven't already done so. Students will be offered automatic remediation or enrichment based on their score.

In *War and Empire*, students learned about the causes and effects of the Spanish-American War, including the U.S. role in the global community. Students learned how the United States became a colonial power and how it ruled its colonies.

Post these questions to the class on the Discussion Board:

Interpret What is the significance of the Spanish-American War to American history? To the history of Cuba, the Philippines, Puerto Rico, and Guam?

Distinguish What is the difference between a colony and a protectorate?

Topic Inquiry

Have students continue their investigations for the Topic Inquiry.

U.S. Power in Latin America

Supporting English Language Learners

Use with the reading, **The Panama Canal.**

Listening

Read aloud the first four paragraphs of *The Panama Canal*. Tell students that they will learn and use academic language that they hear in the reading selection.

Beginning Introduce the words *canal* and *isthmus* and explain what they mean. Ask students to point to them on a map of Latin America. Then have them complete the following sentence frames: A(n) _____ is a waterway dug across land. A(n) _____ is a narrow strip of land that has water at each side with the strip of land connecting two larger bodies of land.

Intermediate Introduce the words *canal* and *isthmus* and explain what they mean. Ask partners to talk about why President Roosevelt wanted to build a canal. Encourage them to identify the body of land across which he wanted to build it on a map. Have them talk about the characteristics of an isthmus.

Advanced Review the meaning of the words *canal* and *isthmus*. Ask partners to talk about who owned the isthmus and what President Roosevelt did to try to get approval to build a canal across it.

Advanced High Read the section titled *Taking the Canal Zone*. Ask partners to talk about what President Roosevelt did to allow him to proceed with the construction of the canal. Encourage them to use the words canal and isthmus in their discussion.

Use with the reading, **Intervention in Latin America.**

Learning

Tell students that they can use learning strategies, such as comparing and contrasting, to help them develop grade-level vocabulary and concepts.

Beginning Use simple spoken language to summarize the section titled *Dollar Diplomacy*. Ask partners to use the sentence frames to compare President Taft's ideas with President Roosevelt's ideas: Roosevelt _____ U.S. intervention in Latin America to preserve law and order. Taft _____ U.S. intervention, but he wanted the U.S. to _____ instead of fight battles.

Intermediate Use simple spoken language to summarize the section titled *Dollar Diplomacy*. Ask partners to compare President Taft's ideas about U.S. intervention in Latin America with the ideas of President Roosevelt.

Advanced Ask students to read the section titled *Dollar Diplomacy* silently. Have partners work together to compare and contrast Roosevelt's and Taft's ideas about U.S. intervention in Latin America.

Advanced High Ask students to read the sections titled *Dollar Diplomacy* and *Moral Diplomacy* silently. Have partners compare and contrast Woodrow Wilson's ideas about U.S. intervention in Latin America with those of Presidents Roosevelt and Taft.

D Differentiate Instruction

Use the Differentiated Instruction notes throughout the lesson plan to support the varied skill sets, levels of readiness, and interests in the mixed-ability classroom.

Challenge These notes include suggestions for expanding the activity for advanced students.

On-Level These notes include suggestions for modifying the activity to address different interests or learning styles.

Extra Support These notes include ideas for providing more scaffolding or reading spuport.

Special Needs These notes provide ideas for adapting instruction to support the needs of various special needs students.

NOTES

PEARSON realize www.PearsonRealize.com

Go online to access additional resources including: Primary Sources • Biographies • Supreme Court cases • 21st Century Skill Tutorials • Maps • Graphic Organizers.

Objectives

Objective 1: Identify why and how the United States built the Panama Canal.

Objective 2: Explain Theodore Roosevelt's "big stick" policy in Latin America.

Objective 3: Summarize the crisis that erupted between the United States and Mexico.

LESSON 3 ORGANIZER — **PACING: APPROX. 1 PERIOD, .5 BLOCKS**

	OBJECTIVES	PACING	RESOURCES Online	RESOURCES Print
Connect				
DIGITAL START UP ACTIVITY **U.S. Interest in Latin America**		5 min.	●	
Investigate				
DIGITAL TEXT 1 **The Panama Canal**	Objective 1	10 min.	●	●
DIGITAL TEXT 2 **Construction Proves Challenging**	Objective 1	10 min.	●	●
INTERACTIVE GALLERY **The Panama Canal**	Objective 1	10 min.	●	
DIGITAL TEXT 3 **Intervention in Latin America**	Objective 2	10 min.	●	●
INTERACTIVE CARTOON **Roosevelt's Big Stick Diplomacy**	Objective 2	10 min.	●	
DIGITAL TEXT 4 **U.S. Involvement in Mexico**	Objective 3	10 min.	●	●
Synthesize				
DIGITAL ACTIVITY **Revising Your Ideas**		5 min.	●	
Demonstrate				
DIGITAL QUIZ **Lesson Quiz and Discussion Board**		10 min.	●	

U.S. Power in Latin America

CONNECT

DIGITAL START UP ACTIVITY

U.S. Interest in Latin America

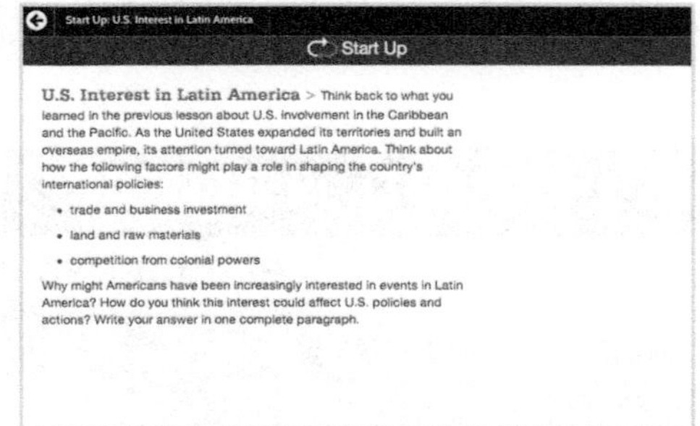

Start Up: U.S. Interest in Latin America
Start Up
U.S. Interest in Latin America > Think back to what you learned in the previous lesson about U.S. involvement in the Caribbean and the Pacific. As the United States expanded its territories and built an overseas empire, its attention turned toward Latin America. Think about how the following factors might play a role in shaping the country's international policies:
• trade and business investment
• land and raw materials
• competition from colonial powers
Why might Americans have been increasingly interested in events in Latin America? How do you think this interest could affect U.S. policies and actions? Write your answer in one complete paragraph.

Project the Start Up Activity Ask students to answer the questions as they enter and get settled. Then ask them to share and discuss their ideas with partners.

Discuss Why might Americans have been increasingly interested in events in Latin America? *(Possible response: Americans might have been concerned about encroaching colonial powers.)* How do you think this interest could affect U.S. policy in the region? *(Possible response: The United States might adopt policies that encourage trade with Latin America or try to colonize parts of the area.)*

Tell students that in this lesson they will be learning about U.S. dealings with Latin America, including the construction of the Panama Canal.

Aa Vocabulary Development: Use the Interactive Reading Notepad to preview the Key Terms and Academic Vocabulary in this lesson with students.

FLIP IT!

Assign the Flipped Video for this lesson.

STUDENT EDITION PRINT PAGES: 657–663

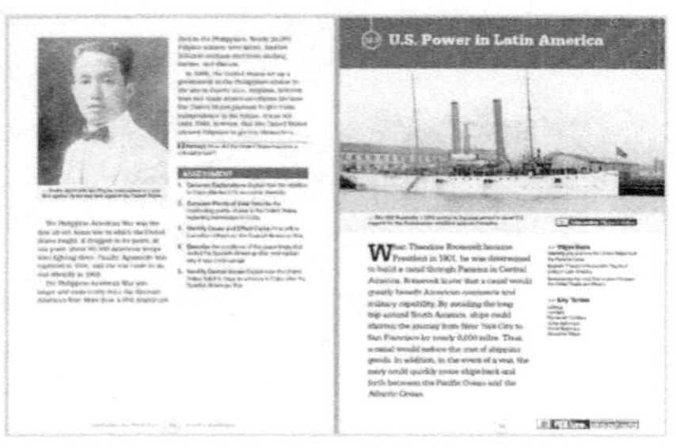

INVESTIGATE

DIGITAL TEXT 1

The Panama Canal

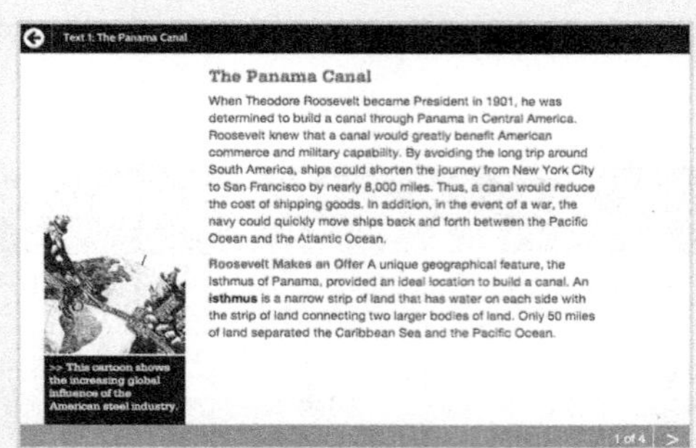

DIGITAL TEXT 2

Construction Proves Challenging

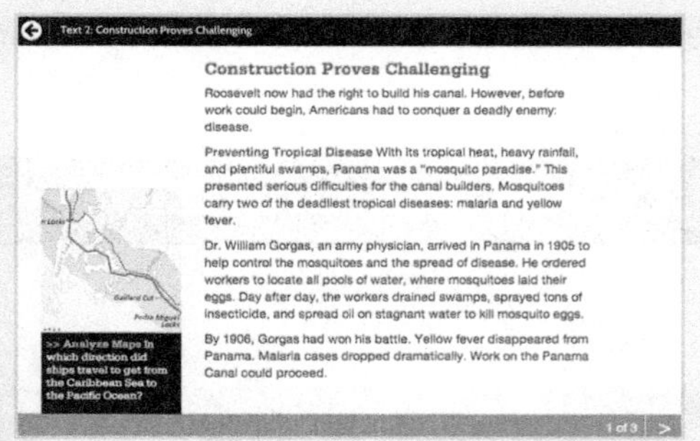

Objective 1: **Identify why and how the United States built the Panama Canal.**

Quick Instruction

Interactive Gallery: The Panama Canal Navigate through the gallery with the class, discussing the difficulties faced in building the canal. Ask: Who was mostly responsible for building the canal? *(people from the West Indies)* Which part of building the canal do you think was the most challenging? Why? *(Possible response: moving so much earth or breaking through the mountains)*

Analyze Maps Display the map of the Panama Canal. Ask: Why was Panama the best place to connect the Caribbean Sea with the Pacific Ocean? *(It was the thinnest stretch of land between the two bodies of water, where it would take the least amount of effort to dig the canal.)* Explain that the United States saw the economic possibilities of a canal, but Colombia was not willing to allow the canal to be built or to lease the land. In response to the Colombian refusal, the U.S. government encouraged a Panamanian rebellion against Colombian rule. The United States was then able to lease the land from the newly-independent nation of Panama and build the canal.

ACTIVE CLASSROOM

Have students use the Conversation with History strategy to investigate the Interactive Gallery. Tell students to imagine they are having a conversation with one of the people pictured in the gallery. Have students write down a question they would like to ask, what they think the person from the photo would say, and then a possible response to the question. Invite volunteers to share their conversations with the class.

ELL Use the ELL activity described in the ELL chart.

Further Instruction

Support a Point of View with Evidence Do you think the way President Roosevelt handled obtaining the land for the Panama Canal was justified? *(Possible responses: No, he did not respect Colombia's decision and had the Colombian government overthrown to get his way. He rallied and supported the Panamanians in their rebellion. Yes, he understood the canal's economic benefits and did what needed to be done to ensure it was built. He was also justified because he was helping the Panamanians.)*

INTERACTIVE GALLERY

The Panama Canal

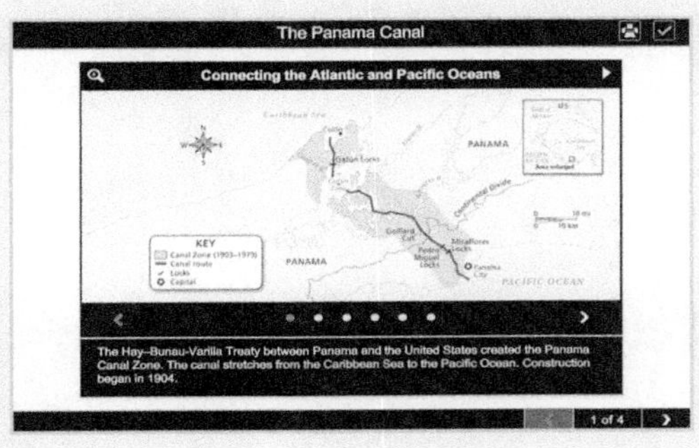

The Panama Canal
Connecting the Atlantic and Pacific Oceans
The Hay-Bunau-Varilla Treaty between Panama and the United States created the Panama Canal Zone. The canal stretches from the Caribbean Sea to the Pacific Ocean. Construction began in 1904.
1 of 4

Identify Cause and Effect What impact did the building of the Panama Canal have on commerce? *(As a result of the canal, American merchants could cheaply ship goods to Asia and South America from the east coast. Also, South Americans received the benefit of access to less expensive imports.)*

DIGITAL TEXT 3

Intervention in Latin America

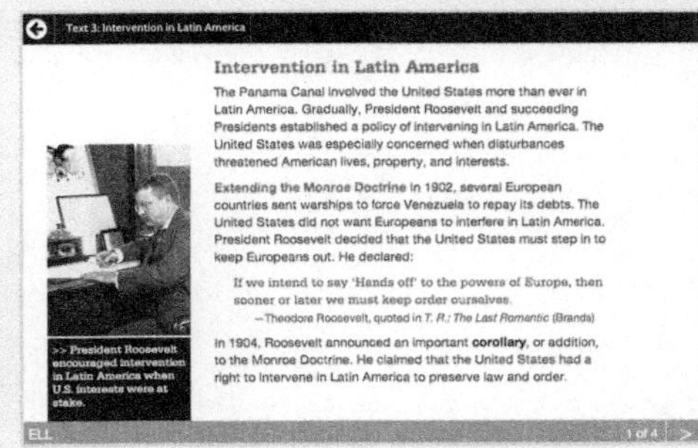

Text 3: Intervention in Latin America
Intervention in Latin America
The Panama Canal involved the United States more than ever in Latin America. Gradually, President Roosevelt and succeeding Presidents established a policy of intervening in Latin America. The United States was especially concerned when disturbances threatened American lives, property, and interests.
Extending the Monroe Doctrine in 1902, several European countries sent warships to force Venezuela to repay its debts. The United States did not want Europeans to interfere in Latin America. President Roosevelt decided that the United States must step in to keep Europeans out. He declared:
If we intend to say 'Hands off' to the powers of Europe, then sooner or later we must keep order ourselves.
—Theodore Roosevelt, quoted in T. R.: The Last Romantic (Brands)
In 1904, Roosevelt announced an important corollary, or addition, to the Monroe Doctrine. He claimed that the United States had a right to intervene in Latin America to preserve law and order.
>> President Roosevelt encouraged intervention in Latin America when U.S. interests were at stake.
ELL
1 of 4

Objective 2: **Explain Theodore Roosevelt's "big stick" policy in Latin America.**

Quick Instruction

Display the proverb, "Speak softly and carry a big stick, and you will go far." Invite a volunteer to explain what the proverb means. Tell students that President Roosevelt was known to quote this proverb and ran the government accordingly. He felt it was appropriate to use force to control Latin American countries and other less powerful nations.

Interactive Cartoon: Roosevelt's Big Stick Diplomacy Project the Interactive Cartoon. Discuss the cartoon with students and guide them through the questions. Ask students to list the issues criticized in this cartoon. *(Possible responses: The cartoon criticizes Roosevelt's use of force, his use of the American military to collect debts, and his disregard for the Caribbean nations' autonomy.)*

INTERACTIVE CARTOON

Roosevelt's Big Stick Diplomacy

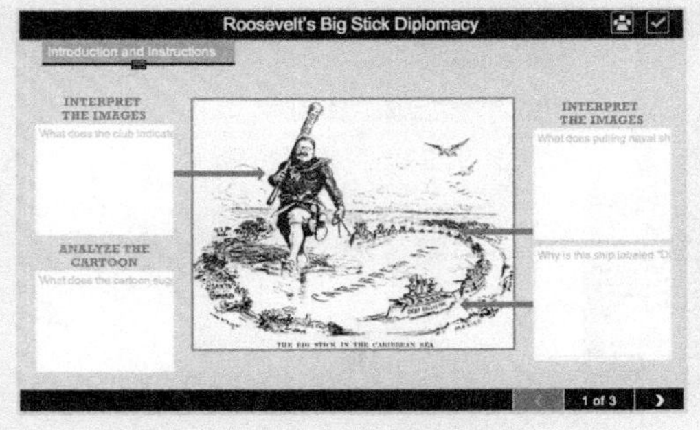

ACTIVE CLASSROOM

Use the A Closer Look strategy to further investigate Roosevelt's big stick diplomacy. Project the Interactive Cartoon and use a whiteboard tool to divide it into four numbered quadrants. Have students count off 1 to 4. Then have them look closely at the part of the image in their quadrant. Have them tell you what they see and what they learned as a result of their focus on this part of the image. Collect insights for each quadrant.

ELL Use the ELL activity described in the ELL chart.

Further Instruction

Assign *Biography: Theodore Roosevelt* to extend the lesson.

Compare and Contrast How did the policies of Roosevelt, Taft, and Wilson differ in their approach to Latin America? What similarities did they share? *(Roosevelt, Taft, and Wilson all took an active role in Latin American politics. Roosevelt focused on using force, while Taft encouraged investment. Wilson wanted to spread democracy and peace, but he took more military action than either of the other two presidents.)*

U.S. Power in Latin America

DIGITAL TEXT 4

U.S. Involvement in Mexico

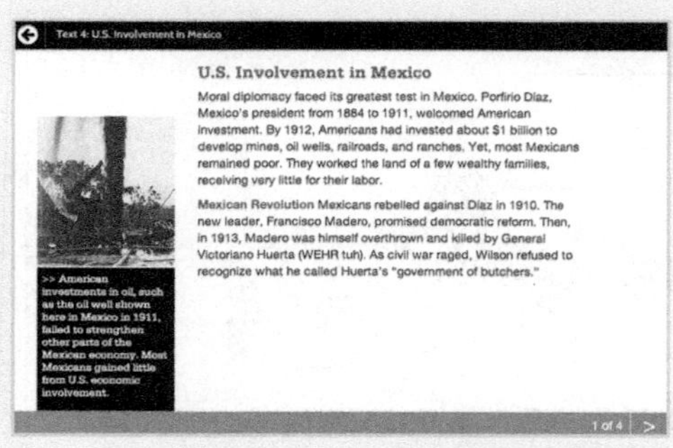

Text 4: U.S. Involvement in Mexico
U.S. Involvement in Mexico
Moral diplomacy faced its greatest test in Mexico. Porfirio Díaz, Mexico's president from 1884 to 1911, welcomed American investment. By 1912, Americans had invested about $1 billion to develop mines, oil wells, railroads, and ranches. Yet, most Mexicans remained poor. They worked the land of a few wealthy families, receiving very little for their labor.
Mexican Revolution Mexicans rebelled against Díaz in 1910. The new leader, Francisco Madero, promised democratic reform. Then, in 1913, Madero was himself overthrown and killed by General Victoriano Huerta (WEHR tuh). As civil war raged, Wilson refused to recognize what he called Huerta's "government of butchers."
>> American investments in oil, such as the oil well shown here in Mexico in 1911, failed to strengthen other parts of the Mexican economy. Most Mexicans gained little from U.S. economic involvement.
1 of 4

Objective 3: **Summarize the crisis that erupted between the United States and Mexico.**

Quick Instruction

Display the photograph of the U.S. occupation of Veracruz, 1914. Remind students that President Wilson embraced a policy of moral diplomacy with the goals of condemning imperialism, spreading democracy, and promoting peace. Explain that when a dictator overthrew the standing Mexican government, Wilson refused to acknowledge the dictator's government. Only when the situation threatened American interests did Wilson respond.

Generate Explanations How might some perceive President Wilson's early response to the crisis in Mexico as a contradiction of his goals to condemn imperialism? *(When a dictator overthrew the standing Mexican government, Wilson refused to acknowledge the dictator. However, it was only when the dictator threatened Americans that Wilson responded with military force.)*

Hypothesize Even though the Mexican government quickly apologized and released the American sailors Huerta's troops had arrested, why did President Wilson still order U.S. troops into Mexico? *(Wilson felt that the instability in Mexico was threatening American interests, leaving him little choice but to respond with military force.)*

D Differentiate: Extra Support To help students better understand the crisis that erupted between the United States and Mexico, focus their attention on these key points: The United States had strong financial ties to Mexico. The dictator Huerta threatened the financial ties and ruled with brutality. President Wilson wanted to oust Huerta to uphold moral democracy and protect the U.S. economy. The Mexican revolutionary Pancho Villa entered the United States and killed people, which incited the U.S. military to cross the border in pursuit when he returned to his country. This "invasion" strained relations between the countries further.

Further Instruction

Sequence Events Have students sequence the Mexican leaders during the civil war there. *(Porfirio Díaz, Francisco Madero, General Victoriano Huerta, Venustiano Carranza)* Point out that the changes of power—four leaders in three years—created serious instability in Mexico.

Predict Consequences How will the United States' new way of approaching global conflict affect its role in World War I? *(Possible response: As a result of setting itself up as a global police force, the U.S. military will likely become one of the key forces in World War I.)*

PEARSON realize™ www.PearsonRealize.com Access your Digital Lesson

SYNTHESIZE

DIGITAL ACTIVITY

Revising Your Ideas

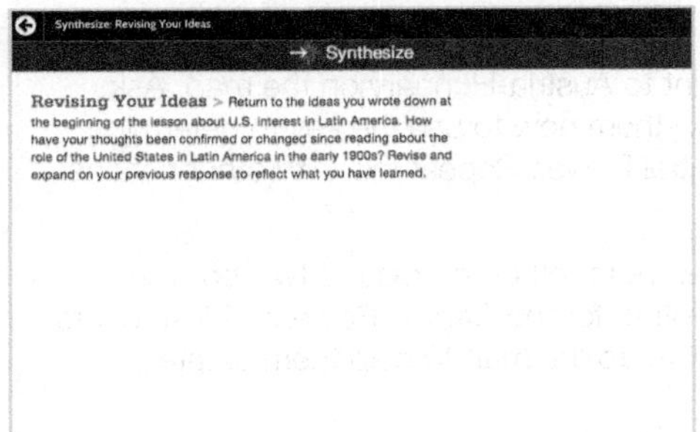

Synthesize: Revising Your Ideas
Synthesize
Revising Your Ideas > Return to the ideas you wrote down at the beginning of the lesson about U.S. interest in Latin America. How have your thoughts been confirmed or changed since reading about the role of the United States in Latin America in the early 1900s? Revise and expand on your previous response to reflect what you have learned.

Allow students time to review their original responses and compare those ideas to what they have learned in the lesson. When students finish revisions, suggest they share their new paragraphs with partners.

Discuss How does the U.S. involvement in Latin America compare to that of the U.S. in the Pacific and Caribbean?

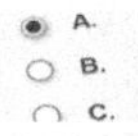

DEMONSTRATE

DIGITAL QUIZ

Lesson Quiz and Discussion Board

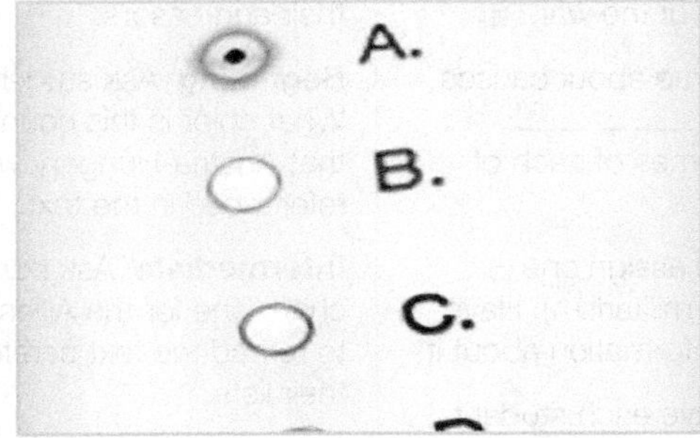

Assign the online Lesson Quiz for this lesson if you haven't already done so. Students will be offered automatic remediation or enrichment based on their score.

In *U.S. Power in Latin America*, students learned the history of the Panama Canal. They were introduced to President Roosevelt's big stick diplomacy, Taft's dollar diplomacy, and Wilson's moral diplomacy. They also learned about the civil war in Mexico that led to tensions between that country and the United States.

Post these questions to the class on the Discussion Board:

Compare and Contrast Consider the foreign policies of Roosevelt, Taft, and Wilson. Compare and contrast the concepts behind the Roosevelt Corollary, dollar diplomacy, and moral diplomacy.

Summarize Summarize the key events that led to the Panama Canal's construction.

Topic Inquiry

Have students continue their investigations for the Topic Inquiry.

A European War

Supporting English Language Learners

Use with the reading, **The Buildup to War.**

Speaking

Read aloud *The Buildup to the War* while students follow along in their book. Read slowly and clearly, and pause to answer any questions. Ask students to listen carefully for information about causes of the war.

Beginning Ask students to complete the sentence frame about causes of the war: The three causes of the war in Europe were ____, ____, and ____. Then have partners take turns saying the names of each of the causes.

Intermediate Divide students into groups of three and assign one cause of the war to each (nationalism, imperialism, and militarism). Have students take turns naming their cause and providing information about it.

Advanced Divide students into groups of three and have each student choose one cause of the war. Have students take turns providing other group members with information about their cause. Then ask students to give information about the allied powers.

Advanced High In groups of three, have students choose one cause of the war and provide the other group members with information about it. Ask them to talk about the alliance system and which countries were allied with each other. Encourage them to talk about the new dangers posed by the alliance system.

Use with the reading, **The Crisis Begins.**

Reading

Read aloud the section titled *Alliances Declare War*. Ask students to study the map carefully as you read about the allied nations and their aggressors.

Beginning Ask students to point to Austria-Hungary on the map. Ask, What color is this country? Show them how to use the key to determine that Austria-Hungary was a Central Power. Repeat this with other nations referenced in the text.

Intermediate Ask partners to work together to create a two-column chart: one for the Allies and the other for the Central Powers. Tell students to reread the text carefully and refer to the map to help them create their lists.

Advanced Ask partners to reread the text for information about the Allies and the Central Powers. Tell them to write the names of the countries in each group. Then have them use the map to check their answers. Encourage them to add other countries to their lists.

Advanced High Ask students to reread the text silently and write two lists: Allies and Central Powers. Encourage students to use the map to help them identify the neutral nations. Ask them to create a third list with the neutral nations.

D Differentiate Instruction

Use the Differentiated Instruction notes throughout the lesson plan to support the varied skill sets, levels of readiness, and interests in the mixed-ability classroom.

Challenge These notes include suggestions for expanding the activity for advanced students.

On-Level These notes include suggestions for modifying the activity to address different interests or learning styles.

Extra Support These notes include ideas for providing more scaffolding or reading spupport.

Special Needs These notes provide ideas for adapting instruction to support the needs of various special needs students.

NOTES

PEARSON realize™ www.PearsonRealize.com

Go online to access additional resources including: Primary Sources • Biographies • Supreme Court cases • 21st Century Skill Tutorials • Maps • Graphic Organizers.

Objectives

Objective 1: Identify the causes of World War I.

Objective 2: Describe how war was fought in the trenches.

Objective 3: Explain how Germany's use of submarine warfare affected American neutrality.

LESSON 4 ORGANIZER	PACING: APPROX. 1 PERIOD, .5 BLOCKS			
			RESOURCES	
	OBJECTIVES	PACING	Online	Print
Connect				
DIGITAL START UP ACTIVITY **Nationalism and Militarism**		5 min.	●	
Investigate				
DIGITAL TEXT 1 **The Buildup to War**	Objective 1	10 min.	●	●
DIGITAL TEXT 2 **The Crisis Begins**	Objective 1	10 min.	●	●
INTERACTIVE CHART **Chain of Events, 1914**	Objective 1	10 min.	●	
DIGITAL TEXT 3 **Trench Warfare Leads to Stalemate**	Objective 2	10 min.	●	●
3-D MODEL **Trench Warfare**	Objective 2	10 min.	●	
DIGITAL TEXT 4 **The United States Tries to Stay Neutral**	Objective 3	10 min.	●	●
INTERACTIVE GALLERY **World War I Technology**	Objective 3	10 min.	●	
Synthesize				
DIGITAL ACTIVITY **Causes of World War I**		5 min.	●	
Demonstrate				
DIGITAL QUIZ **Lesson Quiz and Discussion Board**		10 min.	●	

A European War

CONNECT

DIGITAL START UP ACTIVITY

Nationalism and Militarism

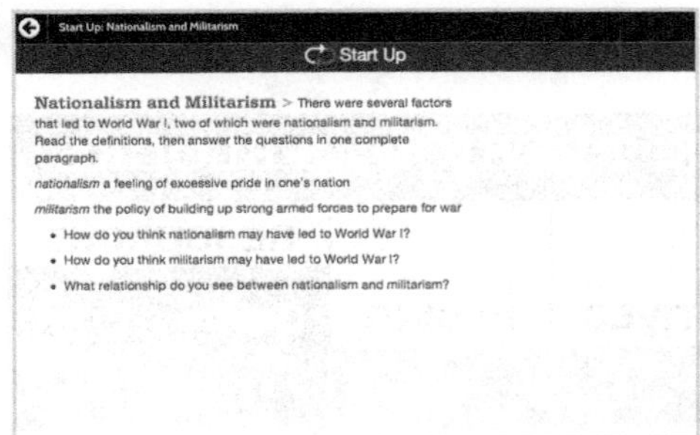

Project the Start Up Activity Have students answer the questions as they enter the classroom. Then ask them to discuss their answers.

Discuss How do you think nationalism may have led to World War I? *(Possible response: Excessive pride in one's nation might lead to a bid to spread its influence over "inferior" nations.)* How do you think militarism may have led to World War I? *(Possible response: Armies and weapons made it easy for war to begin.)* What relationship do you see between nationalism and militarism? *(Possible response: If a nationalistic government had an army, it could annex other countries.)*

Tell students that this lesson examines the causes and early course of World War I.

Aa Vocabulary Development: Use the Interactive Reading Notepad to preview the Key Terms and Academic Vocabulary in this lesson with students.

FLIP IT!

Assign the Flipped Video for this lesson.

STUDENT EDITION PRINT PAGES: 664–671

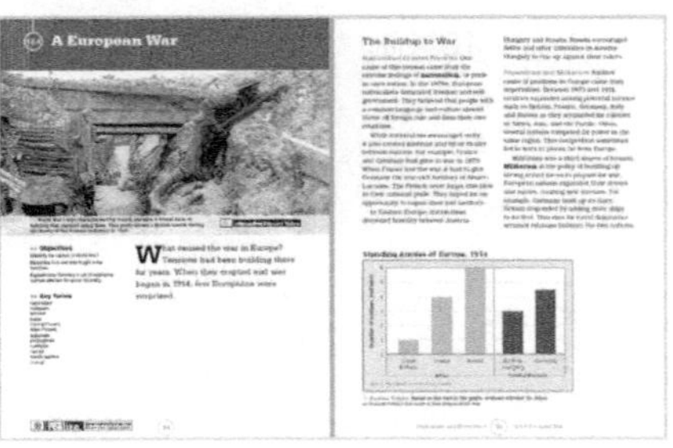

INVESTIGATE

DIGITAL TEXT 1

The Buildup to War

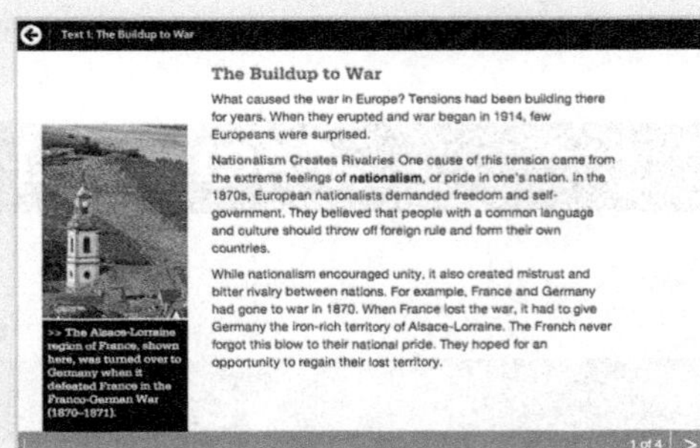

Objective 1: Identify the causes of World War I.

Quick Instruction

Display the timeline showing the events that led up to World War I. To clarify relationships, draw a two-column chart of the Triple Alliance (Germany, Austria-Hungary, Italy) and the Triple Entente (France, Britain, Russia). Make sure students understand that a conflict between any one of these alliances could spark a major war because the countries had pledged to protect each other.

Interactive Chart: Chain of Events, 1914 Display the Interactive Chart. Remind students of the impact of nationalism and militarism on Europe as you discuss the formation of alliances. Guide students through the process of completing the chart. Prompt students to consider which event in the flowchart represented the point from which there was no turning back in the march to war. Ensure students defend the rationale behind their choice.

DIGITAL TEXT 2

The Crisis Begins

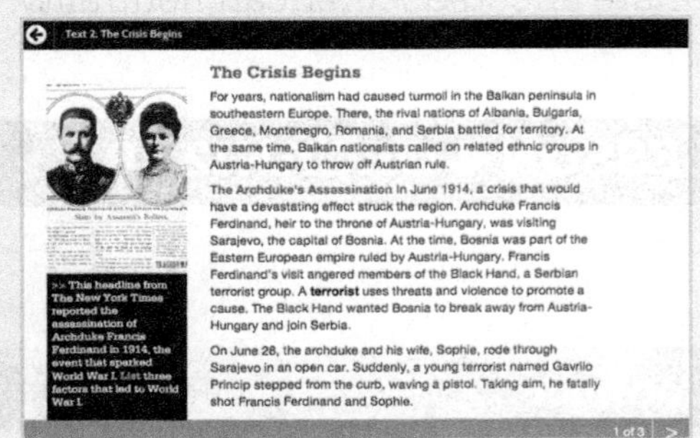

ACTIVE CLASSROOM

Use the Wallpaper strategy to further investigate the chain of events that led to war. Group students together to design a piece of "wallpaper" that depicts the conflicts and connections among countries. Post students' wallpaper and conduct a gallery walk. Encourage students to note the similarities and differences between depictions.

D Differentiate: Extra Support Explain the buildup to World War I with a simple cause and effect chart that summarizes the causes (nationalism, imperialism, militarism, and alliances) of World War I.

ELL Use the ELL activity described in the ELL chart.

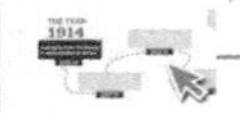

INTERACTIVE CHART

Chain of Events, 1914

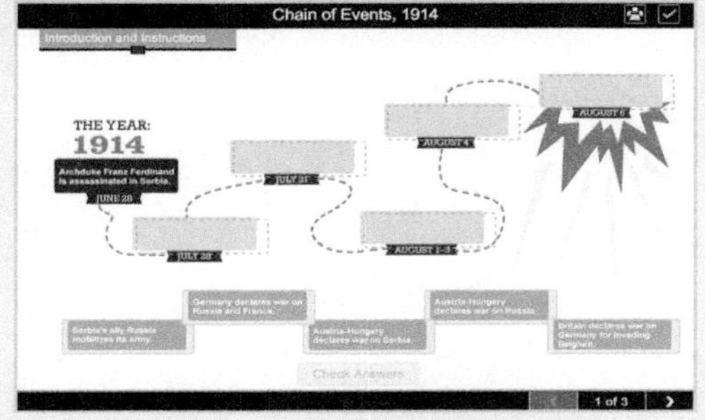

DIGITAL TEXT 3

Trench Warfare Leads to Stalemate

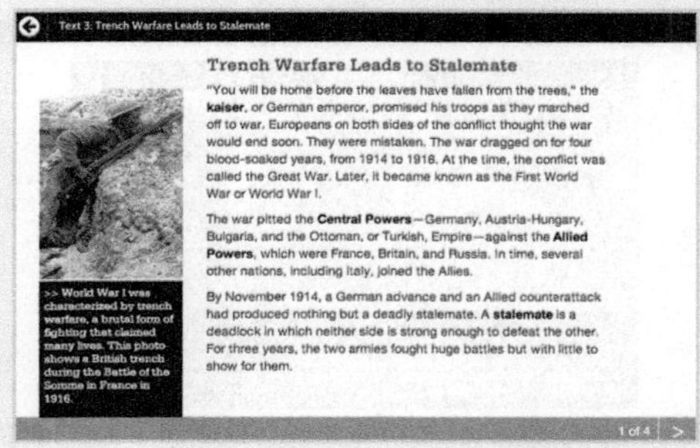

3-D MODEL

Trench Warfare

Further Instruction

Infer Why did Austria-Hungary accuse the Serbian government of organizing Archduke Ferdinand's assassination? *(Austria-Hungary knew that Serbia wanted more control over territory in the Balkans, and they assumed Ferdinand's assassination might prompt a Serbian takeover of Bosnia.)* How did this event ignite war? *(With accusations came threats of war, which led Russia to support Serbia and Germany to support Austria-Hungary. Other allies then fell in with their respective alliances.)*

Objective 2: **Describe how war was fought in the trenches.**

Quick Instruction

3-D Model: Trench Warfare Project the 3-D Model and navigate around the image. Discuss the planning that went into establishing the trenches and the experience of the soldiers living and fighting in these trenches.

Draw Conclusions What were the benefits of fighting from trenches? *(The trenches provided a barrier that served as protection from enemy fire and attack, allowing the soldiers to defend the line effectively.)* What were the drawbacks of trench warfare? *(Because both sides used trenches for protection, any advances were difficult, which resulted in stalemates for long periods of time. Conditions in the trenches were often miserable from mud, rats, and tight spaces.)*

ACTIVE CLASSROOM

Use the See-Think-Wonder strategy to further investigate the 3-D Model. Pair students and ask: What do you see? What does that make you think? What are you wondering about now that you have seen this? Allow partners time to discuss their responses. Reconvene as a class and have pairs share any thoughts that have gone unanswered. Discuss possible answers as a class.

Further Instruction

Predict Consequences How do you predict the use of trench warfare will affect the outcome of World War I? *(It will likely make it a long, drawn out war that ends with little territorial gains or losses.)*

A European War

DIGITAL TEXT 4

The United States Tries to Stay Neutral

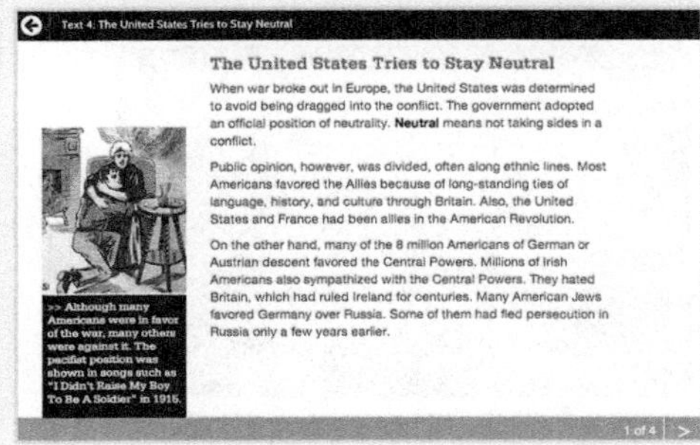
Text 4: The United States Tries to Stay Neutral

The United States Tries to Stay Neutral

When war broke out in Europe, the United States was determined to avoid being dragged into the conflict. The government adopted an official position of neutrality. **Neutral** means not taking sides in a conflict.

Public opinion, however, was divided, often along ethnic lines. Most Americans favored the Allies because of long-standing ties of language, history, and culture through Britain. Also, the United States and France had been allies in the American Revolution.

On the other hand, many of the 8 million Americans of German or Austrian descent favored the Central Powers. Millions of Irish Americans also sympathized with the Central Powers. They hated Britain, which had ruled Ireland for centuries. Many American Jews favored Germany over Russia. Some of them had fled persecution in Russia only a few years earlier.

>> Although many Americans were in favor of the war, many others were against it. The pacifist position was shown in songs such as "I Didn't Raise My Boy To Be A Soldier" in 1915.

1 of 4

INTERACTIVE GALLERY

World War I Technology

Objective 3: **Explain how Germany's use of submarine warfare affected American neutrality.**

Quick Instruction

Interactive Gallery: World War I Technology Project the Interactive Gallery and navigate through the photographs of World War I technology. Prompt students to understand that these technological innovations, such as the U-boat and the airplane, changed the nature of warfare.

Identify Central Issues Why were German U-boat attacks considered unacceptable by the United States? *(First, they violated international law, which stated that the countries had the right to search neutral and passenger ships but not to bomb them. Second, the attacks cost thousands of lives of innocent people.)*

ACTIVE CLASSROOM

Use the Rank It strategy to further investigate the technology of World War I. Have students review the list of new technologies available during World War I and rank them in order of their impact. Instruct students to be prepared to provide justification for their rankings. Then, group students and have them compare rankings and justifications. End with a poll of the class to see if there is agreement.

Further Instruction

Express Ideas Clearly How was the United States able to stay out of World War I after the German U-boat bombing of the *Lusitania*, which took the lives of 128 American citizens? *(Germany agreed to restrict U-boat bombings in an effort to appease the United States because Germany understood that angering the United States would draw them into the war and strengthen Allied power.)*

Support Ideas with Evidence What evidence from the text supports the idea that the United States was not entirely neutral in the early years of the war? *(Trade with the Allies increased significantly as American manufacturers and farmers increased production to support Allied needs early in the war.)*

SYNTHESIZE

DIGITAL ACTIVITY

Causes of World War I

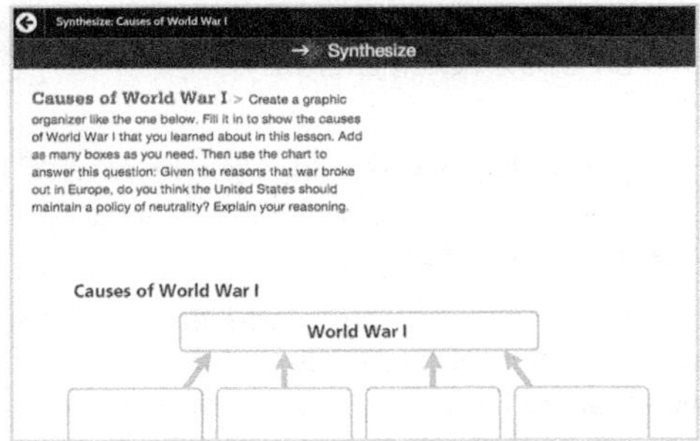

Have students complete the graphic organizers and discuss whether the causes of World War I involved the United States in any way. Then, allow them time to write their paragraphs.

Discuss Lead a class discussion in which students share their opinions about American neutrality. To spur discussion, ask: Would you consider the United States a member of the Allies before the country officially joined the war? Why or why not?

DEMONSTRATE

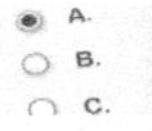

DIGITAL QUIZ

Lesson Quiz and Discussion Board

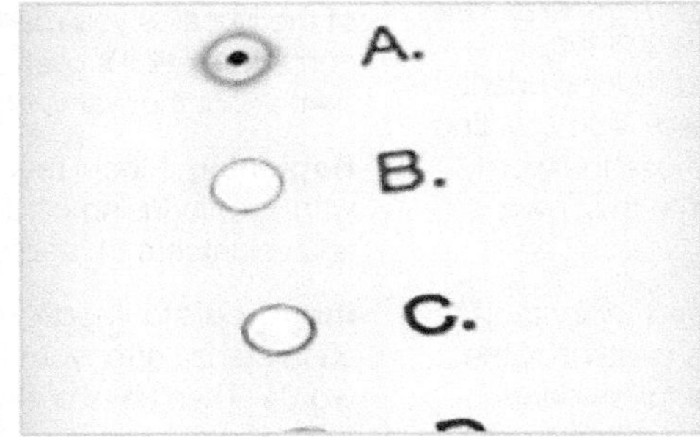

Assign the online Lesson Quiz for this lesson if you haven't already done so. Students will be offered automatic remediation or enrichment based on their score.

In *A European War*, students learned about the nationalism, imperialism, militarism, and alliances that caused World War I. They also learned about the assassination of Francis Ferdinand that started the war. They were introduced to the difficulties and outcomes of trench warfare, and they investigated the American reaction to German U-boats bombing neutral and civilian ships.

Post these questions to the class on the Discussion Board:

Express Problems Clearly Explain the problematic nature of the alliances that formed before World War I began.

Determine Relevance How did an assassination in Austria-Hungary begin a war that spread across Europe?

Topic Inquiry

Have students continue their investigations for the Topic Inquiry.

Entering the War

Supporting English Language Learners

Use with the reading, **The U.S. Moves Toward War.**

Writing

Prompt students to write using content-based grade-level vocabulary.

Beginning Read the first paragraph of the section titled *Diplomacy Ends* and explain the definition of *blockade* based on the content of the paragraph. Draw a picture of a blockaded port on the board for students to better understand the context in which the word is used. Model writing simple sentences on the board for students in which you use the word *blockade*, then have students work in small groups to write their own sentences based on the models.

Intermediate Read the first paragraph of the section titled *Diplomacy Ends* and explain the definition of *blockade* based on the content of the paragraph. Model writing simple sentences on the board for students in which you use the word *blockade*, then have students work in small groups to write their own sentences based on the models. Ask volunteers to share their sentences with the class.

Advanced Read the first paragraph of the section titled *Diplomacy Ends* and explain the definition of *diplomacy* based on the content of the paragraph. Model writing simple sentences on the board for students in which you use the word *diplomacy*, then have students individually write their own sentences based on the models. Ask volunteers to share their sentences with the class.

Advanced High Read the third paragraph of the reading *The U.S. Moves Toward War* and explain the definition of *warmonger* based on the content of the paragraph. Ask students to write individually write their own sentences in which they use the word *warmonger*. Ask volunteers to share their sentences with the class.

Use with the reading, **Preparing for War.**

Listening

Read aloud the lyrics to the song *Over There* written by George M. Cohan in 1917. Explain that “over there” refers to Europe. Emphasize the rhythm of the lyrics as you read them. Point out that the last words “we won’t come back till it’s over over there” means “the Americans will not return home until the war is over in Europe.”

Beginning Model reading the lyrics line by line. Have students echo read with you, focusing on the rhythm and intonation of the words. Choose a few volunteers to read a stanza using the correct intonation.

Intermediate Model reading the lyrics line by line. Have students repeat each stanza after you, focusing on the rhythm and intonation of the words. Then have partners practice reading the first verse, focusing on the rhythm and intonation of the words.

Advanced Ask partners to practice reading the lyrics, focusing on the rhythm and intonation of the words. Partners should correct each other as needed. Then ask a few students to read the lyrics to the class.

Advanced High Ask more proficient students to model the rhythm and intonation of the words for beginners. Then ask them to read the lyrics chorally with the beginners.

D Differentiate Instruction

Use the Differentiated Instruction notes throughout the lesson plan to support the varied skill sets, levels of readiness, and interests in the mixed-ability classroom.

Challenge These notes include suggestions for expanding the activity for advanced students.

On-Level These notes include suggestions for modifying the activity to address different interests or learning styles.

Extra Support These notes include ideas for providing more scaffolding or reading spuport.

Special Needs These notes provide ideas for adapting instruction to support the needs of various special needs students.

NOTES

Objectives

Objective 1: Summarize how President Wilson tried to bring about peace.

Objective 2: Explain why the United States chose to declare war.

Objective 3: Describe how the government prepared for and managed the war effort.

Objective 4: Identify the impact of the war on the home front.

LESSON 5 ORGANIZER	PACING: APPROX. 1 PERIOD, .5 BLOCKS		RESOURCES	
	OBJECTIVES	PACING	Online	Print
Connect				
DIGITAL START UP ACTIVITY **Arguments for War**		5 min.	●	
Investigate				
DIGITAL TEXT 1 **The U.S. Moves Toward War**	Objectives 1, 2	10 min.	●	●
INTERACTIVE TIMELINE **Buildup to War**	Objectives 1, 2	10 min.	●	
DIGITAL TEXT 2 **Preparing for War**	Objective 3	10 min.	●	●
DIGITAL TEXT 3 **Overseeing the War Effort**	Objective 3	10 min.	●	●
DIGITAL TEXT 4 **Americans on the Home Front**	Objective 4	10 min.	●	●
INTERACTIVE GALLERY **World War I Home Front**	Objective 4	10 min.	●	
Synthesize				
DIGITAL ACTIVITY **Effects of World War I**		5 min.	●	
Demonstrate				
LESSON QUIZ **Lesson Quiz and Class Discussion Board**		10 min.	●	

Entering the War

CONNECT

DIGITAL START UP ACTIVITY
Arguments for War

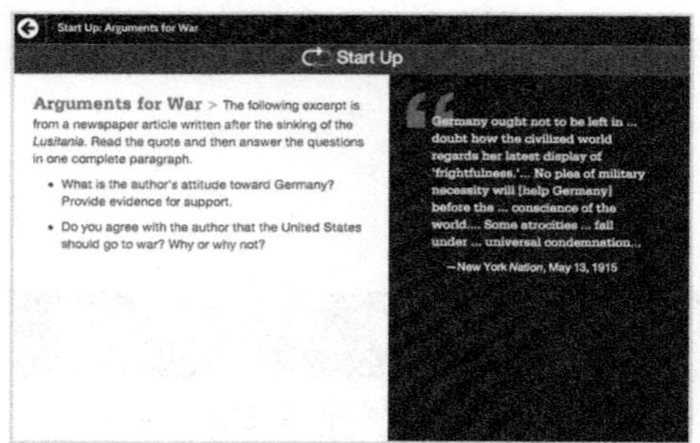

Project the Start Up Activity Ask students to read the quote and answer the questions as they enter and get settled. Have students share their paragraphs with a partner.

Discuss What is the author's attitude toward Germany? Do you agree with the author that the United State should go to war? Why or why not? *(The author has a negative attitude toward Germany, as shown by the use of the words "atrocities" and "condemnation" to describe their actions. Possible responses: Yes, I agree with the author. Or: No, diplomacy should be given more time.)*

Tell students that in this lesson they will be learning about America's involvement in World War I.

Aa Vocabulary Development: Use the Interactive Reading Notepad to preview the Key Terms and Academic Vocabulary in this lesson with students.

FLIP IT!
Assign the Flipped Video for this lesson.

STUDENT EDITION PRINT PAGES: 672–680

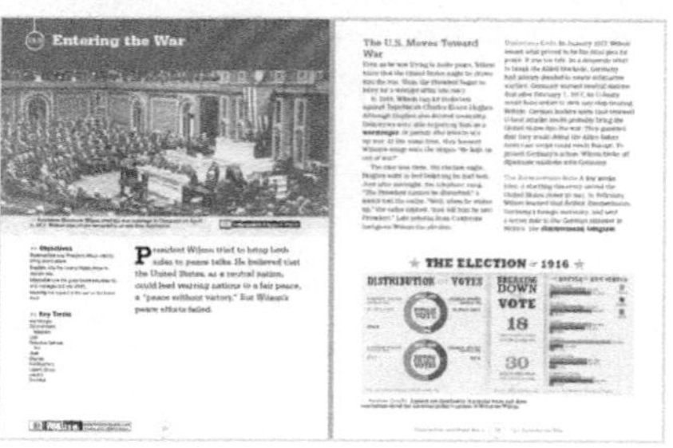

INVESTIGATE

DIGITAL TEXT 1
The U.S. Moves Toward War

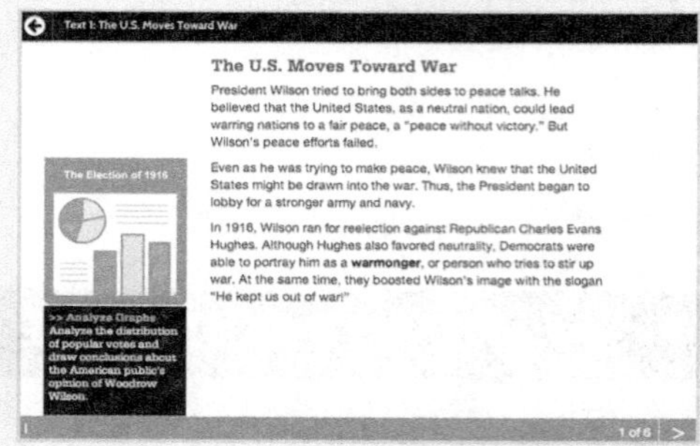

INTERACTIVE TIMELINE
Buildup to War, 1918

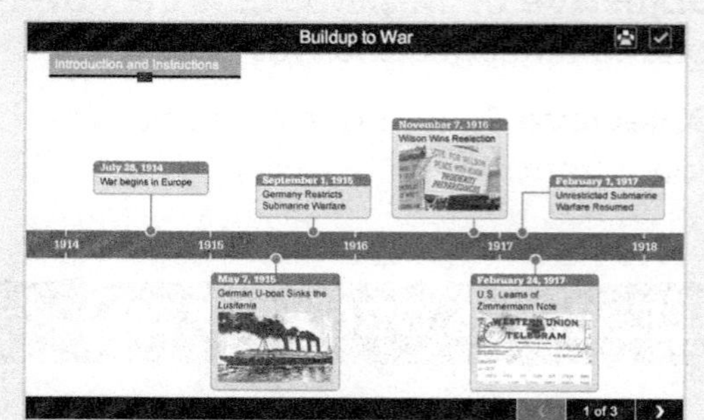

Objectives 1: **Summarize how President Wilson tried to bring about peace; 2: Explain why the United States chose to declare war.**

Quick Instruction

Interactive Timeline: Buildup to War, 1918 Project the interactive timeline and click through the images. Have students identify the key events leading up to the American declaration of war. Prompt students to identify patterns in the timeline that help explain why the United States was drawn into the war, such as the escalation of German hostilities and unrestricted submarine warfare.

Make Predictions Based on the timeline, why do you think President Wilson will be unable to bring about peace? *(German aggression will make it impossible for the United States to remain neutral. The United States will have to respond to submarine attacks. The Zimmerman note will also make the public want to go to war.)*

ACTIVE CLASSROOM

Have students break into groups and use the Circle Write strategy to answer the question, Why did the United States enter World War I? Have students write as much as they can for 1 minute, then switch with the person on their right. Have the next person improve or elaborate the response. Tell students to continue to switch until the paper comes back to the first person. Have the group decide which is the best response and share it with the class.

Further Instruction

Identify Cause and Effect How did the Russian Revolution affect Wilson's decision to ask for a declaration of war? *(The Russian Revolution seemed to indicate a shift towards democracy. Wilson now felt he could ally with Russia against Germany without appearing to support an absolute ruler.)*

Evaluate Arguments When Wilson asked for a declaration of war, he said, "The world must be made safe for democracy." How did the idea of protecting democracy influence his decision to go to war? *(Wilson decided to ask Congress for a declaration of war to protect democratic nations from German aggression and to prevent Germany from spreading its rule. He also looked to support new democratic reforms in Russia by keeping Russia from falling to Germany.)*

www.PearsonRealize.com
Access your Digital Lesson

DIGITAL TEXT 2

Preparing for War

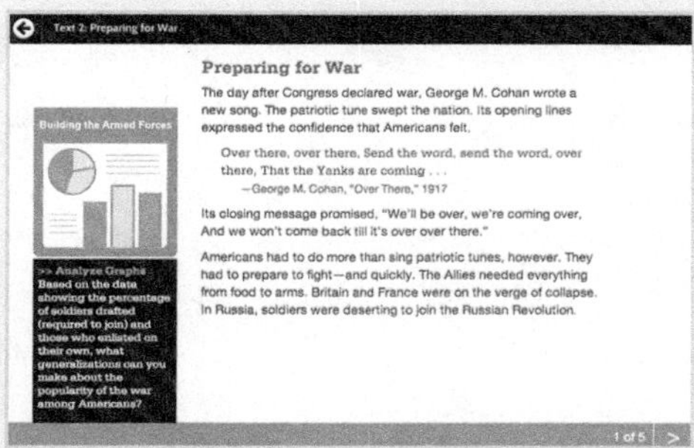

Objective 3: **Describe how the government prepared for and managed the war effort.**

Quick Instruction

Project the image of the recruitment poster. Prompt students to discuss why many Americans were eager to fight in the war. Ask how posters such as this one helped support U.S. entry into the war.

Hypothesize What is a draft and how do you think it impacted military service? *(A draft is a law that requires people of a certain age to enlist in the military. Men ages 21 to 30 had to register for the military draft. This requirement served to increase the number of men available to serve in the armed forces, allowing the U.S. military to expand.)*

ELL Use the ELL activity described in the ELL chart.

Further Instruction

Identify Central Issues Why did the United States require new government agencies when it entered the war? *(The United States needed to reorganize its economy. It had to produce food to feed its armies and supply the arms and other goods needed to fight. New government agencies oversaw these changes. The Food Administration increased production and sent food to the Allies. The War Industries Board oversaw factories to determine production, share resources, and set prices.)*

DIGITAL TEXT 3

Overseeing the War Effort

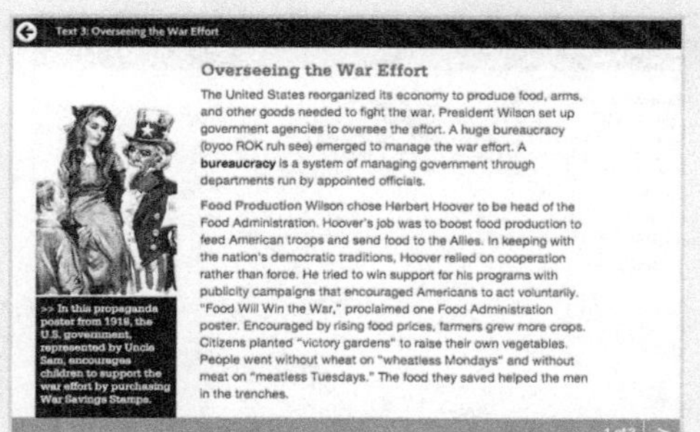

Support Ideas with Evidence What evidence in the text supports the claim that World War I boosted the nation's economy? *(The war increased demand for food and manufactured goods, especially for U.S. allies in Europe. The nation increased production to meet this need. The United States produced more food, which made money for farmers. It also manufactured more goods such as arms and ammunition.)*

Identify Cause and Effect What factors caused Wilson to support unions during the war? What effects did his support have? *(Causes—industries needed workers to meet the increased demand for production; workers were in short supply because many men were off fighting in the war; Wilson wanted to avoid strikes and other unrest that would negatively affect production. Effects—union membership rose; labor unrest decreased; workers won better pay and shorter work days.)*

DIGITAL TEXT 4

Americans on the Home Front

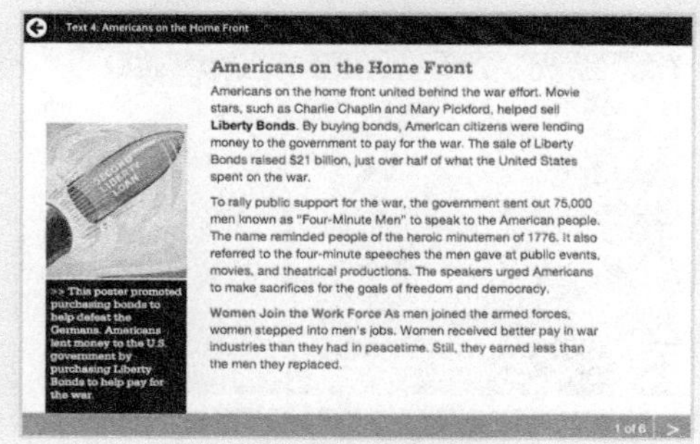

Objective 4: **Identify the impact of the war on the home front.**

Quick Instruction

Interactive Gallery: World War I Home Front Project the Interactive Gallery and click through the images. Prompt students to brainstorm ways that civilians could support the military, such as growing food, manufacturing goods, raising money, and making sacrifices to send products to the armed forces overseas.

Analyze Images Project the image of the women working in a manufacturing plant. Ask students to explain how the work the women are doing in the factory contributed to the war effort. Discuss why women were called upon to do this work. *(Factories produced the arms and other materials that soldiers needed to fight in the war. With many men fighting overseas, women had greater opportunities to work outside the home.)*

Entering the War

INTERACTIVE GALLERY

World War I Home Front

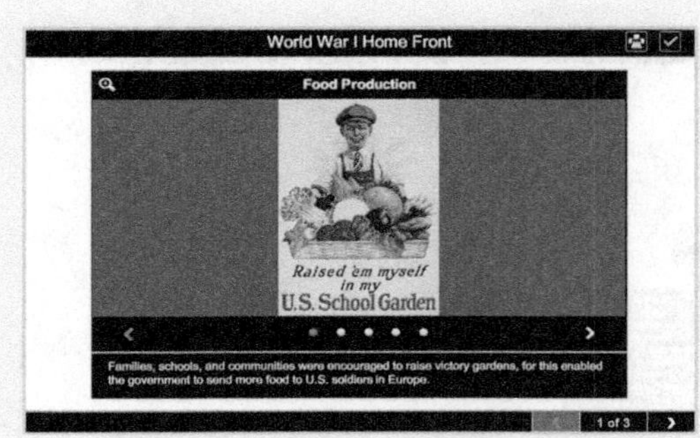

ACTIVE CLASSROOM

Conduct an If Images Could Talk activity. Have students select one of the images in the Interactive Gallery. Ask them what the person or people in the image might say if they could talk. Have them provide evidence supporting their views.

Further Instruction

Discuss the ways that the war affected life on the home front. In particular, be sure students can explain how the war affected immigrants, minorities, and women in the United States.

Compare and Contrast the views of those for and against the war. Why did many Americans support the war? Why were others opposed? *(For—patriotism; anti-German sentiment; desire to spread democracy. Against—opposed all war; believed the war benefited factory owners instead of workers.)*

Generate Explanations Explain why the war spurred migration within the nation. *(Immigration had slowed significantly, and cities and factories needed workers after men went abroad to fight. Newcomers from the South, Southwest, and Mexico came to cities in the North to find jobs related to the war industries.)*

SYNTHESIZE

DIGITAL ACTIVITY

Effects of World War I

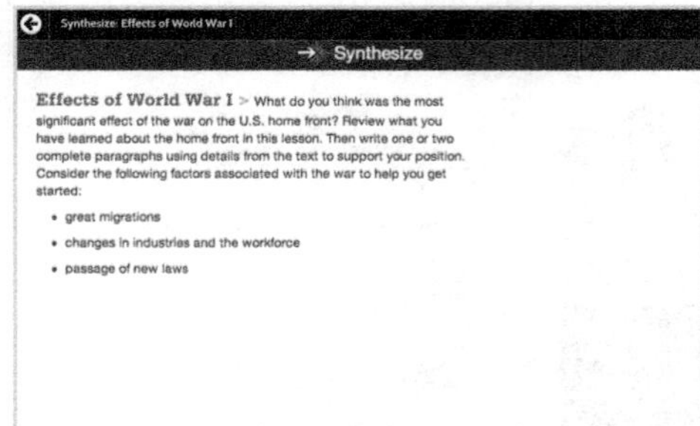

Have students share the rationale for their answers with a partner and discuss their responses.

Discuss Prompt the class to summarize the different effects of the war on the home front. Ask them to make predictions about how these effects will continue to impact the nation after the war.

DEMONSTRATE

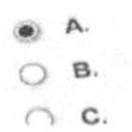

LESSON QUIZ

Lesson Quiz and Class Discussion Board

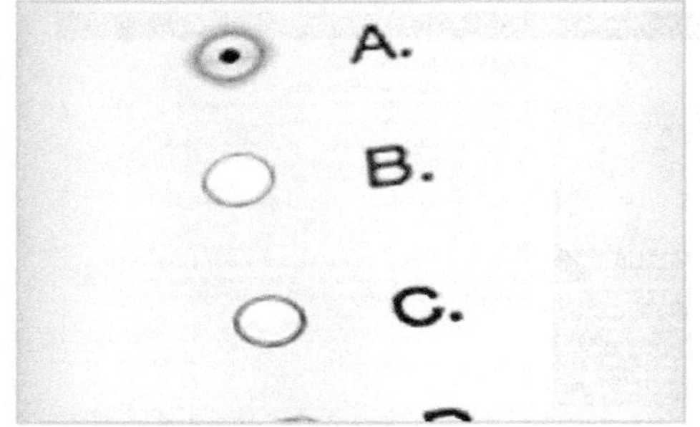

Assign the online Lesson Quiz for this lesson if you haven't already done so. Students will be offered automatic remediation or enrichment based on their score.

Pose these questions to the class on the Discussion Board:

Identify Cause and Effect What social and economic changes took place in the United States as a result of the decision to enter World War I?

Draw Conclusions Do you believe Congress was right to pass laws making it a crime to criticize the government or interfere with the war effort? Why or why not?

Topic Inquiry

Have students continue their investigations for the Topic Inquiry.

Winning the War

Supporting English Language Learners

Use with the reading, **Allied Victory.**

Speaking

Have students read *Allied Victory* silently. Then ask students to get partners to talk about the Allied victory. Beginners will speak using a few words. Encourage more proficient students to discuss the victory with increasing specificity and detail.

Beginning Ask students to reread the first paragraph. With a partner, have them use the following sentence frame to talk about the Americans' entrance into the war: With help from _____, the Allies forced the _____ to retreat.

Intermediate Ask partners to reread the first two paragraphs. Then they can take turns talking about the German retreat and how the Americans took the offensive.

Advanced Ask partners to reread the first two paragraphs. Then they can take turns talking about the German retreat and the American offensive in the areas between the Meuse River and the Argonne Forest. Encourage them to add as many details as they can.

Advanced High Ask partners to reread the section titled *The Final Offensive*. Have them take turns talking about the advance of the American soldiers in great detail, including the number of days they fought and detailed information about the battle they won.

Use with the reading, **The Costs of War.**

Reading

Before reading the section titled *The Costs of War*, say the words *epidemic* and *influenza*. Ask students to raise their hand if they know the meaning. If not, explain the words and point out that in English we often say flu for influenza. Then have students preview the graph of the war casualties.

Beginning Ask students to point to the tallest column and tell which country had the most casualties. Ask them to read the first paragraph and compare this information with the information in the chart.

Intermediate Ask partners to look at the chart to determine the number of casualties the Allied Powers and Central Powers had. Ask them to read the first two paragraphs and use the information in the chart to help them understand the huge number of civilians who also died in the war.

Advanced Ask partners to look at the chart to determine how many German casualties there were. Then have them read the text. Ask them to use the information from the chart to help them figure out approximately how many civilian casualties there were among the Germans.

Advanced High Ask students to study the chart carefully before reading the text. Have them use the information they learned to understand the vast number of casualties among the Allied and Central Power troops. Ask them to talk about how the spread of influenza increased the amount of casualties among civilians.

D Differentiate Instruction

Use the Differentiated Instruction notes throughout the lesson plan to support the varied skill sets, levels of readiness, and interests in the mixed-ability classroom.

Challenge These notes include suggestions for expanding the activity for advanced students.

On-Level These notes include suggestions for modifying the activity to address different interests or learning styles.

Extra Support These notes include ideas for providing more scaffolding or reading spuport.

Special Needs These notes provide ideas for adapting instruction to support the needs of various special needs students.

NOTES

Topic 12 Lesson 6

Winning the War

Objectives

Objective 1: Identify the setbacks the allies suffered in 1917 and early 1918.

Objective 2: Explain how the American Expeditionary Force helped the Allies win the war.

Objective 3: Describe the toll on human life caused by the war.

LESSON 6 ORGANIZER	PACING: APPROX. 1 PERIOD, .5 BLOCKS		RESOURCES	
	OBJECTIVES	PACING	Online	Print
Connect				
DIGITAL START UP ACTIVITY **Asking Questions**		5 min.	●	
Investigate				
DIGITAL TEXT 1 **Allied Setbacks**	Objective 1	10 min.	●	●
DIGITAL TEXT 2 **American Forces in France**	Objective 2	10 min.	●	●
INTERACTIVE MAP **Key Battles Fought by Americans in World War I**	Objective 2	10 min.	●	
DIGITAL TEXT 3 **Allied Victory**	Objective 2	10 min.	●	●
INTERACTIVE GALLERY **Life of American Soldiers in World War I**	Objective 2	10 min.	●	
DIGITAL TEXT 4 **The Costs of the War**	Objective 3	10 min.	●	●
Synthesize				
DIGITAL ACTIVITY **Answering Your Questions**		5 min.	●	
Demonstrate				
LESSON QUIZ **Lesson Quiz and Class Discussion Board**		10 min.	●	

PEARSON realize™ www.PearsonRealize.com

Go online to access additional resources including:
Primary Sources • Biographies • Supreme Court cases • 21st Century Skill Tutorials • Maps • Graphic Organizers.

CONNECT

DIGITAL START UP ACTIVITY

Asking Questions

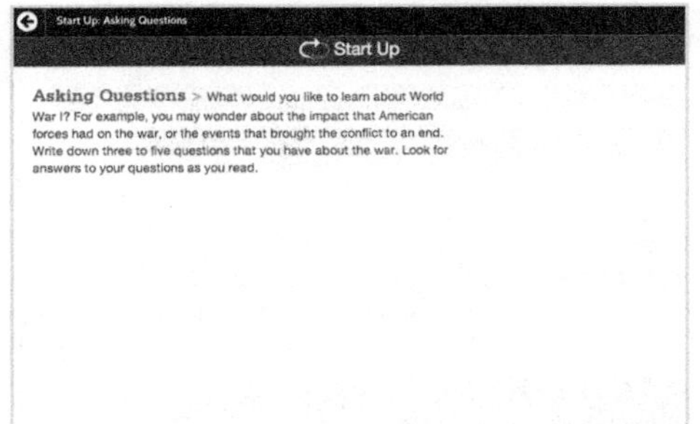

Project the Start Up Activity Ask students to write down their questions as they enter and get settled. Have students share their questions with a partner, either in class or through a blog space.

Tell students that in this lesson they will be learning about the challenges the Allies faced later in the war, the way in which the American Expeditionary Force helped the Allies win, and the human cost of the war.

Aa Vocabulary Development: Use the Interactive Reading Notepad to preview the Key Terms and Academic Vocabulary in this lesson with students.

FLIP IT!

Assign the Flipped Video for this lesson.

STUDENT EDITION PRINT PAGES: 681–687

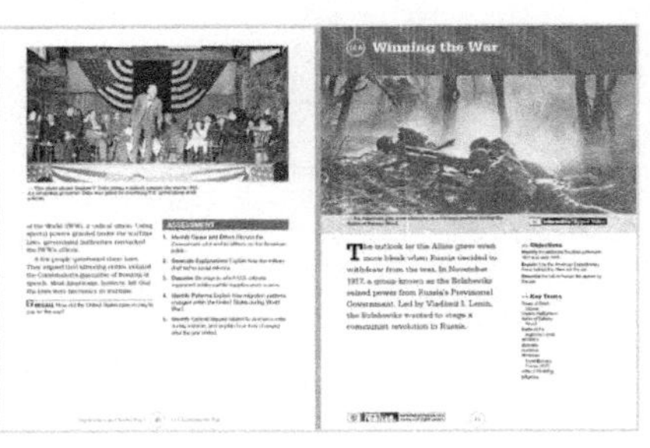

INVESTIGATE

DIGITAL TEXT 1

Allied Setbacks

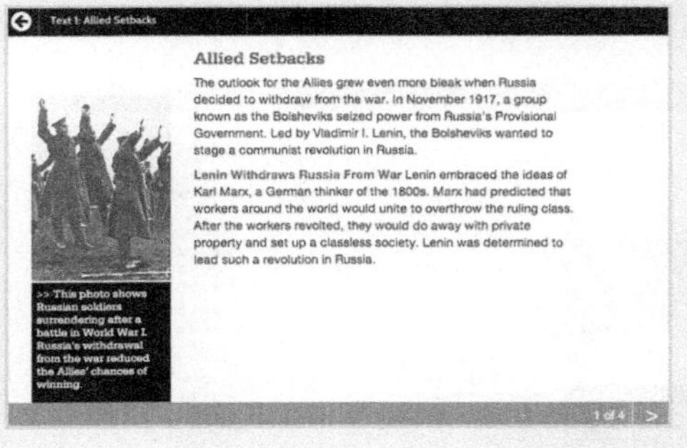

Objective 1: **Identify the setbacks the Allies suffered in 1917 and early 1918.**

Quick Instruction

Project the image of Russian soldiers surrendering during World War I. Explain that the Allies faced a number of setbacks in 1917 and 1918. The Allies had lost millions of soldiers, and then Russia decided to withdraw from the war.

Identify Cause and Effect How did Russia's surrender and the Treaty of Brest-Litovsk affect the Allies? *(The Allies viewed the treaty as a betrayal. It gave land and valuable resources to Germany. It also let Germany remove its troops from the eastern front to focus on the west.)*

Further Instruction

Review the state of the Allied troops leading up to America's entry into the war. Prompt students to recall the reasons the United States entered the war and discuss the conditions American troops faced when they arrived in France.

Cite Evidence from the text explaining why Russia withdrew from World War I. *(The Bolshevik party wanted to stage a communist revolution in Russia, and the party's leader, Vladimir Lenin, argued that further Russian participation in World War I would only benefit the ruling class.)*

Make Predictions How do you think the entry of the Americans into the war will affect the German peace offensive? *(The Americans will contribute more soldiers and resources to the Allied troops. Therefore, they will be able to help push back the German offensive.)*

DIGITAL TEXT 2

American Forces in France

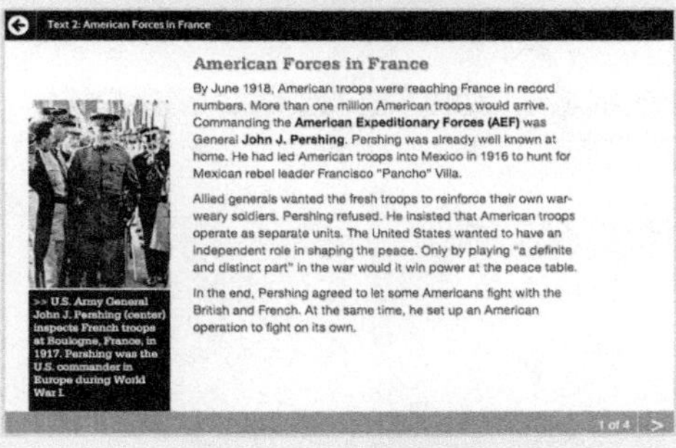

Objective 2: **Explain how the American Expeditionary Force helped the Allies win the war.**

Quick Instruction

Tell students that part of the American Expeditionary Force fought alongside the Allies and part fought as an independent unit. Life for the soldiers was difficult. In addition to the dangers of battle, they also faced hunger and disease. Hundreds of thousands of American soldiers died.

Interactive Map: Key Battles Fought by Americans in World War I Project the Interactive Map and click through the battles. Have students identify the Allied front line. Discuss how American forces helped the Allies push back the German forces, using examples from the activity for support.

Interactive Gallery: Life of American Soldiers in World War I Project the Interactive Gallery and click through the images. Draw students' attention to the pie chart showing causes of death in the trenches, and prompt students to understand the role disease played in World War I casualty rates.

Winning the War

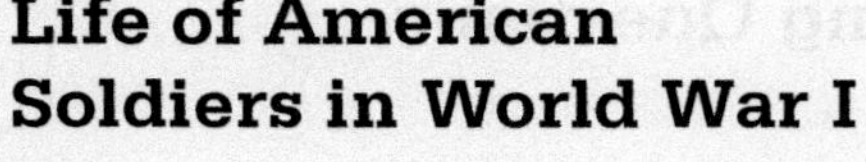

INTERACTIVE MAP

Key Battles Fought by Americans in World War I

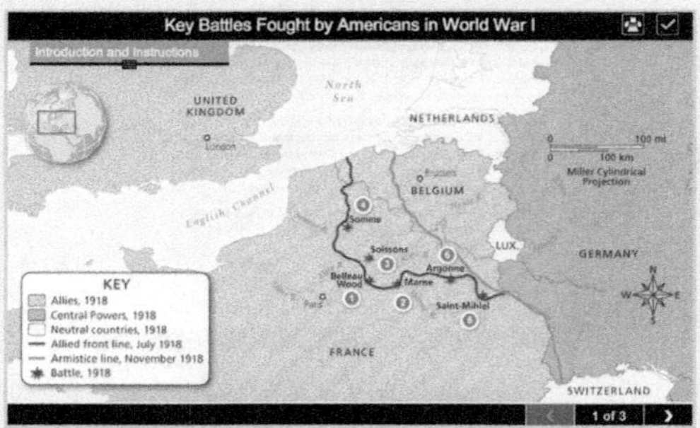

Sequence Events from July 1918 to November 1918. *(Germany launched an attack to take Paris. The Allies forced them to retreat. Allies attacked from Verdun to the North Sea. Americans fought in the Battle of Argonne Forest. Allied forces broke through German lines of defense. The head of the German cabinet secretly cabled Wilson about armistice. The German emperor resigned and fled. New German leaders agreed to the armistice terms, ending the war.)*

ACTIVE CLASSROOM

Conduct a Make Headlines activity. Have students write a headline that captures the overall flow of action in the Interactive Map. Ask: If you were to write a headline that captured the most important aspect of this map, what would it be? Ask students to exchange their headlines with a partner for revision, then ask for volunteers to share their headline with the class.

DIGITAL TEXT 3

Allied Victory

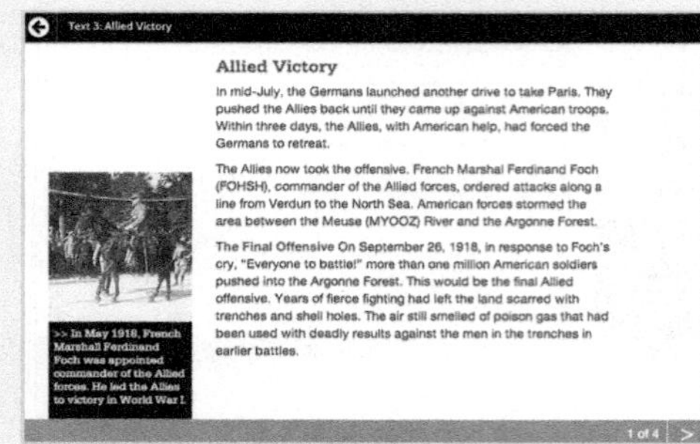

ACTIVE CLASSROOM

Conduct a My Metaphor activity using the Interactive Gallery. Give students the following prompt so they can create a metaphor based on the content of one of the gallery images: This image shows that _____ is like _____ because _____. Ask students to exchange their metaphors with a partner for revision, then ask for volunteers to share their metaphor with the class.

ELL Use the ELL activity described in the ELL chart.

Further Instruction

Have students review the major battles in which Americans fought. Be sure they understand the key events leading to armistice.

Generate Explanations Explain the significance of the Battle of Belleau Wood. *(Belleau Wood was outside Paris. The victory meant Germany could not advance and capture the city. This was the Americans' first major battle in the war. The victory likely helped bolster the troops and the country's image.)*

INTERACTIVE GALLERY

Life of American Soldiers in World War I

Hypothesize Explain Wilson's conditions for armistice. Why do you think these were his terms? *(Wilson required Germany to agree to his plan for peace and made the emperor abdicate power. Wilson may have wanted to change German leadership and make sure Germany would not be able to launch future attacks.)*

DIGITAL TEXT 4

The Costs of the War

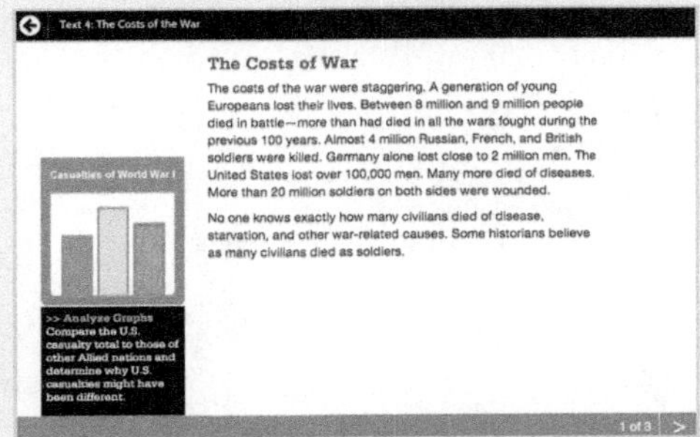

Objective 3: **Describe the toll on human life caused by the war.**

Quick Instruction

Project the war casualties by nation. Have students read the chart and identify the nations with the most casualties. Ask what factors they think caused the numbers to be so high. Explain that in addition to battle, soldiers also died from starvation and disease.

Summarize What were the human costs of World War I, in addition to the number of soldiers lost in battle? *(A generation of young people died in battle and from injuries sustained during fighting. Civilians also lost their lives. Homes were destroyed, children orphaned, and many left starving. Much of the land where battles were fought was ruined.)*

Identify Cause and Effect What was the epidemic of 1918 and what effect did it have following the war? *(An epidemic is the rapid spread of a contagious disease among large numbers of people. A flu epidemic around the world killed more than 30 million people after the war.)*

ELL Use the ELL activity described in the ELL chart.

Further Instruction

Draw Conclusions Why was northern France in ruins after the war? *(Much of the fighting on the western front had been in France. The areas where battles raged would have been burned out and ruined by trenches, bombs, and other effects of the war. Many buildings and homes were destroyed, as well as farms and factories.)*

Make Predictions What difficulties do you think Europe and the United States will face following the war? Why? *(It will be expensive for countries in Europe to rebuild. It will also be difficult for Germany to recover from its defeat. Negotiating a peace plan to prevent future wars will be difficult. The United States went through many changes on the home front. It may be difficult for soldiers to return home from battle. Women, African Americans, and other minorities may not be able to hold on to the opportunities they had in the workforce and in the military during the war.)*

Winning the War

SYNTHESIZE

DIGITAL ACTIVITY

Answering Your Questions

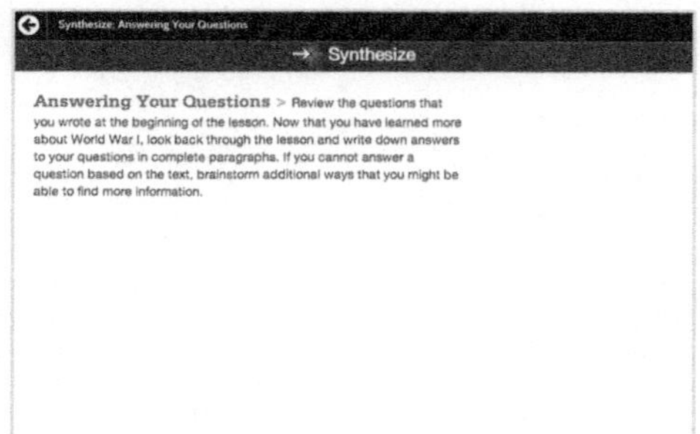

Have students review the questions they wrote at the beginning of the lesson and write down their answers. Have students share their questions and answers with a partner and discuss their responses.

Discuss Ask students what questions they still have about World War I and the aftermath of the war. See if the class can answer the questions based on the text and their prior knowledge. Discuss where else students might look to answer their questions.

DEMONSTRATE

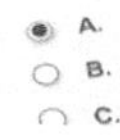

LESSON QUIZ

Lesson Quiz and Class Discussion Board

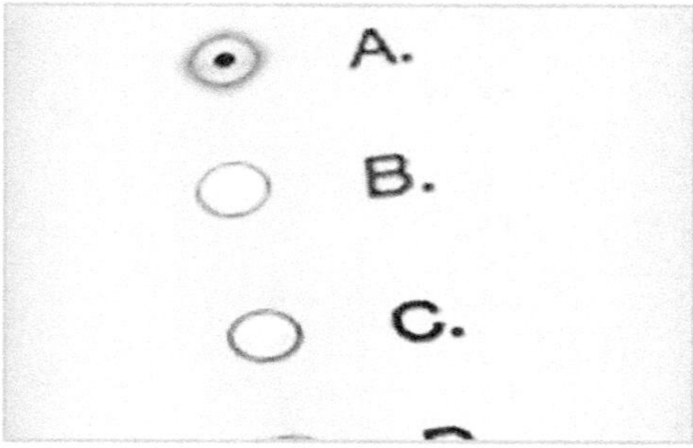

Assign the online Lesson Quiz for this lesson if you haven't already done so. Students will be offered automatic remediation or enrichment based on their score.

Pose these questions to the class on the Discussion Board:

Support Ideas with Evidence What evidence supports the claim that the entry of the United States into World War I helped the Allies win against Germany?

Identify Central Issues What were the main challenges American troops faced during the war?

Topic Inquiry

Have students continue their investigations for the Topic Inquiry.

PEARSON realize™ www.PearsonRealize.com Access your Digital Lesson

Wilson and Isolationism

Supporting English Language Learners

Use with the reading, **Wilson's Fourteen Points.**

Learning

Explain to students that monitoring what they say and using self-correcting techniques when they speak will help them improve their oral language skills.

Beginning Use simple spoken language to summarize the first three paragraphs. Ask partners to use the following sentence frame to talk about President Wilson's trip to Europe: Allied leaders _____ agree with President Wilson. Encourage them to monitor their own pronunciation and intonation.

Intermediate Use spoken language to summarize the first three paragraphs. Ask partners to talk about why President Wilson went to Europe and what the Allied leaders thought of his ideas. Tell students to self-monitor their speech for correct word use and grammar. Have them self-correct any errors.

Advanced Use spoken language to summarize the first three paragraphs. Ask partners to talk about President Wilson's trip to Europe. Encourage them to include what he wanted to achieve and why the Allied leaders disagreed. Remind students to self-monitor for correct word use, grammar, and pronunciation. Have them self-correct any errors.

Advanced High Ask students to read *Wilson's Fourteen Points*. With a partner, have students talk about Wilson's peace plan. Encourage them to say what it was called and name a few details of the plan. Suggest that they use sequence words to explain. Remind students to self-monitor their use of sequence words and correct errors as needed.

Use with the reading, **The Paris Peace Conference.**

Listening

Read aloud the first four paragraphs of *The Paris Peace Conference*. Pause at the end of each sentence to clarify language or concepts. Have students seek clarification about any unfamiliar words. Encourage them to ask questions about word meaning and/or content.

Beginning Pause after the word *reparations* and ask students if they know what it means. Model pronunciation and have them repeat. Then explain that reparations are cash payments for losses during the war.

Intermediate Ask volunteers to name the Big Four. Encourage them to ask for help pronouncing the names of the foreign leaders, if needed.

Advanced Ask students to summarize what President Wilson's aim was. If needed, have them ask for help to explain what "peace without victory" means.

Advanced High Read aloud the fourth paragraph. Ask students to explain what Clemenceau had to say about Wilson's Fourteen Points. Encourage them to ask questions to clarify the meaning of the statement.

D Differentiate Instruction

Use the Differentiated Instruction notes throughout the lesson plan to support the varied skill sets, levels of readiness, and interests in the mixed-ability classroom.

Challenge These notes include suggestions for expanding the activity for advanced students.

On-Level These notes include suggestions for modifying the activity to address different interests or learning styles.

Extra Support These notes include ideas for providing more scaffolding or reading spuport.

Special Needs These notes provide ideas for adapting instruction to support the needs of various special needs students.

NOTES

Topic 12 Lesson 7

Wilson and Isolationism

Objectives

Objective 1: Describe Wilson's fourteen-point peace plan.

Objective 2: Explain what Wilson achieved at the Paris Peace Conference.

Objective 3: Summarize why the Versailles Treaty and League of Nations failed to win support in the United States.

LESSON 7 ORGANIZER	PACING: APPROX. 1 PERIOD, .5 BLOCKS		RESOURCES	
	OBJECTIVES	PACING	Online	Print
Connect				
DIGITAL START UP ACTIVITY **Peace at Last!**		5 min.	●	
Investigate				
DIGITAL TEXT 1 **Wilson's Fourteen Points**	Objective 1	10 min.	●	●
DIGITAL TEXT 2 **The Paris Peace Conference**	Objective 2	10 min.	●	●
BEFORE AND AFTER **Europe Before and After World War I**	Objective 2	10 min.	●	
DIGITAL TEXT 3 **Wilson Fights for the Treaty of Versailles**	Objective 3	10 min.	●	●
INTERACTIVE GALLERY **Woodrow Wilson**	Objective 3	10 min.	●	
Synthesize				
DIGITAL ACTIVITY **America's New Role**		5 min.	●	
Demonstrate				
LESSON QUIZ **Lesson Quiz and Class Discussion Board**		10 min.	●	

Go online to access additional resources including: Primary Sources • Biographies • Supreme Court cases • 21st Century Skill Tutorials • Maps • Graphic Organizers.

CONNECT

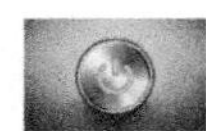

DIGITAL START UP ACTIVITY

Peace at Last!

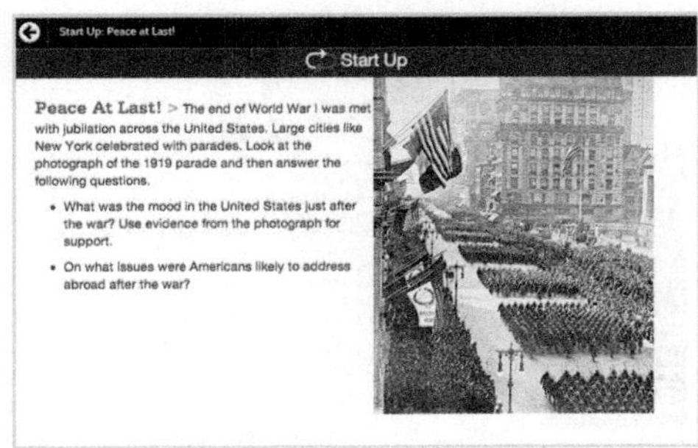

Project the Start Up Activity Ask students to look at the photograph and answer the questions as they enter and get settled. Have students share their answers with a partner.

Discuss What was the mood in the United States just after the war? Use evidence from the photograph for support. *(The mood was happy and celebratory, as shown by the parade and people cheering.)* On what were Americans likely to focus in addressing the aftermath of World War I? *(rebuilding Europe; preventing another world war)*

Tell students that in this lesson they will be learning about President Wilson's efforts to secure peace after World War I.

Aa Vocabulary Development: Use the Interactive Reading Notepad to preview the Key Terms and Academic Vocabulary in this lesson with students.

FLIP IT!

Assign the Flipped Video for this lesson.

STUDENT EDITION PRINT PAGES: 688–694

INVESTIGATE

DIGITAL TEXT 1

Wilson's Fourteen Points

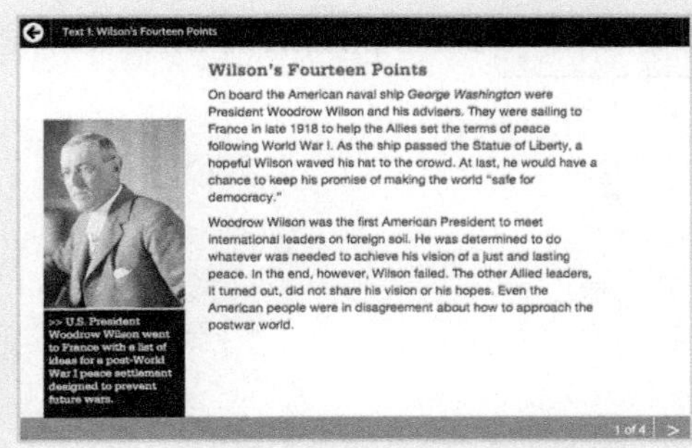

Objective 1: Describe Wilson's fourteen-point peace plan.

Quick Instruction

Project the table outlining the main elements of the Fourteen Points. Explain that the Fourteen Points listed President Wilson's goals for peace. Prompt students to explain the key parts of Wilson's plan in their own words. What did Wilson hope to accomplish with his Fourteen Points? *(He hoped to prevent future international problems from turning into wars.)*

Identify Central Issues Identify the central issues Wilson faced in implementing his peace plan. *(Not everyone agreed with his vision. Europeans wanted to punish Germany for the war. Many nations were more concerned with protecting their interests than working together to prevent future conflicts. Some of Wilson's points were vague or impossible to implement. Even Americans had conflicting ideas about what to do.)*

D Differentiate: Extra Support Explain to students that a *league* is a collection of people or countries that come together for a shared purpose. Prompt students to understand President Wilson's perspective by asking them to think about the ways in which a league provides protection and encourages cooperation.

ELL Use the ELL activity described in the ELL chart.

Further Instruction

Evaluate Arguments What did Wilson mean when he argued for "peace without victory"? *(Wilson meant that the victors should not punish the losing side. Instead they should work to make a lasting peace.)*

Hypothesize Why do you think Wilson called for freedom of the seas, free trade, and self-determination? What were the benefits of these three freedoms? *(Wilson believed these freedoms would reduce conflict. Allowing nations to trade freely across oceans that were safe would promote economic growth without encouraging dangerous alliances. Self-determination would allow national groups to form their own governments. These freedoms were intended to prevent nations from dictating policies and limiting the opportunities of less powerful groups.)*

Wilson and Isolationism

DIGITAL TEXT 2

The Paris Peace Conference

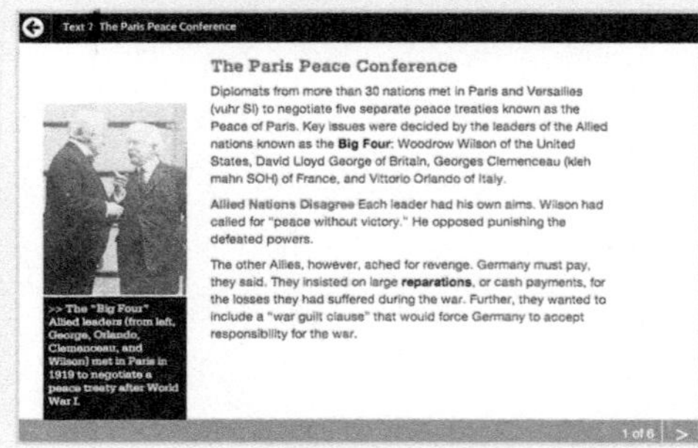

BEFORE AND AFTER

Europe Before and After World War I

DIGITAL TEXT 3

Wilson Fights for the Treaty of Versailles

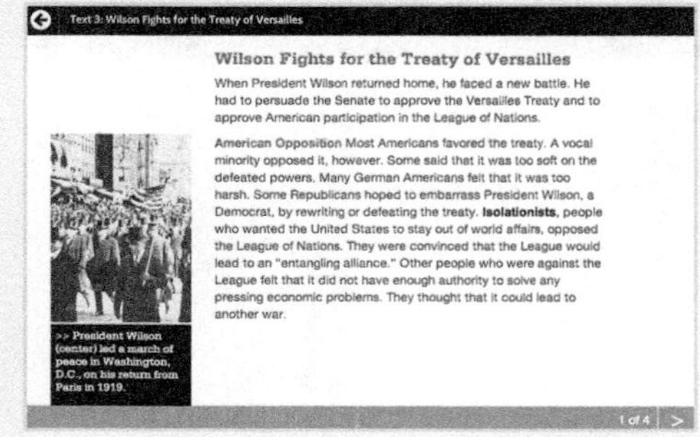

Text 3: Wilson Fights for the Treaty of Versailles
Wilson Fights for the Treaty of Versailles
When President Wilson returned home, he faced a new battle. He had to persuade the Senate to approve the Versailles Treaty and to approve American participation in the League of Nations.
American Opposition Most Americans favored the treaty. A vocal minority opposed it, however. Some said that it was too soft on the defeated powers. Many German Americans felt that it was too harsh. Some Republicans hoped to embarrass President Wilson, a Democrat, by rewriting or defeating the treaty. Isolationists, people who wanted the United States to stay out of world affairs, opposed the League of Nations. They were convinced that the League would lead to an "entangling alliance." Other people who were against the League felt that it did not have enough authority to solve any pressing economic problems. They thought that it could lead to another war.
>> President Wilson (center) led a march of peace in Washington, D.C., on his return from Paris in 1919.
1 of 4

Objective 2: **Explain what Wilson achieved at the Paris Peace Conference.**

Quick Instruction

Interactive Map: Europe Before and After World War I Project the Interactive Map and move the slider to show European political boundaries before and after the war. Connect the changes students see to the Paris Peace Conference in which new nations were created, mandates for governing territories were given, and Germany was stripped of its colonies.

Support Ideas with Examples What examples from the text indicate that the Treaty of Versailles humiliated and weakened Germany? *(It forced Germany to take blame for starting the war, took away Germany's overseas colonies and other territory, made Germany pay expensive reparations, and limited the German military.)*

Apply Concepts How did Wilson's principle of self-determination, outlined in the Fourteen Points, change the map of Europe after the war? *(Self-determination allowed national groups to have their own territory and government. It resulted in the creation of new nations in Eastern Europe, including Czechoslovakia and Yugoslavia.)*

ACTIVE CLASSROOM

Conduct a Make Headlines activity. Have students write headlines announcing the signing of the Treaty of Versailles that also incorporate a change in the Interactive Map. The headlines should be from the perspective of an American newspaper, a German newspaper, and a British newspaper. Have students share their headlines and discuss the differences in perspective.

ELL Use the ELL activity described in the ELL chart.

Further Instruction

Have students summarize the key issues discussed at the Paris Peace Conference. Be sure they understand the terms of the Treaty of Versailles.

Evaluate Arguments Why did Wilson think the League of Nations was "a guarantee of peace"? Do you think this view will prove correct? Why or why not? *(Wilson thought the League would prevent war by bringing nations together to talk over conflicts. If negotiations failed, there would be a united group of nations to fight aggressors.)*

Generate Explanations Describe the "war guilt clause." Why was it included in the Treaty of Versailles? *(The clause made Germany take full responsibility for the war and its losses. It was intended to humiliate Germany and punish it for the war.)*

Objective 3: **Summarize why the Versailles Treaty and League of Nations failed to win support in the United States.**

Quick Instruction

Interactive Gallery: Woodrow Wilson Project the Interactive Gallery and click through the images. Have students study the cartoon in the fourth image. Discuss the difficulties Wilson faced gaining support for his plan in the United States.

Identify Central Issues that some Americans had with the Treaty of Versailles. What were their reasons for opposing Wilson's plan? *(Some thought it was too soft on Germany. Others thought it was too harsh. Some Republicans wanted to embarrass the President by defeating the treaty. Isolationists wanted to stay out of world affairs. They feared the League of Nations could lead to another war.)*

ACTIVE CLASSROOM

Conduct a Cartoon It activity with students. Have students create a political cartoon based on the image of George, Clemenceau, and Wilson at the Paris Peace Conference that reflects similarities or differences between the three.

INTERACTIVE GALLERY

Woodrow Wilson

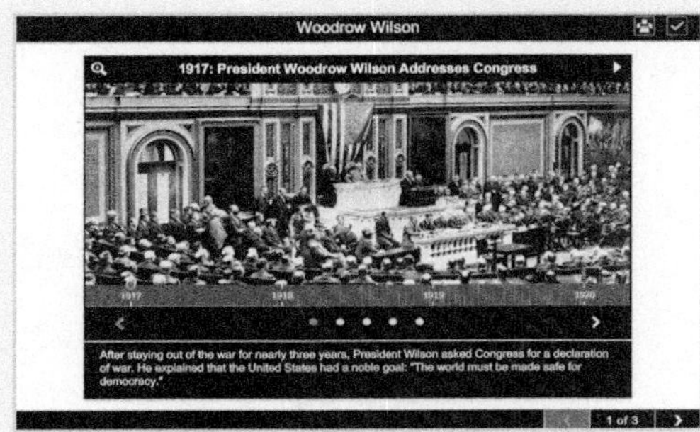

Woodrow Wilson
1917: President Woodrow Wilson Addresses Congress
After staying out of the war for nearly three years, President Wilson asked Congress for a declaration of war. He explained that the United States had a noble goal: "The world must be made safe for democracy."
1 of 3

Further Instruction

Review the reasons the United States failed to pass the Treaty of Versailles and discuss the effects this had on President Wilson. Be sure students understand the opposition to the treaty and the League of Nations. Ask what outcome they think this decision may have on the United States and Europe in the coming decades.

Determine Point of View Why did Henry Cabot Lodge disagree with the idea of the United States joining the League of Nations? *(Lodge thought that the League of Nations would cause the United States to lose its independence. He feared that the United States could become entangled in another war if it had to protect member states.)*

Identify Cause and Effect What were the effects of America's decision not to join the League of Nations? *(The League of Nations was not as strong as it could have been with U.S. support. It had less authority and was less able to protect its members from aggression.)*

SYNTHESIZE

DIGITAL ACTIVITY

America's New Role

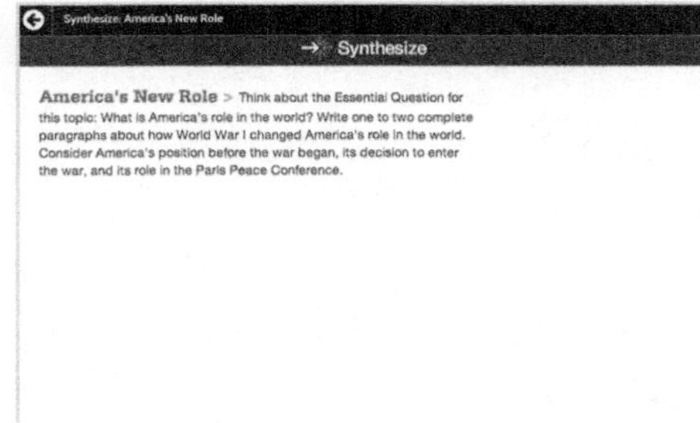

Have students review the Essential Question for the topic and write one to two complete paragraphs about how World War I changed America's role in the world. Have students share their paragraphs with a partner.

Discuss Ask students what factors they think contributed most to America's changed role. Ask them to make a prediction about what the role of the United States will be in the years following the war.

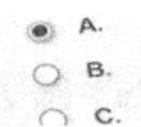

DEMONSTRATE

LESSON QUIZ

Lesson Quiz and Class Discussion Board

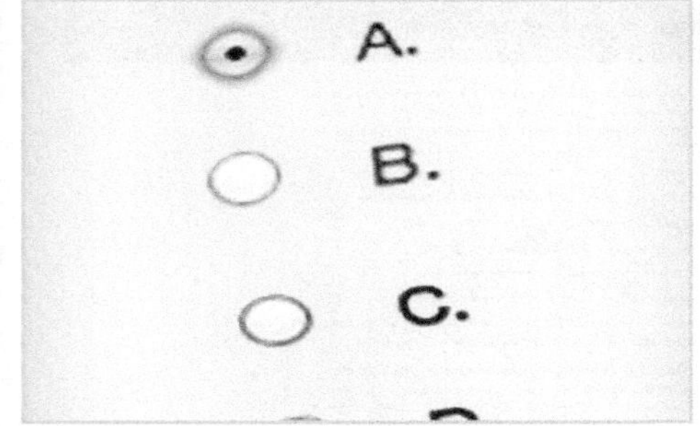

Assign the online Lesson Quiz for this lesson if you haven't already done so. Students will be offered automatic remediation or enrichment based on their score.

Pose these questions to the class on the Discussion Board:

Draw Conclusions Identify the victories and compromises Wilson made in Paris to draw a conclusion about the success of his efforts at the Conference.

Generate Explanations Did the United States Senate make the right decision when it rejected the Treaty of Versailles? Why or why not?

Topic Inquiry

Have students continue their investigations for the Topic Inquiry.

Imperialism and World War I

SYNTHESIZE

DIGITAL ACTIVITY

Reflect on the Essential Question and Topic

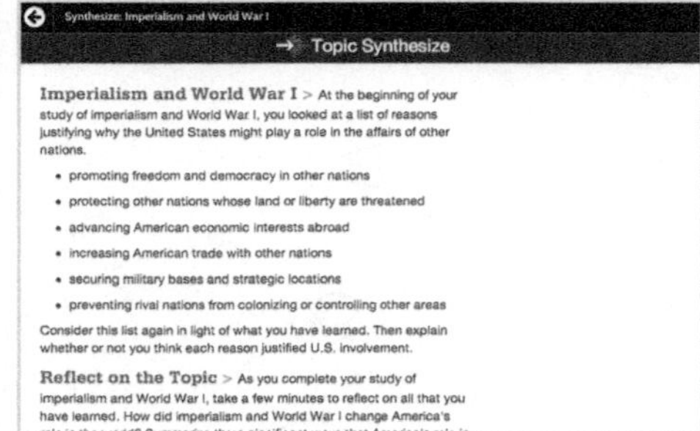

First ask students to reconsider the Essential Question for this Topic: What is America's role in the world? Have them review the list of reasons why the United States might become involved in the affairs of other nations.Then have them explain whether or not they think each reason justified U.S. involvement in the affairs of other nations in the late 1800s and early 1900s.

Ask students, "How would you characterize America's new role at the end of World War I?" Have students give examples from the topic. Discuss their responses as a class or ask students to post their answers on the Class Discussion Board.

Next, ask students to reflect on the topic as a whole and summarize three significant ways that imperialism and World War I changed America's role in the world, while supporting their claims with evidence from the text.

Topic Inquiry

Have students complete Step 3 of the Topic Inquiry.

DEMONSTRATE

DIGITAL TOPIC REVIEW AND ASSESSMENT

Imperialism and World War I

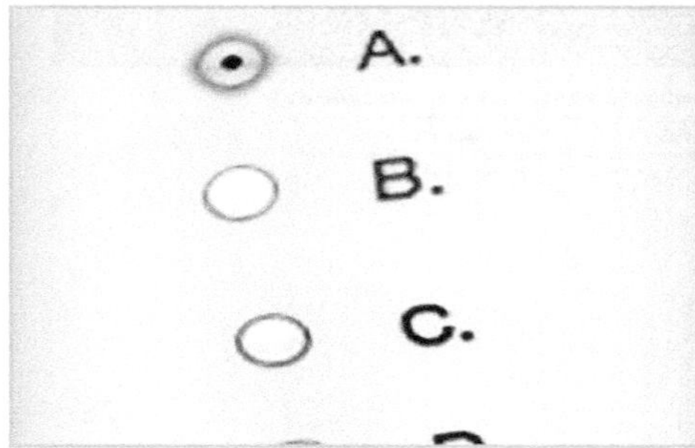

Students can prepare for the Topic Test by answering the questions in the Topic Review and Assessment online or the Assessment questions in the Print Student text. They can also prepare by reviewing their answers to the Interactive Reading Notepad questions or reviewing their notes in the Reading and Notetaking Study Guide.

DIGITAL TOPIC TEST

Imperialism and World War I

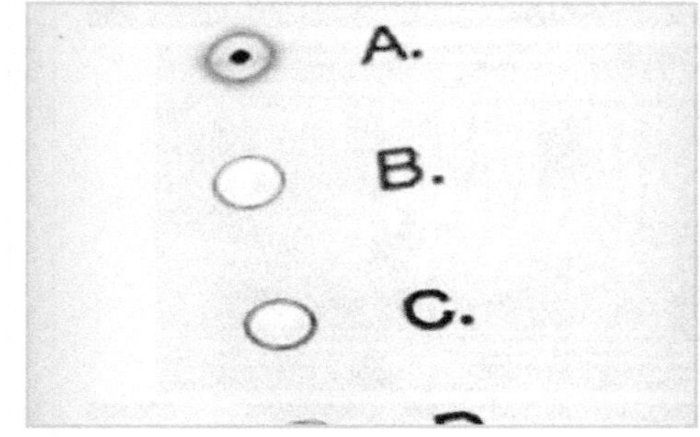

TOPIC TEST

Assign the Topic Test to assess students' understanding of topic content.

BENCHMARK TESTS

Assign these benchmark tests as you complete the relevant topics to monitor student progress toward mastering the course content and as preparation for the End-of-Course Test.

Benchmark Test 1: Topics 1–2

Benchmark Test 2: Topics 3–4

Benchmark Test 3: Topics 5–6

Benchmark Test 4: Topics 7–9

Benchmark Test 5: Topics 10–12

Benchmark Test 6: Topics 13–14

Benchmark Test 7: Topics 15–17

Prosperity and Depression

TOPIC 13 ORGANIZER	PACING: APPROX. 10 PERIODS, 5 BLOCKS
	PACING
Connect	1 period
MY STORY VIDEO **Billie Holiday, Lady Day**	10 min.
DIGITAL ESSENTIAL QUESTION ACTIVITY **What Should Governments Do?**	10 min.
DIGITAL OVERVIEW ACTIVITY **Timeline: Prosperity and Depression**	10 min.
TOPIC INQUIRY: DOCUMENT-BASED QUESTION **The Role of the Government in the Economy**	20 min.
Investigate	3–7 periods
TOPIC INQUIRY: DOCUMENT-BASED QUESTION **The Role of the Government in the Economy**	Ongoing
LESSON 1 Harding and Coolidge	30–40 min.
LESSON 2 Social Change	30–40 min.
LESSON 3 Roaring Twenties Culture	30–40 min.
LESSON 4 Division and Inequality	30–40 min.
LESSON 5 Entering the Great Depression	30–40 min.
LESSON 6 Roosevelt's New Deal	30–40 min.
LESSON 7 Life During the Depression	30–40 min.
Synthesize	1 period
DIGITAL ACTIVITY **Reflect on the Essential Question and Topic**	10 min.
TOPIC INQUIRY: DOCUMENT-BASED QUESTION **The Role of the Government in the Economy**	20 min.
Demonstrate	1–2 periods
DIGITAL TOPIC REVIEW AND ASSESSMENT **Prosperity and Depression**	10 min.
TOPIC INQUIRY: DOCUMENT-BASED QUESTION **The Role of the Government in the Economy**	20 min.

TOPIC INQUIRY: DOCUMENT-BASED QUESTION

The Role of the Government in the Economy

In this Topic Inquiry, students work independently to analyze documents that express various viewpoints on government involvement in the economy and write essays in which they respond to the prompt, "In times of economic distress, what should governments do to help or support their citizens?" Learning about government involvement in the economy and citizens' lives will contribute to students' understanding of the Topic Essential Question: **What should governments do?**

STEP 1: CONNECT

Develop Questions and Plan the Investigation

Launch the DBQ Writing Activity

Discuss some of the actions the government takes to help or support citizens. Then, have students read the introduction to the activity in the Student Instructions.

Generate Questions

Pair students and allow them time to share their ideas about the photograph and the caption. Have partners work together to generate their own questions and answer the Questions to Discuss from Step 1B of the Student Instructions.

Suggestion: If time is limited, conduct the entirety of Step 1B as small group work. Walk around the room as students talk and clarify any unfamiliar or difficult concepts related to the inquiry topic.

Resources

- Project Launch
- Student Instructions

PROFESSIONAL DEVELOPMENT

Document-Based Question

Be sure to view the Document-Based Question Professional Development resources in the online course.

STEP 2: INVESTIGATE

Apply Disciplinary Concepts and Tools

Analyze the Documents

As students read the documents, they should keep their lists of questions in hand, recording answers as they go. Students might find it helpful to categorize documents based on point of view. For example, they might divide the documents into pro- and anti-intervention or they might categorize them based on the kind of government involvement discussed. Students can organize their essays in the same way.

Suggestion: Remind students to clearly identify the sources of the ideas they include in their essays.

Check Your Understanding

Students can reconvene with their partners to share and discuss the answers they provided to the questions attached to each document. Partners should share their interpretations of the central ideas of each document, taking time to discuss and possibly resolve discrepancies in interpretation.

Resources

- Student Instructions
- Document A: Excerpt from Dear Mrs. Roosevelt, letter written by M.I. to First Lady Eleanor Roosevelt, 1936
- Document B: Excerpt from It's a Great Life, letter by CCC employee Robert L. Miller, 1937
- Document C: Excerpts from Conversations with Alice Paul: Women Suffrage and the Equal Rights Amendment, by Alice Paul, 1975
- Document D: Excerpt from the Statement on Public vs. Private Financing of Relief Efforts, by President Herbert Hoover, 1931
- Document E: Excerpt from Acceptance of the Presidential Nomination at the Democratic National Convention, by Franklin D. Roosevelt, 1932
- Document F: Excerpt from Acceptance of the Republican Presidential Nomination, by Wendell Willkie, 1940

STEP 3: SYNTHESIZE

Evaluate Sources and Use Evidence to Formulate Conclusions

Write Your Essay

Display the Rubric for a DBQ Essay for the class and review the Criteria for an Excellent essay. Post the inquiry question: In times of economic distress, what should governments do to help or support their citizens? Review the bulleted list in the Student Instructions that guides students through the writing process.

Suggestion: Allow students time to write their thesis statements in which they share their opinions in response to the question. Have partners exchange statements and work together to refine their ideas. Once students have their final theses, they can begin their writing in support of their opinions.

Resources

- Student Instructions
- Rubric for a DBQ Essay

STEP 4: DEMONSTRATE

Communicate Conclusions and Take Informed Action

Reflect on the Project

After students have completed and submitted their essays, lead a class discussion in which students reflect on what they have learned and share the reasoning behind their opinions. Ask students how they predict this new-found understanding of government involvement in the economy will inform their future study of history or sociology.

Suggestion: As an extension activity, have students research government involvement in the economy before and after the recession of 2008 and synthesize what they learned from the Topic Inquiry.

Resources

- Student Instructions

INTRODUCTION

Prosperity and Depression

The decades of the 1920s and 1930s were polar opposites in many ways. The 1920s was a time of great economic growth. Pro-business Republicans ran the country, while corporations made record profits and many Americans' standard of living improved. However, many banks made questionable loans, many investors made questionable investments in the stock markets, and many consumers bought goods on credit. In 1929, the stock market crash was the first sign that these unstable financial practices had caught up with the American public. Within months, many Americans felt the effects of the economic downturn. Unemployment hit record highs, banks failed, factories closed, and drought hit the Great Plains. With little response from the Hoover administration, Americans turned to the Democratic candidate Franklin D. Roosevelt. In the first hundred days FDR was in office, Congress passed fifteen major laws that formed the basis of the New Deal programs.

CONNECT

MY STORY VIDEO

Billie Holiday, Lady Day

Watch a video about the life of Billie Holiday.

Check Understanding Who was Billie Holiday *(a famous jazz singer of the mid-twentieth century)*

Determine Point of View What was Holiday's purpose in writing "Strange Fruit"? *(to decry the discriminatory obstacles she and other African-Americans faced)*

FLIP IT!

Assign the My Story Video.

DIGITAL ESSENTIAL QUESTION ACTIVITY

What Should Governments Do?

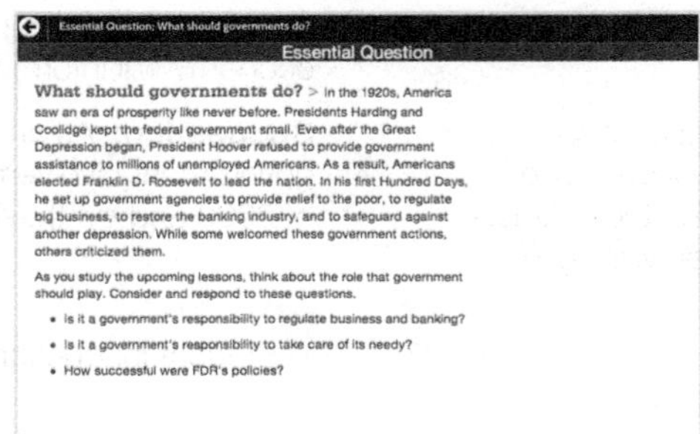

Ask students to think about the Essential Question for this topic: What should governments do? Some people believe the government should play an active role in the economic and social lives of its citizens. Others believe government's role should be more limited.

If students have not already done so, have them consider and answer the questions.

Evaluate Arguments What happened when the U.S. government refused to intervene during the Depression? What happened as a result of government intervention in the economy, especially in the banking industry?

Support Ideas with Evidence Should the government regulate business and banking industries today in the same manner as it did during the Great Depression? Why or why not?

DIGITAL OVERVIEW ACTIVITY

Prosperity and Depression

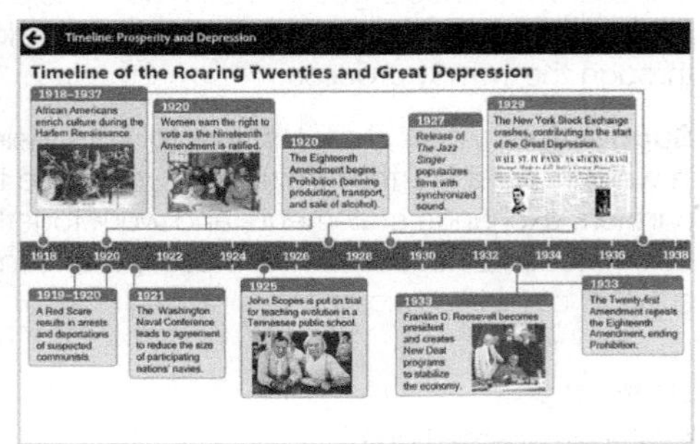

Display the timeline of the Roaring Twenties and the Great Depression. During this topic, students will learn about all these events and many more. This timeline will provide a framework into which students can place the events they learn about as they study the Topic.

Analyze Information What do the entries suggest about the American sensibility at the time? *(Possible response: Americans were beginning to claim their voices as the Harlem Renaissance celebrated the African American experience, women won suffrage, and Scopes dared to teach evolution.)*

Topic Inquiry

Launch the Topic Inquiry with students after introducing the topic.

PEARSON realize www.PearsonRealize.com Access your Digital Lesson

Harding and Coolidge

Supporting English Language Learners

Use with the reading, **Economic Growth Under President Coolidge**.

Learning
Discuss how pictures (drawn, seen, or imagined) can help students to understand and remember the meanings of words, phrases, and abstract concepts.

Beginning Display the word *consumer* and pronounce it together. Explain its meaning using words and a simple drawing. Then have students draw their own representation of the word on paper. Repeat this process for the word *income*.

Intermediate Display the word *debt*, pronounce it together, and discuss its meaning. Have students independently draw a picture representing the word. Then, in small groups, invite students to share and describe their pictures using a sentence that includes the word *debt*. Repeat this process for the noun *demand*.

Advanced Ask students to draw pictures that represent the following words: prosperity, debt, demand. Then invite partners to share, compare, and describe their pictures. Ask: Did you and your partner depict each word in the same way? Why do you think that is? How were your pictures similar and different?

Advanced High Invite students to draw pictures on separate pieces of paper that represent the following terms: prosperity, consumer, income, demand, debt, stock market. Then have students hold up each "flash card" so a partner can guess the related term and use it in a sentence to describe the picture.

Use with the reading, **A Return to Isolationism**.

Listening
Discuss the following questions with students: Why is it important to understand what people say? How do you know if you have understood what someone says?

Beginning Recite (two times) a linguistically accommodated version of the text's first paragraph. Then display a list of several simple sentences, some that you said and some that you did not say. Together, sort the sentences into a two-column chart.

Intermediate Recite the first paragraph of the text. Then display several sentence starters based on the paragraph. Invite students to complete them using information they heard you say.

Advanced Use a conversational tone to summarize the text. Then invite students to write down all the details they heard you say. Ask: How well were you able to understand and recall what I said? How might you improve your listening skills?

Advanced High Place students in three-person small groups and ask students to take turns defining these terms: isolationism, communism, disarmament. Have the two listeners restate each speaker's definition and assess their ability to do so.

D Differentiate Instruction

Use the Differentiated Instruction notes throughout the lesson plan to support the varied skill sets, levels of readiness, and interests in the mixed-ability classroom.

Challenge These notes include suggestions for expanding the activity for advanced students.

On-Level These notes include suggestions for modifying the activity to address different interests or learning styles.

Extra Support These notes include ideas for providing more scaffolding or reading spupport.

Special Needs These notes provide ideas for adapting instruction to support the needs of various special needs students.

NOTES

Harding and Coolidge

Objectives

Objective 1: Describe how corruption hurt Harding's presidency.

Objective 2: Explain why the economy grew under Coolidge.

Objective 3: Identify the role the United States played in international politics during the 1920s.

LESSON 1 ORGANIZER	PACING: APPROX. 1 PERIOD, .5 BLOCKS		RESOURCES	
	OBJECTIVES	PACING	Online	Print
Connect				
DIGITAL START UP ACTIVITY **Draw Conclusions**		5 min.	●	
Investigate				
DIGITAL TEXT 1 **Republicans Regain the White House**	Objective 1	10 min.	●	●
DIGITAL TEXT 2 **Economic Growth Under President Coolidge**	Objective 2	10 min.	●	●
INTERACTIVE CHART **Economic Expansion in the 1920s**		10 min.	●	
DIGITAL TEXT 3 **A Return to Isolationism**	Objective 3	10 min.	●	●
INTERACTIVE CHART **Points of View on Foreign Affairs in the 1920s**		10 min.	●	
Synthesize				
DIGITAL ACTIVITY **Republican Leadership in the 1920s**		5 min.	●	
Demonstrate				
DIGITAL QUIZ **Lesson Quiz and Discussion Board**		10 min.	●	

CONNECT

DIGITAL START UP ACTIVITY

Draw Conclusions

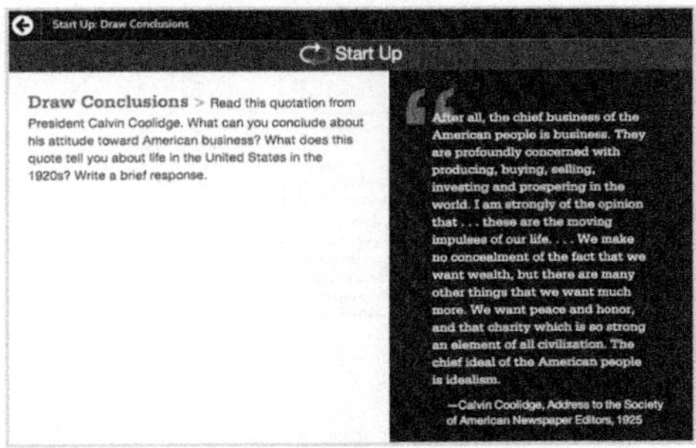

Project the Start Up Activity Have students read the quotation and complete the writing as they enter the classroom. Then ask them to share and discuss their ideas with partners.

Discuss What can you conclude about President Coolidge's attitude toward business? *(President Coolidge supported business as long as it aligned with American ideals.)*

Tell students that this lesson examines how political corruption hurt Harding's presidency and how President Calvin Coolidge ushered in an era of economic expansion and a return to isolationism.

Aa Vocabulary Development: Use the Interactive Reading Notepad to preview the Key Terms and Academic Vocabulary in this lesson with students.

FLIP IT!
Assign the Flipped Video for this lesson.

STUDENT EDITION PRINT PAGES: 700–705

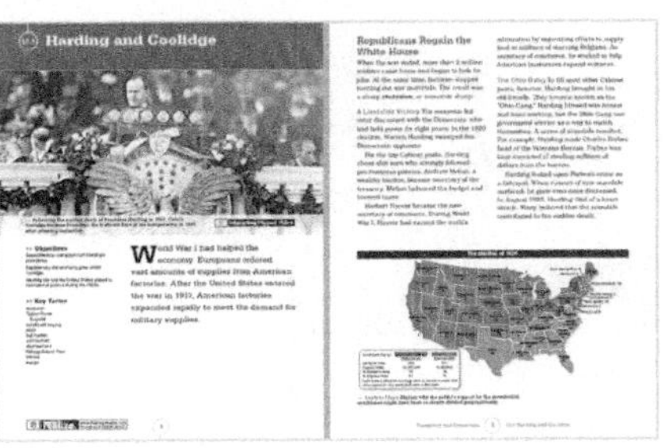

INVESTIGATE

DIGITAL TEXT 1

Republicans Regain the White House

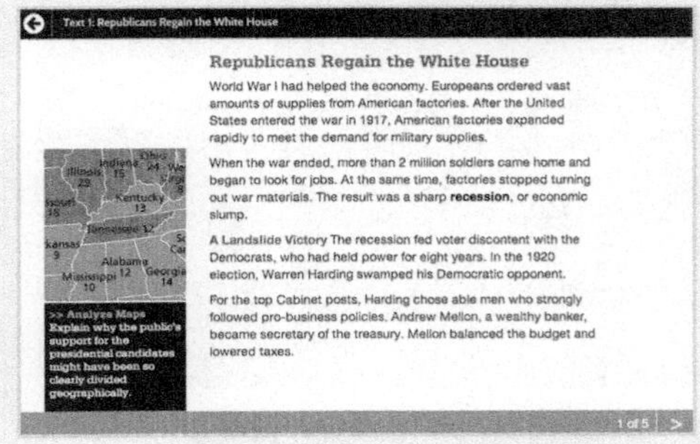

Objective 1: Describe how corruption hurt Harding's presidency.

Quick Instruction

Explain that when Harding became President, he appointed some well-qualified officials as well as friends from his home state Ohio. These friends proved to be untrustworthy as scandal after scandal plagued Harding's presidency. These appointees became known as the Ohio Gang. Harding, who was an honest man and strong business leader, was distraught over his friends' betrayal. Ask: How did the behavior of the Ohio Gang likely affect people's opinion of Harding's presidency? *(Possible response: It likely reflected on the President himself, making Americans less trusting of his leadership abilities.)*

Summarize How did President Coolidge deal with members of the Ohio Gang who were involved in scandals during Harding's presidency? *(He forced them to resign from office.)* How did his response to the scandal affect citizen's confidence? *(It helped them regain confidence in him as evidenced by his re-election.)*

Compare Presidents Harding and Coolidge. *(Both were Republicans who supported big business. After Harding died, Coolidge cleaned up much of the scandal involving the previous administration, gaining enough voter support to win his own election in 1924.)*

Further Instruction

Infer How did economic conditions in the country most likely affect the 1920 presidential election? *(After World War I, economic production declined and unemployment rose. High unemployment led to voter discontent with the Democratic party, and the Republicans claimed the Presidency for the first time in eight years.)*

Hypothesize In light of the scandals associated with the Harding administration, would Republicans have retained control of the White House in the next election had Harding not died? *(The many scandals associated with the Harding administration may have made it difficult for him to win election if he did not resolve the scandals in a manner that satisfied the public.)*

Harding and Coolidge

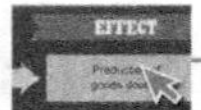

DIGITAL TEXT 2

Economic Growth Under President Coolidge

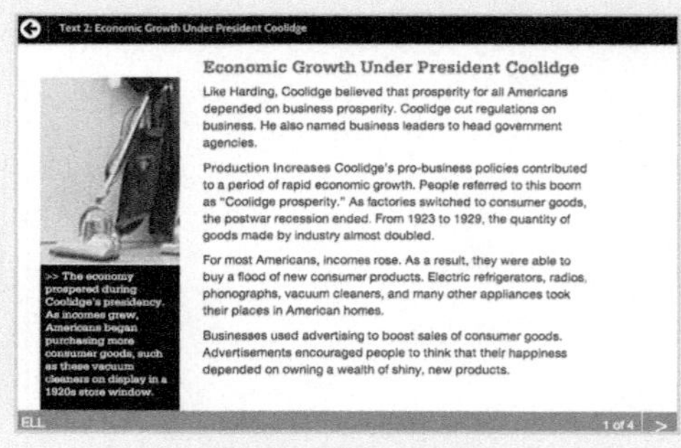

INTERACTIVE CHART

Economic Expansion in the 1920s

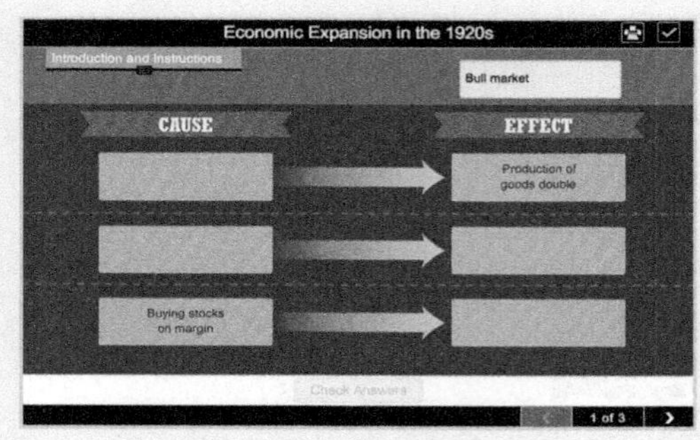

DIGITAL TEXT 3

A Return to Isolationism

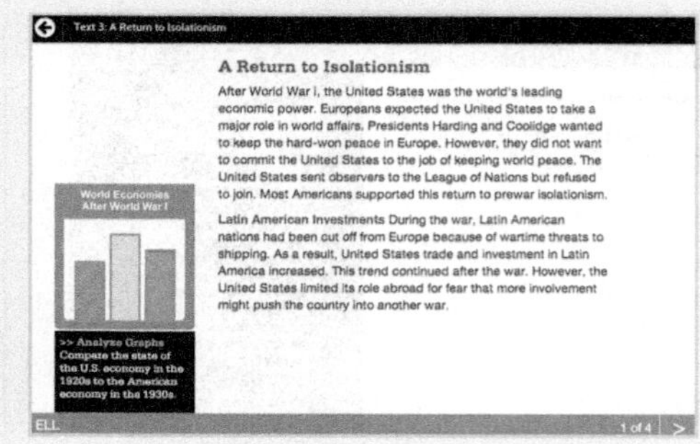

Objective 2: Explain why the economy grew under Coolidge.

Quick Instruction

Interactive Chart: Economic Expansion in the 1920s Project the Interactive Chart and prompt students to complete it. Discuss Coolidge's belief that American prosperity depended on the success of business. Coolidge advocated deregulation of business practices and appointed businessmen to official positions. Point out that industries transitioned from wartime production to domestic production for consumers.

Summarize What role did installment buying play in the robust economy of the 1920s? *(As production of goods increased, many businesses offered consumers the option of paying for goods in monthly installments rather than paying the full purchase price at once. Consumer purchases increased significantly, which further stimulated economic growth.)*

Summarize Although installment buying stimulated economic growth, what potential negative consequence did the practice have for consumers? *(Many consumers purchased more than they could afford with installment buying. As a result, consumer debt increased.)*

ACTIVE CLASSROOM

Conduct a Sticky Notes activity. Ask students to jot down questions or comments about each cause-and-effect relationship in the interactive chart. Then, have them post their stickies together by topic. Discuss the questions and comments, guiding students to understand the relationship between each cause and effect.

D Differentiate: Extra Support Before completing the chart, review the key terms *installment buying, margin,* and *bull market.* Make sure students understand that installment buying is similar to purchasing something with a credit card only the store held the loan, not a bank. Explain the process of buying stock on margin, pointing out that if stocks lost value, then the holder would owe more than the stock was worth.

ELL Use the ELL activity described in the ELL chart.

Further Instruction

Draw Conclusions What would happen if a stock bought on margin lost value? *(The person holding the stock would owe more than the stock was worth so would have to pay for something that was worthless.)*

Predict Consequences What will happen as a result of stock prices rising faster than the actual value of businesses? *(Many people, especially those who bought stock on margin, will lose money on their purchases.)*

Objective 3: Identify the role the United States played in international politics during the 1920s.

Quick Instruction

Interactive Chart: Points of View on Foreign Affairs in the 1920s Project the Interactive Chart and guide students as they compare and contrast the primary source quotes. Remind students that World War I, which had recently ended, was fresh in the minds of Americans. Though the United States was the leading power in the world, Americans did not want to take on the role of global police. Instead, President Coolidge guided the country back to pre-war isolationism. In the meantime, Secretary of State Frank Kellogg worked to create the Kellogg-Briand Pact in order to avoid another war.

Summarize What foreign challenges confronted the United States in the 1920s? *(In Latin America, American investments were threatened by governments, and the Soviet Union was going through a civil war and famine, both of which led the United States to increase its involvement in foreign affairs despite intentions otherwise.)*

SYNTHESIZE

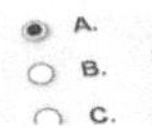

DEMONSTRATE

INTERACTIVE CHART

Points of View on Foreign Affairs in the 1920s

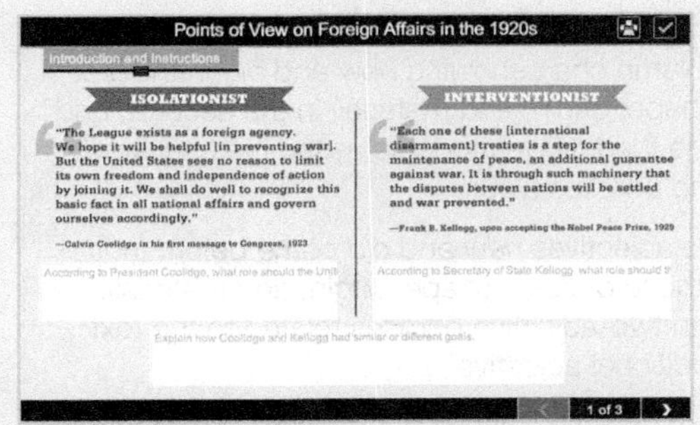

ACTIVE CLASSROOM

Conduct a Circle Write strategy. Ask students which point of view seems most reasonable and divide them into groups based on their opinions. Have students write the reasons for their opinions for a minute and then switch with the person on their right. The next student should try to improve or elaborate on the first response. Continue to write and exchange the paper until it returns to the first person. At the end, the group should decide which is the best response and share it with the class.

ELL Use the ELL activity described in the ELL chart.

Further Instruction

Connect How did the recent experience of World War I affect the way President Coolidge dealt with concerns in Mexico? *(President Coolidge was hesitant to draw the American military into another foreign conflict so soon after World War I. Rather than sending troops when Mexico threatened to take over American companies, Coolidge tried diplomacy to work out a solution.)*

Identify Central Issues Why did the United States decide against active participation in the League of Nations? *(The United States chose not to participate in the League of Nations because many did not want to give up the government's autonomy to the organization and preferred to return to a pre-war isolationism.)*

DIGITAL ACTIVITY

Republican Leadership in the 1920s

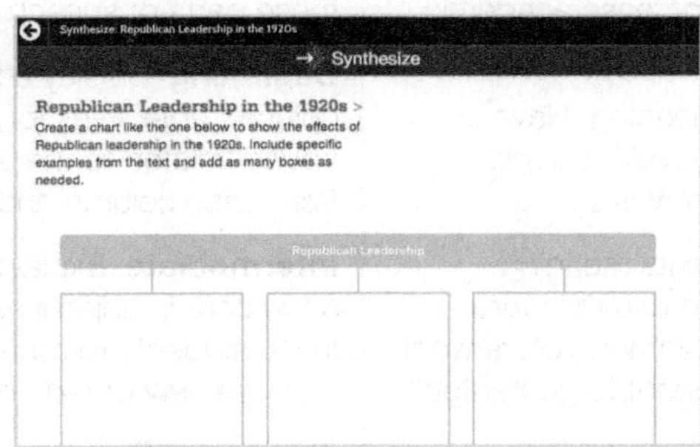

Before students begin their charts, review the policies and economics that are traditionally associated with Republican leadership, such as pro-business policies and deregulation. Then, have students complete the charts independently.

Discuss Invite students to share their completed charts with the class or post them on the Class Discussion Board. Challenge students to hypothesize how leadership would have differed if a Democrat were in office.

DIGITAL QUIZ

Lesson Quiz and Discussion Board

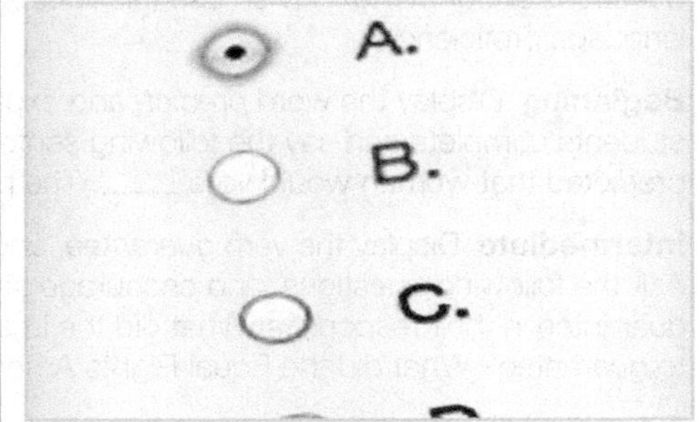

Assign the online Lesson Quiz for this lesson if you haven't already done so. Students will be offered automatic remediation or enrichment based on their score.

In *Harding and Coolidge*, you learned about a recession that led voters to elect Warren Harding and the scandals that plagued his presidency, economic growth under Calvin Coolidge, and some foreign policy challenges of the 1920s.

Post these questions to the class on the Discussion Board:

Identify Cause and Effect What caused the economic growth that marked the 1920s?

Express Problems Clearly What potential economic problems might result from stock market speculation and increasing consumer debt in the 1920s?

Topic Inquiry

Have students continue their investigations for the Topic Inquiry.

Topic 13 Lesson 2

Social Change

Supporting English Language Learners

Use with the reading, **Changes in Women's Lives**.

Speaking

Facilitate students' use of content-area vocabulary by having them answer questions about the text. Then use this vocabulary to increase academic language proficiency.

Beginning Display the word *predict*, and explain its meaning. Have students complete and say the following sentences: In 1920, people predicted that women would vote _____. The prediction was _____.

Intermediate Display the verb *guarantee*, and discuss its meaning. Ask the following questions, and encourage students to use the word guarantee in their responses: What did the League of Women Voters want to guarantee? What did the Equal Rights Amendment want to guarantee?

Advanced Display the verbs *guarantee* and *deny*. Discuss their meanings and how they are related to each other (as antonyms). Have pairs of students use these words as they discuss how American women's rights were guaranteed and/or denied in the 1920s and beyond.

Advanced High Display the words guarantee, deny, professional, and convention. Invite pairs of students to locate these words (or their related word forms) in the text and determine their meanings. Then have them use each of these words as they discuss the rights of American women in the 1920s.

Use with the reading, **A New National Culture**.

Reading

Display the title of the text. Identify its adjectives and noun, and review these parts of speech.

Beginning Display a three-column chart showing *new* and *old* in the first column, *adjectives* (of color, shape, origin, and material) in the second, and *nouns* (related to the text) in the third. Have students assemble one word from each column and read the phrases aloud.

Intermediate Explain that the adjectives *new* and *old* come before (not after) certain adjectives (e.g., those of color, shape, origin, and material). Invite students to come up with two-adjective phrases related to the text that use *new* or *old* and an additional adjective.

Advanced Explain the order of adjective placement (opinion, dimension, age, shape, color, origin, material). Discuss how this order is reflected in the title and other two-adjective phrases from the text (e.g., warm, sunny climate; red velvet seats; tiny derby hat).

Advanced High Explain the order of adjective placement (opinion, dimension, age, shape, color, origin, material). Ask pairs of students to locate at least three other examples of two-adjective phrases in the text and examine the order of those adjectives (e.g., warm, sunny climate; red velvet seats; tiny derby hat).

D Differentiate Instruction

Use the Differentiated Instruction notes throughout the lesson plan to support the varied skill sets, levels of readiness, and interests in the mixed-ability classroom.

Challenge These notes include suggestions for expanding the activity for advanced students.

On-Level These notes include suggestions for modifying the activity to address different interests or learning styles.

Extra Support These notes include ideas for providing more scaffolding or reading spuport.

Special Needs These notes provide ideas for adapting instruction to support the needs of various special needs students.

NOTES

PEARSON realize™ www.PearsonRealize.com

Go online to access additional resources including: Primary Sources • Biographies • Supreme Court cases • 21st Century Skill Tutorials • Maps • Graphic Organizers.

Objectives

Objective 1: Identify Prohibition.

Objective 2: Describe how life changed for women.

Objective 3: Explain the impact of the automobile and mass culture on American life.

LESSON 2 ORGANIZER	OBJECTIVES	PACING	RESOURCES Online	RESOURCES Print
Connect				
DIGITAL START UP ACTIVITY **Women Continue to Fight for Equality**		5 min.	●	
Investigate				
DIGITAL TEXT 1 **The Noble Experiment**	Objective 1	10 min.	●	●
INTERACTIVE GALLERY **The Prohibition Era**	Objective 1	10 min.	●	
DIGITAL TEXT 2 **Changes in Women's Lives**	Objective 2	10 min.	●	●
DIGITAL TEXT 3 **The Automobile Changes America**	Objective 3	10 min.	●	●
DIGITAL TEXT 4 **A New National Culture**	Objective 3	10 min.	●	●
INTERACTIVE GALLERY **Changes in American Life in the 1920s**	Objective 3	10 min.	●	
Synthesize				
DIGITAL ACTIVITY **Cultural Change after World War I**		5 min.	●	
Demonstrate				
DIGITAL QUIZ **Lesson Quiz and Discussion Board**		10 min.	●	

PACING: APPROX. 1 PERIOD, .5 BLOCKS

Social Change

CONNECT

DIGITAL START UP ACTIVITY

Women Continue to Fight for Equality

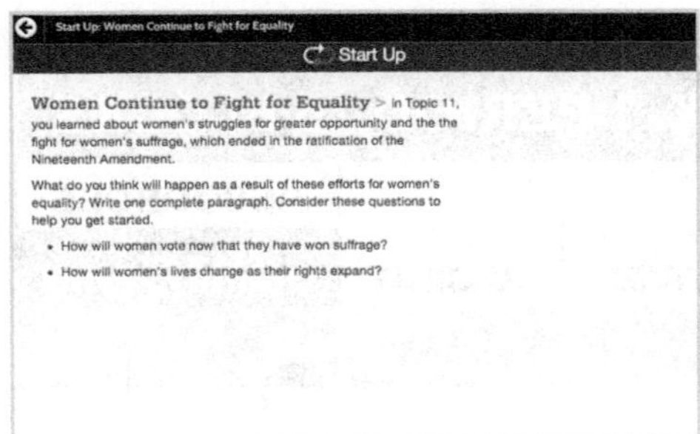

Start Up: Women Continue to Fight for Equality
Start Up
Women Continue to Fight for Equality > In Topic 11, you learned about women's struggles for greater opportunity and the the fight for women's suffrage, which ended in the ratification of the Nineteenth Amendment.
What do you think will happen as a result of these efforts for women's equality? Write one complete paragraph. Consider these questions to help you get started.
• How will women vote now that they have won suffrage?
• How will women's lives change as their rights expand?

Project the Start Up Activity Have students complete the activity as they enter the classroom. Then ask them to share and discuss their ideas with partners.

Discuss How will women vote now that they have won suffrage? *(They will likely vote for officials who support equality and the causes they espouse.)* How will women's lives change as their rights expand? *(Women will have more job opportunities outside the home and will be given more freedoms and respect.)*

Tell students that this lesson examines social change in 1920s America, including the introduction and repeal of Prohibition, the expansion of women's rights, and the impact of the automobile and mass culture.

Aa Vocabulary Development: Use the Interactive Reading Notepad to preview the Key Terms and Academic Vocabulary in this lesson with students.

FLIP IT!

Assign the Flipped Video for this lesson.

STUDENT EDITION PRINT PAGES: 706–713

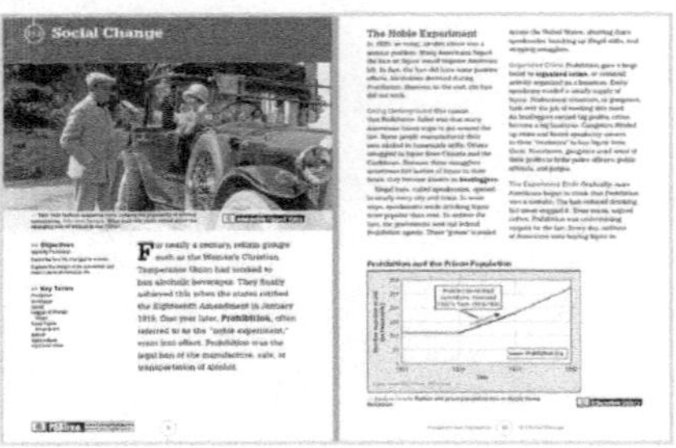

INVESTIGATE

DIGITAL TEXT 1

The Noble Experiment

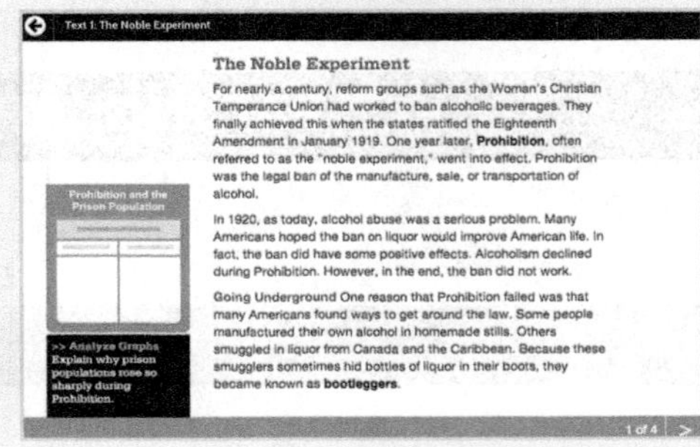

INTERACTIVE GALLERY

The Prohibition Era

Objective 1: Identify Prohibition.

Quick Instruction

Interactive Gallery: The Prohibition Era Project the Interactive Gallery and guide students through the images. Prompt students to understand that, although rates of alcoholism did somewhat decline, an unintended effect of Prohibition was the illegal production and distribution of alcohol. Why did Prohibition fail to achieve its planned outcomes? *(People refused to give up drinking and the social life surrounding it, so Prohibition led to an illegal, underground network that supplied the continued demand for alcohol.)*

ACTIVE CLASSROOM

Conduct an If Photos Could Talk activity. Instruct students to choose an image from the gallery. Then, ask: What do you think the person pictured would say if they could talk? What's your evidence? Group students and have them share their answers.

Further Instruction

Draw Conclusions How did Prohibition undermine the authority of the government? *(It turned average citizens who enjoyed social drinking into criminals. Instead of obeying the law and respecting the ban, they purchased illegal alcohol supplied by organized crime.)*

DIGITAL TEXT 2
Changes in Women's Lives

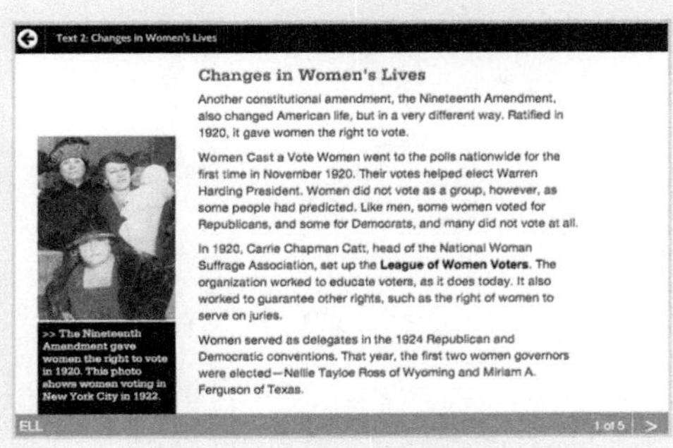

Text 2: Changes in Women's Lives

Changes in Women's Lives

Another constitutional amendment, the Nineteenth Amendment, also changed American life, but in a very different way. Ratified in 1920, it gave women the right to vote.

Women Cast a Vote Women went to the polls nationwide for the first time in November 1920. Their votes helped elect Warren Harding President. Women did not vote as a group, however, as some people had predicted. Like men, some women voted for Republicans, and some for Democrats, and many did not vote at all.

In 1920, Carrie Chapman Catt, head of the National Woman Suffrage Association, set up the **League of Women Voters**. The organization worked to educate voters, as it does today. It also worked to guarantee other rights, such as the right of women to serve on juries.

Women served as delegates in the 1924 Republican and Democratic conventions. That year, the first two women governors were elected—Nellie Tayloe Ross of Wyoming and Miriam A. Ferguson of Texas.

>> The Nineteenth Amendment gave women the right to vote in 1920. This photo shows women voting in New York City in 1922.

ELL 1 of 5 >

DIGITAL TEXT 3
The Automobile Changes America

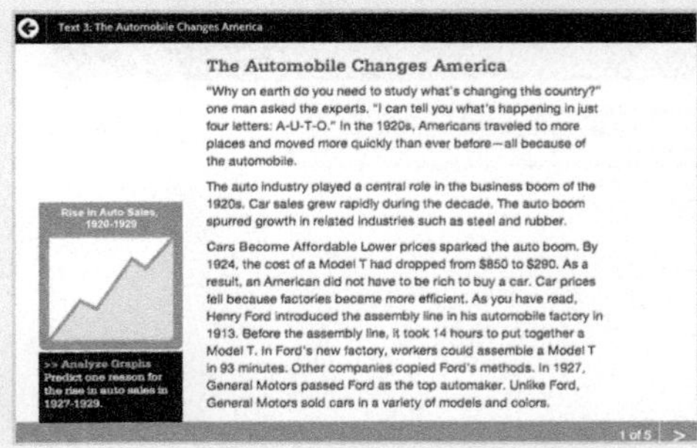

Text 3: The Automobile Changes America

The Automobile Changes America

"Why on earth do you need to study what's changing this country?" one man asked the experts. "I can tell you what's happening in just four letters: A-U-T-O." In the 1920s, Americans traveled to more places and moved more quickly than ever before—all because of the automobile.

The auto industry played a central role in the business boom of the 1920s. Car sales grew rapidly during the decade. The auto boom spurred growth in related industries such as steel and rubber.

Cars Become Affordable Lower prices sparked the auto boom. By 1924, the cost of a Model T had dropped from $850 to $290. As a result, an American did not have to be rich to buy a car. Car prices fell because factories became more efficient. As you have read, Henry Ford introduced the assembly line in his automobile factory in 1913. Before the assembly line, it took 14 hours to put together a Model T. In Ford's new factory, workers could assemble a Model T in 93 minutes. Other companies copied Ford's methods. In 1927, General Motors passed Ford as the top automaker. Unlike Ford, General Motors sold cars in a variety of models and colors.

Rise in Auto Sales, 1920–1929

>> Analyze Graphs Predict one reason for the rise in auto sales in 1927-1929.

1 of 5 >

DIGITAL TEXT 4
A New National Culture

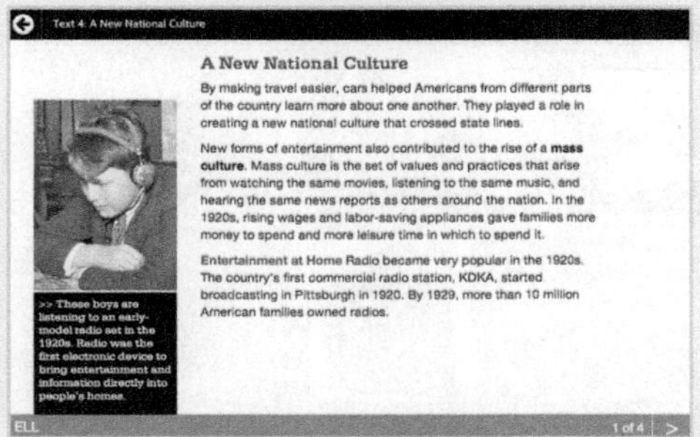

Text 4: A New National Culture

A New National Culture

By making travel easier, cars helped Americans from different parts of the country learn more about one another. They played a role in creating a new national culture that crossed state lines.

New forms of entertainment also contributed to the rise of a **mass culture**. Mass culture is the set of values and practices that arise from watching the same movies, listening to the same music, and hearing the same news reports as others around the nation. In the 1920s, rising wages and labor-saving appliances gave families more money to spend and more leisure time in which to spend it.

Entertainment at Home Radio became very popular in the 1920s. The country's first commercial radio station, KDKA, started broadcasting in Pittsburgh in 1920. By 1929, more than 10 million American families owned radios.

>> These boys are listening to an early-model radio set in the 1920s. Radio was the first electronic device to bring entertainment and information directly into people's homes.

ELL 1 of 4 >

Objective 2: **Describe how life changed for women.**

Quick Instruction

Display the photograph of women at the polls. Point out that having the vote gave women a stronger voice in American politics. It also encouraged women to seek more rights, including the right to serve on juries, enter colleges and universities, and have a wider choice of careers.

Support Ideas with Evidence What evidence supports the idea that many Americans supported women's suffrage and increased participation in politics? *(The Nineteenth Amendment gave women the right to vote in 1920, which reflected many Americans' belief that women should be active citizens. Women were subsequently chosen as delegates at national conventions and elected to statewide office for the first time.)*

ELL Use the ELL activity described in the ELL chart.

Further Instruction

Compare Points of View How were viewpoints concerning the Equal Rights Amendment divided? *(Those in favor of the amendment believed it protected women by guaranteeing equal treatment, whereas those opposed to it thought it threatened the legal protections set in place for women in the workplace and undermined women's traditional societal roles.)*

Infer How did World War I expand employment opportunities for women? *(Many women filled positions left by men fighting in the war in Europe; however, some women remained in the workforce following the war.)*

Objective 3: **Explain the impact of the automobile and mass culture on American life.**

Quick Instruction

Interactive Gallery: Changes in American Life in the 1920s Project the Interactive Gallery and navigate through the images with students. Prompt students to understand that innovations such as cars, radios, and movies allowed common cultural attributes to be shared across the country. The automobile let people travel farther more easily than ever before. Radios and movies broadcast trends and fashions across the country. Americans were not so geographically isolated any longer.

ACTIVE CLASSROOM

Conduct an Act It Out activity. Group students and have them choose a photograph and discuss what happened before or after the photograph was taken. Then, have group members write a conversation or script based on the event they chose and ask volunteers to act out the event.

D Differentiate: Extra Support Draw a cause-effect chart with one cause—the automobile—and boxes for multiple effects. Ask students to identify some changes that occurred as a result of the rise in popularity of the car. Guide students to connect this event to the growth of the economy; jobs in the auto industry, the steel industry, the rubber industry, and so on; changes to the American landscape, including paved roads and gas stations; the birth of the hotel industry and mechanic shops; growth of the suburbs.

ELL Use the ELL activity described in the ELL chart.

Social Change

INTERACTIVE GALLERY

Changes in American Life in the 1920s

Further Instruction

Identify Central Issues How did increased automobile production affect other industries and stimulate economic growth throughout the country? *(Other industries developed concurrently with the increasing popularity of the automobile, such as steel and rubber production and oil refineries. Highway construction also grew exponentially. All of these industries created jobs for Americans, which further stimulated economic growth.)*

Identify Cause and Effect What technological innovations led to the birth of a mass culture in the United States? *(National entertainment in the form of radio and movies contributed to the birth of mass culture by spreading ideals and fashions to moviegoers and listeners across the nation.)*

SYNTHESIZE

DIGITAL ACTIVITY

Cultural Change after World War I

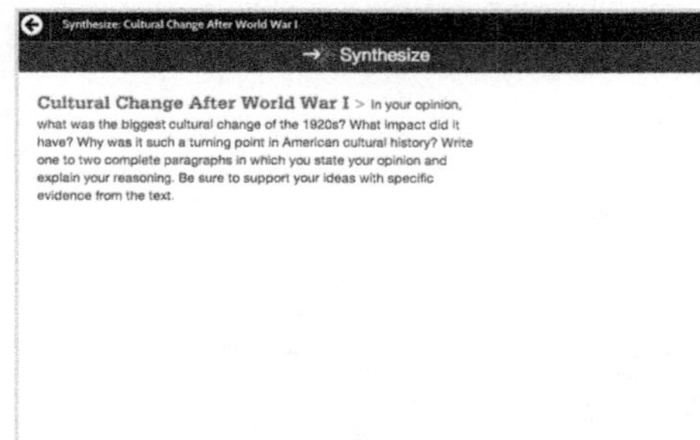

Synthesize: Cultural Change After World War I
→ Synthesize
Cultural Change After World War I > In your opinion, what was the biggest cultural change of the 1920s? What impact did it have? Why was it such a turning point in American cultural history? Write one to two complete paragraphs in which you state your opinion and explain your reasoning. Be sure to support your ideas with specific evidence from the text.

Before students write their opinion paragraphs, convene as a class and brainstorm a list of cultural changes from the 1920s. Then, allow students time to form their opinions and complete the writing.

Discuss Invite volunteers to share their opinion paragraphs. Take a class poll to see if one particular cultural change was ranked most important overall. Prompt students to discuss the rationale behind their rankings.

DEMONSTRATE

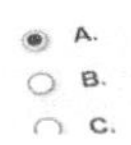

DIGITAL QUIZ

Lesson Quiz and Discussion Board

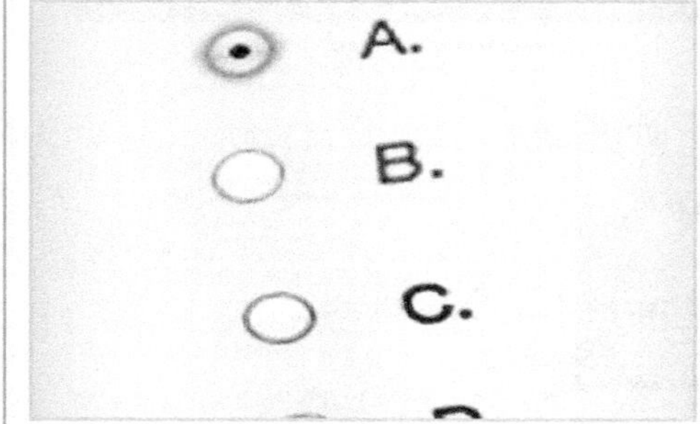

Assign the online Lesson Quiz for this lesson if you haven't already done so. Students will be offered automatic remediation or enrichment based on their score.

In *Social Change*, you learned about Prohibition, changes in women's political and societal roles, the effects of the automobile, and the birth of mass culture.

Post these questions to the class on the Discussion Board:

Summarize the social changes that occurred in the 1920s and how they affect American life.

Determine Relevance How did the rise in the popularity of the automobile effect social change?

Topic Inquiry

Have students continue their investigations for the Topic Inquiry.

PEARSON realize™ www.PearsonRealize.com Access your Digital Lesson

Roaring Twenties Culture

Supporting English Language Learners

Use with the reading, **Trends of the 1920s**.

Learning

Explain that when students encounter unfamiliar words (or familiar words in unfamiliar contexts), their prior knowledge can help them to determine the words' meanings.

Beginning Ask: What does the word *crazy* mean? Then display this sentence based on the text: The Charleston was a dance craze. Guide students to see how knowledge of the word *crazy* can help them to understand this sentence and define *craze*.

Intermediate Point out the use of *crazes* and *craze* in the text's third paragraph. Ask: What familiar word is similar to *craze*? What does crazy mean? How can thinking about *crazy* help you to understand the word *craze*?

Advanced Display images of a marathon race (e.g., runners, race course, spectators). Have partners describe this type of marathon and then use that knowledge to define *dance marathon*.

Advanced High Point out the term *old-fashioned* in the text. Ask students to explain in writing how considering the individual parts *old* and *fashioned* helps define the entire term. Then have partners share and discuss their ideas.

Use with the reading, **A New Generation of Writers**.

Listening

Ask students when and how they have heard the word *popular* used at school. Point out three uses of *popular* in the text.

Beginning Say several sentences, either true or false, that use the word *popular* and refer to the text (e.g., Hemingway was a popular writer; Sinclair Lewis was popular in small towns). Have students listen to each sentence and identify it as true or false.

Intermediate Invite students to use the word *popular* as they describe the United States in the 1920s. Then ask students questions about which people, things, and ideas might have been more or less popular than others.

Advanced Invite students to use the word *popular* as they describe the United States in the 1920s. Then have pairs of students use the word *popular* as they compare the popularity of Hemingway, Fitzgerald, et al., in the 1920s and today.

Advanced High Have pairs of students examine the three uses of *popular* in the text. Ask them to discuss these questions: How would you define *popular* in each example? What synonyms could replace *popular* in each example? What else was popular in the 1920s?

D Differentiate Instruction

Use the Differentiated Instruction notes throughout the lesson plan to support the varied skill sets, levels of readiness, and interests in the mixed-ability classroom.

Challenge These notes include suggestions for expanding the activity for advanced students.

On-Level These notes include suggestions for modifying the activity to address different interests or learning styles.

Extra Support These notes include ideas for providing more scaffolding or reading spuport.

Special Needs These notes provide ideas for adapting instruction to support the needs of various special needs students.

NOTES

Roaring Twenties Culture

Objectives

Objective 1: Identify fads and fashions of the 1920s.

Objective 2: Explain the origins and effects of jazz music.

Objective 3: Identify new kinds of writing during the 1920s, including the Harlem Renaissance.

Objective 4: Identify heroes of the 1920s.

LESSON 3 ORGANIZER	PACING: APPROX. 1 PERIOD, .5 BLOCKS		RESOURCES	
	OBJECTIVES	PACING	Online	Print
Connect				
DIGITAL START UP ACTIVITY **A Flight Across the Atlantic**		5 min.	●	
Investigate				
DIGITAL TEXT 1 **Trends of the 1920s**	Objective 1	10 min.	●	●
INTERACTIVE GALLERY **American Culture in the 1920s**	Objective 1	10 min.	●	
DIGITAL TEXT 2 **A New Generation of Writers**	Objective 3	10 min.	●	●
DIGITAL TEXT 3 **The Harlem Renaissance**	Objective 3	10 min.	●	●
INTERACTIVE GALLERY **Key Figures of the Harlem Renaissance**	Objective 3	10 min.	●	
Synthesize				
DIGITAL ACTIVITY **1920s Culture**		5 min.	●	
Demonstrate				
DIGITAL QUIZ **Lesson Quiz and Discussion Board**		10 min.	●	

CONNECT

DIGITAL START UP ACTIVITY

A Flight Across the Atlantic

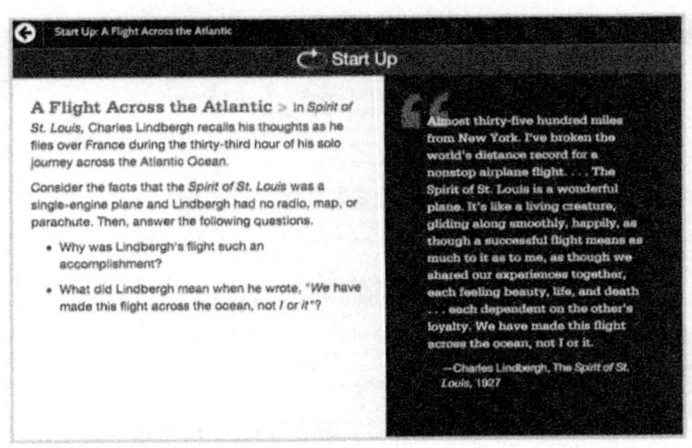

Project the Start Up Activity Have students read the quotation and answer the questions as they enter the classroom.

Discuss Why was Lindbergh's flight such an accomplishment? *(It broke the record for the longest distance for a nonstop flight, which he took alone across the Atlantic Ocean.)* What did Lindbergh mean when he wrote, "We have made this flight across the ocean, not *I* or *it*"? *(Possible response: He considers the flight a joint effort by his airplane and himself. He sees his airplane as a partner of sorts.)*

Tell students that this lesson examines the culture of the Roaring Twenties, including fashions and fads, music, literature, and the emergence of national heroes.

Aa Vocabulary Development: Use the Interactive Reading Notepad to preview the Key Terms and Academic Vocabulary in this Lesson with students.

FLIP IT!

Assign the Flipped Video for this lesson.

STUDENT EDITION PRINT PAGES: 714–720

INVESTIGATE

DIGITAL TEXT 1

Trends of the 1920s

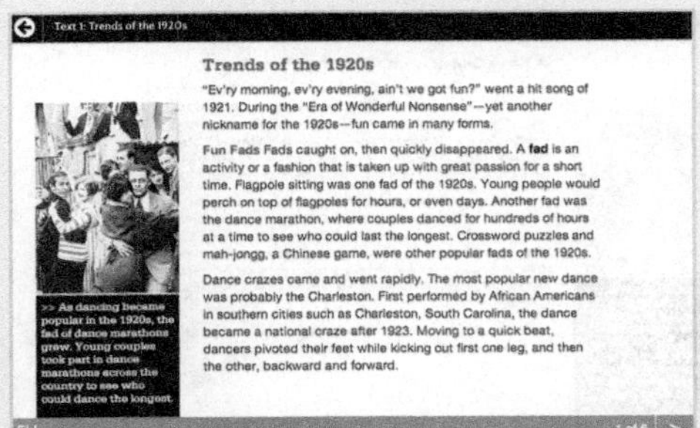

INTERACTIVE GALLERY

American Culture in the 1920s

Objective 1: **Identify fads and fashions of the 1920s.**

Quick Instruction

Interactive Gallery: American Culture in the 1920s Project the Interactive Gallery and navigate through the images with students. As you display the photograph of the two flappers dancing the Charleston, explain that their clothing is an example of a bold new fashion of the 1920s. Point out that dancing in various forms was a popular pastime and with its popularity came the rise in popularity of music. Movies were another popular form of entertainment.

Connect How did the dance fads and clothing fashions of flappers symbolize a "new sense of freedom" in the 1920s? *(The dance and clothing styles of the time represented a bold departure from the values of the previous generation. The fads and fashions were a symbol of women's evolving role in society and gradually increasing social and educational opportunities.)*

ACTIVE CLASSROOM

Conduct a My Metaphor activity. Give students the following prompt: This gallery/photograph shows that _____ is like _____ because _____. Provide students with an example to get them started: This gallery shows that *fads* are like *waves in the ocean* because *they regularly come and go*. After students have completed their metaphors, invite volunteers to share their metaphors with the class.

ELL Use the ELL activity described in the ELL chart.

Further Instruction

Express Ideas Clearly Instruct students to draw an idea web to record the key ideas from this text. Tell students to label the center circle "Trends of the 1920s." They should then list the major trends in the next layer of circles: Fashion, Fads, Music, Heroes. Finally, they should list details about each of these categories. *(Details should include: Fashion: flappers, bobbed hair, short skirts; Fads: dance marathons, flagpole sitting, mah-jongg; Music: jazz, Louis Armstrong; Heroes: sports heroes, Charles Lindbergh)*

Roaring Twenties Culture

Generate Explanations What role did the media play in creating celebrity sports heroes who were popular around the country? *(Innovations such as radio and movies supplemented newspapers and kept Americans across the country informed about sporting events. So, sports heroes such as Babe Ruth, who generally played in the east and midwest regions of the country, were also well-known in the far west, creating a fanbase that stretched nationwide.)*

DIGITAL TEXT 2

A New Generation of Writers

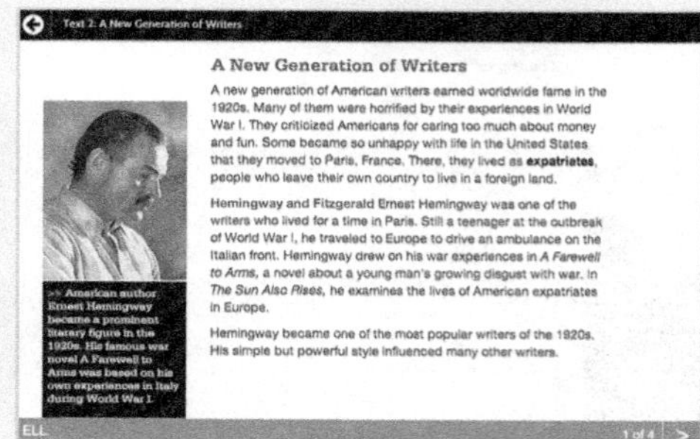

Objective 3: **Identify new kinds of writing during the 1920s, including the Harlem Renaissance.**

Quick Instruction

Interactive Gallery: Key Figures of the Harlem Renaissance Project the Interactive Gallery and navigate through the images with students. Prompt students to understand that the Harlem Renaissance was a literary and artistic movement in which African Americans celebrated their heritage and fought prejudice and racism.

Synthesize Many African American soldiers returned home hoping for increased political and social equality after fighting for the United States in World War I. How might this hope connect to the Harlem Renaissance? *(The return of African American soldiers from World War I may have underscored the importance of the underlying themes present in much of the Harlem Renaissance's artistry: a celebration of African American heritage and a strong statement against racism in the same country for which African American soldiers fought.)*

DIGITAL TEXT 3

The Harlem Renaissance

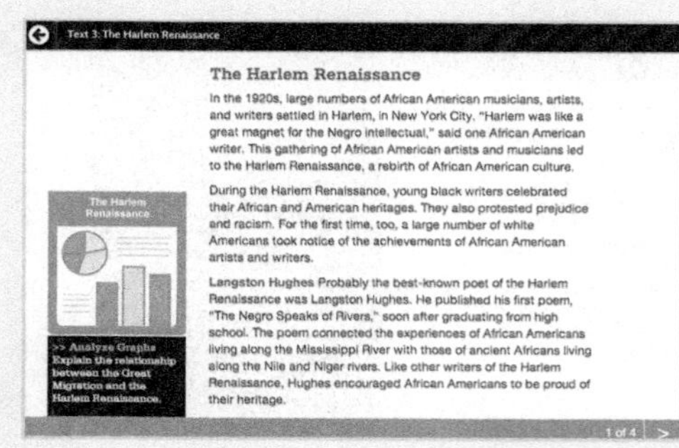

ACTIVE CLASSROOM

Conduct a Conversation with History activity. Tell students to imagine they are having conversations with one of the people pictured. Instruct students to write down a question to ask, what that person would likely say, and how they would respond. Invite students to share their conversations with the rest of the class.

INTERACTIVE GALLERY

Key Figures of the Harlem Renaissance

ELL Use the ELL activity described in the ELL chart.

Further Instruction

To further explore the concepts of the Harlem Renaissance, assign Primary Sources: Two Poems (Langston Hughes).

Connect How did many of F. Scott Fitzgerald's stories about wealth and happiness connect to American life in the 1920s? *(Although many Americans saw their standard of living improve during the prosperous 1920s, Fitzgerald questioned how much happiness an increase in material possessions could really bring.)*

SYNTHESIZE

DIGITAL ACTIVITY

1920s Culture

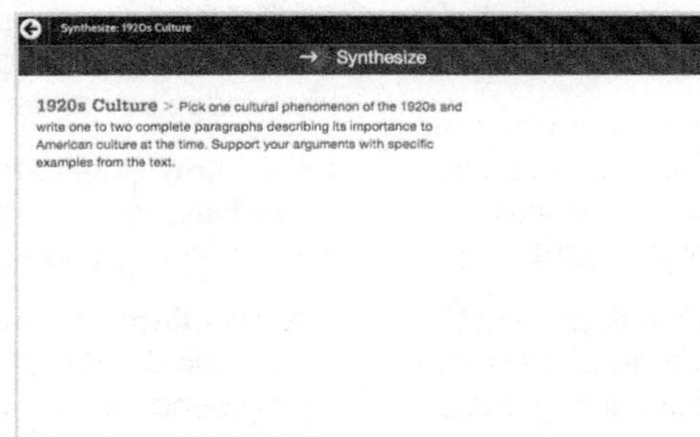

Synthesize
1920s Culture > Pick one cultural phenomenon of the 1920s and write one to two complete paragraphs describing its importance to American culture at the time. Support your arguments with specific examples from the text.

Work as a class to brainstorm a list of cultural phenomena of the 1920s before students choose one to discuss in writing. Then, allow students time to complete their paragraphs.

Discuss Invite students to share their paragraphs with the class. Lead a class discussion in which you consider the impact of the cultural phenomenon and how it paved the way for a cultural phenomenon of today.

DEMONSTRATE

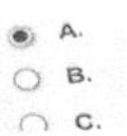

DIGITAL QUIZ

Lesson Quiz and Discussion Board

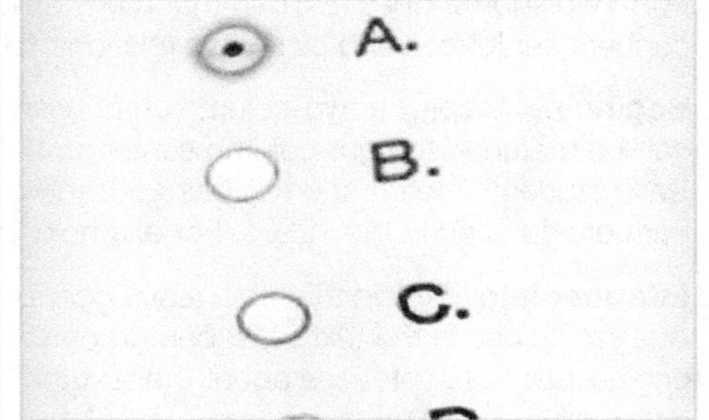

Assign the online Lesson Quiz for this lesson if you haven't already done so. Students will be offered automatic remediation or enrichment based on their score.

In *Roaring Twenties Culture*, you learned about fads and fashions of the 1920s, including flappers, dances, and music. You were introduced to athletic heroes and learned about the new generation of writers that expressed their discontent through fiction. You learned about the Harlem Renaissance and some of its key participants.

Post these questions to the class on the Discussion Board:

Compare and Contrast How did the atmosphere created by fads and fashions of the 1920s differ from those created by the new generation of writers of the time?

Determine Relevance Why was the Harlem Renaissance so important to African American culture and the whole of American culture?

Topic Inquiry

Have students continue their investigations for the Topic Inquiry.

Division and Inequality

Supporting English Language Learners

Use with the reading, **The Downside of the 1920s**.	Use with the reading, **Cultural Clashes**.
Speaking Review how words such as *and* and *but* can create a longer sentence from two shorter ones. Explain that many other words and phrases also connect sentences and clarify the relationship between them. **Beginning** Display a two-column chart, with left-column sentences that can be matched to right-column sentences beginning with "for example." Have students match and say pairs of sentences about the text (e.g., Farmers suffered in the 1920s. For example, many went into debt.). **Intermediate** Explain that *as a result* connects a cause with an effect. Analyze its use in the text's last paragraph. Then invite students to create original pairs of sentences about the text that use this connecting phrase. **Advanced** Point out *in return* in the text's fourth paragraph. With students, create a list of alternative phrases with a similar meaning (e.g., in exchange). Invite pairs to create an original example of *in return* in pairs of sentences about the text. **Advanced High** Explain that *at the same time* can mean "simultaneously" or "on the other hand." Have pairs of students determine its meaning in the text's last paragraph. Then have them use the phrase both ways as they discuss the content of the text.	**Reading** Explain that to grasp both Charles Darwin's theory of evolution and various Biblical interpretations of creation can be daunting. Encourage students to recognize what they do not understand and seek additional background knowledge as needed. **Beginning** Reread the second and third paragraphs of the text, pausing periodically to model asking questions in order to obtain additional information. Encourage students also to ask questions about the material. **Intermediate** Provide a brief written summary of the conflicting positions involved in the Scopes Trial. After students have read this additional background knowledge, ask: How has your understanding or perspective of the Scopes Trial changed? What other background knowledge would be helpful? **Advanced** Invite pairs of students to use books or the Internet to develop their background knowledge of the conflicting positions in the Scopes Trial. Then invite them to discuss how their research has helped them to better understand the text. **Advanced High** Provide pairs of students with brief primary texts related to the Scopes Trial (e.g., Biblical passages, Darwin's writings, transcripts from the trial). Invite pairs to read the primary texts and discuss how they add to their understanding of the text *Cultural Clashes*.

D Differentiate Instruction

Use the Differentiated Instruction notes throughout the lesson plan to support the varied skill sets, levels of readiness, and interests in the mixed-ability classroom.

Challenge These notes include suggestions for expanding the activity for advanced students.

On-Level These notes include suggestions for modifying the activity to address different interests or learning styles.

Extra Support These notes include ideas for providing more scaffolding or reading spuport.

Special Needs These notes provide ideas for adapting instruction to support the needs of various special needs students.

NOTES

Objectives

Objective 1: Identify Americans who faced economic hardship during the 1920s.

Objective 2: Explain the significance of the Scopes Trial and the Red Scare.

Objective 3: Describe the causes and effects of limits on immigration.

Objective 4: Identify the impact of racial tensions during the 1920s.

Objective 5: Describe the election of 1928.

LESSON 4 ORGANIZER — **PACING: APPROX. 1 PERIOD, .5 BLOCKS**

	OBJECTIVES	PACING	RESOURCES Online	RESOURCES Print
Connect				
DIGITAL START UP ACTIVITY **America's Outsiders in the 1920s**		5 min.	●	
Investigate				
DIGITAL TEXT 1 **The Downside of the 1920s**	Objective 1	10 min.	●	●
DIGITAL TEXT 2 **Cultural Clashes**	Objective 2	10 min.	●	●
DIGITAL TEXT 3 **Tensions Divide Americans**	Objectives 4, 5	10 min.	●	●
INTERACTIVE GRAPH **Limiting Immigration**	Objective 3	10 min.	●	
INTERACTIVE GALLERY **Contrasts in American Society**		10 min.	●	
Synthesize				
DIGITAL ACTIVITY **What Should Governments Do?**		5 min.	●	
Demonstrate				
DIGITAL QUIZ **Lesson Quiz and Discussion Board**		10 min.	●	

Topic 13 Lesson 4

Division and Inequality

CONNECT

DIGITAL START UP ACTIVITY

America's Outsiders in the 1920s

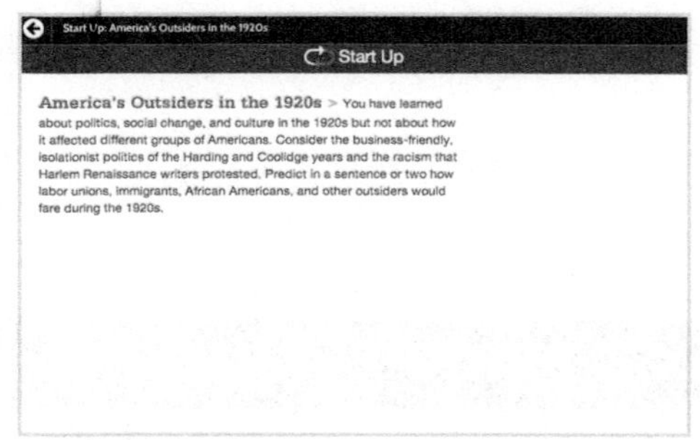

Project the Start Up Activity Have students record their predictions as they enter the classroom. Then ask them to share and discuss their ideas with partners.

Discuss Invite volunteers to share the reasoning behind their predictions with the class. Encourage students to revisit their predictions after the lesson to verify and adjust them as needed.

Tell students that this lesson examines the division and inequality that Americans experienced during the 1920s. Economic hardship, racism, and intolerance were part of the 1920s experience.

Aa Vocabulary Development: Use the Interactive Reading Notepad to preview the Key Terms and Academic Vocabulary in this lesson with students.

FLIP IT!

Assign the Flipped Video for this lesson.

STUDENT EDITION PRINT PAGES: 721–727

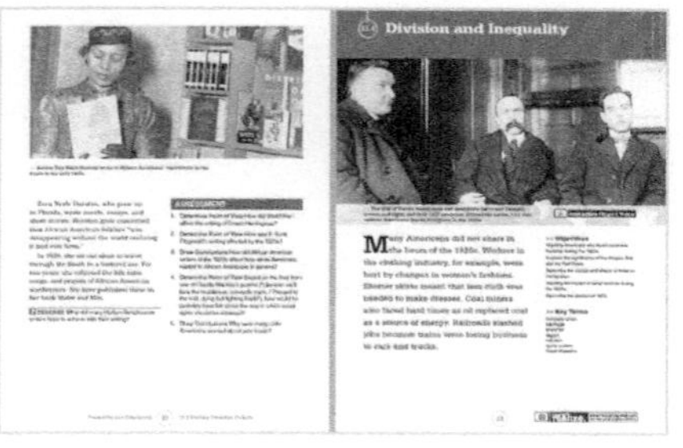

INVESTIGATE

DIGITAL TEXT 1

The Downside of the 1920s

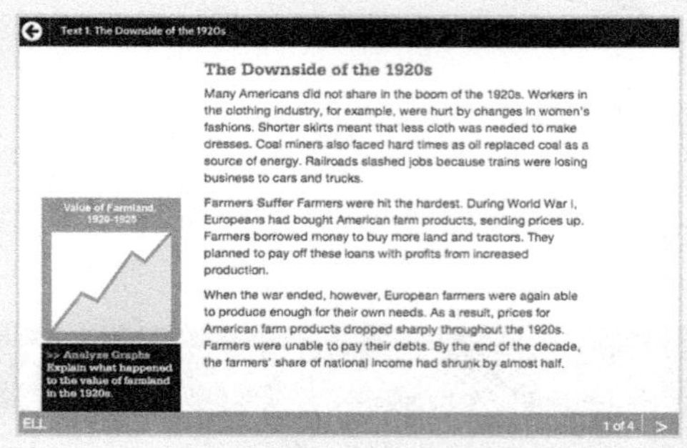

Objective 1: Identify Americans who faced economic hardship during the 1920s.

Quick Instruction

Display the graph depicting the changes in farmland value and help students analyze it. Explain that farmers were not the only people who suffered financial losses during the 1920s. Workers in the clothing industry, coal miners, railroad workers, and factory workers all faced economic challenges as trends shifted and jobs disappeared.

Identify Cause and Effect How did the rise in popularity of the automobile affect the railroad industry? *(The automobile made it possible for people to travel independently, so not as many people rode trains. As a result, the railroad industry lost customers and money.)*

ELL Use the ELL activity described in the ELL chart.

Further Instruction

Prompt students to recall the impact labor unions had in the late 1800s and early 1900s, pointing out that labor unions won shorter work days, higher pay, and improved workplace safety for many workers across the country.

Summarize What effect did unsuccessful worker strikes have on public support of labor unions? *(Public support decreased significantly when strikes were unsuccessful and the government did not step in to resolve issues in favor of labor unions.)*

Infer Why were companies eager to undermine labor unions and their efforts? *(Because unions gave power to the workers, companies felt threatened and lost power. This would equate to a loss in profit if workers won in negotiations.)*

DIGITAL TEXT 2

Cultural Clashes

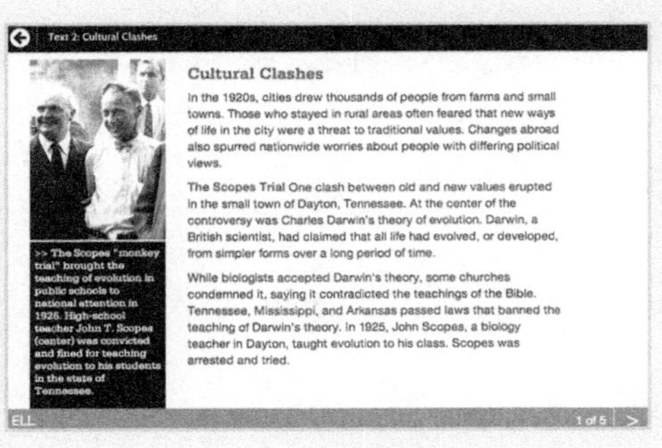

DIGITAL TEXT 3

Tensions Divide Americans

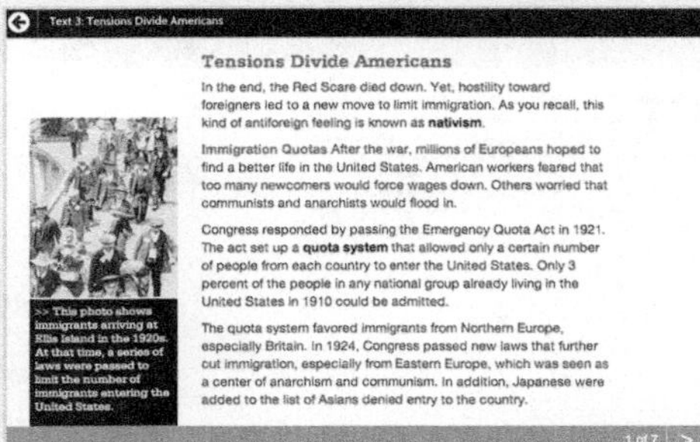

INTERACTIVE GRAPH

Limiting Immigration

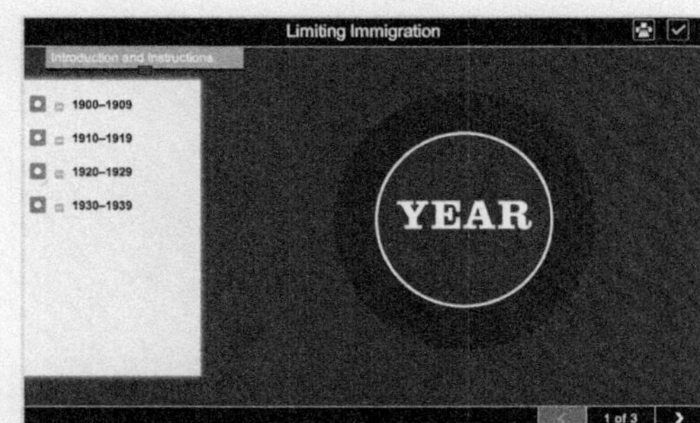

Objective 2: Explain the significance of the Scopes Trial and the Red Scare.

Quick Instruction

As you discuss the Scopes Trial, explain that the trial was not over Scope's guilt or innocence. Scopes had broken Tennessee state law when he taught evolution in his science classroom, which was beyond debate. At issue was the role of religion and science in public schools.

Express Problems Clearly Why did some believe that evolution should not be taught in public schools? *(Some argued that the Darwin's theory of evolution contradicted biblical teachings.)*

ELL Use the ELL activity described in the ELL chart.

Further Instruction

Support Ideas with Evidence What evidence from the text shows that fear of communists was visible in American society? *(Some Americans were concerned that labor union strikes were actually part of a communist revolution.)*

Cite Evidence What details about the Sacco and Vanzetti case symbolize anti-foreign feeling in the 1920s? *(Both men were sentenced to death despite little evidence against them, and the judge was openly prejudiced against them during the trial.)*

Objective 3: Describe the causes and effects of limits on immigration.

Objective 4: Identify the impact of racial tensions during the 1920s.

Objective 5: Describe the election of 1928.

Quick Instruction

Interactive Graph: Limiting Immigration Project the Interactive Graph and navigate through the features with students. Review the quota system for students, explaining that World War I had ravaged parts of Europe, leading to an influx of immigrants to the United States. Ask: What effect did some believe a large immigrant population would have on wages? *(Some thought immigrants would drive down wages by creating a surplus of workers.)*

ACTIVE CLASSROOM

Conduct a Take a Stand activity to further investigate the immigration quota system. Ask students to take a stand on the following question: Was the quota system a fair way to limit immigration? Divide students into groups based on their responses. Have them discuss the reasons for their answers. A representative from each group should present and defend the group's answers.

Interactive Gallery: Contrasts in American Society Project the Interactive Gallery and navigate through the images with students. Prompt students to point out specific evidence that contrasts the differences in economic class between the families.

ACTIVE CLASSROOM

Conduct an If Photos Could Talk activity. Have students choose one of the photos in the gallery. Then, ask them to consider what one of the people in the photos would say if they could talk. Ask students to support their idea with specific evidence.

Division and Inequality

INTERACTIVE GALLERY

Contrasts in American Society

Further Instruction

Despite the hardships some Americans experienced, the country considered the Republican leadership of the 1920s a success. When President Coolidge decided not to run in the 1928 election, Herbert Hoover took his place and easily won against Democratic opponent Alfred Smith. A Catholic and a grandson of immigrants, Smith took the large American cities, but Protestant Midwesterner Hoover, who was a self-made millionaire, won the rest of the country.

Generate Explanations How did the differences in candidates reflect the difference in culture across the nation? *(As an immigrant and a Catholic, Smith won votes from the majority of the population in large urban areas. Hoover was a self-made millionaire from the Midwest. He won votes from rural areas and business leaders.)*

SYNTHESIZE

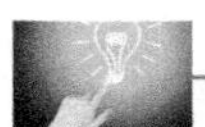

DIGITAL ACTIVITY

What Should Governments Do?

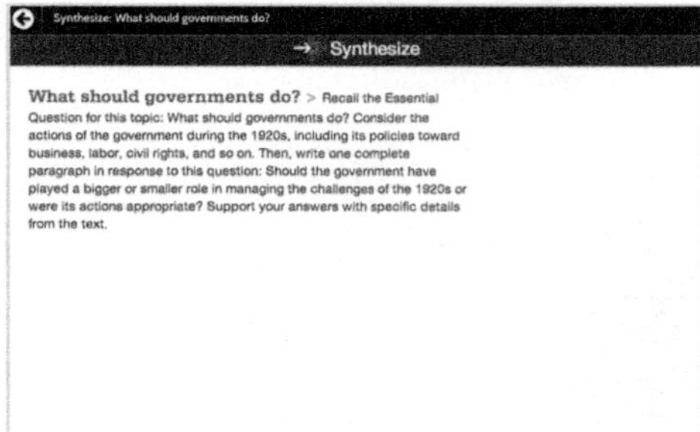

Synthesize: What should governments do?
Synthesize
What should governments do? > Recall the Essential Question for this topic: What should governments do? Consider the actions of the government during the 1920s, including its policies toward business, labor, civil rights, and so on. Then, write one complete paragraph in response to this question: Should the government have played a bigger or smaller role in managing the challenges of the 1920s or were its actions appropriate? Support your answers with specific details from the text.

Display the Essential Question for this Topic: What should governments do? Guide students to consider the role the government should take in addressing such issues as economic hardship, racism, discrimination, and immigration. Then, allow students time to write their paragraphs in response to the question.

Discuss Divide the class into groups based on their responses to the question and allow students time to share their central ideas as a group. Have each group present their ideas to the class.

DEMONSTRATE

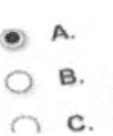

DIGITAL QUIZ

Lesson Quiz and Discussion Board

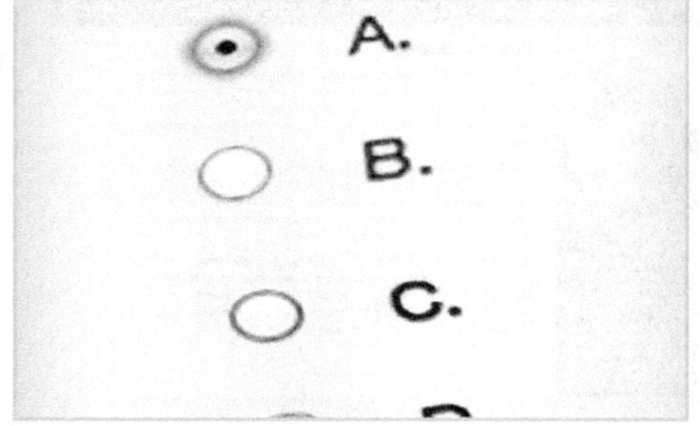

Assign the online Lesson Quiz for this lesson if you haven't already done so. Students will be offered automatic remediation or enrichment based on their score.

In *Division and Inequality*, you learned about the divisions and inequality that Americans experienced in the 1920s. You were introduced to the racial, cultural, and ideological tensions caused by immigration and migration. You also learned about the growth of new organizations that fueled racism, such as the new Ku Klux Klan, and those that fought it, such as the NAACP.

Post these questions to the class on the Discussion Board:

Distinguish Which groups suffered economic hardships during the 1920s? Why?

Identify Central Issues What factors led to congressional passage of an immigration quota system?

Topic Inquiry

Have students continue their investigations for the Topic Inquiry.

Entering the Great Depression

Supporting English Language Learners

Use with the reading, **Causes of the Crash**.

Learning

Explain that when students need to explain something, it may be helpful to use non-verbal cues, synonyms, and/or circumlocution. Review these strategies as needed.

Beginning Ask: What does *crash* mean? What things crash? Then display this sentence: The stock market crashed. Encourage students to explain how a stock market "crashes," using non-verbal cues or pictures as support.

Intermediate Display the first sentence of the text's second paragraph. Ask: What is a stock market? How can it crash? How are a stock market crash and an airplane crash alike and different? Encourage students to use synonyms and circumlocution as they answer the questions.

Advanced Display this sentence from the text: When Hoover took office in 1929, he saw a growing economy. Ask pairs to discuss these questions: How does an economy grow? How is this like and unlike a plant growing? What is another way of saying that Hoover could "see" the economy grow?

Advanced High Invite students to read the text's second sentence. Have them answer these questions and then share their ideas with a partner: What is another way to say that Hoover "served" in the Cabinet? How is this kind of serving like and unlike serving a tennis ball or serving food?

Use with the reading, **The Great Depression Sets In**.

Listening

Brainstorm with students how to increase listening comprehension when someone is speaking about statistics or other detailed facts. Explain that they will practice retelling or summarizing statistics in this activity.

Beginning Using simple language, tell students about the banking system during the Great Depression, including that more than 5,000 banks closed between 1929 and 1932. Ask: How many banks closed? When did they close?

Intermediate Give students an overview of the Great Depression, including that it lasted from 1929 to 1941. Then ask them to restate that detail by asking: About how many years did the Great Depression last?

Advanced Tell students about the gap between rich and poor before the Great Depression, including that over one third of American assets were owned by one percent of Americans. Have pairs of students work together to restate this statistic in their own words.

Advanced High Tell students about the gap between rich and poor before the Great Depression, including that over one third of American assets were owned by one percent of Americans. Invite students to summarize this statistic by drawing a graph or picture of it. Have partners explain and compare their work.

D Differentiate Instruction

Use the Differentiated Instruction notes throughout the lesson plan to support the varied skill sets, levels of readiness, and interests in the mixed-ability classroom.

Challenge These notes include suggestions for expanding the activity for advanced students.

On-Level These notes include suggestions for modifying the activity to address different interests or learning styles.

Extra Support These notes include ideas for providing more scaffolding or reading spuport.

Special Needs These notes provide ideas for adapting instruction to support the needs of various special needs students.

NOTES

Entering the Great Depression

Objectives

Objective 1: Identify the causes of the stock market crash of 1929 and the Great Depression.

Objective 2: Explain how hard times affected Americans.

Objective 3: Describe and evaluate Hoover's response to the Depression.

LESSON 5 ORGANIZER	PACING: APPROX. 1 PERIOD, .5 BLOCKS			
			RESOURCES	
	OBJECTIVES	PACING	Online	Print
Connect				
DIGITAL START UP ACTIVITY **Soaring Unemployment**		5 min.	●	
Investigate				
DIGITAL TEXT 1 **Causes of the Crash**	Objective 1	10 min.	●	●
DIGITAL TEXT 2 **The Great Depression Sets In**		10 min.	●	●
INTERACTIVE CHART **The Great Depression—Causes and Effects**		10 min.	●	
DIGITAL TEXT 3 **Life During the Great Depression**	Objective 2	10 min.	●	●
INTERACTIVE GALLERY **The Impact of the Great Depression**		10 min.	●	
DIGITAL TEXT 4 **The President Responds**	Objective 3	10 min.	●	●
Synthesize				
DIGITAL ACTIVITY **Causes of the Great Depression**		5 min.	●	
Demonstrate				
DIGITAL QUIZ **Lesson Quiz and Discussion Board**		10 min.	●	

Go online to access additional resources including:
Primary Sources • Biographies • Supreme Court cases • 21st Century Skill Tutorials • Maps • Graphic Organizers.

CONNECT

DIGITAL START UP ACTIVITY

Soaring Unemployment

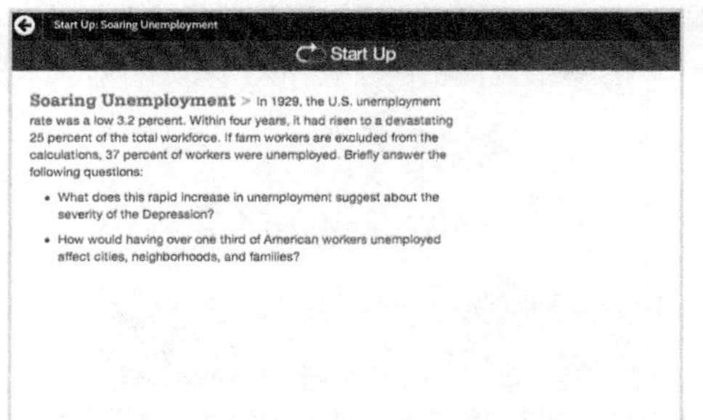

Project the Start Up Activity Have students complete the activity as they enter the classroom. Then ask them to share and discuss their ideas with partners.

Discuss What does this rapid increase in unemployment suggest about the severity of the Depression? *(It suggests that the Depression affected jobs across all industries and the financial security of many Americans.)*

Tell students that in this lesson they will be learning about the causes and initial effects of the Great Depression, as well as the government's response to it.

Aa Vocabulary Development: Use the Interactive Reading Notepad to preview the Key Terms and Academic Vocabulary in this lesson with students.

FLIP IT!

Assign the Flipped Video for this lesson.

STUDENT EDITION PRINT PAGES: 728–735

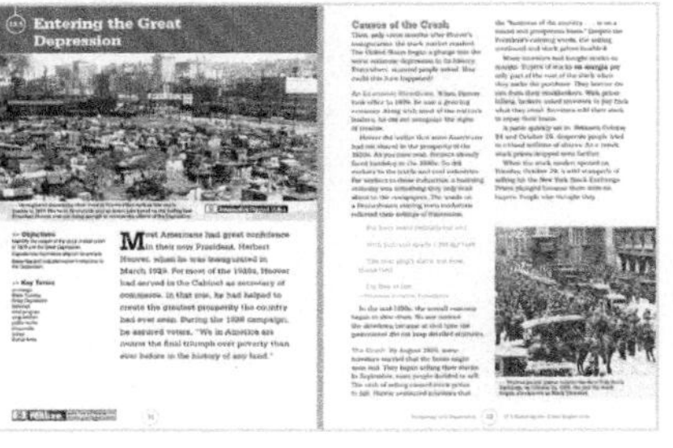

INVESTIGATE

DIGITAL TEXT 1

Causes of the Crash

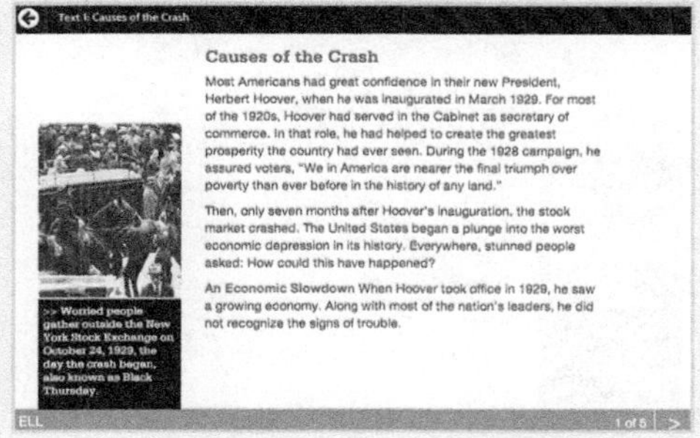

Objective 1: **Identify the causes of the stock market crash of 1929 and the Great Depression.**

Quick Instruction

Interactive Chart: The Great Depression—Causes and Effects Project the Interactive Chart and guide students as they drag and drop answers in the appropriate column. Point out that many of the causes and effects of the Great Depression are closely related. For example, high unemployment led to the Depression and also was an effect of the depression. Ask: How are bank failures connected with people losing their savings? *(When a bank failed, those who had deposited their money in that bank lost the money.)*

DIGITAL TEXT 2

The Great Depression Sets In

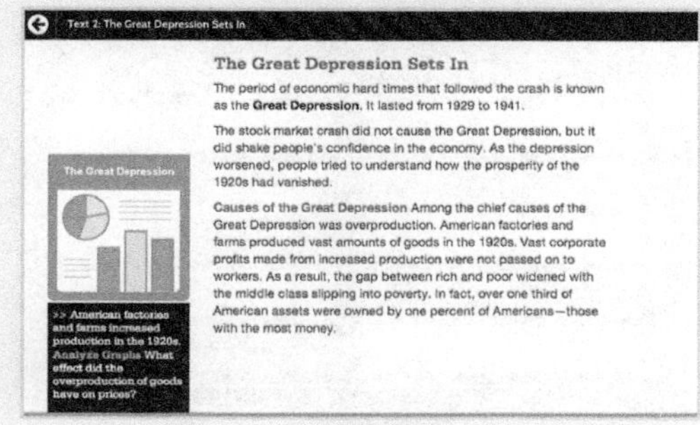

ACTIVE CLASSROOM

Conduct a Sequence It activity. Display a list of key events leading up to and resulting from the Great Depression, including those listed in the Interactive Chart. Have the class work together to create a sequential list of events on the board or butcher paper. Discuss which of the events in the sequence share both a cause and effect relationship and a sequential relationship.

D Differentiate: **Extra Support** To support students' understanding, draw a causal chain to depict the events described in the quote from the interactive activity. Connect the events with arrows, making sure students understand that one event (i.e., factories produced too many goods) led to another (prices fell) that, in turn, led to another (factories closed and workers were laid off).

ELL Use the ELL activity described in the ELL chart.

Entering the Great Depression

INTERACTIVE CHART

The Great Depression—Causes and Effects

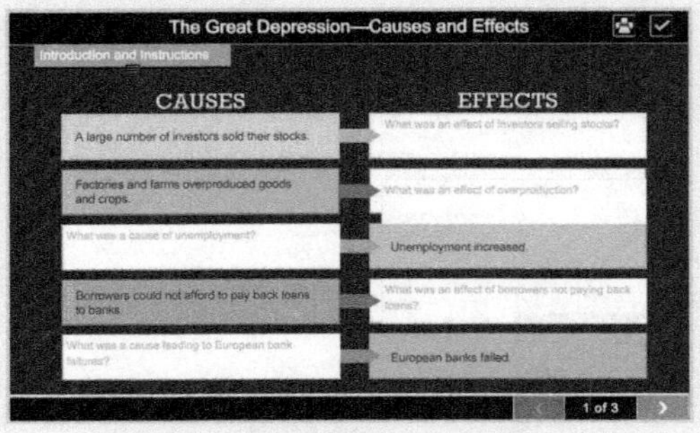

DIGITAL TEXT 3

Life During the Great Depression

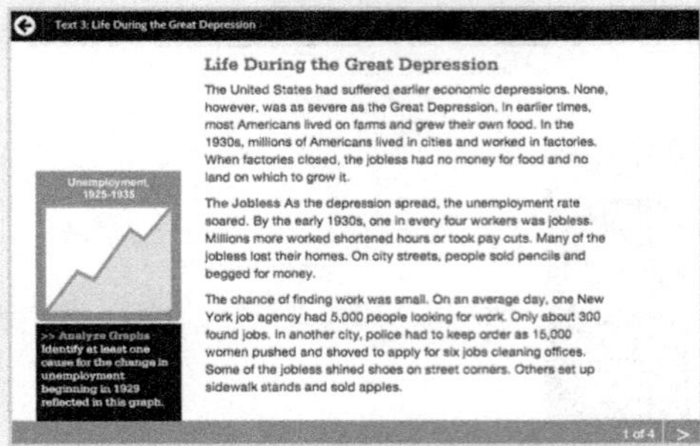

INTERACTIVE GALLERY

The Impact of the Great Depression

Further Instruction

To make sure students understand the economic factors that contributed to the Great Depression, assign *Economic Core Concepts: Economic Systems.*

Generate Explanations In the mid-1920s, production of goods and corporate profits increased significantly. Why did production of goods begin to decrease in the late 1920s even if businesses were profitable? *(Profits from increased production were not passed on to workers in the form of higher wages. As a result, workers could not afford to purchase as many goods, causing production to slow and businesses to begin laying off workers.)*

Cite Evidence What evidence from the text explains why banks were unable to give depositors their money back? *(Many banks made unwise loans to investors in the stock market. When the stock market crashed, these investors were unable to pay back their loans to banks, leaving many banks with little money to return to depositors.)*

Objective 2: **Explain how hard times affected Americans.**

Quick Instruction

Interactive Gallery: The Impact of the Great Depression Project the Interactive Gallery and navigate through the images with students, pausing on the photos of the employment agency, the soup kitchen, and the children. Explain that people were so impoverished during this time that many were malnourished and starving.

Support Ideas with Evidence What evidence from the text supports the idea that competition for available jobs was high during the Great Depression? *(One out of every four workers was unemployed. Thousands of workers would apply for a few available positions, meaning employers had to turn away most applicants.)*

ACTIVE CLASSROOM

Conduct a PMI activity. Group students and have each group construct a three-column chart with the headings *Plus*, *Minus*, and *Interesting*. Instruct them to study each image and record their responses to the following questions in the chart: What are the positive ideas about this? What are the negative ideas about this? What is interesting about this? Invite groups to share their overall responses to each image.

Further Instruction

Use Context Clues What does the phrase "ride the rails" mean in the context of the Great Depression? *(Many American had lost their homes, leaving them little choice but to travel in search of work or shelter. Sometimes that meant hitching rides on freight trains.)*

Make Generalizations Why might many Americans have lost faith in themselves during the Great Depression? *(Many people's self-worth is based partly on their ability to be productive members of society and provide for themselves and those around them. Without work, many felt a sense of failure during the Great Depression.)*

Go online to access additional resources including: Primary Sources • Biographies • Supreme Court cases • 21st Century Skill Tutorials • Maps • Graphic Organizers.

DIGITAL TEXT 4

The President Responds

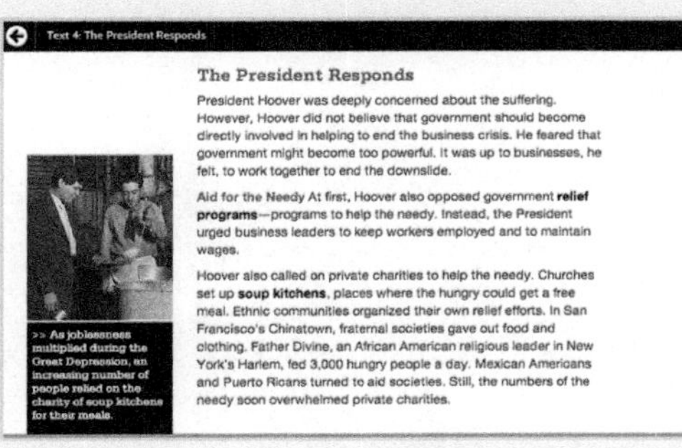

Text 4: The President Responds

The President Responds

President Hoover was deeply concerned about the suffering. However, Hoover did not believe that government should become directly involved in helping to end the business crisis. He feared that government might become too powerful. It was up to businesses, he felt, to work together to end the downslide.

Aid for the Needy At first, Hoover also opposed government **relief programs**—programs to help the needy. Instead, the President urged business leaders to keep workers employed and to maintain wages.

Hoover also called on private charities to help the needy. Churches set up **soup kitchens**, places where the hungry could get a free meal. Ethnic communities organized their own relief efforts. In San Francisco's Chinatown, fraternal societies gave out food and clothing. Father Divine, an African American religious leader in New York's Harlem, fed 3,000 hungry people a day. Mexican Americans and Puerto Ricans turned to aid societies. Still, the numbers of the needy soon overwhelmed private charities.

>> As joblessness multiplied during the Great Depression, an increasing number of people relied on the charity of soup kitchens for their meals.

Objective 3: **Describe and evaluate Hoover's response to the Depression.**

Quick Instruction

Project the photos of the soup kitchen and the Hoover Dam. Explain that President Hoover did little to address the economic depression or the desperation that plagued the nation until it was too late. As the situation worsened, Hoover began public works projects like the Hoover Dam, which offered some opportunities for work, but his efforts proved ineffective.

Determine Point of View Why did President Hoover initially not use the resources of the U.S. government to improve the economic situation in the country? *(Although he did encourage the development of some public works programs, such as the Hoover Dam, to put people back to work, he declined to establish a federal welfare program. President Hoover believed that it was not the government's role to directly regulate the economy and help the unemployed. He felt that private businesses were best suited to end the crisis.)*

Further Instruction

Identify Central Issues Why did many Americans refer to the shacks where the homeless lived as "Hoovervilles"? *(These shacks were called Hoovervilles because many people were not satisfied with the government's response to the Depression. They felt that President Hoover held some responsibility for the continuing economic difficulties.)*

Infer Why were many people upset by President Hoover's decision to use military force to stop veterans from protesting for their World War I bonuses? *(The Bonus Army were veterans who had fought to defend the country. President Hoover used military force to stop their unarmed protest.)*

Entering the Great Depression

SYNTHESIZE

DIGITAL ACTIVITY

Causes of the Great Depression

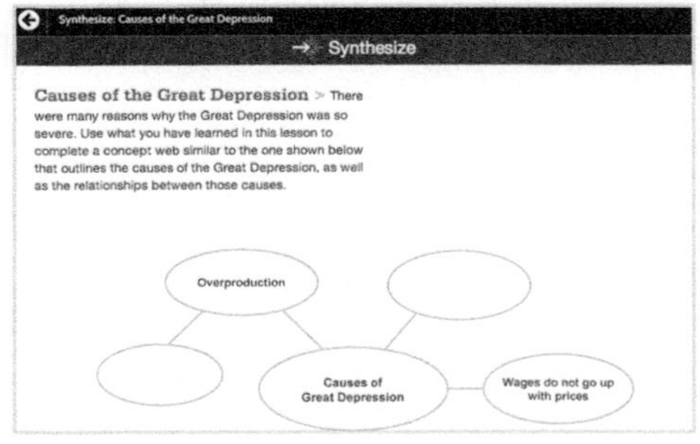

Invite students to brainstorm lists of causes of the Great Depression. Then, allow them time to consider the relationships among those causes and complete their graphic organizers. After students have completed their graphic organizers, invite them to share their work with partners.

Discuss Lead a class discussion in which students consider the economic practices that led to the Great Depression and how those practices had a far-reaching impact on the American and world economy.

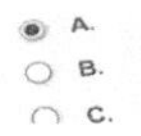

DEMONSTRATE

DIGITAL QUIZ

Lesson Quiz and Discussion Board

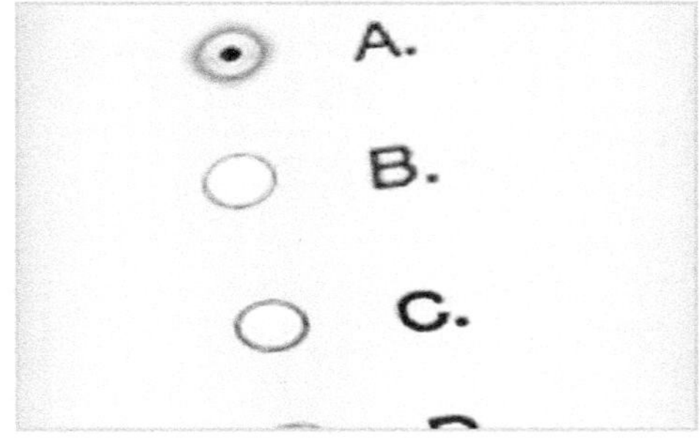

Assign the online Lesson Quiz for this lesson if you haven't already done so. Students will be offered automatic remediation or enrichment based on their score.

In *Entering the Great Depression*, you learned about the causes and effects of the Great Depression. You also learned how the government responded to the desperation that ensued as a result of the Depression.

Post these questions to the class on the Discussion Board:

Summarize the main causes of the Great Depression.

Generate Explanations Explain how the Great Depression impacted daily life for millions of Americans.

Topic Inquiry

Have students continue their investigations for the Topic Inquiry.

Roosevelt's New Deal

Supporting English Language Learners

Use with the reading, **Roosevelt's Path to the Presidency**.

Speaking

Give students a simple set of directions that use sequence words (e.g., first, next, last). Explain that words denoting sequence can highlight and clarify the relationship of events to one another.

Beginning Display three short sentences that begin with sequence words and that describe events from Roosevelt's life. Ask students to use their knowledge of Roosevelt and sequence words to put the sentences in order and say them aloud.

Intermediate Display the following: Roosevelt was assistant secretary of the navy. Then he ____. Ask students to identify the sequence word, complete the second sentence, and read both sentences aloud. Repeat this process with another pair of sentences.

Advanced Brainstorm time and sequence words with students. Then have pairs of students ask and answer questions about Roosevelt's life using these words (e.g., What happened after Roosevelt returned to public life? First, he was elected governor. Then he ran for president.).

Advanced High Have students use content from the text to create a timeline of Roosevelt's life. Then have partners take turns telling each other the "story" of FDR, using time and sequence words and phrases to do so.

Use with the reading, **Reforming the Economy**.

Reading

Explain that when confronted with a text that includes many definitions, students can improve their comprehension and retention by summarizing this information.

Beginning Display the term *Tennessee Valley Authority* with three possible definitions of this program, and ask students to choose the correct one. Repeat this process for other New Deal programs, such as the NIRA and PWA.

Intermediate Display a list of each program from the text (e.g., NIRA, NRA, PWA, AAA, REA, TVA, FDIC). Invite students to volunteer one-sentence summaries for the different programs. Record each summary next to its respective program on the list.

Advanced Invite pairs of students to create a three-column chart summarizing the programs mentioned in the text. The three column titles should be as follows: Program, Abbreviation, Brief Description. Ask: How does organizing information from the text in this way help you to better understand it?

Advanced High Invite students to write a brief summary of five programs from the text they found most difficult. Then have partners compare and discuss their work. Ask: How did summarizing the programs help you to better understand them? What questions do you still have?

D Differentiate Instruction

Use the Differentiated Instruction notes throughout the lesson plan to support the varied skill sets, levels of readiness, and interests in the mixed-ability classroom.

Challenge These notes include suggestions for expanding the activity for advanced students.

On-Level These notes include suggestions for modifying the activity to address different interests or learning styles.

Extra Support These notes include ideas for providing more scaffolding or reading spuport.

Special Needs These notes provide ideas for adapting instruction to support the needs of various special needs students.

NOTES

Roosevelt's New Deal

Objectives

Objective 1: Explain why Roosevelt won the election in 1932.

Objective 2: Describe the impact of the New Deal, including the Hundred Days, jobless relief, labor reforms,Social Security, and other programs.

Objective 3: Explain why critics objected to the New Deal.

Objective 4: Describe Roosevelt's conflict with the Supreme Court.

Objective 5: Evaluate the effects of the New Deal.

LESSON 6 ORGANIZER — PACING: APPROX. 1 PERIOD, .5 BLOCKS	OBJECTIVES	PACING	RESOURCES Online	RESOURCES Print
Connect				
DIGITAL START UP ACTIVITY **Responding to the Homeless**		5 min.	●	
Investigate				
DIGITAL TEXT 1 **Roosevelt's Path to the Presidency**	Objective 1	10 min.	●	●
DIGITAL TEXT 2 **Seeking Relief and Recovery**	Objective 2	10 min.	●	●
DIGITAL TEXT 3 **Reforming the Economy**	Objective 2	10 min.	●	●
DIGITAL TEXT 4 **Supporting Workers and the Elderly**	Objective 2	10 min.	●	●
INTERACTIVE MAP **New Deal Programs**	Objective 2	10 min.	●	
DIGITAL TEXT 5 **Critics Attack the New Deal**	Objectives 3, 4	10 min.	●	●
DIGITAL TEXT 6 **Evaluating the New Deal**	Objective 5	10 min.	●	●
INTERACTIVE CARTOON **The New Deal Political Cartoon**	Objective 5	10 min.	●	
Synthesize				
DIGITAL ACTIVITY **Revisiting Hoovervilles**		5 min.	●	
Demonstrate				
DIGITAL QUIZ **Lesson Quiz and Discussion Board**		10 min.	●	

PEARSON realize™ www.PearsonRealize.com

Go online to access additional resources including: Primary Sources • Biographies • Supreme Court cases • 21st Century Skill Tutorials • Maps • Graphic Organizers.

CONNECT

DIGITAL START UP ACTIVITY

Responding to the Homeless

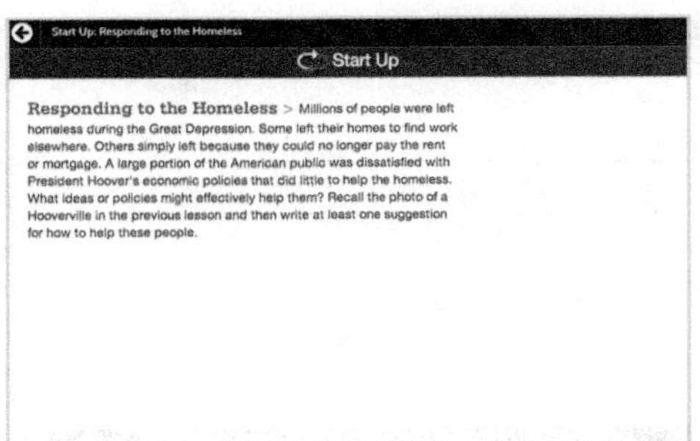

Project the Start Up Activity Ask students to answer the questions as they enter and get settled. Then have them share their ideas.

Discuss What ideas or policies might effectively have helped the homeless? *(Possible answers include opening public shelters, providing food, or government jobs programs.)*

Tell students that in this lesson they will be learning about President Roosevelt's election and his New Deal policies during the Great Depression. Students will learn about criticism of the New Deal and Roosevelt's attempt to increase the size of the Supreme Court.

Aa Vocabulary Development: Use the Interactive Reading Notepad to preview the Key Terms and Academic Vocabulary in this lesson with students.

FLIP IT!

Assign the Flipped Video for this lesson.

STUDENT EDITION PRINT PAGES: 736–747

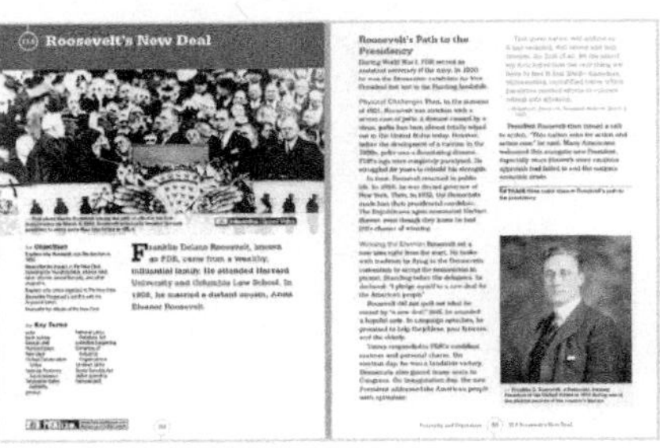

INVESTIGATE

DIGITAL TEXT 1

Roosevelt's Path to the Presidency

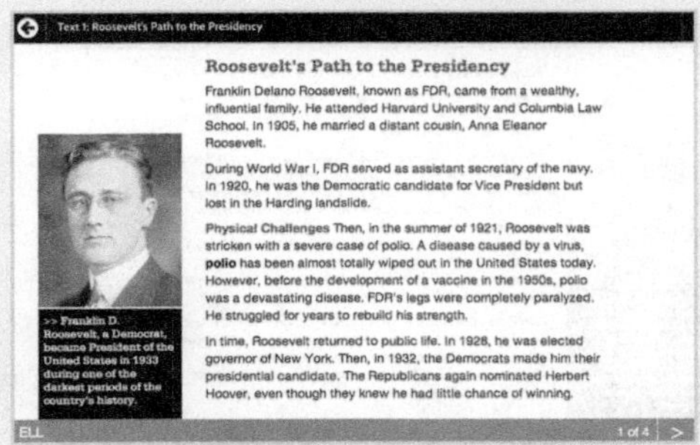

Objective 1: Explain why Roosevelt won election in 1932.

Quick Instruction

Display the photograph of Roosevelt's inauguration and summarize FDR's accomplishments for students. He attended Harvard and Columbia to become a lawyer and pursued a career in politics. Even after contracting polio, he won the governorship of New York and later, the presidency.

Infer Why did FDR choose to accept the Democratic nomination for president in person, becoming the first candidate to do so? *(Possible response: He wanted to show the American people that he would be present and engaged with the nation's problems if elected president.)*

ELL Use the ELL activity described in the ELL chart.

Further Instruction

Support Ideas with Examples When FDR spoke at the Democratic Convention, he promised Americans a "new deal." What examples from the text show that he would encourage the government to deal more directly with the economic crisis? *(In campaign speeches, he promised to help the jobless, poor farmers, and the elderly, indicating that the government would play a direct role in aid to those in need.)*

DIGITAL TEXT 2

Seeking Relief and Recovery

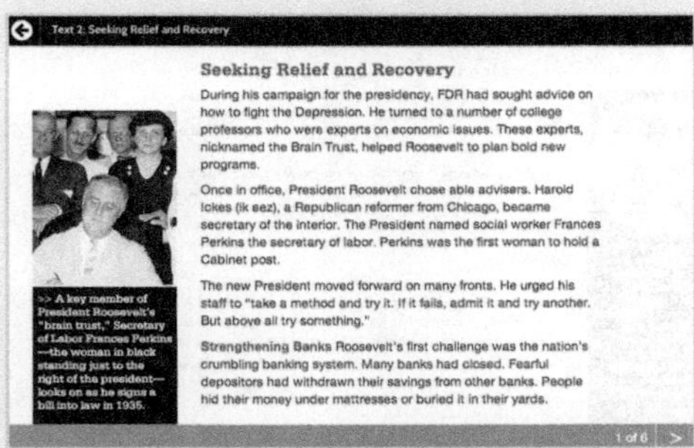

Objective 2: Describe the impact of the New Deal, including the Hundred Days, jobless relief, labor reforms, Social Security, and other programs.

Quick Instruction

Explain to students that the *Hundred Days* refers to the first hundred days of Roosevelt's presidency, in which Congress passed fifteen major laws. These laws aimed to address the three goals of Roosevelt's New Deal: provide relief for the jobless, plan for economic recovery, and create reforms intended to avoid another depression.

Interactive Map: New Deal Programs Project the Interactive Map and navigate through the layers showing New Deal projects with students. Connect each program with Roosevelt's stated purpose of providing jobs and encouraging economic growth.

Summarize What was the purpose of Social Security? *(The program gave financial assistance to the unemployed, the disabled, and the elderly.)*

Roosevelt's New Deal

DIGITAL TEXT 3

Reforming the Economy

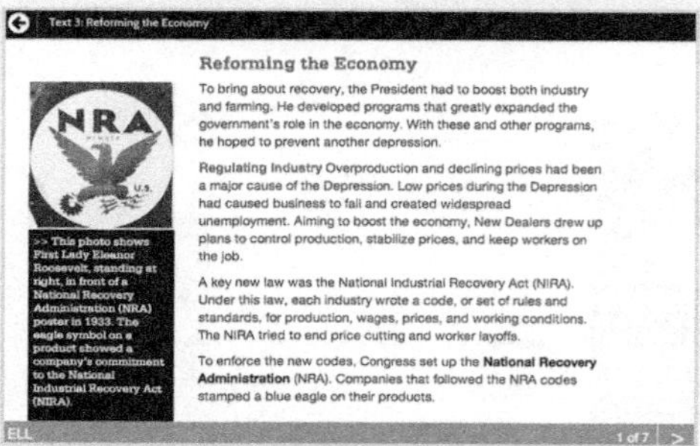

DIGITAL TEXT 4

Supporting Workers and the Elderly

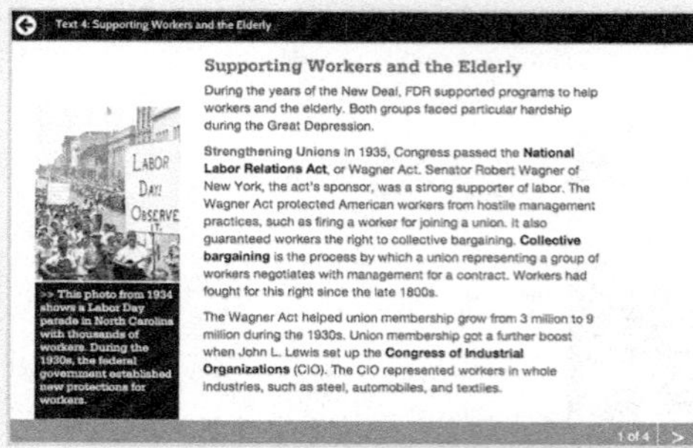

INTERACTIVE MAP

New Deal Programs

ACTIVE CLASSROOM

Conduct a Rank It activity. List the projects and ask students to rank them based on their economic and social impact. Ask students to justify their rankings, and then have them share their ideas in pairs. Poll the class to see if there is agreement on rankings.

D Differentiate: Challenge Ask students to choose a New Deal project to further investigate. Instruct students to research the project, providing information about it and commonly held opinions about its success or failure. Invite students to share their research with the class.

ELL Use the ELL activity described in the ELL chart.

Further Instruction

Summarize Why did the Agricultural Adjustment Act pay farmers to produce less crops and livestock? *(Prices for crops and livestock were too low for farmers to make a profit. If farmers produced less, supply would decrease, which in turn would raise prices and enable farmers to run a profitable business again.)*

Infer What was the purpose of Roosevelt's "fireside chats"? *(Roosevelt wanted to explain the reasoning behind new New Deal programs and to reassure the American public that the government was taking steps to improve the nation's economy.)*

Identify Central Issues What goal did the majority of New Deal programs have in common? *(Although not all the programs were successful, the goal of the New Deal programs was to provide relief for the jobless and improve the economy.)*

DIGITAL TEXT 5

Critics Attack the New Deal

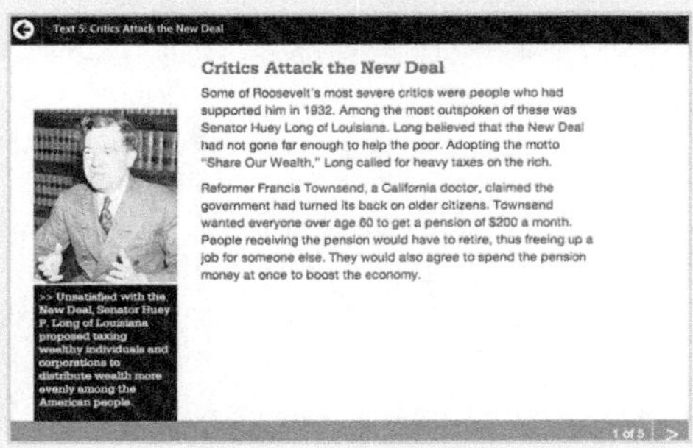

Text 5: Critics Attack the New Deal
Critics Attack the New Deal
Some of Roosevelt's most severe critics were people who had supported him in 1932. Among the most outspoken of these was Senator Huey Long of Louisiana. Long believed that the New Deal had not gone far enough to help the poor. Adopting the motto "Share Our Wealth," Long called for heavy taxes on the rich.
Reformer Francis Townsend, a California doctor, claimed the government had turned its back on older citizens. Townsend wanted everyone over age 60 to get a pension of $200 a month. People receiving the pension would have to retire, thus freeing up a job for someone else. They would also agree to spend the pension money at once to boost the economy.
>> Unsatisfied with the New Deal, Senator Huey P. Long of Louisiana proposed taxing wealthy individuals and corporations to distribute wealth more evenly among the American people.
1 of 5

Objective 3: **Explain why critics objected to the New Deal.**

Objective 4: **Describe Roosevelt's conflict with the Supreme Court.**

Quick Instruction

Project the political cartoon satirizing FDR and the New Deal, and explain its elements, including the Trojan horse metaphor. Point out that both liberals and conservatives were critical of New Deal programs and that the cartoon was a conservative criticism arguing that the programs would give the federal government too much power.

Summarize What opposition, from both liberals and conservatives, did Roosevelt face as he tried to address the social and economic issues created by the Depression? *(Roosevelt faced opposition from liberals, who claimed he did too little; conservatives, who claimed he did too much; big business, which balked at the regulations newly enacted; and the Supreme Court, which ruled against many of Roosevelt's plans.)*

Further Instruction

Express Ideas Clearly Why did Roosevelt want to increase the number of Supreme Court Justices from 9 to 15? *(The Supreme Court ruled that some of the New Deal programs were unconstitutional, so he thought that nominating six Justices would sway future Court decisions in favor the programs.)*

Infer Why did Roosevelt wait until after his re-election to attempt to increase the number of Justices on the Court? *(He knew the plan would be unpopular because his motivation for doing so was transparently obvious.)*

Identify Central Issues What was the essential argument behind conservative opposition to FDR's idea to expand the Supreme Court? *(Many conservatives saw Roosevelt's plans as a threat to the separation of powers, or the principle that each branch of government has distinct responsibilities, because Roosevelt was trying to influence the decisions of the judicial branch.)*

DIGITAL TEXT 6

Evaluating the New Deal

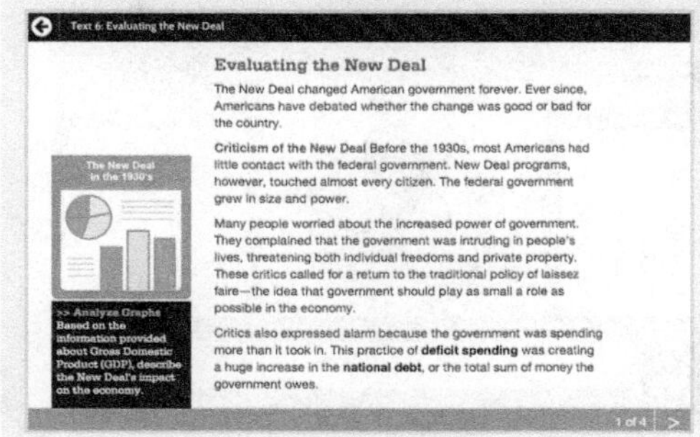

Text 6: Evaluating the New Deal
Evaluating the New Deal
The New Deal changed American government forever. Ever since, Americans have debated whether the change was good or bad for the country.
Criticism of the New Deal Before the 1930s, most Americans had little contact with the federal government. New Deal programs, however, touched almost every citizen. The federal government grew in size and power.
Many people worried about the increased power of government. They complained that the government was intruding in people's lives, threatening both individual freedoms and private property. These critics called for a return to the traditional policy of laissez faire—the idea that government should play as small a role as possible in the economy.
Critics also expressed alarm because the government was spending more than it took in. This practice of deficit spending was creating a huge increase in the national debt, or the total sum of money the government owes.
The New Deal in the 1930's
>> Analyze Graphs Based on the information provided about Gross Domestic Product (GDP), describe the New Deal's impact on the economy.
1 of 4

Objective 5: **Evaluate the effects of the New Deal.**

Quick Instruction

Interactive Cartoon: The New Deal Political Cartoon Project the Interactive Cartoon for students. Discuss the opinion conveyed by the laughing children playing "Ring Around a Roosevelt." Explain the allusion to the children's rhyme "Ring Around the Rosie." Guide students as they complete the graphic organizer to analyze the cartoon. After students study the second cartoon, ask them to compare and contrast the messages expressed in each. *(The first gives a positive message by showing children who represent Roosevelt's programs frolicking around their creator, while the second presents a negative opinion of Roosevelt by depicting him as an animal trainer who cannot control the chimpanzee, which represents angry tax payers.)*

ACTIVE CLASSROOM

Conduct a Make Headlines activity. Have students write a headline that captures the importance of the New Deal and reflects the opinion expressed in one of the cartoons from the Interactive Activity. Ask: If you were to write a headline that captured the most important aspect of the New Deal, what would that headline be? Divide students into groups based on the cartoon chosen and have them compare headlines. Invite groups to share two or three headlines they evaluate as best.

Topic 13 Lesson 6

Roosevelt's New Deal

INTERACTIVE CARTOON

The New Deal Political Cartoon

Further Instruction

Summarize What were the essential arguments in favor of and against New Deal programs? *(Supporters of New Deal programs argued that the government had a responsibility to provide opportunities for its citizens and direct assistance in difficult economic times. Opponents of New Deal programs argued that government should play a minimal role in the economy and its citizens lives.)*

SYNTHESIZE

DIGITAL ACTIVITY

Revisiting Hoovervilles

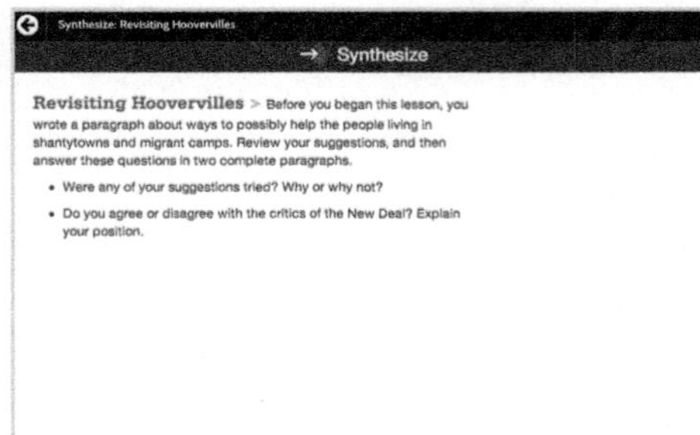

Synthesize: Revisiting Hoovervilles
Synthesize
Revisiting Hoovervilles > Before you began this lesson, you wrote a paragraph about ways to possibly help the people living in shantytowns and migrant camps. Review your suggestions, and then answer these questions in two complete paragraphs.
• Were any of your suggestions tried? Why or why not?
• Do you agree or disagree with the critics of the New Deal? Explain your position.

Allow students time to revisit their ideas from the Start Up Activity before responding. After they write their paragraphs, invite them to share their writing with partners.

Discuss Lead a class discussion in which students share their opinions of the New Deal. Prompt students to provide specific justification that supports their opinions.

DEMONSTRATE

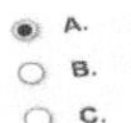

DIGITAL QUIZ

Lesson Quiz and Discussion Board

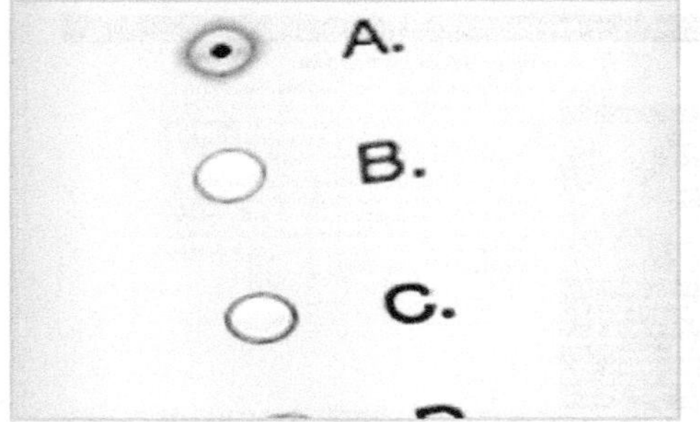

Assign the online Lesson Quiz for this lesson if you haven't already done so. Students will be offered automatic remediation or enrichment based on their score.

In *Roosevelt's New Deal*, you learned about the Hundred Days and the goals of the New Deal. You read about the projects and programs enacted to reach these goals, as well as public response to the President's new plans.

Post these questions to the class on the Discussion Board:

Summarize What were the three main goals of Roosevelt's New Deal?

Compare and Contrast How did Roosevelt's approach to the problems of the Great Depression differ from his predecessor President Hoover's?

Topic Inquiry

Have students continue their investigations for the Topic Inquiry.

Life During the Depression

Supporting English Language Learners

Use with the reading, **The Dust Bowl**.

Learning
Display the term *migrant worker*, and review that it means "a person who moves from place to place in search of work." Ask: Which part of the definition relates to *worker*? Which relates to *migrant*?

Beginning Explain that in the term *migrant worker*, the word *migrant* is an adjective, and that the verb *migrate* is related to it. Ask: Do you think *migrate* means to work hard, to move from one place to another, or to look for something?

Intermediate Explain that a word related to the adjective *migrant* is the verb *migrate* and ask students to guess its meaning. Then practice using it in different contexts (related and unrelated to the text).

Advanced Display these words along with their parts of speech: migrate (verb), migration (noun). Have pairs of students discuss the words' possible meanings and check their answers in a dictionary. Then ask them to create a sentence using each word.

Advanced High Ask students to write down possible meanings of these words: migrate (verb), migration (noun), migratory (adjective). Have them check their answers in a dictionary and write sentences that correctly use these words. Have them share their sentences with a partner.

Use with the reading, **Literature and Arts During the Depression**.

Listening
Remind students that an idiomatic expression is not to be taken literally, but sometimes its literal meaning can hint at its intended meaning.

Beginning Tell students about *Gone With the Wind* portraying the Civil War "in a romantic light." Explain that this phrase means "in a romantic way." Ask: What else might you see "in a romantic light"?

Intermediate Tell students about *Gone With the Wind* portraying the Civil War "in a romantic light." Invite students to guess what the expression means. Then discuss another light in which a war could be portrayed.

Advanced Discuss how *Gone With the Wind* portrays the Civil War "in a romantic light." Ask: What is another way to say "in a romantic light"? Tell students that "in a favorable light" and "in an unfavorable light" are also common expressions. Invite students to use these phrases to describe various things during the Great Depression.

Advanced High Discuss how *Gone With the Wind* portrays the Civil War "in a romantic light." Ask: What is another way to say "in a romantic light"? Then have pairs of students use the expression "in a(n) _____ light" as they discuss different aspects of the Great Depression.

D Differentiate Instruction

Use the Differentiated Instruction notes throughout the lesson plan to support the varied skill sets, levels of readiness, and interests in the mixed-ability classroom.

Challenge These notes include suggestions for expanding the activity for advanced students.

On-Level These notes include suggestions for modifying the activity to address different interests or learning styles.

Extra Support These notes include ideas for providing more scaffolding or reading spupport.

Special Needs These notes provide ideas for adapting instruction to support the needs of various special needs students.

NOTES

Life During the Depression

Objectives

Objective 1: Identify the causes and effects of the Dust Bowl.

Objective 2: Explain how the Depression affected women.

Objective 3: Describe the Depression's impact on African Americans and other groups.

Objective 4: Explain how the arts reflected life during the Depression.

LESSON 7 ORGANIZER	PACING: APPROX. 1 PERIOD, .5 BLOCKS			
			RESOURCES	
	OBJECTIVES	PACING	Online	Print
Connect				
DIGITAL START UP ACTIVITY **Mary McLeod Bethune**		5 min.	●	
Investigate				
DIGITAL TEXT 1 **The Dust Bowl**	Objective 1	10 min.	●	●
INTERACTIVE GALLERY **The Dust Bowl**		10 min.	●	
DIGITAL TEXT 2 **The Depression Affects Women**	Objective 2	10 min.	●	●
DIGITAL TEXT 3 **African Americans During the Depression**	Objective 3	10 min.	●	●
DIGITAL TEXT 4 **Other Americans Weather the Depression**		10 min.	●	●
INTERACTIVE CHART **The Great Depression's Impact**		10 min.	●	
DIGITAL TEXT 5 **Literature and Arts During the Depression**	Objective 4	10 min.	●	●
Synthesize				
DIGITAL ACTIVITY **America During the Depression**		5 min.	●	
Demonstrate				
DIGITAL QUIZ **Lesson Quiz and Discussion Board**		10 min.	●	

PEARSON realize™
www.PearsonRealize.com

Go online to access additional resources including:
Primary Sources • Biographies • Supreme Court cases • 21st Century Skill Tutorials • Maps • Graphic Organizers.

CONNECT

DIGITAL START UP ACTIVITY

Mary McLeod Bethune

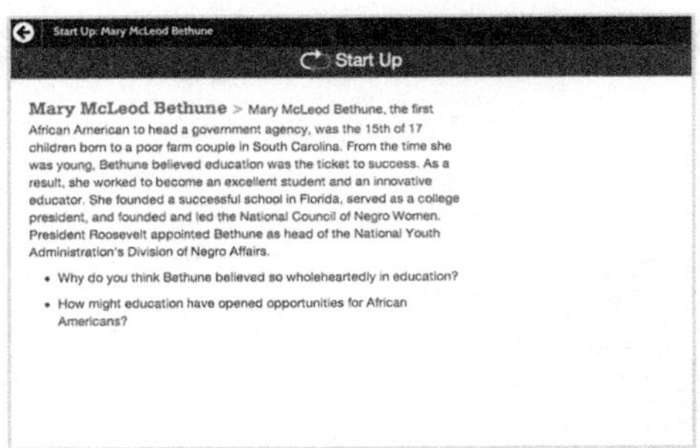

Project the Start Up Activity Have students read the biography and answer the questions as they enter the room. Then ask them to discuss their ideas with partners.

Discuss Why do you think Bethune believed so whole-heartedly in education? *(She knew that an education would lead to better job opportunities than farming, which had left her parents and family impoverished.)* How might education have opened opportunities for African Americans? *(Education would have opened up employment opportunities.)*

Tell students that this lesson examines life during the Great Depression.

Aa Vocabulary Development: Use the Interactive Reading Notepad to preview the Key Terms and Academic Vocabulary in this lesson with students.

FLIP IT!

Assign the Flipped Video for this lesson.

STUDENT EDITION PRINT PAGES: 748–755

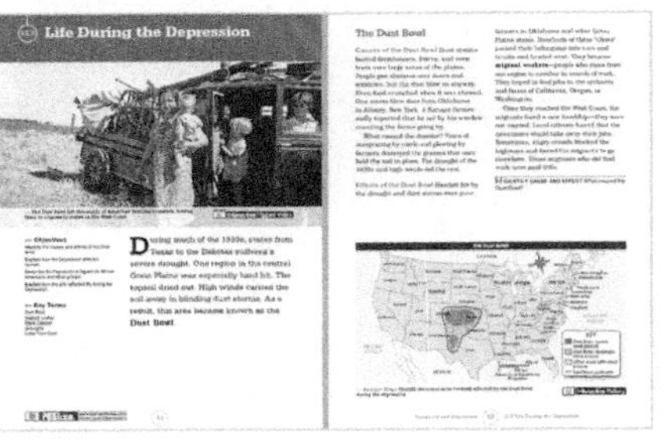

INVESTIGATE

DIGITAL TEXT 1

The Dust Bowl

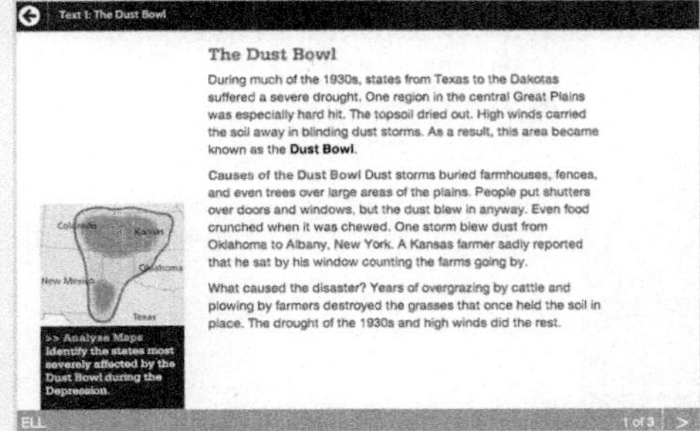

INTERACTIVE GALLERY

The Dust Bowl

Objective 1: Identify the causes and effects of the Dust Bowl.

Quick Instruction

Interactive Gallery: The Dust Bowl Project the Interactive Gallery and navigate through the images with students. Define the Dust Bowl for students, making sure that they understand that it refers to the Great Central Plains, the area of the country most affected by drought in the 1930s. Navigate the hot spots with students, leading a discussion of what it must have been like to live in such an environment.

Express Problems Clearly What environmental events and human choices created "dust bowl" conditions in the Great Plains? *(Overgrazing and plowing had destroyed the prairie grass that held the soil in place. These choices, combined with the severe drought that hit in the 1930s, created the Dust Bowl.)*

ACTIVE CLASSROOM

Conduct a Closer Look activity. Project the map and divide it into four numbered quadrants, making sure that each quadrant has at least one hot spot. Have students count off 1 to 4 and look closely at the part of the map in their quadrant. Instruct students to describe in writing what they see. Invite volunteers to share what they learned as a result of their focus on this part of the image.

ELL Use the ELL activity described in the ELL chart.

Further Instruction

Draw Conclusions Why did the residents of the Dust Bowl leave? *(Most had lost their homes as a result of their inability to pay the mortgages, and there was no work in the area. In addition, the environment was hazardous to one's health.)* Why did many Americans living in the Dust Bowl choose to migrate west instead of east? *(The western region of the country offered more farming opportunities for migrant workers than the East.)*

Generate Explanations Why were migrants from the Dust Bowl unwanted on the West Coast? *(Residents of the West Coast believed that this influx of workers would harm their economy, take their jobs, and drive wages down because there would be a surplus of workers.)*

Life During the Depression

DIGITAL TEXT 2

The Depression Affects Women

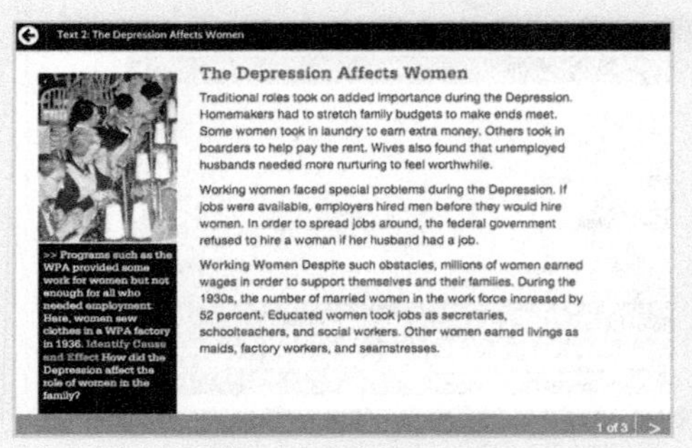

DIGITAL TEXT 3

African Americans During the Depression

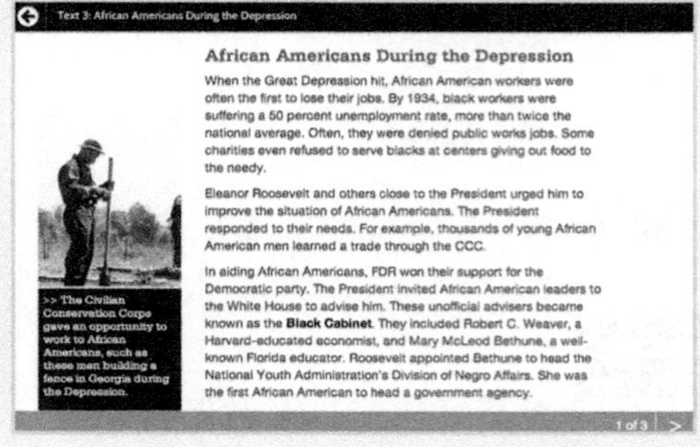

DIGITAL TEXT 4

Other Americans Weather the Depression

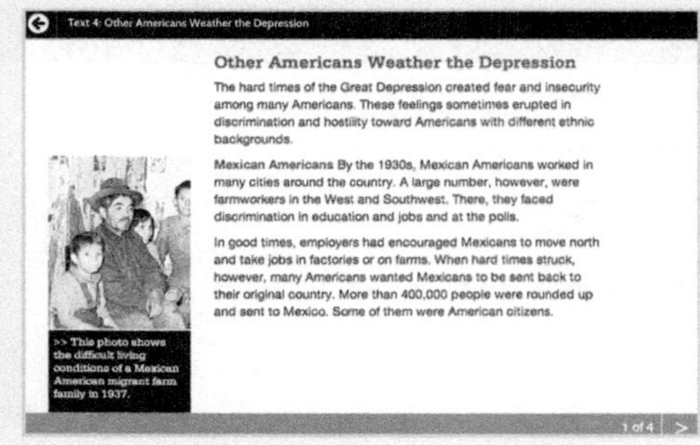

Objective 2: **Explain how the Depression affected women.**

Quick Instruction

Project the photo of the women working in the clothing factory. Explain that as before, women still worked in such jobs during the Depression. However, they found it more difficult to obtain work. If a job was available, the first candidate was usually a man. In addition, the government would not hire a married woman if her husband already had a job. Despite these challenges, the number of married women who worked increased to 52 percent during the 1930s.

Make Generalizations How did the Depression affect many women? *(In addition to experiencing the same hardships as all Americans, women faced the extra challenge of finding work when the few jobs available went to men. Some women worked outside the home for the first time.)*

Further Instruction

Support Ideas with Examples How did Eleanor Roosevelt redefine the role of First Lady? *(She traveled the country speaking for equal rights for all and helped the President determine how well people were actually doing.)*

Objective 3: **Describe the Depression's impact on African Americans and other groups.**

Quick Instruction

Interactive Chart: The Great Depression's Impact Project the Interactive Chart and navigate the chart with students, identifying each of the groups. Then, work together with students to identify the impact of the Depression on each. When the chart is complete, ask students to compare the economic impact of the Depression across groups. *(Possible response: Unemployment rates were higher in these groups than in the general population.)*

ACTIVE CLASSROOM

Conduct a Quick Write activity. Allow students to review the completed chart and then have them quick write their observations and conclusions based on the information in the chart for one minute. When students finish, invite volunteers to share their ideas with the class.

D Differentiate: Extra Support Remind students that the Great Depression occurred when racism, segregation, and discrimination were the norm for minority groups and women. As a result, these groups suffered even more when the Depression threatened the economic well-being of most Americans.

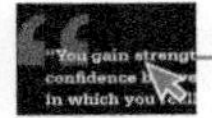

INTERACTIVE CHART

The Great Depression's Impact

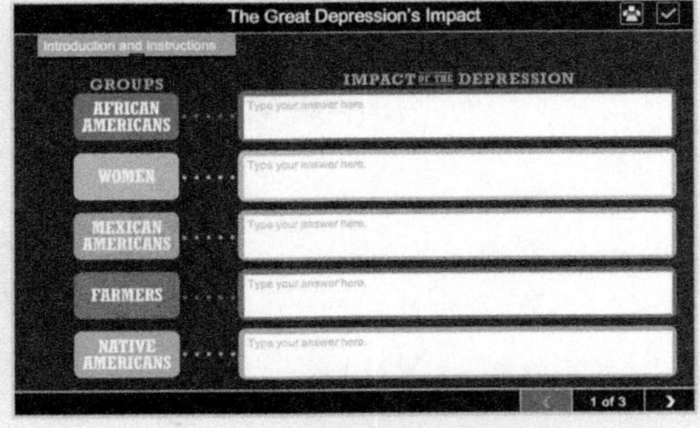

DIGITAL TEXT 5

Literature and Arts During the Depression

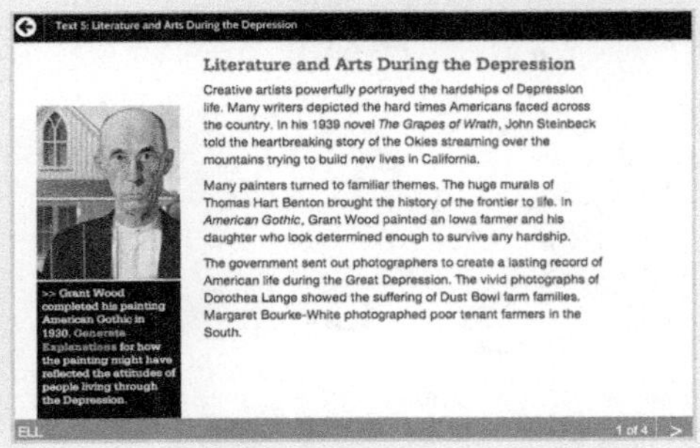

Further Instruction

Summarize What did President Roosevelt do to help minority groups, such as African Americans and American Indians? *(He established the Indian New Deal, which included programs and projects to help American Indians. Many African Americans learned new trades through the CCC. He also established the Black Cabinet, a group of African American advisers to help him address issues particular to that group of people.)*

Distinguish How were many Mexican and Asian Americans affected by the Depression? *(Unlike the African Americans and American Indians, Mexican and Asian Americans were not helped by the U.S. government. Instead, thousands of Mexican Americans were sent back to Mexico while many Asian Americans were provided with a free trip home as long as they promised not to return.)*

Objective 4: **Explain how the arts reflected life during the Depression.**

Quick Instruction

Display the image of moviegoers from the 1930s. Explain that despite the poverty people experienced during the Depression, movie attendance was a popular form of entertainment. Many movies expressed themes of hope and fortitude that inspired Americans to keep going, while others provided laughter and escape from the daily hardships of the time. On the other hand, many art forms, including photography, painting, and literature, echoed and reflected the struggles Americans faced.

Interpret Why would Americans be interested in making or experiencing art that depicted the economic hardships many experienced? *(Possible response: Art was a reflection of the reality in which many Americans lived. Perhaps for some it was a validation of their own difficulties during the economic downturn.)*

ELL Use the ELL activity described in the ELL chart.

Further Instruction

Display the infographic on discussing mass entertainment in the 1930s. Ask students to analyze the information, drawing conclusions about what the figures suggest about the American public at the time.

Analyze Graphs Based on the information about mass entertainment in the 1930s, approximately how many more households owned a radio in 1939 than in 1929? *(Approximately 17 million more households owned a radio.)* Why were more households able to purchase a radio in the middle of the Depression? *(The price of radios fell dramatically, making radios more affordable for many people.)*

Analyze Data What does the increasing amount of box office receipts between 1940 and 1944 suggest about the economic health of the country? *(The increasing amount of box office receipts suggests that Americans had more money to spend in the early 1940s, indicating that the country's economy had improved.)*

Life During the Depression

SYNTHESIZE

DIGITAL ACTIVITY

America During the Depression

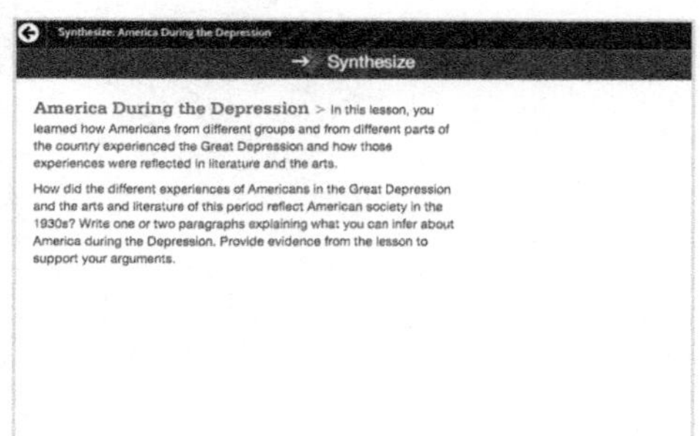

Synthesize: America During the Depression
→ Synthesize
America During the Depression > In this lesson, you learned how Americans from different groups and from different parts of the country experienced the Great Depression and how those experiences were reflected in literature and the arts.
How did the different experiences of Americans in the Great Depression and the arts and literature of this period reflect American society in the 1930s? Write one or two paragraphs explaining what you can infer about America during the Depression. Provide evidence from the lesson to support your arguments.

After students have completed their writing, invite them to share their work with partners.

Discuss the diversity of American culture and the American experience of the Great Depression. Also, discuss the common experiences of the Depression. Ask students to consider the ways that the hardships divided and united the country.

DEMONSTRATE

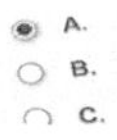

DIGITAL QUIZ

Lesson Quiz and Discussion Board

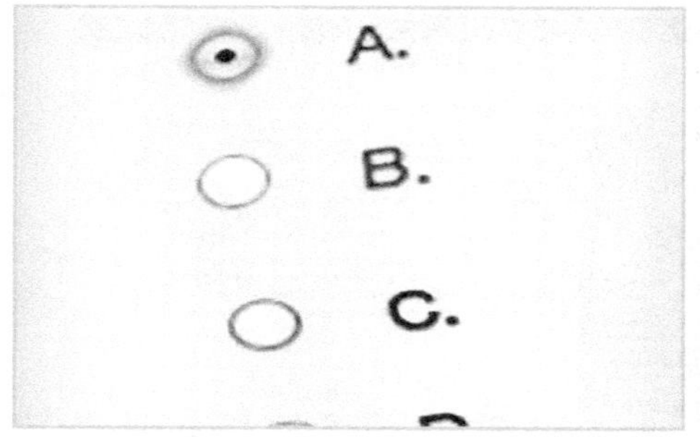

Assign the online Lesson Quiz for this lesson if you haven't already done so. Students will be offered automatic remediation or enrichment based on their score.

In *Life During the Depression*, you learned what life was like during the Great Depression. You examined the impact the Depression had on specific groups of people, including farmers, women, and various minority groups. You also learned how the economic challenges of the time impacted arts and literature.

Post these questions to the class on the Discussion Board:

Summarize How did the Great Depression impact women, farmers, and minority groups? How did the U.S. government respond to each of these groups of people?

Infer What evidence from the text indicates that literature and art produced during the Great Depression reflected the economic challenges of the era?

Topic Inquiry

Have students continue their investigations for the Topic Inquiry.

PEARSON realize

www.PearsonRealize.com
Access your Digital Lesson

Prosperity and Depression

SYNTHESIZE

DIGITAL ACTIVITY

Reflect on the Essential Question and Topic

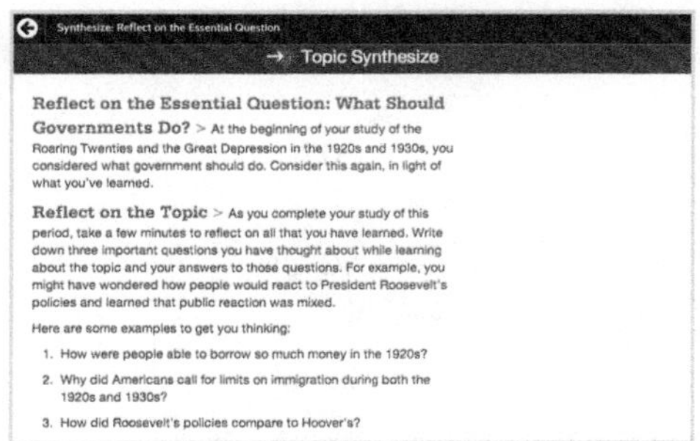

Ask students to reconsider the Essential Question for the topic: What should government do? Remind students of the possibilities they considered at the start of the topic. For example, government can

- regulate business
- regulate banking
- intervene in the economy
- take care of the needy

After students have responded to the questions, ask volunteers to share their writing with the class. Encourage discussion and debate as students share their reflections. Invite students to post their answers on the Class Discussion Board.

Next, ask students to reflect on the topic as a whole and jot down three questions about the topic content and the answers to those questions. Review the sample questions and encourage students to share their own questions with the class. Invite students to post their questions and answers on the Class Discussion Board.

Topic Inquiry

Have students complete Step 3 of the Topic Inquiry.

DEMONSTRATE

DIGITAL TOPIC REVIEW AND ASSESSMENT

Prosperity and Depression

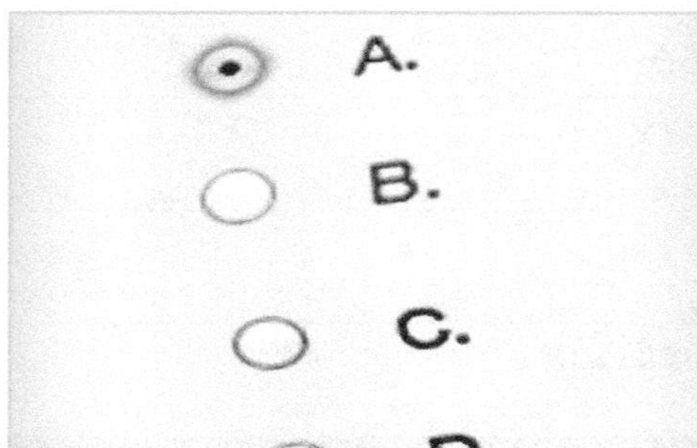

Students can prepare for the Topic Test by answering the questions in the Topic Review and Assessment online or the Assessment questions in the Print Student text. They can also prepare by reviewing their answers to the Interactive Reading Notepad questions or reviewing their notes in the Reading and Notetaking Study Guide.

DIGITAL TOPIC TEST

Prosperity and Depression

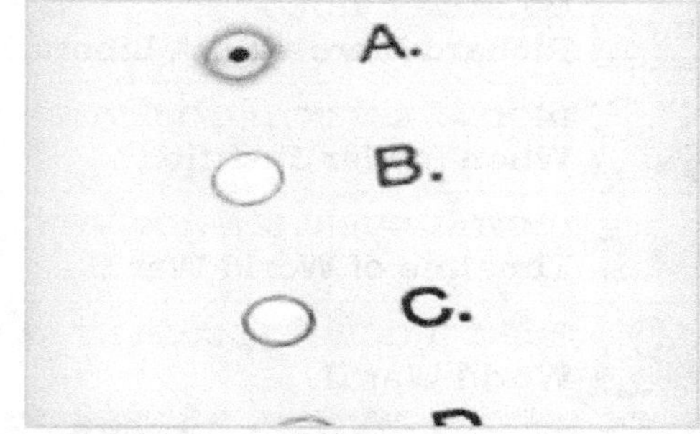

TOPIC TEST

Assign the Topic Test to assess students' understanding of topic content.

BENCHMARK TESTS

Assign these benchmark tests as you complete the relevant topics to monitor student progress toward mastering the course content and as preparation for the End-of-Course Test.

Benchmark Test 1: Topics 1–2
Benchmark Test 2: Topics 3–4
Benchmark Test 3: Topics 5–6
Benchmark Test 4: Topics 7–9
Benchmark Test 5: Topics 10–12
Benchmark Test 6: Topics 13–14
Benchmark Test 7: Topics 15–17

Topic 14

World War II

TOPIC 14 ORGANIZER	PACING: APPROX. 7 PERIODS, 3.5 BLOCKS
	PACING
Connect	1 period
MY STORY VIDEO **Richard Marowitz, A Liberation Story**	10 min.
DIGITAL ESSENTIAL QUESTION ACTIVITY **When Is War Justified?**	10 min.
DIGITAL OVERVIEW ACTIVITY **Timeline of World War II**	10 min.
TOPIC INQUIRY: DOCUMENT-BASED QUESTION **World War II**	20 min.
Investigate	2–4 periods
TOPIC INQUIRY: DOCUMENT-BASED QUESTION **World War II**	Ongoing
LESSON 1 Aggression Overseas and Isolationism at Home	30–40 min.
LESSON 2 Entering World War II	30–40 min.
LESSON 3 The Home Front	30–40 min.
LESSON 4 Winning a Deadly War	30–40 min.
Synthesize	1 period
DIGITAL ACTIVITY **Reflect on the Essential Question and Topic**	10 min.
TOPIC INQUIRY: DOCUMENT-BASED QUESTION **World War II**	20 min.
Demonstrate	1–2 periods
DIGITAL TOPIC REVIEW AND ASSESSMENT **World War II**	10 min.
TOPIC INQUIRY: DOCUMENT-BASED QUESTION **World War II**	20 min.

TOPIC INQUIRY: DOCUMENT-BASED QUESTION

World War II

In this Topic Inquiry, students will investigate primary source documents to evaluate the decision made by President Truman to use an atomic bomb in the war against Japan. At the conclusion of the inquiry, each student will write an essay in response to the question: Was President Truman justified in his decision to drop the atomic bomb? This investigation will help students explore and answer the Topic Essential Question: **When is war justified?**

STEP 1: CONNECT

Develop Questions and Plan the Investigation

Launch the Document-Based Question Activity

Remind students that the war in Europe had ended on May 8, 1945, following the surrender of Germany on May 7. However, the war in the Pacific continued. Assessments of the planned invasion of Japan were grim. They forecast huge losses in American lives. At the same time, the Manhattan Project in the United States announced that it had a devastating new weapon—a weapon that could end the war.

Ask students to read the Student Instructions for Step 1. Then, project the embedded C-Span video segment entitled "President Truman Speech After the Bombing of Hiroshima."

Suggestion: Pause the video periodically and pose questions to the class such as the following: How does Truman describe the bomb dropped on Hiroshima? Why does Truman say that the United States dropped the bomb? What does Truman say that the United States has the power to do? To what ultimatum does Truman refer, and why? Why does Truman refer to Pearl Harbor?

Generate Questions

Tell students that in this Topic Inquiry they will explore primary source documents to evaluate President Truman's decision to drop atomic weapons on the cities of Hiroshima and Nagasaki in Japan. Organize students into small groups. Have them begin their investigation by discussing the video segment. Emphasize that the speech by Truman was the first time that many Americans learned about the Manhattan Project and atomic weapons.

Display the Document-Based Question: Was President Truman justified in his decision to drop the atomic bomb? Point out that Japan did surrender soon after the use of atomic weapons. However, point out that the weapons themselves resulted in massive casualties and loss of life, largely among civilians. Challenge student groups to brainstorm reasons both for dropping the bombs and for not using nuclear weapons.

Resources

- Topic Inquiry DBQ Student Instructions
- Embedded video segment from C-Span "President Truman Speech After the Bombing of Hiroshima"

STEP 2: INVESTIGATE

Apply Disciplinary Concepts and Tools

Analyze the Documents

Project the list of the primary source documents, and have students refer to their Student Instructions. Direct students to work in pairs to review each of the six primary sources and to answer the questions that follow each source. Prompt students to evaluate the validity of each source as they read and answer the questions. You may wish to model for them how to identify bias in written material.

Check Your Understanding

As a class, review and discuss answers to the questions for each source. Allow students to make any corrections necessary. Then, tell students to review the documents for evidence to support or oppose President Truman's decision. Pose the question: Which documents suggest that the decision was justified? Which documents suggest or imply that it was not?

Suggestion: Advise students to divide a sheet of paper into two columns labeled "Justified" and "Not Justified." Have them record evidence from the documents in the appropriate columns.

Resources

- Topic Inquiry DBQ Student Instructions
- Document A: The Potsdam Declaration, containing Allied surrender terms for Japan
- Document B: A petition sent to President Truman from atomic scientists
- Document C: Photographs of the bombing of Hiroshima
- Document D: A transcript of a meeting between Japanese emperor Hirohito and his advisers
- Document E: A letter from President Truman explaining his decision
- Document F: A letter from Douglas MacArthur giving his opinion of the bombing

PROFESSIONAL DEVELOPMENT

Document-Based Question

Be sure to view the Document-Based Question Professional Development resources in the online course.

 TOPIC INQUIRY: DOCUMENT-BASED QUESTION

World War II *(continued)*

STEP 3: SYNTHESIZE
Evaluate Sources and Use Evidence to Formulate Conclusions

Write Your Essay
Project the Student Instructions and the Rubric. Review the directions for the essay and the expectations from the rubric as a class. Tell students to be sure to use evidence from at least three documents to support their conclusions. Remind them to address at least one counter-argument to their position in the essay.

Suggestion: Review the components of a complete essay, including an introduction with a thesis, or position statement; the body, with evidence to support the position and discussion of counter-arguments; and the conclusion, with a restatement of the thesis. You may wish to model for students how to outline their ideas for the essay.

Resources
- Topic Inquiry DBQ Student Instructions
- Topic Inquiry DBQ Rubric

STEP 4: DEMONSTRATE
Communicate Conclusions and Take Informed Action

Complete Your Essay
Have students revise and submit their essays. Remind students to read over their essays for any errors before turning it in.

Suggestion: When students finish drafting their essays, have them read aloud their work individually. Reading aloud will help them identify errors, problems with flow, and misconceptions. Tell students to use their Student Instructions and Rubrics like a checklist to ensure that they have included all required elements.

Assess Your Work
Tell students to reflect on the investigation and writing process. Challenge them to assess how well they did and to suggest what they might do differently on a future topic inquiry.

Evaluate the Bombings of Hiroshima and Nagasaki
Ask students to evaluate the impact of the bombings on international relations and on the status of the United States in the world. Organize students into small groups to discuss and present their ideas. Encourage them to consider what lasting legacy the decision might have had not only for the United States but also for nations and peoples around the world. Then, take a thumb vote: Did President Truman make the right decision? Organize students into groups based on their responses and have them discuss and share their reasoning.

Resources
- Topic Inquiry DBQ Student Instructions
- Topic Inquiry DBQ Rubric
- Self-Assessment

INTRODUCTION

World War II

In the years following World War I, economic challenges and a desire to disengage from world affairs encouraged a trend toward isolationism in the United States. Many people began to fear becoming overly involved in overseas conflicts again. As totalitarian governments gained power and aggressively expanded their borders in Europe and Asia, the United States slowly increased its involvement in global affairs; however, the attack on Pearl Harbor propelled the United States into World War II. The war's economic and social impact was felt at home, and its conclusion found the course of world history irrevocably changed.

CONNECT

MY STORY VIDEO

Richard Marowitz, A Liberation Story

Watch a video about the liberation of Dachau, near the end of World War II.

Check Understanding What shock did Richard Marowitz and his fellow Americans receive as they entered the camp at Dachau? *(Assuming the foul odor in the air was of dead animals, they soon realized they were surrounded by the bodies of dead prisoners.)*

Identify Patterns What is the value of teaching about disturbing historical events that happened some seventy years ago? *(Most students will mention that the value in teaching about disturbing historical events is to understand what happened and to work to ensure that they never take place again.)*

DIGITAL ESSENTIAL QUESTION ACTIVITY

When Is War Justified?

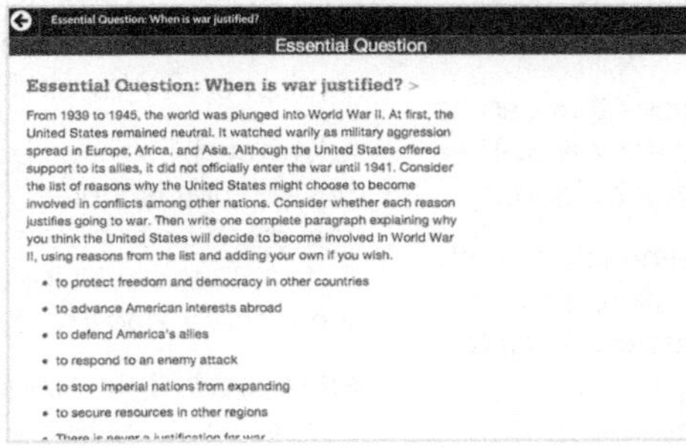

Essential Question: When is war justified?
Essential Question
Essential Question: When is war justified? >
From 1939 to 1945, the world was plunged into World War II. At first, the United States remained neutral. It watched warily as military aggression spread in Europe, Africa, and Asia. Although the United States offered support to its allies, it did not officially enter the war until 1941. Consider the list of reasons why the United States might choose to become involved in conflicts among other nations. Consider whether each reason justifies going to war. Then write one complete paragraph explaining why you think the United States will decide to become involved in World War II, using reasons from the list and adding your own if you wish.
• to protect freedom and democracy in other countries
• to advance American interests abroad
• to defend America's allies
• to respond to an enemy attack
• to stop imperial nations from expanding
• to secure resources in other regions

Project the Digital Essential Question Activity. Organize students into groups and have them read through the activity. Ask them to work in pairs to rank the list of reasons for going to war. Then, have students work individually to write several lines in which they explain why they think the United States will become involved in World War II. Remind them that they may use the reasons listed as well as reasons of their own. Have students share their responses with partners.

Apply Concepts Many Americans opposed U.S. involvement in World War II. Look again at the list of reasons. For each reason, offer a response from an opposing, or counter, point of view. *(Possible answers: The United States should worry about maintaining democracy and freedom within its own borders. The United States would do better to develop its resources and economy at home. The United States can offer economic and other types of support to its allies.)*

Make Generalizations To justify something is to show that it is right, fair, or reasonable. How does one determine if war is justified? *(Answers will vary. Students might respond that to justify war, the reasons for going to war should be weighed against potential outcomes. They might cite religious values or ethical standards to determine whether a particular reason is or is not justifiable.)*

DIGITAL OVERVIEW ACTIVITY

Timeline of World War II

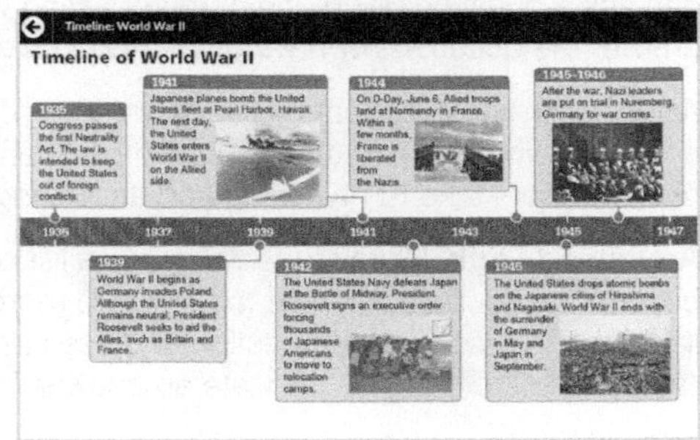

Project the Timeline of World War II. Call attention to the outbreak of war in Europe in 1939, and explain that despite its neutrality, the United States did provide economic and other assistance to its allies from World War I, Britain and France. The United States had a vested interest in helping these nations stop imperialist and militaristic regimes in Germany and Italy from gaining too much power over Europe. Ask students to identify the turning point at which the United States became involved in the war. Guide them to understand that the attack on Pearl Harbor represented a direct assault on U.S. territory and American lives.

Discuss How do you think the United States went from avoiding war to taking decisive actions to win the war in Europe and the Pacific? *(Once Japan attacked the United States, it was committed to the war effort on the side of the Allies. As it entered the war, the United States engaged its military and economic resources to aid the Allies in Europe and to defeat Japan in the Pacific.)*

Topic Inquiry

Launch the Topic Inquiry with students after introducing the topic.

Aggression Overseas and Isolationism at Home

Supporting English Language Learners

Use with the reading, **Totalitarian Soviet Union and Militarist Japan**.

Speaking

Discuss why it is important to ask questions as we read (e.g., to maintain our interest, to engage with the text, to help us think critically). Say that students will practice asking questions aloud about the text as they reread it.

Beginning Display and explain these question frames: What does ____ mean? Where is ____? Why did ____? Then reread the text together, pausing periodically so students can ask a question using one of the frames above.

Intermediate Review the question words *who*, *what*, *when*, *where*, *why*, and *how*. Then reread the text together, pausing periodically so students can ask a question using one of the question words above. If possible, answer the questions or have other students do so.

Advanced Have students write down a list of five questions that can be answered from the text (and require more than one-word answers). Then have partners take turns asking and answering the questions aloud.

Advanced High Have students create a list of five questions that reach beyond the scope of the text (and require more than one-word answers). Invite them to select one question and use appropriate search terms to "ask" the search engine to locate an answer.

Use with the reading, **Isolationism in the United States**.

Reading

Highlight the geographical locations mentioned in the text. Explain that having a greater familiarity with this vocabulary will increase students' comprehension.

Beginning Display a map showing political boundaries during the World War II era with labels for the Soviet Union, Japan, and other countries in East Asia. (Or refer to the Pacific Theater map in Lesson 4.) Reread the last sentence of the text. Use the map to show how improved relations with the Soviet Union might inhibit Japanese expansion in Asia. Ask: What does *expansion* mean?

Intermediate Display maps of the eastern and western hemispheres. With students, label Asia, Europe, the United States, and Argentina. Reread the text's second-to-last paragraph together, and ask: What is a hemisphere? Why did FDR use that word?

Advanced Provide pairs of students with maps of the eastern and western hemispheres. Ask pairs to reread the text's second-to-last paragraph and discuss: Why did Roosevelt see Argentina and the United States as united? How is that expressed in language such as *hemisphere*, *consult together*, and *mutual safety*?

Advanced High Ask students to label a world map with the locations mentioned in the text. Have them reread the text, referring to the map as necessary. Ask: How does the map help you to visualize the concept and difficulties of American isolationism?

D Differentiate Instruction

Use the Differentiated Instruction notes throughout the lesson plan to support the varied skill sets, levels of readiness, and interests in the mixed-ability classroom.

Challenge These notes include suggestions for expanding the activity for advanced students.

On-Level These notes include suggestions for modifying the activity to address different interests or learning styles.

Extra Support These notes include ideas for providing more scaffolding or reading spuport.

Special Needs These notes provide ideas for adapting instruction to support the needs of various special needs students.

NOTES

Objectives

Objective 1: Explain how fascist governments came to power in Italy and Germany.

Objective 2: Identify the communist dictatorship Stalin set up in the Soviet Union.

Objective 3: Describe how military rulers took power in Japan.

Objective 4: Explain why the United States adopted a policy of isolationism as European and Asian nations moved toward war.

LESSON 1 ORGANIZER	PACING: APPROX. 1 PERIOD, .5 BLOCKS		RESOURCES	
	OBJECTIVES	PACING	Online	Print
Connect				
DIGITAL START UP ACTIVITY **Totalitarianism in the 1920s and 1930s**		5 min.	●	
Investigate				
DIGITAL TEXT 1 **Political Changes in Italy and Germany**	Objective 1	10 min.	●	●
DIGITAL TEXT 2 **Totalitarian Soviet Union and Militarist Japan**	Objectives 2, 3	10 min.	●	●
INTERACTIVE GALLERY **Characteristics of Totalitarianism**	Objectives 2, 3	10 min.	●	
DIGITAL TEXT 3 **Isolationism in the United States**	Objective 4	10 min.	●	●
Synthesize				
DIGITAL ACTIVITY **Comparing Totalitarian Regimes**		5 min.	●	
Demonstrate				
DIGITAL QUIZ **Lesson Quiz and Class Discussion Board**		10 min.	●	

Aggression Overseas and Isolationism at Home

CONNECT

DIGITAL START UP ACTIVITY

Totalitarianism in the 1920s and 1930s

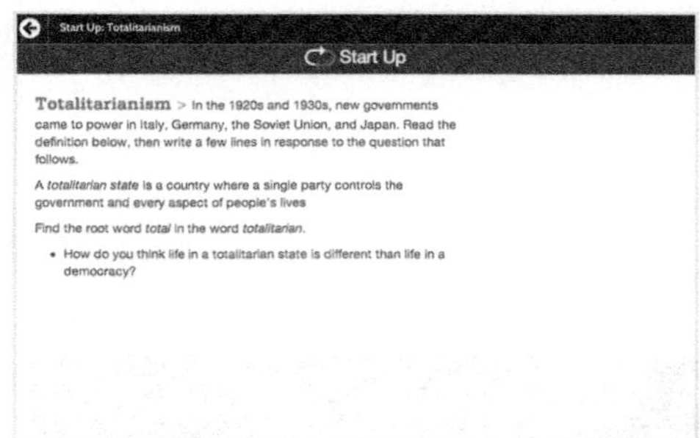

Start Up: Totalitarianism
Start Up
Totalitarianism > In the 1920s and 1930s, new governments came to power in Italy, Germany, the Soviet Union, and Japan. Read the definition below, then write a few lines in response to the question that follows.
A totalitarian state is a country where a single party controls the government and every aspect of people's lives
Find the root word total in the word totalitarian.
• How do you think life in a totalitarian state is different than life in a democracy?

Project the Start Up Activity Ask students to answer the question as they enter and get settled. Then have them share their ideas with another student, either in class or online.

Discuss How would you expect the national government of a totalitarian state to be structured? *(A totalitarian state would have one central leader or central group of leaders who would hold all government power.)*

Tell students that in this lesson they will explore how totalitarian states rose to power in several European and Asian nations in the 1930s. They will compare the different totalitarian governments, examine how the ambitions of those governments led to world war, and investigate the reasons behind American isolationism.

Aa Vocabulary Development: Use the Interactive Reading Notepad to preview the Key Terms and Academic Vocabulary in this lesson with students.

FLIP IT!

Assign the Flipped Video for this lesson.

STUDENT EDITION PRINT PAGES: 760–765

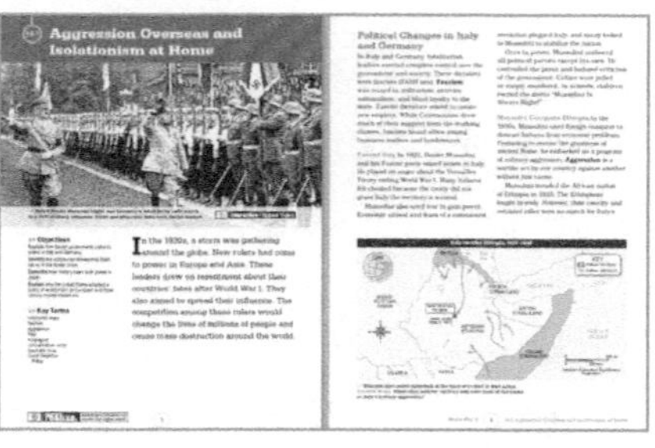

INVESTIGATE

DIGITAL TEXT 1

Political Changes in Italy and Germany

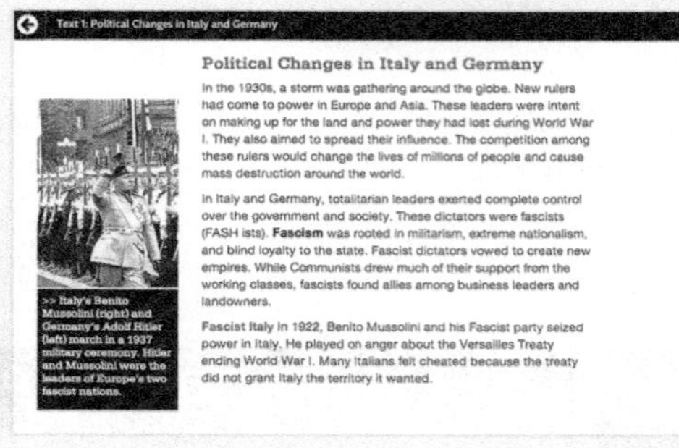

Objective 1: Explain how fascist governments came to power in Italy and Germany.

Quick Instruction

To begin, prompt students to recall how World War I ended and how different European nations fared at the end of that war. Remind students that Germany faced harsh penalties and economic losses as a result of its defeat in World War I. Point out that the United States and much of the industrialized world was in the midst of the Great Depression in the 1930s.

Compare and Contrast the manner in which Mussolini and Hitler rose to power. *(Both leaders were fascists who relied on militarism, extreme nationalism, and blind loyalty to the state. Both played on fear of economic hardship and political unrest to gain power. Hitler specifically targeted Jews and other minority groups in his efforts to rally Germans behind his leadership.)*

Summarize How did the fascists differ from the communists? *(Communists rallied the working class to support their cause while fascists found allies among business leaders and landowners.)*

D Differentiate: Extra Support Ask students to write the following key words on note cards: *fascism* and *totalitarianism*. Tell them to record words related to each term on the cards as they move through the reading. Point out that many words might repeat. Then, have student partners work together to write a definition for each term. Finally, ask students to write a sentence in which they use both key words.

Further Instruction

Begin by projecting the infographic on German economic problems after World War I. Conduct a Think-Pair-Share with students, asking them to relate the economic hardship in the graphic with how these circumstances might have made the German people vulnerable, or open, to new types of leadership.

Draw Conclusions How might invasion and war have distracted people in Germany and Italy from their economic problems? *(Many citizens would have served in the military rather than remained at home looking for jobs and struggling with economic burdens. The nations' media would have diverted attention to political and military affairs. The national economies, too, might have been boosted by a surge in production to support invasion and war efforts.)* Why were Jewish people and other minority populations persecuted in Germany? *(Many German citizens and Hitler's government targeted Jews and other people. They were blamed for Germany's problems and their persecution served to unite the Germans in a common cause and sentiment.)*

Hypothesize Why might charismatic leaders be able to gain increasing levels of power during difficult economic times? *(During economic hardship, many people would have been looking for change to improve their conditions. They would have been more open to new leaders offering solutions and promises, especially as they would likely blame existing leadership for their difficulties.)*

DIGITAL TEXT 2

Totalitarian Soviet Union and Militarist Japan

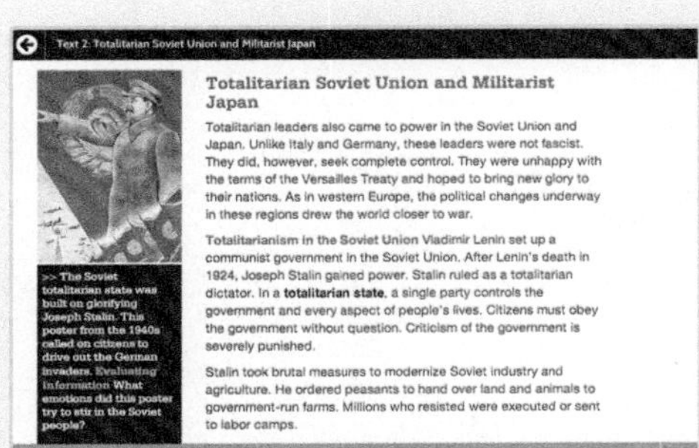

INTERACTIVE GALLERY

Characteristics of Totalitarianism

Objectives 2: Identify the communist dictatorship Stalin set up in the Soviet Union; 3: Describe how military rulers took power in Japan.

Quick Instruction

Begin by pointing out Europe, the Soviet Union, and Japan on a world map of the World War II era. Explain that the Soviet Union and Japan also suffered economic hardship during the era of the Great Depression. Remind students, too, that the Soviet Union was recovering not only from its part in World War I but also from its own Russian Revolution.

Interactive Gallery: Characteristics of Totalitarianism Project the Interactive Gallery and navigate through the images as you prompt students to connect each to the larger ideas of charismatic leaders, youth indoctrination, propaganda, militarism, and lack of civil rights. Why was propaganda important to leaders of totalitarian states? *(Propaganda spread what totalitarian leaders wanted their citizens to believe and helped build up support and legitimacy for their governments. It helped make their authority more about a specific message and image, and used strong symbols to unite and motivate people.)*

ACTIVE CLASSROOM

Conduct a Quickdraw activity. Organize students into groups, and assign each group one of these nations: Japan, Germany, Italy,and the Soviet Union. Ask students to design counter-propaganda posters meant to combat the messages used by totalitarian leaders in their countries to amass power. Ask volunteers to discuss the metaphors or symbolism used in their posters with the class. Display completed posters in the class.

ELL Use the ELL activity described in the ELL chart.

Further Instruction

Compare What similarities did Japan share with Germany and Italy during this time? *(Like Italy and Germany, Japan was suffering economic challenges. Military leaders were able to take power over government, and they preached racial superiority over other Asians and non-Asians, just as Hitler had launched the persecution of the Jews and other select groups. Like Italy, Japan also sought to gain economic resources by invading other nations, such as China. It proved as aggressive militarily as both European nations.)*

Apply Why might nations in Europe and North America hesitate to take military action against Japan? *(Japan and China were located in East Asia. This likely presented logistical issues. It would have been difficult and costly for other nations, especially in Europe and the United States, from taking military action against Japan.)*

Aggression Overseas and Isolationism at Home

DIGITAL TEXT 3

Isolationism in the United States

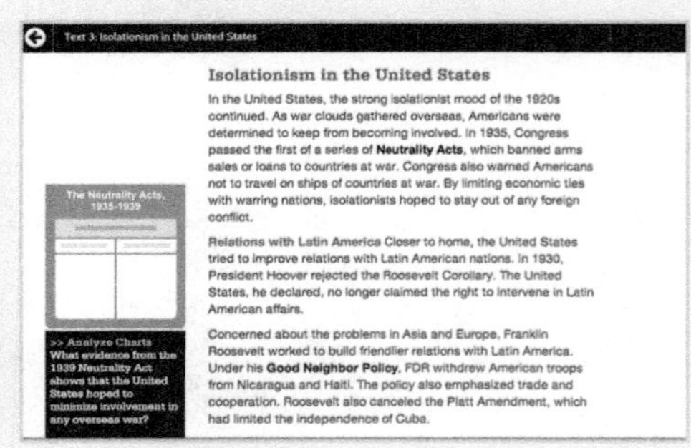

Text 3: Isolationism in the United States

Isolationism in the United States

In the United States, the strong isolationist mood of the 1920s continued. As war clouds gathered overseas, Americans were determined to keep from becoming involved. In 1935, Congress passed the first of a series of **Neutrality Acts**, which banned arms sales or loans to countries at war. Congress also warned Americans not to travel on ships of countries at war. By limiting economic ties with warring nations, isolationists hoped to stay out of any foreign conflict.

Relations with Latin America Closer to home, the United States tried to improve relations with Latin American nations. In 1930, President Hoover rejected the Roosevelt Corollary. The United States, he declared, no longer claimed the right to intervene in Latin American affairs.

Concerned about the problems in Asia and Europe, Franklin Roosevelt worked to build friendlier relations with Latin America. Under his **Good Neighbor Policy**, FDR withdrew American troops from Nicaragua and Haiti. The policy also emphasized trade and cooperation. Roosevelt also canceled the Platt Amendment, which had limited the independence of Cuba.

The Neutrality Acts, 1935-1939

>> Analyze Charts What evidence from the 1939 Neutrality Act shows that the United States hoped to minimize involvement in any overseas war?

Objective 4: **Explain why the United States adopted a policy of isolationism as European and Asian nations moved toward war.**

Quick Instruction

Project the chart titled *The Neutrality Acts, 1935–1939*. Prompt students to suggest reasons that account for the provisions in the chart and why the United States might want to remain neutral in European and East Asian conflicts. List their ideas on the board, and revisit and revise the list as you move through the text.

Connect How might World War I and the Great Depression have contributed to the isolationist mood of the American people and their leaders? *(World War I had already involved the United States in an overseas conflict that drew many resources and cost many American lives. The Great Depression resulted in poverty, unemployment, and other hardship for many Americans. Many people would have been more interested in resolving these domestic issues rather than committing money, citizens, and resources to more overseas conflict.)*

ELL Use the ELL activity described in the ELL chart.

Further Instruction

Ask students to work in small groups to write a few sentences explaining why many Americans preferred the country to take a more isolationist position in world affairs. Have each group share their ideas. Be sure that students recall the farm crisis, the stock market crash, the Great Depression, and the rise in immigration and nativism.

Evaluate Information In what way did the United States not behave in an isolationist fashion during this time period? *(Events in Europe and Asia encouraged the United States to seek closer ties with its more immediate neighbors in the Western Hemisphere, especially in Latin America. President Roosevelt adopted his Good Neighbor Policy so that the United States and its neighbors might be better prepared to join together if an attack came from Europe or Asia. The United States also reached out to the Soviet Union and restored diplomatic relations.)*

Make Predictions Given the previous way in which the United States entered World War I, what circumstances might motivate the U.S. government to abandon its position of neutrality in the war in Europe? *(an attack on or a more serious threat to American lives, property, territory or interests)*

SYNTHESIZE

DIGITAL ACTIVITY

Comparing Totalitarian Regimes

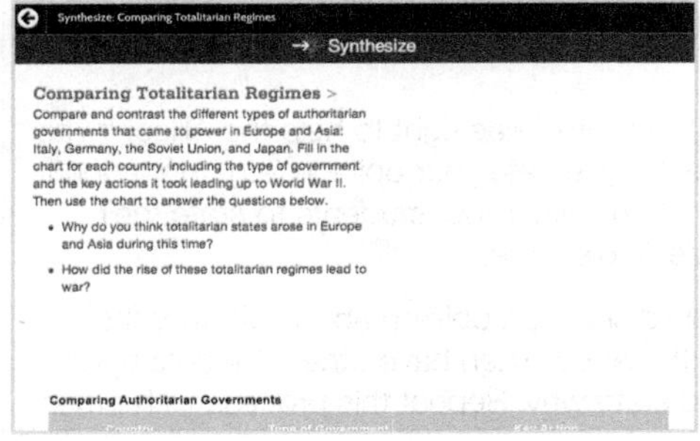

Project the Digital Activity Ask students to work in pairs to complete the charts. Then, have them answer the questions individually. Call on volunteers to share their responses.

Discuss If Italy, Germany, the Soviet Union, and Japan had stronger economies in the 1920s and 1930s, would totalitarian regimes have been able to take power? Why or why not? How do you think economics influenced the response of Americans to these events?

DEMONSTRATE

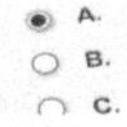

DIGITAL QUIZ

Lesson Quiz and Class Discussion Board

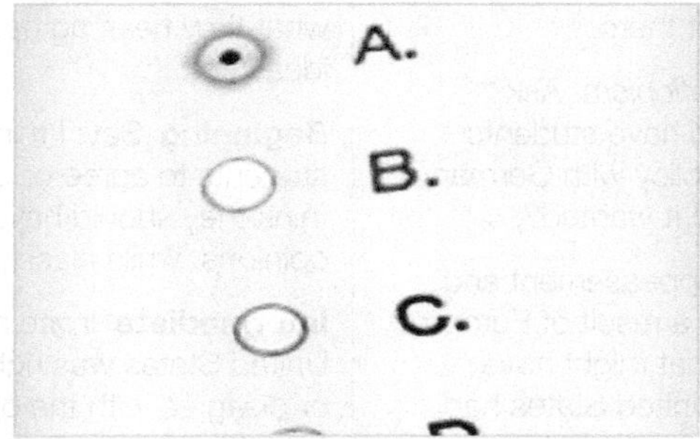

Assign the online Lesson Quiz for this lesson if you haven't already done so. Students will be offered automatic remediation or enrichment based on their score.

Pose these questions to the class on the Discussion Board:

In *Aggression Overseas and Isolationism at Home*, you learned how totalitarian governments came to power in Japan, Germany, Italy, and the Soviet Union. You also evaluated the reasons behind American isolationism in response to these changes in world affairs.

Draw Conclusions Why might American isolationism prove difficult to maintain in the face of totalitarian regimes overseas?

Integrate Information Would you have supported an isolationist point of view toward Europe at the onset of World War II? Why or why not? Explain your position.

Topic Inquiry

Have students continue their investigations for the Topic Inquiry.

Entering World War II

Supporting English Language Learners

Use with the reading, **The Beginnings of War**.

Learning

Explain that appeasement and isolationism are two stances that were taken by nations at the beginning of World War II. To better understand these terms, it can be helpful to compare and contrast them.

Beginning Display the words *appeasement* and *isolationism*. Ask questions pertaining to one, both, or neither term, and have students identify the relevant words (e.g., What was France's policy with Germany? Which policy (or policies) allowed Germany to do what it wanted?).

Intermediate Compare and contrast the impact of appeasement and isolationism on Sudetenland. Ask: What happened as a result of Europe's appeasement and the United States' isolationism? What might have happened if Europe had been isolationist and/or the United States had adopted an appeasement policy?

Advanced Display a chart with the following content, and ask pairs of students to copy and complete it: show two columns titled *Appeasement* and *Isolationism* and three rows titled *Who used it?*, *Why did they use it?*, and *What happened as a result?*

Advanced High Invite pairs of students to discuss the similarities and differences between appeasement and isolationism, including their definitions, supporters, causes, and effects. Have pairs record their ideas on a Venn diagram.

Use with the reading, **The United States Assists the Allies**.

Listening

Tell students that they can demonstrate listening comprehension by responding directly to what someone says. This can be done by restating what they hear, agreeing or disagreeing with it, and/or linking their own ideas to it.

Beginning Say: I think the United States was right to help the Allies. Invite students to agree or disagree as they restate your opinion (e.g., no, I don't think they should have helped). Then invite other students to state their opinions, while classmates agree or disagree.

Intermediate Invite a volunteer to share an opinion about whether the United States was right to help the Allies. Then have other students agree or disagree with the opinion and state why. Repeat this process with other volunteers.

Advanced Ask pairs of students to construct a case for American isolationism or for assisting the Allies. During this process, students should listen to their partner's ideas and build on them to create a solid argument.

Advanced High Invite pairs of students to take opposite sides and debate whether the United States should have assisted the Allies. Encourage them to restate each other's comments, agree or disagree with them, and then add their own thoughts.

D Differentiate Instruction

Use the Differentiated Instruction notes throughout the lesson plan to support the varied skill sets, levels of readiness, and interests in the mixed-ability classroom.

Challenge These notes include suggestions for expanding the activity for advanced students.

On-Level These notes include suggestions for modifying the activity to address different interests or learning styles.

Extra Support These notes include ideas for providing more scaffolding or reading spuport.

Special Needs These notes provide ideas for adapting instruction to support the needs of various special needs students.

NOTES

PEARSON realize www.PearsonRealize.com

Go online to access additional resources including: Primary Sources • Biographies • Supreme Court cases • 21st Century Skill Tutorials • Maps • Graphic Organizers.

Objectives

Objective 1: Explain how aggression led to war in Asia and Europe.

Objective 2: Describe how the United States responded to the outbreak of World War II.

Objective 3: Explain why the United States finally entered the war.

LESSON 2 ORGANIZER	PACING: APPROX. 1 PERIOD, .5 BLOCKS		RESOURCES	
	OBJECTIVES	PACING	Online	Print
Connect				
DIGITAL START UP ACTIVITY **U.S. Involvement in Europe**		5 min.	●	
Investigate				
DIGITAL TEXT 1 **The Beginnings of War**	Objective 1	10 min.	●	●
INTERACTIVE MAP **Axis and Allied Nations in Europe, 1939–1942**	Objective 1	10 min.	●	
DIGITAL TEXT 2 **Germany Attacks France and Britain**	Objective 2	10 min.	●	●
DIGITAL TEXT 3 **The United States Assists the Allies**	Objective 2	10 min.	●	●
DIGITAL TEXT 4 **The United States Declares War**	Objective 3	10 min.	●	●
INTERACTIVE MAP **Surprise Attack on Pearl Harbor**	Objective 3	10 min.	●	
INTERACTIVE CHART **The United States Debates Going to War**	Objective 3	10 min.	●	
Synthesize				
DIGITAL ACTIVITY **Answer Your Questions**		5 min.	●	
Demonstrate				
DIGITAL QUIZ **Lesson Quiz and Class Discussion Board**		10 min.	●	

Entering World War II

CONNECT

DIGITAL START UP ACTIVITY

U.S. Involvement in Europe

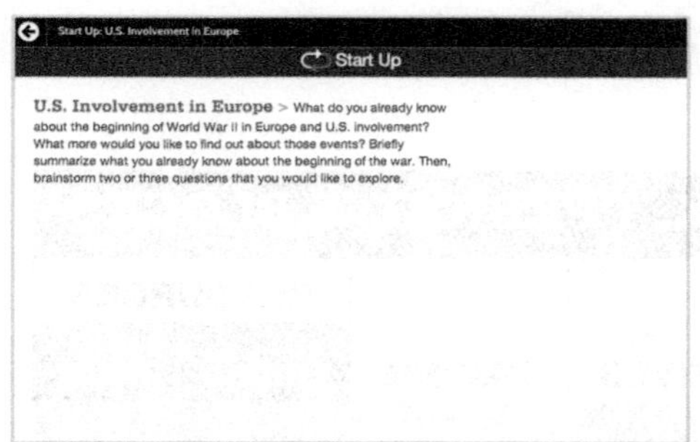

Project the Start Up Activity Have students complete the activity as they enter and get settled. Invite volunteers to share what they think they know and want to learn. Record ideas and questions on the board to revisit.

Discuss Why would the United States want to stay out of a second world war? *(The United States might not want to risk more lives, property, and money fighting in another war or become more entangled in world affairs that might have a negative impact on business at home.)*

Tell students that in this lesson, they will learn how aggression among nations led to war and how the United States responded to the outbreak of World War II.

Aa Vocabulary Development: Use the Interactive Reading Notepad to preview the Key Terms and Academic Vocabulary in this lesson with students.

FLIP IT!

Assign the Flipped Video for this lesson.

STUDENT EDITION PRINT PAGES: 766–774

INVESTIGATE

DIGITAL TEXT 1

The Beginnings of War

INTERACTIVE MAP

Axis and Allied Nations in Europe, 1939–1942

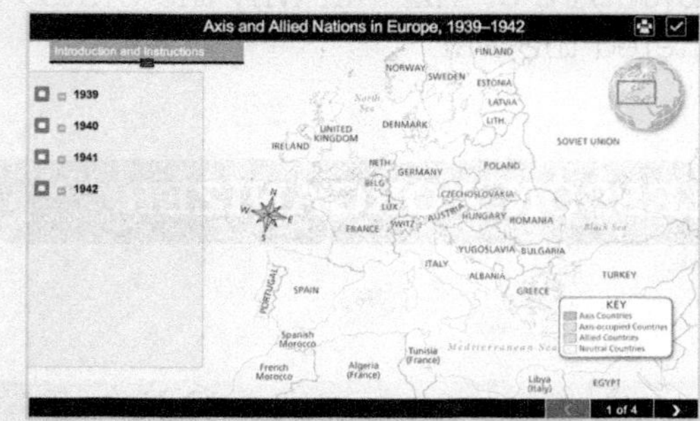

Objective 1: Explain how aggression led to war in Asia and Europe.

Quick Instruction

Remind students that totalitarian governments had taken power in Germany, Japan, Italy, and the Soviet Union, and ask them to consider why this posed a threat to other nations in Europe and Asia. Have students Think-Pair-Share their responses.

Interactive Map: Axis and Allied Nations in Europe, 1939–1942 Project the Interactive Map and navigate through the layers with students. Pause at each layer and ask students to identify changes in alliances and territory. Based on the map, when did Germany become a direct threat to Britain? *(In 1940, when Germany occupied Belgium, Denmark, Norway, and France, all of which lie across the sea from Britain. Belgium and France in particular are located very close to Britain, just across the English Channel.)*

Draw Conclusions Why did Britain and France tolerate German aggression for so long in favor of appeasement? *(Both nations hoped to avoid war and a clear threat to their own citizens. They hoped that Germany would settle for smaller conquests without engaging in war with their nations. Also, both nations were still recovering from World War I and the Great Depression.)*

ACTIVE CLASSROOM

Conduct a Make Headlines activity. Organize students into groups, and assign each group one level of the map. Ask each group to write two different headlines that relate to the changes shown on their level of the map. Ask volunteers to share their headlines with the class.

D Differentiate: Extra Support Preview the content by having students skim the text for keywords. As they move through the text, have them write down definitions for the keywords. When they have finished the text, ask students to write one sentence that corresponds to the content using each word. Then, ask students to share and revise their sentences with a partner.

ELL Use the ELL activity described in the ELL chart.

Further Instruction

Review the instructions for the Interactive Reading Notepad. Have students work in pairs to read the text and answer the questions. Then, combine pairs into small groups to share their responses. Call on each group to answer one or more questions.

DIGITAL TEXT 2

Germany Attacks France and Britain

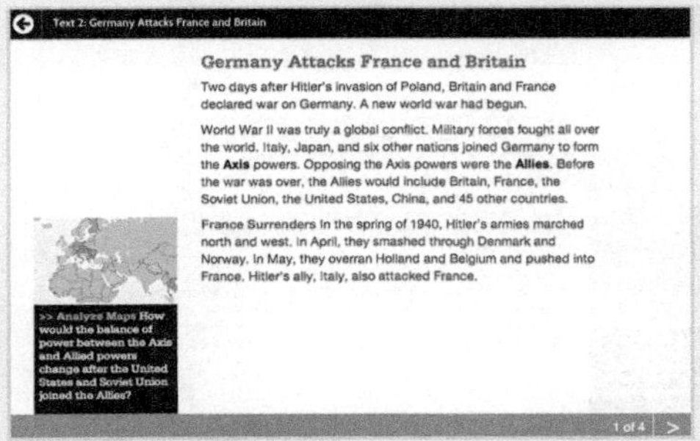

DIGITAL TEXT 3

The United States Assists the Allies

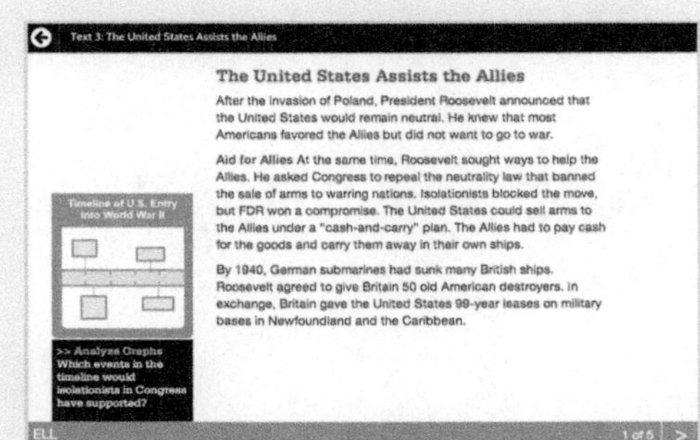

Generate Explanations Why did conflict in Asia and Europe concern the United States? *(The United States had economic interests and trade relations in both parts of the world. Conflict threatened to upset its trade and economy, both of which were still recovering from the Great Depression. Moreover, the spread of totalitarian regimes abroad, especially militaristic and imperialist ones, posed a potential long-term threat to U.S. interests.)*

Connect How do events in other parts of the world affect the United States today? *(The United States has political and economic interests in many parts of the world today; events in one part of the world oftentimes affect other parts of the world as well. The world's nations are more closely connected than ever, and the Internet and mass media encourage global awareness of events that would otherwise have remained relatively unknown to many. Moreover, because of alliances and interests, conflict in other nations can easily involve the United States.)*

Objective 2: **Describe how the United States responded to the outbreak of World War II.**

Quick Instruction

Project the political cartoon from Dr. Seuss. Introduce the cartoon by recalling the background of Dr. Seuss, as the renowned children's author of books such as *The Cat in the Hat* and *Green Eggs and Ham*. Point out that Dr. Seuss was also a cartoonist and that he took a great deal of interest in American politics and world affairs. Call on students to describe elements of the cartoon and to read aloud the caption. Be sure to draw attention to symbols such as the Nazi swastika and the American stars and stripes.

Analyze Images What is the significance of the trees in the forest? *(The trees all stand in one forest, illustrating the connection between each. All of the trees except for England and the one on which the bird in Uncle Sam's hat is sitting have been toppled. The Nazi vulture is pecking away at England, and the implication is that England will fall, too. This will leave only the American tree standing.)* What does the bird's statement, in quotations, suggest about American policy? *(It suggests that the United States believes that Germany will be too exhausted and spent with war in Europe to come after the United States next.)* What does Dr. Seuss appear to think about the United States' position? *(Dr. Seuss does not seem to agree with the position of the United States. He suggests that the United States is okay with letting Germany tear down the other trees, or nations, and that the United States feels secure in its position. However, the implication is that the United States will ultimately share the same fate.)*

Draw Conclusions Why did the conflict in Europe spread to become a world war? *(The conflict spread in part because of the imperial ambitions of European nations and in part because of their system of alliances. Many European countries already had overseas empires, which were inevitably drawn into the conflict. They also maintained alliances with one another that drew more and more countries into conflict.)*

ELL Use the ELL activity described in the ELL chart.

Further Instruction

Analyze Maps Based on the maps that show the progression of the Axis Powers, what do you think was Germany's ultimate goal? *(to conquer all of Europe and perhaps regions beyond Europe, including North Africa)*

Generate Explanations Why did Germany choose to invade Britain by air? *(Britain, as an island, had long had the most powerful naval forces in the world. By air, Germany could bombard Britain while risking few of its own soldiers. This would keep the pressure on Britain and hopefully trap the British on the isles, preventing them from engaging more directly on the continent.)*

Entering World War II

Support Ideas with Evidence Did providing war supplies to the Allies involve the United States in the war even though the United States was not taking part in the fighting? Why might Germany have felt it was fair to fire on U.S. ships? Support your ideas with evidence from the lesson. *(By providing economic and military aid to the Allies, the United States had in effect given its support to the Allies and taken sides in the conflict. Though the United States was not fighting in the war at this time, it was operating against Germany and the Axis Powers.)*

DIGITAL TEXT 4

The United States Declares War

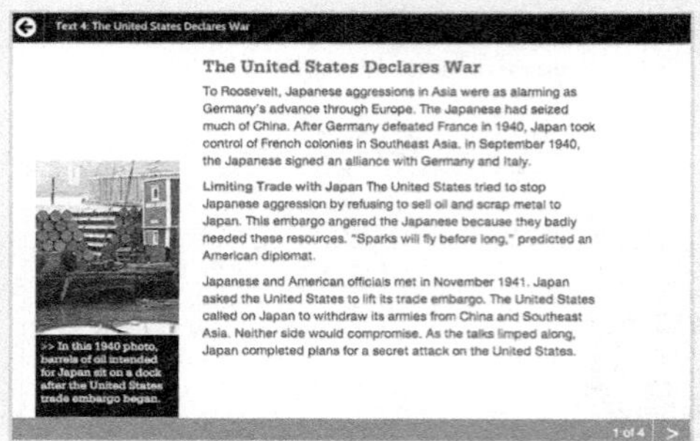
Text 4: The United States Declares War

The United States Declares War

To Roosevelt, Japanese aggressions in Asia were as alarming as Germany's advance through Europe. The Japanese had seized much of China. After Germany defeated France in 1940, Japan took control of French colonies in Southeast Asia. In September 1940, the Japanese signed an alliance with Germany and Italy.

Limiting Trade with Japan The United States tried to stop Japanese aggression by refusing to sell oil and scrap metal to Japan. This embargo angered the Japanese because they badly needed these resources. "Sparks will fly before long," predicted an American diplomat.

Japanese and American officials met in November 1941. Japan asked the United States to lift its trade embargo. The United States called on Japan to withdraw its armies from China and Southeast Asia. Neither side would compromise. As the talks limped along, Japan completed plans for a secret attack on the United States.

>> In this 1940 photo, barrels of oil intended for Japan sit on a dock after the United States trade embargo began.

1 of 4

Objective 3: **Explain why the United States finally entered the war.**

Quick Instruction

To begin, write the words *Pearl Harbor* on the board. Ask the class to brainstorm everything they think they know about Pearl Harbor. Write their answers on the board in a concept web. Revisit and revise the concept web on the board as you move through the text.

Interactive Map: Surprise Attack on Pearl Harbor Project the Interactive Map and click through the hotspots. Then, pose the question from the text: What evidence from the map indicates the attack on Pearl Harbor was carefully planned? Have students Think-Pair-Share their responses.

ACTIVE CLASSROOM

Conduct an Audio Tour activity. Pair students. Have the first student give a verbal "tour" of the Interactive Map detailing the attack on Pearl Harbor—what does it show? Have the second give the first an explanation of the significance of each hotspot.

INTERACTIVE MAP

Surprise Attack on Pearl Harbor

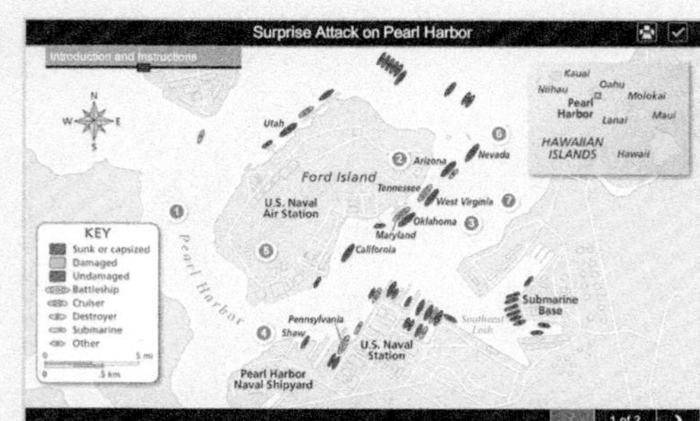

Interactive Chart: The United States Debates Going to War Project the Interactive Chart. Prompt students to discuss the reasoning for and against U.S. entry into the war.

ACTIVE CLASSROOM

Conduct a Take a Stand activity. Ask students to take a stand on the U.S. decision to declare war against Japan. Ask students to divide into two groups based on their answer and move to separate areas of the classroom. Ask students to talk with each other and compare their reasons for answering the way they did. Ask a representative from each side to present and defend the group's point of view.

Draw Conclusions Why would an alliance with Japan benefit Germany? *(Germany knew that the United States supported the Allies and may have suspected that U.S. involvement in the war was inevitable. However, Germany knew that the United States was concerned about Japan in the Pacific as well. If the United States entered the war, a German alliance with Japan would force it to fight a war on two fronts, which would somewhat limit the number of forces allied against Germany in Europe.)*

INTERACTIVE CHART

The United States Debates Going to War

United States Debates Going to War

Introduction and Instructions

REASONS FOR	REASONS AGAINST
Japan's military aggression in Asia.	Conflict was far away from United States.

1 of 3

Further Instruction

Project the photo of the attack on Pearl Harbor. Point out that video and photographic footage of the attack was shown to the American public. Discuss whether the U.S. government could have reasonably avoided entering the war after those images were made public. If time allows, take a thumb vote and divide students according to their answers. Then, ask each group to discuss and defend their position.

Hypothesize Would the United States have entered the war even if Japan had not attacked Pearl Harbor? Explain. *(Possible answer: U.S. entry into the war was inevitable. The United States had already taken sides by supporting the Allies, and it had a vested interest in ensuring that Germany and Japan did not continue their territorial expansion. If Pearl Harbor hadn't occurred, another event would have served as a justifiable reason to trigger U.S. military engagement.)*

SYNTHESIZE

DIGITAL ACTIVITY

Answer Your Questions

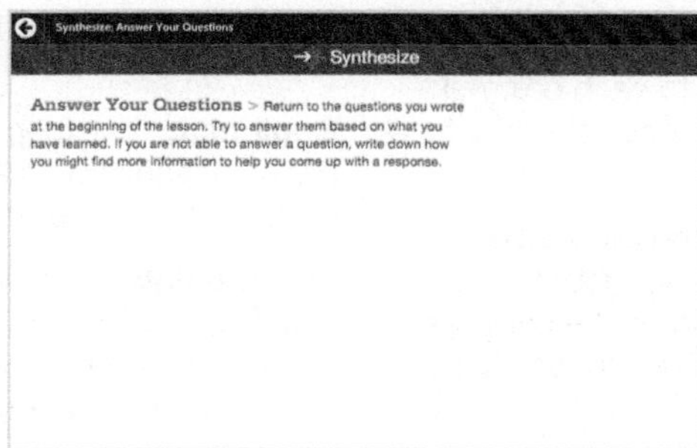

Instruct students to review their ideas and questions from the Digital Start Up Activity. Have them revise what they thought they knew and answer their own questions. If they cannot answer their questions, tell them to record ways in which they can find the answers.

Discuss What was the most surprising piece of information that you learned about the onset of World War II, and why? Do you think that the United States made the right decision in going to war? Why or why not?

DEMONSTRATE

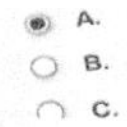

DIGITAL QUIZ

Lesson Quiz and Class Discussion Board

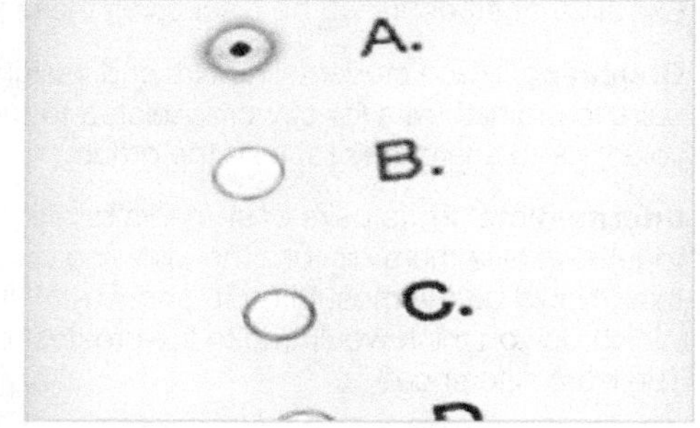

Assign the online Lesson Quiz for this lesson if you haven't already done so. Students will be offered automatic remediation or enrichment based on their score.

Pose these questions to the class on the Discussion Board:

In *Entering World War II*, you learned how World War II erupted in Europe and Asia. You also explored the reasons why the United States initially stayed out of the war and then elected to join the Allies in 1941.

Make Predictions How will the entry of the United States affect the progress of the war?

Draw Conclusions What do you think the United States hoped to gain from entering World War II?

Topic Inquiry

Have students continue their investigations for the Topic Inquiry.

The Home Front

Supporting English Language Learners

Use with the reading, **Mobilizing for War**.

Speaking

With students, create a list of wartime jobs listed in the text (including those in military, manufacturing, government, and domestic sectors). Explain that students will be discussing these jobs with one another.

Beginning Place students in pairs and assign one job to each pair. Ask pairs to brainstorm a list of words related to their job. Encourage pairs to volunteer to share their list with the group.

Intermediate Invite pairs of students to read through the list of jobs together. Have them discuss the following questions: Which job do you think would be the most difficult, and why? Which would be the easiest? Which do you think would make the greatest difference during wartime? The least difference?

Advanced Place students in pairs and assign two jobs to each pair. Ask pairs to compare and contrast the skills needed to carry out each job. Have them record their ideas in a Venn diagram.

Advanced High Invite individual students to rank the jobs in order of importance to the war effort. Next to each job on the list, have them write down a reason to support the ranking. Then have pairs of students compare and discuss their lists.

Use with the reading, **Women and African Americans Join the War Effort**.

Reading

Remind students that when they read in the classroom, their teacher and classmates can help them understand more. Ask: What kind of assistance might a teacher or classmate provide for you?

Beginning Together, read aloud the first two paragraphs of the text. Pause periodically to ask students direct questions in order to confirm their understanding and emphasize important information.

Intermediate Invite volunteers to take turns reading paragraphs of the text. Pause periodically to let students ask clarifying questions about the content. Additionally, ask students questions that prompt them to think more analytically about the information presented.

Advanced Have pairs of students read the text aloud together. At the end of each paragraph, encourage partners to ask each other questions to confirm or enhance understanding of what was read.

Advanced High Invite students to read the text silently and, as they do so, to create a list of questions that arise. Then have students share and discuss their question list with a partner.

D Differentiate Instruction

Use the Differentiated Instruction notes throughout the lesson plan to support the varied skill sets, levels of readiness, and interests in the mixed-ability classroom.

Challenge These notes include suggestions for expanding the activity for advanced students.

On-Level These notes include suggestions for modifying the activity to address different interests or learning styles.

Extra Support These notes include ideas for providing more scaffolding or reading spupport.

Special Needs These notes provide ideas for adapting instruction to support the needs of various special needs students.

NOTES

Go online to access additional resources including: Primary Sources • Biographies • Supreme Court cases • 21st Century Skill Tutorials • Maps • Graphic Organizers.

PEARSON realize™ www.PearsonRealize.com

Objectives

Objective 1: Describe how Americans mobilized the economy to provide materials and funds for World War II.

Objective 2: Summarize how women in the workforce helped the war effort.

Objective 3: Describe the impact the war had on African Americans.

Objective 4: Explain how and why Japanese Americans and other groups faced wartime restrictions.

LESSON 3 ORGANIZER	PACING: APPROX. 1 PERIOD, .5 BLOCKS		RESOURCES	
	OBJECTIVES	PACING	Online	Print
Connect				
DIGITAL START UP ACTIVITY **The United States at War**		5 min.	●	
Investigate				
DIGITAL TEXT 1 **Mobilizing for War**	Objective 1	10 min.	●	●
DIGITAL TEXT 2 **Women and African Americans Join the War Effort**	Objectives 2, 3	10 min.	●	●
INTERACTIVE GALLERY **Life on the Home Front During World War II**		10 min.	●	
DIGITAL TEXT 3 **Problems for Other Americans at Home**	Objective 4	10 min.	●	●
INTERACTIVE GALLERY **The Experience of Japanese Internment**		10 min.	●	
Synthesize				
DIGITAL ACTIVITY **Changes at Home**		5 min.	●	
Demonstrate				
DIGITAL QUIZ **Lesson Quiz and Class Discussion Board**		10 min.	●	

The Home Front

CONNECT

DIGITAL START UP ACTIVITY

The United States at War

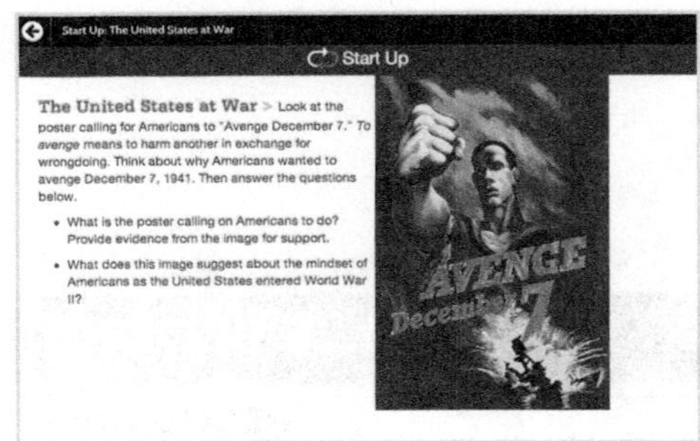

Project the Start Up Activity Have students study the poster and respond to the questions as they enter and get settled. Be sure to point out key aspects of the image.

Discuss What is the tone or feeling conveyed by the poster? *(anger, darkness, retribution, fury, intensity)* Why do you think the poster calls for vengeance, not justice? *(Vengeance is a more powerful word likely to invoke a fighting spirit in the American public.)*

Explain that in this lesson, students will learn about the impact of World War II on Americans at home.

Aa Vocabulary Development: Use the Interactive Reading Notepad to preview the Key Terms and Academic Vocabulary in this lesson with students.

FLIP IT!
Assign the Flipped Video for this lesson.

STUDENT EDITION PRINT PAGES: 775–781

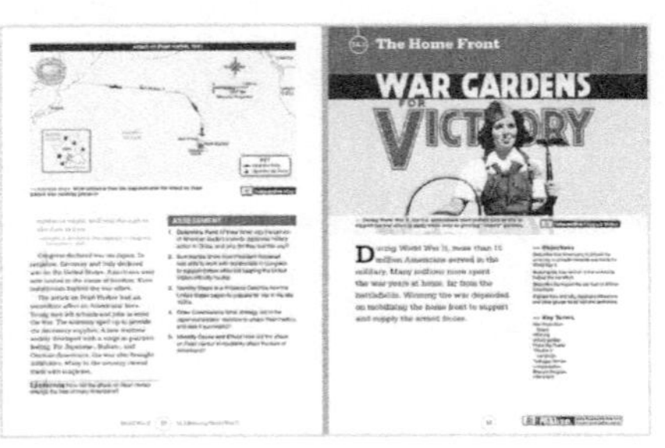

INVESTIGATE

DIGITAL TEXT 1

Mobilizing for War

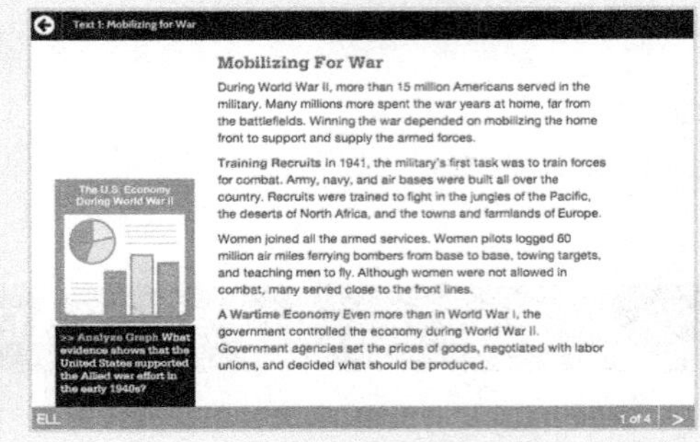

Objective 1: Describe how Americans mobilized the economy to provide materials and funds for World War II.

Quick Instruction

Project the infographic titled *The U.S. Economy During World War II*. Prompt students to understand how elements in the section titled *Ramping Up Production* reflected the U.S. economy's shift towards the war effort. Point out the sacrifices many Americans made in their daily lives, such as rationing food, in support of the war effort. What does the rapid mobilization of the U.S. economy for war suggest about the importance of the nation's agricultural and industrial base? *(It suggests that the nation had a strong foundation in agriculture and manufacturing with sufficient natural, human, and capital resources to support a shift to massive wartime production.)*

Draw Conclusions Would the United States have been able to engage in World War II effectively without its economic resources? Explain. *(No, without sufficient workers, farms, and factories already in place, the United States would not have been able to mobilize and support its armed forces efficiently enough.)*

D Differentiate: Challenge Direct students to the National Archives and Library of Congress websites for World War II propaganda posters. Ask students to analyze each poster to determine its relevance to the war effort. Then, have them assemble the posters and their analyses into a slideshow to present to the class.

ELL Use the ELL activity described in the ELL chart.

Further Instruction

Draw Conclusions Why did the U.S. government produce propaganda posters, film clips, and other materials? *(World War II required contributions from all Americans. To support the war, the nation needed its citizens to produce goods and crops, ration materials, buy war bonds, and volunteer. This meant that it had to convince U.S. citizens of the necessity to actively support the war efforts by any means possible, and posters and films were used to accomplish this goal.)*

Connect If the United States suddenly decided that rationing was necessary today because of a conflict overseas, how do you think Americans would react? How would you react? *(Sample answer: Some people today might be less likely to accept such rationing, while others would be willing to help. I would do what is asked of me, even if it would mean having to make due with less.)*

www.PearsonRealize.com
Access your Digital Lesson

DIGITAL TEXT 2

Women and African Americans Join the War Effort

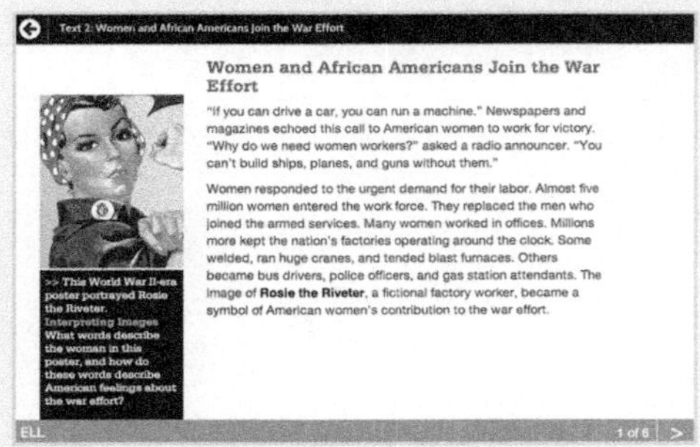

INTERACTIVE GALLERY

Life on the Home Front During World War II

DIGITAL TEXT 3

Problems for Other Americans at Home

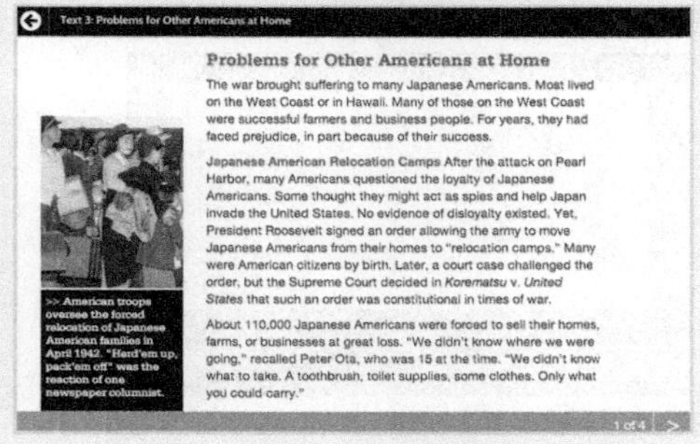

Objectives 2: Summarize how women in the workforce helped the war effort; 3: Describe the impact the war had on African Americans.

Quick Instruction

Interactive Gallery: Life on the Home Front During World War II Project the Interactive Gallery and navigate through the images with students. Prompt students to connect each image to the efforts of Americans to support the war on the home front. What sacrifices for the war effort do you see Americans making? *(Citizens bought war bonds, professional athletes such as Ted Williams joined the military, and women went to work in factories.*

Cite Evidence How did the United States fall short in equal treatment of women and African Americans during World War II? *(The United States employed women and African Americans when it needed them but did not treat them as full and equal citizens. It did not pay them fair wages, and it continued to discriminate against them. African Americans experienced segregation even in service.)*

ACTIVE CLASSROOM

Organize students into pairs or small groups. Assign each pair or group one of the images from the gallery or the text. Tell them to use the Conversation with History strategy to write a dialogue or an interview Q&A with the people in their images. Post the completed writings on the class blog. If time permits, have students act out their conversations.

ELL Use the ELL activity described in the ELL chart.

Further Instruction

Before you begin, tell students to divide a sheet of paper into two columns labeled "Women" and "African Americans." Have them record details about the roles of each in the war effort as they read the text. Then, instruct students to read the text. When they have finished, have them work in pairs to answer the questions in the Interactive Reading Notepad. Organize them into groups to review and revise their responses. Be sure that students understand that wartime mobilization and production depended heavily on women and African Americans who worked on farms and in industry. Point out, too, that the government actively recruited women and African Americans to contribute and to serve.

Apply What arguments might women and African Americans have used from this period to support claims to equal rights and greater protection of their civil liberties? *(Women and African Americans would most likely point out that they behaved as full and equal citizens during the war, contributing their service, their labor, and their resources to support the war effort. For that reason, they would argue that they were entitled to equal rights and protections with that of white male citizens.)*

Objective 4: Explain how and why Japanese Americans and other groups faced wartime restrictions.

Quick Instruction

Interactive Gallery: The Experience of Japanese Internment Project the Interactive Gallery and navigate through the images with students. Be sure that students understand that the Japanese, German, and Italian Americans held in internment camps were not prisoners of war (POWs). Separate camps existed for housing POWs. Internment camps imprisoned American citizens of Japanese, German, and Italian ancestry solely on the basis of that ancestry. These were men, women, and children who lived, worked, and went to school with other American citizens. Many of them actively supported the war effort and some even had family members serving in the American armed forces during the war. Why did the United States feel justified treating Japanese Americans in this fashion? *(because the United States was at war with Japan and people feared that Japanese Americans might act on Japan's behalf)*

Compare and Contrast How was internment of the Japanese in the United States similar to and different from Nazi treatment of Jewish people and others in its concentration camps? *(It was similar in that it was discrimination and imprisonment based on race or ethnicity. It was different because the United States did not set out to exterminate people of Japanese heritage like the Germans did to the Jews.)*

The Home Front

INTERACTIVE GALLERY

The Experience of Japanese Internment

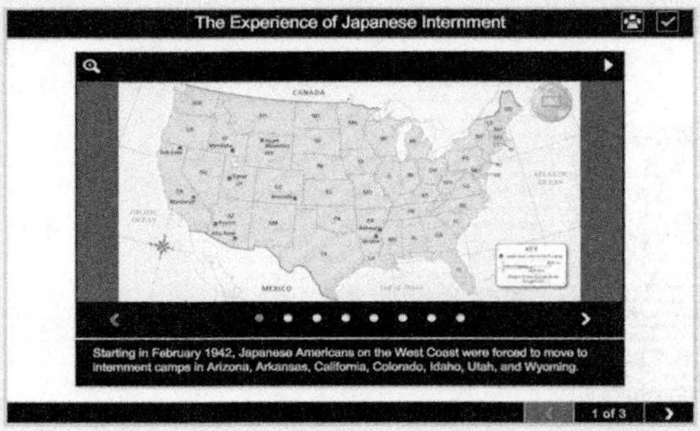

Support Ideas with Evidence What argument might you have made against Japanese internment? *(Possible answer: There was no evidence of spying among Japanese Americans and many Japanese Americans served in the U.S. military. Internment violated many constitutional rights and freedoms.)*

ACTIVE CLASSROOM

Instruct students to use the Quick Write strategy to write a letter to the editor in response to Japanese internment. Tell them to work individually. They may address internment as it was happening or they may choose to address government reparations to Japanese Americans after the war. Share their work on the class blog.

D Differentiate: Extra Support Explain that *bracero* is Spanish for "manual laborer" (a man who does physical work). Have students make a flash card explaining the meaning and significance of the Bracero Program. Then, challenge partners to discuss how the Bracero Program resembles other incidents in American history, such as the African slave trade, the use of Chinese laborers on the railroads, and the recruitment of European immigrants to work in factories in the 19th century.

Further Instruction

Connect Reread Eleanor Roosevelt's statement regarding discrimination against Mexicans. What do you think is the source of that discrimination, specifically against Mexican Americans? *(Possible answer: I think the discrimination against Mexicans had its origins in historical conflicts over territory, as the United States and Mexico each competed for land and resources in the American Southwest. The discrimination may also have deeper roots in ethnic and political differences among American colonists and American Indians and among the English and the Spanish.)*

Make Generalizations Why do you think discrimination, against any group of people, has been an ongoing social issue in the United States? *(Possible answer: I think that discrimination has been such a widespread issue in the United States because the United States has been such a "melting pot." So many people have contributed to the nation's culture, from American Indians to Spanish, Dutch, French, and English colonists to enslaved Africans to immigrants from all corners of the globe. These many groups of people have often come into conflict for land, jobs, and other resources, as well as for political power and economic wealth. When in conflict, it's easier for people to organize along readily identifiable group lines.)*

SYNTHESIZE

DIGITAL ACTIVITY

Changes at Home

Synthesize: Changes at Home

Synthesize

Changes at Home > In this lesson, you learned about how World War II changed the lives of millions of Americans on the home front. Fill in the chart with the groups of people you learned about in this lesson. Then write down the changes they experienced and the reasons for each change. When you have finished your chart, select one of the changes you have listed and write one complete paragraph explaining why it was a key development in United States history.

The Home Front in World War II

People on the Home Front	Changes on the Home Front	Reasons for Change

Project the Digital Activity Instruct student pairs to work together to complete the first part of the Digital Activity. Then, tell students to work independently as they write responses to the charts. Have students post their responses to the class discussion board, and ask students to respond to two other postings.

Discuss What do you think was the most significant impact of World War II on the home front, and why?

DEMONSTRATE

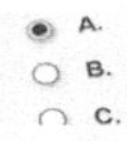

DIGITAL QUIZ

Lesson Quiz and Class Discussion Board

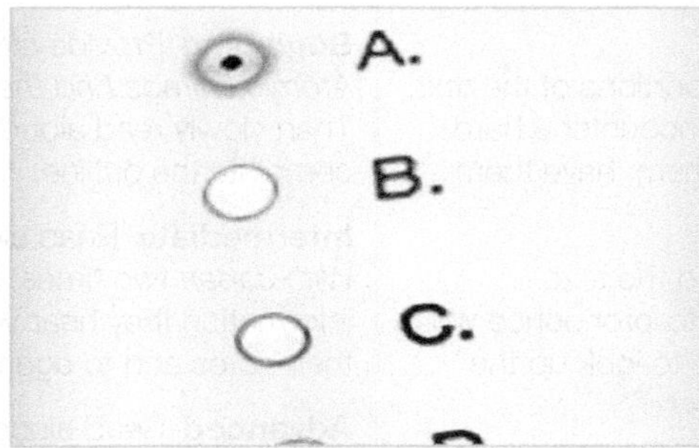

Assign the online Lesson Quiz for this lesson if you haven't already done so. Students will be offered automatic remediation or enrichment based on their score.

Pose these questions to the class on the Discussion Board:

In *The Home Front*, you learned how World War II impacted Americans at home. You examined the role of the economy and of citizens in supporting the war effort. You also looked at the impact of the war on specific groups, such as women, African Americans, and Japanese Americans.

Connect How did World War II help the United States recover from the Great Depression?

Make Predictions African Americans not only worked to support the war effort but also served in the war. Women, too, worked for industry and served in the war. How might you expect the end of the war to impact their roles and status in society?

Topic Inquiry

Have students continue their investigations for the Topic Inquiry.

Winning a Deadly War

Supporting English Language Learners

Use with the reading, **The Allies Agree on a Strategy**.

Learning

Whether students are reading aloud or speaking in everyday conversations, they should prepare as much as they can beforehand, as well as monitor and correct themselves as they speak.

Beginning Invite students to take turns reading aloud portions of the text. Encourage them to pause and ask for help when they encounter a hard-to-pronounce word. After you pronounce the word for them, have them repeat it and continue reading.

Intermediate Invite partners to take turns reading aloud the text. Encourage them to pause when they encounter a hard-to-pronounce word and ask their partner to say it for them—or, if necessary, to look up the pronunciation in a dictionary.

Advanced Ask students to read aloud the text to themselves and make a list of hard-to-pronounce words as they encounter them. Have them look up and practice the pronunciation of these words. Then have partners read aloud the text to each other and assess their improvement.

Advanced High Have students list important and hard-to-remember terms about D-Day and the liberation of France. Then invite partners to take turns narrating this piece of history. Encourage them to reference their list as needed, whether to jog their memory or to correct a misstatement.

Use with the reading, **Japan Surrenders**.

Listening

Tell students that when they take notes they should not be concerned about spelling and can correct any mistakes after the speaker has finished.

Beginning Provide students with a brief outline of the section titled *Atomic Bombs End the War With Japan* that has a few words omitted. Then slowly read aloud the section twice, giving students an opportunity to complete the outline.

Intermediate Read aloud the section titled *Atomic Bombs End the War With Japan* two times. Have students write down the most important information they hear you say. Then ask them to share information from their notes and to aggregate their responses into a model outline.

Advanced Read aloud the first six paragraphs of the text. After each paragraph, pause so students can write down a key point from it. Then ask: What information in your notes do you think might be incomplete or incorrect? Address students' concerns so they can make corrections.

Advanced High Read aloud the first six paragraphs of the text, while students take notes on the important points they hear. Then have them share their notes with a partner, both to compare the information they wrote down and to make any necessary corrections.

D Differentiate Instruction

Use the Differentiated Instruction notes throughout the lesson plan to support the varied skill sets, levels of readiness, and interests in the mixed-ability classroom.

Challenge These notes include suggestions for expanding the activity for advanced students.

On-Level These notes include suggestions for modifying the activity to address different interests or learning styles.

Extra Support These notes include ideas for providing more scaffolding or reading spuport.

Special Needs These notes provide ideas for adapting instruction to support the needs of various special needs students.

NOTES

PEARSON realize™ www.PearsonRealize.com

Go online to access additional resources including: Primary Sources • Biographies • Supreme Court cases • 21st Century Skill Tutorials • Maps • Graphic Organizers.

Objectives

Objective 1: Identify the early defeats and hardships the Allies suffered.

Objective 2: Explain how changes to Allied tactics later in the war turned the tide of the war in Europe.

Objective 3: Summarize how the war in Europe ended.

Objective 4: Explain why Japan finally surrendered.

Objective 5: Describe what made World War II the deadliest war in history.

LESSON 4 ORGANIZER	PACING: APPROX. 1 PERIOD, .5 BLOCKS		RESOURCES	
	OBJECTIVES	PACING	Online	Print
Connect				
DIGITAL START UP ACTIVITY **Two Theaters**		5 min.	●	
Investigate				
DIGITAL TEXT 1 **The Allies Suffer Early Defeats**	Objective 1	10 min.	●	●
DIGITAL TEXT 2 **The Allies Agree on a Strategy**	Objective 2	10 min.	●	●
DIGITAL TEXT 3 **Germany's Defeat**	Objective 3	10 min.	●	●
3-D MODEL **The B-24 Liberator**	Objective 3	10 min.	●	
DIGITAL TEXT 4 **Japan Surrenders**	Objective 4	10 min.	●	●
BEFORE AND AFTER **Hiroshima**	Objective 4	10 min.	●	
DIGITAL TEXT 5 **The Devastation of World War II**	Objective 5	10 min.	●	●
INTERACTIVE GALLERY **Holocaust Aftermath and Remembrance**	Objective 5	10 min.	●	
Synthesize				
DIGITAL ACTIVITY **Review of Two Theaters**		5 min.	●	
Demonstrate				
LESSON QUIZ **Lesson Quiz and Class Discussion Board**		10 min.	●	

Topic 14 Lesson 4

Winning a Deadly War

CONNECT

DIGITAL START UP ACTIVITY

Two Theaters

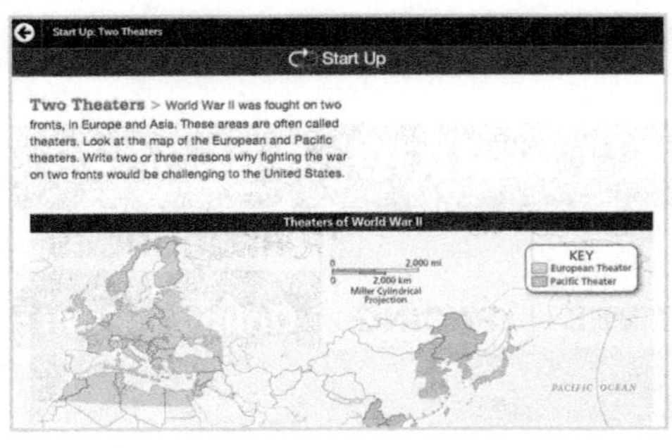

Start Up: Two Theaters
Start Up
Two Theaters > World War II was fought on two fronts, in Europe and Asia. These areas are often called theaters. Look at the map of the European and Pacific theaters. Write two or three reasons why fighting the war on two fronts would be challenging to the United States.
Theaters of World War II
0 2,000 mi
0 2,000 km
Miller Cylindrical Projection
KEY
European Theater
Pacific Theater
PACIFIC OCEAN

Project the Start Up Activity Have students study the map and write their responses as they get settled. Call on students to share.

Discuss Which theater might the United States have considered most important, and why? *(the Pacific theater; because Japan first attacked American territory and forces)*

Explain that in this lesson students will identify early hardships and defeats suffered by the Allies, and Allied tactics. They will examine the conduct of the war in the Pacific and in the European theaters. They will also learn how the war ended in each theater.

Aa Vocabulary Development: Use the Interactive Reading Notepad to preview the Key Terms and Academic Vocabulary in this lesson with students.

FLIP IT!

Assign the Flipped Video for this lesson.

STUDENT EDITION PRINT PAGES: 782–793

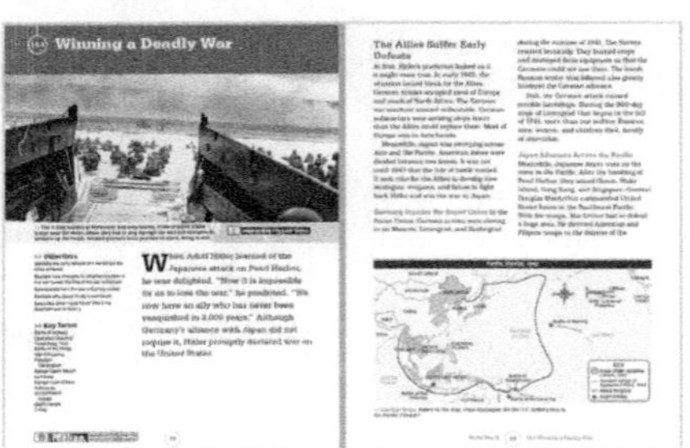

INVESTIGATE

DIGITAL TEXT 1

The Allies Suffer Early Defeats

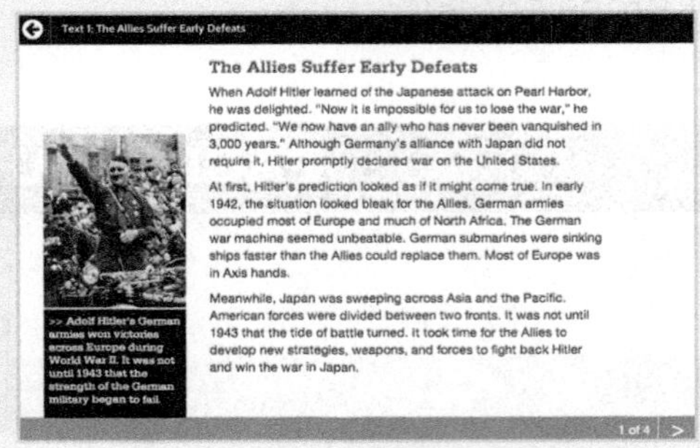

Text 1: The Allies Suffer Early Defeats
The Allies Suffer Early Defeats
When Adolf Hitler learned of the Japanese attack on Pearl Harbor, he was delighted. "Now it is impossible for us to lose the war," he predicted. "We now have an ally who has never been vanquished in 3,000 years." Although Germany's alliance with Japan did not require it, Hitler promptly declared war on the United States.
At first, Hitler's prediction looked as if it might come true. In early 1942, the situation looked bleak for the Allies. German armies occupied most of Europe and much of North Africa. The German war machine seemed unbeatable. German submarines were sinking ships faster than the Allies could replace them. Most of Europe was in Axis hands.
Meanwhile, Japan was sweeping across Asia and the Pacific. American forces were divided between two fronts. It was not until 1943 that the tide of battle turned. It took time for the Allies to develop new strategies, weapons, and forces to fight back Hitler and win the war in Japan.
>> Adolf Hitler's German armies won victories across Europe during World War II. It was not until 1943 that the strength of the German military began to fail.
1 of 4

Objective 1: **Identify the early defeats and hardships the Allies suffered.**

Quick Instruction

Begin by displaying the map of the Pacific theater in 1942. Prompt students to distinguish between the Japanese advances and controlled territory and other areas claimed by the United States. What significant challenge did the United States face in defending its Pacific territories and fighting Japan? *(The fighting in the Pacific theater was spread out over thousands of miles, most of it at sea. U.S. territories on Pacific islands were spread out, far from one another and from the continental United States. U.S. forces were divided and often cut off from resources and reinforcements as they sought to engage Japan.)*

Draw Conclusions Why was it important, strategically, to the United States to hold onto territories in the Pacific? *(The United States needed islands in the Pacific at which to base its forces, where it could store resources, house troops, and replenish its forces and supplies as needed. The United States could not fight a war in the Pacific without places in the Pacific from which to launch attacks and to which its forces might retreat when needed.)*

Further Instruction

Review the instructions for the Interactive Reading Notepad. Have students read the text. Then, answer the questions in the notepad as a class. Be sure that students understand that Germany and its allies had already conquered much of Europe by the time the United States entered the war. Point out that the United States was largely committed in the Pacific theater at first.

Analyze Primary Sources Read aloud the quotation from Adolf Hitler: "Now it is impossible for us to lose the war. We now have an ally who has never been vanquished in 3,000 years." Why did Hitler feel confident in declaring war on the United States? *(Hitler thought that Japan was strong enough to take on and defeat the United States. He counted on the United States being too busy in the Pacific theater to engage in Europe and attack German forces with any great strength.)*

www.PearsonRealize.com
Access your Digital Lesson

DIGITAL TEXT 2

The Allies Agree on a Strategy

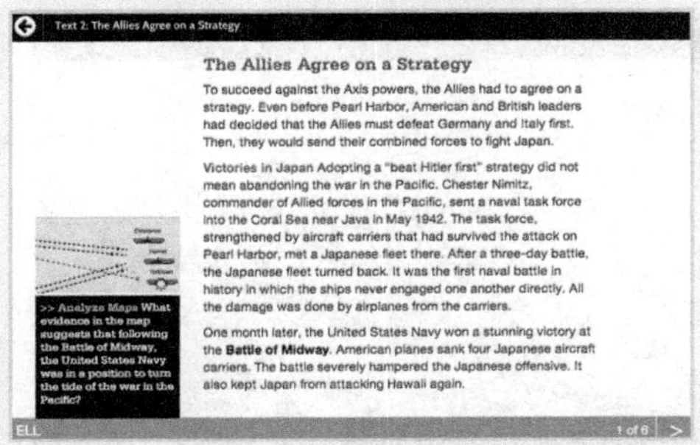

Objective 2: **Explain how changes to Allied tactics later in the war turned the tide of the war in Europe.**

Quick Instruction

Project the map of Europe and Africa during World War II. Draw attention to territories held by the Axis Powers and the Allied Powers in Europe and North Africa. Point out North Africa on the map. Note that although Germany and its allies did not have troops throughout the region, Allied forces still moved in from east and west in an attempt to control the North African coastline. Why would the Allies want to gain control of North Africa? *(Victory in North Africa would allow the Allies to attack the Axis Powers from the south as well as from the west and the east. Axis Powers in Europe would be surrounded on multiple fronts.)*

D Differentiate: Extra Support Help students identify key events in the text. Have them record these events on slips of paper. For Extra Support, guide students to arrange the events in order. If time permits, ask students to paste the events in a sequence chart or timeline on a poster and have them write one or two sentences that explains the significance of each event.

ELL Use the ELL activity described in the ELL chart.

Further Instruction

Direct students to work in pairs to read the text and answer the questions in the Interactive Reading Notepad. Then, organize pairs into groups to review and revise their answers. You may wish to point out that the designation *D-Day* is actually a military term used to refer to the designated day on which a secret attack is planned to take place. For the invasion of Normandy by the Allied Powers, D-Day was June 5, 1944, but bad weather forced the Allies to wait an extra day. The attack took place on June 6, 1944, the date that has since become known as D-Day.

Draw Conclusions What key mistake in strategy did Germany make that likely cost it the war? *(Germany made a mistake by invading the Soviet Union. Germany underestimated not only Soviet forces and resistance but also the impact of the Soviet winter and the size of the nation. Germany suffered great losses in the Soviet Union and was forced to retreat.)*

Make Inferences The United States and Britain waited a long time to open a western front. What does this suggest about their strategy regarding the role of the Soviet Union? *(The United States and Britain wanted to secure North Africa and Italy while the Soviet Union engaged German forces on the eastern front. Once the south was secure and Germany was somewhat weakened from fighting on the eastern front, the United States and Britain opened a western front in France in 1944.)*

DIGITAL TEXT 3

Germany's Defeat

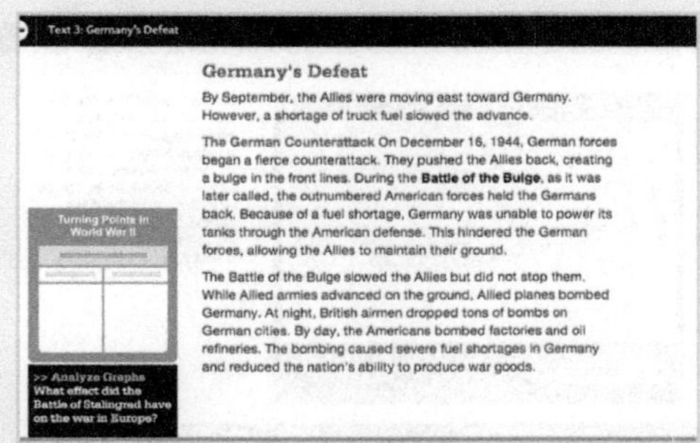

Objective 3: **Summarize how the war in Europe ended.**

Quick Instruction

3-D Model: The B-24 Liberator Project the 3-D Model and navigate through the image. Discuss the questions associated with the model. What does the model of the B-24 Liberator suggest about its use during World War II? *(Fighting took place not only on land and at sea but also by air. Air attacks and bomb raids were crucial to winning the war.)*

Explain What strategic benefit did air support and air attacks give Allied forces in Europe? *(The Allies not only kept German forces harried by attacking from the air as well as on land but also used air forces to destroy supply trains, factories, and fuel sources, weakening German troops by destroying their arteries for food, weapons, fuel, medical aid, and reinforcements. Air attacks also weakened the resolve of the German people and helped clear the way for ground attacks.)*

ACTIVE CLASSROOM

Conduct a Sticky Notes Activity. Have students take three minutes to answer the following question: How might World War II have been different without the use of air technology? When students have finished, ask them to share their responses with a partner. Then, have students post their sticky notes on a wall in the classroom, and have students take a tour of the notes. Ask them to respond to at least two other notes. Discuss their ideas and questions as a class.

Winning a Deadly War

3-D MODEL

The B-24 Liberator

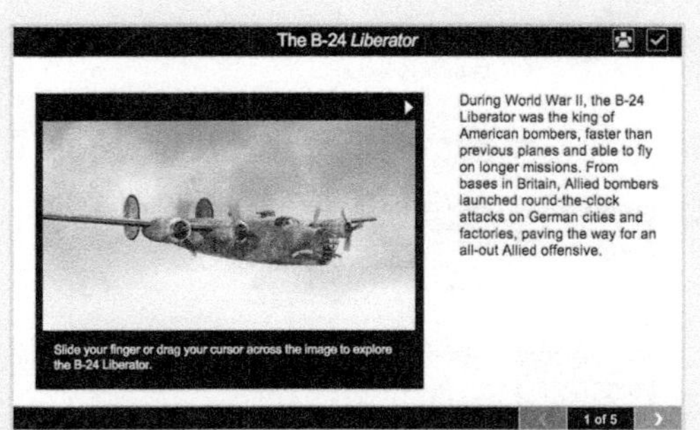

Further Instruction

Direct student pairs to read the text and answer the questions in the Interactive Reading Notepad. Then, call on students to share their responses. Be sure that students understand that once the Allies attacked from the east, the south, and the west, Germany and the other Axis forces in Europe had to fight on multiple fronts.

Draw Conclusions Why do you think the Allies wanted to win the European theater of war before the Pacific theater? *(The Allies were largely concerned about losses to Hitler in Europe. They wanted to stop Hitler there first before turning attention to East Asia, where they had fewer immediate interests. Also, the other Allies might have worried that they would lose the advantage offered by the entry of the United States if American forces stayed concentrated on the Pacific theater.)*

DIGITAL TEXT 4

Japan Surrenders

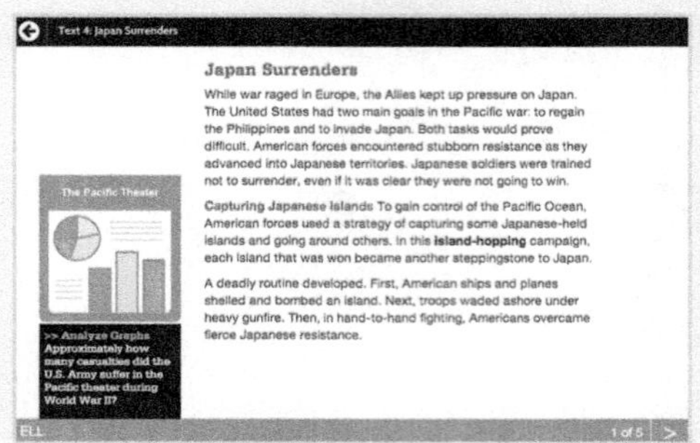

Text 4: Japan Surrenders
Japan Surrenders
While war raged in Europe, the Allies kept up pressure on Japan. The United States had two main goals in the Pacific war: to regain the Philippines and to invade Japan. Both tasks would prove difficult. American forces encountered stubborn resistance as they advanced into Japanese territories. Japanese soldiers were trained not to surrender, even if it was clear they were not going to win.
Capturing Japanese Islands To gain control of the Pacific Ocean, American forces used a strategy of capturing some Japanese-held islands and going around others. In this island-hopping campaign, each island that was won became another steppingstone to Japan.
A deadly routine developed. First, American ships and planes shelled and bombed an island. Next, troops waded ashore under heavy gunfire. Then, in hand-to-hand fighting, Americans overcame fierce Japanese resistance.
The Pacific Theater
>> Analyze Graphs Approximately how many casualties did the U.S. Army suffer in the Pacific theater during World War II?
ELL
1 of 5

Objective 4: **Explain why Japan finally surrendered.**

Quick Instruction

Before and After: Hiroshima Project the Before and After, and move the slider from left to right to illustrate the damage of the atomic bomb on Hiroshima. Write the number of casualties from Hiroshima and Nagasaki on the board *(about 70,000 and 40,000 respectively)*. Explain that these numbers account for the lives lost as a result of the initial impacts of the two atomic bombs. Tell students that thousands more people died after the bombs were dropped as a result of injuries sustained and illnesses contracted from radiation leftover from the attacks. Estimates put total deaths as a result of the atomic bombs around 200,000.

Infer How did the strategy of "island hopping" help American forces gain control of much of the Pacific region? *(American forces chose to fight for islands in strategic locations while bypassing others. This strategy allowed a general progression towards Japan.)*

ACTIVE CLASSROOM

Conduct a See-Think-Wonder activity. Project the Before and After images of Hiroshima. Ask: What do you see? What does that make you think? What are you wondering about now that you've seen this? Prompt volunteers to share their insights with the class.

ELL Use the ELL activity described in the ELL chart.

BEFORE AND AFTER

Hiroshima

Further Instruction

Review the instructions for the Interactive Reading Notepad. Have students work in small groups to read the text and answer the questions. Then, go over their answers as a class. Point out that in 1945 the United States seemed well positioned to defeat Japan. However, many Allied leaders believed that Japan would not surrender without even greater loss of life.

Summarize What role did the Navajo "code-talkers" play in the American military's victory in the Pacific? *(The U.S. military was concerned that Japanese forces would intercept and break the codes of their radio communications. Navajo soldiers, however, radioed messages to each other on different islands using their native language. This gave American forces a means of secure communication because the Japanese never understood the Navajo were simply speaking their own language.)*

Connect What was the relationship between the Navajo code-talkers and the U.S. military's island-hopping strategy? *(The code-talkers provided secure radio communication for the U.S. military to discuss troop movements among the islands without fear of the Japanese discovering their plans.)*

DIGITAL TEXT 5

The Devastation of World War II

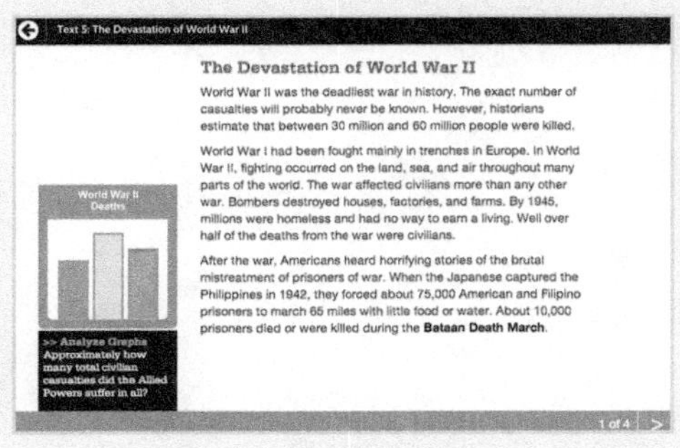

INTERACTIVE GALLERY

Holocaust Aftermath and Remembrance

Objective 5: **Describe what made World War II the deadliest war in history.**

Quick Instruction

Interactive Gallery: Holocaust Aftermath and Remembrance Project the Interactive Gallery and navigate through the images with students. Point out the image of the Nuremberg Trials and the image related to more recent genocides. Prompt students to connect the two as you discuss international efforts to stop genocides.

ACTIVE CLASSROOM

Conduct a Circle Write activity. Organize students into groups to answer the following question: Were the Nuremberg Trials a sufficient response to the Holocaust? Why or why not? Have each group share their ideas with the class.

Further Instruction

Have students read the text and answer the questions in the Interactive Reading Notepad. Call on volunteers to share their responses.

Summarize What was the purpose of the Nuremberg Trials? *(The Nuremberg Trials were conducted to try people suspected of war crimes, to expose the brutality of the Holocaust, and to establish that war crimes could be tried under international law.)*

Winning a Deadly War

SYNTHESIZE

DIGITAL ACTIVITY

Review of Two Theaters

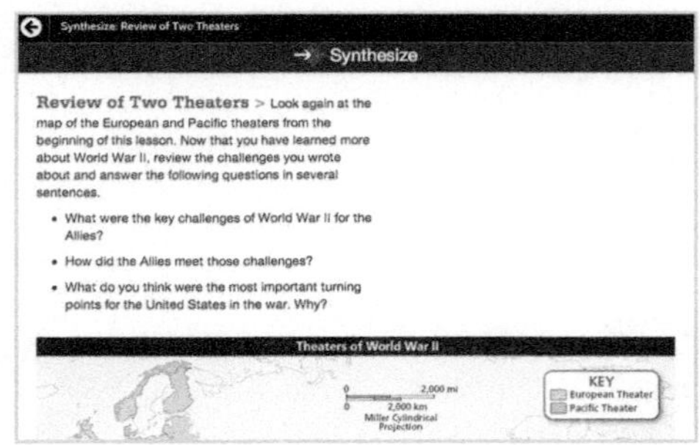

Synthesize: Review of Two Theaters
→ Synthesize
Review of Two Theaters > Look again at the map of the European and Pacific theaters from the beginning of this lesson. Now that you have learned more about World War II, review the challenges you wrote about and answer the following questions in several sentences.
• What were the key challenges of World War II for the Allies?
• How did the Allies meet those challenges?
• What do you think were the most important turning points for the United States in the war. Why?
Theaters of World War II
0 2,000 mi
0 2,000 km
Miller Cylindrical Projection
KEY
European Theater
Pacific Theater

Instruct students to work with partners or in small groups to review their Start Up Activities and to answer the questions in the Digital Activity. Call on pairs and groups to share their responses.

Discuss At what point did it become inevitable that Germany would lose World War II? What about Japan? Cite evidence from the lesson to support your answer.

DEMONSTRATE

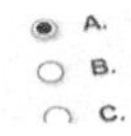

LESSON QUIZ

Lesson Quiz and Class Discussion Board

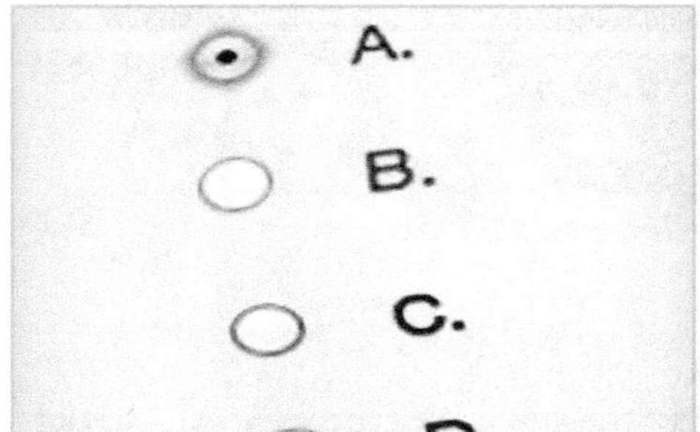

Assign the online Lesson Quiz for this lesson if you haven't already done so. Students will be offered automatic remediation or enrichment based on their score.

Pose these questions to the class on the Discussion Board:

In *Winning a Deadly War*, you explored how the Allies conducted a war in two theaters and what strategies they used to win the war. You learned about the ends of the war in the European and Pacific theaters. In addition, you read about the devastating effects of World War II.

Support Ideas with Evidence What evidence do you see in the text that shows the Allied victory in World War II came at significant human cost?

Make Predictions What efforts to maintain peace do you think the Allies would take following the conclusion of World War II?

Topic Inquiry

Have students continue their investigations for the Topic Inquiry.

World War II

SYNTHESIZE

DIGITAL ACTIVITY

Reflect on the Essential Question and Topic

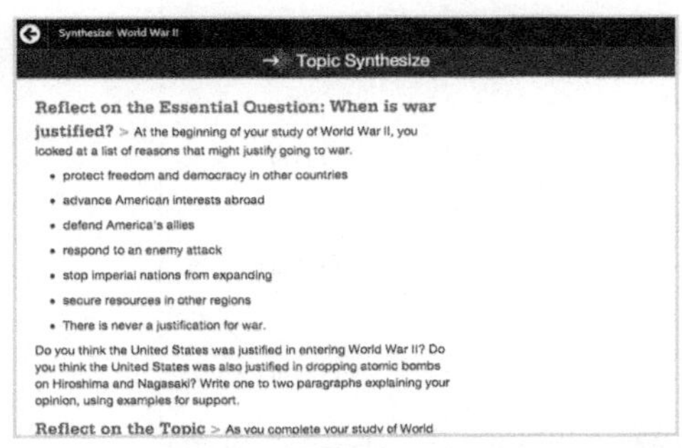

Ask students to consider the Essential Question for the topic: When is war justified? Remind students of the list of reasons that they evaluated at the start of the topic. Recall that reasons the United States might go to war included the following:

- protect freedom and democracy in other countries
- advance American interests abroad
- defend America's allies
- respond to an enemy attack
- stop imperial nations from expanding
- secure resources in other regions
- There is never a justification for war.

Take a thumb poll for the following questions:

- Do you think the United States was justified in entering World War II?
- Do you think the United States was justified in dropping atomic bombs?

For each poll, divide the class into groups according to their responses. Have the groups discuss and prepare a written statement in which they defend their position. If time allows, ask individual students to write their own responses to share on the class discussion board.

Next, ask students to reflect on the topic as a whole. Remind students the United States had many reasons to stay out of World War II and to join. Tell them to work individually to list three reasons the United States decided to join the war. Then, have them discuss their reasons with a partner and explain whether each reason was justified.

Topic Inquiry

Have students complete Step 3 of the Topic Inquiry.

DEMONSTRATE

DIGITAL TOPIC REVIEW AND ASSESSMENT

World War II

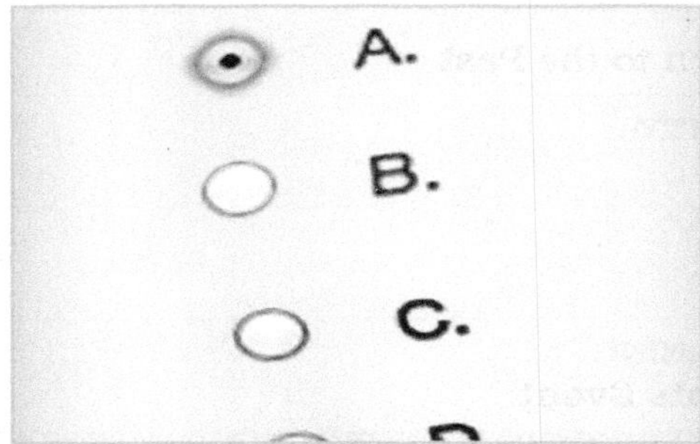

Students can prepare for the Topic Test by answering the questions in the Topic Review and Assessment online or the Assessment questions in the Print Student text. They can also prepare by reviewing their answers to the Interactive Reading Notepad questions or reviewing their notes in the Reading and Notetaking Study Guide.

DIGITAL TOPIC TEST

World War II

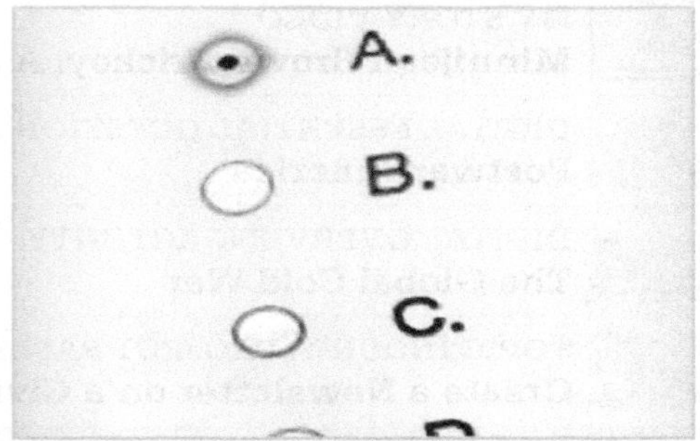

TOPIC TEST

Assign the Topic Test to assess students' understanding of topic content.

BENCHMARK TESTS

Assign these benchmark tests as you complete the relevant topics to monitor student progress toward mastering the course content and as preparation for the End-of-Course Test.

Benchmark Test 1: Topics 1–2

Benchmark Test 2: Topics 3–4

Benchmark Test 3: Topics 5–6

Benchmark Test 4: Topics 7–9

Benchmark Test 5: Topics 10–12

Benchmark Test 6: Topics 13–14

Benchmark Test 7: Topics 15–17

Topic 15

Postwar America

TOPIC 15 ORGANIZER	PACING: APPROX. 9 PERIODS, 4.5 BLOCKS
	PACING
Connect	**1 period**
MY STORY VIDEO **Minnijean Brown-Trickey, A Sojourn to the Past**	10 min.
DIGITAL ESSENTIAL QUESTION ACTIVITY **Postwar America**	10 min.
DIGITAL OVERVIEW ACTIVITY **The Global Cold War**	10 min.
TOPIC INQUIRY: PROJECT-BASED LEARNING **Create a Newsletter on a Civil Rights Event**	20 min.
Investigate	**3–6 periods**
TOPIC INQUIRY: PROJECT-BASED LEARNING **Create a Newsletter on a Civil Rights Event**	Ongoing
LESSON 1 The Beginning of the Cold War	30–40 min.
LESSON 2 Korea and Other Postwar Conflicts	30–40 min.
LESSON 3 Eisenhower and Postwar America	30–40 min.
LESSON 4 Civil Rights	30–40 min.
LESSON 5 Kennedy, Johnson, and Vietnam	30–40 min.
LESSON 6 The Nixon Years	30–40 min.
Synthesize	**1 period**
DIGITAL ACTIVITY **Reflect on the Essential Question and Topic**	10 min.
TOPIC INQUIRY: PROJECT-BASED LEARNING **Create a Newsletter on a Civil Rights Event**	20 min.
Demonstrate	**1–2 periods**
DIGITAL ACTIVITY **Reflect on the Essential Question and Topic**	10 min.
TOPIC INQUIRY: PROJECT-BASED LEARNING **Create a Newsletter on a Civil Rights Event**	20 min.

Create a Newsletter on a Civil Rights Event

In this Topic Inquiry, students work in small teams to study one particular event during the civil rights era by researching facts and analyzing both primary and secondary reports about it. Students will then create a newsletter in which they analyze the influence various reports may have had on public opinion about the event or the larger civil rights movement. Students will base their explorations on the following guiding question: **How do the different ways a story is told and reported influence public opinion about social movements?**

STEP 1: CONNECT

Develop Questions and Plan the Investigation

Launch the Project and Generate Questions

Display the Project Launch: Public Opinion and the 20th Century American Civil Rights Movement. Tell students that they will study primary and secondary sources about an event during the civil rights movement and write a newsletter about these events. The goal will be to understand how an event was reported affected public opinion.

Suggestion: Answer questions and explain terms in the Launch Letter.

Organize students into teams. Distribute and review the Student Instructions, Information Organizer, and Rubric for a Newsletter on a Civil Rights Event. Review the tasks for Step 1 of the Student Instructions to ensure students' understanding of the task.

Prepare the Investigation

Distribute the Project Contract, Project Tracker, and Need-to-Know Questions. Instruct teams to assign tasks using the Project Tracker. Guide teams to discuss expectations and roles for all group members.

Suggestion: Before students get started on their research, review the Guiding Question: How do the different ways a story is told and reported influence public opinion about social movements? Discuss the questions in the Student Instructions to help guide teams during their explorations.

Resources

- Student Instructions
- Project Launch
- Information Organizer
- Rubric for a Newsletter on a Civil Rights Event
- Project Contract
- Need-to-Know Questions

PROFESSIONAL DEVELOPMENT

Project-Based Learning

Be sure to view the Project-Based Learning Professional Development resources in the online course.

STEP 2: INVESTIGATE

Apply Disciplinary Concepts and Tools

Research Your Civil Rights Era Event

Provide opportunities for teams to review the Skills Tutorials: Analyze Media Content and Distinguish Between Fact and Opinion, and Identify Bias. Tell students that now they are ready to research basic facts and details about their assigned event.

Suggestion: Lead a brief discussion about appropriate primary and secondary sources. Review the differences between a primary and secondary source and encourage students to examine the validity and appropriateness of a source they are considering for the project.

Research Primary and Secondary Source Reports on Your Civil Rights Era Event

Review the Student Instructions and emphasize that teams must select and analyze at least five primary and secondary sources about their event. Encourage students to review the suggested websites. Guide groups to the most appropriate websites for their specific events. Meet as a class and discuss the project's paragraph format, ensuring students' understanding.

Suggestion: If students are having difficulty identifying bias, prompt them to ask questions about what the author is saying, how the author is saying it, and why the author is expressing this viewpoint.

Research Information for Sidebars

Point out the possible formats and requirements for the sidebar features for the newsletters:

- map
- timeline
- short biography
- photo with caption
- "where-are-they-now" paragraph

Consider providing visual examples from appropriate magazines or newspapers to aid teams in developing their own sidebars.

Resources

- Project Tracker

TOPIC INQUIRY: PROJECT-BASED LEARNING

Create a Newsletter on a Civil Rights Event *(continued)*

STEP 3: SYNTHESIZE

Evaluate Sources and Use Evidence to Formulate Conclusions

Create Your Newsletter

Students will now use the sources they have gathered to write and create their newsletters on the following topic: How do the different ways a story is told and reported influence public opinion about social movements? Have students review the Rubric for a Newsletter on a Civil Rights Event before they begin.

Suggestion: Meet with each team individually to review the requirements for the newsletters: an introduction which gives a summary of the event, an analysis of each of the five sources, and two sidebars.

STEP 4: DEMONSTRATE

Communicate Conclusions and Take Informed Action

Present Your Newsletter

Advise teams to review their newsletters one last time using the Rubric for a Newsletter on a Civil Rights Event as a checklist. Then, ask each team to present their newsletters to the class or to another appropriate audience. Encourage students in the audience to post questions to facilitate a discussion for each newsletter.

Suggestion: Match teams. Have each team practice their presentation for another team, and vice versa. Each team should give feedback to their partner team.

Reflect on the Project

Ask project teams to discuss what they thought went well and what they thought could be done better. Then, have them complete Team/Peer Assessments. Advise students to use the Rubric when completing their assessments.

Suggestion: As a final activity, direct students to work individually to answer the guiding question: How do the different ways a story is told and reported influence public opinion about social movements? Give students five minutes to write summary paragraphs in response to the question.

Resources

- Team/Peer Assessment

PEARSON realize™ www.PearsonRealize.com Access your Digital Lesson

INTRODUCTION

Postwar America

Following World War II, the United States experienced steady economic growth. Postwar prosperity at home, however, was shadowed by heightened tensions around the world. The alliance between the United States and the Soviet Union broke down. The Cold War, a struggle which pitted the Soviet Union and its Communist allies against the United States and its non-Communist allies, began. Cold War conflicts erupted around the world, including two major wars in Korea and Vietnam. During the postwar years, African Americans and other American minorities fought their own battle, struggling for equal rights and fair treatment.

CONNECT

MY STORY VIDEO

Minnijean Brown-Trickey, A Sojourn to the Past

Watch a video about the lessons Minnijean Brown-Trickey teaches to students today about a historical event in which she participated.

Check Understanding What was Minnijean Brown-Trickey's brush with history? *(She was one of the "Little Rock Nine," the nine black students who desegregated Little Rock's schools in 1957.)*

Identify Patterns What was the importance of Brown-Trickey's actions in 1957? *(She and her fellow students provided inspiration for many of the participants in the civil rights movement in the decade that followed. She continues to teach lessons about the civil rights movement today.)*

DIGITAL ESSENTIAL QUESTION ACTIVITY

Postwar America

Ask students to think about the Essential Question for this Topic: What is America's role in the world? Point out that the first half of the 1900s was rocked by the two most destructive wars the world had ever experienced. What lessons did American leaders learn from these events?

Express Ideas Clearly What ideals or principles should the United States try to promote? Why? *(Sample response: The United States should promote ideals such as democracy and human rights because they improve people's lives.)*

Generate Explanations What strategies or methods are most effective in spreading the ideals or principles you listed? *(Sample response: The United States can provide aid to governments that protect human rights or can send troops to protect people from being mistreated.)*

DIGITAL OVERVIEW ACTIVITY

The Global Cold War

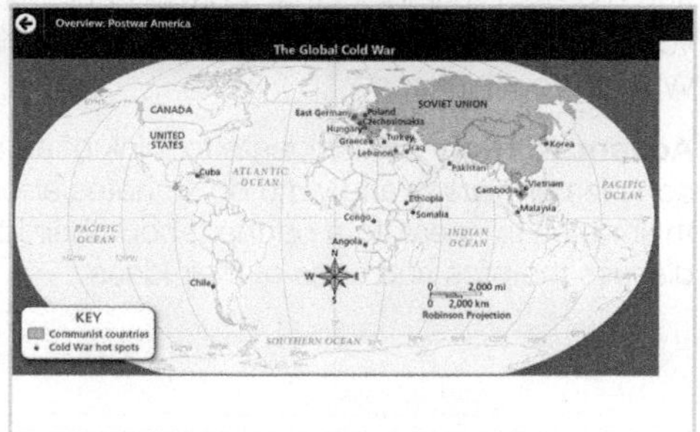

Display the map showing the conflicts of the Cold War. Explain that nations shaded orange are Communist countries. Each red circle represents a conflict, or "hot spot," in which Communists and non-Communists clashed. They include wars between nations or armies, as in Vietnam and Korea, as well as internal struggles and rebellions, as in Hungary and Czechoslovakia. The map will provide a visual framework to help students better understand where Cold War conflicts occurred.

Analyze Maps Why might so many of the "hot spots" have been located in Eastern Europe? *(The Soviet Union occupied this area during World War II, and conflicts broke out when it tried to control the region after the war ended.)*

Express Problems Clearly What problems might the United States face in dealing with the Cold War conflicts? *(Most of the conflicts were located thousands of miles from the United States, making it difficult to send military aid and to use influence.)*

Topic Inquiry

Launch the Topic Discussion with students after introducing the topic.

The Beginning of the Cold War

Supporting English Language Learners

Use with the reading, **The Aftermath of War**.

Speaking

Ask: What are the main reasons we have for speaking? Tell students that they will develop the skill of expressing ideas in the activities below.

Beginning Ask students to suggest words and phrases that describe the idea of Truman's containment policy. Display these responses in a list. Then guide students to say these words and phrases in complete sentences (e.g., Truman's containment policy was ____).

Intermediate Have students discuss the following questions: What was Truman's idea of containment? Can you think of other ideas Truman might have tried to deal with the Soviet influence? What are they? Support students' efforts to suggest ideas and expand on the ideas of others.

Advanced Invite pairs of students to define Truman's containment policy and discuss other ideas that Truman could have tried instead. Ask: Would your ideas have been more or less effective than the one Truman chose? Why do you think that?

Advanced High Ask students to think of an alternative idea to Truman's containment policy and write down notes about it. Then have them use their notes to speak to a partner about their idea. Encourage partners to discuss the pros and cons of their ideas.

Use with the reading, **Postwar Alliances**.

Reading

Invite students to read or reread the text if necessary (independently, with a partner, or as a group). Then invite them to demonstrate their reading comprehension by responding to the questions below.

Beginning Ask students simple, direct questions, such as: Was the United States part of the Warsaw Pact? Which organization helped to improve health and education around the world? As students respond to each question, check their answers in the text together.

Intermediate Ask students questions that require full-sentence answers, such as: What is NATO? What has the United Nations had a hard time doing? As students respond to each question, check their answers in the text together.

Advanced Provide pairs of students with several open-ended questions for them to discuss, such as: How were NATO and the Warsaw Pact similar and different? What are the strengths and weaknesses of the United Nations? Encourage students to double-check their answers in the text.

Advanced High Place students in pairs and invite partners to quiz each other on the content of the text. Have them take turns skimming the text and creating questions for their partner to answer. Encourage them to start their questions with the words why and how.

D Differentiate Instruction

Use the Differentiated Instruction notes throughout the lesson plan to support the varied skill sets, levels of readiness, and interests in the mixed-ability classroom.

Challenge These notes include suggestions for expanding the activity for advanced students.

On-Level These notes include suggestions for modifying the activity to address different interests or learning styles.

Extra Support These notes include ideas for providing more scaffolding or reading spuport.

Special Needs These notes provide ideas for adapting instruction to support the needs of various special needs students.

NOTES

Objectives

Objective 1: Explain why the United States took a leadership role in the world after World War II.

Objective 2: Summarize how the Cold War began.

Objective 3: Describe U.S. response to Soviet expansion.

Objective 4: Analyze how the crisis over Berlin led to new Cold War alliances.

Objective 5: Identify the events during 1949 that increased Cold War tensions.

LESSON 1 ORGANIZER	PACING: APPROX. 1 PERIOD, .5 BLOCKS			
			RESOURCES	
	OBJECTIVES	PACING	Online	Print
Connect				
DIGITAL START UP ACTIVITY **Former Allies**		5 min.	●	
Investigate				
DIGITAL TEXT 1 **The Causes of the Cold War**	Objectives 1, 2	10 min.	●	●
DIGITAL TEXT 2 **The Aftermath of War**	Objective 3	10 min.	●	●
INTERACTIVE CHART **Cold War—Cause and Effect**		10 min.	●	
DIGITAL TEXT 3 **Postwar Alliances**	Objectives 4, 5	10 min.	●	●
INTERACTIVE MAP **Early Cold War Alliances**		10 min.	●	
Synthesize				
DIGITAL ACTIVITY **A Cold War Begins**		5 min.	●	
Demonstrate				
DIGITAL QUIZ **Lesson Quiz and Class Discussion Board**		10 min.	●	

Topic 15 Lesson 1

The Beginning of the Cold War

CONNECT

DIGITAL START UP ACTIVITY

Former Allies

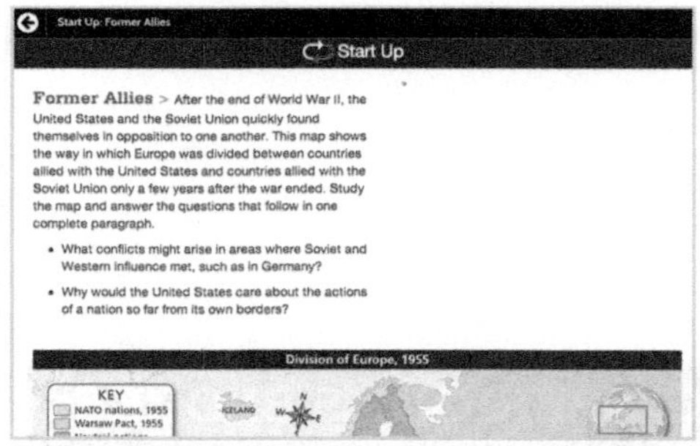

Start Up: Former Allies
Start Up
Former Allies > After the end of World War II, the United States and the Soviet Union quickly found themselves in opposition to one another. This map shows the way in which Europe was divided between countries allied with the United States and countries allied with the Soviet Union only a few years after the war ended. Study the map and answer the questions that follow in one complete paragraph.
• What conflicts might arise in areas where Soviet and Western influence met, such as in Germany?
• Why would the United States care about the actions of a nation so far from its own borders?
Division of Europe, 1955
KEY
NATO nations, 1955
Warsaw Pact, 1955

Ask students to think about how the United States and the Soviet Union became rivals in the Cold War. Present the map and encourage students to review the information on it. Have students share their ideas with a partner.

Discuss Take a moment to reflect on why U.S. leaders might have felt threatened by growing Soviet power. *(Possible responses: they were worried about the spread of communism; they did not want another world war to break out.)*

Tell students that in this lesson they will be learning about tensions between the Soviet Union and the United States that led to the Cold War.

Aa Vocabulary Development: Use the Interactive Reading Notepad to preview the Key Terms and Academic Vocabulary in this lesson with students.

FLIP IT!

Assign the Flipped Video for this lesson.

STUDENT EDITION PRINT PAGES: 798–803

INVESTIGATE

DIGITAL TEXT 1

The Causes of the Cold War

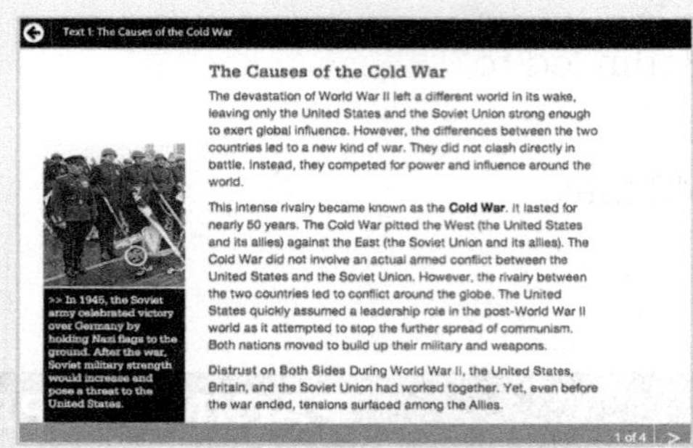

Text 1: The Causes of the Cold War
The Causes of the Cold War
The devastation of World War II left a different world in its wake, leaving only the United States and the Soviet Union strong enough to exert global influence. However, the differences between the two countries led to a new kind of war. They did not clash directly in battle. Instead, they competed for power and influence around the world.
This intense rivalry became known as the Cold War. It lasted for nearly 50 years. The Cold War pitted the West (the United States and its allies) against the East (the Soviet Union and its allies). The Cold War did not involve an actual armed conflict between the United States and the Soviet Union. However, the rivalry between the two countries led to conflict around the globe. The United States quickly assumed a leadership role in the post-World War II world as it attempted to stop the further spread of communism. Both nations moved to build up their military and weapons.
Distrust on Both Sides During World War II, the United States, Britain, and the Soviet Union had worked together. Yet, even before the war ended, tensions surfaced among the Allies.
>> In 1945, the Soviet army celebrated victory over Germany by holding Nazi flags to the ground. After the war, Soviet military strength would increase and pose a threat to the United States.
1 of 4

Objectives 1: Explain why the United States took a leadership role in the world after World War II; 2: Summarize how the Cold War began.

Quick Instruction

Direct students' attention to the digital image of the Soviet Army with captured Nazi flags. Invite volunteers to describe the overall tone and purpose of the image. *(The photo's tone is one of victory or triumph. The Soviet soldiers are holding the Nazi flags to the ground to symbolize the Nazi's defeat. The photo looks like propaganda to highlight Soviet power.)* Encourage students to reflect on how Soviet leaders might respond to changing post-war relationships with other Allied countries.

Infer Why would the Soviet Union want to expand its power into Eastern Europe after World War II? *(The Soviet Union had been invaded by Germany in World War II. Controlling Eastern Europe would give more protection from future German or other threats.)*

Identify Central Issues Why did Stalin break his promise to hold free elections in Eastern Europe? How did this affect Eastern European countries? *(Stalin refused to hold free elections because he believed Eastern Europeans would elect anti-Soviet governments. Instead, he imposed Communist governments loyal to the Soviet Union on the people of Eastern Europe.)*

Further Instruction

Go through the Interactive Reading Notepad questions and use appropriate questions to begin a discussion in which you ask: what were the differences between the countries of the West and the Soviet Union. *(The Soviet Union's communist government rejected religion, freedom of speech, and private property, while the countries of the West supported religious freedom, freedom of speech, and free enterprise.)* Pair students and have them discuss how these issues created a great sense of distrust between the Soviet Union and the United States leading to the start of the Cold War. Have student pairs share their thoughts with the class.

Draw Conclusions Why did western nations consider Stalin's actions in the years after World War II a threat? *(Stalin wanted to spread communism and make the Soviet Union the dominant power in the world. They feared he would try to spread Communism to countries like Italy and Greece that were outside of Eastern Europe.)*

Generate Explanations What factors led the United States to become the world's most powerful nation after World War II? *(The United States had the most powerful military, and the country was much stronger economically than the European countries because it did not experience the destruction of the war as others had.)*

DIGITAL TEXT 2

The Aftermath of War

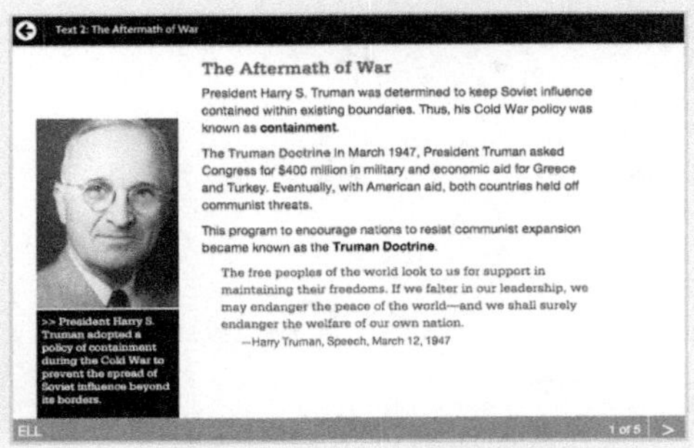

Objective 3: Describe U.S. response to Soviet expansion.

Quick Instruction

Interactive Chart: Cold War—Cause and Effect Project the Interactive Chart and prompt students to reflect on the relationship between the events as they complete the graphic organizer. Discuss the excerpts from Churchill's "Iron Curtain Speech", connecting both to the larger theme of the impending Cold War.

Summarize the key goal of the Truman Doctrine. *(The main goal of the Truman Doctrine was to contain, or stop, the expansion of Soviet influence beyond its borders.)*

ACTIVE CLASSROOM

Conduct a Conversation with History activity. Tell students to imagine that they are having a conversation with Winston Churchill as he is writing a draft of what will become known as the "Iron Curtain Speech." Direct each student to write down a question he or she would like to ask, then how Churchill would respond, and then what the student would say in response.

ELL Use the ELL activity described in the ELL chart.

INTERACTIVE CHART

Cold War—Cause and Effect

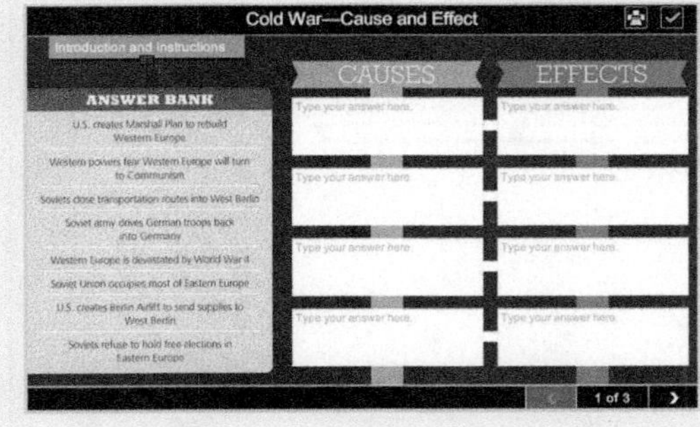

Further Instruction

Identify Cause and Effect Describe the reasons behind the creation of the Marshall Plan and its effects on Europe. *(World War II had left Europe's homes, roads, and factories in ruins. Millions of Europeans were homeless, hungry refugees. By helping these nations rebuild their economies, the Marshall Plan reduced the threat of communist revolutions in Western Europe.)*

Support a Point of View with Evidence What evidence in the text shows that the Berlin Airlift was a success? *(American and British planes carried tons of food, fuel, and other supplies to West Berliners every day. Stalin found that the West would not abandon West Berlin so he lifted the blockade.)*

DIGITAL TEXT 3

Postwar Alliances

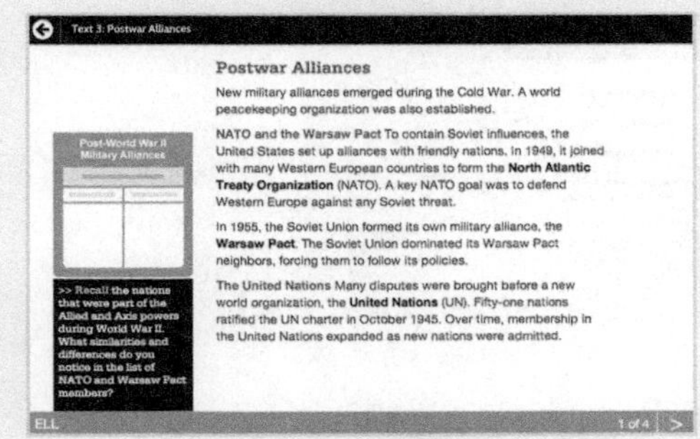

Objectives 4: Analyze how the crisis over Berlin led to new Cold War alliances; 5: Identify the events during 1949 that increased Cold War tensions.

Quick Instruction

Interactive Map: Early Cold War Alliances Project the Interactive Map and prompt students to connect the political divisions in Europe with the events of the early Cold War. Ask: What factors might make it difficult for Yugoslavia to maintain its neutral status? *(Yugoslavia was located between NATO and Warsaw Pact countries.)*

Determine Relevance Why was the Soviet Union's successful test of an atomic bomb significant for the United States? *(When the United States was the only nation with atomic weapons, it had an advantage. Now the Soviet Union was more evenly matched with the United States.)*

ACTIVE CLASSROOM

Conduct a Graffiti Concepts activity. Ask students to reflect on the causes of the Cold War and the key differences in the NATO and Warsaw Pact goals and to create a visual image and/or phrase that represents each organization. (Allow approximately 3–5 minutes.) Then ask students to post their "graffiti" on the board or on chart paper and ask students to look at all the various causes then discuss them as a group.

The Beginning of the Cold War

INTERACTIVE MAP

Early Cold War Alliances

D Differentiate: On-Level To aid students in keeping track of which organizations European countries belonged to, have students complete a two-column chart that lists NATO and Warsaw Pact organizations. Have students list the member nations and the purpose of the organization. Students can use their charts as a study aid for the Lesson.

ELL Use the ELL activity described in the ELL chart.

Further Instruction

Initiate a discussion about the United Nations. Ask students to describe the purpose of the UN. *(to maintain peace and settle international disputes)* Challenge students to identify the successes of the United Nations. *(The UN has succeeded in fighting hunger and disease and in improving education. UN relief programs have provided food, medicine, and supplies to victims of famine, war, and other disasters. The UN has not been as successful in preserving peace because some countries have rejected United Nations resolutions.)* To extend the discussion and provide more depth, assign Primary Source: Charter of the United Nations.

Express Problems Clearly How did the communist takeover of China present a foreign policy challenge for the United States? *(Communist China and the Soviet Union now controlled almost a quarter of the globe and many Americans feared that communism would spread still farther.)*

SYNTHESIZE

DIGITAL ACTIVITY

A Cold War Begins

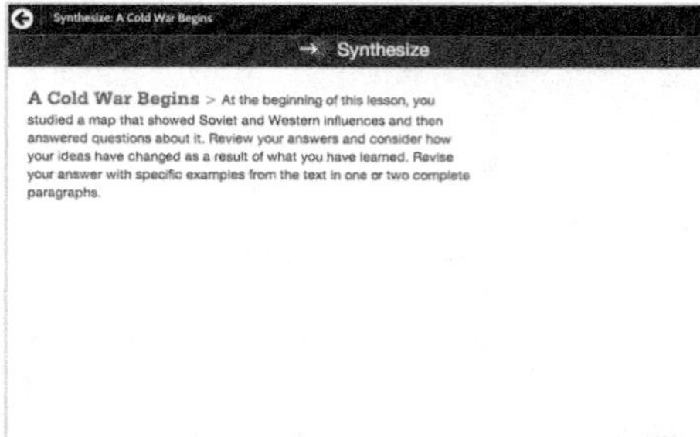

Discuss Ask students to think about the Lesson Start Up Activity and their answers to the questions they answered at the beginning of this lesson. Ask if they would change any of their responses now that they have learned more about the Cold War. When students have finished writing their revised paragraphs, invite volunteers to share them with the class.

Have students think about the following question: How did the United States' role in the world change from the beginning of World War II through the Cold War? Have students use evidence from the text to support their ideas.

DEMONSTRATE

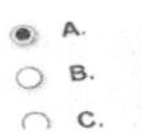

DIGITAL QUIZ

Lesson Quiz and Class Discussion Board

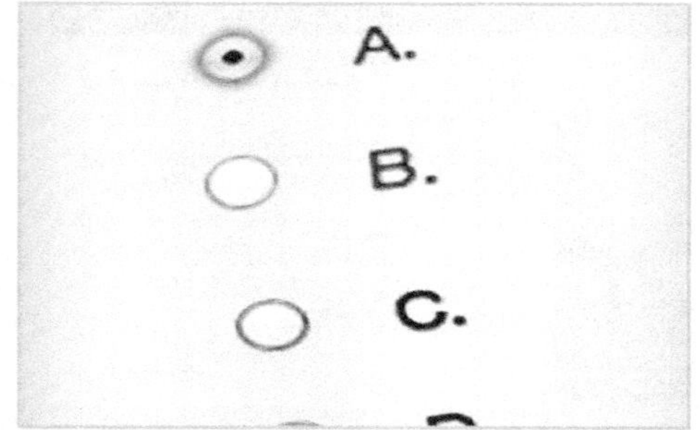

Assign the online Lesson Quiz for this lesson if you haven't already done so. Students will be offered automatic remediation or enrichment based on their score.

In *The Beginning of the Cold War*, you read about the events and issues that launched the Cold War between the United States and the Soviet Union. To halt the spread of communism, the United States and other western nations formed NATO. It aimed to contain communism within the Soviet's current borders. Countries around the world also created the United Nations to help settle international disputes in the wake of World War II.

Pose these questions to the class on the Discussion Board:

Infer After World War I, the United States refused to join the League of Nations. Why do you think it joined the United Nations after World War II?

Make Predictions How might American foreign policy have changed as a result of the shocks of 1949?

Topic Inquiry

Have students continue their investigations for the Topic Inquiry.

PEARSON realize™ www.PearsonRealize.com Access your Digital Lesson

Korea and Other Postwar Conflicts

Supporting English Language Learners

Use with the reading, **War on the Korean Peninsula.**

Learning

Explain that in the following activities students will use a chart to help them understand and analyze information from the text.

Beginning Display a two-column chart with columns titled *Countries* and *Reasons for Involvement*. Work together with students to use essential information from the text to summarize why the United States and China were involved in the Korean War.

Intermediate Display a partially completed two-column chart with columns titled *Country* (Soviet Union, United States, China, South Korea, North Korea) and *Reasons for Involvement*. Work together with students to use essential information from the text to summarize why the Soviet Union, United States, China, South Korea, and North Korea were involved in the Korean War.

Advanced Provide pairs of students with a three-column chart with columns titled *Country*, *Reasons for Involvement*, and *Desired Outcome*. Guide students to use essential information from the text to summarize why the Soviet Union, United States, China, South Korea, and North Korea were involved in the Korean War.

Advanced High Provide individual students with a three-column chart with columns titled *Country*, *Reasons for Involvement*, and *Desired Outcome*. Guide students to use essential information from the text to summarize why the Soviet Union, United States, China, South Korea, and North Korea were involved in the Korean War.

Use with the reading, **A Cold War Around the Globe.**

Listening

Point out the phrase *both openly and secretly* in the text's fifth paragraph and explain the *both . . . and* language structure.

Beginning Using intonation to stress the use of *both . . . and*, say: Both the Soviet Union and the United States were part of the Cold War. Ask: What two countries were part of the Cold War? Repeat this process with other *both . . . and* sentences.

Intermediate Display these sentence parts: Soviet Union/United States/ part of the Cold War. Add *both . . . and* to create a complete sentence and say it aloud. Have students repeat the sentence. Then have students create a *both . . . and* sentence with these parts: Somalia/Ethiopia/were in a long war.

Advanced Talk to students about the impact of the Cold war in Africa, using *both . . . and* at least twice. Ask students to explain the meaning of the *both . . . and* sentences. Then guide them to create their own *both . . . and* sentence.

Advanced High Invite pairs of students to talk about the impact of the Cold War around the world, with each partner using *both . . . and* sentences at least twice. When one student says a *both . . . and* sentence, encourage the other to explain the sentence in other words.

D Differentiate Instruction

Use the Differentiated Instruction notes throughout the lesson plan to support the varied skill sets, levels of readiness, and interests in the mixed-ability classroom.

Challenge These notes include suggestions for expanding the activity for advanced students.

On-Level These notes include suggestions for modifying the activity to address different interests or learning styles.

Extra Support These notes include ideas for providing more scaffolding or reading spuport.

Special Needs These notes provide ideas for adapting instruction to support the needs of various special needs students.

NOTES

Topic 15 Lesson 2

Korea and Other Postwar Conflicts

Objectives

Objective 1: Explain why the United States became involved in the conflict in Korea.

Objective 2: Summarize how the fighting in Korea ended.

Objective 3: Explain why the Cold War spread to Africa and other parts of Asia.

Objective 4: Explain why there were hunts for Communists at home and identify the results of the hunts.

LESSON 2 ORGANIZER		PACING: APPROX. 1 PERIOD, .5 BLOCKS	RESOURCES	
	OBJECTIVES	PACING	Online	Print
Connect				
DIGITAL START UP ACTIVITY **A "Cold" War**		5 min.	●	
Investigate				
DIGITAL TEXT 1 **War on the Korean Peninsula**	Objective 1	10 min.	●	●
INTERACTIVE MAP **Phases of the Korean War**	Objective 1	10 min.	●	
DIGITAL TEXT 2 **The Fighting Ends**	Objective 2	10 min.	●	●
DIGITAL TEXT 3 **A Cold War Around the Globe**	Objective 3	10 min.	●	●
INTERACTIVE CHART **Cold War Actions—The United States and the Soviet Union**	Objective 3	10 min.	●	
DIGITAL TEXT 4 **Concern about Communism at Home**	Objective 4	10 min.	●	●
Synthesize				
DIGITAL ACTIVITY **The Cold War at Home**		5 min.	●	
Demonstrate				
DIGITAL QUIZ **Lesson Quiz and Class Discussion Board**		10 min.	●	

Go online to access additional resources including:
Primary Sources • Biographies • Supreme Court cases • 21st Century Skill Tutorials • Maps • Graphic Organizers.

CONNECT

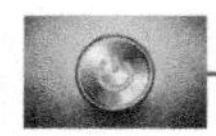

DIGITAL START UP ACTIVITY

A "Cold" War

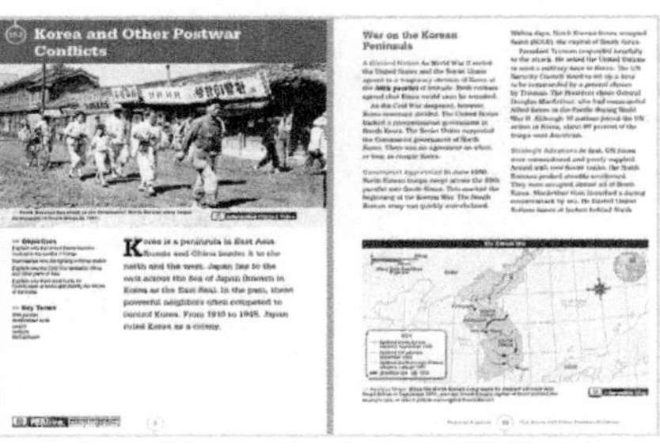

Project the Start Up Activity Ask students to consider the activity as they enter and get settled. Then have them share their responses with another student.

Discuss If you were an American during the Cold War, how would you have felt about communist aggression against noncommunist nations? *(Possible answers: threatened, angered, frightened)*

Tell students that in this lesson they will be learning about the causes and effects of the communist invasion of South Korea and the increasing concerns over the spread of communism.

Aa Vocabulary Development: Use the Interactive Reading Notepad to preview the Key Terms and Academic Vocabulary in this lesson with students.

FLIP IT!

Assign the Flipped Video for this lesson.

STUDENT EDITION PRINT PAGES: 804–811

INVESTIGATE

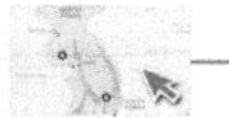

DIGITAL TEXT 1

War on the Korean Peninsula

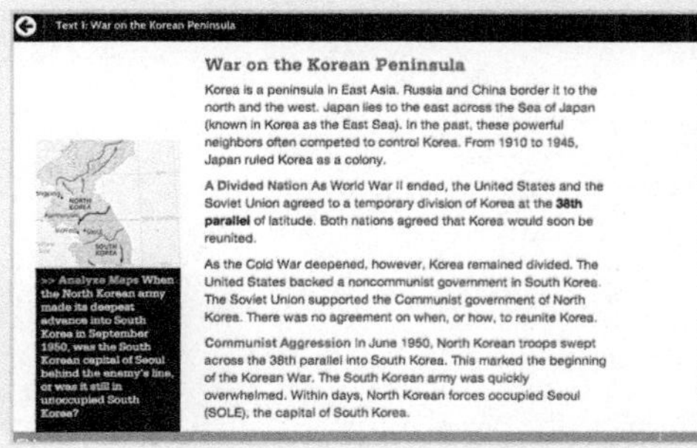

INTERACTIVE MAP

Phases of the Korean War

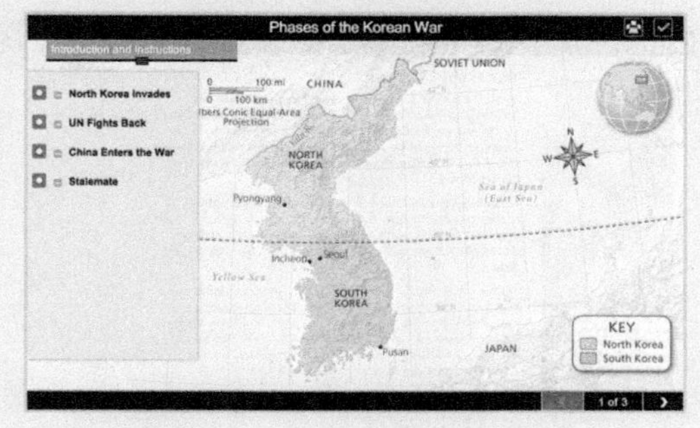

Objective 1: **Explain why the United States became involved in the conflict in Korea.**

Quick Instruction

Interactive Map: Phases of the Korean War Project the Interactive Map and navigate through the layers to reveal the phases of the Korean War. Point out that conditions in the war changed repeatedly. First, North Korea made large advances, then United Nations and South Korean troops pushed back nearly to North Korea's border with China. Finally, Chinese troops intervened and forced United Nations and South Korean troops to withdraw to the south. After all the bitter fighting, loss of life, and destruction, the North-South border remained approximately where it had been before the war. Ask: Which side gained the most from the war? *(Possible response: The South Koreans and the UN, because they stopped the communist takeover of South Korea.)*

Infer What was China's impact on the outcome of the Korean War? *(Chinese troops entered the war when UN forces neared the Chinese border. They pushed UN troops back far to the south, though UN forces were able to regroup and fight the Chinese and North Koreans to a standstill.)*

ACTIVE CLASSROOM

Conduct a Make Headlines activity. Ask: If you were to write a headline that captured the most important aspect of the Korean War, what would that headline be? Allow students to use subheadings to communicate more information. Encourage them to use their headlines to present the Korean War within the context of the larger Cold War. Have students pass their headlines to a partner for them to review.

ELL Use the ELL activity described in the ELL chart.

Further Instruction

Go through the Interactive Reading Notepad questions and use appropriate questions to initiate a discussion about why the United States became involved in the conflict in Korea. Use a world map or globe to show students the location of Korea. Point out its proximity to China and the Soviet Union and remind students that the Soviet Union and China were communist countries.

Summarize President Truman's response to the North Korean aggression in 1950. *(Truman responded forcefully to the attack. He asked the United Nations to send a military force to Korea. The UN Security Council voted to set up a force that included troops from 16 nations. Truman chose General Douglas MacArthur who had commanded Allied forces in the Pacific during World War II to command UN forces.)*

Korea and Other Postwar Conflicts

DIGITAL TEXT 2
The Fighting Ends

Text 2: The Fighting Ends

The Fighting Ends

During the deadlock, a serious disagreement arose between General MacArthur and President Truman. MacArthur felt that to win the war, UN forces must attack China. Truman feared that an attack on China might lead to a world war. He hoped to limit the war and restore the border between North Korea and South Korea at the 38th parallel.

Disagreement at the Top A frustrated MacArthur complained publicly that politicians in Washington were holding him back. "We must win," he insisted. "There is no substitute for victory." Angry that MacArthur was defying orders, Truman fired the popular general.

Truman's action outraged many Americans. They gave MacArthur a hero's welcome when he returned home. Truman, however, defended his decision. Under the Constitution, he pointed out, the President is commander in chief, responsible for key decisions about war and peace. MacArthur's statements, said Truman, undermined attempts to reach a peace settlement.

>> General Douglas MacArthur (far right), a World War II veteran, assumed command of the UN forces in Korea at President Truman's request.

1 of 4

Objective 2: Summarize how the fighting in Korea ended.

Quick Instruction

Summarize Who was Douglas MacArthur and what role did he play in the fighting of the Korean War? *(MacArthur was considered a hero for his command of Allied forces in the Pacific during World War II. He was placed in command of the UN forces fighting against the communist forces of North Korea and China.)*

Explain Problems Clearly What disagreements led to President Truman removing Douglas MacArthur from command of UN forces? *(MacArthur was determined to win the Korean War above all else. In order to do this, he believed it was necessary to attack China. MacArthur complained publicly that politicians in Washington were holding him back. Truman was angry that MacArthur was defying orders, so he fired the general.)*

Further Instruction

Initiate a discussion about the terms of the Korean War armistice. Make sure students understand that it ended the fighting, redrew the border between North and South Korea near the original, and set up a demilitarized zone between the two nations.

Generate Explanations Why do you think the United States accepted an armistice? *(Possible answers: There were too many lives lost already; the war was at a stalemate and did not seem winnable; to prevent further conflict with China.)*

Support a Point of View with Evidence In your opinion, was the Korean War worth fighting? Explain. *(Possible answers: No. Millions of people were killed and the Korean political situation did not change because the border was essentially unchanged at the end of the war; Yes. The U.S. military achieved President Truman's goal of containing communism.)*

DIGITAL TEXT 3
A Cold War Around the Globe

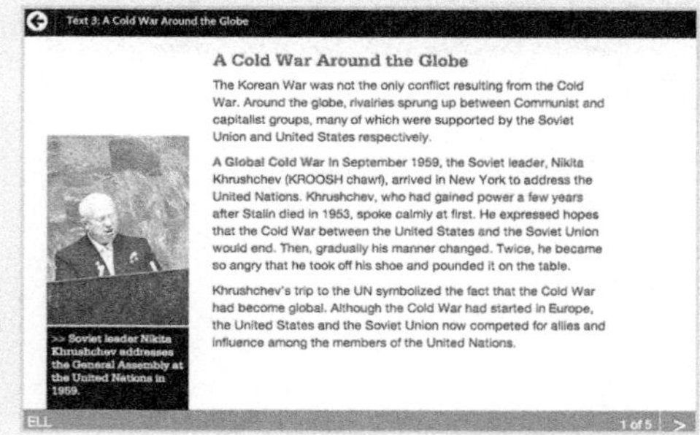
Text 3: A Cold War Around the Globe

A Cold War Around the Globe

The Korean War was not the only conflict resulting from the Cold War. Around the globe, rivalries sprung up between Communist and capitalist groups, many of which were supported by the Soviet Union and United States respectively.

A Global Cold War In September 1959, the Soviet leader, Nikita Khrushchev (KROOSH chawf), arrived in New York to address the United Nations. Khrushchev, who had gained power a few years after Stalin died in 1953, spoke calmly at first. He expressed hopes that the Cold War between the United States and the Soviet Union would end. Then, gradually his manner changed. Twice, he became so angry that he took off his shoe and pounded it on the table.

Khrushchev's trip to the UN symbolized the fact that the Cold War had become global. Although the Cold War had started in Europe, the United States and the Soviet Union now competed for allies and influence among the members of the United Nations.

>> Soviet leader Nikita Khrushchev addresses the General Assembly at the United Nations in 1959.

ELL 1 of 5

Objective 3: Explain why the Cold War spread to Africa and other parts of Asia.

Quick Instruction

Interactive Chart: Cold War Actions—The United States and the Soviet Union Project the Interactive Chart and prompt students to place the tiles in the correct categories and answer the questions. Ask: Based on the information in the interactivity, how do you think the Cold War affected African and Asian nations? *(Sample response: The Cold War harmed African and Asian nations, as the United States and the Soviet Union intervened in conflicts between countries like India and Pakistan or Ethiopia and Somalia.)*

ACTIVE CLASSROOM

Conduct a Closer Look activity. Use a whiteboard tool to divide a map of the world into four quadrants. Direct students to look closely at each quadrant and use information from the interactivity to locate the nations affected by Cold War conflicts. Ask students what they can learn or infer about how and why the Cold War spread around the globe.

INTERACTIVE CHART

Cold War Actions—The United States and the Soviet Union

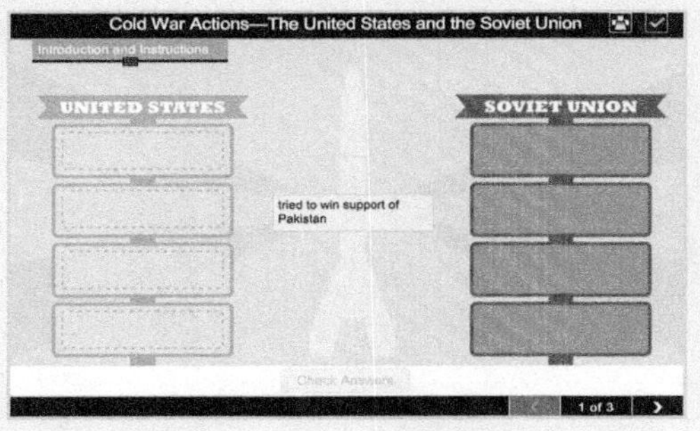

D Differentiate: Challenge Challenge students to research another Cold War conflict from the mid 20th century. Have students use the information they gather to connect this conflict with the Cold War themes they have already learned.

ELL Use the ELL activity described in the ELL chart.

Further Instruction

Infer Why were nations in Africa and Asia frequently the center of political and military conflicts during the Cold War? *(For years, many of these nations had been governed as colonies of European and other foreign powers. After World War II, many of these nations gained independence but then faced ethnic conflict or wars with neighbors. The United States and the Soviet Union intervened in some of these conflicts.)*

Identify Patterns How did India and Pakistan handle relations with the two Cold War superpowers? How did India break the pattern followed by some other newly independent countries? *(Pakistan allied with the United States, while India accepted both American and Soviet aid but stayed neutral. This made it different from other countries, which chose sides.)*

DIGITAL TEXT 4

Concern about Communism at Home

Text 4: Concern About Communism at Home

Concern about Communism at Home

For many Americans, the Korean War increased worries about Communists at home. Communist sympathizers and spies, they feared, might be secretly working to overthrow the government. These concerns helped spark a hunt for Communists within American society.

During the Great Depression, some Americans had turned against democracy and free enterprise. They had rejected the efforts of the New Deal as ineffective. To them, communism offered the only solution to the nation's deep economic troubles. In time, however, many American Communists recognized that Soviet leader Joseph Stalin was a brutal dictator, and they left the party.

Hunting Spies Still, some remained avid Communists. Between 1946 and 1950, several people in the United States, Canada, and Britain were arrested as Soviet spies. In the United States, Ethel and Julius Rosenberg were sentenced to death for passing atomic secrets to the Soviets. Despite protests, both were executed in 1953. The Rosenberg case made many Americans wonder if other Soviet spies were living among them as ordinary citizens.

>> In 1953, some Americans celebrated the execution of Julius and Ethel Rosenberg—two Americans charged as spies working for the Soviets. Generate Explanations What does this say about the atmosphere in the United States in the 1950s?

Objective 4: **Explain why there were hunts for Communists at home and identify the results of the hunts.**

Quick Instruction

Identify Patterns How did the Alger Hiss and Rosenberg cases heighten Cold War tensions in the United States? *(These two cases of communist spying seemed to prove the communists were, in fact, infiltrating the United States, making other accusations of communist activity seem more credible.)*

Draw Conclusions How did Joseph McCarthy's actions affect the United States? *(His exaggerated claims and reckless accusations spread suspicion and fear of communism across the nation. Not only the government but colleges and businesses as well questioned the loyalty of their employees.)*

Further Instruction

Go through the Interactive Reading Notepad questions and use appropriate questions to continue the discussion of the hunts for Communists in the United States during the Cold War and identify and explore the results of the hunts.

Generate Explanations Why might fears of communism have increased in the United States after the Korean War? *(Communist forces fought the United States to a stalemate in Korea. This may have frightened Americans who were worried about growing Communist power.)*

Korea and Other Postwar Conflicts

SYNTHESIZE

DIGITAL ACTIVITY

The Cold War at Home

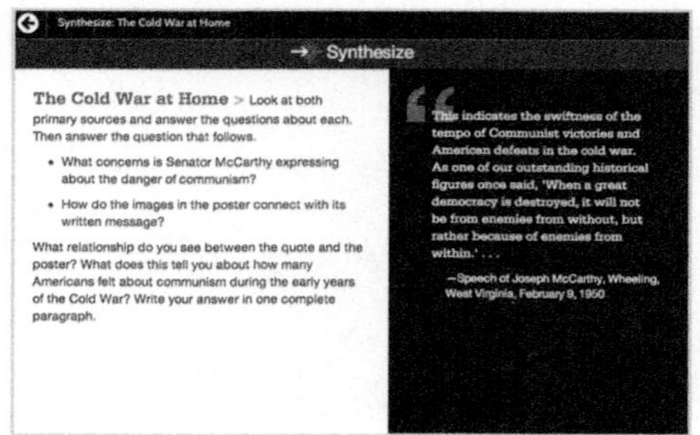

Discuss Before students begin reviewing the primary sources, lead a brief review about how Cold War fear and tensions were intensified by each of the following:

- communist aggression
- the Korean War
- Nikita Khrushchev's speech to the General Assembly at the United Nations
- the Alger Hiss and Rosenberg cases
- McCarthyism

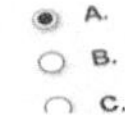

DEMONSTRATE

DIGITAL QUIZ

Lesson Quiz and Class Discussion Board

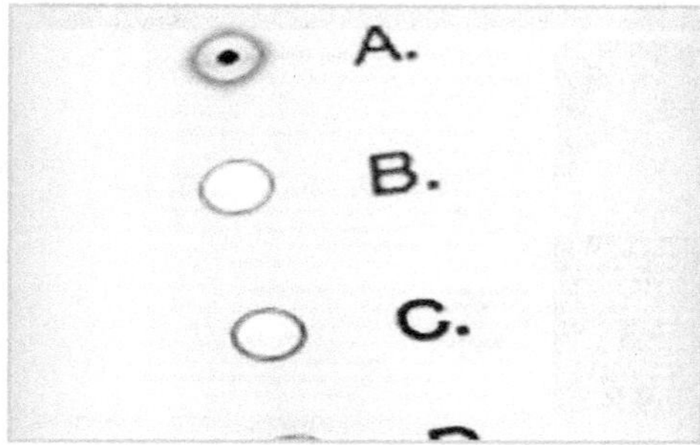

Assign the online Lesson Quiz for this lesson if you haven't already done so. Students will be offered automatic remediation or enrichment based on their score.

Pose these questions to the class on the Discussion Board:

In *Korea and Other Postwar Conflicts*, you read about how the Korean War was directly linked to the Cold War. It soon involved not only Koreans but also the United Nations, the United States, China, and other powers. The Cold War intensified after the war as the United States and the Soviet Union competed for power around the world, which created great fear and tension among Americans at home.

Evaluate Information How effective do you think the United States was in containing the spread of communism? Explain.

Apply Concepts How did the Cold War play out in different places around the world, including Asia and Africa?

Topic Inquiry

Have students continue their investigations for the Topic Inquiry.

PEARSON realize™ www.PearsonRealize.com Access your Digital Lesson

Eisenhower and Postwar America

Supporting English Language Learners

Use with the reading, **Postwar Prosperity.**

Speaking

Review the four sentence types with students (declarative, interrogative, exclamatory, imperative). Demonstrate how intonation changes with each type.

Beginning Say these sentences and prompt students to identify their type: *After World War II, the United States got bigger and stronger. The population exploded!* Then have students complete these declarative and exclamatory sentences: The U.S. economy _____. It was really _____ !

Intermediate Say this sentence and have students identify its type: *After World War II, the United States got bigger and stronger.* Then have students create a question based on it. Repeat the activity, this time providing a question and having students create a declarative sentence based on it.

Advanced Ask pairs of students to take turns saying declarative, interrogative, and exclamatory sentences about the text. Challenge them to create a set of all three sentence types that are logically connected to one another.

Advanced High Invite pairs of students to use all four types of sentences as they discuss the political, economic, and social climate of the United States after World War II. Suggest that they create an imperative sentence by using direct speech (e.g., hypothetical quotes of Truman).

Use with the reading, **Life in the 1950s.**

Reading

Explain that some verbs (i.e., some phrasal verbs) must be followed by a preposition. Without the preposition, the verb has a different meaning.

Beginning Display this sentence: Empty lots turned into housing developments. Explain that *turned into* means *became*. Then read the text's eighth paragraph together (beginning with *As millions* . . .). Ask: What was the country becoming, or turning into?

Intermediate Together, read the text's seventh paragraph (beginning with *Shopping centers* . . .). Ask: What is the verb in the first sentence? What does *sprang up* mean? Support students in using words and gestures to describe how stores might *spring up*.

Advanced Point out the text's two uses of *put up* (in the fifth and sixth paragraphs). Have pairs of students discuss the meaning of *put up* and think of alternate ways to say the same thing. Ask: How is the meaning of *put up* different than *put*?

Advanced High Challenge pairs of students to locate phrasal verbs in the text, such as *put up*, *sprang up*, *was turning into*, *called for*, and *caught on*. Ask pairs to define each phrasal verb they find and discuss how its meaning is different than the verb without the preposition.

D Differentiate Instruction

Use the Differentiated Instruction notes throughout the lesson plan to support the varied skill sets, levels of readiness, and interests in the mixed-ability classroom.

Challenge These notes include suggestions for expanding the activity for advanced students.

On-Level These notes include suggestions for modifying the activity to address different interests or learning styles.

Extra Support These notes include ideas for providing more scaffolding or reading spupport.

Special Needs These notes provide ideas for adapting instruction to support the needs of various special needs students.

NOTES

Topic 15 Lesson 3

Eisenhower and Postwar America

Objectives

Objective 1: Discuss postwar problems in America.

Objective 2: Identify the factors that contributed to the economic and baby booms of the 1950s.

Objective 3: Explain how American lifestyles changed in the 1950s.

LESSON 3 ORGANIZER	PACING: APPROX. 1 PERIOD, .5 BLOCKS		RESOURCES	
	OBJECTIVES	PACING	Online	Print
Connect				
DIGITAL START UP ACTIVITY **An Improved Economy**		5 min.	●	
Investigate				
DIGITAL TEXT 1 **Postwar Prosperity**	Objectives 1, 2	10 min.	●	●
BEFORE AND AFTER **The Baby Boom Changes the Nation**		10 min.	●	
DIGITAL TEXT 2 **Life in the 1950s**	Objective 3	10 min.	●	●
INTERACTIVE GALLERY **Life in the 1950s**		10 min.	●	
Synthesize				
DIGITAL ACTIVITY **Life in Postwar America**		5 min.	●	
Demonstrate				
DIGITAL QUIZ **Lesson Quiz and Class Discussion Board**		10 min.	●	

Go online to access additional resources including:
Primary Sources • Biographies • Supreme Court cases • 21st Century Skill Tutorials • Maps • Graphic Organizers.

PEARSON realize™ www.PearsonRealize.com

CONNECT

DIGITAL START UP ACTIVITY

An Improved Economy

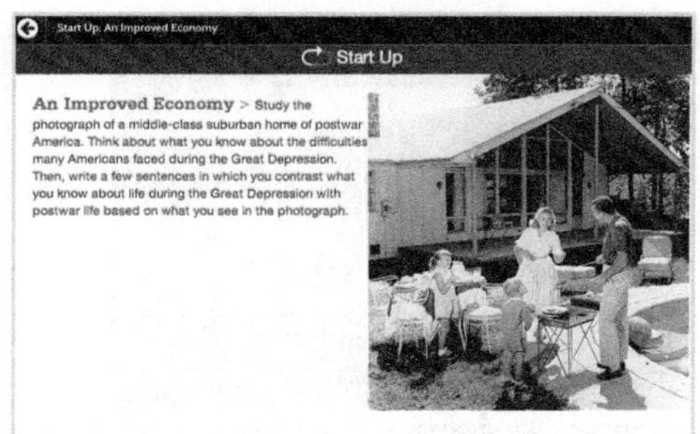

Project the Start Up Activity Ask students to take a few minutes to view the image and then answer the question as they enter and get settled. Then have them share their ideas with another student, either in class or through a chat or blog space.

Discuss What other changes might the postwar prosperity bring to Americans in the 1950s? *(Americans will have had more economic, educational, and entertainment opportunities due to the strong economy.)*

Tell students that in this lesson they will explore important economic, social, and political changes that were transforming the United States during the Cold War era of the 1950s.

Aa Vocabulary Development: Use the Interactive Reading Notepad to preview the Key Terms and Academic Vocabulary in this lesson with students.

FLIP IT!

Assign the Flipped Video for this lesson.

STUDENT EDITION PRINT PAGES: 812–818

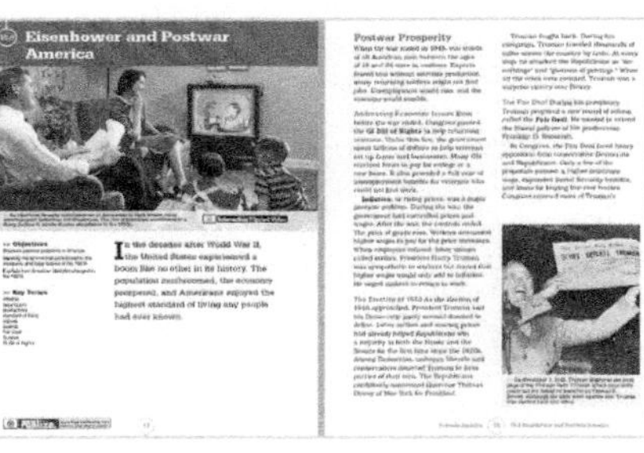

INVESTIGATE

DIGITAL TEXT 1

Postwar Prosperity

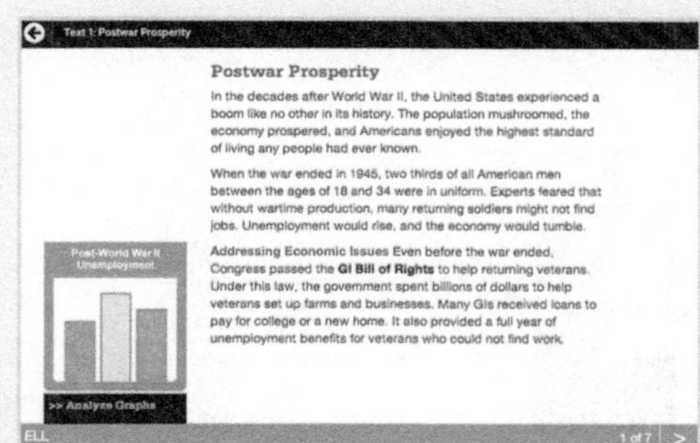

Objectives 1: **Discuss postwar problems in America; 2: Identify the factors that contributed to the economic and baby booms of the 1950s.**

Quick Instruction

Before and After: The Baby Boom Changes the Nation Project the Before and After and navigate the slider to compare aspects of U.S. society before and during the Baby Boom. Prompt students to explain how each of the following improved life in the United States: birth rates, educational success, increase in labor force. Ask: What effects did the baby boom have on the nation's economy? *(The dramatic population jump increased consumer spending and demand for products, such as homes, clothing, food, and services, which in turn encouraged companies to increase production and hire more workers.)*

Summarize how government and private sector actions that helped boost the American economy. *(The government created the GI Bill to help millions of returning soldiers get college educations, which increased productivity and wages. Private businesses and agricultural industries put into action new technology—many developed during the war—to create new products and increase productivity and consumer spending.)*

BEFORE AND AFTER

The Baby Boom Changes the Nation

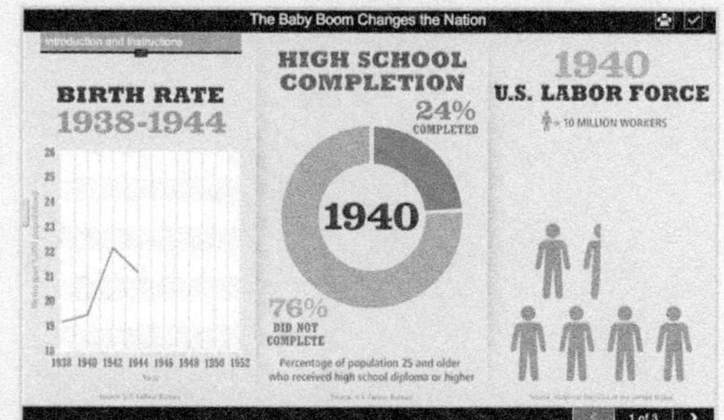

ACTIVE CLASSROOM

Conduct a Circle Write activity. Break students into groups and provide this question as a writing prompt: How did the Baby Boom improve life in postwar America? Have students write as much as they can for one minute then switch with the person on their right. The next person tries to improve or elaborate the response where the other person left off. Continue to switch until the paper comes back to the first person. The group then decides which is the best composition (or response) and shares that with the larger group.

ELL Use the ELL activity described in the ELL chart.

Further Instruction

Summarize What economic and political challenges did the United States face in the years immediately following World War II? *(Inflation, or rising prices, was a major postwar problem. Workers demanded higher wages to pay for the price increases but employers refused, pushing labor unions to call for strikes. Political divisions emerged between liberals and conservatives, who stopped many of President Truman's Fair Deal programs.)*

Contrast How did President Eisenhower differ from President Truman on how to boost the economy? *(Eisenhower believed in limiting federal spending and reducing federal regulation of the economy.)*

Eisenhower and Postwar America

Draw Conclusions What was the impact of technological innovations, such as the computer, on business and labor? *(Technology and computers made workers and companies more efficient and productive. High productivity allowed the United States to manufacture and consume more goods.)*

DIGITAL TEXT 2

Life in the 1950s

Text 2: Life in the 1950s

Life in the 1950s

The economic boom raised Americans' **standard of living**, a measurement that determines how well people live based on the amount of goods, services, and leisure time people have. Americans bought washing machines, vacuum cleaners, televisions, automobiles, and many other consumer goods.

Public confidence in the United States replaced much of the financial worries associated with the Great Depression and World War II. Because so many of their purchases revolved around home and family, few Americans worried that they were saving little. Instead, most Americans enjoyed a life in which they had more money to spend. This consumer spending reshaped the country.

The New Suburbs With their newfound wealth, many people bought homes in the **suburbs**, or communities outside the cities. The GI Bill encouraged home building in the suburbs by offering low-interest loans to veterans. During the 1950s, suburbs grew 40 times faster than cities.

Homeownership, 1940-1960

>> Analyze Graphs Explain how the data on homeownership relates to standard of living.

ELL 1 of 7

Objective 3: Explain how American lifestyles changed in the 1950s.

Quick Instruction

Interactive Gallery: Life in the 1950s Project the Interactive Gallery and navigate through the images with students to reveal some of the significant changes in American society in the 1950s. Invite volunteers to share what they know about elements of American society shown in the gallery.

Generate Explanations What impact did increased automobile usage have on the American family and society in the 1950s? *(Cars allowed people to move to the suburbs and drive to work. As American suburbs grew, cities entered a long decline. Cars also created new ways of shopping, such as the mall. Drive-in theaters became popular. New roads and highways created better and more efficient transportation networks and brought regions closer together.)*

ACTIVE CLASSROOM

Conduct a Wallpaper activity. Have each student design a piece of "wallpaper" that encapsulates a significant change in American society in the 1950s. Post student work on the walls and have the class take a gallery walk to note what others have written or illustrated. Ask volunteers to defend the rationale for their wallpaper to further class discussion.

INTERACTIVE GALLERY

Life in the 1950s

D Differentiate: Challenge Encourage students to do additional research on Chuck Berry or another early pioneer of rock-and-roll. Suggest that they locate photographs and write a few lines describing the performer's key contributions. Have students present their findings.

ELL Use the ELL activity described in the ELL chart.

Further Instruction

Identify Central Issues What economic effect did the development of suburbs have on many cities throughout the United States? *(Urban populations began to decrease as more people moved to suburbs, leaving cities with less businesses and tax revenue from residents.)*

Make Generalizations How did the emergence and popularity of rock-and-roll and the Beatniks influence young Americans? *(Rock-and-roll and the views of the Beatniks provide opportunities and role models for young Americans to embrace their individuality.)*

SYNTHESIZE

DIGITAL ACTIVITY

Life in Postwar America

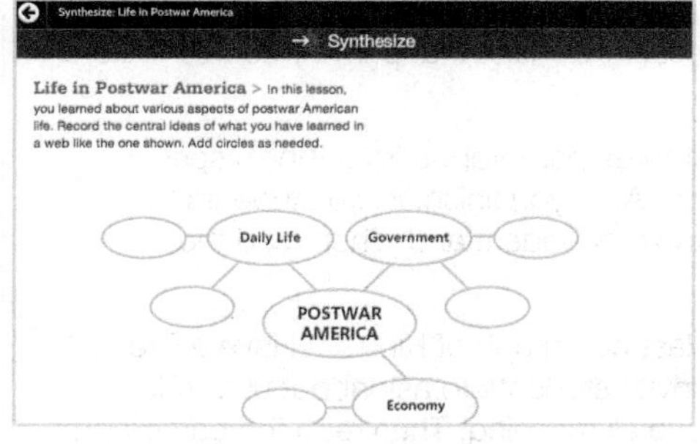

Synthesize: Life in Postwar America
→ Synthesize
Life in Postwar America > In this lesson, you learned about various aspects of postwar American life. Record the central ideas of what you have learned in a web like the one shown. Add circles as needed.
Daily Life
Government
POSTWAR AMERICA
Economy

Discuss Before students begin their graphic organizers, lead a brief discussion about how the United States transitioned from a wartime to a peacetime economy. Then ask students to reflect on the following questions to help them get started:

- How did inflation affect the postwar economy?
- What was the relationship between cars and the suburbs?
- How did the changes of the 1950s improve the lives of most Americans?

DEMONSTRATE

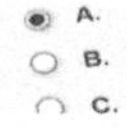

DIGITAL QUIZ

Lesson Quiz and Class Discussion Board

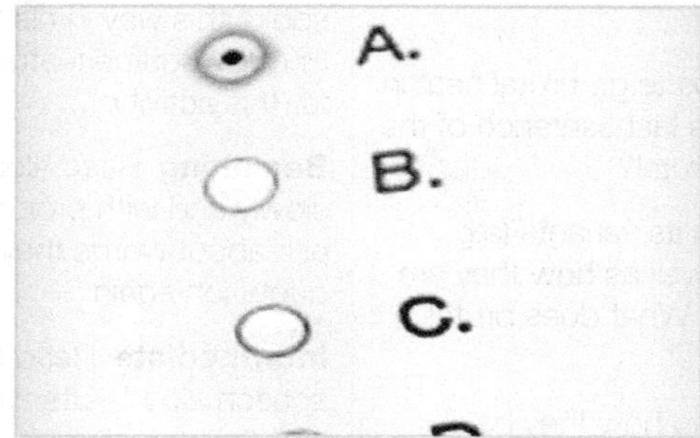

Assign the online Lesson Quiz for this lesson if you haven't already done so. Students will be offered automatic remediation or enrichment based on their score.

Pose these questions to the class on the Discussion Board:

In *Eisenhower and Postwar America*, you read about how American transitioned from a wartime to a peacetime economy and how the actions the government and private sector took created a changing yet robust economy. By enacting the GI Bill of Rights and spending more money to build new roads, houses, and schools, the government helped boost the economy. New technologies and the emergence of the automobile led to increased consumerism.

Make Predictions How long will America's economy continue to grow and what factors might impact it in the 1950s?

Make Predictions What will be the political impact of millions of Americans migrating to the Sunbelt?

Topic Inquiry

Have students continue their investigations for the Topic Inquiry.

Topic 15 Lesson 4

Civil Rights

Supporting English Language Learners

Use with the reading, **Discrimination Continues.**

Learning

Explain that students can sometimes determine a word's meaning by using what they already know, such as word variants, context clues, and word parts.

Beginning Explain the word *brutal* in a familiar context (e.g., brutal heat in summer). Then have them apply this knowledge to the last sentence of the text's first paragraph. Ask: What is another word for brutal?

Intermediate Display the word *brutal* and brainstorm its variants (e.g., brute, brutality). Discuss what these words mean, as well as how they are related. Then reread the first paragraph together. Ask: What does brutal mean in this context?

Advanced Ask pairs of students to discuss where and how they have heard the word *coordinated* used (e.g., to describe clothing). Then have them locate the phrase *coordinated demonstrations* and apply their prior knowledge to defining it.

Advanced High Have pairs of students read the first two sentences of the text's third paragraph and discuss these questions: What does the prefix *sub-* mean? What might it mean to be *subject* to a law? Invite students to consider whether all of their prior knowledge (e.g., of school subjects) would have been helpful in this situation.

Use with the reading, **The Crusade for Equality Continues.**

Listening

Explain that sometimes a speaker is not only trying to communicate but to do so in a poetic or moving way. Explain that Martin Luther King, Jr., spoke this way in his "I Have a Dream" speech, part of which appears as a Primary Source feature in this lesson. Consult that primary source feature for this activity.

Beginning Read aloud the first three paragraphs from King's speech slowly and with proper intonation. After you finish, invite students to ask about words they did not know or understand. Then read the quotation again.

Intermediate Read the entire last paragraph of King's "I Have a Dream" speech aloud. After you finish, invite students to ask about unfamiliar words, confusing phrasing, or overall meaning. Then read the paragraph again.

Advanced Read the full selection from King's "I Have a Dream" speech. Pause periodically so students can ask clarifying questions about what you said. After you finish, invite them to ask general questions about the speech's overall meaning.

Advanced High Play a recording of some or all of King's "I Have a Dream" speech. Encourage students to jot down confusing words or phrases as they listen to the speech and to ask questions about their notes after the recording has played.

D Differentiate Instruction

Use the Differentiated Instruction notes throughout the lesson plan to support the varied skill sets, levels of readiness, and interests in the mixed-ability classroom.

Challenge These notes include suggestions for expanding the activity for advanced students.

On-Level These notes include suggestions for modifying the activity to address different interests or learning styles.

Extra Support These notes include ideas for providing more scaffolding or reading spuport.

Special Needs These notes provide ideas for adapting instruction to support the needs of various special needs students.

NOTES

Objectives

Objective 1: Explain how discrimination affected the lives of minorities in the United States.

Objective 2: Summarize how the courts, protests, and boycotts helped minority groups achieve greater rights.

Objective 3: Describe the role of Martin Luther King, Jr., in the Civil Rights movement.

Objective 4: Compare how different minority groups tried to achieve equal rights.

LESSON 4 ORGANIZER — PACING: APPROX. 1 PERIOD, .5 BLOCKS	OBJECTIVES	PACING	RESOURCES Online	RESOURCES Print
Connect				
DIGITAL START UP ACTIVITY **Segregation in the United States**		5 min.	●	
Investigate				
DIGITAL TEXT 1 **Discrimination Continues**	Objective 1	10 min.	●	●
DIGITAL TEXT 2 **The Legal Struggle for Equality**	Objectives 2, 3	10 min.	●	●
DIGITAL TEXT 3 **The Montgomery Bus Boycott**	Objectives 2, 3	10 min.	●	●
DIGITAL TEXT 4 **The Crusade for Equality Continues**	Objectives 2, 3	10 min.	●	●
INTERACTIVE GALLERY **Nonviolent Strategies in the Civil Rights Movement**	Objectives 2, 3	10 min.	●	
DIGITAL TEXT 5 **Other Minorities Fight for Equality**	Objective 4	10 min.	●	●
DIGITAL TEXT 6 **The Women's and Gay Rights Movements**	Objective 4	10 min.	●	●
INTERACTIVE GALLERY **Leaders for Change**	Objective 4	10 min.	●	
Synthesize				
DIGITAL ACTIVITY **Steps Toward Equality**		5 min.	●	
Demonstrate				
DIGITAL QUIZ **Lesson Quiz and Class Discussion Board**		10 min.	●	

Topic 15 Lesson 4

Civil Rights

CONNECT

DIGITAL START UP ACTIVITY

Segregation in the United States

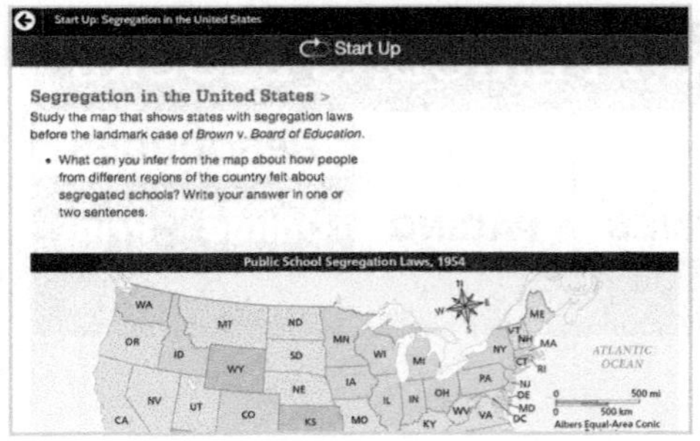

Project the Start Up Activity Ask students to analyze the map as they enter and get settled. Then have them answer the question. Have students share their ideas with a partner.

Discuss Take a moment to reflect on how segregation has affected African Americans over time. *(Student responses should show their understanding about how views of segregation have evolved over the last several decades.)*

Tell students that in this lesson they will be learning about the development of the civil rights movement.

Aa Vocabulary Development: Use the Interactive Reading Notepad to preview the Key Terms and Academic Vocabulary in this lesson with students.

FLIP IT!

Assign the Flipped Video for this lesson.

STUDENT EDITION PRINT PAGES: 819–835

INVESTIGATE

DIGITAL TEXT 1

Discrimination Continues

Text 1: Discrimination Continues

Discrimination Continues

From the late 1940s to the 1970s, the United States witnessed profound changes in civil rights. Mass protests and coordinated demonstrations made it clear that discrimination against minorities would no longer be tolerated. But full equality would take time, and the struggle to get there would often be brutal.

Discrimination Against African Americans and Mexican Americans Throughout the nation, discrimination limited the lives of millions of Americans. Qualified African Americans found themselves barred from good jobs and decent housing in the North. In the South, laws enforced strict **segregation**, or separation, of the races in schools, theaters, restaurants, and other public places. Facilities for blacks were inferior to those for whites.

Discrimination also limited Mexican Americans and other Latinos. They were not subject to strict segregation laws. However, other laws—as well as traditions—worked against them. In the Southwest, all-white schools closed their doors to Mexican American children. Instead, poorly equipped "Mexican schools" served them. Custom kept Mexican Americans from living in certain neighborhoods or using certain hotels or restaurants. Often, better-paying jobs were not open to them.

>> Racial discrimination took on many forms. African Americans were forced to use segregated bathrooms and water coolers as seen in this 1939 photo.

Objective 1: Explain how discrimination affected the lives of minorities in the United States.

Quick Instruction

Project the digital image of the segregated water cooler. Ask: What does the image tell you about life in the South for African Americans? *(Sample answers: segregation was widespread; it affected every part of life.)* Review the words *segregation* and *discrimination*.

Support Ideas with Examples What examples in the text support the idea that discrimination existed throughout the country? *(African Americans were barred from good jobs and decent housing in the North. In the South, laws enforced strict segregation in schools, theaters, restaurants, and other public places. In the Southwest, all-white schools closed their doors to Mexican American children, and many Mexican Americans were denied better paying jobs and were unable to live in certain neighborhoods or attend certain schools.)*

ELL Use the ELL activity described in the ELL chart.

Further Instruction

Go through the Interactive Reading Notepad questions and use appropriate questions to discuss key leaders and events in the Civil Rights Movement. Be sure students can trace the historical development of the Civil Rights Movement beginning in the 1940s and 1950s.

Infer Why did Thurgood Marshall and the NAACP go to court to fight against segregation? *(Marshall and the NAACP wanted to end segregation by challenging existing laws. Their long-term goal was to achieve equality for African Americans.)*

DIGITAL TEXT 2

The Legal Struggle for Equality

DIGITAL TEXT 3

The Montgomery Bus Boycott

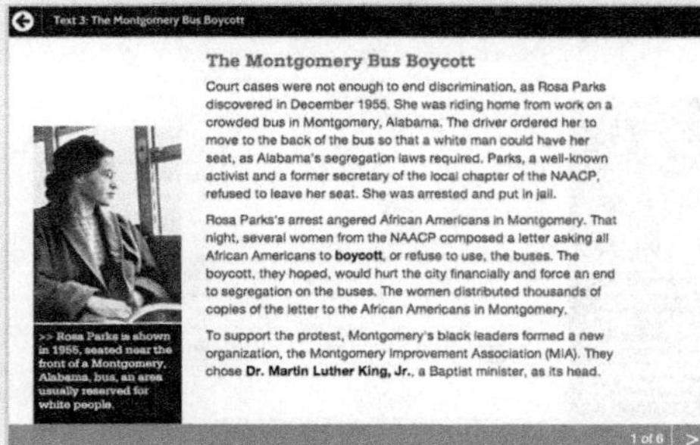

Text 3: The Montgomery Bus Boycott
The Montgomery Bus Boycott
Court cases were not enough to end discrimination, as Rosa Parks discovered in December 1955. She was riding home from work on a crowded bus in Montgomery, Alabama. The driver ordered her to move to the back of the bus so that a white man could have her seat, as Alabama's segregation laws required. Parks, a well-known activist and a former secretary of the local chapter of the NAACP, refused to leave her seat. She was arrested and put in jail.
Rosa Parks's arrest angered African Americans in Montgomery. That night, several women from the NAACP composed a letter asking all African Americans to boycott, or refuse to use, the buses. The boycott, they hoped, would hurt the city financially and force an end to segregation on the buses. The women distributed thousands of copies of the letter to the African Americans in Montgomery.
To support the protest, Montgomery's black leaders formed a new organization, the Montgomery Improvement Association (MIA). They chose Dr. Martin Luther King, Jr., a Baptist minister, as its head.
>> Rosa Parks is shown in 1955, seated near the front of a Montgomery, Alabama, bus, an area usually reserved for white people.
1 of 6

DIGITAL TEXT 4

The Crusade for Equality Continues

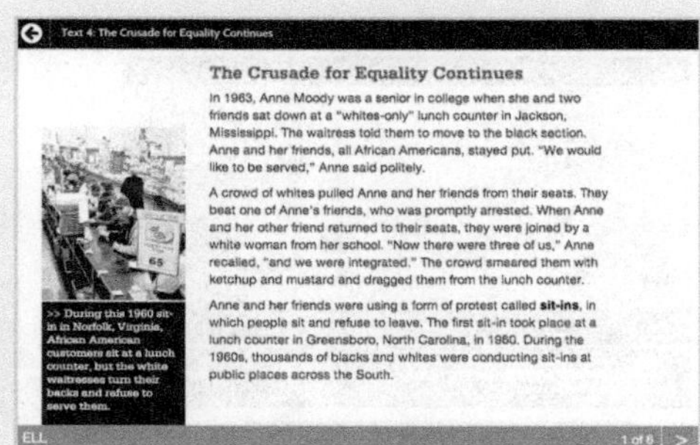

Text 4: The Crusade for Equality Continues
The Crusade for Equality Continues
In 1963, Anne Moody was a senior in college when she and two friends sat down at a "whites-only" lunch counter in Jackson, Mississippi. The waitress told them to move to the black section. Anne and her friends, all African Americans, stayed put. "We would like to be served," Anne said politely.
A crowd of whites pulled Anne and her friends from their seats. They beat one of Anne's friends, who was promptly arrested. When Anne and her other friend returned to their seats, they were joined by a white woman from her school. "Now there were three of us," Anne recalled, "and we were integrated." The crowd smeared them with ketchup and mustard and dragged them from the lunch counter.
Anne and her friends were using a form of protest called sit-ins, in which people sit and refuse to leave. The first sit-in took place at a lunch counter in Greensboro, North Carolina, in 1960. During the 1960s, thousands of blacks and whites were conducting sit-ins at public places across the South.
>> During this 1960 sit-in in Norfolk, Virginia, African American customers sit at a lunch counter, but the white waitresses turn their backs and refuse to serve them.
ELL
1 of 6

Objectives 2: Summarize how the courts, protests, and boycotts helped minority groups achieve greater rights; 3: Describe the role of Martin Luther King, Jr., in the Civil Rights Movement.

Quick Instruction

Interactive Gallery: Nonviolent Strategies in the Civil Rights Movement Project the Interactive Gallery and navigate through the images as you prompt students to identify specific nonviolent strategies. What details in some of the images suggest that some of the protests may have been threatened by violence? *(Soldiers or police are present at several protests, indicating a threat of violence or arrest. The sit-in protesters are surrounded by a hostile crowd and look to be covered in food thrown by those opposed to the sit-in.)*

Express Problems Clearly How were many states and local school boards able to delay integrating their schools? *(In the Brown decision, the Court ordered the schools to be desegregated "with all deliberate speed." In turn, many school boards decided that the phrase "with all deliberate speed" could mean they could take years to integrate their schools or refuse to obey the decision at all.)*

Determine Relevance What was the significance of the case of *Hernández* v. *Texas*? *(The Court ruled that Mexican Americans in Texas were denied equality under the law because they were excluded from juries. In the future, other minority groups would use this decision to help win their civil rights.)*

ACTIVE CLASSROOM

Conduct an Act It Out activity. Review the images and information about protest strategies. Then challenge students to create a short sketch using one of the images from the gallery that "brings the picture to life" by depicting appropriate challenges faced by the protesters (e.g., counter-demonstrations, threat of violence or arrest). Encourage students to emphasize the power of nonviolent protests in their actions.

ELL Use the ELL activity described in the ELL chart.

Civil Rights

INTERACTIVE GALLERY

Nonviolent Strategies in the Civil Rights Movement

Nonviolent Strategies in the Civil Rights Movement
Picketing
FREEDOM
Picketing was part of an overall civil disobedience strategy used during the civil rights movement. These picketers are carrying signs for equal rights, integrated schools, decent housing, and an end to bias.
1 of 3

DIGITAL TEXT 5

Other Minorities Fight for Equality

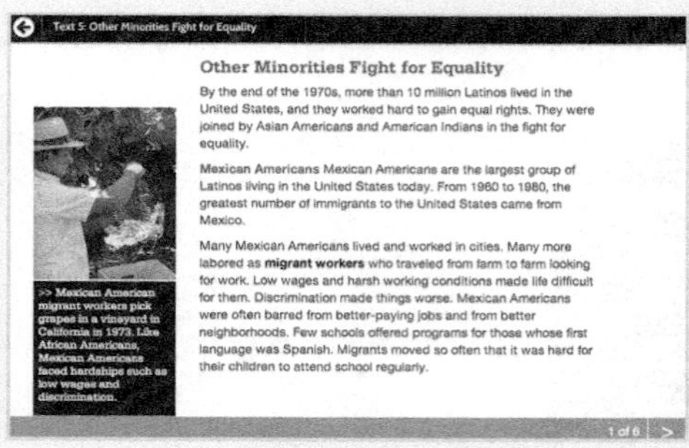

Text 5: Other Minorities Fight for Equality
Other Minorities Fight for Equality
By the end of the 1970s, more than 10 million Latinos lived in the United States, and they worked hard to gain equal rights. They were joined by Asian Americans and American Indians in the fight for equality.
Mexican Americans Mexican Americans are the largest group of Latinos living in the United States today. From 1960 to 1980, the greatest number of immigrants to the United States came from Mexico.
Many Mexican Americans lived and worked in cities. Many more labored as migrant workers who traveled from farm to farm looking for work. Low wages and harsh working conditions made life difficult for them. Discrimination made things worse. Mexican Americans were often barred from better-paying jobs and from better neighborhoods. Few schools offered programs for those whose first language was Spanish. Migrants moved so often that it was hard for their children to attend school regularly.
>> Mexican American migrant workers pick grapes in a vineyard in California in 1973. Like African Americans, Mexican Americans faced hardships such as low wages and discrimination.
1 of 6

DIGITAL TEXT 6

The Women's and Gay Rights Movements

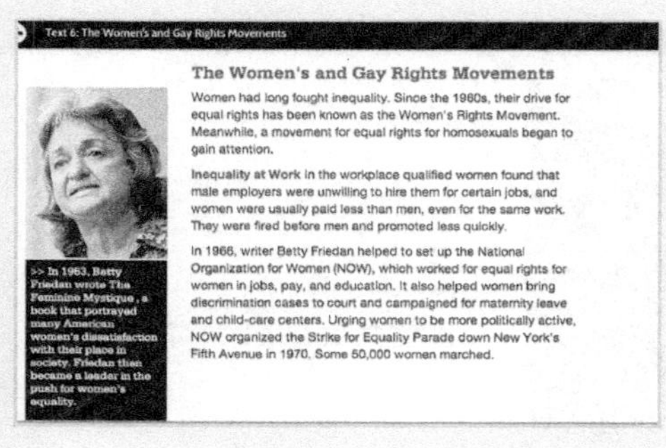

Further Instruction

Draw Conclusions Why do you think the Montgomery bus boycott used both nonviolent protesting and litigation as methods of expanding civil rights? *(Nonviolent protesting drew public attention to the injustices of segregation, putting social and economic pressure on the city. Bringing the issue to court provided a legal means for segregation laws to change.)*

Generate Explanations What qualities led Martin Luther King, Jr., to become an influential leader in the civil rights struggles? *(King was well educated and served as pastor of an African American church in Montgomery. He built his following by promoting social change through peaceful means.)*

Contrast How were Malcolm X's early ideas different from those of Martin Luther King, Jr.? *(Malcolm X advocated separation of races, while King believed in integration.)*

Objective 4: **Compare how different groups tried to achieve equal rights.**

Quick Instruction

Interactive Gallery: Leaders for Change Project the Interactive Gallery and navigate through the images as you prompt students to identify the political, social, and economic contributions of civil rights leaders to American society. Initiate a discussion about the various minority groups fighting for equal rights. Ask: What issues did Latinos face in the United States? *(Immigrants from Mexico, Puerto Rico, and Cuba, faced harsh working conditions. Mexican Americans were often barred from better-paying jobs and from better neighborhoods. Puerto Ricans faced discrimination in housing and jobs. Immigrants from Cuba were unskilled; they had a hard time making a living.)*

Express Problems Clearly What issues led many American Indians to push for full rights? *(Although the federal government had agreed to many treaties with American Indian groups, it failed to honor them. The government also tried to break up tribal governments and encouraged American Indians to leave the reservations. Traditional Indian customs were weakened because more than half of all American Indians lived off the reservations.)*

ACTIVE CLASSROOM

Conduct a Rank It activity. List the following names of reform leaders on the board: Cesar Chavez, Harry Hay, Rosa Parks, Russell Means, Betty Friedan, and Lyndon B. Johnson. Ask students to rank the leaders according to who had the greatest impact. Ask students to provide a justification for the ranking decisions they made. Then ask students to work in pairs to share their rankings and justifications. Poll the class to see if there is agreement on the ranking.

D Differentiate: Extra Support To help students remember the groups that struggled for their rights that they have learned about in this lesson, have them create a table listing each group in one column and important details about each group's struggle in a second column.

Further Instruction

Evaluate Arguments What arguments did opponents of the ERA make? Why might some have disagreed with those arguments? *(Opponents of the ERA argued that the amendment would lead to women being drafted into the military and would harm the traditional family. Proponents of the law may have argued that women would not be drafted or that if they were drafted it would be a positive step. Opponents of the law argued that it would harm the traditional family. Proponents of the law may have argued that it would be good to change some aspects of traditional family life.)*

INTERACTIVE GALLERY

Leaders for Change

Connect What happened at the Stonewall Inn in 1969? How does this event continue to affect life in the United States today? *(In 1969, the New York City police raided a bar that was a gathering place for homosexuals. Bar patrons resisted, rioting against the police. Their actions were controversial at the time. This riot encouraged others to fight for gay rights. gay, lesbian, bisexual, and transgender Americans continue to fight for equality today. That fight remains controversial.)*

SYNTHESIZE

DIGITAL ACTIVITY

Steps Toward Equality

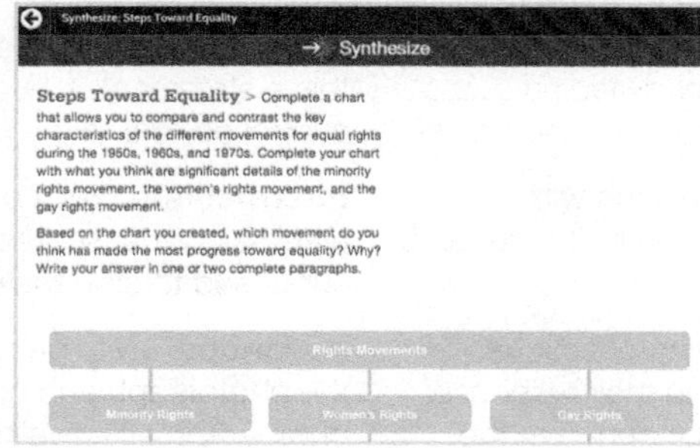

Synthesize: Steps Toward Equality
Synthesize
Steps Toward Equality > Complete a chart that allows you to compare and contrast the key characteristics of the different movements for equal rights during the 1950s, 1960s, and 1970s. Complete your chart with what you think are significant details of the minority rights movement, the women's rights movement, and the gay rights movement.
Based on the chart you created, which movement do you think has made the most progress toward equality? Why? Write your answer in one or two complete paragraphs.
Rights Movements
Minority Rights
Women's Rights
Gay Rights

Provide time for students to review the lesson to aid them in creating their charts. Inform them that their charts are not expected to be comprehensive but should instead reflect the most important details of the three civil rights movements.

Discuss Invite volunteers to share some of the details from their charts, focusing on the impact of the details. As a class, try to develop a list of details that reflect a consensus in thinking. Encourage students to revise their paragraphs using information from the class discussion.

DEMONSTRATE

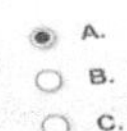

DIGITAL QUIZ

Lesson Quiz and Class Discussion Board

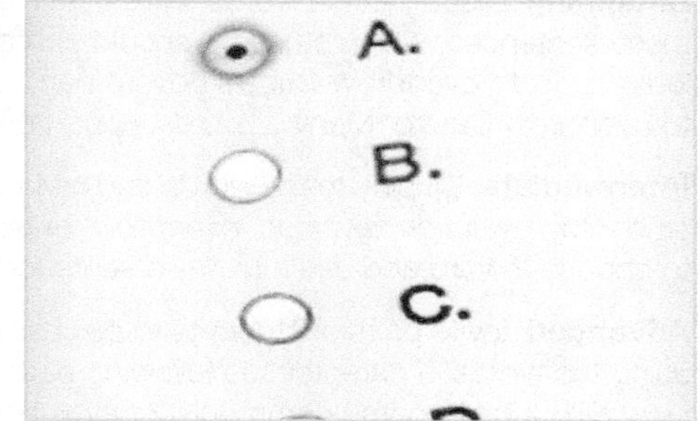

Assign the online Lesson Quiz for this lesson if you haven't already done so. Students will be offered automatic remediation or enrichment based on their score.

Pose these questions to the class on the Discussion Board:

In *Civil Rights*, you learned about how the growing discontent with inequality after World War II accelerated the civil rights movement in the United States. Significant steps towards equality for all Americans were made during this period.

Hypothesize Although laws and Constitutional amendments *legally* ended segregation and explicit discrimination, why did minorities continue to face challenges in gaining full equality?

Support Ideas with Examples Why are boycotts an effective means of protest?

Topic Inquiry

Have students continue their investigations for the Topic Inquiry.

Kennedy, Johnson, and Vietnam

Supporting English Language Learners

Use with the reading, **Communist Cuba.**

Speaking

Remind students that one of the best ways to grasp new and challenging vocabulary words is to practice using them.

Beginning Display these words: *exiles, revolution, invasion.* Then display these sentences, which students should complete and say aloud: Castro led a _____ to overthrow Cuba's government. Then Kennedy led an _____ to overthrow Castro. Many _____ escaped from Cuba to the United States.

Intermediate Display these words and review their meanings with students: *revolution, invasion, overthrow, exiles, crisis*. Then invite students to choose a word and use it to say a sentence about the text.

Advanced Invite pairs of students to discuss the following questions, using the words in parentheses following each question in their response: How did Cuba become communist? *(revolution)* What happened at the Bay of Pigs? *(invasion, overthrow)* What happened when the Soviet Union became involved with Cuba? *(crisis)*

Advanced High Display these words: *revolution, invasion, overthrow, exiles, crisis*. Invite students to use all of these words in describing the key events involving Cuba, the United States, and the Soviet Union during the Kennedy Administration.

Use with the reading, **Protests at Home.**

Reading

Display the photograph of young men and women protesting the Vietnam War. Review background facts about this photograph (e.g., the protest was directed at the U.S. government; it took place at the White House).

Beginning Point out the text in the rightmost sign: *End the draft!* Ask: Is this a statement, a question, or a command? Who is speaking? Who is supposed to end the draft? What is a draft?

Intermediate Point out the text in the leftmost sign: *No more . . . Stop the war!* Ask: What sentence type is *Stop the war!*? Who is speaking? Who is supposed to stop the war?

Advanced Invite pairs of students to read each of the three signs in the photograph and discuss their meanings. Ask: Are the signs in the photograph effective? Why or why not?

Advanced High Ask pairs of students to discuss the meaning of the middle sign. Then have them research Eartha Kitt and the Vietnam War and answer these questions: What does the sign mean to you now? Do you think Eartha Kitt's comments were well known in 1968? Why or why not?

D Differentiate Instruction

Use the Differentiated Instruction notes throughout the lesson plan to support the varied skill sets, levels of readiness, and interests in the mixed-ability classroom.

Challenge These notes include suggestions for expanding the activity for advanced students.

On-Level These notes include suggestions for modifying the activity to address different interests or learning styles.

Extra Support These notes include ideas for providing more scaffolding or reading spuport.

Special Needs These notes provide ideas for adapting instruction to support the needs of various special needs students.

NOTES

Go online to access additional resources including: Primary Sources • Biographies • Supreme Court cases • 21st Century Skill Tutorials • Maps • Graphic Organizers.

PEARSON realize
www.PearsonRealize.com

Objectives

Objective 1: Summarize the accomplishments of President Kennedy.

Objective 2: Summarize the accomplishments of President Johnson, including his "Great Society."

Objective 3: Explain why the United States became involved in the Vietnam War.

Objective 4: Describe the early years of the Vietnam War.

Objective 5: Describe American protests of the Vietnam War and explain the counterculture that developed during this era.

LESSON 5 ORGANIZER — **PACING: APPROX. 1 PERIOD, .5 BLOCKS**

	OBJECTIVES	PACING	RESOURCES Online	RESOURCES Print
Connect				
DIGITAL START UP ACTIVITY **Nuclear Missiles Close to Home**		5 min.	●	
Investigate				
DIGITAL TEXT 1 **A New President**	Objective 1	10 min.	●	●
DIGITAL TEXT 2 **Communist Cuba**	Objective 1	10 min.	●	●
DIGITAL TEXT 3 **Reforms and Progress**	Objective 1	10 min.	●	●
INTERACTIVE TIMELINE **Confronting Cuba**	Objective 1	10 min.	●	
DIGITAL TEXT 5 **The Vietnam War Begins**	Objectives 3, 4	10 min.	●	●
INTERACTIVE CHART **Hawks and Doves**	Objectives 3, 4	10 min.	●	
DIGITAL TEXT 4 **Johnson's Great Society**	Objective 2	10 min.	●	●
DIGITAL TEXT 6 **Protests at Home**	Objective 5	10 min.	●	●
Synthesize				
DIGITAL ACTIVITY **Implications of the Vietnam War**		5 min.	●	
Demonstrate				
DIGITAL QUIZ **Lesson Quiz and Class Discussion Board**		10 min.	●	

Kennedy, Johnson, and Vietnam

CONNECT

DIGITAL START UP ACTIVITY

Nuclear Missiles Close to Home

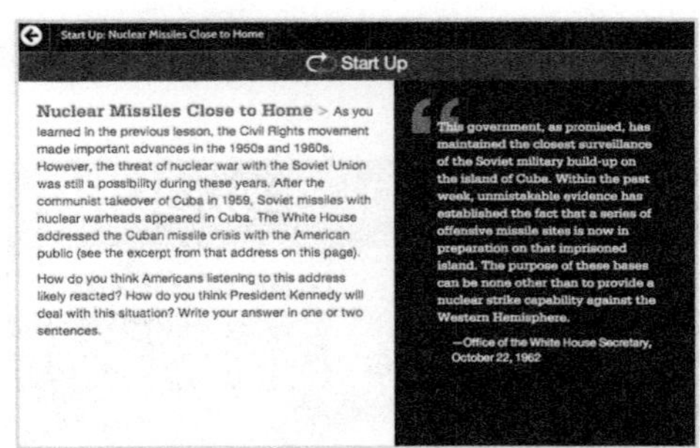

Project the Start Up Activity Ask students to answer the questions as they get settled. Then have them share their ideas with another student.

Discuss How does the White House Secretary's quote relate to many American's fears during the early years of the Cold War? *(Many Americans were concerned about the spread of communism and the potential of military conflict.)*

Tell students that in this lesson they will be learning about President Kennedy's and President Johnson's domestic and foreign policies, and the early course of the Vietnam War and its effects on the nation.

Aa Vocabulary Development: Use the Interactive Reading Notepad to preview the Key Terms and Academic Vocabulary in this lesson with students.

FLIP IT!

Assign the Flipped Video for this lesson.

STUDENT EDITION PRINT PAGES: 836–848

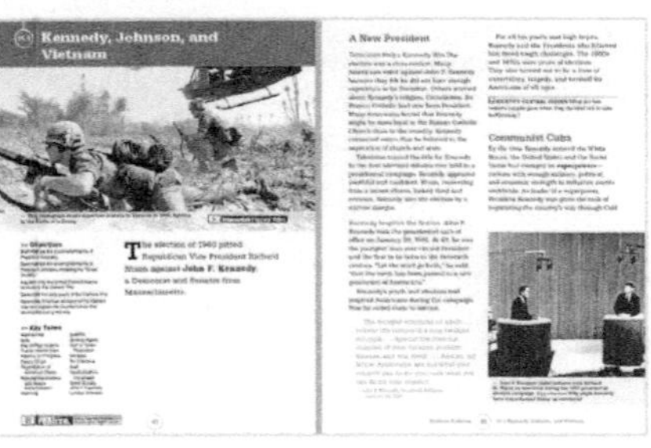

INVESTIGATE

DIGITAL TEXT 1

A New President

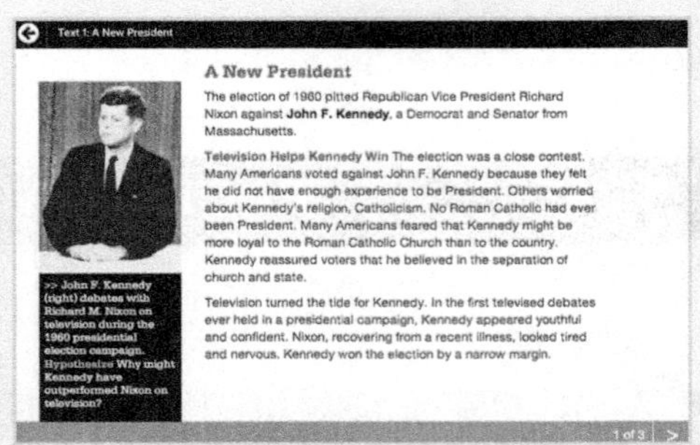

DIGITAL TEXT 2

Communist Cuba

Text 2: Communist Cuba

Communist Cuba

By the time Kennedy entered the White House, the United States and the Soviet Union had emerged as **superpowers**—nations with enough military, political, and economic strength to influence events worldwide. As leader of a superpower, President Kennedy was given the task of negotiating the country's way through Cold War crises. In fact, the rivalry between the superpowers led to clashes in many places, including Cuba, an island in the Caribbean very close to the United States.

In 1959, Fidel Castro led a revolution that set up a communist state in Cuba. Castro's government took over private companies, including many owned by American businesses. Thousands of Cubans, especially those from the upper and middle classes, fled to the United States.

>> Fidel Castro (center) was a revolutionary leader who turned Cuba into the first communist state in the western hemisphere. Here, Castro is seen giving a speech on January 8, 1959, after entering Havana to take control of the Cuban government.

ELL 1 of 4 >

Objective 1: Summarize the accomplishments of President Kennedy.

Quick Instruction

Interactive Timeline: Confronting Cuba Project the Interactive Timeline and navigate through the images as you prompt students to understand the conflict's escalation and eventual resolution. How did the failed Bay of Pigs invasion heighten tensions between the United States and the Soviet Union? *(The failed invasion strengthened Castro in Cuba and motivated the Soviet Union to give Cuba more weapons, eventually leading to the Cuban Missile Crisis.)*

Infer How did televised coverage of the 1960 election change political campaigns and presidential elections? *(Television coverage forced campaigns to direct more focus on how their candidates looked.)*

Interpret What do you think Kennedy meant when he said, "the torch has been passed to a new generation of Americans"? *(As the youngest person ever elected president, Kennedy wanted to set an optimistic and forward-looking tone to continue the progress the nation had made since the end of World War II.)*

ACTIVE CLASSROOM

Direct students to have a "Conversation with President Kennedy." Tell students to imagine that they are having a conversation with Kennedy as he is developing a plan to confront the Soviet Union over the Cuban Missile Crisis. Direct each student to write down a question he or she would like to ask, then how Kennedy would respond, and then what the student would say in response.

ELL Use the ELL activity described in the ELL chart.

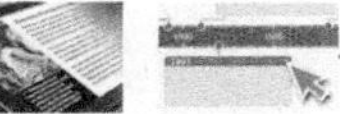

DIGITAL TEXT 3

Reforms and Progress

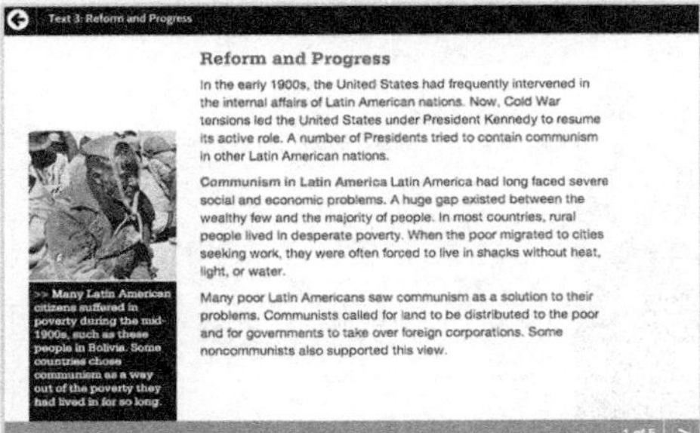

INTERACTIVE TIMELINE

Confronting Cuba

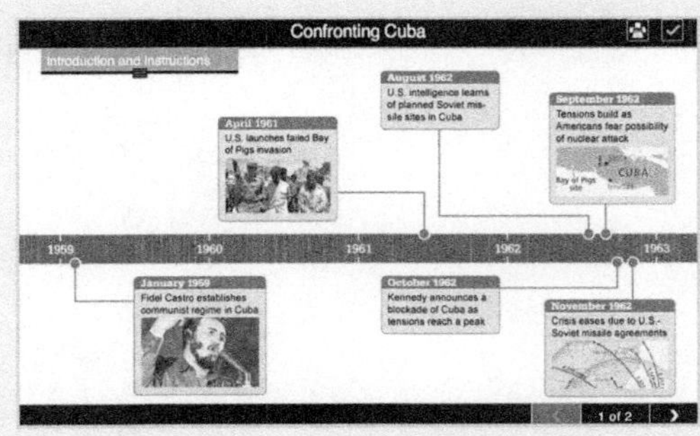

DIGITAL TEXT 5

The Vietnam War Begins

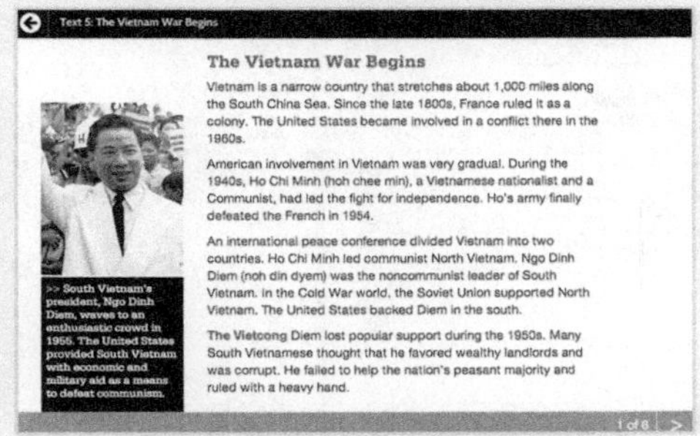

Further Instruction

Summarize the issues that led President Kennedy to get involved in Latin America. *(Latin America had long faced severe social and economic problems. Many rural people lived in poverty, and the gap between the wealthy few and the majority of people was huge. Kennedy and other U.S. leaders thought that many people in Latin America would turn to communism to try to overthrow governments.)*

Analyze Information How's does the creation of the Peace Corps reflect the vision Kennedy expressed in his inaugural address? *(The Peace Corps was made up of American volunteers who worked in developing countries as teachers, engineers, and technical advisers. Peace Corps workers had answered Kennedy's "trumpet call" to bear the burden of a long twilight struggle . . . against the common enemies of man: tyranny, poverty, disease, and war itself.)*

Objectives 3: **Explain why the United States became involved in the Vietnam War;** 4: **Describe the early years of the Vietnam War.**

Quick Instruction

Interactive Chart: Hawks and Doves Project the Interactive Chart and connect the terms *hawks* and *doves* with the quotes from Nixon and Kerry. Then prompt students to fill in the graphic organizer to interpret the quotes and compare the viewpoints of the hawks and doves. What generalizations can you make about doves and hawks? *(Hawks were concerned with America's status in the world, while doves viewed military action in Vietnam as unnecessary and hypocritical.)*

Connect Explain the relationship between the Domino Theory and American involvement in Vietnam. *(Many American leaders believed that if Vietnam became communist, other countries in the region would follow—like a row of falling dominoes. The United States became involved in Vietnam to try to stop the communists from taking control of the country and to prevent other countries from falling to communism.)*

Kennedy, Johnson, and Vietnam

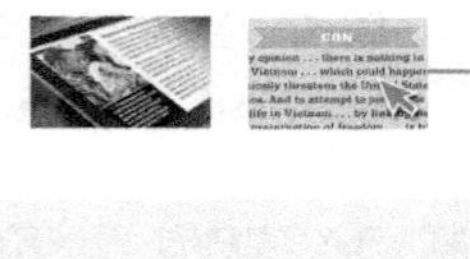

INTERACTIVE CHART

Hawks and Doves

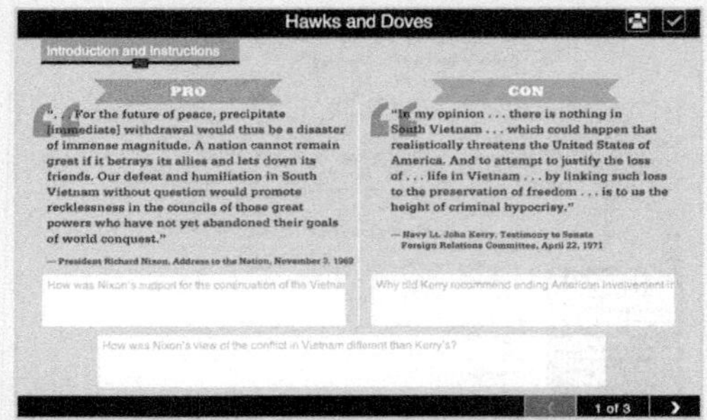

DIGITAL TEXT 4

Johnson's Great Society

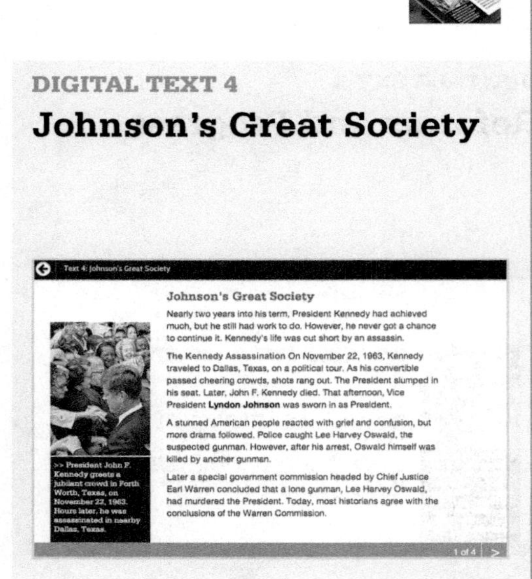

ACTIVE CLASSROOM

Conduct a Take a Stand activity. Ask students to take a stand on the following question: Were the doves justified in protesting against the Vietnam War? Ask students to divide into two groups based on their answers and move to separate areas of the classroom. Engage students in talking with each other to compare their reasons for answering yes or no. Ask a representative from each side to present and defend the group's point of view.

D Differentiate: On Level Encourage students to connect debate over American involvement in Vietnam with contemporary events, such as the wars in Iraq and Afghanistan, and the way in which U.S. foreign policy has been influenced by the different perspectives of hawks and doves.

Further Instruction

Draw Conclusions How did the Gulf of Tonkin Resolution change the scope of the war in Vietnam? *(After the resolution, the American role in the conflict expanded. Where previously President Johnson had provided military aid and advisers to South Vietnam, after the passage of the resolution he ordered the bombing of North Vietnam and Vietcong-held areas in the south and then sent more than 500,000 troops to fight in Vietnam.*

Summarize the challenges American troops faced fighting against guerilla tactics in the jungle. *(Because they used guerilla tactics and operated in the jungle, the Vietcong were hard to pin down. When Americans found an enemy stronghold, the guerrillas disappeared into the forest. When the Americans left, the Vietcong returned. American soldiers often could not distinguish between civilians and Vietcong.)*

Objective 2: **Summarize the accomplishments of President Johnson, including his "Great Society."**

Quick Instruction

Compare the domestic legislative records of Kennedy and Johnson in their first two years in office. *(Congress did not support Kennedy's poverty programs. However, Johnson was more persuasive. Johnson pushed 50 new laws through Congress in his first two years.)*

Draw Conclusions How would you describe Johnson's political skills based on the amount of legislation Congress passed during his first two years in office? *(Johnson was a skilled politician who knew how to get votes for his projects by persuading Congress using various methods.)*

Further Instruction

Generate Explanations What does Johnson's Great Society tell you about his views on the role of government? *(It suggests that Johnson thought the federal government should play a larger role in directly reducing poverty throughout the nation.)*

www.PearsonRealize.com
Access your Digital Lesson

DIGITAL TEXT 6

Protests at Home

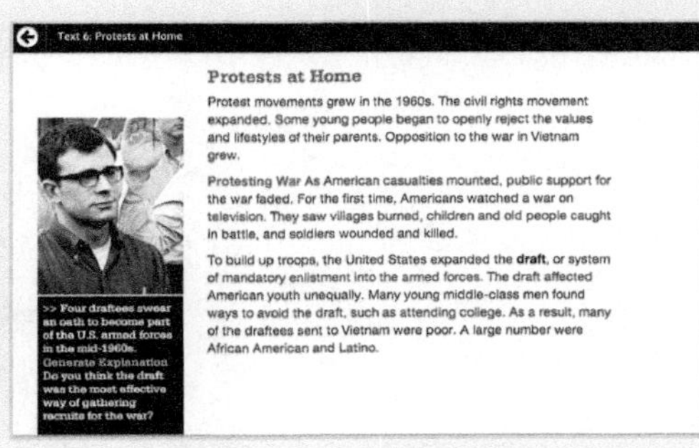

Text 6: Protests at Home
Protests at Home
Protest movements grew in the 1960s. The civil rights movement expanded. Some young people began to openly reject the values and lifestyles of their parents. Opposition to the war in Vietnam grew.
Protesting War As American casualties mounted, public support for the war faded. For the first time, Americans watched a war on television. They saw villages burned, children and old people caught in battle, and soldiers wounded and killed.
To build up troops, the United States expanded the draft, or system of mandatory enlistment into the armed forces. The draft affected American youth unequally. Many young middle-class men found ways to avoid the draft, such as attending college. As a result, many of the draftees sent to Vietnam were poor. A large number were African American and Latino.
>> Four draftees swear an oath to become part of the U.S. armed forces in the mid-1960s.
Generate Explanation
Do you think the draft was the most effective way of gathering recruits for the war?

Objective 5: **Describe American protests of the Vietnam War and explain the counterculture that developed during this era.**

Quick Instruction

Project the digital image of Vietnam War protesters outside the White House. Ask students to identify the issues that motivated many Americans to protest the war. *(increasing American casualties; television and other media coverage of the war; the inequalities of the draft)* Point out to students that the antiwar movement included many Americans who protested against the draft.

Determine Point of View Why did some American believe the draft unfairly targeted minorities and the poor? *(Critics of the draft thought that it was unfair because a large number of those drafted were working-class or poor men, many of whom were African American and Latino. Many young middle-class men found ways to avoid the draft, such as attending college.)*

Interpret What did Richard Nixon most likely mean when he promised "peace with honor" in Vietnam? *(Nixon probably wanted to end the war with a peace settlement, but did not want the United States to lose or appear to betray its allies or South Vietnam.)*

ELL Use the ELL activity described in the ELL chart.

Further Instruction

Generate Explanations Why might young Americans who joined the counterculture movement not want to mimic their parents' lifestyles? *(For some young Americans, their parents were seen as part of an establishment that supported escalating the war in Vietnam and opposed the Civil Rights movement. These young Americans rejected competition, the drive for personal success, and many traditional values.)*

Summarize the problems Democrats faced in the presidential election of 1968, leading to defeat. *(The antiwar movement was growing, resulting in a large drop in President Johnson's popularity. To avoid angry protesters, Johnson stayed in the White House and finally decided not to run for reelection. In addition, Robert Kennedy, a strong contender for the Democratic nomination was assassinated.)*

Kennedy, Johnson, and Vietnam

SYNTHESIZE

DIGITAL ACTIVITY

Implications of the Vietnam War

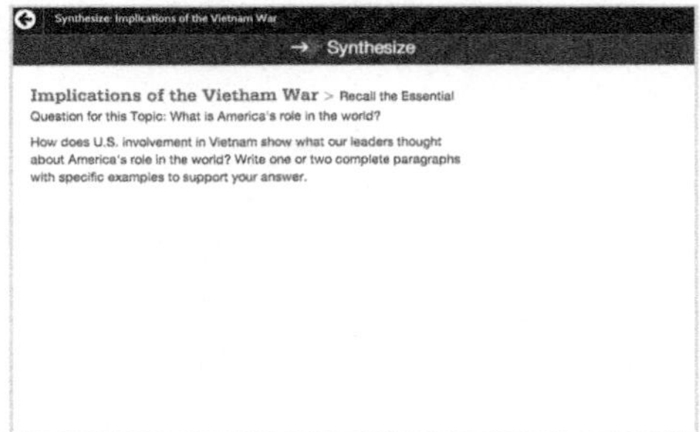

Ask students to recall the Topic Essential Question, "What is America's role in the world?" Have them use the Think Pair Share strategy to reflect on the question in the Activity. Encourage them to locate specific information in the Lesson to support their ideas. Provide time for students to individually write a response to the question using specific examples to support their answers. Have students share their answers with a talking partner.

Discuss Have partners think about the following question: Do you think American leaders were justified in sending American troops to fight in Vietnam? Have pairs share their answers with the class.

DEMONSTRATE

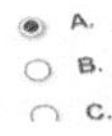

DIGITAL QUIZ

Lesson Quiz and Class Discussion Board

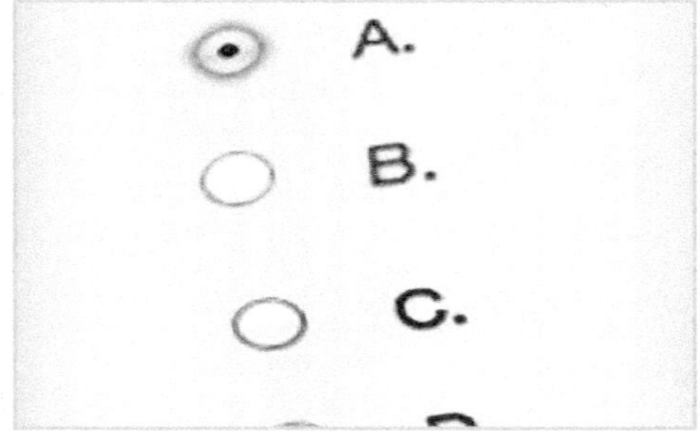

Assign the online Lesson Quiz for this lesson if you haven't already done so. Students will be offered automatic remediation or enrichment based on their score.

Pose these questions to the class on the Discussion Board:

In *Kennedy, Johnson, and Vietnam*, you learned that as Cold War tensions were increasing, Presidents John F. Kennedy and Lyndon Johnson supported reforms that transformed the nature of American society. Eventually, the threat of communism spreading led the United States into a long, deadly conflict in Vietnam. A deep divide opened between Americans who supported the war and those who opposed it.

Predict Consequences What impact do you think America's antiwar movement will have on the war effort and the military's ability to win?

Express Ideas Clearly Do you think the federal government should support programs to help the poor, even if they are expensive? Why or why not?

Topic Inquiry

Have students continue their investigations for the Topic Inquiry.

PEARSON realize www.PearsonRealize.com Access your Digital Lesson

The Nixon Years

Supporting English Language Learners

Use with the reading, **Nixon's Presidency.**

Learning

Remind students that when they cannot think of adequate words to express themselves, they can use non-verbal cues, synonyms, and circumlocution to help them communicate. Additionally, they can ask for assistance from others.

Beginning Reread the second paragraph of the text together. Ask: In your own words, what do you think *silent majority* means? Encourage students to support their speaking efforts by asking for assistance and using non-verbal gestures.

Intermediate With students, discuss the term *silent majority*. Encourage them to use language accessible to them, even if it is not as direct and efficient as they would like. If necessary, they can also ask for assistance.

Advanced Discuss stagflation and its relationship to inflation and stagnation with students. Encourage them to use synonyms and circumlocution as they define and compare these three words.

Advanced High Ask pairs of students to discuss the effects of stagflation on a nation and its citizens: How might daily life be affected? How might the government need to act? Encourage students to use gestures, synonyms, and circumlocution as they speak.

Use with the reading, **The Watergate Scandal.**

Listening

Explain that in the following activities, students will need to be engaged listeners so that they can answer questions and requests by the speaker as they arise.

Beginning Begin telling the events of the Watergate scandal using simple sentences. Then stop and ask students what happens next. Provide them with three possibilities from which to choose.

Intermediate Begin narrating the Watergate scandal. Then stop and ask students what happens next. After students have provided the next detail, continue your narration for a few sentences. Then stop and ask students what happens next. Repeat this process until the end of the narration.

Advanced Arrange students in a circle. Have a student begin narrating the Watergate scandal with one sentence and then ask the student to his or her right, "What happens next?" Continue this process of students adding sentences until the narration has finished or all students have contributed.

Advanced High Ask pairs of students to narrate the Watergate scandal together. Have one student begin with a few sentences and then ask his or her partner, "What happens next?" Have partners take turns narrating until the end of the narration is reached.

D Differentiate Instruction

Use the Differentiated Instruction notes throughout the lesson plan to support the varied skill sets, levels of readiness, and interests in the mixed-ability classroom.

Challenge These notes include suggestions for expanding the activity for advanced students.

On-Level These notes include suggestions for modifying the activity to address different interests or learning styles.

Extra Support These notes include ideas for providing more scaffolding or reading spuport.

Special Needs These notes provide ideas for adapting instruction to support the needs of various special needs students.

NOTES

The Nixon Years

Objectives

Objective 1: Summarize the accomplishments of President Nixon.

Objective 2: Explain how the Vietnam War ended and identify the results of the war.

Objective 3: Explain the Watergate scandal and why Nixon resigned from office.

LESSON 6 ORGANIZER	PACING: APPROX. 1 PERIOD, .5 BLOCKS		RESOURCES	
	OBJECTIVES	PACING	Online	Print
Connect				
DIGITAL START UP ACTIVITY **U.S. Troops in Vietnam**		5 min.	●	
Investigate				
DIGITAL TEXT 1 **Nixon's Presidency**	Objective 1	10 min.	●	●
DIGITAL TEXT 3 **Foreign Policy Decreases Tension**	Objective 1	10 min.	●	●
INTERACTIVE GALLERY **Apollo 11**	Objective 1	10 min.	●	
DIGITAL TEXT 2 **Nixon Addresses Vietnam**	Objective 2	10 min.	●	●
DIGITAL TEXT 4 **The Watergate Scandal**	Objective 3	10 min.	●	●
INTERACTIVE TIMELINE **Watergate**	Objective 3	10 min.	●	
Synthesize				
DIGITAL ACTIVITY **The Nixon Administration**		5 min.	●	
Demonstrate				
DIGITAL QUIZ **Lesson Quiz and Class Discussion Board**		10 min.	●	

Go online to access additional resources including: Primary Sources • Biographies • Supreme Court cases • 21st Century Skill Tutorials • Maps • Graphic Organizers.

CONNECT

DIGITAL START UP ACTIVITY

U.S. Troops in Vietnam

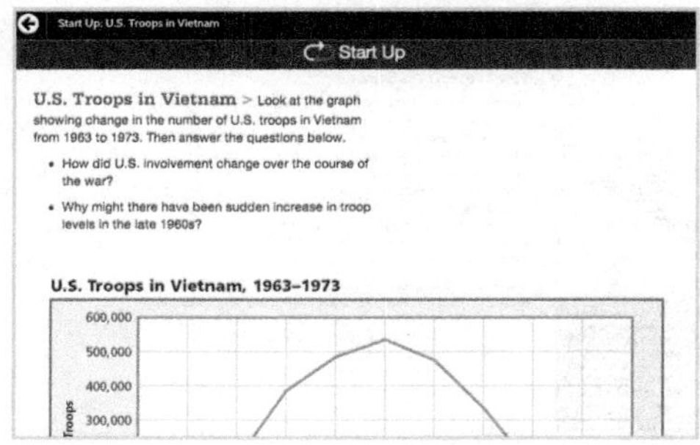

Project the Start Up Activity As students enter and get settled, draw their attention to the graph. Encourage them to take a few minutes to digest the information before they write down their answers to the questions. When they have completed their answers, consider working together as a group to reach a consensus answer for why might there have been a sudden increase in troop levels in the late 1960s.

Tell students that in this lesson they will be learning about the Nixon administration, President Nixon's handling of the Vietnam War, and the Watergate scandal.

Aa Vocabulary Development: Use the Interactive Reading Notepad to preview the Key Terms and Academic Vocabulary in this lesson with students.

FLIP IT!

Assign the Flipped Video for this lesson.

STUDENT EDITION PRINT PAGES: 849–855

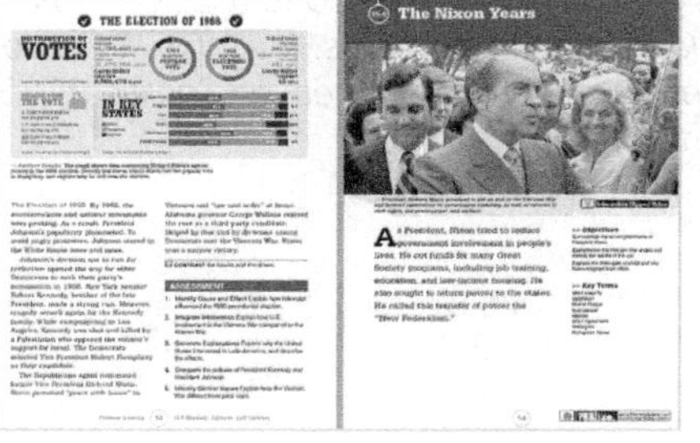

INVESTIGATE

DIGITAL TEXT 1

Nixon's Presidency

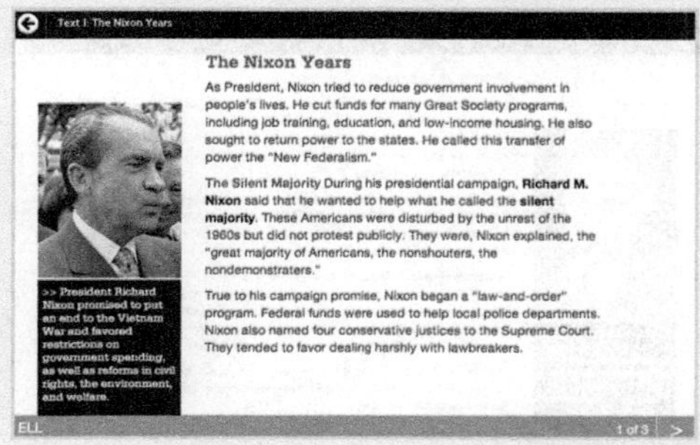

DIGITAL TEXT 3

Foreign Policy Decreases Tension

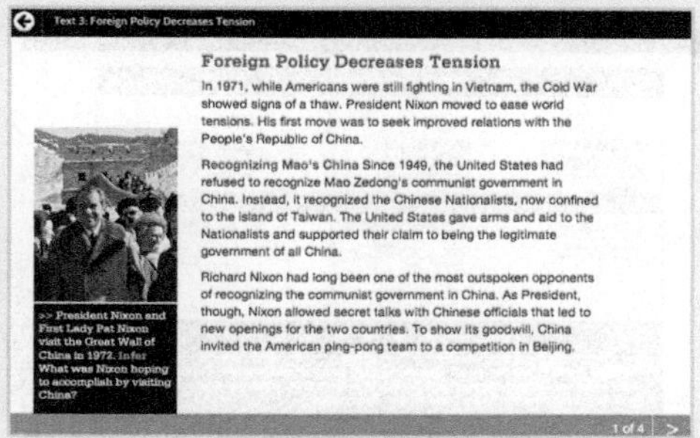

Objective 1: **Summarize the accomplishments of President Nixon.**

Quick Instruction

Interactive Gallery: Apollo 11 Project the Interactive Gallery and navigate through the images. Spend a few minutes reviewing the timeline showing the development of the space program. Prompt students to understand the connection between the U.S. space program and to the larger context of the Cold War between the United States and the Soviet Union. What might be the Soviet Union's response to the Apollo 11 moon landing? *(The Soviet Union might have stepped up their space program in the hope of matching the U.S. space program's accomplishment.)*

Summarize the economic conditions that led to the Nixon administration's economic policies. *(Military spending for the Vietnam War had fed inflation and economic growth had stalled, resulting in stagflation—a combination of rising prices, high unemployment, and slow economic growth. To halt inflation, Nixon froze wages and prices. To stimulate economic growth, he increased federal spending.)*

ACTIVE CLASSROOM

Conduct a Make Headlines activity. Ask: If you were to write a headline that captured the most important aspect of the Apollo 11 moon landing, what would that headline be? Allow students to use subheadings to communicate more information. Encourage students to connect the Apollo 11 moon landing with events of the larger Cold War era. Have students pass their headlines to a partner for them to review.

D Differentiate: Challenge Encourage interested students to research one of the other five moon landings in the Apollo program. Invite students to share their findings, focusing on significant achievements and lasting effects of the mission.

ELL Use the ELL activity described in the ELL chart.

The Nixon Years

INTERACTIVE GALLERY

Apollo 11

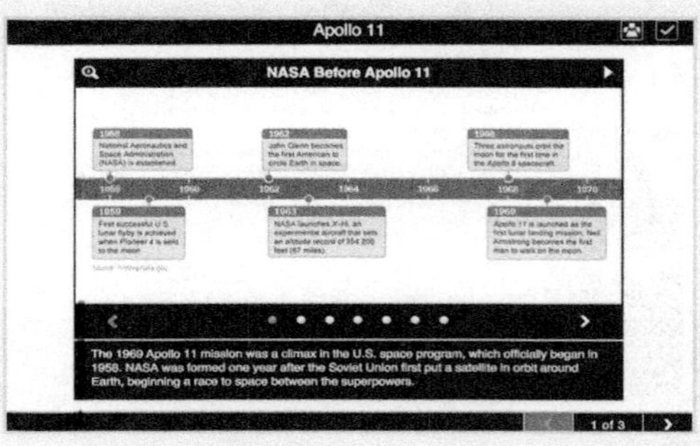

Further Instruction

Initiate a brief discussion about the challenges Richard Nixon faced as President. *(Possible responses: a weak economy; the ongoing war in Vietnam; Cold War tensions with the Soviet Union and China)* Encourage students to critique Nixon's handling of these issues and to describe whether he was successful in handling them. Assign Biographies: Richard Nixon to extend the discussion.

Draw Conclusions What evidence from the text indicates that President Nixon didn't entirely agree with expanding the federal government's power? *(Nixon cut funds for many Great Society programs and sought to return power to the states. He called this transfer of power the "New Federalism.")*

Infer Why might Nixon's support of détente and his goal to improve relations with China have been surprising to many Americans? *(Nixon had long been an outspoken opponent of recognizing the communist government in China.)*

DIGITAL TEXT 2

Nixon Addresses Vietnam

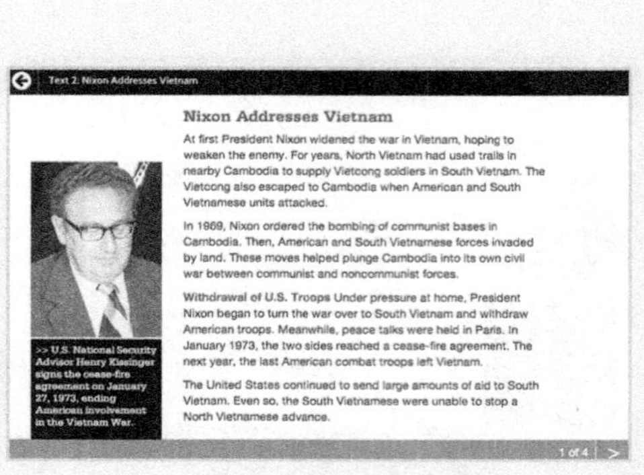
Text 2: Nixon Addresses Vietnam

Nixon Addresses Vietnam

At first President Nixon widened the war in Vietnam, hoping to weaken the enemy. For years, North Vietnam had used trails in nearby Cambodia to supply Vietcong soldiers in South Vietnam. The Vietcong also escaped to Cambodia when American and South Vietnamese units attacked.

In 1969, Nixon ordered the bombing of communist bases in Cambodia. Then, American and South Vietnamese forces invaded by land. These moves helped plunge Cambodia into its own civil war between communist and noncommunist forces.

Withdrawal of U.S. Troops Under pressure at home, President Nixon began to turn the war over to South Vietnam and withdraw American troops. Meanwhile, peace talks were held in Paris. In January 1973, the two sides reached a cease-fire agreement. The next year, the last American combat troops left Vietnam.

The United States continued to send large amounts of aid to South Vietnam. Even so, the South Vietnamese were unable to stop a North Vietnamese advance.

>> U.S. National Security Advisor Henry Kissinger signs the cease-fire agreement on January 27, 1973, ending American involvement in the Vietnam War.

1 of 4

Objective 2: **Explain how the Vietnam War ended and identify the results of the war.**

Quick Instruction

Present the digital image of Henry Kissinger signing the cease-fire agreement that ended American involvement in the Vietnam War. Challenge students to review key events or aspects of the Vietnam War. *(Possible events might include, assassination of Diem; guerilla warfare; Tet Offensive; Gulf of Tonkin Resolution; antiwar protests)* Review the costs and aims of the Vietnam War, then encourage students to share their thoughts and opinions about its lasting impact. How did the Vietnam War affect the Vietnamese people in both North and South Vietnam? *(The war killed more than one million Vietnamese soldiers and perhaps half a million civilians died. Many millions were left homeless. Their economies were destroyed. Many Vietnamese had to flee the country in search of better lives.)*

Categorize In his efforts to end the Vietnam War, Nixon first increased U.S. involvement, then decreased it. What examples from the text show each type of policy? *(Nixon increased involvement by ordering the bombing and invasion of Cambodia. He also supported continued aid to South Vietnam. He lessened involvement by turning the war over to South Vietnam and withdrawing American troops.)*

Further Instruction

Evaluate Nixon's decision to bomb Cambodia. *(Sample response: Nixon's decision to bomb Cambodia had unintended consequences. Cambodia was soon caught up in its own civil war that resulted in the Khmer Rouge's brutal government.)*

DIGITAL TEXT 4

The Watergate Scandal

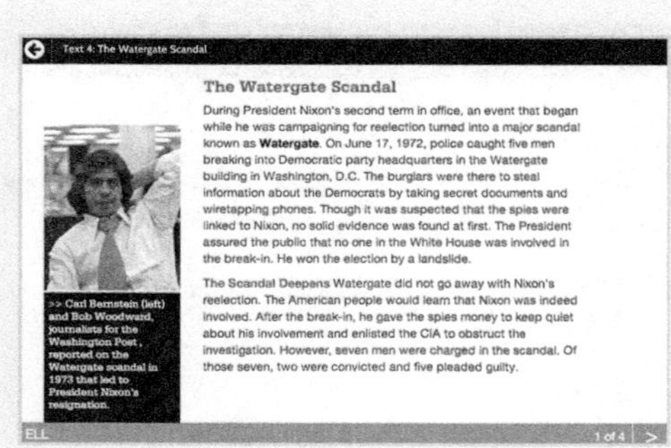
Text 4: The Watergate Scandal

The Watergate Scandal

During President Nixon's second term in office, an event that began while he was campaigning for reelection turned into a major scandal known as **Watergate**. On June 17, 1972, police caught five men breaking into Democratic party headquarters in the Watergate building in Washington, D.C. The burglars were there to steal information about the Democrats by taking secret documents and wiretapping phones. Though it was suspected that the spies were linked to Nixon, no solid evidence was found at first. The President assured the public that no one in the White House was involved in the break-in. He won the election by a landslide.

The Scandal Deepens Watergate did not go away with Nixon's reelection. The American people would learn that Nixon was indeed involved. After the break-in, he gave the spies money to keep quiet about his involvement and enlisted the CIA to obstruct the investigation. However, seven men were charged in the scandal. Of those seven, two were convicted and five pleaded guilty.

>> Carl Bernstein (left) and Bob Woodward, journalists for the Washington Post, reported on the Watergate scandal in 1973 that led to President Nixon's resignation.

ELL 1 of 4

Objective 3: **Explain the Watergate scandal and why Nixon resigned from office.**

Quick Instruction

Interactive Timeline: Watergate Project the Interactive Timeline and navigate through the images with students. Ensure students understand that burglars attempted to steal secrets from the Democratic party headquarters before the 1972 election. When they were discovered, President Nixon adamantly denied any involvement in the affair. Later, it became clear that he had been involved, and he resigned before he could be impeached.

Infer What does Nixon's statement, "If the president does it, that means it is not illegal . . . ." tell you about his view of the presidency? *(Nixon believed that the executive branch has the power to act without Congressional approval in certain circumstances and that presidential actions are not subject to review by the legal system.)*

Draw Conclusions How might President Nixon's scandal and resignation have affected how Americans view government? *(Possible answer: Watergate and Nixon's resignation could have led to a lack of trust or faith in elected officials. It also might have strengthened divisions between political parties.)*

INTERACTIVE TIMELINE

Watergate

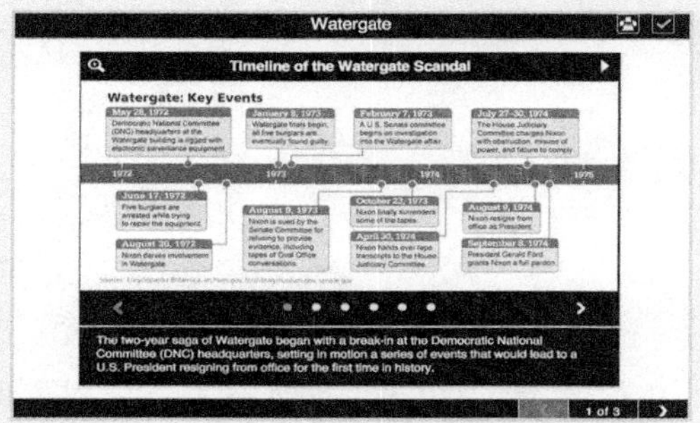

ACTIVE CLASSROOM

Conduct a Cartoon It activity. Use Nixon's quote, "If the president does it, that means it is not illegal . . . ." to prompt student thinking about the powers of the executive branch. Have students create a quick copy of one compelling image on a piece of paper and turn it into a political cartoon that illustrates a key concept or main idea.

ELL Use the ELL activity described in the ELL chart.

Further Instruction

Hypothesize why might many Americans have been upset that President Ford pardoned Nixon? *(Many Americans probably thought that Nixon broke the law and should have faced a trial just like a regular citizen would have.)*

Summarize the challenges Gerald Ford faced as he assumed the presidency. *(Ford had to deal with the fallout of the Watergate scandal and to continue improving relations with the Soviet Union. Also, the country was facing troubling domestic economic problems.)*

SYNTHESIZE

DIGITAL ACTIVITY

The Nixon Administration

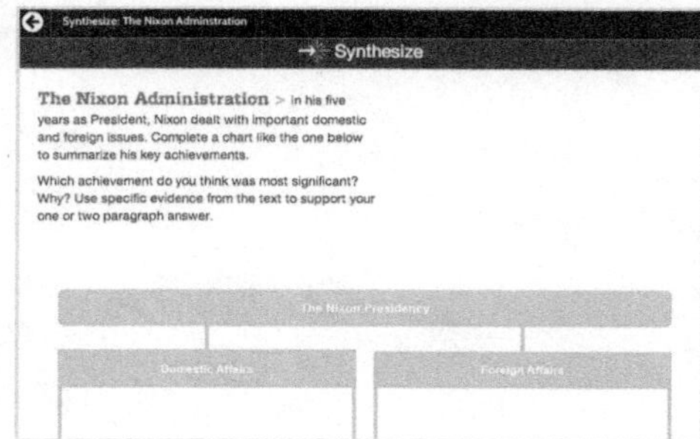

Before students begin their charts and write their paragraphs, lead a brief discussion to ensure student understanding of the challenges Richard Nixon faced when he became President. Encourage students to look beyond the Watergate scandal and to reflect on the full scope of Nixon's presidency.

Discuss Meet as a class and have students think about the following question: For what will Richard Nixon be best remembered? Encourage students to support their answers with specifics from their paragraphs and information from the lesson.

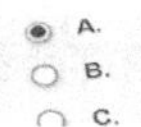

DEMONSTRATE

DIGITAL QUIZ

Lesson Quiz and Class Discussion Board

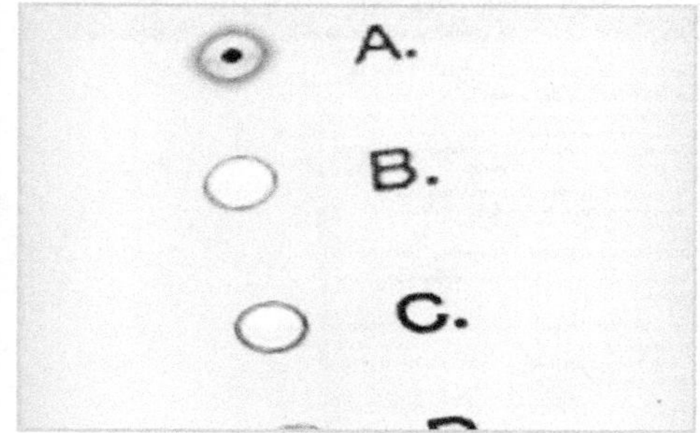

Assign the online Lesson Quiz for this lesson if you haven't already done so. Students will be offered automatic remediation or enrichment based on their score.

Pose these questions to the class on the Discussion Board:

In *The Nixon Years*, you learned how President Nixon dealt with other challenging issues besides the Vietnam War. He eased Cold War tensions and improved relations with Communist China. However, a destructive scandal marred his presidency, leading him to become the first U.S. President to resign from office.

Predict Consequences What effect did the Vietnam War have on many American's view of their country's role in the world? How might the war affect American leaders when dealing with future conflicts around the world?

Draw Conclusions Was the Watergate scandal a test of American democracy? Why or why not?

Topic Inquiry

Have students continue their investigations for the Topic Inquiry.

Postwar America

SYNTHESIZE

DIGITAL ACTIVITY

Reflect on the Essential Question and Topic

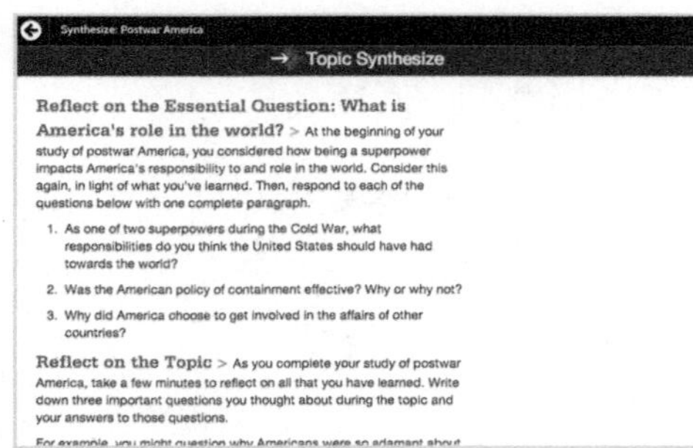
Synthesize: Postwar America

→ Topic Synthesize

Reflect on the Essential Question: What is America's role in the world? > At the beginning of your study of postwar America, you considered how being a superpower impacts America's responsibility to and role in the world. Consider this again, in light of what you've learned. Then, respond to each of the questions below with one complete paragraph.

1. As one of two superpowers during the Cold War, what responsibilities do you think the United States should have had towards the world?
2. Was the American policy of containment effective? Why or why not?
3. Why did America choose to get involved in the affairs of other countries?

Reflect on the Topic > As you complete your study of postwar America, take a few minutes to reflect on all that you have learned. Write down three important questions you thought about during the topic and your answers to those questions.

First ask students to reconsider the Essential Question for the Topic: What is America's role in the world? Ask students to recall their thoughts about how the status of the United States as a super power affects its responsibilities and its role in the world. Provide time for students to consider this again, in light of what they've learned. Invite student volunteers to share their ideas. Review the questions in the activity and direct students to write their paragraphs.

Next ask students to reflect on the Topic as a whole and jot down 1–3 questions they've thought about during the Topic. Have students read over the sample questions to help generate ideas. You may ask students to share their questions and answers on the Class Discussion Board.

Topic Inquiry

Have students complete Step 3 of the Topic Inquiry.

DEMONSTRATE

DIGITAL TOPIC REVIEW AND ASSESSMENT

Postwar America

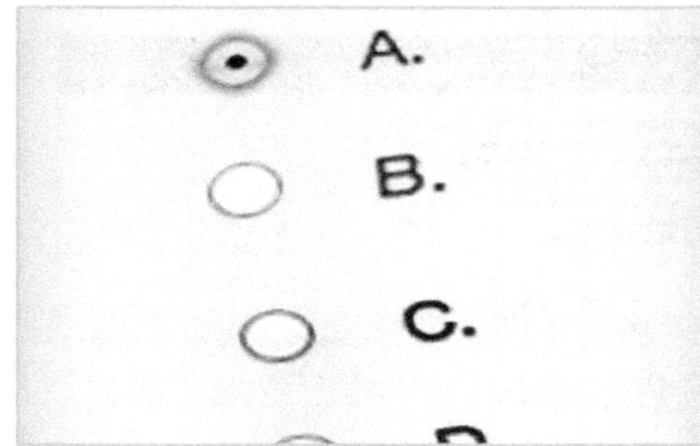

Students can prepare for the Topic Test by answering the questions in the Topic Review and Assessment online or the Assessment questions in the Print Student text. They can also prepare by reviewing their answers to the Interactive Reading Notepad questions or reviewing their notes in the Reading and Notetaking Study Guide.

DIGITAL TOPIC TEST

Postwar America

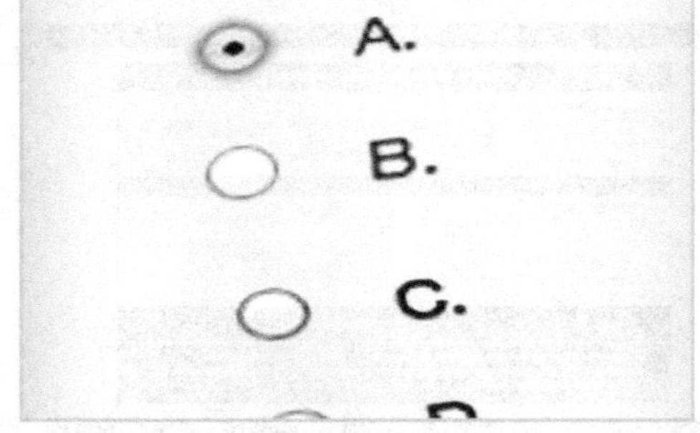

TOPIC TEST

Assign the Topic Test to assess students' understanding of topic content.

BENCHMARK TESTS

Assign these benchmark tests as you complete the relevant topics to monitor student progress toward mastering the course content and as preparation for the End-of-Course Test.

Benchmark Test 1: Topics 1–2

Benchmark Test 2: Topics 3–4

Benchmark Test 3: Topics 5–6

Benchmark Test 4: Topics 7–9

Benchmark Test 5: Topics 10–12

Benchmark Test 6: Topics 13–14

Benchmark Test 7: Topics 15–17

A Global Superpower Facing Change

TOPIC 16 ORGANIZER	PACING: APPROX. 6 PERIODS, 3 BLOCKS
	PACING
Connect	1 period
MY STORY VIDEO **Irene Zoppi, Gulf War Veteran**	10 min.
DIGITAL ESSENTIAL QUESTION ACTIVITY **How Should We Handle Conflict?**	10 min.
DIGITAL OVERVIEW ACTIVITY **A Global Superpower Facing Change**	10 min.
TOPIC INQUIRY: DOCUMENT-BASED QUESTION **Analyzing the Reagan Conservative Movement**	20 min.
Investigate	1–3 periods
TOPIC INQUIRY: DOCUMENT-BASED QUESTION **Analyzing the Reagan Conservative Movement**	Ongoing
LESSON 1 The Conservative Revolution	30–40 min.
LESSON 2 The End of the Cold War	30–40 min.
LESSON 3 Regional Conflicts	30–40 min.
Synthesize	1 period
DIGITAL ACTIVITY **Reflect on the Essential Question and Topic**	10 min.
TOPIC INQUIRY: DOCUMENT-BASED QUESTION **Analyzing the Reagan Conservative Movement**	20 min.
Demonstrate	1–2 periods
DIGITAL ACTIVITY **Reflect on the Essential Question and Topic**	10 min.
TOPIC INQUIRY: DOCUMENT-BASED QUESTION **Analyzing the Reagan Conservative Movement**	20 min.

TOPIC INQUIRY: DOCUMENT-BASED QUESTION

Analyzing the Reagan Conservative Movement

In this Topic Inquiry, students work independently to analyze documents that express various viewpoints on Reaganomics and write an essay in which they respond to the question, "How did conservative Reaganomics differ from liberals' and moderates' beliefs about the best way to achieve a healthy economy in the 1980s?" Learning about differing opinions concerning economic policies and theories will contribute to students' understanding of the Topic Essential Question: **How should we handle conflict?**

STEP 1: CONNECT

Develop Questions and Plan the Investigation

Launch the DBQ Writing Activity

Discuss the basics of Reaganomics as a class. Display the guiding question to which students will respond. Inform students that they will write an essay in which they share their analyses of several documents pertaining to opinions of Reaganomics. Play the video for the class, encouraging students to take notes as they watch.

Generate Questions

Pair students and allow them time to share their notes and reflections on the video. Have partners work together to generate their own questions and answer the Questions to Discuss from Step 1B of the Student Instructions.

Suggestion: Allow time for partners to share their ideas and answers with the whole class. Encourage students to record ideas they find original or interesting to discuss in their writing.

Resources

- Project Launch
- Student Instructions
- Video

PROFESSIONAL DEVELOPMENT

Document-Based Question

Be sure to view the Document-Based Question Professional Development resources in the online course.

STEP 2: INVESTIGATE

Apply Disciplinary Concepts and Tools

Analyze the Documents

As students read the documents, they should keep their lists of questions in hand, recording answers as they go. Students might find it helpful to categorize documents based on point of view. For example, they might divide the documents into conservative, moderate, and liberal economic perspectives. Students can use this categorization as a starting point for the organization of their essays.

Suggestion: Remind students that they must give credit when they cite specific ideas in their analyses, even when they do not use direct quotations from the sources.

Check Your Understanding

Students can reconvene with their partners to share and discuss the answers they provided to the questions attached to each document. Partners should share their interpretations of the central ideas of each document, taking time to discuss and possibly resolve discrepancies in interpretation.

Resources

- Student Instructions
- Document A: Excerpt from a debate between Republican presidential candidates, George H. W. Bush and Ronald Reagan, 1980
- Document B: Excerpt from the *State of the Union Address,* President Jimmy Carter, 1981
- Document C: Excerpt from an *Address to the Nation on the Economy,* President Ronald Reagan, February 1981
- Document D: Excerpt from *Remarks on Signing the Economic Recovery Tax Act of 1981,* President Ronald Reagan, August 1981
- Document E: Excerpt from *Mondale's Acceptance Speech,* Walter Mondale, 1984
- Document F: Excerpt from the *Democratic National Convention Keynote Address,* Mario Cuomo, 1984
- 21st Century Skills: Evaluate Existing Arguments
- 21st Century Skills: Distinguish Between Fact and Opinion

STEP 3: SYNTHESIZE

Evaluate Sources and Use Evidence to Formulate Conclusions

Write Your Essay

Review the *Rubric for a DBQ Essay* with the class. Post the guiding questions: How did conservative Reaganomics differ from liberals' and moderates' beliefs about the best way to achieve a healthy economy in the 1980s? and review the bulleted list in the Student Instructions that guides students through the writing process.

Suggestion: Suggest that students use a graphic organizer, such as an idea web or three-column chart, to categorize ideas and organize information before they begin writing. Students can consult their graphic organizers as they draft their essays.

Resources

- Student Instructions
- Rubric for a DBQ Essay

STEP 4: DEMONSTRATE

Communicate Conclusions and Take Informed Action

Reflect on the Project

After students have completed and submitted their essays, lead a class discussion in which students reflect on what they have learned and share the opinions they have formed and the reasoning behind those opinions. Ask students how they predict this new-found understanding of economic policy will inform their future study of history or sociology.

Suggestion: As an extension activity, have students research contemporary economic policies and compare their implementation and success with Reaganomics.

Resources

- Student Instructions

Topic 16

INTRODUCTION

A Global Superpower Facing Change

The 1970s, 1980s, and 1990s were rife with change. The 1970s were plagued by inflation and an oil crisis. As the decade came to an end, the Iran hostage crisis took front stage while Cold War tensions escalated with the Soviet invasion of Afghanistan. The 1980s brought in the conservative era of Presidents Reagan and George H. W. Bush associated with economic growth, significant budget deficits, and eventually a recession. The Cold War came to an end during this era as well, leaving the United States to negotiate unfamiliar terrain as the world's lone superpower. As President Clinton took office in 1993, the economy turned around and the budget deficit became a surplus partly as a result of his moderate policies.

CONNECT

MY STORY VIDEO

Irene Zoppi, Gulf War Veteran

Watch a video about a military officer's experiences in the Gulf War.

Check Understanding What was the Gulf War? *(The first U.S. war after the Cold War, the Gulf War was the response of the United States and its allies to Iraq's invasion of neighboring Kuwait.)*

Determine Point of View What, according to Irene Zoppi, were the benefits of serving in the military? *(Irene Zoppi left Puerto Rico to join the military. She gained proficiency in English and, during her years of service, was able to learn leadership skills, discipline, and a better understanding of people. She was able to serve while marrying and raising a family.)*

DIGITAL ESSENTIAL QUESTION ACTIVITY

How Should We Handle Conflict?

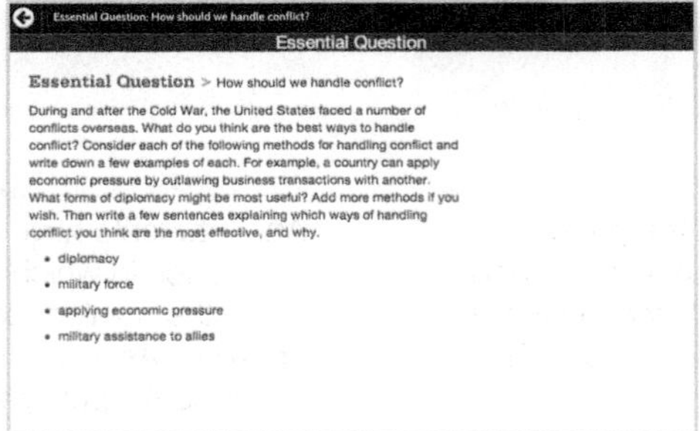

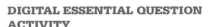

Ask students to think about the Essential Question for this Topic: How should we handle conflict? Just like people, countries respond to conflict in different ways.

Have students complete the activity. Discuss students' responses and the additional means of conflict resolution they suggest.

Apply Concepts Should the type of conflict resolution depend upon the nature of the conflict? Give at least two examples. *(Possible response: Yes. If a country has violated a treaty but done no physical harm, economic pressure and diplomacy might be the best tactics. However, when a country commits serious human rights violations, military force may be the best way to address the conflict.)*

Hypothesize How would the world be different if the United States did not get involved in international conflicts? *(Possible response: Democracy would not have made as many gains, and the U.S. economy would have suffered, especially as a result of Middle Eastern conflicts over oil.)*

DIGITAL OVERVIEW ACTIVITY

A Global Superpower Facing Change

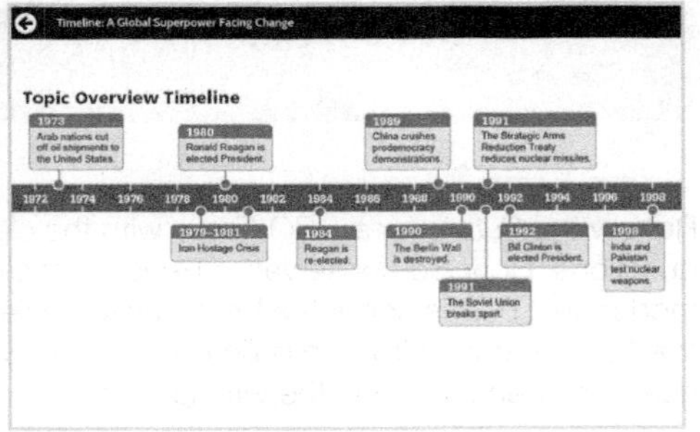

Display the timeline of major events in the late 1900s. In this topic, students will learn about all these events and many more. This timeline will provide a framework into which students can place the events they learn about as they study the topic.

Analyze Information Which administration saw the greatest change based on the events listed in the timeline? *(Possible response: The Bush administration saw the greatest change with the destruction of the Berlin Wall and the end of the Cold War.)*

Topic Inquiry

Launch the Topic Inquiry with students after introducing the topic.

PEARSON realize™ www.PearsonRealize.com Access your Digital Lesson

The Conservative Revolution

Supporting English Language Learners

Use with the reading, **President Carter's Administration.**

Speaking

With students, discuss techniques for presenting information to others in a clear and logical way.

Beginning Display the following sentences: Inflation happens when prices _____. To fight inflation, President Carter cut _____. Invite students to complete each sentence with the correct information (referring to the text if needed) and say it aloud.

Intermediate Ask students questions about the work and impact of President Carter, such as: How did Carter deal with the problem of high inflation? Why did Iranian revolutionaries take 53 Americans hostage? Encourage students to provide their answers in thought-out complete sentences.

Advanced Provide pairs of students with this list of issues related to Carter's presidency: inflation, transportation industry, Iran, oil. Ask partners to take turns providing information about issues from the list.

Advanced High Invite students to prepare a mock news story about Carter's presidency for a (hypothetical) audience. Encourage students to present the information in a clear, compelling, and organized way. Have partners practice reciting their reports to each other.

Use with the reading, **The Reagan and Bush Presidencies.**

Reading

Say that when reading, two major tasks are understanding content and understanding language. When reading *The Budget Deficit*, encourage students to focus more on comprehension and less on language-related challenges. Group students by ability level.

Beginning Rewrite *The Budget Deficit*, presenting key points using basic language and simple sentences. Distribute this simplified text to students and have them read the text in pairs. Then ask students close-ended questions so they can demonstrate comprehension.

Intermediate Provide students with the simplified version of *The Budget Deficit*. Have them read the course text and refer to the simplified version when they reach a passage that they find difficult. In pairs, have them ask each other clarifying questions as needed. Ask: What is a balanced budget?

Advanced Make a dictionary available to students. Have them read *The Budget Deficit* independently, referring to the dictionary to look up any difficult words.Have them discuss the following question with a partner: What happened to the budget under Reagan?

Advanced High Make a dictionary available to students. Have them read *The Budget Deficit* independently and discuss the importance of a balanced budget with a partner.

D Differentiate Instruction

Use the Differentiated Instruction notes throughout the lesson plan to support the varied skill sets, levels of readiness, and interests in the mixed-ability classroom.

Challenge These notes include suggestions for expanding the activity for advanced students.

On-Level These notes include suggestions for modifying the activity to address different interests or learning styles.

Extra Support These notes include ideas for providing more scaffolding or reading spupport.

Special Needs These notes provide ideas for adapting instruction to support the needs of various special needs students.

NOTES

Topic 16 Lesson 1

The Conservative Revolution

Objectives

Objective 1: Identify the challenges faced by the administration of Jimmy Carter.

Objective 2: Describe Ronald Reagan's conservative agenda.

Objective 3: Identify the challenges faced by the administration of George H. W. Bush.

Objective 4: Explain the issues that Bill Clinton faced as President.

LESSON 1 ORGANIZER	PACING: APPROX. 1 PERIOD, .5 BLOCKS		RESOURCES	
	OBJECTIVES	PACING	Online	Print
Connect				
DIGITAL START UP ACTIVITY **Liberals and Conservatives**		5 min.	●	
Investigate				
DIGITAL TEXT 1 **President Carter's Administration**	Objective 1	10 min.	●	●
INTERACTIVE CARTOON **Reacting to Crises Under Carter**		10 min.	●	
DIGITAL TEXT 2 **The Conservative Movement Takes Hold**	Objectives 2, 3	10 min.	●	●
DIGITAL TEXT 3 **The Reagan and Bush Presidencies**		10 min.	●	●
DIGITAL TEXT 4 **President Clinton Turns Toward the Center**	Objective 4	10 min.	●	●
INTERACTIVE CHART **Compare Four Presidents**		10 min.	●	
Synthesize				
DIGITAL ACTIVITY **Liberal and Conservative Policies**		5 min.	●	
Demonstrate				
DIGITAL QUIZ **Lesson Quiz and Discussion Board**		10 min.	●	

CONNECT

DIGITAL START UP ACTIVITY

Liberals and Conservatives

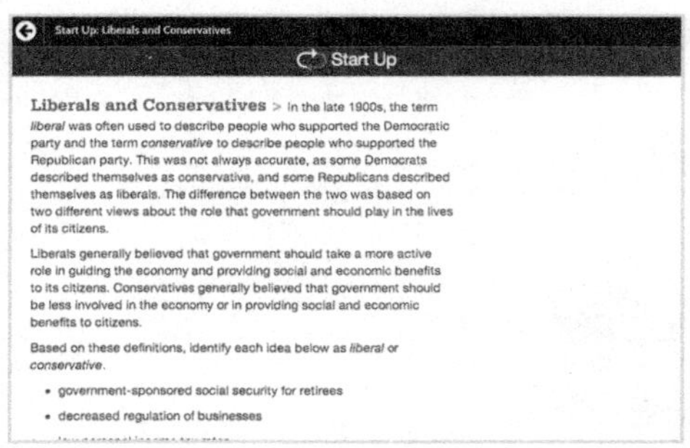

Project the Start Up Activity Have students complete the activity as they enter the classroom. Then ask them to share and discuss their ideas with partners.

Discuss Lead a class discussion in which students explain their reasoning for identifying each idea as liberal or conservative.

Tell students that in this lesson they will be learning about the challenges and issues associated with the presidencies of Carter, Reagan, Bush, and Clinton.

Aa Vocabulary Development: Use the Interactive Reading Notepad to preview the Key Terms and Academic Vocabulary in this lesson with students.

FLIP IT!

Assign the Flipped Video for this lesson.

STUDENT EDITION PRINT PAGES: 860–869

INVESTIGATE

DIGITAL TEXT 1

President Carter's Administration

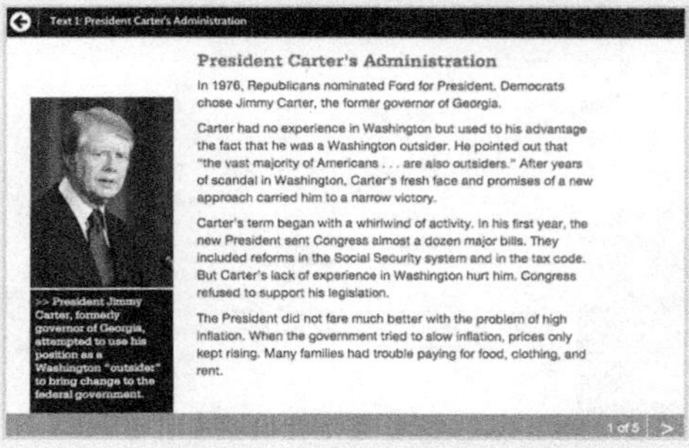

INTERACTIVE CARTOON

Reacting to Crises Under Carter

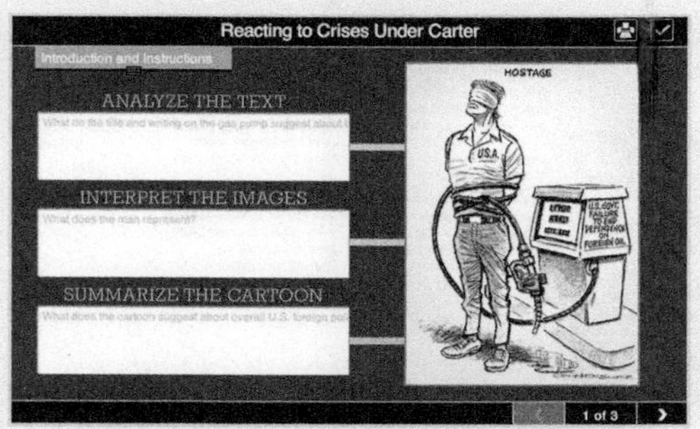

Objective 1: Identify the challenges faced by the administration of Jimmy Carter.

Quick Instruction

Interactive Cartoon: Reacting to Crises Under Carter Project the Interactive Cartoon and prompt students to analyze the text and interpret the images. Ask: What events led up to the Iran hostage crisis? *(When the religious regime led by Ayatollah Khomeini ousted the Shah from power, relations between the United States and Iran became tense. When President Carter granted the Shah admission to the United States for medical treatment, the new regime's supporters seized hostages from the American embassy in Iran.)*

Identify Cause and Effect What effect did the crisis have on life in the United States? *(The crisis isolated Iran from other countries. Many U.S. citizens blamed President Carter's foreign policy choices for both the crisis and the reduced supply of oil, which in turn drove up gas prices. The crisis cost President Carter the chance of reelection.)*

ACTIVE CLASSROOM

Conduct a Make Headlines activity. Have students write a headline that captures the perspective of the crisis presented in the cartoon. Ask: If you were to write a headline that summarized the most important aspect of the cartoon, what would that headline be? When students finish writing, have them exchange papers with partners and discuss their ideas. Invite volunteers to share their headlines with the class.

ELL Use the ELL activity described in the ELL chart.

Further Instruction

Summarize How did Carter's role as an outsider affect his ability to run the country? *(Because he did not have many political allies, Congress blocked a majority of the legislation he proposed.)*

Determine Point of View Why did Ayatollah Khomeini and his supporters disagree with both the Shah and the United States? *(The United States had long supported the Shah. In turn, the Shah encouraged policies that would draw Iran closer to the United States and embrace some U.S. values. Khomeini on the other hand did not approve of the Shah's policies and was strongly anti-American. He preferred Iran to be governed under a strict, old-fashioned interpretation of Islam.)*

Topic 16 Lesson 1

The Conservative Revolution

DIGITAL TEXT 2
The Conservative Movement Takes Hold

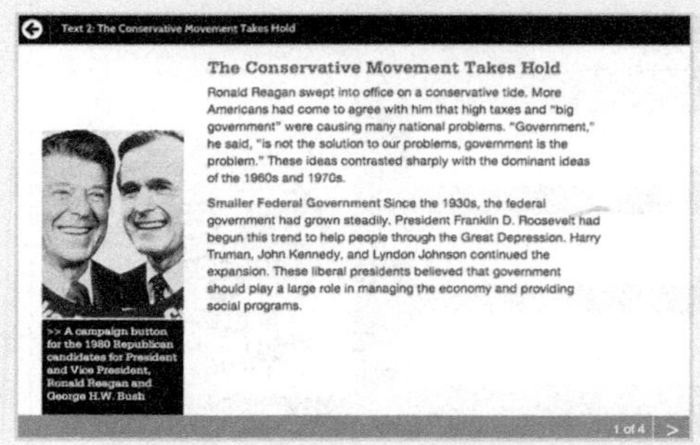

Text 2: The Conservative Movement Takes Hold
The Conservative Movement Takes Hold
Ronald Reagan swept into office on a conservative tide. More Americans had come to agree with him that high taxes and "big government" were causing many national problems. "Government," he said, "is not the solution to our problems, government is the problem." These ideas contrasted sharply with the dominant ideas of the 1960s and 1970s.
Smaller Federal Government Since the 1930s, the federal government had grown steadily. President Franklin D. Roosevelt had begun this trend to help people through the Great Depression. Harry Truman, John Kennedy, and Lyndon Johnson continued the expansion. These liberal presidents believed that government should play a large role in managing the economy and providing social programs.
>> A campaign button for the 1980 Republican candidates for President and Vice President, Ronald Reagan and George H.W. Bush
1 of 4

DIGITAL TEXT 3
The Reagan and Bush Presidencies

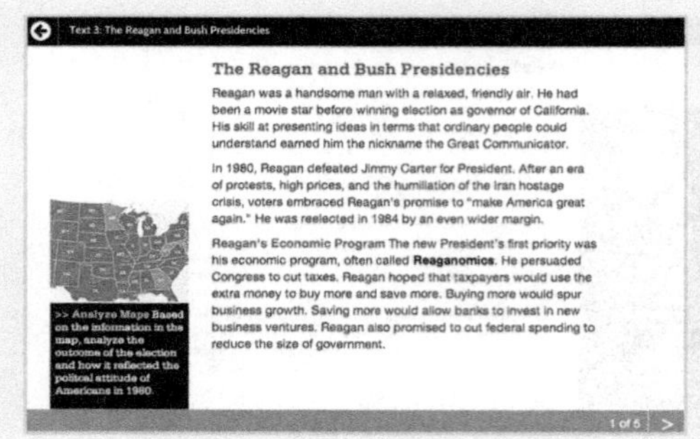

Text 3: The Reagan and Bush Presidencies
The Reagan and Bush Presidencies
Reagan was a handsome man with a relaxed, friendly air. He had been a movie star before winning election as governor of California. His skill at presenting ideas in terms that ordinary people could understand earned him the nickname the Great Communicator.
In 1980, Reagan defeated Jimmy Carter for President. After an era of protests, high prices, and the humiliation of the Iran hostage crisis, voters embraced Reagan's promise to "make America great again." He was reelected in 1984 by an even wider margin.
Reagan's Economic Program The new President's first priority was his economic program, often called Reaganomics. He persuaded Congress to cut taxes. Reagan hoped that taxpayers would use the extra money to buy more and save more. Buying more would spur business growth. Saving more would allow banks to invest in new business ventures. Reagan also promised to cut federal spending to reduce the size of government.
>> Analyze Maps Based on the information in the map, analyze the outcome of the election and how it reflected the politcal attitude of Americans in 1980.
1 of 5

DIGITAL TEXT 4
President Clinton Turns Toward the Center

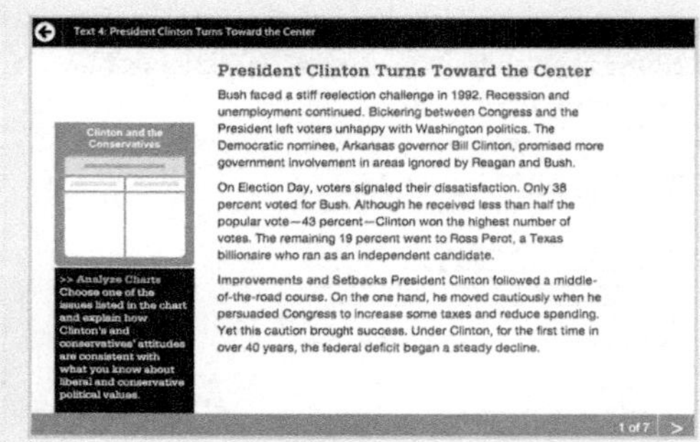

Text 4: President Clinton Turns Toward the Center
President Clinton Turns Toward the Center
Bush faced a stiff reelection challenge in 1992. Recession and unemployment continued. Bickering between Congress and the President left voters unhappy with Washington politics. The Democratic nominee, Arkansas governor Bill Clinton, promised more government involvement in areas ignored by Reagan and Bush.
On Election Day, voters signaled their dissatisfaction. Only 38 percent voted for Bush. Although he received less than half the popular vote—43 percent—Clinton won the highest number of votes. The remaining 19 percent went to Ross Perot, a Texas billionaire who ran as an independent candidate.
Improvements and Setbacks President Clinton followed a middle-of-the-road course. On the one hand, he moved cautiously when he persuaded Congress to increase some taxes and reduce spending. Yet this caution brought success. Under Clinton, for the first time in over 40 years, the federal deficit began a steady decline.
Clinton and the Conservatives
>> Analyze Charts Choose one of the issues listed in the chart and explain how Clinton's and conservatives' attitudes are consistent with what you know about liberal and conservative political values.
1 of 7

Objectives 2: **Describe Ronald Reagan's conservative agenda; 3: Identify the challenges faced by the administration of George H. W. Bush.**

Quick Instruction

Identify Central Issues How did President Reagan's economic policies, known collectively as "Reaganomics," show his conservative ideas? *(President Reagan persuaded Congress to lower taxes when he first took office. He also wanted to reduce the size of the government and deregulate businesses to spur economic growth.)*

Express Problems Clearly Why did President Reagan's economic policies increase the budget deficit? *(President Reagan encouraged Congress to cut taxes, which reduced the amount of money the government took in. While Congress cut some spending on social and education programs, it significantly increased spending on the military. Because the government was spending more money than it was taking in, the budget deficit quickly grew.)*

ELL Use the ELL activity described in the ELL chart.

Further Instruction

Summarize What did President Bush do to address the growing budget deficit soon after he took office? *(The government was unable to pay for some popular federal programs, so he agreed to increase some taxes despite his promise not to do so.)*

Identify Cause and Effect What impact did Reagan's deregulation of businesses have on the nation's economy? *(Deregulation of the banking industry allowed banks to make increasingly profitable but risky loans, which in turn contributed to the banking crisis and the economic recession that developed during Bush's presidency.)*

Objective 4: **Explain the issues that Bill Clinton faced as President.**

Quick Instruction

Interactive Chart: Compare Four Presidents Display the Interactive Chart and prompt the students to associate the events and issues with the appropriate President. Review some of the economic and domestic policies of each President.

Summarize President Clinton's achievements during his time in office. *Throughout his presidency, the economy boomed and the government finally had a budget surplus instead of a deficit. Trade further opened up between Canada, the United States, and Mexico under the agreements associated with NAFTA, a remnant of Bush's administration that Clinton embraced.*

INTERACTIVE CHART

Compare Four Presidents

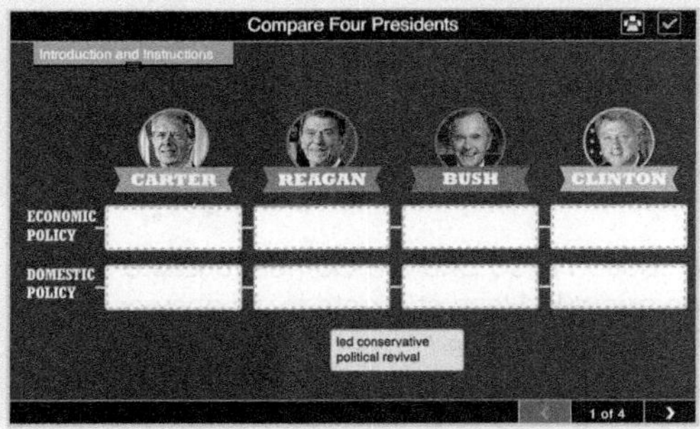

ACTIVE CLASSROOM

Conduct a Sticky Notes activity. Ask students to jot down questions, comments, or observations on Sticky Notes and post them in columns that mirror the Interactive Chart. Challenge students to record the impact of the policies of each President on their Stickies. Discuss students' notes as a group.

Further Instruction

Support Ideas with Evidence What examples from the text show that Clinton's policies were "middle of the road"? *(Though he promoted the liberal policy of government intervention in healthcare, he also sponsored NAFTA, a treaty supported by President Bush. In addition, he supported the conservative goal of welfare reform, while also raising some taxes to provide the government with more revenue and decrease the budget deficit.)*

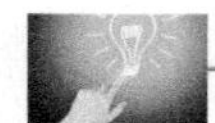

SYNTHESIZE

DIGITAL ACTIVITY

Liberal and Conservative Policies

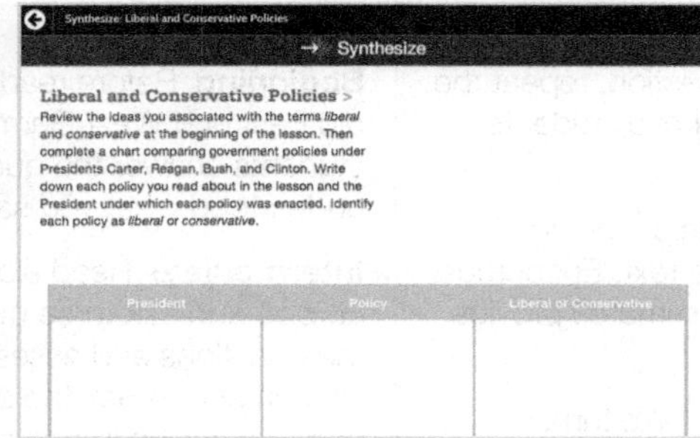

Synthesize: Liberal and Conservative Policies
Synthesize
Liberal and Conservative Policies
Review the ideas you associated with the terms liberal and conservative at the beginning of the lesson. Then complete a chart comparing government policies under Presidents Carter, Reagan, Bush, and Clinton. Write down each policy you read about in the lesson and the President under which each policy was enacted. Identify each policy as liberal or conservative.
President
Policy
Liberal or Conservative

Begin the activity by working as a class to list the policies students learned about in this lesson. Then, allow students time to complete their graphic organizers. Have students post their completed charts on the Class Discussion Board.

Discuss Invite students to compare their graphic organizers as a class. Discuss whether all the policies under Democrats were liberal and Republicans were conservative. Ask students whether the policies associated with each President were in keeping with his party and why.

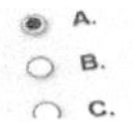

DEMONSTRATE

DIGITAL QUIZ

Lesson Quiz and Discussion Board

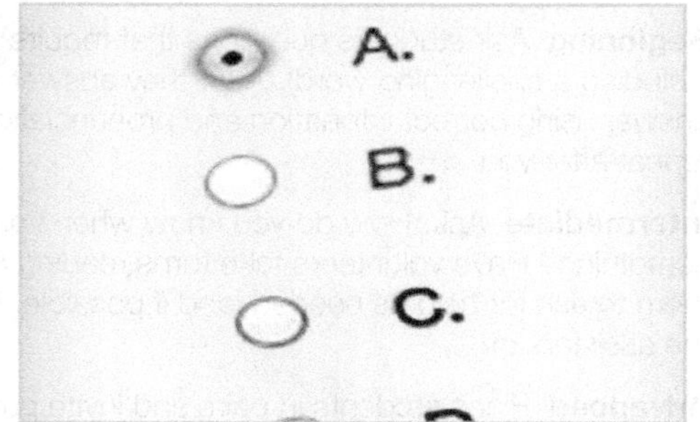

Assign the online Lesson Quiz for this lesson if you haven't already done so. Students will be offered automatic remediation or enrichment based on their score.

In *The Conservative Revolution*, you learned about the issues Presidents Carter, Reagan, Bush, and Clinton had to address and how they did so.

Post these questions to the class on the Discussion Board:

Compare and Contrast What is the fundamental difference between conservative and liberal economic policies?

Identify Cause and Effect What factors contributed to the economic boom during President Clinton's administration?

Topic Inquiry

Have students continue their investigations for the Topic Inquiry.

The End of the Cold War

Supporting English Language Learners

Use with the reading, **The End of Détente.**

Learning

With students, brainstorm how to monitor the quality and effectiveness of one's speaking, as well as correct oneself when needed.

Beginning Ask students questions that require short answers (preferably including a challenging word). After they answer each question, repeat the answer using correct intonation and pronunciation Then have students repeat after you.

Intermediate Ask: How do you know when you need help reading something? Have volunteers take turns reading aloud the text. Encourage them to ask for help as needed (and if possible, have classmates provide the assistance).

Advanced Place students in pairs and invite partners to take turns reading aloud the text. Have students refer to an online dictionary's audio pronunciation tool to help them with challenging words.

Advanced High Place students in pairs, and invite them to discuss how the policy of détente ended and what that meant for the United States. Encourage students to aim for accuracy as they speak, as opposed to speed. Also provide them with a print dictionary that they can use to look up the pronunciation of challenging words.

Use with the reading, **The Soviet Empire Crumbles.**

Listening

With students, brainstorm answers to these questions: How can you tell if you are listening well to a speaker? What can you do to increase your comprehension?

Beginning Before reading aloud the text's last paragraph, ask: When did East and West Germany come back together? After reading, have students answer the question. Ask students to assess how well they understood what you said.

Intermediate Read aloud the section titled *Change Comes to Eastern Europe* and ask three questions about it. Have students try to answer the questions and assess how well they listened. Then reread the section and re-ask the same questions. Have students assess how their comprehension improved.

Advanced Facilitate a group discussion in which students sit in a circle and take turns speaking about the text. Encourage students to remark on the previous student's comment, as well as cite other students' comments when possible. Ask: How well were you able to connect your ideas to others that you heard?

Advanced High Invite pairs of students to discuss the fall of the Soviet Empire. Encourage them to use certain phrases to help them monitor understanding of what their partner says, such as *I agree that...*, *Like you, I think...* and *However....*

D Differentiate Instruction

Use the Differentiated Instruction notes throughout the lesson plan to support the varied skill sets, levels of readiness, and interests in the mixed-ability classroom.

Challenge These notes include suggestions for expanding the activity for advanced students.

On-Level These notes include suggestions for modifying the activity to address different interests or learning styles.

Extra Support These notes include ideas for providing more scaffolding or reading spuport.

Special Needs These notes provide ideas for adapting instruction to support the needs of various special needs students.

NOTES

PEARSON realize www.PearsonRealize.com

Go online to access additional resources including: Primary Sources • Biographies • Supreme Court cases • 21st Century Skill Tutorials • Maps • Graphic Organizers.

Objectives

Objective 1: Describe the new Cold War tensions that developed after 1979.

Objective 2: Explain why communism fell in Eastern Europe and the Soviet Union.

Objective 3: Identify Americans' reaction to the end of the Cold War.

LESSON 2 ORGANIZER	PACING: APPROX. 1 PERIOD, .5 BLOCKS			
			RESOURCES	
	OBJECTIVES	PACING	Online	Print
Connect				
DIGITAL START UP ACTIVITY **Tear Down This Wall**		5 min.	●	
Investigate				
DIGITAL TEXT 1 **The End of Détente**	Objective 1	10 min.	●	●
DIGITAL TEXT 2 **The Soviet Empire Crumbles**	Objective 2	10 min.	●	●
BEFORE AND AFTER **The Berlin Wall**		10 min.	●	
INTERACTIVE MAP **Shifting Alliances in Europe**		10 min.	●	
DIGITAL TEXT 3 **The Aftermath of the Cold War**	Objective 3	10 min.	●	●
Synthesize				
DIGITAL ACTIVITY **How the Cold War Ended**		5 min.	●	
Demonstrate				
DIGITAL QUIZ **Lesson Quiz and Discussion Board**		10 min.	●	

The End of the Cold War

CONNECT

DIGITAL START UP ACTIVITY
"Tear Down This Wall"

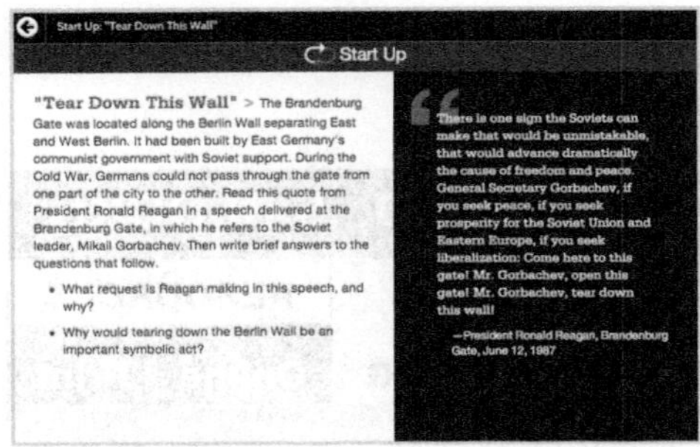

Project the Start Up Activity Have students read the quotation and answer the questions. Then ask them to discuss their ideas with partners.

Discuss What request is Reagan making in this speech, and why? *(He requests that the Soviet Union take down the wall between East and West Berlin to free movement between the two parts of the divided city.)* Why would tearing down the Berlin Wall be an important symbolic act? *(The wall stood as a divider between the communist and Western world.)*

Tell students that in this lesson they will examine escalating Cold War tensions, the fall of the Soviet Union, and the American reaction to the end of the Cold War.

Aa Vocabulary Development: Use the Interactive Reading Notepad to preview the Key Terms and Academic Vocabulary in this lesson with students.

FLIP IT!

Assign the Flipped Video for this lesson.

STUDENT EDITION PRINT PAGES: 870–876

INVESTIGATE

DIGITAL TEXT 1
The End of Détente

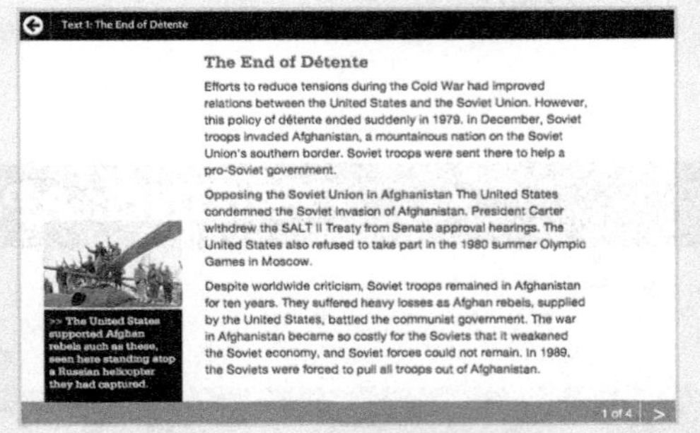

Objective 1: Describe the new Cold War tensions that developed after 1979.

Quick Instruction

Support Ideas with Examples What examples from the text help explain why tensions between the United States and the Soviet Union increased? *(Soviet troops invaded Afghanistan in 1979 in support of a newly formed pro-Soviet government. President Carter responded by withdrawing the SALT II treaty, funding Afghan rebels, and boycotting the 1980 Olympic Games hosted in Moscow. When Reagan took office, tensions escalated further as he took a tough anti-communist stance and referred to the Soviet Union as "evil.")*

Generate Explanations How did President Reagan address escalating Cold War tensions with the Soviet Union? *(He championed increased military spending in order to develop a new missile defense system named Star Wars, continued funding Afghan rebels, and sponsored economic sanctions against Poland, which enacted martial law under Soviet pressure.)*

ELL Use the ELL activity described in the ELL chart.

Further Instruction

Determine Point of View Why did Reagan address the Cold War situation by increasing military spending? *(Reagan wanted to approach the Soviet Union from a position of military strength.)*

DIGITAL TEXT 2
The Soviet Empire Crumbles

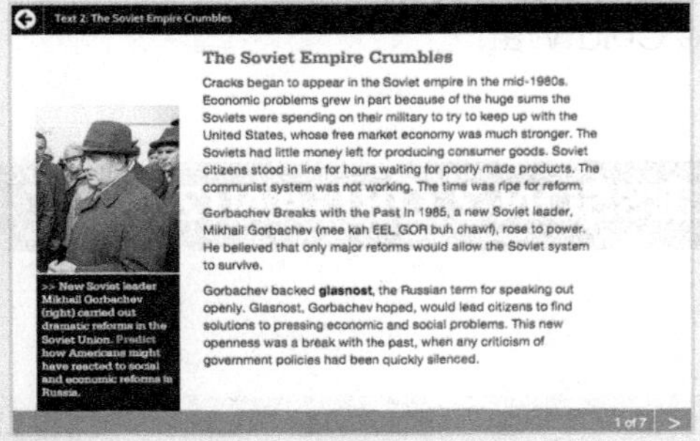

Objective 2: Explain why communism fell in Eastern Europe and the Soviet Union.

Quick Instruction

Before and After: The Berlin Wall Project the Before and After and use the slider to navigate between the two contrasting images of the Brandenburg Gate and the two contrasting images of Checkpoint Charlie. Prompt students to draw conclusions about the post-Soviet era of freedom based on the images. Review with students the function of the Berlin Wall as a literal separation between East and West Berlin, as well as a symbolic separation between Communism and the West.

ACTIVE CLASSROOM

Conduct a See-Think-Wonder activity. Pair students and have them respond to the following questions: What do you see? What does that make you think? What are you wondering about now that you have seen this? Invite volunteers to share their insights with the rest of the class.

BEFORE AND AFTER

The Berlin Wall

INTERACTIVE MAP

Shifting Alliances in Europe

DIGITAL TEXT 3

The Aftermath of the Cold War

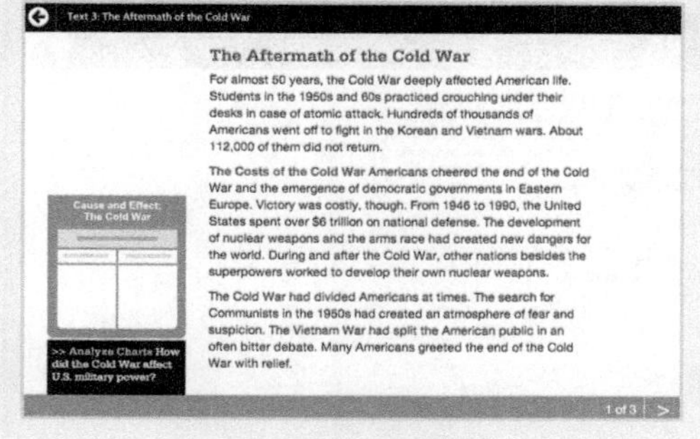

The Aftermath of the Cold War

For almost 50 years, the Cold War deeply affected American life. Students in the 1950s and 60s practiced crouching under their desks in case of atomic attack. Hundreds of thousands of Americans went off to fight in the Korean and Vietnam wars. About 112,000 of them did not return.

The Costs of the Cold War Americans cheered the end of the Cold War and the emergence of democratic governments in Eastern Europe. Victory was costly, though. From 1946 to 1990, the United States spent over $6 trillion on national defense. The development of nuclear weapons and the arms race had created new dangers for the world. During and after the Cold War, other nations besides the superpowers worked to develop their own nuclear weapons.

The Cold War had divided Americans at times. The search for Communists in the 1950s had created an atmosphere of fear and suspicion. The Vietnam War had split the American public in an often bitter debate. Many Americans greeted the end of the Cold War with relief.

Interactive Map: Shifting Alliances in Europe Project the Interactive Map and navigate through the layers with students, pointing out the increase in NATO members and the disappearance of the Warsaw Pact as the Soviet Union gradually lost control and broke apart. Remind students that NATO represented democratic and free-trade countries, whereas the Warsaw Pact was an alliance among Communist countries.

ACTIVE CLASSROOM

Conduct an Audio Tour activity. Pair students and have the first student give the second a verbal tour of the map, describing what it shows. Then, have the second student give the first an explanation of what it means. Continue the exercise for each layer of the map, having partners switch roles each time. Then, have partners work together to create an audio tour of the layers in their entirety. Invite volunteers to share their final tour with the class.

ELL Use the ELL activity described in the ELL chart.

Further Instruction

Interpret Why was the term *glasnost* an appropriate way to describe Soviet reform efforts? *(The term was a Russian word meaning to speak out openly. Gorbachev thought that the economic and social problems required more open, honest political dialogue, something that the one-party Soviet system had previously resisted.)*

Draw Conclusions Why would former communist countries, such as Poland and Hungary, be interested in joining NATO? *(NATO pledged to protect its member countries, and membership would encourage social and economic ties among countries as well.)*

Generate Explanations Why did the United States offer economic aid to former communist countries that had been part of the Soviet empire? *(The United States wanted to encourage a smooth transition to a free-market system and strengthen these nations to become trading partners.)*

Objective 3: **Identify Americans' reaction to the end of the Cold War.**

Quick Instruction

Summarize How did the end of the Cold War benefit many Americans? *(The U.S. government was able to decrease its military spending after the Cold War. The decreased spending in turn made it easier to address the budget deficit. Also, the threat of war seemed increasingly remote after the demise of the Soviet Union.)*

Further Instruction

Make Generalizations Why were many Americans relieved at the end of the Cold War? *Many Americans were relieved to live with a reduced threat of devastating nuclear war, as well as the constant tensions between East and West. The domestic debates over Cold War conflicts such as Vietnam seemed behind the country.)*

The End of the Cold War

SYNTHESIZE

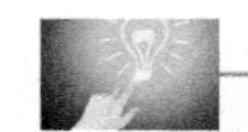

DIGITAL ACTIVITY

How the Cold War Ended

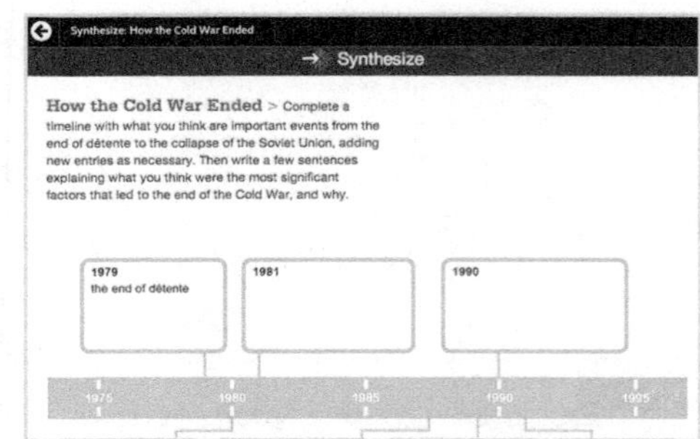

Work as a class to list important events within the given time period. Then, allow students time to complete their timelines and evaluations.

Discuss Poll the class to see if there is agreement on the events listed as having the most impact. Then, invite volunteers to share their reasoning. Discuss as a class students' ideas about the importance of events.

DEMONSTRATE

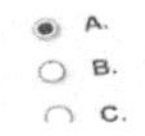

DIGITAL QUIZ

Lesson Quiz and Discussion Board

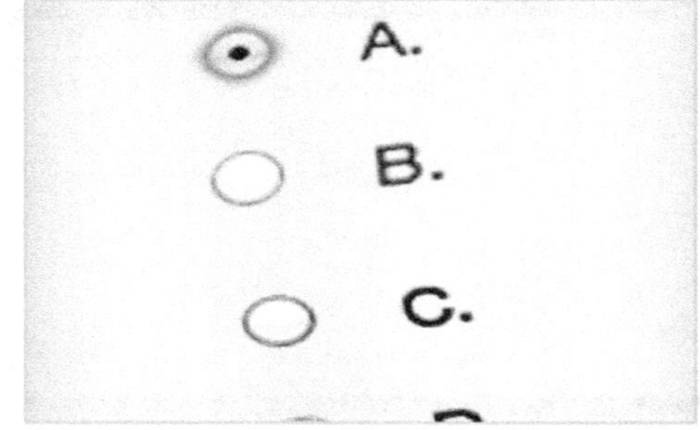

Assign the online Lesson Quiz for this lesson if you haven't already done so. Students will be offered automatic remediation or enrichment based on their score.

In *The End of the Cold War*, you learned about escalating Cold War tensions in the 1980s, the downfall of the Soviet Empire, and the aftermath of the Cold War.

Post these questions to the class on the Discussion Board:

Compare and Contrast How did Gorbachev's policies differ from the leaders' before him?

Express Problems Clearly Why did Cold War tensions escalate in 1979 and through the 1980s?

Topic Inquiry

Have students continue their investigations for the Topic Inquiry.

PEARSON realize™ www.PearsonRealize.com Access your Digital Lesson

Regional Conflicts

Supporting English Language Learners

Use with the reading, **A Post-Cold War World**.

Speaking

Review the difference between a fact and an opinion. Explain that students will express opinions in the activities below.

Beginning Provide students with phrases that express agreement, disagreement, or uncertainty, such as *Yes, I agree with that/him, No, I don't agree,* and *I'm not sure what I think*. Then read the Gingrich quotation "The United States must lead, period," and ask students to share their opinion about it.

Intermediate Ask: Do you think it is important that the world stop developing nuclear weapons? Why or why not? Invite students to express their opinion, as well as support that opinion with a reason.

Advanced Ask pairs of students to discuss: Do you believe that spreading freedom and democracy around the world is something the United States should do, or should it avoid intervening overseas? Why? Encourage students to use information from the text to support their opinions.

Advanced High Ask pairs of students to discuss: What roles and responsibilities do you think the United States should have around the world, and why? Invite students to use information from the text, from previous texts, and from current events in order to express their opinions.

Use with the reading, **Challenges in Russia and Eastern Europe.**

Reading

Explain that visuals can help students learn new words. The visuals can be literal representations or suggest meanings in less direct ways.

Beginning Point out the word *faltered* in the text's second paragraph. Act out the word for students and then read the paragraph together. Ask: Was Yeltsin successful in Chechnya or did he make mistakes?

Intermediate Display the word *faltered* and explain its meaning to students. Then have students look for visuals in the classroom or on the Internet that represent this word for them. Display and discuss their findings and then read the text's second paragraph together.

Advanced Invite pairs of students to look up and discuss the meaning of *faltered*. Then have them act out the word together before reading the text's second paragraph. Ask: How did the visual of acting out *faltered* help you to understand it when you read it?

Advanced High Invite students to look up the meaning of *faltered*, draw a picture representing it, and read the text's second paragraph. Then have partners compare their pictures and discuss how visuals—even if not directly related to the context—can help with reading comprehension.

D Differentiate Instruction

Use the Differentiated Instruction notes throughout the lesson plan to support the varied skill sets, levels of readiness, and interests in the mixed-ability classroom.

Challenge These notes include suggestions for expanding the activity for advanced students.

On-Level These notes include suggestions for modifying the activity to address different interests or learning styles.

Extra Support These notes include ideas for providing more scaffolding or reading spuport.

Special Needs These notes provide ideas for adapting instruction to support the needs of various special needs students.

NOTES

Regional Conflicts

Objectives

Objective 1: Describe how the end of the Cold War changed America's role in the world.

Objective 2: Explain why nuclear arms remained a threat.

Objective 3: Describe how the United States helped promote democracy.

Objective 4: Explain the role of the United States in conflicts in Russia and Eastern Europe, Latin America, the Middle East, and elsewhere.

LESSON 3 ORGANIZER	PACING: APPROX. 1 PERIOD, .5 BLOCKS		RESOURCES	
	OBJECTIVES	PACING	Online	Print
Connect				
DIGITAL START UP ACTIVITY **Fighting for Democracy**		5 min.	●	
Investigate				
DIGITAL TEXT 1 **A Post–Cold War World**	Objectives 1, 2	10 min.	●	●
BEFORE AND AFTER **Nuclear Arms Reductions**		10 min.	●	
DIGITAL TEXT 2 **Democratic Gains Around the Globe**	Objective 3	10 min.	●	●
DIGITAL TEXT 3 **Challenges in Russia and Eastern Europe**	Objective 4	10 min.	●	●
DIGITAL TEXT 4 **Intervention in Latin America, Africa, and Europe**		10 min.	●	●
DIGITAL TEXT 5 **Conflict in the Middle East**		10 min.	●	●
INTERACTIVE CHART **U.S. Engagement Around the World**		10 min.	●	
Synthesize				
DIGITAL ACTIVITY **American Responses to Conflict**		5 min.	●	
Demonstrate				
DIGITAL QUIZ **Lesson Quiz and Discussion Board**		10 min.	●	

PEARSON realize™ www.PearsonRealize.com

Go online to access additional resources including:
Primary Sources • Biographies • Supreme Court cases • 21st Century Skill Tutorials • Maps • Graphic Organizers.

CONNECT

DIGITAL START UP ACTIVITY

Fighting for Democracy

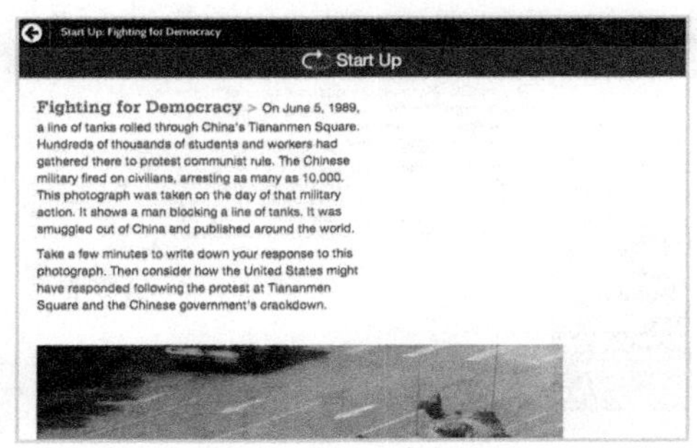

Start Up: Fighting for Democracy
Start Up
Fighting for Democracy > On June 5, 1989, a line of tanks rolled through China's Tiananmen Square. Hundreds of thousands of students and workers had gathered there to protest communist rule. The Chinese military fired on civilians, arresting as many as 10,000. This photograph was taken on the day of that military action. It shows a man blocking a line of tanks. It was smuggled out of China and published around the world.
Take a few minutes to write down your response to this photograph. Then consider how the United States might have responded following the protest at Tiananmen Square and the Chinese government's crackdown.

Project the Start Up Activity Have students view the photograph and complete the activity as they enter the classroom. Then ask them to share and discuss their ideas with partners.

Discuss Lead a class discussion in which students share their responses to the photograph, as well as their opinions about how the United States should respond to the events in Tiananmen Square.

Tell students that this lesson examines the post–Cold War era, including nuclear disarmament and proliferation, the spread of democracy, and U.S. involvement in conflicts around the globe.

Aa Vocabulary Development: Use the Interactive Reading Notepad to preview the Key Terms and Academic Vocabulary in this lesson with students.

FLIP IT!
Assign the Flipped Video for this lesson.

STUDENT EDITION PRINT PAGES: 877–887

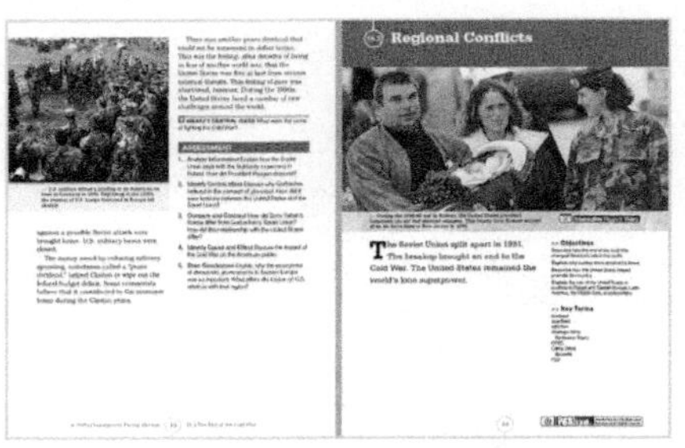

INVESTIGATE

DIGITAL TEXT 1

A Post–Cold War World

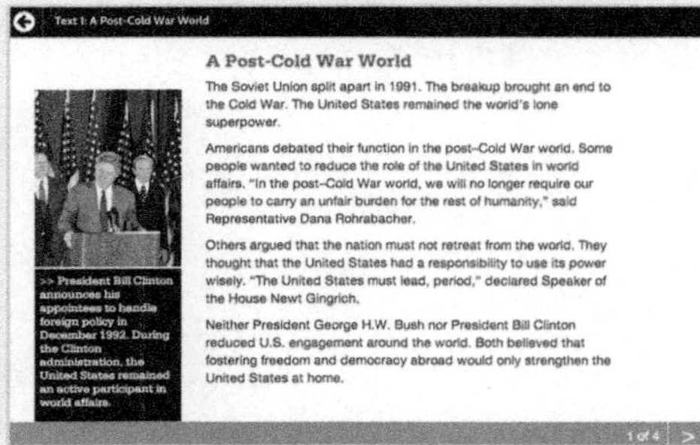

Text 1: A Post-Cold War World
A Post-Cold War World
The Soviet Union split apart in 1991. The breakup brought an end to the Cold War. The United States remained the world's lone superpower.
Americans debated their function in the post-Cold War world. Some people wanted to reduce the role of the United States in world affairs. "In the post-Cold War world, we will no longer require our people to carry an unfair burden for the rest of humanity," said Representative Dana Rohrabacher.
Others argued that the nation must not retreat from the world. They thought that the United States had a responsibility to use its power wisely. "The United States must lead, period," declared Speaker of the House Newt Gingrich.
Neither President George H.W. Bush nor President Bill Clinton reduced U.S. engagement around the world. Both believed that fostering freedom and democracy abroad would only strengthen the United States at home.
>> President Bill Clinton announces his appointees to handle foreign policy in December 1992. During the Clinton administration, the United States remained an active participant in world affairs.
1 of 4

BEFORE AND AFTER

Nuclear Arms Reductions

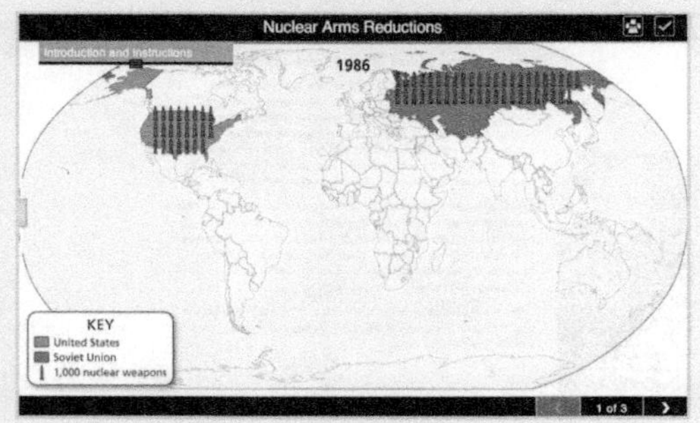

Objectives 1: **Describe how the end of the Cold War changed America's role in the world; 2: Explain why nuclear arms remained a threat.**

Quick Instruction

Before and After: Nuclear Arms Reductions Project the Before and After and use the slider to navigate between the two contrasting images. Prompt students to place the contrasting numbers of nuclear armaments in historical context. In 1986, the United States and Soviet Union were still engaged in the Cold War arms race; in 1996, it was apparent to both sides that the number of nuclear weapons could be reduced without sacrificing security. Ask: How did these two nations arrive at an agreement to cut their nuclear stockpiles so drastically? *(Nuclear arms reduction began with a treaty—START. Then, in 1993, further agreements were made to reduce nuclear weaponry.)*

ACTIVE CLASSROOM

Conduct a Cartoon It activity. Discuss the importance of nuclear arms reductions and then have students create a political cartoon that depicts one of the key issues or leaders of the time. Tell students to be sure their cartoons share a clear point of view about the chosen subject. Invite students to display their cartoons in the classroom or scan their cartoons to place on a class blog.

ELL Use the ELL activity described in the ELL chart.

Further Instruction

Generate Explanations Why did nuclear arms remain a threat despite international treaties promoting disarmament? *(Not all countries agreed to sign the nuclear non-proliferation treaties and others continued to develop nuclear weapons, including India and Pakistan. The capability to develop nuclear technology is also a concern.)*

Regional Conflicts

DIGITAL TEXT 2

Democratic Gains Around the Globe

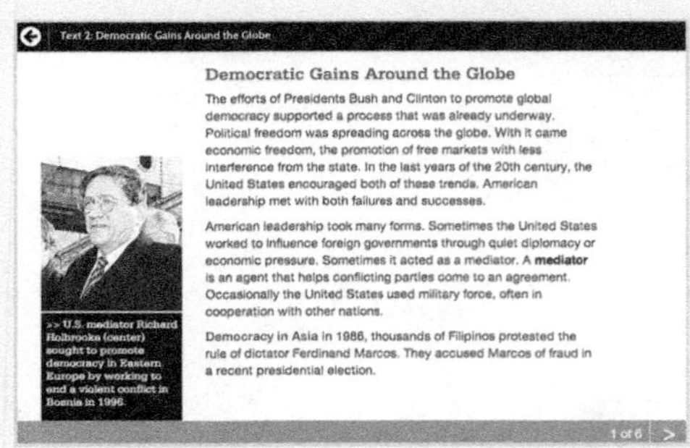

Objective 3: Describe how the United States helped promote democracy.

Quick Instruction

Project the digital image depicting apartheid in South Africa. Prompt students to understand the relationship between economic and political freedom. Identify countries in which democratic gains were realized, including South Africa and the Philippines. Also discuss those that resisted change, including Cuba and North Korea.

Distinguish Which elements of westernization did China adopt? Which did China ignore? *(Chinese Communist leaders adopted economic reforms and began to create a free-market economy; however, they did not open up their political system.)*

Infer Why did Presidents George H. W. Bush and Bill Clinton choose to not take strong action in response to the Chinese government's crackdown on the Tiananmen Square protests? *(Both Presidents hoped stronger diplomatic and economic connections to China would influence the Chinese government's position on human rights violations.)*

Further Instruction

Support Ideas with Evidence How did the United States use economic pressure to encourage political change in South Africa? *(The U.S. government approved sanctions against South Africa in 1986. American businesses were not allowed to invest in South Africa, and South African goods were not imported to the United States. Both measures were designed to create economic difficulty that would encourage South Africa to end its policy of apartheid.)*

DIGITAL TEXT 3

Challenges in Russia and Eastern Europe

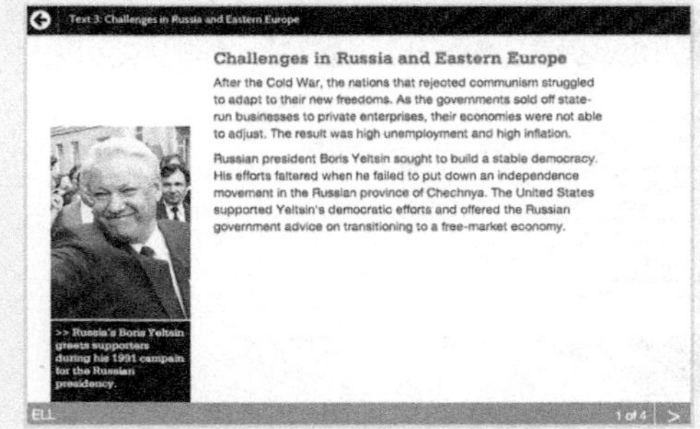

Objective 4: Explain the role of the United States in conflicts in Russia and Eastern Europe, Latin America, the Middle East, and elsewhere.

Quick Instruction

Interactive Chart: U.S. Engagement Around the World Project the Interactive Chart and guide students to identify the U.S. response to each event and drag the icons to the appropriate conflict. As you discuss each conflict, prompt students to explicitly consider the reasons why the United States chose to intervene. *(Possible responses: to promote democracy, to stop communism, to protect economic interests)*

Determine Point of View Why did the Reagan administration support a group attempting to overthrow the elected government in Nicaragua? *(Members of the administration did not want to see a socialist government in Latin America that was somewhat similar to Cuba.)*

DIGITAL TEXT 4

Intervention in Latin America, Africa, and Europe

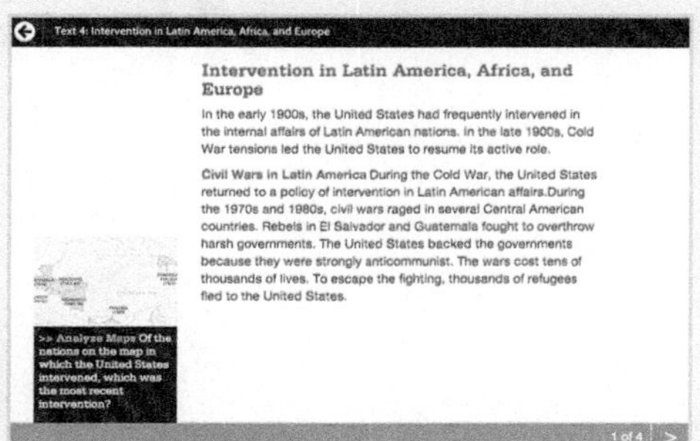

DIGITAL TEXT 5

Conflict in the Middle East

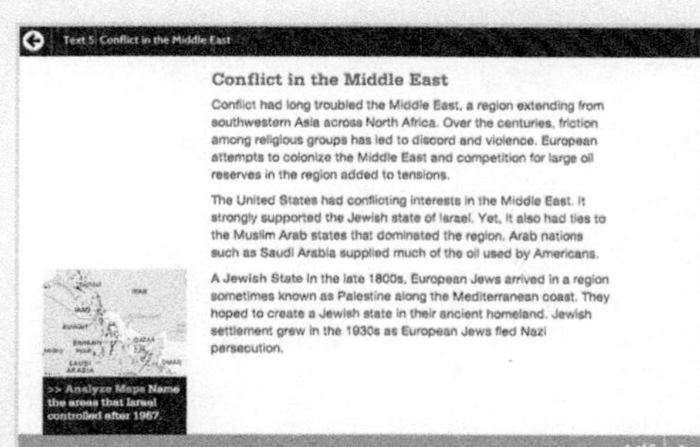

INTERACTIVE CHART

U.S. Engagement Around the World

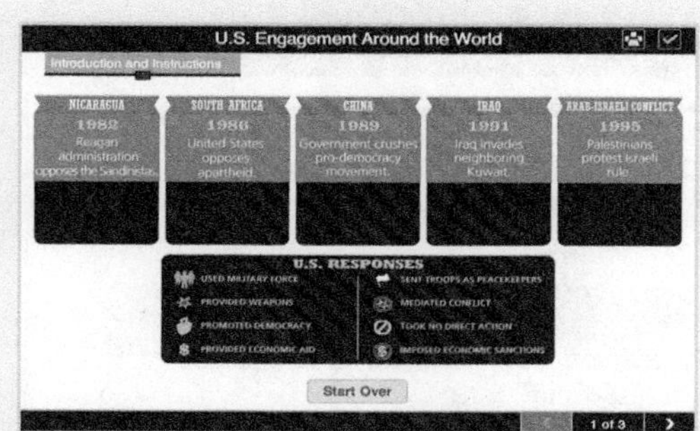

ACTIVE CLASSROOM

Conduct a Take a Stand activity. Ask students to take a stand on the following question: In which conflict was it most clearly in the interests of the United States to intervene? Divide students into groups based on their chosen conflict and allow them time to discuss the reasons for their responses. Instruct each group to choose a representative to present and defend the group's point of view. After the presentations, discuss whether anyone changed their opinion.

D Differentiate: Challenge Have students choose one of the international conflicts to investigate. Suggest students research the cause of the conflict, the level of U.S. involvement, and analyses suggesting the motivations for involvement. Allow students time to present their research to the class.

ELL Use the ELL activity described in the ELL chart.

Further Instruction

Cite Evidence What factors best explain why the United States and other UN allies chose to take military action after Iraq invaded Kuwait in 1990? *(Many countries were concerned that Iraq was trying to control a greater percentage of oil production in the Middle East. There were also concerns over Iraq's chemical and biological weapon programs.)*

Identify Patterns What role did the United States repeatedly take in international conflicts? *(Possible responses: The United States sent troops around the globe to stop civil wars in Eastern Europe, Africa, and Latin America. The United States was a peacekeeper, stationing troops in areas to protect and enforce treaties. The United States also continued to support anti-communist movements around the globe.)*

Identify Central Issues What common issues are related to the conflicts in Eastern Europe, Africa, and the Middle East? *(Most of the conflicts were over land and self-rule and were motivated by factors such as ethnicity and/or religion.)*

Regional Conflicts

SYNTHESIZE

DIGITAL ACTIVITY

American Responses to Conflict

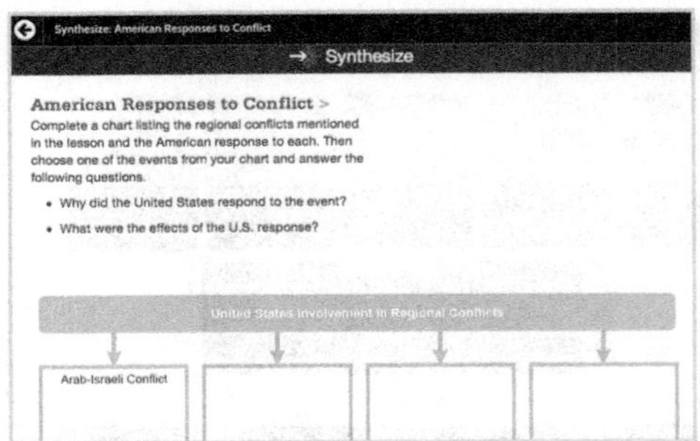

After students have completed their graphic organizers, invite them to share their work with partners before responding to the questions. Allow students time to consider their answers based on what they have learned and construct paragraphs in response.

Discuss Lead a class discussion in which students consider the impact of U.S. involvement in foreign affairs. Challenge students to consider the impact abroad and at home.

DEMONSTRATE

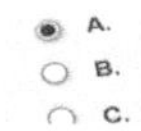

DIGITAL QUIZ

Lesson Quiz and Discussion Board

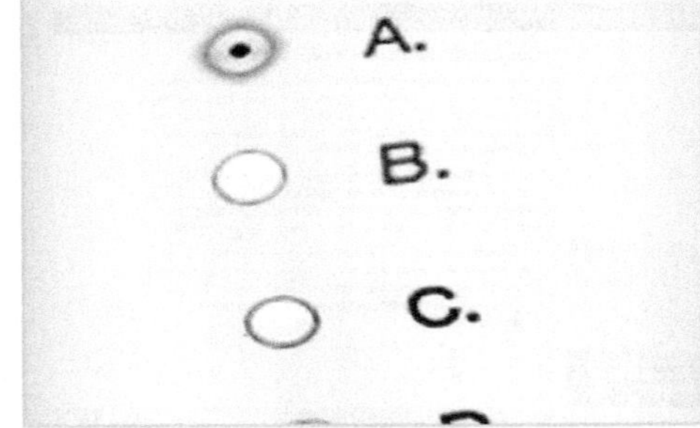

Assign the online Lesson Quiz for this lesson if you haven't already done so. Students will be offered automatic remediation or enrichment based on their score.

In *Regional Conflicts*, you learned about issues related to nuclear weapons in a post–Cold War world. You learned of democratic gains around the globe and about international conflicts and the role the United States took in those conflicts.

Post these questions to the class on the Discussion Board:

Support Ideas with Examples Should the United States get involved in other countries' civil wars? Why or why not? Provide examples from the text to support your opinion.

Summarize Choose one conflict in the Middle East and summarize the key events in that conflict, including U.S. involvement and its impact.

Topic Inquiry

Have students continue their investigations for the Topic Inquiry.

www.PearsonRealize.com
Access your Digital Lesson

A Global Superpower Facing Change

SYNTHESIZE

DIGITAL ACTIVITY

Reflect on the Essential Question and Topic

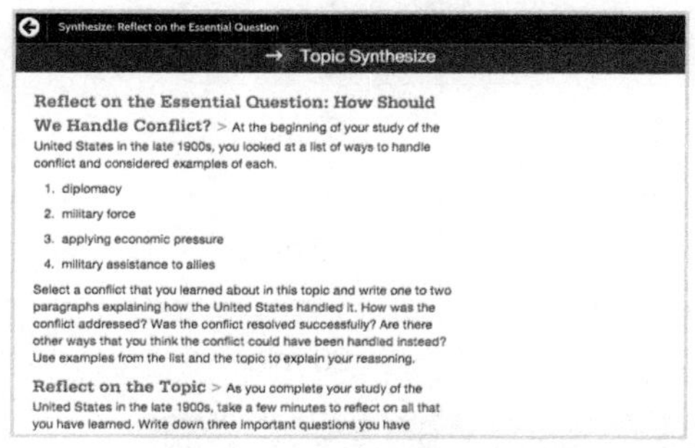

Ask students to reconsider the Essential Question for the Topic: How should we handle conflict? Remind students of the possibilities they considered at the start of the Topic:

- diplomacy
- military force
- applying economic pressure
- military assistance to allies

After students have chosen a conflict and responded to the questions in a paragraph or two, ask volunteers to share their writing with the class. Encourage discussion and debate as students share their ideas. Invite students to post their answers on the Class Discussion Board.

Next, ask students to reflect on the Topic as a whole and jot down three questions about the Topic content and the answers to those questions. Review the sample questions and encourage students to share their own questions with the class. Invite students to post their questions and answers on the Class Discussion Board.

Topic Inquiry

Have students complete Step 3 of the Topic Inquiry.

DEMONSTRATE

DIGITAL TOPIC REVIEW AND ASSESSMENT

A Global Superpower Facing Change

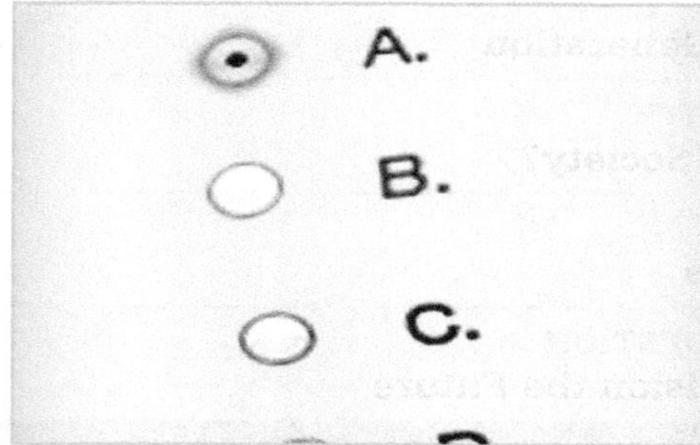

Students can prepare for the Topic Test by answering the questions in the Topic Review and Assessment online or the Assessment questions in the Print Student text. They can also prepare by reviewing their answers to the Interactive Reading Notepad questions or reviewing their notes in the Reading and Notetaking Study Guide.

DIGITAL TOPIC TEST

A Global Superpower Facing Change

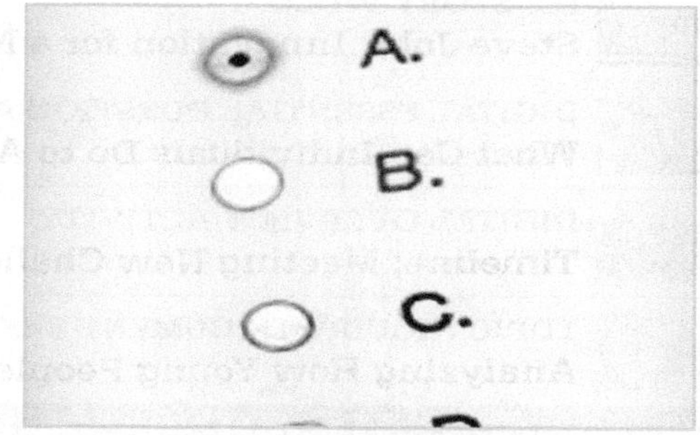

TOPIC TEST

Assign the Topic Test to assess students' understanding of topic content.

BENCHMARK TESTS

Assign these benchmark tests as you complete the relevant topics to monitor student progress toward mastering the course content and as preparation for the End-of-Course Test.

Benchmark Test 1: Topics 1–2
Benchmark Test 2: Topics 3–4
Benchmark Test 3: Topics 5–6
Benchmark Test 4: Topics 7–9
Benchmark Test 5: Topics 10–12
Benchmark Test 6: Topics 13–14
Benchmark Test 7: Topics 15–17

Meeting New Challenges

TOPIC 17 ORGANIZER	PACING: APPROX. 8 PERIODS, 4 BLOCKS
	PACING
Connect	1 period
MY STORY VIDEO **Steve Jobs: Innovation for a New Generation**	10 min.
DIGITAL ESSENTIAL QUESTION ACTIVITY **What Can Individuals Do to Affect Society?**	10 min.
DIGITAL OVERVIEW ACTIVITY **Timeline: Meeting New Challenges**	10 min.
TOPIC INQUIRY: DOCUMENT-BASED QUESTION **Analyzing How Young People Envision the Future**	20 min.
Investigate	2–5 periods
TOPIC INQUIRY: DOCUMENT-BASED QUESTION **Analyzing How Young People Envision the Future**	Ongoing
LESSON 1 Terrorism and Wars Overseas	30–40 min.
LESSON 2 An Unstable World	30–40 min.
LESSON 3 A Global Economy	30–40 min.
LESSON 4 Advances in Science and Technology	30–40 min.
LESSON 5 Challenges at Home	30–40 min.
Synthesize	1 period
DIGITAL ESSENTIAL QUESTION ACTIVITY **Reflect on the Essential Question and Topic**	10 min.
TOPIC INQUIRY: DOCUMENT-BASED QUESTION **Analyzing How Young People Envision the Future**	20 min.
Demonstrate	1–2 periods
DIGITAL ESSENTIAL QUESTION ACTIVITY **Reflect on the Essential Question and Topic**	10 min.
TOPIC INQUIRY: DOCUMENT-BASED QUESTION **Analyzing How Young People Envision the Future**	20 min.

TOPIC INQUIRY: DOCUMENT-BASED QUESTION

Analyzing How Young People Envision the Future

In this Topic Inquiry, students work independently to examine documents that were created using digital media—such as blogs and social media posts—in which young people consider the state of the world and their hopes and concerns for the future. Students will then select two additional primary digital media sources from social media or blogs reflecting young Americans' attitudes today. Students will use these documents to write an essay in which they answer the Guiding Question: What do young Americans envision for themselves and their future? Thinking about how young Americans perceive the future and their role within it will help students to clarify and address important issues. The Topic Inquiry will also develop students' understanding of the Topic Essential Question: **What can individuals do to affect society?**

STEP 1: CONNECT

Develop Questions and Plan the Investigation

Launch the DBQ Writing Activity

Display the guiding question to which students will respond and tell them to keep it in mind as they embark on this Topic Inquiry. Make sure students understand that they will write an essay in which they share their analyses of several documents presenting opinions of young people about the state of the world and their hopes and concerns for the future. Play the audio clip for the class, encouraging students to take notes as they listen.

Generate Questions

Pair students and allow them time to share their notes and reflections on the audio clip. Have partners work together to generate their own questions and answer the Questions to Discuss from Step 1B of the Student Instructions.

Suggestion: Allow time for partners to share their ideas and answers with the whole class. Encourage students to record ideas they find original or interesting to discuss in their writing.

Resources

- Student Instructions
- Project Launch

PROFESSIONAL DEVELOPMENT

Document-Based Question

Be sure to view the Document-Based Question Professional Development resources in the online course.

STEP 2: INVESTIGATE

Apply Disciplinary Concepts and Tools

Analyze the Documents

As students read the documents, they should keep their lists of questions in hand, recording answers as they go. Students might find it helpful to categorize documents based on point of view. For example, they might divide the documents into optimistic outlooks, pessimistic outlooks, and unclear outlooks. Students can use this categorization to help organize their essays.

Before students explore additional contemporary primary sources, review the suggested sources provided in the Student Instructions. Review all student choices for appropriateness.

Suggestion: Remind students that they must give credit when they cite specific ideas in their analyses, even when they do not use direct quotations from the sources.

Check Your Understanding

Students can meet with a partner to share and discuss the answers they provided to the questions attached to each document. Partners should discuss their interpretations of the central ideas of each document.

Resources

- 21st Century Skills Tutorial: Evaluate Websites
- 21st Century Skills Tutorial: Analyze Media Content
- Document A: Excerpt from *We are the next Generation,* article by WriterFanatic
- Document B: Excerpt from *Learning to Fail,* speech by Tara Suri and Niha Jain, 2011
- Document C: Excerpt from *Forever,* editor's letter, by Tavi Gevinson, 2013
- Document D: Excerpt from *Young Adults: Can You Picture Your Retirement,* interview with Asha Richardson, Ashley Williams, and Sayre Quevedo, 2013

TOPIC INQUIRY: DOCUMENT-BASED QUESTION

Analyzing How Young People Envision the Future *(continued)*

STEP 3: SYNTHESIZE

Evaluate Sources and Use Evidence to Formulate Conclusions

Write Your Essay

Display the Rubric for a DBQ Essay for the class and review key criteria. Post the guiding question: What do young Americans envision for themselves and their future? Spend a few minutes reviewing the bulleted list in the Student Instructions that guides students through the writing process.

Suggestion: Suggest that students use a graphic organizer, such as an idea web or three-column chart, to categorize ideas and organize information before they begin writing. Students can consult their graphic organizers as they draft their essays.

Resources

- Rubric for a DBQ Essay

STEP 4: DEMONSTRATE

Communicate Conclusions and Take Informed Action

After students have completed and submitted their essays, lead a class discussion in which students reflect on what they have learned and share the opinions they have formed and the reasoning behind those opinions. Ask students to predict how this new-found understanding of the opinions of young Americans will change society in the future. Encourage students to discuss how the opinions of others will affect how they personally will work to affect society.

Suggestion: As an extension activity, have students research contemporary American youth groups and organizations to find out how they are working to affect positive changes in American society and the successes and failures of the groups.

INTRODUCTION

Meeting New Challenges

America in the twenty-first century faces both challenges and opportunities. Globalization has connected the United States more closely with the rest of the world, bringing economic growth as well as competition. Technology accelerates these changes as innovations in computers, Internet-based communications, and biotechnology impact American life. The terrorist attacks of September 11, 2001, ushered in a new era of domestic and foreign policy, raising questions about security and civil rights. In addition, new immigration trends and other changing social patterns continue to shape America's diverse society.

CONNECT

MY STORY VIDEO

Steve Jobs: Innovation for a New Generation

Watch a video about Steve Jobs's career.

Check Understanding With what company was Steve Jobs associated? *(Apple)*

Make Generalizations What is the most important lesson that Steve Jobs's career reveals? *(that innovation in consumer products, especially in the field of technology, is essential)*

FLIP IT!
Assign the My Story video.

DIGITAL ESSENTIAL QUESTION ACTIVITY

What Can Individuals Do to Affect Society?

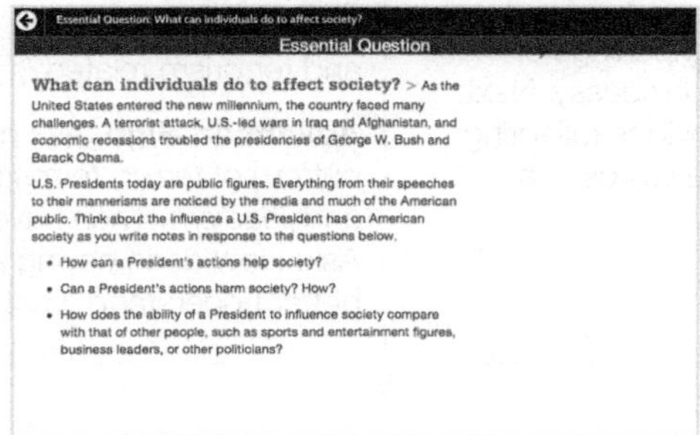

Ask students to think about the Essential Question for this topic: What can individuals do to affect society? Have students reflect on the influence a U.S. President has on American society. What responsibility does the President have in promoting freedom, national pride, or economic opportunity?

If students have not already done so, ask them to respond to the questions.

Compare Think about your answer to the question, How does the ability of a President to influence society compare with that of other people? What qualities or characteristics determines a prominent person's influence on society? *(Answers will vary but should mention factors such as legal powers, public support, and economic and political influence.)*

Support Ideas with Examples Has the increase in mass communication technology increased the influence of U.S. Presidents? Explain. *(Answers will vary but should be supported with examples. Students may respond that by increasing a President's audience, modern communications have increased his or her influence. Students may also respond that modern communications decrease a President's influence by publicizing his or her failings.)*

DIGITAL OVERVIEW ACTIVITY

Timeline: Meeting New Challenges

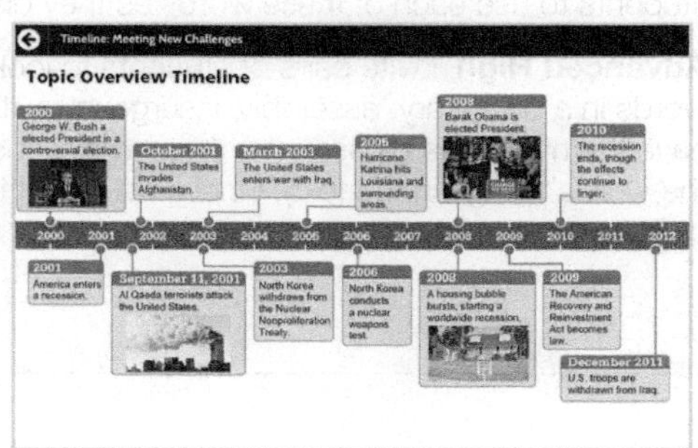

Display the timeline showing the major events that occurred in the 2000s. During this topic, students will learn about all of these events and many more, but this timeline will provide a contextual framework into which they can place events.

Identify Patterns What trends do you notice that might create more uncertainty in the world? *(terrorist attacks, wars in the Middle East, North Korea's nuclear arms ambitions)*

Identify Cause and Effect How did the September 11 attacks shape American foreign policy in the 2000s? *(The attacks led America to go to war in Afghanistan and to fight terrorism.)*

Topic Inquiry

Launch the Topic Inquiry with students after introducing the Topic.

Terrorism and Wars Overseas

Supporting English Language Learners

Use with the reading, **The Iraq War**.

Learning

Review how a glossary or dictionary can help students learn new words by explaining them in more familiar language.

Beginning Display a "glossary" with simple definitions of these four words from the text: assembly, insurgency, withdrawal, embassy. Read aloud the glossary together. Then have students answer questions that demonstrate their understanding of these words' meanings.

Intermediate Display a "glossary" with simple definitions of these four words from the text: assembly, insurgency, withdrawal, embassy. Invite students to ask clarifying questions about the words and their meanings. Then have them use the words in sentences related to the text.

Advanced Ask pairs of students to look up these words in a dictionary and discuss them: assembly, insurgency, withdrawal, embassy. Then invite students to use each of these words as they discuss the text.

Advanced High Invite pairs of students to look up the meanings of these words in a dictionary: assembly, insurgency, withdrawal, embassy. Next, have them create a glossary for these words (using definitions reflecting the words' usage in the text). Finally, ask them to use the words in a discussion about the text.

Use with the reading, **The Continuing Challenges of Jihadism**.

Listening

Display the words *jihad*, *jihadist*, and *jihadism*. Review the differences in their meanings and pronunciation.

Beginning Say a sentence that uses the word *jihad*, *jihadist*, or *jihadism*. Have students identify which word you used. Then ask them a question to confirm their understanding of the sentence. Repeat this process for all three words.

Intermediate Summarize the text aloud, making sure to use the words *jihad*, *jihadist*, and *jihadism*. Then use these words in questions to confirm students' understanding (e.g., What is "external jihad"? What do jihadists do? What do Muslims think of jihadism?).

Advanced Next to *jihad*, *jihadist*, and *jihadism*, display the words *terror*, *terrorist*, and *terrorism*. Discuss how the language patterns of these word groups are similar. Then use all six words to ask questions that confirm and enhance students' comprehension of the text (e.g., How are jihadism and terrorism related?).

Advanced High Ask pairs of students to discuss how the language pattern of *terror*, *terrorist*, and *terrorism* is similar to that of *jihad*, *jihadist*, and *jihadism*. Then have them use all six words as they discuss the text. Ask: How does paying attention to these words' endings help you to better understand what you hear?

D Differentiate Instruction

Use the Differentiated Instruction notes throughout the lesson plan to support the varied skill sets, levels of readiness, and interests in the mixed-ability classroom.

Challenge These notes include suggestions for expanding the activity for advanced students.

On-Level These notes include suggestions for modifying the activity to address different interests or learning styles.

Extra Support These notes include ideas for providing more scaffolding or reading spupport.

Special Needs These notes provide ideas for adapting instruction to support the needs of various special needs students.

NOTES

PEARSON realize™ www.PearsonRealize.com

Go online to access additional resources including: Primary Sources • Biographies • Supreme Court cases • 21st Century Skill Tutorials • Maps • Graphic Organizers.

Objectives

Objective 1: Describe the terrorist attacks of September 11, 2001, and their impact on the United States.

Objective 2: Explain why the United States went to war in Afghanistan and describe the course of that war.

Objective 3: Assess the impact of the U.S. intervention in Iraq.

Objective 4: Reflect on the treatment of prisoners following the September 11 attacks.

Objective 5: Identify the continuing challenges posed by jihadism.

LESSON 1 ORGANIZER	PACING: APPROX. 1 PERIOD, .5 BLOCKS		RESOURCES	
	OBJECTIVES	PACING	Online	Print
Connect				
DIGITAL START UP ACTIVITY **A Response to September 11**		5 min.	●	
Investigate				
DIGITAL TEXT 1 **The United States Responds to an Attack**	Objectives 1, 2	10 min.	●	●
INTERACTIVE GALLERY **September 11, 2001**	Objectives 1, 2	10 min.	●	
DIGITAL TEXT 2 **The Iraq War**	Objective 3	10 min.	●	●
INTERACTIVE TIMELINE **War in Iraq, 2003–2011**	Objective 3	10 min.	●	
DIGITAL TEXT 3 **The Continuing Challenges of Jihadism**	Objectives 4, 5	10 min.	●	●
Synthesize				
DIGITAL ACTIVITY **Guantanamo Bay**		5 min.	●	
Demonstrate				
DIGITAL QUIZ **Lesson Quiz and Class Discussion Board**		10 min.	●	

Terrorism and Wars Overseas

CONNECT

DIGITAL START UP ACTIVITY

A Response to September 11

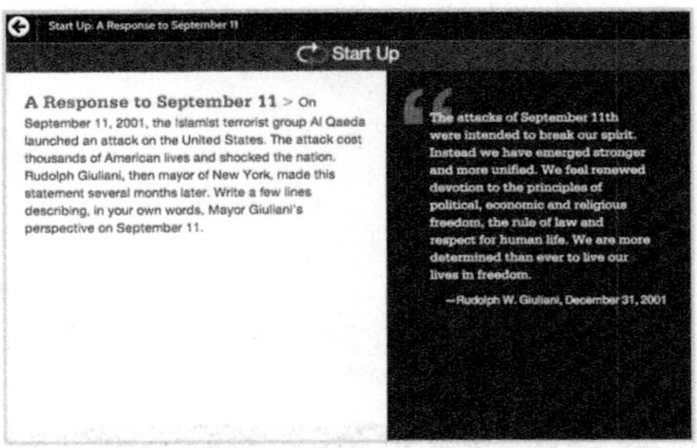

Project the Start Up Activity Ask students to read the quote from Mayor Giuliani as they enter and have them write a paragraph reflecting on it. Have students share their ideas with a partner.

Discuss Take a moment to reflect on how the September 11 attacks would have affected Americans. Invite students to share how they think Americans will emerge to be "stronger and more unified." *(Possible response: Americans will show more support for our leaders; Many Americans might join the armed forces to serve the country.)*

Tell students that in this lesson they will explore the September 11, 2001, terrorist attacks and the wars that followed them.

Aa Vocabulary Development: Use the Interactive Reading Notepad to preview the Key Terms and Academic Vocabulary in this Lesson with students.

FLIP IT!

Assign the Flipped Video for this lesson.

STUDENT EDITION PRINT PAGES: 892–898

INVESTIGATE

DIGITAL TEXT 1

The United States Responds to an Attack

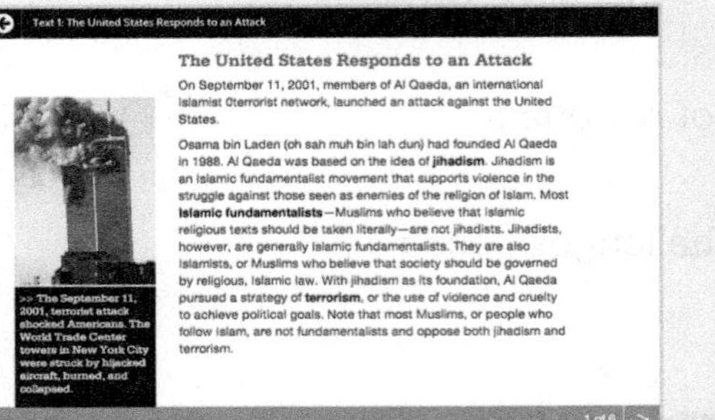

INTERACTIVE GALLERY

September 11, 2001

Objectives 1: Describe the terrorist attacks of September 11, 2001, and their impact on the United States; 2: Explain why the United States went to war in Afghanistan and describe the course of that war.

Quick Instruction

Interactive Gallery: September 11, 2001 Project the Interactive Gallery. Introduce the activity by writing the word *terrorism* on the board. Have the class brainstorm the effect of terrorism on the nation since 2001. *(Possible responses: People have died or been injured. The country has waged war in Afghanistan and Iraq and has had to deal with attacks in other countries. Security has tightened domestically. Americans do not feel as safe as they once did before the September 11th attacks.)* Navigate through the images with students to reveal more information about key aspects of the September 11 attacks and their aftermath.

Generate Explanations How were the September 11 attacks also an attack on American symbols of power? *(Al Qaeda attacked symbols of American power—an important financial center in the country's largest city and the Pentagon, the headquarters of the U.S. military.)*

Draw Conclusions In what ways were the September 11 attacks a turning point for the nation? *(The attacks caused a shift in U.S. foreign policy. Americans united to defend the nation. The nation eventually went to war in Afghanistan and pursued a global war on terrorism.)*

ACTIVE CLASSROOM

Conduct a Wallpaper Activity. Have students design a piece of "wallpaper" with text and images that encapsulate a key aspect of the September 11 attacks. Post each student's wallpaper and have the class take a gallery walk in which they note what others have written or illustrated.

Further Instruction

Connect How was the invasion and war in Afghanistan related to the September 11 attacks? *(The Taliban in Afghanistan was protecting Osama Bin Laden and others responsible for the September 11 attacks.)*

Cite Evidence What evidence suggests that initial U.S. efforts in Afghanistan were not entirely successful? *(Afghanistan's government, supported by the United States, has never been in complete control of the country, and the Taliban regained some of its power.)*

www.PearsonRealize.com
Access your Digital Lesson

DIGITAL TEXT 2

The Iraq War

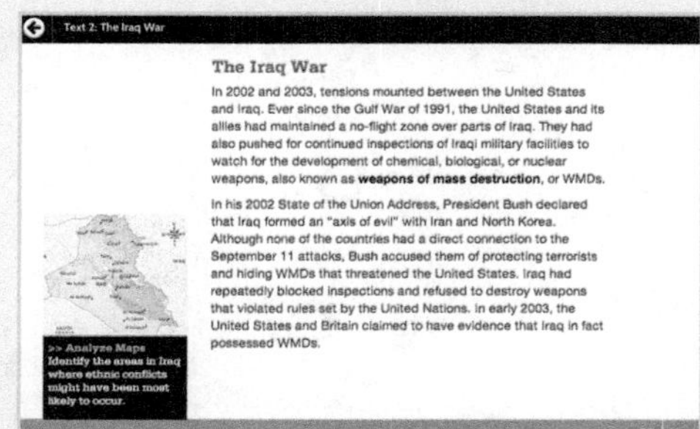

INTERACTIVE TIMELINE

War in Iraq, 2003–2011

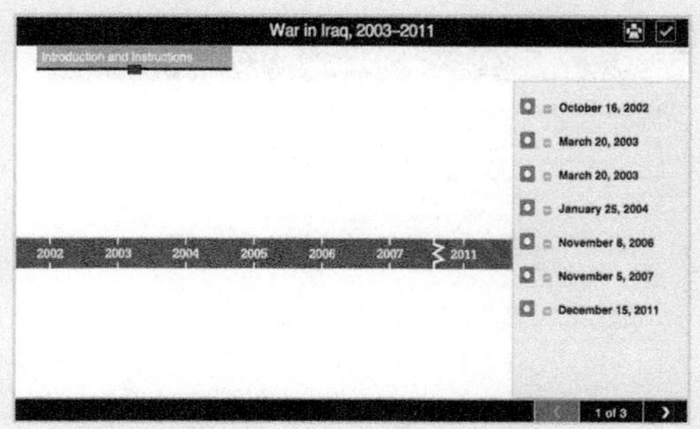

DIGITAL TEXT 3

The Continuing Challenges of Jihadism

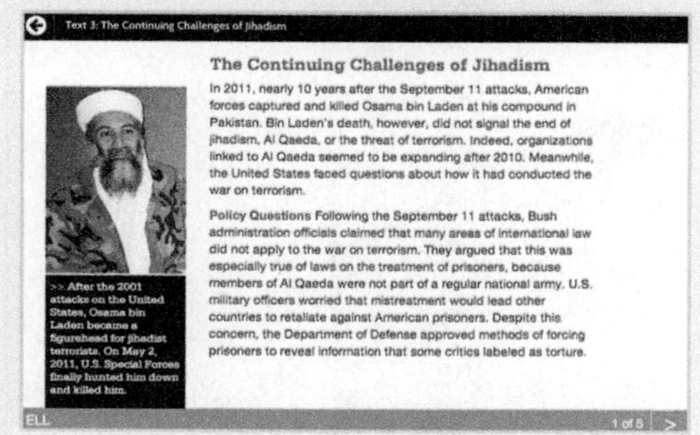

Objective 3: Assess the impact of the U.S. intervention in Iraq.

Quick Instruction

Interactive Timeline: War in Iraq, 2003–2011 Project the Interactive Timeline and navigate through the images with students. Point out that in May of 2003, President Bush declared that combat operations were over, yet the peak year for U.S. combat deaths was 2007. Challenge students to describe what they can infer from that fact. *(Other problems and threats must have developed that made the war much more difficult than U.S. leaders anticipated.)*

Summarize Why did President Bush and other world leaders consider Saddam Hussein a threat? *(President Bush accused Saddam Hussein of protecting terrorists and hiding WMDs that threatened the United States and its allies.)*

ACTIVE CLASSROOM

Conduct a Make Headlines activity. Have students choose an event represented on the Interactive Timeline for which they can write a headline. Ask: If you were to write a headline that describes this event, what would that headline be? When students finish writing, have them exchange papers with partners and discuss their ideas. Invite volunteers to share their headlines with the class.

D Differentiate: Extra Support Pair students to review the text and Interactive Timeline and write down the reasons for the U.S. invasion of Iraq and the key events. Have pairs go through their lists and discuss why each reason was a factor in the conflict.

ELL Use the ELL activity described in the ELL chart.

Further Instruction

Express Problems Clearly How did differences among the Iraqi people make the task of the occupying U.S. forces more difficult? *(Iraq's three distinct groups—Sunni Muslim Arabs, Shiite Muslim Arabs, and ethnic Kurds—often fought among themselves. The new Iraqi government was too weak to manage the country.)*

Draw Conclusions Why might many Americans have thought the Iraq War was unwinnable? *(U.S. leaders continued to send more troops to Iraq; however, violence against U.S. military forces and among different Iraqi factions continued to erupt throughout the country.)*

Objectives 4: Reflect on the treatment of prisoners following the September 11 attacks; 5: Identify the continuing challenges posed by jihadism.

Quick Instruction

Project the digital image of Osama Bin Laden and prompt students to identify the role he played in the War on Terror? *(Bin Laden was the leader of Al Qaeda, the terrorist group responsible for the September 11 attacks. American and other forces invaded Afghanistan to capture Bin Laden, who was hiding there with protection from the Taliban.)*

Draw Conclusions Why did some criticize the treatment of jihadist prisoners? *(Many of the prisoners at Guantanamo had not been tried in court or proven to have acted illegally. Also, some critics considered that the methods used to try to force prisoners to reveal information were torturous.)*

Summarize how President Bush and other American leaders justified the imprisonment of prisoners at Guantanamo Bay. *(Bush administration officials claimed that international law regarding the treatment of war prisoners applied only to soldiers fighting for nations and did not apply to prisoners accused of terrorism, because members of Al Qaeda and other terrorist groups were not part of a recognized nation.)*

ELL Use the ELL activity described in the ELL chart.

Terrorism and Wars Overseas

Further Instruction

Generate Explanations Why have jihadist groups and terrorists around the world been difficult to defeat? *(Many jihadist groups and other terrorist organizations are relatively small and do not have the explicit support of a recognized nation, which makes it challenging to locate and defeat them.)*

SYNTHESIZE

DIGITAL ACTIVITY

Guantanamo Bay

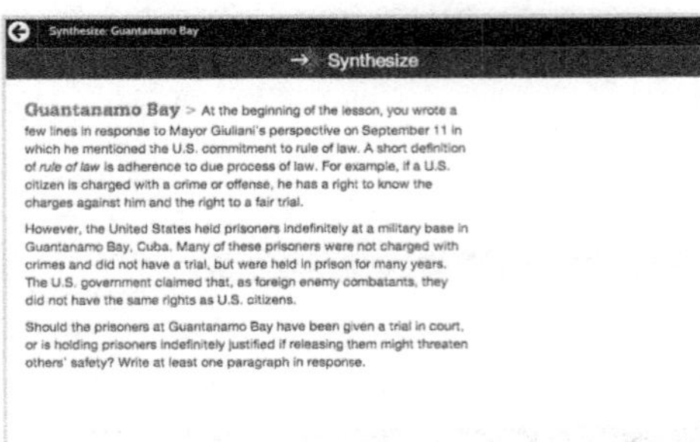

Before students begin writing their paragraphs, review the definition of rule of law *(adherence to set laws and to due process of law)*. Be sure students understand the concept and its connection to American civil liberties and the Constitution *(the Fifth and Fourteenth Amendments)*. Also explain that courts have ruled that the protections of the Constitution apply only on American soil or to American citizens and that the Guantanamo prisoners, on a U.S. base in Cuba, technically fall within neither category. When completed, invite volunteers to share their paragraphs with a partner or the class.

Discuss Is the U.S. government obligated to give the prisoners at Guantanamo Bay the civil liberties described in the Constitution during time of war? *(Possible responses: Yes, the government should maintain its principles and give the prisoners their time in court to determine their guilt or innocence. No, prisoners accused of terrorism do not deserve the same rights as American citizens and can be held without trial to protect American interests.)*

DEMONSTRATE

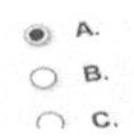

DIGITAL QUIZ

Lesson Quiz and Class Discussion Board

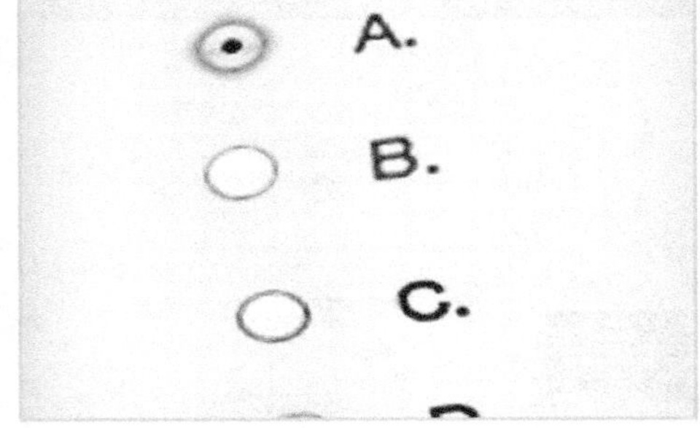

Assign the online Lesson Quiz for this lesson if you haven't already done so. Students will be offered automatic remediation or enrichment based on their score.

In *Responding to Terrorism*, you read about how members of Al Qaeda attacked the United States, igniting a global war against terrorism, as well as some of the challenging decisions the U.S. government had to make in time of war against jihadists.

Pose these questions to the class on the Discussion Board:

Summarize How has the United States tried to remain safe and to defend democracy?

Make Predictions Will there ever be an end to the challenges posed by jihadism? Why or why not?

Topic Inquiry

Have students continue their investigations for the Topic Inquiry.

PEARSON realize™ www.PearsonRealize.com Access your Digital Lesson

An Unstable World

Supporting English Language Learners

Use with the reading, **Unrest in Southwest Asia and North Africa**.

Speaking

Explain that as their English language proficiency increases, students will be able to explain issues and ideas in greater detail. Ask students why this skill is important.

Beginning Ask: How do Arabs and Israelis get along? Whether students answer with a word, a phrase, or a complete sentence, follow up with another question that encourages them to expand on their initial answer.

Intermediate Ask students to volunteer a detail about President Bush's "roadmap to peace" or its outcome. Record and display the details provided by students. Then organize the details for cohesion and read them aloud together.

Advanced Invite pairs of students to take turns telling each other details about Arab-Israeli relations. Encourage them to continue for as long as possible (that is, until all the details they know have been exhausted).

Advanced High Place students in pairs, and have partners separately prepare a talk about either Arab-Israeli relations or the Arab Spring. Encourage students to research extra details for their talk, which should last a few minutes. Then have partners present their talks to each other. Ask: How did hearing extra details about a topic help your understanding of it?

Use with the reading, **Assisting Other Nations**.

Reading

Display these commonly found words from the text: declare, assist, monitor, confirm. With students, define them using familiar synonyms (e.g., say, help, watch, prove).

Beginning Display a simple sentence about the text using the word *declare*. Invite students to read aloud the sentence and restate it in their own words. Repeat this process for the words *assist*, *monitor*, and *confirm*.

Intermediate Display a paragraph about the text that uses the words *declare*, *assist*, *monitor*, and *confirm*, except with write-on-lines where the words would otherwise be. Invite students to read the paragraph and use context clues to determine where each words goes. Then read aloud the paragraph together and discuss its meaning.

Advanced Invite students to locate the words *declared*, *assisted*, *monitored*, and *confirmed* in the text. For each word, have them restate the meaning of the sentence in their own words.

Advanced High Invite students to write a paragraph about the text that uses the words *declare*, *assist*, *monitor*, and *confirm*. Then have partners read each other's paragraphs and discuss their meanings. Ask: Why is it important to both read and write with the words you want to learn?

D Differentiate Instruction

Use the Differentiated Instruction notes throughout the lesson plan to support the varied skill sets, levels of readiness, and interests in the mixed-ability classroom.

Challenge These notes include suggestions for expanding the activity for advanced students.

On-Level These notes include suggestions for modifying the activity to address different interests or learning styles.

Extra Support These notes include ideas for providing more scaffolding or reading spupport.

Special Needs These notes provide ideas for adapting instruction to support the needs of various special needs students.

NOTES

An Unstable World

Objectives

Objective 1: Explain international concerns about nuclear proliferation in North Korea and Iran.

Objective 2: Describe the Israeli-Palestinian conflict and U.S. efforts to mediate it.

Objective 3: Identify U.S. responses to the Arab Spring and the Syrian Civil War.

Objective 4: Describe U.S. relationships with international allies.

LESSON 2 ORGANIZER	PACING: APPROX. 1 PERIOD, .5 BLOCKS		RESOURCES	
	OBJECTIVES	PACING	Online	Print
Connect				
DIGITAL START UP ACTIVITY **U.S. Foreign Policy After September 11**		5 min.	●	
Investigate				
DIGITAL TEXT 1 **Opposing the Spread of Nuclear Weapons**	Objective 1	10 min.	●	●
DIGITAL TEXT 2 **Unrest in Southwest Asia and North Africa**	Objectives 2, 3	10 min.	●	●
INTERACTIVE POLITICAL CARTOON **The U.S. Role in the Middle East**		10 min.	●	
DIGITAL TEXT 3 **Assisting Other Nations**	Objective 4	10 min.	●	●
INTERACTIVE GALLERY **Pivot to Asia**		10 min.	●	
Synthesize				
DIGITAL ACTIVITY **Working with Allies**		5 min.	●	
Demonstrate				
DIGITAL QUIZ **Lesson Quiz and Class Discussion Board**		10 min.	●	

Go online to access additional resources including:
Primary Sources • Biographies • Supreme Court cases • 21st Century Skill Tutorials • Maps • Graphic Organizers.

CONNECT

DIGITAL START UP ACTIVITY

U.S. Foreign Policy After September 11

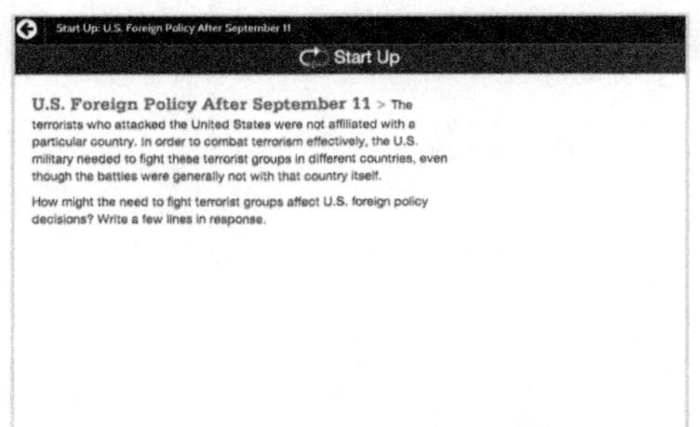
Start Up: U.S. Foreign Policy After September 11

Start Up

U.S. Foreign Policy After September 11 > The terrorists who attacked the United States were not affiliated with a particular country. In order to combat terrorism effectively, the U.S. military needed to fight these terrorist groups in different countries, even though the battles were generally not with that country itself.

How might the need to fight terrorist groups affect U.S. foreign policy decisions? Write a few lines in response.

Project the Start Up Activity Ask students to read the information and answer the question as they get settled. Have students share their response with a partner.

Discuss Provide students with examples of the methods, policies, and actions American leaders have used in the past to protect the country's interests. Prompt students to speculate whether any of these methods might effectively combat terrorism.

Tell students that in this lesson they will be learning about foreign policy challenges the United States faced in different regions of the world in the early twenty-first century.

Aa Vocabulary Development: Use the Interactive Reading Notepad to preview the Key Terms and Academic Vocabulary in this lesson with students.

FLIP IT!

Assign the Flipped Video for this lesson.

STUDENT EDITION PRINT PAGES: 899–904

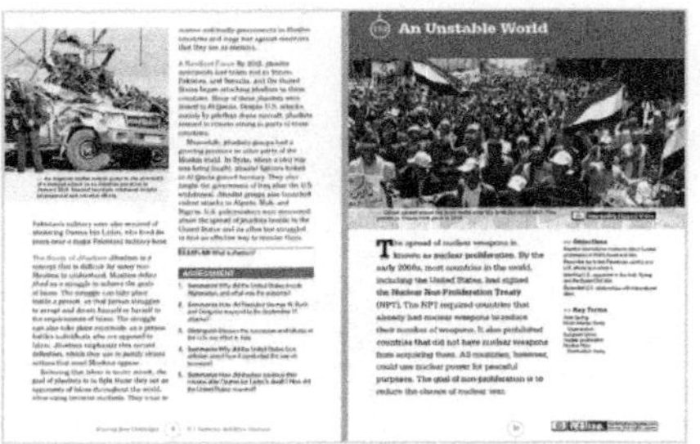

INVESTIGATE

DIGITAL TEXT 1

Opposing the Spread of Nuclear Weapons

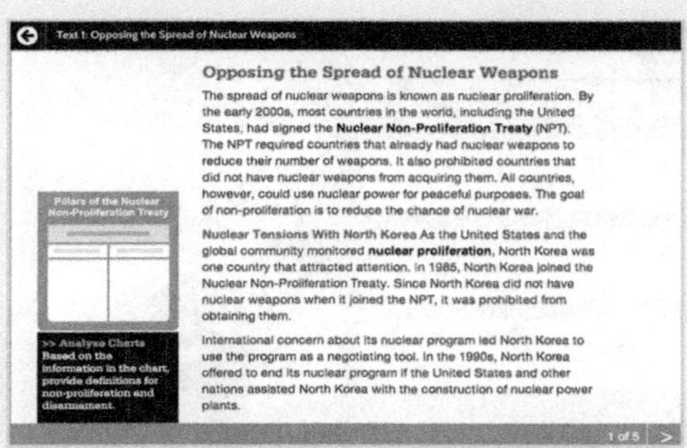
Text 1: Opposing the Spread of Nuclear Weapons

Opposing the Spread of Nuclear Weapons

The spread of nuclear weapons is known as nuclear proliferation. By the early 2000s, most countries in the world, including the United States, had signed the **Nuclear Non-Proliferation Treaty** (NPT). The NPT required countries that already had nuclear weapons to reduce their number of weapons. It also prohibited countries that did not have nuclear weapons from acquiring them. All countries, however, could use nuclear power for peaceful purposes. The goal of non-proliferation is to reduce the chance of nuclear war.

Nuclear Tensions With North Korea As the United States and the global community monitored **nuclear proliferation**, North Korea was one country that attracted attention. In 1985, North Korea joined the Nuclear Non-Proliferation Treaty. Since North Korea did not have nuclear weapons when it joined the NPT, it was prohibited from obtaining them.

International concern about its nuclear program led North Korea to use the program as a negotiating tool. In the 1990s, North Korea offered to end its nuclear program if the United States and other nations assisted North Korea with the construction of nuclear power plants.

Pillars of the Nuclear Non-Proliferation Treaty

>> Analyze Charts Based on the information in the chart, provide definitions for non-proliferation and disarmament.

1 of 5 >

Objective 1: Explain international concerns about nuclear proliferation in North Korea and Iran.

Quick Instruction

Project the table titled *Pillars of the Nuclear Nonproliferation Treaty*. Prompt students to discuss the relationship between nuclear power and nuclear weapons *(Nuclear power is used in a beneficial manner in fields such as energy and medicine; however, byproducts of nuclear power generation can be used in nuclear weapons development.)* and why many nations are closely scrutinized as they develop nuclear capability. How did the United States respond to North Korea's nuclear weapons program? *(The United States and its allies were concerned that North Korea would develop nuclear weapons. They responded with diplomatic efforts, including a UN Security Council vote to condemn North Korea's nuclear testing, and imposed sanctions, or restrictions, on trade with North Korea.)*

Draw Conclusions Why are American leaders threatened by a nuclear-armed Iran? *(Iranian governments have expressed strong hostility toward Israel, a U.S. ally. With the other conflicts in the region, a new Iranian-Israeli conflict would be devastating to stability in the region and around the world. Also, a nuclear-armed Iran could be a threat to other nations in the world's main oil-producing region, threatening the global economy.)*

Further Instruction

To continue the discussion on nuclear nonproliferation, use a world map or digital tool to have students locate Iran. Have students spend a few minutes analyzing Iran's location and surrounding countries. Ask: Based on what you have learned, why might Iran have strategic significance to the United States? *(Iran is located right between Iraq to the west and Afghanistan on the east, two countries in which American forces have fought.)*

Infer Why do you think American and other world leaders imposed economic sanctions on Iran? *(Limiting Iran's ability to sell oil and restricting its access to the international financial system may create economic hardship and prompt Iranian officials to forego their nuclear program.)*

An Unstable World

DIGITAL TEXT 2

Unrest in Southwest Asia and North Africa

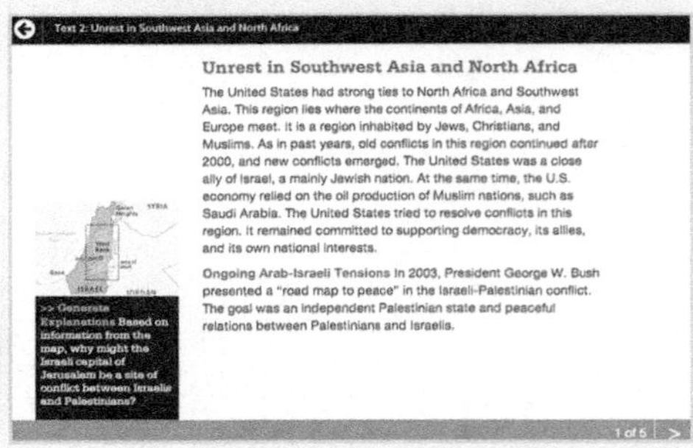

Text 2: Unrest in Southwest Asia and North Africa
Unrest in Southwest Asia and North Africa
The United States had strong ties to North Africa and Southwest Asia. This region lies where the continents of Africa, Asia, and Europe meet. It is a region inhabited by Jews, Christians, and Muslims. As in past years, old conflicts in this region continued after 2000, and new conflicts emerged. The United States was a close ally of Israel, a mainly Jewish nation. At the same time, the U.S. economy relied on the oil production of Muslim nations, such as Saudi Arabia. The United States tried to resolve conflicts in this region. It remained committed to supporting democracy, its allies, and its own national interests.
Ongoing Arab-Israeli Tensions In 2003, President George W. Bush presented a "road map to peace" in the Israeli-Palestinian conflict. The goal was an independent Palestinian state and peaceful relations between Palestinians and Israelis.
SYRIA
ISRAEL
JORDAN
>> Generate Explanations Based on information from the map, why might the Israeli capital of Jerusalem be a site of conflict between Israelis and Palestinians?
1 of 5

Objectives 2: Describe the Israeli-Palestinian conflict and U.S. efforts to mediate it; 3: Identify U.S. responses to the Arab Spring and the Syrian Civil War.

Quick Instruction

Interactive Chart: The U.S. Role in the Middle East Project the Interactive Chart and prompt students to reflect on the issues with which countries in the Middle East have been dealing before they study the cartoon and complete the questions. *(Possible responses: Arab-Israeli tensions; war in Iraq; increasing use of terrorism in the region)*

Summarize the United States' relationship with different countries in the Middle East. *(The United States is a close ally of Israel and has long supported Israel and its security. Arab countries have fought against the establishment of the Jewish state in the past; however, the U.S. economy relies on the oil production of Arab nations, such as Saudi Arabia. The United States has to maintain productive relationships with several countries in the region.)*

ACTIVE CLASSROOM

Conduct a Cartoon It activity. Have students create a political cartoon of their own based on one compelling image from this lesson that shows U.S. involvement in the Israeli-Palestinian conflict. Have students share their cartoons with a partner for feedback, and ask volunteers to share their cartoons with the class.

INTERACTIVE POLITICAL CARTOON

The U.S. Role in the Middle East

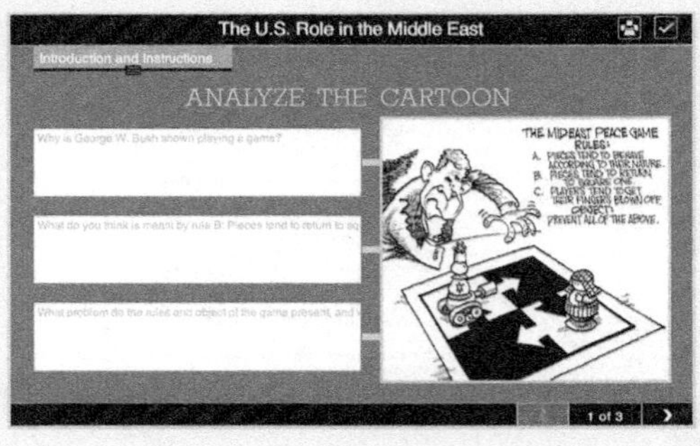

D Differentiate: Challenge Encourage interested students to conduct research on the current state of affairs in Libya, Syria, Egypt, or Gaza. Invite students to share what they learn with the rest of the class, focusing on how American foreign policy has changed or evolved.

ELL Use the ELL activity described in the ELL chart.

Further Instruction

Go through the Interactive Reading Notepad questions and use appropriate questions to initiate a discussion about the Arab Spring. Use a world map or digital tool to locate the countries involved to provide students with a better understanding of the region's conflicts and how they might be related.

Infer Even though the revolts in the Middle East created havoc within the region, why were they still referred to as the *Arab Spring*? *(The movements and revolts represented the flowering or emergence of pro-democracy ideals that had been repressed by previous autocratic governments in the region.)*

Generate Explanations Why did the Obama administration keep U.S. forces out of the Arab Spring conflicts in the Middle East? *(The United States had recently been involved in two wars in Southwest Asia that cost thousands of American lives and a great amount of money. The political situations in both countries were still uncertain. Public support for more American intervention in the region was probably very low.)*

DIGITAL TEXT 3

Assisting Other Nations

Objective 4: Describe U.S. relationships with international allies.

Quick Instruction

Interactive Gallery: Pivot to Asia Project the Interactive Gallery and navigate through the images with students. Discuss the different strategies and policies enacted by the United States to develop closer ties to countries in Asia. Discuss the pros and cons of greater American economic and military involvement in Asia. How does the U.S. "pivot to Asia" strategy affect China? *(U.S. military cooperation in the region with nations involved in disputes with China weakens China's influence and may seem threatening to the Chinese, because the U.S. has offered military support to those Asian countries and can better monitor China's actions.)*

Make Generalizations In what ways might the U.S. "pivot to Asia" strategy have benefited the American economy? *(More than a quarter of all U.S. exports went to the East Asia-Pacific region. Increasing exports would in turn boost domestic production and encourage higher employment.)*

INTERACTIVE GALLERY

Pivot to Asia

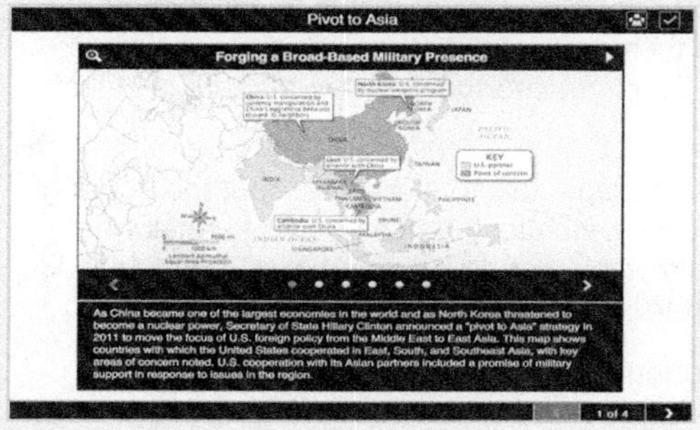

SYNTHESIZE

DIGITAL ACTIVITY

Working with Allies

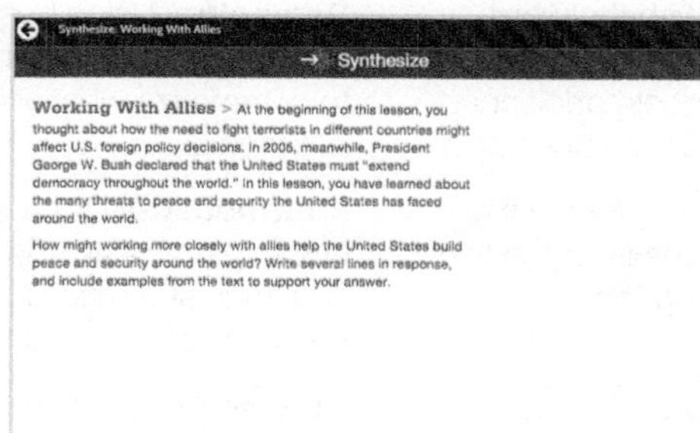

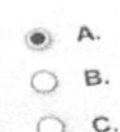

DEMONSTRATE

DIGITAL QUIZ

Lesson Quiz and Class Discussion Board

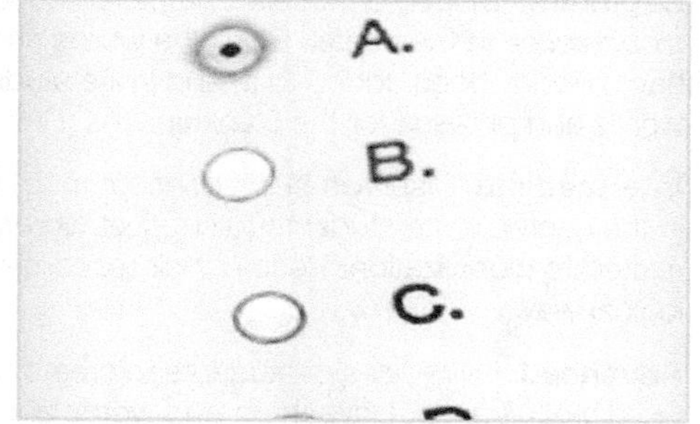

ACTIVE CLASSROOM

Conduct a PMI activity. Have student groups evaluate the pros and cons of an increased U.S. presence in the East Asia-Pacific region. Give each group a three-column organizer with the headings Plus/Minus/Interesting. Have students use the organizer to record responses to the following questions: 1. What are the positive economic effects of increased commerce with the East Asia-Pacific region? 2. What are the negative effects of this? 3. What is interesting about this? Ask volunteers to share their group's responses with the class.

ELL Use the ELL activity described in the ELL chart.

Further Instruction

Continue the discussion of U.S. involvement around the world. Ensure students' understanding of the increased role in Asia, the issues off the coast of Somalia, and eastern Europe. To extend the discussion and provide more depth, assign Government and Civics Core Concepts: Conflict and Cooperation.

Connect Considering that Russians once dominated a much larger Soviet Union, why might the modern-day leaders of Russia have opposed NATO expanding its membership to include countries that were under Soviet rule during the Cold War? *(Russian leaders probably viewed this as a loss of influence and power in the region. Russia and the Soviet Union historically sought to create a buffer zone to protect their borders.)*

Before students write their responses, have them reflect on how the need to fight terrorists in different countries might affect U.S. foreign policy decisions. Then direct student partners to use the Think Pair Share strategy to discuss other threats to peace and security the United States has faced around the world. Have students share their ideas with the class.

Discuss Have students review their responses to the Working with Allies activity. Has the United States successfully built peace and security? Why or why not?

Assign the online Lesson Quiz for this lesson if you haven't already done so. Students will be offered automatic remediation or enrichment based on their score.

In *Global Challenges*, you explored how peace and security around the world has been threatened in the post-September 11 era. To effectively deal with the threat of emerging nuclear-armed countries and conflicts in the Middle East, the United States has often assumed the role of mediator, all the while trying to balance self-interests with those of its international allies and others.

Pose these questions to the class on the Discussion Board:

Synthesize The United States has pursued policies with the goal of building stronger relationships with international allies for a variety of reasons. What policies might countries like China and Russia pursue to counter U.S. influence?

Support a Point of View with Evidence Does the United States have a responsibility to "extend democracy throughout the world"? Why or why not?

Topic Inquiry

Have students continue their investigations for the Topic Inquiry.

Topic 17 Lesson 3

A Global Economy

Supporting English Language Learners

Use with the reading, **A Worldwide Economy Develops**.	Use with the reading, **A World Economic Crisis**.
Learning Review the process of filling out a concept map, as well as why it can be a useful learning technique. **Beginning** Display a partially completed concept map with the word *globalization* in the center. Read the words and phrases (from the text) that have already been added to it, and invite students to suggest additional words and phrases for the blank spaces. Record students' responses. **Intermediate** Display a blank concept map with the word *globalization* in the center. Invite students to suggest words and phrases from the text related to globalization. Record their responses, organizing them in a logical way. **Advanced** Invite pairs of students to create a concept map for the word *globalization*. Have them add words and phrases from the text that are connected to the center term, and encourage them to organize the information in a way that shows its interrelatedness. **Advanced High** Invite students to create a concept map for the word *globalization*. Have them add information from the text that is related to the center term, while also using connecting lines to show how this information is interrelated. Provide time for partners to share, compare, and revise their concept maps.	**Listening** Explain that if students are able to retell or summarize what someone else says, it is proof that they have listened well. **Beginning** Using basic vocabulary, explain to students how subprime mortgages worked. Then ask them to complete these sentences in order to summarize what you said: Subprime mortgages were affordable at first, but then ____. **Intermediate** Using simpler language, talk to students about the housing crisis described in the first section of the text. Ask students to retell what you said, and record and display their responses. Then give your talk again so students can add to their retelling as needed. **Advanced** Read aloud to students the first section about the housing crisis. Then invite pairs of students to collaborate in retelling what you said. Encourage students to ask each other questions in order to clarify information or fill in gaps. **Advanced High** Tell students about the housing crisis, using information from the text as well as from other sources. Then invite students to write a paragraph summarizing what you said in as much detail as possible. Provide time for partners to share and compare their paragraphs.

D Differentiate Instruction

Use the Differentiated Instruction notes throughout the lesson plan to support the varied skill sets, levels of readiness, and interests in the mixed-ability classroom.

Challenge These notes include suggestions for expanding the activity for advanced students.

On-Level These notes include suggestions for modifying the activity to address different interests or learning styles.

Extra Support These notes include ideas for providing more scaffolding or reading spuport.

Special Needs These notes provide ideas for adapting instruction to support the needs of various special needs students.

NOTES

PEARSON realize™ www.PearsonRealize.com

Go online to access additional resources including: Primary Sources • Biographies • Supreme Court cases • 21st Century Skill Tutorials • Maps • Graphic Organizers.

Objectives

Objective 1: Explain the connections between the U.S. economy and the global economy.

Objective 2: Describe the reasons for the 2007 recession.

Objective 3: Identify reasons for the U.S. economy's slow recovery after the 2007 recession.

LESSON 3 ORGANIZER — PACING: APPROX. 1 PERIOD, .5 BLOCKS	OBJECTIVES	PACING	RESOURCES Online	RESOURCES Print
Connect				
DIGITAL START UP ACTIVITY **Economic Connections**		5 min.	●	
Investigate				
DIGITAL TEXT 1 **A Worldwide Economy Develops**	Objective 1	10 min.	●	●
3-D MODEL **The World Today**	Objective 1	10 min.	●	
DIGITAL TEXT 2 **A World Economic Crisis**	Objective 2	10 min.	●	●
BEFORE AND AFTER **Effects of the Recession**	Objective 2	10 min.	●	
DIGITAL TEXT 3 **A Weak Recovery**	Objective 3	10 min.	●	●
INTERACTIVE CHART **Economic Challenges in the 2000s—Causes and Effects**	Objective 3	10 min.	●	
Synthesize				
DIGITAL ACTIVITY **Globalization**		5 min.	●	
Demonstrate				
DIGITAL QUIZ **Lesson Quiz and Class Discussion Board**		10 min.	●	

A Global Economy

CONNECT

DIGITAL START UP ACTIVITY
Economic Connections

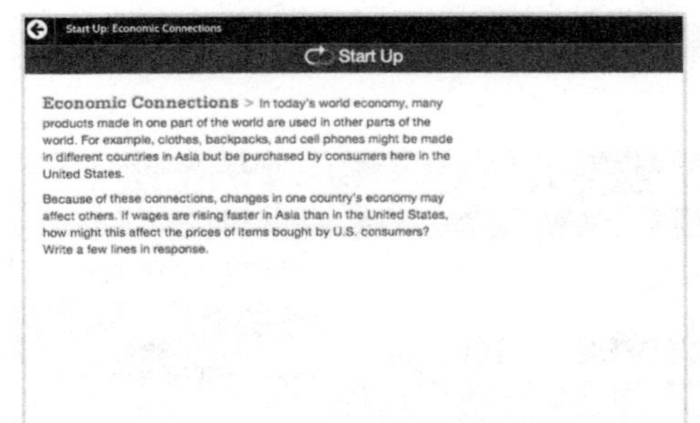

Project the Start Up Activity Ask students to read the information and answer the question as they get settled. Have students share their response with a partner.

Discuss Challenge students to suggest what might affect the prices of goods they purchase. *(cost and availability of materials; the cost of labor; transportation to market; taxes or tariffs imposed by a trade partner)* Pair students and encourage them to reflect on the advantages and disadvantages of international trading partnerships.

Tell students that in this lesson they will be learning about the connections between the U.S. and global economies, and the 2007 recession.

Aa Vocabulary Development: Use the Interactive Reading Notepad to preview the Key Terms and Academic Vocabulary in this lesson with students.

FLIP IT!

Assign the Flipped Video for this lesson.

STUDENT EDITION PRINT PAGES: 905–913

INVESTIGATE

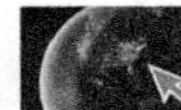

DIGITAL TEXT 1
A Worldwide Economy Develops

3-D MODEL
The World Today

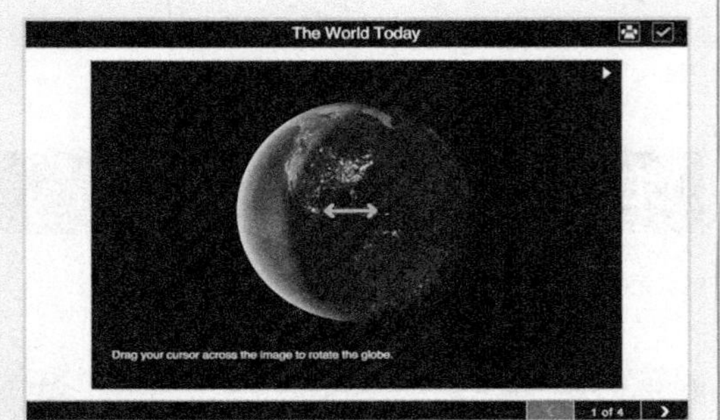

Objective 1: Explain the connections between the U.S. economy and the global economy.

Quick Instruction

3-D Model: The World Today Project the 3-D Model and navigate through the images with students. Review key terms from the activity *(population density, human development, standard of living)* and discuss each to ensure students' understanding. Contrast the standards of living between people in London and the nomadic people of Central Asia. *(Many people in London have a high standard of living. They have access to educational opportunities, technology, and the ability to buy goods and services. Based on the image, the nomadic people of Central Asia would have a much lower standard of living, mainly because they live in a sparsely populated region that lacks comparable economic development.)*

Draw Conclusions Why do American manufacturers often face a disadvantage in a global economy? *(Some costs of doing business in other countries are lower than in the United States. Workers overseas are paid less than American workers and environmental regulations are weaker. Foreign businesses can often produce and sell goods at lower prices.)*

ACTIVE CLASSROOM

Conduct a Connect Two activity. Select ten or twelve words or phrases you think are important for students to know prior to reading, such as: standard of living, population density, human development, globalization, free trade, shared currencies, trade agreements, and market bubbles. Have students choose two words from the list and explain why they belong together, e.g. "I would connect ____ and ____ because . . . ." During reading, have students look for evidence to support or refute their connections.

ELL Use the ELL activity described in the ELL chart.

Further Instruction

Make Generalizations How do U.S. international trade policies promote free trade? *(They reduce trade restrictions, encourage trade relationships with other countries, and create trade groups that stimulate growth among their members.)*

Summarize the advantages and disadvantages of increased American financial ties to the European Union. *(The creation of the EU attracted American investment and opened large markets and trade opportunities for American businesses. However, problems in any nation's economy affected others. If euro-zone countries had less money to invest, Americans would have less money to grow new or existing businesses. If people and businesses in the euro zone had less money to spend, they would buy fewer products from American exporters.)*

DIGITAL TEXT 2

A World Economic Crisis

Text 2: A World Economic Crisis

A World Economic Crisis

As you read, to help the United States economy recover from the 2001 recession, the Federal Reserve System lowered interest rates. This enabled people to pay less to borrow money. Low interest rates encouraged Americans to increase the amount of money that they borrowed and spent.

It also allowed more Americans to buy homes, and low interest rates made larger **mortgages** affordable. Mortgages are loans to buy a piece of property that allow the lender to claim the property if the mortgage is not paid. As the demand for homes and mortgages increased, home prices also increased. This created a housing bubble much like the dot-com bubble that the stock market had experienced.

Banks and mortgage companies thought that home prices would keep increasing. As a result, they offered mortgages to people who were considered lending risks because they could not easily afford the payments. These loans were known as **subprime mortgages**.

The Housing Bubble, 2000–2009

>> Analyze Graphs Describe how the housing bubble affected the prices of homes, and draw conclusions about how that might have affected the U.S. economy.

ELL 1 of 5

BEFORE AND AFTER

Effects of the Recession

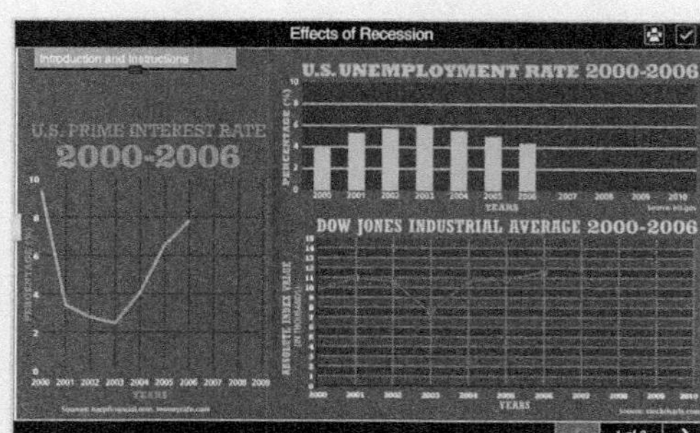

Objective 2: **Describe the reasons for the 2007 recession.**

Quick Instruction

Before and After: Effects of the Recession Project the Before and After and move the slider to compare the contrasting economic data. Explain that the Dow Jones Average is the most widely used indicator of the overall condition of the stock market. The Dow Average is made up of 30 of the most influential companies in the U.S. economy, making it a good indicator of general stock market trends. What can you infer from the fact that housing prices took years to begin to rise again, while the stock market, as reflected in the graphs, rebounded more quickly? *(Many corporations rebounded from the recession fairly quickly. Housing prices, however, are somewhat dependent on demand, which meant many consumers did not feel confident taking on mortgages even as the stock market was recovering, so housing prices remained depressed for a longer period of time.)*

Draw Conclusions What does the U.S. interest rate graph suggest about the strength of the American economy in January 2008? *(The consistently low interest rates suggests that the government wanted to encourage borrowing to strengthen the economy. Low interest rates allow people to pay less to borrow money, which encourages Americans to increase borrowing and spending.)*

ACTIVE CLASSROOM

Conduct a Sticky Notes activity. Have students address the question: How might the recession of 2007 have been avoided? Have students post their Sticky Notes on the board or on chart paper and look at the various responses. Discuss similarities and differences in the responses as a group. Ask students to suggest reasons why the recession was inevitable at the time.

D Differentiate: Extra Support Highlight the unemployment rate graph. Prompt students to understand why the unemployment rate is an important measure of the economy's overall health.

ELL Use the ELL activity described in the ELL chart.

Further Instruction

Go through the Interactive Reading Notepad questions and use appropriate questions to further explore the recession of 2007 and crisis of 2008 and how the U.S. leaders responded.

Identify Patterns How do recessions create a negative economic cycle? *(Recessions occur when an economy produces less goods and services. This is caused by a decline in spending. When spending drops, businesses fail, and more people become unemployed. Because unemployed people have less money to spend, even fewer goods and services are produced, and the cycle continues.)*

Make a Prediction about the effects of the 2007 recession and 2008 financial crisis. *(The economy may be slow to recover; there may be controversial steps taken to stimulate the economy; voters may elect candidates they see as unassociated with the economic downturn; there may be new financial reforms to banks and increased regulation of mortgages and lending practices.)*

Topic 17 Lesson 3

A Global Economy

DIGITAL TEXT 3

A Weak Recovery

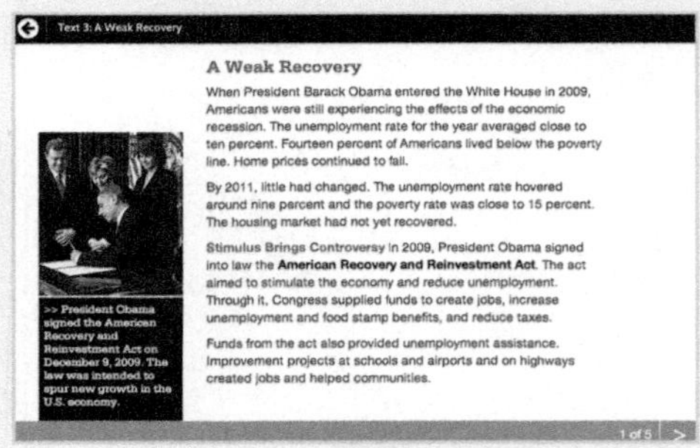

INTERACTIVE CHART

Economic Challenges in the 2000s—Causes and Effects

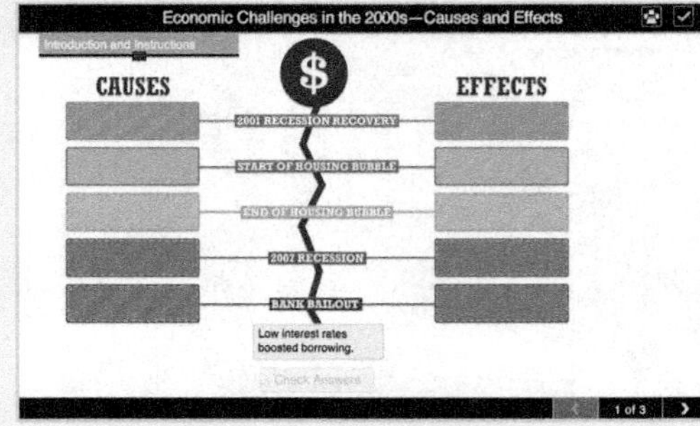

Objective 3: **Identify reasons for the U.S. economy's slow recovery after the 2007 recession.**

Quick Instruction

Interactive Chart: Economic Challenges in the 2000s—Causes and Effects Project the Interactive Chart showing the economic challenges that the United States faced in the 2000s. Prompt students to drop the tiles in the correct locations and discuss responses together. Explain how a "housing bubble" contributed to the United States sliding into a financial crisis in 2008. *(Banks made subprime home mortgage loans to risky borrowers and then sold the loans to investors. As the economy slid into a recession and Americans lost their jobs, they couldn't pay back these mortgages. Foreclosures increased, housing prices fell, and investments lost their value.)*

Cite Evidence What is the function of the U.S. debt ceiling, and why is congressional action necessary when the country nears it? *(The debt ceiling limits the amount of debt that the United States can owe. When the country nears the debt ceiling, Congress must vote to raise the limit, or the country risks default, or failure to repay the debt, and a possible financial crisis.)*

ACTIVE CLASSROOM

Conduct a Take a Stand activity with the following question: Should people have the opportunity to take a subprime mortgage if they don't qualify for a loan with better terms? Ask students to divide into two groups based on their answer and move to separate areas of the classroom. Ask students to talk with each other to compare their reasons for answering yes or no. Ask a representative from each side to present and defend the group's point of view.

Further Instruction

Continue the discussion about the weak economic recovery following the financial crises of 2007 and 2008 and focus on the American Recovery and Reinvestment Act. Challenge students to explain the purpose for the act *(It was a $787 billion stimulus package that cut taxes, provided aid to state and local governments, and funded infrastructure projects. The act put money into the public sector to boost the economy after the financial crisis of 2008.)* and the positions of those who opposed it. *(Some people criticized the act because they thought that it had been ineffective, was too expensive, and had increased the federal deficit for no purpose. Some claimed that it increased unemployment.)* Assign Economic Core Concepts: Trade to provide depth to the discussion.

Draw Conclusions How did political differences complicate the debate over how best to pull out the United States from the recession? *(Democrats and Republicans had sharply divided ideas about an appropriate response to the recession. Although the American Recovery and Reinvestment Act was passed by Congress, all Republicans in the House of Representatives voted against it and only three Republican senators voted in favor of it. In addition, when President Obama asked Congress to raise the debt ceiling in 2011 and 2013, Republicans refused unless the President agreed to a compromise.)*

SYNTHESIZE

DIGITAL ACTIVITY

Globalization

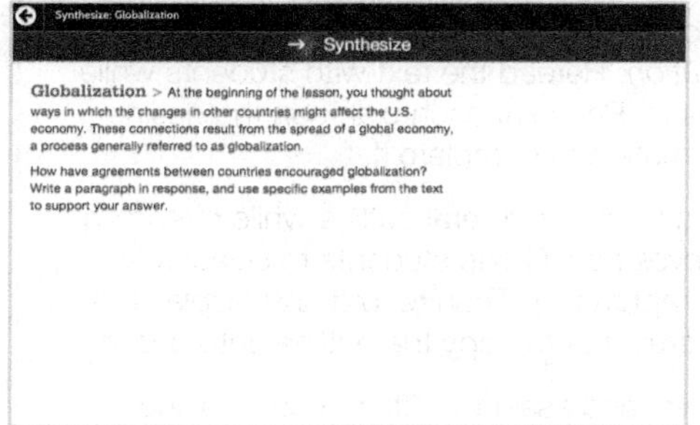

Have students review their responses to the question in the Startup Activity and use information from the lesson or additional research to answer the question, How have agreements between countries encouraged globalization? Direct students to use specific examples from the text to support their answers.

Discuss Have students share their paragraphs and then discuss the advantages and disadvantages to globalization. Ask students whether they think a global economy has made economies around the world more stable and have led to beneficial human development and rising standards of living for citizens of all nations. Have students explain their reasoning.

DEMONSTRATE

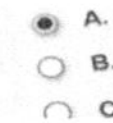

DIGITAL QUIZ

Lesson Quiz and Class Discussion Board

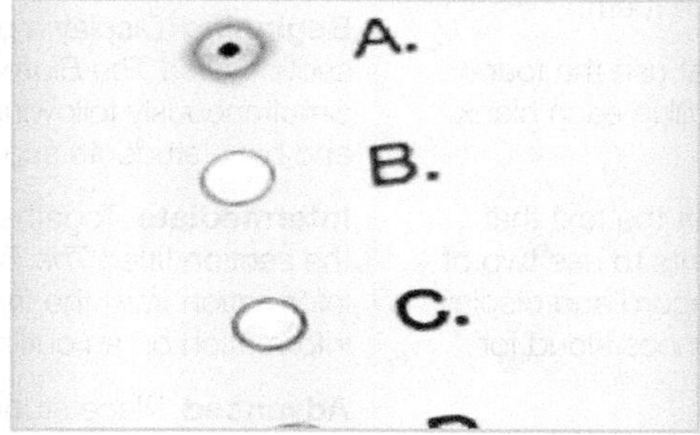

Assign the online Lesson Quiz for this lesson if you haven't already done so. Students will be offered automatic remediation or enrichment based on their score.

In *A Global Economy*, you read about how trade alliances and connected financial markets have created a global economy. As a result, the economies of countries around the globe are interconnected.

Pose these questions to the class on the Discussion Board:

Analyze How did international trade change the world economy?

Support a Point of View with Evidence What are the benefits and drawbacks of free trade on American businesses?

Topic Inquiry

Have students continue their investigations for the Topic Inquiry.

Advances in Science and Technology

Supporting English Language Learners

Use with the reading, **New Discoveries**.

Speaking

Display several challenging, content-area vocabulary words from the text (e.g., orbiter, terrain, rover, laboratory). Explain to students that they will practice speaking with these words in order to internalize them.

Beginning Display simple sentences about the text that use the four words above but have them omitted. Invite students to fill in each blank with the appropriate word and say the sentence aloud.

Intermediate Invite students to make statements about the text that use one of the four words above. Then challenge students to use two of the above words in a single sentence about the text. Record and display all of their responses, and have students read the sentences aloud for reinforcement.

Advanced Invite pairs of students to use the four words above as they discuss the following questions about the text: Which NASA programs mentioned in the text seem most interesting to you, and why? What kind of space exploration do you think will take place in the future?

Advanced High Place students in pairs and have each partner do further research on either orbiters or rovers used by NASA. Then have them use all four of the above words as they tell each other about their findings.

Use with the reading, **Advances in Biology and Medicine**.

Reading

Brainstorm different note-taking methods, such as bullet-point lists, Roman numeral outlines, and concept maps.

Beginning Display a partially completed Roman numeral outline for the section titled *The Biotech Revolution*. Reread the text with students while simultaneously following the outline. Pause at each blank on the outline and have students suggest information to complete it.

Intermediate Together, create a Roman numeral outline while rereading the section titled *The Biotech Revolution*. Guide students to select key information from the text and paraphrase it. Then record and display the information on an outline. Invite students to copy the outline onto paper.

Advanced Place students in pairs and assign a different note-taking method to each pair. Have pairs reread the section titled *The Biotech Revolution* and take notes on it. Then invite pairs who used different note-taking methods to share and compare their notes.

Advanced High Place students in pairs and invite each pair to reread the section titled *The Biotech Revolution* twice, each time using a different method to take notes on it. Then have them discuss these questions: Which note-taking method was easier to use, and why? Which did a better job of capturing the text's content, and why?

D Differentiate Instruction

Use the Differentiated Instruction notes throughout the lesson plan to support the varied skill sets, levels of readiness, and interests in the mixed-ability classroom.

Challenge These notes include suggestions for expanding the activity for advanced students.

On-Level These notes include suggestions for modifying the activity to address different interests or learning styles.

Extra Support These notes include ideas for providing more scaffolding or reading spuport.

Special Needs These notes provide ideas for adapting instruction to support the needs of various special needs students.

NOTES

PEARSON realize™ www.PearsonRealize.com

Go online to access additional resources including: Primary Sources • Biographies • Supreme Court cases • 21st Century Skill Tutorials • Maps • Graphic Organizers.

Objectives

Objective 1: Describe the results of recent NASA research.

Objective 2: Identify environmental challenges and explain the ways in which those challenges are being addressed.

Objective 3: Describe the impact of advances in biotechnology and medicine.

Objective 4: Identify the effects of advances in digital technology and communication.

LESSON 4 ORGANIZER — **PACING: APPROX. 1 PERIOD, .5 BLOCKS**

	OBJECTIVES	PACING	RESOURCES Online	RESOURCES Print
Connect				
DIGITAL START UP ACTIVITY **Innovations and Modern American Life**		5 min.	●	
Investigate				
DIGITAL TEXT 1 **New Discoveries**	Objective 1	10 min.	●	●
DIGITAL TEXT 2 **Responding to Environmental Challenges**	Objective 2	10 min.	●	●
INTERACTIVE GALLERY **Advances in Energy Technology**		10 min.	●	
DIGITAL TEXT 3 **Advances in Biology and Medicine**	Objective 3	10 min.	●	●
DIGITAL TEXT 4 **A Networked World**	Objective 4	10 min.	●	●
INTERACTIVE GALLERY **Technology in the 21st Century**		10 min.	●	
Synthesize				
DIGITAL ACTIVITY **New Ways to Communicate**		5 min.	●	
Demonstrate				
DIGITAL QUIZ **Lesson Quiz and Class Discussion Board**		10 min.	●	

Topic 17 Lesson 4

Advances in Science and Technology

CONNECT

DIGITAL START UP ACTIVITY

Innovations and Modern American Life

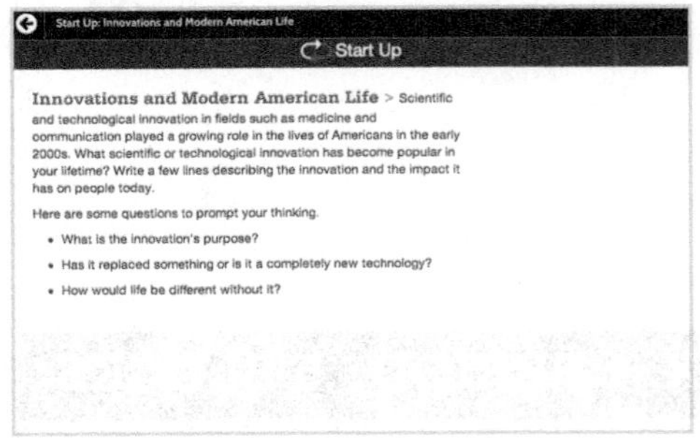

Project the Start Up Activity Ask students to review the activity and reflect briefly on the question. Before students begin their responses, review the three question prompts and discuss students' responses as a class. Have students individually write their answers to the Activity question and share their ideas with another student, either in class or through a chat or blog space.

Tell students that in this lesson they will explore how scientific discoveries and technological innovations continue to transform the world in which we live.

Aa Vocabulary Development: Use the Interactive Reading Notepad to preview the Key Terms and Academic Vocabulary in this lesson with students.

FLIP IT!

Assign the Flipped Video for this lesson.

STUDENT EDITION PRINT PAGES: 914–923

INVESTIGATE

DIGITAL TEXT 1

New Discoveries

Objective 1: Describe the results of recent NASA research.

Quick Instruction

Cite Evidence What evidence from the text shows the focus of NASA's exploration of Mars? *(Spacecraft took photographs of Mars, recorded the weather, mapped the terrain, and sent the information back to Earth. The Opportunity and Spirit rovers traveled across the planet's surface and sent images back to Earth. The Curiosity science laboratory collected and analyzed Martian soil and rocks.)*

Determine Relevance Why did NASA make it a goal to increase our knowledge of the solar system? *(Possible response: Learning about other planets in the solar system might help scientists gain a better understanding of the origins of Earth and how better to protect it.)*

ELL Use the ELL activity described in the ELL chart.

Further Instruction

Generate Explanations Why do you think NASA has paid special attention to Mars? *(Mars is the second-closest planet to Earth, making exploration easier than more distant planets. Also, because of its distance from the sun, it is the most likely planet to have supported life as we know it.)*

Contrast How is the Kepler mission different from other solar system explorations? *(The Kepler mission uses a space-based telescope rather than rovers and orbiters.)*

DIGITAL TEXT 2

Responding to Environmental Challenges

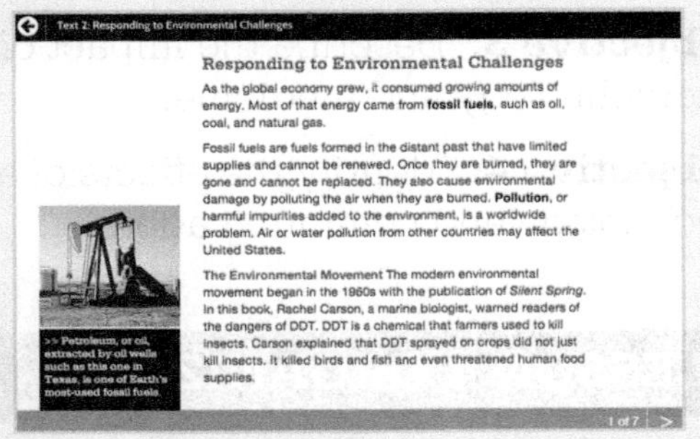

Objective 2: Identify environmental challenges and explain the ways in which those challenges are being addressed.

Quick Instruction

Interactive Gallery: Advances in Energy Technology Project the Interactive Gallery and navigate through the images with students. Discuss the economic, environmental, and safety factors involved in developing and improving energy technologies. Prompt students to weigh the costs and benefits of each innovation. Why might many people question the long-term viability of fracking, clean coal, and gasification technologies? *(These technologies are being developed to access fossil fuels that have limited supplies and cannot be renewed.)*

Contrast Identify opposing viewpoints on how to best address global warming. *(Some people call for the increased use of renewable energy sources instead of fossil fuels. Renewable energy sources have the potential to decrease America's dependence on foreign oil, diminish greenhouse gas emissions, and reduce pollution. Critics, however, claim that these sources are often more expensive than fossil fuels and that relying on them could harm the economy.)*

www.PearsonRealize.com
Access your Digital Lesson

INTERACTIVE GALLERY

Advances in Energy Technology

ACTIVE CLASSROOM

Conduct a Take a Stand activity. Have students take a stand on the following question: Should we invest in clean energy technology or improve the way we use fossil fuels? Have students move to different sides of the room and group up with others with the same opinion. Have groups create a justification or opening statement defending their position to the class.

D Differentiate: Challenge Encourage interested students to do additional research on the energy technologies described in the gallery to see if and how their community is using these technologies. Invite students to share their findings.

Further Instruction

Summarize the steps the federal government has taken to protect the environment. *(Congress has passed laws restricting the use of dangerous chemicals, such as DDT. In 1970, President Richard Nixon created the Environmental Protection Agency (EPA). The EPA has worked to reduce greenhouse gas emissions. The EPA also worked with international partners to limit pollution and slow climate change. The U.S. government has also encouraged the use of renewable energy sources. Beginning in 2005, federal law required a percentage of the gasoline sold in the United States to be mixed with at least small quantities of ethanol.)*

Determine Relevance In your opinion, why was the Three Mile Island incident significant? *(The accident highlighted the potential dangers of nuclear energy, leading to unresolved debates about to how to safely manage nuclear power and the best way to dispose of nuclear waste.)*

DIGITAL TEXT 3

Advances in Biology and Medicine

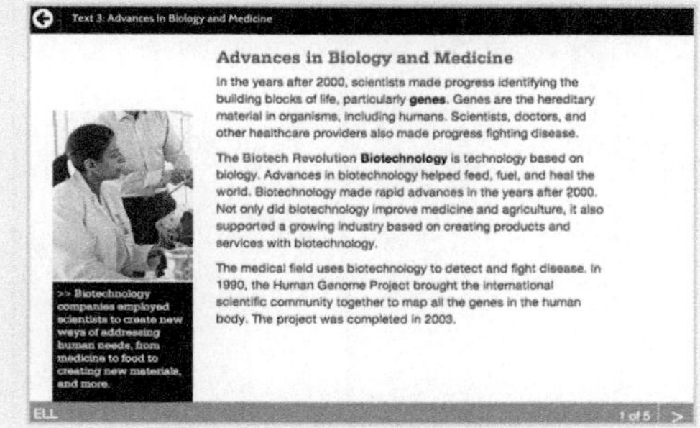

Objective 3: Describe the impact of advances in biotechnology and medicine.

Quick Instruction

Display the digital image of the scientists working in a biotechnology lab. Invite volunteers to analyze the image and describe what they see as a way to prompt students to understand what biotechnology involves. *(Possible responses: scientists using plants or other natural materials; computers and other technical equipment. Biotechnology is technology based on biology and the use of living or natural organisms.)* Ask students to predict how new technologies might aid the development of new medicines and the identification of diseases.

Make Generalizations Make a generalization about the impact of biotechnology on American society. *(Scientists, doctors, and other healthcare providers have used biotechnology to fight diseases and make Americans healthier. Farmers use biotechnology to increase crop production, develop crops that are resistant to insects, and to enhance food nutrition.)*

ELL Use the ELL activity described in the ELL chart.

Advances in Science and Technology

DIGITAL TEXT 4

A Networked World

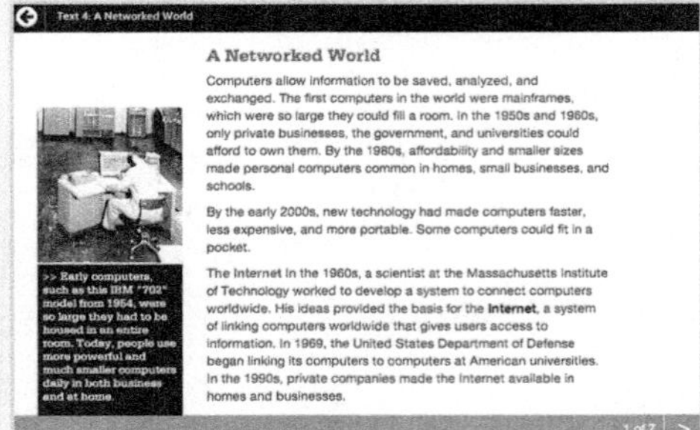

INTERACTIVE GALLERY

Technology in the 21st Century

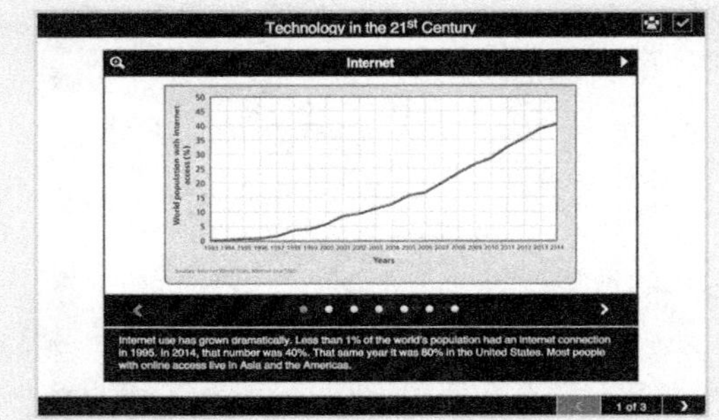

Further Instruction

Contrast Identify opposing viewpoints on genetically modified foods. *(Supporters have shown that using biotechnology can create genetically modified foods and varieties of crops that produce more food or that are resistant to drought, insects, and other agents that harm crops. Critics claim that relying on genetically modified organisms, including crops or livestock, will lead to dependence on biotechnology companies. They also express concerns about possible dangers to the environment or human health.)*

Evaluate the role of the U.S. government in fighting illnesses and diseases throughout the world. *(The government's Centers for Disease Control and Prevention (CDC) has successfully worked with governments around the world to address the rapid spread of diseases, including helping other countries learn how to detect and prevent the spread of potential disease epidemics. Other federal institutions have developed improved treatments for cancer.)*

Objective 4: **Identify the effects of advances in digital technology and communication.**

Quick Instruction

Interactive Gallery: Technology in the 21st Century Project the Interactive Gallery and navigate through the images. Prompt students to think about the role that computers play in everyday life and then to discuss how computer technology has spread to other fields, such as biomedicine and agriculture.

Identify Cause and Effect Have students reflect on what they learned about globalization. How has the Internet sped up the pace of globalization? *(The Internet and its related technologies have made the sharing and accessing of information almost instantaneous. Companies and customers can communicate and work together from anywhere in the world.)*

ACTIVE CLASSROOM

Conduct a Graffiti Concepts activity. Ask students to reflect on the technological innovations of the 2000s and create a visual image and/or phrase that represents each innovation. (Allow approximately 3–5 minutes.) Then ask students to post their "graffiti" on the board or on chart paper and ask students to discuss them as a group.

Further Instruction

Review with students the development of key technological innovations such as the computer, the Internet, and mobile communications devices. Prompt students to think about how these technological innovations have affected the economic development of the United States. *(Digital technologies improve standards of living, create new industries, and increase American business productivity and efficiency and their economic competitiveness.)*

Determine Relevance What role has the U.S. private sector played in the surge in computer and Internet technologies? *(In the 1990s, private companies led the movement to make computers smaller and more affordable, allowing many Americans to use computer technology and the Internet in homes and businesses. Private companies and software engineers were also driven by public demand to develop apps for games, magazines and books, banking, and shopping.)*

Analyze Information What does the creation of the Department of Defense's cyberwarfare unit suggest about the nation's security in the digital age? *(The nation's security depends on computer networks that maintain infrastructure such as electrical power grids, financial markets, and other vital operations.)*

SYNTHESIZE

DIGITAL ACTIVITY

New Ways to Communicate

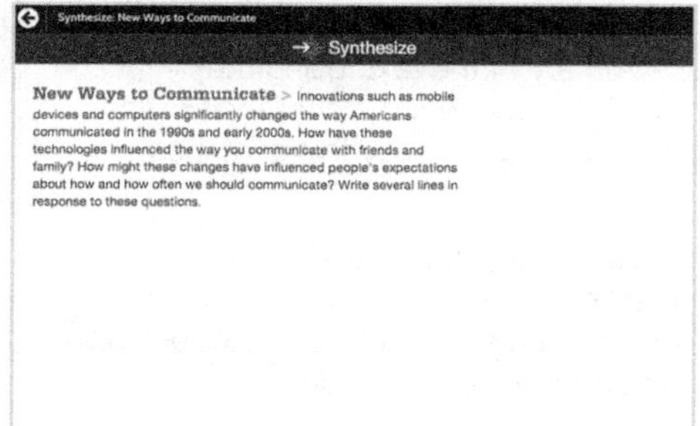

Have partners use the Think Pair Share strategy to discuss how mobile devices and computers changed the way Americans communicated in the 1990s and early 2000s. Ask them to take five minutes to individually create a list, then share it with the class.

Discuss After students have responded to the New Ways to Communicate activity questions, have them share their answers with the class. Ask: What are the advantages and disadvantages of being in constant communication with family and friends?

DEMONSTRATE

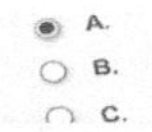

DIGITAL QUIZ

Lesson Quiz and Class Discussion Board

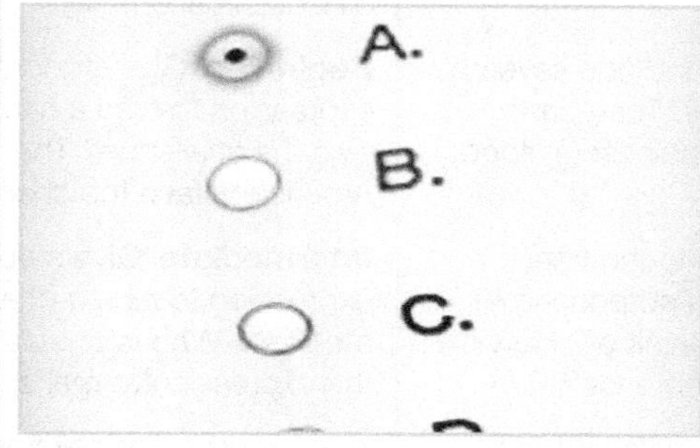

Assign the online Lesson Quiz for this lesson if you haven't already done so. Students will be offered automatic remediation or enrichment based on their score.

In *Advances in Science and Technology*, you read about how technologies like computers and mobile communication devices have improved communication. In addition, the emergence of biotechnology has led to advancements in the fields of energy and medicine, enabling people to lead healthier and more productive lives.

Pose these questions to the class on the Discussion Board:

Analyze How will advances in technology make the job market different in the future?

Draw Conclusions How have advances in telecommunications and the rise of the Internet affected the standard of living in the United States?

Topic Inquiry

Have students continue their investigations for the Topic Inquiry.

Challenges at Home

Supporting English Language Learners

Use with the reading, **The Bush Era**.	Use with the reading, **Social Change**.
Learning Discuss how students' prior knowledge can help them understand unfamiliar words (e.g., examining word parts, thinking about alternate meanings).	**Listening** Display the first sentence of the text, and point out the expression *faced new challenges*. Explain that to face a challenge means "to deal with a difficult situation."
Beginning Read the sentence in which *outpouring* is found (the seventh paragraph). Discuss what it means to pour something out. Then have students identify the meaning of outpouring from these choices: (a) flood, (b) accident, (c) emptying.	**Beginning** Give students an oral summary of the text, using the expression *to face a challenge* once. Ask: Who faced a challenge? What was the challenge? Then have them complete and say this sentence: Americans face the challenge of ____.
Intermediate Read the sentence in which *outpouring* is found (the seventh paragraph). Ask: What two words can you find in outpouring? What does the phrase *pouring something out* make you think of? How can that knowledge help you understand *outpouring* in this sentence?	**Intermediate** Give students an oral summary of the text using the expression *to face a challenge* at least once. Ask: What challenges did I mention? Who is or was facing those challenges? Then have students use the expression to make a statement about American society.
Advanced Display the word *initial*. Ask: What are your initials? What is an initial? Guide students toward the definition of an initial coming at the beginning of a word. Then locate *initial* in the text (the second paragraph) and have students determine the word's meaning in this context.	**Advanced** Invite pairs of students to refer to the text in creating a chart of (1) challenges faced in American society and (2) why they are challenges. Then have students use their chart to help them construct sentences with the expression *to face a challenge*.
Advanced High Discuss how a paper's margin is the space around the edges, and initials are the letters at the beginning of words. Then have pairs of students locate these words in the text (the first and second paragraphs) and use their prior knowledge to infer the words' meanings in these new contexts.	**Advanced High** In addition to the expression *to face a challenge*, also discuss *to face the consequences* and *to face (the) facts*. Invite pairs of students to use all three expressions to discuss American society, referring to both the text and their own observations.

D Differentiate Instruction

Use the Differentiated Instruction notes throughout the lesson plan to support the varied skill sets, levels of readiness, and interests in the mixed-ability classroom.

Challenge These notes include suggestions for expanding the activity for advanced students.

On-Level These notes include suggestions for modifying the activity to address different interests or learning styles.

Extra Support These notes include ideas for providing more scaffolding or reading spupport.

Special Needs These notes provide ideas for adapting instruction to support the needs of various special needs students.

NOTES

PEARSON realize
www.PearsonRealize.com

Go online to access additional resources including: Primary Sources • Biographies • Supreme Court cases • 21st Century Skill Tutorials • Maps • Graphic Organizers.

Objectives

Objective 1: Describe significant events in George W. Bush's presidency.

Objective 2: Describe significant events in Barack Obama's presidency.

Objective 3: Describe the recent effects of immigration and expanded civil rights on American society.

Objective 4: Identify the domestic and foreign challenges Americans will face in the future.

LESSON 5 ORGANIZER	PACING: APPROX. 1 PERIOD, .5 BLOCKS		RESOURCES	
	OBJECTIVES	PACING	Online	Print
Connect				
DIGITAL START UP ACTIVITY **Gridlock in Congress**		5 min.	●	
Investigate				
DIGITAL TEXT 1 **The Bush Era**	Objective 1	10 min.	●	●
DIGITAL TEXT 2 **Obama's Presidency**	Objective 2	10 min.	●	●
DIGITAL TEXT 3 **Social Change**	Objective 3	10 min.	●	●
BEFORE AND AFTER **America's Changing Demographics**		10 min.	●	
DIGITAL TEXT 4 **America's Promise**	Objective 4	10 min.	●	●
INTERACTIVE CHART **Turning Points in U.S. History**		10 min.	●	
Synthesize				
DIGITAL ACTIVITY **Compare and Contrast**		5 min.	●	
Demonstrate				
DIGITAL QUIZ **Lesson Quiz and Class Discussion Board**		10 min.	●	

Challenges at Home

CONNECT

DIGITAL START UP ACTIVITY

Gridlock in Congress

Start Up: Gridlock in Congress

Start Up

Gridlock in Congress > In order for Congressional legislation to become law, both the House of Representatives and the Senate must approve the same bill, which then goes to the President. Many bills, however, never make it to the President's desk, because the House and Senate do not agree on them.

If the House and Senate are unable to agree on legislation, what effect does this have on Congress's ability to address the needs of U.S. citizens? Write a few lines in response.

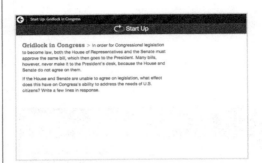

Project the Start Up Activity Ask students to read the information as they get settled. Engage students in individually answering the question and invite them to share their responses with a partner.

Discuss Prompt students to think about Congress's productivity. *(Possible answer: Congress may have difficulty passing legislation if members are not willing to compromise. This leads to gridlock and inaction.)*

Tell students that in this lesson they will be learning about significant events in the Bush and Obama presidencies, the effects of immigration, and the challenges Americans may face in the future.

Aa Vocabulary Development: Use the Interactive Reading Notepad to preview the Key Terms and Academic Vocabulary in this lesson with students.

FLIP IT!

Assign the Flipped Video for this lesson.

STUDENT EDITION PRINT PAGES: 924–933

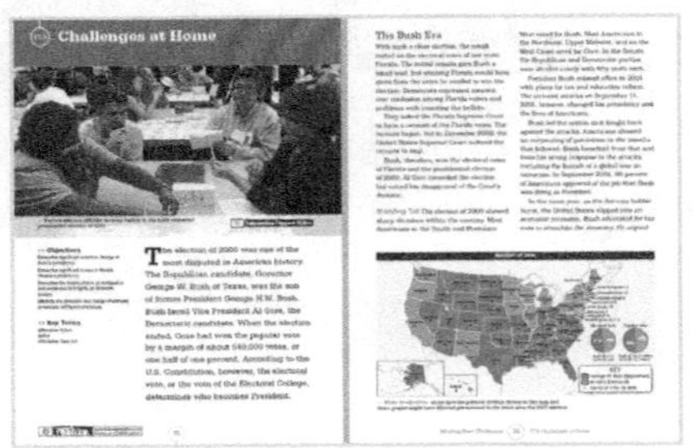

INVESTIGATE

DIGITAL TEXT 1

The Bush Era

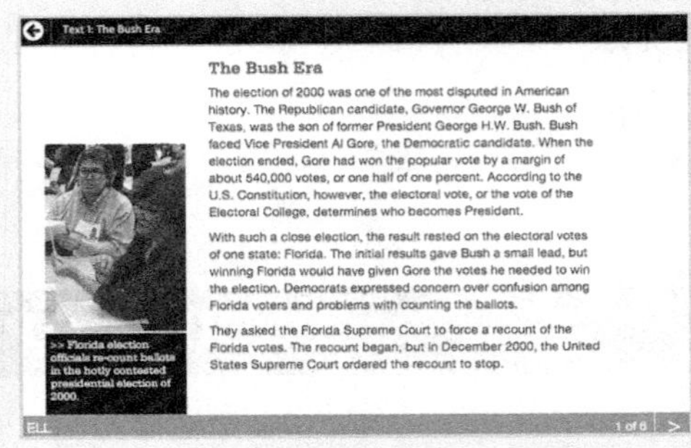

Text 1: The Bush Era

The Bush Era

The election of 2000 was one of the most disputed in American history. The Republican candidate, Governor George W. Bush of Texas, was the son of former President George H.W. Bush. Bush faced Vice President Al Gore, the Democratic candidate. When the election ended, Gore had won the popular vote by a margin of about 540,000 votes, or one half of one percent. According to the U.S. Constitution, however, the electoral vote, or the vote of the Electoral College, determines who becomes President.

With such a close election, the result rested on the electoral votes of one state: Florida. The initial results gave Bush a small lead, but winning Florida would have given Gore the votes he needed to win the election. Democrats expressed concern over confusion among Florida voters and problems with counting the ballots.

They asked the Florida Supreme Court to force a recount of the Florida votes. The recount began, but in December 2000, the United States Supreme Court ordered the recount to stop.

Florida election officials re-count ballots in the hotly contested presidential election of 2000.

ELL 1 of 6

Objective 1: Describe significant events in George W. Bush's presidency.

Quick Instruction

Explain that the framers of the Constitution created the Electoral College as a compromise between election of the President by a vote in Congress and election of the President by a popular vote of qualified citizens. How does the electoral college work? *(Each state has a number of electors equal to its number of congressional representatives. If a presidential candidate wins the popular vote in a state, that state's electors will generally vote for that candidate. If a candidate has the most electoral votes, then he or she wins the presidency.)*

Summarize Why did Al Gore win the overall popular vote but lose the presidency? *(Al Gore had fewer electoral votes than George W. Bush based on the result in each state, so Gore lost the presidency even though he won more popular votes across the country.)*

Generate Explanations Explain why the judicial branch became involved in the presidential election of 2000. *(Neither candidate had enough votes to win the Electoral College without the electoral votes from Florida, but the popular vote in Florida was very close. Democrats asked the Florida Supreme Court to force a recount of the Florida votes. The recount began, but in December 2000, the U.S. Supreme Court ordered the recount to stop.)*

ELL Use the ELL activity described in the ELL chart.

Further Instruction

Analyze Information Although Hurricane Katrina was a natural disaster, why was the aftermath of the storm especially challenging? *(The government was slow to respond, and the Federal Emergency Management Agency (FEMA) was not prepared to deal with the effects of Katrina.)*

Draw Conclusions What domestic challenges did the Bush administration face before the 2006 midterm elections? *(Unemployment remained relatively high and the percentage of people living in poverty increased. The Bush administration also received heavy criticism for its handling of Hurricane Katrina.)* What impact did they have on the election? *(Bush's popularity declined and Democrats took control of Congress for the first time since 1994.)*

DIGITAL TEXT 2

Obama's Presidency

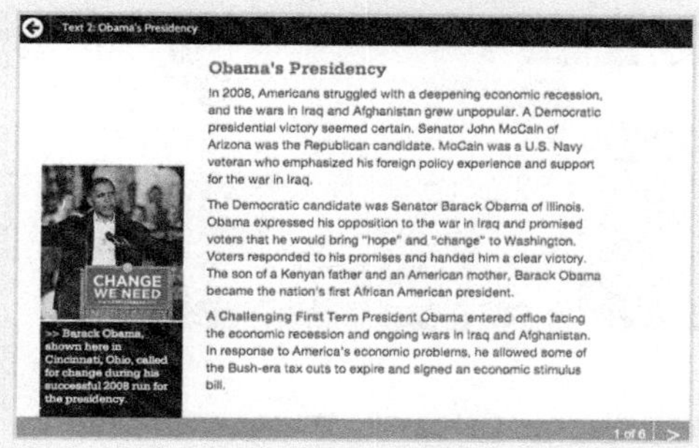
Text 2: Obama's Presidency

Obama's Presidency

In 2008, Americans struggled with a deepening economic recession, and the wars in Iraq and Afghanistan grew unpopular. A Democratic presidential victory seemed certain. Senator John McCain of Arizona was the Republican candidate. McCain was a U.S. Navy veteran who emphasized his foreign policy experience and support for the war in Iraq.

The Democratic candidate was Senator Barack Obama of Illinois. Obama expressed his opposition to the war in Iraq and promised voters that he would bring "hope" and "change" to Washington. Voters responded to his promises and handed him a clear victory. The son of a Kenyan father and an American mother, Barack Obama became the nation's first African American president.

A Challenging First Term President Obama entered office facing the economic recession and ongoing wars in Iraq and Afghanistan. In response to America's economic problems, he allowed some of the Bush-era tax cuts to expire and signed an economic stimulus bill.

>> Barack Obama, shown here in Cincinnati, Ohio, called for change during his successful 2008 run for the presidency.

1 of 6

Objective 2: Describe significant events in Barack Obama's presidency.

Quick Instruction

Project the digital image of Barack Obama campaigning for President in 2008. Direct students' focus to the campaign sign on the podium stand. Challenge students to suggest what changes Obama might be proposing in light of challenging domestic and foreign issues during the Bush administration. *(policy changes in Afghanistan and Iraq; a different approach to strengthening the economy)*

Determine Relevance Discuss the historical significance of the 2008 presidential election. Why was this a historic moment for the country? *(Obama was the first African American to be nominated for President by a major party and the first African American to be elected President.)*

Contrast the opposing viewpoints of Republicans and Democrats on how to best address the federal deficit. *(Republicans wanted to cut spending and reduce taxes. Democrats wanted to protect federal programs, and to pay for them, they supported tax increases on wealthy Americans.)*

Further Instruction

Summarize how and why Congress fell into political gridlock following the 2010 midterm elections. *(In the 2010 elections, Republicans gained control of the House of Representatives. Republicans also won seats in the Senate and several state governorships. Democrats, however, still controlled the Senate. Republicans in Congress blocked passage of bills Obama supported. But neither side had enough control to push through legislation, and neither side was willing to meet the demands of the other to do so.)*

Compare Points of View What arguments existed for and against passage of the Affordable Care Act? *(Supporters of the Affordable Care Act wanted to expand access to healthcare for the millions in the nation without health insurance, as well as reform insurance practices unfavorable to consumers such as term limits and pre-existing conditions. Critics argued that the Affordable Care Act would cost a significant amount of money and increase costs for consumers who already had health insurance.)*

DIGITAL TEXT 3

Social Change

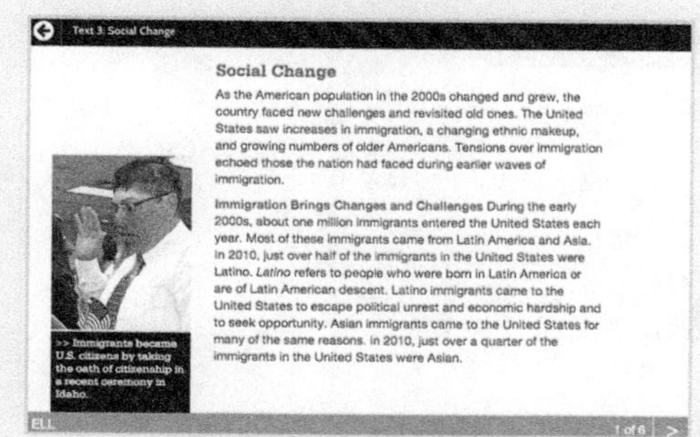
Text 3: Social Change

Social Change

As the American population in the 2000s changed and grew, the country faced new challenges and revisited old ones. The United States saw increases in immigration, a changing ethnic makeup, and growing numbers of older Americans. Tensions over immigration echoed those the nation had faced during earlier waves of immigration.

Immigration Brings Changes and Challenges During the early 2000s, about one million immigrants entered the United States each year. Most of these immigrants came from Latin America and Asia. In 2010, just over half of the immigrants in the United States were Latino. *Latino* refers to people who were born in Latin America or are of Latin American descent. Latino immigrants came to the United States to escape political unrest and economic hardship and to seek opportunity. Asian immigrants came to the United States for many of the same reasons. In 2010, just over a quarter of the immigrants in the United States were Asian.

>> Immigrants became U.S. citizens by taking the oath of citizenship in a recent ceremony in Idaho.

ELL 1 of 6

Objective 3: Describe the recent effects of immigration and expanded civil rights on American society.

Quick Instruction

Interactive Chart: America's Changing Demographics Project the Interactive Chart and navigate the slider with students to contrast the changing demographics of American society. Discuss the trends with students. How do the data on languages spoken in U.S. homes reflect demographic changes in the U.S. population? *(The increase in Spanish and Asian languages spoken at home indicates that more Americans are Latino and Asian.)*

Determine Point of Views Identify viewpoints both for and against immigration. *(Some Americans support immigration because of immigrants' strong work ethic and the cultural diversity that they bring to the country. Other Americans are concerned that increased immigration will create competition for jobs and depress wages. They also worry that the country cannot afford the cost of providing education, healthcare, and other services to immigrants.)*

Challenges at Home

BEFORE AND AFTER

America's Changing Demographics

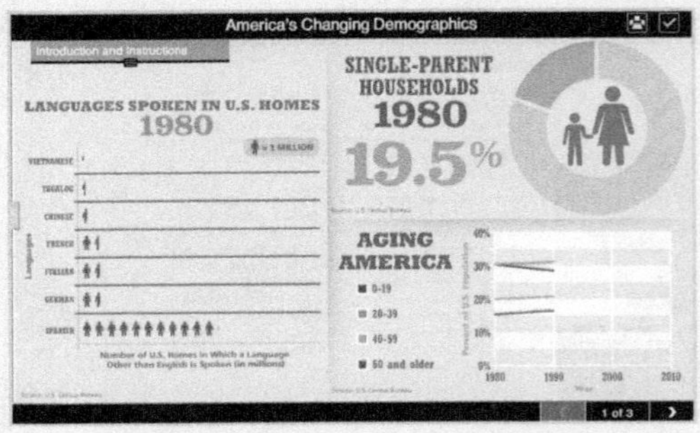

ACTIVE CLASSROOM

Conduct a Take a Stand activity. Have students debate the following question: Should the United States impose stronger legislation to limit immigration? Have students move to opposite sides of the room and group up with others with similar views. Have groups create a justification or opening statement defending their position to the class.

D Differentiate: Extra Support Define demography as the study of how populations change over time, and prompt students to understand that demographics are characteristics of groups of people, such as age, gender, and income.

ELL Use the ELL activity described in the ELL chart.

Further Instruction

Evaluate Arguments In 2003, the Supreme Court ruled that colleges and universities had the right to consider race when deciding whether to admit a student. Do you agree with this idea? Why or why not? *(Possible answers: Yes, college-educated leaders should reflect the nation's increasing diversity and the economic realities of globalization. No, colleges should admit students solely on the basis of merit.)*

DIGITAL TEXT 4

America's Promise

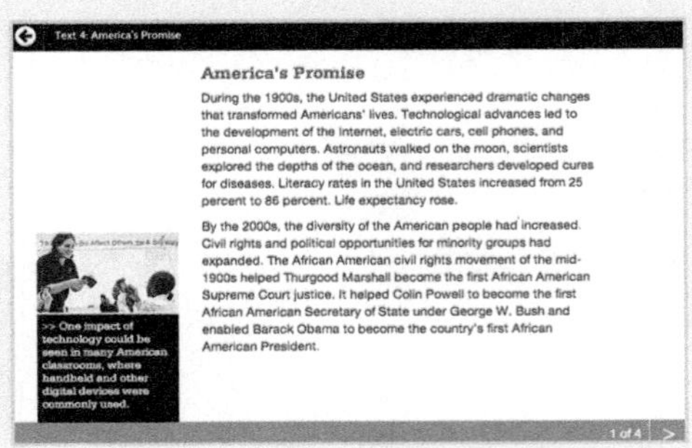

Objective 4: Identify the domestic and foreign challenges Americans will face in the future.

Quick Instruction

Interactive Chart: Turning Points in U.S. History Project the Interactive Chart and navigate through the events as you prompt students to classify each based on historical type and significance. Pair students and have each pair create a list of the five most significant turning points in American history. Ask volunteers to justify their decisions for the class.

Support Ideas with Evidence What evidence from the text supports the idea that opportunities for women and minorities have improved since the modern civil rights era? *(Thurgood Marshall become the first black Supreme Court justice; Colin Powell became the first black Secretary of State; Barack Obama was elected the country's first African American President. Women served as governors and on the Supreme Court; Madeleine Albright served as the first female Secretary of State; Nancy Pelosi became the first female speaker of the House of Representatives.)*

INTERACTIVE CHART

Turning Points in U.S. History

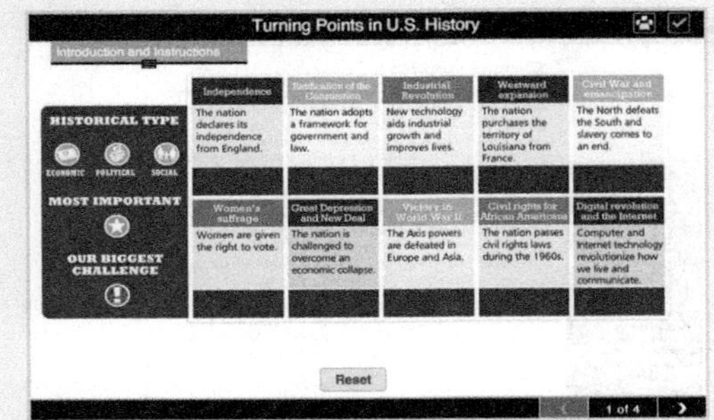

ACTIVE CLASSROOM

Conduct a Circle Write activity. Break into groups and provide the following question as a writing prompt: What is the most significant challenge facing the United States? Have students write as much as they can for one minute then switch with the person on their right. The next person tries to improve or elaborate the response where the other person left off. Continue to switch until the paper comes back to the first person. The group then decides which is the best composition (or response) and shares that with the larger group.

Further Instruction

Generate Explanations By the early 2000s, more than half of medical school and law school students were women. What factors encouraged this shift in higher education? *(Expanded and equal early educational opportunities for young females help level educational outcomes. Greater acceptance of expanded roles for women also contributed significantly. Equal opportunity laws and policies that allowed and encouraged women to pursue careers once dominated by men also helped.)*

SYNTHESIZE

DIGITAL ACTIVITY

Compare and Contrast

Synthesize: Compare and Contrast

→ Synthesize

Compare and Contrast > In this lesson, you learned about the presidencies of George W. Bush and Barack Obama. Complete a graphic organizer similar to the one shown here in which you compare and contrast how these two Presidents responded to terrorism, immigration, and the federal budget deficit.

	PRESIDENT BUSH	PRESIDENT OBAMA
Terrorism		
Immigration		

Provide time for student pairs to review information from the lesson and discuss how Presidents Bush and Obama responded to war, immigration, and the federal budget deficit. When students have completed their graphic organizers, have them share their thoughts with the class.

Discuss Ask students to recall the Topic Essential Question, "What can individuals do to affect society?" Lead the class in a brief review of the duties and responsibilities of the U.S. President. Challenge students to suggest other roles a President might perform or be asked—explicitly or implicitly—to do. Invite students to share their opinions on how Bush and Obama positively affected society in their responses to the challenges they faced in their presidencies.

DEMONSTRATE

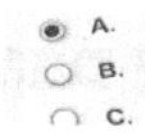

DIGITAL QUIZ

Lesson Quiz and Class Discussion Board

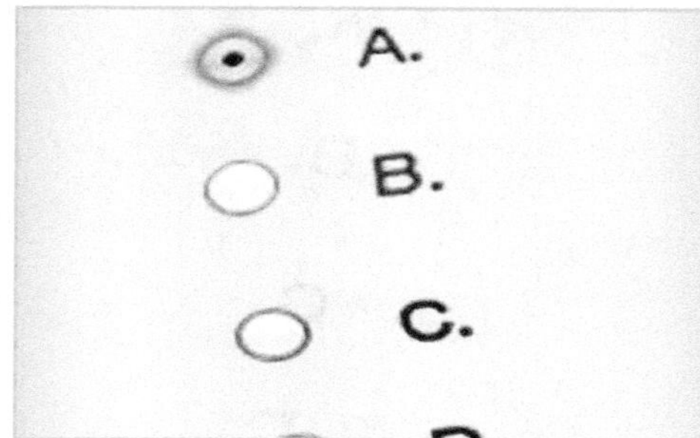

Assign the online Lesson Quiz for this lesson if you haven't already done so. Students will be offered automatic remediation or enrichment based on their score.

In *Challenges at Home*, you read about the issues Presidents Bush and Obama faced, as well as the challenges and opportunities that await Americans.

Pose these questions to the class on the Discussion Board:

Predict Consequences What are the potential effects of rising income inequality?

Make Predictions How will the United States provide leadership in the future in dealing with issues such as climate change, reliance on fossil fuels, and economic crises?

Topic Inquiry

Have students continue their investigations for the Topic Inquiry.

Topic 17

Meeting New Challenges

SYNTHESIZE

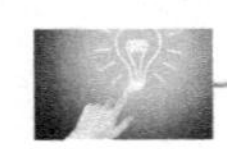

DIGITAL ESSENTIAL QUESTION ACTIVITY

Reflect on the Essential Question and Topic

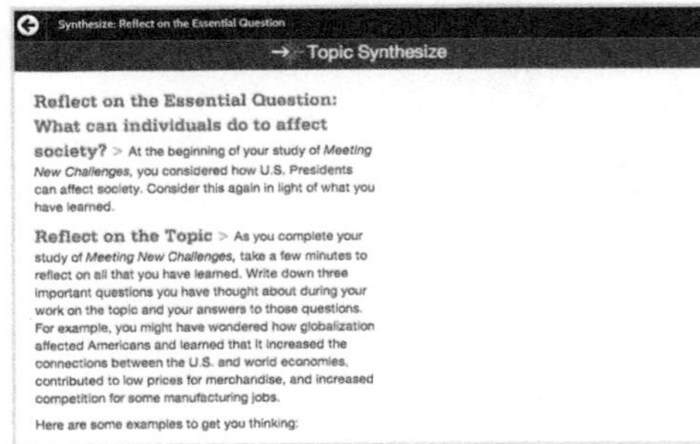

First ask students to reconsider the Essential Question for this topic: What can individuals do to affect society? Have students reflect on their responses to how they think U.S. Presidents can affect society. Have students work with a partner to consider the question again in light of what they have learned. Encourage students to write a revised response to the question.

Next ask students to reflect on the Topic as a whole. Before students write their questions, discuss the example question prompts if students need help getting started.

You may ask students to share their questions and answers on the Class Discussion Board.

Topic Inquiry

Have students complete Step 3 of the Topic Inquiry.

DEMONSTRATE

DIGITAL TOPIC REVIEW AND ASSESSMENT

Meeting New Challenges

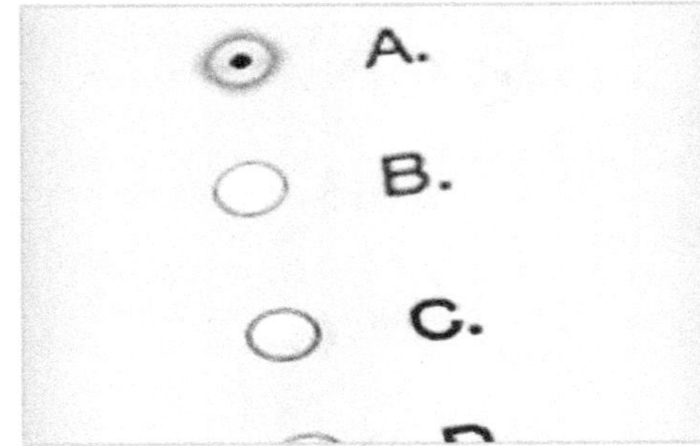

Students can prepare for the Topic Test by answering the questions in the Topic Review and Assessment online or the Assessment questions in the Print Student text. They can also prepare by reviewing their answers to the Interactive Reading Notepad questions or reviewing their notes in the Reading and Notetaking Study Guide.

DIGITAL TOPIC TEST

Meeting New Challenges

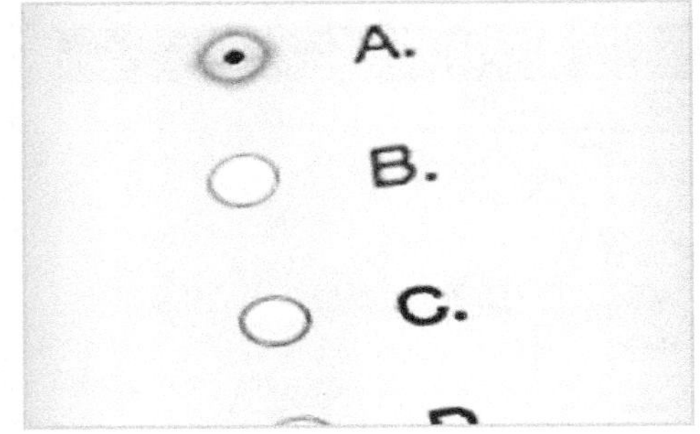

TOPIC TEST

Assign the Topic Test to assess students' understanding of topic content.

BENCHMARK TESTS

Assign these benchmark tests as you complete the relevant topics to monitor student progress toward mastering the course content and as preparation for the End-of-Course Test.

Benchmark Test 1: Topics 1–2

Benchmark Test 2: Topics 3–4

Benchmark Test 3: Topics 5–6

Benchmark Test 4: Topics 7–9

Benchmark Test 5: Topics 10–12

Benchmark Test 6: Topics 13–14

Benchmark Test 7: Topics 15–17